Oxford
Learner's Pocket
Thesaurus

OXFORD
UNIVERSITY PRESS

OXFORD
UNIVERSITY PRESS

Great Clarendon Street, Oxford OX2 6DP

Oxford University Press is a department of the University
of Oxford. It furthers the University's objective of excellence
in research, scholarship, and education by publishing
worldwide in

Oxford New York

Auckland Cape Town Dar es Salaam Hong Kong Karachi
Kuala Lumpur Madrid Melbourne Mexico City Nairobi
New Delhi Shanghai Taipei Toronto

With offices in

Argentina Austria Brazil Chile Czech Republic France
Greece Guatemala Hungary Italy Japan Poland Portugal
Singapore South Korea Switzerland Thailand Turkey
Ukraine Vietnam

OXFORD and OXFORD ENGLISH are registered trade marks
of Oxford University Press in the UK and in certain other
countries

ISBN: 978 0 19 475204 6

Text capture, processing and typesetting
by Oxford University Press

Printed in China

ACKNOWLEDGEMENTS

Edited by: Diana Lea
Assisted by: Victoria Bull

Aa

abandon verb

1 [T, often passive] ■ *They were abandoned by their parents.*

desert • **leave** • **turn your back on sb/sth** | *infml* **walk out (on sb)** • **dump**

▶ abandon/desert/leave/walk out on/dump your **husband/wife**
▶ abandon/desert/leave/dump your **lover**
▶ abandon/leave/dump your **child**

● **ABANDON OR DESERT?** Use **abandon** for leaving people who are unable to support themselves; use **desert** for being disloyal, for example leaving friends without help.

2 [T] ■ *abandon a building/vehicle*

desert • **leave** • **evacuate** | *fml* **vacate**

▶ abandon/desert/leave/evacuate/vacate a **building/house/home**

3 [T] ■ *abandon an attempt*

give sth up • **stop** • **drop** | *infml* **pack sth in** | *esp. AmE, infml* **quit** | *fml* **discontinue**

■ OPP **continue, take sth up**
▶ abandon/give up/stop/drop/quit **what** you are doing
▶ abandon/give up/pack in/quit your **job**
▶ abandon/give up **hope**

abandoned adj.

■ *an abandoned car*

deserted • **disused** • **unoccupied** • **uninhabited**

▶ a/an abandoned/deserted/disused/unoccupied **building**
▶ a/an abandoned/deserted **village**
▶ a/an abandoned/disused **mine**

ability noun

1 [sing., U] ■ *the ability to learn*

capability • **capacity** • **power**

■ OPP **inability**
▶ the ability/capability/capacity/power **to do sth**
▶ **beyond/within** your ability/capability/capacity/power

2 [U, C] ■ *a child's natural abilities*

talent • **gift** • **skill** • **expertise** • **aptitude** • **competence** • **proficiency** • **art** • **flair** | *infml* **knack** • **know-how** | *fml* **prowess**

▶ a **natural** ability/talent/gift/skill/aptitude/flair
▶ (a) **special** ability/talent/gift/skill/expertise/aptitude

be about sb/sth phrase

■ *What's his new book about?*

deal with sth • **cover** • **be concerned with sth** • **concern** • **have/be to do with sth** • **refer to sth** • **relate to sb/sth**

▶ a **book** is about/deals with/covers/is concerned with sth
▶ a **chapter** is about/deals with/covers/is concerned with sth
▶ a **film** is about/deals with/is concerned with sth

● **BE ABOUT STH, DEAL WITH STH OR CONCERN STH?** Be about sth is a more general expression; deal with sth and concern both suggest a formal, serious or thorough discussion of a subject.

about adv.

1 ■ *It costs about $10.*

approximately • **roughly** • **around** • **round about** • **something like** • **more or less**

■ OPP **exactly**

2 ■ *about the best we can hope for*

almost • **nearly** • **virtually** • **more or less** • **practically** | *spoken* **pretty much** • **pretty well**

▶ just about/almost/nearly/virtually/more or less/practically/pretty much **ready**

absolute adj.

1 ■ *a class for absolute beginners* ■ *He must earn an absolute fortune.*

complete • **total** • **real** • **utter** • **outright** • **perfect** • **positive** • **downright** • **pure** • **sheer** • **unqualified** • **undivided**

▶ a/an absolute/complete/total/real/utter **disaster**
▶ absolute/complete/total/real/utter/pure/sheer **joy**
▶ absolute/complete/total/utter/perfect **silence**

2 ■ *absolute proof*

definite • **firm** • **positive** • **concrete** • **hard** • **final** • **conclusive** • **proven** • **undeniable** • **unquestionable** • **definitive**

▶ absolute/definite/firm/positive/hard/conclusive/undeniable/unquestionable/definitive **evidence**
▶ absolute/definite/firm/positive/concrete/final/conclusive/undeniable/definitive **proof**

absolutely adv. (esp. spoken)

■ *You're absolutely right.*

abuse

completely • totally • utterly • entirely • fully • definitely • undeniably • indisputably | *esp. BrE* quite | *esp. spoken* perfectly | *infml* dead

► absolutely/completely/totally/ utterly/entirely/fully/definitely/ quite/perfectly/dead **sure**
► I absolutely/completely/totally/ entirely/fully/definitely/quite/ perfectly/dead **agree**
● **WHICH WORD?** The main differences between these words are in register not meaning. **Completely**, **entirely** and **fully** are used more in written and formal English. **Totally**, **quite**, **absolutely** and **perfectly** are used more in spoken and informal English. **Utterly** is often used to express failure or impossibility: *She utterly failed to convince them.*

abuse *verb*

1 [T] ■ *abuse your position* ■ *abuse drugs*

exploit • use | *fml* misuse

► abuse/exploit your **position**
► abuse/misuse your **power/ authority**
► abuse/misuse **drugs/alcohol**

2 [T, often passive] ■ *sexually abused*

molest • assault • rape | *infml* grope

► sexually abuse/molest/assault sb

3 [T] ■ *verbally abused*

insult • swear at sb • curse • slander | *fml* vilify • malign | *esp. journ.* smear

■ **OPP** compliment, flatter

academic *adj.* [usu. before noun]

■ *academic research/ability*

educational • scholarly • intellectual

► a/an educational/academic/ scholarly **career**
► academic/educational/scholarly/ intellectual **standards/excellence**
► academic/scholarly/intellectual **debate**

accelerate *verb* [I, T]

■ *a car accelerates* ■ *Exposure to the sun can accelerate the ageing process.*

speed (sth) up | *written* speed • hasten

■ **OPP** *fml* retard, decelerate
► accelerate/speed up/speed/ hasten the **pace/progress** (of sth)
► accelerate/speed up/hasten the **death** of sth
● **SPEED UP OR SPEED?** Use **speed up**, not **speed**, to talk about vehicles moving faster:

✔*The train soon speeded up.* ✗ ~~The train soon speeded.~~

accent *noun* [C, U]

■ *a broad/strong Scottish accent*

voice • pronunciation | *phonetics* intonation

► speak in a ... accent/voice
► have (a/an) **excellent/good/poor** accent/pronunciation/intonation
► (a/an) **English/foreign** accent/ pronunciation/intonation

accept *verb*

1 [I, T] ■ *She decided to accept the job.*

take • take sb/sth on • take sth up • take sb up on sth

■ **OPP** refuse, (*fml*) decline
► accept/take/take on a **job/post/ position/role/responsibility**
► accept/take/take up an **offer**
► accept/take up a/an **invitation/ suggestion**
► accept/take on/take up a **challenge**

2 [T] ■ *accept a cheque*

get • receive • collect

► accept/get/receive/collect sth **from** sb
► accept/get/receive/collect a/an **medal/award/prize**
► accept/get/receive **treatment/ payment/help**

3 [T] ■ *He accepted all the changes we proposed.*

agree • approve • go along with sb/ sth • take sth on board | *fml* consent • acquiesce

► agree/consent/acquiesce **to** sth
► accept/agree to/approve/go along with/consent to a **plan/ scheme/proposal**
► accept/agree to/approve/go along with/acquiesce in a **decision**
► accept/agree to/approve/take on board a **suggestion**

4 [T] ■ *She accepts full responsibility for what happened.*

take • carry • shoulder | *fml* assume • bear

► accept/take/carry/shoulder/ assume/bear sth **for** sb/sth
► accept/take/carry/shoulder/ assume/bear the **responsibility**
► accept/take/carry/shoulder/bear the **blame**
► accept/take/bear the **consequences**

5 [T] ■ *He could not accept the fact that he was wrong.*

face • face up to sth • come to terms with sth • live with sth • make the best of sth • resign yourself to sth | *fml* reconcile sb/yourself to sth

account

▶ accept/face/face up to/come to terms with/live with/resign yourself to/reconcile yourself to **the fact that…**
▶ accept/face/come to terms with/make the best of a **situation**
▶ to accept/face/face up to/come to terms with **the truth/the reality of sth**

6 [T] ■ *She had never felt accepted into their world.*

welcome ◆ receive

▶ accept/welcome/receive sb **as** sth
▶ accept/welcome/receive sb **into** sth

7 [T] ■ *The college he applied to has accepted him.*

esp. BrE **enrol** | *AmE usu.* **enroll** | *fml* **admit**

▶ accept/enrol/admit sb **into** sth
▶ accept/enrol/admit sb **as** sth
▶ accept/enrol/admit a **candidate/member/student**

acceptable adj.

1 ■ *an acceptable way to behave*

right ◆ proper ◆ decent ◆ justified ◆ justifiable

■ OPP **unacceptable**
▶ acceptable/right/proper/justified/justifiable **to do sth**
▶ acceptable/right/proper **that…**
▶ acceptable/proper/decent **behaviour**
● ACCEPTABLE OR PROPER? **Proper** is more approving. Use **proper** if you approve of sth; use **acceptable** if you do not disapprove.

2 ■ *a solution that is acceptable to everyone*

satisfactory ◆ fair ◆ reasonable | *esp. spoken* **all right** | *infml, esp. spoken* **OK**

■ OPP **unacceptable**
▶ be acceptable/satisfactory/fair/reasonable/all right/OK **to do sth**
▶ be acceptable/satisfactory/fair/reasonable/all right/OK **that…**
▶ a/an acceptable/satisfactory/fair/reasonable **solution**

3 ■ *The food was just about acceptable.*

adequate ◆ reasonable | *esp. spoken* **all right** | *infml, esp. spoken* **OK**

▶ be acceptable/adequate/reasonable/all right/OK **for sb/sth**
▶ an acceptable/adequate/reasonable **level/degree/standard** of sth
▶ barely/scarcely acceptable/adequate

access noun [U]

■ *Doors give access to the terrace.*

entry ◆ admission ◆ entrance

▶ access/entry/admission/entrance **to** sth
▶ refuse/deny (sb) access/entry/admission/entrance
▶ gain access/entry/admission/entrance

accident noun [C]

■ *an accident on the main road*

crash ◆ collision | *AmE* **wreck** | *esp. journ.* **pile-up**

▶ in a/an accident/crash/collision/wreck/pile-up
▶ have a/an accident/collision
▶ cause a/an accident/crash/collision/wreck/pile-up

accommodate verb [T]

■ *The hotel can accommodate up to 80 guests.*

house ◆ put sb up ◆ take sb in

▶ accommodate/house/take in **refugees**
▶ accommodate/put up/take in **guests**

accommodation noun [U]

■ *live in rented accommodation*

housing ◆ quarters ◆ lodging ◆ a place to stay | *AmE* **accommodations**

▶ (a) temporary accommodation/housing/quarters/place to stay/accommodations
▶ permanent/comfortable accommodation/housing/quarters/accommodations
▶ provide accommodation/housing/lodging/accommodations
▶ look for accommodation/housing/a place to stay/accommodations

accompany verb [T] (fml)

■ *His wife accompanied him on the trip.*

go with sb ◆ take ◆ escort ◆ walk ◆ guide ◆ tag along

▶ accompany/take/escort/walk/guide/go with sb **to…**
▶ accompany/take/go with sb **everywhere/on a trip/on a journey**

account noun [C]

■ *She paid the money into her account.*

fund ◆ budget ◆ savings

▶ pay sth **from/out of** a/an account/fund/budget/savings
▶ have sth **in** a/an account/fund/budget
▶ have/manage a/an/your account/fund/budget/savings

accurate

accurate adj.
■ Accurate records must be kept.

precise • exact • correct • right • reliable • authentic • factual • true

■ OPP inaccurate
▶ accurate/precise/correct/right **about** sb/sth
▶ an accurate/a precise/an exact/ the correct/the right/the true **answer**
▶ (the) accurate/precise/exact/ correct/right **instructions/ measurements**
▶ a/an accurate/precise/exact/ correct/reliable/authentic/ factual/true **account**
● **ACCURATE, PRECISE OR EXACT?** A description that is *not very exact/ precise* lacks details; a description that is *not very accurate* gives details, but the details are wrong.

accuse verb [T]
■ accused of murder

charge • prosecute • indict

▶ accuse sb **of** sth
▶ charge/indict sb **with** sth
▶ prosecute/indict sb **for/on charges of/on a charge of** sth

achieve verb [T]
■ She finally achieved success.

manage • succeed • reach • accomplish | BrE **fulfil** | AmE **fulfill** | infml **pull sth off** | fml **attain • effect**

▶ achieve/succeed in/reach/ accomplish/fulfil/attain a/an **goal/objective**
▶ achieve/succeed in/accomplish/ fulfil/attain an **aim**
▶ achieve/reach/fulfil/attain a **target**
▶ achieve/accomplish/fulfil an **ambition**

achievement noun [C]
■ This is probably his greatest scientific achievement.

accomplishment • feat • work • triumph

▶ a **great/remarkable** achievement/ accomplishment/feat/work/ triumph
▶ a **real** achievement/ accomplishment/feat/triumph
▶ a **major/spectacular** achievement/feat/work/triumph
● **ACHIEVEMENT OR ACCOMPLISHMENT?** Achievement is used esp. for academic, professional, artistic or sporting success. Accomplishment often refers to success which has benefited others, such as an important invention.

acknowledge verb [T]
■ He did not acknowledge that he had done anything wrong.

recognize • admit • concede • confess

▶ acknowledge/recognize/admit/ concede/confess **that…**
▶ It is/was (generally) acknowledged/recognized/ admitted/conceded **that…**
▶ acknowledge/recognize/admit **the truth**

acquire verb
1 [T] (esp. written) ■ I have recently acquired a taste for olives.

earn | esp. spoken **get** | esp. written **gain • obtain** | infml **pick sth up**

▶ acquire/get/obtain/pick up sth **from** sb/sth
▶ acquire/earn/gain a **reputation**

2 [T] (esp. written) ■ He was extremely proud of his newly acquired computer skills.

learn • pick sth up • master

▶ acquire/learn/pick up/master a **skill**

acquit verb [T]
■ The jury acquitted him of murder.

clear | fml **exonerate • absolve • vindicate**

■ OPP convict
▶ acquit/clear/exonerate/absolve sb **of** sth
▶ a **defendant** is acquitted/cleared/ exonerated
● **ACQUIT OR CLEAR?** Acquit is more formal than clear. Clear is used for sb who succeeds in having a conviction overturned (= cancelled): Throughout his years in prison, he fought to clear his name.

act noun
1 [C] ■ an act of kindness

action • gesture • move • step • measure | fml **deed**

▶ a/an act/action/gesture/move/ step/measure/deed **by** sb
▶ a **kind/charitable/generous** act/ action/gesture/deed
▶ **do/perform** a/an act/action/ deed

2 [C] ■ Don't believe her—it's all an act.

front • mask • cover | BrE **pretence** | AmE **pretense**

▶ **put on** a/an act/front/mask/ pretence
▶ **keep up** a/an act/front/pretence

act verb

1 [I] ■ *They had to act quickly to save the girl's life.*

esp. journ. **take action** • **move** | *esp. spoken* **do something** | *esp. written* **take steps**

▶ act/take action/move/take steps **against** sb/sth
▶ act/take action/move/do something/take steps **to do sth**

2 [I] ■ *Ben's been acting very strangely.*

behave • **treat** | *fml* **conduct yourself**

▶ act/behave/treat sb **as if/though/like…**
▶ act/behave/treat sb/conduct yourself **properly**
▶ act/behave/treat sb **reasonably/accordingly/differently/with dignity**

● **ACT OR BEHAVE? Behave** is used to talk about how well sb has behaved, but not how fairly or legally:
✔ *behave well/sensibly* x *behave unfairly/illegally*
Act is used to talk about how sensibly, fairly or legally sb has behaved, but not how well:
✔ *act fairly/unlawfully* x *act well/badly*

3 [I] ■ *I decided to act dumb.*

pretend | *fml* **feign**

▶ pretend/feign **interest/indifference**

4 [I, T] ■ *She is acting the role of Juliet.*

play • **perform**

▶ act/play/perform a **role/part**
▶ act/play/perform in a **play/show/production**
▶ act/play/perform sth **well/together**

● **ACT OR PLAY? Play** must take an object, but **act** can also be used without an object:
✔ *He just can't act.* x *He just can't play.*
A play or film is **acted**, not played:
✔ *The film was well acted.* x *The film was well played.*

action noun

1 [C, U] ■ *We shall take whatever actions are necessary.*

measure • **step** • **move** • **act** • **gesture** • **stunt** | *fml* **deed**

▶ a/an **action/measure/step/move/act/gesture/stunt/deed** by sb
▶ a **heroic/brave/daring action/step/move/act/gesture/deed**
▶ **do/perform** a/an **action/act/stunt/deed**
▶ **take action/measures/steps**
● **ACTION OR ACT? Action** often

combines with **take** but **act** does not:
✔ *Firefighters took action immediately.* x *Firefighters took act immediately.*
Act is often followed by *of*, but **action** is not:
✔ *a heroic act of bravery* x *a heroic action of bravery*

2 [U] ■ *films with plenty of action*

activity • **excitement**

▶ **great/intense action/activity/excitement**
▶ **be involved in/stop** the **action/activity**

active adj.

1 ■ *a physical and active lifestyle*

energetic • **vigorous** • **mobile** | *approv.* **dynamic**

▶ a/an **active/energetic/dynamic person/man/woman**
▶ a/an **active/energetic member** of sth
▶ a/an **active/vigorous supporter/opponent** of sb/sth

2 ■ *They were both politically active.*

engaged • **involved** • **busy**

■ OPP **inactive**, **passive**
▶ **active/engaged/involved** in sth
▶ **keep** sb **active/involved/busy**

activist noun [C]

■ *Gay activists marched in London to protest against the new law.*

campaigner • **crusader** • **reformer** • **lobbyist** • **champion** • **advocate** • **supporter**

▶ a/an **activist/campaigner/crusader/lobbyist/champion for** sth
▶ a **leading/great activist/campaigner/crusader/reformer/advocate/champion/supporter**
▶ a **political activist/campaigner/reformer/lobbyist**
● **ACTIVIST OR CAMPAIGNER?** Use either word for sb who belongs to an organization but use **campaigner** for sb who works as an individual: *student/disabled/union/party activists* • *a tireless campaigner against education cuts*

activity noun

1 [U] ■ *The streets were noisy and full of activity.*

action • **bustle** • **rush**

■ OPP **inactivity**
▶ (a) **great activity/action/bustle/rush**
▶ (a) **frantic activity/action/rush**

actor

▶ **be involved in/stop** the activity/
action

2 [C] ■ ideas for classroom activities

occupation • pursuit • exercise •
project • venture

▶ a **worthwhile** activity/
occupation/pursuit/exercise/
project/venture
▶ **set up/run/support** a/an activity/
project/venture
▶ **carry out/supervise** a/an activity/
exercise/project
● **ACTIVITY, PURSUIT OR OCCUPATION?**
Activity can relate to business,
government, the military,
education or sport and leisure. An
occupation can be a gentle activity
to pass the time, such as *knitting,
walking in the countryside* or
watching people. **Pursuit** is used for
sporting, cultural or intellectual
activities.

actor, actress noun [C]

■ *She is one of the country's leading
actors.*

performer • artist • comedian •
entertainer | *esp. AmE* movie star |
BrE usu. film star | *esp. BrE* artiste

▶ a **young** actor/actress/performer/
artist/comedian/entertainer/
artiste
▶ a **famous** actor/actress/
performer/artist/comedian/
entertainer/movie star/film star
▶ a/an **talented/aspiring** actor/
actress/performer/artist/
comedian/entertainer

actual adj.

1 [only before noun] ■ in actual fact

real • true

▶ a real/ the actual/ the true **reason**
▶ the real/actual/true **cost** of sth

2 [only before noun] ■ What were his
actual words?

very • exact • precise

▶ the actual/very/exact/precise
moment
▶ sb's actual/very/exact **words**
▶ the actual/exact/precise **nature** of
sth

adapt verb [T]

■ adapt equipment for disabled people

alter • modify • tailor • vary •
change • adjust

▶ adapt/alter/modify/tailor/change
sth **for** sb
▶ adapt/alter/modify/change/
adjust your **behaviour**
▶ adapt/vary/change/adjust your
routine

▶ adapt/alter/modify/adjust
equipment

add verb [T]

■ Add these numbers together.

count • total • calculate • work
out • tally | *AmE* figure | *BrE, infml* **tot
sth up** | *infml* compute

■ OPP take away, subtract
▶ add/count/total/tally/tot **up**
▶ add/count up/total up/
calculate/work out/tally/figure/
tot up/compute up **how much/
many**
▶ add up/calculate/work out/
figure/tot up/compute the **cost/
amount** (of sth)
▶ add/count/total/calculate/
work out/tally/tot up/compute
sb's **score**

add up to sth phrasal verb

■ The numbers add up to exactly 100.

amount to sth • make • number |
esp. busin. total

▶ add up to/make a **total**
▶ add up to/amount to/make/
number/total **50/3 million, etc.**
▶ add up to/amount to/make/total
$250/75%
● **WHICH WORD? Amount to sth** and
total focus more on the number/
amount; **add up to sth** and
number focus more on the process
of arriving at the result. **Amount to
sth** and **total** are used esp. when
describing the performance of a
company or business. **Number** usu.
refers to people, and **total** can also
be used in this way:
✔*The crew numbered/totalled
sixteen.* ✗ *The crew amounted to/
added up to sixteen.*

adequate adj.

■ The room was small but adequate.

acceptable • satisfactory •
reasonable • decent • respectable •
solid • sound | *esp. spoken* all right •
not bad | *infml, esp. spoken* OK

■ OPP inadequate
▶ adequate/acceptable/
satisfactory/reasonable/all right/
not bad/OK **for** sb/sth
▶ a/an adequate/acceptable/
satisfactory/reasonable/decent/
respectable **level/degree/
standard**
▶ a/an adequate/acceptable/
satisfactory/reasonable/decent/
respectable **performance**
▶ The **level/standard/performance**
is all right/not bad/OK.

admiration noun [U]

■ I have great admiration for her as a
poet.

respect • awe • recognition • appreciation | *fml* esteem

▶ admiration/respect/recognition **for** sb
▶ do sth **in** admiration/awe/ recognition/appreciation
▶ win/gain/deserve admiration/ respect/recognition
● ADMIRATION OR RESPECT? **Admiration** suggests that you like sb and would like to be like them. You can have **respect** for sb even if you do not like them: *She had a lot of respect for him as an actor, but she didn't like the way he behaved in public.*

admire verb [T]
■ *I admire your determination.*

look up to sb • respect • be/stand in awe of sb/sth | *fml* esteem

▶ admire/look up to/respect/ esteem sb **as/for** sth
▶ admire/respect **the way** sb does sth
● ADMIRE OR RESPECT? You can **admire** a person or their good qualities, but not their opinions. You can **respect** a person or their opinions, but not their good qualities:
✓*I really admire her (for her) courage.* ✗ ~~I admire Jack's opinion on most subjects.~~
✓*I respect Jack's opinion on most subjects.* • *I respect him for his honesty.* ✗ ~~I respect his honesty.~~

admit verb

1 [I, T] ■ *Admit it! You were terrified!*

confess • recognize • accept • concede • acknowledge • grant

■ OPP deny
▶ admit/confess **to** sth
▶ admit/confess/concede sth **to** sb
▶ admit/confess/recognize/accept/ concede/acknowledge/grant **that...**
▶ It is/was (generally) admitted/ recognized/accepted/conceded/ acknowledged/granted **that...**
● ADMIT OR CONCEDE? When sb **admits** sth, they agree that sth wrong or bad has happened, often sth that relates to their own actions; when sb **concedes** sth, they accept unwillingly that a fact or statement is true: *She admits to being strict with her children.* • *He was forced to concede (that) there might be difficulties.*

2 [I, T] ■ *She admitted to the theft.*

confess • own up

■ OPP deny
▶ admit/confess/own up **to** sth
▶ admit/confess/own up **that...**

adopt verb [I, T]
■ *She adopted her sister's child.*

take sb in • bring sb up | *esp. AmE* raise | *esp. BrE* foster

▶ adopt/take in/bring up/raise/ foster a **child**
▶ adopt/bring up/raise a **daughter/ son/family/baby**

adult noun [C]
■ *Can't you two act like civilized adults?*

grown-up

■ OPP child, minor
▶ act/behave/talk/eat **like** a/an adult/grown-up
▶ a **responsible** adult/grown-up
● ADULT OR GROWN-UP? **Grown-up** is often used by or to children: *Ask a grown-up to help you.*

adult adj.
■ *preparing young people for adult life*

grown • grown-up • mature

■ OPP juvenile, childish
▶ a/an adult/grown/mature **man/ woman**
▶ a grown-up/mature **child/boy/ girl**
● ADULT OR MATURE? **Adult** most often refers to physical development; **mature** most often refers to mental development: *an adult male* • *adult education* (= for adults, not children) • *a mature conversation/attitude* (= sensible, not childish)

advance noun [C, U]
■ *recent advances in medical science*

progress • development • breakthrough

▶ (a/an) advance/progress/ development/breakthrough **in** sth
▶ (a) scientific/technical/ technological/political advance/ progress/development/ breakthrough
▶ (a/an) economic/social advance/ progress/development

advance verb

1 [I] ■ *The army was given the order to advance.*

move • go | *fml* proceed

▶ advance/move/go/proceed **from... to...**
▶ advance/move/go/proceed **to/ towards** sb/sth

2 [I] ■ *Medical science has advanced considerably in recent years.*

progress • develop • improve

► advance/progress/develop **towards/beyond** sth
► advance/progress/develop/improve **rapidly/slowly/steadily**

advanced adj.

■ *a technologically advanced society*

modern • up-to-date • state of the art • futuristic • avant-garde

■ OPP **primitive**
► a/an advanced/modern/up-to-date/state of the art/futuristic/avant-garde **design**
► advanced/modern/up-to-date/state of the art/futuristic **technology**
► advanced/modern/up-to-date/state of the art **techniques**
● ADVANCED OR MODERN? **Advanced** is used esp. in the contexts of technology and economics; **modern** is used in the contexts of technology, society, art, fashion and ideas.

advantage noun

1 [sing.] ■ *Being tall gave him an advantage over the other players.*

edge • lead • the upper hand • head start

■ OPP **disadvantage**
► an advantage/an edge/a lead/the upper hand/a head start **over** sb/sth
► an advantage/an edge/a lead/the upper hand/a head start **in** sth
► **have/give** sb an advantage/an edge/a lead/the upper hand/a head start

2 [C, U] ■ *the advantages of having a degree*

benefit • strength • good • asset • good point | *infml* **plus**

■ OPP **disadvantage**
► some/any/no advantage/benefit **in** sth
► be **to** sb's advantage/benefit
► **considerable/great/real/relative** advantages/benefits/strengths/good/assets
● ADVANTAGE OR BENEFIT? A **benefit** is sth that you get or that comes from sth that you do. An **advantage** is sth that a person, thing, plan or action has as a quality.

advertise verb [T, I]

■ *The cruise was advertised as 'the journey of a lifetime'.*

market • promote • publicize | *infml* **push • plug** | *infml, disapprov.* **hype** | *busin.* **merchandise**

► advertise/market/promote/push/plug/hype/merchandise sth **as** sth

► advertise/market/promote/publicize/push/plug/hype/merchandise a **product**
► advertise/market/promote/publicize/plug/hype a **book/film/movie**
► advertise/publicize a/an **event**
► advertise/promote/publicize a/an **fact**
● ADVERTISE OR PUBLICIZE? People usu. **advertise** jobs or events in print, e.g. in newspapers, notices or on the Internet. People **publicize** events or information by talking about them or holding special events, which are then reported on TV, in newspapers or on the Internet.

advertisement noun [C]

■ *I saw your advertisement in the paper.*

publicity • commercial • promotion • blurb | *esp. BrE* **trailer** | *infml* **plug • ad** | *BrE, infml* **advert**

► (a/an) advertisement/publicity/commercial/promotion/blurb/trailer/plug/ad/advert **for** sth
► (a) **TV/television/radio/cinema** advertisement/commercial/promotion/ad/advert
► **run/show** a/an advertisement/commercial/trailer/ad/advert
► **put/place/take out** an advertisement/ad/advert

advice noun [U]

■ *Let me give you some advice.*

guidance • tip | *BrE* **counselling** | *AmE* **counseling**

► advice/guidance/tips/counselling **on** sth
► **professional** advice/guidance/counselling
► **give sb** advice/guidance/a tip/counselling

advise verb [T, I]

■ *I'd advise you not to tell him.*

recommend • urge | *fml* **advocate**

► advise/recommend/urge/advocate **that...**
► advise/recommend/urge **sb to do** sth
► advise/recommend/advocate **doing** sth
► **strongly** advise/recommend/advocate sth
● ADVISE OR RECOMMEND? **Advise** is stronger than **recommend**. Use **advise about** sb in a position of authority:
✔*Police are advising fans without tickets to stay away.* ✗ ~~Police are recommending fans without tickets to stay.~~
Use **recommend** about possible benefits; use **advise** about possible dangers:

✔ I recommend reading the book before seeing the movie. ✗ ~~I advise reading the book before seeing the movie.~~

✔ I would advise against going out on your own. ✗ ~~I would recommend going out on your own.~~

adviser (also advisor) noun [C]

■ an adviser on environmental issues

consultant • aide • mentor • guide | esp. BrE **counsellor** | AmE usu. **counselor**

- ▶ a/an adviser/consultant/aide/ mentor to sb
- ▶ a/an adviser/consultant on sth
- ▶ a **political** adviser/consultant/ aide/mentor
- ▶ a **spiritual** adviser/mentor/guide/ counsellor
- ● ADVISER OR CONSULTANT? An **adviser** may be employed permanently by an organization; a **consultant** is usu. brought in to work on a project for a fixed period.

affair noun

1 [C] ■ current affairs ■ The debate was a pretty disappointing affair.

event • incident • episode • experience • development • business • proceedings • phenomenon | fml **occurrence** • **eventuality**

- ▶ the **whole** affair/event/incident/ episode/experience/business/ phenomenon/proceedings
- ▶ a **strange** affair/event/incident/ experience/development/ business/phenomenon/ occurrence

2 [C] ■ They had a passionate affair.

relationship • love affair • romance • liaison

- ▶ a/an affair/relationship/love affair/romance/liaison with sb
- ▶ a/an affair/relationship/love affair/romance/liaison between A and B
- ▶ have a/an affair/relationship/love affair/romance/liaison
- ● AFFAIR OR LOVE AFFAIR? A **love affair** is usu. more romantic than an **affair** and need not involve sex.

affect verb [T]

■ How will these changes affect us?

influence • involve • concern • act on sth • leave your/a/its mark | BrE **colour** | AmE **color** | esp. journ. or busin. **impact**

- ▶ affect/influence **what** happens
- ▶ affect/influence **how/why/ when/where** sth happens
- ▶ affect/influence/colour sb's **judgement/attitude**

affection noun [U, sing.]

■ Children need lots of love and affection.

love • liking • tenderness • care • devotion • attachment • friendship • intimacy • sentiment

- ▶ affection/love/liking/tenderness/ care/friendship **for** sb
- ▶ affection/love/tenderness/ devotion/intimacy **between** A and B
- ● **show** affection/love/tenderness/ devotion/friendship
- ● AFFECTION OR LOVE? **Love** can be a mild feeling or a very strong one:
  ✔ Bob sends his love (= best wishes/ regards). • There is nothing greater than a mother's love for her children. ✗ ~~There is nothing greater than a mother's affection for her children.~~
  Affection is a gentle feeling, often shown in the way sb talks to, looks at or touches sb else:
  ✔ She spoke/treated him/looked at him/hugged him with great affection.

afraid adj.

■ He was afraid of the dark.

frightened • scared • terrified • alarmed • nervous • paranoid • petrified • intimidated • cowardly • apprehensive | infml **chicken** | fml **fearful**

- ● OPP **brave, confident**, (fml) **unafraid**
- ▶ afraid/frightened/scared/ terrified/nervous/petrified/ apprehensive/fearful **of** sb/sth
- ▶ frightened/scared/alarmed/ nervous/paranoid/apprehensive/ fearful **about** sth
- ▶ afraid/frightened/scared/ terrified/alarmed/petrified/ apprehensive/fearful **that...**
- ▶ afraid/frightened/scared **to do** sth
- ● AFRAID, FRIGHTENED OR SCARED? **Scared** is more informal, more common in speech, and often describes small fears. **Afraid** cannot come before a noun:
  ✔ a frightened child / a scared expression ✗ ~~an afraid child/ expression~~

be against sb/sth phrase

■ I'm strongly against animal testing.

opposed • hostile • resistant | fml **antagonistic**

- ■ OPP **be for sb/sth**
- ▶ opposed/hostile/resistant/ antagonistic to sb/sth
- ▶ hostile/antagonistic **towards** sb/ sth
- ▶ against/opposed to/hostile to/ resistant to **the idea of** sth

age

age noun [C, U]

1 ■ *children of different ages*

generation • age group

▶ people **of** your own age/
generation
▶ people **of** all ages/generations/
age groups
▶ the **younger/older** generation/
age group

2 [C] ■ *in the nuclear age*

era • period • time • day • century • generation | *fml* **epoch**

▶ **in the...** age/era/period
▶ **(the) modern** age/era/period/
times/day
▶ the **end of a/an** age/era/period/
century/epoch
● **WHICH WORD?** **Age, era** and **epoch** are used more for a period in history; **times** and **days** are often used for the present: *modern times • these days*

agent noun [C]
■ *a secret agent*

spy • double agent | *esp. journ.* **mole**

▶ a/an **agent/spy/double agent for** sb
▶ a/an **enemy/foreign/**
government agent/spy
▶ **work/act/recruit** sb **as a/an**
agent/spy/double agent
● **AGENT OR SPY?** An **agent** usu. works for a government; a **spy** can work for a government, commercial company, political organization, etc.

ages noun [pl.] *(esp. BrE, infml)*
■ *I waited for ages.*

years • months • hours | *infml* **an eternity** | *esp. BrE, infml* **an age** | *esp. BrE, fml* **aeon** | *esp. AmE, fml* **eon**

▶ **for** ages/years/months/hours/an
eternity/an age/aeons
▶ ages/years/months/hours/an
eternity/aeons **ago**
▶ **spend/take/wait** ages/years/
months/hours/an eternity/an age

aggressive adj.

1 ■ *aggressive behaviour*

violent • hostile • warlike • militant

▶ aggressive/violent/hostile
towards sb/sth
▶ aggressive/violent/hostile
behaviour/feelings
▶ a/an aggressive/hostile/warlike/
militant **attitude**

2 ■ *They are very aggressive in their strategy.*

competitive • ambitious • vigorous | *often approv.* **forceful • assertive** | *infml, disapprov.* **pushy**

▶ aggressive/competitive/
ambitious/assertive **in** sth
▶ aggressive/vigorous/forceful/
assertive **in doing** sth
▶ a/an aggressive/competitive/
vigorous/forceful/assertive
approach/manner
▶ a/an aggressive/competitive/
ambitious/forceful/assertive
person
● **WHICH WORD? Aggressive** and **pushy** often describe sb who is trying too hard and may appear rude. **Forceful** and **assertive** describe sb who is strong and confident, but in a more respectful and appropriate way.

agree verb

1 [I, T] ■ *'That's true,' she agreed.*

fml **concur**

■ **OPP disagree**
▶ agree/concur **with** sb/sth
▶ agree/concur **that...**
▶ agree/concur **with** sb's
assessment/conclusion/idea/
view

2 [I, T] ■ *I asked for a pay rise and she agreed.*

accept • approve • go along with sb/sth • grant | *fml* **consent • acquiesce**

■ **OPP refuse**
▶ agree/consent/acquiesce **to** sth
▶ agree/accept/approve/go
along with/consent to a **plan/**
scheme/proposal
▶ agree/accept/approve/go
along with/acquiesce in a **decision**
▶ agree/accept/approve/grant a
request

3 ■ *Can we agree a price?*

settle • negotiate • do a deal • understand • broker • hammer sth out | *infml* **thrash sth out** | *fml* **conclude**

▶ agree/settle/negotiate/do a deal/
broker/hammer out/thrash out/
conclude sth **with** sb
▶ agree/be understood **that...**
▶ agree/settle/negotiate/do/
broker/hammer out/conclude a
deal
▶ negotiate/broker/hammer out/
thrash out/conclude an
agreement

agreement noun

1 [C] ■ *An agreement was reached between management and employees.*

deal • settlement • arrangement •
pact • bargain • understanding •
contract • treaty • accord •
convention

▶ a/an agreement/deal/settlement/
  arrangement/pact/bargain/
  understanding/contract/treaty/
  accord **with** sb
▶ a/an agreement/deal/
  arrangement.pact/bargain/
  understanding/contract/treaty/
  accord/convention **between** A
  and B
▶ reach a/an agreement/deal/
  settlement/arrangement/
  understanding
▶ a/an agreement/deal/settlement/
  arrangement/pact/
  understanding/treaty/accord/
  convention **on** sth
▶ a/an agreement/arrangement/
  pact/understanding **that**...
▶ a/an agreement/arrangement/
  pact/contract/treaty/accord **to
  do** sth
▶ reach a/an agreement/deal/
  settlement/arrangement/
  understanding

2 [U] ■ *Are we in agreement?*

consensus • consent • harmony •
unity • solidarity • unanimity | *fml*
accord

■ **OPP** disagreement
▶ **by** agreement/consensus/consent
▶ **in** agreement/harmony/unity/
  accord
▶ agreement/consensus/harmony/
  unity/solidarity/unanimity **among**
  people

3 [U] ■ *He still hopes to get his father's
agreement to the plan.*

consent • permission • acceptance •
approval • blessing | *infml* thumbs
up | *fml* assent • acquiescence

■ **OPP** refusal
▶ agreement/consent/assent **to** sb
▶ permission/approval/the thumbs
  up **for** sth
▶ **give** your/the agreement/
  consent/permission/approval/
  blessing/thumbs up

aid *noun*

1 [U] ■ *£8 million in foreign aid has
been promised.*

relief • help • handout • charity •
welfare | *BrE* social security

▶ government/state aid/relief/
  help/handouts/welfare
▶ emergency/direct/immediate/
  financial/medical aid/relief/help
▶ **get/receive** aid/relief/help/
  handouts/charity/welfare/social
  security
● **AID OR RELIEF?** **Aid** is used esp.
about money given to countries in
financial need. **Relief** refers to
money, medicine, food, etc. given
in response to a sudden emergency
such as a war or natural disaster.

2 [U] ■ *Two other swimmers came to
his aid.*

help • support | *fml* assistance

▶ **without** aid/help/support/
  assistance
▶ **with** the aid/help/support/
  assistance **of** sb/sth
▶ **get/call for/enlist/come to** sb's
  aid/help/support/assistance

aim *noun* [C]

■ *Our main aim is to increase sales.*

purpose • intention • objective •
goal • idea • point | *fml or law* intent

▶ **with** the aim/purpose/intention/
  objective/goal/idea/intent **of**
  doing sth
▶ **have** a/an aim/purpose/
  intention/objective/goal/point/
  intent
▶ **achieve** a/an aim/purpose/
  objective/goal
● **AIM OR PURPOSE?** Your **aim** in
doing sth is what you want to
achieve; your **purpose** is your
reason for doing it.

aim *verb*

1 [T, i] ■ *We aim to be there by six.*

plan • intend • mean | *fml* propose

▶ aim/plan/intend/mean/propose
  to do sth
▶ intend/propose **doing** sth

2 [T] ■ *measures aimed at preventing
crime*

be designed • be intended • be
meant

▶ be designed/intended **for/as** sth
▶ be designed/intended/meant **to
  do/be/have**, etc. sth
▶ be specifically/primarily/mainly/
  principally/largely aimed at/
  designed for/intended for sth

3 [T, i] ■ *He aimed the gun at her
head.*

point • direct • turn • focus

▶ aim/point/direct (sth) **at** sb
▶ aim/point/direct/focus **a** camera
▶ aim/direct/focus (a) **light**
▶ aim/point **a gun at** sb
▶ turn **a gun on** sb

4 ■ *be aimed at a young audience*

target • direct • *esp. busin.* pitch | *fml*
address

▶ be aimed/target sth/direct sth/
  pitch sth **at** sb/sth
▶ primarily aimed at/targeted at/
  directed at/pitched at/addressed
  to sb/sth
▶ **directly** aimed at/targeted at/
  pitched at/addressed to sb/sth

alarm noun

1 [U] ■ *a feeling of alarm*

fright • fear • panic
- ▶ in alarm/fright/fear/panic
- ▶ alarm/fear/panic **that...**
- ▶ be filled with alarm/fear/panic

2 [C] ■ *raise the alarm*

warning • alert | *fml* **caution**
- ▶ a flood/bomb/health warning/alert
- ▶ sound a/an alarm/warning/alert/note of caution

3 [C, usu. sing.] ■ *a burglar alarm*

siren • horn
- ▶ hear a/an alarm/siren/horn
- ▶ a/an alarm/siren/horn **sounds**

alarm verb [T]

■ *It alarms me that no one takes this problem seriously.*

scare • frighten • startle • worry • trouble • disturb • concern • bother
- ▶ It alarms/scares/frightens/startles/worries/troubles/disturbs/concerns/bothers me **that...**
- ▶ It alarms/scares/frightens/startles/worries/troubles/disturbs/concerns/bothers me **to** think, see, etc.

alarmed adj.

■ *She was alarmed at the prospect of travelling alone.*

scared • frightened • afraid • startled • worried • concerned • disturbed • nervous • anxious
- ▶ alarmed/startled/disturbed **by** sb/sth
- ▶ scared/frightened/afraid/nervous **of** sb/sth
- ▶ alarmed/scared/frightened/afraid/startled/worried/concerned/disturbed/nervous/anxious **that...**

alarming adj.

■ *There has been an alarming increase in the disease.*

worrying • disturbing • frightening • unsettling • unnerving | *infml* **scary**

■ OPP **reassuring**
- ▶ alarming/worrying/disturbing/frightening/unsettling/unnerving/scary **for** sb
- ▶ a/an alarming/worrying/frightening/unsettling/scary **prospect**
- ▶ a/an alarming/worrying/disturbing/frightening/scary **thought**
- ▶ a/an alarming/disturbing/frightening/unsettling/unnerving/scary **experience**

alcohol noun [U]

■ *There was no alcohol at the party.*

drink | *esp. BrE* **spirits** | *esp. AmE* **liquor** | *infml* **booze**
- ▶ drink alcohol/spirits/liquor/booze
- ▶ turn to/keep off/stay off (the) alcohol/drink/booze
- ▶ a/an alcohol/drink/booze **problem**

alive adj.

■ *Is he alive or dead?*

living • live | *fml* **animate**

■ OPP **dead**
- ▶ a living/live animal/plant/bird
- ▶ a living/live organism/creature
- ▶ still alive/living
- ● ALIVE, LIVING OR LIFE? Alive is never used before a noun:
  ✓ *all living things* ✗ *all alive things*
  Living can be used after *be* but is not usu. used after other linking verbs:
  ✓ *She stole just to stay alive.* ✗ *She stole just to stay living.*
  Use living to talk about people/animals in a wide context:
  ✓ *the finest living pianist* (= out of all pianists alive today)
  Use live to talk about animals or a person in a particular situation:
  ✓ *I need to talk to a live person* (= not a recorded message).

allocate verb [T]

■ *They allocated more places to mature students last year.*

set • assign • allot • share sth out • provide • issue
- ▶ allocate/set/assign/allot/provide/issue sth **for** sth
- ▶ allocate/assign/allot/issue sth **to** sb
- ▶ allocate/assign/allot/share out/provide **resources**
- ▶ allocate/assign/allot (a) **room/space/seats/time/day/task**
- ● ALLOCATE OR ALLOT? Allocate is used more in business-related contexts. Allot is used more in general, everyday situations: *allocate money/funds/a percentage of the budget • allot space/classrooms/tasks*

allow verb

1 [T] ■ *I'm not allowed to stay out late.*

let • entitle • authorize • license • clear • grant | *infml* **OK/okay** | *fml* **permit • sanction • empower**

■ OPP **forbid**
- ▶ allow/entitle/authorize/license/clear/permit/empower sb **to do** sth

▶ let sb do sth
▶ allow/let/permit **yourself** sth/(to) do sth

2 [T] ■ *Wear clothing that allows easy movement.*

enable ◆ *fml* **permit**

■ OPP **prevent**
▶ allow/enable/permit sb **to do sth**
▶ allow/enable/permit **access**
▶ allow/enable/permit the **creation/development/expansion** of sth
● ALLOW OR PERMIT? Permit is more formal than **allow** and is used esp. in the fixed phrases *if time permits* and *weather permitting*.

all right *adj.*

1 [not usu. before noun] *(esp. spoken)* ■ *I hope the kids are all right.*

safe ◆ **unharmed** ◆ **alive and well** ◆ **unhurt** ◆ **uninjured** ◆ **secure** ◆ **out of harm's way** | *infml, esp. spoken* **OK** ◆ **in one piece** | *written* **unscathed**

▶ remain all right/safe/unharmed/ alive and well/secure/ok/in one piece/unscathed
▶ **perfectly** all right/safe/secure/OK
● ALL RIGHT OR OK? Both are rather informal but OK is slightly more informal than all right.

2 [not before noun] *(esp. spoken)* ■ *I'm feeling all right now.*

strong ◆ **healthy** ◆ **fine** ◆ **well** | *infml, esp. spoken* **OK** | *esp. BrE* **fit** | *AmE, infml* **good**

▶ all right/OK/fit **for** sth
▶ all right/OK/fit **to do** sth
▶ **feel/look** all right/strong/ healthy/fine/well/OK/fit/good
● ALL RIGHT OR OK? These words are slightly less positive than the other words in this group. OK is more informal than all right.

3 [not before noun] *(esp. spoken)* ■ *Is the coffee all right?*

acceptable ◆ **satisfactory** ◆ **fair** ◆ **reasonable** ◆ **adequate** | *esp. spoken* **fine** ◆ **not bad** | *infml, esp. spoken* **OK** | *fml* **in order**

▶ all right/acceptable/satisfactory/ reasonable/adequate/fine/not bad/OK **for** sb/sth
▶ all right/acceptable/satisfactory/ satisfactory/fine/OK/in order **to do** sth
▶ all right/acceptable/satisfactory/ fair/reasonable/fine/OK/in order **that...**
▶ **just (about)** all right/acceptable/ adequate/OK

ally *noun* [C]

■ *a friend and ally of the prime minister*

associate ◆ **colleague** ◆ **partner** ◆ **friend** ◆ **contact** ◆ **collaborator** | *BrE, infml* **mate** | *AmE, infml* **buddy**

■ OPP **enemy**
▶ a **close** ally/associate/colleague/ partner/friend/contact/ collaborator
▶ an **old** ally/associate/colleague/ friend/mate/buddy
▶ a **business** ally/associate/ colleague/partner/contact
▶ a **political** ally/associate/ colleague/contact

almost *adv.*

■ *Dinner's almost ready.*

nearly ◆ **virtually** ◆ **more or less** ◆ **not quite** | *esp. spoken* **practically** ◆ **pretty much/well**

▶ almost/nearly/virtually/more or less/not quite/practically/about/ pretty much **every**
▶ almost/nearly/virtually/more or less/ practically/about/pretty much **any/anything**
▶ almost/nearly/virtually/more or less/practically **always**
▶ almost/virtually/more or less/ practically **impossible**
● ALMOST OR NEARLY? In many cases you can use either word. **Almost**, but not **nearly**, can be used before words like *any, anybody, anything, no, nobody* and *never*: They'll eat almost anything.
Nearly is more common with numbers: There were nearly 200 people in the room.

alone *adj., adv.*

■ *She loved to walk alone by the sea.*

on your own ◆ **by yourself/ yourselves** ◆ **solitary** ◆ **solo** | *fml* **unattended** ◆ **unaided** ◆ **unaccompanied** | *often approv.* **single-handed/single-handedly**

▶ **do** sth alone/on your own/by yourself/unaided/single-handed
▶ **live** alone/on your own/by yourself
▶ **all** alone/on your own/by yourself
▶ a solitary/lonely **existence/life/ walk**

alter *verb*

1 [T] ■ *It doesn't alter the way I feel.*

change ◆ **adapt** ◆ **tailor** ◆ **vary** ◆ **adjust** ◆ **modify** ◆ **revise** ◆ **shift** ◆ **amend**

▶ alter/change/adapt/tailor/ adjust/modify/revise/amend sth **for** sb/sth
▶ alter/change/adapt/adjust/ modify/revise/amend a **plan/ story**

▶ alter / change / vary / shift **the emphasis**

● **ALTER OR CHANGE?** Change has a much wider range and many particular collocations such as *change your mind/name, change colour/tack* and *change the subject.* Change often suggests a complete change; **alter** can suggest a smaller change: *The law needs to be altered* (= changed slightly in order to improve it). ◆ *The law needs to be changed* (= changed completely or got rid of).

2 [I] ■ *Prices did not significantly alter last year.*

---

change ◆ **vary** ◆ **fluctuate** | *esp. journ.* **shift** ◆ **swing**

▶ change / vary / fluctuate / shift / swing **dramatically**
▶ change / vary / fluctuate / shift **significantly**
▶ **hardly/never** alter / change / vary
● **ALTER OR CHANGE?** Alter is often used when sth has changed only slightly or not at all: *The party's policies have scarcely altered, but public opinion has.*
Change can suggest a complete change to sth important: *Her life changed completely when she won the lottery.*

---

alternative *noun* [C]
■ *We had no alternative but to* (= had to) *fire him.*

option ◆ **choice** ◆ **possibility**

▶ a **real/realistic/practical** alternative / option / choice / possibility
▶ a/an **good/acceptable/ reasonable** alternative / option / choice
▶ **have no** alternative / option / choice **(but to** do sth)
▶ **look at/limit** the alternatives / options / choices / possibilities
● **ALTERNATIVE, CHOICE OR OPTION?** Alternative is slightly more formal than **option** or **choice**, and is more frequently used to talk about choosing between two things rather than several.

---

amaze *verb* [T]
■ *The size of the place amazed her.*

astonish ◆ **astound** ◆ **stagger** ◆ **bowl sb over** ◆ **surprise** ◆ **startle** ◆ **stun** | *written* **take sb aback**

▶ It amazes sb / astonishes sb / astounds sb / staggers sb / surprises sb / startles sb / stuns sb / bowls sb over / takes sb aback
▶ **What** amazes / astonishes / astounds / staggers / surprises / startles / stuns sb **is...**

▶ amaze / astonish / astound / surprise / startle / stun sb **that...**
▶ amaze / astonish / astound / surprise / startle / stun sb **to know/ find/learn/see/hear...**
● **AMAZE OR ASTONISH?** In most cases you can use either word, but for sth that both surprises you and makes you feel ashamed, use **astonish**: *He was astonished by his own stupidity.*

---

amazing *adj.*
■ *I made an amazing discovery today.*

astonishing ◆ **awesome** ◆ **breathtaking** ◆ **miraculous** ◆ **sensational** ◆ **remarkable** ◆ **extraordinary** ◆ **exceptional** ◆ **phenomenal** ◆ **surprising** | *infml* **staggering** ◆ **stunning** ◆ **incredible** ◆ **unbelievable**

▶ amazing / astonishing / miraculous / remarkable / extraordinary / not surprising / staggering / incredible / unbelievable **that...**
▶ amazing / astonishing / remarkable / extraordinary / surprising / staggering / incredible / unbelievable **how...**
▶ a/an amazing / astonishing / awesome / remarkable / extraordinary / exceptional / staggering / incredible **achievement**
▶ a/an amazing / astonishing / miraculous / astounding / remarkable / extraordinary / phenomenal / stunning / incredible **success**

---

ambition *noun*
1 [C] ■ *Her ambition is to become a writer.*

dream ◆ **aspiration** ◆ **hope** | *esp. written* **desire** ◆ **wish**

▶ aspirations / hopes / a desire / a wish **for** sth
▶ an ambition / aspirations / the desire / the wish **to do** sth
▶ **have** an ambition / a dream / aspirations / hope / a desire / a wish
● **AMBITION OR ASPIRATION?** Aspirations are more general than **ambitions**. An **ambition** is often connected with success in your career.

2 [U] ■ *a man of driving ambition*

ambition ◆ **drive**

▶ the ambition / drive **to do/be** sth
▶ **personal** ambition / drive
▶ **have/lack** ambition / drive

---

amount *noun* [C, U]
■ *huge amounts of data* ■ *a bill for the full amount*

quantity ◆ **number** ◆ **sum** ◆ **volume**

▶ the amount / quantity / number / volume **of** sth

► a/an amount/quantity/volume of **information**
► a/an amount/sum of **money**
► a/an small/reasonable/ considerable/large/huge amount/quantity/number/sum/ volume
● AMOUNT, QUANTITY OR NUMBER? **Amount** is usu. used with uncountable nouns; **number** is used with plural countable nouns: *a large amount of time/money/ information* ♦ *a number of books/ dogs/people*
Quantity can be used with both countable and uncountable nouns and is slightly more formal.

amount to sth *phrasal verb*
■ *His earnings are said to amount to £400 000 per annum.*

add up to sth • run to sth • number • be • make • equal | *esp. busin.* **total**

► amount to/add up to/run to/ number/equal/be/make/total 50/3 million, etc.
► amount to/add up to/run to/ equal/be/make/total $250/75%
► **profits/scores** amount to/add up to/total sth
► **income** amounts to/adds up to/ totals sth
● WHICH WORD? **Amount to sth** and **total** focus more on the number/ amount; **add up to sth** and **number** focus more on the process of arriving at the result. **Amount to sth** and **total** are used esp. when describing the performance of a company or business. **Number** usu. refers to people, and **total** can also be used in this way:
✓*The crew numbered/totalled sixteen.* ✗ *The crew amounted to/ added up to sixteen.*

amuse *verb* [T]
■ *The visitors amused themselves with sightseeing and picnics.*

entertain

► amuse/entertain sb **with** sth
► keep sb **amused/entertained**

amusing *adj.*
■ *He writes such amusing letters.*

funny • entertaining • witty • humorous • comic • light-hearted • hilarious

► a/an amusing/funny/ entertaining/witty/humorous/ comic/light-hearted **story**
► a/an amusing/funny/ entertaining/witty/humorous/ light-hearted **speech**
► a/an amusing/funny/witty **guy/ man/woman**
► a/an amusing/funny/hilarious **joke**
● WHICH WORD? **Amusing** is the most

general of these words and can be used to describe events, activities and occasions:
✓*an amusing party/game/evening* ✗ *a funny/humorous/comic party/ game/evening*
Funny can describe people, jokes and stories, things that happen or anything that makes people laugh. **Comic** is used esp. to talk about writing and drama. **Humorous** is not quite as strong as **funny** or **comic**.

analyse *(BrE)* *(AmE* analyze*)* *verb* [T]
■ *We need to analyse what went wrong.*

examine • review • study • take stock of | *esp. spoken* **go into sth**

► analyse/examine/review/study/ take stock of/go into **what/how/ whether…**
► analyse/examine/review/study/ take stock of the **situation**
► analyse/examine/review/study a/ an **proposal/idea**

analysis *noun* [U, C]
■ *The information is based on statistical analysis.*

research • examination • study • exploration • enquiry/inquiry | *fml* **scrutiny**

► **scientific** analysis/research/ examination/study/exploration/ enquiry/scrutiny
► **carry out/conduct/undertake** (a/ an) analysis/research/ examination/study/exploration
► **do** analysis/research/a study
► analysis/research/examination/ the study/exploration/scrutiny **reveals** sth
● ANALYSIS OR RESEARCH? When you do **research** you try to find out new information; when you do **analysis** you look in more detail at the information you already have, in order to understand it better.

analyst *noun* [C]
■ *City analysts forecast pre-tax profits of £40 billion.*

commentator • critic • observer | *esp. journ.* **watcher**

► a/an analyst/commentator/critic **for** sb/sth
► a/an **media/industry** analyst/ commentator/observer/watcher
► a/an **political/military** analyst/ commentator/observer
● WHICH WORD? **Analysts, critics** and **commentators** are usu. employed by an organization to do a job: *The*

bank employs a team of investment analysts.
Observers and **watchers** are informed people who may be paid to give advice, but are not usu. employed on a regular basis.

ancient *adj.*
■ *an ancient monument*

old • historic • antique • long-standing

■ OPP **modern**
▶ a/an ancient/old/historic **building/monument**
▶ an ancient/old/antique **chair/clock/coin**
▶ a/an ancient/old/long-standing **tradition/belief/method/problem**

anger *noun* [U]
■ *Jan slammed the door in anger.*

rage • outrage • indignation | *written* **fury**

▶ do sth in anger/rage/outrage/indignation/fury
▶ be filled/shake/tremble/seethe with anger/rage/outrage/indignation/fury
▶ express anger/rage/outrage/indignation/fury

anger *verb* [T]
■ *The question clearly angered him.*

infuriate • antagonize • outrage • incense • annoy • irritate • rile | *infml* **drive sb crazy/mad** | *taboo, slang* **piss sb off**

▶ What really angers/infuriates/incenses/annoys/irritates/riles/enrages me is...
▶ What drives me crazy/mad/pisses me off/is the way/the fact that...
▶ It infuriated/incensed/annoyed/irritated/riled/enraged him that...

angle *noun* [C]
■ *The plane came in at a steep angle.*

slope | *esp. BrE* **gradient** | *esp. AmE* **grade**

▶ at a/an angle/slope/gradient
▶ a slight/steep/gentle angle/slope/gradient

angry *adj.*
■ *Please don't be angry with me.*

indignant • irate • furious • incensed • outraged • fuming • seething • annoyed • irritated | *esp. BrE* **cross** | *esp. AmE, infml* **mad** | *written* **enraged** | *taboo, slang* **pissed off** | *AmE, taboo, slang* **pissed**

▶ angry/furious/annoyed/irritated/cross/pissed off **with** sb

▶ angry/indignant/furious/incensed/outraged/fuming/seething/annoyed/irritated/cross/mad/pissed off/pissed **at/about** sth
▶ angry/indignant/furious/incensed/outraged/cross/mad/pissed off/pissed **that...**
▶ get angry/annoyed/irritated/cross/mad/pissed off/pissed
● ANGRY OR MAD? **Mad** is the usual word for **angry** in informal *AmE*. When used in *BrE*, esp. in the phrase *go mad*, it can mean 'very angry': *Dad'll go mad when he sees what you've done.*

get **angry** *phrase*
■ *Please don't get angry with me. I'm trying my best.*

lose your temper • lose patience | *AmE, infml* **get mad** | *BrE, infml* **go mad • go berserk**

▶ get angry/lose your temper/lose patience/get mad **with** sb
▶ get angry/lose your temper/get mad/go mad **at** sth
▶ get angry/lose your temper **over** sth
● GET ANGRY OR LOSE YOUR TEMPER? If you **lose your temper** you show it in your behaviour: *She lost her temper and shouted at him.*
If you **get angry** the emphasis is more on your feelings and less on your behaviour.

animal *noun* [C]
■ *Strange animals inhabit the forest.*

creature • being • living thing | *old-fash. or fml* **beast** | *fml or biology* **organism**

▶ a living animal/creature/thing/being/organism
▶ a wild animal/creature/thing/beast
▶ a mythical creature/beast

anniversary *noun* [C]
■ *It's our wedding anniversary tomorrow.*

jubilee • birthday • commemoration

▶ a silver/golden/diamond anniversary/jubilee
▶ a first/second/fiftieth anniversary/birthday
▶ Happy Anniversary/Birthday!
● ANNIVERSARY OR BIRTHDAY? Your **birthday** is the day of the year on which you were born; an **anniversary** is a date that is an exact number of years after the date of an important event.

announce *verb* [T]
■ *Has our flight been announced yet?*

declare • state | fml proclaim • pronounce

- announce/declare/state/proclaim/pronounce sth **to** sb
- **It was** announced/declared/stated/proclaimed **that...**
- announce/declare/state/proclaim/pronounce sth **formally/officially**

● **ANNOUNCE OR DECLARE?** Announce is used more often for giving facts; **declare** is used more often for giving judgements:
  ✔ They haven't formally announced their engagement yet. ✗ ~~They haven't formally declared their engagement yet.~~
  ✔ The painting was declared to be a forgery. ✗ ~~The painting was declared to be a forgery.~~

annoy verb [T]
■ It really annoys me when people don't say thank you.

irritate • exasperate • frustrate • rile | infml **get on sb's nerves • bug** | BrE, infml **wind sb up** | fml **displease** | taboo, slang **piss sb off**

- It annoys me/irritates me/gets on my nerves/bugs me **that/when...**
- **What** annoys me/irritates me/frustrates me/riles me/gets on my nerves/bugs me/pisses me off **is...**
- **really** annoy sb/irritate sb/rile sb/get on sb's nerves/bug sb/wind sb up/piss sb off

annoyed adj.
■ I was annoyed with myself for giving in so easily.

irritated • exasperated | cross | esp. BrE **spoken put out** | taboo, slang **pissed off** | AmE, taboo, slang **pissed**

- annoyed/irritated/put out/pissed off/pissed **at** sth
- annoyed/cross/put out/pissed off/pissed **about** sth
- annoyed/irritated/exasperated/cross/pissed off/pissed **with** sb

● **ANNOYED OR IRRITATED?** You are usu. **irritated** by things other people do or say. You can be **annoyed** with yourself or at things you have to do.

annoying adj.
■ I find her untidy habits extremely annoying.

irritating • trying • frustrating • infuriating • maddening • galling | AmE, infml **pesky** | esp. written **tiresome**

- annoying/irritating/trying/frustrating/infuriating/galling/tiresome **for** sb
- a/an annoying/irritating/infuriating/pesky/tiresome **man**

- a/an annoying/irritating/infuriating/maddening/tiresome **habit**
- **find** sb/sth annoying/irritating/frustrating/infuriating/galling/tiresome

● **ANNOYING OR IRRITATING?** Irritating is often used to describe people and their habits; **annoying** is also used to describe facts and situations that make you feel annoyed.

answer noun

1 [C] ■ Have you had an answer to your letter?

reply • response • acknowledgement | written **retort**

- a/an answer/reply/response/retort **to** sb/sth
- a/an answer/reply/response/acknowledgement **from** sb
- **in** answer/reply/response **to** sb/sth
- a/an **sharp/angry/curt** reply/response/retort
- **give/write/elicit/produce/wait for** an answer/reply/response

● **ANSWER, REPLY OR RESPONSE?** Response is slightly more formal than answer and reply. It is used esp. in written or business English.

2 [C] ■ It's the answer to all our problems.

solution • key • resolution • remedy • way out | infml **fix**

- the answer/solution/key/resolution/remedy/fix **to** sth
- the answer/solution/remedy/fix **for** sth
- **find/provide** an answer/a solution/the key/a resolution/a remedy

answer verb [I, T]
■ You haven't answered my question.

reply • respond • write back • acknowledge | infml **get back to sb** | written **retort**

- reply/respond/write back/get back **to** sb/sth
- reply/respond/acknowledge sth/get back to sb/retort **with** sth
- answer/reply/respond/write back/retort **that...**
- answer/reply to/respond to/acknowledge a/an **question/letter/email**

● **ANSWER, RESPONSE OR REPLY?** You can answer sb/sth or just answer, but not 'answer to sb/sth'; you can reply/respond to sb/sth or just reply/respond, but not 'reply/respond to sth'. For some uses you can only use **answer:**

anticipate

✔ *answer the phone/door/sb's prayers* ✗ ~~reply/respond to the phone/the door/sb's prayers~~
You can *answer/respond to a call* but not 'reply to a call'.

anticipate verb

1 [T] ■ *We don't anticipate any major problems this year.*

expect • look forward to sth • bargain for/on sth | *fml* **await**

▶ anticipate/expect **that…**
▶ anticipate/look forward to/ bargain **on doing sth**
▶ anticipate/expect/look forward to/await **results/a reply**
▶ **eagerly** anticipate/look forward to/await **sth**
● ANTICIPATE OR EXPECT? **Anticipate** is slightly more formal than **expect**, and often used in business or official statements.

2 [T] (*fml*) ■ *Try and anticipate the questions the interviewer will ask.*

pre-empt | *fml* **forestall**

▶ anticipate/pre-empt **what…**
▶ anticipate/pre-empt/forestall a **problem/question/possibility/ plan**
▶ pre-empt/forestall **criticism/ discussion**

anxiety noun [U, C]

■ *Some patients experience high levels of anxiety.*

worry • unease • concern • agitation • angst • apprehension

▶ anxiety/worry/unease/concern/ angst/ apprehension **over/about** sth
▶ anxiety/worry/unease/concern/ apprehension **that…**
▶ **great/considerable/growing** anxiety/worry/unease/concern/ agitation/apprehension
▶ **cause** anxiety/unease/concern/ apprehension

anxious adj.

1 ■ *He grew increasingly anxious as time went on.*

worried • nervous • concerned • uneasy • disturbed • agitated • unsettled • bothered | *fml* **apprehensive • fearful** | *written* **troubled**

▶ anxious/worried/nervous/ concerned/uneasy/disturbed/ bothered/apprehensive/fearful/ troubled **about** sth
▶ anxious/worried/nervous/ concerned/disturbed/bothered/ apprehensive/fearful **that…**
▶ a/an anxious/worried/nervous/ concerned/uneasy/apprehensive/ troubled **look/smile**
● ANXIOUS, WORRIED OR NERVOUS? **Worried** is the most frequent word; **anxious** is more formal and can describe a stronger feeling. **Nervous** can describe sb's personality; **worried** describes feelings, not personality. **Anxious** describes feelings or personality.

2 ■ *There were a few anxious moments during the games.*

tense • stressful • strained • nerve-racking/nerve-wracking • worrying • unsettling • upsetting • painful | *esp. BrE* **fraught**

▶ a/an anxious/tense/stressful/ worrying/unsettling/upsetting/ painful/fraught **time**
▶ a/an anxious/tense **wait**

3 ■ *She was anxious to put the past behind her.*

impatient • eager | *esp. BrE* **keen**

▶ anxious/impatient/eager/keen **for** sth
▶ anxious/impatient/eager/keen **to do sth**
▶ anxious/eager/keen **that…**

apartment noun [C] (esp. AmE)

■ *an apartment building*

suite • penthouse | *BrE* **flat** | *esp. AmE* **condominium** | *AmE, infml* **condo**

▶ a **luxury** apartment/suite/ penthouse/flat/condominium/ condo
▶ **live in** a/an apartment/suite/ penthouse/flat/condominium/ condo
▶ **rent** a/an apartment/suite/flat
● APARTMENT OR FLAT? The usual word is **apartment** in AmE and **flat** in BrE. If **apartment** is used in BrE it may mean a place that is larger, finer or more expensive than an ordinary flat.

apologize (BrE also -ise) verb [I]

■ *Go and apologize to her.*

say sorry | *fml, esp. written* **regret** | *esp. BrE, fml, spoken* **beg sb's pardon**

▶ apologize/say sorry **to** sb
▶ apologize/say sorry/beg sb's pardon **for** sth
▶ apologize/regret **that…**

apparent adj.

1 ■ *For no apparent reason the train suddenly stopped.*

evident • obvious • clear • plain • self-evident • visible | *fml* **discernible**

▶ apparent/evident/obvious/clear/ plain/self-evident/visible/ discernible **to** sb/sth

▶ apparent/evident/obvious/clear/ plain/self-evident/visible/ discernible **from/in** sth
▶ apparent/evident/obvious/clear/ plain/self-evident/visible/ discernible **that...**
● **WHICH WORD? Apparent** and **evident** are both rather formal. In the expressions for *no apparent reason*, for *obvious reasons*, *clear majority* and *plain to see*, none of the other words can be used instead.

2 [usu. before noun] ■ *an apparent lack of enthusiasm*

outward • superficial | *fml* seeming • ostensible • alleged • purported | *usu. disapprov.* supposed • so-called

■ OPP **genuine**
▶ a/an apparent/seeming/alleged/ supposed **contradiction/failure/ inability**
▶ a/an apparent/superficial/ alleged/supposed **similarity**
▶ the apparent/ostensible/alleged/ supposed **purpose/reason**

apparently *adv.*
■ *He paused, apparently lost in thought.*

outwardly • it seems (that)... • so it seems • by/from all accounts • to all appearances | *infml* on the face of it • so I'm told | *fml* seemingly • it would seem (that)... • it appears (that)... • it would appear (that)... • ostensibly • allegedly • purportedly | *usu. disapprov.* supposedly

appeal *noun*
1 [C, U] ■ *to lodge/file an appeal with the high court*

retrial • case • hearing
▶ a legal/criminal/civil appeal/ case/hearing
▶ win a/an appeal/retrial/case
▶ lose a/an appeal/case

2 [U, sing.] ■ *Her stories have a universal appeal.*

attraction • interest • fascination • charm • glamour • magic • spell
▶ a/an appeal/attraction/interest/ fascination/charm for sb/sth
▶ have a/an appeal/attraction/ interest/fascination/charm/ glamour/magic
▶ hold a/an appeal/attraction/ interest/fascination/charm/magic

3 [C] ■ *a TV appeal for donations to the charity*

request • petition | *fml* plea | *esp. journ.* call
▶ a/an appeal/request/petition/ plea/call for sth

▶ a/an **personal/urgent** appeal/ request/plea
▶ **make** a/an appeal/request/plea

appeal *verb*
1 [I] ■ *It's a book that appeals to people of all ages.*

attract • interest • fascinate • charm • delight • intrigue • enchant • captivate
▶ a **question/subject** interests/ fascinates sb
▶ **really** appeal to/attract/interest/ fascinate/delight/intrigue/ enchant/captivate sb

2 [I] ■ *Organizers appealed to the crowd not to panic.*

ask • beg • plead • petition • press (sb) for sth | *fml* request • implore | *esp. journ.* call for sth
▶ appeal/ask/beg/plead/petition/ press/call for sth
▶ appeal for/ask for/beg for/ request/call for sth from sb
▶ appeal/ask/beg/plead/appeal with/ petition/request/implore/call for sb to do sth

appear *verb*
1 linking verb (not used in the progressive tenses) ■ *She didn't appear at all surprised.*

seem • look • sound • feel • come across • come over • strike sb (as sth)
▶ appear/seem/look/sound/feel odd/OK/nice, etc.
▶ appear/seem/look **to be** sth
▶ It appears/seems/strikes sb **that...**
▶ It would appear/seem **that...**

2 [I] (usu. used with an adv. or prep.) ■ *She suddenly appeared in the doorway.*

emerge • show • come out • form • materialize • come to light • pop up, out, etc. • crop up | *fml* manifest itself | *written* loom

■ OPP **disappear**
▶ appear/emerge/come out **from** sth
▶ appear/emerge/come/pop/loom **out of** sth
▶ **suddenly** appear/emerge/show/ come out/materialize/pop up/ loom
▶ **gradually** appear/emerge/form/ manifest itself

3 [I] ■ *By ten o'clock Lee still hadn't appeared.*

arrive • come • come in • land | *esp. spoken* turn up • get here • get in • get into sth | *infml* show up • roll in • show

▶ appear/arrive/land/turn up/show up **at/in/on** a place
▶ appear/arrive/come/land/turn up/get/show up/show **here/there**
▶ have **just** appeared/arrived/come/come in/landed/turned up/got here/got there/got in/shown up

appearance noun

1 [C] ▪ *The dog was similar in general appearance to a spaniel.*

look • looks • air

▶ (a) **striking/distinctive** appearance/look/looks
▶ have a ... appearance/look/air
▶ **lose** your/its ... appearance/looks/air
● **APPEARANCE OR LOOK?** Appearance is used about how sb/sth seems in contrast to how they really are; it is also used about how people make themselves look attractive: *To all appearances he was dead.* ◆ *She was always very particular about her appearance.*
Look is used esp. in the phrases *by the look of it/him/her, etc.* and *(not) like the look of sb*: *I don't like the look of that guy* (= I don't trust him, judging by his appearance).
Looks usu. means 'physical appearance': *She has her mother's good looks.*

2 [C, usu. sing.] ▪ *They were startled by the young man's sudden appearance.*

arrival • entrance • coming • approach • advent

▪ OPP **disappearance**
▶ a **sudden/dramatic** appearance/arrival/entrance
▶ sb/sth's **imminent** appearance/arrival/approach
▶ **await** sb/sth's appearance/arrival/coming/approach

appetite noun

1 [U, C, usu. sing.] ▪ *He has a healthy appetite.*

hunger • palate

▶ **satisfy** sb's appetite/hunger
● **APPETITE OR HUNGER?** Appetite is a positive, healthy desire for food; **hunger** is a less pleasant feeling.

2 [C] ▪ *an insatiable appetite for knowledge*

craving • hunger • longing | written yearning

▶ a/an appetite/craving/hunger/longing/yearning **for** sth
▶ sb's **sexual** appetite/hunger/longings

▶ **have/satisfy** a/an appetite/craving/hunger/longing/yearning
● **APPETITE OR CRAVING?** People have an **appetite** for things they enjoy; they have **cravings** for things they feel ill without.

application noun

1 [C] ▪ *Where can I get an application form?*

request • order • claim

▶ a/an application/request/order/claim **for**
▶ a/an **successful/unsuccessful** application/claim
▶ **put in** a/an application/request/order/claim
▶ **make/grant/refuse/reject** a/an application/request/claim

2 [U, C] ▪ *the application of new technology to teaching*

use • exercise • practice

▶ **effective/proper/continued/normal** application/use/exercise/practice
▶ **full/constant** application/use/exercise
▶ sth **has** an application/a use

apply verb

1 [I] ▪ *apply for a job/passport/grant*

ask • try for sth • bid • claim • petition | esp. BrE put in for sth | fml seek • request

▶ apply/ask/try/bid/petition/put in for sth
▶ apply/ask/bid **to do** sth
▶ **formally** apply for/ask for/bid for/claim/petition for/seek/request sth

2 [T] ▪ *apply the new technology to farming* ▪ *apply political pressure*

use • make use of sth • exert • impose • put sth into practice • put sth into effect | fml exercise • employ • utilize

▶ apply/use/make use of/impose/put into practice/put into effect/utilize **ideas**
▶ apply/use/make use of/employ/utilize a **method/technique**
▶ apply/impose/put into practice/put into effect/employ/utilize **measures**
▶ apply/impose/put into practice/utilize a **law/principle**

3 [I, T] (not used in the progressive tenses) ▪ *What I am saying applies only to some of you.*

relate to sb/sth • concern • affect • involve • refer to sb/sth • cover • have/be to do with sth

▶ a **rule/law** applies to/concerns/affects/refers to/covers sth
▶ **directly** apply to/relate to/

concern / affect / involve / refer to sth / have to do with sth

appoint verb [T]

■ They have appointed a new school principal.

name • recruit • employ • take sb on • co-opt • nominate | *esp. AmE* hire | *fml* designate | *esp. BrE, fml* engage

● OPP dismiss

▶ appoint / name / recruit / employ / take on / nominate / hire / designate / engage sb **as** sth
▶ appoint / name / nominate sb **to** sth
▶ appoint / recruit / employ / take on / co-opt / nominate / hire / designate / engage sb **to do** sth

appointment noun [C]

■ I made an appointment to see a doctor.

meeting • engagement • consultation • interview • date • audience

▶ a / an appointment / meeting / engagement / consultation / interview / date / audience **with** sb
▶ **have** a / an appointment / meeting / engagement / consultation / interview / date / audience
▶ **keep** a / an appointment / engagement / date
▶ **cancel** a / an appointment / meeting / engagement / interview

appreciate verb

1 [T] (not used in the progressive tenses) ■ Her family doesn't appreciate her.

value • prize • treasure • admire • respect | *fml* cherish • esteem

▶ value / prize sb / sth **as / for** sth
▶ value / prize / treasure a **friendship**
▶ **really** appreciate / value / treasure / admire / respect / cherish sb / sth
● APPRECIATE OR VALUE? Use value for things that are important to you, for example your *friends, health* or *freedom*. If you appreciate sb/sth, you recognize its value, even if it is not important to you personally.

2 [T] (not used in the progressive tenses) ■ I'd appreciate some help

welcome • be grateful for sth • thankful for sth

▶ appreciate / welcome / be grateful for / be thankful for sb's **support / help**
▶ appreciate / welcome / be grateful for sb's **comments / suggestions**
▶ appreciate / welcome / be grateful for / be thankful for the **chance / opportunity**

approach noun

1 [C] ■ Try a different approach to the problem.

way • method • technique • strategy • tactic • procedure | *fml* manner • methodology

▶ a **traditional / conventional / different** approach / way / method / technique / strategy / tactic / procedure / manner / methodology
▶ **adopt** a / an approach / way / method / technique / strategy / tactic / procedure / manner / methodology
▶ **change** your approach / way / method / strategy / tactics / procedure / methodology

2 [sing.] ■ She hadn't heard his approach. ■ They felt apprehensive about the approach of war.

arrival • coming • entrance • appearance • advent

▶ sb / sth's **imminent** approach / arrival / appearance
▶ **signal** sb / sth's approach / arrival / coming / entrance / advent
▶ the approach / arrival / coming / advent of **spring**

approach verb

1 [I, T] ■ We could hear the train approaching.

come • close in • converge on sth • advance on / towards sth | *written* draw near • near | *fml* proceed towards sth

▶ **slowly** approach / come / close in / advance on sth / draw near / proceed towards sth

2 [I, T] ■ The deadline was fast approaching.

come | *written* draw near • near

▶ spring / summer / autumn / fall / winter approaches / comes / draws near
▶ the **day / time** approaches / comes / draws near

3 [T] ■ They have announced profits approaching $30 million.

border on sth • verge on sth • touch | *esp. BrE* be getting on for sth | *fml* approximate

▶ approach / be getting on for **midnight / three o'clock / lunchtime**
▶ border on / verge on **paranoia / hysteria / contempt**
▶ border on / verge on the **insane / obsessive**

4 [T] ■ What's the best way of approaching this problem?

appropriate

tackle • set about sth • go about sth • deal with sb/sth • handle • get to grips with sth | *fml* address | *written* grapple with sth

▸ approach/tackle/set about/go about/deal with/handle/get to grips with/address a **task**
▸ approach/tackle/deal with/handle/get to grips with/address/grapple with a **problem**

appropriate *adj.*

■ *Jeans are not appropriate for a formal interview.*

suitable • apt • fit • right • acceptable • satisfactory | *esp. BrE* proper | *esp. spoken* all right | *infml, esp. spoken* OK | *fml* fitting

■ OPP inappropriate

▸ appropriate/suitable/apt/fit/ right/acceptable/satisfactory/all right/OK/fitting **for** sb/sth
▸ appropriate/suitable/acceptable/ satisfactory/all right/OK **as** sb/sth
▸ appropriate/suitable/apt/fit/ right/acceptable/satisfactory/ proper/all right/OK/fitting **that**...
▸ appropriate/suitable/fit/right/ acceptable/satisfactory/proper/all right/OK/fitting **to do sth**

● APPROPRIATE, SUITABLE OR RIGHT? How **appropriate** or **suitable** sb/ sth is is a matter of judgement; how **right** sb/sth is is more a matter of fact:
✓ *Do you think she would be an appropriate/a suitable person to ask?*
✗ *a right person to ask*
✓ *She's definitely the right person to ask.* ✗ *She's definitely the appropriate/suitable person to ask.*

approval *noun*

1 [U] ■ *She wanted to win her father's approval.*

praise • admiration • respect • recognition • appreciation • acclaim | *infml* a pat on the back | *fml* adulation • esteem

■ OPP disapproval

▸ approval/praise/admiration/ respect/recognition/acclaim/a pat on the back **for** sth
▸ earn/win approval/praise/ admiration/respect/recognition/ appreciation/acclaim/esteem

2 [U] ■ *The treaty requires approval by the Senate.*

acceptance • agreement • blessing • permission • consent • authorization • clearance | *BrE* favour | *AmE* favor | *infml* thumbs up • the go-ahead | *fml* assent • leave

▸ official approval/acceptance/

---

blessing/permission/ authorization/clearance
▸ give your/the approval/ agreement/blessing/permission/ consent/authorization/clearance/ thumbs up/go-ahead/assent/ leave
▸ get sb's/the approval/ acceptance/agreement/blessing/ permission/consent/ authorization/clearance/thumbs up/go-ahead/assent/leave

approve *verb*

1 [I] (not used in the progressive tenses) ■ *Do you approve of my idea?*

agree with sth • support • back • believe in sth | *BrE* be in favour of sb/sth | *AmE* be in favor of sb/sth | *infml* be all for sth • subscribe to sth

■ OPP disapprove

▸ approve of/agree with/support/ back/believe in/be in favour of/be all for/subscribe to a/an **idea/ view**
▸ approve of/agree with/support/ back/be in favour of/be all for a **plan/policy/suggestion**

2 [T] ■ *The committee approved the plan.*

agree to sth • accept | *fml* consent

■ OPP reject

▸ approve/agree to/accept/consent to a **plan/change/proposal**
▸ approve/agree to/accept a **decision/suggestion/request**

3 [T, often passive] ■ *The course is approved by the Department for Education.*

recognize • certify • uphold • ratify | *fml* validate

▸ approve/recognize/certify/ uphold/ratify/validate sth **as** sth
▸ approve/recognize/validate a **course**
▸ approve/uphold/ratify a **treaty**

approving *adj.*

■ *He gave me an approving nod.*

admiring • appreciative • complimentary • positive • glowing • flattering | *BrE* favourable | *AmE* favorable

■ OPP disapproving

▸ approving/admiring/appreciative of sb/sth
▸ a/an approving/appreciative/ complimentary/positive/ flattering/favourable **comment**
▸ a/an approving/appreciative/ complimentary/positive/flattering **remark**

approximate adj.

■ *The cost given is only approximate.*

rough • imprecise • inexact • vague • general • broad | *AmE* ballpark

■ OPP exact

▶ a/an approximate/rough/vague/ general/broad **idea**
▶ a/an approximate/rough/ballpark **figure/estimate**

● **APPROXIMATE OR ROUGH?**
Approximate most often describes the *number*, *amount*, *cost*, etc. of sth. **Rough** more often describes an *estimate*, *idea* or *guess*:
✓*Construction was completed at an approximate cost of $4.1 million.* • *There were about 20 people there, at a rough guess.*
Rough, but not **approximate** can describe a piece of writing or a drawing:
✓*a rough draft/sketch of sth* ✗ *an approximate draft/sketch of sth*

approximately adv.

■ *The trip takes approximately seven hours.*

roughly • about • around • round about • something like • more or less • imprecisely

■ OPP exactly

area noun

1 [C] ■ *The whole area was flooded.*

region • part • zone • district • quarter | *BrE* neighbourhood | *AmE* neighborhood

▶ a/an eastern/northern/ southern/western area/region/ parts/zone/district/quarter
▶ an industrial area/region/zone/ district/quarter
▶ a residential area/zone/district/ quarter/neighbourhood

● **AREA OR REGION?** **Area** has a wide range of meaning and can refer to a part of sth as large as a continent or smaller than a room. A **region** refers to a large area of a country or continent, esp. in terms of its geographical, political or economic importance.

2 [C] ■ *The big growth area of recent years has been in health clubs.*

sector • field • domain • sphere • realm • subject • branch • specialism | *esp. AmE* specialty | *fml* discipline

▶ within/outside the area/sector/ field/domain/sphere/realm/ discipline
▶ the public/private/domestic sector/domain/sphere/realm
▶ work in the area/sector/field/ domain of sth

argue verb

1 [I] ■ *We're always arguing about money.*

quarrel • fall out • bicker • squabble | *AmE* fight | *BrE, infml* row | *esp. journ.* clash

▶ argue/quarrel/fall out/bicker/ squabble/fight/row/clash **with** sb
▶ argue/quarrel/fall out/bicker/ squabble/fight/row/clash **over** sth
▶ argue/quarrel/fall out/bicker/ squabble/fight/row **about** sth

2 [I, T] ■ *She argued that they needed more time.*

insist • protest • maintain • claim • assert | *fml* contend • allege

▶ argue/insist/protest/maintain/ claim/assert/contend/allege **that…**
▶ It is argued/maintained/claimed/ asserted/contended/alleged **that…**
▶ argue/insist/protest/assert sth **strongly**

argument noun

1 [C, U] ■ *He got into an argument with the teacher.*

quarrel • dispute • debate • disagreement • squabble • controversy • shouting match | *esp. AmE* fight | *BrE, infml* row | *infml* tiff

▶ a/an argument/quarrel/ disagreement/squabble/shouting match/fight/row/tiff **with** sb
▶ (a/an) argument/quarrel/ dispute/debate/disagreement/ squabble/controversy/shouting match/fight/row/tiff **between** A and B
▶ (a/an) argument/quarrel/ dispute/debate/disagreement/ squabble /controversy/fight/row **about/over** sth
▶ a bitter argument/quarrel/ dispute/debate/disagreement/ controversy/row
▶ (a/an) argument/quarrel/ dispute/controversy/row/fight **breaks out**

● **WHICH WORD?** A **quarrel**, **fight** or **row** is usu. only between people who know each other:
✓*We had an argument with the waiter about the bill.* ✗ *We had a quarrel/fight/row with the waiter about the bill.*
A **quarrel** is less violent than a **fight** or **row**, but it can continue for a period of time; an **argument** can be violent or it can be a serious discussion.

2 [C] ■ *arguments for and against nuclear power*

aristocratic

case • reason • justification | BrE
defence | AmE defense | law plea

▶ a/an argument/case/reason/
justification/defence **for** sth
▶ a/an argument/case/reason/
defence **against** sth
▶ a **strong/legal** argument/case/
defence/reason/justification
▶ **put forward** a/an argument/
case/reason/justification
▶ **strengthen** a/an argument/case/
defence

aristocratic adj.

■ a rare glimpse of aristocratic society

noble • upper-class | BrE, infml,
sometimes disapprov. **posh**

▶ a/an aristocratic/noble/upper-
class **family**
▶ a/an aristocratic/noble **origins/
blood/connections**
▶ a/an upper-class/posh **voice/
person/accent**
● ARISTOCRATIC OR NOBLE? Noble is
only used to talk about the family
that sb is born into. Aristocratic
can also be used to talk about the
society, manners, appearance, etc.
of people from such families.

arms noun [pl.]

■ Rebels took up arms against the
state.

weapons • armaments • munitions

▶ **nuclear/conventional** arms/
weapons/armaments
▶ **carry** arms/weapons
▶ a/an arms/weapons/armaments/
munitions **factory**

army noun [C+sing./pl. v.]

■ The armies faced each other across
the battlefield. ■ Mike is in the army.

force • legion • unit

▶ a/the **enemy/rebel/British/
French, etc.** army/forces/unit
▶ a/an army/force/legion **invades** a
place
▶ a/an army/force/legion/unit
advances/retreats

arrange verb

1 [T, I] ■ A news conference was
hastily arranged. ■ We met at six, as
arranged.

organize • plan • agree | esp. spoken
sort sth **out** | written **orchestrate**

▶ arrange/plan **for** sth
▶ arrange/plan/agree/sort out
how/who/when/where...
▶ arrange/plan/agree **that...**
▶ arrange/plan/agree **to do** sth

2 [T] ■ The books were arranged in
alphabetical order.

organize • set sth out • lay sth out •
line sb/sth up • manage • align |
infml **sort** sth **out**

▶ arrange/organize/set out/sort out
your **thoughts/ideas**
▶ arrange/organize/set out/manage
information/data
▶ arrange/organize/manage/sort
out your **affairs**

arrangement noun

1 [C, usu. pl.] ■ Have you finalized
your travel arrangements?

preparation • planning • provision •
organization

▶ arrangements/preparations/
planning/provision/organization
for sb/sth
▶ arrangements/preparations/
planning/provision **to do** sth
▶ **make** arrangements/
preparations/provsision

2 [C, U] ■ We can come to an
arrangement over the price.

agreement • understanding • deal

▶ a/an arrangement/agreement/
understanding/deal **with** sb
▶ a/an arrangement/agreement/
understanding/deal **between** A
and B
▶ a/an arrangement/agreement/
understanding/deal **on/over** sth
▶ **have** a/an arrangement/
agreement/understanding

arrest verb [T, often passive]

■ You could get arrested for doing that.

catch • capture • take | infml **bust** |
fml **apprehend**

▶ arrest/take/bust/apprehend sb
for sth

arrival noun

1 [C, usu. sing., U] ■ Her arrival was a
complete surprise. ■ the arrival of
new technology

appearance • coming • entrance •
approach • advent

■ OPP departure
▶ a **sudden/dramatic** arrival/
appearance/entrance
▶ **await** sb/sth's arrival/appearance/
coming/approach
▶ the arrival/coming/advent of
television/the railways

2 [C] ■ The arrivals are coming
through immigration now.

newcomer • latecomer

▶ an arrival/a newcomer **at/in** sth
▶ a newcomer/latecomer **to** sth

arrive verb [I]

1 ■ What time did they arrive?

come • come in • land • appear | *esp. spoken* get here/there • get in • get in to sth • turn up | *infml* show up • roll in • show • hit | *esp. written* reach

■ **OPP** leave, depart
▶ arrive/land/appear/turn up/show up **at/in/on** a place
▶ be the **first/last** to arrive/come/ come in/land/get here/get in/turn up/show up/roll in/ reach a place
▶ arrive/come in/land/get here/get in/turn up **on time**

2 [I] (*written*) ■ *The day of the wedding finally arrived.*

come
▶ the **day/time** arrives/comes
▶ arrive/come **early/late**
▶ **finally** arrive/come

article noun [C]
■ *Have you seen that article about street crime?*

feature • piece • editorial • column • paper • essay
▶ a/an article/feature/piece/ editorial/column/paper/essay **on/ about** sth
▶ a **newspaper** article/feature/ editorial/column
▶ a **magazine** article/feature/piece/ column
▶ **write/read/publish** a/an article/ feature/piece/editorial/column/ paper/essay

articulate adj.
■ *an unusually articulate ten-year-old*

fluent • eloquent • coherent
■ **OPP** inarticulate
▶ a/an articulate/fluent/eloquent/ coherent **answer/response**
▶ articulate/fluent/eloquent/ coherent **speech**
▶ articulate/fluent/eloquent **language**

artificial adj.
1 ■ *free from artificial colours and flavours*

synthetic • man-made • false • fake • imitation
■ **OPP** natural
▶ artificial/synthetic/man-made **fabrics/fibres/materials/ products**
▶ artificial/synthetic/fake/imitation **fur/leather**
▶ artificial/synthetic/false/fake/ imitation **diamonds/pearls**

2 ■ *A job interview is a very artificial situation.*

disapprov. **forced • strained • laboured • contrived**

▶ a/an artificial/contrived **situation/ example**
▶ a **forced/strained smile**
▶ **sound** forced/strained/laboured/ contrived

artist noun
1 [C] ■ *an exhibition of work by contemporary Danish artists*

painter • sculptor
▶ a **contemporary/talented/ famous** artist/painter/sculptor
▶ a/an **abstract/impressionist/ portrait/landscape** artist/painter

2 [C] ■ *After the duo split up, Kit became a successful solo artist.*

performer • entertainer • artiste • musician • singer • dancer
▶ a **famous/talented/aspiring** artist/performer/entertainer/ musician/singer/dancer

artistic adj.
■ *Victoria's very artistic—she paints and draws beautifully.*

creative • imaginative • original
▶ artistic/creative **ability/ achievement/skill/talent**
▶ a/an artistic/creative/ imaginative/original **mind**

ashamed adj.
■ *She was deeply ashamed of her behaviour at the party.*

sorry • guilty • apologetic | *spoken* **bad**
■ **OPP** shameless, unabashed, unashamed
▶ feel ashamed/sorry/guilty/ apologetic/bad **about** sth
▶ feel ashamed/sorry/guilty/bad **that...**
▶ feel ashamed/guilty/apologetic/ bad

ask verb
1 [T, I] ■ *She asked where he lived.*

enquire/inquire • demand
▶ ask/enquire **about/after** sb/sth
▶ ask/enquire/demand sth **of** sb
▶ ask/enquire/demand **what/who/ how...** etc.
▶ ask/enquire/demand **angrily**

2 [I, T] ■ *He asked me for a job.*

apply • appeal • claim • beg • plead | *fml* **request • seek • invite • petition** | *esp. journ.* **call for** sth
▶ ask/apply/appeal/beg/plead/ petition/call **for** sth
▶ ask for/appeal for/claim/beg/ seek/request/invite/call for sth **from** sb

asleep

▶ ask/appeal for/beg/plead with/
request/invite/petition/call for sb
to do sth

3 [T] ■ Shall we ask Rachel and Mark
to dinner?

invite

▶ ask/invite sb **to/for** sth
▶ ask/invite sb **in/round/along/
over/out**
▶ ask/invite sb **to do** sth
● **ASK OR INVITE?** Ask is used esp. to
talk about informal social
meetings. **Invite** can be used for a
more formal event, such as a
wedding or party. A written
invitation may be given.

fall asleep *phrase*
■ After reading for hours, she finally fell
asleep.

go to sleep • get to sleep | *esp. BrE*
drift off | *infml* **crash** | *esp. BrE, infml*
nod off

■ OPP **wake, wake up**
▶ fall asleep/go to sleep/nod off
during/in the middle of sth
▶ sb **must have** fallen asleep/gone
to sleep/drifted off/nodded off
▶ drift off/nod off **to sleep**

aspect *noun* [C]
■ The talk will cover all aspects of city
life.

**side • respect • dimension •
element • strand • component**

▶ a/an aspect/side/dimension/
element/strand/component **to** sth
▶ an **important** aspect/respect/
dimension/element/strand/
component
▶ a **political/social/cultural/
religious/spiritual/moral/human**
aspect/side/dimension/element/
component

assembly (also Assembly) *noun*
[C+sing./pl. v.]
■ Power was handed over to provincial
and regional assemblies. ■ the 51-seat
National Assembly

**parliament • congress • council •
senate • house • chamber** | *fml*
legislature

▶ an **elected** assembly/parliament/
council/senate/house/chamber/
legislature
▶ the **national/federal** assembly/
parliament/council/legislature
▶ a **local/regional** assembly/
parliament/council
▶ the **upper/lower** house/chamber
(**of the** parliament/legislature, etc.)

assess *verb* [T]
■ The committee assesses whether a
building is worth preserving.

evaluate • rate • judge • gauge |
infml **size sb/sth up**

▶ assess/evaluate/rate/judge/gauge
sb/sth **as/on**
▶ assess/evaluate/rate/judge/gauge
how...
▶ assess/evaluate/judge/gauge **the
extent/significance/success/
effectiveness/effect/impact of**
sth
▶ assess/evaluate/judge/**size up the
situation**
● **ASSESS OR EVALUATE?** You **assess**
sb/sth in order to make a
judgement to see if it is satisfactory.
You **evaluate** sb/sth to understand
it better so that more informed
decisions can be made.

assessment *noun* [C, U]
■ Make an assessment of the risks
involved. ■ written and oral exams and
other forms of assessment

**evaluation • appraisal • review •
commentary • critique • criticism**

▶ **in** a/an assessment/evaluation/
appraisal/review/commentary/
critique
▶ **give** a/an assessment/appraisal/
review/critique
▶ **carry out/make** a/an assessment/
evaluation/appraisal

assignment *noun* [C]
■ to complete a written assignment

**project • homework • exercise •
task • essay • paper • work**

▶ (a/an) project/homework/
exercise/essay/paper/work **on** sth
▶ **do** an assignment/a project/your
homework/an exercise/a task/an
essay/a paper/some work
▶ **give sb/set (sb)** an assignment/
their homework/an exercise/a
task/an essay/some work

assist *verb*
1 [T, I] (*fml*) ■ We'll do all we can to
assist you.

help • help (sb) out • support | *infml*
lend (sb) a hand | *fml* **aid** | *fml,
spoken* **be of service**

▶ assist/help/help out/lend a hand
with sth
▶ assist/help/support/aid sb **in** sth
▶ assist/help/aid sb **in doing** sth/**to
do** sth

2 [I, T] (*fml*) ■ ways to assist the
decision-making process

help • ease | *fml* **facilitate • aid**

▶ assist/help/aid **in (doing)** sth
▶ assist/help/ease/facilitate/aid **the
process**

▶ assist / ease / facilitate the **flow / transition / transfer / passage / introduction** of sth
● ASSIST, FACILITATE OR AID? Assist and **facilitate** have a wider range of collocates than **aid**, including many nouns that describe a process. Both words are usu. used to describe making helpful processes easier; **aid** can also be used to talk about unhelpful processes: *Aided by strong winds, the fire quickly spread.*

assistance noun [U] (fml)
■ technical/economic/military assistance ▪ *Can I be of any assistance, sir?*

help ▸ support ▸ backup ▸ cooperation | fml aid ▸ service

▶ assistance / help / support / cooperation **in doing** sth
▶ **with** the assistance / help / support / cooperation **of** sb / sth
▶ **need** assistance / help / support / sb's cooperation / sb's services
▶ **get** assistance / help / support / backup / cooperation / aid / sb's services
▶ **come to / enlist** sb's assistance / help / support / aid

assistant noun [C]
■ a research / teaching assistant

aide ▸ helper ▸ right-hand man | infml sidekick

▶ a / an assistant / aide / right-hand man / sidekick **to** sb
▶ a **trusted** assistant / aide / sidekick
▶ a **senior / personal / junior** assistant / aide

associate verb [T]
■ *I always associate the smell of baking with my childhood.*

relate ▸ connect | esp. journ. link

▶ associate / relate / connect / link sth **with** sth
▶ associate / relate / link / connect (sth) **directly**
● ASSOCIATE, RELATE OR CONNECT? When you **associate** two things in your mind, it often just happens because of previous experiences. When you **relate** or **connect** them it requires more effort, because the connection is not so obvious or natural to you:
✗ *I always relate/connect the smell of baking with my childhood.*
✓ *I found it hard to relate/connect the two things in my mind.* ✗ *I found it hard to associate the two things in my mind.*

associated adj.
■ *Salaries and associated costs are rising fast.*

related ▸ connected ▸ resulting ▸ ensuing | fml attendant ▸ resultant ▸ consequent

▶ associated / connected **with** sth
▶ associated / related / resulting / ensuing / attendant / resultant / consequent **problems / changes**
▶ associated / connected / attendant **risks**
● ASSOCIATED OR RELATED? Related is a more general word. Associated is used esp. in business contexts and to talk about risks: *a related issue / question / problem / field / area / subject / matter / theme* • *the risks associated with taking drugs*

association noun
1 [C+sing./pl. v.] ■ *Do you belong to any professional or trade associations?*

society ▸ club ▸ alliance ▸ league ▸ union ▸ guild ▸ organization ▸ institute

▶ a **national** association / society / club / league / union / organization / institute
▶ a **local / professional** association / society / club / union
▶ **form / join** a/an association / society / club / alliance / league / union
● ASSOCIATION, SOCIETY OR CLUB? These words are all used for groups of people who have a shared interest or purpose. Often, but not always, an **association** relates to professional interests, a **society** to academic interests, and a **club** to leisure interests.

2 [C, U] ■ *his alleged association with terrorist groups*

tie ▸ link | fml affiliation | esp. busin. contact

▶ an association / ties / links / an affiliation / contacts **with** sb / sth
▶ an association / ties / links / an affiliation **between** A and B
▶ (a) **political / personal** association / ties / links / affiliation / contacts

3 [C, usu. pl.] ■ *The seaside had pleasant associations with my childhood.*

connotation ▸ overtone ▸ nuance ▸ undercurrent

▶ associations / connotations / overtones / nuances / undercurrents **of** sth
▶ **negative / unpleasant / pejorative** associations / connotations / overtones
▶ **take on / have** associations / connotations / overtones

4 [C] ■ *Is there a proven association between smoking and cancer?*

connection • link • relationship • relation • correlation

■ the association/connection/link/relationship/relation/correlation **between** A and B

■ in association/connection **with** sb/sth

■ a **direct/clear/strong/definite/possible** association/connection/link/relationship/relation/correlation

▶ **show/examine** the association/connection/link/relationship/relation/correlation

assume verb [T]

■ Let's assume that the plan will succeed.

suppose • imagine • presume | esp. spoken **take it** | esp. BrE, spoken **expect** | esp. AmE, spoken **guess**

■ assume/suppose/imagine/presume/take it/expect/guess that...

▶ **Let's/Let us** assume/suppose/imagine/presume/take it...

▶ **can only** assume/suppose/imagine/presume/take it (that)...

atmosphere noun [C, U]

■ The hotel has a friendly atmosphere.

mood • feeling • feel • aura • spirit • climate • tone | BrE **flavour** | AmE **flavor**

■ a **general** atmosphere/mood/feeling/feel/spirit/climate/tone/flavour

■ an **international** atmosphere/feel/climate/flavour

▶ **create** a/an atmosphere/mood/feeling/feel/aura/spirit/climate/mood

▶ **capture** the atmosphere/mood/feeling/spirit/tone/spirit/flavour of sth

● **ATMOSPHERE OR MOOD?** An atmosphere belongs to a place; a mood belongs to a group of people:
✗ The hotel has a friendly mood.
✓ a leader who can gauge the popular mood ✗ a leader who can gauge the popular atmosphere

attach verb [T]

■ Attach the rope securely to a tree.

fasten • tie • stick • strap • tape • glue | esp. BrE **fix** | fml **secure**

■ OPP **detach**

▶ attach/fasten/tie/stick/strap/tape/glue/fix/secure sth **to** sb/sth

▶ fasten/tie/stick/strap/tape/glue/fix sth **on** sth

▶ attach/tie/stick/fix/secure **firmly**

attack noun

1 [C] ■ a vicious knife attack

assault • rape

▶ an attack/assault **on/against** sb

▶ a/an **violent/brutal/savage/vicious/alleged** attack/assault/rape

▶ **carry out** an attack/assault

2 [C, U] ■ He ordered his men to mount an attack on the city.

raid • assault • strike • invasion • offensive | fml **incursion**

▶ a/an attack/raid/assault/strike/offensive **against** sb/sth

▶ a/an attack/assault/strike/offensive/incursion **on** sb/sth

▶ a **military** attack/raid/assault/strike/invasion/offensive/incursion

▶ **plan/launch** a/an attack/raid/assault/strike/invasion/offensive

3 [C, U] ■ She launched a scathing attack on the government's policies.

assault • criticism • condemnation | fml **denunciation • censure**

▶ an attack/assault **on** sb/sth

▶ **come under** attack/assault/criticism/censure

● **ATTACK OR ASSAULT?** Attack is used more frequently, but an assault can be more severe and damaging.

4 [C] ■ recovering from an attack of food poisoning

bout • fit • outburst • burst • flurry

▶ a/an attack/bout/fit/outburst/burst/flurry **of** sth

▶ **suffer from/have/bring on** a/an attack/bout/fit (of sth)

▶ **trigger** an attack/fit/outburst (of sth)

● **ATTACK OR BOUT?** You can use either to describe a period of illness, but attack describes a shorter and more sudden illness than bout.

attack verb

1 [T, I] ■ He was attacked with a knife.

assault • beat sb up • mug • strike

▶ attack/assault/beat sb up **with** sth

▶ **get** beaten up/mugged

▶ **violently** attack/assault/beat up sb

2 [T, I] ■ At dawn the army attacked the town.

raid • strike • charge • storm

▶ attack/strike/charge **the enemy**

▶ attack/storm a/an **house/building/embassy**

▶ **soldiers/troops/police** attack/raid/strike/storm sth

▶ **aircraft** attack/raid/strike sth

3 [T] ■ The studio audience repeatedly attacked the minister for her stance.

**criticize + condemn + denounce | fml
censure + berate + castigate**

▶ attack/criticize/condemn/
denounce/censure/berate/
castigate sb **for** sth
▶ attack/criticize/condemn/
denounce/censure/berate/
castigate a **decision**
▶ attack/criticize/condemn/
denounce/censure/berate/
castigate sb **publicly**

attempt noun [C, U]
■ *I passed my driving test at the first attempt.*

effort + try | BrE **go** | infml **shot + stab**

▶ a/an attempt/try/go/shot/stab
at sth
▶ an attempt/try/effort **to do** sth
▶ **make** a/an attempt/effort/stab
▶ **have** a try/go/shot/stab
● ATTEMPT OR EFFORT? Attempt
emphasizes the event or action
involved in trying to do sth; effort
emphasizes the work that sb puts
into doing sth:
✓a/an assassination/suicide attempt
✗ a/an assassination/suicide effort
✓a great/enormous/strenuous effort
✗ a great/enormous/strenuous
attempt

attempt verb [T]
■ *He was shot while attempting to escape.*

try | fml **seek + strive** | BrE, fml
endeavour | AmE, fml **endeavor**

▶ attempt/try/seek/strive/
endeavour **to do** sth
● ATTEMPT OR TRY? Attempt is more
formal than try and places the
emphasis on the act of starting to
do sth rather than on the effort of
achieving it.

attend verb

1 [T, I] (fml) ■ *Over 600 people attended the conference.*

come + go + come along + make it + get

▶ come/go/come along/make it/
get to sth
▶ attend/come to/go to/come
along to/make it to/get to a
meeting/party

2 [T] (fml) ■ *The children attended the local school.*

go to sth

▶ attend/go to **school/college/a
clinic/church/the mosque**
▶ **regularly/occasionally** attend/go
to sth

attention noun [U]
■ *Films with big stars always attract attention.*

**interest + notice + concentration +
care** | fml **regard**

▶ **catch/get/grab/lose** sb's
attention/interest
▶ **attract/bring sth to/come to/
escape** sb's attention/notice
▶ **hold/focus** sb's attention/
interest/concentration

pay attention phrase
■ *Can you all pay attention, please?*

listen | fml **heed**

■ OPP ignore
▶ pay attention/listen **to** sb/sth
▶ pay attention/listen to a
conversation
▶ pay attention/listen to/heed
sb's **words/what sb says**

attitude noun [C]
■ *What is your attitude towards the job as a whole?*

**view + point of view + stance +
position + stand + perspective +
outlook + line + angle + opinion +
feeling**

▶ a **personal** attitude/view/point of
view/stance/position/
perspective/angle/opinion/feeling
▶ a **positive/negative** attitude/
view/point of view/stance/
perspective/outlook/angle/
opinion/feeling
▶ **take** a/an attitude/view/point of
view/stance/position/stand/
perspective/line
▶ **change** your attitude/view/point
of view/stance/position/
perspective/outlook/opinion

attorney noun [C] (esp. AmE)
■ *He remained silent, on the advice of his attorney.*

lawyer + barrister + advocate | BrE
solicitor | law **counsel**

▶ (a/an) attorney/lawyer/barrister/
advocate/solicitor/counsel **for** sb
▶ (a) **defence** attorney/lawyer/
barrister/advocate/solicitor/
counsel
▶ (a) **prosecuting/prosecution**
attorney/lawyer/barrister/
solicitor/counsel
▶ **appoint/hire/instruct/consult**
(a/an) attorney/lawyer/barrister/
advocate/solicitor/counsel
● WHICH WORD? Lawyer (and also
attorney in AmE) is the general
term for sb who is qualified to
advise people about the law. A
lawyer who speaks in the higher
courts in England and Wales and an
advocate in Scotland. A solicitor
gives legal advice, prepares

documents and sometimes has the right to speak in court.

attract verb

1 [T, usu. passive] ■ *I was attracted by the idea of working abroad.*

interest • tempt • appeal • intrigue • charm • captivate • enchant • fascinate

■ OPP repel
▶ be attracted/tempted/intrigued/ charmed/captivated/enchanted/ fascinated **by** sb/sth
▶ really attract/interest/appeal to/ intrigue/fascinate **sb**

2 be attracted to sb [T, passive] ■ *It was obvious that Kit was attracted to her.*

want • have a crush on sb | *infml* go for sb | *BrE, infml* fancy | *AmE, infml* be into sb

attraction noun

1 [U] ■ *She felt an immediate attraction for him.*

desire • love • passion • crush • infatuation | *often disapprov.* lust

▶ attraction/desire/love/passion/ infatuation/lust **for** sb
▶ sexual/physical/mutual attraction/desire/love/passion/ lust

2 [U, C] ■ *I can't see the attraction of sitting on the beach all day.*

appeal • charm • interest • fascination • glamour • spell

▶ a/an attraction/appeal/interest/ fascination **for** sb/sth
▶ have/hold a/an attraction/ appeal/charm/interest/fascination
▶ sth loses its attraction/appeal/ charm/fascination/glamour

attractive adj.

1 ■ *She was a tall, attractive woman.*

good-looking • handsome • pretty • beautiful • striking | *esp. BrE* lovely | *esp. AmE, infml* cute

■ OPP unattractive
▶ a/an attractive/good-looking/ handsome/pretty/beautiful/ striking/lovely/cute **girl/woman/ face**
▶ a/an attractive/good-looking/ handsome/pretty/beautiful/ lovely/cute **boy**
▶ a/an attractive/good-looking/ handsome/beautiful/cute **man**
● ATTRACTIVE OR GOOD-LOOKING? **Attractive** often describes sb's personality as well as their appearance; **good-looking** only describes sb's appearance.

2 ■ *a large house with an attractive garden*

pretty • charming • beautiful • picturesque • impressive | *esp. BrE* lovely

■ OPP unattractive
▶ a/an attractive/pretty/charming/ beautiful/picturesque/lovely **place/town/village**
▶ attractive/beautiful/picturesque/ impressive/lovely **scenery/views**
▶ a/an attractive/charming/ beautiful/lovely **smile**

3 ■ *attractive career opportunities for graduates*

appealing | *fml* desirable

■ OPP unattractive
▶ attractive/appealing **to** sb
▶ an attractive/appealing **idea/ prospect**
▶ highly attractive/desirable

audience noun

1 [C+sing./pl. v.] ■ *An audience of millions watched the match.*

viewers • spectators • listeners

▶ in front of/before (an) audience/ spectators
▶ attract the audience/viewers/ spectators/listeners
▶ a/an audience/viewer/spectator **sees/watches** sb/sth

2 [C] ■ *The target audience was mainly teenagers.*

market • public • clientele

▶ a/an audience/market **for** sth
▶ reach a/an audience/market/wide public
▶ attract/build up a/an audience/ market/clientele

author noun [C]

■ *Who is your favourite author?*

writer • novelist • poet • playwright • dramatist • scriptwriter • screenwriter • biographer

▶ an award-winning author/writer/ novelist/poet/playwright/ screenwriter
▶ a best-selling/romantic author/ writer/novelist/poet
▶ a/an author/writer/novelist/ poet/playwright/dramatist/ scriptwriter/screenwriter/ biographer **writes** sth

authoritarian adj.

■ *an authoritarian style of leadership*

authoritative | *disapprov.* autocratic • overbearing • dictatorial • repressive • oppressive • undemocratic • tyrannical • bossy

▶ a/an authoritarian/authoritative/ autocratic/overbearing/dictatorial **manner**

► a/an authoritarian/authoritative/
bossy **attitude**
► a/an authoritarian/autocratic/
dictatorial/repressive/oppressive/
undemocratic/tyrannical **regime**
● AUTHORITARIAN, AUTHORITATIVE OR
AUTOCRATIC? Autocratic always
shows disapproval; **authoritative**
often shows approval that sb is in
control; **authoritarian** is usu.
simply a descriptive term, showing
neither approval nor disapproval.

authority noun

1 [U] ■ No one in authority takes the
matter seriously enough.

power ◆ control ◆ command ◆ rule ◆
fml jurisdiction

► authority/power/control/
command/rule/jurisdiction **over**
sb/sth
► be **in** authority/power/control/
command
► authority/power/jurisdiction **to do**
sth

2 [U] ■ Only the manager has the
authority to sign cheques.

power ◆ right

► the authority/power/right **to do**
sth
► **have** the authority/power/right
► **use/exercise** your authority/
power/rights
● AUTHORITY OR POWER? (to have) the
authority to do sth usu. refers to
what sb is allowed to do within a
company or other organization.
The power to do sth and special
powers often refer to what sb is
allowed to do within the law or
government of a country:
✗ Only the manager has the power
to sign cheques.
✓ The powers of the police must be
clearly defined. ✗ The authority of
the police must be clearly defined.

3 [U] ■ The council was accused of
selling the land without formal
authority.

authorization ◆ permission ◆
clearance ◆ approval | *BrE* licence |
AmE license | *fml* leave | *infml, esp.
journ.* the go-ahead

► authority/authorization/
permission/clearance/approval/a
licence **for** sth
► **without** sb's authority/
authorization/permission/leave
► **have** (sb's) authority/
authorization/permission/
clearance/a licence/leave
► **receive** authorization/permission/
clearance/approval
● AUTHORITY OR AUTHORIZATION?
Authorization is nearly always
permission for a particular action;
authority can be more general.:

✓ It was done under his authority.
✗ under his authorization

4 the authorities [pl.] ■ The
authorities are investigating the
problem.

the establishment ◆ bureaucracy ◆
the system | *BrE* the top brass | *AmE*
the brass | *disapprov.* officialdom

► the **military** authorities/
establishment/bureaucracy/top
brass/brass
► the **political/medical** authorities/
establishment/bureaucracy
► the **local/government/federal/
state** authorities/bureaucracy

automatic adj.

■ fully automatic driverless trains

automated ◆ computerized ◆
electronic ◆ digital ◆ mechanical ◆
robotic

■ OPP manual

► a/an automatic/automated/
computerized/electronic/digital/
robotic **system**
► a/an automatic/automated/
computerized/electronic/robotic
machine
► a/an automatic/electronic/
mechanical/robotic **device**
● AUTOMATIC OR AUTOMATED?
Automatic usu. describes the
machines themselves; **automated**
more often describes a process, or
the place where such machines are
used.

available adj.

1 ■ They were the only tickets
available.

for sale ◆ on the market ◆ on sale

► available/on sale **from** sb/sth
► **go** on the market/on sale
► **now/still** available/for sale/on the
market/on sale

2 ■ The director was not available for
comment.

free ◆ spare

► available/free **for** sth
► available/free **to do** sth
► available/free/spare **time**
► a free/spare **afternoon/morning/
weekend/moment**

average adj.

1 ■ The route is for walkers of average
ability.

normal ◆ ordinary ◆ typical ◆
common

► the average/normal/ordinary/
common **man**
► a/an average/normal/ordinary
person

avoid

▶ a/an average/normal/ordinary/
typical **working day**

2 (often *disapprov.*) ■ *The quality has been pretty average.*

unremarkable | *disapprov.* **ordinary**

▶ an average/unremarkable/
ordinary **person**
▶ average/ordinary **players**
▶ an average/ordinary **sort of
person/thing**

avoid verb [T]

1 ■ *The accident could have been avoided.*

prevent • stop | *fml* **preclude** | *written* **avert**

▶ avoid/prevent/stop/preclude **doing sth**
▶ avoid/prevent/stop/avert a/an **crisis/accident**
▶ avoid/prevent/avert a **disaster/catastrophe/tragedy/conflict**

2 [T] ■ *He's been avoiding me all week.*

stay away • boycott • steer clear • keep your distance | *written* **shun**

▶ avoid/shun **publicity/the limelight**
▶ deliberately avoid/stay away from/steer clear of **sb/sth**

award noun [C]

■ *nominated for the best actor award*

prize • reward • title • medal • trophy • cup | *BrE* **honour** | *AmE* **honor**

▶ a/an award/prize/reward/medal/trophy/cup **for sth**
▶ a **coveted/prestigious** award/prize/title/trophy
▶ a/an **top/academic** award/prize/honour
▶ **win** a/an award/prize/reward/title/medal/trophy/cup/honour

award verb [T]

■ *The judge awarded equal points to both finalists.*

present • give | *fml* **confer • grant • accord • bestow**

▶ award/present/give/grant/accord sth **to sb**
▶ confer/bestow sth **on sb**
▶ award/give/accord/grant **sb sth**
▶ award/present/give **a prize**

aware adj.

■ *Were you aware that something was wrong?*

conscious • alert to sth | *fml* **mindful**

■ OPP **unaware**

▶ aware/conscious/mindful **of sth**

▶ aware/conscious/mindful **that...**
▶ keenly **aware/conscious/alert**

awareness noun [U, sing.]

■ *There is growing awareness of the link between diet and health.*

consciousness • knowledge • realization | *fml* or *tech.* **perception**

▶ awareness/consciousness/knowledge/realization/perception **of sth**
▶ awareness/consciousness/knowledge/realization/perception **that...**
▶ **public** awareness/consciousness/knowledge/perception

awful adj.

1 (*esp. spoken*) ■ *The weather was awful.*

terrible • bad • foul • revolting • nasty • grim | *esp. spoken* **horrible • disgusting** | *esp. BrE, esp. spoken* **dreadful** | *infml* **vile • horrendous • lousy • ghastly** | *written* **wretched**

▶ a/an awful/terrible/bad/nasty/horrible/dreadful **thought/feeling**
▶ a/an awful/terrible/horrible/dreadful **noise/shock**
▶ awful/terrible/bad/foul/nasty/grim/horrible/dreadful/vile/lousy/ghastly/wretched **weather**
▶ a/an awful/terrible/bad/foul/revolting/nasty/horrible/disgusting/vile **smell**

2 [only before noun] (*infml, esp. spoken*) ■ *The whole thing has been an awful nuisance.*

terrible

▶ an awful/a terrible **mistake/mess/nuisance/disappointment**
▶ an awful/a terrible **fool/snob**

3 ■ *the awful horrors of war*

terrible • horrible • dreadful • horrific • horrifying • gruesome | *BrE* or *fml, AmE* **appalling**

■ OPP **great**

▶ a/an awful/terrible/horrible/dreadful/horrific/horrifying/gruesome/appalling **scene/sight**
▶ a/an awful/terrible/horrible/dreadful/horrific/horrifying/appalling **accident/incident**
▶ awful/terrible/horrible/dreadful/horrific/appalling **pain/suffering**
● AWFUL, TERRIBLE OR APPALLING?
Awful is more often used to describe events or experiences. In BrE appalling is used to describe accidents, crimes and their results, and also bad social conditions. You can use terrible for all of these, although appalling is stronger.

awkward adj.

1 ■ She is awkward with people she doesn't know.

uncomfortable • embarrassed • self-conscious • sheepish

▶ awkward/uncomfortable/embarrassed/self-conscious/sheepish **about** sth
▶ an awkward/uncomfortable/embarrassed **silence**
▶ a/an embarrassed/self-conscious/sheepish **smile**
● AWKWARD, UNCOMFORTABLE OR EMBARRASSED? Embarrassed is used esp. to describe how sb feels; **uncomfortable** can describe a situation; **awkward** often describes sb's personality or bad behaviour.

2 ■ You've put me in an awkward position.

problematic • delicate • sensitive | infml **tricky**

▶ a/an awkward/problematic/delicate/sensitive/tricky **matter/situation**
▶ a/an awkward/problematic/delicate/sensitive **relationship**
▶ a/an awkward/problematic/delicate/sensitive/tricky **question/subject/problem**

3 ■ Please don't be awkward about letting him come.

difficult • perverse • obstructive • uncooperative • unhelpful

▶ be awkward/difficult **about** sth
▶ an awkward/a difficult **customer**
▶ **deliberately** awkward/perverse/obstructive

Bb

baby noun

1 [C] ■ He cried like a baby.

child | fml or tech. **infant**

▶ a **newborn** baby/child/infant
▶ **have/give birth to** a baby/child/infant
▶ a/an baby/child/infant **is born**

2 [C] ■ What do you call a baby kangaroo?

offspring • young

▶ **produce/rear/raise** babies/offspring/young
▶ **give birth to** a(a) baby/offspring/young
● BABY, OFFSPRING OR YOUNG? Offspring and young are more scientific, technical words. The parent animal must be mentioned or understood when using them:
✓The females stay close to their offspring/young. • Oh, look! That one's just a baby! ✗ Oh, look! That one's just an offspring/young.

back verb [T]

■ Her parents backed her in her choice of career.

support • second • champion • side with sb • vote | BrE **(be) in favour (of sb/sth) |** AmE **(be) in favor (of sb/sth)**

▶ back/support/side with sb **in** sth
▶ back/support/second/vote for/be in favour of a **plan/proposal/motion/resolution**
▶ back/support/champion/be in favour of **reform/an idea**

background noun

1 [C] ■ The job would suit sb with a design background.

record • past • history • upbringing • origin/origins • roots • parentage • track record • life history

▶ sb has a background/history/record/track record **of** sth
▶ sb has a/their background/history/record/track record/origins/roots **in** sth
▶ (a) **working class/middle class** background/upbringing/origins/roots
▶ sb's **ethnic/social/cultural** background/origin/roots

2 [C, usu. sing., U] ■ the complex historical background to the war

context • setting | written **backdrop |** fml **milieu**

▶ **against** a background/backdrop
▶ the **cultural/historical/economic/political** background/context/setting/milieu
▶ **describe** the background/context/setting
● BACKGROUND OR BACKDROP? Background has a much wider range than backdrop, which is used esp. in more literary texts and in the phrase against a backdrop of sth: It was against this background/backdrop of racial tension that the civil war began. • Can you give me some more background? • background information

3 [C, usu. sing.] ■ snow-capped mountains in the background

setting • surroundings | written **backdrop**

■ OPP the **foreground**
▶ **against** a/the background/backdrop **of** sth
▶ a **dramatic** background/setting/backdrop
▶ **provide/create** (a) background/setting/surroundings/backdrop

bad *adj.*

1 ■ *I'm having a really bad day.*

unpleasant • nasty • grim • terrible |
esp. spoken awful • horrible | *infml*
lousy • ghastly • vile | *written*
wretched | *esp. BrE, esp. spoken*
dreadful

■ OPP **good**
► a/an bad/unpleasant/nasty/
terrible/awful/ghastly/dreadful
experience/feeling
► a/an bad/grim/terrible/awful/
lousy/wretched/dreadful **day/
night/time**
► bad/unpleasant/nasty/grim/
terrible/awful/lousy/ghastly/vile/
wretched/dreadful **weather**
► bad/grim/terrible/awful/ghastly/
dreadful **time**

2 ■ *It was a bad time for her.*

hard • difficult • tough • rough •
adverse | *fml* disadvantageous | *BrE,
fml* unfavourable | *AmE, fml*
unfavorable

► bad/hard/difficult/tough/
disadvantageous/unfavourable **for
sb**
► a/an bad/hard/difficult/tough/
rough/unfavourable **situation**
► bad/hard/difficult/tough/rough/
adverse/unfavourable **conditions**
► a bad/hard/difficult/tough/rough
time/day/week/year

3 ■ *I thought it was a very bad article.*

poor • cheap • second-rate • low •
inferior | *infml* dismal | *BrE, infml*
hopeless | *BrE, taboo, slang* crap |
AmE, taboo, slang crappy •
shitty

■ OPP **good**
► a/an bad/poor/cheap/second-
rate/inferior **copy/imitation**
► a/an bad/poor/inferior/dismal/
crap/shit/crappy/shitty
performance
► a bad/cheap/second-rate/crap/
shit/crappy/shitty **product**
► bad/poor/second-rate/low/
inferior **quality**
● BAD OR POOR? **Bad** is used more in
informal spoken English; **poor** is
more frequent in written English. Some
words do not collocate with
both:
✔*a poor standard of living* ✗ ~~a bad
standard of living~~
✔*I don't think it's a bad school.* ✗ ~~I
don't think it's a poor school.~~

4 (*esp. spoken*) ■ *I've always been bad
at maths.*

poor • incompetent • inept | *infml*
useless • rotten

■ OPP **good**

► bad/poor/inept/useless/rotten **at
sth**
► a/an bad/poor/incompetent/
useless/rotten **teacher/driver**
► a/an bad/poor/inept/useless/rotten **mother/
father/parent**

5 (*infml, esp. spoken*) ■ *Their
engagement was a bad mistake.*

serious • severe | *fml* grave

► a bad/serious/severe/grave
problem/injury
► a bad/serious/severe **attack/bout**
► a bad/serious/grave **mistake**
► bad/severe **weather**

6 [only before noun] ■ *a bad time to
ask for help*

awkward • inconvenient • wrong •
inappropriate

■ OPP **good**
► a bad/an awkward/an
inconvenient/the wrong/an
inappropriate **time**

7 ■ *The hero gets to shoot all the bad
guys.*

wicked • evil | *fml* sinful

■ OPP **good**
► a/an bad/wicked/evil/sinful **man/
woman/person/life/act/deed/
thought**
► a bad/wicked **child**
► a bad/wicked **omen/influence**
● WICKED OR EVIL? These are very
strong words to describe people or
actions that are very bad. **Evil** is
stronger than **wicked** and is often
connected with the Devil. *Spirits,
forces, minds* and *masterminds* are
evil. *Children,
witches* and *stepmothers* are
bad, esp. in children's stories.

8 [usu. before noun] ■ *I will not
tolerate this bad behaviour.*

naughty • disobedient • rebellious •
defiant

■ OPP **good**
► a bad/naughty/disobedient/
rebellious/defiant **child**
► a bad/naughty/disobedient **boy/
girl**
► a bad/rebellious/defiant **attitude**

9 (*esp. spoken*) ■ *Sugary drinks are
bad for your teeth.*

damaging • negative • unhealthy |
fml harmful

■ OPP **good**
► bad/damaging/harmful **for sth**
► (a) bad/damaging/negative/
harmful **effect/influence/
publicity**
► a bad/an unhealthy **diet**

10 [usu. before noun] ■ *complaints
about bad language*

offensive • abusive • filthy • foul •
insulting | *esp. BrE* rude

> bad / offensive / abusive / filthy / foul / rude / insulting **language**

11 ■ *The meat had gone bad.*

rotten • off • sour • rancid • stale | *BrE* mouldy | *AmE* moldy

> bad / rotten **eggs**
> stale / mouldy **bread**
> **go** bad / off / rotten / sour / rancid / stale / mouldy

bad-tempered *adj.*

■ *Her husband is a bad-tempered man.*

irritable • moody • sulky • sullen • temperamental | *infml* grumpy | *written* morose • petulant

> a bad-tempered / irritable / moody / sullen / temperamental / grumpy / morose **man / woman**
> a sulky / petulant **child**

bag *noun* [C]

■ *I got my bag down from the rack.*

handbag • backpack • suitcase • case | *BrE* rucksack | *AmE* purse | *AmE or old-fash.* knapsack

> **carry** a bag / handbag / backpack / suitcase / case / rucksack / purse / knapsack
> **put on / take off** a backpack / rucksack / knapsack
> **pack / unpack** a bag / backpack / suitcase / case / rucksack / knapsack

baggage *noun* [U] (*esp. AmE*)

■ *Please do not leave baggage unattended.*

bags • suitcase | *esp. BrE* luggage

> **carry** baggage / bags / a suitcase / luggage
> **check (in)** your baggage / bags / suitcase / luggage
> **search** sb's baggage / bags / suitcase / luggage

bake *verb* [T, I]

■ *I'm baking a cake for Gloria.*

make • cook • roast

> bake / make **bread / a cake**
> bake / cook / roast **potatoes**
> cook / roast **meat / a chicken**

balance *verb* [I, I]

■ *How long can you balance on one leg?*

steady • stand • poise • lean • prop • rest

> balance / stand / lean / prop / rest (sth) **on** sth
> steady / stand / lean / prop / rest (sth) **against** sth
> steady / poise / prop **yourself** somewhere

ban *noun* [C]

■ *a total ban on smoking in the office*

embargo • veto • moratorium • boycott • taboo | *fml* prohibition

> a / an ban / embargo / veto / moratorium / boycott / taboo / prohibition **on** sth
> a / an ban / embargo / veto / taboo / prohibition **against** sb / sth
> **impose** a ban / embargo / veto / moratorium / boycott / prohibition
> **lift** a ban / embargo / veto / boycott / prohibition

ban *verb* [T]

■ *plans to ban smoking in public places* ■ *He was banned from the meeting.*

forbid • outlaw • bar • exclude • expel • keep sb/sth out • shut sb/sth out • blacklist | *fml* prohibit

■ OPP permit

> ban / bar / exclude / expel / prohibit sb **from** sth
> ban / forbid / bar / prohibit sb **from doing** sth
> ban / forbid / outlaw / prohibit the **practice / use / sale** of sth

band *noun*

1 [C+sing./pl. v.] ■ *a small band of volunteers*

group • team • party • gang • contingent • crew • squad • corps • detachment • ring | *infml* bunch • crowd | *often disapprov.* pack

> a band / group / team / party / gang / contingent / crew / squad / corps / detachment / bunch / crowd / pack **of** sth
> **join** a band / group / team / party / group / gang / crew / corps

2 [C] ■ *She always ties her hair back in a band.* ■ *The plate was white with a blue band around the edge.*

ribbon • stripe • strip

> a band / ribbon / strip **of** sth
> a narrow / wide / broad band / ribbon / stripe / strip
> **wear** a band / ribbon

bandage *noun* [C, U]

■ *Make sure the bandage isn't too tight.*

dressing • compress • tourniquet | *BrE* plaster | *esp. AmE* Band-Aid™

> **apply** a bandage / dressing / compress / tourniquet
> **put on / take off** a bandage / plaster / Band-Aid

bang *noun* [C]

■ *The door swung shut with a bang.*

crash • clang • thud • thump • crack

▶ **with** a bang/crash/clang/thud/thump/crack
▶ a **loud** bang/crash/clang/thud/thump/crack
▶ **hear** a bang/crash/clang/thud/thump/crack

bang verb [T, I]

1 ■ *The baby was banging the table with a spoon.*

knock • hit • bump | *infml* bash | *fml* strike

▶ bang/knock/hit/bump/bash **against** sb/sth
▶ bang/knock/hit/bump/bash **into** sb/sth

2 [T, I] ■ *The door banged shut behind her.*

crash • clash • explode • crack

▶ a door bangs/crashes
▶ **thunder** crashes/cracks/explodes
▶ bang/crash/explode/crack **loudly**

3 [T] ■ *She fell and banged her head.*

bump • hit • crack • knock

▶ bang/bump/hit/crack/knock your head/knee, etc. **on/against** sth
▶ bang/bump/hit/crack/knock your **head/forehead**
▶ bang/bump/hit/knock your **arm/knee/elbow**

bankrupt adj.

■ *The firm went bankrupt in 2008.*

destitute | *infml* bust • broke | *lit.* penniless | *finance* insolvent

▶ go bankrupt/bust/broke
▶ declare sb bankrupt/insolvent
● **BANKRUPT, BUST, BROKE OR INSOLVENT?** In general English **bankrupt** is preferred. *Go bust* and *go broke* are informal ways of saying *go bankrupt*. **Insolvent** is used more about businesses than individuals.

banned adj.

■ *Traces of a banned pesticide were detected.*

forbidden • taboo | *fml* prohibited

▶ banned/forbidden/taboo/prohibited **areas**
▶ banned/prohibited **substances/weapons**
▶ banned/forbidden/prohibited **by law**

bar noun [C]

■ *Let's have a drink in the bar.*

BrE pub | *BrE, infml* local | *BrE, fml* public house | (in the past) inn • tavern • saloon

▶ go to a bar/the pub/a public house/an inn/a tavern/a saloon

bare adj.

1 ■ *walking in bare feet*

naked • nude • undressed • in the nude

▶ sb's bare/naked **skin/flesh/shoulder/thigh/torso**
▶ **completely/almost** bare/naked/nude

2 ■ *They spent a cold night on the bare mountainside.*

bare • exposed • bleak • windswept | *written* desolate

▶ bare/bleak/desolate **countryside/landscape/mountains**
▶ a/an exposed/bleak/windswept/desolate **coast/hillside**

3 ■ *bare wooden floorboards*

plain | *usu. approv.* simple • austere | *often disapprov.* stark • severe

▶ a bare/plain/simple **interior**
▶ bare/plain/simple/stark **white...**
▶ plain/simple/stark/severe **black...**

4 ■ *Bare shelves greeted anxious shoppers.*

empty • vacant

▶ bare/empty **of** sth
▶ a/an bare/empty/vacant **room**
▶ a/an bare/empty **cupboard**

bargain noun [C]

■ *The car was a bargain at that price.*

good buy | *esp. BrE* value | *infml* giveaway | *BrE, infml* a snip | *esp. AmE, infml* steal

▶ **be** (a) bargain/good buy/good value/giveaway/snip/steal **at** a particular price
▶ bargain/giveaway **prices**

barrel noun [C]

■ *They got through two barrels of beer.*

keg • drum • cylinder • tank • vat • tub

▶ a beer barrel/keg
▶ an oil barrel/drum/tank
▶ fill a barrel/drum/cylinder/tank/vat/tub

barrier noun

1 [C] ■ *Crowds stood behind the barriers.*

obstacle • barricade • roadblock • hurdle | *written* obstruction

▶ a **physical** barrier/obstacle/obstruction
▶ a **police** barrier/barricade/roadblock
▶ **erect/set up** a barrier/barricade/roadblock

► **hit** a/an barrier/obstacle/hurdle/
obstruction

2 [C] ■ *a psychological barrier to
success*

**obstacle • hurdle • handicap •
hindrance •** *fml* **impediment** | *esp.
journ.* **stumbling block** | *AmE, esp.
journ.* **roadblock**

► a/an barrier/obstacle/handicap/
hindrance/impediment/stumbling
block **to** sth
► **remove** a/an barrier/obstacle/
impediment/stumbling block/
roadblock
► **overcome** a/an barrier/obstacle/
hurdle/handicap
● **BARRIER OR OBSTACLE?** A **barrier**
makes sth impossible to do or
achieve; an **obstacle** makes sth
difficult but not impossible.

base *noun*

1 [C, usu. sing.] ■ *The statue has a
solid concrete base.*

bottom • foundation • foot

► **at/near/towards** the base/
bottom/foot of sth
► **on** the base/bottom of sth
► (a) **firm/solid/strong** base/
foundations

2 [C, usu. sing.] ■ *His arguments have
a sound economic base.*

basis • foundation

► the base/basis/foundation **for/of**
sth
► a/an **ideological/intellectual/
philosophical/theoretical/
economic** base/basis/foundation
► **form/have** sth as/**establish/use**
sth as a/the base/basis/
foundation of sth

3 [C] ■ *The company has its base in
New York.*

headquarters • office

► (a/an) **permanent/temporary/
main/local/regional/
administrative** base/
headquarters/office
► (a/an) **army/military/enemy/
rebel/operational/business**
base/headquarters
► **have/establish/set up** a/an base/
headquarters/office

base *verb* [T, often passive]

■ *She works for a company based in
Chicago.*

site | *esp. written* **locate** | *fml* **be
situated**

► be based/sited/located/situated
in/at/close to sth
► be based/sited/located/situated
between A and B
► **conveniently** based/sited/
located/situated

basement *noun* [C]

■ *Kitchen goods are sold in the
basement.*

cellar • bunker • crypt

► **in** a basement/cellar/bunker/
crypt
► the basement/cellar **door/stairs/
steps**
● **BASEMENT OR CELLAR?** A **basement**
is usu. an underground level in a
large modern building; a **cellar** is
usu. an underground room for
storing things, esp. in an older
building.

basic *adj.*

■ *the most basic information* ■ *basic
human rights*

**essential • fundamental •
elementary • underlying** | *fml*
rudimentary

► basic/fundamental **to** sth
► a/an basic/essential/
fundamental/underlying
**assumption/aim/problem/
cause/reason/need/weakness**
► a/an basic/fundamental/
elementary/rudimentary **skill/
understanding/knowledge/level**
● **BASIC OR ESSENTIAL?** **Basic** looks at
things from a practical point of
view; **essential** looks at things from
a more philosophical point of view,
considering the very nature of
things.

basics *noun* [pl.]

■ *the basics of computer programming*

**fundamentals • essentials •
introduction • practicalities**

► a/the **basic** fundamentals/
essentials/introduction
► **teach/grasp** the basics/
fundamentals/essentials
► **understand/know/cover/
concentrate on** the basics/
essentials
● **BASICS, ESSENTIALS OR
FUNDAMENTALS?** **Basics** are usu. the
most practical, **essentials** are often
more theoretical and
fundamentals are the most
theoretical, concerned with ideas
and beliefs: *the basics of survival/
good nutrition* • *the essentials of
arithmetic/how we communicate
using language* • *the fundamentals
of Christian belief/the western
concept of law*

basis *noun*

1 [sing.] ■ *She was chosen on the
basis of her qualifications.*

**reason • grounds • justification •
cause • argument • case**

bath

▶ **(a/an)** basis/reason/grounds/
justification/cause/argument/case
for sth
▶ **on the** basis/grounds **of/that...**
▶ the basis/reason/grounds/
justification/argument/case
that...

2 [C, usu. sing.] ■ *The basis for a good
marriage is trust.*

foundation ◆ base

▶ a/the foundation/base of/
for sth
▶ **have** a/the foundation/base as/**establish/use** sth as/
form a/the basis/foundation/base
of sth
▶ **have no** basis/foundation **in fact**
● **BASIS OR FOUNDATION?** Foundation
is often used to talk about more
important things than a **basis**: *He laid
the foundation of
Japan's modern economy. • These
figures formed the basis of their pay
claim.*

bath *noun* [C]

■ *I think I'll have a bath.*

shower ◆ wash

▶ a **hot/cold** bath/shower
▶ **have** a bath/shower/wash
▶ **take** a bath/shower

bathroom *noun* [C]

■ *I have to go to the bathroom.*

BrE **toilet** | *AmE* **restroom ◆ ladies'
room ◆ men's room** | *BrE, infml* **loo** |
BrE, fml **lavatory**

▶ **use/go to the** bathroom/toilet/
restroom/ladies'room/men's
room/loo/lavatory
▶ **need the** bathroom/toilet/loo/
lavatory
● **BATHROOM OR TOILET?** In *BrE*
bathroom means a room with a
bath or shower in it. It may also
contain a toilet. In *AmE* **bathroom**
often means a room with a toilet in
it, even if there is no bath or
shower. In *AmE* **toilet** is used only
for the toilet itself, not for the room
in which it is found.

battle *noun*

1 [C, U] ■ *Napoleon was defeated at
the Battle of Waterloo.*

**fighting ◆ combat ◆ campaign ◆
skirmish ◆ war ◆ conflict** | *esp. journ.*
action ◆ hostilities

▶ **(a/an)** battle/fighting/combat/
campaign/skirmish/war/conflict/
action/hostilities **with/between/
against** sb/sth
▶ **in** battle/fighting/combat/war/
conflict/action/hostilities
▶ **win/lose** a battle/campaign/
skirmish/war/conflict

▶ **fight** a battle/campaign/war

2 [C] ■ *the legal battle for
compensation*

**struggle ◆ fight ◆ campaign ◆
crusade ◆ war ◆ drive**

▶ a battle/struggle/fight/
campaign/crusade/drive **for** sth
▶ a battle/struggle/fight/
campaign/crusade/drive/war
against sth
▶ **win/lose** the battle/struggle/
fight/war
● **BATTLE OR STRUGGLE?** A **struggle** is
always about things that seem
absolutely necessary. A **battle** can
also be about things that are
desirable but not absolutely
necessary:
*✓the battle/struggle between good
and evil/man and nature* x *a legal
struggle for compensation*
✓a battle of wills/wits x *a struggle of
wills/wits*

be *linking verb*

1 (*esp. spoken*) ■ *How much is that
dress?*

cost ◆ sell ◆ go | *infml* **set sb back** sth
| *busin.* **trade ◆ retail**

▶ **How much** does this cost/is this?
▶ That costs/ will set you back **a lot
of money.**
▶ sth sells/goes/retails **for £9.95**
▶ sth sells/trades/retails **at £9.95**

2 ■ *Three and three is six.*

equal ◆ make ◆ add up to sth ◆
amount to sth ◆ **run to** sth ◆ **number**
| *esp. busin.* **total**

▶ be/equal/make/add up to/
amount to/run to/number/total
50/5,000/5 million, etc.
▶ be/equal/make/add up to/
amount to/run to/total **$50/75%**
▶ be/add up to/amount to/run to/
number/total **about/around/
approximately/nearly/almost/
over/more than/at least** sth
● **BE OR EQUAL?** Equal is not usu. used
in questions and is only used in
exact sums:
*✓How much is a thousand pounds in
Euros?* x *How much does a thousand
pounds equal in Euros?*
*✓A metre is about/around/
approximately 40 inches.* x *A metre
equals about/around/approximately
40 inches.*

beach *noun* [C]

■ *They were sunbathing on the beach.*

**seashore ◆ sand ◆ shoreline ◆
lakeside ◆ shore ◆ coast ◆ coastline** |
esp. BrE **seaside ◆ sea** | *AmE* **ocean**

▶ **on the** beach/seashore/sand/
shoreline/lakeside/shore/coast/
coastline

► **at** the beach/seashore/coast/
seaside
► **by** the seashore/lakeside/shore/
coast/seaside/sea/ocean
► **go to** the beach/seashore/coast/
seaside/sea/ocean
● **BEACH OR SEASHORE?** Beach is usu.
used about a sandy area next to
the sea, where people lie in the sun
or play. **Seashore** is used more to
talk about the area by the sea
where people walk for pleasure: He
liked to look for shells on the
seashore.

bear verb

1 [I, T] (not used in the progressive
tenses) ■ How can you bear this
awful noise?

stand • take | esp. written **tolerate** |
esp. spoken **put up with sb/sth** | fml
endure

► (can't/not) bear/stand/endure
doing sth
► (can't/not) bear/stand/put up
with sb/sth doing sth
► bear/stand/put up with/endure
pain
► sb can hardly bear/stand sth
● **BEAR OR STAND?** Bear is slightly
stronger and more formal than
stand. Stand is used with can/could
in negative statements and
questions, but not in positive
statements:
✔ She bore it with her usual patience.
✗ She stood it with her usual
patience.

2 can't bear [T] (not used in the
progressive tenses) ■ She couldn't
bear the thought of losing him.

can't stand • hate • loathe • detest

► can't bear/can't stand/hate/
loathe/detest doing sth
► can't bear/hate to do sth
► can't bear/can't stand/hate it
when...

3 [T] (fml) ■ She had to bear the
blame for his mistakes.

accept • take • shoulder • carry | fml
assume

► bear/accept/take/shoulder/
carry/assume sth for sb/sth
► bear/accept/take/shoulder/
carry/assume the **responsibility**
► bear/accept/take/shoulder/carry
the **blame**

4 [T] ■ The ground was too soft to
bear his weight.

hold • support • carry

► bear/hold/support/carry the
weight of sb/sth
● **BEAR OR HOLD?** Bear is slightly more
formal and can also be used
figuratively:
✔ He seemed unable to bear the

weight of responsibility. ✗ He seemed
unable to hold the weight of
responsibility.

beat noun [C]

■ I like dancing to music with a strong
beat.

rhythm | music **tempo**

► regular/strong/throbbing
beat/rhythm
► have/lack a beat/rhythm/tempo
► clap/dance/sway to the beat/
rhythm

beat verb

1 [T] ■ He beat me at chess.

defeat • get the better of sb | esp.
BrE, infml **thrash** | AmE, infml **whip** |
written **overcome** • rout • trounce |
fml **best** • prevail | lit. **vanquish**

► beat/defeat/thrash/rout/trounce
sb by 10 points/4 goals, etc.
► beat/defeat/get the better of/
thrash/whip/overcome/rout/
trounce/vanquish an **opponent**
► beat/defeat/overcome/rout/
vanquish an **enemy**
● **BEAT OR DEFEAT?** You can use beat
to talk about winning against one
or several opponents in a
competition or race; use **defeat** to
talk about one opponent in a battle
or contest: She won the 100 metres,
beating a number of top Europeans.
• He defeated the incumbent
president.
Beat is more common in spoken
and **defeat** in written English.

2 [I, T] ■ beating a drum

batter • pound • hammer • pummel
• hit • thump • lash • dash

► beat/batter/pound/hammer/
pummel/hit/lash sb/sth **with** sth
► beat/batter/pound/hammer/
lash/dash sb/sth **against** sth
► beat/batter/pound/hammer/
lash/dash sb **to death**
► the rain/wind/sea beats/batters/
pounds/lashes/dashes (at) sth

3 [I] ■ Her heart began to beat faster.

pulse • throb • pound | written
flutter

► sb's **heart** beats/pulses/throbs/
pounds/flutters
► sb's **blood** beats/pulses/throbs/
pounds
► sb's **pulse** beats/throbs/pounds/
flutters
● **BEAT, PULSE OR THROB?** Pulse and
throb are stronger than **beat** but
are not used to talk about drums.
Music and pain can **pulse** or **throb**.
Machines **throb** but don't **pulse**.

4 [T] ■ *Beat the eggs until they are frothy.*

whisk • whip • stir • mix • blend

▸ beat/whisk/stir/mix/blend sth **into** sth
▸ beat/whisk/stir A and B **together**
▸ beat/whisk/whip **cream/eggs/ egg whites**

beat sb up *phrasal verb*

■ *He was badly beaten up by a gang of thugs.*

attack • assault • mug

▸ beat up/attack/assault sb **with** sth
▸ **get** beaten up/mugged
▸ **violently** beat up/attack/assault sb

beautiful *adj.*

1 ■ *What a beautiful baby!*

pretty • handsome • good-looking • attractive • striking | *esp. BrE* lovely | *infml* gorgeous • stunning | *esp. AmE, infml* cute

■ OPP **ugly**
▸ a/an beautiful/pretty/handsome/ good-looking/attractive/striking/ lovely/gorgeous/stunning/cute **girl/woman**
▸ a/an beautiful/pretty/handsome/ good-looking/attractive/lovely/ gorgeous/cute **boy**
▸ a/an beautiful/handsome/good-looking/attractive/lovely/ gorgeous/cute **man**
▸ a/an beautiful/pretty/handsome/ good-looking/attractive/lovely/ cute **child**

2 ■ *What a beautiful sight!*

pretty • attractive • charming • picturesque • scenic • glorious • magnificent • spectacular • exquisite | *esp. BrE* lovely

■ OPP **ugly**
▸ a/an beautiful/attractive/ charming/picturesque/scenic/ glorious/magnificent/spectacular/ exquisite/lovely **view**
▸ beautiful/attractive/picturesque/ glorious/magnificent/spectacular/ lovely **countryside**
▸ a/an beautiful/pretty/attractive/ charming/picturesque/lovely **place/town/village**
▸ a/an beautiful/pretty/attractive/ exquisite/lovely **design**
● **BEAUTIFUL or LOVELY?** Something that is *lovely* always has a warm quality that appeals not only to the eyes but also to the heart; *beautiful* things often have this quality, but they do not have to: ✔*The designs were pure, austere and coldly beautiful.* ✗ ~~The designs were pure, austere and coldly lovely.~~

become *linking verb*

■ *She was becoming confused.*

get • go • grow • turn • come

▸ become/get/go/grow/turn **cold/ warm/chilly**
▸ become/get/grow **fat/old/ angry/hungry/tired**
▸ become/get **annoyed/confused/ involved/worried**
▸ become/come **loose**
● **BECOME OR GET?** You can often use either word, but there are some cases where you can only use one of them: *I became/got hungry/upset* (= verb + adjective). • *She became Queen/a teacher/a member of the club* (= verb + noun). • *Don't get your dress dirty* (= verb + noun + adjective)!
Use *get* for changes that are the result of deliberate actions by you or sb else: *get dressed/married/killed*
Use *become* with adjectives connected with ability, knowledge, availability and clarity: *become able/skilled/aware/convinced/ available/useful/clear/obvious*

beg *verb* [I, T]

■ *beg for mercy*

plead • ask • appeal | *fml* implore • request

▸ beg/plead/ask **for** sth
▸ beg/plead with/ask/appeal to/ implore/request **sb to do sth**

beggar *noun* [C] (*often disapprov.*)

■ *beggars sleeping in doorways*

tramp | *esp. AmE* drifter | *esp. AmE, infml* bum | *esp. BrE, infml* scrounger | *fml or law* vagrant

● **WHICH WORD?** All these words are disapproving. Neutral terms are **homeless person/man/woman** and **the homeless** [pl.]: *the plight of the homeless in the city*

begin *verb* [T, I]

■ *We began work on the project in May.* ■ *What time does the concert begin?*

start • open • take sth up • set about sth • go about sth • start off • set/put sth in motion | *infml* kick off | *fml* embark on/upon sth • commence • initiate • institute | *esp. busin. or journ.* launch

■ OPP **end**
▸ begin/start/take up/set about/go about/commence **doing sth**
▸ begin/start **to do** sth
▸ begin/start/open/start off/kick off/commence **by doing sth**
▸ begin/start/open/start off/kick off/commence **with sth**
● **BEGIN OR START?** Compare:
✔*'Ladies and gentlemen,' he began.*
✗ ~~'Ladies and gentlemen,' he started.~~

✓Who started the fire? • I can't start the car ✗ *Who began the fire?* • *I can't begin the car.*

beginner noun [C]
■ *Japanese for beginners*

novice • newcomer | *esp. AmE, infml* rookie

■ OPP expert, veteran
▶ a beginner/novice in sth
▶ a/an absolute/complete beginner/novice

beginning noun

1 [C, usu. sing.] ■ *the beginning of July/the movie*

start • opening • birth | *fml* outset • onset | *lit.* dawn | (in football) kick-off

■ OPP end, ending
▶ at the beginning/start/opening/ outset/onset/birth/dawn (of sth)
▶ in the beginning
▶ from the (very) beginning/start/ outset
● BEGINNING OR START? Compare:
✓We missed the beginning of the movie (= the first few scenes). • We'll miss the start of the game (= the moment when it starts; the kick-off). • *from start to finish* • *from beginning to end* ✗ *from start to finish* • *from beginning to finish*
✓*the beginning/start of the day/ week/year/century/a new era* • *at the beginning of July/summer /the 90s* ✗ *at the start of July/summer/the 90s*
✓*I want to make an early start* ✗ *I want to make an early beginning.*

2 beginnings [pl.] ■ *From these small beginnings it grew into the vast company we know today.*

origin/origins • source • root • starting point

■ OPP end, ending
▶ have its beginnings/origin/ source/roots in sth
▶ from these/this beginnings/ source/starting point

behave verb [I]
■ *They behaved very badly towards their guests.*

act • treat | *fml* conduct yourself

▶ behave/act/treat sb/conduct yourself as if/as though/like...
▶ behave/act/conduct yourself well
▶ behave/treat sb badly
● BEHAVE OR ACT? Behave is used to talk about how well, sensibly or normally sb has behaved, but not how fairly or legally. Act is used to talk about how sensibly, normally, fairly or legally sb has behaved, but not how well.

behaviour (*BrE*) (*AmE* behavior) noun [U]
■ *His behaviour towards her was becoming more aggressive.*

treatment • manners | *fml* conduct

▶ your behaviour/manners/conduct towards sb
▶ good/bad behaviour/treatment/ manners/conduct

belief noun

1 [U] ■ *belief in God/a cause*

faith • trust • confidence • conviction

■ OPP disbelief, doubt
▶ belief/faith/trust/confidence in sb/sth
▶ shake sb's belief/faith/ confidence/conviction
▶ destroy sb's belief/faith/trust/ confidence

2 [C, U] ■ *It's my belief that she's telling the truth.*

opinion • view • feeling • judgement • conviction • theory | *fml* contention • hypothesis • thesis

▶ the belief/opinion/view/idea/ point of view/feeling/judgement/ conviction/theory/contention/ hypothesis/thesis that...
▶ a strong belief/opinion/view/ feeling/conviction
▶ a popular belief/opinion/view/ feeling

3 [C, usu. pl.] ■ *You need to examine your own attitudes and beliefs.*

values • principles • ideal • ethics • conviction • teaching • doctrine • philosophy • code | *sometimes disapprov.* ideology | *fml* ethos • tenet

▶ religious beliefs/values/ principles/ideals/conviction/ teaching/doctrine/philosophy/ code/ethos/tenets
▶ political beliefs/values/principles/ ideals/ethics/convictions/ doctrine/philosophy/code/ ideology/ethos/tenets
▶ hold beliefs/values

believe verb

1 [T, I] ■ *I don't believe you!* ■ *Do you believe in God?*

trust • have confidence in sb/sth • have faith in sth

■ OPP doubt, (*fml*) disbelieve
▶ believe/trust/have confidence in/ have faith in sb/sth

2 [T] ■ *She believes that eating meat is wrong.*

believe in sth

think • feel • consider • be under the impression that... | *esp. BrE, infml* reckon | *fml* hold

▶ believe/think/feel/consider/be under the impression/reckon/hold that...

● **BELIEVE OR THINK?** When you are talking about an idea of what is true or possible, use **believe** to talk about other people and **think** to talk about yourself: *Police believe (that) the man may be armed.* • *I think this is their house, but I'm not sure.*
Use **believe** to talk about matters of principle; use **think** to talk about practical matters or matters of personal taste: *I believe we have a responsibility towards the less fortunate in society.* • *I think we should reserve seats in advance.* • *I don't think he's funny at all.*

believe in sth *phrasal verb*
■ *I don't believe in hitting children*

approve of sb/sth | *BrE* be in favour of sb/sth | *AmE* be in favor of sth | *infml* be all for sth | *fml* subscribe to sb/sth

▶ believe in/approve of/be in favour of/be all for **doing sth**

bend *noun* [C]
■ *a sharp bend in the road*

curve • turn • corner • twist • zigzag • hairpin | *BrE* hairpin bend | *AmE* hairpin curve/turn

▶ around/round the bend/corner
▶ a sharp bend/turn/corner/twist

bend *verb*

1 [I, T] ■ *He bent and kissed her.*

stoop • bow • duck • bend down • bend over • crouch • hunch • squat • kneel | *esp. AmE* hunker down

■ OPP straighten up
▶ bend/stoop/bow/duck/crouch/hunch/squat/kneel/hunker **down**
▶ bend/bow/duck your **head**

2 [T] ■ *He bent the wire into the shape of a square.*

twist • deform • buckle • warp

■ OPP straighten
▶ be bent/twisted **out of shape**
▶ bend/buckle **under the weight of sth**

benefit *noun*

1 [U, C] ■ *She had the benefit of a good education.*

advantage • merit • good • reward • strength • asset • good point • good thing • bonus • help • virtue | *infml* plus

■ OPP disadvantage, drawback
▶ There's no benefit/advantage/merit/virtue in sth.
▶ be to sb's benefit/advantage
▶ be for sb's benefit/good
▶ reap the benefits/rewards

2 [usu. pl.] ■ *The company offers generous pay and benefits.*

bonus • perk

▶ tax-free benefits/bonuses/perks
▶ receive/enjoy benefits/a bonus/perks

benefit *verb*

1 [T] ■ *We should spend the money on something that will benefit everyone.*

help • serve | *fml* assist • aid • be of use to sb • profit

■ OPP disadvantage

2 [I] ■ *Who stands to benefit from these changes?*

gain | *fml* profit | *disapprov.* cash in

▶ benefit/gain/profit **from/by** sth
▶ stand to benefit/gain/profit

bent *adj.*
■ *a piece of bent wire* ■ *a small, bent old woman*

twisted • deformed • crooked • gnarled

■ OPP straight
▶ twisted/gnarled roots/branches
▶ deformed/gnarled hands
▶ a twisted/crooked smile

best *adj.*
■ *the best way to cook steak* ■ *It's best if you go now.*

ideal • optimum • wise • sensible • preferred | *fml* desirable • advisable | *fml, BrE* favoured | *fml, AmE* favored

■ OPP worst
▶ be best/wise/sensible/desirable/advisable **to do sth**
▶ the best/the optimum/a wise/a sensible/an ideal/the preferred **choice**
▶ the best/a wise/a sensible **thing to do**

bet *verb*

1 [I, T] ■ *She bet me £20 that I wouldn't do it.*

gamble • stake • risk

▶ bet/gamble/stake/risk sth **on** sth

2 [T] ■ *I bet we're too late.*

be sure • be certain • know • guarantee

> ► bet/be sure/be certain/know/
> guarantee that...
> ► You can bet/be sure/guarantee...

betray verb [T] (disapprov.)
■ She betrayed my trust. ■ He betrayed his country.

disapprov. **deceive** • **cheat** • **let sb down** • **stab sb in the back** | infml, disapprov. **tell** • **blab** | fml, often disapprov. **inform on sb** | BrE **turn King's/Queen's evidence** | AmE **turn State's evidence** | AmE, infml **finger** | BrE, slang, disapprov. **grass** | infml, approv., esp. journ. **blow the whistle on sb**
> ► betray sb/blab/grass to sb
> ► tell/inform/grass/blow the whistle on sb
> ► feel betrayed/cheated/let down

betrayal noun [U, C]
■ I saw her actions as a betrayal of trust.

disloyalty • treason • infidelity | fml or law **bad faith**
■ OPP loyalty, (fml) fidelity, good faith
> ► a betrayal of sb/sth
> ► disloyalty/infidelity to sb/sth

better adj.
■ Her new movie is much better than her last one.

superior • preferable
■ OPP worse
> ► better than sb/sth
> ► superior/preferable to sb/sth
> ► far/greatly/vastly/infinitely better/superior/preferable

get better verb
1 [I] ■ Things got better after my husband found a job.

improve • pick up • progress • advance | infml **look up** • **come along/on**
■ OPP get worse
> ► things get better/improve/pick up/progress/are looking up/are coming along
> ► technology is getting better/improves/progresses/advances

2 [I] ■ He is finally getting better after a long illness.

recover • heal • get well • shake sth off • pull through | fml **recuperate** • convalesce
■ OPP get worse
> ► recover/recuperate from sth
> ► gradually get better/recover/heal

bias noun [U, C, usu. sing.] (usu. disapprov.)
■ They were accused of political bias.

prejudice • discrimination • intolerance • bigotry • racism • chauvinism • nationalism • sexism • ageism | BrE favouritism | AmE favoritism
■ OPP balance, objectivity, impartiality
> ► bias/prejudice/favouritism/discrimination/intolerance/bigotry/racism towards/toward sb/sth
> ► bias/prejudice/discrimination/bigotry/racism against sb/sth
> ► bias/prejudice/discrimination in favour of sb/sth
> ► racial/religious bias/prejudice/discrimination/intolerance

bias verb [T] (usu. disapprov.)
■ The newspapers have biased people against her.

influence • sway | disapprov. **prejudice** • **poison** | BrE **colour** | AmE **color**
> ► bias/influence/sway/prejudice/poison sb/sth against sb/sth
> ► bias/influence/sway sb/sth in favour of sb/sth
> ► bias/influence/sway the result of sb/sth

biased adj. (disapprov.)
■ They admit that they are biased towards the governing party.

prejudiced • partisan • one-sided • unbalanced • intolerant • bigoted • racist • sexist | fml **discriminatory**
■ OPP unbiased, balanced, objective, impartial
> ► biased/prejudiced/discriminatory against sb/sth
> ► biased/prejudiced in favour of sb/sth
> ► a/an biased/prejudiced/partisan/one-sided/unbalanced/bigoted/racist/sexist view

big adj.
1 ■ a big house/company/increase

large • great • tall • spacious • extensive • huge • massive • vast • enormous • sizeable • hefty • bumper
■ OPP little, small
> ► a/an big/large/tall/spacious/huge/massive/vast/enormous building
> ► a/an big/large/great/extensive/spacious/huge/massive/vast/enormous/sizeable area
> ► a/an big/large/great/huge/massive/vast/enormous/sizeable/hefty increase
● **BIG, LARGE or GREAT?** Compare: a **big** man/house/car/boy/dog/smile (a) **large** numbers/part/volume/

population ◆ *great interest/ importance/difficulty/pleasure*
Large is slightly more formal than **big** and is used more in writing. It is not usu. used to describe people, except to avoid saying 'fat'. **Great** often suggests quality and not just size; it describes the physical size of objects or people.

2 (*infml*) ■ *You are making a big mistake.*

important ◆ great ◆ major ◆ significant ◆ serious ◆ momentous

■ OPP little
▶ a/an big/important/great/major/ significant/serious/momentous **decision**
▶ a/an big/important/great/major/ significant/serious **difference**
▶ a/an big/important/great/major/ momentous **day**
▶ a big/great/major/significant/ serious **mistake**

bill *noun* [C]
■ *We ran up a massive hotel bill.*

invoice ◆ account ◆ statement ◆ tab | *AmE* check

▶ the bill/invoice/check/tab **for** sth
▶ **pay/settle** the bill/invoice/ account/check
▶ **pick up** the bill/tab/check
▶ **put sth on** the bill/(sb's) account/ the tab
● BILL OR INVOICE? You get a **bill** in a restaurant, bar or hotel; from a company that supplies you with gas, electricity, etc.; or from sb whose property you have damaged. An **invoice** is for goods supplied or work done as agreed between a customer and a supplier.

bit *noun* [C] (*esp. BrE*)
■ *a bit of pizza/shopping/luck*

piece ◆ scrap ◆ slice ◆ morsel ◆ fragment ◆ sliver ◆ particle ◆ speck ◆ pinch ◆ drop ◆ grain ◆ length | *BrE, infml* spot

▶ a bit/piece/scrap/slice of **meat**
▶ a bit/piece/scrap of **paper/ information/news**
▶ a **small/tiny** bit/piece/scrap/ morsel/fragment/sliver/particle/ speck/drop

bite *verb* [I, T]
■ *She bit into a ripe, juicy pear.*

chew ◆ munch ◆ crunch ◆ nibble ◆ gnaw

▶ bite/chew/munch/crunch/gnaw **through** sth
▶ bite/chew/munch/crunch/nibble **on** sth

▶ bite/chew/munch/nibble/gnaw **at** sth

bitter *adj.*

1 ■ *bitter coffee/chocolate*

sharp ◆ acid ◆ pungent ◆ acrid ◆ sour

■ OPP sweet
▶ a/an bitter/sharp/acid/pungent/ acrid/sour **taste/flavour/smell/ odour**
▶ a/an bitter/sharp/acid/sour **fruit**
▶ a/an bitter/sharp/pungent/acrid **scent**
● WHICH WORD? A **bitter** taste is usu. unpleasant, but some people enjoy the bitter flavour of coffee or chocolate; no other word can describe this flavour. A **sharp** or **pungent** flavour is more strong than unpleasant, esp. when describing cheese. **Sharp, sour** and **acid** all describe the taste of a lemon or a fruit that is not ripe. An **acrid** smell is strong and unpleasant, esp. the smell of smoke or burning, but not the smell of food.

2 ■ *He is bitter about losing his job.*

resentful ◆ sour ◆ disgruntled | *fml* embittered ◆ aggrieved ◆ acrimonious

▶ bitter/resentful/disgruntled/ aggrieved **about** sth
▶ bitter/resentful **towards** sb
▶ a/an bitter/sour/embittered **man**
▶ a bitter/an acrimonious **dispute/ divorce**
● BITTER, RESENTFUL OR SOUR? **Bitter** feelings are the strongest and most openly expressed; if you feel **resentful** or **sour** it may be less obvious: *feeling extremely/intensely/ very bitter* ◆ *a bitter laugh/smile* ◆ *vaguely/silently resentful* ◆ *resentful eyes* ◆ *a sour face*

bitterness *noun* [U]
■ *The pay cut caused great bitterness among the workers.*

resentment ◆ grudge ◆ bad feeling | *esp. AmE* bad feelings | *fml* acrimony

▶ the bitterness/resentment/bad feeling/bad feelings/acrimony **between** them
▶ bitterness/resentment/a grudge/ bad feelings/acrimony **about** sth
▶ resentment/a grudge **against** sb
● BITTERNESS OR RESENTMENT? **Bitterness** can be sudden and can last a long or short time: *she felt touched with a momentary/sudden bitterness.* ◆ *The long occupation of the island has left a legacy of bitterness.*
Resentment may be a less obvious feeling: people try or fail to hide it. It grows more slowly, but it may be shared by many people: *his*

growing/increasing/mounting/
smouldering resentment • popular/
public/widespread resentment

45

block

black adj.

1 ■ *It's pitch black outside tonight.*

dark • **unlit**

■ OPP **light**
▶ a black/dark **night**
▶ go black/dark
▶ pitch black/dark

2 (*esp. BrE*) ■ *a black girl*

African American • **non-white** •
mixed race | *AmE* **of color**

▶ black/African American/non-
white/mixed race **people**
▶ **people** of mixed race/color
▶ black/African American **culture**
● BLACK OR AFRICAN AMERICAN? **Black**
is the mostly widely used and
accepted term in Britain; a **black**
person from the US is **African
American**. **Black** can also be used
as a noun, but it is only acceptable
in the plural. Use the adjective for
singular use: *equality for blacks and
whites • a black man/woman*

blame noun [U]

■ *He refused to take the blame for their
mistakes.*

responsibility • **guilt** • **fault**

■ OPP **credit**
▶ the blame/responsibility/guilt for
sth
▶ accept/share/absolve sb from/
shift the blame/responsibility/
guilt
▶ the blame/responsibility/guilt/
fault lies with sb

blame verb [T]

■ *She blamed the police for failing to
respond quickly.*

criticize • **attack** • **condemn** •
denounce | *fml* **censure** • **rebuke** •
castigate

▶ blame/criticize/attack/condemn/
denounce/censure/rebuke/
castigate sb/sth **for** sth
▶ blame/criticize/attack/condemn/
denounce/censure the
government/president
▶ blame/criticize/attack/condemn/
denounce/censure/rebuke/
castigate sb/sth **publicly**

to blame adj.

■ *For once Ed was not to blame.*

responsible • **at fault** • **in the wrong**
• **guilty**

■ OPP **blameless**
▶ to blame/responsible/at fault **for**
sth
▶ feel to blame/responsible/guilty

▶ consider/hold sb to blame/
responsible/at fault/guilty

blank adj.

■ *She stared at me with a blank
expression.*

expressionless • **impassive** •
inscrutable • **glazed** • **bland** •
unreadable

■ OPP **expressive**
▶ a/an blank/impassive/
inscrutable/glazed/bland/
unreadable **expression**
▶ a/an blank/expressionless/
impassive/inscrutable/bland/
unreadable **face**
▶ blank/expressionless/inscrutable/
glazed/unreadable **eyes**
▶ a/an blank/inscrutable/glazed
look

block noun [C]

■ *a wall made from blocks of stone*

piece • **lump** • **slab**

▶ a block/piece/lump/slab of **ice**
▶ a block/piece/lump of **wood**
▶ a block/piece/slab of **stone**/
marble

block verb

1 [T] ■ *If you pour fat down the sink,
you will block the drain.*

clog • **choke** • **block sth up** • **stop** •
plug • **dam** • **seal**

■ OPP **unblock**
▶ block/clog/choke/stop/plug/
dam/seal sth up
▶ block/clog/choke/stop/seal sth
with sth
▶ block/plug/block up/seal a **hole**
▶ a **road** is blocked/clogged/choked
(with sth)

2 [T] ■ *A large building blocked the
view.*

be/get in sb's/the way • **cut sth off** •
block sth off • **bar** • **barricade** • **seal**
| *fml* **obstruct**

▶ block/bar/obstruct an **entrance**
▶ block/bar sb's **progress/exit**
▶ block/block off/barricade a **road**

3 [T] ■ *He accused them of trying to
block the agreement.*

interfere with sth • **hamper** • **hinder**
• **hold sb/sth back** • **disrupt** • **hold
sb/sth up** • **delay** • **stall** | *fml* **inhibit**
• **obstruct** • **retard**

▶ block/interfere with/hamper/
hinder/hold back/hold up/delay/
inhibit/obstruct/retard **progress**
▶ block/interfere with/hamper/
hinder/hold up/delay/inhibit/
obstruct/retard **development**
▶ block/interfere with/hinder/

blow

delay / stall / inhibit / obstruct / retard
a **process**
● **BLOCK OR INTERFERE WITH STH?**
People usu. **block** things such as
plans or *efforts* deliberately. Things
usu. **interfere with** sth without
anyone particularly intending it.

blow noun [C]
■ *Losing his job was a terrible blow.*

shock • disaster • catastrophe •
calamity • setback • knock •
disappointment

▶ a blow / shock / disaster /
catastrophe / calamity / setback /
disappointment **for** sb
▶ a blow / shock / setback /
disappointment **to** sb
▶ **suffer** a blow / shock / disaster /
catastrophe / calamity / setback /
knock / disappointment

blow verb
1 [I, T] ■ *You're not blowing hard
enough.*

puff • breathe out | *fml* exhale

■ **OPP** suck
▶ blow out / puff / breathe out / exhale
smoke
▶ blow / puff **hard**

2 [I, T] ■ *My hat blew away in the
wind.*

drift • flutter • fly • flap • waft • wave

▶ blow / drift / flutter / flap / waft / wave
gently
▶ blow / drift / flutter / fly / flap / wave
in the wind / breeze
▶ a flag flutters / flies / flaps / waves

3 [T, I] ■ *The referee blew his whistle.*

sound • play • blast • blare • honk •
toot

▶ blow / sound / blast / blare / honk /
toot a **horn**
▶ a **horn** blows / sounds / blasts /
blares / honks / toots
▶ blow / sound / play / blast a **trumpet**
▶ a **trumpet** blows / sounds / plays /
blasts / blares
▶ blow / sound a **whistle**
▶ a **whistle** blows / sounds

blow sth out phrasal verb
■ *She blew the candle out.*

put sth out • snuff • douse | *fml*
extinguish

■ **OPP** light
▶ blow / put / snuff sth **out**
▶ blow out / put out / snuff (out) /
douse / extinguish a **flame / flames**
▶ blow out / put out / snuff (out) /
extinguish a **candle**

blow (sth) up phrasal verb
■ *A man was killed when his car blew
up.*

explode • go off • burst • detonate

▶ a **bomb** blows up / explodes / goes
off / bursts / detonates
▶ a **car / plane / vehicle** blows up /
explodes

board noun
1 [C] ■ *The exam results are on the
board.*

sign • notice • plaque • plate | *BrE*
noticeboard | *AmE* bulletin board

▶ **on** a board / sign / notice / plaque /
plate / noticeboard / bulletin board
▶ **put up / see / read** a board / sign /
notice / plaque / plate /
noticeboard / bulletin board
▶ a board / sign / notice / plaque
appears / goes up

2 [C+sing./pl. v.] ■ *The project will go
to the board for discussion.*

committee • council • commisson •
panel • jury • delegation • body

▶ a/an **advisory / consultative**
board / committee / council / panel /
body
▶ a/an **executive / management**
board / committee / council / body
▶ **serve on / sit on** a board /
committee / council / commisson /
panel / jury / body

board verb [T, I] *(fml)*
■ *Passengers were waiting to board.*

get on • get in | *fml* embark

▶ board / get on / get in a **bus / train**
▶ board / get on a **plane / ship**

boast verb [I] *(usu. disapprov.)*
■ *She's always boasting about her
children.*

congratulate yourself • pride
yourself on sth | *disapprov.* brag •
show off • gloat

▶ boast / brag / show off / gloat **about**
sth
▶ boast / brag **of** sth
▶ boast / brag / congratulate yourself / brag
that...

boat noun [C]
■ *We spent the day on the boat.*

ship • yacht • dinghy • ferry • barge
• canoe • raft • cruiser | *fml* craft •
vessel

▶ **aboard / on board** a boat / ship /
yacht / ferry / barge / cruiser / vessel /
craft
▶ **travel / go / come by** boat / ship /
ferry / barge / canoe
▶ a boat / ship / yacht / ferry / cruiser /
dinghy / vessel / craft **sails / sets sail**
● **BOAT OR SHIP?** You can use boat,

but not **ship**, as a general term for any vehicle that travels on water; a **ship** only travels by sea.

body noun

1 [C] ■ *The heart pumps blood around the body.*

figure • build • anatomy • skeleton | *often approv.* **physique**

▶ the **human/male/female** body/ figure/anatomy/skeleton
▶ **have** a **good, large, slim,** etc. body/figure/build/physique
▶ a **part** of the body/anatomy

2 [C] ■ *a dead body*

corpse • carcass • remains

▶ **identify/bury** a body/a corpse/ remains
● BODY OR CORPSE? **Corpse** is a more unpleasant and direct word than **body**. It is often used when you do not know or care who the dead person was.

bomb noun [C]

■ *Bombs were dropped on the city.*

explosive • device • missile • mine • grenade • rocket

▶ **plant/set off** a bomb/explosives/ a device/a mine
▶ a/an bomb/explosive/device/ mine/grenade/rocket **goes off/ detonates**
▶ a bomb/device/missile/mine/ grenade/rocket **explodes**

bomb verb [T, I]

■ *The city was heavily bombed.*

blow sth up • shell • bombard • strafe

▶ bomb/blow up/strafe a **building**
▶ bomb/shell/bombard/strafe a **village/town**
▶ bomb/shell/bombard/a an **city/ area**

bond noun [C]

■ *the special bond between mother and child*

rapport • relationship • empathy • tie • link • partnership | *fml* **affinity**

▶ a/an bond/rapport/relationship/ empathy/tie/link/partnership/ link/affinity **between** A and B
▶ **(a) close** bond/rapport/ relationship/tie/link/partnership/ affinity
▶ **have** a/an bond/rapport/ relationship/empathy/tie/link/ partnership/affinity
● BOND OR RAPPORT? **Bond** is more general than **rapport**, and describes relationships between countries and groups, as well as individuals. A **bond** is stronger and more important than a **rapport**,

and may be **forged** over a period of time; you can have an *instant* rapport with sb that just happens without effort.

book noun [C]

■ *I'm reading a book by Robert Shea.*

work • title • publication • novel • textbook | *AmE* **text |** *fml* **volume**

▶ a book/work/publication/novel/ textbook/text/volume **about** sb/ sth
▶ **read/write** a book/work/ publication/novel/textbook/text/ volume
▶ **publish** a book/work/title/novel/ textbook/volume

book verb [T, I] (*esp. BrE*)

■ *I've booked seats on the 9.30 flight.*

reserve • order • charter | *esp. AmE* **rent |** *BrE* **hire**

▶ book/reserve a **place/seat/table/ ticket**
▶ book/reserve/rent/hire a **room/ hall**
▶ book/reserve/order sth **for eight o' clock/midday/this evening,** etc.
● BOOK OR RESERVE? If you **book** sth you usu. pay at the same time; if you **reserve** sth you usu. pay later, unless it is for a seat on a train.

border noun [C]

■ *Thousands try to cross the border every day.*

boundary • line | *BrE* **frontier**

▶ **across/along/on/over** a/the border/boundary/line/frontier
▶ **inside/within/beyond/outside** the borders/boundaries/frontiers
▶ the border/boundary/line/frontier **between** one place and another
▶ the border/boundary/frontier **with** a place
● WHICH WORD? The **border** is the point where you cross from one country into another. In BrE you can use **frontier**, although this often suggests wildness or danger. In Britain a **boundary** divides one county from another; in the US a **line** divides counties and states. A **boundary** can also be a physical line between two places, marked by a fence or wall.

bored adj.

■ *The children were bored with staying indoors.*

infml **fed up • sick of sth**

■ OPP **interested**
▶ bored/fed up/sick **of** sth
▶ bored/fed up **with** sth

boring

boring adj. (disapprov.)
■ She found her job very boring.

dull • tedious • uninteresting • monotonous • repetitive • dry

■ OPP interesting
▶ boring / dull / tedious / repetitive / monotonous **jobs/work**
▶ a/an boring / dull / uninteresting **place**
▶ a boring / dull **man/woman/ person**

borrow

borrow verb [T, I]
■ Can I borrow your pen?

beg | infml, disapprov. scrounge

■ OPP lend
▶ borrow / beg / scrounge (sth) **from** sb
▶ borrow / scrounge sth **off** sb
▶ borrow / beg **for money**

boss

boss noun [C] (infml)
■ Ask your boss for a rise. ■ huge bonuses paid to company bosses

manager • employer • supervisor • director • head • chief executive • chairman • chair • chairwoman • leader • president | BrE managing director • governor | esp. journ. chief

▶ a **company** boss / manager / director / chairman / chairwoman / president / chief
▶ a **party/union** boss / chief / chairman / chairwoman / leader / president

bother

bother verb
1 [T] ■ The noise doesn't bother me.

worry • disturb • trouble • concern • unsettle • alarm

▶ It bothers / worries / disturbs / troubles / concerns / alarms sb **that…**
▶ Is **there** something bothering / worrying / disturbing / troubling **you?**
▶ bother / worry / trouble / concern sb **with** sth
▶ bother / worry / trouble / concern **yourself about** sth
● WHICH WORD? **Bother** is the most informal of these words, esp. in spoken phrases such as It doesn't bother me and I'm not bothered. **Concern** is the most formal and is not usu. used in the progressive tenses.

2 [T] (esp. spoken) ■ Sorry to bother you.

disturb • interrupt | fml trouble

▶ bother / disturb / interrupt / trouble sb **with** sth

▶ be **sorry to** bother / disturb / interrupt / trouble sb
● BOTHER, DISTURB OR INTERRUPT? You can **bother** or **disturb** sb who is trying to do sth by talking to them. You **interrupt** sb who is speaking by speaking yourself. You can also **disturb** sb by making a lot of noise.

bottom

bottom noun [C, usu. sing.]
■ There are notes at the bottom of each page.

base • foot • foundation

■ OPP top
▶ **at/near/towards** the bottom / base / foot of sth
▶ **on** the bottom / base of sth
● BOTTOM OR FOOT? **Foot** is used in more literary contexts, and esp. with tree, hill, mountain, stairs, steps and page. **Bottom** is used for a much wider range of things.

bound

bound adj. [not before noun]
■ You've worked hard—you're bound to pass.

certain • sure • guaranteed | fml destined | written assured

▶ bound / certain / sure / guaranteed / destined **to do sth**

bowl

bowl noun [C]
■ a salad/sugar/fruit bowl

dish • plate • platter

▶ a bowl / dish / plate / platter **of** sth
▶ **in** a bowl / dish
▶ **on** a dish / plate / platter

box

box noun [C]
■ a cardboard box

crate • tin • carton • container • case | esp. AmE package

▶ a box / crate / tin / carton / case / package **of** sth
▶ **in** a box / crate / tin / carton / container / package
▶ **fill** a box / crate / tin / carton / container / case

boy

boy noun [C]
1 ■ The older boys teased him.

child • youth • teenager | infml kid • youngster • adolescent | esp. BrE, infml lad | esp. AmE, infml teen | fml or law juvenile • minor

■ OPP girl
▶ a **young** boy / child / teenager / adolescent / kid / lad
▶ a **little** boy / child / kid
▶ a **local** boy / child / youth / teenager / kid / youngster / lad

2 [C] ■ Her eldest boy has just started school.

son • child • baby | infml kid

- OPP **girl**
  - ▸ a **newborn** boy/son/child/baby
  - ▸ sb's **eldest/oldest/youngest/only** boy/son/child/kid
  - ▸ **have/give birth to** a boy/son/child/baby/kid

boyfriend noun [C]
- ▪ Emma's got a new boyfriend.

partner • **man** • **lover** • **fiancé** • **admirer** | esp. AmE **date** | becoming old-fash. **sweetheart** | old-fash. **suitor**
- ▸ sb's **new** boyfriend/partner/man/lover/admirer
- ▸ sb's **ex-** boyfriend/partner/lover/fiancé
- ▸ sb's **former/current** boyfriend/partner/lover
- ▸ **have** a/an boyfriend/partner/man/lover/fiancé/admirer/date
- ● **BOYFRIEND OR PARTNER?** A **partner** is usu. sb you live with but are not married to and suggests a more long-term relationship. Young people often prefer to use the words **boyfriend/girlfriend**.

brain noun [C]

1 ▪ The scan showed no damage to the brain.

mind • **head** • **subconscious**
- ▸ the **human** brain/mind
- ▸ **deep in** the brain/your mind/your subconscious

2 [U, C, usu. pl.] ▪ She must have inherited her mother's brains.

intelligence • **intellect** • **wits** • **mind** • **genius** | AmE, infml **smarts**
- ▸ (a) **great** intelligence/intellect/mind/genius
- ▸ **have** (a) ... brain/intelligence/intellect/...wits/... mind/genius/smarts
- ▸ **use** your brain/intelligence/wits/mind/smarts

branch noun [C]
- ▪ Contact our New York branch.

department • **division** • **unit** • **section** • **arm**
- ▸ an **administrative** branch/department/division/section/arm
- ▸ a **regional** branch/department/division/unit

brand noun [C]
- ▪ a leading brand of toothpaste

make • **model** • **label**
- ▸ a brand/make/model **of** car
- ▸ a **popular/leading/major/famous/well-known** brand/make/model/label

brave adj.
- ▪ a brave fight against cancer

courageous • **heroic** • **daring** • **adventurous** • **bold** | infml **gutsy** | written **fearless** | old-fash. or lit. **gallant**
- ■ OPP **cowardly**
  - ▸ a **brave/courageous/heroic/daring/bold/gallant attempt/action**
  - ▸ a **brave/courageous/daring/bold decision**
  - ▸ a **brave/courageous/heroic/gallant resistance/struggle**
  - ▸ a **brave/courageous/fearless/gallant soldier**

break noun

1 [C] ▪ Have a break for lunch.

rest • **breathing space** | infml **breather** • **time out** | fml **respite** | BrE **break time** | AmE or law **recess**
- ▸ a break/a rest/time out/respite **from** sth
- ▸ **have/take** a break/a rest/a breather/time out
- ▸ **give sb** a break/rest/breathing space/breather/time out
- ● **BREAK OR RECESS?** In BrE **break time** or **break** [U] is a period of time between lessons at school. The AmE word for this is **recess**.

2 [C] ▪ a break in your routine

lull • **gap** • **interruption** • **pause**
- ▸ a/an break/lull/gap/interruption/pause **in** sth
- ▸ **after** a/an break/lull/gap/interruption/pause
- ▸ a **short** break/lull/gap/interruption/pause
- ▸ a **long** break/lull/gap/pause
- ● **BREAK, LULL OR GAP?** A **break** is often planned. A **lull** or **gap** usu. just happens without planning: There was a gap/lull in the conversation.

3 [C] ▪ a weekend break

trip • **excursion** • **outing** | BrE **holiday** • **day out** | AmE **vacation** | infml **getaway**
- ▸ a **great/relaxing** break/trip/holiday/day out/vacation/getaway
- ▸ a **summer/winter** break/trip/holiday/vacation/getaway
- ▸ **take** a break/trip/holiday/vacation
- ▸ **go on** (a/an) trip/excursion/outing/day out/holiday/vacation

break verb

1 [I, T] ▪ She fell and broke her arm.

crack • **fracture** • **snap** • **break (sth) up** • **smash** • **shatter** • **splinter**
- ▸ break/crack/fracture/smash/shatter/splinter a **bone**

break down

▶ crack/fracture/smash/shatter your skull
▶ break/crack/smash a cup/mirror
▶ a branch/rope/cable breaks/snaps

2 [I, T] ■ My watch has broken.

break down • go wrong • fail • crash • go down

▶ a watch/video/DVD player breaks/goes wrong
▶ a washing machine breaks down/goes wrong
▶ a system fails/crashes/goes down

3 [T] ■ Don't break the law by speeding.

fml breach • infringe • violate

■ OPP obey
▶ break/breach/infringe a regulation
▶ break/breach/violate a rule/law/treaty
▶ break/violate a ceasefire/truce

4 [T] ■ He wouldn't break a promise, would he?

go back on sth • backtrack | infml, esp. journ. **do a U-turn**

■ OPP keep
▶ break/go back on a promise/your word/an agreement

break down phrasal verb
■ The agreement broke down almost immediately.

fail • collapse • go wrong • fall through | written **founder**

▶ talks break down/fail/collapse/fall through/founder
▶ a relationship/marriage breaks down/fails/collapses/goes wrong

break out phrasal verb
■ Trouble broke out again in the city last night.

erupt • develop | esp. journ. **blow up**

▶ (a) crisis/storm/row/trouble breaks out/erupts/develops/blows up
▶ a/an argument/controversy/dispute breaks out/erupts/develops
▶ (a) fight/fighting/riot/violence/war breaks out/erupts
● BREAK OUT OR ERUPT? **Erupt** is not used to talk about diseases or disasters:
✔A cholera epidemic broke out. ✗ A cholera epidemic erupted.
Erupt but not **break out** can be used when an argument or violence suddenly becomes worse:
✔The unrest erupted into revolution. ✗ The unrest broke out into revolution.

break up phrasal verb
■ My sister has broken up with her boyfriend.

split up • separate • divorce • get divorced • disband | infml, esp. journ. **split**

■ OPP get together
▶ break up/split up/split with sb
▶ split up/separate/split from sb
▶ a couple breaks up/splits up/separates/divorces/gets divorced/splits
▶ a group breaks up/splits up/disbands/splits
● BREAK UP OR SPLIT UP? Only people can **split up**, but a relationship (personal or business) or people can **break up**: My parents split up when I was five. • The company broke up last year.

breath noun [C]
■ I took a deep breath and began.

gulp • gasp • sniff

▶ take a breath/gulp/sniff
▶ let out a breath/gasp/sniff
▶ give a gulp/gasp/sniff

breed verb [T]
■ Sally breeds sheep for their wool.

rear • raise • keep

▶ breed/rear/keep sth for sth
▶ breed/rear/raise/keep animals/cattle/horses/sheep
▶ breed/rear/raise/keep sth in captivity

bribe noun [C]
■ She was offered a large bribe to drop the charges.

inducement • bait | esp. AmE **kickback** | infml, usu. disapprov. **pay-off**

▶ a £1000/$500, etc. bribe/pay-off
▶ offer (sb) a/an bribe/inducement/pay-off
▶ take bribes/the bait/kickbacks

brief adj.
1 ■ It was only a brief visit.

short • quick • momentary • passing • temporary • short-lived • hasty • hurried | written **fleeting**

■ OPP long
▶ a brief/short/temporary stay
▶ a brief/passing/fleeting moment
▶ a brief/quick/momentary/passing glance/glimpse
● BRIEF OR SHORT? **Brief** is used more frequently than **short** to describe a look, glance, glimpse, smile or sigh. **Short** is used to describe books, lists, projects, etc. that take only a short while to complete, and is

used more often in informal and spoken English.

2 ■ *Please be brief.*

short ◆ **concise** ◆ **economical** | *approv.* **succinct** ◆ **pithy** | *sometimes disapprov.* **terse** | *usu. disapprov.* **curt** ◆ **brusque**

■ OPP **long-winded**
▶ a **brief/short/concise/succinct/ terse/curt answer/statement**
▶ a **brief/short/concise/succinct/ terse summary/account**
▶ a **brief/short/concise version**
● **BRIEF OR SHORT?** A *mention* is usu. **brief**; an *answer* is more likely to be **short**. **Brief** is often used when talking about speech:
✗ *Please be short.*

bright *adj.*

1 ■ *a bright green dress* ■ *a bright morning*

brilliant ◆ **bold** ◆ **strong** ◆ **dazzling** | *BrE* **colourful** ◆ *AmE* **colorful** | *approv.* **vivid** ◆ **vibrant** ◆ **flamboyant** | *disapprov.* **glaring** ◆ **lurid** ◆ **gaudy** ◆ **garish** ◆ **harsh** ◆ **loud**

■ OPP **dull, dim, faint, grey, gloomy**
▶ **bright/brilliant/bold/strong/ dazzling/vivid/vibrant/lurid/ gaudy/garish/harsh/loud colours**
▶ **bright/brilliant/strong/dazzling/ glaring/harsh light**
▶ **bright/brilliant/strong/dazzling/ glaring sunshine**
▶ **bright/colourful/flamboyant/ gaudy/loud clothes**
● **BRIGHT OR BOLD? Bold** emphasizes how easy it is to see a colour. It can be used with a wider range of colours than **bright**, which is usu. used with light colours.

2 ■ *He felt bright and cheerful and full of energy.*

cheerful ◆ **jolly** ◆ **in a good mood** | *infml* **cheery**

▶ **bright/cheerful/jolly/cheery face**
▶ **bright/cheerful/jolly/cheery smile**
● **BRIGHT OR CHEERFUL?** You can use **bright** after the verbs *to be* or *to feel*: *I was not feeling very bright this morning.*
You can say a *cheerful boy/girl*, but a *bright boy/girl* is intelligent, not cheerful.

brilliant *adj.*

1 ■ *a brilliant young scientist*

intelligent ◆ **bright** | *esp. AmE* **smart** | *esp. BrE* **clever**

■ OPP **stupid**
▶ **brilliant/clever at sth**
▶ a/an **brilliant/bright/intelligent/ smart/clever child/boy/girl/ man/woman**

▶ a/an **brilliant/intelligent/smart/ clever thing to do/move**

2 (*BrE, infml*) ■ *The show was brilliant!*

excellent ◆ **outstanding** ◆ **perfect** ◆ **first-rate** ◆ **classic** ◆ **superb** ◆ **tremendous** | *infml* **great** ◆ **fantastic** ◆ **fabulous** ◆ **terrific** ◆ **cool** | *esp. AmE, infml* **awesome** | *slang* **wicked**

■ OPP **rubbish**
▶ a/an **brilliant/excellent/ outstanding/perfect/superb/ great/fantastic/fabulous/terrific/ cool/awesome/wicked place**
▶ **have** a/an **brilliant/excellent/ great/fantastic/fabulous/terrific/ cool/awesome time**
▶ a/an **brilliant/excellent/ outstanding/superb/tremendous/ great/fantastic/terrific/awesome achievement**

bring *verb* [T]

■ *Bring your books with you.*

take ◆ **carry** ◆ **deliver** ◆ **leave** ◆ **transport** ◆ **fly** ◆ **ferry**

▶ **bring/take/carry/deliver/ transport/fly/ferry sb/sth to/from sb/sth**
▶ **bring/take/carry/transport/fly/ ferry sb/sth back/home**
▶ **bring/take/carry/deliver/ transport/ferry sb/sth by car, rail, truck, etc.**
● **BRING OR TAKE? Take** is used from the point of view of the person who is going somewhere with sth; **bring** is used from the point of view of sb who is already in the place the person is going to.

bring sb up *phrasal verb* [often passive]

■ *He was brought up by his aunt.*

rear ◆ **be born and bred** ◆ **adopt** | *esp. AmE* **raise** | *esp. BrE* **foster**

▶ **be brought up/reared/born and bred/raised in a place**
▶ **bring up/rear/adopt/raise/foster a child**
▶ **bring up/rear/adopt/raise a son/ daughter/family**

broad *adj.*

1 (*often approv., esp. written*) ■ *He's got broad shoulders.*

wide

■ OPP **narrow**
▶ a **broad/wide road/street/river/ stream/staircase**
▶ a **broad/wide mouth/smile/grin**
● **BROAD OR WIDE? Broad** is often used to suggest that sth is wide in an attractive way; it is also used rather than **wide** to talk about parts of the body: *a broad avenue*

lined with trees • a broad back/
chest/face/forehead

2 ■ *The course caters for a broad
spectrum of interests.*

wide • extensive • widespread •
general • universal • diverse • mass
• large-scale • sweeping • far-
reaching | *written* wide-ranging |
often approv. varied

■ OPP narrow
► a/an broad/wide/extensive **range**
► a/an broad/extensive/general/
diverse/mass/large-scale/
sweeping/far-reaching/wide-
ranging/varied **programme**
► broad/wide/extensive/
widespread/general/universal/
mass **support**
● BROAD OR WIDE? Broad is used
more to talk about the effect of sth
on a large number of people:
✓have a broad appeal • attract
broad support
Broad also often relates to
knowledge, education and
business:
✓a broad curriculum • broad
experience/knowledge
Wide is used more to talk about a
choice or a range of things or
people and also for a geographical
area:
✓The festival attracts people from a
wide area. ✗ The festival attracts
people from a broad area.

3 ■ *the broad outline of a proposal*

general • sweeping • overall •
rough • approximate

► a broad/general/rough **outline**
► a broad/general/sweeping
assertion/conclusion/statement
► in broad/general/overall **terms**
► a broad/sweeping **generalization**

broadcast *noun* [C]
■ *a live broadcast of the speech*

transmission • showing • podcast •
webcast • show | *BrE* programme |
AmE program

► a broadcast/transmission/webcast
from somewhere
► a radio/**television/TV** broadcast/
transmission/show/programme
► a live broadcast/transmission/
webcast/show/programme
► see/watch a broadcast/
transmission/showing/podcast/
webcast/show/programme

brood *verb* [I] (*sometimes
disapprov.*)
■ *Try not to brood about last night.*

disapprov. mope • sulk • pout

► brood/mope/sulk/pout **about** sth

► brood/sulk **over** sth

brush *verb* [T]
■ brush your hair/teeth/shoes

clean • scrub • sweep • dust •
groom • comb

► brush/clean/sweep/dust sth **off/
from** sth
► brush/sweep sth **away**
► brush/scrub sth **clean**

budget *noun* [C, U]
■ *The hospital faces severe budget
cuts.*

fund • allocation • allowance •
purse • pocket • account • savings |
finance reserves

► pay sth **from/out of** a budget/a
fund/an allocation/an allowance/
the public purse/your own
pocket/an account/your savings/
your reserves
► have a budget/a fund/an
allocation/an allowance/an
account/savings/reserves
► manage a budget/a fund/an
allocation/an account/your
savings/your reserves

build *verb*

1 [T, I] ■ *a house built of stone*

construct • assemble • put sth up •
set sth up | *fml* erect

■ OPP demolish
► build/construct sth **from/out of/
of** sth
► build/construct/put up/erect a
house/shelter/wall/fence
► build/construct a **road/railway/
railroad/tunnel/nest**

2 [T] ■ *She's built a new career for
herself.*

make • create • form • develop |
written, esp. busin. evolve

► build/make/create/form sth **from
out of** sth
► build/create/form a **picture** of
past societies
► build/develop/evolve a **theory/
framework/programme**

building *noun*

1 [C] ■ *a tall/high-rise/ten-storey
building*

property • structure • premises •
complex | *esp. BrE* block

► a commercial/residential
**building/property/premises/
complex/block**
► erect a **building/structure/
complex/block**
► demolish a **building/property/
structure/complex/block**

2 [U] ■ *There's building work going on
next door.*

construction • assembly

■ OPP demolition
▶ house/road building/construction
▶ building/construction companies/
  costs/firms/jobs/materials/work
▶ the building/construction industry
● BUILDING OR CONSTRUCTION?
Construction is a more technical
word, used in business and
industrial contexts. **Building** is
used to talk about building work
on a smaller scale.

build up phrasal verb
■ He had no work and debts began to
build up.

**accumulate • pile up • mount up •
multiply** | fml **accrue**
▶ build up/mount up/multiply to a
  large number/amount, 50000,
  etc.
▶ debts build up/accumulate/pile
  up/mount up
▶ problems build up/accumulate/
  multiply

bullet noun [C]
■ There were bullet holes in the door.

**ammunition • shell • shot • gunshot
• round • cartridge**
▶ live bullets/ammunition/rounds/
  cartridges
▶ fire bullets/ammunition/shells/
  rounds/cartridges
▶ bullet/gunshot wounds

bully verb [T]
■ He was bullied at school.

**victimize • pick on sb • push
around • terrorize • intimidate** | BrE
steamroller | AmE **steamroll** | written
tyrannize • cow
▶ bully/terrorize/intimidate/
  steamroller/cow sb into
  doing sth
▶ get bullied/picked on/pushed
  around

bunch noun [C]
■ a bunch of flowers/grapes/keys

bouquet • cluster • clump • set
▶ a bunch/bouquet/cluster of
  flowers
▶ a bunch/set of keys
▶ grow in bunches/clusters/clumps

bureaucracy noun [U] (often
disapprov.)
■ We aim to eliminate unnecessary
bureaucracy.

paperwork • rules and regulations |
disapprov. **red tape**
▶ unnecessary/too much/endless
  bureaucracy/paperwork/red tape
▶ reduce/cut bureaucracy/
  paperwork/red tape

▶ deal with bureaucracy/paperwork

burn verb
1 [I] ■ The whole city was burning.

be on fire • go up • blaze | BrE
smoulder | AmE **smolder**
▶ a fire/bonfire/log burns/blazes/
  smoulders
▶ a building/house burns/is on fire/
  goes up
▶ burn/blaze fiercely

2 [T, I] ■ He burned all her letters.

**set fire to sth • set sth on fire • torch
• scorch • singe • char • sear • scald
• cremate** | fml **incinerate**
▶ burn/set fire to/torch/scald
  yourself
▶ burn/set fire to/scorch/singe your
  hair/clothes
▶ burn/set fire to/torch a car/
  building

burst noun [C]
■ a sudden burst of energy

**spurt • outburst • fit • flurry • bout
• attack**
▶ a sudden burst/spurt/outburst/
  fit/flurry/bout/attack
▶ a/an burst/spurt/outburst/fit/
  bout of anger
▶ a/an burst/outburst/fit/attack of
  laughter/temper
▶ a burst/spurt/flurry of activity

burst verb [I, T]
■ a dam bursts ■ burst a blood vessel

explode | fml or med. **rupture**
▶ a shell bursts/explodes
▶ a pipe/tank bursts/ruptures
▶ a burst/ruptured appendix/artery

bury verb [T]
■ looking for buried treasure ■ She
learned to bury her feelings.

hide • cover • disguise • mask | fml
conceal
▶ bury/hide/conceal sth under sth
▶ bury/hide/disguise/mask/conceal
  your feelings

bus noun [C]
■ Shall we go by bus?

BrE **coach • minibus** | AmE **van**
▶ by bus/coach/minibus/van
▶ get on/off a bus/coach/minibus
▶ get in/out of a minibus/van
● BUS OR COACH? In BrE a bus that
carries passengers over a long
distance is called a **coach**.

business

business noun

1 [U] ■ *It's a pleasure to do business with you.*

trade • trading • commerce • enterprise • dealing • operation • market • marketplace

▶ business/trade/trading/ commerce/enterprise/dealing **between** people/countries
▶ business/trade/trading/ commerce/dealing **with** sb/a country
▶ **encourage/promote** business/ trade/commerce/enterprise
▶ business/trade/the market **grows/is booming/picks up/ declines**
● **BUSINESS OR TRADE?** Trade is used slightly more to talk about buying and selling goods rather than services. Business is used when sb is trying to emphasize the more personal aspects, such as discussing things and working together to provide goods or services.

2 [C] ■ *He works in the oil business.*

industry • trade • service

▶ the **book/tourist/car/catering/ hotel/construction** business/ industry/trade
▶ the **energy/oil/food/computer/ advertising/insurance/music** business/industry
▶ **work in/be in** a particular business/industry/trade/service

3 [U] ■ *She's away on business.*

work • job • assignment • duty • duties • mission • task

■ OPP **pleasure**

▶ (a) **routine** business/work/job/ assignment/duties/mission/task
▶ **do** business/your work/a job/an assignment/a task
▶ **be on** business/a job/a mission

4 [C] ■ *start your own business*

company • firm • operation • corporation • partnership • practice • cooperative • syndicate • house | *infml* **outfit** | *busin.* **group • conglomerate • consortium** | *busin., journ.* **enterprise**

▶ a **multinational** business/ company/firm/operation/ corporation/group/ conglomerate/consortium/ enterprise
▶ a **family** business/company/firm/ operation/partnership/practice/ … house
▶ **set up** a/an business/company/ firm/operation/corporation/ partnership/practice/cooperative/ syndicate/…house/outfit/ consortium/enterprise

▶ **run** a/an business/company/ firm/operation/corporation/ cooperative/syndicate/…house/ group/conglomerate/ consortium/enterprise

5 ■ *It's my business who I invite to the party.*

affair • preserve | *fml* **concern**

▶ a **private/personal** business/ affair/concern
▶ sth is sb's **own** business/affair/ concern
▶ **be none of** sb's business/affair/ concern
● **BUSINESS OR CONCERN?** You can only use **business**, not **concern**, in the phrases *make it your business to do sth* and *sth is the business of sth*:
✓ *I shall make it my business to find out who is responsible.* ✗ ~~I shall make it my concern to find out who is responsible.~~
✓ *It is the business of the police to protect the community.* ✗ ~~It is the concern of the police to protect the community.~~

businessman, businesswoman noun [C]

■ *a highly successful businessman*

business person • executive • entrepreneur • industrialist • magnate | *sometimes disapprov.* **tycoon**

▶ a **local/leading** businessman, etc./ executive/entrepreneur/ industrialist/magnate/tycoon
▶ a **successful/wealthy** businessman, etc./entrepreneur/ industrialist

busy adj.

1 ■ *The principal is a very busy man.*

active • hard-pressed • occupied • at work • involved | *fml* **engaged**

▶ busy/occupied/involved **with** sth
▶ active/occupied/involved/ engaged **in** sth
▶ **keep** sb busy/active/occupied/ involved

2 ■ *a busy airport*

crowded • full • packed • crammed | *approv.* **lively** | *approv., written* **bustling • vibrant** | *disapprov.* **overcrowded • congested**

▶ busy/crowded/packed/ crammed/bustling **with** people
▶ a/an busy/crowded/lively/ bustling/overcrowded **place/ town/market/bar**
▶ the **place/town/market/bar** is full/packed

3 ■ *a busy time of year*

hectic • full • eventful

■ OPP **quiet**

▶ a/an busy/hectic/full/eventful
day/weekend/week/life
▶ a/an busy/hectic/full
programme/schedule/timetable
● BUSY, HECTIC OR FULL? Busy is the
most general of these words. Full
often describes a period of time,
esp. sb's life, that is busy in a good
way. Hectic usu. describes a period
of time or an activity that is too
busy.

button noun [C]
■ Press the red button.

key ◆ control ◆ switch ◆ lever ◆ knob
◆ dial

▶ (a) button/key/the controls/
switch/lever/knob/dial on sth
▶ press a button/key/switch/lever
▶ push a button/key/switch/lever
▶ turn a knob/dial

buy verb [T]
■ I bought a new coat.

esp. spoken get | infml pick sth up ◆
snap sth up | fml purchase ◆ acquire

■ OPP sell
▶ buy/get/snap up/purchase/
acquire (a) property/company/
house
▶ buy/get/purchase/acquire land/
premises/a site/tickets
▶ get/pick up/snap up a bargain

buyer noun [C]
■ We've found a buyer for our house.

customer ◆ shopper ◆ consumer ◆
end-user ◆ regular ◆ client | BrE, infml
punter | fml purchaser ◆ patron

■ OPP seller
▶ have/deal with/get/lose a
buyer/customer/client
▶ attract buyers/customers/
shoppers/consumers/clients/
punters
▶ buyers/customers/shoppers/
consumers/clients/purchasers
buy/spend sth

buzz verb

1 [I] ■ Bees were buzzing amongst the
flowers.

hum ◆ drone ◆ whine | esp. BrE whirr
| AmE usu. whir

▶ bees buzz/hum/drone
▶ a helicopter buzzes/whirrs
▶ an engine hums/drones/whines
▶ a machine hums/whines/whirrs

2 [I] ■ The doorbell buzzed loudly.

ring ◆ sound ◆ chime ◆ jangle

▶ the doorbell buzzes/rings/
sounds/chimes/jangles
▶ buzz/ring/sound/chime/jangle
loudly

Cc

cable noun [C, U]
■ Roads have to be dug up to lay
underground cables.

wire | esp. AmE cord | BrE lead ◆ flex

▶ an electric/electrical cable/wire/
cord/lead/flex
▶ a telephone cable/wire/cord/lead
▶ connect/disconnect a cable/wire/
cord/lead/flex

calculate verb

1 [T, I] ■ Use the formula to calculate
the volume.

work sth out ◆ figure sth out ◆ tally
◆ count ◆ add ◆ total ◆ quantify ◆ put
a figure on sth | AmE figure | fml
compute | BrE, infml tot sth up

▶ calculate/work out/figure out/
tally up/count up/add up/total
up/quantify/put a figure on/
figure/compute/tot up how
much/how many...
▶ calculate/work out/figure out/add
up/quantify/put a figure on/
figure/compute/tot up the cost/
amount
▶ calculate/work out/figure out/
tally up/count up/add up/
quantify/put a figure on/figure/
compute/tot up the number
● CALCULATE, COMPUTE OR WORK STH
OUT? Calculate is the most frequent
word in written English, but work
sth out is the most frequent term in
spoken English. Compute is used in
written English, esp. to describe
calculations done by machine.

2 [T] ■ It is impossible to calculate the
number of species affected.

estimate ◆ judge ◆ reckon ◆ guess ◆
gauge | esp. AmE figure | fml
extrapolate

▶ calculate/estimate/judge/reckon/
guess/gauge/extrapolate from
sth
▶ calculate/estimate/judge/reckon/
guess/figure/extrapolate that...
▶ calculate/estimate/judge/reckon/
guess/gauge the amount/size/distance

calculation noun [C, U]
■ a rough calculation of the numbers

reckoning ◆ count ◆ tally ◆ estimate

▶ By my/his, etc. calculations/
reckoning/estimate...
▶ a/an accurate/precise/rough/
quick/approximate calculation/
count/estimate
▶ make a/an calculation/estimate

call verb

1 [T] ■ *They decided to call the baby Mark.*

name • entitle • dub • nickname • christen • address | *fml* term • designate | *sometimes disapprov.* label • brand

- ▶ call/name/dub/nickname/ christen sb **Mary, Ali,** etc.
- ▶ call/dub/nickname sb **captain, the wizard,** etc.
- ▶ call/address sb **by** their full name, their first name, etc.
- ▶ address/designate/label/brand sb/sth **as** sth

2 [T] ■ *I wouldn't call German an easy language.*

describe • consider • regard • see • view • count

- ▶ describe/consider/regard/see/ view/count sb/sth **as** sth
- ▶ call/describe/consider/regard/ see/view/count **yourself** (as) sth
- ● **CALL OR DESCRIBE? Call** is used with a noun or adjective complement, without *as*. **Describe** is used with *as* and an adjective or a noun phrase. Adjectives are more frequent with **describe** than nouns: longer noun phrase are possible, but with shorter noun phrases use **call**:
  ✓ *Jim was described by his colleagues as an unusual man.* • *Are you calling me a liar?* ✗ *Are you describing me as a liar?*

3 [I, T] ■ *He called out for help.*

cry out (sth) • shout • yell • scream | *written* exclaim • cry

- ▶ call/cry out/shout/yell/scream/ exclaim/cry (sth) **to** sb
- ▶ call/cry out/shout/yell/scream **for** sb/sth

4 [T, I] ■ *My sister called me from Spain last night.*

dial | *esp. AmE, infml* call sb up | *esp. BrE, fml* telephone | *BrE, esp. spoken* ring • phone

- ▶ call/telephone/ring/phone **from** somewhere
- ▶ call/dial/telephone/ring/phone **a number/a hotline/the switchboard/reception**
- ▶ call/telephone/ring/phone **the doctor/fire brigade/police/ hospital**
- ● **CALL, RING OR PHONE? Call** is the only one of these three words used in *AmE*. **Ring** and **phone** are the most frequent words in spoken *BrE*, but **call** is preferred in an emergency: *Call the police/fire brigade.*

You **call/ring/phone** a person, place or institution; you **call** *a cab/ a taxi/an ambulance.*

5 [T] ■ *He called a meeting to discuss the changes.*

hold • have • give • host | *fml* convene

- ▶ call/hold/have/give/host/ convene a **conference**
- ▶ call/hold/have/convene a **meeting**
- ▶ call/hold/have an **election**

calm noun

1 [U, sing.] ■ *in the calm of the evening*

peace • quiet • hush • silence | *esp. BrE* tranquillity | *AmE usu.* tranquility

- ▶ **absolute/total/relative** calm/ peace/quiet/silence/tranquillity
- ▶ a **sudden** calm/quiet/hush/ silence
- ▶ **break** the calm/peace/quiet/ silence

2 [U, sing.] ■ *The police appealed for calm.*

peace • order

- ▶ an **uneasy** calm/peace
- ▶ **relative/comparative** calm/peace
- ▶ calm/peace/order **prevails**

calm verb [T]

■ *Have a drink to calm your nerves.*

soothe • calm sb down • pacify • placate | *fml, usu. disapprov.* appease

- ■ OPP **agitate**
- ▶ calm/soothe/calm down/pacify/ placate/appease sb **with** sth
- ▶ calm/soothe **your nerves**

calm adj.

■ *Keep calm in an emergency.*

cool • relaxed • placid • composed • controlled • unperturbed • unfazed • easy-going • patient | *infml* laid-back | *sometimes disapprov.* casual

- ■ OPP **agitated, excitable**
- ▶ calm/cool/easy-going/patient/ laid-back/casual **about** sth
- ▶ a/an calm/cool/relaxed/ controlled/easy-going/laid-back/ casual **manner**
- ▶ a calm/cool/relaxed/placid/ controlled **voice**
- ● **CALM, COOL OR RELAXED? Relaxed** describes how you feel about sth. **Cool** is used more to describe how sb behaves when they don't let their feelings affect their behaviour. **Calm** can describe feelings or behaviour.

calm down phrasal verb

■ *Calm down! We'll find her.*

relax • pull yourself together • cool

▶ calm / cool down
▶ things calm down / cool off
● **CALM DOWN OR RELAX?** People can **relax**; people or a situation can **calm down**. To **relax** is to stop feeling worried. **Calm down** is more about behaviour than feelings: you may still feel worried but you manage to behave in a calm way.

campaign noun [C]
■ the campaign for parliamentary reform

drive • crusade • fight • battle • struggle • war

▶ a campaign / drive / crusade / fight / battle / struggle **for** sth
▶ a campaign / drive / crusade / fight / battle / struggle / war **against** sth
▶ a / an **national / international** campaign / drive / crusade / battle / struggle
● **CAMPAIGN OR DRIVE?** A **campaign** may be larger, more formal and more organized than a **drive**. It is usu. aimed at getting other people to do sth. A **drive** may be an attempt by people to get themselves to do sth:
 ✓We're going on an economy drive (= we are going to spend less). ✗ an economy campaign

campaign verb [I]
■ The group campaigns on environmental issues.

fight • lobby • work • agitate

▶ campaign / fight / lobby / work / agitate **for** sth
▶ campaign / lobby / agitate **against** sth
▶ campaign / fight / lobby **on behalf of** sb
● **CAMPAIGN OR FIGHT?** Campaigning is often to persuade people that a political or social change is needed, or a practice needs to be stopped. **Fight** is often used about achieving justice for yourself, for example gaining the right to do sth.

campaigner noun [C]
■ a leading human rights campaigner

activist • crusader • reformer • lobbyist • champion • advocate • supporter

▶ a / an campaigner / activist / crusader / lobbyist / champion **for** sth
▶ a **leading / great** campaigner / activist / crusader / reformer / advocate / champion / supporter
▶ a **political** campaigner / activist / reformer / lobbyist
● **CAMPAIGNER OR ACTIVIST?** Use either word for sb who belongs to an organization but use **campaigner** for sb who works as an

individual: student / disabled / union / party activists • a tireless campaigner against education cuts

can noun [C]
■ a can of beans / beer / paint

jar • pot | BrE tin

▶ a can / tin of **beans / paint**
▶ a jar / pot of **honey / jam / marmalade**
● **CAN OR TIN?** In AmE use **can**. In BrE you can also use **tin** for food, paint, etc. but not for drinks:
 ✓a can of Coke ✗ a tin of Coke

cancel verb
1 [T] ■ All flights have been cancelled because of bad weather.

call sth off • abolish • shelve | esp. journ. scrap | BrE, journ. axe | AmE, journ. ax

▶ cancel / call off a / an **game / match / engagement**
▶ cancel / abolish / scrap / axe a **service**
▶ cancel / shelve / scrap / axe **plans**

2 [T, I] ■ Is it too late to cancel my order?

lift • repeal • invalidate • annul | fml revoke

▶ cancel / revoke an **agreement**
▶ cancel / invalidate a **contract**
▶ lift / revoke / repeal a **ban**
▶ invalidate / annul a **marriage**

candidate noun [C]
■ the best candidate for the job

applicant • nominee • contender • contestant • challenger • entrant

▶ a / an candidate / applicant / nominee / contender / contestant / challenger / entrant **for** sth
▶ a **Democratic / Republican / presidential** candidate / nominee / contender / challenger
▶ **interview / choose / select / shortlist / reject** a candidate / an applicant
● **CANDIDATE OR NOMINEE?** A **candidate** is a person who is suggested or who has suggested themselves for a prize or job. A **nominee** is always sb who was suggested for sth by other people. In political elections one of several **nominees** is chosen by a party to become its **candidate** to take part in the election against other candidates.

capable adj.
■ an extremely capable teacher

competent ∙ able ∙ skilled ∙ good ∙ talented ∙ gifted ∙ proficient ∙ accomplished | *BrE* skilful | *AmE* skillful

■ OPP incompetent
▶ a/an capable/competent/able/skilled/good/talented/gifted/skilful **teacher**
▶ a/an capable/skilled/good/talented/accomplished/skilful **performer**
▶ a capable/competent/good **manager**

car noun

1 [C] ■ *We came by car.*

fml vehicle | *AmE*, becoming old-fash. or humorous **automobile**

2 [C] (*esp. AmE*) ■ *This train has no buffet car.*

compartment | *BrE* carriage ∙ coach ∙ truck ∙ wagon ∙ van | *esp. AmE* freight car
▶ a railway compartment/carriage/coach/truck/wagon
▶ a railroad car
▶ a sleeping car/compartment/coach
▶ a passenger car/compartment/carriage/coach

care noun [U]

■ *She chose her words with care.*

caution ∙ attention | *fml* prudence ∙ regard

■ OPP carelessness
▶ do sth with care/caution/attention to sth/prudence
▶ need/call for care/caution/attention
▶ use/exercise care/caution/prudence

care verb [I]

■ *I don't care what he thinks!*

mind | *esp. BrE, infml, spoken* be bothered
▶ care/mind/be bothered about sth
▶ care/mind/be bothered that...
▶ not care/mind/be bothered what people think
● CARE OR MIND? Mind is used in polite questions and answers. When answering a question *I don't mind* is polite; *I don't care* is very rude.

career noun

1 [C] ■ *a career in journalism*

profession ∙ occupation ∙ vocation ∙ work ∙ employment ∙ job
▶ have/pursue (a/an) career/

profession/occupation/vocation/work/employment
▶ find (a/an) career/occupation/vocation/work/employment/job
▶ go back/return to (a/an) career/profession/work/employment/job

2 [C] ■ *the best tennis of his career*

life ∙ lifetime
▶ in/during sb's career/life/lifetime
▶ sb's school career/life
▶ a career/life/lifetime of doing sth

care for sb *phrasal verb*

■ *He gave up work to care for his wife.*

take care of sb ∙ attend to sb ∙ nurse | *esp. BrE* look after | *written* tend
▶ care for/take care of/nurse/look after/tend to **the sick**
▶ care for/take care of/look after **the children/the elderly/an elderly relative**
● CARE FOR, TAKE CARE OF OR LOOK AFTER SB? To **care for sb** is often a long-term, full-time occupation; you can **take care of sb** or **look after sb** for a short time.

careful *adj.*

■ *After careful consideration they offered the job to Neil.*

thorough ∙ close ∙ rigorous ∙ minute ∙ detailed ∙ comprehensive ∙ in-depth ∙ exhaustive

■ OPP careless
▶ a/an careful/thorough/close/rigorous/detailed/comprehensive/in-depth/exhaustive **study/investigation**
▶ a/an careful/thorough/close/rigorous/minute/detailed/exhaustive **examination** of sth
▶ careful/thorough/close/rigorous/detailed/comprehensive/in-depth/exhaustive **research**

careless *adj.*

1 ■ *It was careless of me to leave the window open.*

forgetful ∙ absent-minded | *fml* or *law* negligent

■ OPP careful

2 (*disapprov.*) ■ *making careless mistakes*

lax ∙ shoddy ∙ sloppy

■ OPP careful

take care of sb/sth *phrase*

■ *Celia will take care of the travel arrangements.*

deal with sb/sth ∙ handle ∙ tackle | *esp. BrE* look after sth | *fml* address | *spoken* see to sth

▶ take care of/deal with/handle/tackle/look after/address/see to **the matter**
▶ take care of/deal with/handle/tackle/look after/address **a problem**
▶ take care of/deal with/handle/tackle/look after the **paperwork**

take **care of yourself** phrasal verb

■ He's old enough to take care of himself.

fend for yourself • stand on your own (two) feet | esp. BrE **look after yourself**

▶ be able to take care of yourself/fend for yourself/stand on your own feet/look after yourself
▶ be capable of taking care of yourself/fending for yourself/looking after yourself
● TAKE CARE OF YOURSELF, FEND FOR YOURSELF OR LOOK AFTER YOURSELF? **Take care of yourself** and **look after yourself** are used to talk about care, health and safety. **Fend for yourself** is used for more practical matters, such as finding food, money or accommodation, and is used about animals as well as people.

cargo noun [C, U]

■ A tanker has spilt its cargo of oil.

load • shipment • consignment | BrE **goods** | busin. **freight**

▶ a cargo/load/shipment/consignment **of** sth
▶ carry (a) cargo/load/goods/freight
▶ send/deliver/receive (a) cargo/load/shipment/consignment/goods

carriage noun

1 [C] (BrE) ■ All the second-class carriages were full.

compartment | BrE **coach** | AmE **car**

▶ a **railway** carriage/compartment/coach
▶ a **railroad** car
▶ a **first-class/second-class**, etc. carriage/compartment/coach
▶ a **passenger** carriage/compartment/coach/car
● CARRIAGE, COACH OR COMPARTMENT? **Coach** is the word used in official language by train companies; **carriage** is used more in everyday speech: Your seats are in Coach D. • I had to go to the end of the carriage to find a seat. A **compartment** is a separate section of a carriage.

2 [C] ■ A horse and carriage awaited the happy couple.

cart • wagon • stagecoach

▶ **in** a carriage/wagon/stagecoach
▶ **on** a cart/wagon
▶ a **horse-drawn** carriage/cart/wagon

carry verb

1 [T] ■ I'll carry your bags.

infml **lug • cart** | esp. AmE, infml **tote** | old-fash. or fml **bear**

▶ carry/lug/cart/tote/bear sth **to/from/up/along** sth
▶ carry/lug/cart/tote sth **around**
▶ carry/bear sth **on your back**

2 [T] ■ a train carrying hundreds of commuters

transport • take • bring • ferry • deliver

▶ carry/transport/take/bring/ferry/deliver sb/sth **to/from** sb/sth
▶ carry/transport/take/bring/ferry sb/sth **back/home**
▶ carry/transport/take/bring/ferry/deliver sb/sth **by car/rail/truck**, etc.
● CARRY OR TRANSPORT? **Carry** is used esp. to talk about people, **transport** to talk about goods.

carry on phrasal verb (esp. BrE, esp. spoken)

1 ■ Carry on until you get to the junction.

continue | esp. spoken **go on • keep on**

▶ carry on/continue/go on/keep on **for** hours/a week/two years, etc.
▶ carry on/continue/go on/keep on **until** morning/next year, etc.

2 (esp. spoken) ■ Carry on with your work.

carry sth on • continue • go on • proceed • keep sth up • keep up with sth • keep • press ahead • press on | infml **stick with sth** | fml **pursue**

▶ carry on/continue/go on/proceed/keep up/press ahead/press on/stick **with** sth
▶ carry on/continue/go on/keep/press ahead/press on with/press on with **doing** sth
▶ carry on/continue/go on/proceed/keep up/press ahead/press on/pursue (with) your **work**

carry sth out phrasal verb

1 ■ You must carry out all orders immediately.

follow • act on/upon sth • obey | fml **implement** | fml, BrE **fulfil** | AmE **fulfill**

▶ carry out/follow/act on/obey/fulfil **orders**
▶ carry out/follow/act on/obey **instructions**
▶ carry out/follow/implement a **policy/recommendation**

2 ■ *They never actually carried out their plan.*

keep | *AmE* **follow through** | *fml, BrE* **honour** | *AmE* **honor** | *esp. journ. busin.* **deliver**

▶ carry out/keep/follow through on/honour/deliver on a **promise**
▶ carry out/keep/follow through/deliver on a **plan**
▶ carry out/follow/follow through on a **threat**

3 ■ *The team carried out over 200 interviews.*

do • **commit** • **go through sth** • **perform** | *fml* **conduct** • **undertake** | *BrE* **practise** | *fml, AmE* **practice**

▶ carry out/do/perform/conduct/undertake a/an **activity/analysis/investigation/review/assessment/evaluation**
▶ carry out/do/perform/conduct/undertake the **work**
▶ carry out/do/perform/conduct/go through a **test**
● **CARRY OUT OR PERFORM?** Carry out places emphasis on the amount of work and can also be used to talk about negative actions, such as *attack, abuse* and *killing*. Perform often emphasizes the skill involved: *She performs an important role in our organization.*

case noun

1 [C] ■ *a classic case of bad planning*

example • **instance** • **illustration**

▶ **in** a particular case/instance
▶ a **typical/classic** case/example/instance/illustration
▶ **cite/take/highlight** a/an case/example/instance

2 [sing.] ■ *It's simply not the case that conditions are improving.*

so • **a fact** • **the situation** • **the truth** • **the position** • **the state of affairs**

3 [C] ■ *They never solved the Jones murder case.*

investigation • **inquiry/enquiry** | *journ.* **probe**

▶ a **murder** case/investigation/inquiry
▶ a/an **police/official** investigation/inquiry/probe

4 [C] ■ *The case will be heard next week.*

suit • **lawsuit** • **action** • **proceedings** • **prosecution** • **litigation** • **appeal** • **trial** • **hearing** • **court martial**

▶ (a) **legal** case/action/proceedings/appeal/hearing
▶ **bring** (a/an) case/suit/lawsuit/action/proceedings/prosecution **(against** sb/sth)
▶ **win/lose** a/an case/suit/lawsuit/action/appeal

5 [C, usu. sing.] ■ *the case for/against private education*

argument • **reason** • **grounds** • **basis** • **need** • **justification** | *BrE* **defence** | *AmE* **defense**

▶ (a/an) case/argument/reason/grounds/basis/need/justification/defence **for** sth
▶ a/an case/argument/reason/defence **against** sth
▶ (a) **strong/legal** case/argument/reason/grounds/basis/need/justification/defence
▶ **put forward** (a/an) case/argument/reason/grounds/justification/defence

6 [C] ■ *a pencil/packing case*

crate • **container** • **box**

▶ a case/crate/box **of** sth
▶ **in** a case/crate/container/box
▶ **fill** a case/crate/container/box

7 [C] ■ *The most serious cases were treated first.*

patient • **victim** • **sufferer** • **invalid** • **the sick**

▶ a **chronic** case/patient/sufferer/invalid
▶ a/an **AIDS/cancer** case/patient/victim/sufferer
▶ **treat** a case/patient/victim/sufferer/the sick

cash noun

1 [U] ■ *Payments can be made by cheque or in cash.*

money • **change**

▶ **draw out/get out/take out/withdraw** cash/money
▶ **ready** cash/money (= money that you have to spend immediately)
● **CASH OR MONEY?** If it is important to contrast money in the form of coins and notes and money in other forms, use **cash**:
✔ *How much money/cash do you have on you?* ✗ ~~Payments can be made by cheque or in money.~~

2 [U] (*infml*) ■ *She refused to part with her hard-earned cash.*

funds • **money** • **capital**

▶ **have/be short of/lack** (the) cash/funds/money/capital
▶ **spend/borrow/invest** cash/funds/money/capital

▶ **get/obtain/lend** cash/funds/money

● **CASH OR FUNDS?** You can use either word in personal or business contexts, although **cash** is more informal than **funds**. **Cash** can be used like an adjective before other nouns:
✔ *The company is having cash flow problems.* ✗ ~~The company is having funds flow problems.~~

cash *verb* [T]
■ *The company cashed my cheque.*

change • exchange • cash sth in • clear

▶ **cash/change** traveller's cheques
▶ **cash/clear** a cheque
▶ **change/exchange** your currency/pounds/dollars for/into pounds/dollars/the local currency

castle *noun* [C]
■ *the ruins of a medieval castle*

fort • fortress • stronghold • tower • garrison

▶ an **old/ancient** castle/fort/fortress/stronghold/tower
▶ **build** a castle/fort/fortress/stronghold/tower/garrison

casual *adj.* [usu. before noun] (sometimes disapprov.)
■ *He tried to sound casual, but I knew he was worried.*

relaxed • calm • cool • easy-going • laid-back • detached • indifferent • uninterested • half-hearted • lukewarm | *disapprov.* **offhand • blasé**

▶ **casual/relaxed/calm/easy-going/laid-back/indifferent/half-hearted/lukewarm/offhand/blasé about** sth
▶ **a/an casual/relaxed/calm/cool/easy-going/laid-back/detached/indifferent/half-hearted/offhand manner**
▶ **a/an casual/relaxed/calm/cool/easy-going/laid-back/detached/indifferent/lukewarm/blasé attitude**

catch *verb*

1 [T] ■ *She caught the ball.*

grab • seize • take • snatch

■ **OPP** drop, throw
▶ **grab/seize/take** hold of sb/sth

2 [T] ■ *Police are trying to catch the culprits.*

capture • arrest • take | *fml* **apprehend** | *infml* **bust**

▶ **police** catch/capture/arrest/take/apprehend/bust sb

3 [T] ■ *How many fish did you catch?*

trap • capture

▶ **catch/trap** sth **in** sth
▶ **catch/trap** a/an **bird/animal**

4 [T] ■ *I caught him smoking at work.*

find • discover • come across sb/sth

▶ **catch/find/discover/come across** sb **doing** sth

5 [T, no passive] ■ *catch a train*

get • go by sth | *esp. written* **take**

■ **OPP** miss
▶ **catch the/get the/go by/take the** bus/train/plane/boat
▶ **catch/get** a **flight**
▶ **get** a **go by/take** a **taxi**

6 [T] ■ *She caught my cold.*

get • come down with sth • develop • have • suffer from | *esp. BrE, esp. spoken* **have got** | *fml* **contract**

▶ **catch/get/develop/have/suffer from/have got/contract** a/an **disease/illness**
▶ **catch/get/come down with/have/suffer from/have got** a **bug/cold**
▶ **catch/get/have/suffer from/have got/contract** the **flu**
▶ **catch/get/have/suffer/contract** a **virus/HIV/malaria**

category *noun* [C]
■ *Which subject category do the documents belong to?*

class • classification • heading • bracket • group • set • league • kind • type • variety | *esp. BrE* **sort** | *fml* **genre**

▶ **be in/within** a category/class/classification/bracket/group/set/league/genre
▶ a **different/the same** category/class/classification/heading/bracket/group/set/league/kind/type/variety/sort/genre
▶ a **broad/separate** category/class/classification/heading/group/set/kind/type/variety/genre

cause *noun*

1 [C] ■ *the cause of the problem*

source • origin • root

■ **OPP** effect
▶ a **common** cause/source/origin/root
▶ **have** a cause/a source/origins/roots
▶ **find/locate/discover/investigate/trace** the cause/source/origin/roots of sth

2 [U] ■ *There is no cause for alarm.*

cause

reason • basis • need • grounds • excuse • case • justification

▪ (a/an) cause/reason/grounds/ basis/need/excuse/case/ justification **for** sth
▶ a **good/valid** cause/reason/ grounds/excuse/case/justification
▶ **have** (a/an) cause/reason/ grounds/excuse/case/justification

cause verb [T]

▪ *The bombing caused an international outcry.*

result in sth • lead (sth) to sth • produce • bring sth about • create • prompt • provoke • trigger • set sth off • stir sth up | *fml* give rise to sth • induce | *esp. journ.* spark • fuel • stoke

▶ cause/result in/lead to/produce/ bring about/prompt/provoke/ trigger/give rise to/fuel/stoke **a/an change/increase**
▶ cause/result in/lead to/produce/ give rise to/create **problems/ difficulties**
▶ cause/result in/lead to/prompt/ provoke/stir up/spark/fuel/stoke **anger**

cease verb [I, T] (*fml*)

▪ *The company ceased trading in May.*

stop • give sth up • abandon • drop | *infml* leave off • knock off (sth) | *esp. AmE, infml* quit | *fml* discontinue

▪ OPP start, continue
▶ cease/stop/give up/leave off/quit **doing sth**
▶ cease/stop/give up/abandon/ drop/leave off/quit **what** you are doing
▶ cease/stop/give up/abandon/ leave off/knock off **work**

celebration noun [C, usu. pl.]

▪ *We're preparing for his 80th birthday celebrations in May.*

festivities • party • function • reception • event • occasion | *infml, esp. journ.* bash

▶ (a) **special** celebration/festivities/ party/reception/event/occasion
▶ (a) celebrations/festivities/party/ function/reception/event/bash **is/are held**
▶ (a) celebrations/festivities/party/ reception/event **takes place/take place**

central adj.

▪ *The central issue is that of widespread racism.*

key • main • principal • chief • prime • primary • major • first • foremost | *infml* number one

▪ OPP **peripheral**
▶ be central/key **to** sth
▶ a/the central/key/main/ principal/chief/prime/primary/ major/first/foremost **aim/ purpose/factor/consideration/ concern/role**
▶ a/the central/key/main/ principal/chief/prime/primary/ major/first **focus/function/ objective**

centre (BrE) (AmE center) noun

1 [C] ▪ *the centre of a circle*

the middle

▪ OPP edge
▶ the centre/middle **of** sth
▶ **in** the centre/middle
● THE CENTRE OR THE MIDDLE? The **centre** of an area may be a more precise area than the **middle**: *the centre of a circle* is the point in the exact middle. **Middle** but not **centre** can be used to describe a situation or a period of time:
✔ *When they quarrel, I am often caught in the middle.* ✗ *When they quarrel, I am often caught in the centre.*

2 [C] ▪ *a centre for people with epilepsy*

institute • institution • organization • association • club

▶ a/an centre/institute/institution/ organization/association/club **for** sth
▶ a **local** centre/institute/ institution/organization/ association/club
▶ a **research/training** centre/ institute/institution/organization

3 [C, usu. sing.] ▪ *Children like to be the centre of attention.*

focus • heart • hub • focal point

▶ the centre/focus **of** attention
▶ the **commercial** centre/heart/hub of sth
▶ **act/serve as** a centre/focus/focal point

ceremony noun [C]

▪ *They were married in a simple ceremony.*

ritual • rite • service • sacrament • liturgy

▶ **at** a ceremony/ritual/rite/service
▶ a **religious** ceremony/ritual/rite/ service
▶ a/an **ancient/primitive/ traditional/pagan** ceremony/ ritual/rite
▶ **perform** a ceremony/ritual/rite

certain adj.

1 ▪ *She looks certain to win an Oscar.*

bound • sure • guaranteed • conclusive • undeniable • indisputable • unquestionable | *fml* destined | *written* assured | *esp. spoken* definite

■ OPP uncertain
► certain/sure/assured **of** sth
► certain/sure/bound/guaranteed/ destined **to do sth**
► certain/conclusive/undeniable/ indisputable/unquestionable **that…**

2 ■ *Are you certain about this?*

sure • confident • convinced • clear • satisfied | *esp. spoken* positive

■ OPP uncertain
► certain/sure/confident/ convinced/clear/positive **about** sth
► certain/sure/confident/ convinced/satisfied **of** sth
► certain/sure/confident/ convinced/satisfied/clear/positive **that…**
► certain/sure/clear/satisfied **who/ what/how…**
● **CERTAIN OR SURE? Certain** is slightly more formal and less frequent than **sure**. Both words are often used in negative statements and questions.

3 ■ *Certain people might disagree.*

particular • specific

► a certain/particular/specific **event/incident/occasion/date**
► certain/particular/specific **needs/ requirements**
► a certain/particular/specific **type/ kind of sth**

certainty noun [C]
■ *The only certainty is change.*

inevitability • a foregone conclusion • necessity | *esp. AmE, infml* a sure thing

■ OPP uncertainty
► a certainty/an inevitability **about** sth
► an **absolute** certainty/necessity
► the **one/only** certainty/necessity

certificate noun [C]
■ *She showed her certificate of insurance.*

documentation • papers • ID • credentials • permit • pass • authorization | *BrE* licence | *AmE* license

► get/obtain (a) certificate/ documentation/papers/ credentials/permit/pass/ authorization/licence
► issue/give (sb) (a) certificate/ documentation/papers/permit/ pass/licence
► see/check sb's certificate/ documentation/papers/ID/

credentials/permit/pass/ authorization/licence

chain noun [C]
■ *It was all part of a chain of events.*

series • sequence • string • succession • line | *esp. BrE* catalogue

► a chain/series/sequence/string/ succession/line/catalogue **of** sth
► a chain/series/sequence/string/ succession **of events**
► a/an **long/endless/continuous/ unbroken** chain/series/sequence/ string/succession/line

chain verb [T]
■ *Protesters chained themselves to the railings.*

tie • fasten • strap • handcuff • restrain • tether | *fml* bind • secure

► chain/tie/fasten/strap/handcuff/ tether/bind/secure sth **to** sth
► chain/tie/fasten/strap/handcuff/ bind sb/sth **together**

chair noun [C]
■ *Sit on your chair!* ■ *a wheelchair/ deckchair/high chair/rocking chair*

seat • armchair • throne • stool

► **in/into/out of** a/an chair/seat/ armchair
► **on/onto/off** a chair/seat/throne/ stool
● **CHAIR OR SEAT?** A **chair** is a piece of furniture designed for sitting on; a **seat** is anywhere that you can sit:
  ✔ *a set of dining/kitchen chairs* ✗ ~~a set of dining/kitchen seats~~
  ✔ *We used the old tree stump as a seat.* ✗ ~~We used the old tree stump as a chair.~~
  Seat is also used for the place where you sit in a vehicle:
  ✔ *the passenger seat/driver's seat* (= in a car) • *an aisle/a window seat* (= in a bus/plane/train)

chairman, chairwoman noun [C]
■ *He was recently appointed chairman of the company.*

chair • leader • head • president • chief executive • director | *BrE* managing director • governor | *infml* boss | *esp. journ.* chief

► a **company/club** chairman/ chairwoman/president/chief executive/director/managing director/boss/chief
► be **appointed** (as) chairman/ chairwoman/chair/leader/head/ president/chief executive/ director/managing director/ governor/chief
► **resign/stand down/step down** as

challenge noun [C]

■ the challenges of a new job

chairman / chairwoman / chair /
leader / head / president / chief
executive / director / managing
director / governor / chief

● **WHICH WORD?** The **chairman** or
chairwoman of a company is usu.
the most senior member of its
board (= group of directors).
President is a title given to the
most senior person in some
companies. The **chief executive** or
managing director is the person in
charge of making decisions about a
business, and is often also the
chairman.

challenge noun [C]

■ the challenges of a new job

problem • **difficulty** • **trouble** • **issue**

▶ (a/an) challenge / problem /
difficulty / trouble / issue **for** sb
▶ (a) **serious** / **real** challenge /
problem / difficulty / trouble / issue
▶ (a) **major** / **minor** challenge /
problem / difficulty / issue

challenge verb

1 [T] ■ The story was successfully
challenged in court.

contest • **question** • **query** • **dispute**
• **doubt**

▶ challenge / question / query /
dispute / doubt **whether…**
▶ challenge / contest / question /
query / dispute a **decision**
▶ challenge / question / doubt the
wisdom of sb/sth

2 [T] ■ Jo challenged me to a game of
chess.

dare • **throw down the gauntlet**

▶ challenge / dare sb to do sth

chance noun

1 [C, U] ■ Is there any chance of
getting tickets now?

possibility • **prospect** • **odds** •
likelihood • **probability**

▶ a chance / a possibility / the
prospect / the odds / the likelihood /
a probability **of / that…**
▶ **little** / **no** chance / possibility /
prospect / likelihood
▶ the chances / odds / likelihood /
probability **is / are that…**
▶ **increase** / **reduce** the chance /
possibility / odds / probability /
likelihood

2 [C] ■ This is your big chance.

opportunity • **start** • **possibilities** |
infml **break** | *esp. spoken* **moment** |
esp. busin. **window**

▶ a chance / the opportunity **to do**
sth

▶ **have** a/an chance / opportunity /
break / moment / window
▶ **get** / **give** sb a/an chance /
opportunity / break / moment / start
▶ **take advantage of** a chance / an
opportunity / the possibilities / a
window

● **CHANCE OR OPPORTUNITY?**
Opportunity tends to be more
formal. In some cases only one of
the words can be used:
✔ I won't give him a second chance.
✗ I won't give him a second
opportunity.
✔ job/equal opportunities ✗ job/
equal chances

3 [C] ■ The manager took a chance on
a young, inexperienced player.

gamble • **risk**

▶ **take** a chance / gamble / risk **on** sb/
sth
▶ **take** a chance / risk **with** sth
▶ a **big** chance / gamble / risk
● **CHANCE, GAMBLE OR RISK? Risk** is
used esp. when there is danger to
life or sb's safety; **gamble** is used
about less serious danger, or when
you risk money. When you decide
to give/not to give sb the
opportunity to do sth, you **take a
chance / take no chances**.

4 [U, sing.] ■ We met by chance at the
airport.

coincidence • **accident** • **luck**

▶ **by** chance / coincidence / accident /
luck
▶ **pure** / **sheer** chance / coincidence /
accident / luck
▶ a/an **happy** / **unfortunate** / **strange**
chance / coincidence / accident

change noun

1 [C, U] ■ a change in the weather

variation • **swing** • **fluctuation** •
alternation | *written* **variability** | *esp.
journ.* **shift**

▶ (a/an) change / variation / swing /
fluctuation / alternation / variability /
shift **in** sth
▶ (a) **rapid** change / fluctuation /
alternation / shift
▶ **cause** (a) change / variation /
swing / fluctuations / variability / shift

2 [C, U] ■ a couple of minor changes
to the opening paragraph

alteration • **conversion** •
amendment • **adjustment** •
modification • **revision** • **adaptation**
• **transition** | *esp. journ.* **switch**

▶ a/an change / alteration /
conversion / amendment /
adjustment / modification /
revision / adaptation / transition /
switch **to** sth
▶ a/an change / alteration /

adjustment/modification/switch in sth

► **make** a/an change/alteration/ amendment/adjustment/ modification/revision/adaptation/ transition/switch

change verb

1 [I] ■ Rick hasn't changed much in 20 years.

alter • vary • alternate • fluctuate | *esp. journ.* **shift • swing**

► change/shift/swing **from** sth **to** sth
► vary/alternate/fluctuate/swing **between** A **and** B
► change/alter/vary/fluctuate/ shift/swing **dramatically/sharply**
● CHANGE OR ALTER? Alter is often used when sth has changed only slightly; **change** is more frequent and has a much wider range, often suggesting a complete change to sth important, or sth which is in the process of changing:
✔Her life changed completely when she won the lottery. ✗ Her life altered completely.
✔changing attitudes to education ✗ altering attitudes to education

2 [T] ■ IT has changed the way people work.

alter • adapt • shift • vary • adjust • revise • tailor • modify • amend

► change/alter/adapt/adjust/ revise/modify your **ideas**
► change/alter/shift/adjust/revise/ modify your/sb's **attitude/opinion**
► change/alter/shift/vary the **emphasis**
► change/alter/adapt/revise/ modify/amend a **text**
● CHANGE OR ALTER? Alter is often used when sth does not change: It doesn't alter the way I feel.
Change has a much wider range of uses, including particular collocations such as change your mind, change your name and change the subject.

3 [I, T] ■ Caterpillars change into butterflies.

turn • transform • convert • translate | *fml* **metamorphose |** *biology* **evolve • mutate**

► change/turn/transform sth/ convert/metamorphose/evolve/ mutate **from** sth **into** sth
► change/turn/transform sth/ convert/evolve/mutate **rapidly** (into sth)
► change/turn/transform sth/ convert/evolve **quickly/slowly/ gradually** (into sth)
● CHANGE OR TURN? Change is only used in cases where sth occurs naturally, automatically or by magic. Turn can also be used when

---

chaos

people use their effort or skill to change one thing or situation into sth different, or when circumstances change a situation:
✔There are plans to turn the old station into a hotel. ✗ There are plans to change the old station into a hotel.

✔A minor disagreement turned into a major crisis. ✗ A minor disagreement changed into a major crisis.

4 [T] ■ Can I change seats with you?

exchange • swap/swop • switch • replace • substitute • reverse • barter | *esp. AmE or journ.* **trade**

► change/exchange/swap/switch/ substitute/barter/trade A **for** B
► change/exchange/swap/trade **places**
► change/replace a **battery/bulb/ fuse/tyre/wheel**

5 [T] (esp. spoken) ■ Where can I change my traveller's cheques?

exchange • cash • cash in

► change/cash **traveller's cheques**
► change/exchange your **currency/ pounds/dollars** into **pounds/ dollars/the local currency**

channel noun

1 [C] ■ a movie/sports channel

station • network | *tech.* **frequency**

► a **television** channel/station/ network
► a **radio** channel/station/frequency
► **tune to** a channel/station/ frequency

2 [C] ■ Music is a channel for releasing emotions.

vehicle • medium

► a channel/vehicle/medium **of/for** sth
► the **proper/appropriate/right** channels/vehicle/medium
► channels/a vehicle/a medium of **communication/expression**
● CHANNEL OR VEHICLE? Channel is used esp. to talk about a way of giving information or expressing feelings that might otherwise become difficult to deal with. Vehicle is used more to talk about a way of getting creative or political ideas across to people.

chaos noun [U]

■ Flooding has caused chaos across the country.

confusion • havoc • mayhem • pandemonium • commotion • mess | *infml* **shambles**

■ OPP **order**

▶ the character/role/part of sb
▶ a **major/minor** character/role/part
▶ **play** a character/role/part

characteristic noun [C]

■ The species have several characteristics in common.

feature • quality • trait • point • attribute | *tech.* property

▶ a/an **essential/desirable/ individual** characteristic/feature/ quality/trait/attribute/property
▶ a/an **important/natural/special/ useful** characteristic/feature/ quality/attribute/property
▶ **possess/display/share** (a) characteristic/feature/quality/ trait/... points/attribute/property

characteristic adj.

■ with her characteristic modesty

typical • representative • classic • usual • habitual • normal

■ OPP uncharacteristic

▶ characteristic/typical/ representative **of** sb/sth
▶ a characteristic/typical/ representative/classic **example** of sth
▶ characteristic/typical/usual/ habitual/normal **behaviour**
● **CHARACTERISTIC OR TYPICAL?** When it is used to mean that sb behaves as you would expect, *typical* often shows disapproval, while *characteristic* usu. shows approval: *It was typical of her to forget.* • *Such kindness was characteristic of Mike.*

charge noun

1 [C] ■ There will be a small charge for refreshments.

fee • price • rate • terms • dues • toll • fare • rental • cost

▶ (a/the) charge/fee/price/rate/ terms/dues/toll/fare/rental **for** sth
▶ **at** a charge/fee/price/rate/fare/ rental/cost **of...**
▶ **pay** (a/the) charge/fee/price/ rate/dues/toll/fare/rental/cost
▶ **increase/reduce** the charge/fee/ price/rate/dues/toll/fare/rental/ cost
● **CHARGE OR FEE?** *Charge* rather than *fee* is used for smaller services in less formal contexts:
✗ *There will be a small fee for refreshments.*
✓ *legal/school/professional fees*
When you visit a museum, etc. you pay an *admission* charge or *admission/entrance fee*, (but never an 'entrance charge').

2 [C] ■ The investigation led to criminal charges against three employees.

character noun

1 [C, usu. sing.] ■ He revealed his true character.

nature • personality • temperament • self • make-up | *fml* disposition • persona

▶ **in** sb's character/nature
▶ a **violent** character/nature/ personality/temperament
▶ an **aspect of** sb's character/ nature/personality/temperament/ disposition
● **WHICH WORD?** *Character* is used esp. about sb's moral behaviour; *nature* is used esp. about sb's normal way of behaving; *personality* is used esp. about whether sb is confident, shy, etc. with other people; *temperament* is used esp. about whether sb normally stays calm, or gets angry, etc.

2 [U] ■ the special character of the neighbourhood

nature • essence • spirit

▶ **in** character/nature/essence/spirit
▶ the **real/true** character/nature/ essence/spirit of sth
▶ **preserve/capture/convey/ reflect/consider/understand/ reveal/define** the character/ nature/essence of sth
● **CHARACTER OR NATURE?** *Character* is used more to talk about the qualities and features of physical things such as buildings; *nature* is used more to talk about the basic qualities of abstract things, such as a problem, work or society.

3 [U] (*approv.*) ■ Everyone admires her strength of character.

personality • charisma • presence • charm

▶ **great** character/charisma/ presence/charm
▶ **lack** character/personality/ charisma/charm

4 [C] ■ the main characters in the novel/film/play

role • part

accusation • recrimination | *esp. AmE* **indictment • impeachment**

▶ (a/an) charge/accusation/ recriminations/indictment **against** sb
▶ **face** a charge/an accusation/an indictment/impeachment
▶ **make/deny** a charge/an accusation

charge verb

1 [T, I] ■ *He only charged me half-price.*

ask • fine • bill • invoice • levy

▶ charge (sb)/ask sth/fine sb/bill sb/invoice sb **for** sth
▶ charge/bill sth **to** sb's account
▶ charge/ask a high/low **price/fee/ commission/rent**

2 ■ *He was charged with murder.*

accuse • impeach • prosecute | *law* **indict**

▶ charge/indict sb **with** sth
▶ impeach/prosecute/indict sb **for** sth
● **CHARGE OR INDICT?** In Britain the Crown Prosecution Service decides whether to **charge** sb with a crime. In the US **charge** is used when this is done by a prosecutor (= a public official) and **indict** when this is done by a Grand Jury (= 23 people).

3 [I] (always used with an adv. or prep.) ■ *The kids were charging around outside.*

tear • stampede • gallop • pound • bound • run • hurtle | *esp. BrE* **career** | *written* **race**

▶ charge/tear/gallop/pound/ bound/run/race **after** sb/sth
▶ charge/stampede/hurtle/career **into** sth
▶ charge/tear/run/race **around/ round**

charity noun

1 [C] ■ *helping local charities*

cause • foundation | *law* **trust**

▶ a charity/foundation/trust **for** sth
▶ a **national/private/independent/ family/educational/ conservation/housing** charity/ foundation/trust
▶ **help/support** a charity/cause/ foundation/trust

2 [U] ■ *raising money for charity*

aid • relief • welfare | *sometimes disapprov.* **handout**

▶ **ask for/get/receive** charity/aid/ relief/welfare
▶ **give (sb)** charity/aid/relief/ handouts

▶ **rely/depend on** charity/welfare/ handouts

charm noun [U] (*usu. approv.*)
■ *a man of great charm*

charisma • magnetism

▶ **great** charm/charisma/ magnetism
▶ **have/lack** charm/charisma/ magnetism

chart noun [C]
■ *A chart showed sales figures for the year.*

pie chart • bar chart • flow chart • flow diagram • graph • table • diagram | *written* **figure**

▶ **in** a chart/pie chart/fbar chart/ flow chart/flow diagram/graph/ table/diagram/figure
▶ **on** a chart/graph/diagram
▶ **draw** a chart/pie chart/bar chart/ flow chart/flow diagram/graph/ diagram

chase verb [T, I]
■ *My dog likes chasing rabbits.*

hunt • follow | *fml* **pursue**

▶ chase/hunt/follow/pursue an **animal**
▶ chase/follow/pursue a **person**
▶ chase/hunt/pursue a **criminal**

chat noun [U, C] (*esp. BrE*)
■ *We had a chat about the kids.*

conversation • talk • gossip • discussion • chatter

▶ (a) chat/conversation/talk/ gossip/discussion/chatter **about** sth
▶ a chat/conversation/talk/gossip/ discussion **with** sb
▶ **have** a chat/conversation/talk/ gossip/discussion

chat verb [I]
■ *We spent hours chatting on the phone.*

chatter • talk • speak | *sometimes disapprov.* **gossip**

▶ chat/chatter/talk/speak **to** sb/ gossip **about** sth
▶ chat/chatter/talk/speak/gossip **to/with** sb
▶ chat/chatter/gossip **away**

cheap adj.

1 ■ *You can get incredibly cheap fares on the Internet.*

budget • economical • affordable • reasonable • half-price • inexpensive | *esp. busin.* **competitive**

■ OPP **expensive**

cheat

▶ cheap/budget/economical/
affordable/reasonable/
competitive **prices/rates/fares**
▶ cheap/economical/affordable/
inexpensive/competitive
products/services
▶ cheap/affordable/inexpensive
goods

2 (*disapprov.*) ■ *cheap and nasty
bottles of wine*

poor • **bad** • **second-rate** • **inferior** |
BrE, taboo, slang **crap** • **shit** |
AmE, taboo, slang **crappy** • **shitty**

▶ a/an cheap/poor/bad/second-
rate/inferior **imitation**
▶ a/an cheap/bad/second-rate/
inferior/crap/shit/crappy/shitty
product

---

cheat *noun* [C] (*disapprov.*)
■ *You cheat! You looked at my cards!*

AmE **cheater** | *infml* **con man** | *esp.
AmE, infml* **hustler** | *esp. journ.*
swindler

---

cheat *verb* [T, I] (*disapprov.*)
■ *She is accused of cheating the
taxman.*

con • **dupe** • **deceive** • **trick** • **fool** •
take sb in • **swindle** • **short-change**
• **defraud** | *infml* **rip sb off** • **fleece** |
esp. AmE, infml **bilk** | *slang* **screw**

▶ cheat/con/dupe/trick/defraud/
fleece/bilk/screw sb **out of** sth
▶ cheat/con/dupe/trick/
fool sb **into doing** sth
▶ cheat/con/trick **your way** into sth
▶ cheat/con/dupe/deceive/trick/
fool/short-change/defraud/rip
off/fleece/bilk **customers**

---

check

check *noun* [C]
■ *Carry out regular safety checks of the
equipment.*

inspection • **examination** • **check-up**

▶ a **thorough/routine/regular**
check/inspection/examination/
check-up
▶ a **medical** check/inspection/
examination/check-up
▶ **carry out/do** a/an check/
inspection/examination

---

check

check *verb*

1 [T] ■ *Check your work before
handing it in.*

inspect • **examine** • **go over sth** •
check over sb/sth • **check through**
sth • **look at sth** | *busin.* **audit**

▶ check/inspect/examine/go
over/check through sth **for** sth
▶ check/inspect/examine/look at
sth **to see if/whether...**
▶ check/inspect/examine/go over/

check over/check through/look at
sth **carefully**
● **CHECK, INSPECT OR EXAMINE?** These
words can all be used when you
are looking for possible problems.
Only **check** is used about looking
for mistakes:
✗ *Inspect/Examine your work before
handing it in.*
Only **examine** is used when
looking for the cause of a problem:
✔ *The doctor examined her but could
find nothing wrong.* ✗ *The doctor
checked/inspected her but could
find nothing wrong.*

2 [I, T] ■ *Go and check that I've locked
the windows.*

make sure | *fml* **verify** • **assure**
yourself

▶ check/verify sth **with** sb
▶ check/make sure/verify/assure
yourself **that...**
▶ check/verify **what/whether...**

---

cheerful *adj.*

■ *He tried to sound cheerful and
unconcerned.*

bright • **in a good mood** • **jolly** |
infml **cheery**

● **OPP** **gloomy, miserable**

▶ cheerful/bright/jolly/cheery **face**
▶ cheerful/cheery/jolly/cheery
person/manner
▶ in a cheerful/good/jolly/cheery
mood
● **bright** and cheerful/jolly/cheery
● **CHEERFUL OR BRIGHT?** You can use
bright after the verbs *to be* or *to
feel*: *I was not feeling very bright that
morning.*
You can say *a cheerful boy/girl*, but
a bright boy/girl is intelligent, not
cheerful.

---

chemical *noun* [C]

■ *a chemical used in cleaning products*

substance • **material** • **gas** • **element**

▶ a **natural** chemical/substance/
material/gas
▶ **radioactive** chemicals/
substances/materials/gases/
elements
▶ a **toxic** chemical/substance/
material/gas/element

---

chew *verb* [T, I]

■ *Chew your food up well.*

munch • **gnaw** • **nibble** • **bite** •
crunch

▶ chew/munch/nibble/bite/crunch
on sth
▶ chew on/gnaw/crunch a **bone**
▶ chew/bite **your nails/lip**

---

chief *adj.*

1 ■ *her chief rival for the gold medal*

main • principal • prime • primary • central • key • major | infml **number one**

▶ the chief/main/principal/prime/primary/central/key/major/number one **concern**
▶ the chief/main/principal/prime/primary/key/major/number one **cause**
▶ the chief/main/prime/number one **suspect**

2 [only before noun] ■ the Chief Education Officer

top • senior • superior • leading • high-ranking

▶ a chief/top/senior/superior/leading/high-ranking **officer**
▶ a chief/top/senior/leading **adviser/aide/economist/lawyer**
▶ a chief/top/senior/high-ranking **executive**

child noun

1 [C] ■ a child of three/a three-year-old child

boy • girl • toddler • baby | infml **kid • youngster • lad** | fml or tech. **infant** | infml, disapprov. **brat** | law **minor • juvenile**

■ OPP **adult, grown-up**
▶ a young **child/boy/girl/baby/kid/infant**
▶ a little **child/boy/girl/baby/kid/brat**
▶ **look after/take care of** a child/baby/kid
● CHILD OR KID? **Kid** is much more frequent in informal and spoken AmE. **Child** is not often used of sb older than about 12; above that age you can call them sb kids, teenagers, young people, girls, youths or lads.

2 [C] ■ She has three children

son • daughter • boy • girl • baby • kid

▶ a newborn **child/son/daughter/boy/girl/baby/kid**
▶ **have/give birth to** a child/son/daughter/boy/girl/baby/kid
▶ **bring up/raise** a child/son/daughter/boy/girl/kid

childhood noun [U, C]
■ He had a happy childhood.

youth • infancy

■ OPP **old age**
▶ in/during/from/since/throughout sb's childhood/youth/infancy
▶ a/an happy/unhappy childhood/youth
▶ **spend** your childhood/youth...

childish adj. (sometimes disapprov.)
■ written in childish handwriting ■ Don't be so childish!

youthful • girlish | usu. approv. **childlike • boyish** | disapprov. **immature**

■ OPP **adult**
▶ childish/childlike/immature **behaviour**
● CHILDISH OR CHILDLIKE? **Childish** is disapproving and used to describe an adult who is being silly; **childlike** is usu. approving and suggests the simple and innocent qualities of a child.

choice noun

1 [C] ■ Many women make a choice between family and career.

selection | infml **pick**

▶ **make** a choice/selection
▶ **have/take** a/your choice/pick
▶ **get** first choice/pick

2 [U, C, usu. sing.] ■ If I had the choice, I'd give up work tomorrow. ■ He had no choice but to (= he had to) leave.

option • alternative • possibility

▶ a real/realistic/practical **choice/option/alternative/possibility**
▶ a/an good/acceptable/reasonable **choice/option/alternative**
▶ **have** no choice/option/alternative (but to do sth)
▶ **look at/limit** the choices/options/alternatives/possibilities
● CHOICE, OPTION OR ALTERNATIVE? **Alternative** is slightly more formal than **option** or **choice**, and is more frequently used to talk about choosing between two things rather than several.

3 [C] ■ She is the first choice for the job.

preference • selection | BrE **favourite** | AmE **favorite** | esp. AmE, infml **pick**

▶ sb's choice/favourite/pick **for** sth
▶ sb's choice/selection/pick **as** sth
▶ an obvious **choice/selection/favourite**

4 [sing., U] ■ a good choice of desserts

range • variety • selection • assortment • array

▶ a wide **choice/range/variety/selection/assortment/array**
▶ a/an good/interesting/limited **choice/range/variety/selection**
▶ **have/offer/provide** (a/an) **choice/range/variety/selection/array/assortment** (of sth)

choose verb [I, T]

1 ■ *We have to choose a new manager.*

select • decide • opt • single sb/sth out • adopt | *infml* **pick • go for sth**

► choose/select/decide/pick **between** A and/or B
► choose/select/opt for sb/sth/adopt/pick/go for sb/sth **as** sb/sth
► choose/select/single out/pick sb/sth **for** sb/sth
► choose/select/opt for/single out/adopt/pick/go for sb/sth **to do sth**
● **CHOOSE, SELECT OR PICK?** When you **select** sth you usu. choose it carefully, unless you actually say that it is *selected randomly/at random.* **Pick** is a more informal word that describes a less careful action. **Choose** is the most general of these words and the only one that can be used without an object:
✔ *You choose—I can't decide* ✗ *You select/pick—I can't decide.*

2 [I, T] ■ *Many people choose not to marry.*

decide • make up your mind | *fml* **determine • elect • resolve**

► choose/decide/make up your mind/determine/elect/resolve **to do sth**
► choose/decide/make up your mind **whether/what/how...**
► **be free to** choose/decide/determine

chop verb [T]

■ *Roughly chop the herbs.*

cut • slice • dice

► chop/cut/slice sth **off** sth
► chop/cut/slice sth **up**
► chop/slice **an onion**

cinema noun [U, sing.] (*esp. BrE*)

■ *one of the great successes of British cinema*

film | *esp. AmE* **movies**

► British/French/classic/avant-garde cinema/film
► work **in** cinema/film/movies
► the cinema/film/movie **industry**
● **CINEMA, FILM OR MOVIES?** **Movie** is more frequent in *AmE.* In *BrE* **cinema** often emphasizes the business side of making films; **film** emphasizes the artistic side.

circle noun [C]

■ *They stood in a circle.*

ring • hoop • disc | *esp. AmE* **disk**

► **in** a circle/ring

► **through** a circle/hoop/disc/disk
► **concentric** circles/rings

circumstance noun [C, usu. pl.]

■ *She did the job very well in the circumstances.*

conditions • situation • position • the case • state of affairs | *infml, esp. spoken* **things**

► **in** the/a circumstances/particular situation/position/state of affairs
► the **general/current/present/real** circumstances/conditions/situation/position/state of affairs
► sb's **economic/financial/social** circumstances/conditions/situation/position
► **describe/explain** the circumstances/situation/position/state of affairs/things
● **CIRCUMSTANCES OR CONDITIONS?** **Circumstances** refers to sb's financial situation; **conditions** refers to things such as food, shelter, or the working environment. The **circumstances** that affect an event are the facts surrounding it; the **conditions** are usu. physical things, such as the weather.

citizen noun

1 [C] ■ *She's French by birth, but is now a British citizen.*

national • subject • native • voter • taxpayer

► a citizen/native/national **of** a country
► a **British** citizen/national/subject/native/voter/taxpayer
► a **US/Australian, etc.** citizen/national/native/voter/taxpayer
► an **ordinary/average** citizen/voter/taxpayer

2 [C] ■ *The crime shocked all law-abiding citizens.*

resident • inhabitant | *fml* **householder |** *written* **dweller**

► **local** citizens/residents/inhabitants/householders
► **private** citizens/householders

city noun [C]

■ *It is one of the world's most beautiful cities.*

town • metropolis • borough | *fml* **municipality • conurbation**

► **in** a city/town/metropolis/borough/municipality/conurbation
► a **major** city/town/metropolis/conurbation
► a city/town/borough **council**
● **CITY OR TOWN?** A **city** is usu. bigger and more important than a **town**.

claim noun

1 [C] ■ *The report examines claims of corruption.*

allegation • assertion | *fml* **contention**

■ **OPP denial**
▶ a/an **claim/allegation/assertion/ contention that...**
▶ a/an **claim/allegation/assertion about/of** sth
▶ **make/deny** a/an **claim/ allegation/assertion**
● **CLAIM OR ASSERTION?** When the point in doubt is a matter of opinion, not fact, use **assertion**:
✔*She made sweeping assertions about the role of women in society.*
✘ ~~She made sweeping claims about the role of women in society.~~

2 [C, U] ■ *She renounced her claim to the throne.*

right | *esp. BrE, fml* **entitlement |** *law* **title**

▶ **claim/right/entitlement/title to** sth
▶ **have** a/an **claim/right/title/ entitlement**
▶ **give up/renounce** your **claim/ right/title**

3 [C] ■ *a three per cent pay claim*

request • application • demand

▶ a/an **claim/request/application/ demand for** sth
▶ a **formal claim/request/ application/demand**
▶ **make/put in/withdraw/refuse/ reject** a **claim/request/ application/demand**

claim verb

1 [T] ■ *He claims that he was not given a fair hearing.*

argue • insist • protest • assert • maintain | *fml* **allege • contend • affirm**

▶ **claim/argue/insist/protest/ assert/maintain/allege/contend/ affirm that...**
▶ **It is claimed/argued/asserted/ maintained/alleged/contended/ affirmed that...**

2 [T, I] ■ *He is not entitled to claim benefit.*

ask • apply • demand | *fml* **request • seek**

▶ **claim/ask for/demand/request/ seek sth from** sth
▶ **formally claim/ask for/apply for/ request/seek** sth

class noun

1 [C+sing./pl. *v*.] ■ *We were in the same class at school.*

grade | *esp. BrE* **year • stream |** *BrE* **set |** *AmE* **track**

▶ **in** a **class/grade/set/year/stream**

2 [C, U] ■ *I have an English class at 11.*

lesson • seminar • session • workshop • tutorial • period

▶ a **class/lesson/seminar/session/ workshop/tutorial on** sth
▶ **in/during** a **class/lesson/seminar/ session/workshop/tutorial/period**
▶ **at** a **class/lesson/seminar/session/ workshop/tutorial**
▶ **go to/attend/give/conduct** a **class/lesson/seminar/session/ workshop/tutorial**
● **CLASS OR LESSON?** A **class** is always for a group of people; a **lesson** can be for a group or for just one person.

3 [C] ■ *The college runs specialist language classes.*

curriculum | *BrE* **programme |** *AmE* **program |** *BrE or fml, AmE* **course**

▶ **in** a/the **class/curriculum/ programme/course**
▶ a **day/evening class/programme/ course**
▶ **run/take/do/enrol on/sign up for** a **class/programme/course**

4 [C+sing./pl. *v*., U] ■ *ideas that appeal to all classes of society*

level • rank • position • status • standing

▶ sb's **class/level/position/rank/ status/standing in/within** sth
▶ a/the **low/lower class/level/ rank/position/status/standing**
▶ the **middle/upper class/level/rank**

5 [C] ■ *It is cheap for this class of hotel.*

category • league • classification • kind • type • bracket | *esp. BrE* **sort**

▶ **be in/within** a **class/category/ league/classification/bracket**
▶ the **same class/category/league/ classification/kind/type/bracket/ sort**
▶ a **different class/category/ league/classification/kind/type/ bracket/sort**

6 [U] (*approx.*) ■ *There's a real touch of class about her.*

style • elegance • glamour • flair • grace

▶ **have/lack class/style/elegance/ glamour/flair/grace**
▶ **give sb/sth class/style/elegance/ glamour/grace**
▶ a **touch of class/style/elegance/ glamour**

classic

classic adj.

1 [usu. before noun] ■ *This classic novel was first published in 1968.*

great ♦ fine ♦ excellent ♦ outstanding ♦ superb ♦ perfect

▶ a/an classic/great/fine/excellent **novel**
▶ a/an classic/great/fine/excellent/ outstanding/superb **work**
▶ a/an classic/great/fine/excellent/ superb/perfect **goal**

2 ■ *a classic example of poor communication*

typical ♦ characteristic ♦ representative | written **archetypal** | fml **quintessential**

▶ a/an classic/typical/ characteristic/representative/ archetypal **example** of sth

3 ■ *wearing a classic little black dress*

elegant ♦ stylish | esp. BrE **smart** | infml **classy**

▶ a/an classic/elegant/stylish/smart **suit/dress**
▶ a/an classic/elegant/stylish **cut/ design**
▶ classic/elegant/smart **style**

classify verb [T]

■ *books classified according to subject*

sort ♦ categorize ♦ group ♦ file ♦ bracket ♦ class

▶ classify/sort/categorize/group/file/ bracket/class sb/sth **according to/into/by** sth
▶ classify/categorize/group/file/ bracket/class sb/sth **as** sth
▶ classify/sort/categorize/group/ file/class sb/sth **under** sth

clean verb [T, I]

■ *I spent all day cooking and cleaning.*

wash ♦ dust ♦ wipe ♦ mop ♦ sponge ♦ scrub ♦ brush ♦ sweep ♦ cleanse ♦ bathe ♦ rinse ♦ hose ♦ dry-clean ♦ shampoo

■ OPP **dirty**, **soil**
▶ clean/wash/mop/scrub/sweep the **floor**
▶ clean/wash/dust/wipe/scrub the **table/surfaces**
▶ clean/wash/cleanse/bathe a **wound**

clean adj.

■ *Are your hands clean?*

pure ♦ sterile ♦ hygienic ♦ spotless

■ OPP **dirty**
▶ clean/pure/sterile **(drinking) water**
▶ clean/sterile/hygienic **conditions**
▶ keep sth clean/pure/sterile/ **spotless**

clear verb

1 [T] ■ *You should be able to clear the building within three minutes.*

evacuate

▶ clear/evacuate a **place/building**
▶ police clear/evacuate a **place**

2 [I] ■ *As the smoke cleared, a plane came into view.*

disappear ♦ vanish ♦ fade ♦ dissolve

▶ cloud/smoke/mist clears/ disappears
▶ clear/disappear/fade/dissolve **gradually**

clear adj.

1 ■ *She gave clear and precise directions.*

plain ♦ explicit ♦ unambiguous ♦ accessible ♦ intelligible | fml **comprehensible ♦ express** | written **lucid**

■ OPP **unclear**, **confusing**
▶ clear/explicit/unambiguous **about** sth
▶ clear/plain/intelligible/ comprehensible **language/English**
▶ make sth clear/plain/explicit/ unambiguous/intelligible/ comprehensible **(to sb)**

2 ■ *It's clear to me that she's lying.*

plain ♦ obvious ♦ apparent ♦ evident ♦ self-evident ♦ noticeable ♦ distinct ♦ definite ♦ decided ♦ conspicuous ♦ unmistakable | esp. written **marked ♦ pronounced** | fml **discernible**

■ OPP **unclear**
▶ clear/plain/obvious/apparent/ evident/self-evident/noticeable/ discernible **to/from/in** sb/sth
▶ clear/plain/obvious/apparent/ evident **who/how/where/why…**
▶ clear/plain/obvious/apparent/ evident/noticeable/distinct/ definite/marked/pronounced/ discernible **difference**
● **WHICH WORD?** You make sth clear or **plain** deliberately, but you make sth **obvious** without meaning to:
✓ *I hope I make myself clear/plain.*
✗ *I hope I make myself obvious.*
✓ *Try not to make your dislike so obvious.* ✗ *Try not to make it so clear/plain.*
Apparent and **evident** are rather formal and can be replaced by **obvious**.

3 ■ *I'm still not clear what the job entails.*

sure ♦ certain

■ OPP **vague**
▶ clear/sure/certain **about** sth
▶ clear/sure/certain **that…**
▶ clear/sure/certain **who/what/ how**, etc.

4 ■ Items must be carried in a clear plastic bag. ■ The beach was perfect —white sand and clear blue water.

transparent • **see-through** | BrE **colourless** | AmE **colorless** | written **translucent**

■ OPP **opaque, cloudy**
► clear/transparent/translucent **glass**
► clear/transparent/see-through **plastic**
► clear/transparent/colourless **varnish**
● **CLEAR OR TRANSPARENT?** Clear is the word most often used to describe water. **Transparent** is used to describe solid things or materials, not liquids (except *varnish*).

clear (sth) up *phrasal verb*

1 ■ Who's going to clear up this mess?

clean (sth) up • **sort sth out** | esp. BrE **tidy**

■ OPP **mess sth up**
► clear up/clean up/tidy up **after** sb
► clear up/clean up/tidy up the **mess**
► clear up/sort out/tidy a **room/ house**

2 ■ Police are desperate to have this murder cleared up.

solve • **resolve** • **crack** • **figure sth out** | esp. BrE **work sth out**

► clear up/solve/resolve/crack a **case/mystery**
► clear up/solve/resolve a **crime/ question**

clever *adj.* (esp. BrE, sometimes disapprov.)

■ How clever of you to work it out!

intelligent • **brilliant** • **bright** | esp. AmE **smart**

■ OPP **stupid**
► clever/brilliant **at** sth
► a/an clever/intelligent/brilliant/ bright/smart **child/boy/girl/ man/woman**
► a/an clever/intelligent/brilliant/ smart **thing to do/move**

client *noun* [C]

■ a well-known lawyer with famous clients

customer • **buyer** • **shopper** • **consumer** • **end-user** • **regular** | fml **patron** • **purchaser** | BrE, infml **punter**

► have/deal with/get/lose a **client/customer/buyer**
► attract **clients/customers/buyers/ shoppers/consumers/punters**
► encourage **clients/customers/ buyers/shoppers/consumers**

climate *noun*

1 [C, U] ■ the harsh climate of the Arctic

weather

► in (a) good, mild, etc. **climate/ weather**
► (a) **hot/cold/warm/good/mild/ harsh/severe climate/weather**
► have (a) good, mild, etc. **climate/ weather**

2 [C] ■ New policies created a climate of fear.

atmosphere • **mood** • **feeling**

► a **hostile climate/atmosphere**
► the **political climate/atmosphere/ mood**
► create/reflect a/an **climate/ atmosphere/mood/feeling** (of sth)

climb *verb*

1 [T, I] ■ The boys climbed over the wall.

go (sth) • **scramble** • **clamber** | fml **mount** • **ascend** | written **scale**

► climb/go/scramble/clamber **up** sth
► climb/scramble/clamber **over** sth
► climb/go up/scramble/scale a **mountain**
► climb/go up/scramble up/ clamber up/ascend/scale a **ladder**
● **CLIMB OR GO UP?** To **climb** sth usu. takes more effort than to **go up**.

2 [I] ■ The path climbs steeply to the summit.

slope • **rise**

■ OPP **descend**
► climb/slope/rise **towards** sth
► a **road/path climbs/slopes**
► climb/slope/rise **steeply**

close *verb*

1 [T, I] ■ She closed the gate behind her.

shut • **draw** • **slam** • **lock** • **bolt**

■ OPP **open**
► close/shut/slam/lock/bolt a **door/gate**
► close/shut/lock a **window/ drawer/case/suitcase**
► close/shut a/an **box/lid/ eyes/mouth/flap/valve/book/ umbrella**
► close/draw the **curtains/blinds**
● **CLOSE OR SHUT?** Close often suggests a more slow or gentle action than shut: *Close your eyes and go to sleep.*

2 [I, T] ■ It was a pity the business closed.

close (sth) down • fail • collapse • go bankrupt • fold • crash • *infml* **go bust • flop |** *fml, busin.* **cease trading**

■ **OPP open**
▶ a **firm/company** closes/closes down/fails/collapses/goes bankrupt/folds/crashes/goes bust/ceases trading
▶ an **industry** closes/closes down/collapses
▶ an **factory/newspaper/operation/shop** closes/closes down
● a **play/show** closes/folds/flops
● **CLOSE OR CLOSE DOWN?** Both these two words can be used to talk about a business or service, but only **close** can be used to talk about a play or show:
✓ *The play closed after just two nights.* ✗ ~~The play closed down after just two nights.~~

3 [T, I] ■ *The offer closes at the end of the week.*

end • finish • wind (sth) up | *fml* **conclude**

■ **OPP open**
▶ close/end/finish/wind up/conclude a **meeting**

close *adj.*

1 ■ *Take a close look at this photograph.*

careful • detailed • minute • thorough • in-depth

▶ a close/careful/detailed/minute/thorough **examination**
▶ a close/careful/detailed/minute/thorough/in-depth **look/study/investigation/analysis**

2 ■ *His feeling for her was close to hatred.*

like • similar

▶ close/similar **to** sth
▶ close/like sth/similar **in** size, amount, etc.

3 ■ *The organizers of the race are predicting a close finish.*

even • hard-fought • narrow • neck and neck | *esp. BrE* **level**

▶ a/an close/even/hard-fought **contest**
▶ a close/hard-fought **battle/finish**
▶ a close/narrow **vote**

closet *noun* [C] (*esp. AmE*)
■ *a walk-in closet for her clothes*

cupboard • wardrobe • pantry • cabinet • unit

▶ a **walk-in** closet/cupboard/wardrobe/pantry
▶ a **built-in** closet/cupboard/wardrobe

▶ a **wall/storage/kitchen** closet/cupboard/cabinet/unit

cloth *noun* [U]
■ *They used to export cotton cloth.*

fabric • material • textile

▶ **woven/cotton/woollen** cloth/fabric/material/textiles
▶ **make/produce/weave/dye** cloth/fabric/textiles
▶ a **length/piece/strip/roll/scrap** of cloth/fabric/material

clothes *noun* [pl.]
■ *I bought some new clothes for my trip.*

clothing • dress • wear • costume • wardrobe | *AmE* **apparel |** *infml* **gear |** *fml* **garment**

▶ **casual** clothes/clothing/dress/wear/apparel/gear
▶ **summer/winter** clothes/clothing/wear/wardrobe/apparel
▶ **designer/sports** clothes/clothing/wear/apparel/gear
● **CLOTHES OR CLOTHING?** Clothing is more formal than **clothes**. You can use it to talk about one thing that you wear, such as a dress or a shirt: *a/an piece/item/article of clothing*

cloud *noun* [C, U]

1 ■ *The sun went behind a cloud.* ■ *Thick cloud hung over the moor.*

fog • mist | *written* **haze**

▶ **in/through** (a) cloud/fog/mist/haze
▶ (a) **thick/heavy/dense/grey/swirling** cloud/fog/mist
▶ **be shrouded in** cloud/fog/mist

2 [C, U] ■ *The car disappeared in a cloud of dust.*

written plume • haze

▶ a cloud/plume/haze **of** sth
▶ a cloud/plume/haze **of smoke/dust/steam**
▶ **in/through** a cloud/haze

cloudy *adj.*
■ *The sky was cloudy when we set off.*

misty • foggy • overcast • dull | *esp. BrE, usu. disapprov.* **grey |** *AmE usu.* **gray |** *often disapprov.* **murky**

■ **OPP clear, sunny**
▶ cloudy/foggy/dull/grey **weather**
▶ a cloudy/misty/overcast/dull/grey **day**
▶ a cloudy/misty/murky **night**
● **WHICH WORD?** If it is **cloudy** there may be a lot of clouds about while the rest of the sky is blue. **Overcast**, **dull** and **grey** suggest that the whole sky is covered with clouds.

club noun

1 [C+sing./pl. v.] ■ *He joined the local drama club.*

society • association • organization

▶ form/set up/belong to/join a/an club/society/association/organization

▶ a/an club/society/association/organization **meets**

▶ a **member of** a/an club/society/association/organization

● CLUB, ASSOCIATION OR SOCIETY? These words are all used for groups of people who have a shared interest or purpose. Often, but not always, a **club** relates to leisure interests, a **society** to academic interests, and an **association** to professional interests. A **club** can be quite informal.

2 [C] (*BrE*) ■ *a Premier League football club*

team • squad • line-up | *BrE* **side**

▶ a **football/rugby/cricket** club/team/squad/side

▶ a/an **Irish/French** club/team/squad/side

▶ the **England/Ireland** team/squad/side/line-up

▶ a club/team/side **plays/wins/loses** (a game/match)

● CLUB, TEAM OR SIDE? Club refers to the organization that includes players, owner and manager; **team** and **side** usu. refer just to the players, often at a particular time: *This team is arguably even better than the Welsh side of the seventies.*

coach noun

1 [C] ■ *Who's the team coach?*

trainer • instructor • teacher

▶ a/an **qualified/experienced** coach/trainer/instructor/teacher

▶ **work as** a coach/trainer/instructor/teacher

2 [C] ■ *They went from London to Berlin by coach.*

bus

▶ **by** bus/coach

▶ **on** a bus/coach

▶ **get on/off** a bus/coach

● BUS OR COACH? In *BrE* a **bus** that carries passengers over a long distance is called a **coach**.

3 [C] (*BrE*) ■ *The train only had two coaches.*

compartment | *BrE* **carriage** | *AmE* **car**

▶ a **railway** coach/carriage/compartment

▶ a **railroad** car

▶ a **first-class/second-class, etc.** coach/carriage/compartment

▶ a **passenger** coach/carriage/compartment/car

● COACH, CARRIAGE OR COMPARTMENT? Coach is the word used in official language by train companies; **carriage** is used more in everyday speech: *Your seats are in Coach D.* • *I had to go to the end of the carriage to find a seat.* A **compartment** is a separate section of a carriage.

coarse adj.

■ *The monks wore coarse linen habits.*

rough • bristly • scratchy • leathery • scaly • prickly

■ OPP **soft, fine**

▶ coarse/rough/leathery/scaly **skin**

▶ coarse/rough/scratchy **cloth/fabric/material**

▶ coarse/bristly **hair**

● COARSE OR ROUGH? Coarse is a more literary word than **rough** for talking about skin or fabric. **Coarse**, but not **rough**, can also describe *hair, sand, salt* or *gravel*.

coast noun [C, usu. sing., U]

■ *We walked along the coast for miles.*

coastline • beach • seashore • shoreline • seaboard • sea • ocean | *esp. BrE* **seaside**

▶ **along** the coast/coastline/beach/seashore/shoreline/seaboard

▶ a **long/beautiful/rocky** coast/coastline/beach/shoreline

▶ **go to** the coast/beach/seashore/sea/ocean/seaside

coat noun [C]

■ *Take your coat off if you're hot.*

jacket | *BrE* **anorak • mac**

▶ a **long** coat/jacket/mac

▶ **wear/put on/take off/remove/do up/undo** a/an coat/jacket/anorak/mac

● COAT OR JACKET? Jacket can describe a piece of clothing worn indoors or one worn outdoors; a **coat** is usu. only worn outdoors. A **jacket** usu. comes down to the waist or hips, but not below; a **coat** is usu. hip-length or longer.

cold adj.

1 ■ *A cold wind blew.*

chilly • freezing • frozen • icy | *written* **chill** | *usu. approv.* **cool • crisp** | *often disapprov.* **bitter • lukewarm • tepid**

■ OPP **hot, warm, mild**

▶ a/an cold/chilly/freezing/icy/chill/cool/crisp **day/night/morning**

▶ cold/chilly/freezing/icy/cool/bitter **weather**

▶ cold/lukewarm/tepid **tea/coffee/food**

2 ■ *Her manner was cold and distant.*

unfriendly • cool • frosty • chilly • impersonal • remote • distant | *written* **aloof**

■ OPP **warm**

▶ a/an **cold/unfriendly/cool/frosty look**
▶ a/an **cold/unfriendly/cool/frosty/impersonal/aloof manner**
▶ a/an **cold/unfriendly/cool/frosty voice/glance**

collapse noun [C, usu. sing., U]

■ *the collapse of the national airline*

breakdown • failure

▶ a/an **complete/total/general/apparent collapse/breakdown/failure**
▶ (an) **economic collapse/breakdown/failure**
▶ **contribute to/lead to/result in/cause/avoid the collapse/breakdown/failure (of sth)**

collapse verb

1 [I] ■ *The roof collapsed under the weight of the snow.*

cave in • give way • disintegrate • crumble

▶ the **ceiling/roof/tunnel/wall collapses/caves in**
▶ the **pillars/supports collapse/give way**
▶ **collapse/cave in/give way under the weight of sth**
● **COLLAPSE, CAVE IN OR GIVE WAY?** Whole buildings **collapse**; roofs and walls **collapse** or **cave in**; supports **collapse** or **give way**; a door or the ground may **give way** or **cave in**.

2 [I] ■ *He collapsed and was taken to hospital.*

faint • pass out | *infml* **drop**

▶ **collapse/faint/pass out/drop from exhaustion/hunger/loss of blood/the heat, etc.**

3 [I] ■ *Talks between the two parties have collapsed.*

break down • fail • fall through • get/go nowhere • come to nothing | *fml* **founder**

▶ a **relationship/marriage collapses/breaks down/fails**
▶ **talks collapse/break down/fail/fall through/founder**
▶ a **project collapses/fails/falls through/founders**

4 [I] ■ *His firm collapsed and he went bankrupt.*

fail • go bankrupt • crash • fold • close down • close | *infml* **go bust** | *fml, busin.* **cease trading**

▶ a **firm/company collapses/fails/goes bankrupt/crashes/folds/closes down/closes/goes bust/ceases trading**
▶ a **business collapses/fails/folds/closes down/closes/crashes/goes bust/ceases trading**
▶ **shares/prices/markets collapse/crash**
● **COLLAPSE OR CRASH?** Crash is more informal and can suggest an even more sudden event. An *economy* can **collapse** but not **crash**.

colleague noun [C]

■ *a colleague of mine from the office*

partner • contact • co-worker • collaborator • teammate • ally • associate | *esp. BrE* **workmate**

▶ a **business colleague/partner/contact/ally/associate**
▶ a **political colleague/contact/ally/associate**
▶ a **junior/senior colleague/partner/associate**
● **COLLEAGUE OR ASSOCIATE?** Colleague is the most frequently used, and is the general word for sb you work with; **associate** is used to describe sb you have a business connection with.

collect verb

1 [T, I] ■ *We collected data from various sources.*

gather • accumulate • amass

▶ **collect/gather/accumulate/amass data/evidence/information**
▶ **dirt/dust/debris collects/accumulates**
▶ **gradually/slowly/steadily collect/gather/accumulate (sth)**
● **COLLECT OR GATHER?** When talking about things, use **gather** for *things, belongings* or *papers* when the things are spread around within a short distance; use **collect** to talk about getting examples of sth from different people or places.

2 [T] ■ *Your package is ready to be collected.*

esp. spoken **pick sb/sth up • get** | *BrE, esp. spoken* **fetch**

▶ **collect/pick up/get/fetch sb/sth from sth/somewhere**
▶ **collect/pick up/get/fetch sth for sb**
▶ **go/come to collect/pick up/get/fetch sb/sth**

3 [I, T] ■ *We're collecting for local charities.*

raise

▶ **collect/raise money for sth**

▶ collect/raise **money**
● **COLLECT OR RAISE?** If you want to **raise** money for sth you organize events or approach organizations; if you want to **collect** money you usu. ask people directly.

college noun [C, U]
■ He's hoping to go to college next year.

university ◆ academy ◆ seminary ◆ school

▶ **at/in** college/university/school
▶ **go to/attend** college/university/an academy/a seminary/school
▶ **graduate from** a/an college/university/academy/seminary/high school
● **COLLEGE OR UNIVERSITY? College** is used in BrE and AmE to describe a place where you do further study after leaving school. In BrE the usual word for an institution where you study for a degree is **university**; in AmE it is **college**: (BrE) She's at university. ◆ (AmE) She's in college.
Some British universities, such as Oxford and Cambridge, are divided into **colleges**: Emmanuel College, Cambridge

colour (BrE) (AmE color) noun [C, U]
■ What's your favourite colour?

shade ◆ tint ◆ tinge | lit. or tech. **hue**

▶ a **bright/vivid/vibrant/dark/deep** colour/shade/hue
▶ a **pale/pastel/soft/subtle/delicate** colour/shade/hue
▶ **have** a colour/shade/tint/tinge/hue

coloured (BrE) (AmE colored) adj.
■ brightly coloured balloons

BrE, often approv. **colourful** | AmE, often approv. **colorful** | disapprov. **gaudy ◆ garish ◆ lurid**

● **COLOURED OR COLOURFUL? Coloured** is either used in compounds, or on its own to describe things which are usu. white or clear; **colourful** is always used on its own: brightly coloured ◆ coloured glass/lights/paper ◆ a small but colourful garden

colouring (BrE) (AmE coloring) noun [U]
■ She inherited her mother's fair colouring.

complexion ◆ pigment | BrE colour | AmE color | tech. **coloration**

▶ **have** a dark/fair, etc. complexion/pigment/colouring/coloration
● **COLOURING OR COMPLEXION? Complexion** only describes a

person's skin; **colouring** describes their skin, hair and eyes.

column noun [C]
■ a temple with marble columns

pillar ◆ post ◆ support

▶ a **stone/concrete** column/pillar
▶ a **wooden/steel/iron** column/pillar/post/support
▶ a column/pillar/post **supports** sth

combination noun [C]
■ an unusual combination of flavours

mixture ◆ blend ◆ cocktail ◆ concoction ◆ assortment ◆ composite | often approv. **mix** | chemistry **compound**

▶ a combination/mixture/blend/cocktail/assortment/composite/mix **of** sth
▶ a/an **interesting/wonderful/strange** combination/mixture/blend/cocktail/concoction/assortment/mix
▶ a **special** mixture/blend/concoction/mix
● **COMBINATION OR MIXTURE?** A **combination** is usu. put together deliberately; a **mixture** usu. just happens.

combine verb [I, T]
■ The trip will combine business with pleasure.

mix ◆ unite ◆ merge ◆ blend ◆ mingle ◆ unify ◆ integrate | fml or tech. **fuse** | busin. or tech. **consolidate**

■ OPP **separate**
▶ combine/mix/unite/merge/blend/mingle/unify/integrate/fuse/consolidate (sth) **with** sth
▶ combine/mix/merge/blend/mingle/integrate/fuse/consolidate (sth) **into** sth
▶ combine/mix/merge/blend/mingle/integrate/fuse (sth) **together**

come verb

1 [I] ■ Come in and shut the door.

come along | written **draw** | fml **approach ◆ near**

■ OPP **go**
▶ come/draw **in/into** sth
▶ come/draw **up/up to** sb/sth
▶ come/draw **close/near/closer/nearer**

2 [I] ■ I've come to get my book.

arrive ◆ appear ◆ come in ◆ land | esp. spoken **get here/there ◆ get in ◆ turn up** | infml **show up ◆ roll in ◆ show**

▶ come/arrive **for** sb

► come/arrive/appear/land/turn
up/ show up/show **here/there**
► **be the first/last to** come/arrive/
appear/come in/land/get here/
turn up/get in/show up/roll in

3 [I] ■ *The time came to leave.*

arrive • approach | written **near •
draw near**

■ OPP **go**
► **spring/summer/autumn/fall/
winter** comes/approaches/
approaches/draws near
► the **day/time** comes/arrives/
approaches/draws near
► come/arrive **early/late**

4 [I] ■ *I'm sorry, I can't come to the
party.*

go • come along • make it | *fml*
attend

► come/go/go to/come along to/
make it to/attend a **meeting/
wedding/party**
► come/go to/go to/attend a
conference

5 [I, T] ■ *He came to England by ship*

go • travel

► come/go/travel **from/to** sth
► come/go/travel **with** sb
► come/go/travel by **air/sea/boat/
ship/train/car**
● **COME OR GO?** Use **come** if you are
at the place where the journey
ends; use **go** if you are at the place
where it starts: *I hope you can come
to France to visit us.* ◆ *We're going to
France to visit our son.*

6 ■ *In time she came to love him.*
■ *The handle came loose.*

grow • get • become

► come/grow/get **to know/like** sb/
sth
► come/become **loose**
● **GROW AND COME** In this meaning,
these two verbs are either followed
by an adjective (*come loose/grow
calm*) or by 'to' + infinitive (*I came/
grew to realize/understand, etc.*)

come back *phrasal verb*
■ *I asked him to come back to London
with me.*

**return • go back • get back • turn
back**

■ OPP **go away**
► come back/return/go back/get
back **to/from/with** sth
► come back/return/go back/get
back/turn back **again**
► come back/return/go back/go
back **home/to work**

come down *phrasal verb*
■ *The price of gas is coming down.*

fall • drop • decline | *fml* **decrease** •
esp. busin. **slump • plunge • tumble •
plummet**

■ OPP **go up**
► come down/fall/drop/decline/
decrease/slump/plunge/tumble/
plummet **by** 100, 25%, a half, etc.
► come down/fall/drop/decline/
decrease/slump/plunge/tumble/
plummet **from** 15000 **to** 1 000
► come down/decline/decrease/
plunge/plummet **in value**

comedy *noun* [C, U]
1 ■ *a romantic comedy starring Tom
Hanks*

farce • play • drama • sketch

► a comedy/farce/play/drama/
sketch **by** sb
► a **television/radio/
Shakespearean** comedy/play/
drama
► **write** a comedy/farce/play/
drama/sketch

2 [U] ■ *He didn't see the comedy of the
situation.*

funny side | *BrE* **humour** | *AmE*
humor

► **gentle/wry/dry/deadpan/black**
comedy/humour
► **see/appreciate** the comedy/funny
side/humour of sth

come in *phrasal verb*
■ *Tell her to come in.*

go in • set foot in/on sth | *fml* **enter**

■ OPP **go out**
► come in/go in/enter **by/through**
sth
► come in/go into/enter/set foot
in a **room/building/country/
town**
● **COME IN OR GO IN?** Go in is used
from the point of view of the
person who is moving; come in is
used from the point of view of sb
who is already in the place that the
person is moving to.

come round *phrasal verb*
■ *'Is she still unconscious?' 'She's just
coming round.'*

come to | *esp. AmE* **come around**

► come round/come to/come
around **from** sth
► come round/come to/come
around **slowly**
● **COME ROUND, COME AROUND OR
COME TO?** With come round/
around the emphasis is more on
the process of becoming
conscious, less on the moment.
You usu. *come around/round slowly*
but you can *come to suddenly.*

■ He's come up with a brilliant idea.

devise • hatch • work sth out • invent • make sth up • coin | *infml* **hit on sth • think sth up • dream sth up** | *fml* **conceive • conceive of sth**

▶ come up with/devise/hatch/work out/hit on/think up/dream up/ conceive a **plan/scheme**
▶ come up with/devise/hatch/hit on/think up/dream up/conceive **an idea/ the idea of doing sth**
▶ come up with/invent/make up/ think up/dream up an **excuse**

comfort *noun*

1 [U] ■ shoes designed for comfort

ease

■ **OPP** *fml* **discomfort**
▶ **comparative/relative** comfort/ ease
▶ a **life of** comfort/ease

2 [U, sing.] ■ a few words of comfort
■ It's a comfort to know that he is safe.

consolation • reassurance • sympathy • relief • compassion • condolence

▶ a comfort/consolation/relief **to** sb
▶ **find** comfort/consolation/relief/ reassurance/relief **in** sth
▶ **seek/find/bring** (sb) comfort/ consolation/reassurance/relief
▶ **offer** (sb) comfort/consolation/ reassurance/relief/your sympathy/ your condolences
● **COMFORT OR CONSOLATION?** These words are used in many of the same patterns but there is a slight difference in meaning. You might find **consolation** after a disappointment, such as losing a competition; you find **comfort** when sth has made you feel unhappy or worried: *consolation prizes include £5 vouchers ◇ Chocolate is a great comfort food.*

comfort *verb* [T]

■ She was being comforted today by family and friends.

console • cheer sb up • cheer • reassure • put/set sb's mind at rest

▶ comfort sb/console sb/cheer sb up/reassure sb/put sb's mind at rest **with** sth
▶ be **greatly** comforted/cheered/ reassured
▶ It comforts/consoles/reassures sb **to know (that)...**
● **COMFORT OR CONSOLE?** Both verbs can be used when sb is unhappy or upset about sth: *I didn't know how to comfort/console her when her baby died.*
You can **comfort** sb who is worried by putting your arm round them,

etc. You can **console** sb who is disappointed by saying that a situation is not as bad as they think: *' Never mind,' she consoled him, 'You can try again next year.'*

comfortable *adj.* (approv.)

■ Wear loose, comfortable clothing.

snug | *infml* **comfy** | *BrE* **cosy • homely** | *AmE* **cozy** | *AmE, infml* **homey/homy**

■ **OPP uncomfortable**
▶ a comfortable/snug/comfy/cosy/ cozy **bed**
▶ a comfortable/comfy/cosy/cozy **chair**
▶ a comfortable/cosy/homely/ cozy/homey **atmosphere**

command *noun*

1 [C] ■ Obey the captain's commands.

order • instruction

▶ (a) **clear/direct/final** command/ order/instructions
▶ **give/issue** a command/an order/ instructions
▶ **receive/obey/carry out/ignore** a command/an order/instructions

2 [U] ■ Who's in command here?

authority • control • power

▶ command/authority/control/ power **over** sb/sth
▶ be **in** command/authority/ control/power
▶ **assume/lose** command/ authority/control/power
▶ **take** command/control

command *verb*

1 [C] ■ He commanded his men to retreat.

order • instruct • tell • rule • decree | *fml* **direct**

▶ command/order/instruct/tell/ direct sb **to do sth**
▶ command/order/instruct/rule/ decree/direct **that...**
▶ command/order/instruct/tell/ direct sb **sb that...**
● **COMMAND OR ORDER?** Command is a slightly stronger word than order and is the normal word to use about an army officer; it is less likely to be said about a parent or teacher.

2 [T] ■ He was the officer commanding the troops in the Western region.

be in charge • direct • be responsible for sb/sth • control

comment *noun* [C]

■ She made helpful comments on my work.

comment

remark ♦ statement | *fml*
observation

▶ a/an comment/remark/
observation/statement **about** sth
▶ a/an comment/observation/
statement **on** sth
▶ **make** a comment/remark/
observation/statement
● COMMENT, REMARK OR
OBSERVATION? A **comment** can be
official or private. An **observation**
may be more considered than a
remark, but both are always
unofficial.

comment verb [I, T]

■ *They commented on how well she
looked.*

remark | *fml* **observe ♦ note**

▶ comment/remark **on** sth
▶ comment/remark/observe **to** sb
▶ comment/remark/observe/note
that...
● COMMENT, REMARK OR OBSERVE?
You can only use **refuse to** with
comment:
✔ *He refused to comment until after
the trial.* ✗ *He refused to remark/
observe until after the trial.*

commercial adj.

1 [usu. before noun] ■ *banks in the
commercial heart of the city*

economic ♦ financial | *finance*
monetary ♦ budgetary

▶ commercial/economic/financial/
monetary/budgetary **policy/
arrangements/systems/problems**
▶ commercial/economic/financial/
monetary **gain/loss/value/
affairs/consequences**
▶ the commercial/economic/
financial **side/status** of sth

2 [only before noun] ■ *They are an
educational charity, not a
commercial publisher.*

**profitable ♦ profit-making ♦
economic ♦ lucrative**

■ OPP **non-profit**
▶ a commercial/profitable/profit-
making/lucrative **enterprise**

commitment noun

1 [C, U] ■ *The company made a
commitment to lower prices.*

**promise ♦ guarantee ♦ assurance ♦
vow |** *esp. journ.* **pledge**

▶ a commitment/promise/
guarantee/vow/pledge **to do** sth
▶ a **formal** commitment/guarantee/
assurance
▶ **make** a commitment/promise/
guarantee/vow/pledge

2 [C] (*esp. busin.*) ■ *Buying a house is
a big commitment.*

**responsibility ♦ obligation ♦ burden
♦ duty |** *esp. busin. or law* **liability**

▶ a/an commitment/obligation/
burden/duty **to** sb/sth
▶ **financial** commitments/
responsibilities/obligations/
burdens/duties
▶ **professional/social/family**
commitments/responsibilities/
obligations/duties
▶ **fulfil/meet** a/an commitment/
responsibility/obligation/duty

committee noun [C+sing./pl. v.]

■ *They have set up an advisory
committee.*

**council ♦ commission ♦ board ♦ body
♦ jury ♦ panel ♦ delegation ♦ task
force ♦ mission**

▶ a committee/council/
commission/board/body/
delegation **for** sth
▶ a/an **joint/independent**
committee/council/commission/
board/body/delegation/task
force/mission
▶ **head** a committee/council/
commission/board/delegation/
task force/mission
▶ **serve/sit on** a committee/
council/commission/board/
body/jury/panel
● COMMISSION, COUNCIL OR
COMMITTEE? **Committee** is the most
general word and refers to a group
of people within an organization
who make decisions. A **council** is
more often an independent group
of experts concerned with arts,
sports, academic research, etc. A
commission is usu. a group of
important politicians with
responsibility for a particular area:
*the United Nations High Commission
for Refugees (UNHCR)*

common adj.

1 ■ *The most common complaint was
of late deliveries.*

**widespread ♦ universal ♦ general ♦
commonplace |** *fml* **prevalent**

■ OPP **rare, uncommon**
▶ a/the common/widespread/
universal/general/prevalent **view/
problem**
▶ a common/widespread/universal/
general **feeling**
▶ **violence** is common/widespread/
commonplace

2 [usu. before noun] ■ *a decision
taken for the common good* (= the
advantage of everyone)

**joint ♦ collective ♦ communal ♦
shared ♦ popular ♦ public ♦
cooperative**

► common/joint/collective/communal/shared/public **property**

► common/joint/collective/communal/shared **ownership/responsibility**

► a common/joint/collective/communal/cooperative **enterprise**

► common/collective/popular **opinion**

3 [only before noun] ▪ *She was nothing more than a common criminal.*

ordinary • normal • average • typical

► common/normal for sb to do sth/for sth to happen

► the common/ordinary/normal/average **man**

► the common/ordinary/normal **sort**

communicate verb

1 [I, T] ▪ *We only communicate by email.*

talk • speak • discuss • consult • debate | *fml* confer

► communicate/talk/speak/discuss sth/consult/debate/confer **with sb**

► communicate/talk/speak/discuss sth/debate **openly**

2 [T, I] ▪ *He communicated his ideas to the group.*

convey • tell • get sth across • repeat • break • send • pass sth on • relay | *fml* impart

► communicate/convey/tell/get across/repeat/break/send/pass on/relay/impart sth **to sb**

► communicate/convey/repeat/break it/relay to sb **that...**

► communicate/convey/get across/repeat/send/pass on/relay/impart **a message**

● **COMMUNICATE OR CONVEY?** You can **convey** sth to one person, to a group or to people in general. You can **communicate** sth to a group but not usu. to only one person.

communication noun [U]

▪ *We are in regular communication by letter.*

contact • dealings | *fml* correspondence

► communication/contact/dealings/correspondence **with sb**

► communication/contact/dealings/correspondence **between people**

► **be in** communication/contact/correspondence (with sb)

community noun

1 [sing.] ▪ *The local community was shocked by the murders.*

population • society • the public • the country • the nation

► the community/the population/society/the public/the country/the nation **at large/as a whole**

► **shock** the community/public/country/nation

► **a section/cross-section/member of** the community/society/the public

2 [C+sing./pl. v.] ▪ *representatives of the city's Asian community*

society • culture • world • race • civilization

► an/the **English-speaking** community/culture/world

► (the) **Arab/Islamic** community/society/culture/world

► **European/American/African, etc.** society/culture/civilization

► a **traditional/mainstream** community/society/culture

company noun [C+sing./pl. v.]

▪ *one of the largest computer companies in the world*

firm • business • corporation • operation • enterprise • practice • house • partnership • cooperative | *infml* outfit

► a **multinational** company/firm/business/corporation/operation/enterprise

► a **family** company/firm/business/operation/enterprise/practice/...house/partnership

► **set up** a/an company/firm/business/corporation/operation/...practice/...house/partnership/cooperative/outfit

► **own/run** a/an company/firm/business/corporation/operation/enterprise/...house/cooperative

● **COMPANY OR FIRM?** Company can be used to talk about any kind of organization. Firm is often used to talk about a small organization or one that has been operating for a long time, sometimes by members of the same family: *a/an old-established/reputable/family firm*

compare verb

1 [T] ▪ *We compared the two reports carefully.*

contrast • balance sth against sth • match sth against sth | *fml* juxtapose

► compare/contrast/juxtapose A **and/with** B

► compare/contrast sth **unfavourably/favourably** with sth

2 [I] ■ *Nothing compares with oak for strength.*

match • rival • equal • be on a par with sb/sth

▶ compare with/match/rival/be on a par with sth **in terms of** sth
▶ compare with/match/equal sb's **achievements**

comparison *noun* [U, C]

■ *His problems seemed trivial by comparison.* ■ *In terms of price there's no comparison.*

analogy • contrast • similarity • parallel • resemblance | *fml* **correspondence**

▶ a/an comparison/analogy/ contrast/similarity/parallel/ resemblance/correspondence **between** A and B
▶ a/an comparison/analogy/ contrast/similarity/parallel/ correspondence **between** A and B
▶ **draw/make/suggest** a/an comparison/analogy/contrast/ parallel

compensate *verb* [I, T]

■ *Nothing can compensate for the death of a loved one.*

make up for sth • counter • counteract • balance | *sometimes disapprov.* **cancel sth out** | *esp. busin.* **offset**

▶ compensate/counter/counteract sth **with** sth
▶ compensate/make up **for** sth
▶ compensate for/counter/ counteract/cancel out/offset the **effect** of sth
● **COMPENSATE OR MAKE UP FOR STH?** Compensate is more formal than make up for sth but can be used with a wider range of structures, with or without *for*:
✔ *You should be able to eat more on this diet without having to compensate by going hungry.* ✗ ~~You should be able to eat more on this diet without having to make up for going hungry.~~

compensation *noun* [U, C]

■ *She received a cash sum in compensation.*

refund • award • rebate | *fml* **reimbursement** | *fml or law* **restitution**

▶ (a/an) compensation/refund/ award/rebate/reimbursement/ restitution **from** sb **to** sb
▶ (a/an) compensation/refund/ award/rebate/reimbursement/ restitution **for** sb
▶ **seek/demand** (a) compensation/ refund/reimbursement/restitution

▶ **receive** (a/an) compensation/ refund/award/rebate/ reimbursement/restitution

compete *verb*

1 [I] ■ *Travel firms are competing fiercely on price.*

fight • struggle • contest • vie | *esp. journ.* **battle**

▶ compete/fight/struggle/vie/ battle **for** sth
▶ compete/struggle/vie/battle **with** sb
▶ compete/fight/struggle/vie for **power**

2 [I] ■ *He's hoping to compete in the Olympics.*

play • enter • go in for sth • take part

▶ compete/play **against** sb
▶ compete in/enter/ go in for/take part in a **competition/contest/ race**
▶ compete in/enter/take part in a **tournament**

competition *noun*

1 [U] ■ *There is intense competition between schools to attract students.*

rivalry • competitiveness | *esp. journ.* **race • contest**

▶ (a) competition/rivalry/race/ contest **for** sth
▶ (a) competition/rivalry/ competitiveness/race/contest **between** people
▶ **in** (a) competition/rivalry/race/ contest **with** sb
▶ (a) **fierce** competition/rivalry/ competitiveness/contest

2 [C] ■ *He won a prize in a competition.*

contest • quiz • race • championship • tournament • event

▶ an **international** competition/ contest/race/championship/ tournament/event
▶ **hold/enter** a/an competition/ contest/quiz/race/tournament/ event
▶ **win** a/an competition/contest/ quiz/race/championship/ tournament/event

competitive *adj.*

1 (*esp. busin.*) ■ *They sell cameras at competitive prices.*

affordable • reasonable • cheap • budget • economical • inexpensive

■ OPP **uncompetitive**
▶ competitive/affordable/ reasonable/cheap/budget/ economical **prices/rates/fares**
▶ competitive/affordable/

reasonable/cheap/economical/
inexpensive **products/services**
▸ highly competitive/**economical**

2 ▪ He has a strong competitive streak.

ambitious | often approv. **assertive** |
sometimes disapprov. **aggressive** |
infml, disapprov. **pushy**

▸ competitive/ambitious/assertive/
aggressive **in sth**
▸ (a/an) competitive/assertive/
aggressive **approach/attitude/
manner/behaviour**
▸ a/an competitive/ambitious/
assertive/aggressive **person**

complain verb [I, T]

▪ He complained that he had been
unfairly treated.

protest • object | disapprov. **grumble
• whine • carp** | infml, disapprov.
moan

▸ complain/protest/grumble/
whine/carp/moan **about sth**
▸ complain/protest/grumble/moan
at sth
▸ complain/protest/object/
grumble/whine/moan **that…**

complaint noun [C, U]

▪ They have received complaints about
the noise.

grievance | infml **gripe**

▸ a complaint/grievance/gripe
about sb/sth
▸ a complaint/grievance **against sb/
sth**
▸ **have** a complaint/grievance/gripe
▸ **register/voice/deal with/
handle/investigate/hear/resolve**
a complaint/grievance
● **COMPLAINT OR GRIEVANCE?** You can
make a **complaint** to sb, or more
formally file or lodge a **complaint**,
often in writing. If you nurse or
harbour a **grievance**, you develop a
strong feeling of unfairness over a
period of time.

complete verb [T, often passive]

▪ The project should be completed
within a year.

finish • follow (sth) through | BrE
round sth off | AmE **round sth out** |
esp. AmE, esp. business **be done** | esp.
busin. **finalize** | infml, esp. busin. or
sport **wrap sth up**

▸ complete/finish/finalize **the
preparations/arrangements**
▸ complete/finish/round off/round
out/wrap up an **discussion/
evening/meal**
▸ complete/finalize/wrap up a **deal**
● **COMPLETE OR FINISH?** Complete is
more frequent in written English;
finish is more frequent in spoken
English. You can finish doing sth but
you cannot complete doing sth:

✔He hasn't finished speaking. ✗ He
hasn't completed speaking.

complete adj.

1 [usu. before noun] ▪ We were in
complete agreement.

**total • outright • utter • perfect •
pure • sheer** | infml **positive** | esp.
spoken **real • absolute** | usu.
disapprov. **downright**

▸ a/an complete/total/utter/real/
absolute **disaster**
▸ complete/total/utter/absolute/
perfect/pure **silence**
▸ complete/total/utter/absolute/
pure/sheer **nonsense**
● **COMPLETE OR TOTAL?** In most cases
you can use either of these words,
although total war is a fixed
collocation that cannot be
changed. **Total** is only used before
a noun.

2 ▪ I collected the complete set.

whole • entire • full • total

▪ OPP **incomplete**
▸ a/an complete/whole/entire/full
day/set
▸ the complete/whole/full **truth/
story**
▸ complete/full **details**

completely adv.

▪ We were completely broke.

totally • utterly • entirely • fully |
esp. BrE **quite** | esp. spoken
absolutely • perfectly

▪ OPP **partly**
▸ completely/totally/utterly/fully/
quite/absolutely **sure/convinced**
▸ completely/totally/entirely/quite/
absolutely/perfectly **normal**
▸ completely/totally/fully/quite/
perfectly **understand**
● **WHICH WORD?** The main differences
between these words are in register
not meaning. **Completely, entirely**
and **fully** are used more in written
and formal English. **Totally, quite,
absolutely** and **perfectly** are used
more in spoken and informal
English. **Utterly** is often used to
express failure or impossibility: She
utterly failed to convince them.

complicate verb [T]

▪ To complicate matters further, there
will be no transport available.

confuse • blur • cloud

▪ OPP **simplify**
▸ complicate/confuse/cloud **the
issue**
▸ complicate/confuse **matters/
things/the situation**
● **COMPLICATE OR CONFUSE?**
Something complicates a situation

by being an additional problem. With **confuse** the emphasis is on the fact that it is difficult to recognize or understand what needs to be done.

complicated adj.

■ *The instructions look very complicated.*

complex • elaborate • intricate • involved • tangled | *written, usu. disapprov.* **convoluted • tortuous**

■ OPP **uncomplicated, straightforward**
▶ a/an complicated/complex/ elaborate/intricate/convoluted **story/plot**
▶ a/an complicated/complex/ elaborate/intricate **design/ structure/network/system**
▶ a/an complicated/complex/ intricate/tangled **web/ relationship**
● **COMPLICATED OR COMPLEX?**
Complex is often used to describe academic, scientific or technical issues, esp. in written English; **complicated** is used more to describe everyday situations: *a complex mathematical equation/ formula • I'll send you a map of how to get here—it's a bit too complicated to describe.*

composure noun [U]

■ *She lost her composure and started shouting.*

poise • self-control • calm • restraint | *infml* **cool**

▶ **lose** your composure/poise/self-control/cool
▶ **keep** your composure/self-control/cool
▶ **recover** your composure/poise

compromise noun [C, U]

■ *In any relationship you have to make compromises.*

concession • trade-off • middle ground • give and take • sop

▶ (a) compromise/concession/ trade-off/middle ground/give and take **between** sb/sth and sb/sth
▶ **make** a compromise/concession/ trade-off
▶ **look for/seek/offer/reject** a compromise/concession

concentration noun [U]

■ *The noise had disturbed his concentration.*

attention • care

▶ **full/total/undivided** concentration/attention

▶ **hold/focus** sb's concentration/ attention
▶ **turn** your concentration/attention **to** sth

concept noun [C]

■ *basic concepts of right and wrong*

idea • notion • thought | *fml* **abstraction**

▶ the concept/idea/notion/thought **that...**
▶ **understand/grasp** a/an concept/ idea/notion/abstraction
▶ **discuss/consider/explore** a/an concept/idea/notion

concern noun

1 [U, C] ■ *There is concern for her safety.*

anxiety • worry • apprehension • unease

▶ concern/anxiety/worry/ apprehension/unease **over/about** sth
▶ **express** concern/anxiety/your worries/apprehension/unease
▶ **cause** concern/anxiety/ apprehension/unease
● **CONCERN, ANXIETY OR WORRY?**
Worry is a more informal word than **concern** and **anxiety**. **Worry** and **anxiety** are used to refer to personal matters; a **concern** often affects many people.

2 [U] ■ *I appreciate your concern at this difficult time.*

sympathy • compassion • understanding

▶ concern/sympathy/compassion **for** sb/sth
▶ **do** sth **with** concern/sympathy/ compassion/understanding
▶ **show (sb)** concern/sympathy/ compassion/understanding

3 [C] ■ *What are your main concerns as a writer?*

issue • matter • question • theme • topic • subject

▶ a/an **important/key/major/ serious/general** concern/issue/ matter/question/theme/topic/ subject
▶ a/an **political/ethical** concern/ issue/matter/question/theme/ topic/subject
▶ a **technical/practical** concern/ issue/matter/question/topic/ subject
▶ **discuss/consider/deal with/ tackle/examine/explore/focus on** a/an concern/issue/matter/ question/theme/topic/subject

concern verb

1 [T, often passive] ■ *Don't interfere with what doesn't concern you.*

involve ↔ affect

▶ be concerned/involved **in** sth
▶ **directly/indirectly** concern/
involve/affect sb/sth
● CONCERN OR INVOLVE? Involve
suggests a greater degree of
physical activity. Concern suggests
a greater degree of interest or
responsibility.

2 [T] ■ *The story concerns the prince's
efforts to rescue Pamina.*

be concerned with sth ↔ be about
sth ↔ deal with sth ↔ have/be to do
with sth ↔ relate to sb/sth ↔ refer to
sb/sth ↔ treat

▶ a **chapter/poem** concerns/is
concerned with/is about/deals
with/refers to sth
▶ a **book/film** concerns/is
concerned with/is about/deals
with/refers to sth
▶ a **rule/law** concerns/is
concerned with/deals with/relates to/refers
to sth
● CONCERN, BE ABOUT OR DEAL
WITH STH? Be about sth is the most
general of these expressions;
concern and deal with sth both
suggest a formal, serious or
thorough discussion of a subject.

3 [T] ■ *What concerns me is our lack of
preparation.*

worry ↔ trouble ↔ disturb ↔ alarm ↔
bother

▶ It concerns/worries/troubles/
disturbs/alarms/bothers sb that...
▶ concern/worry/trouble/bother
yourself about sth
▶ sth **doesn't** concern/worry/bother
sb in the slightest/least
● WHICH WORD? Concern is the most
formal of these words and is not
usu. used in the progressive tenses.
Bother is the most informal, esp. in
spoken phrases like *It doesn't bother
me.* and *I'm not bothered.*

concerned *adj.*

■ *The President is deeply concerned
about this issue.*

worried ↔ anxious ↔ alarmed ↔
uneasy ↔ nervous ↔ bothered | *fml*
apprehensive | *written* disturbed ↔
troubled

■ OPP **unconcerned**

▶ concerned/worried/anxious/
alarmed/uneasy/nervous/
bothered/apprehensive/
disturbed/troubled **about** sth
▶ be concerned/worried/anxious
for sb
▶ be concerned/worried/anxious/
nervous/apprehensive/bothered/
disturbed **that**...
● CONCERNED OR WORRIED? Use
concerned or worried to talk
about a problem that affects
society, the world, another person,

etc. Use worried to talk about
more personal matters.

concert *noun* [C]
■ *They performed a concert of music by
Tallis.*

recital | *esp. BrE* **gig** | *AmE, infml*
show

▶ at a concert/recital/gig/show
▶ a rock/charity/live concert/gig/
show
▶ a/an piano/organ/classical
concert/recital
▶ give/play/do/put on a concert/
recital/gig/show

conclude *verb*

1 [T] (not used in the progressive
tenses) ■ *What do you conclude
from that?*

infer ↔ deduce ↔ read sth into sth ↔
understand ↔ reason ↔ gather | *infml*
figure

▶ conclude/infer/deduce/
understand/reason/gather/
figure **from** sth
▶ conclude/infer/deduce/
understand/gather/figure sth
about sth
▶ conclude/infer/deduce/
understand/reason/gather/figure
that ...

2 [I, T] (*fml*) ■ *The programme
concluded with Handel's 'Zadok the
Priest'.*

finish ↔ end ↔ close ↔ wind (sth) up ↔
stop | *BrE* round sth off | *AmE* round
sth out | *fml* terminate | *infml, esp.
busin. or sport* wrap sth up

■ OPP **begin**

▶ conclude/finish/end/round sth
off/round sth out **by/with** sth
▶ conclude/finish/end/close/wind
up a **meeting**
▶ a play/show/film concludes/
finishes/ends

conclusion *noun*

1 [C] ■ *We can draw some conclusions
from our discussion.*

inference ↔ deduction ↔ finding ↔
judgment/judgement ↔ verdict ↔
ruling

▶ the conclusion/inference/
deduction/finding/judgment/
verdict/ruling **that** ...
▶ a logical/reasonable/valid
conclusion/inference/deduction
▶ base your conclusion/findings/
judgment/verdict/ruling **on** sth

2 [C, usu. sing.] ■ *The meeting was
brought to a hasty conclusion.*

end ↔ finish ↔ ending ↔ finale | *fml,
esp. busin.* **close** ↔ termination

■ OPP **beginning**
▶ at the **conclusion/end/finish/ finale/close**
▶ **provide** a/an (...) **conclusion/ finish/ending/finale**
▶ **bring** sth to a/an **conclusion/end/ close**

condition noun

1 [U, sing.] ■ *The car was in perfect condition.*

state • repair • shape

▶ (a) **good/poor/bad condition/ state/(state of) repair/shape**
▶ **keep** sth in (a) ... **condition/state/ repair/shape**
▶ **get** (sth) **into** a ... **condition/ state/shape**
● **CONDITION OR STATE?** Condition is mainly used to talk about the appearance or working order of sth; **state** is a more general word used to describe the quality sth has at a particular time.

2 [U, sing.] ■ *Her condition is said to be stable.*

health • fitness • shape

▶ sb's **general/physical condition/ health/fitness**
▶ sb's **condition/health/fitness deteriorates/improves**

3 [C] ■ *Does he suffer from any kind of medical condition?*

complaint • disease • illness • trouble • ailment • ill health | *med.* **disorder**

▶ a **serious/common/rare condition/disease/illness/ ailment/disorder**
▶ (a) **heart condition/disease/ trouble**
▶ **suffer from** (a/an) **condition/ complaint/disease/illness/heart, etc. trouble/ailment/ill health/ disorder**
▶ **diagnose/treat/cure** a/an **condition/complaint/disease/ illness/ailment/disorder**

4 **conditions** [pl.] ■ *The children are living in appalling conditions.*

circumstances • situation • state of affairs | *infml, esp. spoken* **things**

▶ (a) **normal/unusual/ideal conditions/circumstances/ situation/state of affairs**
▶ (a/an) **favourable/difficult/ exceptional conditions/circumstances/ desperate conditions/circumstances/situation**
▶ **look at/review conditions/ circumstances/the situation/things**
● **CONDITIONS OR CIRCUMSTANCES?** Circumstances refers to sb's financial situation; **conditions** refers to things such as food,

shelter, or the working environment. The **circumstances** that affect an event are the facts surrounding it; the **conditions** are usu. physical things, such as the weather.

5 [C] ■ *They will give us the car provided their conditions are met.*

terms • qualification • provision | *fml* **requirement • proviso • prerequisite |** *BrE* **the small print |** *AmE* **the fine print**

▶ **under** the **condition/terms/ provisions of** sth
▶ **lay down conditions/terms/ provisions/requirements**
▶ **accept/observe/comply with** the **conditions/terms/provisions/ requirements**

conference noun [C, U]

■ *A three-day conference was held in Glasgow.*

convention • summit • session • gathering • assembly • meeting | *esp. AmE* **caucus**

▶ an **annual** conference/ convention/summit/session/ gathering/assembly/meeting
▶ an **international** conference/ convention/summit/gathering/ assembly/meeting
▶ **hold** a/an **conference/ convention/summit/session/ gathering/assembly/meeting/ caucus**
▶ **attend** a/an **conference/ convention/summit/session/ gathering/assembly/meeting**

confidence noun

1 [U] ■ *The players all have confidence in the new manager.*

faith • belief • trust

▶ **confidence/faith/belief/trust in** sb/sth
▶ **have/show confidence/faith/trust**
▶ a **lack of confidence/faith/belief/ trust**
● **CONFIDENCE OR FAITH?** Faith is used esp. in the context of human relationships; **confidence** is used esp. in business contexts.

2 [U] ■ *He answered the questions with confidence.*

self-confidence • assurance • assertiveness | *fml, approv.* **aplomb**

▶ **with confidence/self-confidence/ assurance/aplomb**
▶ **have/show confidence/self- confidence/assurance**
▶ **lose/be lacking in/lack confidence/self-confidence**
● **CONFIDENCE, SELF-CONFIDENCE OR ASSURANCE?** Confidence or **self- confidence** is what you feel when you believe in yourself. **Assurance**

is the manner and behaviour that shows this feeling.

confident *adj.*

1 ■ Beneath his confident exterior, he's very insecure.

self-confident • independent | *disapprov.* brash

■ OPP insecure
► very confident/self-confident/independent
● CONFIDENT OR SELF-CONFIDENT? Confident can describe a person or what describes a person; self-confident only describes a person.

2 ■ The team feels confident of winning.

sure • certain • convinced • positive

► confident/sure/certain/convinced/positive **about** sth
► confident/sure/certain/convinced **of** sth
► confident/sure/certain/convinced/positive **that...**

confined *adj.* [usu. before noun]

■ It is cruel to keep animals in confined spaces.

tight | *disapprov.* cramped | *approv.* compact

■ OPP open
► a confined/cramped/compact **place**
► a confined/tight/cramped **space**
► confined/cramped **conditions**

confine sb/sth to sth *phrasal verb* [usu. passive]

■ The work will not be confined to the Boston area.

limit • restrict • curb • rein sb in | *written* contain

► confine/limit/restrict sb/sth **to** sth
► confine/limit/restrict **yourself to** sth
► confine/restrict **a discussion/your attention to** sth

confirm *verb*

1 [T] ■ His guilty expression confirmed my suspicions.

support | *fml* substantiate • validate • corroborate • authenticate

■ OPP disprove, (*fml*) refute
► confirm/validate/authenticate sth **as** sth
► confirm/support/substantiate/corroborate **that...**
► confirm/support/substantiate/validate/corroborate/authenticate **a claim**

2 [T] ■ Rumours of job losses were later confirmed.

back sb/sth up | *esp. BrE* bear sb/sth out | *fml* verify • certify • testify • vouch for sb/sth

■ OPP deny
► confirm/verify/certify sth **as** sth
► confirm/bear out/verify/certify/testify **that...**
► confirm/back up/bear out/verify a **claim/statement/theory/story/point**

3 [T] ■ He was confirmed as captain for the season.

approve • recognize | *fml* uphold • ratify

► confirm/approve/recognize/uphold/ratify sb/sth **as** sth
► confirm/uphold/ratify a/an **decision/agreement**
► officially confirm/approve/recognize/ratify sth

conflict *noun*

1 [C, U] (*usu. disapprov.*) ■ a bitter conflict between management and unions

dispute • controversy • war • disagreement • argument • difference | *BrE, infml* row | *usu. approv.* debate

► conflict/dispute/controversy/war/disagreement/argument/difference/contention/row/debate **about/over/between** sb/sth
► resolve a conflict/dispute/controversy/disagreement/sb's differences/debate
► a conflict/dispute/controversy/disagreement/debate **arises**
● CONFLICT OR DISPUTE? A conflict is generally more serious than a dispute and often lasts a long time.

2 [C, U] ■ Conflict between the groups has left more than 800 dead.

war • fighting • combat • warfare • battle | *esp. journ.* hostilities • action

► (a) conflict/war/fighting/combat/warfare/battle/hostilities/action **with/against/between** sb/sth
► (a) fierce/bloody conflict/fighting/combat/warfare/action
► (a) war/conflict/fighting/hostilities **breaks out/break out**

3 [C, U] ■ the conflict between love and duty

clash • contradiction | *fml* opposition • collision

■ OPP harmony, agreement
► a conflict/clash/collision **with** sb/sth
► **in** conflict/contradiction/opposition

conflict

▶ **resolve** a conflict/clash/
contradiction

conflict verb [I]

■ *These results conflict with earlier
findings.*

**contradict • be at odds • go against
sth • contrast • clash**

■ OPP **agree**
▶ conflict/be at odds/contrast/clash
with sth
▶ **stories/versions** conflict/
contradict each other/are at odds
▶ conflicting/contrasting **opinions/
personalities/emotions**

confront verb

1 [T] ■ *She had to confront her fears.*

**face • tackle • get/come to grips
with sth** | *fml* **address** | *written* **brave
• grapple with sth**

▶ be confronted/faced **with** sth
▶ confront/face/tackle/get to grips
with/address/grapple with a
problem/challenge/situation
▶ a **problem/dilemma/challenge/
difficulty/situation** confronts/
faces sb
● CONFRONT OR FACE? If you **confront**
a situation, you actively decide to
deal with it. If you **face** sth, the
problem already exists and you
have no choice but to deal with it.

2 [T] ■ *Would you confront an armed
robber?*

tackle • challenge

▶ confront/tackle/challenge sb
directly

confrontation noun [U, C]

■ *confrontations between employers
and unions*

showdown • clash | *esp. BrE, infml,
journ.* **row**

▶ a confrontation/showdown/
clash/row **with/between/over**
sb/sth
▶ a **major/bitter** confrontation/
clash/row
▶ **avoid** a confrontation/
showdown/clash/row

confuse verb

1 [T] ■ *Doctors love to confuse us with
obscure Latin terms.*

**puzzle • baffle • bewilder • mystify
• perplex • defeat** | *infml* **stump •
beat**

▶ It puzzles/baffles/beats **me how/
why ...**
▶ It puzzles/baffles **me that ...**
▶ What puzzles/baffles/mystifies/
beats **me is ...**

2 [T] ■ *People often confuse me and
my twin sister.*

mistake sb/sth for sb/sth • take |
esp. spoken **mix sb/sth up**

■ OPP **distinguish**
▶ confuse sb/sth/mix sb/sth up
with sb/sth
▶ mistake/take sb/sth **for** sb/sth
▶ be **easily** confused with/mistaken
for sb/sth

3 [T] ■ *Just to confuse matters, all the
street names have changed.*

complicate • cloud • blur

■ OPP **clarify**
▶ confuse/complicate/cloud **the
issue**
▶ confuse/complicate **matters/
things/the situation**
● CONFUSE OR COMPLICATE?
Something **complicates** a situation
by being an additional problem.
With **confuse** the emphasis is on
the fact that it is difficult to
recognize or understand what
needs to be done.

confused adj.

1 ■ *I'm confused—say all that again.*

**puzzled • at a loss • bemused •
dazed • bewildered • perplexed •
disoriented** | *esp. BrE* **muddled**

▶ confused/puzzled/perplexed/
muddled **about** sth
▶ confused/puzzled/at a loss/
perplexed **as to how/why ...**
▶ a confused/puzzled/bemused/
dazed/bewildered/perplexed
expression/look

2 ■ *The child gave a confused account
of the day's events.*

jumbled • disjointed | *fml* **discursive**
| *often disapprov.* **rambling • woolly •
incoherent**

■ OPP **clear**
▶ confused/jumbled/disjointed/
rambling/incoherent **thoughts**
▶ a confused/rambling **account of**
sth

confusing adj.

■ *The news bulletins were confusing,
giving different versions of what had
happened.*

**puzzling • baffling • bewildering •
incomprehensible**

■ OPP **clear**
▶ confusing/puzzling/baffling/
bewildering/incomprehensible **to**
sb
▶ confusing/puzzling/baffling/
bewildering **for** sb
▶ confusing/puzzling/baffling/
bewildering/incomprehensible
that...

confusion noun

1 [U, C] ■ There was confusion as to what to do next.

uncertainty • doubt

▶ confusion/uncertainty/doubt **over/about/as to** sth
▶ **clear up/dispel** confusion/uncertainty/doubt

2 [U] ■ Smoke bombs created confusion and panic.

chaos • havoc • mayhem • pandemonium • commotion • mess • *infml* shambles

▶ **in (the)** confusion/chaos/the mayhem/pandemonium/the commotion/a mess/a shambles
▶ **(a) complete/total** confusion/chaos/mayhem/pandemonium/mess/shambles
▶ **cause** confusion/chaos/havoc/mayhem/pandemonium/a commotion/a mess
● **CHAOS OR CONFUSION?** Chaos generally describes a total lack of order in a system or situation; **confusion** is mainly used when a group of people don't know what to do.

congress (also Congress) noun [C +sing./pl.v., usu. sing., U]

■ Congress will vote on the proposals.

parliament • assembly • senate • house • chamber • council | *fml* legislature

▶ **convene** congress/parliament/the legislature
▶ **the** congress/parliament/assembly/senate/house/chamber/council/legislature **votes (for/on)** sth
▶ **the** congress/parliament/assembly/senate/house/council/legislature **passes a resolution/bill/law**, etc.
● **CONGRESS OR PARLIAMENT?** A **parliament** makes laws, which are then put into effect by a group of people selected from within it; a **congress** makes laws, which are put into effect by a separate group of people.

connect verb [T, I]

1 ■ I'm looking for jobs connected with the environment.

link • couple sth with sth

▶ **be** connected/linked/coupled **with** sb/sth
▶ **be closely/intimately/directly/necessarily/loosely/somehow/in some way** connected/linked
● **CONNECT OR LINK?** Link is often used when the connection between two things is stronger, in a way that makes it impossible to separate

them; **connect** means that two things belong to the same general area. People can be **connected** with each other, but not linked:
✓They were connected by marriage.
✗ They were linked by marriage.

2 [T] ■ There was nothing to connect him with the crime.

relate • associate • match | *esp. journ.* link

▶ connect/relate/match/link sth **to** sth
▶ connect/associate/match/link sth **with** sth
▶ connect/relate/associate/match/link sth **directly**
● **CONNECT, RELATE OR ASSOCIATE?** When you **associate** two things in your mind, it often just happens because of previous experiences. When you **relate** or **connect** them it requires more effort, because the connection is not so obvious or natural to you:
✓I always associate the smell of baking with my childhood. ✗ I always relate/connect the smell of baking with my childhood.
✓I found it hard to relate/connect the two things in my mind. ✗ I found it hard to associate the two things in my mind.

connected adj.

■ There was no connected sequence of events.

related • associated

■ OPP unconnected
▶ **closely** connected/related/associated **with** sth
▶ **closely** connected/related/associated

connection noun [C]

■ The connection between smoking and cancer is well known.

link • relationship • correlation • association • relation | *fml* interdependence

▶ **the** connection/link/relationship/correlation/association/relation/interdependence **between** A and B
▶ **a** connection/link/relationship/correlation/association/relation **with** sb/sth
▶ **a direct/clear/strong/definite/possible** connection/link/relationship/correlation/association/relation
▶ **show/examine the** connection/link/relationship/correlation/association/relation
● **CONNECTION OR LINK?** Link is slightly more informal than **connection** and is often used in newspapers.

conscientious adj.

■ She was a popular and conscientious teacher.

hardworking • meticulous • painstaking • thorough • industrious | fml diligent

■ OPP casual, slapdash
► conscientious/meticulous about sth
► a/an conscientious/hardworking/ industrious/diligent person
► conscientious/meticulous/ painstaking/thorough/diligent work

conscious adj.

1 ■ We are very conscious of the issues involved.

aware • alert to sth | fml mindful

► conscious/aware/mindful of sth
► conscious/aware/mindful that...
► keenly conscious/aware/alert

2 ■ He made a conscious effort to be there on time.

deliberate • intentional • calculated • purposeful | often disapprov. premeditated | esp. BrE, fml, disapprov. or law wilful | AmE usu. willful

■ OPP unconscious
► a/an conscious/deliberate/ intentional/calculated/ purposeful/premeditated/wilful act
► a/an conscious/deliberate/ intentional/calculated/purposeful action
► conscious/deliberate/calculated attempts/manipulation

consequence noun [C]

■ This decision could have serious consequences.

result • outcome • effect • impact • implication • upshot | written repercussion

■ OPP cause
► have consequences/implications/ repercussions for sb/sth
► with the consequence/result/ outcome/effect that...
► have (a/an) consequences/result/ outcome/effect/impact/ repercussions
► show/observe/assess/examine/ measure the consequences/ results/outcome/effect/impact

conservative adj.

■ They were conservative in their political outlook. ■ She was dressed neatly in conservative black.

traditionalist • traditional • orthodox | often disapprov. conventional • conformist

■ OPP radical, progressive
► conservative/traditionalist/ traditional/conventional thinkers/ values
► conservative/traditionalist/ traditional/orthodox/conventional views

consider verb

1 [T, I] ■ He was considering what to do next.

think • look at sth • take • wonder • mull sth over • reflect | esp. written ponder | fml deliberate • contemplate • meditate

► think/mull/ponder/deliberate/ meditate over sth
► consider/think/look at/wonder/ reflect/ponder/deliberate/ contemplate how/what/ whether...
► consider/think/reflect that...

2 [T] (not used in the progressive tenses) ■ He considers himself an expert on the subject.

regard • view • see • count • call • describe • think • believe • feel | fml hold | esp. BrE, infml reckon

► consider/regard/view/see/count/ describe sb/sth/yourself as sth
► consider/regard/view/see sth from a particular point of view
► consider/think/believe/feel/hold/ reckon that...
● CONSIDER OR REGARD? In this meaning consider must be used with a complement or clause. You can consider sb/sth as sth/to be sth. Often the to be or as is left out:
✔ They are considered a high-risk group.
You can regard sb/sth as sth but not to be sth, and as cannot be left out:
✔ I regard him as a close friend. ✗ I regard him to be a close friend. • ✗ I regard him a close friend.

considerable adj.

■ Considerable amounts of money were wasted.

substantial • large • sizeable • extensive • great • big • huge • vast • enormous • tremendous

■ OPP negligible
► a/an considerable/substantial/ large/sizeable/extensive/great/ big/huge/vast/enormous/ tremendous amount
► a/an considerable/substantial/ large/sizeable/great/big/huge/ vast/enormous sum/profit
► a/an considerable/substantial/ extensive/great/big/huge/vast/

enormous/tremendous **change/improvement/influence**

● **CONSIDERABLE OR SUBSTANTIAL? Considerable** is not used to talk about solid things, such as meals or buildings. **Substantial** is not used to talk about emotions or personal qualities, such as anger, concern or efficiency.

✔ Caring for elderly relatives requires considerable moral courage.

✗ ~~substantial moral courage~~

✔ He ate a substantial breakfast. ✗ ~~a considerable breakfast~~

consideration noun

1 [U, C, usu. sing.] ■ Give the matter some consideration.

thought • look • reflection | fml deliberation • meditation • contemplation

▶ after (some, etc.) thought/reflection/deliberation/contemplation
▶ be for sb's consideration/deliberation/contemplation
▶ give sth some consideration/some thought/a look

2 [C] ■ Financial considerations play a big part.

factor • point

▶ a consideration/factor in sth
▶ a/an/the main/major/important/key/essential consideration/factor/point
▶ considerations/factors/points to be taken into account

consist of sb/sth phrasal verb

[no passive] (not used in the progressive tenses)

■ Their diet consists mainly of fruit.

make up/be made • have made up • have got | comprise • be composed of sb/sth • constitute

▶ The group consists of/is made up of/comprises/is composed of ten people.
▶ Ten people make up/comprise/constitute the group.

● WHICH WORD? Consist of sb/sth is the most general of these terms, and is the only one that can be used with the -ing form of a verb: My life consisted of feeding the baby and washing nappies.

conspiracy noun [C, U]

■ a conspiracy to overthrow the government

plot • scheme | esp. AmE sting | esp. written intrigue | fml collusion

▶ a/an conspiracy/plot/intrigue against sb
▶ (an) alleged conspiracy/plot/scheme/intrigue/collusion
▶ be involved in (a/an) conspiracy/

plot/scheme/sting/intrigue/collusion

constant adj.

1 [usu. before noun] ■ Her constant chatter was starting to annoy him.

continuous • continual • persistent • perpetual • frequent • habitual

▶ constant/continuous/continual/persistent/frequent/habitual **use**
▶ a constant/continuous/continual/persistent/frequent/perpetual **problem**
▶ constant/continuous/continual/persistent/frequent **attacks**
▶ a constant/continuous/continual/perpetual **source** of sth

2 ■ Store the samples at a constant temperature.

steady • even • consistent • regular | usu. approv. stable | written unchanging | sometimes disapprov., esp. busin. static

■ OPP variable

▶ a/an constant/steady/even/stable **temperature**
▶ a constant/steady/consistent **trend/rate**
▶ a constant/steady **speed/stream/trickle**
▶ remain constant/steady/even/consistent/stable/unchanging/static

construct verb [T, often passive]

■ When was the bridge constructed?

build • assemble • put sth up • set sth up | fml erect

■ OPP demolish

▶ construct/build sth **from/out of/of** sth
▶ construct/build/assemble a/an **machine/engine**
▶ construct/build/put up/erect a **house/shelter/wall/fence**
▶ construct/build a **road/railway/railroad/tunnel/nest**

construction noun

1 [U] ■ the construction of the new airport

building • assembly • making • production • manufacturing • manufacture

■ OPP demolition

▶ commercial/industrial construction/building/production/manufacturing/manufacture
▶ construction/building/assembly/production/manufacturing methods/processes/systems/techniques
▶ construction/building/

manufacturing **companies/costs/
firms/jobs/materials/work**

● CONSTRUCTION OR BUILDING?
Construction is a more technical
word and is used more in business
and industrial contexts.

2 [U] ■ *ships of steel construction*

structure • composition • form

▶ **basic** construction/structure/
composition/form **of** sth

contact noun

1 [U] ■ *He doesn't have much contact
with his son.*

communication • dealings | *fml*
correspondence

▶ contact/communication/
dealings/correspondence **with** sb
▶ contact/communication/
dealings/correspondence
between people
▶ **be in** contact/communication/
correspondence (with sb)
▶ **have** contact/dealings with sb

2 [C] ■ *He has several contacts in
Paris.*

associate • colleague • partner • ally

▶ a **business** contact/associate/
colleague/partner/ally
▶ a **political** contact/associate/
colleague/ally
▶ a **new/close** contact/associate/
colleague/partner/ally

contain verb [T]

■ *a drink that doesn't contain
alcohol* ■ *Her statement contained one
or two inaccuracies.*

include • incorporate

▶ contain/include/incorporate sth **in**
sth
▶ contain/include/incorporate
particular **features/material**

contemporary adj.

■ *life in contemporary Britain*

modern • present-day • modern-
day • present • current • new •
advanced • up-to-date • recent

▶ contemporary/modern/present-
day/modern-day/new **society**
▶ contemporary/modern/current/
recent **trends**
▶ (a) contemporary/modern/
present-day/new **art/artist/music**
● CONTEMPORARY OR MODERN? You
can use either word when talking
about art, culture or society, but
only **modern** is used to talk about
science or technology: *modern/
contemporary art/dance/fiction/
politics • modern technology/
warfare/techniques*

contempt noun [U, sing.]

■ *I'll treat that remark with the
contempt it deserves.*

scorn • disdain • disrespect •
mockery • ridicule • derision

■ OPP respect
▶ contempt/scorn/disdain /
disrespect **for** sb/sth
▶ **treat** sb/sth with contempt/
disdain/disrespect/ridicule
▶ **risk/invite** (sb's) contempt/scorn/
ridicule/derision
● WHICH WORD? Contempt, scorn
and disdain put the emphasis on
showing that you have no respect
for sb/sth. Mockery, ridicule and
derision put the emphasis on
making sb/sth look silly.

contemptuous adj.

■ *They showed a contemptuous
disregard for his complaints.*

scornful • disdainful • mocking •
scathing • withering • derisive

▶ contemptuous/scornful/
disdainful/scathing **of** sb/sth
▶ a contemptuous/scornful/
disdainful/mocking/scathing/
withering **look/glance**
▶ a contemptuous/scornful/
mocking/scathing **tone**

contest noun

1 [C] ■ *a beauty/talent contest*

competition • quiz • championship
• tournament • cup • match • race

▶ an **international** contest/
competition/championship/
tournament/match/race
▶ **enter/hold** a contest/
competition/quiz/championship/
tournament/race
▶ **win** a contest/competition/quiz/
championship/tournament/cup/
match/race

2 [C] (*esp. journ.*) ■ *a contest for the
leadership of the party*

race • competition • rivalry

▶ (a) contest/race/competition/
rivalry **for** sth
▶ **in** (a) contest/race/competition/
rivalry **with** sb
▶ **enter/win/lose** the contest/race
● CONTEST OR RACE? In many cases
you can use either word to talk
about political contests. However,
contest usu. refers to the election
itself; **race** covers the whole period
of campaigning for an election
which can last months. **Race** can
also be used to talk about the drive
to achieve sth: *The race is on* (= has
begun) *to find a cure for this disease.*

context noun [C, U]

■ *His remarks need to be understood in
context.*

background • setting | *fml* milieu | *written* backdrop

▸ in (a) context/setting/milieu
▸ the cultural/historical/economic/political context/background/setting/milieu
▸ provide (sb with) a context/background/setting/backdrop

continue verb

1 [I] ■ *The rain will continue into the evening.*

last | *esp. spoken* go on • keep on | *esp. BrE, esp. spoken* carry on | *disapprov.* drag on

■ OPP suspend

▸ continue/last/go on/keep on/carry on/drag on **for** hours/a week/two years, etc.
▸ continue/last/go on/keep on/carry on/drag on **until** morning/next year, etc.
▸ continue/last **into** the night/next week, etc.

2 [T, I] ■ *He continued to ignore what I said.*

go on with sth/go on doing sth • keep sth up/keep up with sth • proceed • press on • press ahead | *esp. spoken* keep • carry (sth) on | *infml* stick with sb/sth | *fml* pursue

▸ continue/go on/keep up/proceed/press on/press ahead/keep on/carry on/stick with sth
▸ continue/go on/proceed with/press on with/press ahead with/carry on with/pursue **plans**
▸ continue/go on/keep on/carry on **fighting/working/talking/believing** sth

3 [I] ■ *The path continued over rocky ground.*

go • stretch • lead • extend

▸ continue/go/stretch/lead/extend **beyond/across** sth
▸ continue/go/stretch/lead/extend **from** sth **to** sth
▸ continue/stretch/extend **for** sth

4 [I] (*esp. written*) ■ *She will continue in her present job.*

stay • keep • last | *fml* remain

5 [I, I] ■ *Please continue with the work you were doing before.*

return to sth • reopen • restart | *esp. spoken* go on • take sth up | *fml* resume | *esp. journ.* renew

▸ continue/go on **with** sth
▸ continue/go on/resume **doing** sth
▸ continue/return to/reopen/restart/resume/renew **talks**
▸ continue/return to/take up/resume a **conversation**

continuous adj.

1 ■ *It was a week of almost continuous sunshine.*

continual • unbroken • uninterrupted • endless • perpetual • never-ending • persistent • round-the-clock • non-stop | *disapprov.* relentless • incessant

■ OPP intermittent

▸ a/an continuous/uninterrupted/endless/never-ending/relentless/incessant **flow** of sth
▸ a/an continuous/unbroken/uninterrupted/endless/never-ending **succession/series**
▸ (a/an) continuous/continual/relentless/endless/never-ending **struggle**
● CONTINUOUS OR CONTINUAL? **Continuous** is more frequent and has a wider range of uses than **continual**. **Continual** is used *esp.* to describe states of mind or body; collocates include *state, fear, pain* and *delight*.

2 ■ *The soldiers suffered continuous attacks.*

continual • constant • persistent • frequent • regular • habitual | *esp. written* perpetual

▸ continuous/continual/constant/persistent/frequent/regular/habitual **use/attacks**
▸ a continuous/continual/constant/persistent/frequent/perpetual **problem**
▸ a continuous/continual/constant/frequent/perpetual **source** of sth
● WHICH WORD? **Persistent** is often used to talk about medical problems or problems in society; **perpetual** tends to talk about annoying personal habits. **Continuous** and **continual** are used more in spoken English and less formal contexts.

contract noun [C]

■ *a contract between buyer and seller*

agreement • deal • settlement

▸ a/an contract/agreement/deal **between** sb and sb
▸ a/an contract/agreement/deal/settlement **with** sb
▸ **under** a/an contract/agreement

contract verb [I, T] (*fml*)

■ *Glass contracts as it cools.*

shrink • narrow • shorten

■ OPP expand

▸ contract/shrink/narrow/shorten (sth) **to** a particular size
▸ contract/shrink/narrow/shorten (sth) **by** a particular amount

contrast

contrast noun [C, U]
■ *the contrast between East and West*

difference • variation • distinction | *fml* **disparity**

▶ a contrast/difference/variation/distinction/disparity **between** A and B
▶ a contrast/difference/variation/distinction/disparity **in** sth
▶ **see/be aware of/look at** a contrast/difference/variation/distinction

contrast verb

1 [T] ■ *The poem contrasts youth and age.*

compare | *fml* **juxtapose**

■ OPP **liken**
▶ contrast/compare/juxtapose A **and/with** B
▶ contrast/compare sth **unfavourably/favourably** with sth

2 [I] ■ *Her actions contrasted sharply with her promises.*

conflict • contradict • be at odds with sth

■ OPP **match**
▶ contrast/conflict/be at odds **with** sth
▶ contrasting/conflicting **opinions/personalities/emotions**

contribute verb [I, T]
■ *People contributed generously to the earthquake fund.*

donate • give | *infml* **chip in (sth)**

▶ contribute/donate/give (sth) **to** sth
▶ contribute/donate/give **cash/a sum**
▶ contribute/donate/give/chip in **£10/$1000**, etc.
● CONTRIBUTE OR DONATE? Contribute suggests that a number of people are all giving money, food, etc. to a charity or fund. Donate places the emphasis on the individual. You can **donate**, but not **contribute**, blood.

contribution noun [C, U]
■ *a contribution to charity*

donation • gift

▶ a contribution/donation/gift **for/to/from** sb

▶ a generous/large/small contribution/donation/gift
▶ make a contribution/donation/gift
● CONTRIBUTION OR DONATION? Contributions are often expected or asked for; donations are seen more as voluntary gifts.

control noun

1 [U] ■ *The city is under enemy control.*

power • rule • authority • command • hold • grasp • discipline | *fml* **jurisdiction**

▶ **in** control/power/authority/command
▶ **be under** sb's control/rule/authority/command/jurisdiction
▶ **have/give sb** control/power/authority/command/a hold/jurisdiction **over** sb/sth

2 [U, C] ■ *government controls on trade and industry*

limit • limitation • restriction • constraint • restraint • check • ceiling • curb

▶ controls/limits/limitations/restrictions/constraints/restraints/checks/a ceiling/curbs **on** sth
▶ **without** controls/limits/limitations/restrictions/constraints/restraints/checks
▶ **impose** controls/limits/limitations/restrictions/constraints/restraints/checks/a ceiling/curbs

3 [C, usu. pl.] ■ *the controls of an aircraft*

button • switch • dial • wheel • lever • knob

▶ **be at/take** the controls/wheel
▶ **adjust** the controls/dial
▶ the controls/wheel **operates** sth

control verb

1 [T] ■ *By the age of 25 he controlled the company.*

run • manage • be in charge • direct • be responsible for sb/sth • administer • command

▶ control/run/manage a/an **company/business/organization**
▶ control/run/manage/direct/be responsible for/administer a **project**
▶ control/run/manage/be in charge of/direct/be responsible for **operations**

2 [T] ■ *Can't you control your dog?*

manage • handle

▶ control/manage a **child**
▶ **be easy/difficult** to control/manage/handle
▶ control/manage/handle sb/sth **properly**

3 [T] ■ *new measures to control immigration*

limit • restrict • curb • check • keep/ hold sth in check • rein sth in | *esp. BrE* **cap** | *written* **contain • suppress**

► control/limit/restrict/curb/check/ rein in/cap **spending**
► keep/hold **spending** in check
► control/limit/check/contain the **spread** of sth
► control/limit/restrict the **size/ number/extent/amount** of sth

4 [T] ■ *She was given drugs to control the pain.*

overcome • bring/get/keep sth under control • get over sth | *infml* **beat** | *written* **conquer**

► control/overcome/get over/beat/ conquer a **problem**
► control/overcome/get over/ conquer a **fear**
► control a **fire**/bring a **fire** under control

5 [T] ■ *The lights are controlled by a computer.*

operate • run | *esp. spoken* **work** | *fml* **manipulate**

► control/operate/run/work a **machine**
► control/operate/run a/an **engine/motor**
● **CONTROL, OPERATE OR RUN?** A person **operates** or **runs** a machine; machines are often **controlled** by the controls, such as a computer, knob or lever.

6 [T] ■ *She struggled to control her temper.*

restrain • hold sth back • suppress • repress • stifle • curb | *written* **contain • check**

► control/restrain/contain/check **yourself**
► control/restrain/contain/hold back/ suppress/repress/contain/check your **anger**
► control/restrain/suppress/ repress/stifle/curb/check an **impulse**
► control/curb/contain your **temper**

controversial *adj.*

■ *a controversial plan to build a new road*

contentious • debatable • questionable • dubious | *fml* **arguable**

■ OPP **uncontroversial**
► a controversial/contentious/ questionable/dubious **decision**
► a controversial/debatable/dubious **issue/subject/question**
► a controversial/contentious **matter/view/opinion**
● **CONTROVERSIAL OR CONTENTIOUS?** Controversial has a wider range of

---

meaning than **contentious** and can describe people and things as well as issues and opinions:
✔*a controversial figure/book/film/ play/plan/building* ✗ *a contentious figure/book/film/play/plan/building*

convenient *adj.*

■ *I can't see them now. It's not convenient.*

appropriate • suitable • good

■ OPP **inconvenient**
► convenient/appropriate/suitable/ good for **sb/sth**
► convenient/appropriate/suitable/ good **to do sth**
► a/an convenient/appropriate/ suitable/good **time** to do sth/a/an convenient/appropriate/ suitable/good **place** for sth

convention *noun* [C, U]

■ *The handshake is a social convention.*

custom • practice • tradition • norms

► a convention/custom/tradition **that …**
► follow a convention/custom/ practice/tradition/… norms
► break with convention/a practice/tradition
► a convention/custom/tradition **demands** sth

conventional *adj.*

1 (*often disapprov.*) ■ *a conventional piece of theatre*

conservative • traditionalist | *often disapprov.* **conformist**

■ OPP **unconventional**
► conventional/conformist **behaviour**
► conventional/conservative/ traditionalist **thinkers/views/ values**

2 [usu. before noun] ■ *Use a microwave or cook it in a conventional oven.*

traditional • mainstream • orthodox • classical

■ OPP **alternative**
► conventional/traditional/ mainstream/orthodox/classical **views/theories/methods/ approaches/economics**
► conventional/traditional/ mainstream/classical **ideas/ thinking/education**
► conventional/traditional/orthodox **medicine**
● **CONVENTIONAL OR TRADITIONAL?** Traditional emphasizes how old a method or idea is; conventional emphasizes how usual it is now. Traditional medicine is actually a

form of *alternative medicine*, which is the opposite of modern *conventional medicine*.

conversation noun [C, U]

■ *The conversation turned to politics.*

discussion • talk • chat • debate • consultation • dialogue | *written* **exchange**

▶ a/an conversation/discussion/talk/chat/debate/consultation/dialogue/exchange **about** sth
▶ a/an conversation/discussion/talk/chat/debate/consultation/dialogue/exchange **with** sb
▶ a/an conversation/discussion/debate/dialogue/exchange **between** two people/groups
▶ **have** a/an conversation/discussion/talk/chat/debate/consultation/dialogue/exchange
▶ **get into** (a) conversation/discussion with sb

convey verb [T]

■ *He tried to convey how urgent the matter was.*

communicate • tell • get sth across • send • repeat • break • pass sth on • relay | *fml* **impart**

▶ convey/communicate/tell/get across/send/repeat/break/pass on/impart sth **to** sb
▶ convey/communicate/tell/break it/relay **(to)** sb **that…**
▶ convey/communicate/get across/send/repeat/pass on/relay/impart a **message**
● **CONVEY OR COMMUNICATE?** You can *convey* sth to one person, to a group or to people in general. You can *communicate* sth to a group but not usu. to only one person.

convince verb

1 [T] ■ *I wasn't convinced by her arguments.*

persuade | *fml* **satisfy**

▶ convince/persuade/satisfy sb **of** sth
▶ convince/persuade/satisfy sb **that…**
▶ convince/persuade/satisfy **yourself**

2 [T] ■ *I convinced him to see a doctor.*

persuade • get • talk sb into sth • win sb over • coax • cajole

▶ convince sb/persuade sb/get sb/be coaxed/be cajoled **to do sth**
▶ **try to** convince sb/persuade sb/get sb to do sth/talk sb into sth/win sb/coax sb
● **CONVINCE OR PERSUADE?** You can *persuade sb to do sth* in many ways,

for example by making them believe it is right, or by showing them that they will gain sth from it: *He was persuaded by bribes to reverse his judgement.*
When you **convince sb to do sth** you usu. make them believe that it is the right or the best thing to do: *He convinced me to get legal advice.* This meaning of **convince** is used more in *AmE* than *BrE*; many speakers of *BrE* prefer always to use **persuade** in this meaning.

convincing adj.

■ *Is there convincing evidence that the vaccine is safe?*

compelling • strong • persuasive • forceful | *fml* **cogent**

■ OPP **unconvincing**

▶ a convincing/compelling/strong/persuasive/forceful/cogent **argument**
▶ a convincing/compelling/strong/persuasive/cogent **evidence**
▶ a convincing/compelling/strong/persuasive/cogent **reason/case**
▶ a convincing/compelling/cogent **explanation**

cook verb [T, I]

■ *There are various ways to cook fish.*

make • bake • roast • toast • fry • grill • barbecue | *AmE* **broil** | *esp. AmE* **fix** | *esp. spoken* **get** | *esp. written* **prepare**

▶ cook/make/fix/get/prepare breakfast/lunch/dinner
▶ cook/roast/fry/grill/barbecue/broil/prepare **chicken**
▶ cook/bake/roast/fry **potatoes**

cooker noun [C] (BrE)

■ *All the flats are fitted with gas cookers.*

oven • microwave (oven) | *AmE* **stove** | *BrE* **hob**

▶ **on** the cooker/stove/hob
▶ **in** the oven/microwave
▶ a/an **gas/electric** cooker/oven/stove/hob

cooking noun [U]

■ *My husband does all the cooking.*

baking | *BrE* **cookery** | *fml* **cuisine**

▶ French/Chinese, etc. cooking/cookery/cuisine
▶ **excellent/superb/traditional/local** cooking/cuisine
▶ **home** cooking/baking

cool verb [I, T]

■ *Glass contracts as it cools.*

cool (sb/sth) down • chill • freeze | *fml* **refrigerate**

■ OPP **warm, heat**

► leave sth to/allow sth to/let sth
cool/cool down
► keep sth chilled/frozen/
refrigerated
● COOL OR COOL (SB/STH) DOWN? Cool
down is used more in spoken
English. It can be used with *myself,
yourself, himself, etc.*: *How about a
swim to cool ourselves down?*
Use **cool** in technical language: *The
cylinder is cooled by a jet of water.*

cool *adj.*

1 (*usu. approv.*) ■ Store medicines in a
cool dry place.

cold • chilly • chill | *approv.* **crisp** |
often disapprov. **lukewarm** • **tepid**

■ OPP **warm, hot**
► a cool/cold/chilly/chill/crisp **day/
morning**
► cool/cold/chilly/chill/crisp **air**
► (a) cool/cold/lukewarm/tepid
water/shower

2 ■ *You must try to stay cool, even in
an emergency.*

calm • relaxed • unperturbed •
composed • controlled | *infml*
unfazed

► cool/calm/relaxed **about** sth
► unperturbed/unfazed **by** sth
► a cool/calm/relaxed/controlled
manner/voice/way
● COOL, CALM OR RELAXED? Relaxed
describes how you feel about sth.
Cool is used more to describe how
sb behaves when they don't let
their feelings affect their behaviour.
Calm can describe feelings or
behaviour.

3 ■ *He's been cool towards me ever
since we had the argument.*

cold • unfriendly • frosty • chilly •
remote • distant | *written* **aloof**

■ OPP **warm, friendly**
► cool/cold/unfriendly **to/towards**
sb
► a/an cool/cold/unfriendly/frosty/
distant/aloof **manner**
► a cool/frosty/chilly **reception**

4 (*infml*) ■ *a really cool new video
game*

infml **great • fantastic • fabulous •
terrific** | *BrE, infml* **brilliant** | *esp. AmE*
infml **awesome** | *slang* **wicked**

■ OPP **uncool, rubbish**
► a/an cool/great/fantastic/
fabulous/terrific/brilliant/
awesome/wicked **place**
► have a/an cool/great/fantastic/
fabulous/terrific/brilliant/
awesome/wicked **time**
► a cool/great/fantastic/fabulous/
terrific/brilliant **guy/girl**

cope *verb* [I]

■ *He finds it hard to cope with stress.*

manage • get by • get on | *esp. BrE*
muddle through

► cope/manage/get by/get on/
muddle through **without** sth
► manage/get by/get on
► cope/manage/get by/get on **on your
own**
● COPE OR MANAGE? The subject of
manage in this meaning is always a
person; the subject of **cope** may be
a person, thing or system:
✔ *In heavy rain the drainage system
can't cope.* ✗ *In heavy rain the
drainage system can't manage.*

copy *noun*

1 [C] ■ *I'll send you a copy of the
report.*

photocopy • printout • transcript |
computing **hard copy**

► make a copy/photocopy/
transcript
► attach/enclose a copy/
photocopy/printout/hard copy
► keep a copy/photocopy/
printout/transcript
● COPY OR PHOTOCOPY? A **copy** can
be any kind of printed
reproduction of a document. A
photocopy is a copy made on a
photocopier.

2 [C] ■ *The thieves replaced the
original painting with a copy.*

replica • duplicate • facsimile •
reproduction • model •
reconstruction • mock-up

► an exact copy/replica/duplicate/
facsimile/reproduction/
reconstruction
► a/an good/accurate copy/
facsimile/reproduction/model/
reconstruction
► make a copy/replica/facsimile/
reproduction/model/
reconstruction/mock-up
► keep a copy/duplicate

copy *verb*

1 [T] ■ *Copy the files onto a memory
stick.*

reproduce • photocopy • duplicate |
computing **write • burn • rip**

► to copy/reproduce/photocopy/
write/burn/rip sth **from** sth
► to copy/write/burn/rip (sth) **to** a
disk/CD
► to copy/reproduce/photocopy/
duplicate a **letter/document**
► to copy/reproduce/duplicate sth
exactly

2 [T] ■ *She copied the phone number
into her address book.*

write sth down • write sth out • transcribe • take sth down • put sth down

▶ to copy/write/take/put sth **down**
▶ to copy/write sth **out**
▶ to copy/transcribe sth **into** sth
▶ to copy/write down/write out/transcribe/take down **information/notes**

3 [T] ■ *She copies everything her older sister does.*

follow • imitate | written **model yourself/sth on sb/sth** | fml **mimic • emulate** | esp. busin. or journ. **follow suit**

▶ to copy/follow/imitate/emulate a **style**
▶ to copy/mitate/mimic sb/sth's **movements**
▶ to copy/follow/mimic sb/sth **exactly**

core noun [sing.]

■ *The report goes to the core of the argument.*

heart • crux • nucleus • body

▶ **at** the core/heart/crux of sth
▶ **form** the core/heart/nucleus/body of sth
▶ **lie at/go to** the core/heart/crux of sth
● **CORE OR HEART? Heart** is often used to talk about the most important part of a problem when considered in moral or emotional terms, esp. in the phrase *the heart of the matter/problem*; **core** is often used about the most important part of a problem when considered in logical terms. **Core** is also used to talk about the most important activities in education or business: *the core subjects/curriculum/activities*

corner noun [C]

■ *There was a group of youths standing on the street corner.*

bend • turn • twist • zigzag | BrE **hairpin bend** | AmE **hairpin curve/turn**

▶ **around/round/at/on** a corner/bend/hairpin bend/hairpin curve
▶ a **sharp** corner/bend/turn/twist
▶ **round/take** a corner/bend/turn/hairpin bend

correct verb [T]

■ *He corrected all the mistakes in the report.*

correct • cure • remedy • fix • set sb/sth straight | esp. BrE **put sth right** | fml **rectify • redress**

▶ correct/cure/remedy/fix/put right/rectify/redress **what…**

▶ correct/cure/remedy/fix/put right/rectify/redress a **problem**
▶ correct/remedy/fix/put right/rectify a/an **mistake/error/fault**

correct adj.

1 ■ *You are 48 years old, is that correct?*

right • true

■ OPP **incorrect, wrong**
▶ correct/right **about** sth
▶ the correct/right/true **answer**
▶ the correct/right/true **time**
● **RIGHT OR CORRECT? Correct** is more formal than **right** and is more likely to be used in official instructions or documents.

2 ■ *What's the correct way to shut the machine down?*

right | esp. BrE **proper**

■ OPP **wrong**
▶ correct/right **about** sb/sth
▶ correct/right **to do** sth
▶ correct/right **in thinking/believing/saying** sth
● **CORRECT, RIGHT OR PROPER?** People can be **correct** or **right** about sth, but not **proper**:
✔*You're right to be cautious in this situation.* ✗ *You're proper to be cautious.*
✔*Am I correct in thinking…?* ✗ *Am I proper in thinking…?*
Correct and **proper** are more often used to talk about methods; **right** is more often used to talk about beliefs and decisions.

corridor noun [C] (esp. BrE)

■ *Go along the corridor and turn left.*

hall • hallway • passage • aisle | esp. AmE **passageway**

▶ **in** the corridor/hall/aisle/passage/walkway/hallway/passageway/entryway
▶ **along/down** the corridor/hall/aisle/passage/walkway/hallway/passageway/entryway/catwalk
▶ **through** the corridor/hall/passage/hallway/passageway/entryway
● **CORRIDOR, HALL OR HALLWAY?** A **corridor** is usu. long and straight, and is normally used when talking about large public buildings. **Hall** and **hallway** can be used when talking about both public buildings and houses.

corrupt adj.

■ *a corrupt regime*

unscrupulous • amoral | fml **fraudulent • unprincipled** | infml **dirty • rotten** | esp. journ. **crooked**

■ OPP **honest**
▶ corrupt/unscrupulous/amoral/

fraudulent/unprincipled behaviour

► a/an corrupt/unscrupulous/ crooked **businessman/lawyer/ politician**
► a corrupt/rotten/crooked **system**
● **CORRUPT OR UNSCRUPULOUS?** **Corrupt** is often used to talk about the authorities or a system and people who work for them. **Unscrupulous** is often used to talk about people who manage their own businesses: *unscrupulous dealers/landlords*

corruption *noun* [U]

■ *There were allegations of bribery and corruption among senior officials.*

bribery • extortion • blackmail

► alleged corruption/bribery/ extortion
► attempted bribery/extortion/ blackmail
► be involved in corruption/ bribery/extortion

cost *noun*

1 [C, U] ■ *The roof had to be repaired at a cost of £7000.*

price • value • expense • rate • charge • worth

► the high cost/price/value/rate/ charge
► the real/true cost/price/value/ rate/worth
► increase/reduce the cost/price/ value/expense/rate/charge
● **COST, PRICE OR VALUE?** The **price** is what sb asks you to pay for an item or service:
    ✓to ask/charge a high price
    ✗to ask/charge a high price/value
Obtaining sth may have a **cost**; the **value** of sth is how much money people would pay for it:
house prices • the cost of moving house • The house now has a market value of twice what we paid for it.

2 costs [pl.] ■ *They use cheap labour to keep their costs down.*

expenses • spending • expenditure • outlay | *esp. BrE* **overheads** | *esp. AmE* **overhead**

► government/public/education/ health/defence/military/ household **costs/expenses/ spending/expenditure**
► increase/reduce **costs/expenses/ spending/expenditure/outlay/ overheads/overhead**
► control/cover/cut **costs/ expenses/spending/expenditure/ overheads/overhead**

cost *verb* [T]

■ *Calls cost 40p per minute.*

be • sell • go | *infml* **set sb back** | *busin.* **retail • trade**

► How much does this cost/is this?
► That costs/will set you back a lot of money.
► sth sells/retails/trades **at £9.95**
► sth sells/goes/retails **for £9.95**

costume *noun* [C, U]

■ *Did you see that guy in the giant chicken costume?*

disguise • camouflage | *BrE* **fancy dress**

► in costume/disguise/camouflage/ fancy dress
► to wear (a) costume/disguise/ camouflage/fancy dress
► put on a costume/disguise
● **COSTUME OR DISGUISE?** You wear a **costume** for fun, or to take part in a performance; you wear a **disguise** in order to trick people so that they do not recognize you.

count *verb* [T, I]

■ *She counted up how many guests had been invited.*

add • calculate • total • tally • work sth out • figure sth out | *AmE* **figure** | *BrE, infml* **tot sth up** | *fml* **compute**

► count/add/total/tally/tot up
► count/add up/calculate/total up/tally/tot up/work out/figure out/ figure/tot up/compute **how much/how many …**
► count/add/calculate/tally/work out/figure out/figure/tot up/ compute the **number of** sth
► count/add up/calculate/total/ tally/tot up sb's **points/score**

country *noun*

1 [C] ■ *I like travelling to different countries.*

nation • state • power • superpower | *lit.* **land**

► a foreign country/nation/state/ power/land
► rule a country/nation/state/land
► govern a country/nation/state
● **COUNTRY, NATION OR STATE?** You can use all these words to refer to a country as a political unit or to its government. **Country** and **nation** can also refer to an area where people live, its economy, culture, etc. **Country** is the only word which can be used to refer to a country as a geographical area: *a newly independent nation/country/ state • a wealthy nation/country • a hot country*

2 [U] ■ *She lives in the country.* ■ *We came to an area of wooded country.*

courage

countryside • landscape • the land • scenery | *written* terrain | *tech.* topography

▶ the **surrounding** country/ countryside/landscape/land/ scenery/terrain
▶ **mountain/mountainous/wild/ rugged** country/countryside/ landscape/scenery/terrain
▶ **beautiful/glorious/stunning/ dramatic/magnificent/ spectacular** country/countryside/ landscape/scenery

3 the country [sing.] ■ *This issue has divided the country.*

the nation • population • the public • community • society

▶ the country/the nation/the population/the community/society **at large/as a whole**
▶ the **entire** country/nation/ population/community
▶ **shock** the country/nation/public/ community
● **THE COUNTRY OR THE NATION? The country** is used slightly more to talk about political issues; the **nation** is used slightly more when talking about cultural issues.

courage noun [U]

■ *He showed great courage in the face of danger.*

bravery • heroism • nerve • audacity • daring | *infml* guts | *lit.*, *BrE* valour | *AmE* valor

■ **OPP** cowardice
▶ **have** the courage/bravery/nerve/ audacity/guts **to do sth**
▶ **show** courage/bravery
▶ doing sth **takes** courage/bravery/ nerve/guts
▶ an **act** of courage/bravery/ heroism/valour
● **COURAGE OR BRAVERY? Courage** is often about facing opposition; **bravery** is more often about facing physical danger or pain: *They lack the moral courage to speak out.* • *He received the medal as an award for bravery.*

course noun [C]

■ *an evening course in Art and Design*

class • curriculum • syllabus | *BrE* programme | *esp. AmE* program

▶ **in** a/the course/class/curriculum/ syllabus/programme
▶ **on** a/the course/curriculum/ syllabus/programme
▶ **follow/teach/offer** a/the course/ curriculum/syllabus/programme
▶ **run/take/do/enrol on/sign up for** a course/class/programme

● **COURSE, CLASS OR PROGRAM?** In *AmE*, **course** is only used in formal language; in everday language use **class** or **classes**. In *BrE* you can use **course** in formal and informal language. A period of study that leads to an exam or qualification is a **course** in British and a **program** in *AmE*.

court noun [C, U]

■ *She will appear in court tomorrow.*

courtroom • court of appeal • appeal court • tribunal | *BrE* law court | *AmE* courthouse | *fml* court of law

▶ **in** a court/courtroom/tribunal/ law court/courthouse/court of law
▶ **take sb to/come before/set up/ apply to** a court/tribunal/court of appeal
▶ **go to/refer sth to/appear before/attend/tell/preside over** a court/tribunal
● **WHICH WORD? Court** is the most general of these words and is used to talk about both the building where a trial takes place and the process of holding, attending and judging legal cases. **Court of law** is more formal and refers more to the place than the process. A **courtroom** is the actual room where the trial takes place. **Law courts** (in *BrE*) and **courthouse** (in *AmE*) refer to the building or place where the courts are located.

courtyard noun [C]

■ *The windows look down into a small courtyard.*

court • quad • square • compound • cloister | *BrE* yard | *fml* quadrangle • precinct

▶ **in** the courtyard/court/quad/ square/compound/cloister/yard/ quadrangle/… precincts
▶ **across** the courtyard/court/quad/ square/compound/yard/ quadrangle
▶ the **central/main** courtyard/ square/yard/quadrangle

cover noun [C]

■ *The buggy had a plastic waterproof cover.*

wrapper • wrapping • sheath • casing • covering • wrap

▶ a **protective** cover/wrapper/ wrapping/sheath/casing/ covering
▶ a **plastic** cover/wrapper/ wrapping/sheath/casing/ covering/wrap
▶ **take off/remove** the cover/ wrapper/wrapping/covering/ wrap

cover verb

1 [T] ■ *She covered her face with her hands.*

hide • mask • disguise | *fml* **conceal**

▶ cover/hide/mask/disguise/conceal your **disappointment/surprise**
▶ cover/hide/conceal your **embarrassment**
▶ **completely/partly** cover/hide/disguise/mask/conceal sth

2 [T, often passive] ■ *The players were covered in mud.*

coat • cake • spread • rub • smear • daub

▶ cover/coat/cake/spread/rub/smear/daub sth **with** sth
▶ be covered/coated/smeared in/with **grease/oil**
▶ be covered/caked/smeared/daubed in/with **blood**
▶ be covered/coated/spread with **chocolate**

3 [T] ■ *The survey covers all aspects of the business.*

include • take sth in • contain • incorporate | *fml* **embrace • encompass**

▶ cover/contain/incorporate/embrace/encompass particular **aspects** of sth
▶ cover/contain/incorporate/embrace/encompass a (**wide**) **range** of things
▶ cover/include/contain/incorporate/embrace/encompass **the whole** of sth

coward noun [C]

■ *I'm a real coward when it comes to going to the dentist.*

infml **wimp • sissy • chicken • wuss**

■ OPP **hero**
▶ You're such a/Don't be a coward/wimp/sissy/chicken/wuss!
▶ You coward/wimp/sissy/chicken/wuss!

crack noun [C]

■ *Cracks began to appear in the wall.*

chink • crevice • cleft | *tech.* **fissure**

▶ a crack/chink/crevice/cleft/fissure **in** sth
▶ a **narrow** crack/chink/crevice/cleft/fissure
▶ a crack/fissure **opens**

crack verb [I, T]

■ *The ice cracked as I stepped on it.*

break • snap • fracture

▶ crack/break/fracture a **bone/rib**
▶ crack/fracture your **skull**
▶ crack/break a/an **cup/egg/mirror**
▶ a cracked/broken/fractured **pipe**
● **CRACK, BREAK OR FRACTURE?** Any of

these words can be used for bones; **break** or **fracture** can be used for joints; only **break** can be used for arms and legs. **Fracture** is the usual word used for skulls, though **crack** can also be used.

cramped adj. (disapprov.)

■ *It's difficult working in such cramped conditions.*

confined • tight | *approv.* **compact**

■ OPP **spacious**
▶ a cramped/confined/compact **place**
▶ a cramped/confined/tight **space**
▶ cramped/confined **conditions**

crash noun

1 [C] ■ *A man was killed in a crash involving a stolen car.*

collision • accident | *AmE* **wreck** | *esp. journ.* **pile-up**

▶ **in** a/an crash/collision/accident/wreck/pile-up
▶ a **major** crash/collision/accident/wreck/pile-up
▶ a **car/train** crash/accident/wreck
▶ a **plane** crash/accident/wreck

2 [C, usu. sing.] ■ *The tree fell with a great crash.*

bang • clang • thump • thud • crack

▶ a **loud** crash/bang/clang/thump/thud
▶ **hear** a crash/bang/clang/thump/thud/crack
▶ a crash/crack **of thunder**

crash verb

1 [I, T] ■ *He crashed the car into a wall.*

smash • slam • bang into sth • collide • wreck | *BrE* **write sth off • plough into sth** | *AmE* **plow into sth** | *AmE, infml* **total**

▶ crash/smash/slam/bang/plough **into** sth
▶ **two vehicles** crash/collide
▶ **two vehicles** crash/smash/slam/bang **into each other**
▶ crash/smash/wreck/write off/total a **car/truck/vehicle**
● **WHICH WORD?** When used to talk about vehicles **smash** and **slam** always take a prep., but **crash** and **collide** do not have to:
✔ *We're going to crash/collide!*
✗ *We're going to smash/slam!*

2 [I] ■ *Thunder crashed overhead.*

bang • explode • crack • clash

▶ a **door** crashes/bangs
▶ **thunder** crashes/explodes/cracks
▶ **cymbals** crash/clash

crazy adj.

1 (*esp. AmE, infml, usu. disapprov.*)
■ Are you *crazy*? We could get killed doing that.

stupid ◆ **idiotic** ◆ **reckless** | *esp. spoken* **silly** | *infml* **insane** | *esp. AmE, infml* **dumb** | *esp. BrE, infml* **mad** | *esp. written* **foolish**

▶ crazy/stupid/idiotic/reckless/silly/insane/dumb/mad/foolish **to do sth**
▶ crazy/stupid/idiotic/silly/insane/dumb/mad/foolish **of sb** to do sth
▶ a/an crazy/stupid/idiotic/reckless/silly/insane/dumb/mad/foolish **thing to do**
▶ **Are you** crazy/stupid/dumb/mad/insane?
● **WHICH WORD? Stupid, silly, foolish** and **dumb** describe people or their actions. **Crazy** usu. describes a person, but it can also be used to describe a deliberate and dangerous action. All these words are usu. disapproving and can be offensive.

2 (*esp. AmE, infml, sometimes offens.*)
■ The noise was driving her *crazy*.

sometimes offens. **mad** ◆ **out of your mind** ◆ **(not) in your right mind** | *infml* **nuts** | *esp. BrE, infml* **batty**

▶ be crazy/mad/out of your mind/not in your right mind/nuts **to do sth**
▶ go crazy/mad/nuts/batty
▶ drive sb crazy/mad/nuts/batty
● **WHICH WORD?** These are all rather informal words used to suggest that sb's behaviour is very strange, often because of extreme emotional pressure. They can be offensive if used to describe sb suffering from a real mental illness; use **mentally ill** instead.

create verb

1 [T] ■ There are lots of different myths about how the world was *created*. ■ We need to *create* more jobs for young people.

make ◆ **produce** ◆ **form** ◆ **build** ◆ **generate** ◆ **develop** ◆ **manufacture** | *esp. spoken* **do**

■ **OPP destroy**
▶ create/make/produce/form/build/generate/develop/manufacture sth **from/out of sth**
▶ create/make/produce/do a **drawing/painting**
▶ create/produce/generate **income/profits/wealth**
● **CREATE OR MAKE? Make** is a more general word, used esp. for

physical objects: make a table/dress/cake ◆ create jobs/wealth Use **create** to emphasize how unusual or original sth is: *a new dish, created by our chef*

2 [T] ■ The news *created* widespread confusion.

cause ◆ **produce** ◆ **stimulate** ◆ **arouse** ◆ **result in sth** ◆ **lead to sth** ◆ **bring sth about** ◆ **provoke** ◆ **prompt** | *fml* **give rise to sth**

▶ create/cause/produce/stimulate/arouse/result in/lead to/provoke/prompt/give rise to **speculation**
▶ create/cause/produce/result in/lead to/provoke/give rise to **problems**
▶ create/cause/arouse/lead to/provoke/give rise to **resentment**

creative adj.

■ She's very *creative*—she writes poetry and paints.

artistic ◆ **imaginative** ◆ **inventive** ◆ **original** ◆ **innovative** ◆ **ingenious**

▶ a/an creative/artistic/imaginative/inventive/original/innovative/ingenious **mind**
▶ a/an creative/imaginative/inventive/original/innovative/ingenious **idea/design/solution**
▶ creative/imaginative/original/innovative **thinking**
▶ creative/artistic **ability/achievement/skill/talent**

creature noun [C]

■ The dormouse is a shy *creature*.

animal ◆ **being** ◆ **thing** | *old-fash. or fml* **beast** | *fml or biology* **organism**

▶ a **living** creature/animal/being/thing/organism
▶ a **strange** creature/animal/being/beast
▶ a **mythical** creature/beast

credit noun

1 [U] ■ We offer two months' interest-free *credit*.

loan ◆ **overdraft**

▶ credit/a loan/an overdraft **from sb/an organization**
▶ a/an (low-interest/interest-free) credit/loan/overdraft
▶ obtain/arrange/apply for/refuse sb/deny sb credit/a loan
● **CREDIT OR LOAN? A loan** is an official agreement to borrow money and pay it back later; **credit** is a general term for any money that a bank makes available to a customer who does not have that amount in their account.

2 [U] ■ At least give him some *credit* for trying.

■ OPP **blame**

▶ **credit**/**praise**/**approval**/**acclaim**/a pat on the back **for** sth/doing sth
▶ **deserve** credit/praise/acclaim/a pat on the back
▶ **receive** credit/praise/approval/acclaim
▶ **give sb** credit/praise/approval/a pat on the back

● **CREDIT OR PRAISE? Praise** describes what you actually say, for example: *Well done! That's wonderful!* **Credit** refers to an opinion or feeling of admiration; it can also suggest a reward: *We should give credit to the organizers.* • *Credit is given in the exam for good spelling.*

crime *noun*

1 [U] ■ *This month's figures show an increase in violent crime.*

vice • delinquency | *fml* **wrongdoing • misconduct**

▶ **serious** crime/delinquency/wrongdoing/misconduct
▶ **sexual** crime/vice/misconduct
▶ **juvenile** crime/delinquency
▶ **cause**/**tackle**/**control**/**prevent** crime/delinquency

2 [C] ■ *Many crimes are never reported.*

sin • outrage • atrocity | *BrE* **offence** | *AmE* **offense** | *BrE, fml* **misdemeanour** | *AmE, law* **misdemeanor • felony** | *fml* **wrong**

▶ a/an crime/sin/outrage/atrocity/offence **against** sb/sth
▶ **commit** a/an crime/sin/outrage/atrocity/offence/misdemeanour/felony
▶ **forgive** a/an crime/sin/outrage/offence/misdemeanour/wrong

● **CRIME OR OFFENCE?** In everyday language **crime** is used more often than **offence** for more serious illegal acts, such as murder or rape. **Offence** is used more frequently for illegal activities such as driving too fast, carrying a gun or using drugs. However, in legal contexts, **offence** is the preferred technical term for all illegal acts.

criminal *noun* [C]

■ *I was treated like a common criminal.*

culprit • delinquent | *infml* **crook** | *fml* **offender • sinner** | *esp. AmE, law* **felon**

▶ a **convicted**/**habitual** criminal/offender/felon
▶ **catch** a criminal/the culprit/a crook/an offender
▶ **convict**/**sentence** a criminal/an offender
▶ **punish** criminals/the culprits/offenders/sinners/felons

● **CRIMINAL OR OFFENDER? Criminal** suggests that not only has sb committed a crime, but that they have a tendency to commit crimes. **Offender** simply means that sb has broken the law at least once. **Offender** is the word preferred by people whose job involves dealing with people who break the law.

crisis *noun* [C, U]

■ *help in times of crisis*

emergency • disaster • catastrophe • calamity • tragedy

▶ **in** a crisis/an emergency
▶ a **major**/**national** crisis/emergency/disaster/catastrophe/calamity/tragedy
▶ **deal with**/**cope with** a/an crisis/emergency/disaster

criterion *noun* [C]

■ *What are the criteria used in evaluating student performance?*

standard • measure • benchmark • yardstick • guide • guideline • gauge

▶ a criterion/measure/benchmark/yardstick **for** sth
▶ **by** any criteria/standard/measure/yardstick
▶ **provide** a criterion/standard/measure/benchmark/yardstick/guide

critical *adj.*

1 ■ *They issued a critical report on the government's handling of the crisis.*

disapproving • damning | *disapprov.* **judgemental**

■ OPP **uncritical**

▶ critical/disapproving **of** sb/sth
▶ critical/disapproving/damning/judgemental **comments**
▶ a critical/disapproving/judgemental **tone**/**attitude**

2 ■ *The decision is critical to our future.*

crucial • vital • essential • of the essence • decisive • important • significant • pivotal | *fml* **imperative**

▶ critical/crucial/vital/essential/of the essence/decisive/important/significant/imperative **for** sth
▶ critical/crucial/vital/essential/pivotal **to** sth
▶ **be** critical/crucial/vital/essential/important/significant/imperative **that…**
▶ a critical/crucial/vital/decisive/pivotal **moment**

● **CRITICAL OR CRUCIAL?** There is no real difference in meaning between these words. However, **critical** is often used to talk about technical matters; **crucial** is often used for emotional matters.

criticism noun

1 [U, C] ■ *There is widespread criticism of the airline's fees.*

disapproval • attack • assault • condemnation | *fml* censure • denunciation | *infml* flak | *AmE, infml* rap

▶ criticism/disapproval/
condemnation/censure/
denunciation of sth
▶ criticism/an attack/
condemnation/flak **from** sb/sth
▶ (a) **public** criticism/disapproval/
attack/condemnation/
denunciation
▶ **make** a/an criticism/attack/
assault/denunciation

2 [U] ■ *a book of art/literary/music criticism*

critique • review • assessment • evaluation • appraisal

▶ a/an **objective/careful** criticism/
assessment/evaluation/appraisal
▶ a/an **searching** criticism/critique/
assessment/appraisal
▶ **give** a/an critique/review/
assessment/appraisal

criticize (*BrE also* -**ise**) *verb* [T, I]
■ *The decision was criticized by environmental groups.*

attack • condemn • denounce • blame | *fml* censure • castigate • rebuke

■ **OPP** praise
▶ criticize/attack/condemn/
denounce/blame/censure/
castigate/rebuke sb/sth **for** sth
▶ criticize/attack/condemn/
denounce/blame/censure the
government/president
▶ criticize/attack/condemn/
denounce/censure a **decision**

cross *verb* [I, T]
■ *They crossed the mountains into France.*

cut across sth • cut through sth | *fml* negotiate

▶ cross/cut through the **hills/
mountains**
▶ cross/negotiate a **road/bridge**
▶ cross/cut across a **field**

cross sth out *phrasal verb*
■ *She crossed out 'Miss' and wrote 'Ms'.*

strike sth out • cross sb/sth off (sth) • cut • delete

▶ cross out/strike out/delete a **word**
▶ cross out/cut/delete a **sentence**

▶ cross out/strike out/cut/delete a
paragraph

crowd *noun* [C+sing./pl. v.]
■ *Crowds of people lined the streets.*

drove | *sometimes disapprov.* horde • crush • mob | *disapprov.* rabble | *written* throng

▶ crowds/droves/hordes/a crush/a
throng **of people**
▶ **push/fight/force your way
through** the crowd/hordes/
crush/mob/throng
▶ a crowd/mob/throng **gathers**

crowd *verb* [I, T]
■ *We all crowded into her office.*

herd • cluster • flock • huddle • pack • cram | *written* throng

▶ crowd/herd/cluster/flock/
huddle/be packed/be crammed/
throng **together**
▶ crowd/cluster/flock/huddle/
throng **round/around** somewhere
▶ **people** crowd/cluster/flock/
huddle/throng somewhere

crowded *adj.*
■ *We made our way through the crowded streets.*

busy • packed • crammed | *disapprov.* overcrowded • congested | *approv.* lively • bustling • vibrant

▶ crowded/busy/packed/
crammed/overcrowded/
congested/bustline **with** sb/sth
▶ a/an crowded/busy/packed/
overcrowded/congested/lively/
bustling/vibrant **city**
▶ crowded/busy/packed/
congested/lively/bustling **streets**

crucial *adj.*
■ *It is crucial that we get this right.*

critical • vital • essential • of the essence • decisive • important • significant • pivotal | *fml* imperative

▶ crucial/critical/vital/essential/of
the essence/decisive/important/
significant/imperative **for** sth
▶ crucial/critical/vital/essential/
pivotal **to** sth
▶ be crucial/critical/vital/essential/
important/significant/imperative
that…
▶ the crucial/critical/decisive/
pivotal **moment**
● **CRITICAL OR CRUCIAL?** There is no
real difference in meaning between
these words. However, **critical** is
often used to talk about technical
matters; **crucial** is often used for
emotional matters.

cruel *adj.*
■ *He was a cruel dictator.*

brutal • savage • barbaric • vicious • sadistic • inhuman • inhumane • ruthless • callous • cold-blooded

■ OPP **kind, humane**

► cruel/brutal/savage/barbaric/vicious/sadistic/inhuman/inhumane/ruthless/callous **treatment**
► a/an **cruel**/brutal/savage/barbaric/vicious/sadistic/inhuman/ruthless/callous/cold-blooded **act**
► cruel/brutal/sadistic **torture**
► a brutal/savage/vicious/ruthless/cold-blooded **attack**

● **CRUEL OR BRUTAL? Brutal** is usu. used to talk about murders or physical attacks. **Cruel** can also describe acts which cause mental pain. **Cruel** can vary in strength: it can mean 'deliberately causing extreme pain' or it can just mean 'rather unkind'; **brutal** is always much stronger than 'unkind'.

cruise noun [C]

■ *They are going on a Mediterranean cruise.*

sail • crossing | esp. written voyage • passage

► a cruise/sail/crossing/voyage/passage **from/to** sth
► **take** a cruise/sail/crossing/voyage/passage
► **go for** a cruise/sail

crumple verb [T, I]

■ *He wore a crumpled linen suit.*

rumple • crease • scrunch • crush • ruffle

► crumple/scrunch/ruffle sth **up**
► a bed/sheets/bedclothes **is/are** crumpled/rumpled
► **fabric**/material crumples/creases

cry verb

1 [I] ■ *The child fell over and started to cry.*

be in tears • sob • whimper • whine | fml or lit. weep | disapprov. snivel

► cry/be in tears/whimper/whine/snivel **about** sth
► cry/sob/whimper/weep **with** an emotion
► cry/sob/weep **a little**/silently/bitterly/loudly/uncontrollably/hysterically

● **CRY OR BE IN TEARS? Be in tears** is slightly more formal than **cry**, and is often used to talk about adults crying.

2 [I, T] (written) ■ *She ran to the window and cried for help.*

shout • yell • scream • cry out • call • wail • shriek • howl

► cry/shout/yell/cry out/call **to** sb

► cry/shout/yell/scream/call **for** help
► shout/yell/scream/cry out/call/wail/shriek/howl **in** pain/anguish/rage, etc.

cultural adj. [usu. before noun]

■ *Teachers need to be aware of cultural differences.*

ethnic • racial • national • folk

► a cultural/ethnic/racial/national **group**
► sb's cultural/ethnic/racial/national **identity**/origin
► cultural/national/folk **traditions**
► cultural/ethnic/racial **differences**/factors/background/diversity/minorities

culture noun [U, C]

■ *These ideas are central to Western culture.*

society • civilization • world • community • race

► European/American/African, etc. culture/society/civilization
► (the) **Arab**/Islamic culture/society/world/community
► a/an/the **ancient**/modern/contemporary culture/society/world/civilization
► a **primitive** culture/society/community/race

cupboard noun [C]

■ *The kitchen has built-in cupboards.*

cabinet • unit • wardrobe • locker • pantry | esp. BrE larder | esp. AmE closet

► a kitchen/wall/storage cupboard/cabinet/unit/closet
► a bathroom cupboard/cabinet/closet
► a walk-in cupboard/wardrobe/pantry/larder/closet

cure noun [C]

■ *The only real cure is rest.*

remedy • antidote • medicine • treatment • therapy

► a/an cure/remedy/antidote/medicine/treatment/therapy **for** sth
► a herbal cure/remedy/medicine
► **find** a/an cure/remedy/antidote

cure verb [T]

■ *The doctors couldn't cure him.*

heal • resuscitate • rehabilitate | esp. spoken make sb better

► cure sb/heal sb/rehabilitate sb/make sb better **by** doing sth
► cure/heal sb **of** sth

curious adj.

1 ■ *I was curious as to why Ben was leaving.*

intrigued • inquisitive | *infml, disapprov.* nosy/nosey

► curious/inquisitive **about** sth
► curious/intrigued **as to** sth
► curious/intrigued **to do** sth

2 ■ *There was a curious mixture of people at the party.*

strange • odd • bizarre | *BrE or fml* peculiar | *esp. spoken* funny • weird

► curious/strange/odd/bizarre/peculiar/funny/weird **that...**
► curious/strange/odd/peculiar/funny/weird **how/what...**
► a/an curious/strange/odd/bizarre/peculiar/funny/weird **feeling**
► curious/strange/odd/bizarre/peculiar **behaviour**

curl verb [I, T]

■ *The paper started to curl up in the heat.*

roll • coil • wind • twist

► curl/roll/coil sth **into** a ball
► curl/roll/coil **up**
► curl/coil/wind sth/twist sth **around/round** sb/sth

current noun [C]

■ *ocean/air currents*

flow • circulation | *fml* passage

► **against/with** the current/flow
► a current/the flow/the circulation/the passage of **air/water**
► a current/the flow/the passage of **electricity**
► the flow/circulation of **blood**

current adj. [only before noun]

■ *You will need a reference from your current employer.*

present • latest • recent • contemporary • modern • new

■ OPP former, previous, ex-, then
► current/present/recent/contemporary **events**
► the current/present/latest/contemporary **situation**
► current/present/the latest/recent/contemporary **trends**
● **CURRENT OR PRESENT?** Current is used esp. in financial contexts; present is used more often with lengths of time: *current spending/expenditure • the present day/century/moment*

curse verb [I, T]

■ *He cursed under his breath.*

swear • abuse • blaspheme | *infml* damn

► curse/swear loudly/quietly/softly/silently/under your breath
● **CURSE OR SWEAR?** You can curse a person or a thing but swear never takes an object in this meaning. Swear is much more frequent in everyday spoken English.

curtain noun [C]

■ *It was ten in the morning but the curtains were still drawn.*

blind • hanging | *esp. AmE* drape • screen | *AmE* drapery • shade

► **draw/close/open** the curtains/blinds/drapes/shades
► **pull back/pull** the curtains/drapes/draperies

curve noun [C]

■ *The pattern was made up of straight lines and curves.*

arc • loop • crescent • arch • semicircle | *tech.* parabola • curvature

► (a/an) **downward/upward/slight/graceful** curve/arc/curvature
► **form** a/an curve/arc/loop/arch/semicircle
► **draw** a/an curve/arc/semicircle/parabola

curve verb [I, T]

■ *The road curved around the bay.*

bend • turn • wind • twist • snake | *written* snake | *tech.* arc

► curve/bend/wind/twist/snake **around/round** sth
► curve/bend/turn **(to the) left/right/south/north,** etc.
► the road/path curves/bends/turns/winds/twists/snakes

curved adj.

■ *A ball follows a curved path as it travels through the air.*

round • rounded • convex • concave • domed • arched | *architecture* vaulted

■ OPP straight
► a curved/rounded/convex/concave **surface**
► a/an curved/domed/arched/vaulted **ceiling/roof**
► a curved/convex/concave **mirror/lens**

custom noun [C, U]

■ *It is the custom here to put flowers on the graves at Easter.*

convention • tradition • practice

► **by** custom/convention/tradition
► a custom/convention/tradition **that...**

▶ a **local/British** custom/tradition/practice

customer noun [C]

■ He's one of our best customers.

client • shopper • consumer • buyer • end-user • regular | fml **patron • purchaser** | BrE, infml **punter** ▸

▶ **have/deal with/get/lose** a customer/client/buyer
▶ **attract** customers/clients/shoppers/consumers/buyers/punters
▶ customers/clients/shoppers/consumers/buyers/purchasers **buy/spend** sth

cut noun

1 [C] ■ Blood poured from the cut on his arm.

gash • graze • scratch • wound ▸

▶ **cuts/a gash/a wound to** a part of the body
▶ a **deep** cut/gash/scratch/wound
▶ **clean** a cut/wound

2 [C] ■ They had to take a 20% cut in pay.

reduction • cutback ▸

■ OPP **increase, rise, raise**
▶ a cut/reduction/cutback **in** sth
▶ **big/huge/large/significant/ major/massive** cuts/reductions/cutbacks
▶ **make** cuts/reductions/cutbacks
● **CUT OR REDUCTION?** Reduction can be used for things that become less or smaller by themselves, or things that are reduced deliberately by sb. A **cut** is always made by sb. A **cut** is usu. a negative thing and happens at one point in time; a **reduction** can be gradual:
✔job/salary/pay cuts • a gradual reduction in output ✗ ~~a gradual cut in output~~

cut verb

1 [T] ■ She cut her finger on a piece of glass.

slash • slit • nick • split • gash ▸

▶ cut/slash/slit **sb's throat/your wrists**
▶ cut/split **your head/lip**
▶ cut/nick **yourself**

2 [T] ■ He cut two slices of bread.

chop • slice • carve • dice ▸

▶ cut/chop/slice/carve **into** sth
▶ cut/chop/slice **sth off** sth
▶ cut/chop/slice/carve/dice **meat**
▶ cut/slice **bread/cake**
▶ chop/slice **an onion**

3 [T] ■ She had her hair cut really short.

trim • snip • clip • crop • shear • shave • lop • mow ▸

▶ cut/trim/snip/clip/shear/shave/ lop sth **off**
▶ cut/trim/snip/clip/crop/shear/ shave **hair**
▶ cut/trim/clip a **hedge**
▶ cut/clip **your/sb's nails**
▶ cut/mow **the grass/lawn**

4 [T] ■ His party promises to cut taxes.

cut sth back/cut back on sth • cut sth down/cut down on sth • reduce • lower • bring sth down | esp. AmE or busin. **scale sth back** | busin. **downsize** | infml, journ. **slash** | BrE **axe** | AmE **ax** ▸

■ OPP **increase.**
▶ cut sth/cut sth back/cut sth down/reduce sth/lower sth/bring sth down/downsize sth **from** €50 000 **to** €40 000
▶ cut sth back/cut sth down/reduce sth/lower sth **by** half, 50, etc.
▶ cut/cut back on sth/cut down on sth/reduce/lower/scale back/slash **spending/production**
● **CUT, CUT STH BACK, CUT STH DOWN OR SCALE STH BACK? Cut** is the most general of these words. **Cut back** and **scale sth back** are both used esp. to talk about money or business. **Cut sth down** is more general and not used to talk about things other than business.

cut sb/sth off phrasal verb

1 ■ The army was cut off from its base.

isolate • separate ▸

▶ cut off/isolate/separate sb/sth **from** sb/sth else
▶ cut **yourself** off/isolate **yourself**
▶ a **community** is cut off/isolated

2 ■ Their escape route was cut off by the rising tide.

block • bar • block sth off ▸

▶ cut off/block/bar **sb's retreat**
▶ cut off/block **sb's escape**

cycle noun [C]

■ This cycle of events continually repeats itself.

pattern • rhythm ▸

▶ a/an **regular/irregular** cycle/ pattern/rhythm
▶ a **natural** cycle/rhythm
▶ **break** a cycle/pattern/rhythm
▶ the cycle/rhythm of the **seasons**
● **CYCLE, PATTERN OR RHYTHM? Pattern** is used esp. to talk about people's work and behaviour; **cycle** is used esp. to talk about events in the natural world; **rhythm** is used esp.

to talk about how people's bodies
adapt to changing conditions.

Dd

dad noun [C] (infml, esp. spoken)
■ Do you live with your mum and dad?

father • stepfather • parent | infml,
esp. spoken **daddy**

▸ a good/bad/caring/loving/
devoted/proud dad/father/
parent
▸ take after/inherit sth from your
dad/father/parents/daddy
▸ become a/sb's dad/father/
stepfather/parent
● **DAD OR FATHER?** In spoken English
dad is much more frequent. It can
sound formal to say *my father*.

daily adj. [only before noun]
■ The equipment is used on a daily
basis.

everyday • day-to-day | disapprov.
routine • mundane

▸ daily/everyday/day-to-day/
routine/mundane existence/
work/tasks/activities
▸ daily/everyday/day-to-day/
routine business/use/problems
▸ (a) daily/everyday/day-to-day/
mundane life

damage noun [U]
■ The earthquake caused damage to
hundreds of properties.

harm | fml **detriment**

▸ damage/harm/detriment to sth
▸ great/serious/severe/lasting/
long-term/environmental
damage/harm/detriment
▸ cause/do/inflict/suffer/escape/
prevent harm
● **DAMAGE OR HARM?** Use **damage** to
talk about the effect of fire, floods,
etc. on buildings and other objects:
storm/flood/fire/smoke/bomb/
structural damage
Use **damage** to talk about the
physical state of unhealthy organs
in the body: liver/kidney/lung/brain
damage
Use **damage** or **harm** to talk about
mental or emotional suffering:
emotional/psychological/social
damage/harm

damage verb [T]
■ Smoking seriously damages your
health.

hurt • harm • compromise | fml
impair

▸ damage/hurt/harm/
compromise/impair sb's chances
▸ damage/hurt/harm/compromise
sb's reputation
▸ damage/hurt/harm/sb's interests/
image
▸ damage/harm/compromise/
impair sb's health
● **HARM OR DAMAGE? Harm** is used
esp. to talk about bad effects on
the environment or sb's health;
damage can also be used in this
way, but is used most frequently
about bad effects on objects:
✔The car was badly damaged in the
crash. ✗ The car was badly harmed
in the crash.

damp adj. (sometimes disapprov.)
■ The cottage was cold and damp.

wet | often approv. **moist** | usu.
disapprov. **soggy**

▸ damp/wet/moist with sth
▸ damp/wet/moist/soggy ground
▸ damp/wet/moist earth/soil

dance noun [C]
■ We hold a dance every year to raise
money for charity.

disco • ball • party • rave • function
| infml, esp. spoken **bash**

▸ a charity dance/ball/function/
bash
▸ have/hold/go to/attend a
dance/disco/ball/party/rave/
function/bash
▸ dance/disco/party/rave music

danger noun
1 [U, C] ■ animals in danger of
extinction

risk • threat

▸ OPP safety
▸ the danger/risk/threat of sth
happening
▸ pose a danger/risk/threat
▸ put sth in danger/at risk/under
threat

2 [C] ■ Police said the man was a
danger to the public.

threat • risk • hazard • menace

▸ a danger/threat/risk/hazard/
menace to sb/sth
▸ pose a danger/threat/risk/
hazard/menace
▸ a danger/threat/risk/hazard to
health
▸ a danger/threat/risk to the public
▸ a danger/threat/menace to
society
● **WHICH WORD?** A **danger** is the
possibility of physical or moral
harm and can come from a person
or a thing; a **risk** or **hazard** is the
threat of physical harm from a
thing but not a person. A **threat** is
usu. a probability, not just a

possibility, and is most often used in the phrase *a threat to sth*.

dangerous *adj.*

■ *Flu can be a dangerous illness.*

risky • high-risk • unsafe • hazardous | *fml* **perilous**

■ OPP **safe, harmless**
▶ dangerous/hazardous/perilous **to sb/sth**
▶ dangerous/risky/unsafe/hazardous/perilous **for sb (to do sth)**
▶ dangerous/risky/unsafe/hazardous/perilous **to do sth**
▶ a dangerous/risky/unsafe/hazardous/perilous **business/situation**
▶ a dangerous/high-risk/hazardous **occupation/operation**

dare *verb*

1 [I] (not usu. used in the progressive tenses) ■ *He didn't dare (to) say what he thought.*

risk • hazard • go so/as far as to… | *usu. approv.* **pluck up (the/your) courage • presume |** *infml* **chance • stick your neck out |** *fml* **venture**

▶ dare/go so far as/pluck up (the/your) courage/presume/venture **to do sth**
▶ risk/chance **(doing) sth**

2 [T] ■ *The older boys dared him to steal the sweets.*

challenge • throw down the gauntlet

▶ dare/challenge sb **to do sth**

dark *adj.*

1 ■ *It was getting very dark outside.*

black • shady • shadowy • unlit

■ OPP **light**
▶ a dark/black **night**
▶ a dark/shady/shadowy **place/corner**
▶ a/an dark/shadowy/unlit **room**
▶ a dark/an unlit **road**

2 ■ *I prefer darker colours for a bedroom.*

deep • rich • warm

■ OPP **light, pale**
▶ a dark/deep/rich/warm **colour/tone/shade**
▶ dark/deep/rich/warm **red/orange**
▶ dark/deep/rich/warm **blue/green/purple**

darkness *noun* [U]

■ *After a few minutes our eyes got used to the darkness.*

the dark • blackness • shadows | *lit.* **gloom**

■ OPP **light**

▶ in/into/out of/through (the) darkness/dark/blackness/shadows/gloom
▶ peer into (the) darkness/dark/blackness/shadows/gloom
▶ your eyes adjust to/become accustomed to the darkness/dark/gloom

darling *noun* [C] (*esp. BrE*)

■ *I love you so much, darling.*

love • dear | *infml* **sweetheart • sweetie |** *esp. AmE, infml* **honey |** *slang* **babe |** *esp. AmE, slang* **baby |** *esp. written* **loved one |** *old use or lit.* **beloved**

▶ thank you/hello/yes, etc. darling/love/dear/sweetheart/sweetie/honey/babe/baby
▶ my darling/love/dear/sweetheart/baby/beloved

data *noun* [U]

■ *This computer holds data on all customer accounts.*

information • figures • details • facts • material • intelligence • statistics | *infml* **info • stats |** *fml* **particulars**

▶ data/information/figures/material/intelligence/statistics/info **on sb/sth**
▶ hard data/information/figures/facts/intelligence
▶ have/provide data/information/figures/details/facts/material/intelligence/statistics/info/stats/particulars
▶ collect/gather data/information/figures/details/facts/material/intelligence/statistics/info/statistics

date *noun*

1 [sing., U] ■ *The details can be discussed at a later date.*

time • occasion • point • moment

▶ on that date/occasion
▶ from/until that date/time/point/moment

2 [C] ■ *I've got a date with Lucy tomorrow night.*

meeting • appointment • engagement

▶ a/an date/meeting/appointment/engagement **with sb**
▶ have a/an date/meeting/appointment/engagement
▶ make/keep a/an date/appointment/engagement

daughter *noun* [C]

■ *She gave birth to a daughter.*

girl • child • baby | *infml* kid | *fml*
offspring

■ OPP son
▸ a **young** daughter/girl/child/
baby/kid
▸ a **teenage** daughter/girl/child/kid
▸ **have/give birth to/bring up/**
raise a daughter/girl/child/baby/
kid

dawn noun [U, C]

■ The plane arrived in Sydney at dawn.

sunrise • first light • daybreak • first
thing

■ OPP dusk
▸ **at/before/since/by/until/till**
dawn/sunrise/first light/daybreak

day noun [U, C]

1 ■ Owls sleep by day and hunt by
night.

daytime • morning • afternoon

■ OPP night, night-time
▸ **in/during** the day/daytime/
morning/afternoon
▸ **all/every/each** day/morning/
afternoon
▸ **spend** the day/morning/
afternoon **doing** sth
● DAY OR DAYTIME? Day can either
mean a particular completed
period, or a period of time that is
continuing; daytime never refers
to a particular completed period:
✓during the day/daytime • Did you
have a good day? ✗ Did you have a
good daytime?
Daytime is used esp. in
compounds:
✓daytime television/temperatures
✗ a day television/temperatures

2 [C, usu. pl.] ■ a history of Europe
from 1492 to the present day

period • time • age • century • era |
fml epoch

▸ **in/during …** day(s)/a period/the
time of…/…times/the… century/
the age of…/an era/an epoch
▸ **(the) present** day/period/time/
century/era/epoch
▸ **(the) medieval/Victorian/post-**
war, etc. days/period/time/era
● WHICH WORD? Era, age and epoch
are used more often to mean a
period in history. Day and time are
often used, esp. in the plural, to
talk about the present: these days •
modern times
When day or time is used after a
person's name, it is often used
in history: The battle happened
in King Alfred's day.

dead adj.

■ There was a dead cat lying in the
road.

fml late • deceased | *written* lifeless •
at peace

■ OPP alive, living, live
▸ a dead/late/deceased wife/
husband/mother/father/
brother/sister/relative
▸ a/sb's dead/lifeless **body**
▸ **lie** dead/lifeless/in peace

deal noun [C]

■ The unions are willing to do a deal
over pay.

agreement • bargain • pact •
settlement • arrangement •
understanding

▸ a/an deal/agreement/pact/
settlement/arrangement/
understanding **on** sth
▸ **under** a/an deal/agreement/
pact/arrangement
▸ **reach** a/an deal/agreement/
settlement/arrangement/
understanding
▸ **make/sign** a/an deal/agreement/
pact

dealer noun [C]

■ an antiques dealer

trader • supplier • merchant •
distributor • wholesaler • seller •
retailer • vendor • shopkeeper

▸ **buy/sell** sth **through** a dealer/
distributor/wholesaler
▸ a **local** dealer/trader/supplier/
merchant/distributor/wholesaler/
retailer/vendor/shopkeeper
▸ an **international** dealer/merchant/
supplier/merchant/distributor/
wholesaler

deal in sth phrasal verb

■ The company deals in computer
software.

trade • sell • export • import •
handle • deal • stock • carry | *busin.*
retail | *old-fash.* or *disapprov.* peddle
• hawk

▸ deal/trade **in** sth
▸ deal in/trade/sell/export/import/
handle/stock/retail **goods**
▸ deal in/trade/sell **shares/futures/**
stocks/bonds/securities
▸ deal in/sell/import/deal **drugs**
● DEAL IN STH OR TRADE IN STH? Trade
in sth is often used to talk about
buying and selling raw materials
such as *animals, coal* and *sugar*, as
well as textiles; deal in sth is used
about manufactured products such
as *cars* and *antiques*. Deal in sth
also often refers to criminal buying
and selling; typical collocates are
drugs, guns and *stolen goods*.

deal with sb/sth phrasal verb

1 ■ *The government refused to deal with 'terrorists'.*

negotiate ■ **hold talks** ■ **bargain** ■ **do a deal** ■ **haggle**

▶ deal ■ negotiate/hold talks/ bargain/do a deal/haggle with sb/sth
▶ deal with sb/hold talks/bargain/ do a deal/haggle **over** sth

2 ■ *She dealt with the problem easily.*

handle ■ **take care of sth** ■ **look after sth** ■ **see to sth** ■ **contend with sb/ sth**

▶ deal with/handle/take care of/ look after/see to **the matter**
▶ deal with/handle/take care of/ look after/contend with a **problem**
▶ deal with/handle/take care of/ look after/a/the **correspondence/ paperwork/customers**
● DEAL WITH STH or HANDLE? Handle often suggests control and calmness: *Leave it to Terri—she can handle it.*
Deal with sth is usu. used to discuss *ways, methods* and *means* of **dealing with** problems.

3 ■ *Her poems often deal with the subject of death.*

be about sth ■ **concern** ■ **be concerned with** ■ **have/be to do with sth** ■ **treat** ■ **relate to sb/sth** ■ **refer to sb/sth**

▶ a **chapter/poem** deals with/is about/is concerned with/refers to sth
▶ a **book/film** deals with/is about/is concerned with sth
● DEAL WITH STH, BE ABOUT STH OR CONCERN? Be about sth is the most general of these expressions; concern and deal with sth both suggest a formal, serious or thorough discussion of a subject.

dear adj. (written or becoming old-fash.)

■ *He's one of my dearest friends.*

much loved ■ **precious** ■ **prized** ■ **cherished** ■ **treasured** | *infml* **darling** | *fml* **beloved**

▶ dear/precious **to** sb
▶ a/sb's **dear/much loved/darling/ beloved daughter/son**
▶ a much **loved/prized/cherished/ treasured possession**
▶ **dear/darling Jack/Grace**, etc.

debate noun

1 [C] ■ *After a long debate, Congress approved the proposal.*

discussion ■ **conversation** ■ **dialogue** ■ **talk** ■ **consultation** ■ **exchange**

▶ a/an **debate/discussion/ conversation/dialogue/talk/ consultation/exchange about** sth
▶ a/an **debate/discussion/ conversation/dialogue/talk/ consultation/exchange with** sb
▶ a/an **debate/discussion/ conversation/dialogue/talk/ consultation/exchange between** two people/groups
▶ **have** a/an **debate/discussion/ conversation/dialogue/talk/ consultation/exchange**

2 [C, U] (*usu. approv.*) ■ *There has been much debate in the media about the war.*

argument ■ **dispute** ■ **controversy** ■ **disagreement** | *usu. disapprov.* **conflict**

▶ (a/an) **debate/argument/dispute/ controversy/disagreement/ conflict about/over/between** sb/ sth
▶ a **bitter debate/argument/ dispute/controversy/disagreement/ conflict**
▶ **resolve** a/an **debate/argument/ dispute/controversy/disagreement/ conflict**

debate verb [T, I]

■ *Politicians will be debating the issue next week.*

discuss ■ **talk** ■ **speak** ■ **consult** | *fml* **confer**

▶ **debate/talk/discuss** sth/**speak/ consult/confer with** sb
▶ **talk/speak to** sb/**consult** sb/**confer about** sth
▶ **debate/discuss what/how/ whether/when/who...**

debt noun [C, U]

■ *He had debts of thousands of dollars.*

loss | *finance* **arrears** ■ **liability** ■ **debit**

■ OPP **credit**
▶ **in debt/arrears/debit**
▶ **mortgage/tax/outstanding debts/arrears/liabilities**
▶ **fall/get into/pay off debts/ arrears**
▶ **have debts/liabilities**

decide verb [I, T]

■ *They have decided to take legal action.*

choose ■ **make up your mind/make your mind up** ■ **opt** ■ **select** | *infml* **pick** | *fml* **determine** ■ **elect** ■ **resolve**

▶ **decide/determine/resolve on** sth
▶ **decide/choose/select/pick between** A and/or B
▶ **decide/choose/make up your**

mind / opt / determine / elect /
resolve **to do sth**
▶ decide / determine / resolve **that...**
▶ decide / choose / **make up your
mind whether / what / how...**

declare verb [T]

■ *The president declared a state of
emergency.*

announce • state • say | *fml*
proclaim • pronounce | *esp. journ.*
indicate

▶ declare / announce / state / say /
proclaim / indicate sth **to** sb
▶ declare / announce / state / say /
proclaim / indicate **that...**
▶ declare / announce / state / proclaim
sb / sth **to be** sth
▶ declare / announce / state /
proclaim / pronounce sth **formally /
officially**
● **DECLARE OR ANNOUNCE?** Declare is
used more often for giving
judgments; **announce** is used more
often for giving facts:
✔*The painting was declared to be a
forgery.* ✗ *The painting was
announced to be a forgery.*
✔*They haven't formally announced
their engagement yet.* ✗ *They
haven't formally declared their
engagement yet.*

decline noun [C, usu. sing., U]

■ *the country's continuing economic
decline*

fall • drop • decrease • downturn •
slump • reduction

■ **OPP** rise, increase
▶ a decline / fall / drop / decrease /
downturn / slump / reduction **in** sth
▶ a **20%** decline / fall / drop /
decrease / reduction
▶ a decline / fall / drop / decrease /
reduction **of 20%**
▶ **see** a decline / fall / drop /
downturn / reduction
● **DECLINE, FALL OR DROP?** These
words all describe a process that
happens, not a deliberate action by
sb: *We've seen a steady decline in
profits this year.* **Fall** and **decline**
can happen over time, but a **drop**
cannot:
✔*a gradual decline / fall* ✗ *a gradual
drop*

decline verb

1 [I] ■ *Factory output declined by 15%
last year.*

fall • drop • come down • diminish |
fml decrease | *esp. busin.* sink •
slump • plunge • plummet • tumble

■ **OPP** rise, increase
▶ decline / fall / drop / come down /
diminish / decrease / sink / slump /

plunge / plummet / tumble **by** 100,
25%, a half, etc.
▶ decline / fall / drop / come down /
diminish / decrease / sink / slump /
plunge / plummet / tumble **from**
1 500 **to** 1 000
▶ decline / diminish / decrease **with**
age, time, experience, etc.
▶ prices decline / fall / drop / come
down / decrease / sink / slump /
plunge / plummet / tumble
▶ decline / fall / drop / decrease /
slump / plunge **dramatically**
● **DECLINE, FALL OR DROP?** All these
words can be used about numbers,
levels, prices, profits and sales. Use
decline to talk about a loss of
economic strength in an area:
✔*The city / industry has declined (in
importance).*
A person's health or people's
support for sth **declines**. Voices
and temperatures also **fall** or **drop**.
Things can **fall** or **decline** over a
period of time, but **drop** cannot be
used in the progressive tenses:
✔*Sales have been falling / declining.*
✗ *Sales have been dropping.*

2 [I] (*fml*) ■ *Her health is gradually
declining.*

weaken • fail • worsen • deteriorate
• degenerate • relapse | *esp. spoken*
get worse | *esp. busin.* slip

■ **OPP** improve
▶ sb's **health** declines / fails / worsens /
deteriorates / gets worse
▶ **sales** decline / weaken / deteriorate /
slip
▶ decline / weaken / worsen /
deteriorate **significantly / steadily**

3 [T, I] (*fml*) ■ *We politely declined her
invitation.*

refuse • reject • turn sb / sth down |
fml, often disapprov. rebuff

■ **OPP** accept
▶ decline / refuse / reject / turn down /
rebuff a / an **offer / request**
▶ decline / refuse / reject / turn down
a / an **chance / opportunity /
invitation**
▶ **politely** decline / refuse / reject sth

decorate verb [T]

■ *The cake was decorated with
chocolate buttons.*

garnish • edge • trim • hang • deck •
illustrate | *fml* adorn • ornament | *lit.*
festoon

▶ decorate / garnish / edge / trim /
hang / deck / illustrate / adorn /
ornament / festoon sth **with** sth
▶ decorate / deck / festoon sth **in** sth
▶ **richly** decorated / adorned /
ornamented

decoration noun

1 [C] ■ *Christmas decorations*

ornament • tinsel | *BrE* bauble | written trinket | *sometimes disapprov.* knick-knack

▶ a **little** decoration/ornament/ trinket/knick-knack
▶ a **glass** decoration/ornament/ bauble
▶ (a) **Christmas** decoration/ ornament/tinsel/bauble

2 [C, U] ■ *the elaborate decoration on the carved wooden door*

design • pattern • motif • frills • garnish | *fml* ornament

▶ a decoration/design/pattern/ motif **on** sth
▶ **without** decoration/frills
▶ **little/no** decoration/ornament

---

decorative *adj.*

■ *The mirror is functional yet decorative.*

fancy • ornamental

■ OPP functional, plain
▶ a/an decorative/fancy/ ornamental **design**
▶ **highly/purely/merely** decorative/ ornamental

● **DECORATIVE OR ORNAMENTAL?** Both these words can describe sth that is only used as a decoration rather than for practical purposes, but **decorative** is also used to describe anything that is highly decorated. **Ornamental** is used esp. to describe parts of a building or garden: *an ornamental garden/ fountain/lake/pond/pool/plant/tree/ shrub*

---

decrease *noun* [C, U]

■ *There has been a decrease of 6% in visitor numbers.*

reduction • fall • drop • decline • downturn • slump • cut • cutback

■ OPP increase
▶ a decrease/reduction/fall/drop/ decline/downturn/slump/cut/ cutback **in** sth
▶ a **20%** decrease/reduction/fall/ drop/decline/cut
▶ a decrease/reduction/fall/drop/ decline/cut/cutback **of 20%**
▶ **see** a decrease/reduction/fall/ drop/decline/downturn
● **WHICH WORD? Decrease** looks like the most direct opposite of **increase**, but it is not nearly as frequent. For deliberate reductions use **reduction** or **cut**. For reductions that happen, **fall** or **drop** are often preferred, esp. in business situations.

---

decrease *verb*

1 [I] (*fml*) ■ *The number of students has decreased this year.*

fall • drop • decline • come down • diminish | *esp. busin.* sink • slump • plunge • plummet • tumble

■ OPP increase
▶ decrease/fall/drop/decline/come down/diminish/sink/slump/ plunge/plummet/tumble **by** 100, 25%, a half, etc.
▶ decrease/fall/drop/decline/come down/diminish/sink/slump/ plunge/plummet/tumble **from** 1 500 **to** 1 000
▶ decrease/decline/diminish **with** age, time, experience, etc.
▶ **prices** decrease/fall/drop/ decline/come down/sink/slump/ plunge/plummet/tumble
▶ decrease/fall/drop/decline/ slump/plunge **dramatically**

2 [T] (*fml*) ■ *People should decrease the amount of sugar in their diets.*

reduce • cut • lower • bring sth down • cut sth back/cut back sth • cut sth down/cut down on sth • minimize • turn sth down | *esp. AmE* or busin. scale sth back | *journ.* slash

■ OPP increase
▶ decrease/reduce/cut/lower/bring down/cut back/cut down/scale back sth **from** 100 **to** 75
▶ decrease/reduce/cut/lower/bring down/cut back/cut down/scale back sth **by** half, 50, etc.
▶ decrease/reduce/cut/lower/bring down/minimize the **risk/rate** of sth
● **DECREASE OR REDUCE? Decrease** is more formal and less frequent than its opposite, **increase**; it is used esp. in the contexts of health and medicine. The more usual opposite of **increase** is **reduce**.

---

deep *adj.*

1 ■ *his deep warm voice*

low | *approv.* rich | *fml, approv.* sonorous | *music* bass

■ OPP high
▶ a deep/low/rich/sonorous/bass **voice**
▶ a deep/low/rich/bass **sound**
▶ a deep/low **groan/roar/rumble**
● **DEEP OR LOW?** A **low** voice or sound is one that is near the bottom of the musical scale and is quiet. A **deep** voice or sound is near the bottom of the musical scale and can be loud or quiet.

2 ■ *the old woman's deep brown eyes*

dark • rich • warm

■ OPP pale
▶ a deep/dark/rich/warm **colour/ tone/shade**
▶ (a) deep/dark/rich/warm **red/ orange**

► (a) deep / dark / rich **blue** / **green** / **purple**

3 ■ *None of the insights in the book was particularly deep.*

serious • profound

► (a) deep / serious / profound **question** / **issue** / **analysis**
► (a) deep / serious **conversation** / **discussion**
► (a) deep / profound **understanding** / **insight**
● **DEEP OR PROFOUND?** Profound is more formal than deep. Deep is sometimes used in a slightly humorous or ironic way to suggest that a comment or discussion may not be as serious and important as it seems.

4 ■ *a deep sense of loss*

real • genuine • sincere • heartfelt • from the heart

■ **OPP** superficial

► deep / real / genuine / sincere / heartfelt **sympathy** / **concern**
► deep / real / genuine / sincere **affection** / **respect** / **regret**
► a deep / real / genuine **sense** of sth

deep-seated adj.

■ *a deep-seated fear of failure*

deep-rooted • entrenched • ingrained

► deep-seated / deep-rooted / entrenched / ingrained **prejudices**
► deep-seated / deep-rooted / entrenched **problems**
► (a) deep-seated / deep-rooted **fear** / **hatred** (of sb / sth)
● **DEEP-SEATED OR DEEP-ROOTED?** These words both usu. describe negative feelings or beliefs that are held so deeply they are difficult to examine or change. Deep-rooted is slightly more positive and can be used about beliefs or practices that have existed for a long time: *a deep-rooted tradition*.

defeat verb [T]

■ *The Scots defeated the English at the Battle of Bannockburn.*

beat • get the better of sb | *esp. BrE, infml* **thrash** | *AmE, infml* **whip** | *written* **overcome • rout • trounce** | *fml* **best • prevail** | *lit.* **vanquish**

■ **OPP** lose to sb

► defeat / beat / thrash / whip / rout / trounce sb **by 10 points** / **4 goals**, etc.
► defeat / beat / get the better of / thrash / whip / overcome / rout / trounce / vanquish an **opponent**
► defeat / beat / overcome / rout / vanquish an **enemy**
● **DEFEAT OR BEAT ?** Defeat is more

often used to talk about winning against one opponent in a particular contest, vote or battle: *The government were defeated by 198 votes to 70.*
Beat is more often used to talk about winning against one or many opponents in a game, competition or race: *She won the 100 metres, beating a number of top European runners.*

defect noun [C]

■ *The drug is known to cause birth defects.*

fault • flaw • imperfection • bug • virus | *infml* **glitch**

► a/an defect / fault / flaw / imperfection / bug / virus / glitch **in sth**
► a **technical** / **mechanical** defect / fault / glitch
► a **computer** / **software** fault / bug / virus / glitch
► **have** a/an defect / fault / flaw / imperfection / bug / virus / glitch
► **identify** / **correct** a defect / fault / flaw
● **DEFECT OR FAULT?** A fault can only exist in sth that has been made by people. It can be permanent or temporary and can be present from the beginning or develop later. A defect can exist in sth that has been made by people or in a part of the body. It is present from the beginning or from birth and is not temporary, although it may be repaired or treated:
✔ *If a fault develops in the equipment…* ✗ *If a defect develops…*
✔ *a birth defect* ✗ *a birth fault*

defence (BrE) (AmE defense) noun [C, U]

■ *The body has natural defence mechanisms.*

protection • shield • safeguard • cover • screen • precaution • security • buffer

► (a) defence / protection / shield / safeguard / precaution / buffer **against sth**
► **as** (a) defence / protection / shield / cover / screen / precaution / buffer
► (an) **adequate** defence / protection / safeguard / precaution / security
► **provide** (a) defence / protection / shield / safeguard / cover / screen / precaution / security / buffer

defend verb [T, I]

1 ■ *He had to defend himself against a knife attack.*

protect • guard • shield • shelter • save • preserve • secure | *fml* **safeguard**

- OPP **attack**
▶ defend/protect/guard/shield/
shelter/save/preserve/secure/
safeguard sb/sth **from** sth
▶ defend/protect/guard/secure/
safeguard sb/sth **against** sth
▶ defend/protect/save **yourself**
▶ **heavily** defended/protected/
guarded

2 [T] ■ *She defended herself against
the criticisms.*

justify • explain • stand up for sb/
sth • account for sth | *infml* stick up
for sb/sth

- OPP **attack**
▶ defend/justify/explain/account
for sth **to** sb
▶ defend/justify/explain/stand up for/stick
up for/explain **yourself**
▶ defend/justify/explain/account
for a/your/sb's **decision/
behaviour**
▶ defend/stand up for/stick up for
sb's **rights**

define verb [T]

■ *The term 'mental illness' is difficult to
define.*

explain • interpret • spell sth out •
fml clarify • expound

▶ define/explain/spell out/clarify
how/what…
▶ define/explain/clarify the
position/role/nature/meaning of
sth
▶ **clearly** define/explain/spell out/
expound sth

definite adj.

1 ■ *I can't give you a definite answer.*

certain • sure • conclusive • bound •
guaranteed | *written* assured

▶ definite/certain/sure/conclusive
that…
▶ certain/sure/bound/guaranteed
to do sth
▶ **seem** definite/certain/sure/
conclusive/bound/assured to…/
guaranteed/assured

2 ■ *There was a definite feeling that
things were getting worse.*

distinct • clear • noticeable •
unmistakable • decided • obvious •
striking • sharp | *esp. written* marked
• pronounced

▶ a definite/distinct/clear/
noticeable/decided/obvious/
striking/sharp/marked/
pronounced **improvement**
▶ a definite/distinct/clear/
noticeable/obvious/striking/
sharp/marked/pronounced
difference
▶ a definite/distinct/clear/obvious/
unmistakable **sense of** sth
● DEFINITE, MARKED OR PRONOUNCED?
Definite is used most often to talk
about things that you can see or

feel; **marked** is used most often in a
business context; **pronounced** is
used most often to talk about
physical or personal characteristics:
a definite smell of gas • *a marked
effect on sales* • *a pronounced limp*

definition noun [C, U]

■ *What's your definition of happiness?*

interpretation • understanding •
reading

▶ a clear/precise/narrow/broad/
wide/conventional definition/
interpretation/understanding
▶ **different** definitions/
interpretations/understandings/
readings
▶ **give/provide** a/an definition/
interpretation
● WHICH WORD? **Definition** is used
most often to talk about an
explanation of the meaning of a
word, esp. in a dictionary.
Interpretation is used esp. to talk
about understanding what
happened or what sth means:
*interpretation of data/information/
results/the law/dreams*
Understanding is used esp. to talk
about understanding how sth
works or what problems are
involved: *an understanding of a
process/a relationship/an issue*
Reading is used esp. to talk about
understanding a written text: *my
reading of the text/poem/novel*

defraud verb [T, I]

■ *They defrauded the company of
$900 000.*

swindle • cheat • con | *infml* rip sb
off • fleece | *esp. AmE, infml* bilk |
slang screw

▶ defraud/swindle/cheat/con/
fleece/screw/bilk sb **out of** sth
▶ defraud/swindle/cheat/rip off/
fleece/bilk **customers**
▶ defraud/swindle/cheat/fleece/
bilk **investors**
▶ cheat/rip off/fleece **tourists**

degree noun [C]

■ *To what degree was he responsible?*

extent • level • scale • size | *fml*
magnitude

▶ **to what** degree/extent
▶ **to a greater/lesser** degree/extent
▶ **assess/judge/realize** the degree/
extent/level/scale/size/
magnitude of sth

delay verb

1 [T] ■ *He delayed telling her the news
until the next day.*

▶ deliberate / conscious / wilful
neglect

postpone ◆ put sth off ◆ reschedule
◆ suspend ◆ shelve | *fml* defer ◆
adjourn

■ OPP advance, hasten
▶ delay / postpone / put off / suspend /
shelve / defer / adjourn sth **for** a few
days / the time being, etc.
▶ delay / postpone / put off / defer
adjourn sth **until** sth
▶ delay / postpone / put off / defer
doing sth
▶ delay / postpone / reschedule /
adjourn a **meeting**
▶ delay / postpone / put off / defer a
decision

2 [I] ■ *Don't delay—call us today!*

stall ◆ drag your feet ◆ take your
time ◆ dawdle ◆ buy time | *fml*
procrastinate

■ OPP hurry
▶ stall / take your time / dawdle **over**
sth

3 [T] ■ *Bad weather delayed the flight.*

hold sb/sth up ◆ block ◆ hinder ◆
hold sb/sth back ◆ stall ◆ be/get
bogged down ◆ set sb/sth back ◆
stunt ◆ *esp. spoken* keep | *fml* detain ◆
retard ◆ inhibit

■ OPP accidental
▶ be delayed / held up / blocked /
stalled / set back **by / for hours /
days**, etc.
▶ delay / block / hinder / hold back /
stunt / retard / inhibit the
development / growth of sth
▶ delay / hold up (a) **flight / traffic /
work**

delete verb [T]

■ *She deleted all her emails.*

erase ◆ cut ◆ wipe ◆ cross sth out ◆
strike sth out ◆ cross sb/sth off (sth)
| *BrE* rub sth out

■ OPP add, insert
▶ delete / erase / cut / wipe sth **from**
sth
▶ delete / erase / cut / cross out / strike
out / rub out a **word**
▶ delete / erase / wipe a **file** (on a
computer)

deliberate adj.

■ *Her speech was a deliberate attempt
to embarrass the government.*

intentional ◆ calculated ◆ conscious
| *often disapprov.* premeditated | *esp.
BrE, fml, disapprov. or law* wilful | *AmE*
willful

■ OPP accidental
▶ a/an deliberate / intentional /
calculated / conscious /
premeditated **act**
▶ deliberate / calculated / conscious
attempts / manipulation

delicate adj.

■ *a delicate china cup* ■ *the delicate
ecological balance of the rainforest*

fragile ◆ brittle

▶ delicate / fragile / brittle **bones /
glass**
▶ (a) delicate / fragile **china / thread**
▶ the delicate / fragile **ecology**
● **DELICATE OR FRAGILE?** Delicate
fabrics, like silk, need special care:
Use a cool wash for delicate fabrics.
Fragile fabrics need even more
care, usu. because they are very
old.

delicious adj.

■ *Who cooked this? It's delicious.*

tasty ◆ mouth-watering ◆
appetizing | *spoken* yummy

▶ delicious / tasty / appetizing /
yummy **food**
▶ delicious / tasty / mouth-watering
dishes
▶ a delicious / tasty **meal / lunch**
▶ look delicious / tasty / appetizing /
mouth-watering / yummy

delight noun [U]

■ *Alex squealed with delight when he
saw the monkeys.*

joy ◆ ecstasy ◆ bliss | *esp. written*
euphoria

■ OPP dismay, horror
▶ sb's delight / joy / euphoria **at** sth
▶ sheer / pure delight / joy / ecstasy /
bliss
▶ feel / be filled with delight / joy /
ecstasy
● **DELIGHT, JOY OR BLISS?** Delight and
joy are livelier feelings than bliss:
you can *dance / jump / sing / weep* for
joy or *scream / squeal / whoop* with
delight. Bliss is more peaceful:
married / wedded / domestic bliss

delight verb [T, I]

■ *This news will delight his fans.*

please ◆ charm ◆ fascinate | *esp.
written* captivate ◆ entrance ◆
enchant ◆ bewitch | *BrE* enthral |
AmE enthrall

■ OPP dismay, disgust
▶ be delighted / pleased / charmed /
fascinated / captivated / enthralled /
enchanted / bewitched **by** sb/sth

delighted adj.

■ *I'm absolutely delighted by your
news.*

overjoyed ◆ thrilled ◆ glad ◆ happy ◆
pleased

■ OPP disappointed, horrified

- ▶ delighted/overjoyed/thrilled/
  glad/happy/pleased **about** sth
- ▶ delighted/overjoyed/thrilled/
  pleased **at/with/by** sth
- ▶ delighted/overjoyed/thrilled/
  glad/happy/pleased **that...**
- ▶ delighted/overjoyed/thrilled/
  glad/happy/pleased **to see/hear/
  find/know...**
- ● **DELIGHTED, OVERJOYED OR THRILLED?**
  Overjoyed or *thrilled* may express
  a stronger feeling than *delighted*,
  but *delighted* can be made
  stronger with *absolutely*, *more than*
  or *only* too. *Overjoyed* can be made
  negative and ironic
  with *not exactly* or *less than*: *He's
  less than thrilled at the prospect of
  moving house.*

deliver verb [T, I]

■ *10 000 leaflets have been delivered
to households in the area.*

take • bring • ship • carry •
transport • fly • ferry • leave

■ OPP **collect**
- ▶ deliver/take/bring/ship/carry/
  transport/fly/ferry sb/sth **to/from
  sb/sth**
- ▶ deliver/take/bring/carry/
  transport/ferry sb/sth **by car/rail/
  truck, etc.**
- ▶ deliver/take/bring/transport sb/
  sth **by air/sea/land**

delivery noun [U, C]

■ *Buy online and get free delivery.*

shipment • shipping • freight •
transit | *esp. BrE* transport | *esp. AmE*
transportation | *BrE* haulage | *fml*
handling | *busin.* distribution

■ OPP **collection**
- ▶ **for** delivery/shipment/shipping/
  freight/transport/transportation/
  haulage/distribution
- ▶ delivery/shipping/freight/transit/
  transport/transportation/
  haulage/handling/distribution
  costs
- ▶ a/the delivery/freight/handling
  charge
- ▶ a delivery/shipping/freight/
  transport/haulage/distribution
  company/business

demand noun

1 [C] ■ *a demand for higher pay*

request • call • claim • order
- ▶ a/an demand/request/call/claim/
  order **for** sth
- ▶ **on** demand/request/order
- ▶ a demand/request **that...**
- ▶ **make/withdraw** a/an demand/
  request/claim
- ▶ **refuse/reject** a/an demand/
  request/call/claim

2 demands [pl.] ■ *the demands of
children/work*

pressure • stress • strain | *esp. journ.*
heat
- ▶ demands/pressure/stress/heat **on**
  sb
- ▶ **social/economic/financial**
  demands/pressure/stress
- ▶ **cope with** the demands/pressure/
  stress/strain

3 [U, sing.] *(esp. busin.)* ■ *an
increased demand for organic food*

(no) call for sth | *busin.* market • a
run on sth
- ▶ demand/(no) call/a market **for** sth
- ▶ (a) **potential/growing/buoyant/
  steady/changing/falling**
  demand/market
- ▶ (the) **consumer/domestic/local/
  export/foreign/worldwide**
  demand/market
- ▶ **create** a demand/market
- ▶ **stimulate/boost/increase**
  demand/the market
- ● **DEMAND OR MARKET?** *Market* is a
  more specialist business term.
  People talk about the *housing/
  labour market* but they talk about
  demand for housing/labour. When a
  business has trouble producing
  enough goods because so many
  people want them, people talk
  about **demand** rather than the
  market:
  ✔*We're struggling to meet the
  demand.* ✗ *We're struggling to meet
  the market.*

demand verb

1 [T] ■ *She demanded an explanation.*

ask • expect • insist • call for sth •
claim • press (sb) for sth • hold out
for sth | *fml* require • request • exact
| *BrE* clamour | *AmE* clamor
- ▶ demand/ask/expect/call for/
  claim/require/request/exact sth
  from sb
- ▶ demand/ask/expect/require/
  request **of** sb
- ▶ demand/ask/expect/insist/
  require/request **that...**
- ▶ demand/ask/expect **a lot/too
  much/a great deal**
- ● **DEMAND, ASK OR EXPECT?** *Ask* is not
  as strong as *demand* or *expect*,
  both of which can be more like a
  command.

2 [T, I] ■ *'What's your name?' he
demanded.*

ask | *fml* enquire/inquire
- ▶ demand/ask/enquire **of** sb
- ▶ ask/enquire **about/after** sb/sth
- ▶ demand/ask/enquire **what/who/
  how...**, etc.

demolish verb [T]

■ *The old factory has been demolished.*

knock sth down • pull sth down • raze • level • flatten | *sometimes disapprov.* bulldoze • tear sth down

- OPP **build, construct**
- demolish/knock down/pull down/level/flatten/tear down a **building/house**
- demolish/knock down/pull down/tear down a **factory/wall**
- raze/level/flatten/bulldoze an area
- ● WHICH WORD? **Demolish, knock sth down** and **pull sth down** are all neutral terms; **tear sth down** can suggest that unnecessary violence was used, or that the speaker has negative feelings about what was done.

demonstrate *verb* [T]

■ *The experiment demonstrated that our theory was right.*

show • prove • indicate • illustrate

- demonstrate/show/prove/indicate sth **to sb**
- demonstrate/show/prove/indicate/illustrate **that/what/how…**
- **figures/studies** demonstrate/show/prove/indicate/illustrate sth
- demonstrate/show/prove sth **conclusively/beyond doubt**
- ● DEMONSTRATE, INDICATE OR ILLUSTRATE? **Demonstrate** is the strongest of these words and **indicate** is the weakest. **Demonstrate** can take a person as subject; **indicate** and **illustrate** cannot:
  - ✓*Let me demonstrate to you some of the difficulties we face.* ✗ *Let me indicate/illustrate to you some of the difficulties we face.*

demonstration *noun* [C]

■ *We went on several peaceful demonstrations.*

protest • march | *BrE, infml* demo

- a demonstration/protest/march/demo **against** sth
- a/an **anti-war/pro-democracy/anti-government** demonstration/protest/march/demo
- **hold/organize/stage/go on/join/participate in/take part in** a demonstration/protest/march/demo
- ● DEMONSTRATION OR PROTEST? A **demonstration** can be for or against sb/sth; a **protest** is always against sb/sth. A **demonstration** is usu. about a more public, wider issue that may affect a whole country; a **protest** can be about a more private matter, for example by workers against their employers.

denial *noun* [C, U]

■ *The minister issued a denial of any official involvement.*

fml disclaimer • rebuttal • refutation • retraction

- OPP **claim**
- a denial/disclaimer/rebuttal/refutation/retraction **of** sth
- a **firm** denial/rebuttal/refutation
- **issue/publish** a denial/disclaimer/rebuttal/retraction

deny *verb* [T]

■ *He has denied the accusations.*

contradict | *fml* disclaim • repudiate | *esp. journ.* refute

- OPP **admit, confirm**
- deny/contradict/repudiate/refute a **report/suggestion**
- deny/repudiate/refute a **claim**
- deny/disclaim **knowledge/responsibility**
- **flatly** deny/contradict sth

department *noun* [C]

■ *I work in the sales department.*

division • branch • unit • arm

- an **administrative** department/division/branch/arm
- a **research** department/division/unit/arm
- the **finance/marketing** department/division/arm
- a **regional** department/division/branch/unit

departure *noun* [C, U]

■ *His sudden departure came as a shock.*

exit | *fml* going

- OPP **arrival**
- departure/exit **from** sth
- sb's **sudden/unexpected/abrupt** departure/exit
- **make** a departure/an exit

depend on/upon sb/sth
phrasal verb

1 ■ *Does the quality of teaching depend on class size?*

hang on sth | *esp. written* rest on sth | *esp. journ.* hinge on/upon sth

- It depends (on)/rests on/hinges on **what/how/who/where/whether…**
- **entirely/solely/largely/mainly/partly/ultimately** depend on/rest on sth
- It all depends on/hinges on sth.

2 ■ *He's the sort of person you can depend on.*

rely on/upon sb/sth • trust • count on sb/sth

- depend on/trust/rely on/count on sb **to do sth**

▶ depend on/rely on/count on **sb's support**
▶ trust/rely on **sb's judgement/advice**
● **DEPEND ON/UPON SB/STH, TRUST OR RELY ON/UPON SB/STH?** You can **trust** a person, but not a thing or a system:

✔ *The local transport system can't be depended on/relied on.* ✘ *The local transport system can't be trusted.*

Rely on is used esp. with *you can/could* or *you should* to give advice or a promise:

✔ *You can't really rely on his judgement.* ✘ *I don't really rely on his judgement.*

depress verb [T]

■ *It depresses me to see so many young girls smoking.*

demoralize • discourage • daunt • oppress | *fml* **sadden** | *infml* **get sb down**

■ OPP **cheer sb up**
▶ a thought **depresses/daunts/oppresses/saddens sb**

depressed adj.

■ *She felt depressed about the future.*

gloomy • demoralized • glum • unhappy • sad | *infml* **down** | *esp. written* **despondent • dejected**

■ OPP **cheerful**
▶ depressed/gloomy/glum/sad/unhappy/despondent **about sth**
▶ feel **depressed/gloomy/demoralized/sad/unhappy/down/despondent/dejected**
▶ get **depressed/gloomy/demoralized**

depressing adj.

■ *He found the whole visit a depressing experience.*

miserable • gloomy • bleak • dark • negative • pessimistic • black | *infml* **downbeat**

■ OPP **uplifting**
▶ depressing/gloomy/dark/negative/black **thoughts**
▶ a depressing/gloomy/negative/pessimistic **conclusion**
▶ paint a **depressing/gloomy/bleak/negative/pessimistic picture (of sth)**
● **DEPRESSING OR MISERABLE?** **Depressing** is used esp. to show feelings of sympathy for other people's problems or the bad state of the world; **miserable** usu. describes your unhappy feelings about your own situation: *The report on the state of water pollution paints a depressing picture.* • *My schooldays were thoroughly miserable.*

describe verb [T]

■ *They described seeing strange lights in the sky.* ■ *Can you describe him to me?*

report • tell • portray | *fml* **recount • relate • depict**

▶ describe/portray/depict **sb/sth as sth**
▶ describe/report/tell/recount/relate **what/how...**
▶ describe/report/portray/recount/relate/depict **events/a series of events**
▶ describe/report/recount/relate **your adventures**

description noun [C, U]

■ *Police issued a description of the missing boy.*

picture • portrait • profile • account • report • portrayal | *fml* **depiction** | *written* **evocation**

▶ an accurate **description/picture/portrait/profile/account/report/portrayal/depiction/evocation**
▶ a vivid **description/picture/account/portrayal/depiction/evocation**
▶ give a/an **description/picture/account/report**

descriptive adj.

■ *She read out some descriptive passages in the novel.*

explanatory | *fml* **illustrative • interpretative**

▶ for descriptive/explanatory/illustrative/interpretative **purposes**
▶ (a/an) descriptive/explanatory/interpretative **notes/statement/passage**
▶ descriptive/explanatory/illustrative **material**

desert verb

1 [T] ■ *She was deserted by her husband.*

abandon • leave • turn your back on sb/sth | *infml* **dump • walk out**

▶ desert/abandon/leave/dump/walk out on a **husband/wife**
▶ desert/abandon a **child**
▶ sb's boyfriend/girlfriend **deserts/dumps them**
● **DESERT OR ABANDON?** **Desert** is used more to talk about disloyal acts such as deserting friends without help; **abandon** is used more to talk about leaving people who are unable to support themselves.

2 [T, often passive] ■ *The villages had been deserted.*

abandon • evacuate | *fml* **vacate**

▶ desert/abandon/evacuate/vacate
  a building/house/home
▶ evacuate/vacate the office/
  premises
▶ abandon/evacuate/vacate sth
  immediately

deserted *adj.*
■ *He walked through the deserted
building.*

**abandoned ◆ disused ◆ unoccupied
◆ uninhabited**

▶ a/an deserted/abandoned/
  unoccupied/uninhabited **area**
▶ a/an deserted/abandoned/
  disused/unoccupied **building**
▶ a/an deserted/abandoned/
  unoccupied **house**

deserve *verb* [T]
■ *You deserve a rest after all that work.*

earn | *fml* **merit**

▶ deserve/earn a **rest/drink**
▶ deserve/merit a **mention**
▶ deserve/merit **attention/
  consideration/recognition**
● **DESERVE OR EARN?** Deserve can be
used to talk about either sth
pleasant sb should have for doing
good, or a punishment for sth bad;
earn is only used to talk about sth
good.

design *noun*
1 [U, C] ■ *It's a house built to a
traditional design.*

layout ◆ format ◆ arrangement | *fml
or tech.* **configuration**

▶ a design/layout/format/
  configuration **for** sth
▶ a/the **basic/simple/complex/
  traditional** design/layout/format/
  arrangement
▶ the **standard** design/layout/
  format/arrangement/
  configuration

2 [U, C] ■ *the design and development
of new products*

**creation ◆ development ◆ invention
◆ innovation**

▶ sb's **new/latest** design/creation/
  invention/innovation
▶ a **brilliant** design/invention/
  innovation
▶ **product** design/development

3 [C] ■ *The original designs were
stolen.*

plan ◆ draft ◆ blueprint

▶ a design/plan/blueprint **for** sth
▶ the **original/first/final** design/
  plan/draft/blueprint
▶ **draw up/produce** a design/plan/
  draft

4 [C] ■ *The tiles come in a range of
colours and designs.*

pattern ◆ motif ◆ decoration

▶ a design/pattern/motif/
  decoration **on** sth
▶ **in** a design/pattern
▶ **have/make** a design/pattern/
  motif
▶ **print/produce/weave** a design/
  pattern
● **DESIGN OR PATTERN?** A pattern is
regular and repeated, and is either
created deliberately or formed by
chance; a **design** is either repeated
or single, and is always created
deliberately.

design *verb*
1 [T] ■ *a badly designed kitchen*

engineer ◆ invent

▶ design/engineer/invent a **new
  kind of motor**
▶ design/invent a **new product**
▶ design/engineer a **new car/bridge**
● **DESIGN, ENGINEER OR INVENT?**
When you **invent** sth it is
completely new and nothing of
that kind has existed before. You
design or **engineer** a new version
of sth that already exists.

2 [T] ■ *design a new training course*

plan ◆ make ◆ formulate

▶ design/plan/make/formulate sth
  to do sth
▶ design/plan/formulate a **strategy**

3 [T, usu. passive] ■ *instruments
designed for use in cold conditions*

**be aimed at sth ◆ be intended for/
as/to be sth ◆ mean**

▶ be designed/intended/meant **for/
  as** sth
▶ be designed/intended/meant **to
  be/do** sth

designer *noun* [C]
■ *a fashion/graphic/industrial/theatre
designer*

**developer ◆ planner ◆ architect ◆
engineer ◆ inventor ◆ craftsman**

▶ a **chief/senior** designer/planner/
  architect/engineer
▶ a **leading** designer/developer/
  architect/engineer
▶ **train/work as** a designer/
  architect/engineer

desire *noun* [C, U] (*esp. written*)
■ *She felt an overwhelming desire to
return home.*

**need ◆ urge ◆ temptation ◆ impulse
◆ inclination ◆ want ◆ ambition** | *esp.
written* **wish ◆ compulsion** | *often
disapprov.* **whim**

▶ a/an desire/need/urge/
  inclination/wish **for** sth

- ▶ the desire/need/urge/temptation/impulse/inclination/ambition/wish **to do sth**
- ▶ **have** (a/an) desire/need/urge/temptation/impulse/inclination/wants/ambition/wish/compulsion
- ▶ **feel** a/an desire/need/urge/temptation/impulse/inclination/compulsion
- ● **DESIRE, WISH OR NEED?** These words all refer to sth you want. **Need** is the strongest and usu. refers to sth you feel you must have. When used with adjectives such as *deep, great, urgent*, etc. **desire** expresses a stronger feeling than **wish**.

desire verb [T] (not used in the progressive tenses) (*fml*)
■ *The house had everything you could desire.*

want • wish • like | *fml, esp. spoken* **would like sth** | *infml, esp. spoken* **feel like sth** | *BrE, infml, esp. spoken* **fancy**
- ▶ sb desires/wants/wishes/likes/would like to do sth
- ▶ sb **really** desires/wants/wishes/would like/feels like/fancies sth

despair noun [U]
■ *Driven to despair, he threw himself under a train.*

desperation • hopelessness | *written* **desolation**
- ■ **OPP** hope
- ▶ utter despair/desperation **at** sth
- ▶ **in** despair/desperation
- ▶ **utter** despair/desperation/hopelessness

despair verb [I]
■ *Don't despair! We'll think of a way out of this.*

give up hope • lose hope • lose heart
- ■ **OPP** hope
- ▶ despair/give up hope/lose hope of sth
- ▶ despair/give up hope **that...**
- ▶ **Don't** despair/give up hope.

desperate adj.

1 ■ *I felt desperate about my future.*

in despair • hopeless • suicidal | *written* **despairing**
- ■ **OPP** hopeful
- ▶ desperate/in despair/despairing **about** sth
- ▶ a desperate/despairing **cry/look**
- ▶ **feel** desperate/hopeless/suicidal

2 ■ *The villagers are in desperate need of clean water.*

extreme • severe • serious • acute | *fml* **grave** | *esp. BrE, fml* **dire**

- ▶ a/an desperate/extreme/severe/serious/acute/dire **shortage**
- ▶ a/an desperate/extreme/serious/acute/dire **need**
- ▶ desperate/extreme/severe/serious/acute/dire **poverty**
- ▶ a/an desperate/severe/serious/acute/grave **problem**

despicable adj. (*fml*)
■ *a despicable act*

cheap • worthless | *BrE* **dishonourable** | *AmE* **dishonorable** | *fml* **contemptible** | *written* **feckless**
- ■ **OPP** admirable
- ▶ despicable/dishonourable **of** sb
- ▶ despicable/dishonourable **conduct**
- ▶ a despicable/worthless/contemptible/feckless **man/woman**

destroy verb [T]
■ *a mission to destroy the enemy*

devastate • wipe sb/sth out • annihilate • eradicate • decimate • exterminate • stamp sth out | *infml* **zap** | *esp. written* **ravage**
- ■ **OPP** create
- ▶ destroy/devastate/wipe out/decimate/ravage a **village/town/city**
- ▶ destroy/wipe out/decimate/annihilate/exterminate/zap **the enemy**
- ▶ a/an **earthquake/flood/fire** destroys/devastates/ravages sth
- ● **DESTROY OR DEVASTATE?** Devastate is stronger than **destroy**, but is only used about places or buildings, not substances or objects. When used about people it has a different meaning.

detail noun [C]
■ *Tell me all the details.*

point • fact • circumstance • information • data | *infml* **info** | *fml* **particular**
- ▶ (a) detail/point/fact/information/data/info/particulars **about/relating** to sb/sth
- ▶ **precise** details/facts/circumstances/information/data/info
- ▶ **give (sb)/have** details/the facts/information/data/info/particulars

detailed adj.
■ *He gave detailed instructions on what to do in an emergency.*

minute • in-depth • comprehensive • thorough • exhaustive • careful • close • rigorous
- ▶ a/an detailed/minute/in-depth/comprehensive/thorough/

exhaustive / careful / close / rigorous
analysis / study / investigation
▶ a/an detailed / minute /
comprehensive / thorough /
exhaustive / careful / close / rigorous
examination of sth
▶ detailed / in-depth / thorough /
comprehensive / careful / rigorous
research

determination *noun* [U]

■ She fought the illness with courage
and determination.

persistence ◆ spirit ◆ perseverance ◆
purpose | *fml* resolve ◆ tenacity

▶ determination / resolve **to do sth**
▶ **sheer / dogged** determination /
persistence / perseverance
▶ **show (your)** determination /
persistence / spirit / resolve / tenacity

determine *verb*

1 [T] (*fml*) ■ *An inquiry was set up to
determine the cause of the accident.*

discover ◆ find ◆ establish ◆ identify
| *fml* ascertain

▶ determine / establish / identify /
ascertain **what / how / when /
where / why / whether...**
▶ determine / discover / find /
establish / identify / ascertain the
cause
▶ determine / discover / find /
establish / identify the **correlation**

2 [T, often passive] (*fml*) ■ *Female
employment was determined by
economic factors.*

decide ◆ dictate ◆ govern ◆ shape ◆
form | *often disapprov.* rule

▶ determine / decide / dictate /
govern / shape **how...**
▶ determine / decide / dictate / shape
the **outcome / result** (of sth)
▶ determine / dictate / shape the
course / direction / future (of sth)

determined *adj.*

1 [not before noun] ■ *I'm determined
to succeed.*

bent on sth ◆ insistent | *fml* resolved
◆ intent on / upon sth

▶ determined / insistent / resolved
that...
▶ determined / resolved **to do sth**

2 ■ *I made a determined effort to stop
smoking.*

persistent ◆ resolute | *usu. approv.*
dogged | *approv.* heroic | *sometimes
disapprov.* single-minded | *fml*
tenacious

▶ determined / persistent / resolute /
single-minded / tenacious **in sth**

▶ determined / persistent / resolute /
heroic **opposition** to sth
▶ a determined / persistent / heroic
struggle / effort / attempt
▶ dogged / heroic / single-minded
determination

develop *verb*

1 [I] ■ *It developed from a small fishing
village into a thriving resort.*

progress ◆ evolve ◆ advance ◆
mature ◆ move | *infml* come along /
on | *esp. journ.* shape up

▶ develop / evolve / mature **into** sth
▶ develop / progress / evolve /
advance / move **towards / beyond**
sth
▶ a/an **idea / style / theory** develops /
evolves

2 [T] ■ *The company develops and
markets new software.*

create ◆ build ◆ pioneer | *written, esp.
busin.* evolve

▶ develop / create / build / pioneer a
model / technology / new product
▶ develop / create / pioneer / evolve a
technique / method / policy / plan
▶ develop / pioneer / evolve an **idea**

3 [T, no passive] ■ *She developed lung
cancer at the age of forty.*

get ◆ have ◆ suffer from sth | *esp.
BrE, esp. spoken* have got | *fml*
contract

▶ develop / get / have / suffer from /
have got / contract a/an **disease /
illness**
▶ develop / get / have / suffer from /
have got / contract **cancer / AIDS**
▶ develop / get / have / suffer from /
have got **a condition / arthritis /
diarrhoea**
▶ develop / have / suffer from / have
got a/an **allergy / disorder**

4 ■ *A crisis was rapidly developing.*

break out ◆ erupt | *esp. journ.* blow
up

▶ (a) **crisis / row / storm / trouble**
develops / breaks out / erupts / blows
up
▶ a/an **argument / controversy /
dispute** develops / breaks out /
erupts
▶ (a) **fight / fighting / riot / violence**
breaks out / erupts

development *noun*

1 [U] ■ *opportunities for career
development*

progress ◆ advance ◆ rise ◆
promotion ◆ progression | *fml*
advancement

▶ development / progress / advance /
advancement **in** sth
▶ **scientific / technical /
technological / economic /**

political/social development/
progress/advances/advancement
► **achieve** development/progress/
advances/promotion/progression
► **chart/halt** the development/
progress/rise/progression of sth

2 [U, C] ■ *the design and development
of new products*

design • innovation • creation •
invention

► product development/design/
innovation
► the development/design **process**

device noun

1 [C] ■ *labour-saving devices in the
home*

gadget • tool • instrument • aid | *fml*
implement • utensil

► a **useful** device/gadget/tool/aid
► an **electrical/electronic** device/
gadget
► a **measuring/navigation/**
navigational device/tool/
instrument

2 [C] ■ *Direct mailing can be
successful as a marketing device.*

tactic • *BrE* manoeuvre | *AmE*
maneuver | *often disapprov.* ploy •
ruse

► a **device/tactic/ploy/ruse for**
(doing) sth
► a **clever** device/manoeuvre/ploy/
ruse
► **use** a device/tactic/manoeuvre/
ploy

devote verb [T]

■ *She devoted two hours a day to the
project.*

dedicate • commit • give sth over to
sth

► **devote/dedicate/commit/give**
over **to** sb/sth
► **devote/dedicate/commit/give**
over your **life/time** to sb/sth
► **devote/dedicate/commit** (your)
resources/funds to sth
● **DEVOTE OR DEDICATE?** Devote can
be used with a slightly larger range
of nouns, including *thoughts* and
attention:
✔He devoted all his attention to his
mother. ✗ He dedicated all his
attention to his mother.
The most frequent collocates of
dedicate are *yourself* and your *life*.

devoted adj.

■ *They are devoted to their children.*

loving • caring • adoring •
affectionate

■ OPP indifferent
► a/an devoted/loving/caring/
adoring/affectionate **mother/**

father/parent/husband/wife/
family
► a/an devoted/loving/caring/
affectionate **friend**
► a/an devoted/loving/affectionate
son/daughter/brother/sister

diagram noun [C]

■ *a diagram of an electrical circuit*

chart • illustration • drawing •
picture • graph | *written* figure

► **in** a/an diagram/chart/
illustration/drawing/picture/
graph/figure
► **on** a diagram/chart/graph
► a chart/diagram/illustration/
drawing/picture/graph/figure
shows sth

diary noun

1 [C] (*BrE*) ■ *I'll check the date in my
diary.*

calendar • schedule | *BrE* timetable

► be/put sth **in** your/the diary/
calendar/schedule/timetable
► a **busy/full/packed** diary/
calendar/schedule/timetable
► **look at /check/consult** your/the
diary/calendar/schedule/
timetable

2 [C] ■ *She wrote her thoughts in her
diary each night.*

journal • blog • log • record

► a **daily** diary/journal/blog/log/
record
► **keep** a diary/journal/blog/log/
record
► **read** sb's diary/journal/blog
● **DIARY OR JOURNAL?** A **diary** is often
more personal than a **journal** and
not usu. intended for anyone else
to read. **Journal** often refers to
records of personal experience that
have become historical
documents.

dictate to sb phrasal verb

■ *She refused to be dictated to by
anyone.*

push sb around/about • order sb
around/about • lay down the law •
bully | *written* tyrannize

► sb **will not** be dictated to/pushed
around/bullied/tyrannized (by sb)
► **allow yourself** to be dictated to/
pushed around/bullied
► sb **thinks they can** push/order sb
around
● **DICTATE TO SB, PUSH SB AROUND OR
ORDER SB AROUND?** These
expressions all mean to tell sb what
to do, because you believe you are
more important or powerful than
they are. Sb who **pushes sb
around/about** may use threats or

dictator

violence. Sb who **orders sb around/about** may or may not be obeyed.

dictator *noun* [C]

■ *The country was ruled by a series of military dictators.*

tyrant • despot • autocrat

▶ a/an **cruel/brutal/evil/ruthless** dictator/tyrant/despot
▶ a **benevolent** dictator/despot
▶ a dictator/tyrant/despot **rules** a country

die *verb* [I]

■ *He died of cancer.*

pass away | *lit.* perish

■ **OPP live, survive**
▶ die/perish **of/from** sth
▶ die/perish **in** an accident, fire, etc.
▶ die/pass away **peacefully**
● **DIE OR PASS AWAY?** People say **pass away** to avoid saying 'die'.

differ *verb* [I]

■ *The two languages differ in this respect.*

vary • range | *fml* diverge

■ **OPP**
▶ differ/vary/range/diverge **in** size, shape, etc.
▶ differ/diverge **from** sth
▶ differ/vary/range **between** things/A and B

difference *noun* [C, U]

■ *There are significant differences between the two systems.*

contrast • variation • distinction | *fml* disparity • variance • divergence | *tech.* imbalance

■ **OPP similarity**
▶ a/an difference/contrast/variation/distinction/disparity/variance/divergence/imbalance **between** A and B
▶ a/an difference/contrast/variation/disparity/variance/divergence/imbalance **in** sth
▶ **show** a/an difference/contrast/distinction/disparity/variance/divergence/imbalance
▶ **see/be aware of/look at** a difference/contrast/variation/distinction

different *adj.*

■ *The room looks different without the furniture.*

unlike • unequal • contrasting • varied • mixed • diverse • assorted | *fml* disparate • dissimilar

■ **OPP the same, similar**
▶ different/dissimilar **from** sth

▶ different/contrasting/varied/diverse/disparate **ways**
▶ different/contrasting/mixed/diverse **/disparate views**
▶ **look** different/unlike sth/dissimilar

difficult *adj.*

1 ■ *The exam questions were too difficult for her.*

hard • demanding • taxing • testing | *approv.* challenging

■ **OPP easy, simple**
▶ difficult/hard/demanding/taxing/challenging **for** sb
▶ difficult/hard **to do/believe/see/tell/say** (sth)
▶ a difficult/hard/demanding/taxing/challenging **time/week/year**
▶ a difficult/hard/demanding/challenging **task/target**
● **DIFFICULT OR HARD? Hard** is slightly less formal than **difficult**. It is used esp. in the structure *hard to believe/say/find*, etc.

2 ■ *My boss was making life difficult for me.*

tough • hard • bad • rough • adverse | *fml* disadvantageous | *BrE, fml* unfavourable | *AmE, fml* unfavorable

■ **OPP easy**
▶ difficult/tough/hard/bad/disadvantageous/unfavourable **for** sb
▶ a/an difficult/tough/hard/bad/rough/unfavourable **situation**
▶ difficult/tough/hard/bad/rough/adverse/unfavourable **conditions**
▶ a/an difficult/tough/hard/bad/adverse/disadvantageous/unfavourable **position**

3 ■ *How do you deal with difficult customers?*

awkward • obstructive • uncooperative • perverse • unhelpful

▶ **be** difficult/awkward **about** sth
▶ a/an difficult/awkward/uncooperative **child**
▶ a/an difficult/awkward **customer**

difficulty *noun*

1 [C, usu. pl., U] ■ *We soon ran into difficulties with the project.*

problem • trouble • complication • issue | *usu. approv.* challenge | *esp. spoken* the matter

▶ (a/an/the) difficulty/problem/trouble/complication/issue/matter **with** sth
▶ **have** difficulties/problems/trouble/issues
▶ **cause/avoid** difficulties/problems/trouble/complications
● **DIFFICULTY OR PROBLEM?** To talk about one thing that is difficult to

deal with use **problem**; to talk about more than one thing use either word: *The problem first arose in 2008.* • *The project has been fraught with difficulties/problems from the start.*

2 [U] ■ *I had difficulty making myself heard.*

trouble | *BrE* **bother** • **job** | *infml* **hassle**

■ **OPP** ease
▶ difficulty/trouble/bother/hassle with sth
▶ have difficulty/trouble/a job
▶ cause (sb) difficulty/trouble/bother/hassle

dignity *noun* [U]

■ *He needed a way to retreat without loss of dignity.*

pride • **self-respect** • **self-esteem** • **feelings** | *sometimes disapprov.* **ego**

▶ personal dignity/pride/self-esteem/feelings
▶ damage sb's dignity/pride/self-respect/self-esteem/ego
▶ lose/keep sb's dignity/pride/self-respect

dim *adj.*

1 ■ *The light was too dim to read by.*

faint • **weak** • **soft** | *lit.* **thin**

■ **OPP** bright
▶ dim/faint/weak/soft/thin light
▶ a dim/faint/soft glow
▶ a dim/faint outline
● **DIM, FAINT OR WEAK?** Dim describes light in a room or place when it is not bright enough to see clearly; **faint** describes a particular point of light which is hard to see; **weak** usu. describes sunlight that is not bright.

2 ■ *They stepped into the dim and cluttered shop.*

gloomy • **dreary** • **dingy**

■ **OPP** bright
▶ a dim/gloomy/dreary/dingy room
▶ a dim/gloomy **corridor/interior/street**
▶ a dim/gloomy/dreary **place/day**

dinner *noun* [U, C]

■ *They invited us to dinner.*

lunch • **supper** • **meal** • **banquet** • **feast** | *BrE* **tea** | *fml* **luncheon**

▶ have/invite sb for/to dinner/lunch/supper/a meal/a banquet/a feast/tea/luncheon
▶ eat/serve dinner/lunch/supper/a meal/tea/luncheon
▶ get dinner/lunch/supper/tea/a meal
● **WHICH WORD?** A main or formal meal eaten in the evening is usu.

called **dinner**. **Lunch** is eaten in the middle of the day; in Britain some people call this **dinner** if it is the main meal of the day. **Tea** is usu. a light afternoon meal with a cup of tea, but it can also refer to an evening meal, esp. one for children. **Supper** is an informal evening meal or a light meal before bedtime.

direct *verb* [T]

1 ■ *The machine directs a beam of light on the area.*

aim • **point** • **focus**

▶ direct/aim/point sth **at** sb/sth
▶ direct/aim/focus (a) **light**

2 [T] ■ *She was appointed to direct a new campaign.*

manage • **run** • **be in charge** • **control** • **administer**

▶ direct/manage/run/be in charge of/control/administer a **project**
▶ direct/manage/be in charge of/control **operations**
▶ be centrally directed/managed/run/controlled/administered

direct *adj.*

■ *You'll have to get used to his direct manner.*

blunt • **forthright** • **outspoken** | *often approv.* **frank** • **open** • **honest** • **straight** • **straightforward** | *fml* **unequivocal**

■ **OPP** indirect
▶ direct/forthright/outspoken/frank/open/honest/straight/straightforward/unequivocal **about** sth
▶ direct/blunt/frank/open/honest/straight/straightforward **with** sb
▶ a/an direct/blunt/honest/straight/unequivocal **answer**
▶ a direct/blunt/forthright/frank **manner**

direction *noun*

1 [C, U] ■ *They had gone in the wrong direction.*

way • **route** • **path** • **course** | *tech.* **bearing**

▶ the **right/wrong** direction/way/route/path/course
▶ the **opposite/other** direction/way
▶ **take** a direction/way/route/path/course

2 [C, U] ■ *It's a new direction in party policy.*

course • **path** • **road** • **route**

▶ a **new/different** direction/course/path/road/route

director

▶ take a/the... direction/course/path/road/route

▶ change a/the direction/course

● **DIRECTION OR COURSE?** The **direction** of a person or thing usu. refers to the way they are likely to be developing now and are likely to be developing in the future; the **course** is the way that sb/sth developed in the past and up until now: *They are debating the future direction of the party.* • *Her career followed a similar course to her sister's.*

3 directions [pl.] ■ *Directions for use are printed on the box.*

instructions

▶ directions/instructions **for/on/as to** sth

▶ **clear/precise/detailed/step-by-step/careful** directions/instructions

▶ **give** sb/**follow** directions/instructions

director noun [C]

■ *She's on the board of directors.*

manager • *BrE* **managing director** • **governor** • *infml* **boss** • *esp. journ.* **chief**

▶ work **for** a director/manager/boss

▶ a **company** director/manager/managing director/boss/chief

▶ **become/make** sb a director/manager/governor

● **DIRECTOR OR MANAGER?** Both words can be used to talk about sb who is in charge of a department. However, in a large company, a **director** is often in charge of several **managers**.

dirt noun

1 [U] ■ *His clothes were covered in dirt.*

grime • **mud** • **dust** • **soot** • **pollution**

▶ be **covered in/with** dirt/grime/mud/dust/soot

▶ **wash** the dirt/grime/mud/dust **off/from** sth

▶ **clean/brush** the dirt/mud/dust **off/from** sth

2 [U] (*esp. AmE*) ■ *He picked up a handful of dry dirt.*

soil • **earth** • **dust** • **mud** • **clay** • **ground** • **land**

▶ **dry** dirt/soil/earth/dust/mud/clay/ground/land

▶ **wet/soft** dirt/soil/earth/mud/clay/ground

▶ **damp/moist** dirt/soil/earth/clay/ground

dirty adj.

■ *If your hands are dirty, go and wash them.*

grubby • **muddy** • **grimy** • **filthy** • **dusty** • **stained** • **unwashed** • **messy** • *fml* **soiled**

■ OPP **clean**

▶ dirty/grubby/muddy/filthy/dusty/stained/unwashed/soiled **clothes**

▶ dirty/grubby/grimy/filthy/dusty/unwashed **hands**

▶ **get** dirty/muddy/filthy/dusty/stained/messy

disability noun [C, U]

■ *A disability prevents him from working as a labourer.*

old-fash., sometimes offens. **handicap** | *tech.* **impairment**

▶ a **severe** disability/handicap/impairment

▶ a **permanent** disability/handicap/impairment

▶ **have/be born with/suffer from** a/an disability/handicap/impairment

disable verb [T]

■ *The gunfire could kill or disable the pilot.*

cripple • **immobilize** • **put sb/sth out of action** | *BrE* **paralyse** | *AmE* **paralyze** | *fml* **incapacitate**

▶ He was disabled/crippled/paralysed **in** a car accident.

▶ disabled/crippled/incapacitated **by** illness

▶ a disabling/crippling **accident/condition/illness/disease/injury**

disabled adj.

■ *The accident left him severely disabled.*

lame • *old-fash., sometimes offens.* **handicapped**

■ OPP **able-bodied**

▶ a disabled/handicapped **person/child**

▶ **leave** sb disabled/lame/handicapped

▶ **badly/profoundly/seriously/severely/permanently/mentally/physically** disabled/handicapped

● **DISABLED OR HANDICAPPED?** The word **handicapped** should be avoided. Instead of saying sb is *mentally handicapped* say that they are *learning difficulties/a learning disability.*

disadvantage noun [C, U]

■ *There are disadvantages to the plan.*

drawback • **downside** • **pitfall** | *infml* **snag** • **catch**

■ OPP **advantage**

► a/the disadvantage/drawback/
downside/snag **to** sth
► The disadvantage/drawback/
downside/snag **is that...**
► **overcome** a disadvantage/
drawback/pitfall/snag

disagree verb [I]

■ He disagreed with his parents on
most things.

differ • dispute • be at odds • not
see eye to eye with sb | *fml* take
issue with sb

■ OPP agree
► disagree/differ/dispute/be at
odds/not see eye to eye/take issue
with sb/sth
► disagree/differ/be at odds/not see
eye to eye/take issue **on** sth
► disagree/differ/be at odds/take
issue **over** sth

● DISAGREE OR DIFFER? Only people
can disagree; people or their
opinions can differ:
✓Medical opinion differs as to how
to treat the disease. ✗ ~~Medical
opinion disagrees as to how to treat
the disease.~~

disagreement noun [U, C]

■ There is disagreement among
scholars as to the age of the sculpture.

argument • dispute • difference •
quarrel • controversy | *usu. approv.*
debate | *fml* dissent • contention

■ OPP agreement
► (a/an) disagreement/argument/
dispute/differences/quarrel/
controversy/debate/contention
about/over/between sb/sth
► (a) political disagreement/
dispute/differences/debate/
dissent/contention
► resolve a disagreement/dispute/
sb's differences/controversy/
debate

disappear verb [I]

■ She watched as the train
disappeared from sight.

vanish • fade • melt • die out • clear
| *lit.* dissolve

■ OPP appear
► disappear/vanish/fade/melt/
dissolve **into** sth
► disappear/vanish/fade **from
view/sight**
► anger/hope disappears/vanishes/
fades/melts
► a tradition/custom disappears/
dies out
► cloud/smoke/mist disappears/
clears

disappoint verb [T, T]

■ I hate to disappoint you, but I'm not
interested.

fail | *disapprov.* let sb down | *infml,
disapprov.* leave sb in the lurch

■ OPP satisfy
► disappoint/fail/let down your
fans/children/family/
colleagues/friends
► be sorry to disappoint sb/let sb
down/leave sb in the lurch
► sb won't disappoint sb/fail sb/let
sb down/leave sb in the lurch

disappointed adj.

■ They were bitterly disappointed at
the result.

disillusioned • unhappy •
disenchanted • dissatisfied •
discontented

■ OPP pleased, satisfied
► disappointed/disillusioned/
unhappy/disenchanted/
dissatisfied/discontented **with** sb/
sth
► disappointed/disillusioned/
unhappy **about** sth
► feel disappointed/disillusioned/
unhappy/dissatisfied

disappointing adj.

■ They team gave a disappointing
performance.

discouraging • unsatisfactory | *fml*
wanting

■ OPP encouraging, satisfactory
► disappointing/discouraging/
unsatisfactory **that...**
► a/an disappointing/discouraging/
unsatisfactory **result/experience**
► find sth disappointing/
discouraging/unsatisfactory/
wanting

disappointment noun [C]

■ The new restaurant was a big
disappointment.

anticlimax • blow • failure | *infml*
let-down • flop • washout

► a disappointment/blow/failure/
let-down **for** sb
► a real disappointment/blow/
failure/let-down
► a big disappointment/failure/let-
down/flop
► something of a/an
disappointment/anticlimax/let-
down

disapproval noun [U]

■ He shook his head in disapproval.

criticism • condemnation | *fml*
censure

■ OPP approval
► disapproval/criticism/
condemnation/censure **of** sb/sth
► (a) strong disapproval/criticism/
condemnation

disapprove

▶ express disapproval / criticism / condemnation

disapprove verb [T]

■ Her parents disapproved of her choice of career.

object • **frown on/upon sth** | *fml* **deplore**

■ OPP approve
▶ disapprove of/object to/frown on/deplore a/an **practice/action**
▶ disapprove of/object to/frown on/deplore **the use of** sth
▶ disapprove of/object to/deplore **the way** sb does sth

disapproving adj.

■ She gave him a disapproving look.

critical • **damning** • **judgemental** | *esp. AmE*, disapprov. **judgmental**

■ OPP approving
▶ disapproving/critical of sb/sth
▶ disapproving/critical/damning/judgemental **comments**
▶ a disapproving/critical/judgemental **tone/attitude**

disaster noun

1 [C, U] ■ Thousands died in the disaster.

catastrophe • **tragedy** • **calamity** • **crisis** • **emergency**

▶ a major disaster/catastrophe/tragedy/calamity/crisis/emergency
▶ **cause** a disaster/catastrophe/tragedy/crisis
▶ **bring** disaster/catastrophe/tragedy/calamity
● DISASTER OR CATASTROPHE? Use either with words such as *nuclear*, *environmental* and *economic*; use **disaster** for a famous event in which people were killed: *the Chernobyl disaster*

2 [C, U] ■ The play's first night was a total disaster.

failure • **catastrophe** • **debacle** • **disappointment** | *infml* **fiasco** • **flop** • **washout** • **let-down**

■ OPP success
▶ a disaster/failure/catastrophe/disappointment/let-down for sb
▶ a **total** disaster/failure/catastrophe/fiasco/flop/washout
▶ **prove** a disaster/failure/catastrophe/fiasco/flop/let-down

disastrous adj.

■ The church was rebuilt after a disastrous fire.

devastating • **catastrophic**

▶ disastrous/devastating/catastrophic **for** sb/sth
▶ a disastrous/devastating/catastrophic **effect/impact/failure/defeat/fire/storm/flood**
▶ disastrous/devastating/catastrophic **consequences/results/events**

discipline noun [U]

■ Discipline at the school is strict.

order • **control** • **regulation** • **authority**

▶ **strict** discipline/order/control/regulation/authority
▶ **impose** discipline/order/control/regulation/authority
▶ **keep** discipline/order/control

disciplined adj.

■ a well-led and disciplined army

controlled • **restrained** • **moderate** • **sober**

■ OPP undisciplined
▶ a disciplined/moderate/controlled/restrained **approach**
▶ a disciplined/controlled/restrained **manner**
▶ **strictly** disciplined/controlled

discount verb [T, usu. passive]

(esp. busin.)

■ Stock has been discounted by up to 40%.

take sth off sth • **take** • **reduce** • **cut** • **mark sth down** • **subtract** • **deduct** | *infml* **knock sth off (sth)** • **slash**

■ OPP put sth up, increase, add
▶ take/subtract/deduct sth **from** sth
▶ discount/take/subtract/deduct/knock sth off **an amount**
▶ discount/take sth off/reduce/cut/mark down/knock sth off/slash **prices**

discourage verb

1 [T] ■ a campaign to discourage smoking among teenagers

deter • **dissuade** • **put sb off (sth)** • **talk sb out of sth** • **warn sb off (sth)**

■ OPP encourage
▶ discourage/deter/dissuade sb **from doing sth**
▶ **put sb off/talk sb out of/warn sb off doing sth**

2 [T, often passive] ■ Don't be discouraged by failure—try again!

daunt • **demoralize** • **depress** • **crush** | *infml* **get sb down**

■ OPP encourage

discover verb

1 [T] ■ He was discovered hiding in the shed. ■ Cook is credited with discovering Hawaii.

find • come across sb/sth • stumble on/across/upon sb/sth • catch • unearth

▶ discover/find/come across/catch sb **doing sth**
▶ discover/find/stumble upon a **body**
▶ discover/find/unearth the **remains** (of sth)
▶ discover/find/stumble upon sth **by accident**

2 [T] ■ *Scientists are working to discover a cure for AIDS.*

find • identify • establish | *fml* determine • ascertain

▶ discover/find/identify/establish/ determine/ascertain the **cause**
▶ discover/find/identify/establish a **connection**
▶ discover/find **the answer/a cure**

3 [T] ■ *It was a shock to discover that he couldn't swim.*

find • find out (sth) • hear • learn

▶ discover/find/find out/hear/learn **that…**
▶ discover/find/find out/hear/learn **how/what/why…**
▶ discover/find/find out/learn the **facts/truth/secret/details**

discredit verb [T]

■ *The photos were taken to discredit the President.*

slander • libel | *fml* defame • vilify • malign | *esp. journ.* smear

▶ be discredited/vilified/maligned **for/as sth**
▶ discredit/smear the **government**

discrimination noun [U]

■ *The policy forbids discrimination on the grounds of race, sex or sexuality.*

bias • apartheid • prejudice • intolerance • bigotry • racism • sexism • ageism | *BrE* favouritism | *AmE* favoritism | *usu. approv.* affirmative action

▶ discrimination/bias/prejudice/ intolerance/racism/favouritism **towards/toward** sb
▶ discrimination/bias/prejudice/ racism **against** sb/sth
▶ **blatant** discrimination/racism/ prejudice/racism/sexism
▶ **sexual** discrimination/bias/ prejudice/apartheid
▶ **racial/religious** discrimination/ bias/prejudice/intolerance

discuss verb

1 [T] ■ *Have you discussed the problem with anyone?*

talk • debate • speak • consult | *fml* confer

▶ discuss sth/talk/debate/speak/ consult/confer **with** sb
▶ discuss/debate **what/how/ whether/when/how…**
▶ discuss sth/talk/debate/speak **at length/openly**

2 [T] ■ *This topic will be discussed in the next chapter.*

examine • explore • study • survey | *BrE* analyse | *AmE* analyze | *esp. spoken* go into sth

▶ discuss/examine/explore/study/ survey/analyse/go into **what/ how/whether…**
▶ discuss/examine/explore/study/ survey/analyse the **situation/the evidence/sb's work**
▶ discuss/examine/explore/study/ analyse a/an **proposal/idea**
▶ discuss/examine/explore/study/ analyse/go into sth **in depth/in detail**

discussion noun

1 [C, U] ■ *Discussions between the two leaders took place yesterday.*

talk • conversation • consultation • debate • chat • dialogue | *AmE also* dialog | *written* exchange

▶ a/an discussion/talk/ conversation/consultation/ debate/chat/dialogue/exchange **about** sth
▶ a/an discussion/talk/ conversation/consultation/ debate/chat/dialogue/exchange **with** sb
▶ a/an discussion/conversation/ consultation/debate/dialogue/ exchange **between** two people/ groups
▶ be **involved in/join/participate in/take part in/engage in** (a) discussion/conversation/debate/ dialogue

2 [C, U] ■ *There will be further discussion of these issues in the next chapter.*

examination • analysis • study

▶ (a) **detailed** discussion/ examination/analysis/study

disease noun [C, U]

■ *He suffers from a rare blood disease.*

illness • sickness • infection • condition • ailment • complaint | *infml* bug • virus | *med.* disorder

▶ a **serious/chronic** disease/illness/ infection/condition/ailment/ disorder
▶ **have/suffer from** a/an disease/ illness/sickness/infection/ condition/ailment/complaint/ bug/virus/disorder
▶ **diagnose/treat** a/an disease/

illness/infection/condition/
ailment/virus/disorder
▶ **recover from** a/an disease/illness/
sickness/infection/bug/virus/
disorder
● **DISEASE OR ILLNESS?** Disease is used
to talk about more severe medical
problems, esp. those that
affect the organs:
✓heart/kidney/liver **disease** ✗ ~~heart/
kidney/liver illness~~
Illness is used to talk about most
kinds of medical problems,
including *mental illness*. Disease is
not used about a period of illness:
✓He died after a long illness. ✗ ~~He
died after a long disease.~~

disgrace noun

1 [U] ■ *Her behaviour brought
disgrace on her family.*

shame | *fml* **discredit** • **disrepute** |
BrE, fml **dishonour** | *AmE, fml*
dishonor

■ **OPP** honour/honor
▶ **in** disgrace/disrepute
▶ **bring** disgrace/shame/discredit/
dishonour **on** sb/sth
▶ There is **no** sense of disgrace/
shame/dishonour **in** sth.
● **WHICH WORD?** All these words are
used to talk about a public loss of
respect. **Disgrace** is also used to
talk about the loss of respect of
people you are close to.

2 [sing.] ■ *The state of our roads is a
national disgrace.*

infml **crime** | *fml* **evil** • **abomination** •
iniquity

▶ **It's** a disgrace/crime.
▶ **It's** a disgrace/crime **to do** sth.

disgust verb [T]

■ *The constant violence in the film
really disgusted me.*

horrify • **sicken** • **shock** • **repel** | *BrE*
appal | *AmE* **appall**

■ **OPP** please
▶ disgusted/horrified/shocked/
appalled **at** sb/sth
▶ disgust/horrify/sicken/shock/
appal sb **to think/see/hear/find/
learn** sth
▶ It disgusts/horrifies/sickens/
shocks/appals me **that...**

disgusting adj.

1 ■ *Picking your nose is a disgusting
habit.*

revolting • **foul** • **vile** • **horrible** •
nauseating • **repulsive** | *infml,
spoken* **gross** | *fml* **repellent** •
offensive

▶ a/an disgusting/revolting/foul/

vile/horrible/nauseating/gross/
offensive **smell**
▶ a disgusting/revolting/horrible/
nauseating/gross **habit**
▶ a disgusting/revolting/vile/
horrible/repulsive **man/woman/
person**
▶ **find** sb sth disgusting/revolting/
horrible/nauseating/repulsive/
offensive/repellent
● **DISGUSTING OR REVOLTING?** There is
no real difference in meaning, but
disgusting is more frequent, esp.
in spoken English.

2 ■ *That's a disgusting thing to say.*

hateful • **sickening** • **abominable** |
fml **distasteful** • **repugnant**

▶ disgusting/hateful/abominable/
distasteful/repugnant **to** sb
▶ disgusting/hateful/sickening/
abominable/distasteful/repugnant
that...
▶ a/an disgusting/abominable
practice
▶ a/an sickening/abominable **crime**

dish noun [C]

■ *Arrange the salad on a serving dish.*

bowl • **plate** • **platter**

▶ a dish/bowl/plate/platter **of** sth
▶ **on** a dish/bowl/plate/platter
▶ **in** a dish/bowl

dishonest adj.

■ *Beware of dishonest traders.*

hypocritical • **devious** • **underhand** •
lying | *infml* **two-faced** | *fml*
deceitful

■ **OPP** honest
▶ dishonest/hypocritical/devious **of**
sb **to do** sth
▶ a/an dishonest/hypocritical/
devious/underhand **manner/
way**
▶ dishonest/devious/underhand/
deceitful **tactics/means**

dishonesty noun [U]

■ *Two employees were dismissed for
dishonesty.*

deceit • **deception** • **fraud**

■ **OPP** honesty
▶ **be guilty of/accuse** sb **of**
dishonesty/deceit/deception/
fraud
▶ **obtain** sth **by/practise** deceit/
deception/fraud

dislike noun [U, C]

■ *She took an instant dislike to the
house.*

aversion • **hatred** • **hate** | *fml*
loathing

■ **OPP** liking
▶ dislike/hatred/hate/loathing **for/
of** sb/sth

► **deep** dislike/aversion/hatred/
loathing

dislike verb [T]

■ *Why do you dislike him so much?*

hate • despise • can't stand • can't
bear

► OPP **like**
► dislike/hate/despise sb **for** sth
► dislike/hate/despise **about** sb/
sth
► dislike/hate/can't stand/can't bear
doing sth
► they dislike/hate/can't stand/despise/can't
stand **each other**

dismiss verb

1 [T] ■ *I think we can safely dismiss
their objections.*

brush sb/sth aside • shrug sth off/
aside • set sth aside | *infml* laugh sth
off | *fml* discount • *written* banish

► dismiss/brush sth aside/shrug sth
off/set sth aside/discount sth **as**
irrelevant, unimportant, etc.
► dismiss/brush aside/shrug off/
laugh off/discount a **suggestion**
► dismiss/brush aside/laugh off/
discount/banish a **fear**

2 [T, usu. passive] ■ *She was unfairly
dismissed from her job.*

fire • lay sb off • let sb go | *BrE* make
sb redundant | *esp. BrE, infml* sack |
fml discharge | *BrE,
journ.* axe | *AmE* ax

► OPP **appoint**
► dismiss/fire/lay off/make
sb redundant/sack sb/give sb the
sack/discharge sb **from** a job
► dismiss/fire/lay off/axe **staff/
workers/employees**
► make **staff/workers/employees**
redundant
► let **staff employees** go

display noun

1 [C] ■ *The window display changes
once a month.*

show | *esp. BrE* exhibition | *AmE*
exhibit

► be **on** display/show/exhibition/
exhibit
► a **big/major/public** display/
show/exhibition/exhibit
► **see** a/an display/show/
exhibition/exhibit

2 [C] ■ *The firework display is a
popular annual event.*

show • spectacle • performance •
act

► a **magnificent** display/show/
spectacle/performance
► **put on/stage/see** a display/
show/spectacle/performance

display verb

1 [T] ■ *It's an opportunity for local
artists to display their work.*

show • present • hang • put sth up

► display/show/present your **wares**
► display/show/hang/put up a
picture/painting
► display/show **your work/a
collection/a trophy**
● DISPLAY OR SHOW? **Show** is a less
formal and more general word.
Display usu. means that sth has
been arranged in an attractive way
and put where many people will
see it.

2 [T] ■ *He loved to display his
knowledge.*

show • demonstrate • express •
reflect | *fml* exhibit

► display/show/express/reflect
(your) **feelings/emotions**
► display/show/demonstrate/
express **commitment/courage**
► display/show/demonstrate/
exhibit good, anti-social, etc.
behaviour
● DISPLAY OR DEMONSTRATE? You can
display feelings with meaning to:
*display/exhibit signs of emotion/
fatigue*
When you **demonstrate** a quality,
ability or feeling this is always
deliberate, because you want
people to see your good qualities
such as *understanding* and
commitment.

disprove verb [T]

■ *It took over six months to disprove
the allegations.*

discredit • invalidate • demolish •
explode • debunk | *fml* refute •
rebut • confound

► OPP **prove, confirm**
► disprove/discredit/invalidate/
demolish/explode/debunk/refute
a **theory**
► disprove/invalidate/demolish/
explode/debunk/refute a **myth**
► disprove/discredit/invalidate/
demolish/refute/rebut/confound
an **argument**
► disprove/discredit/invalidate/
demolish/explode/refute/rebut a
claim
● DISPROVE, REFUTE OR REBUT?
Disprove is the most frequent of
these words and is used esp. for
scientific or historical matters.
Refute is used to talk about
arguments or accusations; **rebut** is
used esp. to talk about accusations.

disrupt verb [T]

■ *Demonstrators disrupted the
meeting.*

interrupt • upset • interfere with sth

▶ disrupt/interrupt/interfere with **services/work**
▶ disrupt/interrupt a **meeting**
▶ disrupt/upset/interfere with **plans**

disruption noun [U, C]

■ The strike caused serious disruption.

disturbance • turmoil • upheaval | *esp. written* **turbulence • disarray**

▶ disruption/disturbance **to sth**
▶ **economic** disruption/turmoil/ upheaval/turbulence
▶ **cause** disruption/disturbance/ turmoil/an upheaval
● **DISRUPTION OR DISTURBANCE?** A **disruption** usu. affects a thing, such as **work**, a **service** or sb's **life**; a **disturbance** more often affects people or animals, though it can also affect sb's life.

distinguish verb

1 [I, T] ■ It was hard to distinguish one twin from the other.

tell | *esp. written* **differentiate**

▶ distinguish/differentiate/tell **A from B**
▶ distinguish/differentiate **between A and B**
▶ **clearly/sharply/carefully** distinguish/differentiate sb/sth
● **DISTINGUISH OR DIFFERENTIATE? Differentiate** is more formal and is used more in scientific matters than in matters of human judgement:
✔At what age are children able to distinguish between right and wrong? ✗ differentiate between right and wrong

2 [T] ■ What is it that distinguishes her from her classmates?

set sb/sth apart | *esp. written* **differentiate**

▶ distinguish/set apart/differentiate **A from B**
▶ a **feature** distinguishes/sets apart/ differentiates **A from B**
▶ a **factor** distinguishes/ differentiates **A from B**

distort verb [T]

■ Newspapers often distort the truth.

misquote | *fml* **falsify • misrepresent |** *infml* **fix |** *BrE, infml* **fiddle |** *esp. journ.* **rig**

▶ distort/falsify/fix/fiddle/rig **the results**
▶ distort/misrepresent **the truth/ facts**
▶ **fix/rig** an election

distress noun [U]

■ He was obviously in distress after the attack.

pain • suffering • misery • agony | *infml* **hurt • torture |** *fml* **anguish**

▶ distress/pain/misery/hurt/ anguish **at sth**
▶ **in** distress/pain/misery/agony/ anguish
▶ **cause (sb)** distress/pain/suffering/ misery/agony/hurt/anguish
● **DISTRESS, PAIN OR SUFFERING?** These are all words for a feeling of great unhappiness. **Distress** can also be a feeling of worry. **Pain** is often used when the hurt is individual and the cause more personal, such as the death of a loved one. **Suffering** often refers to sth on a large scale that affects many people, such as a war or natural disaster.

distribute verb [T]

■ They distributed food and blankets to the earthquake victims.

hand sth out • give sth out | *esp. AmE* **pass sth out |** *infml* **dole sth out • dish sth out |** *fml* **dispense**

▶ distribute/hand out/give out/dish out/dispense **food**
▶ distribute/hand out/give out/dole out/dispense **money**
▶ distribute/hand out/dish out/give out **awards/prizes**

district noun

1 [C] ■ He lived in an exclusive residential district.

quarter • area • zone • region • part | *BrE* **neighbourhood |** *AmE* **neighborhood**

▶ (a/an) **eastern/northern, etc.** district/quarter/area/zone/ region/parts
▶ the **whole/entire** district/area/ zone/region/neighbourhood
▶ a **residential** district/quarter/ area/zone/neighbourhood

2 [C] ■ The district council granted permission for the development.

county • region • state • province • zone

▶ **in** a district/county/region/state/ province/zone
▶ a **border/coastal** district/county/ region/state/province/zone
▶ the **northern/southern, etc.** districts/counties/region/states/ provinces/zone

disturb verb

1 [T] ■ Don't disturb her when she's working.

interrupt • barge in | *esp. spoken* **bother |** *fml* **trouble • intrude**

> disturb sb/interrupt/bother sb/ trouble sb **with** sth
> be **sorry to** disturb sb/interrupt/ bother sb/trouble sb/intrude
● **DISTURB, INTERRUPT OR BOTHER** You can **disturb** or **bother** sb who is trying to do sth by talking to them. You **interrupt** sb who is speaking by speaking yourself. You can **disturb** sb by making a lot of noise.

2 [T] ■ *It disturbed her to realize how much she was missing him.*

worry • **trouble** • **concern** • **unsettle** • **bother**

> It disturbs/worries/troubles/ concerns/bothers **sb that…**
> What disturbs/worries/troubles/ concerns/bothers me **is that…**
● **WHICH WORD? Bother** is the most informal of these words, esp. in spoken phrases such as *It doesn't bother me.* and *I'm not bothered.* **Concern** is the most formal and is not usu. used in the progressive tenses.

disturbing adj.
■ *This is an extremely disturbing piece of news.*

worrying • **unsettling** • **disconcerting** • **unnerving** • **alarming** • **upsetting** • **distressing**

> disturbing/worrying/unsettling/ disconcerting/unnerving/ alarming/upsetting/distressing **for** sb
> a/an disturbing/worrying/ alarming/distressing **thought**
> a/an disturbing/worrying/ unnerving/alarming/upsetting/ distressing **experience**

ditch noun [C]
■ *The car went off the road and into a ditch.*

trench • **gully/gulley** • **channel** • **moat** • **furrow**

> an **open** ditch/trench/gully/ channel
> a **deep** ditch/trench/gully/ channel/moat/furrow
> **dig** a ditch/trench/channel/moat

diverse adj.
■ *a mix of people from diverse cultures*

mixed • **contrasting** • **wide-ranging** • **assorted** • **miscellaneous** | *fml* **heterogeneous** • **eclectic** • **disparate** | *often approv.* **varied** | *often disapprov.* **motley**

■ OPP **similar**
> a/an diverse/mixed/assorted/ miscellaneous/heterogeneous/ disparate/varied/motley **group**
> diverse/assorted/miscellaneous/ disparate **items**

> **racially/ethnically/culturally/ socially** diverse/mixed/varied

divide verb
1 [I, T] ■ *The report is divided into three parts.*

split • **break (sth) up** • **split (sb) up** • **cut sth up** • **separate (sth) out** • **subdivide**

> divide/break/split/cut sth **up**
> divide/split/break up/subdivide sth **into parts**
> divide/split/split up/subdivide sth **into groups**
● **DIVIDE, SPLIT OR BREAK UP? Divide** is slightly more formal. Things often **break up** because people or circumstances have forced them to. When sth has **broken up** it is no longer one whole thing: *The empire was broken up into four parts* (= it was no longer one empire). • *The empire was divided/split into different parts* (= it was still one empire but contained separate areas).
Things usu. **divide** or **split** because it is natural for them to do so.

2 [T] ■ *King Lear divided his kingdom between his daughters.*

share • **split** | *disapprov.* **carve sth up**

> divide/share/split/carve up sth **between/among** different people
> divide/share/split the **money/ work**
> divide/share/split your **time**
● **DIVIDE, SHARE OR SPLIT?** Things are **shared** between people; things are **divided** between people, uses or places; things are **split** between people, things or places. **Divide** is often used about very important things; **share** is used about less important things:
✓*He shared his sweets out among his friends.* ✗ *He divided his sweets among his friends.*

3 [T] ■ *The issue has bitterly divided the community.*

split • **separate** • **come between sb and sb** • **alienate** | *fml* **be/become estranged**

> be divided/split **over** sth
> **increasingly** divided/split/ separated/alienated/estranged
> **deeply** divided/split
● **DIVIDE OR SPLIT? Divide** suggests a disagreement between two or more people that may be temporary; **split** suggests it may be permanent.

division noun
1 [U, sing.] ■ *a fair division of the money*

separation ✦ split ✦ partition ✦ segregation

▶ division/separation/segregation **from** sb/sth
▶ (a) division/separation/split/segregation **between** A and B
▶ (a) division/separation/split/segregation **into** parts
▶ (a) **clear** division/separation/split

2 [C, U] ■ We must heal the divisions within society.

rift ✦ alienation ✦ distance | *infml* split | *fml* schism ✦ disunity ✦ estrangement

▶ (a) division/rift/split/schism/disunity/estrangement **between** people or groups
▶ (a) division/rift/split/schism/disunity/estrangement **within** a group
▶ (a) split/distance/alienation/estrangement **from** sb
▶ (a/an) **deep/serious/internal/ideological** division/split/rift
▶ **heal** divisions a split/a rift

divorce verb [T, I]

■ She's divorcing her husband.

get divorced ✦ separate ✦ break (sth) up ✦ split up | *infml, esp. journ.* split

■ OPP **marry, get married**
▶ break up/split up/split **with** sb
▶ separate/split/split up/split **from** sb
▶ a couple divorces/gets divorced/separates/breaks up/splits up/splits
● **DIVORCE OR GET DIVORCED?** One person **divorces** another person but **get divorced** usu. refers to an action by two people: *He divorced her husband last year.* ◆ *They got divorced last year.*
You can also use **be divorced from** sb: *She is divorced from the boy's father.*
When there is no object **get divorced** is more common in spoken English.

divorced adj.

■ My parents are divorced.

separated | *fml* estranged

■ OPP **married**
▶ be divorced/separated/estranged **from** sb
▶ a divorced/separated **man/woman/parent/mother/father/couple**

do verb

1 [T] ■ They did an experiment to see if it would work.

carry sth out ✦ commit ✦ go through sth ✦ perform | *fml* conduct ✦ undertake ✦ implement | *BrE, fml* practise | *AmE, fml* practice

▶ do/carry out/perform/conduct/undertake the/a/an **work/activity/analysis/investigation/review/assessment**
▶ do/carry out/go through/perform a **manoeuvre**
▶ do/carry out/implement a **plan/policy/strategy**

2 [I] (always used with an adv. or prep.) (*esp. spoken*) ■ He's doing very well at school.

perform | *BrE* get on/along | *esp. spoken* go | *esp. written* fare

▶ do/perform/get on/go/fare **well**
▶ do/perform/go **brilliantly/excellently/badly**
▶ do/perform/fare **poorly**
● **DO OR GO? Do** is used to talk about the progress or success of either a person or a thing, esp. how popular or profitable a business is; **go** is only used about things, esp. experiences such as an *interview*, a *test* or *life* in general.

3 [T] (*esp. spoken*) ■ She did a drawing of a house.

make ✦ create ✦ produce

▶ do/make/create/produce a **drawing/painting**
▶ do/make/produce a **sketch/copy**

doctor noun

1 [C] ■ I think you should go to the doctor about that cough.

surgeon ✦ paramedic ✦ nurse | *BrE* GP | *AmE* internist | *infml* medic | *esp. AmE, fml* physician

▶ **see** a doctor/the surgeon/a nurse/your GP/your internist/a medic/a physician
▶ **call** a doctor/the paramedics/your GP/a medic/a physician
▶ a doctor/paramedic/surgeon/GP/physician **treats** sb
▶ a doctor/surgeon/GP/physician **examines** sb

2 doctor's [C, usu. sing.] (*esp. spoken*) ■ I have an appointment at the doctor's tomorrow.

BrE surgery ✦ health centre | AmE doctor's office ✦ clinic

▶ **at** the doctor's/surgery/health centre/doctor's office/clinic

document noun [C]

■ This is an important legal document.

file ✦ papers ✦ paperwork ✦ archive ✦ deed | *fml* dossier

▶ a document/a file/the paperwork/a dossier **on** sb/sth
▶ **in** a document/a file/the paperwork/the archives/a dossier
▶ **draw up** a document/papers/the paperwork/a dossier

dominate verb [T, I] (often disapprov.)

■ *United dominated the first half of the game.*

take (sth) over • reign • corner • often disapprov. **monopolize** | infml, disapprov. **hog**

▶ dominate/take over/monopolize/ corner the **market**
▶ dominate/take over/monopolize **the conversation/an industry**

door noun [C]

■ *There was a knock on the door.*

entrance • exit • doorway • way • hatch • gate • gateway

▶ **at the** door/entrance/exit/gate
▶ **through** the door/doorway/ hatch/gate/gateway
▶ **the front/back/side** door/ entrance/exit/way/gate
▶ **open/shut/close/slam** the door/ hatch/gate

doubt noun

1 [U] ■ *If you're in doubt, wear a suit.*

uncertainty • question • a question mark over sth • confusion • indecision

■ OPP **certainty**
▶ doubt/uncertainty/a question mark/confusion/indecision **over** sth
▶ doubt/uncertainty/confusion/ indecision **about/as to** sth
▶ **in** doubt/uncertainty/question
▶ **beyond/without** doubt/question
▶ **come into/be open to** doubt/ question
● **DOUBT OR UNCERTAINTY?** Doubt often refers to a more active state of mind that questions sb/sth; uncertainty refers to a less forceful and more passive lack of certainty about sth.

2 [C] ■ *I have my doubts about his suitability for the job.*

second thoughts • qualm • suspicion • scruple • misgiving | fml **compunction**

▶ doubts/second thoughts/qualms/ suspicions/scruples/misgivings/ compunction **about** sth
▶ **without (a)** doubt/second thought/qualm/scruples/ misgivings/compunction
▶ **have** doubts/second thoughts/ qualms/suspicions/scruples/ misgivings

doubt verb [T]

■ *There's no reason to doubt her story.*

question • challenge • dispute • contest • query

▶ doubt/question/challenge/ dispute/contest/query **whether...**

draft

▶ doubt/dispute **that...**
▶ doubt/question/challenge/ dispute/contest the **validity** of sth
▶ doubt/question/challenge a **story**

do (sth) up phrasal verb (esp. spoken)

■ *I can't do this zip up.*

tie • button • zip • fasten

■ OPP **undo**
▶ sth does/buttons/zips/fastens **up**
▶ do/tie/button/zip/fasten sth **up**
▶ do **up/tie your laces/shoelaces**
▶ do **up/fasten buttons**

do well verb [I] (esp. spoken)

■ *Jack is doing very well at school.*

thrive • blossom • bloom | infml **be going places** | esp. written **flourish • prosper** | esp. journ. **boom**

■ OPP **do badly**
▶ do well/prosper/blossom **as** sth
▶ a **business** does well/thrives/ blossoms/flourishes/prospers/is booming
▶ a **plant/town** does well/thrives/ flourishes

do without (sb/sth) phrasal verb

■ *She went without eating for three days.*

go without (sb/sth) • give sth up | fml **forgo/forego**

▶ do without/go without/forgo **food/sleep**
▶ do without/go without/give up/ forgo your **holiday**

draft noun [C]

■ *This is only the first draft of my speech.*

plan • design • blueprint

▶ a **rough** draft/plan
▶ the **orginal/first/final** draft/plan/ design/blueprint
▶ **draw up/produce** a draft/plan/ design

draft (also **draught**) verb [T]

■ *I'll draft a letter for you.*

draw sth up • put sth together • get sb/sth ready • prepare

▶ draft/draw up/put together/get ready/prepare sth **for** sth
▶ draft/draw up/put together/ prepare a **list/report/paper/ plan/strategy**
▶ draft/draw up/prepare a/an **document/contract/agenda/ budget/treaty**

drag verb

1 [T] ▪ *I dragged the chair over to the window.*

haul • **pull** • **trail** • **tow** • **tug** | *written*
draw

▸ drag/haul/pull/trail/tow/tug/
draw sth **along/down/towards**
sth
▸ drag/haul/pull/trail/tow/tug/
draw sb/sth **behind**
▸ drag/pull/haul/draw a **cart/
sledge/sled**
● pull/haul/tow a **truck**
● DRAG OR HAUL? You usu. **drag** sth
behind you along the ground; you
usu. **haul** sth towards you, often
upwards:
✔ *He reached down and hauled her
up onto the ledge.* ✗ *He reached
down and dragged her up onto the
ledge.*
Dragging sth often needs effort;
hauling sth always needs effort.

2 [T] ▪ *I'm sorry to drag you all this
way in the heat.*

haul • **hustle** • **bundle** • **rush** | *infml*
pack sb off

▸ drag/haul/hustle/bundle sb **off/
away** (from sth)
▸ drag/haul/hustle/bundle/rush sb
out of sth
▸ drag/haul/hustle **yourself**
somewhere

drain noun [C]

▪ *The drain is blocked.*

sewer • **gutter**

▸ an **open** drain/sewer
▸ a drain/gutter is **blocked**
▸ a drain/sewer/gutter **runs** down/
along sth

drama noun

1 [C] ▪ *a courtroom drama serialized
on TV*

play • **comedy** • **tragedy** • **farce**

▸ a **television/radio** drama/play/
comedy
▸ a **historical** drama/play

2 [U] ▪ *Television drama is a powerful
cultural medium.*

acting • **the stage** • **show business** •
the performing arts | *BrE* **theatre** |
AmE **theater** | *infml* **showbiz**

▸ **improvisational/serious** drama/
acting/theatre
▸ **classical/Elizabethan/modern**
drama/theatre
▸ a drama/stage/acting/performing
arts/theatre **school**

dramatic adj.

1 ▪ *The news had a dramatic effect on
house prices.*

sudden • **sharp** • **abrupt**

▸ a/an dramatic/sudden/sharp/
abrupt **increase/rise** (in sth)
▸ a dramatic/sudden/sharp **drop/
fall** (in sth)
▸ a/an dramatic/sudden/abrupt
end

2 ▪ *They watched dramatic pictures of
the police raid on TV.*

exciting • **thrilling** • **stirring** •
exhilarating • **heady**

▸ a/an dramatic/exciting/thrilling/
exhilarating/heady **experience/
moment**
▸ a/an dramatic/exciting/thrilling/
stirring/exhilarating **performance**
▸ a/an dramatic/exciting/stirring
tale

draught (*esp. BrE*) (*AmE, BrE* draft)
verb [T]

▪ *I'll draught a letter for you.*

draw sth up • **put sth together** • **get
sb/sth ready** • **prepare**

▸ draught/draw up/put together/
get ready/prepare sth **for** sth
▸ draught/draw up/put together/
prepare a **list/report/paper/
plan/strategy**
▸ draught/draw up/prepare a/an
**document/contract/agenda/
budget/treaty**

draw noun [C] (*esp. BrE*)

▪ *The match ended in a one-all draw.*

tie | *esp. BrE* **dead heat**

▸ a draw/tie/dead heat **with/
between** sb
▸ a draw/tie **against** sb
▸ **end** in a draw/tie/dead heat
● DRAW OR TIE? In sport, a **draw** is
always between two teams or
players and is the final result of the
game. A **tie** can be between more
than two players and can be used to
describe the situation at any
stage of a game or competition, as
well as the final result.

draw verb [T, I]

▪ *She drew a house in green felt tip.*

sketch • **paint** | *BrE* **colour** | *AmE*
color

▸ draw/sketch/paint/colour a
picture
▸ draw/sketch/paint a **landscape/
portrait**
▸ draw/sketch a **diagram/graph**

drawing noun [C]

▪ *a pencil drawing of a yacht*

sketch • **picture** • **illustration** •
cartoon • **diagram** • **portrait** •
graphics • **artwork**

- ► make/do a/an drawing/sketch/illustration/portrait
- ► draw a/an sketch/picture/illustration/cartoon/diagram/portrait
- ► show/display/exhibit a drawing/picture/portrait

dream noun [C]

1 ■ I had a vivid dream about my old school.

nightmare • hallucination | esp. written vision

- ► a dream/nightmare about sth
- ► have (a) dream/nightmare/hallucinations/vision
- ► a dream/nightmare fades

2 [C] ■ Her lifelong dream was to be a famous writer.

ambition • hope • aspiration • fantasy • expectation | esp. written wish • desire

- ► have (a/an) dream/ambition/aspirations/hopes/fantasy/expectations/wish/desire
- ► harbour a/an dream/ambition/hope/fantasy/wish/desire
- ► fulfil your dreams/ambitions/hopes/aspirations/fantasies/expectations/wishes/desires
- ► abandon/give up a/an dream/ambition/hope

3 [C] ■ She wandered round the house in a dream.

daydream • daze • trance • stupor | fml or lit. reverie

- ► be in a dream/daydream/daze/trance/stupor/reverie
- ► be lost in a dream/daydream/reverie

dress noun [U]

■ All the guests were in evening dress.

clothes • clothing • costume • wear • wardrobe | AmE apparel | infml gear | fml garment

- ► casual dress/clothes/clothing/apparel/wear/gear
- ► evening/formal dress/clothes/wear
- ► wear ...dress/clothes/costume/gear/garments

drink noun

1 [C, U] ■ Food and drinks will be available.

soft drink | fml beverage

- ► a/an hot/cold/alcoholic/non-alcoholic drink/beverage

2 [C, usu. sing.] ■ She took a drink from the glass, then put it down.

sip • gulp

- ► a drink/sip/gulp/swig of sth
- ► have/take a drink/sip/gulp/swig

3 [C, U] ■ Let's go for a drink after work.

alcohol | esp. AmE liquor | esp. BrE spirit | infml booze

- ► alcoholic drinks/liquor
- ► strong drink/liquor
- ► turn to/keep off/stay off (the) drink/alcohol/booze
- ► a/an drink/alcohol/booze problem

drink verb [T, I]

■ He was drinking straight from the bottle.

sip • suck • drain | infml swig • booze

- ► drink/sip/swig from a bottle/glass of sth
- ► drink/sip/drain your drink/pint
- ► drink/sip/swig beer
- ► drink/sip tea/coffee/water

drive noun [C]

■ We went out for a drive.

ride | BrE lift

- ► a drive/ride/lift from/to sth
- ► a drive/ride/lift back/home
- ► take/go on/go for a drive/ride
- ► give sb/hitch a ride/lift

drive verb

1 [I, T] ■ I learned to drive at 17.

steer • handle | BrE manoeuvre | AmE maneuver

- ► drive/steer/handle/manoeuvre a car

2 [I, T] ■ We've driven over 200 miles today.

travel • go • come • do

- ► drive/travel/go/come from/to sth
- ► drive/travel/go/come/do 50 miles/10 kilometres, etc.
- ► drive/travel/come a long distance

3 [T] (sometimes disapprov.) ■ You're driving yourself too hard.

work | disapprov. overwork | usu. approv. push

- ► drive/work/push sb hard
- ► drive/push sb too far/to the limit
- ► drive/work sb into the ground

driver noun [C]

■ She's a good driver.

chauffeur | esp. journ. motorist

- ► speeding drivers/motorists
- ► be sb's driver/chauffeur
- ● DRIVER OR MOTORIST? Motorist is usu. used in journalism to talk about car drivers as a group in

society, often to contrast them
with **pedestrians** and **cyclists**.

drop noun

1 [C] ■ *A few drops of rain fell.*

bead • globule • splash • drip | *infml*
blob

▶ a drop/bead/splash of **blood**
▶ a drop/bead of **moisture/sweat/
perspiration**
▶ a drop/splash of **water**

2 [C, usu. sing.] ■ *The restaurant
suffered a drop in trade.*

fall • decline • cut • reduction •
decrease • downturn

■ OPP **rise**
▶ a drop/fall/decline/cut/
reduction/decrease/downturn **in**
sth
▶ (a) **big/huge/massive/major**
drop/fall/decline/cut/reduction/
downturn
▶ **lead to/result in/cause** a drop/
fall/decline/cut/reduction/
decrease
● DROP, FALL OR DECLINE? These
words all describe a process that
happens, not a deliberate action by
sb. **Fall** and **decline** can happen
over time, but a **drop** cannot:
✓*a gradual decline/fall* x *a gradual
drop*

drop verb

1 [I] ■ *He staggered in and dropped
into a chair.*

fall • sink • crash • tumble • come
down • go down

■ OPP **rise**
▶ drop/fall/sink/crash/tumble/
come/go **down**

2 [I] ■ *The temperature has dropped
considerably.*

fall • decline • come down | *fml*
decrease | *esp. busin.* sink • slump •
plunge • plummet • tumble

■ OPP **rise, climb**
▶ drop/fall/decline/come down/
decrease/sink/slump/plunge/
plummet/tumble **by** 100, 25%, a
half, etc.
▶ drop/fall/decline/come down/
decrease/sink/slump/plunge/
plummet/tumble **from** 1 500 to
1 000
▶ prices drop/fall/decline/
decrease/come down/sink/
slump/plunge/plummet/tumble
▶ the temperature drops/falls
▶ sb's voice drops/falls/sinks
● DROP, FALL OR DECLINE? All these
words can be used about numbers,
levels, prices, profits and sales. Use

decline to talk about a loss of
economic strength in an area:
✓*The city/industry has declined (in
importance).*
A person's or people's
support for sth **declines**. Voices
and temperatures **fall** or **drop**.
Things can **fall** or **decline** over a
period of time, but **drop** cannot be
used in the progressive tenses:
✓*Sales have been falling/declining.*
x *Sales have been dropping.*

drug noun

1 [C] ■ *As a teenager, he
experimented with drugs.*

infml dope | *fml* narcotic • stimulant

▶ **use** drugs/dope/narcotics/
stimulants
▶ **take** drugs/narcotics/stimulants
▶ a drug/dope/narcotics **dealer**

2 [C] ■ *The doctor prescribed drugs for
my son's rash.*

medicine • medication • remedy •
antidote • cure • prescription

▶ (a/an) drug/medicine/
medication/remedy/cure/
antidote/prescription **for** sth
▶ an **effective** drug/medicine/
medication/remedy/cure
▶ **prescribe** drugs/medicine/
medication/a remedy/a cure
▶ **take** your medicine/your
medication/a remedy/the
antidote
● DRUG, MEDICINE OR MEDICATION?
Drug emphasizes what the
substance is made of; **medicine**
and **medication** emphasize what it
is used for.

drunk adj. [not usu. before noun]

■ *They got drunk on vodka.*

drunken • under the influence |
infml tipsy | *fml* intoxicated | *slang*
wasted | *BrE, taboo, slang* pissed

■ OPP **sober**
▶ drunk/tipsy/pissed **on** sth
▶ **get** drunk/tipsy/wasted/pissed

dry adj.

■ *weeks of hot, dry weather*

clear | *approv.* good • sunny | *esp.
BrE, approv.* fine

■ OPP **wet**
▶ dry/clear/good/sunny/fine
weather/conditions
▶ a dry/clear/good/sunny/fine **day/
morning/afternoon/evening**
▶ **remain/stay** dry/sunny/fine

dull adj.

■ *She found her job very dull.*

boring • tedious • uninteresting •
dry • repetitive • monotonous

■ OPP **interesting**

► dull/boring/tedious/repetitive/
monotonous **jobs/work**
► a dull/boring/tedious/dry
subject/book
► a/an dull/boring/uninteresting
place

dump verb [T, I] (disapprov.)
■ Too much toxic waste is being
dumped at sea.

**throw sth away/out ◆ get rid of sth
◆ scrap ◆ dispose of sth** | fml **discard**

► dump/get rid of/dispose of/
discard **waste**
► dump/throw away/dispose of/
discard **rubbish/garbage/trash**
► dump/throw away/dispose of a
(dead) **body**

dust noun
1 [U] ■ A cloud of dust rose as the
truck sped by.

earth ◆ soil | esp. AmE **dirt**

► dry dust/earth/soil/dirt

2 [U] ■ The books were all covered
with dust.

dirt ◆ grime ◆ soot

► covered in/with dust/dirt/grime/
soot
► a **layer** of dust/dirt/grime
► a **speck** of dust/dirt

duty noun
1 [C, U] ■ It is your duty to report this
to the police.

**responsibility ◆ commitment ◆
obligation ◆ burden** | infml **job**

► a/an duty/commitment/
obligation/burden **to** sb/sth
► a duty/responsibility **towards** sb
► a **professional/social** duty/
responsibility/commitment/
obligation
► **fulfil/meet** a/an duty/
responsibility/commitment/
obligation

2 duty/duties [U, pl.] ■ Report for
duty at 8 a.m.

work ◆ task ◆ business ◆ job ◆ chore

► (a) **routine/daily/day-to-day**
duties/work/task/business/job/
chore
► **household/domestic** duties/
work/task/job/chore
► **carry out** your duties/the work/a
task/a job
● **DUTIES OR WORK?** Your **duties** are a
list of tasks that you have to do
because they are your
responsibility; your **work** is all the
activities you do in the course of
doing your job.

Ee

eager adj.
■ Everyone seemed eager to learn.

**enthusiastic ◆ avid ◆ hungry ◆
anxious ◆ impatient** | esp. BrE **keen** |
infml **mad** | fml **zealous**

● OPP **reluctant**
► eager/avid/hungry/anxious/
impatient/keen/mad **for** sth
► eager/enthusiastic/anxious/
impatient/keen **to do** sth
► eager/anxious/keen **that...**
● **EAGER OR ENTHUSIASTIC?** People are
often **eager** about things that they
want for themselves; they are often
enthusiastic about other people
and their ideas and achievements:
The low prices pulled in crowds of
eager buyers. ◆ enthusiastic support/
applause/praise

early adj.
■ Let's make an early start.

punctual ◆ prompt ◆ on time

● OPP **late**
► be early/punctual **for** sth

earn verb
1 [T, I] ■ She earns about £25 000 a
year.

**make ◆ bring (sb) in sth ◆ gross ◆ net
◆ profit** | infml **pull sth in** | often
disapprov. **pocket** | infml, often
disapprov. **rake sth in**

► earn/make/bring in/gross/net/
pull in/pocket/rake in **$100 000 a
year**
► earn/make **money/a living/a
fortune**
● **EARN OR MAKE?** Earn emphasizes
the work you have to do to get the
money. Use **make** if the money
comes as interest or profit, and the
subject is a person; if the subject is
a business, you can use either word: She
made a fortune on the stock market.
◆ The plant will make/earn £95
million for the UK.

2 [T] ■ As a teacher, she earned the
respect of her students.

win ◆ gain ◆ get ◆ secure

► earn/win/gain/get/secure
support/approval
► earn/win/gain **respect/
admiration**
► earn/gain **notoriety/a reputation**

3 [T] ■ I need a rest. I think I've earned
it.

deserve | fml **merit**

► earn/deserve a **rest/drink**
► deserve/merit **attention/**

consideration / recognition / a mention

● EARN OR DESERVE? Deserve can be used to talk about either sth pleasant sb should have for doing good, or a punishment for sth bad; earn is only used to talk about sth good.

earth noun

1 [U, sing.] ■ *The earth revolves around the sun.*

the world • the globe • the planet

▶ around / across / all over the earth / world / globe / planet
▶ on (the) earth / globe / planet
▶ save / destroy the earth / world / planet

● THE EARTH OR THE WORLD? Use **the world** when you are concerned with things that exist in the world and not outside it. Use **the earth** when our planet is being considered in relation to other planets, its place in space, or heaven.

2 [U, sing.] ■ *It was good to feel the earth beneath our feet.*

ground • land | *lit.* **soil**

▶ on / under the earth / ground
▶ bare earth / ground
▶ drop / fall to (the) earth / ground

● EARTH, GROUND OR LAND? **Ground** is the normal word for the solid surface that you walk on. Use **earth** to draw attention to the rock, soil, etc. that the ground is made of. **Land** is only used to contrast sth with the sea: *They fought both at sea and on land.*

3 [U] ■ *The smell of freshly dug earth was in the air.*

soil • clay • mud • ground • peat | *esp. AmE* **dirt**

▶ dry / wet / soft earth / soil / clay / mud / ground / peat / dirt
▶ good / rich earth / soil
▶ dig the earth / soil / clay / mud / ground / peat

ease verb [T, I]

■ *This medicine should help ease the pain.*

relieve • soothe • alleviate • soften • cushion • lighten | *fml* **allay**

■ OPP **aggravate**
▶ ease / relieve / soothe / alleviate the **pain**
▶ ease / relieve / soothe / alleviate / allay sb's **fear / anxiety**
▶ ease / relieve / alleviate **pressure / stress / poverty / suffering**

easy adj.

1 ■ *vegetables that are easy to grow*

simple • straightforward • effortless • uncomplicated • *infml, often disapprov.* **cushy** | *written* **undemanding • painless**

■ OPP **difficult, hard**
▶ easy / simple / straightforward / painless **to do sth**
▶ a / an easy / simple / straightforward / undemanding **task**
▶ a / an easy / simple / straightforward **matter / decision / test / question**

● EASY OR SIMPLE? **Easy** means 'not difficult': an *easy test / task* is one that causes you no difficulties because you have the ability to do it. **Simple** means 'not complicated': a *simple task* is one that needs only very few, basic actions and does not usu. depend on people's abilities.

2 ■ *We set off at an easy pace.*

leisurely • at leisure • lazy | *written* **unhurried • languid**

▶ a / an easy / leisurely / unhurried / languid **manner**
▶ a / an easy / leisurely / unhurried / lazy **day / morning / afternoon / time**
▶ a / an easy / leisurely **trip / stroll / ride / drive**

eat verb

1 [I, T] ■ *Eat your dinner.*

have • swallow • taste • finish | *infml* **wolf • stuff** | *fml* **consume • devour** | *esp. written* **devour** | *BrE, esp. spoken* **tuck in / tuck into sth** | *tech.* **ingest**

▶ eat / swallow / wolf down / stuff yourself with / consume / devour / tuck into your **food**
▶ eat / have / finish / devour / tuck into a **meal**
▶ eat / have / finish / wolf / tuck into your **lunch / dinner**
▶ eat / have / taste / consume some **meat / fruit**

2 [I] ■ *We ate at the new restaurant in town.*

fml **dine • lunch • breakfast** | *written* **feast**

▶ eat / dine / lunch / breakfast **at a place**
▶ dine / lunch / breakfast / feast **on a particular food**
▶ eat / dine **out / well**

echo verb [I, T]

■ *Her footsteps echoed in the empty room.*

reverberate • ring out | *fml* **resonate** | *lit.* **resound • ring**

▶ echo / reverberate / ring out / resonate / resound / ring **through / around** a place

▶ echo/reverberate/ring out/
resonate/resound/ring with sth
▶ a **voice** echoes/reverberates/rings
out/resonates/resounds/rings
▶ **laughter** echoes/reverberates/
rings out/resounds/rings
● ECHO OR REVERBERATE?
Reverberate is often used of loud
sounds made in smaller enclosed
spaces; **echo** can be used for
indoor or outdoor spaces: *Birdcalls
echoed across the lake.*

economic *adj.*

1 [only before noun] ■ *Economic
growth was fastest in Japan.*

financial ◆ commercial | *finance*
monetary ◆ budgetary

▶ economic/financial/commercial/
monetary/budgetary **policy/
systems/problems**
▶ economic/financial/commercial/
monetary **gain/loss/value/affairs**
▶ economic/financial/commercial/
budgetary **data/decisions**

2 (often used in negative sentences)
■ *It is not economic for small farmers
to buy large amounts of fertilizer.*

**profitable ◆ commercial ◆ profit-
making**

■ OPP **uneconomic**

edge *noun* [C]

■ *He stood on the edge of the cliff.*

**end ◆ side ◆ limit ◆ fringe ◆
perimeter** | *fml* **periphery ◆ margin**

■ OPP **the middle**

▶ **at** the edge/end/side/limits/
fringe/perimeter/periphery/
margins
▶ **on** the edge/end/side/fringe/
perimeter/periphery/margins
▶ **along/around** the edge/side/fringe/
perimeter/periphery/margins
▶ **reach** the edge/end/limit/fringe/
perimeter/periphery
● EDGE, END OR SIDE? The **edge** of an
object goes all the way around it.
The **ends** or **sides** are the parts of
the edge that are opposite each
other. **Ends** have the longest
distance between them.

edge *verb* [I, T] (always used with
an adv. or prep.)

■ *She edged a little closer to me.*

inch ◆ crawl ◆ creep ◆ thread

▶ edge/inch/crawl/creep **along/
forwards/closer/nearer**
▶ edge/inch/crawl/creep **towards**
sth
▶ edge/crawl/creep/thread
through sth
● EDGE OR INCH? When you **inch**
somewhere you tend to be moving
forwards or towards sth. You can

use **edge** when you are moving in
any direction.

educate *verb* [T, often passive]

■ *She was educated in the US.* ■ *a
campaign to educate the public about
healthy eating*

**teach ◆ tutor ◆ train ◆ coach ◆
prepare** | *fml* **instruct**

▶ educate/train/coach/instruct sb
in sth
▶ educate/teach sb **about** sth
▶ educate/teach/tutor/train/
instruct **a pupil**
▶ educate/teach/train **a/the
teacher/doctor/nurse/student/
workforce**

educated *adj.*

■ *an educated and articulate
spokesman*

**informed ◆ knowledgeable ◆
thinking ◆ well-read**

■ OPP **uneducated**

▶ educated/informed/
knowledgeable **about** sth
▶ educated/informed/
knowledgeable/thinking/well-
read **people**

education *noun* [U, sing.]

■ *He had little formal education.*

**teaching ◆ training ◆ learning ◆
study** | *BrE* **coaching** | *esp. AmE*
tutoring | *fml* **schooling ◆
instruction ◆ tuition**

▶ education/teaching/training/
coaching/tutoring/schooling/
instruction/tuition **in** sth
▶ **public/state** education/schooling
▶ **private** education/teaching/
study/coaching/tutoring/
schooling/tuition
▶ **have/get/receive** (an) education/
training/coaching/tutoring/
instruction/tuition

educational *adj.*

■ *Is the trip of educational value?*

academic ◆ informational | *often
approv.* **scholarly** | *fml* **instructional ◆
pedagogic ◆ didactic**

▶ educational/academic/
informational/scholarly/
instructional/pedagogic **value/
use**
▶ a/an educational/academic/
informational/instructional/
pedagogic **programme**
▶ educational/academic/scholarly/
pedagogic **practice/methods**

effect *noun* [C, U]

■ *Management changes had little
effect on output.*

impact • influence • result •
outcome • consequence • upshot •
impression • power • force • action

▶ an effect/influence/
impression **on/upon** sb/sth
▶ (a) **considerable/tremendous/
great** effect/impact/influence/
impression/power/force
▶ **have** (a/an) effect/impact/
influence/result/outcome/
consequences

effective adj.

■ a simple but highly effective
treatment

successful • powerful

■ **OPP** ineffective
▶ effective/successful/powerful **in**
sth
▶ effective/successful/powerful **in
doing** sth
▶ a/an effective/successful/powerful
campaign/challenge

efficiency noun [U]

■ She ran the project with great
efficiency.

organization • order • method | fml
coherence

■ **OPP** inefficiency
▶ efficiency/method/coherence **in**
sth
▶ **great** efficiency/coherence
▶ **have/lack** organization/order/
coherence

efficient adj.

■ an incredibly efficient system

systematic • methodical • organized
• orderly • businesslike

▶ efficient/systematic/methodical/
organized/businesslike **in** sth
▶ a/an efficient/systematic/
methodical/organized/orderly/
businesslike **approach/way**
▶ **highly** efficient/systematic/
organized

effort noun

1 [U, C] ■ The long climb to the top is
well worth the effort.

hard work • struggle • energy/
energies • exertion/exertions | BrE,
fml endeavour | AmE, fml endeavor

▶ (a) **great** effort/struggle/exertion/
endeavour
▶ **need** effort/hard work/your
energies/exertion
▶ **put** effort/hard work/your
energies **into** sth
● **EFFORT OR EXERTION?** Effort is used
about the work people do to
achieve sth; exertion refers to the
energy used to carry out an
activity: A lot of effort has gone into

achieving this result. ◆ She was
sweating from the exertion of
housework.

2 [C] ■ I'll make a special effort to
finish on time.

attempt • try | BrE go | infml shot •
stab

▶ an attempt/attempt **to do** sth
▶ a **first/last/good** effort/attempt/
try/go/shot/stab
▶ **make** a/an effort/attempt/stab
● **EFFORT OR ATTEMPT?** Effort
emphasizes the work that sb puts
into doing sth; attempt
emphasizes the event or action
involved in trying to do sth:
✔a great/enormous/strenuous effort
✗ a great/enormous/strenuous
attempt

✔a coup/suicide attempt ✗ a coup/
suicide effort

elderly adj.

■ She is busy caring for two elderly
relatives.

old • mature | fml aged

■ **OPP** young
▶ a/an elderly/old/mature/aged
**man/woman/gentleman/lady/
couple**
▶ sb's elderly/old/aged **father/
mother/aunt/uncle/relative**

elect verb [T]

■ the newly elected government

vote for sb • vote sb in • vote sb
into sth

▶ elect sb/vote for sb/vote sb in **as**
sth

election noun [C, U]

■ Elections take place every four years.

vote • ballot • referendum • show
of hands | esp. journ. poll/the polls

▶ a/an election/vote/ballot/
referendum/poll **on** sth
▶ a **democratic/free** election/vote/
ballot/poll
▶ **hold** an election/vote/ballot/
referendum/poll
▶ **call/lose/win** a/an election/vote/
ballot/referendum

electronic adj. [usu. before
noun]

■ The dictionary is available in
electronic form.

digital • automatic • automated •
computerized • mechanical •
robotic

▶ a/an electronic/digital/
automatic/automated/
computerized/mechanical/robotic
system
▶ a/an electronic/automatic/
mechanical/robotic **device**

► a/an electronic/digital/computerized **database**

elegance noun [U] (approv.)
■ She dresses with casual elegance.

style • grace • class • glamour • flair

► do sth with elegance/style/grace/flair
► give sb/sth elegance/style/grace/class/glamour
► a **touch** of elegance/style/class/glamour

elegant adj.
■ She was tall, slim and elegant.

stylish • well-dressed • graceful • fashionable • glamorous • classic | esp. BrE smart

■ OPP inelegant

► a/an elegant/stylish/well-dressed/graceful/fashionable/glamorous/smart **woman**
► a/an elegant/well-dressed/fashionable/smart **man**
► a/an elegant/stylish/fashionable/glamorous/classic/smart **dress**
► a/an elegant/stylish/fashionable/smart **restaurant**

element noun

1 [C] ■ Cost was a key element in our decision.

component • ingredient • aspect • strand • dimension • part

► a/an element/component/ingredient **in** sth
► an **important** element/component/ingredient/aspect/strand/dimension/part
► a/an **necessary/essential** element/component/ingredient/aspect/dimension/part

2 [C, usu. sing.] (always followed by of) ■ All such activities carry an element of risk.

touch • trace • hint

► a **slight** element/touch/trace/hint of sth
► **detect** a/an element/touch/trace/hint of sth
► **contain** elements/traces/a hint of sth

elite noun [C+sing./pl. v.]
■ Only the elite can afford this kind of education.

the upper class/classes • the nobility • the aristocracy • the gentry • society

► **among** the elite/upper class/nobility/aristocracy/gentry
► the British/French, **etc.** elite/upper class/nobility/aristocracy/gentry
► **belong to** an elite/the upper

classes/the nobility/the aristocracy/the gentry

email (also e-mail) noun [C, U]
■ I check my email daily.

mail • message | fml communication • correspondence

► an email/mail/a message/a communication/correspondence **from/to** sb
► **send/receive** an email/mail/a message/a communication/correspondence
► **open** an email/a message

embarrass verb [T]
■ Her questions about my private life embarrassed me.

humiliate • mortify | written or fml shame

► embarrass/humiliate sb **in front of** sb
► be embarrassed/mortified **at** sth
► embarrass/humiliate/shame **yourself**

embarrassed adj.
■ I've never felt so embarrassed in my life!

uncomfortable • awkward • self-conscious • sheepish

■ OPP unembarrassed

► embarrassed/uncomfortable/awkward/self-conscious/sheepish **about** sth
► an embarrassed/uncomfortable/awkward **silence**
► **feel/look** embarrassed/uncomfortable/awkward/self-conscious/sheepish
● **EMBARRASSED, UNCOMFORTABLE OR AWKWARD? Embarrassed** is used esp. to describe how sb feels; **uncomfortable** can describe a situation; **awkward** often describes sb's personality or usual behaviour.

emerge verb

1 [I] (usu. used with an adv. or prep.) ■ The swimmer emerged from the lake.

appear • come out | written loom | fml manifest itself

■ OPP disappear

► emerge/appear **from** sth
► emerge/appear/loom **out of** sth
► **suddenly** emerge/appear/come out/loom

2 [I] ■ No new evidence emerged during the investigation.

come out • come to light • get out • leak out • turn out | fml transpire

► **news/the truth** emerges/comes out/gets out/leaks out

emergency

▶ It emerges/turns out/transpires that...
▶ emerge/come out/come to light/ turn out/transpire **later**

emergency noun [C, U]

■ A state of emergency has been declared.

crisis • disaster • catastrophe • calamity • tragedy

▶ **in** an emergency/a crisis
▶ a **major/national** emergency/ crisis/disaster/catastrophe/ calamity/tragedy
▶ **deal with/cope with** a/an emergency/crisis/disaster

emotion noun [U, C]

■ She spoke with deep emotion.

feeling • passion • heat | *sometimes disapprov.* **sentiment** | *BrE, written* **fervour** | *AmE, written* **fervor**

▶ **with** emotion/feeling/passion/ heat/fervour
▶ **intense/considerable/profound/ strong/violent** emotion/feelings/ passion
▶ **arouse/stir up** emotion/feelings/ passion/fervour

emotional adj.

1 [usu. before noun] ■ Victims require emotional support.

spiritual • inner

▶ emotional/spiritual/inner **development/needs/strength/ turmoil**
▶ sb's emotional/spiritual/inner **self/state**
▶ emotional/spiritual/inner **growth/support/welfare/well- being**

2 (sometimes disapprov.) ■ They made an emotional appeal for help.

passionate • intense • fierce • heated

■ OPP **unemotional**
▶ emotional/passionate/intense/ fierce/heated **about** sth
▶ a/an emotional/passionate/ intense/fierce/heated **debate**
▶ a/an emotional/passionate/ fierce/heated **argument**

emphasis noun [U, C]

■ The company lays great emphasis on customer care.

stress • priority

▶ (a) **particular/special/equal** emphasis/stress/priority
▶ **put/lay/place** emphasis/stress **on** sb/sth
▶ **have** a ...emphasis/priority

emphasize (*BrE also* -ise) verb [T]

■ The report emphasizes the need for economic stability.

stress • underline • highlight • point sth out | *esp. AmE, esp. busin.* **underscore**

■ OPP **understate, play sth down**
▶ emphasize/stress/underline/ highlight/point out **how...**
▶ emphasize/stress/underline/point out **that...**
▶ emphasize/stress/underline/ highlight/point out/underscore **the fact that ...**
▶ emphasize/stress/underline/ highlight/point out/underscore **the importance** of sth
● **EMPHASIZE OR STRESS? Emphasize** is slightly more formal and is used more in written and academic English, esp. when the subject is not human: *The report emphasizes....* **Stress** is used more in spoken English and journalism, esp. when the subject is human: *I must stress....*

employ verb [T]

■ More people have been employed to deal with the extra work.

take sb on • recruit • contract • appoint • sign | *esp. AmE* **hire** | *esp. BrE, fml* **engage** | *law* **retain**

■ OPP **dismiss**
▶ employ/take on/recruit/appoint/ sign/hire/engage/retain sb **as** sth
▶ employ/take on/recruit/contract/ appoint/sign/hire/engage/retain sb **to do** sth
▶ employ/take on/recruit/contract/ hire **workers/staff**

employee noun [C]

■ The firm has over 500 employees.

worker | *BrE* **member of staff** | *esp. AmE* **staff member**

▶ a/an **full-time/part-time/male/ female/experienced/key** employee/worker/member of staff/staff member
▶ a **permanent/junior/senior** employee/member of staff/staff member
▶ **have/employ/dismiss/fire/sack** a/an employee/worker/member of staff/staff member

employer noun [C]

■ They are very good employers.

manager • director • firm • company • organization | *esp. spoken or journ.* **boss**

▶ **work for** a/an employer/ manager/director/firm/ company/organization/boss
▶ a **good** employer/manager/ director/firm/company/ organization/boss

► **have** a/an employer/manager/ director/boss

employment noun [U]
■ It's difficult for young people to find regular employment.

work • occupation • career • profession • trade • job | esp. BrE **post** | fml **position**

■ OPP **unemployment**
► sb's **chosen** employment/work/ occupation/career/profession/ trade
► (a) **full-time/part-time/ permanent** employment/work/ occupation/career/job/post/ position
► **look for/seek/find** employment/ work/an occupation/a career

empty verb [T]
■ I emptied my pockets but I couldn't find my keys.

clear • drain • unload • unpack

■ OPP **fill**
► empty/clear/drain sth **of** sth
► empty/drain/unload/unpack the **contents** of sth
► empty/unpack a **suitcase/bag**
► empty/drain **water** from sth/your **glass**

empty adj.
■ The theatre was half empty.

bare • free • vacant

■ OPP **full**
► a/an empty/bare/vacant **room**
► a/an empty/free/vacant **seat**
► a/an empty/bare **cupboard**
► a/an empty/vacant **house**

enable verb [T]
■ Insulin enables the body to use and store sugar.

allow | fml **permit**

■ OPP **prevent**
► enable/permit/allow sb **to do** sth
► enable/permit/allow **access**
► enable/permit/allow the **creation/development/ expansion** of sth

encourage verb
1 [T] ■ She was greatly encouraged by his kind words.

cheer • cheer sb up • lift/raise sb's spirits • reassure | fml **uplift**

■ OPP **discourage**
► be **greatly** encouraged/cheered/ reassured
● **ENCOURAGE OR CHEER?** People or events can **encourage** you; you can be **cheered** by events or things. **Cheer** is more about comfort; **encourage** is more about confidence.

2 [T] ■ Banks actively encourage people to borrow money.

urge • spur | infml **put sb up to sth • egg sb on** | fml **exhort** | esp. written **galvanize**

■ OPP **discourage**
► encourage/urge/spur/egg on/ exhort/galvanize sb **to do sth**
► encourage/urge/exhort sb **not to do** sth
► **constantly/repeatedly** encourage/urge/exhort sb to do sth

3 [T] ■ The questions are designed to encourage debate.

stir sth up • whip sb/sth up | approv. **stimulate** | disapprov. **incite** | esp. journ. or busin. **fuel • stoke**

■ OPP **hold sb/sth back**
► encourage/incite sb **to do sth**
► encourage/stir up/whip up/ stimulate/fuel/stoke **interest**
► encourage/stir up/whip up/incite **opposition**

end noun
1 [C] ■ They have called for an end to violence.

conclusion • finish • ending • finale | fml, esp. busin. **close • termination** | fml, esp. journ. **cessation**

■ OPP **beginning**
► a/an (...) end/finish/ending/ finale **to**
► **at the** end/conclusion/finish/ finale/close
► **bring sth to** a/an end/conclusion/ close

2 [C] ■ She sat at the far end of the table.

side • edge • limit

■ OPP **the middle**
► **at the** end/side/edge/limits
► **on the** end/side/edge
► **beyond the** end/edge/limits
● **END, SIDE OR EDGE?** The **edge** of an object goes all the way around it. The **ends** or **sides** are the parts of the edge that are opposite each other. **Ends** have the longest distance between them.

end verb [I, T]
■ How does the story end?

finish • stop • close • wind (sth) up | BrE **round sth off** | AmE **round sth out** | fml **conclude • terminate**

■ OPP **begin**
► end/finish/conclude/round sth off/round sth out **by/with** sth
► end/finish/conclude/close/wind up a **meeting**
► a **play/show/film** ends/finishes/ concludes

endless

▶ a story/letter/note ends/concludes

● END, FINISH, STOP OR CONCLUDE? End, finish and conclude are used esp. about things that you do not expect to start again: *The war ended in 1945.* • *The concert should finish by 10 o'clock.* • *She concluded her speech with a quotation from Shakespeare.*
Stop is used about things that may or will start again: *The rain stopped for a couple of hours.*

endless adj.
■ *He had endless arguments with his father.*

never-ending • perpetual • interminable • continuous • continual • relentless | *often disapprov.* incessant

▶ a/an endless/never-ending/continuous/relentless/incessant **flow** of sth
▶ a/an endless/never-ending/perpetual/continuous/continual/relentless **struggle**
▶ endless/interminable **discussions/meetings**

enemy noun [C]
■ *They used to be friends, but now they are sworn enemies.*

opponent • rival • competitor • the opposition • the competition | *fml* adversary | *old-fash.* or *fml* foe

■ OPP ally, friend
▶ against an enemy/an opponent/a rival/a competitor/the opposition/the competition/an adversary/a foe
▶ a/an **old/dangerous** enemy/opponent/rival/adversary/foe
▶ **face/defeat** an enemy/an opponent/a rival/a competitor/the opposition/the competition/an adversary/a foe

energetic adj.
■ *He's an energetic person who will get things done.*

vigorous • active | *approv.* lively • dynamic • spirited

▶ a/an energetic/active/lively/dynamic/spirited **person/man/woman**
▶ an energetic/active **member** of sth
▶ a/an energetic/vigorous/active/lively/dynamic/spirited **campaign**

● ENERGETIC OR VIGOROUS? Energetic tends to refer more to physical energy and activities; vigorous often refers to business and political activities: *a vigorous opponent/supporter/campaigner*

energy noun

1 [U] ■ *She's always full of energy.*

vitality • dynamism • life • fire • spark • gusto • zest | *BrE* vigour | *AmE* vigor

▶ **do** sth with energy/vitality/dynamism/gusto/zest/vigour
▶ **have** energy/vitality/dynamism/spark/zest/vigour
▶ **lack** energy/vitality/dynamism/spark/vigour
▶ **be full of** energy/vitality/dynamism/life/fire/zest/vigour

2 [U] ■ *The plant provides a fifth of the nation's energy.*

power

▶ electrical/nuclear/atomic/solar/wind/tidal energy/power
▶ generate/produce/provide/supply/use/harness energy/power
▶ an energy/a power **supply**
▶ a **source** of energy/power

● ENERGY OR POWER? Energy is the source of power: the fuel, the light and heat from the sun or a nuclear reaction, etc. Power is energy that has been collected and used to produce electricity, etc. The *energy supply* is all the power that has not yet been used up; the *power supply* is the continuous flow of power to where it is being used: *The world's energy supply is heading for crisis.* • *interruptions in the power supply*

engine noun [C]
■ *Switch the engine off.*

motor • machine • unit

▶ a **powerful** engine/motor/machine
▶ **start/stop** a/an engine/motor/machine
▶ **run/switch on/switch off/turn on/turn off/service** a/an engine/motor/machine/unit
▶ a/an engine/motor/unit **drives** sth

● ENGINE OR MOTOR? Engine is usu. used to talk about vehicles which use thermal (= heat) energy from petrol, diesel or steam; motor is used to talk about machines which run on electricity.

enjoy verb

1 [T] ■ *We thoroughly enjoyed our time in New York.*

relish • revel in sth | *sometimes disapprov.* wallow in sth | *BrE, esp. written* savour | *AmE, esp. written* savor

▶ enjoy/relish/revel in **doing** sth
▶ enjoy/relish/revel in/savour **the moment**
▶ enjoy/relish/revel in **the attention/your freedom**

► enjoy/relish a **challenge**

2 enjoy yourself ■ *The kids really enjoyed themselves at the party.*

have fun | *infml* **have a good/great time**

► Let's enjoy ourselves/have fun/ have a good time.

enjoyable *adj.*
■ *Swimming is an enjoyable way of keeping fit.*

good ◆ **pleasant** ◆ **satisfying** | *esp. spoken* **fun** ◆ **nice** ◆ **lovely** | *fml* **pleasurable**

► a/an enjoyable/good/pleasant/ satisfying/fun/nice/lovely/ pleasurable **experience/thing** (to do)
► a/an enjoyable/good/pleasant/ fun/nice/lovely **time/evening/ party**
► a/an enjoyable/pleasant/fun/ pleasurable **task**

enjoyment *noun* [U]
■ *I get a lot of enjoyment from gardening.*

pleasure ◆ **entertainment** ◆ **fun** | *esp. spoken* **good time** ◆ **great time**

► do sth for enjoyment/pleasure/ entertainment/fun
► get/derive enjoyment/pleasure/ entertainment **from** sth
► spoil sb's enjoyment/sb's pleasure/the fun

● **ENJOYMENT OR PLEASURE?**
Enjoyment usu. comes from an activity that you do; **pleasure** can come from sth that you do or sth that happens:
✓He beamed with pleasure at seeing her. ✗ He beamed with enjoyment at seeing her.

enormous *adj.*
■ *The work cost an enormous amount of money.*

huge ◆ **vast** ◆ **tremendous** ◆ **massive** ◆ **immense** ◆ **great** ◆ **colossal** ◆ **giant** ◆ **gigantic** ◆ **monumental**

■ OPP **tiny**
► a/an enormous/huge/vast/ tremendous/massive/great/ colossal **amount of** sth
► enormous/huge/tremendous/ massive/immense/great **pressure**
► be a/have enormous/huge/ tremendous/massive/immense/ great **significance/importance**
► on a/an enormous/huge/vast/ massive/great/colossal/ monumental **scale**

● **ENORMOUS OR HUGE?** **Huge** is used slightly more to talk about the physical size of sth; **enormous** is used slightly more to talk about the degree of sth: *a huge chunk/pile/*

boulder/slab/mound/expanse ◆ *enormous fun/pleasure/importance/ significance/flexibility/scope*

enquiry (also **inquiry**) *noun*

1 [C] ■ *Police have launched a murder enquiry.*

investigation ◆ **survey** ◆ **inquest** ◆ **check** | *journ.* **probe**

► a/an enquiry/investigation/ survey/inquest/probe **into** sth
► conduct a/an enquiry/ investigation/survey/inquest/ check
► carry out a/an enquiry/ investigation/survey/check
► the **results/findings** of a/an enquiry/investigation/survey/ inquest

2 [C] ■ *We received over 300 enquiries about the job.*

query ◆ **question**

► a/an enquiry/query/question **about/as to/concerning/on** sth
► address/direct a/an enquiry/ query/question to sb
► have/deal with/handle/reply/ respond to/answer a/an enquiry/ query/question

ensure *verb* [T]
■ *The book ensured his success.*

make sure ◆ **guarantee** ◆ **assure** ◆ **see to it that...**

► ensure/make sure/guarantee/see to it **that...**
► ensure/guarantee/assure the **success/survival/quality** of sth
► **absolutely/virtually** ensure/ guarantee/assure sth

● **WHICH WORD?** **Ensure** and **make sure** are often used in orders or instructions:
✓Please ensure/make sure that the gas is switched off. ✗ Please guarantee/assure that the gas is switched off.
Guarantee and **assure** can suggest that feelings of worry or doubt are removed.

enter *verb* [I, T] (*fml*)
■ *He was refused permission to enter the country.*

go in ◆ **come in** ◆ **set foot in/on** sth

■ OPP **exit, leave**
► enter/go in/come in **by/through** sth
► enter/go into/come into/set foot in a **room/building/country/ town**

entertain

entertain verb

1 [I, T] ▪ *The job involves a lot of entertaining.*

welcome | *fml* **receive**

▶ entertain/welcome/receive a **guest/visitor**
▶ **be there to** entertain/welcome/receive sb

2 [T, I] ▪ *He entertained us for hours with his stories.*

amuse

▶ entertain/amuse sb **with sth**
▶ **keep sb** entertained/amused

entertainer noun [C]

▪ *Covent Garden is famous for its street entertainers.*

performer • **artist** • **comedian** | *esp. BrE, sometimes ironic* **artiste**

▶ a **young** entertainer/performer/ artist/comedian/artiste
▶ a/an **famous/talented/aspiring** entertainer/performer/artist/ comedian

entertaining adj.

▪ *He was a charming and entertaining companion.*

amusing • **funny** • **witty** • **humorous** • **comic** • **light-hearted**

■ OPP **boring**
▶ a/an entertaining/amusing/ funny/witty/humorous/comic **story**
▶ a/an entertaining/amusing/ funny/witty/humorous/light-hearted **speech**
▶ a/an entertaining/funny/witty/ humorous **speaker**

entertainment noun [U]

▪ *The entertainment was provided by a folk band.*

amusement • **play** • **pleasure** • **fun** • **recreation** • **relaxation**

▶ **do sth for** entertainment/ amusement/pleasure/fun/ recreation/relaxation
▶ **do sth for sb's** entertainment/ amusement
▶ **provide** entertainment/ amusement/fun/recreation/ relaxation

enthusiastic adj.

▪ *They gave her an enthusiastic welcome.*

eager • **avid** • **hungry** | *esp. BrE* **keen** | *infml* **mad** | *fml* **zealous**

■ OPP **unenthusiastic, apathetic**
▶ enthusiastic/mad **about sth**
▶ a/an enthusiastic/avid/keen **collector/fan**

▶ a/an enthusiastic/keen **supporter/admirer**
● **ENTHUSIASTIC OR EAGER?** People are often **eager** about things that they want for themselves; they are often **enthusiastic** about other people and their ideas and achievements: *The low prices pulled in crowds of eager buyers.* • *enthusiastic support/ applause/praise*

entire adj. [only before noun]

▪ *The entire village was destroyed.*

whole • **total** • **full** • **complete**

■ OPP **partial**
▶ a/an entire/whole/full/complete **day/set**
▶ the entire/whole/total **population**
▶ your entire/your whole/a full **life**
● **ENTIRE OR WHOLE?** **Entire** emphasizes sth more strongly than **whole** and is used esp. to emphasize how bad sth is: ✓I wasted an entire/a whole day on it. • We spent the whole day on the beach. ✗ *We spent the entire day on the beach.*

entirely adv.

▪ *I entirely agree with you.*

totally • **completely** • **fully** • **utterly** | *esp. BrE* **quite** | *esp. spoken* **absolutely** • **perfectly**

■ OPP **partly**
▶ entirely/totally/completely/quite/ absolutely/perfectly **normal**
▶ entirely/totally/completely/ utterly/quite **different**
▶ entirely/totally/completely/quite **forget**
● **WHICH WORD?** The main differences between these words are in register not meaning. **Completely**, **entirely** and **fully** are used more in written and formal English. **Totally**, **quite**, **absolutely** and **perfectly** are used more in spoken and informal English. **Utterly** is often used to express failure or impossibility: *They utterly failed to convince them.*

entrance noun [C]

▪ *I'll meet you at the main entrance.*

door • **gate** • **doorway** • **gateway** • **mouth** • **way**

■ OPP **exit**
▶ **at the** entrance/door/gate/mouth
▶ **in the** entrance/doorway/gateway
▶ **front/back/side** entrance/door/ gate/way

entry noun [U]

▪ *Entry to the museum is free.*

access • **admission** • **entrance**

▶ entry/access/admission/entrance **to sth**

▶ free entry/access/admission/entrance
▶ refuse/deny (sb) entry/access/admission/entrance

environment noun

1 [C] ■ *a pleasant working environment*

setting • surroundings •
background | *written* **backdrop** | *fml*
milieu

▶ in an environment/a setting/surroundings/a milieu
▶ the/sb/sth's **natural** environment/setting/surroundings/backdrop/milieu
▶ **provide/create** a(/an) environment/setting/surroundings/background/backdrop/milieu

2 the environment [sing.] ■ *products that are harmful to the environment*

nature • the natural world •
the wild • ecosystem • life • wildlife

▶ in the environment/nature/the wild/an ecosystem
▶ **protect** the environment/the natural world/…life/wildlife
▶ **damage** the environment/…life/wildlife

equal verb

1 linking verb ■ *A metre equals 39.38 inches.*

be • add up to sth • amount to sth •
run to sth | *esp. busin.* **total**

● EQUAL OR BE? Equal is not usu. used in questions and is only used in exact sums:
✔ *How much is a thousand pounds in Euros?* ✗ *How much does a thousand pounds equal in Euros?*
✔ *A metre is about/around/approximately 40 inches.* ✗ *A metre equals about/around/approximately 40 inches.*

2 [T] ■ *With his last jump he equalled the world record.*

match • rival • compare • be on a
par with sb/sth

▶ equal/match/compare with sb's **achievements**
▶ equal/match/rival the **performance** of sth
▶ be equalled/matched/rivalled **only by** sth

equal adj.

1 ■ *Cut it into four equal parts.*

the same • identical • uniform •
interchangeable • indistinguishable
• synonymous | *fml* **homogeneous** |
written **tantamount to** sth

■ OPP **unequal**

▶ equal/identical/tantamount to sth

▶ identical/interchangeable/synonymous **with** sth
▶ **roughly** equal/the same/synonymous

2 ■ *a desire for a more equal society*

just • fair | *fml* **equitable**

■ OPP **unequal**

▶ a/an equal/just/fair/equitable **division/distribution/share** of sth

equip verb [T]

■ *We travelled in a specially equipped medical jeep.*

arm • stock • *BrE* **fit sb/sth out •** **kit**
sb/sth out | *esp. AmE* **outfit** | *fml*
provision

▶ equip/arm/stock/fit out/kit out/provision sb/sth **with** sth
▶ equip/arm **yourself**
▶ equip/fit out/outfit/provision a **ship**
▶ be **fully/properly/poorly** equipped/armed/stocked

equipment noun [U]

■ *Put the camping equipment in the car.*

gear • kit • apparatus • material •
hardware • tackle | *infml* **stuff** | *esp.*
BrE, infml **things**

▶ **basic** equipment/kit/apparatus/materials/hardware
▶ **state-of-the-art/up-to-date/the**
latest equipment/gear/kit/hardware
▶ **have/use** (the right) equipment/gear/kit/apparatus/materials/hardware/stuff/things
▶ a **piece** of equipment/gear/kit/apparatus/hardware

equivalent noun [C]

■ *This tradition has no equivalent in our culture.*

parallel • counterpart | *esp. BrE, infml*
your opposite number

▶ a/an equivalent/parallel/counterpart **to** sb/sth
▶ the/your **American/Chinese, etc.** equivalent/counterpart/opposite number
▶ a **modern/direct** equivalent/parallel/counterpart
▶ **have** a/an equivalent/parallel/counterpart/opposite number

equivalent adj.

■ *Eight kilometres is roughly equivalent to five miles.*

comparable • corresponding •
matching | *fml* **analogous**

▶ equivalent/comparable/corresponding/analogous **to** sth

eradicate

► equivalent/comparable **in** size, amount, etc.
► an equivalent/a comparable **size/ amount/proportion**

eradicate verb [T]

■ *Polio has been virtually eradicated from Brazil.*

stamp sth out • root sb/sth out • wipe sb/sth out • eliminate • get rid of sb/sth • weed sb/sth out

► eradicate/eliminate/get rid of/ weed out **from** sth
► eradicate/stamp out/root out **corruption/drug abuse**
► eradicate/stamp out a **disease**
► eradicate/root out **inefficiency**

error noun [C]

■ *She made a serious error in her calculations.*

mistake • blunder • slip • inaccuracy • misprint • gaffe • oversight | *fml* omission | *esp. BrE, infml* howler

► due to a/an error/mistake/ blunder/oversight/omission
► a simple error/mistake/blunder/ slip/misprint
► a stupid/dreadful/terrible/fatal/ tragic error/mistake/blunder
► make a/an error/mistake/ blunder/slip/gaffe/howler

escape verb [I, T, no passive]

■ *She managed to escape from the burning car.*

get away • lose • elude • evade

► escape/get away **from** sb/sth
► escape/evade **being** captured, killed, hit, etc.
► escape/get away from/lose/ elude/evade your **pursuers**
► escape/elude/evade **capture/ detection/the police**

essay noun [C]

■ *Write an essay on the causes of the First World War.*

paper • article • piece • thesis • dissertation • assignment | *sometimes disapprov.* tract | *tech.* monograph

► a/an essay/paper/article/piece/ thesis/dissertation/tract/treatise/ monograph **on/about**
► a research paper/article/ thesis/dissertation/assignment/ monograph
► write/read a/an essay/paper/ article/piece/thesis/dissertation/ assignment/tract/treatise/ monograph
► submit a/an essay/paper/ piece/thesis/dissertation/ assignment

essential noun

1 [C, usu. pl.] *Agencies are trying to provide food and other basic essentials.*

need | *fml* necessity • want • requirement

► basic essentials/needs/necessities/ wants/requirements
► the bare essentials/necessities
● ESSENTIALS, NECESSITIES OR WANTS?
Wants are the most basic and physical of these; essentials are often more practical; necessities can cover both physical and practical needs: *human/bodily wants* • *The studio had all the essentials like heating and running water.*

2 essentials [pl.] ■ *the essentials of English grammar*

basics • practicalities • introduction | *esp. written* fundamentals

► a/the basic essentials/ introduction/fundamentals
► teach/grasp the essentials/basics/ fundamentals
► understand/know/cover/ concentrate on the essentials/ basics
● BASICS, ESSENTIALS OR FUNDAMENTALS? Basics are usu. the most practical; essentials are often more theoretical; fundamentals are the most theoretical, concerned with ideas and beliefs: *the basics of survival/good nutrition* • *the essentials of arithmetic/how we communicate using language* • *the fundamentals of Christian belief/the western concept of law*

essential adj.

1 ■ *Experience is essential for this job.*

vital • crucial • critical • indispensable • of the essence • key • necessary • compulsory • important | *fml* imperative • mandatory • obligatory

■ OPP inessential

► essential/vital/crucial/critical/ indispensable/key/necessary/ important **to** sth
► be essential/vital/crucial/critical/ necessary/compulsory/ important/imperative/ mandatory/obligatory **that...**
► be essential/vital/crucial/critical/ necessary/compulsory/ important/imperative/ mandatory/obligatory **to do** sth
► a/an essential/vital/crucial/ critical/indispensable/key/ necessary/compulsory/ important/mandatory **part**

2 ■ *The essential difference between us is our attitude to money.*

basic • ultimate • elementary | *esp. written* **fundamental • underlying**

▶ a/an essential/basic/ fundamental/underlying **difference/distinction**
▶ a/an essential/basic/elementary/ fundamental/underlying **rule/ principle**
▶ an essential/a basic/the ultimate/a fundamental/an underlying **truth/ cause/reason**
● **ESSENTIAL OR BASIC? Basic** looks at things from a practical point of view; **essential** looks at things from a more philosophical point of view, considering the very nature of things.

establish verb

1 [T] (*esp. written*) ■ *The company was established in 1766.*

set sth up • form • start | *esp. written* **found**

▶ establish/set up/form/start/found a/an **group/club/company/ movement/colony**
▶ establish/set up/form a/an **government/committee/ network**
▶ establish/set up/start a/an **fund/ project**

2 [T] (*fml*) ■ *We need to establish the truth.*

find • discover • identify | *fml* **determine • ascertain**

▶ establish/identify/determine/ ascertain **what/how/when/ where/why/whether...**
▶ establish/ascertain **that...**
▶ establish/find/discover/identify/ determine the **cause**
● **ESTABLISH OR ASCERTAIN?** Both words are used about official or scientific investigations but **ascertain** can also be used when you are trying to find out about sb's intentions and feelings:
✔ *Could you ascertain his position on this matter?* ✗ *Could you establish his position on this matter?*

estate noun

1 [C] ■ *The house is set on a 200-acre estate.*

land | *fml* **lands** | *esp. AmE* **real estate**

▶ **on** (an) estate/land/lands/real estate
▶ **own/buy/sell** (an) estate/land/ lands/real estate

2 [C] (*BrE*) ■ *an industrial estate.*

development | *BrE* **housing scheme** | *AmE* **project**

▶ a **housing** estate/development/ scheme/project
▶ an **industrial/commercial** estate/ development

estimate noun

1 [C] ■ *He gave me a rough estimate of the amount.*

guess • count • calculation • tally • reckoning

▶ a **rough** estimate/guess/count/ calculation
▶ a/an **accurate/precise/quick/ approximate** estimate/count/ calculation
▶ **make** a/an estimate/guess/ calculation
▶ **By** my/his, etc. estimate/ calculations/reckoning...

2 [C] ■ *We got estimates for the work from three different builders.*

valuation | *BrE* **costing** | *fml* **quotation** | *infml, esp. spoken* **quote**

▶ a/an estimate/quotation/quote **for** a piece of work
▶ a **high/low** estimate/valuation/ quotation/quote
▶ **give/provide/get/obtain/accept** a/an estimate/valuation/ quotation/quote
● **ESTIMATE OR COSTING?** An **estimate** usu. gives the total likely cost for a single piece of work. A **costing** or **costings** is/are a detailed list of all the likely costs of a service or product.

estimate verb [T, often passive]

■ *Police estimated the size of the crowd at 50 000.*

judge • guess • reckon • assess • calculate • gauge | *esp. AmE* **figure** | *fml* **extrapolate**

▶ estimate/judge/guess/reckon/ assess/calculate/gauge/ extrapolate sth **from** sth
▶ estimate/reckon/assess/calculate sth **at**
▶ estimate/judge/guess/reckon/ calculate/figure/extrapolate **that...**
▶ estimate/judge/guess/assess/ calculate/figure/gauge **how much/how many/how far**, etc.
● **ESTIMATE OR JUDGE?** People **estimate** future costs and lengths of time which cannot be calculated exactly by thinking carefully about the information available; people **judge** distances and speeds using their experience as a quick guide.

evade verb [T]

■ *She is trying to evade responsibility for her actions.*

avoid • get out of sth • sidestep • fend sb/sth off • skirt | *infml, disapprov.* **dodge • duck • wriggle out of sth • fudge**

■ OPP **face**

▶ evade/avoid/get out of/dodge/
wriggle out of **doing sth**
▶ evade/avoid/dodge/
wriggle out of your **responsibilities**
▶ evade/avoid/sidestep/fend off/
skirt round/dodge/duck a
question
▶ evade/avoid/dodge **taxes**

even adj.

1 ■ Children do not learn at an even
pace.

steady ◆ regular ◆ consistent ◆
constant ◆ stable | *usu. approv.* **stable** |
sometimes disapprov., esp. busin.
static | *written* **unchanging**

■ OPP **uneven, variable**
▶ a/an uneven/steady/constant/stable
temperature
▶ a/an even/steady/constant **flow**
▶ even/steady/regular **breathing**

2 ■ The scores were even at 2–2.

close ◆ neck and neck ◆ hard-fought
| *esp. BrE* **level**

■ OPP **uneven, unequal**
▶ a/an even/close/hard-fought
contest

evening noun [U, C]

■ I'll see you this evening.

night ◆ dusk ◆ twilight ◆ sunset |
esp. AmE, esp. written **sundown** | *fml*
or lit. **nightfall**

■ OPP **morning**
▶ **in the** evening/dusk/twilight
▶ **at** night/dusk/twilight/sunset/
sundown/nightfall
▶ tomorrow/yesterday/Monday,
etc. evening/night
▶ evening/night/dusk **falls**
● **EVENING OR NIGHT? Evening**
emphasizes the earlier hours, from
about 6pm onwards; **night**
emphasizes the later hours and can
include the early hours of the next
day: *We were up late last night and
didn't get to bed till 2am.*
Night can also mean the whole
time until it gets light: *I'm going to
my sister's for the evening* (= and
coming back later in the evening).
• *I'm going to my sister's for the night*
(= and not coming back until the
morning).

event noun

1 [C] ■ The election was the main
event of 2008.

incident ◆ affair ◆ experience ◆
episode ◆ phenomenon ◆
development ◆ business | *fml*
occurrence ◆ eventuality

▶ a **strange** event/incident/affair/
experience/phenomenon/
development/occurrence

▶ a **dramatic** event/incident/
experience/episode/development
▶ **witness** a/an event/incident/
episode/phenomenon
▶ a/an event/incident/experience/
episode/phenomenon **occurs/
takes place**

2 [C] ■ Here is a list of the club's social
events over the summer.

occasion ◆ party ◆ reception ◆
celebration ◆ reunion ◆ function ◆
festivities | *infml* **get-together** ◆
bash

▶ a (a) **special** event/occasion/party/
reception/celebration/reunion/
festivities
▶ a **social** event/occasion/function
▶ a/an event/party/reception/
celebrations/reunion/function/
festivities **is/are held**

evidence noun [U]

■ Do you have any evidence to support
this allegation?

proof ◆ support ◆ demonstration |
fml **testimony**

▶ evidence/support **for sth**
▶ evidence/proof/demonstration/
testimony **that…**
▶ **provide/give** evidence/proof/
support/a demonstration/
testimony
● **EVIDENCE OR PROOF? Evidence** is
what makes you believe that sth is
true; **proof** shows that sth is true in
a way that no one can argue
against.

evil noun [U]

■ the eternal struggle between good
and evil

wrong ◆ wickedness ◆ sin ◆
immorality | *esp. journ.* **vice**

■ OPP **good**
▶ **do** evil/wrong
▶ **turn (away) from** evil/
wickedness/sin

evil adj.

■ the evil effects of racism

wicked ◆ bad ◆ dark ◆ satanic ◆
demonic | *fml* **sinful** ◆ **base**

■ OPP **good**
▶ a/an evil/wicked/bad/sinful **man/
woman/life/act/thought**
▶ a/an evil/wicked **crime**
▶ evil/dark/demonic **forces/powers**
● **EVIL OR WICKED?** Both are very
strong words and should be used
with care. **Evil** is stronger than
wicked. *Children, witches* and
stepmothers can be **wicked**, esp. in
children's stories. *Spirits, forces,
monsters* and *killers* are **evil**, esp. in
stories for adults and popular news
reports.

exact adj.

1 [usu. before noun] ■ *She gave an exact description of the attacker.*

precise • accurate • specific

■ OPP inexact, approximate, rough
- exact/precise/accurate/specific **instructions/details**
- (a/an) exact/precise/accurate **answer/description/measurements**
- an exact/accurate **picture/copy**
- the exact/precise **time**
- ● EXACT, PRECISE OR ACCURATE? A description that is *not very exact/precise* lacks details; if it is *not very accurate* it has details, but they are wrong.

2 ■ *I had the exact same problem as you.*

very • actual • precise

■ OPP approximate
- the exact/very/actual/precise **moment**
- sb's exact/very/actual **words**
- the exact/actual/precise **nature of sth**
- the exact/very **same** sth

exaggerate verb [I, T]

■ *The dangers have been greatly exaggerated.*

overstate • dramatize | *fml* **embellish** | *esp. journ.* **inflate**

■ OPP play sth down, understate
- exaggerate/overstate/inflate the **importance/significance** of sth
- exaggerate/dramatize/embellish a **story**
- greatly/grossly/vastly/wildly/somewhat exaggerate/overstate/inflate sth

exam noun [C]

■ *The geography exam is on Thursday.*

test • assessment • oral | *BrE* **paper • practical** | *esp. AmE* **quiz** | *fml* **examination**

- a/an exam/test/quiz/examination **on** sth
- a **chemistry/geography, etc.** exam/test/paper/practical/quiz/examination
- **take/pass/fail** a/an exam/test/assessment/oral/paper/practical/quiz/examination
- ● EXAM OR TEST? An **exam** is an important test at school or college, usu. at the end of a year, semester or course of study; a **test** is sth that students might be given at any point, covering only part of the material. **Test** is also usu. used for tests of practical skill or physical or mental ability rather than academic knowledge: *an IQ test • (BrE) a driving test • (AmE) a driver's test*

examination noun

1 [U, C] ■ *Careful examination of the roof revealed the cause of the leak.*

inspection • check • observation • surveillance • survey • scan • check-up | *esp. busin.* **audit**

- a **medical** examination/inspection/check/check-up
- **carry out/do** a/an examination/inspection/check/observation/surveillance/survey/scan/audit
- a/an examination/inspection/check/observation/survey/scan/check-up/audit **reveals/shows** sth

2 [U, C] ■ *Your proposals are still under examination.*

research • analysis • exploration • study • discussion • enquiry/inquiry | *fml* **scrutiny**

- **scientific** examination/research/analysis/exploration/study/enquiry/scrutiny
- **carry out/conduct/undertake** (a/an) examination/research/analysis/exploration/study
- (the) examination/research/analysis/exploration/study/scrutiny **reveals** sth
- ● EXAMINATION OR STUDY? In this meaning, **examination** is often practical, in order to make a decision about sth; **study** is usu. academic, in order to find out about a subject.

examine verb

1 [T] ■ *These ideas will be examined in detail in Chapter 10.*

study • discuss • survey • review | *BrE* **analyse** | *AmE* **analyze** | *esp. spoken* **go into sth**

- examine/study/discuss/survey/review/analyse/go into **what/how/whether...**
- examine/study/discuss/survey/review/analyse the **situation**
- examine/study/discuss/review/analyse/go into **in depth/in detail**
- ● EXAMINE OR STUDY? You **examine** sth in order to understand it or to help other people understand it, for example by describing it in a book; you **study** sth in order to understand it yourself.

2 [T] ■ *The police officer examined the package.*

inspect • check • look at sth • go over sth • look over sth • check over sb/sth • check through sth | *busin.* **audit**

- examine/inspect/check/check over/check through (sth) **for** sth
- examine/inspect/check/look at sth **to see if/whether...**

example

▶ examine/inspect/check sth **regularly/daily**

● **EXAMINE, INSPECT OR CHECK?** These words can all be used when you are looking for possible problems, but only **check** is used about looking for mistakes:
✔Check your work before handing it in. ✗ ~~Examine/Inspect your work before handing it in.~~

Only **examine** is used when looking for the cause of a problem:
✔The doctor examined her but could find nothing wrong. ✗ ~~The doctor inspected/checked her but could find nothing wrong.~~

Inspect is used more often about an official:
✔Public health officials were called in to inspect the restaurant.

example noun

1 [C] ▪ *Can you give me an example of what you mean?*

case • instance • illustration • specimen

▶ **for** example/instance
▶ a **typical** example/case/instance/specimen
▶ **give** sb/**provide** a/an example/instance/illustration/specimen
▶ **cite/take/highlight** a/an example/case/instance

2 [C] (*approv.*) ▪ *She is a shining example to the rest of society.*

model • role model • ideal • inspiration | *fml* **embodiment • epitome • archetype**

▶ an example/a model/the embodiment/the epitome/the archetype **of** sth
▶ an example/inspiration **to** sb

excellent adj.

▪ *The rooms are excellent value at $30 a night.*

outstanding • wonderful • first-rate • classic • superb | *BrE, esp. spoken* **marvellous** | *AmE, esp. spoken* **marvelous** | *BrE, infml, spoken* **brilliant** | *esp. BrE, fml* **sterling**

▪ OPP **mediocre**

▶ a/an excellent/outstanding/wonderful/first-rate/perfect/superb/marvellous/brilliant/sterling **performance/job/service**
▶ a/an excellent/outstanding/wonderful/superb/marvellous/brilliant **achievement**
▶ **really** excellent/outstanding/wonderful/first-rate/perfect/superb/marvellous/brilliant

exception noun [C]

▪ *With a few exceptions, all the children can speak good French.*

oddity • anomaly | *fml* **aberration • vagaries** | *sometimes offens.* **freak**

▶ (an) exception/oddity/anomaly/aberration/vagaries **in** sth
▶ a **bit of** an exception/oddity/anomaly/freak
▶ a/an **curious/apparent** exception/anomaly

excess adj. [only before noun]

▪ *Excess food is stored in the body as fat.*

surplus • spare • leftover | *fml* **superfluous**

▶ (a/an) excess/surplus/spare **amount/demand/supply**
▶ excess/surplus/spare **cash/capacity/energy**
▶ excess/surplus/leftover **food**
● **EXCESS, SURPLUS OR SPARE?** **Spare** is the most informal and common of these words. **Surplus** is often used in business contexts: *surplus stock/products, surplus capital/income.* To talk about an extra amount that is seen as a bad thing, **excess** is often used: *excess fat/baggage.*

excessive adj.

▪ *Excessive drinking can damage your health.*

unreasonable • disproportionate | *fml* **undue • inordinate** | *BrE, disapprov.* **over the top** | *infml, disapprov.* **a bit much • extortionate** | *fml, disapprov.* **exorbitant**

▶ a/an excessive/unreasonable/disproportionate/undue/inordinate **amount** of sth
▶ a/an excessive/undue/inordinate **influence**
▶ excessive/unreasonable/extortionate/exorbitant **prices**
● **EXCESSIVE OR UNDUE?** Use **excessive** about matters of fact, when there is too much of sth: *excessive use/heat.* Use **undue** about matters of opinion, when you think sth is unreasonable: *undue delay/hardship.*

exchange noun [C, U]

▪ *Timber was sent to Egypt in exchange for linen.*

replacement • substitution • barter • reversal | *esp. BrE, spoken or journ.* **swap/swop**

▶ a/an exchange/reversal/swap **between** A and B
▶ a **direct** exchange/replacement/substitution
▶ a **straight** exchange/swap

exchange verb

1 [T] ■ *We use the forum to exchange ideas.*

swap/swop • switch • change • reverse • barter • substitute • replace | *esp. AmE or journ.* **trade**

▸ exchange/swap/switch/change/ barter/substitute/trade A **for** B
▸ switch/substitute/replace B **with** A
▸ exchange/swap/switch/reverse A **and** B
▸ exchange/swap/switch/change/ trade **places**
● WHICH WORD? **Exchange** is slightly formal and is often used in fixed phrases when people look at or talk to each other:
✓exchange glances/a few words
✗swap/trade glances/a few words
You can also *exchange information/ ideas.* **Switch** is often used when one thing is exchanged for another without sb knowing about it. **Swap** is used more for physical things, although you can *swap stories/ jokes.* **Trade** is commonly used in *AmE* but in *BrE* it is mostly used just for stories, jokes and insults.

2 [T] ■ *She exchanged her dollars for euros.*

change • cash • cash sth in

▸ exchange/change your **currency/ pounds/dollars for/into** pounds/ dollars/the **local currency**
▸ cash/change **traveller's cheques**

excited adj.

■ *The kids are excited about the trip.*

ecstatic • elated • exhilarated • rapturous • euphoric

▸ excited/ecstatic/elated/euphoric **at** sth
▸ excited/ecstatic/elated/euphoric **about** sth
▸ **feel** excited/elated/exhilarated/ euphoric

excitement noun [U, C]

■ *The good news caused great excitement.*

thrill • exhilaration • charge | *infml* **buzz • high • kick**

▸ (a) **real** excitement/thrill/charge/ buzz/high/kick
▸ **get** a thrill/charge/buzz/kick **out** of sth

exciting adj.

■ *Watching the band play live was incredibly exciting.*

thrilling • exhilarating • dramatic • heady • stirring

● OPP **unexciting**
▸ exciting/thrilling/exhilarating/ dramatic/heady/stirring **stuff**
▸ a/an exciting/thrilling/

exhilarating/dramatic/heady **experience**
▸ a/an exciting/thrilling/ exhilarating/dramatic/stirring **performance**
● EXCITING, THRILLING OR EXHILARATING? **Exciting** is the weakest but most general of these words. **Exhilarating** is the strongest and is often used about physical activities that involve speed and/or danger. **Thrilling** is often used about contests and stories where the ending is uncertain.

exclude verb

1 [T] ■ *We should not exclude the possibility of negotiation.*

rule sb/sth out • eliminate

● OPP **include**
▸ exclude/rule out/eliminate sth **as** sth
▸ exclude/rule out/eliminate sth **from** sth
▸ exclude/rule out/eliminate a/an **possibility/explanation**

2 [T, often passive] ■ *Women are still excluded from some golf clubs.*

keep sb/sth out • shut sb/sth out • blacklist | *fml* **ostracize**

● OPP **admit, accept**
▸ **feel** excluded/ostracized
● EXCLUDE, KEEP SB/STH OUT OR SHUT SB/STH OUT? **Exclude** is slightly more formal and usu. refers to a rule or policy; **keep sb/sth out** and **shut sb/sth out** usu. refer to sth such as a door or barrier which physically stops sb from entering a place.

exclusive adj.

■ *an exclusive hotel*

select • elitist

● OPP **inclusive**
▸ a/an exclusive/select **group/ clientele**
▸ an exclusive/elitist **image**

excuse noun [C]

■ *What's your excuse for being late today?*

explanation • justification • pretext • reason • grounds | *BrE* **defence** | *AmE* **defense** | *law* **plea**

▸ (a/an) excuse/explanation/ justification/pretext/reason/ grounds **for** sth
▸ (a) **good/valid** excuse/ justification/reason/grounds/ defence
▸ **have** (a/an) excuse/explanation/ justification/pretext/reason/ grounds/defence

excuse

excuse verb [T]
■ *Please excuse the mess.*

forgive + pardon + condone

■ OPP **condemn**
► excuse/forgive/pardon/condone sb **for** sth
► excuse/forgive/condone sb's **behaviour**
► Excuse/Forgive/Pardon **my ignorance**.

execution

execution noun [U, C]
■ *She faced execution by hanging for murder.*

the death penalty + capital punishment + hanging + gallows + scaffold + firing squad + the electric chair | *AmE, infml* **the chair**

► a **public/mass** execution/hanging
► **face** execution/the death penalty/ the firing squad/the electric chair/ the chair
► **abolish/bring back** the death penalty/capital punishment/ hanging/the electric chair

executive

executive noun [C]
■ *He's a senior executive in a computer firm.*

businessman + businesswoman + business person + entrepreneur + industrialist

► a **local/leading** executive/ businessman, etc./entrepreneur/ industrialist
► a **business/media/property** executive/entrepreneur
► an **ambitious** executive/ businessman, etc./entrepreneur

exempt

exempt verb [T] (*fml*)
■ *Charities are exempted from paying the tax.*

excuse + pardon + let sb off | *lit.* **spare**

► exempt/excuse/spare sb **from** sth
● **EXEMPT OR EXCUSE?** **Exempt** is usu. used when a whole group or organization is given permission not to do sth; **excuse** is used more about an individual.

exercise

exercise noun

1 [U, C] ■ *Swimming is good exercise.*

training + workout + aerobics | *BrE* **sport + PE** | *AmE* **sports + P.E.**

► **do** exercises/training/a workout/ aerobics/sport/PE

2 [C] ■ *Do one exercise for homework.*

assignment + task + homework

► a/an **easy/difficult** exercise/ assignment/task

► **do** an exercise/a task/your homework
► **give/set (sb)** some exercises/an assignment/a task/their homework

exercise verb [I, T]
■ *How often do you exercise?*

work out + train + warm up | *esp. BrE* **keep fit**

► exercise/train/warm up **properly**
► exercise/train/work out **regularly**
► exercise/train a **horse/dog**
● **EXERCISE OR WORK OUT?** **Exercise** can be any type of physical activity; **working out** usu. involves using equipment in a gym.

exhibition

exhibition noun [C] (*esp. BrE*)
■ *Have you seen the Picasso exhibition?*

show + display + trade show/fair | *AmE* **exhibit + fair**

► **on** exhibition/show/display/ exhibit
► a **big/major/public** exhibition/ show/display/exhibit
► **attend/go to/visit** a/an exhibition/show/trade show/ exhibit/fair
● **EXHIBITION OR SHOW?** An **exhibition** usu. contains works of art, or items of cultural or scientific interest that may be on display for a long time. **Show** is a more general word and usu. refers to a temporary event.

exist

exist verb [I] (not used in the progressive tenses)
■ *Do these creatures still exist in the wild?*

be found + live + occur | *fml* **prevail**

► exist/be found/occur/prevail **in/ among** sth
► **still** exist/be found/occur/prevail
► **never** exist/be found/occur

existence

existence noun [U]
■ *The industry's continued existence is threatened.*

survival + life

► sb/sth's **very/continued/day-to-day** existence/survival
► **threaten** sb/sth's existence/ survival/life
► a **struggle** for existence/survival

exit

exit noun

1 [C] ■ *There is a fire exit on each floor.*

door + gate + way + hatch + turnstile

■ OPP **entrance**
► **at** the exit/door/gate/turnstile
► the **front/back/side** exit/door/ gate/way

▶ the **rear** exit/door

2 [C, usu. sing.] ■ *He made a quick exit to avoid her.*

departure | *fml* **going**

■ OPP **entrance**
▶ a/an exit/departure **from** sth
▶ a **hasty/speedy** exit/departure
▶ **make** an exit/a departure

expand verb

1 [I, T] ■ *Metals expand when they are heated.* ■ *There are plans to expand the local airport.*

grow • extend • enlarge • widen • broaden • lengthen • stretch

■ OPP **contract**
▶ expand/grow/extend/enlarge/ widen/lengthen/stretch (sth) **to** a particular amount
▶ expand/grow/extend/enlarge/ widen/broaden/lengthen (sth) **by** a particular amount
▶ expand/extend/enlarge/widen/ broaden sth's **scope/range**

2 [I, T] (*esp. busin.*) ■ *The company has expanded into the mail order business.*

branch out • broaden | *esp. busin.* **diversify**

▶ expand/branch out/diversify **into** sth
▶ expand/broaden your **horizons**
▶ a/an company/firm/economy **expands/diversifies**

expect verb

1 [T] ■ *They're not expecting to get any money from the government.*

think • look forward to sth • anticipate • bargain for/on sth • look for sth • look ahead • watch for sb/sth | *fml* **await**

▶ expect/think/anticipate **that...**
▶ It **is** expected/thought/ anticipated **that...**
▶ expect/look forward to/ anticipate/look for/await **results**

2 [T] ■ *They expect their children to be high achievers.*

demand • ask • insist • hold out for sth | *fml* **require • stipulate**

▶ expect/demand/ask/require sth **from** sb
▶ expect/demand/ask/insist/ require/stipulate **that...**
▶ expect/ask/require **sb to do sth**
● **EXPECT, DEMAND OR ASK?** Ask is not as strong as **expect** or **demand**, both of which can be more like a command.

3 [T] (*esp. BrE, spoken*) ■ *I expect he'll be late, as usual.*

suppose • imagine • suspect • assume • presume | *esp. spoken* **take it** | *esp. BrE, spoken* **I dare say** | *esp. AmE, spoken* **guess**

▶ expect/suppose/imagine/ suspect/assume/presume/take it/ I dare say/guess **that...**
▶ I expect/suppose/imagine/ suspect/assume/presume/guess **so.**

expectation noun

1 [C, U] ■ *We are confident in our expectation of a rise in prices.*

anticipation • forecast • prediction • projection • prophecy | *approv.* **foresight**

▶ (a/an) expectations/forecast/ prediction/projection/prophecy **about** sth
▶ (a/an) expectation/anticipation/ forecast/prediction/projection/ prophecy **that...**
▶ **in** expectation/anticipation **of** sth

2 [C, usu. pl.,] U ■ *The results exceeded our expectations.*

hope • dream • ambition • aspiration | *esp. written* **desire • wish**

▶ expectations/hopes/aspirations/ desires/wishes **for** sth
▶ **high** expectations/hopes/ ambitions/aspirations
▶ **have** (a/an) expectations/hopes/ dream/ambition/aspiration/ desire/wish

expel verb

1 [T] ■ *The government has expelled all foreign journalists.*

deport • exile • banish • extradite | *fml* **repatriate • displace**

▶ expel/deport/exile/banish/ extradite/repatriate sb **to/from** a country
▶ expel/deport/repatriate/displace **refugees**
▶ expel/deport/repatriate **immigrants**

2 [T] ■ *She was expelled from school for taking drugs.*

evict • throw sb out • drop • excommunicate | *BrE* **exclude** | *infml* **kick sb out** | *esp. BrE, infml* **chuck sb out** | *fml* **eject**

▶ expel/evict/drop/exclude/eject sb **from** a place or organization
▶ throw/kick/chuck sb **out of** a place
▶ a **landlord** evicts/throws out/kicks out/chucks out/ejects sb

expense noun

1 [U, C, usu. sing.] ∎ *They had the house redecorated at great expense.*

price + cost

▸ the **considerable/enormous expense/cost**
▸ **increase/reduce** the **expense/price/cost**

2 [pl.] ∎ *You can claim back your travel expenses.*

costs + spending + expenditure + outlay | *esp. BrE* **overheads** | *esp. AmE* **overhead**

▸ **increase/reduce expenses/costs/spending/expenditure/the outlay/overheads**
▸ **control/cover/cut expenses/costs/spending/expenditure/overheads**
▸ **meet expenses/costs/expenditure/overheads**
▸ **incur expenses/costs/expenditure**

expensive adj.

∎ *I can't afford expensive restaurants.*

costly + overpriced | *infml* **pricey**

∎ OPP **cheap, inexpensive**
▸ **expensive/costly/pricey for sb/sth**
▸ **expensive/costly to do sth**

experience noun

1 [U] ∎ *I have over 10 years' teaching experience.*

knowledge + understanding + learning + wisdom

∎ OPP **inexperience**
▸ **practical experience/knowledge/understanding/wisdom**
▸ **acquire experience/knowledge/understanding/learning/wisdom**
▸ **gain experience/knowledge/understanding/wisdom**

2 [C] ∎ *I had a bad experience with fireworks once.*

event + incident + affair + episode | *esp. spoken* **business**

▸ a **terrible experience/event/incident/affair/business**
▸ an **enjoyable experience/event/affair**
▸ a/an **experience/event/incident/episode occurs/takes place**

experience verb

1 [T] (*esp. written*) ∎ *The country experienced a severe food shortage.*

have + meet + feel + take + go through sth + run into sth | *esp. written* **encounter + suffer + receive + undergo**

▸ **experience/have/meet/run into/encounter problems**

▸ **experience/have/feel/suffer/receive a/the shock**
▸ **experience/go through/suffer/undergo an ordeal**

2 [T] ∎ *I had never experienced such pain before.*

feel + know | *esp. written* **taste + sense**

▸ **experience/feel/know/taste joy**
▸ **experience/feel/know pain/satisfaction/shame**
▸ **experience/feel a need**
▸ **experience/feel a/an sense/emotion/urge/stab**

experienced adj.

1 ∎ *She's a very experienced teacher.*

long-serving | *esp. journ.* **veteran** | *esp. written* **seasoned** | *BrE* **practised** | *AmE* **practiced**

∎ OPP **inexperienced**
▸ **experienced/practised in sth**
▸ a/an **experienced/veteran/seasoned campaigner**
▸ a/an **experienced/veteran actor/politician/soldier**

2 ∎ *Ali is young and not experienced yet in the ways of the world.*

often approv. **sophisticated + suave + urbane**

∎ OPP **inexperienced**
▸ a/an **experienced/sophisticated/suave/urbane man/manner**

experiment noun [C, U]

∎ *an experiment to discover the effects of a low calorie diet*

test + testing + trial + pilot study

▸ (a/an) **experiment/test/testing/trial on sth**
▸ (a/an) **experiment/test/testing/trial/pilot study to do sth**
▸ **carry out/conduct (a/an) experiment/test/testing/trial/pilot study**

experiment verb [I]

∎ *He believes that experimenting on animals is wrong.*

test + try + try sth out + pilot + put sth to the test

▸ **experiment/test/try/try out sth on sb/sth**

experimental adj.

∎ *experimental teaching methods*

modern + modernist + futuristic + avant-garde + postmodernist

▸ a/an **experimental/modern/modernist approach**
▸ **experimental/modern/modernist/avant-garde/postmodernist art/writing/works**

expert noun [C]

■ She's a leading expert in child psychology.

authority • specialist • connoisseur • pundit • buff • afficionado | *infml, esp. journ.* guru

▶ a/an expert/authority/specialist **in/on** sth
▶ a/an expert/authority/specialist **in the field** (of sth)
▶ a **leading** expert/authority/ specialist /pundit
● **EXPERT OR AUTHORITY?** An **expert** is sb who is very skilled at sth and can give useful advice or training. An **authority** is sb who knows a lot about an academic subject, which may be very interesting but may not be useful or relevant.

expert adj.

■ They're all expert in this field.

great • skilled • talented • gifted • professional • impressive • masterly • virtuoso • accomplished • skilful | *BrE* skilful | *AmE* skillful

■ OPP inexpert
▶ expert/great/skilled/ accomplished/skilful **at** sth
▶ expert/skilled/professional **in** sth
▶ a/an expert/great/skilled/ talented/professional/impressive/ masterly/virtuoso/accomplished/ skilful **performance**

explain verb

1 [T, I] ■ Pat explained the rules of the game.

spell sth out • define • interpret • illustrate • shed/cast/throw light on sth | *fml* clarify • expound

▶ explain/spell out/clarify/expound sth **to** sb
▶ explain/spell out/**that...**
▶ explain/spell out/illustrate/shed light on/clarify **how/what/why...**

2 [I, T] ■ The government now has to explain its decision to the public.

justify • defend • account for sth

▶ explain/justify/defend/account for sth **to** sb
▶ explain/justify/account for **what/ why/how...**
▶ explain/justify/defend/account for a **decision/sb's behaviour**
▶ explain/justify/defend **yourself**

explanation noun [C, U]

■ What explanation can you give for your appalling behaviour?

reason • excuse • motive • grounds • justification • cause • pretext | *BrE* defence | *AmE* defense • law plea

▶ a/an explanation/reason/excuse/ motive/grounds/justification/ cause/pretext/defence **for** sth

▶ the **obvious** explanation/reason/ excuse/motive/grounds/ justification/cause/pretext/ defence
▶ **have** a/an excuse/reason/ excuse/motive/grounds/ justification/cause/pretext/ defence

explode verb [I, T]

■ The bomb exploded.

blow (sth) up • go off • burst • erupt • detonate | *fml or med.* rupture

▶ a bomb explodes/blows up/goes off/bursts/detonates
▶ a car/plane/vehicle explodes/ blows up
▶ a volcano explodes/erupts

exploit verb [T] (usu. disapprov.)

■ Some employers are exploiting immigrants.

disapprov. abuse • use | *fml* misuse

▶ exploit/abuse your **position**
▶ abuse/misuse **drugs/alcohol/ solvents**
▶ exploit/use sb/sth **for your own ends**

explore verb

1 [T, I] ■ The city is best explored on foot.

tour • go backpacking

▶ explore/tour **by car**
▶ **go** exploring/touring/ backpacking

2 [T] ■ The police are exploring every possibility.

investigate • look into sth • research • examine • discuss • inquire/enquire into sth • delve into sth | *esp. journ.* probe

▶ explore/investigate/look into/ research/examine/discuss/inquire into **what/why/how/whether...**
▶ explore/investigate/look into/ research/examine/discuss/inquire into a **problem/matter**
▶ explore/investigate/look into/ research/examine/discuss/delve into a **subject**

explorer noun [C]

■ Early European explorers traded with the Native Americans.

discoverer • pioneer • adventurer

▶ a **band** of explorers/pioneers/ adventurers

explosion noun [C]

■ The explosion destroyed the building.

journ. blast

▶ a loud/deafening/powerful/
massive/huge explosion/blast
▶ a bomb/gas/chemical/nuclear
explosion/blast
▶ a/an explosion/blast **rips
through**/rocks sth

expose verb

1 [T] ■ *She was exposed as a liar.*

reveal • uncover • betray • give sb/
sth away • bring sth to light | *fml*
disclose • divulge | *journ.* leak

▶ expose/reveal/betray/give away/
divulge/leak sth to sb
▶ expose/reveal/uncover/disclose
sb/sth **as** sth
▶ expose/reveal/uncover/give
away/disclose **the truth**

2 [T] ■ *They exposed themselves to
unnecessary risks.*

lay sb/sth open to sth • put sb
through sth | *fml* subject sb/sth to
sth

▶ expose sb/lay sb open/subject sb
to sth
▶ expose/subject **yourself** to sth
▶ expose sb to/lay sb open to/
subject sb to **criticism/ridicule/
abuse/attack**

express verb [T]

■ *Teachers have expressed concern
about the new tests.*

say • put • phrase • state • voice •
air | *esp. journ.* indicate

▶ express/state/voice/air your
**thoughts/opinions/views/
concerns**
▶ express/put/phrase/state/
indicate **clearly**
● EXPRESS OR SAY? **Express** is often
followed by a noun describing a
feeling or emotion; **say** cannot be
used in this way: *to express your
dissatisfaction/fear/horror/gratitude
• to say that you are dissatisfied/
afraid/horrified/grateful*

expression noun

1 [C, U] ■ *These riots are an
expression of anti-government
feeling.*

display • show • demonstration |
esp. BrE, fml exhibition

▶ a/an expression/display/show/
demonstration of **support/
affection**
▶ a/an expression/display/show of
concern/emotion
▶ a **public** expression/display/
show/demonstration of sth

2 [C] ■ *There was a worried expression
on her face.*

look • face

▶ an expression/a look **of**
amazement/disbelief/horror, etc.
▶ an expression/a look **on** sb's face
▶ an expression/a look **in** sb's eyes
▶ a/an **happy/sad/worried/angry/
stern/serious** expression/look/
face
● EXPRESSION OR LOOK? Your
expression is usu. a reflection of
what you happen to be thinking or
feeling at any particular moment; a
look is either the expression that
happens to be in your eyes, it can
be a way of deliberately
communicating a thought or
feeling to a particular person: you
can *give* or *throw* sb a look or
exchange looks with sb: *She threw
him a dirty look.*

3 [C] ■ *The novel is full of slang
expressions.*

word • phrase • idiom • term

▶ a/an **new/ambiguous/technical/
colloquial** expression/word/
phrase/term
▶ **use** a/an expression/word/
phrase/idiom/term
▶ **coin** a/an expression/word/
phrase/term

extend verb

1 [T] ■ *We plan to extend the house
next year.*

enlarge • expand • lengthen •
stretch • widen • broaden

▶ extend/enlarge/expand/
lengthen/stretch/widen sth **to** a
particular amount
▶ extend/enlarge/expand/
lengthen/widen sth **by** a particular
amount
▶ extend/expand/widen/broaden
your **knowledge**
● EXTEND OR ENLARGE? Things that
you **extend** are usu. on a larger
scale than things that you **enlarge**:
you extend a house or building,
but enlarge a picture, or an area
within a building.

2 [T] ■ *They've agreed to extend the
deadline.*

prolong • sustain • maintain

■ OPP shorten
▶ extend/prolong/sustain/maintain
(sb's) **life**
▶ extend/prolong/maintain a **visit/stay**
▶ extend/prolong/maintain sth
indefinitely
● EXTEND OR PROLONG? **Extend** is
used esp. in business contexts: *to
extend an overdraft/a trip/a visa*
Prolong is used more to talk about
making experiences last longer: *to
prolong your stay/survival/agony*

extensive adj.

1 ■ *The fire caused extensive damage.*

considerable • substantial • sizeable/sizable • large • big • great • huge • vast • enormous • immense

■ OPP limited
▶ a/an extensive/considerable/substantial/sizeable/large/big/great/huge/vast/enormous/immense **amount**
▶ a/an extensive/considerable/substantial/sizeable/large/big/great/huge/vast/enormous **area**
▶ a/an extensive/considerable/substantial/large/big/great/huge/vast/enormous **collection**
▶ a/an extensive/considerable/substantial/big/great/huge/vast/enormous/immense **change/improvement/gain/loss/influence**

2 ■ *Extensive research has been done into this disease.*

wide • broad • wide-ranging • comprehensive • exhaustive

■ OPP limited
▶ a/an extensive/wide/broad/comprehensive **range**
▶ extensive/wide/broad/wide-ranging **interests**
▶ extensive/wide/broad/comprehensive **knowledge**

extent *noun* [U, sing.]
■ *It is difficult to assess the full extent of the damage.*

scale • degree • level • size • proportions | *fml* **magnitude**

▶ the **full** extent/scale/size of sth
▶ the **true** extent/level/size of sth
▶ **assess/judge** the extent/scale/degree/level/size/magnitude of sth
● **EXTENT OR SCALE?** The **scale** of sth is how large it is; the **extent** is how far it goes. Some qualities, such as *knowledge*, are considered as being wide rather than large, and so have **extent** rather than **scale**:
✓I was amazed at the extent of his knowledge. ✗ I was amazed at the scale of his knowledge.
You are more likely to try to **measure/calculate** the extent of sth, while you simply try to **comprehend/grasp** the scale of sth.

extraordinary *adj.*

1 ■ *What an extraordinary thing to say!*

surprising • unexpected • astonishing • amazing

▶ extraordinary/surprising/unexpected/astonishing/amazing **events/effects/changes/results**
▶ a/an extraordinary/surprising/unexpected/astonishing/amazing **development**

▶ extraordinary/unexpected **circumstances/problems**

2 ■ *He did the work with extraordinary energy.*

remarkable • exceptional • amazing • astonishing • phenomenal • unique | *infml* **incredible • unbelievable • staggering** | *written* **unusual**

■ OPP ordinary
▶ a/an extraordinary/remarkable/amazing/astonishing/unique/incredible/staggering **achievement**
▶ extraordinary/remarkable/exceptional/amazing/astonishing/unique/incredible/unbelievable **beauty**
▶ a/an extraordinary/remarkable/amazing/astonishing/phenomenal/incredible/unusual **success**

extravagant *adj.* (*sometimes disapprov.*)
■ *He bought extravagant presents that he couldn't really afford.*

lavish | *disapprov.* **wasteful**

■ OPP thrifty
▶ the extravagant/lavish/wasteful **use** of sth
▶ extravagant/wasteful **consumption**
▶ an extravagant/a lavish **present/gift/lifestyle**

extreme *adj.*

1 [usu. before noun] ■ *We are still working under extreme pressure.*

intense • maximum • utmost • supreme

■ OPP moderate
▶ extreme/maximum/the utmost/supreme **importance**
▶ extreme/maximum/the utmost **care/difficulty**
▶ extreme/intense/supreme **happiness**
● **EXTREME OR INTENSE?** Intense describes a very strong or deep feeling or quality; extreme describes a feeling, quality, action or state that is at its limit: *intense desire/interest/heat/blue eyes • extreme pain/heat/violence/danger*

2 ■ *It was the most extreme example of cruelty to animals I have ever seen.*

severe • serious • desperate • drastic • acute | *fml* **grave** | *esp. BrE, fml* **dire**

■ OPP slight, mild
▶ (a/an) extreme/severe/serious/desperate/acute/dire **shortage/poverty**

extremely

▶ a/an extreme/serious/desperate/
acute/dire **need**
▶ extreme/severe/serious/acute/
grave **danger**

3 (usu. disapprov.) ■ extreme left-
wing/right-wing views

radical • revolutionary | disapprov.
extremist | usu. approv. **progressive**

■ OPP **moderate**
▶ extreme/radical/revolutionary/
extremist/progressive **ideas/views**

extremely adv. (usu. used with
adjectives and adverbs)
■ This issue is extremely complicated.

highly • very • desperately | esp.
spoken **really • so** | fml **most** | BrE,
taboo, slang **bloody**

■ OPP **slightly, moderately**
▶ extremely/highly/very/really/so
**successful/intelligent/
competitive/critical/sensitive**
▶ extremely/very/desperately/
really/so/most **anxious/
concerned/disappointed/
unhappy/important**
▶ extremely/very/desperately/
really/so **ill/sick/tired/poor/
lonely/hard/close**

Ff

fabric noun [U, C]
■ They sell a wide variety of printed
cotton fabrics.

cloth • material • textile

▶ woven/cotton/woollen **fabric/
cloth/material/textiles**
▶ make/produce/weave/dye
fabric/cloth/textiles
▶ a length/piece/strip/roll/scrap of
fabric/cloth/material

face verb

1 [T] ■ Travelling across the desert,
they faced many dangers.

confront | written **brave**

▶ face/confront sb **with sth**
▶ face/confront **a problem/crisis/
dilemma/challenge/difficulty/
situation**
▶ a **problem/dilemma/challenge/
difficulty/situation** faces/
confronts sb
● FACE OR CONFRONT? If you confront
a situation, you actively decide to
deal with it. If you face sth, the
problem already exists and you
have no choice but to deal with it.

2 [T] ■ It's not always easy to face the
truth.

**accept • face up to sth • come to
terms with sth • live with sth •
make the best of sth • resign
yourself to sth** | fml **reconcile sb/
yourself to sth**

▶ face/accept/face up to/come to
terms with/live with/make the
best of/resign yourself to/reconcile
yourself to **the fact that...**
▶ face/accept/face up to/come to
terms with/live with **the fact
that...**
▶ face/accept/come to terms with/
make the best of **a situation**

facilities noun [pl.]
■ Each room has basic cooking
facilities.

service • resource • amenity | esp.
AmE **utility**

▶ public/basic/local **facilities/
services/resources/amenities/
utilities**
▶ provide/lack **facilities/services/
resources/amenities**
▶ have access to **facilities/services/
resources**

fact noun

1 [sing., U] ■ In actual fact, the work is
very easy.

**the truth • reality • so • the case •
the real world • real life**

■ OPP **fiction**
▶ in fact/reality/the real world/real
life
▶ the fact (of the matter)/the truth
(of the matter)/the case is that...
▶ face/accept/ignore **the fact/the
truth/reality**

2 [C] ■ Let's look at some basic facts
about healthy eating.

**point • detail • information • data •
intelligence • figure • statistics** |
infml **stats • info** | fml **particular**

▶ (a) **fact/point/detail/information/
data/intelligence/stats/info/
particulars about/relating to** sb/
sth
▶ accurate/precise **facts/details/
information/data/intelligence/
figures/statistics/stats/info**
▶ give (sb) the **facts/details/
information/data/figures/
statistics/stats/info/particulars**

factor noun [C]
■ The result will depend on a number
of different factors.

point • consideration

▶ a **factor/consideration in sth**
▶ a/an **additional/main/
important/key/crucial/prime
factor/point/consideration**
▶ political/practical **factors/points/
considerations**

factory noun [C]

■ *The factory closed down last year.*

plant • mill • works • yard • workshop • foundry

▶ a **car/chemical/munitions** factory/plant

▶ **manage/run** a factory/plant/mill/works/yard/workshop/foundry

▶ **work in/at** a factory/plant/mill/yard/workshop/foundry

▶ a factory/plant/mill/works/workshop/foundry **makes/manufactures/produces** sth

fail verb

1 [I, T] ■ *Opponents say it's a policy doomed to fail.*

go wrong • collapse • break down • backfire • fall through • get/go nowhere • come to nothing | *fml* **founder**

■ **OPP** succeed

▶ a **plan** fails/goes wrong/backfires/falls through/comes to nothing/founders

▶ a **relationship/marriage** fails/goes wrong/collapses/breaks down

▶ **talks** fail/collapse/break down/fall through/founder

▶ a **project** fails/collapses/falls through/founders

2 [T, I] ■ *She never fails to email every week.*

forget | *fml* **neglect** | *esp. BrE, fml* **omit**

▶ fail/forget/neglect/omit to do sth

▶ **completely/totally/almost/never/conveniently** fail/forget to do sth

3 [I, T] ■ *He failed his driving test.*

esp. AmE, infml **flunk**

■ **OPP** pass

▶ fail/flunk a/an **exam/examination/test/course**

failure noun

1 ■ *The marriage ended in failure.*

collapse • breakdown

■ **OPP** success

▶ a **failure/collapse/breakdown in** sth

▶ **contribute to/lead to/result in/cause/avoid** the failure/collapse/breakdown (of sth)

▶ **end in** failure/the breakdown (of sth)

2 [C] ■ *The whole thing was a complete failure.*

disaster • catastrophe • debacle | *infml* **fiasco • washout • flop**

■ **OPP** success

▶ a **failure/disaster/catastrophe for** sb

▶ a **total** failure/disaster/

catastrophe/debacle/fiasco/washout/flop

▶ a **financial** failure/disaster/debacle/fiasco

3 [C] ■ *He was a failure as a teacher.*

disappointment | *disapprov.* **incompetent** | *infml, disapprov.* **loser • disaster • no-hoper**

■ **OPP** success

▶ be a failure/disappointment/disaster **as** sth

▶ a **complete** failure/loser/disaster/no-hoper

faint verb [I]

■ *I almost fainted from lack of air.*

pass out • collapse | *infml* **drop**

▶ faint/pass out/collapse/drop **from** exhaustion/hunger/loss of blood/the heat, etc.

● **FAINT OR PASS OUT?** People **faint** because not enough blood is going to the brain. They can **pass out** for this reason, or because they have been hit on the head or because they are drunk.

faint adj.

1 ■ *There was a faint glimmer of light from her window.*

dim • weak • soft | *lit.* **thin**

■ **OPP** bright

▶ faint/dim/weak/soft/thin **light**

▶ a faint/dim/soft **glow**

▶ a faint/dim **outline**

● **DIM, FAINT OR WEAK?** Dim describes light in a room or place when it is not bright enough to see clearly; faint describes a particular point of light that is hard to see; weak usu. describes sunlight that is not bright.

2 ■ *Their voices grew fainter as they walked down the road.*

quiet • soft • muffled • inaudible | *written* **dull**

▶ a/an faint/quiet/soft/muffled/inaudible **voice**

▶ a faint/quiet/soft/muffled/dull **sound**

▶ a faint/soft/muffled/dull **noise/thud/thump**

3 [not before noun] ■ *The walkers were faint from hunger.*

light-headed • dizzy

▶ faint/light-headed/dizzy **from/with** sth

▶ **feel** faint/light-headed/dizzy

● **FAINT OR LIGHT-HEADED?** People usu. **faint** from weakness, pain or fear; they feel **light-headed** from weakness, alcohol or happiness.

fair adj.

■ *We want a fair wage.*

reasonable ◆ equal ◆ even-handed ◆ just | *fml* equitable

▶ OPP **unfair**
▶ be fair/reasonable/just/equitable that…
▶ a/an **fair**/reasonable/just/equitable **division/distribution/share** of sth
▶ a **fair**/reasonable/just **law/punishment/sentence/judgement/person/man/woman**

fairly adv.

■ *The plants are fairly easy to grow.*

reasonably ◆ rather ◆ quite ◆ *esp. BrE* rather ◆ quite ◆ *AmE or infml, BrE* pretty

▶ fairly/reasonably/rather/quite/pretty **good/successful/large/easy/pleased/confident**
▶ fairly/rather/quite/pretty **bad/big/heavy/new/difficult/expensive**
▶ fairly/reasonably/pretty **certain/accurate/happy/safe/sure**
● FAIRLY OR REASONABLY? Fairly is more positive than reasonably, which often suggests that sth is of an acceptable level, but not the best.

faith noun

1 [U, sing.] ■ *I have great faith in you —I know you'll do well.*

confidence ◆ belief ◆ trust ◆ certainty ◆ conviction

▶ faith/confidence/belief/trust in sb/sth
▶ **have/show** faith/confidence/trust
▶ **lack** faith/confidence/belief/conviction
▶ **destroy** sb's faith/confidence/belief/trust
● FAITH OR CONFIDENCE? Faith is used esp. in the context of human relationships; confidence is used esp. in business contexts.

2 [U, C] ■ *people of different faiths*

religion ◆ cult ◆ sect ◆ Church | *fml* denomination

▶ (a) **religious** faith/cult/sect
▶ **practise** your faith/religion
▶ **belong to** a cult/a sect/the Church/a denomination

faithful adj.

■ *He has been a faithful friend to me.*

loyal ◆ dedicated ◆ devoted ◆ true ◆ staunch ◆ reliable ◆ trusted

▶ faithful/loyal/dedicated/true to sb/sth
▶ a faithful/loyal/devoted/true/staunch/reliable/trusted **friend**

▶ faithful/loyal/reliable **service**
● FAITHFUL OR LOYAL? There is only a slight difference of emphasis: a loyal friend/servant remains **loyal** as a matter of principle; a faithful friend/servant remains **faithful** from affection.

fake noun [C]

■ *All the paintings proved to be fakes.*

forgery ◆ imitation ◆ dummy ◆ copy

▶ a **good** fake/forgery/imitation/copy
▶ a **cheap** fake/imitation
▶ a **poor/crude** forgery/imitation
● FAKE OR FORGERY? Forgery usu. refers to things that are written, drawn, painted or printed in order to deceive people. Fake can refer to any object that is made or produced, as well as artificial copies of natural objects (for example, jewels); fakes may or may not be used to deceive people.

fake adj. [only before noun]

■ *There was a stall selling fake designer clothing.*

fake ◆ false ◆ counterfeit ◆ dummy ◆ *disapprov.* bogus ◆ sham | *BrE, infml* phoney | *esp. AmE, infml* phony

▶ OPP **genuine**
▶ fake/false/counterfeit **money/currency/coins**
▶ a fake/false/phony **identity**
▶ a fake/false/phony **document/passport/invoice**
▶ a fake/bogus/sham **marriage**
● FAKE OR FALSE? False is used more frequently to describe documents and parts of the body such as *eyelashes, teeth* or a *beard, moustache* or *nose*. Fake is used more frequently to describe other objects: *fake goods/flowers/pearls/bombs*

fall noun

1 [C] ■ *Share prices suffered a fall yesterday.*

drop ◆ decline ◆ decrease ◆ downturn ◆ slump ◆ reduction

■ OPP **rise**

▶ a **fall/drop/decline/decrease/downturn/slump/reduction in** sth
▶ a **20% fall/drop/decline/decrease/reduction**
▶ a fall/drop/decline/decrease/reduction **of 20%**
▶ **see** a fall/drop/decline/decrease/downturn/reduction
● FALL, DROP OR DECLINE? These words all describe a process that happens, not a deliberate action by sb: *We've seen a steady decline in profits this year.* Fall and decline can happen over time, but a **drop** cannot:

✔ a gradual decline/fall ✗ ~~a gradual drop~~

2 [sing.] ■ *the fall of Rome to the barbarians*

downfall • overthrow

■ **OPP** rise
► bring about/lead to sb's **fall/ downfall/overthrow**

fall *verb*

1 [I] ■ *He fell onto the rocks below.*

drop • tumble • plunge • sink • topple • fall

► fall/drop/tumble/sink/crash **down**
► fall/plunge **to your death**

2 [I] (usu. used with an adv. or prep.) ■ *70 millimetres of rain fell overnight.*

come down • rain • pour

► rain **falls/comes down/pours**
► fall/rain **heavily/lightly/steadily**
● FALL, COME DOWN OR RAIN? Rain is the most frequent verb and is used with the subject *it*. Fall and come down are used with a subject such as *rain* or *snow*.

3 [I] ■ *She slipped and fell on the ice.*

fall down • fall over • stumble • trip • slip

● FALL, FALL DOWN OR FALL OVER? Fall and fall over are only used about people in this meaning. Fall down can be used about people, buildings or other structures that can stand and then suddenly stop standing.

4 [I] ■ *The temperature fell sharply in the night.*

drop • come down • decline • diminish | *fml* **decrease** | *esp. busin.* **sink • slump • plunge • plummet • tumble**

■ **OPP** rise
► fall/drop/come down/decline/ diminish/decrease/sink/slump/ plunge/plummet/tumble **by** 100, 25%, a half, etc.
► fall/drop/come down/decline/ diminish/decrease/sink/slump/ plunge/plummet/tumble **from** 1 500 **to** 1 000
► prices **fall/drop/come down/ decline/decrease/sink/slump/ plunge/plummet/tumble**
► fall/drop/come down/decline/ decrease/slump/plunge **dramatically**
● FALL, DROP OR DECLINE? All these words can be used about numbers, levels, prices, profits and sales. Use **decline** to talk about a loss of economic strength or importance:
✔ *The city/industry has declined (in importance).*
A person's health or people's

support for sth **declines**. Voices and temperatures **fall** or **drop**. Things can **fall** or **drop** over a period of time, but **drop** cannot be used in the progressive tenses:
✔ *Sales have been falling/declining.*
✗ ~~Sales have been dropping.~~

fall asleep *phrase*

■ *I often fall asleep watching TV.*

go to sleep • get to sleep | *esp. BrE* **drift off** | *infml* **crash** | *esp. BrE, infml* **nod off**

■ **OPP** wake, wake up
► fall asleep/go to sleep/nod off **during/in the middle of** sth
► sb **must have** fallen asleep/gone to sleep/drifted off/nodded off
► **finally** fall asleep/go to sleep/get to sleep/drift off

false *adj.*

1 ■ *A whale is a fish. True or false?*

wrong • untrue • incorrect • mistaken • inaccurate • misguided

■ **OPP** true
► false/wrong/untrue/incorrect/ mistaken/inaccurate **information**
► a/an false/mistaken/inaccurate/ misguided **belief**
► **give/get** a false/the wrong/a mistaken/an inaccurate **impression**

2 ■ *a false beard and moustache*

fake • imitation • artificial • synthetic • man-made

■ **OPP** real, genuine
► false/fake/imitation/artificial/ synthetic **diamonds/pearls**
► fake/imitation/artificial/synthetic **fur/leather**
► artificial/synthetic/man-made **fabrics/fibres/materials/ products**

3 ■ *He had been using a false passport.*

fake | *fml* **counterfeit** | *disapprov.* **bogus • sham** | *BrE, infml, often disapprov.* **phoney** | *esp. AmE* **phony**

► a false/fake/bogus **identity**
► a false/fake/phoney **document/ passport/invoice**
► a false/fake/bogus **claim/application**
● FALSE OR FAKE? False is used more frequently to describe documents and parts of the body, such as *eyelashes* or *teeth*; fake is used more to describe other objects: *fake goods/flowers/bombs*

4 ■ *This is no time for false modesty.*

insincere • hollow

■ **OPP** genuine
► false/insincere/hollow **words**

false

fame

▶ a/an false/insincere/hollow **smile**
▶ look/sound/ring false/hollow

fame noun [U]
■ She found fame on the stage.

celebrity • stardom • publicity |
written prominence

■ OPP obscurity
▶ fame/celebrity/prominence **as sth**
▶ **international** fame/celebrity/
stardom/publicity/prominence
▶ **achieve/shoot to** fame/stardom/
prominence
● **FAME OR CELEBRITY?** Fame can refer
to people, places or events and can
last for a long or short time.
Celebrity usu. refers to a sb such as
an actor, model or sportsperson
who is well known at a particular
time, and is often discussed in the
media.

family noun
1 [C+sing./pl.v.] ■ a family of four

household • home • house

▶ a **low-income/poor/high-
income/wealthy** family/
household/home
▶ a **middle-class/working-class/
single parent** family/household/
home
▶ sb's family/home **life/
background/situation**
● **FAMILY OR HOUSEHOLD?** Members
of a **family** are related to each
other; members of a **household**
live together as a group or unit but
need not be related.

2 [C+sing./pl.v.] ■ All our family came
to Grandad's birthday party.

relatives • relations | *old-fash.* or *fml*
kin

▶ **have** family/relatives/relations (in
Australia, abroad, in the car trade,
etc.)
▶ **stay with/visit** family/relatives/
relations
▶ **friends and** family/relatives/
relations

3 [C+sing./pl.v.] ■ He came from an
ancient and noble family.

background • dynasty • parentage •
origin/origins • roots • birth •
ancestry | *fml* descent • lineage •
blood

▶ **Scottish, Italian, etc.** family/
background/parentage/origin/
roots/ancestry/descent/lineage/
blood
▶ of **humble/lowly** family/
background/origins/roots/birth
▶ of **noble** family/origins/roots/
birth/ancestry/descent/lineage/
blood

▶ **trace** your family/origin/roots/
lineage/birth/ancestry

famous adj.
■ He became a world-famous
conductor.

well known • prominent •
renowned • legendary • historic |
written famed • celebrated

■ OPP unknown, obscure
▶ famous/well known/prominent/
renowned/famed/celebrated **as sb**
▶ famous/well known/renowned/
legendary/famed/celebrated **for**
sth
▶ a famous/well known/prominent/
renowned/celebrated **author/
actor/architect/artist/collection**
▶ a famous/well known/renowned
brand

fan noun [C]
■ She's a great fan of Madonna.

enthusiast • admirer • lover •
devotee • follower | *BrE* supporter |
sometimes disapprov. fanatic • addict

▶ a **great** fan/enthusiast/admirer/
lover
▶ a **keen** fan/enthusiast/admirer/
follower/supporter
▶ a **music/art/jazz** fan/enthusiast/
lover/devotee/fanatic
▶ a **sports/football/boxing/cricket,
etc.** fan/enthusiast/devotee/
fanatic

fancy adj. [usu. before noun]
■ They sell a wide range of fancy
goods.

decorative • ornamental • elaborate

■ OPP plain, simple
▶ a/an fancy/decorative/
ornamental/elaborate **design**
▶ fancy/decorative **packaging**

farm noun [C]
■ The children had to work on the
family farm.

ranch • plantation • vineyard •
orchard | *esp. AmE* homestead

▶ **on** a farm/ranch/plantation/
vineyard/homestead
▶ **at** a farm/ranch/plantation/
vineyard
▶ a **5-hectare, 100-acre, etc.** farm/
ranch/plantation/vineyard/
orchard
▶ a **cattle/sheep** farm/ranch

farm verb [I, T]
■ They have farmed in Kent for many
years.

grow • plant • work | *BrE* plough |
AmE plow | *fml* cultivate

▶ farm/plant/work/plough/
cultivate **the land**

▶ grow / plant / cultivate **crops**
▶ be organically / intensively
  farmed / grown / cultivated

fashion noun [C, U]

■ *The stores are full of the spring fashions.*

style • trend • look • craze | *written* vogue | *disapprov.* fad

▶ a fashion / trend / craze / vogue / **fad for sth**
▶ the **latest** fashion / style / trend / look / craze / fad
▶ come (back) into / (be / go) out of fashion / vogue

fashionable adj.

■ *My in-laws live in a very fashionable part of London.*

glamorous | *esp. BrE* smart | *approv.* stylish • elegant | *infml, approv.* classy • hip | *infml, sometimes disapprov.* trendy

■ OPP unfashionable
▶ fashionable / glamorous / smart / stylish / classy / trendy **people**
▶ fashionable / glamorous / smart / stylish / elegant / trendy **clothes**
▶ a / an fashionable / smart / stylish / elegant / classy / trendy **hotel / restaurant**

fast adj.

■ *She loves driving fast cars.*

quick • rapid • brisk • swift • high-speed • express • supersonic • speedy • hurried | *often disapprov.* hasty

■ OPP slow
▶ be fast / quick **at doing sth**
▶ a fast / quick / rapid / brisk / swift **movement / pace**
▶ a fast / quick **reader / worker / learner / rhythm**
▶ a / an fast / high-speed / express **train / link**
● **FAST OR QUICK?** Use **fast** to talk about travelling:
  ✓ *a fast road / car* ✗ *a quick road / car*
  A person may be **fast** or **quick**, but **fast** is not used in expressions where sb does sth in a short time:
  ✓ *a fast / quick reader / runner / learner* • *The kids were quick to learn.* ✗ *The kids were fast to learn.*

fasten verb

1 [T] ■ *Fasten your seat belts please!*

do sth up • tie • button • zip

■ OPP unfasten
▶ sth fastens / does / buttons / zips **up**
▶ fasten / do / tie / button / zip **sth up**
▶ fasten / do up / tie / button / zip **at** the neck, waist, etc.

2 [T] (usu. used with an adv. or a

prep.) ■ *Fasten the papers together with a paper clip.*

attach • tie • stick • tape • chain | *esp. BrE* fix | *fml* secure

▶ fasten / attach / tie / stick / tape / chain / fix / secure sth **to sth**
▶ fasten / tie / stick / tape / fix sth **on sth**
▶ fasten / tie / stick / tape / fix sth **together**

fat noun [U, C]

■ *Cook the meat in shallow fat.*

butter • oil • margarine • lard • spread • blubber | *disapprov.* grease

▶ vegetable fat / oil / margarine
▶ fry / cook sth in fat / butter / oil / margarine / lard
▶ heat the fat / butter / oil

fat adj.

■ *A big fat man walked into the room.*

overweight | *often approv.* plump • chubby | *esp. BrE* stout | *fml or med.* obese

■ OPP thin
▶ a / an fat / overweight / plump / chubby / stout / obese **man / woman / child**
▶ a fat / plump / chubby / stout **body**
▶ fat / plump / chubby **arms / cheeks / fingers / legs / hands**

fatal adj.

■ *The illness could prove fatal.*

deadly • lethal • terminal • incurable • inoperable | *med.* malignant

▶ fatal / deadly / lethal **to sb**
▶ a / an fatal / deadly / lethal / terminal / incurable / malignant **disease**
▶ a / an fatal / terminal / incurable **illness / condition**

father noun [C]

■ *Gary's a wonderful father.*

parent • stepfather • guardian | *infml, esp. spoken* dad • daddy | *esp. AmE, infml* folks

▶ a good / bad / caring / loving father / parent / dad
▶ take after / inherit sth from your father / parents / dad / daddy
▶ become a / sb's father / parent / stepfather / guardian / dad
● **FATHER OR DAD?** In spoken English **dad** is much more frequent. It can sound formal to say *my father*.

fault noun

1 [U] ■ *It was her fault that we were late.*

responsibility • blame • guilt

▶ (not) **without** fault/responsibility/
blame/guilt

▶ **admit** your fault/responsibility/
your guilt

▶ **deny** responsibility/your guilt

▶ the fault/responsibility/blame/
guilt **lies with sb**

● **FAULT OR RESPONSIBILITY?** Fault is
usu. used in the phrases *my/your/
his/her/our/their/sb's (own)* fault or
sb is at fault:
✗ *It was her responsibility that we
were late.*
People typically *accept/share/
admit/claim/deny* responsibility *for
sth*:
✔ *The bank refuses to accept
responsibility for the error.* ✗ *The
bank refuses to accept fault for the
error.*

2 [C] ▪ *She is blind to her son's faults.*

weakness • failing • inadequacy •
flaw • vice | *fml* frailty

▶ (a) fault/weakness/failing/
inadequacies/flaw in sb/sth

▶ **despite/in spite of** sb's faults/
weaknesses/failings/
inadequacies/flaws

▶ **have** faults/weaknesses/failings/
flaws/a vice

● **FAULT OR WEAKNESS?** A fault is
often more serious than a
weakness. You can see a
weakness in yourself, but a **fault** in
sb else.

3 [C] ▪ *The fire was caused by an
electrical fault.*

defect • flaw • imperfection • bug |
infml glitch

▶ a/an fault/defect/flaw/
imperfection/bug/glitch **in** sth

▶ a **technical/mechanical** fault/
defect/flaw/glitch

▶ **have** a/an fault/defect/flaw/
imperfection/bug/glitch

▶ **detect/correct** a fault/defect/flaw

● **FAULT OR DEFECT?** A fault can only
exist in sth that has been made by
people. It can be permanent or
temporary. A **defect** can exist in
sth that has been made by people
or in a part of the body. It is
present from the beginning or
from birth and is not temporary,
although it may be repaired or
treated:
✔ *If a fault develops in the
equipment…* ✗ *If a defect develops…*
✔ *a birth defect* ✗ *a birth fault*

favourite (*BrE*) (*AmE* **favorite**)
noun [C]

▪ *This song is a particular favourite of
mine.*

preference • choice • selection | *esp.
AmE, infml* pick

▶ sb's favourite/choice/pick **for** sth

▶ an **obvious** favourite/choice/
selection

● **FAVOURITE OR PREFERENCE?** Your
favourites are the things you like
best, and that you have, do, etc.
often; your **preferences** are the
things that you would rather have
or do if you can choose.

favourite (*BrE*) (*AmE* **favorite**)
adj.

▪ *Who is your favourite poet?*

best-loved • of choice • pet | *esp.
busin.* preferred | *esp. written*
favoured

▶ sb's favourite/preferred/favoured/
food/activity/method/way/type

▶ sb's favourite/pet subject/topic

▶ sb's favourite/preferred **option/
approach/strategy/version/
location/candidate/idea**

be in **favour** (of sb/sth) (*BrE*)
(*AmE* be in favor (of sb/sth)) *phrase*

▪ *I'm all in favour of equal pay for
equal work.*

approve • agree with sth • support •
back • believe in sth | *infml* **be all
for** sth | *fml* subscribe to sth

▪ **OPP** be opposed (to sb/sth)

▶ be in favour of/approve of/agree
with/support/back/believe in/be
all for/subscribe to/an **idea/
view**

▶ be in favour of/approve of/agree
with/support/back/be all for a
plan/policy/suggestion

● **(BE) IN FAVOUR (OF SB/STH) OR
APPROVE?** In favour is often used
about a policy or strategy that
people might vote on; **approve** is
used to talk about more personal
matters: *All those in favour, please
raise your hand.* • *I don't think your
mother would approve of this
behaviour.*

fear noun [U, C]

▪ *The child was shaking with fear.*

fright • dread • terror • alarm •
panic • phobia

▪ **OPP** hope

▶ a fear/dread/terror **of** sth

▶ **in** fear/dread/terror/
alarm/panic

▶ be **filled with** fear/dread/terror/
alarm/panic

● **FEAR OR FRIGHT?** Fright is a reaction
to sth that is happening or has just
happened. Use **fear** to talk about
things that always frighten you and
things that may frighten you in the
future.:
✔ *She cried out in fear/fright.* • *I have
a fear of spiders.* ✗ *I have a fright of
spiders.*

feature noun [C]

■ Which features do you look for when choosing a car?

characteristic • quality • trait • point • attribute | tech. **property**

▶ a/an **essential/desirable/ individual** feature/characteristic/ quality/trait/attribute/property
▶ a/an **important/natural/special/ useful** feature/characteristic/ quality/attribute/property
▶ **possess/display/share (a/an)** feature/characteristic/quality/ trait/... points/attribute/property

feature verb [T, I]

■ The film features Anne Hathaway as Jane Austen. ■ Garlic features heavily in her cooking.

star • appear • figure

▶ feature/star/appear/figure **in** sth
▶ feature/star/appear/figure **as** sth
▶ a **film/movie** features/stars sb
▶ feature/star/appear **in a film/ movie**

fee noun [C]

■ They spent £20 000 on legal fees.

charge • cost • rate • terms • dues • subscription

▶ (a/the) **fee**/charge/rate/terms/ price/dues/subscription **for** sth
▶ **pay** (a/the) fee/charge/cost/rate/ price/dues/subscription
▶ **charge** (a) fee/rate/dues
▶ **increase/reduce** the fee/charge/ cost/rate/price/dues/subscription
● **FEE OR CHARGE?** Charge is often used for smaller services in less formal contexts: We have to make a small charge for refreshments. • legal/school/professional fees
When you visit a museum, etc. you pay an admission/entrance fee or admission/entrance charge, (but never an 'entrance charge').

feel verb

1 [I, T] ■ I felt the warm sun on my back.

sense • experience • know | esp. written **taste**

▶ feel/experience/know/taste **joy**
▶ feel/sense/experience a **need**
▶ feel/experience **(a/an) sense/ sensation/emotion/urge/pang/ surge/rush/stab**
● **FEEL OR SENSE?** You usu. **feel** your own feelings and emotions but **sense** sb else's: He felt a terrible pain in his chest. • She sensed the pain he was feeling.

2 linking verb (not used in the progressive tenses) ■ It felt strange to be back in my old school.

seem • sound • look • appear

▶ feel/seem/sound/appear/look **odd/OK/nice, etc.**
▶ feel/seem/sound/look **like** sth
▶ feel/seem/sound/look **as if/as though...**
● **FEEL OR SOUND?** Use **sound** to talk about the impression you get from hearing sb/sth; use **feel** to talk about your own or other people's feelings: He sounded happy, but I don't think he felt it.

3 [T] ■ Can you feel the lump on my head?

touch • brush | written **graze**

▶ feel/touch/brush/graze sb/sth **with** sth

4 [T, I] (not used in the progressive tenses) ■ We all felt that we were lucky to win.

think • believe • consider • be under the impression that... | esp. BrE, infml, esp. spoken **reckon** | fml **hold**

▶ feel/think/believe sth **of/about** sb/sth
▶ feel/think/believe/consider/be under the impression/reckon/hold **that...**
▶ be felt/thought/believed/ considered/reckoned/held **to be** sth

5 [I] (always used with an adv. or prep.) ■ He felt in his pockets for some money.

grope • fumble • rummage • fish | esp. BrE **scrabble**

▶ feel/grope/fumble/rummage/ fish/scrabble **around/about**
▶ feel/grope/fumble/rummage/fish around/scrabble **in/for** sth
▶ feel/grope **your way** somewhere
● **FEEL OR GROPE?** You can **feel** or **grope** around in the dark. When you **feel** around you are likely to do it in an easier, more controlled way than if you **grope** around.

feeling noun

1 [C] ■ There was a feeling of sadness in the room.

sense • impression • idea | esp. written **sensation**

▶ a/an **wonderful/warm/ uncomfortable** feeling/sense/ impression/idea/sensation
▶ **have** a/an feeling/sense/ impression/idea/sensation
▶ **have** the feeling/sense/ impression/sensation **that...**
▶ **get/give sb/leave sb with/ convey** a/an feeling/sense/ impression/idea/sensation
● **FEELING OR SENSATION?** A **feeling** may be physical or mental; a

sensation is a physical feeling: *a sensation of falling/ floating/nausea*

2 [sing.] ■ *I had a feeling that we were being followed.*

instinct • suspicion • hunch • intuition • idea | *esp. written* premonition • foreboding

▶ a/an feeling/instinct/suspicion/ hunch/intuition/idea/ premonition/foreboding **about** sth
▶ a/an feeling/instinct/suspicion/ hunch/intuition/idea/ premonition/foreboding **that ...**
▶ **have** a/an feeling/instinct/ suspicion/hunch/intuition/ premonition/foreboding
● FEELING OR INSTINCT? A **feeling** in this meaning is that one particular unpleasant thing is true; your **instincts** may be more general and can be positive or negative: *Her instincts were right—he was a man who could be trusted.*

3 [C, U] ■ *My own feeling is that we should go for the cheaper option.*

view • opinion • belief • idea • point of view • attitude • philosophy • conviction | *fml* sentiment

▶ sb's feelings/views/beliefs/ideas/ conviction/sentiments **about** sb/ sth
▶ the feeling/view/opinion/belief/ idea/point of view/attitude/ philosophy/conviction **that...**
▶ **express** your feelings/view/ opinion/belief/ideas/conviction/ sentiments
● FEELING OR IDEA? An **idea** is based more on principles or beliefs; a **feeling** is based slightly more on emotions.

4 [C, usu. pl., U] ■ *The debate aroused strong feelings.*

emotion • passion • heat | *BrE* fervour • | *AmE* fervor | *sometimes disapprov.* sentiment

▶ **with** feeling/emotion/passion/ heat/fervour
▶ **intense/considerable/profound/ strong/violent** feelings/emotion/ passion
▶ **arouse** feelings/emotion/passion/ fervour
▶ feelings/emotions/passions **are running high**

5 feelings [pl.] ■ *I didn't mean to hurt your feelings.*

dignity • pride • self-esteem • self-respect | *written* sensibilities | *often disapprov.* ego

▶ **injured** feelings/dignity/pride/ self-esteem

▶ **personal** feelings/dignity/pride/ self-esteem
▶ **hurt** sb's feelings/pride

fence noun [C]
■ *Guards with dogs patrolled the perimeter fence.*

railing • wall

▶ a **high/low** fence/wall
▶ (a) **metal/wooden** fence/railings
▶ **put up/build** a fence/wall

fend sb/sth off phrasal verb
■ *She used a chair to fend off her attacker.*

ward sb/sth off • deflect • parry • block | *fml* repel

▶ fend off/ward off/deflect/parry/ block/repel an **attack**
▶ fend off/ward off/deflect/parry/ block a **blow**
▶ fend off/repel an **assault**

fetch verb [T] (*BrE, esp. spoken*)
■ *She's gone to fetch the kids from school.*

collect | *esp. spoken* get • pick sb/sth up

● FETCH OR GET? **Fetch** usu. refers to sb/sth that is in a place and needs to be collected. **Get** can have a wider range of meaning; you can **get** things that need to be prepared or obtained:
✓*Get John a drink.* ✗ *Fetch John a drink.*

fibre (*BrE*) (*AmE* fiber) noun [C]
■ *Synthetic fibres are used in the manufacturing process.*

thread • strand • hair

▶ a **long/single** fibre/thread/ strand/hair
▶ **delicate/cotton** fibres/threads

fictional adj.
■ *a fictional account of life on a desert island*

imaginary • non-existent • virtual | *sometimes disapprov.* fictitious | *infml* pretend

▶ OPP **real-life**
▶ a/an fictional/fictitious/imaginary **story/character**
▶ a/an fictional/imaginary/virtual **world**
● FICTIONAL OR FICTITIOUS? Use either word to talk about characters, places, etc, that are invented for a story. You can also use **fictional** to describe the process of writing fiction; **fictitious** is used when sb has invented sth in order to trick people: *the fictional world of J.K. Rowling • Police said the name John Haydon was fictitious.*

field noun

1 [C] ■ *We camped in a field near the village.*

meadow • paddock • pasture

▶ **in** (a) field/meadow/paddock/pasture
▶ **open/green/lush** fields/meadows/pasture

2 [C] ■ *This discovery opens up a whole new field of research.*

area • domain • sphere • realm • specialism • subject • sector | *esp. AmE* **specialty |** *fml* **discipline**

▶ **within/outside** the field/area/domain/sphere/realm/sector/discipline of sth
▶ **the political** field/domain/sphere/realm
▶ **the scientific** field/sphere/subjects/disciplines
▶ **work in** the field/area/domain/sector

3 [C] (used esp. in compounds or fixed phrases) ■ *a sports field*

playing field • stadium • arena | *BrE* **pitch • ground |** *AmE* **park • ballpark**

▶ **on/off** the field/playing field/pitch
▶ **a sports** field/stadium/arena/pitch/ground
▶ **a football/cricket/rugby** field/stadium/pitch/ground
▶ **a baseball** field/stadium/park
● **FIELD, PITCH OR GROUND?** Both **field** and **pitch** are used to talk about the area of land where a sport is played. **Ground** also includes buildings, seating, etc. around the place where a game is played.

fight noun

1 [C] ■ *He got into a fight in a bar.*

brawl • struggle • scuffle • tussle | *journ.* **clash**

▶ **a** fight/brawl/struggle/scuffle/tussle/clash **with** sb
▶ **a** fight/brawl/struggle/scuffle/tussle/clash **between** people
▶ **a** fight/brawl/struggle/scuffle/tussle/clash **over** sth
▶ **be into/get into/be involved in** a fight/brawl/scuffle/tussle/clash

2 [sing.] ■ *the fight against crime*

war • crusade • battle • struggle • campaign

▶ **a** fight/crusade/battle/struggle/campaign **for** sth
▶ **a** fight/war/crusade/battle/struggle/campaign **against** sth
▶ **a** fight/war/battle/struggle **between** people
▶ **lead/continue** the fight/war/crusade/battle/struggle/campaign
● **FIGHT, WAR OR CRUSADE?** A **war** is

---

about stopping things, like drugs and crime, that everyone agrees are bad. A **fight** can be about achieving justice for yourself. A **crusade** is often about persuading people to share your beliefs about what is right and wrong.

3 [C] (*esp. AmE*) ■ *We had a fight over money.*

argument • quarrel • squabble • shouting match • disagreement • dispute | *BrE, infml* **row • tiff**

▶ **a/an** fight/argument/quarrel/squabble/shouting match/disagreement/row/tiff **with** sb
▶ **a/an** fight/argument/quarrel/squabble/shouting match/disagreement/dispute/row/tiff **between** A and B
▶ **(a/an)** fight/argument/quarrel/squabble/disagreement/dispute/row **about/over** sb/sth
▶ **a/an** fight/argument/quarrel/row/dispute **breaks out**
● **WHICH WORD?** A **quarrel**, **row** or **fight** is usu. only between people who know each other:
✓ *We had an argument with the waiter about the bill.* ✗ ~~We had a quarrel/row/fight with the waiter about the bill.~~
A **quarrel** is less violent than a **row** or **fight**, but it can continue for a period of time; an **argument** can be violent or it can be a serious discussion.

fight verb

1 [I, T] ■ *The soldiers were trained to fight in the jungle.*

wage • skirmish | *fml* **engage • take up arms**

▶ fight/skirmish/engage **with** sb/sth
▶ fight/take up arms **against** sb/sth
▶ fight/wage (a) **war/battle/campaign**

2 [I, T] ■ *She fought her attacker bravely.*

wrestle • struggle • brawl • grapple • box • scuffle | *esp. journ.* **clash**

▶ fight/wrestle/struggle/brawl/grapple/scuffle/clash **with** sb
▶ fight/struggle/box **against** sb
▶ fight/struggle **fiercely/furiously**

3 [I, T] ■ *There are ten parties fighting the election.*

compete • struggle • contest | *fml* **vie |** *esp. journ.* **battle**

▶ fight/compete/struggle/vie/battle **for** sth
▶ fight/compete/struggle/vie for **power**

► fight/compete/struggle/battle **hard**

4 [T, I] ■ *Workers are fighting the decision to close the factory.*

combat • oppose • resist • defy • rebel

► fight/rebel **against** sb/sth
► fight/oppose/resist a **plan/ proposal**
► fight/combat **crime/disease/ pollution/inflation**

5 [I, T] ■ *Campaigners fought to save the school from closure.*

campaign • work • lobby • agitate

► fight/campaign/work/lobby/ agitate **for/to do sth**
► fight/campaign/lobby **on behalf of** sb
► a **group** fights/campaigns/works/ lobbies
● **FIGHT OR CAMPAIGN?** Campaigning is often to persuade people that a political or social change is needed, or a practice needs to be stopped. **Fight** is often used to talk about achieving justice for yourself, for example gaining the right to do sth.

6 [I] *(AmE)* ■ *It's not worth fighting about.*

argue • quarrel • fall out • squabble • bicker | *BrE, infml* row | *esp. journ.* clash

► fight/argue/quarrel/fall out/ squabble/bicker/row/clash **with** sb
► fight/argue/quarrel/fall out/ squabble/bicker/row/clash **over** sth
► fight/argue/quarrel/fall out/ squabble/bicker/row **about** sth

fight back *phrasal verb*
■ *He tried to fight back against the bullies.*

retaliate • strike back • settle a score | *infml* hit back • get back at sb • get even | *fml* or *lit.* avenge

► fight back/retaliate/strike back/ settle a score **against** sb
► fight back/strike back/hit back **at** sb
► fight back/retaliate/hit back **by doing sth**

figure *noun*

1 [C] ■ *the latest unemployment figures*

statistics • number • fraction • data | *infml* stats

► a **high/low/round** figure/number
► **exact** figures/numbers/statistics/ data

► **add/multiply/subtract/divide** figures/numbers/fractions
► **publish** figures/statistics/data
● **FIGURE OR STATISTICS?** In many cases you can use either word:
✓ *official/crime/unemployment figures/statistics*
Statistics can suggest a higher level of science or calculation than **figures**. It is usu. necessary to say which figures:
✓ *Government/Inflation figures show that…* • *Statistics show that…*
✗ *Figures show that…*

2 [C] ■ *Write the figure '7' on the board.*

digit • number • symbol • sign • character

► **write** sth **in** figures/numbers/ symbols
► a **single** figure/digit/symbol/ character
► **double** figures/digits
► a **sequence/series/set/string** of figures/numbers/symbols/digits/ characters
● **FIGURE OR DIGIT?** Use **figure** for amounts of money, but **digit** for: *a series of figures to identify sth* • *a deal for a seven-figure sum* • *a four-digit extension number*
Digit is used more than **figure** for matters of technology and related equipment.

3 [C] ■ *He's a leading figure in the music industry.*

person • individual • character

► a **sad** figure/person/individual/ character
► a **key/powerful/independent** figure/person/individual

4 [C] ■ *I saw a shadowy figure approaching.*

shape • form • shadow • outline • silhouette

► a **tall** figure/shape/form/shadow/ silhouette
► a **black/dark** figure/shape/ shadow/outline/silhouette
► **make out/see** a/an figure/shape/ form/outline/silhouette

5 [C] ■ *She has a good figure.*

body • build | *often approv.* physique

► **have** a good, large, slim, etc. figure/body/build/physique

figure *verb*

1 [I] ■ *Do I still figure in your plans?*

appear • feature

► figure/appear/feature **as** sb/sth
► figure/appear/feature **prominently in** sth

2 [T] *(AmE)* ■ *First we should figure roughly how much it will cost.*

estimate • judge • reckon • calculate • guess • gauge

▶ figure/estimate/judge/reckon/ calculate/guess **that...**
▶ figure/estimate/judge/calculate/ guess/gauge **how much, how many, how far, etc.**
▶ figure/estimate/judge/reckon/ calculate/guess/gauge sth **to be sth**

figure sb/sth out *phrasal verb*

1 (*esp. AmE, esp. spoken*) ■ I can't figure out how to do this.

esp. BrE, esp. spoken **work sth out**

▶ figure out/work out **how/what/ where/how/why...**
● FIGURE SB/STH OUT OR WORK STH OUT? Figure sb/sth out is used more in *AmE* and work sth out is used more in *BrE*. However, if you are talking about understanding sb's character and behaviour, **figure sb out** is used in both: *I've never been able to figure her out.*

2 (*infml*) ■ Can we figure out how much the trip will cost?

work sth out • calculate • put a figure on sth | *AmE* **figure**

▶ figure out/work out/calculate/ put a figure on/figure **how much/ how many...**
▶ figure out/work out/calculate/ figure **that...**
▶ figure out/work out/calculate/ put a figure on/figure the **cost/ number/amount** (of sth)

file *noun*

1 [C] ■ A stack of files lay on my desk.

folder • binder • envelope • portfolio

▶ in a/an file/folder/binder/ envelope/portfolio
▶ open a/an file/folder/binder/ envelope
▶ a/an file/folder/binder/envelope/ portfolio **containing** sth

2 [C] ■ Confidential files on clients are kept for three years.

document • papers • paperwork • archive/archives | *fml* **dossier** | *tech.* **deed**

▶ a file/a document/the paperwork/ a dossier **on** sb/sth
▶ in a file/a document/the paperwork/the archives/a dossier
▶ (a) **personal/secret** file/ documents/papers/archive/ dossier
▶ **keep** a file/a document/papers/ the paperwork/an archive/a dossier/the deeds

fill *verb* [T, I]

■ She filled the kettle.

fill (sth) up • load • pack • refill • restock | *esp. BrE* **top sb/sth up** | *fml* **replenish**

► OPP **empty**

▶ fill/fill up/load/pack/refill/ restock/top up/replenish sth **with** sth
▶ fill/load/pack sth **in/into** sth
▶ fill sth up/refill/top up/replenish sb's **glass**

film *noun*

1 [C] (*esp. BrE*) ■ I watched a film on TV.

DVD • video | *esp. AmE* **movie**

▶ **in** a film/video/movie
▶ **make/produce/direct** a film/ video/movie
▶ **see/watch** a film/DVD/video/ movie
● FILM OR MOVIE? In *BrE* movie can suggest that a film is just entertainment without any artistic value; in *AmE* film can suggest that a film has artistic value:
✓an art film ✗an art movie

2 [U] ■ a film and photography course

esp. BrE **cinema** | *esp. AmE* **movies**

▶ **work** in film/cinema/movies
▶ the film/cinema/movie **industry**

film *verb* [I, T]

■ The show was filmed in Moscow.

shoot | *esp. BrE* **video**

▶ film/shoot sth **on location**

filter *verb* [T]

■ All drinking water must be filtered.

strain • purify • sieve • sift • refine

▶ filter/strain/sieve/sift sth **into** sth
▶ filter/strain/sieve sth **through** sth
▶ filter/purify **air/water**

final *adj.*

1 [only before noun] ■ My final point is the most important.

last • ultimate • eventual • closing • later • latter

► OPP **initial, first**

▶ the final/last/ultimate/closing/ later/latter **stage/phase**
▶ the final/last/ultimate/eventual/ later **aim/goal/outcome**
▶ the final/last/closing **remark/ chapter/minutes**

2 ■ The judge's decision is final.

definitive • absolute • definite • firm | *fml* **categorical**

▶ a final/definitive/definite/firm **decision/conclusion/diagnosis/ agreement/answer**

finance

▶ a final/definitive **judgement/ ruling**

finance noun

1 [U] ■ *Finance for education comes from taxpayers.*

money • **funds** • **funding** • **means** • **capital** | *infml* **cash**

▶ **government/public finance/ money/funds/funding/capital/ cash**
▶ **have/lack (the) finance/money/ funds/funding/means/capital/ cash (to do sth)**
▶ **raise/provide/put up (the) finance/money/funds/funding/ capital/cash (for sth)**

2 [U] ■ *the Minister of Finance*

economics • **banking**

● **FINANCE OR ECONOMICS? Finance** is the practical process of managing money. **Economics** is the theory of how money works.

finance verb [T]

■ *The project will be financed by the government.*

fund • **support** • **sponsor** • **subsidize** • **endow** | *esp. AmE, infml* **bankroll** | *finance* **guarantee** • **underwrite**

▶ **finance/fund/support/sponsor/ subsidize/bankroll/underwrite a project/programme**
▶ **finance/fund/support/sponsor/ subsidize/bankroll a campaign**
▶ **sth is publicly financed/funded/ sponsored/subsidized**

financial adj. [usu. before noun]

■ *They got into financial difficulties.*

economic • **commercial** | *finance* **monetary** • **budgetary**

▶ **financial/economic/commercial/ monetary/budgetary policy/ systems/problems**
▶ **financial/economic/commercial/ monetary gain/loss/value/affairs**
▶ **financial/economic/commercial/ budgetary data/decisions**

find verb

1 [T] ■ *Look what I've found!*

discover • **come across sb/sth** • **stumble on/upon/across sb/sth** • **catch** • **turn sth up** • **unearth** | *fml* **come upon sth**

▶ **find/discover/come across/catch sb doing sth**
▶ **find/discover/unearth the remains (of sth)**
▶ **find/discover/stumble upon sth by accident**

2 [T] ■ *I can't find my keys.*

trace • **track sb/sth down** • **search sb/sth out** • **locate** | *infml* **sniff sb/ sth out**

■ OPP **lose**
▶ **find/track down/search out/ locate sth for sb/sth**
▶ **find/trace/track down/locate the missing...**
▶ **find/trace/track down the killer/ location**

3 [T] ■ *Scientists are still trying to find a cure for cancer.*

discover • **identify** • **establish** | *fml* **determine** • **ascertain**

▶ **find/discover/identify/establish/ determine/ascertain the cause**
▶ **find/discover/identify/establish a connection**
▶ **find/discover a cure/the answer**

4 [T] ■ *Her blood was found to contain poison.*

find (sth) out • **discover** • **hear** • **learn**

▶ **find/find out/hear/discover/learn that...**
▶ **find/discover sb/sth to be/have, etc. sth**
▶ **be surprised/saddened/ delighted/interested to find/ discover/hear/learn sth**

5 [T] ■ *I find watching television so boring.*

consider • **think** • **feel** • **see** • **view** • **count** • **regard** | *esp. BrE, infml* **reckon**

▶ **find/consider/reckon sb/sth to be sth**

6 [T] (not used in the progressive tenses) ■ *These flowers are found only in Africa.*

exist • **live** • **occur** | *fml* **prevail**

▶ **be found/exist/live/occur/prevail in/among sth**
▶ **still be found/exist/live/occur/ prevail**

find (sth) out phrasal verb

■ *She didn't want her parents to find out about her boyfriend.*

find • **discover** • **hear** • **learn**

▶ **find out/hear/learn about sth**
▶ **find out/find/hear/discover/learn that...**
▶ **find out/hear/discover/learn how/what/why...**

fine adj.

1 [usu. before noun] ■ *The church is a fine example of Saxon architecture.*

good • **excellent** • **high quality** • **superior** • **first-rate** • **prime** • **quality** | *infml* **great** | *esp. BrE, fml* **sterling**

OPP **poor**

- (of) fine/good/excellent/ superior/prime/great/sterling **quality**
- (a/an) fine/good/excellent/high quality/superior/first-rate/ quiality/great/sterling **performance/service**
- a/an fine/good/excellent/high quality/superior/quality/great **product**

2 [not before noun] (not used in negative statements; not used in the comparative or superlative) (*esp. spoken*) ■ '*How are you?*' '*Fine thanks.*'

healthy • strong • good | *esp. spoken* **well • all right** | *esp. BrE* **fit** | *infml, esp. spoken* **OK • great**

- feel/look fine/healthy/strong/ good/fit/well/all right/OK/great

3 (*spoken*) ■ *Don't worry, it's fine to ask me questions.*

acceptable • satisfactory • reasonable • right • fair | *esp. spoken* **all right** | *infml, esp. spoken* **OK** | *fml* **in order**

- be fine/acceptable/satisfactory/ reasonable/fair/all right/OK/in order **to do sth**
- be fine/acceptable/satisfactory/ reasonable/fair/all right/OK/in order **that...**
- That's fine/all right/OK **by me.**

4 (*esp. BrE, approv.*) ■ *a week of fine, dry weather*

dry • mild • clear | *approv.* **good • sunny • glorious**

- fine/dry/mild/clear/good/ sunny/glorious **weather**
- a fine/dry/mild/clear/sunny/ glorious **day/morning/evening/ afternoon**
- remain/stay fine/dry/mild/sunny

5 ■ *a brush with a fine tip*

narrow • thin

OPP **thick**

- a fine/narrow/thin **crack/strip**
- (a) fine/narrow/thin **hair/thread/layer**

finish *noun* [C, usu. sing.]

■ *He led the race from start to finish.*

end • ending • finale • conclusion | *fml, esp. busin.* **close**

OPP **start**

- a/an (...) finish/end/ending/ finale **to sth**
- at the finish/end/finale/ conclusion/close
- a dramatic finish/end/ending/ finale/conclusion

finish *verb*

1 [T, I] ■ *He finished his homework as quickly as he could.*

esp. written **complete • finalize** | *esp. spoken* **follow (sth) through** | *esp. AmE, esp. spoken* **be done** | *BrE* **round sth off** | *AmE* **round sth out** | *infml, esp. busin.* or *sport* **wrap sth up**

OPP **start**

- finish/follow through/be done/round sth off/round sth out **with sth**
- finish/complete/round off/round out/wrap up a/an **discussion/ evening/meal**
- finish/complete/finalize the **preparations/arrangements**
- **FINISH OR COMPLETE?** Finish is more frequent in spoken English; complete is more frequent in written English. Note that you can *finish doing sth* but you cannot '*complete doing sth*':
  ✓ *He hasn't finished speaking.* ✗ *He hasn't completed speaking.*

2 [I, T] ■ *The play finished at 10.30.*

end • stop • close • wind (sth) up | *fml* **conclude • terminate**

OPP **start**

- finish/end/conclude **by/with** sth
- finish/end/close/wind up/ conclude **a meeting**
- a **play/show/film** finishes/ends/ concludes
- **WHICH WORD?** Finish, end and conclude are used esp. about things that you do not expect to start again: *The concert should finish by 10 o'clock.* • *The war ended in 1945.* • *She concluded her speech with a quotation.*
  Finish is used more to talk about *when* sth ends; conclude is used more to talk about *how* sth ends.
  Stop is used about things that may or will start again or that cannot ever be 'completed': *The rain stopped for a couple of minutes.*

fire *noun*

1 [U, C] ■ *The car was now on fire.*

flames | *esp. journ.* **blaze • inferno** | *tech.* **combustion**

- start a fire/blaze
- fight/tackle/contain/put out/ extinguish a fire/inferno/a blaze
- a fire/blaze **breaks out/starts**
- a fire/flames/a blaze **spreads/ spread**

2 [C] ■ *Get warm by the fire.*

bonfire • campfire

- build/make/light a fire/bonfire/ campfire
- sit/gather round/around a fire/ bonfire/campfire
- a fire/bonfire/campfire **burns**

fire 176

fire verb

1 [I, T] ■ *The officer ordered his men to fire.*

shoot • open fire • launch

► fire/shoot **at sb**
► fire/open fire **on sb/sth**
► fire/shoot **blanks/bullets/arrows**
► fire/launch **a missile/torpedo**

2 [T, often passive] ■ *We had to fire him for dishonesty.*

lay sb off • let sb go • dismiss | *BrE* **make sb redundant** | *esp. BrE, infml* **sack • give sb the sack** | *fml* **discharge** | *BrE, journ.* **axe** | *AmE, journ.* **ax**

■ OPP **hire**

► fire sb/lay sb off/dismiss sb/make sb redundant/sack sb/give sb the sack/discharge sb **from a job**
► fire/lay off/dismiss/sack/axe **staff/workers/employees**
► make **staff/workers/employees** redundant

firm noun [C]

■ *an engineering firm*

company • business • partnership • house • practice • corporation • operation | *infml* **outfit** | *busin., journ.* **enterprise**

► a **family** firm/company/business/partnership/... house/practice/operation/enterprise
► **manage** a/an firm/company/business/partnership/... house/corporation/operation/outfit/enterprise
► **work for/join/leave/resign from** a/an firm/company/business/partnership/... house/practice/corporation

● FIRM OR COMPANY? **Firm** is often used to talk about a small, often specialized organization, esp. one that sells professional advice or services: *a law/consulting/insurance firm • a firm of accountants*
Firm is also often used about companies that have been operating for a long time or companies run by a family. **Company** is much wider in range.

firm adj.

1 (*approv.*) ■ *four large tomatoes, ripe but firm*

hard • solid • stiff • rigid

■ OPP **soft**

► a firm/hard/solid **surface**
► firm/hard **ground**
● FIRM OR HARD? **Hard** things are harder than **firm** things. **Hard** can mean 'very hard' or 'too hard': *Diamonds are the hardest known mineral. • a hard mattress*

Firm is always a positive word: a *hard mattress* is a bad thing, but a *firm mattress* is good.

2 ■ *Stand the fish tank on a firm base.*

secure • steady • stable

■ OPP **unstable**

► a firm/secure/steady/stable **foundation**
► a firm/secure/stable **base**

first det., adj.

1 ■ *It was the first time they had ever met.*

initial • original • earliest • opening • introductory • preliminary | *esp. BrE, fml* **preparatory** | *fml or tech.* **primary**

■ OPP **last**

► the first/initial/earliest/opening/introductory/preparatory/primary **stage**
► a/an first/initial/original/preliminary **estimate/draft/version**
► a/an first/initial/preliminary **step/appointment/visit**

2 ■ *She won first prize in the competition.*

top • main • key • highest • primary • prime | *infml* **number one** | *esp. written* **foremost** | *esp. written or journ.* **premier**

■ OPP **last**

► the/our first/top/main/key/highest/number one/foremost **priority**
► the/our first/top/main/key/primary/prime/number one/foremost **concern**
► (the) first/top/premier **division/prize**

fit verb [I, T] (not used in the progressive tenses)

■ *The facts certainly fit your theory.*

match • tie in • correspond • agree | *fml* **correlate**

► A ties in/corresponds/agrees/correlates **with B**
► A and B correspond/agree/correlate
► fit/match/tie in/correlate **well**
► not quite fit/match/correlate

fit adj.

1 (*esp. BrE*) ■ *Exercise keeps you fit and healthy.*

healthy • strong • well

■ OPP **unfit**

► keep (sb) fit/healthy/well
► get strong/well
► physically fit/healthy/strong/well
► fit and healthy/strong/well

2 ■ *The food was not fit for human consumption.*

■ **OPP** unfit
▶ fit/suitable/good **for** sb/sth
▶ fit/suitable/good **to do** sth

fix verb

1 [T] (*esp. BrE*) ■ *He fixed the shelf to the wall.*

attach ◆ fasten ◆ tie ◆ strap ◆ tape ◆ stick | *fml* secure
▶ fix/attach/fasten/tie/strap/tape/ stick/secure sth **to** sth
▶ fix/put/fasten/tie/strap/tape/ stick sth **on** sth
▶ fix/fasten/tie/strap/tape/stick sth **together**

2 [T] ■ *The date was fixed well in advance.*

set ◆ schedule ◆ book | *esp. BrE* timetable
▶ fix/set/schedule/book/timetable sth **for** sth
▶ fix/set/schedule/book/timetable sb/sth **to do** sth
▶ fix/set/schedule/book a **time/ date/day**
▶ fix/set/schedule/timetable a **meeting**

3 [T] ■ *I took the car to the garage to get it fixed.*

repair ◆ patch sth up | *esp. BrE* mend
▶ fix/repair/mend a **road/fence/ roof/bike/puncture**
▶ fix/repair a **car/television/fault/ defect/leak**
▶ get sth fixed/repaired/mended
● **FIX OR REPAIR?** The most general word in *BrE* is **repair**. **Fix** is less formal and is used to talk about repairing machines and equipment. In *AmE* **fix** is the usual word to talk about repairing sth that is damaged or broken, and **repair** sounds rather formal.

4 [T] ■ *Don't imagine that the law can fix everything.*

correct ◆ cure ◆ remedy | *esp. BrE* put sth right | *fml* rectify ◆ redress
▶ fix/correct/cure/remedy/put right/rectify/redress **what...**
▶ fix/correct/cure/remedy/put right/rectify/redress a **problem**
▶ fix/correct/cure/remedy/put right/ rectify a **mistake/error/fault**
● **FIX OR PUT STH RIGHT?** These are both rather informal, but **fix** is used more in business contexts and in *AmE*.

fixed adj.

1 ■ *The money has been invested for a fixed period.*

set | *fml* predetermined

■ **OPP** flexible, variable

▶ fixed/set/predetermined **rules**
▶ a fixed/set/predetermined **number/level/quantity/pattern**
▶ a fixed/set **price**

2 ■ *My parents had fixed ideas about my future.*

set ◆ entrenched ◆ ingrained | *disapprov.* rigid ◆ inflexible
▶ fixed/set/entrenched/rigid **views/ideas**
▶ fixed/entrenched/ingrained/rigid **beliefs/habits**

flash verb [I, T]

■ *Lightning flashed in the distance.*

flicker
▶ (a) **light/lightning/bulb/screen** flashes/flickers
▶ sb's **eyes** flash/flicker
▶ flash/flicker **on and off/briefly/ momentarily**

flashy adj. (*infml, usu. disapprov.*)

■ *I just want a reliable car, nothing flashy.*

usu. disapprov. showy ◆ glitzy ◆ ostentatious | *disapprov.* pretentious ◆ grandiose | *infml, often approv.* snazzy
▶ flashy/showy **technique/ footwork**

flat noun [C] (*BrE*)

■ *They rented a large flat near the city centre.*

penthouse ◆ suite | *esp. AmE* apartment ◆ condominium | *AmE, infml* condo
▶ at sb's **flat/apartment**
▶ a one—/two—/three—bedroom **flat/apartment/condominium/ condo**
▶ live in a/an **flat/suite/penthouse/ apartment/condominium/condo**
▶ rent a **flat/suite/apartment**
● **FLAT OR APARTMENT?** Both these words are used in *BrE*, but **flat** is more usual. Some people use **apartment** to mean accommodation that is larger, finer or more expensive than an ordinary **flat**. In *AmE* use **apartment**.

flat adj.

■ *low buildings with flat roofs*

level ◆ horizontal | *often approv.* smooth

■ **OPP** bumpy

▶ a flat/level/horizontal/smooth **surface**
▶ a flat/level/smooth **road/floor**
▶ a flat/smooth **rock/stone**
▶ flat/level **ground/land**

● **FLAT OR LEVEL? Level** is used most often with the words *ground* and *floor; flat* is used more to talk about surfaces that are not rounded or landscapes that do not have any hills: *a flat base/stomach/surface • a flat field/plateau/beach*

flavour (BrE) (AmE flavor) noun
[U, C]

■ *It is stronger in flavour than the other cheeses.*

taste • tang

▶ a **delicious/rich/spicy/bitter/ sour/sweet/taste**
▶ a **sharp/salty/distinctive flavour/ taste/tang**
▶ **have/give sth/add flavour/taste**
▶ **enhance/spoil the flavour/taste of sth**

● **FLAVOUR OR TASTE?** Use either word to talk about how a meal tastes. Use **taste** for food you can find in nature. Use **flavour** for food that has been created by sb: *The tomatoes give extra flavour/taste to the sauce. • I don't like the taste of olives. • Which flavour of ice cream would you like?*

flee verb [I, T]

■ *Refugees fled from the city.*

bolt • make off | *esp. BrE* **run off** | *esp. spoken* **run away • run for it** | *infml* **take off**

▶ flee/bolt/run away **from** sb/sth
▶ flee/bolt/run off/run away **to** sth
▶ flee/bolt/make off/run off/run away/take off **down/into** sth

flexible adj.

1 (*approv.*) ■ *We need a more flexible design.*

adjustable • multi-purpose | *approv.* **adaptable • versatile**

■ OPP **inflexible**
▶ a/an **flexible/adaptable/versatile system**
▶ a **flexible/versatile workforce/ approach**
▶ a **versatile/multi-purpose machine**

2 ■ *a metre of flexible plastic tubing*

elastic • supple • springy

■ OPP **rigid**
▶ **flexible/elastic materials**

flirt verb [I]

■ *He flirts outrageously with his female clients.*

infml **come on to sb • make a pass at sb** | *BrE, infml* **chat sb up** | *disapprov.* **tease**

● **FLIRT OR CHAT SB UP? Chat sb up** only refers to sb's words; **flirt** also

---

includes their behaviour. Usually sb who **chats you up** wants to have a relationship with you, but sb who **flirts** may not.

float verb [I]

■ *A group of swans floated by.*
■ *Beautiful music came floating out of the window.*

drift • hang • hover

■ OPP **sink**
▶ float/drift/hang/hover **over** sth
▶ float/hang/hover **above/ overhead/in the air/in the sky**
▶ a **boat floats/drifts**
▶ **clouds** float/drift/hang/hover

● **FLOAT OR DRIFT?** Float places more emphasis on the idea of sth being supported on the surface of the water or in the air. **Drift** places more emphasis on the fact that sth is moving slowly in a particular direction, often without any control.

flood noun

1 [C, U] ■ *Rain caused floods in many areas.*

flash flood • torrent • tidal wave • tsunami | *esp. written* **deluge**

▶ **cause** a flood/flash flood/tidal wave/tsunami
▶ floods/flash floods/a tidal wave/a tsunami **hit/hits** sth
▶ a flood/tidal wave/tsunami **destroys** sth

2 [C] (usu. followed by 'of') ■ *A flood of phone calls followed the broadcast.*

stream • barrage • torrent | *written* **shower • hail • outpouring**

▶ a flood/stream/torrent of **words**
▶ a flood/stream of **calls**
▶ floods/a torrent of **tears**
▶ **unleash** a flood/barrage/torrent of sth

flood verb

1 [I] ■ *The river flooded, causing immense destruction.*

overflow • burst its banks

▶ a **river floods/overflows/bursts its banks**

2 [I] (always used with an adv. or prep.) ■ *Refugees continued to flood into neighbouring countries.*

pour • stream • surge | *infml* **pile** | *often disapprov.* **swarm**

▶ flood/pour/stream/surge/pile/ swarm **into** sth
▶ flood/pour/stream/swarm **out of** sth
▶ **come** flooding/pouring/streaming **in/out**

● **FLOOD OR POUR?** Flood places more emphasis on the large numbers of people or things involved; **pour** emphasizes that the action continues over a period of time.

floor noun

1 [C, usu. sing.] ■ *She sat on the floor and watched TV.*

ground ◆ earth

■ OPP ceiling
▶ on/under the floor/ground/earth
▶ drop/fall to (the) floor/ground/earth
▶ reach/hit (the) floor/ground

2 [C] ■ *an office on the third floor*

level ◆ deck | *esp. BrE* storey | *AmE usu.* story

▶ on the top, etc. floor/level/deck/storey
▶ the top/upper/lower floor/level/deck/storey
▶ the main floor/deck
● **FLOOR OR STOREY?** Use floor to talk about which level of a building sb lives/works on; use storey to talk about how many floors a building has: *His office is on the fifth floor.* ● *a five-storey house*

flow noun

1 [U, C, usu. sing.] ■ *There was a swift flow of air through the room.*

current ◆ circulation | *fml* passage

▶ against/with the flow/current
▶ a/the flow/current/circulation/passage of water/air
▶ a/the flow/passage of electricity
▶ the flow/circulation of blood

2 [C, usu. sing., U] ■ *an uninterrupted flow of traffic*

stream ◆ tide ◆ trickle

▶ a flow/stream (of sb/sth) into/through sth
▶ a steady/constant flow/stream/trickle
▶ halt/control the flow/tide
▶ go/swim against the flow/tide

flow verb [I]

■ *It's here that the river flows down to the ocean.*

run ◆ stream ◆ pour ◆ circulate ◆ gush ◆ pump ◆ spurt ◆ trickle | *written* cascade

▶ water flows/runs/streams/pours/circulates/gushes/spurts/trickles/cascades
▶ blood flows/runs/streams/pours/circulates/gushes/pumps/spurts/trickles
▶ tears flow/run/stream/pour/gush/trickle
▶ light flows/streams/pours

flush verb [I]

■ *He flushed with anger.*

blush ◆ glow ◆ burn | *BrE* colour | *AmE* color

▶ flush/blush/glow/burn/colour with sth
▶ sb's cheeks flush/glow/burn/colour
▶ sb's face flushes/glows/burns/colours
● **FLUSH OR BLUSH?** A person only blushes when they feel embarrassment or shame. In other situations use **flush**.

fly verb

1 [I] ■ *A wasp flew in through the window.*

glide ◆ flutter | *written* soar

▶ fly/glide/flutter/soar away
▶ fly/glide/soar off/above/over/overhead/up
▶ fly/soar into the air/sky/clouds

2 [I, T] ■ *We're flying from JFK airport.*

go ◆ travel

▶ fly/go/travel from/to sth
▶ fly/go/travel with sb
▶ fly/go/travel 50 miles/1000 km

3 [I, T] ■ *Where did you learn to fly?*

pilot ◆ handle ◆ steer ◆ navigate | *BrE* manoeuvre | *AmE* maneuver

▶ fly/steer/navigate/manoeuvre sth into/out of sth
▶ fly/steer/navigate sth across/through sth
▶ fly/pilot/handle/steer/navigate/manoeuvre a plane

4 [I] (usu. used with an adv. or prep.) ■ *A stone came flying through the window.*

shoot ◆ hurtle ◆ speed ◆ streak | *esp. BrE* career | *infml* zoom | *infml, esp. BrE* whizz | *infml, esp. AmE* whiz

▶ fly/shoot/hurtle/speed/streak/career/zoom/whizz down/across (sth)
▶ fly/shoot/hurtle/speed/streak/career/zoom/whizz past (sb/sth)
▶ fly/shoot/hurtle/speed/streak/career/whizz through sth

foam noun [U]

■ *beer with a good head of foam*

froth ◆ surf ◆ lather ◆ suds

▶ a head of foam/froth

focus noun [U, C, usu. sing.]

■ *His provided a focus for debate.*

focal point ◆ hub ◆ heart | *BrE* centre | *AmE* center

focus

▶ an **important** focus/focal point/
hub
▶ **act/serve** as a focus/focal point/
centre
▶ **give rise/provide** a focus/focal
point

focus verb

1 [I, T] ▪ *The discussion focused on
two main issues.*

target • direct • turn • be aimed at
sb • orient | *fml* address

▶ focus/target/turn **on** sth
▶ efforts/resources/campaigns are
focused on/targeted at/directed at
sb/sth
▶ attention is focused on/directed
at/turned sb/sth

2 [I, T] ▪ *Focus the camera on the
children.*

point • aim • direct • turn

▶ focus/turn sth **on** sth
▶ point/aim/direct sth **at** sb/sth
▶ focus/point/aim **a camera**
▶ focus/aim/direct (a) **light**

fold noun [C]

▪ *The fabric fell in soft folds.* ▪ *Why is
the place I want to find always on the
fold of the map?*

wrinkle • crease • line

▶ a fold/crease **in** sth
▶ a wrinkle/line **on** sth
▶ a **neat** fold/crease
● **FOLD OR WRINKLE?** Fold is used
more about fabric; wrinkle is used
more about skin. Folds in fabric are
tidy but wrinkles are unwanted.
Wrinkles in skin are thin lines;
folds are fatter and usu. occur
because sb is overweight.

follow verb

1 [I, T] ▪ *I think we're being followed.*

chase • tail • trail • track • stalk •
hunt | *fml* pursue

▪ OPP lead
▶ follow/chase/pursue sb/sth **into**
sth
▶ follow/chase/tail/trail/track/
stalk/pursue a **person**
▶ follow/trail/track/stalk/
hunt/pursue an **animal**

2 [T, I] (not used in the progressive
tenses) ▪ *A new proposal followed
on from the discussions.*

result • stem from sth | *fml* ensue •
arise

▶ follow/result/stem/ensue/arise
from sth
▶ follow/result/arise **out of** sth
▶ sth follows/results/stems/arises
from the fact that...

---

3 [T] ▪ *He has trouble following
instructions.*

obey • carry sth out • act on/upon
sth • respect • comply | *fml* adhere
to sth • abide by • observe

▶ follow/obey/carry out/act on
instructions/orders
▶ follow/carry out/act on a
recommendation
▶ follow/obey/respect/comply
with/adhere to/abide by/observe
the **conventions/rules/
regulations/law**

4 [T, I] ▪ *Don't follow my example and
rush into marriage.*

copy • imitate • follow in sb's
footsteps • model yourself on sb/
sth | *fml* emulate • mimic | *esp. busin.
or journ.* follow suit

▶ follow/copy/imitate/emulate a
style
▶ follow/copy/mimic sb/sth **exactly**
▶ follow/copy sb/sth **faithfully/
slavishly**

5 [I, T] (not used in the progressive
tenses) ▪ *Sorry—I don't quite follow.*
▪ *The plot is almost impossible to
follow.*

understand • grasp | *esp. spoken* see
• get | *fml* comprehend

▶ follow/understand/grasp/see/
get/comprehend **what/why/
how...**
▶ follow/understand **instructions**
▶ be **easy/difficult/hard** to follow/
understand/grasp/see/
comprehend

food noun [U, C]

▪ *Do you like French food?*

meal • diet | *fml* refreshment | *fml or
tech.* foodstuff • nourishment |
written, esp. journ. fare

▶ (a) **staple** food/diet/foodstuff
▶ (a/an) **simple/traditional/
vegetarian/English/Chinese, etc.**
food/meal/diet/fare
▶ **provide** food/a meal/a...diet/
refreshment/nourishment
▶ **serve** food/a meal/...fare

fool noun [C] (sometimes offens.)

▪ *Don't be such a fool!*

sometimes offens. idiot | *BrE, infml,
sometimes offens.* prat | *esp. AmE,
infml, sometimes offens.* dork | *offens.*
moron | *esp. AmE, infml, offens.* jerk

▶ a **complete** fool/idiot/prat/dork/
moron/jerk
▶ **feel/look like** a/an fool/idiot/
prat/dork/moron/jerk
▶ **make** a/an fool/idiot/prat/dork
of yourself

forbidden adj.

▪ *Smoking is strictly forbidden.*

banned • taboo | fml prohibited

■ OPP permitted
► forbidden/banned/taboo/prohibited **areas**
► forbidden/banned/prohibited **books**
► a forbidden/taboo **subject**

force noun

1 [U] ■ The rioters were taken away by force.

strength • power | fml **coercion • might**

► **physical** force/strength/power/coercion
► **brute** force/strength
► **use** (your) force/strength/power/coercion/might

2 [U] ■ The force of the blast hurled bodies into the air.

impact • shock

► the force/impact of the **blow/crash**
► the force/shock of the **impact/explosion**
► **feel** the force/shock/impact

3 [U] ■ The force of her argument impressed the committee.

power • impact

► (a) **considerable/tremendous/great** force/power/impact

4 [C+sing./pl. v.] ■ A peace-keeping force was deployed to the area.

army • unit • contingent • legion

► (a/the) **British/French**, etc. forces/army/unit
► (a/an) **enemy/rebel** forces/army/units
► **command/be in command of** a/an enemy/unit/contingent
► a/an force/army/legion **invades**

force verb

1 [T, often passive] ■ The president was forced to resign.

make • drive | fml **oblige • compel • impel**

► force sb/be made/be obliged/drive sb/compel sb/impel sb **to do** sth
● **FORCE OR MAKE? Make** is slightly more informal. It is usu. a person who **makes** sb else do sth: Mum made me eat all my cabbage. **Force** often suggests threats, or a situation where there is no choice about what to do: The hijackers forced the passengers to lie on the ground. • The plane was forced to make an emergency landing.

2 [T] (often used with an adv. or prep.) ■ He forced the lid of his suitcase shut. ■ She forced her way through the crowds.

push • ram • drive • shove • barge • shoulder • elbow | written **thrust**

► force/push/ram/drive/shove/barge/thrust sth **into** sth
► force/push/drive/shove/thrust sth **through** sth
► force/push/shove/thrust sb/sth **away**
► force/push/shove/thrust sth **open/shut**
► force/push/barge/shoulder/elbow **your way** through

forecast noun [C]

■ Sales forecasts are encouraging.

prediction • projection • prophecy • expectation

► (a) forecast/prediction/projection/prophecy/expectations **about** sth
► (a) forecast/predictions/projections/expectations **for** sth
► **make** a forecast/prediction/projection/prophecy

forecast verb [T]

■ Snow is forecast for tomorrow.

predict • foresee • prophesy | esp. busin. **project** | esp. spoken **say**

► forecast/predict/foresee/prophesy/say **that...**
► forecast/predict/foresee/prophesy/say **how/when/who/where/whether...**
► forecast/predict/foresee/prophesy **the future**
● **FORECAST OR PREDICT?** Someone **predicts** what will happen based on the information available, their opinions or using religious or magical powers; someone **forecasts** sth based on the information available and often using scientific methods.

foreign adj.

■ What foreign languages do you speak?

esp. busin. or politics **overseas • external** | often disapprov. **alien**

■ OPP native, domestic, home
► (a/an) foreign/overseas/alien **country/territory**
► foreign/overseas/external **trade/markets/debt/policy**
► a foreign/an overseas **bank/firm/holiday/tour/trip**
► a foreign/an alien **culture/language/species/system**
● **WHICH WORD? Foreign** is the most frequent of these words and has the widest usage. **Overseas** and **external** are factual words with no suggestion of 'strangeness', which **foreign** and **alien** sometimes have. **Alien** can also be used to describe

plants and animals from a foreign country.

forest noun [C, U]

■ *The species is found in both coniferous and deciduous forests.*

wood/woods • woodland • woodlands • rainforest • jungle • plantation

► **dense** forest/wood/woodland/ jungle
► **tropical** forest/rainforest/jungle

forget verb [I, T]

1 ■ *Don't forget to write.*

fail | *fml* **neglect** | *esp. BrE, fml* **omit**

■ OPP **remember**
► forget/fail/neglect/omit **to do sth**
► **completely/totally/almost/ never/conveniently** forget/fail to do sth

2 [T] ■ *I forgot my purse.*

leave • lose | *esp. BrE, fml* **mislay**

■ OPP **remember**
► forget/leave/lose/mislay your **keys/wallet/bag**

3 [I, T] ■ *Try to forget what happened.*

shut sb/sth out • blot sth out • wipe

■ OPP **remember**
► shut sb/sth out of/blot sth out of/ wipe sth from your **mind**
► shut/blot/wipe out a **memory**

forgive verb [T]

■ *I can't forgive that type of behaviour.*

pardon • excuse • condone

■ OPP **condemn, punish**
► forgive/pardon/excuse/condone **sb for sth**
► forgive/excuse/condone sb's **behaviour**
► Forgive/Pardon/Excuse my **ignorance.**

form noun

1 [C] ■ *It's a common form of cancer.*

type • kind • variety • style • brand • version | *esp. BrE* **sort** | *fml* **genre**

► **a** form/type/kind/variety/style/ brand/version/sort/genre **of sth**
► **various** forms/types/kinds/styles/ versions/sorts/genres
► **different** forms/types/kinds/ varieties/styles/versions/sorts/ genres
► **the best/worst** form/type/kind/ sort

2 [C, U] ■ *The disease takes many different forms.*

shape • guise

► **in the** form/shape/guise **of sb/sth**

► **take** a form/shape

3 [C] ■ *This is a standard form sent to all applicants.*

questionnaire • coupon

► **an entry** form/coupon
► **design/draw up/prepare/send out/receive** a form/questionnaire
► **complete/fill in/fill out/return** a form/questionnaire/coupon

4 [C] ■ *They made out a shadowy form in front of them.*

shape • figure • shadow • outline • silhouette

► **a tall** form/shape/figure/shadow/ silhouette
► **a ghostly** form/shape/figure/ shadow
► **make out/see** a/an form/shape/ figure/outline/silhouette

form verb

1 [T, often passive] ■ *Rearrange the letters to form a new word.*

make • create • build

► form/make/create/build sth **from/out of sth**
► form/make sth **into sth**
► form/create/build a **picture** of past societies

2 [T, I] ■ *They hope to form a new government.* ■ *The band formed in 2008.*

set sth up • start | *esp. written* **establish • found**

► form/set up/start/establish/found **a group/society/company/ movement/colony**
► form/set up/start/establish a **partnership/relationship**
► form/set up/establish a **government/team/network/ database**

formal adj.

1 ■ *She has a formal, rather unfriendly manner.*

disapprov. **staid • stuffy • stiff**

■ OPP **informal, casual**
► formal/stuffy **about** sth
► a formal/stiff **manner**

2 ■ *A formal complaint has been made.*

official • authorized

■ OPP **informal**
► a formal/an official **announcement/request/ complaint/apology/agreement**
► formal/official/authorized **institutions**
► a/an formal/official/authorized **body**

former adj.

1 [only before noun] ■ *The palace has been restored to its former glory.*

past • old • previous | *fml* **prior**

■ OPP present, future
● **FORMER, PAST OR OLD?** Use **former** or **past** to talk about times gone by; use **old** to talk about things from your own life: *my old school/ colleagues/friends.* **Former** can also describe sth that has changed: *the former Yugoslav republic.* A *former friend* is sb who is no longer your friend; an *old friend* is sb you have known for a long time.

2 [only before noun] ■ *She's the former world champion.*

ex- • old • then

■ OPP current, future
▶ sb's former/ex-/old/then **partner/ boyfriend/girlfriend**
▶ sb's former/ex-/old/then **husband/ wife**
▶ a/an former/ex-/old **lover/ colleague/member**
▶ a/an former/ex-/old **friend/ally/ enemy**
● **FORMER OR EX-?** Former has a wider range of collocates. **Ex-** is less formal and is preferred in spoken English.

fortune noun

1 [U] ■ *She had the good fortune to work with a top designer.*

luck • chance • fate

▶ **good/bad/ill** fortune/luck
▶ **have the …fortune/luck to do sth**
▶ **a stroke of** fortune/luck/fate

2 [C, usu. sing.] ■ *She inherited the family fortune.*

money • wealth • prosperity | *lit.* **riches**

▶ (a) **personal/family** fortune/ money/wealth/prosperity
▶ **have/possess/accumulate/ acquire/inherit** (a) fortune/ money/wealth/riches
▶ **make a** fortune/money (on/out of sth)

forum noun [C]

■ *Television is an important forum for public debate.*

stage • platform | *written* **arena**

▶ a/an forum/stage/platform/arena **for** sth
▶ a/an **international/global/ political** forum/stage/platform/ arena
▶ **provide** a/an forum/platform/ arena

---

found verb [T] (*esp. written*)

■ *He founded the company 20 years ago.*

form • set sth up • start | *esp. written* **establish**

▶ found/form/set up/start/establish **a group/society/company/ movement/colony**
▶ found/set up/start/establish a **business/firm/programme**
▶ found/establish a/an **dynasty/empire**

foundation noun

1 [C, usu. pl.] ■ *They started to lay the foundations of the new school.*

base • bottom

▶ (a) **firm/solid/strong** foundations/base
▶ **have** (a) foundations/base/ bottom

2 [C, usu. sing.] ■ *Friendship provides a solid foundation for marriage.*

basis • base

▶ the foundation/basis/base **for/of** sth
▶ a/an **ideological/intellectual/ philosophical/theoretical/ economic** foundation/basis/base
▶ **form/have sth as/establish/use sth as** a/the foundation/basis/ base of sth
● **FOUNDATION OR BASIS?** Foundation is often used to talk about larger and more important things than **basis**: *He laid the foundation of Japan's modern economy. • These figures formed the basis of their pay claim.*

fragile adj.

■ *It's fragile, so don't drop it.*

delicate • brittle

■ OPP robust
▶ fragile/delicate/brittle **bones/ glass**
▶ fragile/delicate **china**
▶ (a) fragile/delicate **thread**
▶ the fragile/delicate **ecology**
● **FRAGILE OR DELICATE?** Delicate fabrics, like silk, need special care: *Use a cool wash for delicate fabrics.* **Fragile** fabrics need even more care, usu. because they are very old.

fragment noun [C]

■ *Fragments of glass lay on the floor.*

sliver • splinter • flake • chip • shred • piece | *esp. BrE* **bit |** *written* **shard**

▶ **in** fragments/slivers/flakes/ shreds/pieces/bits/shards
▶ **small** fragments/slivers/splinters/ flakes/chips/pieces/bits/shards

▶ glass / metal fragments / splinters / shards

▶ a fragment / sliver / splinter / shard of glass

● **FRAGMENT OR SLIVER?** A **fragment** is usu. a part of sth that has broken into pieces; a **sliver** may have been cut off sth that is still whole except for this one piece.

frame noun [C]

■ a bicycle frame

body • chassis • shell • hull • bodywork • fuselage

▶ the frame / body / chassis / shell / bodywork of a **car**
▶ the frame / body / fuselage of a / an **aircraft / plane**
▶ the frame / hull of a **ship**
▶ a metal / steel frame / body / chassis / shell / hull / bodywork

fraud noun

1 [U] ■ The property had been obtained by fraud.

dishonesty • deceit • deception

▶ be guilty of / accuse sb of fraud / dishonesty / deceit / deception
▶ practise / obtain sth by fraud / deceit / deception
▶ use / admit / confess to / deny fraud / deception

2 [C] ■ He helped prevent a $100 million fraud.

infml **scam • racket • game • con**

▶ a $100 million fraud / scam / racket
▶ a / an **insurance / financial** fraud / scam
▶ operate / run / be involved in a fraud / scam / racket
▶ control a fraud / racket

free verb

1 [T] ■ Ten prisoners were freed today.

release • set sb/sth free • let sb go • liberate • let sb/sth loose • ransom | *fml* **emancipate**

■ OPP **capture, imprison**
▶ free / release / set sb/sth free / liberate / emancipate sb **from** sth
▶ free / release / set free / let go / liberate / ransom a **prisoner / hostage**
▶ free / release sb **on bail**
● **FREE, RELEASE OR SET FREE? Free** emphasizes the decision to let sb go. **Release** emphasizes the physical act of letting sb go; **set free** also emphasizes this, esp. where force, not authority, is used: *The woman was freed by the Appeal Court this morning. • They were interrogated before being released. • The rioters stormed the prison and set all the prisoners free.*

2 [T] ■ Two men were freed from the wreckage.

release • disentangle • cut | *fml* **disengage |** *esp. spoken* **let (sb) go**

■ OPP **trap**
▶ free / release / disentangle / cut / disengage sb **from** sth
▶ free / release / disentangle / disengage **yourself from** sth
▶ free / release / disentangle / disengage / let go of your / sb's **arm / hand**

3 [T] (always used with *of* or *from*) ■ These exercises help free the body of tension.

fml **rid • purge**

▶ free / rid / purge sb/sth/yourself **of** sth
▶ free / purge sb/sth **from** sth
▶ free / purge **yourself** of sb/sth
● **FREE OR RID? Free** emphasizes the good feeling that follows when you remove sth; **rid** emphasizes how unpleasant that thing was.

free adj.

1 ■ He set the horses free.

loose • at large

■ OPP **captive**
▶ set sb/sth free / loose
▶ break / get / run free / loose
▶ remain free / loose / at large

2 ■ Admission is free.

complimentary • free of charge • for nothing

▶ a free / complimentary ticket / sample / copy / subscription
▶ get sth free / free of charge / for nothing

3 ■ Is this seat free?

empty • vacant • unoccupied • available

■ OPP **taken, engaged**
▶ a / an free / empty / vacant / unoccupied **seat**

4 ■ Are you free for lunch?

available • spare

■ OPP **unavailable, busy**
▶ free / available **for** sth
▶ free / available **to do** sth
▶ free / available **spare** time
▶ a free / spare **morning / afternoon / weekend / moment**

freedom noun [U, C]

■ Branch managers enjoy considerable freedom.

independence • liberty • leeway | *fml* **autonomy**

▶ freedom / liberty / leeway **to do** sth
▶ have freedom / independence / liberty / leeway / autonomy

► enjoy/lose freedom/
independence/liberty/autonomy
► encourage/promote freedom/
independence/autonomy

freezing adj.

■ Expect freezing conditions tonight.

frozen • frosty • icy • snowy •
wintry | *disapprov.* bitter

■ OPP boiling
► freezing/frosty/icy/snowy/
wintry/bitter **weather**
► freezing/frozen/frosty/icy/
snowy/wintry **conditions**
► a/an freezing/frosty/icy/snowy/
wintry **morning/day/night**

frequent adj.

■ He is a frequent visitor to Paris.

regular • constant • persistent •
continual • continuous • habitual •
perpetual

■ OPP infrequent, occasional
► frequent/regular/constant/
persistent/continual/continuous/
habitual **use**
► frequent/regular/constant/
persistent/continual/continuous
attacks
► a frequent/constant/persistent/
continual/perpetual
problem
● FREQUENT OR REGULAR? Use **regular**
in more active examples, when you
are talking about people doing
things, rather than things that
happen:
✔Eat a healthy diet and take regular
exercise. ✗ ~~Take frequent exercise.~~

frequently adv.

■ Trains are frequently cancelled.

often • routinely • habitually | *infml,*
esp. spoken a lot

■ OPP infrequently
► happen frequently/often/a lot
► occur frequently/often
► frequently/routinely/habitually
used
● FREQUENTLY OR OFTEN? **Frequently**
is more formal than **often** and is
used esp. to talk about things that
affect people generally; **often** is
used more to talk about things that
affect sb personally.

friend noun [C]

■ He's one of my best friends.

companion • acquaintance •
confidant • ally | *BrE, infml* mate |
AmE, infml buddy | *infml, old-fash.* pal
| *often disapprov.* crony

■ OPP enemy
► a friend/companion/pal of
mine/yours/his/hers/ours/
theirs/my mother's/Diana's, etc.

► an old friend/acquaintance/ally/
mate/buddy/pal
► a good friend/companion/mate/
buddy/pal
► have friends/acquaintances/
allies/mates/buddies/pals

friendly adj.

1 ■ Jim gave me a friendly smile.

warm • welcoming • good-natured
• pleasant • likeable • hospitable •
approachable | *esp. spoken* nice •
lovely | *written* amiable • genial

■ OPP unfriendly
► friendly/pleasant/welcoming/
hospitable/nice **to sb**
► a/an friendly/warm/good-
natured/pleasant/likeable/
hospitable/approachable/nice/
lovely/amiable/genial **person**
► a friendly/warm/welcoming/
pleasant/hospitable/amiable/
genial **manner**

2 ■ She was on friendly terms with her
employees.

amicable • easy | *fml* cordial

■ OPP hostile
► (a/an) friendly/amicable/easy/
cordial **relationship/relations**
► a/an friendly/amicable/cordial
meeting
► be on friendly/amicable/easy/
cordial **terms (with sb)**

friendship noun [C, U]

■ Her friendship is important to me.

intimacy • togetherness • closeness
| *esp. written* companionship •
camaraderie | *fml* fellowship •
comradeship • acquaintance

■ OPP enmity
► friendship/intimacy/closeness/
companionship/camaraderie/
fellowship/comradeship/
acquaintance **with sb**
► the friendship/intimacy/
closeness/companionship/
camaraderie/fellowship/
comradeship **between** A and B
► develop a/an friendship/
intimacy/closeness/camaraderie
● FRIENDSHIP OR INTIMACY?
Friendship is the more frequent
and general word. **Intimacy**
describes a stronger and closer, or
romantic, relationship.

frighten verb [T]

■ She's not easily frightened.

scare • terrify • alarm • traumatize •
intimidate | *infml* spook | *written*
cow

■ OPP reassure
► frighten/scare **away/off**

▶ frighten / scare / terrify / intimidate /
cow sb **into** doing sth
▶ It frightens / scares / terrifies / alarms
me **that...**
● **FRIGHTEN OR SCARE?** Scare is more
common in spoken English. Both
words can be used without an
object: *He doesn't frighten/scare
easily.*, but it would be more usual
to say: *Nothing frightens/scares him.*

frightened *adj.*

■ *I'm frightened—please stay with me.*

**afraid • scared • terrified • petrified
• paranoid • alarmed • worried •
nervous • anxious • startled •
intimidated** | *fml* **fearful**

▶ frightened / scared / paranoid /
worried / nervous / anxious / fearful
about sth
▶ frightened / afraid / scared /
terrified / petrified / fearful **of** sb / sth
▶ frightened / afraid / scared /
terrified / petrified / worried /
nervous / anxious / fearful **that...**
● **FRIGHTENED, AFRAID OR SCARED?**
Scared is more informal, more
common in speech, and often
describes small fears. Afraid
cannot come before a noun:
✓ *a frightened child* • *a scared
expression* ✗ *an afraid child/
expression*

frightening *adj.*

■ *It is frightening to think that it could
happen again.*

**alarming • terrifying • chilling •
eerie • disturbing • intimidating •
daunting • hair-raising** | *infml* **scary •
spooky • creepy**

■ OPP **comforting**
▶ frightening / alarming / terrifying /
disturbing / intimidating /
daunting / scary **for** sb
▶ frightening / terrifying / disturbing /
daunting / scary **to think...**
▶ a/an frightening / alarming /
terrifying / chilling / disturbing /
daunting / scary **experience /
thought / prospect**
● **FRIGHTENING, ALARMING OR SCARY?**
Alarming describes a situation and
is often a warning for the future.
Frightening and scary can
describe people as well as
situations and refer to a fear about
the now or the future.

the front *noun* [sing.]

■ *The kids pushed to the front.*

**the lead • the forefront • the fore •
the foreground**

■ OPP **the back**
▶ the front / forefront / foreground **of**
sth
▶ **at** the front / forefront / fore

▶ **in** the lead / forefront / foreground

frown *verb* [I, T]

■ *Why are you frowning at me?*

grimace | *disapprov.* **scowl**

■ OPP **smile**
▶ frown / grimace / scowl **at** sb / sth
▶ frown / grimace **in** concentration,
anxiety, etc
▶ frown / scowl **darkly / heavily**

frozen *adj.*

■ *My hands are frozen.*

**freezing • icy • chilly • snowy •
frosty • wintry**

▶ frozen / freezing / icy / snowy /
frosty / wintry **conditions**
▶ a/an frozen / icy / snowy / wintry
landscape
▶ I'm **frozen / freezing.**

frustration *noun* [U, C, usu. pl.]

■ *Joe thumped the table in frustration.*

**irritation • annoyance •
exasperation** | *fml* **displeasure •
chagrin • pique**

■ OPP **satisfaction**
▶ frustration / irritation / annoyance /
exasperation / displeasure **at** sth
▶ **do** sth **in** frustration / irritation /
annoyance / exasperation
▶ **hide** your frustration / irritation /
annoyance / exasperation /
displeasure / chagrin
▶ **show** your frustration / irritation /
annoyance / displeasure

fuel *noun* [U, C]

■ *Fuel bills are set to rise again.*

**oil • gas • coal • fossil fuel • diesel •
petroleum** | *BrE* **petrol** | *AmE*
gasoline

▶ sth **runs on** (a particular kind of)
fuel / oil / gas / diesel / petrol /
gasoline
▶ **run out of** fuel / oil / gas / diesel /
petrol
▶ fuel / oil / gas / coal / fossil fuel /
diesel / petroleum / petrol / gasoline
consumption

full *adj.*

1 ■ *There were boxes full of clothes.*

packed • crammed • crowded | *infml*
stuffed | *disapprov.* **overcrowded •
congested**

■ OPP **empty**
▶ full / packed / crammed / crowded /
overcrowded / congested **with** sb /
sth
▶ packed / crammed / stuffed **full of**
sb / sth

2 ■ *We haven't heard the full story.*

whole • complete • entire • total

■ OPP **partial**

► the full/whole/complete **truth/ story**
► full/complete **details**

3 ■ *He led a very full life.*

busy • hectic • eventful | *esp. BrE* **lively**

■ OPP **empty**
► a/an full/busy/hectic/eventful **day/weekend/week/life**
► a full/busy/hectic/lively **programme**
► a full/busy/hectic **schedule/ timetable**
● **FULL, BUSY OR HECTIC?** Busy is the most general of these words. A period of time that is **full** is busy in a good way; if it is **hectic** then it is usu. too busy.

fumble *verb* [I, T] (usu. used with an adv. or prep.)

■ *She was fumbling around in the dark, looking for the light switch.*

grope • feel • rummage • fish | *esp. BrE* **scrabble**

► fumble/grope/feel/rummage/ fish/scrabble **around/about**
► fumble/grope/feel/rummage/fish/ scrabble **for sth**

fun *noun* [U]

■ *We had a lot of fun at Tim's party.*

entertainment • pleasure • enjoyment • amusement • play • recreation • relaxation | *esp. spoken* **good time • great time** | *AmE, infml* **blast**

► do sth **for** fun/entertainment/ pleasure/enjoyment/amusement/ recreation/relaxation
► **have** fun/a good time/a great time/a blast
► **provide** fun/entertainment/ amusement/recreation/relaxation
► **spoil** the fun/sb's pleasure/sb's enjoyment

function *noun* [C, U]

■ *The committee performs a useful function.*

use • purpose

► sth's **main/primary** function/use/ purpose
► a **useful** function/purpose
► **have** a function/use/purpose
► **serve/fulfil** a function/purpose

function *verb* [I] (usu. used with an adv. or prep.) (*fml*)

■ *The hospital struggled to function during the raids.*

run • operate | *esp. spoken* **work • go**

► function/run/operate/work **efficiently/smoothly/**

independently/successfully/ normally/reliably
► function/run/work **perfectly**
► function/operate/work **effectively/properly/correctly**
● **FUNCTION OR OPERATE?** Function is used more to talk about whether sth works or how well or badly it works; operate is used more to talk about the conditions required for sth to work: *We now have a functioning shower.* • *Solar panels can only operate in sunlight.*

fund *noun*

1 [C] ■ *She made a donation to the cancer relief fund.*

budget • account • savings • pocket • purse | *infml* **stash** | *finance* **reserves**

► pay sth **from/out of** a fund/a budget/an account/your savings/ your own pocket/the purse/your reserves
► a/the **public** fund/budget/purse
► **have** (a/an) fund/budget/ account/savings/reserves/stash
► **manage** a fund/a budget/an account/your savings/your reserves

2 funds [pl.] ■ *The village is raising funds for a new hall.*

money • capital • finance • means | *infml* **cash**

► government/public funds/ money/capital/finance/cash
► **have/lack** (the) funds/money/ capital/finance/cash/means (**to do sth**)
► **raise/provide/put up** funds/ money/capital/finance/cash
► **spend/borrow/invest** funds/ money/capital/cash
● **FUNDS OR CASH?** You can use either word in personal or business contexts, although cash is more informal than funds. Cash can be used like an adjective before other nouns: *The company is having cash flow problems.*

fund *verb* [T]

■ *The museum is privately funded.*

finance • support • sponsor • subsidize • endow | *esp. AmE, infml* **bankroll** | *finance* **guarantee • underwrite**

► fund/finance/support/sponsor/ subsidize/bankroll/underwrite a **project/programme**
► fund/finance/support/sponsor/ bankroll/underwrite a **campaign**
► fund/finance/support/sponsor/ subsidize **research**
● **FUND OR FINANCE?** Fund is used more often than finance for

fundamental

projects that continue or are repeated year after year.

fundamental adj.

■ Living without war is a fundamental freedom.

basic • essential • radical • ultimate • underlying • elementary | *fml* **rudimentary**

▶ fundamental/basic **to** sth
▶ a/an fundamental/basic/ essential/radical/underlying **difference/distinction**
▶ a/an fundamental/basic/ essential/elementary/underlying **rule/principle**
▶ a/an fundamental/basic/ essential/underlying **assumption/ aim/problem/cause/reason/ need/weakness**

funny adj.

1 ■ It's the funniest story you ever heard.

amusing • witty • humorous • comic • hilarious • light-hearted • entertaining

▶ a/an funny/amusing/witty/ humorous/comic/light-hearted/ entertaining **story**
▶ a/an funny/amusing/witty/ humorous/light-hearted/ entertaining **speech**
▶ a/an funny/amusing/witty **guy/ man/woman**
● WHICH WORD? Amusing is the most general of these words and can be used to describe events, activities and occasions. Funny can describe people, jokes and stories, things that happen or anything that makes people laugh. Comic is used esp. to talk about writing and drama. Humorous is not quite as strong as funny or comic.

2 (esp. spoken) ■ The engine's making a very funny noise.

strange • odd • bizarre • mysterious • uncanny • unusual • curious | *esp. spoken* **weird** | *BrE or fml* **peculiar**

▶ funny/strange/odd/bizarre/ uncanny/unusual/curious/weird/ peculiar **that...**
▶ funny/strange/odd/uncanny/ curious/weird/peculiar **how/ what...**
▶ a/an funny/strange/odd/bizarre/ mysterious/unusual/curious/ weird/peculiar **thing**
▶ a/an funny/strange/odd/bizarre/ uncanny/unusual/curious/weird/ peculiar **feeling**

furious adj.

■ I was furious at the way we'd been treated.

outraged • incensed • fuming • seething | *written* **enraged**

▶ furious/outraged/incensed/ fuming/seething **about/at/over** sth
▶ furious/outraged/incensed **that...**
▶ **absolutely** furious/outraged/ incensed/fuming

fuss noun [U, sing.]

■ They made such a fuss about the noise.

outcry • uproar • scene | *BrE* **furore** | *esp. AmE* **furor** | *esp. journ.* **storm**

▶ a/an fuss/outcry/uproar/furore **about** sth
▶ a/an fuss/outcry/uproar/furore/ **storm over** sth
▶ **cause** a/an fuss/outcry/uproar/ scene/furore/storm
▶ **create** a/an fuss/uproar/scene/ furore/storm

future noun [C, U]

■ His future is uncertain

destiny • fate • fortune | *esp. BrE* **lot** | *lit.* **doom**

■ OPP **past**
▶ a **grim** future/destiny/fate/lot
▶ **meet** your destiny/fate/doom
▶ **avoid/escape** your destiny/fate

future adj.

■ He met his future wife at law school.

later • next • coming • following | *fml* **prospective • subsequent**

■ OPP **past, previous, ex-, former**
▶ future/later/coming/subsequent **months/decades/generations/ events**
▶ a **later/a next/the next/a** subsequent **time**
▶ a **later/a next/the next/the** following/a subsequent **stage/ chapter**
● FUTURE OR LATER? Future is used esp. about situations or developments in the future; later is used esp. about a stage in an event, process or account: *future plans/prospects/trends • a later stage/phase/addition*

Gg

gain noun [C, U]

■ Exercise is the best way to prevent weight gain.

increase • rise • growth

■ OPP **loss**
▶ a gain/an increase/a rise/growth **in** sth
▶ a gain/an increase/a rise/growth **of** 20%

gain verb

1 [T] (*esp. written*) ■ The party gained over 50% of the vote.

win • earn • land | *esp. spoken* get | *esp. written* obtain | *fml* secure • procure | *written, esp. journ.* net

■ OPP lose
▸ gain/win/earn/get/obtain/secure/procure sth by (doing) sth
▸ gain/win/earn/get/obtain/secure/procure sth for sb
▸ gain/win/earn/get/obtain/secure approval
▸ gain/win/earn/get respect/admiration

2 [T, I] ■ Who stands to gain from this decision?

benefit | *fml* profit | *disapprov.* cash in

■ OPP lose
▸ gain/benefit/profit from sth
▸ the company/industry/farmer gains/benefits/profits/cashes in
▸ the customer/consumer/individual gains/benefits
▸ stand to gain/benefit/profit
● GAIN OR BENEFIT? Gain is used more often to talk about financial advantages. Benefit cannot be used with an object:
✔ There is nothing to be gained from delaying. ✗ There is nothing to be benefited from delaying.

3 [T] ■ I've gained weight recently.

increase in sth • put sth on

■ OPP lose
▸ gain/increase in/put on weight
▸ gain/increase in strength

gamble noun

1 [sing.]
■ It was the biggest gamble of his political career.

risk • chance | *often disapprov.* lottery

■ OPP safe bet
▸ take a gamble/risk/chance on sth
▸ a huge/major/calculated gamble/risk
▸ something of/a bit of a gamble/risk/lottery
● GAMBLE, RISK OR CHANCE? Risk is used *esp.* when there is danger to life or sb's safety; gamble is used about less serious danger, or when you risk money. When you decide to give/not to give sb the opportunity to do sth, you take a chance/take no chances.

gamble verb [I, T]

■ He gambled all his winnings on the last race.

bet

▸ gamble/bet (sth) on sth
▸ gamble/bet money/£50, etc.

game noun

1 [C] ■ Chess is a game of skill.

sport

▸ play/take part in a game/sport
▸ team/competitive games/sports

2 [C] ■ The team is in training for the big game.

esp. BrE match | *BrE* fixture • tie • test (match)

▸ a game/match/fixture/tie/test against/with sb
▸ a game/match/fixture/tie/test between A and B
▸ a/an international/friendly game/match/fixture
▸ a home game/match/fixture/tie/test
▸ an away game/match/fixture/tie
▸ win/lose a game/match/fixture/test/tie
● GAME OR MATCH? Game has a wider range of uses than match. In BrE match is used to talk about individual or team sports. In AmE match is used for individual sports, but game is used for team sports:
✔ (BrE) a football match • (BrE, AmE) a tennis match • a football game • a game of football ✗ a match of football

gap noun

1 [C] ■ a gap in a hedge/fence/wall

space • hole • opening

▸ a/an gap/space/hole/opening in sth
▸ a gap/space between A and B
▸ leave a/an gap/space/hole/opening

2 [C] ■ I waited for a gap in the conversation.

break • lull • pause

▸ a gap/break/lull/pause in sth
▸ after a gap/break/lull/pause
▸ fill a gap/pause
● GAP, BREAK OR LULL? A gap or lull usu. happens without being planned. A break is often planned.

3 [C] ■ the widening gap between rich and poor

gulf • margin

▸ the gap/gulf/margin between A and B
▸ bridge the gap/gulf
▸ a gap/gulf separates A and B

garbage noun

1 [U] (*esp. AmE*) ■ The canal is full of garbage and bits of wood.

waste • litter • scrap | *esp. BrE*
rubbish | *AmE* trash | *fml* refuse •
debris

▸ **household/domestic** garbage/
waste/rubbish/trash/refuse
▸ **dump** garbage/waste/rubbish/
trash/refuse/debris
▸ **produce** garbage/waste/rubbish/
trash/debris
● **WHICH WORD?** Use **rubbish** in BrE
and **garbage** or **trash** in AmE for
the everyday things that we throw
away. **Waste** is used esp. to talk
about large amounts and in the
context of industry.

2 [U] (*esp. AmE, infml*) ■ Don't believe
all the garbage in the papers!

nonsense • lies • story • fiction | *BrE,
infml* rubbish | *esp. AmE, slang* bull |
taboo, slang bullshit • crap

▸ garbage/nonsense/lies/stories/
rubbish/bull/bullshit/crap **about**
sth
▸ **believe** that/those garbage/
nonsense/lies/story/fiction/
rubbish/bull/bullshit/crap
▸ **a load/lot of** garbage/nonsense/
rubbish/bull/crap

3 [U] (*AmE, infml*) ■ She just watches
garbage on TV all day.

infml trash | *BrE, infml* rubbish |
taboo, slang crap

▸ **absolute/complete/total**
garbage/trash/rubbish/crap
▸ **read/watch/listen to** garbage/
trash/rubbish

garden *noun*

1 [C] (*BrE*) ■ They sat in the garden,
enjoying the sunshine.

grounds | *AmE* yard • backyard | *BrE*
park • parkland

▸ **the front/back** garden/yard
▸ **(a) beautiful/landscaped** garden/
grounds/yard/backyard/park/
parkland

2 [C] (*esp. AmE*) ■ They planted a
garden of woodland plants.

bed • border • patch • kitchen
garden | *esp. BrE* allotment

▸ **a flower/rose** garden/bed
▸ **a vegetable** garden/patch

3 gardens [pl.] ■ The botanical
gardens close at 6 pm.

park • playground | *esp. AmE* garden

▸ **visit the** gardens/park/garden

gas *noun*

1 [C, U] ■ Air is a mixture of gases.

chemical • substance • element

▸ **a natural** gas/chemical/substance

▸ **a toxic** gas/chemical/substance/
element
▸ **a radioactive** gas/chemical/
substance/element

2 [U] (*AmE*) ■ He still had plenty of gas
in the tank.

fuel • diesel | *BrE* petrol | *AmE*
gasoline

▸ **unleaded** gas/fuel/petrol/
gasoline
▸ **sth runs on** gas/fuel/diesel/
petrol/gasoline
▸ **fill the car up with** gas/diesel/
petrol
▸ **run out of** gas/fuel/diesel/petrol

gate *noun* [C]

■ They met at the factory gates.

entrance • exit • gateway • way •
turnstile • door

▸ **at the** gate/entrance/exit/
turnstile/door
▸ **through the** gate/gateway/
turnstile/door
▸ **the front/back/side** gate/
entrance/exit/way/door
▸ **open/shut/close/slam/lock/bolt**
the gate/door

gather *verb* [I]

1 ■ A crowd soon gathered.

mass • assemble • rally • meet |
infml get together | *fml* convene

■ OPP disperse, scatter
▸ gather/mass/assemble/rally/
meet/get together/convene **for**
sth
▸ **crowds/supporters** gather/
assemble/rally
▸ **people** gather/mass/assemble
● **GATHER, MASS OR ASSEMBLE?**
Gather is the most general of these
words. **Mass** emphasizes the large
number of people involved.
Assemble is more formal and refers
to arranged meetings.

2 [T] ■ They gathered their belongings
and left.

collect • accumulate • amass

■ OPP scatter
▸ gather/collect/accumulate/amass
data/evidence/information
● **GATHER OR COLLECT?** When talking
about things, use **gather** for *things,
belongings* or *papers* when the
things are spread around within a
short distance; use **collect** to talk
about getting examples of sth from
different people or places.

gear *noun* [U]

■ Have you brought your walking
gear?

equipment • kit • apparatus •
hardware • material | *infml* stuff |
esp. BrE, infml things

► state-of-the-art/up-to-date/**the latest** gear/equipment/kit/hardware
► **electronic/electrical** gear/equipment/apparatus/hardware/stuff
► **have/use** (the right) gear/equipment/kit/apparatus/materials/stuff/things

general adj.

1 ■ *The general opinion is that a new bridge is needed.*

widespread ∙ common ∙ universal ∙ popular ∙ commonplace ∙ rife | *fml* **prevalent** | *fml or humorous* **ubiquitous**

► **in** general/widespread/common/universal **use**
► **the** general/widespread/universal/common/popular/prevalent **view**
► **a** general/widespread/universal/common/prevalent **problem**

2 ■ *All the machines operate on the same general principle.*

standard ∙ routine ∙ usual ∙ regular ∙ traditional ∙ habitual

► **the** general/standard/routine/usual/regular/traditional **procedure/practice**
► **the** general/standard/routine/usual/regular/traditional/habitual **way**
► **sb's** general/usual/habitual **behaviour**

3 ■ *She read the introduction to get a general idea of the subject.*

broad ∙ overall ∙ sweeping

■ OPP **specific, detailed**
► **the** general/broad/overall **context**
► **a/an** general/broad/overall **conclusion**
► **a** general/broad/sweeping **assertion/statement**
● **GENERAL OR BROAD?** General is used slightly more often when talking about trends; broad is used slightly more often when talking about categories and aims: *a general trend/tendency/direction* ◆ *a broad definition/sense/aim/objective*

generation noun [C+sing./pl. v., U]

■ *People of his generation may be less comfortable with new technology.*

age ∙ age group ∙ peer group

► **the younger/older** generation/age group
► **people of your own** generation/age
► **people of all** generations/ages/age groups

generous adj.

1 ■ *a kind and generous man* ■ *a very generous gift*

written, sometimes disapprov. **liberal ∙ free with sth**

■ OPP **mean**
► **be** generous/liberal/free **with** sth
► **a** generous/liberal **amount** of sth
● **GENEROUS OR LIBERAL?** People can be **generous** with their *money, time* or *help*. If they are **generous** with their money, you can just say that they are **generous** (without stating 'with their money'). People can be **liberal** with their *money, cash, criticism* or *advice*.

2 ■ *He wrote a very generous assessment of my work.*

kind ∙ considerate ∙ thoughtful | *esp. spoken* **nice ∙ good ∙ sweet** | *fml* **benevolent ∙ benign**

■ OPP **mean**
► generous/kind/considerate/nice/good/benevolent **to** sb
► **be** generous/kind/considerate/thoughtful/nice/good/sweet of sb (to do sth)
► **a** generous/kind/considerate/thoughtful/nice/good/sweet/benevolent **man/woman/person**

genius noun [C]

■ *He was a comic genius.*

prodigy ∙ brain ∙ mastermind

■ OPP **dunce**
► **the** genius/brains/mastermind **behind** sth
► **a** true/child genius/prodigy
► **a** great/scientific genius/brain

gentle adj.

1 ■ *Be gentle with her!* ■ *He's such a sweet, gentle man.*

sensitive ∙ sympathetic ∙ understanding ∙ compassionate ∙ humane | *sometimes disapprov.* **soft**

■ OPP **rough**
► gentle/sensitive/sympathetic/understanding/compassionate **towards** sb
► **a** gentle/sensitive/sympathetic/compassionate/humane **manner/man**
► **(in) a** gentle/sensitive/sympathetic/compassionate/humane **way**

2 ■ *Cook over a gentle heat.*

light ∙ mild

■ OPP **vigorous**
► **(a)** gentle/light **breeze/wind/rain**
► gentle/light **work/exercise**
► **a** light/mild **punishment**
● **GENTLE, LIGHT OR MILD?** Gentle is

used esp. to describe weather, temperature, work and exercise. **Light** is used esp. to describe weather, work, exercise and punishments. **Mild** is used esp. to describe weather, diseases, drugs, criticism and punishment.

gentleman noun [C] (fml)

■ There's a gentleman here to see you.

man | infml **guy** | BrE, infml **bloke** | esp. AmE, slang **dude** | fml **male**

● **OPP lady**
▶ a/an young/old gentleman/man/guy/bloke/dude/male
▶ a nice gentleman/man/guy/bloke/dude

genuine adj.

1 ■ Is the painting a genuine Picasso?

authentic • real • true • actual | BrE, spoken **proper**

■ **OPP fake**
▶ a genuine/a real/the true/the actual/a proper **reason**
▶ a/an genuine/authentic/real/true **work of art**
▶ genuine/real **leather/silk/gold**
● **GENUINE OR AUTHENTIC?** Genuine describes sth that really belongs to a group of things of the same type. Authentic describes sth that has really been produced or created by sb/sth. This means that sometimes either word can be used: a/an genuine/authentic Picasso sketch

2 ■ She always showed genuine concern for others.

sincere • real • deep • heartfelt • wholehearted

■ **OPP forced, insincere**
▶ genuine/sincere **about** sth
▶ genuine/sincere/real/deep/heartfelt **sympathy/concern**
▶ a genuine/sincere **person**
● **GENUINE OR SINCERE?** Sincere is more likely to be used by sb about their own feelings and intentions; genuine is more likely to be used to express a judgement on sb else's feelings and intentions:
✓ Please accept our sincere apologies.
✗ Please accept our genuine apologies.
✓ He made a genuine attempt to improve the situation.

get verb

1 [T, no passive] (esp. spoken) ■ I got a letter from Dave today.

collect | esp. written **receive • reap** | fml **derive** sth **from** sth

▶ get/collect/receive/reap/derive sth **from** sb/sth
▶ get/collect/receive a/an **medal/award/prize**

▶ get/receive a/an **reply/letter/shock/prison sentence**
● **GET OR RECEIVE?** Receive is rather formal; get is the more usual word in spoken English. You can **get** or **receive** a sudden feeling such as a **shock** or an **impression**, over a period of time that you experience over a period of time such as enjoyment and satisfaction you usu. **get**.

2 [T, no passive] (not usu. used in the progressive tenses) (esp. spoken) ■ I managed to get three tickets for the concert.

take • get hold of sth • land | infml **pick sth up** | esp. written **obtain • acquire • gain** | fml **procure • secure**

▶ get/take/ pick up/obtain/acquire/gain/procure sth **from** sb/sth
▶ get/take/ pick up/ obtain/acquire/gain/procure **information**
▶ get/ get hold of/land/pick up/ obtain/acquire/procure a **ticket**
▶ get/gain/pick up/acquire a **reputation** for sth

3 [T, no passive] (esp. spoken) ■ Did you get your mother a present?

buy • take | infml **pick sth up • snap sth up** | fml **purchase • acquire**

▶ get/buy/pick up/snap up/ purchase/acquire sth **for £10, $2 million, etc.**
▶ get/buy/pick up/purchase/acquire sth **from** sb/a particular shop
▶ get/buy/take/purchase/acquire **goods**
▶ get/buy/pick up/snap up/ purchase/acquire **shares**

4 [T, no passive] (esp. spoken) ■ We got £220000 for the house.

make • bring (sb) in sth • **fetch • raise** | fml **realize**

▶ get/make/fetch/bring in/raise/ realize **$199/£300000**
● **GET, MAKE OR BRING IN STH?** You can **make** money, a particular amount of money, or a profit or loss. You can **bring in** money or a particular amount of money. You can only **get** a particular amount of money:
✓ The garage sale made/brought in more than we expected. ✗ The garage sale got more than we expected.
✓ The company is making a loss. ✗ The company is getting/bringing in a loss.

5 [T] (esp. spoken) ■ Could you get the blue file from the desk?

bring • collect | esp. spoken **pick sb/sth up** | BrE, esp. spoken **fetch**

▶ get/bring/collect/pick up/fetch sb/sth **from** sth/somewhere

▶ get/bring/collect/pick up/fetch sth **for** sb

▶ get/bring/fetch sb sth

▶ **go/come and** get/bring/fetch/collect/pick up/fetch sb/sth

● **GET OR FETCH?** Get has a wider range of meaning than fetch; you usu. **fetch** sb/sth that is in a place and just needs to be collected; you can **get** sth that needs to be prepared or obtained as well as collected:

✔ Get John a drink. ✗ ~~Fetch John a drink.~~

6 [T, no passive] (*esp. spoken*) ■ *I think I'm getting a cold.*

catch ◆ come down with sth ◆ develop ◆ suffer from sth ◆ have ◆ *esp. BrE, esp. spoken* **have got |** *fml* **contract**

▶ get/catch/develop/suffer from/have/have got/contract a/an **disease/illness**

▶ get/catch/come down with/suffer from/have/have got/contract a **bug**

▶ get/develop/suffer from/have/have got/contract **cancer/AIDS**

7 linking verb (*esp. spoken*) ■ *I soon got used to the climate in Spain.*

become ◆ grow ◆ come ◆ go ◆ turn

▶ get/grow/come **to know/like** sth

▶ get/become/grow/turn **cold/warm/chilly**

▶ get/become/grow **fat/old/angry/hungry/tired**

● **GET OR BECOME?** You can often use either word, but there are some cases where you can only use one of them: *I became/got hungry/upset* (= verb + adjective). ◆ *She became Queen/a teacher/a member of the club* (= verb + noun). ◆ *Don't get your dress dirty* (= verb + noun + adjective)!

Use **get** for changes that are the result of deliberate actions by you or sb else: *get dressed/married/killed*

Use **become** with adjectives connected with ability, knowledge, availability and clarity: *become able/skilled/aware/convinced/available/useful/clear/obvious*

8 [T] (*esp. spoken*) ■ *He got his sister to help him.*

persuade ◆ convince ◆ talk sb into sth ◆ coax ◆ cajole ◆ win sb over

▶ get sb/persuade sb/convince sb/be coaxed/be cajoled **to do** sth

9 [I] (always used with an adv. or prep.) ■ *We got to the party very late.*

arrive ◆ land ◆ *esp. spoken* **get in ◆ make ◆ make it |** *infml* **show up ◆ roll in ◆ hit |** *esp. written* **reach**

▶ get/make **it to** a place

▶ get/arrive/land/make it/show up/reach **here/there**

● **GET OR REACH?** Get is the usual word in spoken English. Get takes no object, but always takes an adv. or adverbial phrase; reach always takes an object and is usu. more specific about the destination: *We'll get there before dinner.* ◆ *It took them three hours to reach the opposite shore.*

10 [I, T] (always used with an adv. or prep.) (*esp. spoken*) ■ *It takes an hour to get from here to the cinema.*

go ◆ move ◆ travel ◆ make your way ◆ pass | *fml* **proceed**

▶ get/go/move/travel/make your way/pass/proceed **from/to** sth/somewhere

▶ get somewhere/go/make your way **by** bus/train/car, etc.

11 [T, no passive] (*esp. spoken*) ■ *I got the bus home from town.*

catch ◆ go by sth | *esp. written* **take**

▶ get/catch/go by/take sth **from/to** sth/somewhere

▶ get the/catch the/go by/take the **bus/train/plane/boat**

▶ get/catch **a flight**

12 [T] (*esp. spoken*) ■ *Can I get you something to eat?*

make ◆ cook | *esp. AmE* **fix |** *esp. written* **prepare**

▶ get/make/cook/fix sth **for** sth

▶ get/make/cook/fix sb/yourself sth

▶ get/make/cook/fix/prepare **breakfast/lunch/dinner**

get angry *phrase*
■ *Please don't get angry with me. I'm trying my best.*

lose your temper ◆ lose patience ◆ *AmE, infml* **get mad |** *BrE, infml* **go mad ◆ go berserk**

▶ get angry/lose your temper/lose patience/get mad **with** sb

▶ get angry/lose your temper/get mad/go mad **at** sb

▶ get angry/lose your temper **over** sth

● **GET ANGRY OR LOSE YOUR TEMPER?** If you **lose your temper** you show it in your behaviour: *She lost her temper with a customer and shouted at him.*

If you **get angry** the emphasis is more on your feelings and less on your behaviour.

get away *phrasal verb*
■ *You'd better get away—the soldiers are coming.*

get (sth) back

escape • lose • elude • evade

▸ get away/escape **from** sb/sth
▸ get away from/escape/lose/elude/evade your **pursuers**

get (sth) back *phrasal verb*

1 ■ *We got back from our trip at midnight.*

return • go back • come back

▸ get back/return/go back/come back **to/from/with** sth
▸ get back/return/go back/come back **again**
▸ get back/return/go back/come back **home/to work**

2 ■ *Sometimes I lend books and don't get them back.*

recover • regain • reclaim | *fml* retrieve • recoup

▸ get back/recover/regain/reclaim/retrieve/recoup sth **from** sb
▸ get back/recover/reclaim/retrieve/recoup your **money**
▸ get back/recover/regain/reclaim **the lead**

get better *verb*

1 [I] ■ *Things got better after my husband found a job.*

improve • pick up • progress • advance | *infml* look up • come along/on

■ OPP **get worse**
▸ **things** get better/improve/pick up/progress/are looking up/are coming along
▸ **technology** is getting better/improves/progresses/advances

2 [I] ■ *He is finally getting better after a long illness.*

recover • heal • get well • shake sth off • pull through | *fml* recuperate • convalesce

■ OPP **get worse**
▸ recover/recuperate **from** sth
▸ **gradually** get better/recover/heal

get by *phrasal verb*

■ *How does she get by on such a small salary?*

cope • manage • get on | *BrE* muddle through

▸ get by/cope/manage/muddle through **without** sth
▸ get by/manage **on** sth
▸ get by/manage/muddle through **somehow**

get in (sth) *phrasal verb*

1 ■ *I got in the car.*

get on | *fml* board • embark • mount

■ OPP **get out (of sth)**
▸ get in/get on/board a **bus/train**
▸ get on/board a **plane/ship**
▸ get on/mount a **horse/bike/bicycle/motorcycle**

2 (*esp. spoken*) ■ *What time did you get in last night?*

get into sth • arrive • land • come in • appear | *esp. spoken* get here/there • make • make it • turn up | *infml* show up | *esp. written* reach

▸ have just got in/arrived/landed/come in/appeared/got here/turned up
▸ get in/arrive/come in/appear/get here/turn up/show up **late**

get off (sth) *phrasal verb*

■ *We'll get off at the next stop.*

get out (of sth) | *fml* disembark • alight • dismount

■ OPP **get on (sth)**
▸ get off/get out/alight **here**

get on (sth) *phrasal verb*

1 ■ *She got on the horse and rode off.*

get in (sth) | *fml* board • embark • mount

■ OPP **get off (sth)**
▸ get on/get in/board a **bus/train**
▸ get on/board a **plane/ship**
▸ get on/mount a **horse/bike/bicycle/motorcycle**

2 (*esp. BrE*) ■ *Jack's getting on very well at school.*

perform | *esp. BrE* get along | *esp. spoken* do • go | *esp. written* fare

▸ get on/perform/get along/do/go/fare **well**

get out (of sth) *phrasal verb*

1 ■ *He got out of the taxi.*

get off | *fml* disembark • alight • dismount

■ OPP **get in (sth)**
▸ get out/get off/alight **here**

2 ■ *I wish I could get out of going to the meeting.*

avoid • evade • sidestep • skirt • skip | *disapprov.* shirk | *infml, disapprov.* duck • wriggle out of sth • dodge | *BrE, infml, disapprov.* skive

▸ get/duck/wriggle **out of** sth
▸ get out of/avoid/evade/dodge/wriggle out of **doing** sth
● GET OUT OF STH OR DUCK? Duck is more disapproving than get out of sth; you might admit to wanting to get out of sth yourself; you would accuse sb else of trying to duck sth.

get over (sth) *phrasal verb*

■ *She can't get over her shyness.*

overcome • control | *infml* **beat** | *written* **conquer**

▶ get over/overcome/control/beat/ conquer a **problem**
▶ get over/overcome/control/ conquer a **fear**
▶ get over/overcome/control/ conquer a **difficulty/ hurdle**

get rid of sb/sth *phrase*
■ *We got rid of all the old furniture.*

dispose of sth • throw sth away/out • dump • scrap • remove • eliminate • eradicate | *esp. spoken* **do away with sth** | *fml* **discard • dispense with sth** | *esp. journ.* **shed**

■ **OPP keep,** (*infml*) **hang on to sth**
▶ get rid of/remove/eliminate/ eradicate sth **from** sth
▶ get rid of/dispose of/dump/ remove/eliminate/discard **waste**
▶ get rid of/dispose of/remove/ eliminate a **problem**

get up *phrasal verb*
1 ■ *He got up and strolled to the window.*

stand up • stand • pick yourself up | *fml* **rise** | *written* **get to your feet**

■ **OPP sit down**
▶ get up/stand up/rise/pick yourself up **from** sth
● **GET UP OR STAND UP?** Get up is the most frequent way of saying 'get into a standing position', and this can be from a sitting, kneeling or lying position. **Stand up** is used esp. to tell sb or a group of people to do this. Use **get up** to tell sb politely that there is no need to rise from their chair:
  ✓*Please don't get up!* ✗ *Please don't stand up!*

2 ■ *She always gets up early.*

get out of bed • wake up | *written* **wake**

■ **OPP go to bed**
▶ get up/get out of bed/wake up/ wake late/early/in the morning/ at seven o'clock, etc.

get well *phrase*
■ *Get well soon!*

get better • recover • come through (sth) • pull through • shake sth off | *fml* **recuperate**

▶ recover/recuperate **from** sth
▶ gradually get better/recover

ghost *noun* [C]
■ *Do you believe in ghosts?*

spirit | *esp. written* **apparition**

▶ see a/an ghost/spirit/apparition
▶ a/an ghost/spirit/apparition **haunts** sth

▶ a ghost/spirit **appears**

gift *noun*
1 [C] ■ *There's a free gift for every reader.*

present • donation • contribution • tip | *fml* **gratuity** | *often disapprov.* **handout**

▶ a gift/present/donation/ contribution/tip/gratuity/ handout **for/from** sb
▶ a gift/present/donation/ contribution **to** sb/sth
▶ a **birthday/wedding/ anniversary/Christmas** gift/ present
▶ **get/receive** a gift/present/ donation/contribution/tip/ gratuity/handout
● **GIFT OR PRESENT?** Especially in *BrE*, **gift** is more formal than **present** and is used more in business contexts. A **present** is usu. an object but a **gift** may be a sum of money, or sth such as the *gift of love/life*.

2 [C] ■ *She has a great gift for music*

talent • ability • flair • aptitude | *infml* **knack**

▶ a/an gift/talent/flair/aptitude/ knack **for** (doing) sth
▶ a **natural/great** gift/talent/ ability/flair/aptitude
▶ **have/develop** a/the gift/talent/ ability/flair/aptitude/knack
● **GIFT OR TALENT?** Gift is used more about people's abilities in the arts, or in relationships; **talent** is used more of sb's abilities in business: *a gift for painting/languages/ friendship* • *a talent for diplomacy/ figures/management*

girl *noun*
1 [C] ■ *A nine-year-old girl was injured.*

child | *infml* **kid • youngster**

■ **OPP boy**
▶ a **little** girl/child/kid
▶ a **bright/local** girl/child/kid/ youngster
▶ a girl/child/kid/youngster **learns sth/plays/grows (up)**

2 [C] ■ *They've had a baby girl.*

daughter • child • baby | *infml* **kid**

■ **OPP boy**
▶ a **newborn** girl/daughter/child/ baby
▶ sb's **eldest/oldest/youngest** girl/ daughter/child/kid
▶ **have/give birth to** a girl/ daughter/child/baby

3 [C] (*sometimes offens.*) ■ *one of the girls at work*

girlfriend

young woman • teenager • adolescent | *infml, esp. AmE* **teen** | *fml or law* **juvenile**

■ OPP **lad, young man**
▶ a **young** girl/woman/teenager/ adolescent
▶ a/an **older/local** girl/teenager

girlfriend noun [C]

■ *He's got a new girlfriend.*

partner • fiancée • mistress • lover | *esp. AmE* **date** | *becoming old-fash.* **sweetheart**

■ OPP **boyfriend**
▶ sb's **new/former/current** girlfriend/partner/mistress/lover
▶ sb's **ex-** girlfriend/partner/fiancée/lover
▶ **have** a girlfriend/partner/fiancée/ mistress/lover/date/sweetheart
● GIRLFRIEND OR PARTNER? A **partner** is usu. sb you live with but are not married to and suggests a more long-term relationship. Young people often prefer to use the words girlfriend/boyfriend.

give verb

1 [T] ■ *Give this letter to your mother.*

hand • hand sb/sth over • pass

■ OPP **take**
▶ give/hand/hand over/pass sth **to** sb
▶ **just** give/hand/hand over/pass sth
▶ give/hand/hand over/pass sth **immediately/promptly**

2 [T, I] ■ *She was given a huge bunch of flowers.*

present • award • transfer | *fml* **bestow • confer • accord**

■ OPP **receive**
▶ give/present/award/transfer/ accord sth **to** sb
▶ bestow/confer/accord sth **on** sb
▶ give/present/bestow **gifts/an award**
▶ give/present/award **a prize**

3 [T] ■ *Could you give me some information?*

provide • supply • issue • lend

▶ give/supply/issue/lend sth **to** sb
▶ provide/supply/issue sb **with** sth
▶ give/provide/supply **equipment/details/information**
▶ give/supply/lend **support/ credibility/weight/credence**
● GIVE OR PROVIDE? **Provide** is often used when sth is being made available to people in general; **give** is more often used about a particular person: *The hospital aims to provide the best possible medical care. • We want to give you the best possible care.*

4 [T, I] ■ *She gave regularly to charity.*

contribute • donate | *infml* **chip in (sth)**

▶ give/contribute/donate (sth) **to** sth
▶ give/contribute/donate **cash/a sum**
▶ give/contribute/donate/chip in **£10/$1000,**

5 [T] ■ *I gave £50 for the lot.*

pay • spend

▶ give/pay £50 **for** sth
▶ spend £50 **on** sth

6 [T] ■ *The judge gave him a £500 fine.*

infml **hand sth out** | *fml* **administer • dispense**

▶ give/hand out/administer/ dispense sth **to** sb
▶ give/hand out/administer **punishment/treatment**
▶ give/administer/dispense **medicine/drugs/medication**
▶ give/hand out/dispense **advice**

7 [T] (*esp. spoken*) ■ *Jack gave me his cold.*

pass sth on • spread • infect | *fml* **transmit**

▶ give/pass on/spread/transmit sth **to** sb
▶ give sb/pass on/spread/infect sb **with/transmit** a/an **disease/ infection/virus**

8 [T] ■ *The dark glasses gave him an air of mystery.*

add | *written* **lend • impart**

▶ give/add/lend/impart sth **to** sb
▶ give/add/lend/impart a/an **sense/feeling/air of** sth
▶ give/add/lend (a) **new dimension/credibility/distinction** (to sth)

give sb/sth away phrasal verb

■ *He gave away state secrets to the enemy.*

reveal • betray • expose | *fml* **divulge • disclose** | *journ.* **leak**

▶ give away/reveal/betray/expose/ divulge/disclose/leak sth **to** sb
▶ give away/reveal/betray/divulge/ disclose **that...**
▶ give away/reveal/betray/divulge/ disclose a **secret**

give sth back phrasal verb

■ *Give me back my pen!*

hand sth back • return • pay sb back • repay • refund | *fml* **restore**

▶ give back/hand back/return/pay back/repay/refund/restore sth to sb/sth

▶ give back/hand back/return/pay back/repay/refund **money**
▶ give back/hand back/return a **book**

give in *phrasal verb*
■ They won't give in to the kidnappers' demands.

bow to sth • back down | *esp. BrE* give way | *fml* submit • yield • relent

■ OPP resist
▶ give in/bow/give way/submit/yield **to sb/sth**
▶ give in/back down/give way/relent **on sth**
▶ give in/bow/give way/submit/yield **to pressure/sb's demands**
● GIVE IN OR GIVE WAY? In many cases you can use either phrase, although you more often give **in** to sb's demands or to pressure, and give **way** to a person.

give sth out *phrasal verb*
■ The teacher gave out the exam papers.

hand sth out • distribute | *esp. AmE* pass sth out | *infml* dole sth out • dish sth out | *fml* dispense

▶ give out/hand out/distribute/pass out/dole out/dish out **leaflets**
▶ give out/hand out/distribute/dispense **food**
▶ give out/hand out/distribute/dispense **money**
▶ give out/hand out/dole out/dish out **punishments**

give sth up *phrasal verb*

1 ■ She didn't give up work when she had the baby.

stop • abandon • drop | *infml* leave off • pack sth in • knock off (sth) | *esp. AmE, infml* quit | *fml* cease • discontinue

■ OPP take sth up
▶ give up/stop/leave off/quit/cease **doing sth**
▶ give up/stop/abandon/drop/leave off/quit/cease **what you are doing**
▶ give up/abandon/pack in/quit/ **your job**
▶ give up/abandon **hope**
▶ give up/quit **smoking**

2 ■ He gave up his claim to the throne.

sacrifice • concede • waive • forfeit • abdicate | *fml* surrender • relinquish • renounce • cede

▶ give up/concede/abdicate/surrender/relinquish/cede sth **to sb**
▶ give up/sacrifice/concede/waive/forfeit/surrender/relinquish/renounce a **right/claim**
▶ give up/abdicate/renounce **the throne**

▶ give up/renounce your **citizenship/nationality**
▶ give up/surrender your **passport/ weapons**

glad *adj.* [not usu. before noun]
■ She was glad the meeting was over.

happy • pleased • relieved • grateful • delighted • proud

■ OPP sorry
▶ glad/happy/pleased/relieved/delighted **about sth**
▶ glad/happy/pleased/relieved/grateful/delighted/proud **that...**
▶ glad/happy/pleased/relieved/grateful/delighted to **see/hear/find/know**
▶ glad/happy/pleased/delighted/proud **to say (that ...)**
● GLAD, HAPPY OR PLEASED? Feeling **pleased** can suggest that you have judged sb/sth and approve of them or that sth has happened that is particularly good for you. Feeling **glad** can be more about feeling grateful for sth. **Happy** can mean glad, pleased or satisfied.

global *adj.* [usu. before noun]
■ The commission is calling for a global ban on whaling.

worldwide • international | *esp. busin. or journ.* multinational | *approv.* cosmopolitan

■ OPP local
▶ global/worldwide/international **attention/campaigns/influence/issues/markets**
▶ a/an global/international/multinational **company/corporation**
▶ a/an global/international/cosmopolitan **outlook**
● GLOBAL OR WORLDWIDE? Global is used more in political contexts and worldwide in business contexts, but in many cases you can use either word.

gloom *noun* [U, sing.]
■ The news filled me with gloom.

depression • sadness • unhappiness • despondency | *infml* the blues | *lit.* melancholy

■ OPP cheerfulness
▶ gloom/sadness/unhappiness/despondency/melancholy **about sth**
▶ deep gloom/depression/sadness/unhappiness/despondency/melancholy
▶ fill sb with/sink into/plunge into gloom/depression
▶ the gloom/depression deepens/lifts

go verb

1 [I] (always used with an adv. or prep.) ■ *She went into her room.*

move • travel • make your way • get • head • make for sth • run • pass • advance | *fml* **proceed**

■ OPP **come**

▶ go/move/travel/make your way/get/run/pass/advance/proceed **from... to...**
▶ go/travel/make your way/head/run/advance/proceed **towards** sb/sth
▶ make your way/get **somewhere by** bus/train/car, etc.

2 [I] ■ *She goes to Turkey every summer.*

travel • come • drive • fly • run • do • cover | *esp. AmE* **ride**

▶ go/travel/come/drive/fly/run/ride **from/to** sth
▶ go/travel/come/drive/fly/ride **with** sb
▶ go/travel/come/drive/fly/do/cover/ride **50 miles/1000 km**
● GO OR COME? **Go** is used from the point of view of sb who is at the place where the journey starts; **come** is used from the point of view of sb who is at the place where the journey ends: *We're going to Australia to visit our daughter. • I hope you can come to Australia to visit me.*

3 [I] ■ *He invited her to go to the concert with him.*

come • come along • make • make it | *fml* **attend**

▶ go/come/come along/make it **to** sth
▶ go/come/come along/attend **with** sb
▶ go to/come to/come along to/make/make it to/attend a **meeting/wedding**
● GO OR COME? **Come** expresses the point of view of sb who arranges an event or attends it; **go** is used when the speaker is talking about other people.

4 [I] ■ *I must be going now.*

leave • go away • get away • go off • set • start | *esp. BrE* **be/go on your way** | *esp. BrE, spoken* **be off** | *esp. AmE, spoken* **get out of here** | *fml* **depart • exit**

■ OPP **stay**

▶ go/leave/go away/get away/set off/start/depart/exit **from** sb/sth
▶ go/leave/go away/get away/go off/set off/start/be on your way/depart **at** 9 a.m./midnight, etc.
▶ **be ready to/about to/going to** go away/get away/set off/start/depart

● **LEAVE OR GO AWAY?** Leave is used in ways that emphasize the act or time of leaving sb/sth; go away emphasizes the need or desire of the speaker to be somewhere else or for another person to be somewhere else.

5 [I] (always used with an adv. or prep.) ■ *Where does this road go?*

lead • continue • reach • stretch • span • extend

▶ go/lead/continue/reach/stretch/span/extend **beyond/across** sth
▶ go/lead/continue/reach/stretch/extend **from** sth **to** sth

6 [I] (esp. spoken) ■ *How did your interview go?*

perform | *esp. BrE* **get on/along** | *esp. spoken* **do** | *esp. written* **fare**

▶ go/perform/get on/fare **well**
▶ go/perform/do **brilliantly/excellently/badly**
● GO OR DO? **Do** is used to talk about the progress or success of either a person or a thing, e.g. how popular or profitable a business is; **go** is only used about things, esp. experiences such as an *interview*, a *test* or *life* in general.

7 linking verb ■ *His hair is going grey.*

become • turn • get • grow

▶ go/become/turn **red/white/blue, etc.**
▶ go/become/turn **blind/crazy/mad**
▶ go/turn **bad/sour**

goal noun [C]
■ *He pursued his goal of becoming a photographer.*

objective • target • aim • object • purpose • plan | *fml* **end**

▶ goals/objectives/targets/aims/plans **for** sth
▶ work **towards** a/an goal/objective/target/aim
▶ the **main/primary/prime/principal** goal/objective/target/aim/object/purpose
● GOAL, OBJECTIVE OR TARGET? Goals usu. relate to a person or organization's long-term plans. Targets are usu. specific figures, such as a number of sales, that are set officially, for example by an employer or a government committee. People often set their own objectives that they wish to achieve, for example as part of a project, campaign or piece of writing.

go away phrasal verb (used esp. in orders)
■ *Just go away and leave me alone!*

leave • go • go off • get away | *esp. BrE* be/go on your way | *esp. BrE, infml* clear out • be off | *esp. AmE, spoken* get out of here | *esp. BrE, written* decamp

■ OPP come back
▶ go away/leave/go/get away/ decamp from sb/sth
▶ go away/leave/go/get away/go off/be on your way/be off/get out of here now/soon
● GO AWAY OR LEAVE? Leave is used in ways that emphasize the act or time of leaving sb/sth; go away emphasizes the need or desire of the speaker to be somewhere else or for another person to be somewhere else or for another.

■ **go by** *phrasal verb*
■ *Things will get easier as time goes by.*

pass • tick away | *written* wear on • progress • elapse

▶ hours/days go by/pass/elapse
▶ a season/a year/time goes by/ passes/elapses
▶ the day/night/season/year/time wears on/progresses
▶ the minutes/seconds go by/pass/ tick away/elapse

good *noun*

1 [U] ■ *the difference between good and evil*

right • goodness • morality • purity | *fml* virtue | *fml, esp. religion* righteousness

■ OPP evil
▶ do good/right
● GOOD OR RIGHT? Questions of right and wrong are about treating people in a fair or unfair way; matters of good and evil are about treating people in a kind or cruel way.

2 [U] ■ *We've made these changes for the good of the whole company.*

benefit • advantage • merit • virtue

▶ do sth for sb's good/benefit
▶ see the good/benefit/advantage/ merit/virtue

good *adj.*

1 ■ *Your work is very good.*

fine • high quality • superior • excellent • first-rate • prime • quality | *infml* great | *esp. BrE, fml* sterling

■ OPP bad
▶ (of) good/fine/high/superior/ excellent/prime/great/sterling quality
▶ a/an good/fine/high quality/ superior/excellent/first-rate/ quality/great/sterling performance/service

▶ a/an good/fine/high quality/ superior/excellent/quality/great product

2 ■ *Did you have a good time in America?*

enjoyable • wonderful • pleasant | *esp. spoken* nice | *esp. BrE, esp. spoken* lovely | *fml* pleasurable

■ OPP bad
▶ a/an good/enjoyable/wonderful/ pleasant/nice/lovely/pleasurable experience/thing (to do)
▶ a/an good/enjoyable/wonderful/ pleasant/nice/lovely time/ evening/party
▶ It's good/wonderful/pleasant/ nice/lovely to be/feel/find/ have/know/meet/see…
● GOOD, NICE OR PLEASANT? All these words can describe times, events, feelings and the weather. Nice and pleasant can also describe places, and nice can also describe sb's appearance.

3 ■ *Let's hope we have good weather for the picnic tomorrow.*

dry • mild • clear • sunny • glorious | *esp. BrE* fine

■ OPP bad
▶ good/dry/mild/clear/sunny/ glorious/fine weather
▶ good/dry/clear/sunny/fine (weather) conditions

4 ■ *Maria made a really good point.*

valid • solid • sound • legitimate • well founded

■ OPP bad
▶ a good/valid/solid/sound/ legitimate reason/basis
▶ good/valid/solid/sound evidence
▶ a good/valid/legitimate question/point/excuse

5 ■ *The school has an extremely good reputation.*

positive • complimentary • approving • appreciative • flattering • glowing • admiring | *BrE* favourable | *AmE* favorable

■ OPP bad
▶ a/an good/positive/ complimentary/approving/ appreciative/flattering/favourable comment
▶ a good/positive/favourable opinion/impression/reaction/ response
▶ show sb/sth in a good/positive/ favourable light
● GOOD OR FAVOURABLE? In some cases good does not mean that sth expresses approval; instead use favourable: a good comment is a clever comment; a favourable comment is a comment expressing

approval. If you are **good to sb** you are kind to them; if sth is *favourable to sb* it expresses approval.

6 ■ *He's a really good cook.*

skilled • **talented** • **gifted** • **capable** • **competent** • **expert** • **proficient** • **accomplished** • **able** | *BrE* **skilful** | *AmE* **skillful** | *esp. spoken* **great**

■ **OPP bad, poor**
▶ good/skilled/gifted/competent/ expert/proficient/accomplished/ skilful/great **at sth**
▶ good/skilled/gifted/competent/ great **with sth**
▶ a/an good/skilled/talented/ gifted/able/skilful/great **teacher**
▶ a/an good/skilled/talented/ capable/accomplished/skilful/ great **performer**

7 ■ *She's such a good person.*

moral • **principled** • **virtuous** • **ethical** • **scrupulous**

■ **OPP bad, evil, wicked**
▶ a good/moral/principled/ virtuous/scrupulous **person**
▶ a good/moral/virtuous **life**
▶ good/moral/ethical **behaviour/ practices/principles**

8 [not usu. before noun] (*esp. spoken*) ■ *She was very good to me when I was ill.*

kind • **generous** • **considerate** • **thoughtful** | *infml* **wonderful** | *esp. spoken* **nice** • **sweet** | *esp. BrE, esp. spoken* **lovely** | *fml* **benign** • **benevolent**

■ **OPP unkind, cruel**
▶ good/kind/generous/nice/ considerate/benevolent **to sb**
▶ be good/kind/generous/ considerate/thoughtful/ wonderful/nice/sweet/lovely **of sb (to do sth)**

9 ■ *He's such a good little boy.*

well behaved • **obedient** | *written* **dutiful**

■ **OPP bad, naughty**
▶ a/an good/well-behaved/ obedient/dutiful **child**
▶ a/an good/obedient/dutiful **daughter/son/wife/servant**
▶ a/an good/obedient **dog**

10 ■ *Vijay gave me some good advice.*

valuable • **helpful** • **worthwhile** • **constructive** • **positive** • **advantageous** | *BrE* **favourable** | *AmE* **favorable** | *fml* **beneficial**

■ **OPP bad**
▶ good/valuable/helpful/ advantageous/favourable/ beneficial **for sb/sth**
▶ good/valuable/helpful/

worthwhile/advantageous/ beneficial **to do sth**
▶ good/valuable/helpful/ constructive/positive **suggestions/advice**

11 ■ *Too much sun isn't good for you.*

healthy • **nutritious** • **nourishing** | *tech.* **nutritional**

■ **OPP bad**
▶ a good/healthy/nutritious/ nourishing/nutritional **meal/diet**
▶ good/healthy/nutritious/ nourishing **food**

12 ■ *Monday morning is a good time to have the meeting.*

appropriate • **right** • **convenient** • **suitable** • **apt** • **fit** | *infml* **cut out for sth/to be sth** | *fml* **fitting**

■ **OPP bad**
▶ good/appropriate/right/ convenient/suitable/apt/fit/cut out/fitting **for sb/sth**
▶ good/appropriate/suitable **as sb/ sth**
▶ good/appropriate/suitable/apt/fit/ fitting **that...**
● **WHICH WORD?** How **appropriate** or **suitable** sb/sth is depends on your judgement. How **good** sb/sth is depends on what you like yourself or what is convenient. How **right** sb/sth is depends on the facts:
✔*Do you think she would be a/an good/appropriate/suitable person to ask?* ✗ *a right person to ask*
✔*She's definitely the right person to ask.* ✗ *She's definitely the good/ appropriate/suitable person to ask.*
Good, **suitable** and **right** can all be used when sth is correct for a particular purpose, but **appropriate** is only used about people or situations.

goods noun

1 [pl.] ■ *luxury goods*

merchandise • **product** • **produce** | *economics* **commodity**

▶ **consumer/industrial** goods/ products/commodities
▶ **household** goods/products
▶ **sell/market** goods/merchandise/ a product/produce/a commodity
● **GOODS OR MERCHANDISE?** Use **goods** if the emphasis is on what the product is made of or what it is for: *leather/household goods*. Use **merchandise** if the emphasis is less on the product itself and more on its brand or the fact of buying/ selling it.

2 [pl.] (*esp. written or law*) ■ *The bag contained all her worldly goods.*

possessions • belongings • valuables • property | *infml* stuff • gear | *esp. BrE, infml* things | *infml, disapprov.* junk | *busin.* asset

▶ **private** goods/possessions/ belongings/property/assets
▶ **buy** goods/property/stuff/things/ assets
▶ **sell** your goods/possessions/ belongings/valuables/property/ stuff/things/assets

good thing noun [C]
■ *Think of all the good things in life.*

blessing • bonus • help • boon • godsend

■ OPP bad thing
▶ a good thing/blessing/bonus/ boon/godsend **for** sb
▶ a good thing/blessing/bonus/ help **that...**
● **GOOD THING OR BLESSING?** A **blessing** is important, that is good from any point of view. A **good thing** can also be important or it can be less important that just you are pleased about: *It's a blessing no one was in the house when the fire started.* ◆ *It's a good thing I remembered the camera.*

go off phrasal verb
■ *The bomb didn't go off.*

explode • blow (sth) up • burst • detonate

▶ a **bomb** goes off/explodes/blows up/bursts/detonates
▶ a **firework/rocket** goes off/ explodes

go on phrasal verb
1 (*esp. spoken*) ■ *The fight for justice goes on.*

continue • last • take | *esp. spoken* keep on | *esp. BrE, esp. spoken* carry on | *disapprov.* drag on

▶ go on/continue/last/keep on/ carry on/drag on **for** hours/a week/two years, etc.
▶ go on/continue/last/keep on/ carry on/drag on **until** morning/ next day, etc.

2 (*esp. spoken*) ■ *Let's stop now, and go on again tomorrow.*

continue • return to sth • restart • reopen | *esp. spoken* take sth up | *fml* resume | *esp. journ.* renew

▶ go on/continue **with** sth
▶ go on/continue/resume **doing** sth
▶ **work** goes on/continues/restarts

go on with sth phrasal verb
■ *She shrugged and went on with her writing.*

---

go on doing sth • continue • keep sth up/keep up with sth • press ahead/on • proceed | *esp. spoken* keep • carry (sth) on • stick with sb/ sth | *fml* pursue

▶ go on/continue/keep on/press ahead/proceed/keep on/carry on/stick **with** sth
▶ go on/continue/press ahead with/keep/carry on **doing sth**
▶ go on with/go on doing/ continue/keep on/press ahead/ proceed/carry on/pursue **your work**

go out phrasal verb (used esp. in the progressive tenses)
■ *Tom has been going out with Lucy for six weeks.*

see | *esp. AmE* date | *esp. spoken* be together | *old-fash.* court • woo

● **GO OUT WITH, SEE OR DATE?** These expressions are all commonly used in the progressive tenses with time expressions such as *how long, for three months*, etc. This suggests a temporary relationship that may or may not become permanent.

go up phrasal verb (esp. spoken)
■ *The price of bread is going up.*

rise • increase • grow • climb • escalate

■ OPP come down
▶ go up/rise/increase/grow **in** price, number, etc.
▶ go up/rise/increase/grow/climb **by** 10%, 2000, etc.
▶ the **price/number** goes up/rises/ increases/climbs/escalates
▶ the **level/cost** goes up/rises/ increases/escalates

govern verb [T, I]
■ *The Liberals had governed the country for 11 years.*

rule • be in power • reign

▶ govern/rule **a country**
▶ a (political) **party** governs/rules/is in power
▶ the governing/ruling **party/ coalition/class/elite**
● **GOVERN OR RULE?** Elected parties and governments **govern**; non-elected groups or individuals such as kings, queens and dictators **rule**.

government noun
1 [C+sing./pl. v.] ■ *The government has cut taxes.*

administration • regime • cabinet • the executive • parliament • reign

▶ **under** a/an government/ administration/regime/sb's reign
▶ the **former/previous/current**

government/administration/
regime

▶ **elect** a government/an
administration

▶ **bring down/overthrow** a/an
government/administration/
regime

● **GOVERNMENT OR ADMINISTRATION?**
Countries with prime ministers usu.
have a **government**; countries with
presidents usu. have an
administration: *during/under the
Bush/Obama administration •
during/under the Blair/Brown
government*

2 [U] ■ *This country needs strong
government.*

**leadership • administration •
management • regulation •
supervision • direction**

▶ **be/work, etc. in** government/
administration/management

▶ **effective** government/
administration/leadership/
management/regulation/
supervision/direction

▶ **firm/strong** government/
leadership/management/direction

go without (sth) *phrasal verb*

■ *I was so busy that I had to go
without lunch.*

do without (sb/sth) • give sth up |
fml **forgo/forego**

▶ go without/do without/forgo
food/sleep

▶ go without/do without/give up/
forgo **your meal/sleep**

▶ **have to/be prepared to/be
willing to** go without/do without/
give up/forgo sth

● **GO WITHOUT OR DO WITHOUT?** Do
without suggests that sb manages
to do sth successfully despite not
having sb/sth; **go without**
suggests more that sb tolerates a
situation where sth is missing.

go wrong *phrase*

■ *The marriage started to go wrong
when he lost his job.*

**break down • fail • collapse •
backfire • fall through • get/go
nowhere • come to nothing |** *fml*
founder

▶ a **plan** goes wrong/fails/backfires/
falls through/comes to nothing/
founders

▶ a **relationship/marriage** goes
wrong/breaks down/fails/
collapses

▶ a **deal** goes wrong/collapses/falls
through

grab *verb* [T, I]

■ *She grabbed his hand and ran.*

snatch • catch • take | *esp. written*
seize

▶ grab/snatch/take/seize sth **from**
sb

▶ grab/snatch **at** sth

▶ grab/catch/take/seize **hold of** sb/
sth

● **GRAB OR SNATCH? Snatch** is most
often used when sb takes sth
directly from a person's hands;
grab has a wider range of uses.

grade *noun* [C]

■ *She got good grades in her exams.*

score • result | *esp. BrE* **mark**

▶ a **high/low/good/poor** grade/
score/mark

▶ a **final** grade/score/result/mark

▶ **get** a grade/a score/your results/a
mark

● **GRADE OR MARK?** In British schools
a **mark** is often more precise than a
grade, expressed as a particular
number out of 10 or 100, for
example; **grade** is often a letter
such as A, B or C, covering a range
of marks. However, in American
schools a **grade** can be a letter or a
number, and **mark** is not usu.
used.

grade *verb*

1 [T, often passive] ■ *Eggs are graded
from small to large.*

rank • rate • place | *fml* **order**

▶ grade/rank/rate/order sb/sth
according to sth

▶ grade/rank/order sb/sth **by** sth

▶ grade/rank/rate/place sb/sth **in**
order of sth

2 [T, I] (*esp. AmE*) ■ *She spent the
evening grading papers.*

correct | *BrE* **mark**

▶ grade/correct/mark a/an **paper/
essay/assignment**

▶ grade/correct/mark sb's **work/
classwork/homework**

▶ grade/mark a/an **test/exam/
examination/project/student/
pupil**

gradual *adj.*

■ *a gradual change in climate*

slow • measured

■ OPP **sudden**

▶ gradual/slow **improvement/
change/acceptance**

grand *adj.*

■ *The wedding was a very grand
occasion.*

**magnificent • majestic • impressive
• imposing • splendid • spectacular**

■ OPP **humble**

▶ a/an **grand/magnificent/**

majestic / impressive / imposing / splendid **building**
- a/an grand / magnificent / majestic / imposing **castle**
- a/an grand / magnificent / imposing **palace / staircase**

grant noun [C]

■ The college has a government grant to buy new equipment.

funding • subsidy | fml **endowment**
- a grant / funding / a subsidy / an endowment **from** sb/sth
- a grant / funding / a subsidy / an endowment **for** sth
- a grant / subsidy **to** sb/sth
- a grant / funding **to do** sth

the grass noun [sing., U]

■ We all sat down on the grass.

lawn • turf • common | BrE **green**
- **on** the grass / lawn / turf / common / green
- **sit on / cut / mow** the grass / lawn

grateful adj.

■ I am grateful to everyone for their help.

thankful • glad • relieved • appreciative | fml **indebted**
■ OPP **ungrateful**
- grateful / thankful **for** sth
- grateful / indebted **to** sb
- grateful / thankful / glad / relieved **that...**

great adj.

1 [usu. before noun] ■ A great crowd had gathered.

large • big • huge • massive • vast • enormous • tremendous • immense • extreme • monumental • substantial • considerable
■ OPP **small, little**
- a/an great / large / big / huge / massive / vast / enormous / tremendous / substantial / considerable **amount**
- a/an great / large / big / huge / massive / vast / enormous / substantial / considerable **area**
- a/an great / large / big / huge / massive / vast / enormous / substantial **crowd**
- great / huge / massive / enormous / tremendous / immense / extreme / considerable **pressure**
● **GREAT, LARGE OR BIG?** Compare: a big man / house / car / boy / dog / smile • (a) large numbers / part / volume / population • great interest / importance / difficulty / pleasure
Large is slightly more formal than **big** and is used more in writing. It is not usu. used to describe people, except to avoid saying 'fat'. **Great** often suggests quality and not just

size; it does not usu. describe the physical size of objects or people.

2 ■ She is one of the world's greatest cellists.

distinguished • eminent • prestigious | ** fml or humorous **exalted
■ OPP **minor**
- a/an great / distinguished / eminent **scientist / painter / writer / historian / philosopher / professor**
- a great / distinguished / prestigious **collection**
- a great / distinguished **achievement / career / position**

3 (infml) ■ That was a great goal!

excellent • classic • superb • tremendous | infml **fantastic • fabulous • terrific |** infml, spoken **cool |** esp. AmE, infml, spoken **awesome |** BrE, infml, spoken **brilliant |** slang **wicked**
■ OPP **awful**
- have a/an great / tremendous / fantastic / fabulous / terrific / cool / awesome / brilliant **time**
- a/an great / excellent / superb / tremendous / fantastic / terrific / awesome / brilliant **achievement**
- a/an great / excellent / classic / superb / fantastic / fabulous / terrific / cool / brilliant **goal**

4 [only before noun] ■ As the great day approached, she grew more and more nervous.

important • significant • momentous | infml **big**
- a/an great / important / significant / momentous / big **day**
- great / important / significant / momentous / big **events / changes / developments**
- a/an great / important / significant / big **difference / feature / achievement / success**

5 (infml) ■ He's great with the kids.

good • capable • talented • gifted • skilled • impressive • expert • accomplished | BrE **skilful |** AmE **skillful**
■ OPP **rotten**
- great / good / gifted / skilled / expert / accomplished / skilful **at** sth
- great / good / gifted / skilled **with** sb/sth
- a great / good / capable / talented / gifted / skilled / skilful **teacher**
- a/an great / good / capable / talented / skilled / accomplished / skilful **performer**
- a/an great / good / talented / gifted / skilled / accomplished / skilful **player**

6 (infml) ■ *This gadget's great for opening jars.*

useful • convenient • practical | infml **handy**

► OPP **rubbish**
► great/useful/convenient/handy **for doing sth**

greedy adj. (disapprov.)
■ *The shareholders are greedy for profit.*

insatiable | disapprov. **grasping • mercenary • materialistic |** fml **voracious |** fml, disapprov. **acquisitive**

► a materialistic/mercenary **attitude**
► a materialistic/an acquisitive **society**
► an insatiable/a voracious **appetite**

greet verb [T]
■ *She greeted her guests with a smile.*

welcome • meet | fml **receive**

► greet/welcome/meet/receive sb **with** a smile, etc.
► greet/welcome/meet/receive a **guest/visitor**
► **be there to** greet/welcome/meet/receive sb
● **GREET OR WELCOME?** You **greet** sb when you say hello to them. You **welcome** sb when they come to visit you or when they return after being away for a long time. You make a special effort to show them that you are happy they are with you.

greeting noun [C, U] (esp. written)
■ *She waved a friendly greeting.*

welcome • reception

► a greeting/welcome/reception **from** sb
► **do sth in** greeting/welcome
► a **warm/friendly** greeting/welcome/reception

grief noun [U, C]
■ *He was overcome with grief at his wife's death.*

sadness • unhappiness • regret • heartache • heartbreak | fml **sorrow |** lit. **melancholy**

► OPP **joy**
► grief/sadness/unhappiness/regret/heartache/heartbreak/sorrow/melancholy **at/about/over** sth
► **be filled with/full of/overcome with** grief/sadness/unhappiness/regret/heartache/heartbreak/sorrow/melancholy
► **express/show/hide** your grief/sadness/unhappiness/regret/sorrow

ground noun

1 [U] ■ *He fell to the ground.*

earth • land • floor | lit. **soil**

► **on/under the** ground/earth/floor
► **drop/fall to (the)** ground/earth/floor
► **reach the** ground/the floor/land
● **GROUND, EARTH OR LAND?** Ground is the normal word for the solid surface that you walk on. Use **earth** to draw attention to the rock, soil, etc. that the ground is made of. **Land** is only used to contrast with the sea: *They fought both at sea and on land.*

2 [U] ■ *Dig a small hole in the ground.*

soil • land • earth • clay • mud

► **dry** ground/soil/land/earth/clay/mud
► **wet/soft** ground/soil/land/earth/clay/mud
► **fertile/infertile/poor/marshy** ground/soil/land
► **dig** the ground/soil/land/earth/clay/mud
► **cultivate/till/fertilize/drain** the ground/soil/land

3 [U, C] ■ *The kids were playing on waste ground near the school.*

land • space • plot | AmE **lot**

► **(an) open** ground/land/space
► **a/an empty/vacant** ground/land/plot/lot
► **waste/derelict** ground/land
► **a burial** ground/land/plot
● **GROUND, LAND OR LOT?** Ground [U] is any area of open land; a **ground** [C] is an area of land used for a particular purpose. **Land** refers to large areas in the country; a **lot** is a smaller piece of land in a town or city.

4 [C] (often in compounds) (BrE)
■ *The council is building a new sports ground in East Oxford.*

field • playing field • arena • stadium | BrE **pitch |** AmE **park • ballpark**

► a **sports** ground/field/arena/stadium/pitch
► a **football/cricket/rugby** ground/field/stadium/pitch
► a **baseball** field/stadium/park
● **GROUND, FIELD OR PITCH?** Both **field** and **pitch** are used to talk about the area of land where a sport is played. **Ground** also includes the buildings, seating, etc. around the place where a game is played.

5 grounds [pl.] ■ *The castle grounds are open to the public.*

gardens | BrE **park • parkland**

► (a) **beautiful/landscaped** grounds/gardens/park/parkland

► (an) **extensive** grounds/gardens/park/parkland

6 grounds [pl.] ■ *You have no grounds for complaint.*

reason • cause • basis • case • motive • excuse • justification • pretext

► (a/an) grounds/reason/cause/basis/case/motive/excuse/justification/pretext **for** sth
► **on the** grounds/basis/pretext **of**/**that**…
► **logical/personal/no apparent** grounds/reason/cause/motive/justification
► **have** (a/an) grounds/reason/cause/case/motive/excuse/justification/pretext

group noun

1 [C+sing./pl.v.] ■ *A group of people sat on the grass.*

set • cluster • bunch • collection • clump

► a group/set/cluster/bunch/collection/clump **of** sth
► **in** a group/set/cluster/bunch/clump
► **divide** sth **into** groups/sets/clusters

2 [C+sing./pl.v.] ■ *The college has a small but active women's group.*

circle • band • party | *infml* bunch • crowd • gang | *often disapprov.* set • clique

► a group/circle/band/party/bunch/crowd/gang/clique **of** sth
► a group/circle/band/party/bunch/crowd/gang/set **of friends**
► **belong to** a group/gang/clique

3 [C+sing./pl.v.] (*busin.*) ■ *This acquisition will make them the largest newspaper group in the world.*

partnership • cooperative • syndicate | *infml* outfit | *busin.* conglomerate • consortium

► a **large** group/partnership/syndicate/outfit/conglomerate/consortium
► an **international** group/partnership/syndicate/conglomerate/consortium
► **form** a/an group/partnership/cooperative/syndicate/outfit/conglomerate/consortium

grow verb

1 [I] ■ *Company profits grew by 5% last year.*

rise • increase • climb • expand • escalate | *esp. spoken* go up

■ OPP **shrink**

► grow/rise/increase/go up **in** price, number, etc.

guarantee

► grow/rise/increase/climb/expand/go up **by** 10%, 2000, etc.
► grow/rise/increase/climb/expand/escalate/go up **from** 20 to 50
► grow/rise/increase/climb/expand/go up **slightly/steadily/slowly/rapidly/dramatically**

2 [T] ■ *I didn't know they grew rice in Spain.*

farm • plant | *fml* cultivate

► grow/plant/cultivate **crops**
► be **organically/intensively** grown/farmed/cultivated

3 *linking verb* ■ *He grew more impatient as time went on.*

become • get • come • turn

► grow/become/get/turn **cold/warm/chilly**
► grow/become/get **fat/old/angry/hungry/tired**
► grow/become/get **used to/accustomed to** sth
► grow/get/come **to know/like** sb/sth

growth noun [U, sing.]

■ *The growth in average earnings has remained constant.*

increase • rise • inflation • gain • surge • spiral • upturn | *infml, esp. journ.* hike

► (a/an) growth/increase/rise/inflation/gain/surge/spiral/upturn/hike **in** sth
► (a/an) growth/increase/rise/inflation/gain/surge/hike **of** 5%
► **lead to/mean/report** (a/an) growth/increase/rise/inflation/gain/surge/hike
● GROWTH, INCREASE OR RISE? Growth is used esp. to talk about size and is often positive; increase and rise are often used to talk about negative things: *the growth in employment/demand* • *an alarming increase/rise in violent crime*

grunt verb [I, T]

■ *He pulled on the rope, grunting with the effort.*

snort • croak • rasp • squawk

► grunt/snort/croak/squawk **at** sb/sth
► grunt/snort/croak/squawk **in**/**with** surprise/pain, etc
► grunt/squawk **loudly**

guarantee noun [C]

■ *The union wants a guarantee that there witll be no job losses.*

promise • assurance • commitment | *esp. journ.* pledge

▶ a guarantee/promise/
commitment/pledge **to do sth**
▶ a/an guarantee/promise/
assurance/pledge **that...**
▶ **give** a/an guarantee/promise/
assurance/commitment/pledge
● **GUARANTEE, PROMISE OR PLEDGE?**
Promise is the most general and
frequent of these words, and the
only one used of personal
relationships:

✔She had forgotten her promise to
call me ✗ She had forgotten her
guarantee/pledge to call me.
Guarantee is used esp. in matters
of business; **pledge** is used esp. in
politics:
✔election/campaign/manifesto
pledges

guarantee verb

1 [T] ■ *We guarantee next day
delivery.*

promise • assure • pledge | *fml or
busin.* undertake

▶ guarantee/promise/pledge/
undertake **to do sth**
▶ guarantee/promise/pledge **that...**
▶ guarantee/promise/pledge **your
support**
● **GUARANTEE OR PROMISE?** When you
promise sth, you make a personal
commitment to do sth. **Guarantee**
is less personal; when you
guarantee sth, you mean that you
will make sure that it happens. You
have a moral duty to do what you
have promised, but you may also
have a legal duty to do what you
have guaranteed.

2 [T] ■ *Getting a degree doesn't
guarantee you a job.*

assure • make sure • ensure • see to
it that...

▶ guarantee/make sure/ensure/see
to it **that...**
▶ guarantee/assure/ensure the
success/survival/quality of sth
● **WHICH WORD?** Ensure and make
sure are often used in orders or
instructions:
✔Please ensure/make sure that the
gas is switched off. ✗ Please
guarantee/assure that the gas is
switched off.
Guarantee and **assure** can suggest
that feelings of worry or doubt are
removed.

guard noun

1 [C] ■ *A guard was posted outside the
building.*

sentry • bodyguard • lookout | *esp.
BrE* minder

▶ a/an **armed/uniformed** guard/
bodyguard

▶ **stand** guard/sentry
▶ **post** a guard/sentry/lookout

2 [U] ■ *He fell asleep on guard duty.*

watch • alert • vigil

▶ **on** guard/watch/alert
▶ **keep** guard/watch/a vigil
▶ **mount** (a) guard/watch

guard verb [T]

■ *Police guarded the palace.*

protect • defend • shield • shelter •
secure • preserve | *fml* safeguard

▶ guard/protect/defend/shield/
shelter/secure/preserve/safeguard
sb/sth **from** sth
▶ guard/protect/defend/secure/
safeguard sth **against** sth
▶ **heavily** guarded/protected/
defended

guerrilla (also guerilla) noun [C]

■ *Two guerrillas were killed in an
attack on a border post.*

rebel • revolutionary • partisan •
bomber • paramilitary | *fml*
insurgent | *disapprov.* terrorist

▶ **armed** guerrillas/rebels/
revolutionaries/insurgents/
terrorists
▶ **support** the guerrillas/rebels/
partisans/paramilitaries/
insurgents/terrorists
▶ guerrilla/rebel/revolutionary/
paramilitary/insurgent/terrorist
activity

guess noun [C]

■ *At a guess, there were about 40
people there.*

estimate • speculation • assumption
• guesswork • presumption | *fml*
conjecture | *fml, disapprov.*
presupposition

▶ (a/an) guess/speculation/
assumption/guesswork/
presumption/conjecture/
presupposition **about** sth
▶ **make** a/an guess/estimate/
assumption/speculation/
conjecture
▶ **base** sth **on** (a/an) guess/
estimate/assumption/
presumption/presupposition

guess verb

1 [I, T] ■ *I guessed from Gina's
expression that something was
wrong.*

fml surmise • conjecture

▶ guess/surmise/conjecture **that...**
▶ guess/surmise/conjecture sth **from** sth
▶ guess/surmise/conjecture **what/
how/why...**

2 [T] ■ *Guess how much these boots
cost.*

estimate • judge • reckon • calculate • gauge | *esp. AmE, infml* figure | *fml* extrapolate

▶ guess/estimate/judge/reckon/calculate/gauge/extrapolate sth **from** sth
▶ guess/estimate/judge/reckon/calculate/figure/extrapolate **that...**
▶ guess/estimate/judge/calculate/gauge/figure **how much/how many/how far, etc.**

3 I guess [T] (*esp. AmE, infml*) ■ *I guess I'm just lucky.*

suppose • imagine • assume • suspect • presume | *esp. spoken* take it | *esp. BrE, spoken* expect • I dare say

▶ I guess/suppose/imagine/assume/suspect/presume/take it/dare say **that...**
▶ I guess/suppose/imagine/assume/suspect/presume **so.**

guest *noun* [C]
■ *She had invited over 100 guests.*

visitor • caller | *fml* company

▶ a/an **frequent/surprise/uninvited** guest/visitor
▶ **have** guests/visitors/company
▶ **be expecting/entertain/invite** guests/visitors

guide *verb* [T]
■ *She guided us through the busy streets.*

take • lead • escort • show • walk • usher

▶ guide/take/lead/escort/show/walk/usher sb **to/out of/into** sth
▶ guide/take/lead/escort/walk/usher sb **there/somewhere**
▶ guide/take/lead/escort/show/walk sb **round/around**

guilt *noun* [U]
■ *The next day she was consumed by guilt.*

shame • regret • remorse

▶ guilt/shame/regret/remorse **at** sth
▶ guilt/regret/remorse **over** sth
▶ **feel (no)** guilt/shame/regret/remorse
● **GUILT OR SHAME?** You feel **guilt** when you have done sth you believe to be wrong; you feel **shame** when other people know that you have done sth wrong or stupid: *He could not bear the guilt of knowing it was his fault.* • *He could not bear the shame of his family knowing what he had done.*

guilty *adj.*

1 ■ *I feel guilty about not visiting my parents more often.*

ashamed • sorry | *esp. spoken* bad

▶ guilty/ashamed/sorry/bad **about** sth
▶ **feel** guilty/ashamed/sorry/bad **that...**

2 ■ *Everyone thought he was guilty, but there was no proof.*

responsible • to blame • at fault • in the wrong

■ OPP **innocent, not guilty**
▶ **feel** guilty/responsible/to blame
▶ **consider/hold** sb guilty/responsible/to blame/at fault
▶ **clearly** guilty/responsible/to blame/at fault

gun *noun* [C]
■ *He pointed his gun at the cashier.*

rifle • shotgun • pistol • revolver • handgun • machine gun • cannon • mortar | *fml* firearm

▶ **be armed with** a gun/rifle/shotgun/pistol/handgun/machine gun/cannon/mortar
▶ **load** a gun/rifle/shotgun/pistol/handgun/cannon
▶ **fire** a gun/rifle/shotgun/pistol/revolver/handgun/machine gun/cannon/mortar
▶ **shoot** sb/sth with a gun/rifle/shotgun/pistol/revolver/handgun/machine gun

guy *noun* [C] (*infml*)
■ *He seemed like a nice guy.*

man | *BrE, infml* bloke | *esp. AmE, slang* dude | *fml* gentleman • male

■ OPP **girl**
▶ a **middle-aged/older** guy/man/bloke/gentleman/male
▶ a **good/great/funny/big/little** guy/man/bloke/dude
▶ a **cool** guy/dude
● **GUY, BLOKE OR DUDE?** Bloke suggests that sb is a nice but ordinary person. **Dude** can suggest that sb is attractive and fashionable. A **guy** can be either.

Hh

habit *noun* [C, U]
■ *I got into the habit of calling my aunt every night.*

practice • ways • ritual • rule | *fml* policy

▶ **be** sb's habit/practice/policy **to do** sth
▶ **the/sb's usual** habit/practice/ritual/policy

habitat

▶ **change** your habit/practice/
policy/ways

habitat noun [C, U]

■ *The tiger's natural habitat is the
forest.*

**territory • home • environment •
haunt**

▶ a/an habitat/home/environment/
haunt **for** sb/sth
▶ a **breeding** habitat/territory
▶ a **native** habitat/home/
environment

hair noun [C]

■ *There's a hair in my soup.*

strand • thread | *BrE* **fibre** | *AmE* **fiber**

▶ a **long/single** hair/strand/thread/
fibre
▶ a **fine** hair/strand/thread

hairy adj.

■ *His unbuttoned shirt revealed a hairy
chest.*

furry • shaggy • bushy • unshaven |
esp. written **bearded**

▶ a/an hairy/unshaven/bearded
man/face
▶ a hairy/furry/shaggy **coat**
▶ a hairy/furry **creature/monster/
body**
▶ hairy/unshaven **armpits**

hall noun

1 [C] ■ *She ran into the hall and up
the stairs.*

lobby • foyer | *esp. BrE* **hallway •
reception** | *AmE* **entry • entryway**

▶ **in** the hall/lobby/foyer/hallway/
reception/entry/entryway
▶ an **entrance** hall/lobby/foyer
● **HALL OR HALLWAY? Hall** is more
frequent and has a broader range;
hallway is used esp. to describe a
long, narrow space.

2 [C] ■ *Her office is just down the hall.*

passage | *esp. BrE* **corridor** | *esp. AmE*
hallway • passageway

▶ **in/along/down/through** the
hall/passage/corridor/hallway/
passageway
▶ a **long/narrow** hall/passage/
corridor/hallway/passageway
▶ **at/to the end of** the hall/passage/
corridor/hallway/passageway
● **HALL, CORRIDOR OR HALLWAY? Hall**
and **hallway** can be used to talk
about a connecting space in public
buildings or large houses. A
corridor is usu. long and straight
and is normally used when talking
about large public buildings.

3 [C] ■ *a concert hall with good
acoustics*

auditorium • chamber | *BrE* **theatre** |
AmE **theater**

▶ a **500-seat** hall/auditorium/
chamber/theatre
▶ a **crowded/packed** hall/
auditorium/theatre
▶ a **conference** hall/chamber

hand verb [T]

■ *My aunt handed me the letter.*

give • hand sb/sth over • pass

▶ hand/give/hand over/pass sth **to**
sb
▶ **just** hand/give/hand over/pass
sth
▶ hand/give/hand over/pass sth
immediately/promptly
● **HAND, GIVE OR PASS? Give** is the
most frequent use, esp. in spoken
English. **Hand** and **pass** are used
esp. in written, literary, English;
pass is also often used in polite
spoken requests.

handle verb [T]

■ *The new office handles 500 calls an
hour.*

**deal with sb/sth • take care of sth •
contend with sb/sth** | *BrE* **look after
sth** | *spoken* **see to sth**

▶ handle/deal with/take care of/
contend with/look after a **problem**
▶ handle/deal with/take care of/
look after/see to **the matter**
▶ handle/deal with/take care of/
look after the **correspondence/
paperwork/customers**
● **HANDLE OR DEAL WITH STH? Handle**
often suggests control and
calmness: *Don't worry—I can
handle the situation.*
Deal with sth is often used to
discuss *ways, methods* and *means*
of *dealing with* problems.

hand sth out phrasal verb

■ *Could you hand these books out,
please?*

give • hand sth over • distribute | *esp. AmE*
pass sth out | *infml* **dish sth out •
dole sth out** | *fml* **dispense**

▶ hand out/give out/distribute/dish
out/dispense **food**
▶ hand out/give out/distribute/dole
out/dispense **money**
▶ hand out/give out/distribute/pass
out/dish out/dole out **leaflets**

hand sth over phrasal verb

■ *She handed over a cheque for
$20000.*

give • hand • pass

▶ hand over/give/hand/pass sth **to**
sb

▶ **just** hand over/give/hand/pass sth

▶ hand over/give/hand/pass sth **immediately/promptly**

hang verb [T, I]
■ *Hang your coat up on the hook.*

put sth up | *fml* **suspend**

▶ hang/suspend sth **from/by** sth
▶ hang/put up a **picture**
● **HANG OR PUT STH UP?** You **hang** a *painting* in a frame, that hangs on a hook; you **put up** a *notice* or *poster* that has no frame and is just stuck to the wall.

hang on phrasal verb [no passive]
1 (spoken) ■ *Hang on tight!*

hold hold on/hold onto sb/sth • **cling** • **clutch** • **grip** • **grasp** | *written* **clasp**

▶ hang on to/hold/hold on to/cling to/clutch/grip/grasp/clasp sb/sth **by/with** sth
▶ hang/hold/cling/clutch/grip/grasp/clasp on to **sth**
▶ hang/hold/cling **on**

2 (spoken) ■ *Hang on a minute—I'm almost ready.*

wait | *spoken* **hold on** | *written* **sit tight**

▶ hang on/wait/hold on/sit tight **until** sth happens
▶ hang on/wait/hold on a **minute/second**

happen verb [I]
■ *How did the accident happen?*

take place • **come about** • **come up** • **present itself** • **turn out** • **materialize** • **crop up** | *fml* **occur** • **arise**

▶ a **change** happens/takes place/comes about/occurs/arises
▶ an **event/accident** happens/takes place/occurs
▶ be **likely to** happen/take place/come about/come up/materialize/crop up/occur/arise

happiness noun [U]
■ *Her eyes shone with happiness.*

joy • **bliss** • **pride** • **satisfaction** • **contentment** | *BrE* **fulfilment** | *AmE* **fulfillment**

■ OPP **sadness, unhappiness**
▶ happiness/pride/satisfaction/contentment/fulfilment **in** sth
▶ **great** happiness/joy/bliss/pride/satisfaction
▶ **bring** sb happiness/joy/bliss/pride/satisfaction/contentment/fulfilment
● **WHICH WORD?** You feel **happiness** when things give you pleasure; you feel **contentment**, which is a

quieter feeling than **happiness**, when you have learned to find pleasure in things. **Joy** and **bliss** are extreme happiness: **joy** is a livelier feeling and **bliss** is a more peaceful feeling. You can feel **satisfaction** at achieving almost anything, small or large; you feel **fulfilment** when you do sth useful and enjoyable with your life.

happy adj.
1 ■ *I was so happy on my wedding day.*

joyful • **blissful** • **overjoyed** • **elated** • **euphoric** • **ecstatic** • **excited** • **exhilarated**

■ OPP **sad, unhappy**
▶ happy/overjoyed/elated/ecstatic/excited **at** sth
▶ happy/overjoyed/elated/ecstatic/exhilarated **with** sth
▶ **feel** happy/joyful/blissful/overjoyed/elated/euphoric/ecstatic/excited/exhilarated

2 ■ *Everyone in the team was happy with the result.*

glad • **satisfied** • **content** • **contented** • **pleased** • **proud** • **delighted** • **thrilled** • **relieved**

■ OPP **disappointed, unhappy**
▶ happy/glad/satisfied/pleased/proud/delighted/thrilled/relieved **about** sth
▶ happy/satisfied/content/contented/pleased/delighted/thrilled **with** sth
▶ happy/glad/pleased/delighted/thrilled **for** sb
● **HAPPY, GLAD OR PLEASED?** Feeling **pleased** can suggest that you have judged sb/sth and approve of them or that sth has happened that is particularly good for you. Feeling **glad** can be more about feeling grateful for sth. **Happy** can mean glad, pleased or satisfied.

harass verb [T, often passive] (disapprov.)
■ *He complained of being harassed by the police.*

nag • **pester** | *BrE* **go on** | *written* **hound** • **harry** • **hector** • **persecute**

▶ harass/nag/pester/go on at/hector sb **about** sth
▶ harass/pester/harry sb **with** sth
▶ harass/nag/harry/hector sb **into doing** sth

hard adj.
1 ■ *Wait for the concrete to go hard.*

solid • **rigid** • **stiff** | *approv.* **firm**

■ OPP **soft**
▶ a hard/solid/firm **surface**

harm

► hard/firm **ground**
► go hard/stiff
● **HARD OR FIRM?** Hard things are harder than firm things. **Hard** can mean 'very hard' or 'too hard': *Diamonds are the hardest known mineral.* • *The mattress was really hard.*
Firm is usually a positive word: *I sleep better with a firm mattress.*

2 ■ *He found it hard to learn a foreign language.*

difficult • demanding • taxing • testing | *approv.* **challenging**

■ OPP **easy**
► hard/difficult/demanding/ taxing/challenging **for sb**
► hard/difficult/demanding/ taxing/challenging **to believe/see/tell/ say/do sth**
► a hard/difficult/demanding/ taxing/testing/challenging **time/ week/year**
● **HARD OR DIFFICULT?** Hard is slightly more informal than **difficult**. It is used esp. in the structure *hard to believe/say/find/take*, etc., although **difficult** can also be used in any of these examples.

3 ■ *My grandmother had a hard life.*

difficult • tough • bad • rough • adverse | *BrE* **unfavourable** | *AmE* **unfavorable** | *fml* **disadvantageous**

■ OPP **easy**
► hard/difficult/tough/bad/ unfavourable/disadvantageous **for sb**
► hard/tough/rough **on sb**
► a/an hard/difficult/tough/bad/ rough/unfavourable **situation**
► hard/tough/difficult/bad/rough/ adverse/unfavourable **conditions**

4 ■ *It's hard work shovelling snow.*

strenuous • arduous • punishing | *esp. BrE* **gruelling** | *AmE usu.* **grueling**

■ OPP **easy**
► hard/strenuous/arduous/gruelling **work**
► a/an hard/strenuous/arduous **climb**
► a hard/punishing/gruelling **schedule**
► a hard/punishing/gruelling **day**

5 (*usu. disapprov.*) ■ *She gave me a hard stare.* ■ *My father was a hard man.*

tough • stern • strict | *usu. disapprov.* **harsh • brutal** | *disapprov.* **callous • heartless • ruthless • cold-blooded • unforgiving** | *esp. written* **severe • steely**

■ OPP **soft**
► be hard/tough/strict/harsh/ severe **on sb**
► a hard/tough/stern/strict/

callous/heartless/ruthless **man/ woman**
► sb has a hard/tough/harsh/ brutal/ruthless **side**

harm noun [U]

■ *Hard work never did anyone any harm.*

damage | *fml* **detriment**

■ OPP **good**
► harm/damage/detriment **to sth**
► harm/damage **from sth**
► **cause/do/inflict/suffer/escape/ prevent** harm/damage
● **HARM OR DAMAGE?** Harm is only used in a number of fixed phrases to express opinions about what or who may cause harm, or whether harm may have been caused: *Luckily, no harm was done.*
Damage is used to talk about the effects of storms, fire, etc. and about the physical state of unhealthy organs in the body: *storm/flood/smoke damage* • *brain/ liver/kidney damage*
Both words can be used to talk about mental or emotional suffering: *psychological damage/ harm*

harm verb [T]

■ *Pollution can harm marine life.*

damage • hurt • compromise | *fml* **impair**

■ OPP **benefit**
► harm/damage/hurt/ compromise/impair sb's **chances**
► harm/damage/hurt/compromise sb's **reputation**
► harm/damage/compromise/ impair sb's **health**
► **seriously** harm/damage/hurt/ compromise/impair sb's/sth
● **HARM OR DAMAGE?** Harm is used esp. to talk about bad effects on the environment or sb's health; **damage** can also be used in this way, but is used most frequently about bad effects on objects:
✔ *The car was badly damaged in the crash.* ✗ *The car was badly harmed in the crash.*

harmful adj. (fml)

■ *the harmful effects of alcohol*

damaging • negative • bad • ill • destructive | *fml* **detrimental • pernicious**

■ OPP **harmless**
► harmful/damaging/detrimental/ destructive **to sb/sth**
► harmful/damaging/bad **for sb/ sth**
► harmful/negative/damaging/ bad/destructive/detrimental/ pernicious **effects**
● **HARMFUL OR DAMAGING?** Harmful is used esp. to talk about bad effects

on the environment or sb's health. **Damaging** can also be used in this way, but is used most frequently about bad effects on sb's wealth or reputation.

harmless adj.

■ Most bacteria are harmless to humans.

safe | fml or med. **benign**

■ OPP harmful
▶ a harmless/benign **substance**
▶ environmentally harmless/safe/ benign

harsh adj. (disapprov.)

■ the harsh glare of the headlights

strong • dazzling | disapprov. **glaring**

■ OPP soft
▶ a harsh/strong/dazzling/glaring **light**
▶ harsh/strong/dazzling **colours**

hat noun [C]

■ She was wearing a straw hat.

cap • headgear • hat • bonnet • helmet • turban • hood

▶ have on/wear (a) hat/cap/ headgear/beret/bonnet/helmet/ turban
▶ put on/take off/remove a/your, etc. hat/cap/headgear/beret/ bonnet/helmet/turban

hate verb [T, I]

■ He hates violence in any form.

can't bear • loathe • despise • dislike • detest | esp. spoken **can't stand** | fml **abhor**

■ OPP love
▶ hate/loathe/despise/dislike/ detest sb/sth **for** sth
▶ hate/can't bear/loathe/dislike/ detest/can't stand **doing** sth
▶ hate/can't bear **to do** sth
▶ hate/can't bear/can't stand/dislike **it when...**
▶ hate/loathe/despise/dislike/ detest/can't stand **each other**

hatred noun [U, C]

■ She felt nothing but hatred for her attacker.

hate • dislike • aversion | fml **loathing**

■ OPP love
▶ hatred/hate/dislike/loathing **for/ of** sb/sth
▶ deep hatred/dislike/aversion/ loathing
▶ be filled with hatred/hate/ loathing
● HATRED OR HATE? **Hatred** is more frequent, slightly more formal and used esp. in writing. Both **hatred** and **hate** can refer to the idea of

have

strong dislike, but **hatred** is more often used to describe a very strong feeling of dislike for a particular person or thing:
✓ a look of pure hatred/hate • His deep hatred of his brother. ✗ His deep hate of his brother.

have verb

1 [T, no passive] (not used in the progressive tenses) ■ He has three cars.

own | esp. BrE, esp. spoken **have got** | fml **possess • hold**

▶ have/own/have got/possess a **car/house**
▶ have/own/have got a **company**
▶ have/own/have got/hold a **driving licence/passport**
● HAVE OR HAVE GOT? **Have got** is common in BrE, esp. in spoken and informal language and esp. in the present tense. In the past tense, a form of **have** is used more often than the forms had got and hadn't got:
✓ He had a house by the sea. ✗ He had got a house by the sea.

2 [T, no passive] (not used in the progressive tenses) ■ In 2006 the party had 10 000 members.

consist of sb/sth • make up sth • constitute | esp. BrE, esp. spoken **have got** | fml **comprise • be composed of sb/sth**

▶ The group has/has got/consists of/is made up of/comprises/is composed of **ten people**.
▶ Ten people make up/constitute/ comprise **the group**.

3 [T, no passive] (not used in the progressive tenses) ■ They have two children.

esp. BrE, esp. spoken **have got** | fml **enjoy • possess • be endowed with sth** | esp. written **be blessed with sth • boast**

▶ have/have got/possess/be blessed with **charm/talent/charisma**
▶ have/have got/enjoy/possess/be endowed with an/the **ability to do sth**
▶ have/have got/be blessed with a **child**

4 [T, no passive] (not used in the progressive tenses) ■ I had a cold yesterday so I wasn't at work.

suffer from sth • get • catch • come down with sth • develop | esp. BrE, esp. spoken **have got** | fml **contract**

▶ have/suffer from/get/catch/ develop/have got/contract a/an **disease/illness**

have (got) sth on

▶ have/suffer from/get/catch/come
down with/have got a **bug**
▶ have/suffer from/get/develop/
have got/contract **cancer/AIDS**

5 [T] ■ *We had a terrible experience on
the journey.*

**meet • take • feel • go through sth •
run into sth** | *esp. written* **suffer •
encounter • experience • undergo •
receive**

▶ have/meet/run into/encounter/
experience **problems**
▶ have/feel/suffer/experience/
receive the **shock**
▶ have/experience/undergo/receive
treatment

6 [T] ■ *Let's have a party.*

hold • give • host • call | *infml* **throw**
| *fml* **convene**

▶ have/hold/give/host/call/
convene a **conference**
▶ have/hold/call/convene a
meeting
▶ have/hold/give/host/throw a
party
▶ have/hold a **conversation/
debate/discussion**

7 [T] ■ *I had an egg salad for lunch.*

eat • taste | *fml* **consume • dine on
sth** | *esp. written* **devour**

▶ have/eat/devour a **meal**
▶ have/eat your **lunch/dinner**
▶ have/eat/taste/consume some
meat/fruit

8 [T] ■ *She's going to have a baby.*

**give birth • produce • breed •
reproduce** | *fml or lit.* **bear**

▶ have/give birth to/produce/bear
a/an **child/son/daughter/heir**
▶ have/give birth to/produce a
baby/litter
● **HAVE OR GIVE BIRTH?** Have is the
verb most commonly used to talk
about the process of being
pregnant and then giving birth.
Give birth is used to talk about the
actual act of making a baby come
out of your body: *She's going to
have a baby* (= she is pregnant). •
She's about to give birth (= the baby
is in the process of being born).

have (got) sth on *phrasal verb*

(not used in the progressive tenses)
■ *She had a red jacket on.*

wear • be dressed in sth

▶ have on/wear a **coat/jacket/suit/
hat/ring/badge/watch**
▶ have on/wear your **glasses**
▶ have on/wear **make-up/lipstick**

head *noun*

1 [C] ■ *I can't get that tune out of my
head.*

mind • brain

▶ a thought **enters** sb's head/mind
● **HEAD OR MIND?** Head is slightly
more informal than **mind**, and is
used to talk about thoughts and
ideas that *get* into your head or that you can't
get out of your head.

2 [C] ■ *The Bishop is head of the
Church in Kenya.*

**leader • president • director •
chairman • chief executive** | *BrE*
governor • managing director |
infml **boss** | *esp. journ.* **chief**

▶ be **appointed** (as) head/leader/
president/director/chairman/
chief executive/governor/
managing director/chief
▶ **take over** as head/leader/
president/director/chairman/
managing director/chief
▶ **resign/stand down/step down** as
head/leader/president/director/
chairman/managing executive/
governor/managing director/chief

head *verb*

1 [I] (always used with an adv. or
prep.) ■ *Where are we heading?*

**make for sth • make your way • go •
get • move • travel**

▶ make/make your way/go/get/
move/travel **to** sb/sth
▶ head/make **for** sb/sth
▶ head/make **for**/make your way/
go/get **home**

2 [T] ■ *He was appointed to head the
research team.*

lead • chair • captain | *fml* **preside**

▶ head/lead/captain a **team**
▶ head/lead a (political) **party/the
government**
▶ head/lead/chair/preside over a/
an **commission/committee/
inquiry**
● **HEAD OR LEAD?** A person who
heads sth has the official position
of being the head of it. A person
who **leads** sth may also have an
official position, but the verb *lead*
emphasizes their leadership
qualities. An individual usu. **heads**
sth, but a group of people can **lead**
sth.

health *noun* [U]

■ *Exhaust fumes are bad for your
health.*

**fitness • condition • shape • well-
being • constitution**

▶ sb's **general/physical** health/
fitness/condition/well-being
▶ sb's health/fitness/condition
deteriorates/improves

▶ **maintain/regain** your health/ fitness
▶ be in good health/shape

healthy adj.

1 ■ *Keep healthy with good food and exercise.*

strong ◆ *esp. BrE* **fit** | *esp. spoken* **well** ◆ **fine**

■ OPP **sickly, unhealthy**
▶ feel/look healthy/strong/fit/ well/fine
▶ keep (sb) healthy/fit/well
▶ fit and healthy/strong/well

2 [usu. before noun] ■ *Many people are adopting a healthy lifestyle.*

good ◆ **nutritious** ◆ **nourishing**

■ OPP **unhealthy**
▶ a healthy/good/nutritious/ nourishing **meal/diet**
▶ healthy/good/nutritious/ nourishing **food**

hear verb

1 [I, T] ■ *She heard a noise.*

listen ◆ **catch** ◆ **tune in (to** sth**)**

▶ hear/listen to/catch/tune in to a **radio show**
▶ hear/listen to/catch **sb's words/ what sb says**
▶ hear/listen to **music/a conversation**

2 [I, T] (not usu. used in the progressive tenses) ■ *I was sorry to hear that you'd been ill.*

find out ◆ **discover** ◆ **find** ◆ **learn**

▶ hear/find out/learn **about** sth
▶ hear/find out/discover/find/learn **that...**
▶ hear/find out/discover/learn **how/what/why...**
▶ be **surprised/saddened/ delighted/interested to** hear/ discover/find/learn sth

heat noun

1 [U, sing.] ■ *He could feel the heat of the sun on his back.*

warmth

■ OPP **cold**
▶ heat/warmth **of/from** sth
▶ gentle/body heat/warmth
▶ feel the heat/warmth

2 [U] ■ *The heat that summer was unbearable.*

heatwave ◆ **drought**

■ OPP **cold weather**
▶ **in** the heat/a drought/a heatwave
▶ a/the **summer** heat/drought/ heatwave
▶ a/the **terrible** heat/drought

heat verb [T]

■ *Heat the oil and add the onions.*

heat (sth) up ◆ **warm** ◆ **warm (sth) up** ◆ **reheat**

■ OPP **cool**
▶ heat/warm up/warm up/reheat **soup**
▶ heat/warm/warm up a **room/ house**
▶ heat/heat up/warm/warm up/ reheat sth **in the oven/microwave**

● HEAT OR HEAT (STH) UP? Heat is is not normally used without an object:
✔*The oven is heating up.* ✗ *The oven is heating.*
Use **heat** in technical language and when talking about buildings:
✔*The system produced enough energy to heat several thousand homes.* ✗ *The system produced enough energy to heat up several thousand homes.*

heavy adj.

■ *The box was too heavy to lift.*

bulky ◆ **massive** | *physics* **dense**

■ OPP **light**
▶ a heavy/bulky **item/object**

height noun [sing.]

■ *She was at the height of her career.*

peak ◆ **top** ◆ **climax** ◆ **high point** ◆ **prime** ◆ **heyday** | *esp. written* **culmination** | *busin. or journ.* **high**

■ OPP **low point**
▶ the height/peak/top/climax/high point/prime/heyday/culmination **of** sth
▶ **at** its height/its peak/the top/its climax/a high point/its culmination/a high
▶ **reach** its height/its peak/the top/ its climax/a high point/its culmination/a high

● HEIGHT OR PEAK? **Peak** is the more frequent and more general of these words. It is used in compounds or before other nouns *(peak hours/ season/demand/rates, etc.)*, but **height** is not. A person can be at *the peak/height of their career/ powers* but otherwise **height** is not used to talk about a person.

hell noun [U, sing.]

■ *Her father made her life hell.*

nightmare ◆ **horror** ◆ **ordeal** ◆ **trauma**

■ OPP **heaven**
▶ a/an **absolute/living** hell/ nightmare
▶ **go through** hell/an ordeal/a trauma

help

help noun

1 [U] ■ *He recovered quickly with the help of his family.*

support • backup • cooperation • service | *fml* **assistance • aid**

▸ help/support/cooperation/ assistance in doing sth
▸ **get** help/support/backup/ cooperation/service/assistance/aid
▸ **offer/need** help/support/sb's services/assistance/sb's cooperation
▸ **come to/enlist** sb's help/support/ assistance/aid

2 [U] ■ *The organization offers practical and financial help.*

aid • relief • welfare • charity

▸ help/aid/relief/welfare/charity for sb
▸ **emergency/direct/immediate/ financial/medical** help/aid/relief
▸ **get/receive** help/aid/relief/ welfare/charity

help verb

1 [I, T] ■ *We must all help each other.*

help (sb) out • support • cooperate | *BrE* **co-operate** | *infml* **lend a hand** | *fml* **assist • aid** | *fml, spoken* **be of service** | *law or humorous* **aid and abet**

■ **OPP** hinder
▸ help/help out/lend a hand/assist with sth
▸ help/support/cooperate/assist/ aid (sb) in sth
▸ help/cooperate/assist/aid (sb) in doing sth
▸ help/aid (sb) to do sth

2 [I, T] ■ *Talking to a counsellor helped her enormously.*

benefit • clear/open the way • ease | *fml* **assist • aid • facilitate**

■ **OPP** hinder, hamper
▸ help/assist in (doing) sth
▸ help/ease/assist/aid/facilitate the development of sth
▸ help/ease/assist/aid/facilitate a process
▸ help/ease/facilitate matters

helpful adj.

1 ■ *Here are some helpful hints for successful revision.*

valuable • good • positive • constructive • advantageous | *fml* **beneficial**

■ **OPP** unhelpful
▸ helpful/valuable/good/ advantageous/beneficial for sb/ sth

▸ helpful/valuable/advantageous/ beneficial to sb/sth
▸ helpful/valuable/good/ advantageous/beneficial to do sth
▸ a helpful/valuable/good/positive/ constructive **suggestions/advice**

2 ■ *The staff were very helpful.*

cooperative • willing | *BrE* **neighbourly** | *AmE* **neighborly** | *fml* **obliging • accommodating**

■ **OPP** unhelpful
▸ helpful/obliging/accommodating to sb
▸ **find sb** helpful/cooperative/ willing
▸ **friendly and** helpful/cooperative/ obliging/accommodating

herd noun [C+sing./pl. v.]

■ *a herd of cows/deer/elephants*

flock • pack • swarm

▸ a herd/flock/pack/swarm of sth
▸ do sth in herds/flocks/packs/ swarms
▸ a herd/flock of sheep
▸ the herd/pack **instinct**

hero noun

1 [C] ■ *He remains one of the country's national heroes.*

heroine • idol • icon • legend • star • superstar | *infml* **great**

▸ a/an hero/heroine idol of mine, his, etc.
▸ a **national** hero/heroine/icon/ legend
▸ a **film/pop** hero/idol/icon/ legend/star/superstar
▸ a **sports** hero/icon/legend/star
● **HERO OR ICON?** Use hero to talk about sth that you admire yourself; use icon to talk about sb who is special to a particular group of people: *a personal hero • a feminist icon*

2 [C] ■ *The hero of the novel is a young artist.*

heroine • lead • star | *fml* **protagonist**

■ **OPP** villain
▸ a **young** hero/heroine/star/ protagonist
▸ a **mythical/fictional/tragic/great** hero/heroine
▸ **play** the hero/heroine/lead
● **HERO, HEROINE OR PROTAGONIST?** Hero and heroine suggest a positive role. Protagonist can be positive or negative, and can refer to a man or woman. It is often used in reviews of films, books, etc.

hesitant adj.

■ *He's hesitant about signing the contract.*

uncertain • unsure • faltering • halting • doubtful • dubious | *written* tentative

■ OPP **confident, certain**
▶ hesitant/uncertain/unsure/doubtful/dubious **about/of** sth
▶ hesitant/uncertain/faltering/halting/tentative **steps**
▶ a/an hesitant/uncertain/faltering/halting **voice**

hesitate *verb*

1 [I] ■ *She hesitated before replying.*

pause | *esp. written* break off | *esp. BrE, disapprov.* dither

▶ hesitate/dither **over** sth
▶ hesitate/pause/break off (for) a **moment**
▶ hesitate/pause **briefly/momentarily/a little**

2 [I] ■ *Please don't hesitate to ask for help.*

hold back • think twice • shy away from sth • shrink from sth

▶ make sb hesitate/hold back/think twice
▶ hesitate/hold back **a little/(for) a moment**
● **HESITATE OR HOLD BACK?** You **hesitate** when you are not sure what to do; you **hold back** when what you want to do may not be what sb else wants.

hide *verb*

1 [T] ■ *He hid the letter in a drawer.* ■ *She couldn't hide her feelings.*

cover • bury • disguise • mask • camouflage | *fml* conceal

■ OPP **reveal**
▶ hide/disguise/mask/camouflage/conceal sth **behind** sth
▶ hide/bury/conceal sth **under** sth
▶ hide/disguise/mask/conceal **the truth/the fact that...**
▶ hide/disguise/mask/conceal your **disappointment/surprise**

2 [I, T] ■ *I hid under the bed.*

lie low • lurk | *infml* hole up/be holed up

▶ hide/lie low/lurk/hole up **in a place**
▶ a **place to** hide/lie low/hole up

high *adj.*

1 ■ *It's the highest mountain in Spain.*

tall • towering • high-rise | *fml or lit.* lofty

■ OPP **low**
▶ a high/tall/towering/lofty **mountain/cliff**
▶ a high/tall/high-rise/lofty **tower/building**
▶ a high/lofty **ceiling**

● **HIGH OR TALL?** Common collocations are: *a high mountain/peak/cliff/wall* • *(a) tall building/tower/tree/grass*
Compare: *The room has high windows* (= the windows are at the top of the wall near the ceiling). • *The room has tall windows* (= the windows stretch from the bottom of the wall to the top).

2 ■ *They charge very high prices for a pretty average service.*

inflated • unreasonable • excessive • disproportionate • expensive • prohibitive | *infml* steep • astronomical | *fml* inordinate | *disapprov.* exorbitant • extortionate

■ OPP **low**
▶ high/inflated/unreasonable/prohibitive/steep/astronomical/exorbitant/extortionate **prices**
▶ a/an unreasonable/excessive/disproportionate **level**
▶ high/excessive/prohibitive/astronomical/exorbitant **costs**

3 ■ *She has a high voice.*

high-pitched • sharp | *disapprov.* shrill • piercing | *music* treble

■ OPP **low, deep**
▶ a high/high-pitched/sharp/shrill/piercing/treble **voice**
▶ a high/high-pitched/sharp/shrill/piercing **sound**
▶ a high/sharp/shrill **note**
● **HIGH OR HIGH-PITCHED?** This meaning of **high** combines with a few frequent nouns for sounds; **high-pitched** is used for most other sounds: *a high voice/note/key* • *a high-pitched noise/scream/whistle/tone*

highlight *noun* [C]

■ *One of the highlights of the trip was seeing the Taj Mahal.*

high point • climax

▶ the highlight/high point/climax **of** sth

highlight *verb* [T]

■ *The report highlights the major problems facing society today.*

point sth out • draw attention to sb/sth • stress • emphasize • point to sth • underline | *esp. AmE, esp. busin.* underscore | *fml* point sth up

■ OPP **play sth down**
▶ highlight/point out/stress/emphasize/point to/underline **how...**
▶ highlight/point out/draw attention to/stress/emphasize/point to/underline/underscore/point up **the fact that...**
▶ highlight/point out/draw

attention to / stress / emphasize / point to / underline / underscore / point up the **importance** / **difference**

highway noun [C] (esp. AmE)
■ The hotel is located off Highway 21.

road | BrE motorway • dual carriageway | AmE interstate (highway) • freeway • turnpike • divided highway

► **on** a road / highway / motorway / dual carriageway / interstate / freeway / turnpike / divided highway
► **get on / off** the road / highway / interstate / freeway
► **join / leave** the road / highway
► **a stretch of** road / highway / motorway / freeway / dual carriageway / divided highway
● HIGHWAY, FREEWAY, INTERSTATE OR TURNPIKE? **Highway** is the most general of these terms and can mean any main road connecting and going through cities in the US . A **turnpike** is a road that you have to pay to use. An **interstate** is a road with two or more lanes of traffic in either direction. This is called a **freeway** in the Western States. The same road may be referred to in different ways in different parts of the country.

hill noun [C]
■ I love walking in the hills.

mountain • fell • highlands • foothills • mound | esp. BrE moor

■ OPP valley
► **on** a hill / a mountain / the fells / a mound / the moors
► **in** the hills / mountains / fells / highlands / foothills
► **climb** a hill / mountain / fell

hire verb
1 [T] (BrE) ■ We hired a car from a local firm.

esp. AmE rent • charter

► hire / rent / charter sth **for** sth
► hire / rent (a) bicycle / boat / car / equipment / movie / car / vehicle / room / hall
► hire / rent / charter a plane / vessel / yacht
● HIRE OR RENT? In BrE you **hire** vehicles or tools, but you rent DVDs or videos. In AmE **rent** is used for all these things. For larger vehicles with paying passengers use **charter**.

2 [T, I] (esp. AmE) ■ The company hired her three years ago.

employ • take sb on • recruit • appoint • sign • contract | BrE, fml engage | law retain

■ OPP fire
► hire / employ / take on / recruit / appoint / sign / engage / retain sb **as** sth
► hire / employ / take on / recruit / appoint / sign / contract / engage / retain sb **to do sth**
► hire / employ / take on / recruit / appoint / contract **staff**
► hire / employ / take on / recruit / contract **workers**

history noun
1 [U, sing.] ■ These events changed the course of history.

the past • the old days

■ OPP the future
► **in** (sth's) history / the past / the old days
► (sth's) colourful / rich / chequered / glorious history / past
► (sth's) recent / ancient / medieval history / past
► **distort / rewrite** (the) past / history

2 a history of sth [C, usu. sing.] ■ She's writing a new history of Europe.

story • chronicle

► **read / write** a history / the story / a chronicle of sth
► **tell** (sb) / **recount / relate** the history / story of sth
● HISTORY OR STORY? The **story of** sth is usu. more popular and less academic than a **history**.

3 [sing.] ■ He has a history of violent crime.

record • background • past • track record • life history

► sb **has** a history / record / background / track record of sth
► sb's **criminal** history / record / background / past
► sb's **medical** history / record

hit noun [C]
■ The series was a big hit with children.

success • best-seller | infml winner

■ OPP infml flop
► **a big** hit / success / winner
► **an instant** hit / success / best-seller
► **have** a hit / success
► **become** a hit / best-seller

hit verb
1 [T] ■ She hit him hard in the stomach.

punch • thump • beat • batter • pound • pummel • slap • spank | esp. BrE smack | infml whack • sock | fml strike

► hit / beat / batter / pound / pummel / whack / strike sb / sth **with** sth
► hit / thump / strike / whack sb **over the head**

► beat/batter sb **around/about the head**
► hit/punch/thump/strike sb **in the stomach/chest**
► hit/punch sb **on the nose**

2 [T, I] ■ *The boy was hit by a speeding car.*

knock • bang • bump | infml bash | fml strike

■ **OPP miss**
► hit/knock/bang/bump/bash **against** sth
► knock/bang/bump/bash **into** sth
► hit/strike the **ground/floor/wall**

3 [T] ■ *He fell, hitting his head on the stone floor.*

bang • knock • crack • bump

► hit/bang/knock/crack/bump your **head/knee**, etc. **on/against** sth
► hit/bang/knock/crack/bump your **head/forehead**
► hit/bang/knock/bump your **arm/knee/elbow**

---

hoarse *adj.*

■ *His voice was hoarse with exhaustion.*

husky • thick | written guttural | often disapprov. harsh • rough • gruff • raucous

■ **OPP mellow, soft**
► hoarse/husky/thick **with** sth
► a hoarse/thick/guttural/hrash/rough/gruff/husky **voice**
► a hoarse/husky/guttural/harsh/gruff/raucous **laugh**
► a hoarse/husky/harsh/gruff **whisper**

---

hobby *noun* [C]

■ *Her hobbies include swimming and cooking.*

interest • pastime

► a **popular** hobby/interest/pastime
► **have/share** hobbies/interests
► **take up/pursue** a/an hobby/interest
● **HOBBY, INTEREST OR PASTIME?** A **hobby** is often more active than an **interest**:
  ✓His main hobby is football (= he plays football). • His main interest is football (= he watches and reads about football, and may or may not play it).
  Pastime is used when talking about people in general; when you are talking about yourself or an individual it is more usual to use **interest** or **hobby**:
  ✓Eating out is the national pastime in France. ✗ ~~Eating out is the national hobby/interest in France.~~
  ✓Do you have any hobbies/interests? ✗ ~~Do you have any pastimes?~~

---

hold *verb*

1 [T] ■ *He held the baby gently in his arms.*

clutch • grip • hold on/hold onto sb/ sth • grasp • cling • hang on • handle | written clasp

■ **OPP drop, release, let go of sth**
► hold/clutch/grip/clasp sth **in your hand/hands/arms**
► hold/clutch/grip/hold on to/ grasp/cling/hang on to/clasp sb/ sth **by/with** sth
► hold/clutch/grip/grasp/hang/ clasp **on to** sth
► hold/clutch/hold onto/ grasp/cling on to/clasp sb's **hand**

2 [T] ■ *Careful, that branch won't hold your weight!*

support • hold sb/sth up • bear • carry • prop sb up

► hold/support/bear/carry the **weight** of sb/sth
● **HOLD OR BEAR? Bear** is more formal and can also be used figuratively:
  ✓ He seemed unable to bear the weight of his responsibility. ✗ ~~He seemed unable to hold the weight of his responsibility.~~

3 [T] ■ *He was held prisoner for two years.*

send sb to prison • intern • detain • imprison | infml lock sb up/away | fml incarcerate | esp. journ. jail

■ **OPP release**
► hold/send to prison/intern/lock up/detain/imprison/jail sb **for** sth
► hold/detain/imprison/ incarcerate sb **in** sth
► hold/detain/imprison/jail sb **without** trial/charge

4 [T] ■ *Your personal records are held on computer.*

keep • store | fml retain

► hold/keep/store/retain **information/data**
► hold/keep a **record/records**
► **still/no longer** hold/keep/store/ retain sth

5 [T, often passive] ■ *The conference was held in Oregon.*

have • host • give • call | infml throw | fml convene

► hold/have/host/give/call/ convene a **conference**
► hold/have/call/convene a **meeting**
► hold/have/host/give/throw a **party**
► hold/have a **conversation/ debate/discussion**

hold sb/sth up *phrasal verb*

■ The launch was held up for two hours by protesters.

delay • hold sb/sth back • set sb/sth back • stall • interfere with sth • hamper • hinder • stunt • block | *esp. spoken* keep | *fml* detain • retard

■ OPP speed sth up

▸ be held up/delayed/set back/stalled **by**/for **hours**/**days**/**months**, etc.

▸ hold up/delay/hold back/interfere with/hamper/hinder/stunt/block the **development**/**growth** of sth

▸ hold up/delay/hold back/interfere with/hamper/hinder/block/retard **progress**

hole *noun*

1 [C] ■ We dug a deep hole in the ground.

pit • crater • hollow | *fml or tech.* cavity

▸ a hole/pit/crater/hollow/cavity **in** sth

▸ a **deep**/**shallow** hole/pit/crater/hollow

▸ **dig** a hole/pit

● HOLE OR PIT? A **pit** is always large and in the ground; a **hole** can be any size and in anything. **Pit**, but not **hole**, is often used with a figurative meaning:
  ✓ (fig.) The human mind is a dark, bottomless pit. ✗ *The human mind is a dark, bottomless hole.*

2 [C] ■ There's a hole in your jeans.

gap • space • opening • slot | *fml or tech.* aperture

▸ a/an hole/gap/space/opening/slot/aperture **in** sth

▸ **leave** a/an hole/gap/space/opening

▸ **make** a/an hole/opening/slot

holiday *noun*

1 [U] ■ She's on holiday this week.

leave • break • time off • day off | *BrE* holidays | *AmE* vacation

▸ **during** the holidays/break/vacation

▸ be **on** holiday/leave/vacation

▸ (the) **summer**/**Christmas** holiday/vacation

2 [C] (*BrE*) ■ The neighbours are away on holiday.

break | *AmE* vacation | *infml* getaway

▸ a **great**/**relaxing** holiday/break/vacation/getaway

▸ **go**/**be on** holiday/vacation

▸ a **week's**/**three-day**, etc. holiday/break/vacation

holy *adj.*

1 [usu. before noun] ■ the holy city of Mecca

sacred • religious

▸ a holy/sacred **shrine**/**temple**/**relic**/**river**/**book**/**thing**

● HOLY OR SACRED? **Holy** is used esp. in connection with the world religions that worship only one god, that is Christianity, Judaism and Islam; **sacred** is used esp. in connection with religions that worship or recognize more than one god, including Hinduism. *Music* and *art* are always **sacred**, not **holy**.

2 (*often approv.*) ■ He gave away all his possessions and became a holy man.

pure • blameless | *sometimes disapprov.* saintly

■ OPP *fml* sinful

▸ a holy/pure/saintly **man**/**woman**/**person**

▸ **live** a holy/pure/blameless/saintly **life**

● HOLY OR SAINTLY? **Holy** means that sb has given their life to religion and is used in a way that is either approving or simply descriptive; **saintly** is either approving or disapproving, and is not used in a simply descriptive way: it can suggest that sb is annoying because they seem too good.

home *noun*

1 [C, U] ■ My home is very near here.

house • address | *BrE* flat | *esp. AmE* apartment | *infml* place | *fml* dwelling • residence | *fml or humorous* abode

▸ **at** home/sb's house/an address/sb's flat/sb's apartment/sb's place/sb's residence

▸ **in** a home/sb's house/sb's flat/sb's apartment/sb's place/a dwelling/a residence

▸ **have** a/an home/house/address/flat/apartment/place of your own

2 [C] ■ 200 new homes are being built in the town.

house • cottage | *BrE* flat • bungalow | *esp. AmE* apartment • townhouse • condominium | *AmE* ranch house

▸ a **detached**/**semi-detached** home/house/cottage/bungalow

▸ a **one-**/**two-**/**three-bedroom** home/house/cottage/flat/bungalow/apartment/townhouse/ranch house

▸ **rent** a/an home/house/cottage/flat/bungalow/apartment

3 [C, U] ■ She left England and made her home in Spain.

homeland • hometown • birthplace

▶ a/an **beloved/adopted** home/ homeland/hometown
▶ a **tribal/traditional/spiritual** home/homeland
▶ **return to** your home/homeland/ hometown/birthplace

4 [C] ■ *a child from a secure and loving home*

family • household • house

▶ a **low-income/poor/high-income/wealthy/rich** home/ family/household
▶ **come from** a ...home/family
▶ sb's home/family **life/ background/situation**

homework noun [U]

■ *I've got geography homework for tomorrow.*

assignment • project • exercise

▶ homework/a project/an exercise **on sth**
▶ **do** your homework/an assignment/a project/an exercise
▶ **give sb/set (sb)** (their) homework/an assignment/some exercises

honest adj. (often approv.)

■ *Give me your honest opinion.*

direct • outspoken • blunt • forthright | often approv. **frank • straight • candid** | approv. **sincere • truthful • open • straightforward**

■ OPP **dishonest**

▶ honest/direct/outspoken/ forthright/frank/straight/candid/ sincere/truthful/open/ straightforward **about sth**
▶ honest/direct/blunt/frank/ straight/candid/truthful/open/ straightforward **with sb**
▶ honest/outspoken/forthright/ frank/candid/sincere **in** your views/criticism, etc.

● WHICH WORD? **Honest**, **frank** and **candid** all refer to *what* you say as much as *how* you say it: *a/an honest/frank/candid admission of guilt*
Direct, **outspoken**, **blunt** and **forthright** all describe sb's manner of saying very clearly what they think, without worrying about other people's reactions. **Forthright** is the most positive of these words. **Open** and **straightforward** both describe sb's character: *She's such an open/ straightforward person.*

honesty noun [U]

■ *I expect total honesty from my employees.*

integrity • sincerity • good faith | BrE **honour** | AmE **honor** | fml **probity**

■ OPP **dishonesty**

▶ **absolute/complete** honesty/ integrity/sincerity
▶ sb's **personal** honesty/integrity/ honour/probity

honour (BrE) (AmE **honor**) noun

1 [sing.] ■ *It was a great honour to be invited here today.*

pleasure • delight • joy • pride • privilege | esp. spoken **treat**

▶ **It's a/an** honour/pleasure/ delight/joy/privilege/treat **to do sth.**
▶ a **great** honour/pleasure/joy/ privilege

2 [U] ■ *Proving his innocence was a matter of honour.*

integrity • honesty | fml **probity**

■ OPP **dishonour**

▶ a man/woman **of** honour/ integrity
▶ sb's **personal** honour/integrity/ honesty/probity

● HONOUR OR INTEGRITY? **Integrity** means being good and honest so that you can approve of yourself; **honour** means being good and honest so that you keep your reputation. **Integrity** is usu. individual; **honour** can be individual or collective:
✓to defend the family honour ✗ to defend the family integrity

3 [U] ■ *She brought honour to her country.*

reputation • image • status • prestige • glory • name • profile | fml **stature • character**

■ OPP **dishonour**

▶ sb's **professional** honour/ reputation/image/status/stature
▶ **personal/national** honour/ reputation/image/prestige/glory
▶ **gain/bring/lose/seek** honour/a reputation/status/prestige/glory
▶ **defend** sb's honour/reputation/ image/status
▶ **restore** sb's honour/reputation/ image/status/prestige/glory

hooligan noun [C]

■ *Police arrested 30 football hooligans after the match.*

vandal • thug | BrE **lout**

▶ a **drunken** hooligan/lout
▶ a **gang of** hooligans/vandals/ thugs

hope noun

1 [U, C] ■ *There is no hope of finding any more survivors.*

optimism • expectancy • wishful thinking

hope

■ OPP despair, hopelessness
► hope/optimism for sth
► hope/optimism that...
► express/share your hope/optimism

2 [C] ■ *They have high hopes for their children.*

dream • ambition • aspiration • expectation • fantasy

■ OPP fear
► hopes/aspirations/expectations for sth
► high hopes/ambitions/aspirations/expectations
► have hopes/a dream/an ambition/aspirations/expectations/a fantasy
► fulfil your hopes/dreams/ambitions/aspirations/expectations/fantasies

hope verb [I, T]
■ *We're hoping for good weather on Sunday.*

wish • aspire • wait • set your heart on sth | *esp. journ.* set your sights on sth

■ OPP despair of sth
► hope/wish/wait for sth
► hope/wish that...
► hope/aspire/wait to do sth

horizontal adj.
■ *Draw a grid of horizontal and vertical lines.*

flat • level • *often approv.* smooth

■ OPP vertical
► a horizontal/flat/level/smooth surface

horn noun [C]
■ *The driver in front honked her horn.*

alarm • siren

► hear a/an horn/alarm/siren
► a/an horn/alarm/siren **sounds**

horror noun
1 [U] ■ *There was a look of horror on his face.*

shock • dismay

■ OPP delight
► horror/shock/dismay at sth
► in/with horror/shock/dismay
► fill sb with horror/dismay

2 [C, usu. pl.] ■ *He witnessed the horrors of civil war.*

nightmare • hell • trauma • ordeal

► a terrible horror/nightmare/ordeal
► suffer a/an horror/nightmare/trauma/ordeal

hospital noun [C]
■ *I'm going to the hospital to visit my brother.*

infirmary • clinic • hospice • sanatorium | *AmE* medical center

► a **private** hospital/clinic/hospice/sanatorium/medical center
► a/an **eye/maternity/psychiatric** hospital/clinic
► **go to/visit** (the) hospital/a clinic

host noun [C] *(esp. AmE)*
■ *a TV game show host*

announcer • anchorman • anchorwoman • broadcaster • newscaster | *esp. AmE* anchor | *esp. BrE* commentator | *BrE* presenter • newsreader

► a **radio/television/TV** host/announcer/anchorman/anchorwoman/broadcaster/newscaster/anchor/commentator/presenter/newsreader
► a **news** anchorman/anchorwoman/anchor
► a **sports** announcer/anchorman/anchorwoman/broadcaster/anchor/commentator/presenter
● WHICH WORD? An **anchor** presents news programmes; a **presenter** *(BrE)* or **announcer** *(AmE)* presents any type of television or radio show. In *BrE* a **host** presents an entertainment show; in *AmE* **host** can also describe sb who presents more serious shows. A **broadcaster** may talk on a variety of shows but is not the presenter for a particular show.

host verb
1 [T] ■ *The President hosted a banquet in her honour.*

have • give • hold • call | *infml* throw | *fml* convene

► host/have/hold/give/give/convene a **conference**
► host/have/give/hold/throw a **party**
► host/have/hold a **competition/contest**

2 [T] ■ *Charlie Rose will be hosting tonight's show.*

BrE present | *esp. spoken* introduce

► host/present/introduce a **programme/show**

hostage noun [C]
■ *The robbers took the bank manager hostage.*

prisoner • detainee • prisoner of war • POW | *lit.* captive

► a **political** hostage/prisoner/detainee

▶ take/hold/keep sb **hostage**/
  prisoner/captive
▶ free/release a **hostage**/**prisoner**/
  detainee/**prisoner of war**/**POW**/
  captive

hot adj.

1 ■ *I'll feel better after a hot bath.*

warm • **heated** • **burning** • **boiling** •
humid • **sultry** • **red-hot**

■ OPP **cold**

▶ hot/warm/humid/sultry
  weather/**conditions**
▶ hot/warm **sunshine**/**water**
▶ hot/burning/red-hot **coals**

2 ■ *a hot curry with plenty of chillies*

spicy • **strong**

■ OPP **mild**

▶ a hot/spicy/strong **flavour**
▶ hot/strong **mustard**
▶ a hot/spicy **curry**

hotel noun [C]

■ *We stayed at a cheap hotel near the
station.*

motel • **guest house** • **bed and
breakfast/B and B/B & B** • **hostel**

▶ stay in/at a **hotel**/**motel**/**guest
  house**/**bed and breakfast**/**hostel**
▶ check in at/check into/check out
  of a **hotel**/**motel**/**bed and
  breakfast**/**hostel**
▶ run a **hotel**/**motel**/**guest house**/
  bed and breakfast/**hostel**

house noun [C]

■ *We live in a two-bedroom house.*

home • **cottage** • *BrE* **bungalow** •
flat | *esp. AmE* **townhouse** •
apartment | *AmE* **ranch house** | *infml*
place | *fml* **residence** • **dwelling**

▶ a detached/semi-detached
  house/**home**/**cottage**/**bungalow**
▶ a one-/two-bedroom, etc. **house**/
  home/**cottage**/**bungalow**/**flat**/
  townhouse/**apartment**/**ranch
  house**
▶ live in a **house**/**cottage**/
  bungalow/**flat**/**townhouse**/
  apartment/**ranch house**
▶ stay in a **house**/**cottage**/
  bungalow/**flat**/**apartment**

household noun [C]

■ *Most households own at least one
car.*

family • **home** • **house**

▶ a low-income/poor/high-
  income/wealthy/rich/one-
  parent **household**/**family**/**home**
▶ an/the **average household**/
  family/**home**
▶ be one of the **household**/**family**
● FAMILY OR HOUSEHOLD? Members
of a **family** are related to each
other; members of a **household**

live together as a group or unit but
need not be related.

housing noun [U]

■ *Health problems are linked to poor
housing.*

lodging | *BrE* **accommodation** | *AmE*
accommodations

▶ temporary/permanent/
  comfortable **housing**/
  accommodation/**accommodations**
▶ have/provide **housing**/**lodging**/
  accommodation/**accommodations**

hug verb [T, I]

■ *They hugged each other warmly.*

cuddle • **cradle** | *fml* **embrace**

▶ hug/cuddle/cradle/embrace a/
  your **child**/**son**/**daughter**
▶ hug/cuddle/embrace your **wife**/
  husband
▶ hug/cuddle/cradle a **baby**/**doll**

huge adj.

■ *The building is huge.* ■ *The party
was a huge success.*

enormous • **massive** • **vast** •
tremendous • **immense** • **great** •
colossal • **giant** • **gigantic** •
monumental

■ OPP **tiny**

▶ a/an huge/enormous/massive/
  vast/tremendous/great/colossal
  amount of sth
▶ a/an huge/enormous/massive/
  vast/great **crowd**/**area**
▶ a/an huge/enormous/massive/
  tremendous/great/monumental
  task
▶ be of/have huge/enormous/
  massive/tremendous/immense/
  great **significance**/**importance**
● HUGE OR ENORMOUS? **Huge** is used
slightly more to talk about the
physical size of sth; **enormous** is
used slightly more to talk about the
degree of sth: *a huge chunk/pile/
boulder/slab/mound/expanse* •
*enormous fun/pleasure/importance/
significance/flexibility/scope*

human noun [C]

■ *Dogs can hear much better than
humans.*

human being • **person** • **individual** |
humorous **mortal**

▶ a/an **average**/**normal**/**ordinary**
  human/**human being**/**person**/
  individual/**mortal**
▶ an **intelligent human**/**human
  being**/**person**
▶ a **rational human**/**human being**/
  person/**individual**
● HUMAN OR HUMAN BEING? **Human**
often refers to the biological

characteristics of people compared with animals or machines. It can also refer to the different stages in the development of the human race; **human being** is often used to talk about sb's ability to think, feel and be social: *early/primitive/modern humans* • *She was not behaving like a rational human being.*

humid adj.

■ These ferns will grow best in a humid atmosphere.

sultry • hot • steamy • stuffy • stifling | written airless

▶ a humid/sultry/stuffy/steamy/stifling **atmosphere**
▶ humid/sultry/hot **weather**
▶ hot and humid/sultry/stuffy/steamy

humorous adj.

■ a humorous look at the world of fashion

amusing • funny • comic • light-hearted • entertaining • witty

■ **OPP** serious
▶ a/an humorous/amusing/funny/comic/light-hearted/entertaining/witty **story**
▶ a/an humorous/amusing/funny/light-hearted/entertaining/witty **speech**
▶ a/an humorous/funny/comic/entertaining/witty **writer**
● WHICH WORD? Amusing is the most general of these words and can be used to describe events, activities and occasions:
✓ an amusing party/evening
✗ *a funny/humorous/comic party/game/evening*
Funny can describe people, jokes and stories, things that happen or anything that makes people laugh. Comic is used esp. to talk about writing and drama. Humorous is not quite as strong as funny or comic.

humour (BrE) (AmE humor) noun [U]

■ She ignored his feeble attempt at humour.

wit • comedy • funny side • banter

■ **OPP** seriousness
▶ gentle/wry humour/wit/comedy
▶ dry/deadpan/black humour/comedy
▶ see/appreciate the humour/comedy/funny side of sth

hungry adj.

■ This talk of food is making me hungry.

starving • ravenous

▶ hungry/starving **for** sth
▶ hungry/starving **children/people**

hunt verb

1 [I, T] ■ Lions sometimes hunt alone.

chase • stalk • track • trail • follow | fml pursue

▶ hunt/chase/stalk/track/trail/follow/pursue **an animal**
▶ hunt/chase/stalk/pursue (its) **prey**
▶ hunt/chase/pursue **a criminal**

2 [T, I] ■ I'm still hunting for a new job.

search • look | fml seek • forage

▶ hunt/search/look/seek/forage **for** sth
▶ hunt/search/look **through** sth
▶ hunt/search/look for **clues**
▶ police/detectives hunt/search for/look for sb/sth

hurry verb [I, T]

■ You'll have to hurry to catch that bus.

rush • dash • fly • run | spoken get a move on | fml or lit. hasten

■ **OPP** dawdle
▶ hurry/rush/run/hasten **to do sth**
▶ hurry/fly/run **along**
▶ hurry/rush **a meal**

hurt verb

1 [T, I] ■ He hurt his back playing squash.

injure • wound • bruise • sprain • strain • pull • tear • twist

▶ hurt/injure/strain **yourself**
▶ hurt/injure/sprain/pull/tear **a muscle**
▶ hurt/injure/sprain/twist your **ankle/foot/knee**
▶ hurt/injure/strain your **back/shoulder/eyes**
● HURT OR INJURE? You can hurt or injure a part of the body in an accident. Hurt emphasizes the physical pain caused; injure emphasizes that the part of the body has been damaged in some way.

2 [I] ■ My feet hurt.

ache • sting • throb • burn • itch

▶ your **eyes** hurt/ache/sting/burn/itch
▶ your **skin** hurts/stings/burns/itches
▶ your **head** hurts/aches/throbs
▶ your **stomach/tummy** hurts/aches

3 [T, I] ■ It hurt me to think that he would lie to me.

upset • distress • break sb's heart | fml sadden • pain | written sting • lit. wound

▶ It hurt/upset/distressed/

saddened/pained **me to see/ think/know...**

▶ It **breaks my heart** to see/think/ know...

▶ hurt/wound sb's **feelings**

▶ not want/not mean to hurt/ upset/distress/wound sb

● HURT OR UPSET? Hurt is used esp. to talk about sb you like or trust doing sth to make you unhappy. Being **upset** can be sth that sb does partly willingly:
✓ Don't upset yourself about it.
✗ Don't hurt yourself about it.
✓ Try not to let him upset you. ✗ Try not to let him hurt you.

4 [T] ■ Hard work never hurt anyone.

harm • damage • compromise | fml **impair**

▶ hurt/harm/damage/ compromise/impair sb's **chances**
▶ hurt/harm/damage/compromise sb's **reputation**
▶ hurt/harm/damage sb's **interests/ image**

● HURT, DAMAGE, OR HARM? Hurt is less formal than **damage** or **harm**. **Harm** is often used to talk about the ways in which things such as *animals, wildlife* and the *environment* are affected by human activity.

hurt adj.

1 [not usu. before noun] ■ None of the passengers was badly hurt.

injured • wounded • bruised • bad

■ OPP unhurt
▶ a/an injured/wounded/bruised/ bad **arm/leg/shoulder/knee**
▶ an injured/a wounded **man/ woman/person**
▶ badly/slightly hurt/injured/ wounded/bruised

2 ■ She was deeply hurt by his remarks.

upset • distressed • devastated • dismayed

▶ hurt/upset/distressed/ devastated **by** sth
▶ hurt/upset/distressed/ devastated/dismayed **that...**
▶ feel/look hurt/upset/distressed/ devastated/dismayed

husband noun [C]

■ He is her second husband.

man • partner | infml **hubby** | infml, esp. spoken, often humorous sb's **other half** | fml or law **spouse**

■ OPP wife
▶ sb's **future** husband/spouse
▶ sb's **former/ex-** husband/partner/ spouse
▶ have/find a husband/partner

hut noun [C]

■ The area is served by a network of mountain huts and refuges.

cabin • shed • shelter • shack • shanty | disapprov. **hovel**

▶ a wooden hut/cabin/shed/ shelter/shack
▶ build a hut/cabin/shed/shelter/ shack
▶ live in a hut/cabin/shack/hovel

hysterical adj.

■ Emma became hysterical and began screaming.

frantic • delirious • beside yourself • panic-stricken • incoherent • overwrought • agitated | infml **panicky • worked up**

■ OPP calm
▶ hysterical/frantic/delirious/beside yourself/incoherent **with** anger, rage, joy, etc.
▶ hysterical/frantic/agitated/ panicky/worked up **about** sth
▶ become hysterical/frantic/ delirious/incoherent/agitated/ worked up

I i

idea noun

1 [C] ■ That's a brilliant idea! ■ I like the idea of living on a boat.

thought • concept • notion • image • prospect • picture | fml abstraction

▶ a/an idea/thought/concept/ notion **about** sth
▶ the idea/thought/concept/notion **that...**
▶ have a/an idea/thought/ concept/notion/image/picture
▶ discuss/consider/explore a/an idea/concept/notion

2 [sing., U] ■ The brochure gives some idea of what the hotel is like.

impression • feeling • sense

▶ a good/definite/distinct/vague idea/impression/feeling/sense
▶ have a/an idea/impression/ feeling/sense
▶ get/give sb/leave sb with a/an idea/impression/feeling/sense

3 [C] ■ He had some very strange ideas about education.

view • opinion • belief • point of view • feeling • attitude • values • conviction | fml **sentiment • ethos** | sometimes disapprov. **ideology**

▶ sb's ideas/view/opinion/beliefs/ feelings/conviction/sentiments **about** sb/sth

ideal

▶ the idea / view / opinion / belief /
point of view / feeling / attitude /
conviction **that...**
▶ **different** ideas / views / opinions /
beliefs / points of view / attitudes /
values / convictions / sentiments /
ideologies
▶ (sb's) **political / religious** ideas /
views / opinions / beliefs / feelings /
values / conviction / sentiments /
ethos / ideology
▶ **change** your ideas / view / opinion /
belief / point of view / attitude

4 [sing.] ■ *I've an idea where it might
be.*

**feeling ∙ instinct ∙ inkling ∙
suspicion ∙ hunch**

▶ a / an idea / feeling / instinct /
inkling / suspicion / hunch **about** sth
▶ a / an idea / feeling / instinct /
inkling / suspicion / hunch **that...**
▶ **have** a / an idea / feeling / instinct /
inkling / suspicion / hunch
▶ **get / give sb** the idea / the feeling /
an inkling

5 [sing.] ■ *The whole idea of going
was to meet her new boyfriend.*

**purpose ∙ object ∙ aim ∙ intention ∙
objective ∙ point** | *fml or law* **intent**

▶ **with** the idea / purpose / object /
aim / intention / intent **of** doing sth
▶ sb / sth's **original** purpose /
object / aim / intention / intent
▶ the **whole** idea / aim / point

ideal noun [C]

■ *It was hard to live up to his high
ideals.*

**principle ∙ standards ∙ values ∙
morals ∙ morality ∙ ethics ∙ ethos**

▶ **political** ideals / principles / values /
morality / ethics / ethos
▶ **have** (no / high, etc.) values /
principles / standards / values /
morals / ethos
▶ **compromise** your ideals /
principles / standards

ideal adj.

■ *This beach is ideal for children.*

perfect ∙ tailor-made ∙ optimum |
spoken **just right**

▶ ideal / perfect / tailor-made / just
right **for** sb / sth
▶ an ideal / a perfect **opportunity /
solution / candidate**
▶ **absolutely** ideal / perfect

identify verb

1 [T] (not used in the progressive
tenses) ■ *She was able to identify
her attacker.*

**recognize ∙ know ∙ name ∙ pick sb /
sth out ∙ make sb / sth out ∙ pinpoint
∙ place** | *fml* **discern ∙ isolate**

▶ identify / recognize / know sb / sth
by sth
▶ identify / recognize / name /
pinpoint sb / sth **as** sb / sth
▶ identify / recognize / know / make
out / pinpoint / discern / isolate
who / what / how...

2 [T] ■ *Scientists have identified a link
between diet and cancer.*

find ∙ discover ∙ establish | *fml*
determine ∙ ascertain

▶ identify / establish / determine /
ascertain **what / how / when /
where / why / whether...**
▶ identify / find / discover / establish /
determine / ascertain the **cause**
▶ identify / find / discover / establish a
connection

identify with sb / sth *phrasal
verb*

■ *I couldn't identify with any of the
characters.*

**relate to sb / sth ∙ empathize ∙
understand**

▶ **try to** identify with / relate to /
empathize (with) / understand sb /
sth
▶ **be able / unable to** identify with /
relate to / empathize (with) /
understand sb / sth
▶ **It's easy / difficult / hard to** identify
with / relate to / empathize (with) /
understand sb / sth

● **IDENTIFY WITH SB / STH OR RELATE TO
SB / STH?** Relate to sb / sth is often
used to talk about personal
relationships between people who
actually know each other. Identify
with sb / sth often describes
people's positive feelings towards
characters in a book or film or
famous people: *He's a successful
and popular teacher because he
really relates to the children.* • *Which
character do you identify with most,
the father or his son?*

identity noun [C, U]

■ *a sense of national / cultural /
personal / group identity*

individuality ∙ uniqueness | *fml* **(the)
self**

▶ **human** identity / individuality /
uniqueness
▶ **express / lose** your identity /
individuality / uniqueness
▶ **sense of** identity / individuality /
uniqueness / self

ignorance noun [U, sing.]
(*sometimes disapprov.*)

■ *There is widespread ignorance about
the disease.*

incomprehension • **inexperience** | often disapprov. **naivety** | approv. **innocence**

■ OPP **knowledge**
▶ ignorance/naivety/innocence **about** sth
▶ **betray/show** (your) ignorance/inexperience
▶ **take advantage of** sb's ignorance/inexperience/naivety/innocence

ignorant adj. (disapprov.)
■ Too many of the staff were badly trained and ignorant.

uninformed • **uneducated** • **untrained** • **illiterate** | infml, disapprov. **clueless**

■ OPP **knowledgeable**
▶ ignorant/uninformed/clueless **about** sth
▶ ignorant/uninformed/uneducated/untrained/illiterate/clueless **people**
▶ an ignorant/uninformed **comment**

ignore verb [T]
■ She ignored him and carried on with her work.

take no notice • **overlook** • **neglect** • **turn a blind eye** • **gloss over** sth | fml **disregard**

■ OPP **pay attention to** sb/sth
▶ ignore/overlook/neglect/turn a blind eye to/gloss over/disregard **the fact that…**
▶ ignore/overlook/neglect/disregard **the importance/need/possibility of** sth
▶ ignore/disregard sb's **advice/rules/wishes**

ill adj. (esp. BrE)
■ Her son is seriously ill in hospital.

sick • **not (very) well** • **unwell** • **sickly** • **unhealthy** | esp. spoken **bad** | fml **ailing**

■ OPP **well**
▶ ill/sick/unwell **with** flu, a fever, etc
▶ seriously ill/sick/sickly/unhealthy **children**
▶ **feel** ill/not (very) well/unwell/bad
▶ **become/get/fall** sick/ill

● ILL OR SICK? In BrE the usual word is **ill**, unless you are taking time off work because of illness:
✓Ellie is off sick/called in sick today.
✗ Ellie is off ill/called in ill today.
In AmE the usual word is **sick**; **ill** is only used about very serious illnesses.

illegal adj.
■ Their action was judged illegal by the court.

illicit • **pirate** • **delinquent** • **unconstitutional** | fml **illegitimate** | fml or law **criminal** • **unlawful**

■ OPP **legal**
▶ a/an illegal/illicit/unconstitutional/delinquent/criminal/unlawful **act**
▶ illegal/illicit/delinquent/criminal/unlawful **activity/conduct**
▶ illegal/illicit/criminal/unlawful **possession** of drugs/weapons

illness noun
1 [U] ■ I missed a lot of school through illness.

sickness • **ill health** • **trouble**

■ OPP **good health**
▶ **due to/owing to/through** illness/sickness/ill health
▶ **chronic** illness/sickness/ill health
▶ **suffer from** illness/sickness/ill health/heart, etc. trouble

● ILLNESS OR SICKNESS? **Sickness** is used esp. in contexts concerning work and insurance. **Illness** is more general and has a wider range of uses.

2 [C] ■ She was recovering from a serious illness.

disease • **sickness** • **infection** • **condition** • **ailment** • **complaint** | infml **bug** • **virus** | med. **disorder**

▶ a **serious/chronic** illness/disease/infection/condition/ailment/disorder
▶ **have/suffer from** a/an illness/disease/sickness/infection/condition/ailment/complaint/bug/virus/disorder
▶ **catch/contract/get/pick up** a/an illness/disease/infection/bug/virus
▶ **diagnose/treat** a/an illness/disease/infection/condition/ailment/virus/disorder
▶ **recover from** a/an illness/disease/sickness/infection/bug/virus/disorder

● ILLNESS OR DISEASE? **Disease** is used to talk about more severe physical medical problems, esp. those that affect the organs:
✓kidney/liver disease ✗ heart/kidney/liver illness
Illness is used to talk about most kinds of medical problems, including mental illness. **Disease** is not used about a period of illness:
✓He died after a long illness. ✗ He died after a long disease.

illusion noun [C]
■ They created the illusion of being a happy family.

myth • **false impression** • **delusion** • **misunderstanding** • **the wrong idea** • **misconception** • **fallacy**

▶ an illusion/a myth/a delusion/a misunderstanding/the wrong

idea / a misconception / a fallacy
about sb / sth
▶ the illusion / myth / false
impression / delusion /
misunderstanding /
misconception / fallacy that...
▶ under a / an illusion / false
impression / delusion

illustrate verb [T]
■ *Two examples serve to illustrate my point.*

explain • demonstrate • clarify •
define | *fml* expound

▶ illustrate / explain / demonstrate /
clarify **how / what / why...**
▶ illustrate / explain / demonstrate /
clarify / expound an **idea**
▶ illustrate / explain / demonstrate /
clarify / define the **position / role /
nature / meaning** of sth

image noun

1 [C, U] ■ *The advertisements improved the company's image.*

reputation • prestige • status •
name • profile | *fml* stature •
character

▶ sb's image / reputation / prestige /
status / name / stature **as** sth
▶ a **bad** image / reputation / name
▶ **damage** sb's image / reputation /
character

2 [C] ■ *I had an image in my head of her standing by the window.*

picture • idea • thought • prospect

▶ **have** a / an image / picture / idea /
thought
▶ **conjure up** a / an image / picture /
idea
▶ a / an image / picture / idea / thought
forms
● IMAGE OR PICTURE? **Image** often
suggests a mental picture of one
person or thing at one moment in
time; **picture** often suggests a
mental picture of a complete scene
and / or events that may take place
over a period of time.

3 [C] ■ *Images of deer decorate the cave walls.*

picture • design • graphics •
artwork • photograph • photo •
painting • drawing • sketch • statue

▶ **make** a / an image / picture /
design / painting / drawing / sketch /
statue

4 [C] ■ *An image appeared on the screen.*

reflection • mirror image

▶ a / an image / reflection **in / on** sth
▶ a **clear / faint / blurred / distorted**
image / reflection

▶ **see / look at / stare at / watch /
study** a / an image / reflection
● IMAGE OR REFLECTION? A picture on
a television or computer screen or
seen through a camera is an
image. An **image** can also be a
picture in a mirror, etc. but this is
quite a literary use; the usual word
is **reflection**.

5 [C] ■ *Her writing is full of poetic images of home.*

metaphor • imagery | *tech.* simile •
figure of speech

▶ a / an **powerful / vivid / poetic /
appropriate / apt** image /
metaphor / imagery
▶ **use** a / an image / metaphor /
imagery / simile / figure of speech

imaginary adj.
■ *I had an imaginary friend when I was a child.*

fictional • fictitious • virtual • non-
existent | *infml* pretend

■ OPP **real**
▶ a / an imaginary / fictional / fictitious
story / character
▶ a / an imaginary / fictional / virtual
world

imagination noun

1 [U, C] ■ *These worries are all in your imagination.* ■ *She has a vivid imagination.*

vision | *sometimes disapprov.* fantasy
• make-believe

■ OPP **reality**
▶ a / an **romantic** imagination / vision /
fantasy
● IMAGINATION OR FANTASY?
Imagination is usu. a more
approving term; **fantasy** is often
used in a disapproving way to
suggest that sb is unwilling or
unable to face reality.

2 [U] ■ *His writing lacks imagination.*

inspiration • creativity • vision •
originality • ingenuity •
inventiveness

▶ **have** imagination / inspiration /
originality / ingenuity
▶ **lack / be lacking in** imagination /
inspiration / vision / originality /
ingenuity
▶ **use** your imagination / ingenuity

imagine verb

1 [T, I] ■ *Imagine you are walking through a forest.*

picture • pretend • think • see •
visualize | *fml* conceptualize •
envision | *esp. BrE* envisage

▶ imagine / picture / see / visualize /
conceptualize / envision / envisage
sb / sth **as** sth

▶ imagine/picture/see/visualize/
envision/envisage **doing** sth
▶ imagine/pretend/think/envision/
envisage **that**...
▶ imagine/picture/think/see/
visualize/envision/envisage **who/
what/how**...
● IMAGINE, PICTURE OR VISUALIZE?
Imagine is the most general of
these words and is used for any
idea that you form of how sb/sth
might look or feel. **Picture** and
visualize are used particularly
for imagining sth as a picture or
series of pictures.

2 [T] ■ 'Will we still be allowed in?' 'I
imagine so.'

suppose • **assume** • **suspect** •
presume | *esp. spoken* **take it** | *esp.
BrE, spoken* **expect** • **I dare say** | *esp.
AmE, spoken* **guess**

▶ imagine/suppose/assume/
suspect/presume/take it/expect/
dare say/guess **that**...
▶ Let's/Let us imagine/suppose/
assume/presume/take it...
▶ I imagine/suppose/assume/
suspect/expect/presume/guess
so.

immediate adj.
■ Her immediate reaction to the news
was to laugh.

instant • **prompt** • **instantaneous**

■ OPP **delayed**
▶ a/an immediate/instant/prompt/
instantaneous **reaction/response/
return**
▶ immediate/instant/prompt
action/attention/payment/relief
▶ an immediate/instant **appeal/
answer/solution/result/effect/
improvement**
● WHICH WORD? **Prompt** describes sth
that you do; **instantaneous**
describes sth that happens;
immediate and **instant** can
describe either. **Prompt** does not
suggest quite as much speed of
reaction as the other words:
✓a very/fairly prompt response
✗a/an very/fairly immediate/
instant/instantaneous response

immoral adj.
■ Is it immoral to want to be rich?

wrong • **unethical** • **improper** •
unfair • **unjust** • **unequal** | *fml*
inequitable

■ OPP **moral**
▶ immoral/wrong/unethical/
improper/unfair/unjust **to do** sth
▶ immoral/unethical/improper
behaviour/conduct

impact noun
1 [C, usu. sing., U] ■ Her speech made
a profound impact on the audience.

effect • **influence** • **impression** •
power • **force** • **consequence** •
implication | *written* **repercussion**

▶ an impact/effect/influence/
impression/on/upon sb/sth
▶ **under** the impact/effect/influence
of sth/sb
▶ **have** (a/an) impact/effect/
influence/consequences/
implications/repercussions

2 [C, usu. sing., U] ■ The impact of
the blow knocked Joe to the ground.

force • **shock**

▶ the impact/force of the **blow/
crash**
▶ **feel** the impact/force/shock of sth
▶ **take** the impact/force of sth

impatient adj.
1 ■ After waiting ten minutes I was
getting impatient.

restless

■ OPP **patient**
▶ **become/get/feel/look**
impatient/restless

2 ■ The people are impatient for
change.

eager • **anxious** • **hungry** | *esp. BrE*
keen

▶ impatient/eager/anxious/
hungry/keen **for** sth
▶ impatient/eager/anxious/keen **to
do** sth

imply verb [T]
■ The fact that she was here implies
she's interested.

suggest • **mean** • **point** • **indicate** |
fml **signify** • **denote** | *esp. journ.*
signal

▶ imply/suggest/mean/indicate/
signify sth **to** sb
▶ imply/suggest/mean/indicate/
signify **that**...
▶ imply/suggest/mean/point/to/
indicate a **great deal/high
degree/lack of** sth
● IMPLY OR SUGGEST? **Imply** is often
used to talk about how facts show
the need for sth or the existence of
sth; **suggest** is often used to talk
about how a piece of research, etc.
shows a link between things: *The
data implies an imminent healthcare
crisis.* ◆ *Research suggests a strong
link between state of mind and the
body's immune system.*

importance noun [U]
■ This project is of great importance.

seriousness • **urgency** • **significance**
| *fml* **consequence** • **substance** •
gravity

▶ be **of importance/significance to**
sb
▶ **have/gain importance/**
significance/substance
▶ **give** sth **importance/urgency/**
significance/substance

important *adj.*

1 ■ *I have an important*
announcement to make.

significant ✦ **great** ✦ **crucial** ✦ **critical**
✦ **vital** ✦ **essential** ✦ **momentous** |
infml **big** | *fml* **notable**

■ OPP **unimportant, trivial**
▶ be **important/significant/crucial/**
critical/vital/essential for/to sb/
sth
▶ be **important/significant/crucial/**
critical/vital/essential/notable
that…
▶ **important/significant/great/**
crucial/critical/vital/momentous/
big/notable events/changes/
developments
● **IMPORTANT OR SIGNIFICANT?**
Important is a more general word.
Things that are **significant** are
important from a particular point
of view, have been measured in
some way, or are great in degree:
✔*These figures are statistically*
significant. ✗ *These figures are*
statistically important.
✔*a significant proportion of the*
population ✗ *an important*
proportion of the population

2 ■ *Being a manager is an important*
job.

powerful ✦ **dominant** ✦ **influential** ✦
great ✦ **high-powered** ✦
instrumental | *approv.* **strong**

■ OPP **unimportant**
▶ **important/dominant/influential/**
instrumental in (doing) sth
▶ a/an **important/powerful/**
dominant/influential/great/
strong figure/leader/position
▶ a/an **important/powerful/**
dominant/great/strong influence
● **WHICH WORD?** Powerful people
such as politicians use their
position to control events.
Influential people change other
people's opinions or behaviour
because they respect and listen
to them. **Important** people
influence other people or events
because people respect them or
because their actions have a
great effect. **Strong** people
are confident and have
leadership qualities.

impose *verb* [T]

■ *A new tax was imposed on fuel.*

apply ✦ **enforce** ✦ **put sth into**
practice ✦ **put sth into effect**

▶ **impose/apply/enforce/put into**
practice/put into effect measures
▶ **impose/apply/enforce a rule/**
restriction/penalty/sanction/
standard

impossible *adj.*

■ *It was an impossible dream.*

out of the question | *esp. written*
unthinkable ✦ **inconceivable** ✦
unattainable

■ OPP **possible**
▶ be **impossible/unthinkable/**
inconceivable to sb
▶ be **impossible/out of the question/**
unthinkable/inconceivable for sb
to do sth
▶ be **impossible/out of the question/**
unthinkable/inconceivable that…

impress *verb* [T, often passive, I]

■ *She was very impressed by his work.*

dazzle ✦ **take sb's breath away** ✦
move ✦ **touch** ✦ **affect**

▶ **impress/dazzle/move sb with** sth
▶ it **impresses/moves/touches sb to**
see/hear sth
▶ **impress/move/touch/affect sb**
deeply

impression *noun*

1 [C] ■ *My first impression of him was*
favourable.

idea ✦ **sense** ✦ **feeling** | *esp. written*
sensation

▶ a **good/definite/distinct/vague**
impression/idea/sense/feeling
▶ **have** a/an **impression/idea/**
sense/feeling/sensation
▶ **get/give/leave sb with/**
convey a/an **impression/idea/**
sense/feeling

2 [C, usu. sing.] ■ *The city made a*
deep impression on him.

effect ✦ **impact** ✦ **influence**

▶ an **impression/effect/impact/**
influence on/upon sb/sth
▶ a **profound/positive/strong/**
big/positive/lasting impression/
effect/impact/influence
▶ **make** an **impression/impact**

impressive *adj.*

■ *He gave a truly impressive*
performance. ■ *The college is an im-*
pressive building with a huge tower.

magnificent ✦ **spectacular** ✦ **expert**
✦ **masterly** ✦ **virtuoso** ✦ **professional**
✦ **grand** ✦ **majestic** ✦ **imposing** ✦
accomplished | *esp. spoken* **great** |
fml **consummate**

■ OPP **unimpressive**
▶ a/an **impressive/magnificent/**

spectacular/expert/masterly/
virtuoso/professional/grand/
accomplished/great
performance/display
▶ impressive/expert/masterly/
virtuoso/professional/great/
consummate **skill**
▶ a/an impressive/magnificent/
spectacular/grand **achievement**
▶ impressive/magnificent/
spectacular/grand/majestic
scenery/views

improve verb

1 [T] ■ *The graphics on the website
have been greatly improved.*

reform • refine • enhance | *written*
enrich

■ OPP *fml* impair
▶ improve/refine/enhance/enrich
your **understanding**
▶ improve/refine/enhance/enrich
your **knowledge**
▶ improve/enhance/enrich your **life**

2 [I] ■ *His quality of life improved after
the operation.*

pick up • advance • progress •
develop • get better | *infml* look up •
come along/on

■ OPP worsen, deteriorate
▶ start/begin/continue to
improve/pick up/advance/
progress/develop/get better/look
up
▶ fail to improve/advance/
progress/get better
▶ improve/pick up/advance/
progress/develop/get better
**slowly/gradually/slightly/
dramatically**

inadequate adj.

■ *The food supplies were quite
inadequate for 1 000 people.*

lacking • scant • paltry | *BrE* meagre
| *AmE* meager | *fml* insufficient •
deficient

■ OPP adequate
▶ inadequate/insufficient **for** sth
▶ inadequate/insufficient **to do** sth
▶ a/an inadequate/meagre/paltry/
insufficient **amount/level/number**
● INADEQUATE OR INSUFFICIENT?
Insufficient emphasizes the
quantity or strength of sth;
inadequate often emphasizes the
quality as well as the quantity:
insufficient money/attention •
inadequate understanding/training

incentive noun [C, U]

■ *Tax incentives are designed to
encourage investment.*

inducement • motivation • impetus
• inspiration • stimulus

■ OPP disincentive
▶ the incentive/motivation/

| **income**

impetus/inspiration/stimulus **for**
sth
▶ the incentive/inducement/
impetus/stimulus **to** sth
▶ the incentive/inducement/
impetus/stimulus **to do** sth
▶ **provide/give (sb/sth)** the
incentive/inducement/
motivation/impetus/inspiration/
stimulus

incident noun [C, U]

■ *There was a shooting incident near
here last night.*

event • episode • affair • experience
• development • business | *fml*
occurrence

▶ a **strange** incident/event/affair/
experience/development/
occurrence
▶ **witness** an incident/event/
episode
▶ an incident/event/episode/
experience **occurs/takes place**

include verb

1 [T] (not usu. used in the
progressive tenses) ■ *Does the price
include tax?*

contain • involve • cover • take sth
in • build sth in(to sth) • incorporate
| *fml* encompass • embrace

■ OPP exclude
▶ include/contain/involve/
incorporate sth **in** sth
▶ be included/covered/
incorporated/encompassed **as** sth
▶ include/contain/cover/
incorporate/encompass **particular
material**

2 [T] ■ *There are 12 in the group,
including students.*

count | *fml* number

■ OPP exclude
▶ include sb/count (sb)/number (sb)
as/among sb/sth
▶ include/count/number **yourself**
as/among sb/sth

income noun

1 [C, U] ■ *Organic food is not
affordable for people on low incomes.*

earnings • wage/wages • pay •
salary

▶ (a) **high/low/basic** income/
earnings/wage/pay/salary
▶ **receive** (a/an) income/earnings/
wage/pay/salary
▶ **pay/give** sb (a/an) income/
wage/salary
● INCOME OR EARNINGS? **Earnings**
may vary from month to month
depending on how many hours sb
works. They do not include
unearned income, for example from

investments. **Income** is typically seen as a regular amount that you can rely on.

2 [C, U] ■ *Paper manufacture is the company's main source of income.*

revenue • **takings** • **proceeds** | *busin.* **turnover** • **receipts** | *esp. AmE, busin.* **take**

▶ the income/revenue/takings/proceeds/turnover/receipts/take **from** sth
▶ **gross/net/total** income/revenue/takings/proceeds/turnover/receipts/take
▶ **increase/boost/reduce** (your) income/revenue/turnover
● **INCOME OR REVENUE?** These words are very similar but **revenue** is used when talking about tax.

incompetent *adj.*

■ *an incompetent manager*

inadequate • **poor** • **inept** | *esp. spoken* | *infml* **rotten** • **useless**

▶ **OPP** competent
▶ a/an incompetent/poor/bad/rotten/useless **teacher/driver**
▶ a/an inadequate/bad/rotten/useless **mother/father/parent**
▶ **hopelessly** incompetent/inept

inconsistent *adj.* [not usu. before noun]

■ *The witness statements were inconsistent.*

at odds • **incompatible** • **contradictory** • **mutually exclusive** | *fml* **irreconcilable**

▶ **OPP** consistent
▶ inconsistent/at odds/incompatible/irreconcilable **with** sth

increase *noun* [C, U]

■ *This year saw an increase of nearly 50% in the number of visitors.*

rise • **growth** • **gain** • **surge** • **upturn** • **spiral** • **inflation** | *AmE* **raise** | *infml, esp. journ.* **hike**

▶ **OPP** cut, reduction, decrease
▶ (a/an) increase/rise/growth/gain/surge/upturn/spiral/inflation/hike **in** sth
▶ (a/an) increase/rise/growth/gain/surge/inflation/hike **of** 20%, 300, £10, a third, etc.
▶ **see** (a/an) increase/rise/growth/gain/surge/upturn/inflation/hike
● **INCREASE, RISE OR GROWTH?** Growth is used more often about sth positive; **increase** and **rise** are used more often about sth negative: *the growth in earnings/employment* • *an*

---

alarming increase/rise in violent crime
Rise is used more for sth that happens to rise, rather than deliberate increases; **increase** is used in both these ways.

increase *verb*

1 [T] ■ *They have increased the price by 50%.*

raise • **heighten** • **intensify** • **step sth up** • **turn sth up** | *often approv., esp. journ.* **boost** | *often disapprov., esp. journ.* **inflate** | *esp. busin.* **maximize**

▶ **OPP** cut, reduce, (*fml*) decrease
▶ increase/raise/step up/boost/inflate sth **by** 15%, 250, £100, a third, etc.
▶ increase/raise/step up/boost/inflate sth **from** 2% **to** 5%
▶ increase/raise/boost/inflate/maximize **prices**
▶ increase/raise/heighten/boost **awareness/interest**
▶ increase/raise/intensify/step up the **pressure**
● **INCREASE OR RAISE?** Increase is used slightly more often about numbers, prices and figures; **raise** is often used about feelings and qualities.

2 [I] ■ *The population increased from 1.2 million to 1.5 million.*

rise • **grow** • **climb** • **escalate** • **jump** • **rocket** | *esp. spoken* **go up** | *written* **soar** | *disapprov.* **spiral** • **shoot up**

▶ **OPP** decline, (*fml*) decrease
▶ increase/rise/grow/climb/jump/go up/soar/shoot up **in** price, number, etc.
▶ increase/rise/grow/climb/jump/rocket/go up/soar/shoot up **(by)** 10%, 200, etc.
▶ increase/rise/grow/climb/escalate/jump/rocket/go up/soar/shoot up **from** 2% **to** 5%
▶ the **price** increases/rises/climbs/escalates/jumps/rockets/goes up/soars/spirals/shoots up
▶ the **level** increases/rises/escalates/jumps/goes up/soars/shoots up
● **INCREASE, RISE OR GROW?** Increase is slightly more formal. **Rise** is the most common and is used more often about the number or level of sth; **increase** and **grow** can also be used about size and strength: *Profits/Numbers have increased/risen/grown.* • *Her confidence increased/grew.*

increase in sth *phrasal verb*

■ *Oil has increased in price.*

gain • **put sth on**

▶ **OPP** lose, (*fml*) decrease in sth
▶ increase in/gain/put on **weight**
▶ increase in/gain **strength**

incredible adj.
■ *It's incredible that only one person was hurt.*

unbelievable • beyond belief • implausible

■ OPP **credible**
▶ incredible/unbelievable **to sb**
▶ be incredible/unbelievable/ beyond belief/implausible **that...**
▶ find sth incredible/unbelievable/ implausible
● INCREDIBLE OR UNBELIEVABLE? If you describe sth as **incredible**, you usu. have accepted that it is true, even though you find it very difficult to believe. If you describe sth as **unbelievable**, you probably don't believe that it is true or possible.

independence noun
1 [U] ■ *Cuba gained independence from Spain in 1898.*

self-government | *fml* **autonomy • sovereignty • self-determination**

■ OPP **dependence**
▶ independence/self-government/ autonomy/sovereignty/self-determination **for sb**
▶ national/political independence/ autonomy/sovereignty/self-determination
▶ have/enjoy/give sb/grant sb/ recognize sth's independence/ autonomy/sovereignty
● INDEPENDENCE OR AUTONOMY? **Independence** usu. means complete freedom for a whole country from outside political control; **autonomy** is usu. a degree of freedom that is less than complete independence.

2 [U] ■ *Young people have more independence these days.*

freedom • liberty • leeway | *fml* **autonomy**

■ OPP **dependence**
▶ complete/individual/personal independence/freedom/liberty/ autonomy
▶ have independence/freedom/ liberty/leeway/autonomy
▶ enjoy/lose independence/ freedom/liberty/autonomy

independent adj.
■ *Two independent research groups reached the same conclusions.*

unrelated • unconnected • self-contained • free-standing

▶ independent/unrelated data
▶ a/an independent/self-contained/ free-standing **unit**

index noun [C]
■ *His name doesn't appear in the index.*

list • table • directory • catalogue | *AmE also* **catalog**

▶ an alphabetical index/list/ directory/catalogue
▶ compile a/an index/list/table/ directory/catalogue
▶ list sth in/look sth up in/consult a/an index/table/directory/ catalogue

indicate verb
1 [T] ■ *Record profits indicate a boom in the economy.*

show • demonstrate • prove • illustrate

▶ indicate/show/demonstrate/ prove sth **to sb**
▶ indicate/show/demonstrate/ prove/illustrate **that/when/ how...**
▶ research indicates/shows/ demonstrates/proves/illustrates sth

2 [T] ■ *Early results indicate success for the party.*

suggest • imply • point • mean | *fml* **signify • denote** | *esp. journ.* **signal**

▶ indicate/suggest/imply/mean/ signify sth **to sb**
▶ indicate/suggest/imply/mean/ signify **that...**
▶ the results indicate/suggest/ imply/point to/mean/signify sth
▶ the facts indicate/suggest/imply/ point to sth

indication noun [C, U]
■ *There are clear indications that the economy is improving.*

sign • signal • suggestion • pointer • hint • symptom | *esp. busin.* **indicator**

▶ a/an indication/sign/signal/ symptom/indicator **of sth**
▶ a/an indication/sign/signal/ suggestion/hint/symptom/ indicator **that...**
▶ an obvious indication/sign/ signal/suggestion/pointer/hint/ symptom/indicator
● INDICATION OR SIGN? An **indication** often comes in the form of sth that sb says; a **sign** is usu. sth that happens or sth that sb does.

indifferent adj. [not usu. before noun]
■ *Public opinion remained largely indifferent to the issue.*

lukewarm • half-hearted • uninterested | *esp. written* **apathetic • detached** | *disapprov.* **casual • offhand**

▶ indifferent/lukewarm/half-

hearted/apathetic/casual/offhand **about** sth
▶ indifferent/lukewarm/apathetic **towards** sb/sth
▶ a/an indifferent/lukewarm/ detached/apathetic/casual **attitude**

individual noun [C]

■ *The average individual watches four hours television a day.*

person • human • human being • soul • figure • character | *humorous* **mortal**

▶ a/an **average/normal/ordinary** individual/person/human/human being/mortal
▶ a/an **key/powerful/independent** individual/person/figure
▶ the individual/person **concerned/ responsible**

individual adj.

1 [only before noun] ■ *The minister refused to comment on individual cases.*

particular • separate • single • specific • certain • respective

■ OPP **collective**
▶ a/an individual/particular/ specific/certain **person**
▶ individual/particular/separate/ single/specific/certain/respective **categories/regions**
▶ individual/particular/specific/ certain/respective **needs/ requirements**

2 [only before noun] ■ *Try to measure in individual portions how much people will eat.*

personal • own • private • subjective

■ OPP **communal**
▶ sb's individual/personal/own/ private/subjective **experience**
▶ sb's individual/personal/own **needs/requirements/objectives/ freedom**

industry noun

1 [U] ■ *Pollution from heavy industry is the worst in Europe.*

manufacturing • production

▶ **local** industry/manufacturing/ production
▶ **large-scale/small-scale** industry/ manufacturing/production

2 [C] ■ *Thousands of jobs were lost in the steel industry.*

trade • business • service

▶ be **in/work in** a particular industry/trade/business/service
▶ the **tourist/car/hotel/**

---

construction industry/trade/ business
▶ the **timber/fur/wool/wine/ motor/building** industry/trade
▶ the **energy/entertainment/ music/hospitality** industry/ business

ineffective adj.

■ *Punishment is largely ineffective as a deterrent.*

inefficient • unproductive • counterproductive • self-defeating | *fml* **ineffectual**

■ OPP **effective**
▶ ineffective/inefficient/ counterproductive **for** sb/sth
▶ ineffective/ineffectual **as** sth
▶ ineffective/inefficient **in/at doing** sth
▶ ineffective/inefficient/ counterproductive/self-defeating **to do** sth

inequality noun [U, C]

■ *new attempts to reduce inequality in our society*

injustice • unfairness | *fml* **inequity**

■ OPP **equality**
▶ inequality/injustice/unfairness/ inequity **in** sth
▶ **social/racial/economic** inequality/injustice/inequity
▶ **fight/tackle/struggle against** inequality/injustice

inevitable adj.

■ *A rise in interest rates seems inevitable.*

unavoidable • inescapable | *written* **necessary** | *fml* **inexorable**

■ OPP **avoidable**
▶ a/an inevitable/unavoidable/ necessary **consequence**
▶ a/an inevitable/inescapable/ necessary **conclusion/fact**
▶ the inevitable/inexorable **slide** into/towards war, fascism, mediocrity, etc.
● INEVITABLE OR UNAVOIDABLE? **Inevitable** is much more frequent and has a wider range of collocates. **Unavoidable** always describes sth unpleasant, such as *delays* and *consequences*.

be in favour (of sb/sth) *(BrE)* *(AmE* be in favor *(of sb/sth))* phrase

■ *I'm all in favour of equal pay for equal work.*

approve • agree with sth • support • back • believe in sth | *infml* **be all for sth** | *fml* **subscribe to sth**

■ OPP **be opposed (to sb/sth)**
▶ be in favour of/approve of/agree with/support/back/believe in/be

All for/subscribe to a/an **idea/
view**
▶ be in favour of/approve of/agree
with/support/back/be all for a
plan/policy/suggestion
● **(BE) IN FAVOUR (OF STH/STH) OR
APPROVE?** In favour is often used
about a policy or strategy when
people might vote on; approve is
used to talk about more personal
matters: *All those in favour, please
raise your hand.* • *I don't think your
mother would approve of this
behaviour.*

infect verb [T]
■ *You cannot infect another person by
kissing.*

**pass sth on • spread | fml transmit |
esp. spoken give**

▶ infect sb with/pass on/spread/
transmit/give sb a/an **disease/
infection/virus**

infection noun [C]
■ *He's off work with a throat infection.*

**illness • disease • ailment | infml bug
• virus**

▶ a **serious/chronic/minor**
infection/illness/disease/ailment
▶ **catch/contract/get/pick up** a/an
infection/illness/disease/bug/
virus
▶ a/an infection/illness/disease/
virus **spreads**

influence noun
1 [U, C] ■ *the influence of television on
children*

effect • impact • impression

▶ an influence/effect/impact/
impression **on/upon** sb/sth
▶ **under the** influence/effect/impact
of sth/sb
▶ a/an **cultural/economic/
political/social** influence/effect/
impact
▶ **have an** influence/effect/impact

2 [C] ■ *That boy is a bad influence on
him.*

force • example • lead

▶ an influence/example **for** sb
▶ an influence/a force **for** sb
▶ a **decisive/positive/strong**
influence/force/lead

influence verb
1 [T] ■ *Many social factors influence
life expectancy.*

**affect • leave your/its/a mark | BrE
colour | AmE color | esp. journ. or
busin. impact**

▶ influence/affect **what/how/
when/where** (sth) happens
▶ influence/affect/colour sb's
judgement/attitude

▶ **adversely/inevitably** influence/
affect/impact on sth

2 [T] ■ *Her parents tried to influence
her in her choice of career.*

sway • prejudice • bias

▶ influence/sway/prejudice/bias sb/
sth **against** sb/sth
▶ influence/sway/bias sb/sth **in
favour of** sb/sth
▶ influence/sway/bias the **result of**
sth

inform verb [T]
■ *Please inform us of any change of
address.*

**tell • report • fill sb in • brief | fml
notify | esp. written or humorous
enlighten**

▶ inform sb/tell sb/report/brief sb/
notify sb **that...**
▶ inform/tell/notify sb **of** sth
▶ inform/tell/enlighten sb
about sth
● **INFORM OR NOTIFY?** Notify is often
used for important facts that the
authorities or public need to know.
It is not used for more personal or
general information:
✓ *I have been reliably informed that
the couple will marry next year.* ✗ ~~I
have been reliably notified that the
couple will marry next year.~~
✓ *The leaflet informs customers
about healthy eating.* ✗ ~~The leaflet
notifies customers about healthy
eating.~~

informal adj.
■ *Discussions are held on an informal
basis.*

casual • relaxed

● OPP **formal**
▶ an informal/a relaxed **atmosphere**
▶ informal/casual **dress**
● **INFORMAL OR CASUAL?** You can use
either word to talk about clothes in
general, but to talk about particular
items of clothing use casual:
✓ *a casual shirt/jacket* ✗ ~~an informal
shirt/jacket~~

information noun [U]
■ *Contact us for further information.*

**data • details • facts • figures •
statistics • intelligence • material •
news • word | infml info • stats | fml
particulars**

▶ information/data/details/facts/
figures/statistics/intelligence/
material/info/particulars **about/
relating to** sb/sth
▶ **(a/an) further/additional**
information/data/details/facts/
figures/statistics/intelligence/
material/info/particulars

▸ **have** information/data/details/
the facts/the figures/the statistics/
intelligence/material/news/word/
info/particulars
▸ a **piece** of information/data/
intelligence/news

informative *adj.*

■ *The talk was both entertaining and informative.*

instructive • educational •
informational • revealing •
illuminating • telling • enlightening
| *fml* instructional

■ OPP uninformative

▸ informative/instructive/revealing/
illuminating/telling/enlightening
about sth
▸ a/an informative/revealing/
illuminating/telling/enlightening
insight/account
▸ **find** sth informative/instructive/
educational/illuminating/
enlightening

● INFORMATIVE OR INSTRUCTIVE?
Things that you read or hear may
be **informative**; things that you do
or experience may be **instructive**.

informed *adj.* [usu. before noun]

■ *The paper's readership was generally well informed and intelligent.*

knowledgeable • educated •
thinking • well read

■ OPP uninformed

▸ informed/knowledgeable/
educated **about** sth
▸ informed/knowledgeable/
educated/thinking/well-read
people

inherit *verb* [T, I]

■ *She inherited a fortune from her father.*

succeed • come into sth

▸ inherit/succeed to the/sb's
throne/crown/title/estate
▸ inherit/come into **money/
property/a fortune**
● INHERIT OR SUCCEED? **Inherit** is used
more to talk about receiving
money or property; **succeed** is
used more to talk about gaining a
title or position, esp. *the throne* (=
the position of king or queen).

initial *adj.* [only before noun]

■ *My initial response was one of anger.*

first • original • preliminary •
opening • introductory •
preparatory | *fml* or *tech.* primary

■ OPP final

▸ the initial/first/earliest/opening/
preliminary/introductory/
preparatory/primary **stage**

▸ a/an initial/first/original/
preliminary **estimate/draft/
version**
▸ a/an initial/first/preliminary **step/
appointment/visit**

injure *verb* [T]

■ *He injured his knee playing hockey.*

hurt • bruise • sprain • strain • twist
• pull • tear • wound • maim

▸ injure/hurt/strain **yourself**
▸ injure/hurt/strain/strain/pull/
tear a **muscle**
▸ inhure/hurt/sprain/twist your
ankle/foot/knee
● INJURE OR HURT? You can **injure** or
hurt a part of the body in an
accident. **Hurt** emphasizes the
physical pain caused; **injure**
emphasizes that the part of the
body has been damaged in some
way.

injured *adj.*

■ *The injured man was struggling to stand.*

hurt • wounded • bruised • bad

■ OPP uninjured

▸ a/an injured/wounded/bruised/
bad **arm/leg/shoulder/knee**
▸ an injured/a wounded **man/
woman/person**
▸ **badly/slightly** injured/hurt/
wounded/bruised

injury *noun* [C, U]

■ *He escaped with only minor injuries.*

wound • cut • bruise • scratch •
gash • graze

▸ (a/an) injury/wound/cuts/bruise/
gash **to** a part of the body
▸ **minor** injuries/wounds/cuts/
bruises
▸ **suffer** (a/an) injury/wound/cuts/
bruises/scratches/gash

in love *adj.*

■ *We're in love!*

besotted • infatuated | *infml* crazy
about sb | *often humorous* smitten

▸ in love/besotted/infatuated/
smitten **with** sb
▸ **totally/completely** in love/crazy
about sb/besotted/infatuated/
smitten

innocent *adj.*

1 ■ *They imprisoned an innocent man.*

blameless | *infml* in the clear | *law*
not guilty

■ OPP guilty

▸ innocent/not guilty **of** sth
▸ **plead** innocent/not guilty
▸ **find** sb innocent/not guilty

2 ■ *the innocent world of childhood*

naive + childlike + inexperienced + impressionable

■ OPP knowing
► an innocent/impressionable child
► a/an innocent/naive belief
► young and innocent/inexperienced/impressionable

inquiry (also **enquiry**) noun

1 [C] ■ Police have launched a murder inquiry.

investigation + **survey** + **inquest** + **check** | journ. **probe**

► a/an inquiry/investigation/survey/inquest/probe into sth
► conduct a/an inquiry/investigation/survey/inquest/check
► carry out a/an inquiry/investigation/survey/check
► the results/findings of a/an inquiry/investigation/survey/inquest

2 [C] ■ We received over 300 inquiries about the job.

query + **question**

► a/an inquiry/query/question about/as to/concerning/on sth
► address/direct a/an inquiry/query/question to sb
► have/deal with/handle/reply/respond to/answer a/an inquiry/query/question

insensitive adj.

■ It was a really insensitive thing to say.

thoughtless + **unsympathetic** + **uncaring** + **tactless** + **inconsiderate** | written **unthinking**

■ OPP **sensitive**
► insensitive/unsympathetic to sb/sth
► a/an insensitive/thoughtless/tactless **remark**
► an unsympathetic/uncaring/inconsiderate **attitude**

insist verb

1 [I, T] ■ She insisted on his wearing a suit.

demand + **expect** | fml **require** + **stipulate**

► insist/demand/expect/require/stipulate **that...**
► insist on/demand/expect/require **high standards**

2 [I, T] ■ He insisted that he was innocent.

protest + **claim** + **argue** + **assert** + **maintain** | fml **affirm** + **contend**

► insist/protest/claim/argue/assert/maintain/affirm/contend **that...**

► insist on/protest/assert/maintain your **innocence**

inspect verb [T]

■ The Tourist Board inspects all recommended hotels.

examine + **check** + **go over sth** + **look sb/sth over** + **check over sb/sth** + **check through sth** + **look at sth** + **visit**

► inspect/examine/check/check over sth
► inspect/examine/check/check through sth for sth
► inspect/examine/check/look at sth to see if/whether...
► inspect/examine/check/visit sth regularly/daily
● INSPECT, CHECK OR EXAMINE? These words can all be used when you are looking for possible problems. Only **check** is used about looking for mistakes:
✓ Check your work before handing it in. ✗ Inspect/Examine your work before handing it in.
Only **examine** is used when looking for the cause of a problem:
✓ The doctor examined her but could find nothing wrong. ✗ The doctor checked/inspected her but could find nothing wrong.

inspection noun [U, C]

■ The documents are available for public inspection.

examination + **check** + **observation** + **survey** | esp. busin. **audit**

► a detailed inspection/examination/check/observation/survey/audit
► carry out/do a/an inspection/examination/check/observation/survey/audit
► a/an inspection/examination/check/observation/survey **confirms** sth

inspector noun [C]

■ The health and safety inspector wrote a worrying report.

regulator + **monitor** + **observer** | esp. AmE **examiner** | esp. journ. **watchdog**

► a/an government/federal/independent inspector/regulator/observer/watchdog
► an **official** inspector/regulator/observer/watchdog
► call a/an inspector/regulator/examiner
► send a/an inspector/monitor/observer/examiner

inspiration noun [U]

■ Dreams are a source of inspiration for many artists.

creativity • vision • imagination • originality • ingenuity • inventiveness

▸ **great** inspiration/creativity/ vision/imagination/originality/ ingenuity/inventiveness
▸ **have** inspiration/imagination/ originality/ingenuity
▸ **lack/be lacking in** inspiration/ vision/imagination/originality/ ingenuity

inspire verb [T]
■ *The actors inspired us to put on our own productions.*

motivate • stimulate • fire sb up

▸ **inspire/motivate/stimulate sb to** sth
▸ **inspire/motivate/stimulate/fire up** sb **to do** sth
▸ **inspire/motivate/fire up** sb **by doing** sth

instinct noun [U, C]
■ *I acted purely on instinct.*

intuition • sixth sense

▸ **a/an instinct/intuition/sixth sense for** sth
▸ **an instinct/intuition that...**
▸ **do** sth **by** instinct/intuition
▸ **have** a/an instinct/intuition/sixth sense
▸ **rely on** your instinct/intuition

institution noun

1 [C] ■ *Loans to financial institutions were disguised as investments.*

institute • organization | *BrE* **centre** | *AmE* **center**

▸ **a/an** institution/institute/ organization/centre **for** sth
▸ **a private** institution/organization
▸ **a government** institution/ institute/organization
▸ **a research/training** institution/ institute/organization/centre
● **INSTITUTION OR INSTITUTE?** Institution can refer to a range of organizations; institute usu. refers to a particular organization or its building: *financial/academic institutions • the Dundee Institute of Technology*

2 [C] (sometimes disapprov.) ■ *He spent years in a mental institution.*

home • orphanage

▸ **live in** a/an institution/home/ orphanage
▸ **move to** an institution/a home

instruction noun

1 instructions [pl.] ■ *Follow the instructions carefully.*

directions

▸ **instructions/directions for/on/as to** sth
▸ **clear/precise/detailed/step-by-step/careful** instructions/ directions
▸ **give sb/follow** instructions/ directions

2 [C, usu. pl.] ■ *I'm under instructions to keep my speech short.*

order • command • directive

▸ **under** sb's instructions/sb's orders/a directive
▸ **issue/obey/ignore** instructions/ an order/a command/a directive
▸ **give/receive/carry out** instructions/an order/a command

instrument noun [C]
■ *This pen is a precision instrument for all your graphic needs.*

tool • gadget • device • aid | *fml* **implement • utensil**

▸ **a measuring/navigation/ navigational** instrument/tool/ device
▸ **a drawing/writing** instrument/ tool/aid/implement
▸ **a medical/surgical** instrument/ device/implement

insult verb [T, often passive]
■ *I've never been so insulted!*

offend • abuse • shock

■ OPP **compliment, flatter**
▸ **feel** insulted/offended/shocked
▸ **deeply** insulted/offended/ shocked
● **INSULT OR OFFEND?** To **insult** sb is to do or say sth rude to them, usu. deliberately. To **offend** sb is to upset them, either because you have insulted them, or because you have been rude or thoughtless about sb/sth that is important to them.

insulting adj.
■ *She was really insulting to me.*

rude • offensive • abusive | *fml* **derogatory • disparaging • pejorative**

■ OPP **complimentary**
▸ **insulting/rude/offensive/abusive/ derogatory to** sb
▸ **a/an insulting/rude/offensive/ abusive/derogatory/disparaging remark/comment**
▸ **a/an insulting/rude/offensive/ abusive/derogatory/disparaging/ pejorative word**

integrity noun [U]
■ *She behaved with absolute integrity.*

honesty • sincerity • good faith | *BrE* **honour** | *AmE* **honor** | *fml* **probity**

- OPP **dishonesty**
▶ a man/woman **of** integrity/honour
▶ sb's **personal** integrity/honesty/honour/probity
▶ sb's **professional** integrity/honour/probity
● INTEGRITY OR HONOUR? **Integrity** means being good and honest so that you can approve of yourself; **honour** means being good and honest so that you keep your reputation. **Integrity** is usu. individual; **honour** can be individual or collective:
✓to defend the family honour ✗ to defend the family integrity

intellectual adj.

1 [usu. before noun] ■ *His approach to art was intellectual rather than practical.*

theoretical • abstract • academic • psychological • mental • philosophical | *fml* **conceptual**

■ OPP **physical**
▶ an intellectual/a theoretical/an abstract/an academic/a psychological/sb's mental/a philosophical/a conceptual **approach**
▶ intellectual/theoretical/abstract/academic/philosophical **discussion/argument/debate**

2 ■ *Not all college students are highly intellectual!*

literary • studious • scholarly | *fml* **learned** | *approv.* **cultured** | *sometimes disapprov.* **highbrow • bookish**

▶ a/an intellectual/literary/studious/scholarly/learned/cultured/bookish **man/woman**
▶ (a/an) intellectual/literary/scholarly/learned/highbrow/cultured **readers/readership**
▶ a/an intellectual/literary/scholarly/cultured **elite**

intelligence noun [U]

■ *a person of average intelligence*

intellect • mind • brain • wits • genius | *AmE, infml* **smarts**

■ OPP **stupidity**
▶ (a) **great** intelligence/intellect/mind/brain/genius
▶ **have** (the) intelligence/wits/smarts **to do** sth
▶ **use** your intelligence/mind/brain/wits/smarts

intelligent adj.

■ *He's a highly intelligent man.*

bright • brilliant | *esp. BrE* **smart** | *esp. BrE, sometimes disapprov.* **clever**

■ OPP **stupid**
▶ a/an intelligent/bright/brilliant/

smart/clever **child/boy/girl/man/woman**
▶ a/an intelligent/brilliant/smart/clever **move/thing to do**

intend verb

1 [I, T] ■ *He intends to retire next year.*

plan • aim • have sb/sth in mind | *esp. spoken* **mean** | *fml* **propose**

▶ intend/plan/aim/have in mind/mean/propose **to do** sth
▶ intend/propose **doing** sth
▶ sb **originally** intended/planned/meant sth

2 **be intended** ■ *The book is intended for children.*

design • be aimed at sth • mean

▶ be intended/designed/meant **for/as** sth
▶ be intended/designed/meant **to be/do** sth

intense adj.

■ *There was an intense relationship between mother and son.*

passionate • fierce • heated • violent • fiery | *sometimes disapprov.* **emotional** | *esp. written* **ardent • fervent**

▶ intense/passionate/fierce/heated/emotional **about** sth
▶ a/an intense/passionate/fierce/heated/fiery/emotional **debate**
▶ intense/fierce/violent **opposition**

intention noun [C]

■ *Our intention is to raise public awareness of this issue.*

plan • aim • goal • objective • object • purpose • idea | *fml or law* **intent**

▶ with the intention/aim/goal/objective/object/purpose/idea **of doing** sth
▶ sb's intention/plan/aim/goal/objective/purpose/idea/intent **that...**
▶ **have** a/an intention/plan/aim/goal/objective/object/purpose/idea/intent
● INTENTION OR PLAN? Your **intentions** are what you want to do, esp. in the near future; your **plans** are what you have decided or arranged to do, often, but not always, in the longer term.

interest noun

1 [sing., U] ■ *She showed no interest in the conversation.*

attention • notice • concentration | *fml* **regard**

▶ close/media/personal/special interest/attention

interest

▶ catch/get/grab/lose sb's interest/
  attention
▶ hold/focus sb's interest/
  attention/concentration

2 [U, sing.] ■ *There are many places of
interest around Oxford.*

**attraction • appeal • fascination •
magic • glamour • charm • spell**

▶ a/an interest/attraction/appeal/
  fascination **for** sb/sth
▶ have (a/an) interest/attraction/
  appeal/fascination/magic/
  glamour/charm
▶ hold (a/an) interest/attraction/
  appeal/fascination/magic/charm

3 [C] ■ *Her main interests are music
and gardening.*

hobby • pastime

▶ a popular interest/hobby/pastime
▶ have/share interests/hobbies
▶ take up/pursue a/an interest/
  hobby
● INTEREST, HOBBY OR PASTIME? A
hobby is often more active than an
interest:
✔*His main hobby is football* (= he
plays football). • *His main interest is
football* (= he watches and reads
about football, and may or may
not play it).
Pastime is used when talking about
people in general; when you are
talking about yourself or an
individual it is more usual to use
interest or **hobby**:
✔*Eating out is the national pastime
in France.* ✗ ~~Eating out is the national
hobby/interest in France.~~

4 [U] (finance) ■ *The Gold Account
pays monthly interest of 5.5%.*

**profit • earnings • dividend • return
• surplus** | often disapprov. **gain**

▶ (a) interest/profit/earnings/
  dividend/return/surplus/gain **on/
  from** sth
▶ pay interest/a dividend
▶ a rate of interest/return

interest verb [T]

■ *Politics just doesn't interest me.*

**appeal • attract • fascinate •
intrigue • absorb • rivet • grip** | esp.
written **captivate • enthral •
entrance**

▶ a question/subject interests/
  fascinates/intrigues sb

interested adj.

■ *I'm very interested in history.*

**fascinated • absorbed • engrossed •
attentive** | written **rapt**

■ OPP **uninterested, bored**

▶ interested/absorbed/engrossed/
  rapt **in** sth
▶ interested/absorbed/engrossed **in
  doing** sth
▶ interested/fascinated **to do** sth

interesting verb

■ *a really interesting book*

**fascinating • gripping • absorbing •
stimulating** | esp. written **compelling •
riveting**

■ OPP **boring, dull, uninteresting**

▶ interesting/fascinating **to** sb
▶ interesting/fascinating **that...**
▶ a/an interesting/fascinating/
  gripping/compelling **story/read/
  book**
▶ a/an interesting/fascinating/
  stimulating **experience/
  discussion/idea**

interfere verb [I] (disapprov.)

■ *I wish my mother would stop
interfering and let me make my own
decisions.*

fml **impinge** | disapprov. **meddle •
pry • invade** | infml, disapprov. **muscle
in** | fml, disapprov. **intrude •
encroach**

▶ interfere/meddle **in** sth
▶ interfere in/impinge on/invade/
  intrude on/encroach on sb's
  privacy
▶ interfere in/impinge on/pry into/
  invade/intrude on sb's **life**

international adj. [usu. before
noun]

■ *international trade*

**global • worldwide •
intercontinental** | approx.
cosmopolitan | esp. busin. or journ.
multinational

■ OPP **national, local**

▶ international/global/worldwide
  **attention/campaigns/influence/
  issues/markets**
▶ a/an international/global/
  multinational **company/
  corporation**
▶ a/an international/global/
  cosmopolitan **outlook**

interpretation verb [C, U]

■ *New evidence has led to a different
interpretation of these events.*

**understanding • reading •
definition**

▶ (a) clear/precise/narrow/broad/
  conventional interpretation/
  understanding/definition
▶ a literal interpretation/
  understanding/reading
▶ give/provide/offer a/an
  interpretation/definition
● INTERPRETATION, UNDERSTANDING
OR READING? **Interpretation** is used
esp. about understanding what

happened or what sth means; **understanding** is used esp. about understanding how sth works or what problems are involved; **reading** is used esp. about understanding a written text: *interpretation of data/results/events/ the law/dreams • an understanding of a process/a relationship/an issue • a different reading of the text/story*

interrupt verb

1 [I, T] ■ *Please stop interrupting me!*

disturb • cut in • barge in | *esp. spoken* **bother |** *infml* **chip in |** *fml* **intrude • trouble**

▶ interrupt/disturb sb/cut in/bother sb/chip in/trouble sb **with** sth
▶ be sorry to interrupt sb/disturb sb/cut in/bother sb/intrude/ trouble sb
● **INTERRUPT, DISTURB OR BOTHER?** You usu. **interrupt** sb who is speaking to you or someone else. You can either **disturb** or **bother** sb who is trying to do sth on their own, by talking to them or asking questions. You can also **disturb** (but not **bother** or **interrupt**) sb who is trying to rest, by making a lot of noise.

2 [T] ■ *The game was interrupted twice by rain.*

disrupt • interfere with sth • hold sb /sth back • hamper • hinder • obstruct • upset

▶ interrupt/disrupt/interfere with/ hamper/hinder/obstruct/upset (sb's) **work**
▶ interrupt/disrupt a **meeting**

interval noun

1 [C] *(esp. written)* ■ *After a brief interval, the door opened.*

lapse • meantime | *esp. written* **interlude |** *esp. busin.* **interim**

▶ an interval/interlude **between** A and B
▶ **in** the meantime/interim
▶ a **brief** interval/lapse/interlude

2 [C, usu. pl.] ■ *She ruled for ten years, except for a brief interval.*

time • period • spell • stint • while • span • season • term • run | *esp. BrE, infml* **patch**

▶ a/an interval/time/period/spell/ stint/span/season/term/run/ patch **of** sth
▶ **for** a/an interval/time/period/ spell/stint/while/span/season/ term/run/patch
▶ **during** a/an interval/time/ period/spell/stint/season/term/ run/… patch

intervene verb [I]

■ *A passerby intervened to stop the fight.*

mediate • arbitrate | *fml* **intercede**

▶ intervene/mediate/intercede **on behalf of** sb
▶ intervene/intercede **with** sb
▶ intervene/mediate/arbitrate **between** A and B
● **INTERVENE OR INTERCEDE?** **Intervene** can refer to actions as well as discussions; **intercede** only refers to discussions.

interview noun

1 [C] ■ *I've got a job interview tomorrow.*

audition • screen test | *BrE* **trial |** *AmE* **tryout**

▶ an interview/an audition/trials/ tryouts a screen test **for** sth
▶ **in** an interview/an audition/trials/ tryouts
▶ **have** an interview/an audition/ trials/tryouts/a screen test

2 [C] ■ *She rarely gives interviews to journalists.*

audience • consultation • interrogation

▶ a/an interview/audience/ consultation **with** sb
▶ **have/request/give** sb **/grant** sb a/an interview/audience/ consultation
▶ **carry out/conduct** an interview/ interrogation

interview verb [T]

■ *The police are waiting to interview the injured man.*

question • interrogate • cross-examine • grill • debrief | *esp. journ.* **quiz**

▶ interview/question/interrogate/ cross-examine/grill/debrief/quiz sb **on** sth
▶ interview/question/interrogate/ cross-examine/grill/quiz sb **about** sth
▶ interview/question/interrogate/ cross-examine a **witness**
▶ interview/question/interrogate a **suspect**

introduce verb

1 [T] ■ *Can I introduce my wife?*

fml **present**

▶ introduce/present sb **to** sb

2 [T] ■ *They are introducing the latest technology into schools.*

bring sth in • set/put sth in motion | fml initiate • institute | esp. BrE, fml instigate | esp. busin. launch • phase sth in

▶ introduce/bring in/set in motion/ initiate/institute/instigate/ launch/phase in a **scheme/reform**
▶ introduce/bring in/set in motion/ initiate/institute/instigate/phase in **changes**
▶ introduce/bring in/initiate (a) **legislation/law**

introduction noun

1 [U] ■ The war led to the introduction of compulsory military service.

formation • creation | fml establishment • foundation

▶ the early/gradual/rapid/recent introduction/formation/creation/ establishment of sth
▶ lead to/result in/see the introduction/formation/creation/ establishment/foundation of sth
▶ call for/support/allow (for)/ enable/announce the introduction/formation/creation/ establishment of sth

2 [sing.] (esp. written) ■ This album was my first introduction to modern jazz.

debut | fml initiation • inauguration • induction

▶ an initiation/induction **into** sth

3 [C, U] ■ The guide book has a short introduction by the local vicar.

preface • foreword • prologue | fml preamble

▶ the introduction/preface/ foreword/prologue/preamble **to** a book, etc.
▶ **in** the introduction/preface/ foreword/prologue/preamble
▶ read/write the introduction/a preface/a foreword/a prologue/a preamble

invade verb [I, T]

■ When did the Romans invade Britain?

occupy • conquer • take • capture • seize • attack • storm | fml annex

▶ invade/occupy/conquer/seize/ attack/annex a **country/region**
▶ invade/occupy/conquer/take/ capture/seize/attack/storm a **town/city**
▶ **troops/soldiers** invade/occupy/ take/capture/seize/attack/storm a place
▶ a **country** invades/occupies/ conquers/attacks/annexes a place

invent verb

1 [T] ■ I wish television had never been invented!

design • engineer

▶ invent/design/engineer a **new kind of motor**
▶ invent/design a **new product**
▶ design/engineer a **new car/bridge**
▶ ● INVENT, DESIGN OR ENGINEER? When you **invent** sth it is completely new and nothing of that kind has existed before. You **design** and **engineer** a new version of sth that already exists.

2 [T] ■ He invented a reason for calling her.

make sth up • fabricate • think sth up • come up with sth • devise • trump sth up • coin

▶ invent/make up/fabricate/think up/come up with/devise a **story**
▶ invent/make up/think up/come up with a/an **excuse/name**
▶ invent/make up/coin a **word**

invention noun [C, U]

■ Fax machines were a wonderful invention at the time. ■ the invention of the printing press

innovation • creation • design • development

▶ sb's **new/latest** invention/ innovation/creation/design
▶ a **brilliant** invention/innovation/ design
▶ a/an **ingenious/wonderful** invention/design

investigate verb [I, T]

■ Police are investigating links between the two murders.

explore • look into sth • research • inquire/enquire into sth • delve into sth | esp. journ. probe

▶ investigate/explore/look into/ research/inquire into **what/why/ how/whether...**
▶ investigate/explore/look into/ research/inquire into a **problem/ matter**
▶ investigate/explore/look into/ research/delve into a **subject**

investigation noun [C, U]

■ Police have launched an investigation into the allegations.

inquiry/enquiry • case • survey • study • review • report • check • inquest | journ. probe

▶ a/an investigation/inquiry/ survey/report/inquest/probe **into** sth
▶ an **official** investigation/inquiry/ survey/probe
▶ **carry out** a/an investigation/

inquiry / survey / study / review /
check
▶ a/an investigation / inquiry /
survey / study / review / report /
inquest **finds** / **shows** / **reveals** sth

investment noun [C, U]

■ The arts need more government
investment.

funding • subsidy • grant • backing • sponsorship | fml endowment

▶ investment / funding / a subsidy / a
grant / backing / sponsorship / an
endowment **from** sb / sth
▶ investment / funding / a subsidy / a
grant / backing / sponsorship / an
endowment **for** sth
▶ **get** investment / funding / a
subsidy / a grant / backing /
sponsorship
▶ **receive** / **increase** investment /
funding / a subsidy / a grant /
sponsorship / an endowment

invisible adj.

■ She felt invisible in the crowd.

out of sight • inconspicuous | fml imperceptible

■ OPP visible
▶ invisible / imperceptible **to** sb / sth
▶ **remain** invisible / out of sight /
inconspicuous
▶ **almost** invisible / out of sight /
imperceptible

invite verb [T]

■ Have you been invited to her party?

ask

▶ invite / ask sb **to** / **for** sth
▶ invite / ask sb **in** / **round** / **along** /
over / **out**
▶ invite / ask sb **to do** sth
● INVITE OR ASK? Ask is used esp. to
talk about informal social
meetings. Invite can be used for a
more formal event, such as a
wedding or party. A written
invitation may be given.

involve verb

1 [T] ■ Any investment involves an
element of risk.

mean • entail | fml necessitate

▶ sth involves / means / entails /
necessitates a/an **increase** /
reduction
▶ sth involves / entails **risk**
▶ sth **ordinarily** / **typically** involves /
means sth
● INVOLVE OR ENTAIL? In many cases
you can use either word. However,
a problem might **involve** an
aspect, such as *drugs* or *violence*,
that is not necessary to achieve sth,
but defines the nature of the
problem. Entail cannot be used in
this way:

---

involvement

✓ Many of the crimes involved drugs/
violence. ✗ ~~Many of the crimes
entailed drugs/violence.~~

2 [T] ■ Try to talk to someone who is
not directly involved.

concern • affect

▶ be involved / concerned **in** sth
▶ **directly** / **indirectly** involve /
concern / affect sb / sth
● INVOLVE OR CONCERN? Involve
suggests a greater degree of
physical activity. Concern suggests
a greater degree of interest or
responsibility.

be/get involved phrase

■ I got involved with politics when I
was at college.

take part • take part in (sth) • have/play a part • join | fml engage in • participate • enter • enter into sth

▶ get involved / take part / play a
part / join sb / engage / participate **in**
sth
▶ get involved / join in / enter into sth
with sb / sth
▶ be / get **actively** / **directly** involved
in sth
▶ **actively** / **directly** take part /
participate / engage in sth
● WHICH WORD? You take part or
participate in a particular activity
or event. Be/get involved is a
more general expression to talk
about the kind of activity or
general interest that sb gives their
time to; you might be involved in
politics but would participate/take
part in a political debate. Engage in
sth is used esp. for activities that
are bad in some way: He continued
to engage in criminal activities.

involved adj. [not usu. before
noun]

■ She was deeply involved with the
local hospital.

occupied • active • busy | fml engaged

▶ involved / occupied / busy **with** sth
▶ involved / occupied / active /
engaged **in** sth
▶ **actively** involved / engaged in sth
● INVOLVED OR OCCUPIED? Involved
usu. suggests a personal or
emotional connection; occupied
suggests that sb has a lot to do.

involvement noun [U, C, usu.
sing.]

■ He denied any involvement in
weapons production.

participation • role • part • interest • contribution • input • stake in sth | fml engagement | esp. journ. hand in sth

ironic

▶ involvement/a role/a part/interest/a stake/engagement/a hand **in** sth
▶ involvement/participation/contribution/input **from** sb
▶ **encourage/increase** involvement/participation
● INVOLVEMENT OR PARTICIPATION? **Participation** requires a greater level of choice from the person who is acting in a situation.

ironic adj.

■ There were ironic cheers from the opposition.

satirical | *disapprov.* sarcastic ◆ sardonic | *approv.* wry ◆ dry

■ OPP **sincere**
▶ a/an ironic/satirical/sarcastic/sardonic/wry/dry **comment**
▶ ironic/satirical/sarcastic/sardonic/wry/dry **humour**
▶ a/an ironic/sarcastic/sardonic/wry/dry **tone/smile**

irrational adj.

■ These are just irrational fears.

illogical ◆ unfounded ◆ groundless ◆ unscientific ◆ unjustified | *fml, sometimes disapprov.* unwarranted

■ OPP **rational**
▶ an irrational/illogical **fear**
▶ sb's fears are unjustified/unwarranted
▶ **totally** irrational/illogical/unfounded/groundless/unscientific/unjustified/unwarranted
● IRRATIONAL OR ILLOGICAL? **Irrational** emphasizes that there is no good reason for sth; **illogical** suggests that sb has used a false line of reasoning from facts that do not support their reasoning.

irrelevant adj.

■ Whether I'm married or not is irrelevant.

immaterial | *fml* extraneous | *esp. spoken* beside the point

■ OPP **relevant**
▶ irrelevant/immaterial/extraneous **to** sth
▶ irrelevant/immaterial/beside the point **whether...**
▶ irrelevant/immaterial **that...**

irritable adj.

■ He was tired and irritable.

bad-tempered ◆ moody ◆ sulky ◆ sullen | *infml* grumpy | *written* morose ◆ petulant

■ OPP **good-humoured**
▶ a/an irritable/bad-tempered/moody/sullen/grumpy/morose **man/woman**
▶ a sulky/petulant **child**

irritate verb [T]

■ The way she puts on that accent really irritates me.

annoy ◆ exasperate ◆ rile ◆ frustrate | *infml* get on sb's nerves ◆ bug | *BrE, infml* wind sb up | *fml* displease

■ OPP **pacify**
▶ It irritates me/annoys me/riles me/gets on my nerves/bugs me **that/when...**
▶ What irritates me/annoys me/riles me/frustrates me/gets on my nerves **is the way that the fact that...**
▶ really irritate sb/annoy sb/rile sb/get on sb's nerves/bug sb/wind sb up

irritated adj.

■ She was getting more and more irritated by his comments.

annoyed ◆ exasperated | *esp. BrE* cross | *esp. spoken* put out

▶ irritated/annoyed/exasperated/cross **with** sb
▶ irritated/annoyed/cross/put out **at** sth
▶ irritated/annoyed/cross/put out **that...**
▶ irritated/annoyed/put out **to find/see...**
● IRRITATED OR ANNOYED? You are usu. **irritated** by things that other people do or say. You can be **annoyed** with yourself or at things you have to do.

irritating adj.

■ The way he stares at me is extremely irritating.

annoying ◆ trying ◆ tiresome ◆ frustrating ◆ infuriating ◆ maddening ◆ galling | *esp. AmE, infml* pesky

▶ irritating/annoying/trying/tiresome/frustrating/infuriating/galling **for** sb
▶ a/an irritating/annoying/tiresome/infuriating/pesky **man**
▶ a/an irritating/annoying/tiresome/infuriating/maddening **habit**
● IRRITATING OR ANNOYING? It is usu. other people or their habits that are **irritating**; **annoying** can also describe facts and situations that make you feel annoyed.

isolate verb [T, often passive]

■ He was isolated from the other prisoners.

cut sb/sth off ◆ quarantine | *fml* segregate

▶ isolate/cut off/segregate sb/sth **from** sb/sth else
▶ isolate **yourself**/cut **yourself** off
▶ isolate/quarantine/segregate a **patient**
▶ a **community** is isolated/cut off/segregated

issue noun

1 [C] ■ *The party was divided on this issue.*

matter • question • concern • subject

▶ a/an issue/matter/question **relating to**/**concerning** sth
▶ a **key**/**major**/**serious**/**general** issue/matter/question/concern/subject
▶ a **political**/**moral**/**technical** issue/matter/question/concern/subject
▶ **raise**/**deal with**/**address**/**tackle**/**discuss**/**consider**/**examine**/**explore**/**focus on** a/an issue/matter/question/concern/subject

2 [C] ■ *Anger is a big issue for her.*

problem • difficulty • complication | *esp. spoken* **the matter |** *disapprov.* **trouble |** *usu. approv.* **challenge**

▶ (a/an) issue/problem/difficulty/complication/the matter/trouble **with** sth
▶ (a/an) issue/problem/difficulty/challenge **for** sb
▶ **have** issues/problems/difficulties/trouble
▶ **make** an issue of sth/difficulties/trouble

3 [C] ■ *The article appeared in issue 25.*

edition • volume • part • unit

▶ the **first**/**second**/**next** issue/edition/volume/part/unit
▶ the **January**/**February**, etc. issue/edition of sth
▶ **produce** a/an issue/edition/volume/part
▶ **bring out** a/an issue/edition/volume
● ISSUE, EDITION OR VOLUME? Use **issue** for magazines and journals; use **edition** for newspapers. All the issues for one year belong to a **volume**.

issue verb

1 [T] ■ *The police issued an appeal for witnesses.*

publish • release • print • circulate

▶ issue/release/circulate sth **to** sb
▶ issue/publish/release/print/circulate a **report**/**details**
▶ issue/publish/release/print a **document**/**statement**/**description**
▶ issue/publish/print an **apology**
● ISSUE, PUBLISH OR RELEASE? Use any of these words to talk about

information being formally made available to the public. **Issue** has the widest range of collocates and is used esp. with words relating to announcements and legal notices. **Publish**, but not issue or release, is also used to talk about letters and articles.

2 [T, often passive] ■ *We can issue a passport within a day.*

supply • provide • give • allocate • equip

▶ issue/supply/give/allocate sth **to** sb
▶ issue/supply/provide/equip sb **with** sth
▶ issue/supply/give/provide **equipment**/**details**/**information**

item noun

1 [C] ■ *What's the next item on the agenda?*

issue • matter • question • topic • subject • concern

▶ a/an item/issue/matter/question/concern **relating to**/**concerning** sth
▶ an **important** item/issue/matter/question/topic/subject/concern
▶ **raise**/**deal with**/**tackle**/**discuss**/**consider** a/an item/issue/matter/question/topic/subject/concern

2 [C] ■ *Can I pay for each item separately?*

thing • object | *fml* **entity • commodity |** *tech.* **artefact/artifact**

▶ a **precious**/**valuable** item/thing/object/commodity/artefact
▶ a **separate** item/thing/object/entity
▶ **produce**/**manufacture** a/an item/thing/object/commodity/artefact

Jj

jab verb [T, I]

■ *She jabbed him in the ribs with her finger.*

prod • poke • nudge

▶ jab/prod/poke/nudge sb/sth **with** your finger/a stick/a rifle
▶ jab/prod/poke **at** sth (with sth)
▶ jab/prod/poke/nudge sb **in** sth

jacket noun [C]

■ *His jacket hung over the back of the chair.*

coat • blazer • tails • raincoat | *BrE* **anorak • mac |** *esp. AmE* **tuxedo |** *esp. AmE, infml* **tux**

jail

▶ a long/short/heavy/light jacket/coat
▶ **wear/put on/take off/remove** a/an jacket/coat/blazer/tails/raincoat/anorak/mac/tuxedo/tux
▶ **do up/undo** a/an jacket/coat/blazer/raincoat/anorak/mac
● JACKET OR COAT? **Jacket** can describe a piece of clothing worn indoors or one worn outdoors; a **coat** is usu. only worn outdoors. A **jacket** usu. comes down to the waist or hips, but not below; a **coat** is usu. hip-length or longer.

jail (*BrE* also **gaol**) *noun* [U, C]
■ She faces jail for child cruelty.

prison • *BrE* **detention centre** | *AmE* **detention center** • **penitentiary** • **jailhouse** • **correctional facility**

▶ **in** jail/prison
▶ **in a** jail/prison/detention centre/penitentiary/jailhouse/correctional facility
▶ **go to/be sent to/be released from/get out of** jail/prison
● JAIL OR PRISON? In *BrE* there is little difference between these words. **Prison** can be used to describe the system, as well as the buildings or institution:
✔ the prison service/system ✗ the jail service/system
In *AmE* a **jail** is usu. smaller than a **prison**.

jail *verb* [T, usu. passive]
■ He was jailed for two months.

send sb to prison • **hold** • **intern** • **imprison** • **detain** | *infml* **lock sb up/away** | *fml* **incarcerate**

▶ jail/send sb to prison/hold/intern sb/imprison sb/detain sb/lock sb up **for** sth
▶ jail/hold/detain/imprison sb **without trial/charge**

jealousy *noun* [U, C]
■ Her promotion aroused intense jealousy among her colleagues.

envy

▶ jealousy/envy **of** sb
▶ **feel/arouse** jealousy/envy
▶ **a feeling/pang/stab/twinge of** jealousy/envy
● JEALOUSY OR ENVY? **Jealousy** is nastier than **envy** and can cause sb to behave in an unkind way. People can enjoy *inspiring/arousing* envy but they do not like to *cause/provoke* jealousy in sb else.

job *noun*
1 [C] ■ He's trying to get a job in teaching.

work • **employment** • **career** • **profession** • **trade** • **vacancy** • **opening** • **occupation** | *esp. BrE* **post** • **appointment** • **posting** | *fml* **position**

▶ (a) **full-time/part-time/permanent** job/work/employment/career/occupation/post/appointment/position
▶ **have** (a/an) job/work/employment/career/profession/trade/vacancy/opening/occupation/occupation/post/appointment/posting/position
▶ **look for** (a/an) job/work/employment/career/occupation/post/posting/position
▶ **apply for** a job/vacancy/post/posting/position

2 [C] ■ I've got various jobs to do around the house.

task • **work** • **duty** • **chore** • **housework** • **errand** • **mission** • **assignment**

▶ (a) **routine** job/task/work/duties/chore/mission/assignment
▶ (a) **household/domestic** job/task/work/duties/chore
▶ **have** a job/a task/work/a chore/the housework/an errand/an assignment **to do**
▶ **get on with** a job/a task/your work/a chore/the housework/an assignment
● JOB OR TASK? A **job** may be one of several small things you have to do, esp. in the home; a **task** may be more difficult and may require more thought.

3 [C, usu. sing.] (*esp. spoken*) ■ It's not my job to lock up!

duty • **responsibility**

▶ **have** the job/a duty/a responsibility

join *verb*
1 [T, I] ■ Join the two sections of pipe together.

connect • **link**

■ OPP **separate**

▶ join/connect/link A **to/and** B
▶ join/link (sth) **up**
▶ join/connect **pieces**
▶ join/connect/link sth **to** a computer

2 [T, I] ■ I've joined a dance class.

be/get involved • **take part** • **join in** (sth) | *fml* **enter** • **participate**

■ OPP **leave**

▶ join sb/get involved/take part/participate **in** sth
● JOIN OR ENTER? When you **join** sth you become a member of an organization or club. You **enter** politics, professions such as law

and medicine, and institutions such as universities and Parliament.

joint adj. [only before noun]
■ The report was a joint effort.

common • collective • communal • shared • cooperative

■ OPP separate
▶ joint/common/collective/communal/shared **ownership/responsibility**
▶ (a) joint/collective/communal/cooperative **effort/action**
▶ a joint/collective/communal **decision**

joke noun [C]
■ She's always cracking jokes.

quip • prank • pun | infml gag • wisecrack • one-liner

▶ a joke/quip/gag/wisecrack **about sb/sth**
▶ make a joke/quip/pun/wisecrack
▶ do sth as a joke/prank
▶ tell/crack a joke/gag

joke verb [I]
■ Don't worry—I was only joking.

quip | infml kid • wisecrack | esp. BrE, infml have sb on | fml or humorous jest

▶ joke/kid/jest/have sb on **about sth**
▶ I'm, he's, etc. **only/just** joking/kidding/having you on.
▶ **You must be** joking/kidding!
● JOKE OR KID? Both words are often used in the progressive tenses, meaning to say sth that is not true. Kid is used more in spoken and AmE.

journalist noun [C]
■ I spoke to a journalist from 'The Guardian'.

reporter • broadcaster • correspondent • columnist • reviewer • contributor • editor • writer | infml, disapprov. hack

▶ a news/sports journalist/reporter/broadcaster/correspondent/columnist/editor/writer
▶ a newspaper/magazine/financial journalist/reporter/correspondent/columnist/editor
▶ an investigative journalist/reporter
▶ tell journalists/reporters/a broadcaster
● JOURNALIST OR REPORTER? A reporter is sb who visits places to write news reports. A journalist is sb who works on a newspaper or magazine, or a radio or television programme, as a reporter, writer, photographer, designer, etc.

journey noun [C]
■ They continued their journey on foot.

trip • tour • expedition • pilgrimage • excursion • outing • travels | esp. BrE day out | esp. written voyage

▶ a/an journey/trip/tour/expedition/pilgrimage/excursion/outing/day out/voyage to sth/somewhere
▶ go on/be on/come back from/return from a/an journey/trip/tour/expedition/pilgrimage/excursion/outing/your travels/day out/voyage
▶ make a/an journey/trip/tour/expedition/pilgrimage/excursion/outing/day out/voyage
● JOURNEY OR TRIP? A trip is usu. a journey to a place and back again and is used esp. when you travel for pleasure or for a particular purpose; a journey is usu. one-way, and is often used when the travelling takes a long time and is difficult: a day/school/business trip • It was a difficult journey across the mountains.

joy noun
1 [U] ■ I'll never forget the pure joy I felt at being free again.

delight • bliss • ecstasy • euphoria • happiness

■ OPP grief
▶ sb's joy/delight/euphoria at sth
▶ sheer/pure joy/delight/bliss/ecstasy/happiness
▶ feel/be filled with joy/delight/ecstasy/happiness
● JOY, DELIGHT OR BLISS? Joy and delight are livelier feelings than bliss. You can jump/weep for joy or scream/whoop with delight. Bliss is more peaceful: married/domestic bliss

2 [C] ■ the joys and sorrows of childhood

delight • pleasure • privilege | BrE honour | AmE honor | esp. spoken treat

■ OPP grief, sorrow
▶ the joys/delights/pleasures of sth
▶ It's a joy/delight/pleasure/privilege/honour/treat to do sth.
▶ a joy/delight/pleasure to see/find/behold/watch
● JOY, PLEASURE OR DELIGHT? A joy or delight is greater than a pleasure; a person, esp. a child, can be a joy or delight but not a pleasure.

judge noun
1 [C] ■ The case comes before a judge next week.

judge

magistrate | *fml* Justice of the Peace/JP | *law* the bench

- before a judge/a magistrate/a Justice of the Peace/a JP/the bench
- appoint sb as a judge/as a magistrate/as a Justice of the Peace/as a JP/to the bench
- a judge/magistrate orders/awards/adjourns/upholds/considers/dismisses/decides/finds sth
- a judge/magistrate sentences sb

2 [C] ■ *The winner was chosen by a panel of judges.*

referee • umpire | *BrE* examiner | *esp. in AmE* moderator | *infml* ref | *fml* arbiter

- an independent judge/examiner
- act as (a/an) judge/referee/moderator/arbiter
- the judge/referee/umpire decides/awards sth

judge verb

1 [I, T] ■ *The tour was judged a great success.*

assess • evaluate • rate • gauge | *infml* size sb/sth up

- judge/assess/evaluate/rate sb/sth as/on/according to sth
- judge/assess/evaluate/rate/gauge how…
- judge/assess/evaluate/gauge what/whether…
- judge/assess/evaluate/gauge the extent/significance/success/effectiveness/effect/impact of sth
- judge/assess/evaluate/gauge sth's progress/performance/quality/merits/potential

2 [T] ■ *It was difficult to judge the speed of the vehicle.*

estimate • gauge • guess • reckon • assess • calculate | *esp. AmE* figure | *fml* extrapolate

- judge/estimate/gauge/guess/reckon/assess/calculate/extrapolate sth from sth
- judge/estimate/gauge/guess/reckon/calculate/figure/extrapolate that…
- judge/estimate/gauge/guess/assess/calculate/figure how much/how many/how far, etc.
- judge/estimate/gauge/guess/assess/calculate the amount/value/size/distance
- ● JUDGE OR ESTIMATE? People estimate future costs and lengths of time which cannot be calculated exactly by thinking carefully about the information available; people judge distances and speeds by

using their experience as a quick guide.

3 [T, I] ■ *He was judged guilty of murder.*

adjudicate | *law* decide

- adjudicate/decide on/in sth
- judge/adjudicate/decide a case
- adjudicate/decide a dispute/matter

judgement (*esp. AmE* judgment) noun [C, U]

■ *In her judgement, it was the wrong thing to do.*

opinion • assessment • evaluation • view • point of view • belief • conviction | *fml* estimation

- sb's judgement/opinion/view/beliefs/conviction about sb/sth
- in sb's judgement/opinion/view/assessment/view/estimation
- the judgement/opinion/assessment/view/point of view/belief/conviction that…

jumble verb [T, usu. passive]

■ *Books, shoes and clothes were jumbled together.*

mix sth up • shuffle | *esp. BrE* muddle

- jumble/mix/muddle things up
- be jumbled/muddled up together
- jumble/mix up the letters in a word/words in a sentence

jump verb

1 [I, T] ■ *He jumped over the fence.*

hurdle • vault • hop • bounce | *written* leap

- jump/hurdle/vault/hop/leap over sth
- jump/hop/bounce/leap up and down
- jump/hurdle/vault/leap a fence/hedge/wall

2 [i] (always used with an adv. or prep.) ■ *She jumped up and ran off.*

leap • spring | *infml* hop

- jump/leap/spring/hop up/down/out
- jump/leap/spring to your feet/into action/in the air
- jump/hop into bed/into your car/onto your bike
- jump/hop on a bus/train/plane
- Do you want a ride? Jump/Hop in.
- ● WHICH WORD? Jump is used most often for quick body movements: *jump up/to your feet.* Leap is used most for longer distances and more figurative actions: *leap into action/to sb's defence.* Spring is used esp. about animals. Hop is usu. used for getting into or out of vehicles.

3 [I] ■ *A loud bang made me jump.*

flinch • cower • cringe | *written*
recoil • shrink

► jump/flinch/cringe/recoil **at** sth
► **make** sb jump/flinch/cower/
  cringe/recoil
● JUMP OR FLINCH? You **jump** with
  your whole body, esp. because you
  are surprised. **Flinching** may be a
  smaller movement of the face or
  part of the body, caused by pain or
  fear.

junction *noun* [C] *(esp. BrE)*
■ *Turn left at the next junction.*

crossroads • exit | *BrE* **turning •**
roundabout | *esp. AmE* **turn |** *AmE or*
fml, *BrE* **intersection**

► the junction/intersection **with...**
► a **busy** junction/crossroads/
  roundabout/intersection
► **come to** a/an junction/
  crossroads/exit/roundabout/
  intersection
► **take** the turning/turn/exit

justice *noun* [U]
■ *Our laws must be based on principles*
of justice.

fairness • fair play • equality | *fml*
equity

■ OPP **injustice**
► justice/fairness/fair play/equality/
  equity **for**
► **social/economic** justice/fairness/
  equality/equity
► **ensure** justice/fairness/fair play/
  equality/equity
► **guarantee** justice/fairness/
  equality/equity

justified *adj.* [not usu. before
noun]
■ *Is the death penalty ever justified?*

justifiable • right • acceptable

■ OPP **unjustified**
► justified/justifiable/right **to do** sth
► justified/right **in doing** sth
► **perfectly** justified/justifiable/
  right/acceptable
● JUSTIFIED OR JUSTIFIABLE? A person
  or action can be **justified**; an
  action, feeling or reason can be
  justifiable.

justify *verb* [T]
■ *How can the banks justify paying*
such huge bonuses?

defend • explain • account for sth

► justify/defend/explain/account
  for sth **to** sb
► justify/explain/account for **what/**
  why/how ...
► justify/defend/explain **yourself**
► justify/defend/explain/account
  for **sb's behaviour/a decision**

K k

keen *adj. (esp. BrE)*
■ *Dan was keen to help.*

eager • enthusiastic • avid • anxious
• hungry | *infml* **mad |** *fml* **zealous**

■ OPP **reluctant**
► keen/eager/avid/anxious/
  hungry/mad **for** sth
► keen/mad **on** sth
► keen/eager/enthusiastic/anxious
  to do sth
► keen/eager/anxious **that...**
► a/an eager/keen/enthusiastic/avid
  collector/fan

keep *verb*

1 [I, T] ■ *We managed to keep warm.*

stay | *fml* **remain**

► keep/stay/remain **awake/calm/**
  cheerful/cool/dry/fine/healthy/
  quiet/silent
► keep/stay **close/still/warm**
► stay/remain **alert/alive/asleep/**
  loyal/safe/the same/a secret/
  shut/sober/upright

2 [T, I] *(esp. spoken)* ■ *Keep smiling!*

continue • go on with sth/**go on**
doing sth **• keep sth up/keep up**
with sth **• press ahead/on |** *esp.*
spoken **carry (sth) on • stick with** sb/
sth

■ OPP **stop, give** sth **up**
► keep/continue/go on/keep
  up/press ahead/carry on/stick
  with sth
► keep/continue/carry on/carry on/
  press ahead with **doing** sth
► keep/continue/go on/carry on
  fighting/working/talking/
  improving sth/**believing/**
  building sth

3 [T] ■ *I've kept all her letters.*

hold onto sth **• save |** *fml* **retain**

■ OPP **lose, throw** sth **away**
► keep/retain **control** (of sth)
► **still** keep/hold onto/retain sth
● KEEP OR RETAIN? **Retain** is formal
  and not used in spoken English. It
  often suggests that the thing that
  you keep will be useful in the
  future. **Keep** is a more general
  word.

4 [T] *(esp. BrE)* ■ *I've kept two seats for*
us at the front.

save • reserve • hold

■ OPP **give** sth **up**
► keep/save/reserve/hold sth **for**
  sb/sth
► keep/save/reserve/hold a **seat/**
  place for sb/sth

▶ keep/save some **food** for sb
● KEEP, SAVE OR RESERVE? Reserve is used esp. when sth is officially saved for sb/sth. Keep and save are more often used if sth is saved for you unofficially, for example by a friend.

5 [T] ■ *Where do you keep the sugar?*

store • hoard • stock up • stockpile | *infml* **stash**
───────────────
▶ keep/store/hoard/stock up on/ stockpile **food**
▶ keep/store/stockpile **weapons**
▶ keep/hoard/stash **money**

6 [T] ■ *My aunt kept chickens in her back yard.*

breed • rear • raise
───────────────
▶ keep/breed/rear/raise sth **for** sb
▶ keep/breed/rear/raise **animals/ cattle/horses/sheep**
▶ keep/breed/rear/raise sth **in captivity**

7 [T] ■ *She kept her promise to visit them.*

carry sth out • stand by sth | *AmE* **follow through** | *BrE, fml* **honour** | *AmE* **honor** | *esp. journ. or busin.* **deliver**
───────────────
■ OPP **break**
▶ carry out/follow through on/honour/deliver on a **promise**
▶ keep/stand by/follow through on/ honour **your word**
▶ keep to/stand by/follow through on/honour an **agreement**
▶ keep to/carry out/stand by/follow through on a **plan**
● KEEP OR HONOUR? Honour is much more formal than keep in most cases. You can **keep** but not **honour** an *appointment* or *engagement*; you can **honour** but not **keep** sb's *wishes*.

8 [T] ■ *Keep a record of your child's illnesses.*

hold • store | *fml* **retain**
───────────────
▶ keep/hold/store/retain **information/data**
▶ keep/hold a **record/records**
▶ still/no longer keep/hold/store/ retain sth

9 [T] (*BrE*) ■ *She doesn't earn enough to keep a family.*

support • provide for sb • maintain
───────────────
▶ keep/support/provide for/ maintain a **family/children/wife/ husband**
▶ keep/support/provide for/ maintain **yourself**
● WHICH WORD? You can **provide for** sb on a continuous basis or by making a large one-off payment. If you **keep, support** or **maintain** sb,

you provide for them on a continuous basis over a period of time.

key *noun*
1 [C, usu. sing.] ■ *The key to success is preparation.*

answer • solution
───────────────
▶ the key/answer/solution **to** sth
▶ look for/find/provide/offer the **key/an answer/a solution**

2 [C] ■ *Press the return key.*

button • switch • control
───────────────
▶ a key/button/switch **on** sth
▶ a **control** key/button/switch
▶ **press/hit** a key/button/switch

key *adj.* [usu. before noun]
■ *The key issue is taxation.*

main • major • essential • central • principal • prime • primary • chief • predominant | *infml* **number one**
───────────────
■ OPP **secondary**
▶ be key/essential/central **to** sth
▶ the key/main/major/essential/ central/principal/prime/primary/ chief/predominant **purpose/ source/factor**
▶ the key/main/major/essential/ central/principal/prime/primary/ chief **aim/function/objective/ task/consideration**

kid *noun* [C] (*infml*)
■ *He's just a kid. You can't expect him to understand.*

child • boy • girl • toddler • baby • teenager | *infml* **youngster** | *esp. BrE, infml* **lad** | *esp. AmE, infml* **teen** | *often disapprov.* **youth** | *infml, disapprov.* **brat** | *fml or tech.* **infant** | *law* **minor • juvenile**
───────────────
■ OPP **grown-up, adult**
▶ a **young** kid/child/boy/girl/ baby/teenager/lad/infant
▶ a **spoiled** kid/child/brat
▶ **look after/take care of** a kid/ child/baby
● KID OR CHILD? Kid is much more frequent in informal and spoken AmE. Child is not often used of sb older than about 12; above that age you can call them *kids, teenagers, young people, girls, youths* or *lads*.

kidnap *verb* [T]
■ *The men were kidnapped by terrorists.*

abduct | *esp. journ.* **seize**
───────────────
▶ kidnap/abduct/seize your/sb's **son/daughter/child**

kill *verb* [T, I]
■ *Two boys were killed in the crash.*

murder • execute • assassinate • shoot | _infml_ **take sb/sth out • finish sb/sth off** | _infml, humorous_ **bump sb off** | _fml_ **eliminate** | _AmE, esp. journ._ **slay**

▸ **kill/murder/assassinate/shoot sb in cold blood**
▸ **brutally kill/murder/slay sb**

killer _noun_ [C]
■ _Police are hunting his killer._

murderer • assassin • serial killer • gunman • sniper | _infml_ **hit man**

▸ a **notorious** killer/murderer/gunman
▸ a **professional/hired/contract** killer/assassin/hit man
▸ **hunt/track down/catch** a killer/murderer

killing _noun_ [C, usu. pl.] (_esp. journ._)
■ _Refugees brought accounts of mass killings._

murder • assassination • massacre • slaughter • bloodshed • carnage • euthanasia • extermination • genocide | _law_ **manslaughter** | _esp. AmE, law_ **homicide** | _esp. AmE, journ._ **slaying**

▸ (a) **mass** killing/murder/slaughter/extermination/slaying
▸ **prevent** (a/an) killing/murder/assassination/massacre/slaughter/bloodshed/genocide
▸ **witness** a/an killing/murder/assassination/massacre/slaughter/carnage/genocide/slaying
● **KILLING OR MURDER? Murder** usu. refers to the killing of one person; **killing** is usu. used in the plural about acts during a war.

kind _noun_ [C, U]
■ _They play music of all kinds._

type • form • variety • style • brand • category • class • version • nature | _esp. BrE_ **sort** | _fml_ **genre**

▸ a **kind**/type/form/variety/style/brand/category/class/version/sort/genre **of** sth
▸ a **different/the same** kind/type/form/variety/style/brand/category/class/version/nature/sort/genre
▸ **various** kinds/types/forms/styles/categories/versions/sorts/genres
▸ a/the/that kind/type/sort **of thing**
● **KIND, TYPE OR SORT? Kind** is the most frequent word in this group; **sort** is used more in BrE. **Type** is slightly more formal and used more in official, scientific or academic contexts.

kind _adj._
■ _It was kind of you to help._

generous • considerate • thoughtful • caring | _esp. spoken_ **good • sweet • nice** | _esp. BrE, esp. spoken_ **lovely** | _fml_ **benevolent • benign**

■ **OPP** unkind, cruel

▸ **kind**/generous/considerate/good/nice/benevolent **to** sb
▸ **be kind**/generous/considerate/thoughtful/good/sweet/nice **of** sb (**to do** sth)
▸ a **kind**/generous/considerate/thoughtful/caring/good/sweet/nice/lovely/benevolent **man/woman/person**

king _noun_ [C]
■ _The King of Spain attended the ceremony._

emperor • monarch • ruler • the crown • regent | _fml_ **sovereign**

▸ **under** a/an king/emperor/monarch/ruler
▸ **become** king/emperor/monarch/ruler/regent
▸ a/an king/emperor/monarch **reigns/rules**

knife _noun_ [C]
■ _A sharp knife is essential for carving._

blade • dagger • scalpel • machete • cleaver • penknife • switchblade

▸ a **sharp** knife/blade/dagger/penknife
▸ **cut** sth with a knife/blade/scalpel/machete/penknife
▸ **stab** sb/sth with a knife/blade/dagger
▸ **chop** sth with a knife/machete/cleaver

knock _verb_
1 [I] ■ _He knocked on the window to get my attention._

rap • tap • drum

▸ **knock**/rap/tap **at** sth
▸ **knock**/rap/tap/drum **on/with** sth
▸ **knock/rap loudly**

2 [T, I] ■ _The blow knocked him senseless._

hit • bang • bump | _infml_ **bash** | _fml_ **strike**

▸ **knock**/hit/bang/bump/bash **against** sb/sth
▸ **knock**/bang/bump/bash **into** sb/sth

knock sth down _phrasal verb_
■ _They knocked the wall down._

demolish • pull sth down • raze • level • flatten | _sometimes disapprov._ **tear sth down • bulldoze**

■ **OPP** build, put sth up

know

▶ knock down/demolish/pull down/level/flatten/tear down a **building/house**

▶ knock down/demolish/pull down/tear down a **factory/wall**

▶ raze/level/flatten/bulldoze an **area**

● **WHICH WORD? Knock sth down**, **demolish** and **pull sth down** are all neutral terms; **tear sth down** can suggest unnecessary violence was used, or that the speaker has negative feelings about what was done.

know *verb*

1 [T] (not used in the progressive tenses) ■ *I know exactly how you feel.*

realize • appreciate

▶ **without** knowing/realizing/appreciating sth

▶ know/realize/appreciate **that...**

▶ know/realize/appreciate **what/how/why...**

● **KNOW OR REALIZE?** To **realize** means to become or be aware of sth. To **know** is to be aware of it: **know** can mean 'become aware' if it happens in a single moment; however, if the process of becoming aware takes any time, use **realize**:
  ✔ *The moment I walked in the room I realized/knew something was wrong.* ■ *I soon/quickly/gradually realized my mistake.* ✗ *I soon/quickly/gradually knew my mistake.*

2 [T,I] ■ *I know my keys are here somewhere.*

guarantee | spoken bet

▶ know/guarantee/bet **that...**

▶ you **can** guarantee/bet (that...)

knowledge *noun*

1 [U, sing.] ■ *He has no specialist knowledge of the subject.*

understanding • experience • learning • scholarship • wisdom • enlightenment • lore

■ OPP **ignorance**

▶ knowledge/learning/wisdom/enlightenment **about** sth

▶ **practical** knowledge/understanding/experience/wisdom

▶ **acquire** knowledge/understanding/experience/learning/wisdom

2 [U] ■ *She sent the letter without my knowledge.*

awareness • consciousness • realization | fml or tech. perception

■ OPP **ignorance**

▶ the knowledge/an awareness/a consciousness/the realization/a perception **of** sth

▶ the knowledge/an awareness/a consciousness/the realization/a perception **that...**

▶ **develop/increase** sb's knowledge/awareness/perception

LI

label *noun* [C]

■ *The label says it's 100% cotton.*

tag • sticker

▶ a price label/tag/sticker

▶ a name label/tag

▶ have/attach/put on/stick on a label/tag/sticker

▶ The label/tag/sticker **says...**

label *verb* [T, often passive]

■ *Each box was labelled with a code number.*

mark • tag • flag

▶ label/mark/tag/flag sth **with** sth

▶ label/mark **boxes/bags**

▶ label/mark sth **clearly/carefully**

● **LABEL OR MARK?** When you say sth is **labelled**, you do not need to give more details if the context is clear; when you use **mark**, you usu. say exactly how sth is marked: *The path is marked on the map in red.* • *Make sure your luggage is clearly labelled* (= with your name and address).

labour *(BrE)* *(AmE* **labor***) noun* [U]

■ *a lifetime of hard manual labour*

work • service | disapprov. drudgery | infml, disapprov. slog | lit. toil

■ OPP **ease**

▶ **hard** labour/work/slog/toil

▶ **manual/physical/honest/unremitting** labour/work/toil

▶ **hours/years/a lifetime of** labour/work/service/drudgery/toil

lack *noun* [U, sing.]

■ *a lack of food/money/skills*

absence • shortage • scarcity • shortfall | fml deficiency • deficit

■ OPP *fml* **abundance**

▶ **have/suffer from** a lack/absence/shortage/deficiency/deficit

▶ **face** a lack/shortage/shortfall/deficit

▶ **There is no** lack/shortage/scarcity/deficiency of sth

lacklustre *(BrE)* *(AmE* **lackluster***) adj.*

■ *a lacklustre performance*

unimaginative • bland • banal • wooden • pedestrian • tired • stale

■ OPP **inspired, dynamic**
▶ a lacklustre/**wooden** performance
▶ a bland/**pedestrian** affair
▶ tired/**stake** jokes

lady noun [C]
■ There's a lady at the door.

woman | fml **female**

■ OPP **gentleman**
▶ a/an young/old/black/white lady/woman/female
▶ a/an middle-aged/old/elderly lady/woman
▶ a/an married/single/unmarried lady/woman

lake noun [C]
■ Let's go for a swim in the lake.

reservoir • loch • lagoon • pond • pool • waters

▶ (a) deep lake/reservoir/loch/lagoon/pond/pool/waters
▶ the edge/surface/bottom/middle of the lake/reservoir/loch/lagoon/pond/pool

lamp noun [C]
■ She switched off the lamp.

light • lantern | BrE **torch** | esp. AmE **flashlight**

▶ switch on/off a lamp/light/torch/flashlight
▶ light a lamp/lantern
▶ a lamp/light/lantern/torch shines
▶ carry a lamp/light/lantern/torch/flashlight

land noun

1 [U] ■ We travelled by land.

earth • ground | lit. **soil**

■ OPP **sea**
▶ reach land/the ground
● LAND, EARTH OR GROUND? Ground is the normal word for the solid surface that you walk on when you are not in a building; earth is used when you want to draw attention to the rock, soil, etc. that the ground is made of; land is only used when you want to contrast it with the sea:
✓the earth/ground beneath our feet
✗ the land beneath our feet
✓feel the earth/ground shake ✗ feel the land shake
✓travel by land ✗ travel by earth/ground

2 [U] ■ an area of rich, fertile land

soil • ground • earth

▶ marshy land/soil/ground
▶ dig the land/soil/ground/earth
▶ cultivate/till/fertilize/drain the land/soil/ground

3 [U] ■ The price of land is rising.

farmland • estate | esp. AmE **real estate** | fml **lands**

▶ on land/farmland/an estate/real estate/sb's lands
▶ own/buy/sell land/farmland/an estate/real estate
▶ a piece of land/farmland/real estate

land verb [I, T]
■ The aircraft landed safely.

touch down • come down • bring sth down • settle • perch | written **come to rest** | lit. **alight**

■ OPP **take off**
▶ land/touch down/come down/bring sth down/settle/perch/come to rest/alight **on** sth
▶ land/touch down/come down/bring sth down/come to rest **at/in** sth
▶ land/touch down/come down/bring sth down/come to rest **safely**

landscape noun [U]
■ The mountains dominate the landscape.

countryside • scenery • country • the land | written **terrain** | tech. **topography**

▶ the surrounding landscape/countryside/scenery/country/land/terrain
▶ open landscape/countryside/country/land/terrain
▶ protect the landscape/countryside/land

lane noun [C]
■ a quiet country lane

road • alley • street • avenue | BrE **terrace** | AmE **boulevard**

▶ in the lane/road/alley/street/avenue
▶ a narrow lane/road/alley/street/terrace
▶ turn into a/an lane/road/alley/street/avenue/boulevard

language noun

1 [C, U] ■ Italian is my first language.

dialect | fml **idiom** | lit. or old-fash. **tongue**

▶ speak **in** a/an language/dialect/idiom/tongue
▶ sb's native language/dialect/tongue
▶ speak/understand/use/learn/study a language/dialect

2 [U] ■ The document was written in very formal language.

► the last/final/closing/later/latter/
  ultimate **stage/phase**
► sb's/sth's last/final/closing/later/
  latter **years**
► the last/final/closing **remark/
  chapter/minutes**

2 ■ *We went to Greece last year.*

past • previous | *fml* **preceding**

■ OPP **first, next**
► the last/past/previous/preceding
  **few days/week/month/year/
  century**
► the last/previous **page/chapter/
  time/visit/meeting/war**
● **LAST OR PAST?** You can only use
  past about a period of time that
  has just gone by; it must be used
  with the or a determiner such as
  this:
  ✓*The past week has been very busy.*
  • *Last week was very busy.*
  Past is not used about particular
  dates, or about things:
  ✓*The critics hated her last book.*
  ✗ *The critics hated her past book.*

late adj. [not usu. before noun]
■ *My flight was an hour late.*

overdue • slow | *written* **belated**

■ OPP **early, on time, punctual**
► late/overdue **for sth**
► late/slow **in doing sth**
► **two weeks/a year** late/overdue

later adj.

1 [only before noun] ■ *The game has
been postponed to a later date.*

future • next • the following | *fml*
subsequent

■ OPP **earlier**
► later/future/subsequent **months/
  decades/generations**
► later/future/subsequent **events**
► a later/a future/the next/a
  subsequent **time**
● **LATER OR FUTURE?** Later is used esp.
  about a stage in an event, process
  or account; **future** is used esp.
  about situations or developments
  in the future: *a later stage/phase/
  addition • future plans/prospects/
  trends*

2 ■ *the later part of the seventeenth
century*

**latter • final • last • closing •
ultimate**

■ OPP **earlier**
► later/latter/final/last/closing/
  ultimate **stage/phase**
► sb's/sth's later/latter/final/last/
  closing **years**

latest adj. [only before noun]
■ *She always wears the latest fashions.*

**wording • terms • vocabulary •
terminology • usage**

► **in...** language/terms/vocabulary/
  terminology/usage
► **formal/informal/everyday**
  language/terms/vocabulary/
  usage
► **use ...** language/wording/terms/
  vocabulary/terminology

large adj.
■ *A thousand pounds seemed like a
large sum of money.*

**big • great • spacious • extensive •
huge • massive • vast • enormous •
substantial • considerable • sizeable
• hefty**

■ OPP **small, little**
► a/an large/big/great/extensive/
  spacious/huge/massive/vast/
  enormous/substantial/
  considerable/sizeable **area**
► a/an large/big/spacious/huge/
  massive/vast/enormous **building**
► a/an large/big/great/extensive/
  substantial/considerable/sizeable/
  handsome **amount**
► a/an large/big/great/huge/
  massive/vast/considerable/sizeable/
  hefty **increase**
● **LARGE, BIG OR GREAT?** Compare: *(a)
  large numbers/part/volume/
  population • a big man/house/car/
  boy/dog/smile • great interest/
  importance/difficulty/pleasure*
  Large is slightly more formal than
  big and is used more in writing. It
  is not usu. used to describe people,
  except to avoid saying 'fat'. **Great**
  often suggests quality and not just
  size; it does not usu. describe the
  physical size of objects or people.

last verb [I] (not used in the
progressive tenses)
■ *Each game lasts about an hour.*

take | *esp. written* **continue** | *esp.
spoken* **go on • keep on** | *esp. BrE,
esp. spoken* **carry on** | *disapprov.* **drag
on**

► last/continue/go on/keep on/
  carry on/drag on **for hours/a
  week/two years, etc.**
► last/continue/go on/keep on/
  carry on/drag on **until morning/
  next year, etc.**
► last/take **a few minutes/an hour/
  all day/years, etc.**

last det., adj.

1 ■ *The last bus leaves at midnight.*

**final • closing • later • latter •
ultimate**

■ OPP **first**

recent • current • present • new • modern • contemporary • modern-day • present-day

- ▶ the latest/current/present/contemporary/present-day **situation**
- ▶ the latest/recent/modern/current/present/contemporary **trends**
- ▶ the latest/recent/current/present/new/modern/contemporary/modern-day **version**

laugh verb [I]
■ It was so funny I laughed out loud.

giggle • chuckle • titter • roar | esp. BrE **snigger** | AmE **snicker** | infml **crack up • be/have sb in stitches**

■ OPP **cry**

- ▶ laugh/giggle/chuckle/titter/roar/snigger/snicker **at** sth
- ▶ laugh/giggle/chuckle/titter/snigger/snicker **about/over** sth
- ▶ laugh/giggle/chuckle/roar/snigger/snicker **with** pleasure/amusement, etc.

laugh at sb/sth phrasal verb
■ The other children laughed at my accent.

tease • make fun of sb/sth • poke fun at sb/sth • mock • sneer • ridicule

- ▶ laugh/poke fun at/mock/sneer **at** sb/sth
- ▶ laugh at/tease/mock/sneer at/ridicule sb/sth **for** sth
- ▶ laugh at/poke fun at **yourself**

law noun

1 the law [U] ■ Driving without insurance is against the law.

legislation • constitution • code • charter

- ▶ (the) **civil/criminal** law/legislation/code
- ▶ **break** the law/a code
- ▶ **be enshrined in** the law/legislation/the constitution/a charter

2 [C] ■ They are introducing tough new laws against gun crime.

legislation • rule • regulation • act • statute • commandment

- ▶ (a) law/legislation/rule **against** sth
- ▶ **pass** (a/an) law/legislation/regulation/act/statute
- ▶ **break** a law/rule/regulation/commandment

3 [C, U] ■ He behaved as though moral laws did not exist.

principle • rule | fml **tenet**

- ▶ the law/principle/rule/tenet **that...**

- ▶ a **basic/fundamental** law/principle/rule/tenet
- ▶ a **moral** law/principle/rule

4 [C] ■ the laws of supply and demand

principle • rule • theory | tech. **theorem**

- ▶ the law/principle/rule/theory/theorem **that...**
- ▶ a **basic/fundamental** law/principle/rule/theory/theorem
- ▶ a law/principle/rule/theory/theorem **states that...**

lawyer noun [C]
■ I advise you to consult a lawyer.

esp. AmE **attorney** | BrE **barrister • solicitor** | fml or ScotE **advocate** | law **counsel**

- ▶ (a/an) lawyer/attorney/solicitor/barrister/advocate/counsel **for** sb
- ▶ **appoint/hire/instruct/consult** (a/an) lawyer/attorney/solicitor/barrister/counsel
- ▶ (a/an) lawyer/attorney/solicitor/barrister/advocate/counsel **represents** sb
- ● **WHICH WORD?** Lawyer (and also **attorney** in AmE) is the general term for sb who is qualified to advise people about the law. A **lawyer** who speaks in the higher courts is called a **barrister** in England and Wales and an **advocate** in Scotland. A **solicitor** gives legal advice, prepares documents and sometimes has the right to speak in court.

lay noun

1 [T] (usu. used with an adv. or prep.) ■ He laid a hand on my arm.

place • put • set • position

- ▶ lay/place/put/set/position sth **on** sth
- ▶ lay/place/put/set sth **down**
- ▶ lay/place/put sth **carefully**
- ● **LAY OR PLACE?** Lay is more gentle and **place** is more deliberate. You **place** things but not people; you can **lay** things or people:
  ✔ A bomb was placed under the seat.
  ✗ A bomb was laid under the seat.
  ✔ She laid the baby on the bed.
  ✗ She placed the baby on the bed.

2 [T] (usu. used with an adv. or prep.) ■ He laid newspaper on the floor.

spread • lay sth out

- ▶ lay/spread/lay out sth **on** sth
- ▶ lay/spread sth **over** sth

lazy adj.

1 ■ I was feeling too lazy to go out.

idle | *fml* **indolent** • **slothful**

2 ■ *We spent a lazy day at the beach.*

leisurely • **unhurried** • **easy** | *written* **languid**

■ OPP **busy**, **active**
► a/an lazy/leisurely/unhurried **way**
► a/an lazy/leisurely/easy **day/ morning/afternoon/time**

lead *noun*

1 the lead [sing.] ■ *The Democrats are in the lead.*

the front • **the forefront** • **the foreground** • **the fore**
► in the lead/forefront/foreground

2 [sing.] ■ *She has a narrow lead over the other runners.*

advantage • **edge** • **the upper hand** • **head start**
► a lead/an edge/the upper hand/a head start **over** sb
► a lead/an advantage/an edge/the upper hand/a head start **in** sth
► **have/give** sb a lead/an advantage/an edge/the upper hand/a head start

lead *verb*

1 [T, I] ■ *The survivors were led to safety.*

take • **escort** • **show** • **walk** • **guide** • **usher** | *fml* **accompany**

■ OPP **follow**
► lead/take/escort/show/walk/ guide/usher/accompany sb **to/ out of/into** sth
► lead/take/escort/walk/guide/ usher/accompany sb **there/ somewhere**
► lead/take/escort/show/walk/ guide sb **round/around**
► lead/show **the way**

2 [I, T] (always used with an adv. or prep.) ■ *A path leads to the beach.*

go • **continue** • **reach** • **stretch** • **extend**
► lead/go/continue/reach/stretch/ extend **beyond/across** sth
► lead/go/continue/reach/stretch/ extend **from** sth **to** sth

3 [T] ■ *What led you to this conclusion?*

prompt • **make** • **motivate** | *fml* **induce** • **predispose**
► lead/predispose sb **to** sth
► lead/prompt/motivate/induce/ predispose sb **to do** sth
► **make** sb **do** sth

4 [I, T] ■ *The champion is leading by*

18 seconds. ■ *They lead the world in cancer research.*

be ahead of sb • **leave** sb/sth **behind** • **get ahead** • **overtake** • **pass** | *written, esp. busin.* **outpace**

■ OPP **trail**
► lead/be ahead of sb/leave sb/sth behind/get ahead/overtake sb **in** sth
► lead/be ahead of/overtake a **rival**

5 [T, I] ■ *He led an expedition to the North Pole.*

head • **chair** • **captain** | *fml* **preside** | *esp. journ.* **spearhead**
► lead/head/captain a **team**
► lead/head a (political) **party/the government**
► lead/head/chair/preside over a/ an **commission/committee/ inquiry**

● **HEAD OR LEAD?** A person who **heads** sth has the official position of being the head of it. A person who **leads** sth may also have an official position, but the verb *lead* emphasizes their leadership qualities. An individual usu. **heads** sth, but a group of people can **lead** sth.

leader *noun*

1 [C] ■ *Business leaders have been in talks with the group.*

head • **director** • **chief executive** • **chairman/chairwoman** • **chair** • **president** | *BrE* **managing director** • **governor** | *infml* **boss** | *esp. journ.* **chief**
► a **deputy** leader/head/director/ chief executive/chairman/chair/ president/managing director/ governor/boss/chief
► be **appointed** (as) leader/head/ director/chief executive/ chairman/chair/president/ managing director/governor/chief
► **resign/stand down/step down** as leader/head/director/chief executive/chairman/president/ managing director/governor/chief

2 [C] ■ *The company is the world leader in electrical goods.*

market leader • **pioneer** • **front runner** • **innovator**
► a leader/market leader/pioneer/ front runner/innovator **in** sth
► **among** the leaders/pioneers/front runners
► a **clear/world** leader/market leader

leading *adj.* [only before noun]
■ *He's a leading business analyst.*

top • senior • high-ranking • chief • major • principal • central • key • main • prime | *esp. written* foremost | *esp. written or journ.* premier

■ OPP junior, secondary
▶ a leading/top/senior/high-ranking/chief **officer**
▶ a leading/top/senior/chief **adviser/aide/economist/lawyer**
▶ a/the leading/top/senior/chief/major/principal/central/key/main/prime **role**

lead to sth *phrasal verb*

■ Eating too much sugar can lead to health problems.

cause • result in sth • bring sth about • produce • create • prompt • provoke • encourage | *fml* give rise to sth • induce | *esp. journ.* fuel • stoke

▶ lead to/cause/result in/bring about/produce/prompt/provoke/give rise to/fuel/a/an **change/increase**
▶ lead to/cause/result in/produce/give rise to/create **problems/difficulties**
▶ lead to/cause/produce/create/prompt/provoke/encourage/give rise to/fuel **speculation**

leaflet *noun* [C]

■ We pick up some leaflets on local places of interest.

flyer • handout • circular • pamphlet • brochure • booklet

▶ a free leaflet/handout/pamphlet/brochure/booklet
▶ produce a leaflet/flyer/handout/circular/pamphlet/brochure/booklet
▶ give out leaflets/flyers/handouts/brochures

leak *verb* [I, T]

■ A pipe was leaking in the bathroom.

seep • drip • ooze • escape | *fml* discharge | *tech.* leach • secrete

▶ leak/seep/drip/ooze/escape/leach **from** sth
▶ leak/escape/discharge/leach **into** sth
▶ water leaks/seeps/drips/escapes
▶ gas leaks/seeps/escapes

lean *verb*

1 [I] (usu. used with an adv. or prep.)
■ I leaned back in my chair.

tilt • tip • angle • slant • slope • bank

▶ lean/tilt/tip/angle/slant/slope (sth) **towards/away** from sth
▶ lean/angle/slant/tip (sth) **across** sth
▶ lean/tilt/tip (sth) **forwards/back/backwards/to one side**

2 [I, T] ■ Lean your bike against the wall.

rest • prop • stand • balance • steady • poise

▶ lean/rest/prop/stand/balance (sth) **on** sth
▶ lean/rest/prop/stand/steady (sth) **against** sth

learn *verb*

1 [T, I] ■ Did you learn German at school?

study • do • memorize • pick sth up • know • master • learn/know sth by heart • get the hang of sth | *fml* acquire

▶ learn/pick up/know sth **from** sb/sth
▶ learn/memorize/pick up/know/master/get the hang of **what...**
▶ learn/study/do/pick up/know/master/acquire a **language**

2 [I, T] (not usu. used in the progressive tenses) ■ I learned the news from a close friend.

discover • find out (sth) • hear

▶ learn/find out/hear **about** sth
▶ learn/discover/find out the **facts/truth/secret/identity**
▶ be **surprised/shocked/delighted/interested** to learn/discover/find out/hear sth

leave *verb*

1 [I, T] ■ Come on—it's time we left.

go • go away • get away • go off • set off • take off • start | *esp. BrE* be/go on your way | *esp. BrE, spoken* be off | *esp. AmE, spoken* get out of here | *fml* depart • exit

■ OPP arrive, enter
▶ leave/go/go away/get away/set off/take off/start/depart/exit **from** sb/sth
▶ leave/go/go away/go off/set off/take off/start/be on your way/depart **at** 9 a.m., midnight, etc.
▶ be **ready/about/going** to leave/go/go away/set off/take off/start/depart

● LEAVE OR GO AWAY? **Leave** is used in ways that emphasize the act or time of leaving sb/sth; **go away** emphasizes the need or desire of the speaker to be somewhere else or for another person to be somewhere else.

2 [T, I] ■ Villagers left to seek work in the towns.

move • move out • quit • relocate • emigrate • migrate

■ OPP stay on

▶ move/move out/relocate/
emigrate/migrate from ... to ...
▶ leave/quit your **home/school/
college/job**
▶ **threaten to** leave/move out/quit
▶ **decide/plan/want to** leave/
move/move out/quit/relocate/
emigrate

3 [I, T] ■ *Workers are threatening to
leave.*

resign • **give in/hand in your notice**
• **retire** • **step down** • **stand down** |
infml **quit** | *AmE or busin.* **depart**

■ OPP **stay on**
▶ leave/resign from/retire from/step
down from/stand down from/
quit/depart a **post/position**
▶ **decide to** leave/resign/hand in
your notice/retire/step down/
stand down/quit
▶ be **ready/going to** leave/resign/
retire/step down/stand down/
quit

4 [T] ■ *She's leaving him for another
man.*

abandon • **desert** • **strand** • **turn
your back on sb** • **neglect** | *infml*
dump • **walk out (on sb)**

▶ leave/desert/dump sb **for** sb else
▶ leave/abandon/desert/neglect/
dump/walk out on a **husband/
wife**
▶ leave/abandon/desert/dump a
lover
▶ abandon/desert/neglect a **child**

5 [T] ■ *I left my bag on the bus.*

lose • **forget** | *esp. BrE, fml* **mislay**

▶ leave/lose/forget/mislay your
keys/wallet/bag

6 [T] ■ *She left £1 million to her
daughter in her will.*

pass sth on | *fml* **bequeath**

▶ leave/pass on/bequeath sth **to** sb
▶ leave/pass on/bequeath a/an
legacy/property/estate
▶ leave/bequeath (sb) your **money/
art collection**

7 [T] ■ *Leave the cooking to me.*

hand sth over • **refer sb/sth to sb/
sth** • **delegate** | *esp. AmE* **turn sth
over to sb** | *fml* **entrust**

▶ leave/hand over/turn over/refer/
delegate/entrust sth **to** sb
▶ leave/entrust sb **with** sth
▶ leave/hand over/turn over/
delegate the **task/job/
responsibility/management** of sth
to sb

leave sb/sth out *phrasal verb*
(*esp. spoken*)
■ *She left out an 'm' in
'accommodation'.*

BrE **miss sth out** | *fml* **omit** | *esp.
spoken* **leave sb/sth off (sth)**

■ OPP **include**
▶ leave out/omit sth **from** sth
▶ leave/miss sth out **of** sth
▶ leave out/omit **the details/a
reference**
● LEAVE STH OUT OR OMIT? Use **leave
sb out** when you are talking about
not including sb in an argument or
social situation; **omit** is only used in
formal contexts.

lecture *noun* [C]
■ *Dr Lee gave a lecture on public art.*

talk • **speech** • **address** • **sermon**

▶ a/an **inaugural/farewell/keynote**
lecture/speech/address
▶ an **informal** lecture/talk
▶ **give/deliver** a/an lecture/talk/
speech/address/sermon
▶ **write/prepare** an lecture/talk/
speech/address/sermon

lecturer *noun* [C]
■ *He's a law lecturer at Exeter
University.*

professor • **fellow** • **teacher** • **tutor** |
BrE **don**

▶ a **lecturer/professor/fellow/
teacher/tutor/don at** sth
▶ a **university** lecturer/professor/
fellow/teacher/tutor/don
▶ a **college** lecturer/professor/
fellow/teacher/tutor
▶ a **French/biology, etc.** lecturer/
professor/fellow/teacher/tutor/
don

legacy *noun* [C]
■ *He received a legacy of £5 000.*

inheritance • **heritage** | *fml* **bequest**
• **birthright** | *law* **estate**

▶ a/an **legacy/inheritance/bequest
from** sb
▶ a/an **cultural/artistic** legacy/
inheritance/heritage
▶ **leave** (sb) a **legacy/an
inheritance/a bequest/your estate**
▶ **bequeath** (sb)/**inherit** a legacy/an
estate

legal *adj.*
■ *Do you know your legal rights?*

statutory • **legitimate** • **valid** •
constitutional | *fml* **lawful**

■ OPP **illegal**
▶ (a) legal/statutory/legitimate/
valid/constitutional/lawful **claim/
means**
▶ a legal/statutory/legitimate/lawful
owner
● LEGAL OR LAWFUL? Both words

mean 'allowed by law': by *legal/ lawful means*. **Legal** also means 'connected with the law': *the US legal system*

legend noun

1 [C] ■ *the legend of Robin Hood*

story • fairy tale • fable • myth • epic

▶ a/an legend/story/fairy tale/ fable/myth/epic **about** sth
▶ an **ancient** legend/story/fable/ epic
▶ a **Greek/Roman** legend/myth/ epic

2 [U] ■ *Legend has it that a giant lived here.*

folklore • myth • mythology

▶ **in** legend/folklore/myth/ mythology
▶ **be part of** legend/folklore/myth/ mythology
▶ **pass into** legend/folklore/ mythology

leisure noun [U]

■ *These days we have more leisure than ever before.*

spare time • free time

▶ **have (more/no)** leisure/spare time/free time
▶ **spend** your spare time/free time **doing** sth
● **WHICH WORD?** Leisure is used when talking about people and society in general, esp. in a business context; when talking about your own or an individual person use **spare time** or **free time**:
✓*What do you do in your spare/free time?* ✗ *What do you do in your leisure?*
✓*the leisure industry* ✗ *the spare/free time industry*

lend verb [T, I]

■ *The bank refused to lend us the money.*

advance | *esp. AmE* **loan**

■ OPP **borrow**
▶ lend/advance/loan sth **to** sb
▶ lend/advance/loan **money**

lenient adj.

■ *The courts were more lenient with female offenders.*

usu. disapprov. **soft** | *usu. approv.* **forgiving** | *esp. written* **merciful**

■ OPP **strict, harsh**
▶ lenient/soft **with/on** sb
▶ lenient/merciful **to** sb
▶ a lenient/soft **approach**

lesson noun [C]

■ *a history lesson on the Civil War*

class • seminar • session • workshop • tutorial • period

▶ a lesson/class/seminar/session/ workshop/tutorial **on** sth
▶ **in/during** a lesson/class/seminar/ session/workshop/tutorial/period
▶ **at** a lesson/class/seminar/session/ workshop/tutorial
▶ **go to/attend/give/conduct** a lesson/class/seminar/session/ workshop/tutorial
● **LESSON or CLASS?** A **class** is always for a group of people; a **lesson** can be for a group or for just one person.

let verb [T]

■ *They won't let him leave the country.*

allow • entitle • authorize • license • grant | *infml* **OK/okay** | *fml* **permit • sanction • empower**

■ OPP **prevent, forbid**
▶ allow/entitle/authorize/license/ permit/empower sb **to do** sth
▶ let sb **do** sth
▶ let/allow/permit **yourself** sth/(to) do sth

let sb down *phrasal verb (disapprov.)*

■ *I'm afraid she let us down badly.*

fail • disappoint | *infml, disapprov.* **leave sb in the lurch**

▶ let down/fail/disappoint your **fans/family/children/ colleagues/friends**
▶ be **sorry to** let sb down/disappoint sb/leave sb in the lurch
▶ sb **won't** let sb down/fail sb/ disappoint sb/leave sb in the lurch

let sb/sth go *phrase*

■ *He begged the kidnappers to let his son go.*

release • free • set sb/sth free • liberate • ransom

▶ let go/release/free/set free/ liberate/ransom a **prisoner/ hostage**
▶ **finally** let sb go/release sb/free sb/liberate sb

letter noun

1 [C] ■ *Many listeners wrote letters of complaint.*

message • note • memo • fax • email/e-mail • mail | *BrE* **post** | *fml* **communication • correspondence • memorandum**

▶ (a/an) letter/message/note/ memo/email/fax/email/ communication/correspondence/ memorandum **from/to** sb
▶ (a) **private/personal** letter/

message/note/email/mail/
communication/correspondence
▶ **write** a/an letter/message/note/
email/memo/memorandum

2 [C] ■ '*Z*' is the last letter of the
alphabet.

character

▶ **print/write** a letter/character
▶ a **sequence/series/set/string** of
letters/characters

level noun

1 [C] ■ *Another cause for concern is
the rising level of crime.*

**degree • extent • scale • size •
proportions | fml magnitude**

▶ the **true** level/extent/size
▶ **assess/judge** the level/degree/
extent/scale/size/magnitude of
sth
▶ **realize** the level/degree/extent/
scale/size of sth

2 [C, U] ■ *These students have a high
level of language ability.*

**standard • grade • quality | BrE
calibre | AmE caliber**

▶ be of a/the ... level/standard/
grade/quality/calibre
▶ **high/highest/low** level/
standard/grade/quality/calibre
▶ **raise/improve** the level/standard/
quality/calibre of sth

3 [C] ■ *He promised reforms at all
levels of government.*

**rank • grade • position • class •
status**

▶ sb's **level/rank/class/position/
status in/within** sth
▶ a/the **low/lower** level/rank/
grade/position/class/status
▶ a/the **high/higher** level/rank/
grade/position/status
▶ a/the **senior** level/rank/grade/
position

4 [C] ■ *The library is all on one level.*

**floor • deck • tier | esp. BrE storey |
AmE usu. story**

▶ on the **top, etc.** level/floor/deck/
tier/storey
▶ the **top/upper/lower** level/floor/
deck/tier/storey

level adj.

1 ■ *Pitch the tent on level ground.*

**flat • horizontal | often approv.
smooth**

■ OPP **uneven, bumpy**
▶ a level/flat/smooth/horizontal
surface
▶ a level/flat/smooth **road/floor**
▶ level/flat **ground**

● **LEVEL OR FLAT?** Level is used most
often with the words *ground* and
floor. Flat is used more often to
talk about surfaces that are not
rounded or landscapes that do not
have any hills: *a flat base/stomach/
surface • flat land • a flat landscape/
field/plateau*

2 [not before noun] (*esp. BrE*) ■ *The
clubs are level on points.*

even • neck and neck

▶ level/neck and neck **with** sb

licence (BrE) (AmE license) noun
[C]

■ *You need a licence to fish in this river.*

**permit • authorization • franchise •
warrant • charter • pass • papers •
documentation • certificate**

▶ **under** (a) licence/franchise/
charter
▶ **grant** (sb) (a) licence/permit/
authorization/franchise/warrant/
charter
▶ **get/obtain** (a) licence/permit/
authorization/franchise/warrant/
charter/pass/papers/
documentation/certificate
▶ **see/check** sb's licence/permit/
authorization/pass/papers/
documentation/certificate

lid noun [C]

■ *a jar with a tight-fitting lid*

top • cap

▶ a **close-fitting/tight-fitting** lid/
top/cap
▶ **put on/screw on/take off/
unscrew/remove** the lid/top/cap

lie noun [C]

■ *The story is a pack of lies.*

**story • nonsense • fiction | infml fib |
BrE, infml, disapprov. rubbish | esp.
AmE, infml. garbage | fml
fabrication • falsehood | law perjury
| taboo, slang, disapprov. bullshit**

▶ (a) **complete** lie/nonsense/fiction/
rubbish/garbage/fabrication/
falsehood/bullshit
▶ **tell** (sb) a lie/story/fib/falsehood
▶ **believe** a lie/a story/that
nonsense/a fiction/that rubbish/
that garbage/that bullshit

lie verb [I] (usu. used with an adv. or
prep.)

■ *A cat was lying in the sun.*

**lie down • sprawl • lounge • bask |
fml recline**

▶ lie/lie down/sprawl **on your back/
side/front**

life noun

1 [U, C] ■ *The body was cold and
showed no signs of life.*

| existence • survival |

- **OPP** death
- ▶ sb's/sth's **very/continued/day-to-day** life/existence/survival
- ▶ **threaten** sb's/sth's life/existence/survival
- ▶ **fight for** your life/survival

2 [C, U] ■ I've lived here all my life.

| lifetime • career • in sb's day |

- ▶ **in/of** sb's life/lifetime/career/day
- ▶ **during** sb's life/lifetime/career/day
- ▶ a life/lifetime/career **of doing sth**

3 [C] ■ How do you find life in America?

| lifestyle • way of life • living • existence |

- ▶ (sb's) **day-to-day** life/living/existence
- ▶ a **comfortable/busy** life/lifestyle/existence
- ▶ **have/lead/enjoy** a … life/lifestyle/existence

4 [U] ■ We need to inject some new life into this project.

| energy • vitality • fire • dynamism • spark • gusto • zest | BrE vigour | AmE vigor |

- ▶ **new** life/energy/vitality/zest/vigour
- ▶ **be full of** life/energy/vitality/fire/dynamism/zest/vigour

lift noun [C] (BrE)

■ He offered me a lift home in his van.

| ride • drive |

- ▶ a lift/ride/drive **in** sth
- ▶ a lift/ride/drive **from/to** sth
- ▶ **give** sb/**hitch** a lift/ride

lift verb [T, I] (usu. used with an adv. or prep.)

■ The suitcase was so heavy I could hardly lift it.

| pick sb/sth up • hoist • scoop • heave | esp. written raise |

- **OPP** put sb/sth down
- ▶ lift/pick/hoist/scoop/raise sb/sth **up**
- ▶ lift/pick up/hoist/scoop/raise a **bag/basket**
- ▶ lift/pick up/hoist/scoop a **child/girl/boy**
- ▶ lift/raise your **hand/arm/head/chin/face/eyes/eyebrows**
- ● **LIFT, PICK SB/STH UP OR RAISE?** Lift can mean to move sb/sth in a particular direction, not just upwards; **pick sb/sth up** is usu. used about sb/sth that is not very heavy and is only used for upwards movement; **raise** is used esp. about parts of the body: *He lifted the suitcase down from the rack. • He picked up the phone and dialled the number. • She raised her eyebrows.*

light noun

1 [U, sing.] ■ She could just see by the light of the candle.

| brightness • lighting |

- **OPP** darkness, the dark, shade
- ▶ light/brightness **from** sth
- ▶ **in** the light/brightness
- ▶ **good/bright/strong/poor/electric** light/lighting
- ▶ **give** light/brightness **to** sth

2 [C] ■ Turn on the lights!

| lamp • candle • lantern | BrE torch | esp. AmE flashlight |

- ▶ **switch on/off** a light/lamp/torch/flashlight
- ▶ **shine** a light/lantern/torch/flashlight **on** sth
- ▶ a light/lamp/lantern/torch/flashlight **shines**

light verb

1 [T] ■ The explorers lit a fire to keep warm.

| set fire to sth/set sth on fire • torch | fml ignite |

- **OPP** put sth out, extinguish
- ▶ light/ignite a **fire/a flame/the gas**
- ▶ a spark lights sth/sets fire to sth/ignites sth
- ● **LIGHT, SET FIRE TO STH OR IGNITE?** Light is used esp. when sb makes sth burn that is supposed to burn. **Set fire to sth** is used about bigger fires, esp. about sth that is not supposed to burn. Sth is usu. **ignited** by a spark or flame, rather than a person: *He lit a candle. • She accidentally set fire to the sofa. • A spark must have ignited the gas.*

2 [T, usu. passive] ■ The stage was lit by spotlights.

| light (sth) up • brighten • flood | fml illuminate |

- ▶ **be** lit/lit up/flooded/illuminated **with** sth
- ▶ light/brighten/flood/illuminate a **room**
- ▶ **well/brightly/dimly/softly** lit/illuminated

light adj.

1 ■ Light colours suit you best.

| pale • soft • pastel • neutral | usu. approv. cool |

- **OPP** dark
- ▶ a light/pale/soft/pastel/neutral/cool **colour/shade**
- ▶ light/pale/soft/pastel/cool **blue/green**
- ▶ light/pale/soft/pastel **pink**
- ▶ light/soft/pale **yellow/brown/red**
- ● **LIGHT OR PALE?** Both words can be

used to describe colours. **Pale** is also used to describe a kind of light that contains a lot of white and is not bright:
✓a pale light/glow/sky ✗ *a thin light/glow/sky*

2 ■ *The forecast is for light showers.*

gentle + mild

► OPP **heavy**
► (a) **light/gentle** breeze/wind/rain
► **light/gentle** work/exercise
► **light/mild** punishment
● **LIGHT, GENTLE OR MILD?** **Light** is used esp. to describe weather, work, exercise and punishment. **Gentle** is used esp. to describe weather, temperature, work and exercise. **Mild** is used esp. to describe weather, diseases, drugs, criticism and punishment.

like verb

1 [T] (not usu. used in the progressive tenses) ■ *Which shirt do you like best?*

love + be fond of sth | infml go for sb/sth + adore | BrE, infml be keen on sth

► OPP **dislike**
► **like/love/be fond of/adore/be keen on doing sth**
► **like/love to do sth**
► **I like/love/adore it here/there/when…**

2 [T] (not usu. used in the progressive tenses) ■ *She's a nice person and I like her a lot.*

be fond of sb + care for sb + love

► OPP **dislike**
► **like/be fond of/care for/love your children/husband/wife/mother/father**
► **like/care for/love sb very much**

3 [T, no passive] (*BrE, infml, esp. spoken*) (not usu. used in the progressive tenses) ■ *Do what you like—I don't care.*

want + wish | fml desire | fml, esp. spoken would like to | BrE, infml, esp. spoken feel like | BrE, infml, esp. spoken fancy

► **sb likes/wants/wishes/desires/would like to do sth**
► **if you like/want/wish**

like prep.

■ *She's wearing a dress like mine.*

similar + close + alike

► OPP **unlike**
► **like sth/similar/close/alike in size, amount, etc.**
► **look like sth/similar/alike**
► **feel/sound/taste like sth/similar**

■ *What is the most likely cause of the infection?*

possible + potential + prospective + prone to sth + inclined to do sth + liable to sth | esp. written probable

► OPP **unlikely**
► **be likely/possible/probable that…**
► **likely/prone/inclined/liable to do sth**
► a **likely/possible/potential/probable cause/effect/consequence/outcome**
● **LIKELY OR PROBABLE?** **Probable** is much more frequent in written than in spoken English. **Likely** is very frequent in both, and used in a far wider range of structures and registers with **probable**:
✓sth/sb is likely to do sth ✗ *sb/sth is probable to do sth*

limit noun

1 [C] ■ *She knew the limits of her power.*

boundary + frontier + bounds | fml parameter + confines

► **beyond the limits/boundaries/frontiers/bounds/parameters/confines of sth**
► **extend the limits/boundaries/frontiers/bounds/parameters of sth**
► **set/define/establish the limits/boundaries/bounds/parameters of sth**

2 [C] ■ *The EU has set strict limits on pollution levels.*

control + limitation + restriction + constraint + restraint + check + ceiling + curb

► **limits/controls/limitations/restrictions/constraints/restraints/checks/a ceiling/curbs on sth**
► **limits/limitations/checks to sth**
► **without limits/controls/limitations/restrictions/restraints/checks**

limit verb

1 [T] ■ *This diet limits your calories to 1 000 a day.*

restrict + control + curb + check + rein sth in + hold/keep sth in check | esp. BrE cap | written contain + suppress

► **be limited/restricted to sth**
► **limit/restrict/control/curb/check/rein in/cap spending**
► **limit/restrict/control the size/number/extent/amount of sth**
● **LIMIT OR RESTRICT?** **Limit** is used both about controlling what people can do and also about controlling the effects of sth; **restrict** is used more often about controlling what people can do:

✔ to limit carbon dioxide emissions
✗ to restrict carbon dioxide emissions

2 [T, often passive] ■ *Free tickets are limited to three per family.*

restrict • confine sb/sth to sth | *fml* **constrain**

▶ limit/restrict/confine sb/sth to sth
▶ limit/restrict/confine **yourself** to sth

limited adj.

1 ■ *Our resources are very limited.*

restricted • scarce • low • in short supply • short | *usu. disapprov.* **narrow**

■ OPP **unlimited**

▶ limited/restricted/narrow **in** sth
▶ a limited/restricted/narrow **range/scope/vocabulary**
▶ **resources** are limited/scarce/low/ in short supply/short

2 ■ *The number of passengers is limited to fifteen.*

restricted • controlled

▶ be limited/restricted **to** sth
▶ limited/restricted/controlled **access**
▶ **strictly** limited/controlled

line noun

1 [C, usu. pl.] ■ *He has fine lines around his eyes.*

wrinkle • crease

▶ lines/wrinkles/creases **around** the/sb's eyes/mouth
▶ **deep** lines/wrinkles/creases
▶ **fine** lines/wrinkles

2 [C] ■ *The ball went over the line.*

boundary • border • frontier

▶ **across/along/on/over** a/the line/boundary/border/frontier
▶ the line/boundary/border/frontier **between** one place and another
▶ **form/mark/cross** a/the line/ boundary/border/frontier

3 [C] ■ *There is a clear dividing line here between fact and fiction.*

boundary • borderline | *fml* **parameter**

▶ the line/boundary/borderline **between** A and B
● **LINE OR BOUNDARY?** A **line** between two areas of thought or behaviour is sth that exists; a **boundary** has to be decided by sb:
✔ *The teacher must set clear boundaries.* ✗ *The teacher must set clear lines.*

4 [C] ■ *The children stood in a line.*

row • file • rank • cordon | *BrE* **queue** | *esp. written* **column**

▶ a line/row/file/rank/queue/ column of sb/sth
▶ **in** (a) line/single file/a row/a queue/a column
▶ **form** a line/cordon/queue
● **LINE, ROW OR QUEUE?** People or things in a **line** can be next to each other from side to side, but are more often one behind the other from front to back; people or things in a **row** are next to each other from side to side. People or vehicles in a **row** are not usu. waiting for anything; those in a **line** usu. are: *a row of parked cars • a line of traffic waiting at the lights* In *BrE* the usual word for people waiting in a line is **queue**; in *AmE* it is **line**.

5 [C, usu. sing.] ■ *This novel is the latest in a long line of thrillers from G. J. Brady.*

series • sequence • string • chain • succession • catalogue | *AmE also* **catalog**

▶ a line/series/sequence/string/ chain/succession/catalogue **of** sth
▶ a/an **long/endless/continuous/ unbroken** line/series/sequence/ string/chain/succession
▶ the **first/last/latest in** a line/ series/sequence/string/succession

link noun

1 [C] ■ *Police suspect a link between the two murders.*

connection • relationship • correlation • association • relation | *fml* **interdependence**

▶ the link/connection/relationship/ correlation/association/relation/ interdependence **between** A and B
▶ (a) link/connection/relationship/ correlation/association **with** sb/ sth
▶ **have** (a) link/connection/ relationship/correlation/ association/relation
● **LINK OR CONNECTION?** Link is slightly more informal than **connection** and is often used in newspapers. Only connection is used in the collocation make the connection:
✔ *How did you make the connection* (= realize that there was a connection between two things)?
✗ *How did you make the link?*

2 [C, U] ■ *They established trade links with China.*

tie • relationship • partnership • relations • association | *fml* **affiliation** | *esp. busin.* **contact**

▶ (a/an) link/ties/relationship/ partnership/relations/association/ affiliation/contact **with** sb/sth
▶ (a/an) links/ties/relationship/

link

partnership/relations/association/
affiliation **between** A and B
► **build/establish/foster** (a) links/
ties/relationship/partnership/
relations/contacts
● **LINK OR TIE?** A **link** is less strong
than a **tie**. **Link** is used more
frequently about practical rather
than emotional connections:
✓trade/business links • family ties
✗ *family links*

link *verb*

1 [T, often passive] ■ *The computers
are linked into the network.*

connect • join

► link/connect/join sth **to** sth
► link/connect/join sth **with** sth
► link/connect/join A **and** B
► link/join A **and** B **together**

2 [T, usu. passive] ■ *The two factors
are directly linked.*

connect • couple sth with sth

► be linked/connected/coupled
  with sb/sth
► be **closely/directly/inextricably/
  obviously/loosely** linked/
  connected
● **LINK OR CONNECT?** **Link** is often used
about a strong connection in
which one causes the other, or
two things which depend on each
other, so that they cannot be
separated:
✓be indissolubly/inescapably/
inextricably linked
Connect is often used about a
looser connection in which two
things belong in the same general
area. People can be connected but
not linked:
✓They are connected by marriage.
✗ *They are linked by marriage.*

3 [T] (esp. *journ.*) ■ *Detectives have
linked the break-in to a series of
recent robberies.*

match • connect • relate • associate

► link/match/connect/relate **to**
  sth
► link/match/connect/associate
  with sth
► link/match/connect/relate/
  associate (sth) **directly**

liquid *noun* [C, U]

■ *The cup contained a dark brown
liquid.*

fml or tech. **fluid**

► a **sticky** liquid/fluid
● **LIQUID OR FLUID?** Although a **fluid**
is usu. a **liquid**, it can be any
substance which can flow, for
example a gas or a liquid
containing small solid pieces.

list *noun* [C]

■ *Is your name on the list?*

**listing • checklist • roll • register •
inventory • index • table • directory
• catalogue** | *AmE also* **catalog**

► **in** a/an list/listing/register/
  inventory/index/table/directory/
  catalogue
► **on** a/an list/checklist/roll/
  register/inventory
► **compile** a/an list/checklist/
  register/inventory/index/table/
  directory
► **draw up** a/an list/checklist/
  register/inventory/table/
  catalogue

list *verb* [T]

■ *They asked us to list our ten favourite
songs.*

**itemize • name • state • detail •
specify**

► list/itemize/state/detail/name/
  specify sth **as/in** sth
► list/itemize/detail/specify sth
  under sth
► list/detail/name/specify **items**

listen *verb* [I]

■ *She listened carefully to the
instructions.*

**pay attention • tune in • hear •
catch** | *fml* **heed**

► listen/pay attention to/tune in to
  sb/sth
► listen to/tune in to/hear/catch a
  radio programme
► listen to/pay attention to/hear/
  catch/heed **sb's words/what sb
  says**
► listen to/hear/heed **advice/a
  warning**

literature *noun* [U]

■ *'Paradise Lost' is a great work of
literature.*

writing • text

► literature/writing **on** sth
► **feminist/scientific/English**
  literature/writing
► a **piece of** literature/writing/text

little *adj.*

1 [usu. before noun] (not usu. used
in the comparative or superlative)
■ *What a dear little baby!*

**small • tiny • miniature • compact •
minute • microscopic**

■ **OPP big, large**
► a little/small/tiny/miniature
  house/town/room
► a little/small/tiny/minute/
  microscopic **detail**
► a little/small/tiny **baby/child**
● **LITTLE OR SMALL?** **Small** is the most
usual opposite of *big* or *large*. **Little**

is often used to show how you feel about sb/sth, esp. after other adjectives such as *ugly*, *nice* or *cute*.

2 [usu. before noun] *(esp. spoken)*
■ *What a fuss over one little mistake!*

small • **slight** • **minimal** • **marginal** • **minor** | *usu. disapprov.* **trivial** • **petty**

■ OPP **big**, **great**
▶ a little/small/slight/minimal/marginal **change/improvement**
▶ a little/small/slight/trivial **error/mistake/problem**
▶ a little/small/slight **defect/accident**

live verb

1 [I] (always used with an adv. or prep.) ■ *I live in a small house near the station.*

fml **inhabit** • **occupy** • **reside** | *written* **people**

▶ live/reside **in/among/near** sth
▶ live **in/inhabit/occupy/reside in** a house
▶ live **in/inhabit/people** the world

2 [I] ■ *Spiders can live for days without food.*

survive • **come through (sth)** • **make it** • **pull through**

■ OPP **die**
▶ live/survive **on** (a diet of) sth
▶ live/survive **for** a few days/many years, etc.
▶ live/survive **without** food/money, etc.
▶ live/survive/come/make it/pull **through** sth

3 [I] (not usu. used in the progressive tenses) ■ *He's the greatest painter who ever lived.*

exist • **be found**

lively adj.

1 (*approv.*) ■ *Her lively personality will be greatly missed.*

spirited • **vivacious** • **animated** • **dynamic** • **energetic** • **active** | *infml* **bubbly** • *written* **exuberant** • *sometimes disapprov.* **ebullient** • **hearty**

▶ a/an lively/vivacious/dynamic/bubbly/exuberant/ebullient **personality**
▶ a lively/spirited/vivacious **young woman**
▶ a/an lively/spirited/dynamic/energetic/exuberant **performance**

2 (*approv.*) ■ *It's a lively resort, popular with young people.*

busy | *written, approv.* **bustling** • **vibrant** | *sometimes disapprov.* **crowded**

■ OPP **quiet**, **dead**

▶ a lively/busy/bustling/vibrant/crowded **city**
▶ a lively/busy/bustling/crowded **place/town/resort/port/harbour/market/bar**
▶ a lively/busy/crowded **pub**

living adj.

■ *one of our finest living musicians*

live • **alive** | *fml* **animate**

■ OPP **dead**
▶ a live/living **animal/plant/bird**
▶ a live/living **organism/creature**
▶ still living/alive
● **LIVING, ALIVE OR LIVE?** Alive is never used before a noun:
✓*all living things* ✗ *all alive things*
Living can be used after *be* but is not usu. used after other linking verbs:
✓*She stole just to say alive.* ✗ *She stole just to stay living.*
Use **living** to talk about people/animals in a wide context:
✓*the finest living pianist* (= out of all pianists alive today)
Use **live** to talk about animals or a person in a particular situation:
✓*I need to talk to a live person* (= not a recorded message).

load noun [C]

■ *A truck had shed its load on the way to the depot.*

cargo • **consignment** | *BrE* **goods** | *fml* **merchandise** | *busin.* **freight**

▶ a load/cargo/consignment **of** sth
▶ carry (a) load/cargo/consignment/goods/burden/freight
▶ send/deliver/receive (a) load/cargo/consignment/goods

load verb [T, I]

■ *We loaded the car in ten minutes.*

fill • **fill (sth) up** • **pack**

■ OPP **unload**
▶ load/fill/fill up/pack sth **with** sth
▶ load/fill/pack sth **in/into** sth

loan noun [C]

■ *He took out a loan to pay for the car.*

credit • **overdraft** • **mortgage** • **advance**

▶ a (an) loan/credit/overdraft/mortgage/advance **from** sb/an organization
▶ a **bank** loan/credit/overdraft/mortgage
▶ obtain/arrange/apply for/refuse sb/deny sb (a) loan/credit/mortgage
● **LOAN OR CREDIT?** A **loan** is an official agreement to borrow money and pay it back later; **credit**

is a general term for any money that a bank makes available to a customer who does not have that amount in their account.

locate verb

1 [T] ■ *Planes tried to locate the missing sailors.*

find • trace • track sb/sth down • search sb/sth out | *infml* **sniff sb/sth out**

▸ locate/find/track down/search out sth **for** sb/sth
▸ locate/trace/track down/sniff out sb's **whereabouts**
▸ locate/find/trace/track down the **missing…**

2 [T, often passive] (*esp. written*) ■ *The offices are located near the station.*

base • site | *fml* **be situated**

▸ be located/based/sited/situated **in/at/close to** sth
▸ be located/based/sited/situated **between** A and B
● **LOCATED, SITUATED OR SITED?** Located and situated are used to talk about where sth is, including a natural feature. Sited is normally only used to describe sth that sb has built, such as a school or hospital.

location noun [C]

■ *The hotel is in a central location.*

position • place • site • venue • spot • point • scene • whereabouts • area

▸ a (good, etc.) location/position/place/site/venue/spot **for** sth
▸ **at a** location/position/place/site/venue/spot/point/scene
▸ the/sb/sth's **exact/precise** location/position/place/site/spot/whereabouts

lock verb [T, I]

■ *Did you lock the door?*

bolt • shut • close

■ OPP **unlock**
▸ lock/bolt/shut/close a **door/gate**
▸ lock/bolt/shut/close a **window/drawer/case/suitcase**
▸ lock/bolt/shut/close sth **behind** you

logic noun [U, sing.]

■ *I fail to see the logic behind his argument.*

reason • reasoning • rationality

▸ the logic/reason/rationality **in** sth
▸ **see/defy** (the) logic/reason
▸ a **lack** of logic/reason/rationality

logical adj.

1 ■ *It was the logical thing to do.*

obvious • natural • understandable

■ OPP **illogical**
▸ logical/obvious/natural/understandable **that …**
▸ logical/natural (for sb) **to do** sth
▸ the logical/obvious/natural **thing to do/choice/conclusion/solution**

2 ■ *A logical rather than an emotional response is needed.*

rational • reasoned • scientific • coherent

■ OPP **illogical**
▸ a logical/rational/reasoned/scientific/coherent **argument/explanation**
▸ logical/rational/reasoned/scientific/coherent **thought**
▸ a logical/rational/reasoned/scientific/coherent **choice/decision/conclusion**

logo noun [C]

■ *blue paper cups bearing the company logo*

symbol • trademark • emblem • crest • arms • coat of arms

▸ **bear/carry/display/feature** a logo/a symbol/an emblem/a crest/the arms

lonely adj.

1 ■ *She lives alone and often feels lonely.*

alone • isolated • desolate | *written* **forlorn**

▸ **feel** lonely/alone/isolated/desolate/forlorn
● **LONELY OR ALONE?** Alone is slightly more informal than lonely and cannot be used before a noun.

2 [usu. before noun] ■ *He thought of those lonely nights watching TV.*

solitary • alone • by yourself • on your own

▸ a lonely/solitary **existence/life/walk**

long verb [I]

■ *He had always longed for a brother.*

hanker | *infml* **be dying for sth/to do sth** | *written* **crave** | *fml or written* **covet** | *lit.* **yearn**

▸ long/hanker/be dying/yearn **for** sb/sth
▸ long/hanker/be dying/yearn **to do** sth
▸ **always/still** long for/hanker/covet/crave/yearn for sth

long adj.

■ *There was a long silence.*

look *noun*

long-lasting | *esp. written* **prolonged**
+ **lengthy** | **extended** | *fml*
protracted

■ OPP **short, brief**

▶ a long/prolonged/lengthy/
extended **period**
▶ a long/prolonged/lengthy/
protracted **delay/dispute/illness**
▶ long/prolonged/lengthy/
extended/protracted **negotiations**

look *noun*

1 [C, usu. sing.] ■ *Have a look at this.*

glance + **glimpse** + **sight** + **stare** +
glare + **gaze**

▶ a look/glance **at** sb/sth
▶ a **hard** look/glance/stare/glare/
gaze
▶ a **cold/penetrating/piercing/
curious/quizzical** look/glance/
stare/gaze
▶ **have/get/take** a look/glance/
glimpse

2 [C, usu. sing.] ■ *Take a close look at
the facts.*

consideration + **thought**

▶ (a) **serious/careful** consideration/
thought/look
▶ **give** sth some consideration/some
thought/a look

3 [C, usu. sing.] ■ *Have a look
downstairs for your keys.*

search + **hunt**

▶ a look/search/hunt **for** sb/sth

4 [C] ■ *He gave me a funny look.*

expression + **face**

▶ a look/an expression **of**
amazement/disbelief/horror, etc.
▶ a look/an expression **on** sb's **face**
▶ a look/an expression **in** sb's **eyes**
▶ a/an **happy/sad/troubled/
angry/stern/serious** look/
expression/face

● **LOOK OR EXPRESSION?** Your
expression is usu. a reflection of
what you happen to be thinking or
feeling at any particular moment; a
look is either the expression of
what happens to be in your eyes, or it
can be a way of deliberately
communicating a thought or
feeling to a particular person: you
can **give** or **throw** a look or
exchange looks with sb.

5 [C, usu. sing.] (also **looks** [pl.])
■ *It's going to rain today by the look
of it.*

appearance + **air**

▶ (a) **striking/distinctive** look/
looks/appearance
▶ **have** a ...look/appearance/air
▶ **improve/like** sb/sth's look/looks/
appearance

● **LOOK, LOOKS OR APPEARANCE?**

Appearance is used about how sb/
sth seems in contrast to how they
really are; it is also used about how
people make themselves look
attractive: *To all appearances he
was dead.* ◆ *She was always very
particular about her appearance.*
Look is used esp. in the phrases *by
the look of it/him/her, etc.* and *(not)
like the look of sb: I don't like the look
of that guy* (= I don't trust him,
judging by his appearance).
Looks usu. means 'physical
appearance': *She has her mother's
good looks.*

6 [sing.] ■ *The punk look is in again.*

fashion + **style** + **trend** | *written*
vogue

▶ a **new** look/fashion/style/trend/
vogue
▶ the **latest** look/fashion/style/
trend
▶ **create** a look/style/trend/vogue

look *verb*

1 [I] ■ *She looked at me and smiled.*

watch + **see** + **glance** + **stare** + **peer** +
glare | *infml* **check** sb/sth **out** | *fml* **view**
+ **observe** + **regard** + **contemplate** |
esp. written **gaze**

▶ look/glance/stare/peer/glare/
gaze **at** sb/sth
▶ look/watch **for** sb/sth
▶ look/watch/stare at/view/
observe/regard/contemplate (sb/
sth) **with** amazement/surprise/
disapproval, etc

2 [I] ■ *Are you still looking for a job?*

search + **hunt** + **scout** | *fml* **seek** |
written **forage** + **cast about/around**
for sth

▶ look/search/hunt/scout/seek/
forage **for** sb/sth
▶ look/search/hunt/scout/forage
around (for sth)
▶ look/search/hunt **through** sth
▶ look for/search for/seek/cast
around for a/an **alternative/way**
▶ look/search/hunt for **clues**

3 *linking verb* (not usu. used in the
progressive tenses) ■ *You look tired.*

seem + **appear** + **sound** + **feel**

▶ look/seem/appear/sound/feel
odd/OK/nice, etc.
▶ look/seem/sound/feel **like** sth
▶ look/seem/sound/feel **as if/as
though** ...
▶ look/seem/appear **to be** sth

look after sb/sth *phrasal verb*

1 (*esp. BrE*) ■ *She stayed at home to
look after a sick child.*

look after yourself

take care of sb • attend to sb •
nurse | written care for sb • tend

▶ look after/take care of/nurse/care
for/tend to **the sick**
▶ look after/take care of/care for **the
children/the elderly/an elderly
relative**
▶ look after/take care of **yourself**
● LOOK AFTER, TAKE CARE OF OR CARE
FOR SB? To **care for sb** is often a
long-term, full-time occupation;
you can **take care of sb** or **look
after sb** for a short time.

2 (*esp. BrE*) ■ *He looks after the team's
sponsorship.*

take care of sb/sth • deal with sb/
sth • handle | *spoken* see to sth

▶ look after/take care of/deal with/
handle/see to **the matter**
▶ look after/take care of/deal with/
handle **a problem**
▶ look after/take care of/deal with/
handle **the correspondence/
paperwork/customers**

look after yourself *phrasal
verb* (esp. BrE)

■ *He's barely able to look after himself.*

take care of yourself • fend for
yourself • stand on your own (two)
feet

▶ be able to **look after yourself/take
care of yourself/fend for yourself/
stand on your own feet**
▶ be capable of **looking after
yourself/taking care of yourself/
fending for yourself**
● LOOK AFTER, TAKE CARE OF OR FEND
FOR YOURSELF? Use **look after
yourself** or **take care of yourself**
to talk about sb who is responsible
for their own care, health and
safety. Use **fend for yourself** to
talk about dealing with more
practical situations, such as finding
food, shelter or money. It is often
used to describe a person or animal
that is in a difficult situation.

look at sth *phrasal verb*

1 ■ *I think a doctor should look at your
swollen ankle.*

examine • check • inspect • look sb/
sth over • check over sb/sth

▶ look at/examine/check/inspect
sth **to see if/whether...**
▶ look at/examine/check/inspect/
look over/check over sth **carefully**
▶ look at/examine/check/inspect
sth **closely**

2 ■ *In this chapter we will look at three
different theories.*

consider • think • reflect • take | *esp.
written* ponder | *fml* contemplate

▶ look at/consider/think/reflect/
ponder/contemplate **how/what/
whether...**
▶ look at/consider/think/reflect/
ponder **carefully/briefly**
▶ look at/think/reflect/ponder
long and hard

3 ■ *I look at it this way:...*

see • view • consider • count | *fml*
regard

▶ look at/see/view/consider/
count/regard sth **as sth**
▶ look at/see/view/consider/regard
sb/sth **from a particular point of
view**
▶ look at/see/view/regard sb/sth
with sth

look forward to sth *phrasal
verb* (often used in the progressive
tenses)

■ *We're looking forward to seeing you
again.*

expect • hope • anticipate | *fml*
await

● OPP **dread**
▶ look forward to/expect/hope for/
anticipate/await **a reply**
▶ look forward to/expect/
anticipate/await **the arrival** of sb/
sth

look into sth *phrasal verb*

■ *The local MP is looking into the
workers' claims.*

investigate • explore • research •
inquire/enquire into sth • delve into
sth | *esp. journ.* probe

▶ look into/investigate/explore/
research/inquire into **what/why/
how/whether...**
▶ look into/investigate/explore/
research/inquire into **a problem/
matter**
▶ look into/investigate/inquire into/
probe **an allegation**

look like sb/sth *phrase* (not
used in the progressive tenses)

■ *She doesn't look at all like her sister.*

take after sb • resemble

▶ look like/take after/resemble your
**mother/father/grandmother/
grandfather/aunt/uncle**
▶ look superficially/(not) remotely
like sb
▶ superficially/(not) remotely
resemble sb

look through sth *phrasal verb*
[no passive]

■ *She looked through her notes before
the exam.*

flick through sth • leaf through sth
• scan • skim • dip into sth • read

► look through/flick through/leaf through/dip into/read a **book**
► look through/flick through/leaf through/scan/skim/read a **newspaper/paper**
► look through/flick through/leaf through/scan/skim **the pages of** sth
● LOOK THROUGH OR FLICK THROUGH STH? If you **flick through** sth you do it more quickly than if you **look through** sth, which is usu. more deliberate.

look sth up *phrasal verb*
■ *I looked it up in a dictionary.*

refer to sb/sth • consult

► look up/refer to/consult a **website**
► look sth up in/refer to/consult a/an **dictionary/encyclopedia/guide/manual**
► refer to/consult the **map/the timetable/the schedule/your notes**
● LOOK STH UP, REFER TO SB/STH OR CONSULT? The object of **look sth up** is usu. the information you want to find, rather than the place where you look to find the information: *Look this word up in the index.* ♦ *Refer to/consult the Help file for more information.*

lord *noun* [C]
■ *He was made a peer and took the title Lord Bellamy.*

peer • noble • nobleman • aristocrat • lady

► a **great/wealthy** lord/noble/nobleman/aristocrat/lady
► a **hereditary** lord/peer/noble
► **become** a lord/peer

lorry *noun* [C] (*BrE*)
■ *The lorry rumbled over the bridge.*

van • vehicle • *esp. AmE* truck

► **by** lorry/vehicle/truck
► a **heavy** lorry/vehicle/truck
► **drive** a lorry/van/vehicle/truck

lose *verb*
1 [T] ■ *I've lost my keys.*

forget • leave | *esp. BrE, fml* mislay

■ OPP **find**
► lose/forget/leave/mislay your **keys/wallet/bag**

2 [I, T] ■ *So far we haven't lost a game.*

trail • come off worse/worst

■ OPP **win**
► lose/trail/come off worse **in** sth
► lose/trail **by** sth
► lose/trail **badly**

3 [T] ■ *Hurry—there's no time to lose.*

---

disapprov. waste • throw sth away • squander | *infml* blow • splurge

■ OPP **save**
► lose/waste/throw away/squander/blow/splurge sth **on** sth
► lose/waste/throw away/squander/blow/splurge **money**
► lose/waste/throw away/squander/blow/splurge a/an **fortune/chance/opportunity**

lose out *phrasal verb*
■ *I just lost out on the first prize.*

miss | *infml* pass sth up

► lose out/miss/pass up a/an **chance/opportunity**

loser *noun*
1 [C] ■ *They were 16–3 losers to New Zealand.*

runner-up | *often disapprov.* also-ran

■ OPP **winner**
► a/an loser/runner-up/also-ran **in** sth
► a loser/runner-up **to** sb
► **winners** and losers/runners-up

2 [C] (*infml, often disapprov.*) ■ *She's one of life's losers.*

failure • underachiever | *disapprov.* incompetent | *infml, disapprov.* no-hoper • disaster

■ OPP **winner**
► a **group/bunch** of losers/incompetents/no-hopers

lose your temper *idiom*
■ *She lost her temper and started shouting.*

get angry • lose patience • go berserk | *BrE, infml* go mad | *AmE, infml* get mad

■ OPP **keep your temper**
► lose your temper/get angry/lose patience/get mad **with** sb
► lose your temper/get angry/get mad **at** sth
► lose your temper/get angry **over** sth
● LOSE YOUR TEMPER OR GET ANGRY? If you **lose your temper** you show it in your behaviour; if you **get angry** the emphasis is more on your feelings and less on your behaviour.

loss *noun* [C]
■ *The bank announced losses of $8 billion.*

debt | *finance* liability • arrears • debit

■ OPP **profit**
► **heavy/massive** losses/debts
► **run up** losses/debts

loss-making adj.

■ *The publisher sold its loss-making magazine business.*

unprofitable • uneconomic • non-profit

■ OPP **profit-making, profitable**
▶ a loss-making/an unprofitable/a non-profit **company**
▶ loss-making/unprofitable/uneconomic **industries**
▶ loss-making/unprofitable **routes/years**

loud adj.

■ *That music's too loud.*

deafening • roaring • ear-splitting | *often disapprov.* **noisy**

■ OPP **quiet, soft**
▶ a/an loud/deafening/roaring/ear-splitting **noise**
▶ loud/deafening/roaring/ear-splitting **applause**
▶ (a) loud/deafening **crash/roar/cheer/shout**

love noun

1 [U] ■ *a mother's love for her children*

affection • tenderness • devotion • attachment • liking

■ OPP **hatred, hate**
▶ love/affection/tenderness/liking **for** sb
▶ love/affection/tenderness/devotion **between** A and B
▶ **show** love/affection/tenderness/devotion
▶ **feel** love/affection/tenderness/an attachment
● LOVE OR AFFECTION? Love can be a mild feeling or a very strong one:
✔ *Bob sends his love* (= best wishes/regards). • *There is nothing greater than a mother's love for her children.* ✗ *There is nothing greater than a mother's affection for her children.*
Affection is a gentle feeling, often shown in the way sb talks to, looks at or touches sb else:
✔ *She spoke/treated him/looked at him/hugged him with great affection.*

2 [U] ■ *He fell madly in love with her.*

passion • desire • romance • attraction • infatuation • crush | *often disapprov.* **lust**

▶ love/passion/desire/attraction/infatuation/lust **for** sb
▶ **sexual/physical/mutual** love/passion/desire/attraction/lust
▶ **find** love/romance
▶ love/passion/attraction/desire **grows**
● LOVE, PASSION OR DESIRE? Love is the most general of these words. Passion and desire are stronger

words and are more to do with physical love and sex.

3 [U, sing.] ■ *We share a love of music.*

passion • liking • taste

▶ a **great** love/passion/liking **for** sth
▶ **have/develop/share** a love/passion/liking/taste **for** sth
● LOVE OR PASSION? Passion is stronger than **love** and may affect the way you live your life: *The family had a passion for art and the house was full of paintings and sculptures.*

love verb

1 [T] (not used in the progressive tenses) ■ *I love you.*

care for sb • be fond of sb • like • be devoted to sb • adore • idolize • dote on/upon sb

■ OPP **hate, loathe, detest**
▶ love/care for/be fond of/like/be devoted to/adore/dote on your **children**
▶ love/care for/be fond of/like/be devoted to/adore your/sb's **husband/wife/father/mother**
▶ **really** love/care for/like/adore/idolize/dote on sb

2 [T] (not usu. used in the progressive tenses) ■ *My dad loves cricket.*

adore • like • be fond of sth | *BrE, infml* **be keen on sth**

■ OPP **hate**
▶ love/adore/like/be fond of/be keen on **doing** sth
▶ I love/adore/like it here/there/when…
▶ love/adore/like **the way** sb does sth
● LOVE OR ADORE? Adore is more informal than **love**, and expresses a stronger feeling.

in love adj.

■ *We're in love!*

besotted • infatuated | *infml* **crazy about sb |** *often humorous* **smitten**

▶ in love/besotted/infatuated/smitten with sb
▶ **totally/completely** in love/crazy about sb/besotted/infatuated/smitten

lovely adj.

1 (*esp. BrE*) ■ *We walked through lovely countryside.*

beautiful • attractive • pretty • scenic • picturesque • charming • exquisite

■ OPP **horrible**
▶ a/an lovely/beautiful/attractive/

pretty / picturesque / charming
place / town / village

▸ a / an lovely / beautiful / attractive / scenic / picturesque / charming / exquisite **setting / view**

▸ lovely / beautiful / attractive / picturesque **countryside / scenery / surroundings**

● LOVELY OR BEAUTIFUL? Something that is **lovely** always has a warm quality that appeals not only to the eyes but also to the heart; **beautiful** things often have this quality, but they do not have to:
✔ The designs were pure, austere and coldly beautiful. ✘ The designs were pure, austere and coldly lovely.

2 (esp. BrE) ■ She was looking lovely.

beautiful • pretty • attractive • good-looking • striking | infml **gorgeous • stunning** | esp. AmE, infml **cute**

■ OPP horrible, ugly

▸ a / an lovely / beautiful / pretty / attractive / good-looking / striking / gorgeous / stunning / cute **girl / woman**

▸ a / an lovely / beautiful / pretty / attractive / good-looking / striking / cute **face**

▸ a / an lovely / beautiful / attractive / gorgeous / cute **body**

3 (esp. BrE, esp. spoken) ■ We had a lovely day.

wonderful • delightful • enjoyable | BrE, esp. spoken **marvellous** | AmE, esp. spoken **marvelous** | lit. **delicious**

■ OPP horrible

▸ a lovely / wonderful / delightful / marvellous / delicious **feeling / sensation**

▸ (a) lovely / wonderful / delightful / marvellous **experience / time / place / scenery / weather**

▸ It's lovely / wonderful / marvellous **to be / feel / find / know / have / see...**

● LOVELY, WONDERFUL OR DELIGHTFUL? **Lovely** is the most frequent in spoken BrE. In AmE **wonderful** is the most frequent, both written and spoken. **Delightful** is used mostly to talk about times, events and places.

4 (esp. BrE, esp. spoken) ■ Her mother's a lovely woman.

wonderful • charming • pleasant • friendly • kind • lovable • charismatic • engaging | esp. BrE **likeable** | esp. AmE **likable** | esp. spoken **nice • sweet**

■ OPP horrible

▸ a / an lovely / wonderful / charming / pleasant / friendly / kind / lovable / charismatic / engaging / likeable / nice / sweet **man**

▸ a / an lovely / wonderful / charming / pleasant / friendly / kind / lovable /

engaging / likeable / nice / sweet **person**

▸ a / an lovely / wonderful / charming / pleasant / friendly / kind / engaging / kind / nice / sweet **woman**

lover noun

1 [C] ■ He denied that they were lovers.

mistress • partner • girlfriend • boyfriend • concubine • gigolo

▸ **have** a lover / mistress / partner / girlfriend / boyfriend / concubine

▸ **be** sb's lover / mistress / partner / girlfriend / boyfriend / concubine / gigolo

● LOVER OR MISTRESS? A **lover** can be male or female, but a **mistress** can only be a woman. **Mistress** is rather old-fashioned and is often used to describe the partners of powerful men: Charles II fathered eight sons by his five mistresses.

2 [C] ■ She was a great lover of opera.

fan • enthusiast • admirer • devotee | sometimes disapprov. **fanatic**

▸ a great lover / fan / enthusiast / admirer

▸ a music / art / jazz lover / fan / enthusiast / devotee / fanatic

loving adj.
■ He came from a warm and loving family.

caring • devoted • affectionate • tender • fond • adoring • romantic

▸ a / an loving / caring / devoted / affectionate / fond / adoring **mother / father / parent**

▸ a / an loving / caring / devoted / affectionate / adoring **husband / wife / family**

▸ a / an loving / caring / devoted / affectionate **friend**

low adj.

1 [not before noun] ■ Our food supplies were running low.

scarce • in short supply • short • limited

■ OPP plentiful

▸ **supplies** are low / limited

▸ **resources** are scarce / in short supply / limited

▸ **food** is scarce / in short supply / short

▸ **time** is short / limited

● WHICH WORD? **Scarce** and **in short supply** are used about resources that are not generally available; **short** is used esp. about time and money; **low** is used esp. about your supplies when you have not got much left.

2 ■ *They spoke in low voices.*

deep | *approv.* **rich** | *music* **bass**

■ OPP **high**
► a low/deep/rich/bass **voice/ sound**
► a low/deep **groan/roar/rumble**
● **LOW OR DEEP?** A **low** voice or sound is one that is near the bottom of the musical scale and is quiet. A **deep** voice or sound is near the bottom of the musical scale and can be loud or quiet.

3 ■ *Sadly, the work was of a low standard.*

poor • bad • second-rate • inferior | *infml* **dismal**

■ OPP **high**
► low/poor/bad/second-rate/ inferior **quality**
► a low/poor/bad **opinion** of sb/sth
► a/an low/poor/inferior/dismal **standard**

loyal *adj.* (*approv.*)

■ *He is one of the president's most loyal supporters.*

faithful • reliable • true • staunch • dedicated • trustworthy • trusted • committed

■ OPP **disloyal**
► loyal/faithful/true/dedicated/ committed **to** sb/sth
► a loyal/faithful/reliable/true/ staunch/trustworthy/trusted **friend**
► a loyal/faithful/dedicated/ staunch/trusted/committed **member** of sth
● **LOYAL OR FAITHFUL?** In many cases you can use either word. However, a loyal *friend/servant* remains loyal as a matter of principle; a *faithful friend/servant* remains faithful from affection.

luck *noun* [U]

■ *It was sheer luck that we met like that.*

chance • coincidence • accident • fortune • fate • destiny | *fml* **providence**

► by ...luck/chance/coincidence/ accident
► bring sb good/bad luck/fortune
► have the... luck/fortune to do sth

lucky *adj.*

1 ■ *Sam knew he was lucky to be alive.*

fortunate • in luck

■ OPP **unlucky**
► lucky/fortunate **that...**
► lucky/fortunate **to do sth**
► feel/consider **yourself/count**

yourself/think yourself lucky/ fortunate

2 ■ *It was lucky for us that he didn't see us.*

fortunate • happy • timely

■ OPP **unlucky**
► lucky/fortunate/timely **for** sb/sth
► lucky/fortunate/timely **that...**
► a lucky/fortunate/happy **coincidence/chance**

luggage *noun* [U] (*esp. BrE*)

■ *Only one item of luggage is allowed in the cabin.*

bags • suitcase | *esp. AmE* **baggage**

► carry luggage/bags/suitcase/ baggage
► check (in) your luggage/bags/ suitcase/baggage
► search sb's luggage/bags/ suitcase/baggage

lump *noun*

1 [C] ■ *He put some lumps of coal on the fire.*

piece • chunk • hunk • cube • wedge • slab • block

► a lump/piece/chunk/hunk/ wedge of **cheese**
► a lump/piece/chunk/hunk/slab of **meat**
► a lump/piece/block/slab of **ice**

2 [C] ■ *I was unhurt except for a lump on my head.*

bump • swelling | *BrE* **tumour** | *AmE* **tumor**

► a lump/bump/swelling/tumour **on** a part of the body
► a lump/swelling/tumour **in** a part of the body
► a painful lump/swelling
► have a lump/bump/swelling/ tumour

lunch *noun* [U, C]

■ *I have a one-hour lunch break.*

dinner • meal | *fml* **luncheon**

► a hot/cold lunch/dinner/meal
► have/eat/serve lunch/dinner/a meal/luncheon
► have sth for lunch/dinner/ luncheon
● **LUNCH OR DINNER?** Lunch is eaten in the middle of the day; in Britain some people call this **dinner** if it is the main meal of the day. A main or formal meal eaten in the evening is usu. called **dinner**.

luxury *noun* [U]

■ *She lived a life of luxury.*

esp. written **grandeur** | *BrE* **splendour** | *AmE* **splendor**

■ OPP **poverty, squalor**

► **sheer** luxury/grandeur/splendour
► **enjoy** the luxury/grandeur/
splendour of sth

271   **magic**

Mm

machine noun [C]
■ *How does this machine work?*

appliance • unit • contraption •
engine • motor

► a/an **electronic/electric/electrical**
machine/appliance/unit/motor
► **operate/run/install/switch on/
switch off/turn on/turn off** a/an
machine/appliance/unit/engine/
motor
► a/an machine/unit/engine/motor
runs/starts/stops/fails/dies

machinery noun [U]
■ *These workshops were built to house
heavy machinery.*

hardware • technology | *tech.* plant

► **existing/modern/new**
machinery/hardware/
technology/plant
► **current/the latest/basic/
advanced/complex/sophisticated**
machinery/hardware/technology
► **have/use/invest in** machinery/
hardware/technology/plant

mad adj.

1 (*esp. BrE, sometimes offens.*) ■ *I'll go
mad if I stay here much longer.*

sometimes offens. **(not) in your right
mind** • **out of your mind** | *infml* nuts
| *esp. AmE, infml* crazy | *esp. BrE, infml*
batty

► **be mad/not in your right mind/
out of your mind/nuts/crazy** to do
sth
► **go** mad/nuts/crazy/batty
► **drive sb/think sb must be** mad/
out of their mind/nuts/crazy/
batty
● **WHICH WORD?** These are all
informal words used to suggest
that sb's behaviour is very strange,
often because of extreme
emotional pressure. They can be
offensive if used to describe sb
suffering from a real mental illness;
use **mentally ill** instead.

2 (*esp. BrE, infml*) ■ *You must be mad
to risk it.*

stupid • idiotic | *infml* insane | *esp.
AmE, infml* crazy • dumb | *esp. spoken*
silly | *esp. written* foolish

■ OPP sensible

► mad/stupid/idiotic/insane/crazy/
dumb/silly/foolish **to do** sth
► a/an mad/stupid/idiotic/insane/

crazy/dumb/silly/foolish **thing to
do/idea**
► **Are you** mad/stupid/insane/
crazy/dumb?

3 [not before noun] (*esp. AmE, infml*)
■ *He's mad at me for being late.*

angry • irate • furious • incensed •
outraged • fuming • seething •
annoyed | *esp. BrE* cross | *written*
enraged | *taboo, slang* pissed off |
AmE, taboo, slang pissed

► mad/angry/furious/incensed/
outraged/fuming/seething/
annoyed/cross/pissed off/pissed
at/about sth
► mad/angry/furious/incensed/
outraged/annoyed/cross/pissed
off/pissed **that...**
► **get** mad/angry/annoyed/cross/
pissed off/pissed
● **MAD OR ANGRY? Mad** is the usual
word for **angry** in informal *AmE.*
When used in *BrE*, esp. in the
phrase **go mad**, it can mean 'very
angry': *Dad'll go mad when he sees
what you've done.*

4 [not usu. before noun] (*infml*)
■ *He's always been mad about
football.*

crazy • enthusiasic • avid | *esp. BrE*
keen

► mad/crazy/enthusiasic **about** sth
► mad/keen **on** sth
► mad/crazy/keen/avid **for** sth

5 ■ *The team won and the fans went
mad.*

wild • crazy • frantic • furious

► a mad/wild/frantic/furious **rush**
► **go** mad/wild/crazy
► mad/wild/crazy **with excitement**

magazine noun [C]
■ *designer clothes from the pages of a
glossy magazine*

journal • supplement • weekly •
comic • fanzine • periodical •
monthly • quarterly | *infml* mag

► **in a** magazine/journal/
supplement/weekly/comic/
fanzine/periodical/monthly/
quarterly/mag
► a **weekly/monthly** magazine/
journal/supplement/comic/
periodical
► **publish** a magazine/journal/
supplement/weekly/comic/
fanzine/periodical/monthly/
quarterly/mag

magic noun [U]
■ *Do you believe in magic?*

witchcraft • black magic • the
supernatural • the occult •
conjuring | *written* sorcery

▶ do sth **by** magic/sorcery
▶ **use** magic/witchcraft/sorcery
▶ a magic/conjuring **trick**

magic *adj.*

■ *a magic spell/charm/potion*

magical • mystical • supernatural |
written enchanted • occult • other-
worldly • transcendental

▶ magic/magical/mystical/
supernatural/occult **powers**

magnificent *adj.*

■ *It was a magnificent performance.*

spectacular • impressive • grand •
glorious • majestic • splendid •
imposing • beautiful • wonderful |
BrE, esp. spoken marvellous | *AmE,
esp. spoken* marvelous

▶ a/an magnificent/spectacular/
impressive/glorious/majestic/
splendid/beautiful/wonderful/
marvellous **sight**
▶ magnificent/spectacular/grand/glorious/
majestic/impressive/grand/glorious/
marvellous **scenery/views**
▶ a/an magnificent/impressive/
grand/majestic/imposing/
beautiful **building**

mail *noun* [U]

■ *There isn't any mail for you today.*

letter • email • message • note •
memo • fax • text | *BrE* post | *fml*
correspondence • communication •
memorandum

▶ (a/an) mail/letter/email/
message/note/memo/fax/text/
post/correspondence/
communication/memorandum
from/to sb
▶ (a) **personal/private** mail/letter/
email/message/note/
correspondence/communication
▶ **send/receive** (a/an) mail/letter/
email/message/note/memo/fax/
text/post/correspondence/
communication/memorandum

mail *verb* [T] (*esp. AmE*)

■ *Don't forget to mail that letter.*

send • forward • send sth on | *BrE*
post | *fml, esp. busin.* dispatch

▶ mail/send/forward/send on/
post/dispatch sth **to** sb
▶ mail/send/forward/send on/
post/dispatch a **letter**
▶ mail/send/forward/send on/
post/dispatch an **invitation/
package/parcel/postcard/reply**

main *adj.* [only before noun]

■ *Health and safety is our main
concern.*

major • key • chief • leading •
central • principal • prime • primary
• predominant | *infml* number one

■ **OPP** secondary, minor
▶ a/the main/major/key/chief/
central/principal/prime/primary/
predominant/number one
concern
▶ a/the main/major/key/chief/
central/principal/prime/primary
**aim/focus/function/objective/
task/reason**
▶ a/the main/major/key/leading/
central/principal **role**
▶ main/major/principal **road/
town/city**

maintain *verb*

1 [T] ■ *We must maintain law and
order.*

keep sth up • preserve • sustain •
extend • prolong | *esp. spoken* keep
sth going | *fml* perpetuate | *often
disapprov., esp. busin.* prop sth up

▶ maintain/keep up/preserve/
sustain **standards/a relationship**
▶ maintain/keep up/sustain **levels/
rates/morale/interest/growth**
▶ maintain/preserve/sustain/
extend/prolong (sb's) **life**
● **MAINTAIN OR SUSTAIN? Maintain** is
used esp. to talk about keeping sth
at its usual level for an unlimited
period of time; **sustain** is used
more to talk about keeping sth at a
higher level than usual for a long
but not unlimited period: *Is the role
of the state simply to maintain the
status quo?* • *How long can such fast
growth be sustained?*

2 [T] ■ *The house and its grounds are
beautifully maintained.*

preserve • service • keep sth up

▶ maintain/preserve a **house**
▶ maintain/service a/an **car/
appliance**
▶ have/keep sth **maintained/
preserved/serviced**

major *adj.* [usu. before noun]

■ *He played a major role in the
handover.*

main • key • chief • leading • central
• principal • prime • primary •
predominant | *infml* number one

■ **OPP** minor
▶ a/the major/main/key/chief/
central/principal/prime/primary/
predominant/number one
concern
▶ a/the major/main/key/leading/
central/principal **role**
▶ a/the major/main/key/chief/
central/principal/prime/primary
**aim/focus/function/objective/
task/reason**
▶ major/main/principal **road/
town/city**

make

make noun [C]
■ *What make of car does he drive?*

brand • model • label

▶ a make/brand/model of car
▶ a popular/leading/major/famous/well-known make/brand/model/label
● MAKE OR MODEL? All cars made by one company are the same **make**. For each make there will be a range of **models** (= designs): *We need to know the make, model and year of your car.*

make verb

1 [T] ■ *Wine is made from grapes.*

create • produce • manufacture • build • develop • generate • form | *esp. spoken* **do**

■ OPP **destroy**
▶ make/create/produce/manufacture/build/develop/generate/form **from/out of** sth
▶ make/develop/form sth **into** sth
▶ make/create/produce/do a **drawing/painting**
● MAKE OR CREATE? **Make** is a more general word and is used esp. about physical things: you would usu. *make a table/dress/cake* but *create jobs/wealth*. You can use **create** about sth physical to emphasize how original it is: *Try this new dish, created by our head chef.*

2 [T] ■ *This cake is very easy to make.*

cook • bake • brew | *esp. written* **prepare** | *esp. spoken* **get** | *esp. AmE* **fix**

▶ to make/cook/bake/prepare/get/fix sth **for** sb
▶ to make/cook/bake/prepare/get/fix sb/yourself sth
▶ to make/cook/prepare/get/fix **breakfast/lunch/dinner**

3 [T] ■ *Who made these unjust laws?*

plan • design • formulate

▶ make/plan/design/formulate sth **to do** sth
▶ make/formulate a **plan/hypothesis**

4 [T] ■ *The rock made a dent in the roof of the car.*

cause • create • produce

▶ make/cause/create/produce a **hole**

5 [T] ■ *Nothing will make me change my mind.*

lead • prompt • motivate • provoke • persuade | *fml* **induce • predispose**

▶ make sb **do** sth
▶ lead/prompt/motivate/provoke/persuade/induce/predispose sb **to do** sth

6 [T] ■ *They made us work very hard.*

force • drive | *fml* **oblige • compel • impel**

▶ be made/force sb/drive sb/be obliged/compel sb/impel sb **to do** sth
● MAKE OR FORCE? **Make** is slightly more informal. It is usu. a person who **makes** sb else do sth: *Mum made me eat all my cabbage.* **Force** often suggests threats, or a situation where you have to do what to do: *The hijackers forced the passengers to lie on the ground.* • *The plane was forced to make an emergency landing.*

7 [T] ■ *50 and 450 make 500.*

be • equal • add up to sth • amount to sth • number • run to sth | *esp. busin.* **total**

▶ make/be/equal/add up to/amount to/number/run to/total **50/2 million/$250/75%, etc.**
▶ make/add up to/amount to/number/run to/total **nearly/almost/about/approximately/over/more than** sth

8 [T] ■ *She sold her foreign investments and made $75 000.*

raise • fetch • bring (sb) in sth | *esp. spoken* **get** | *fml* **realize**

■ OPP **lose**
▶ make/raise/bring in **money**
▶ make/raise/fetch/bring in/get/realize **$199/£300 000**
▶ make/realize **£1 000/$50 000 on** a deal
● MAKE, BRING IN STH OR GET? You can **make** money, a particular amount of money, or a profit or loss. You can **bring in** money or a particular amount of money. You can only **get** a particular amount of money:
✓*The garage sale made/brought in a lot more than we expected.* ✗ ~~The garage sale got a lot more than we expected.~~
✓*The company is making a loss.* ✗ ~~The company is getting/bringing in a loss.~~

9 [T] ■ *She made a fortune on the stock market.*

earn • bring (sb) in sth • **net • gross** | *infml* **pull sth in** | *fml* **profit** | *sometimes disapprov.* **pocket** | *infml, sometimes disapprov.* **rake in**

■ OPP **lose**
▶ make/earn/bring in/net/gross/pull in/pocket/rake in **$100000 a year**
▶ make/earn **money/a living/a fortune**
● MAKE OR EARN? **Earn** emphasizes the work you have to do to get

money. If the money comes as interest or profit, and the subject is a person, use **make**; if the subject is a business, use either word:
✔ The business made/earned the family £3 million last year. ✗ She earned a fortune on the stock market.

maker noun [C] (often in compounds)

■ His father was a watchmaker.

manufacturer • producer • builder • designer • developer • creator • inventor | often approv. craftsman

► a car maker/manufacturer/ producer
► a computer maker/manufacturer
► a steel/wine maker/producer
● MAKER, MANUFACTURER OR PRODUCER? Maker and manufacturer are used esp. about goods such as cars that are put together from different parts; producer is used more about natural materials such as oil that are grown or obtained and then processed. Maker is also used about products for which quality and skill are seen to be important, such as steel and wine.

make sure phrase

1 ■ Make sure (that) no one finds out.

ensure • see to it that ... • guarantee • assure

► make sure/ensure/see to it/ guarantee that...
► make absolutely sure
► absolutely ensure/guarantee/ assure sth

2 ■ Make sure (that) the door's locked.

check | fml verify • assure yourself

► make sure/check/verify/assure yourself that...
► go and make sure/check
► always make sure/check/verify sth

make sth up phrasal verb

1 (not used in the progressive tenses)
■ Women make up over 50% of the student body.

consist of sb/sth • constitute | fml comprise • be composed of sb/sth

► The group is made up of/consists of/has/comprises/is composed of ten people.
► Ten people make up/constitute/ comprise the group.

2 ■ He made up some excuse about his son being sick.

invent • fabricate • come up with sth • trump sth up • coin | infml think sth up

► make up/invent/fabricate/come up with/think up a story
► make up/invent/come up with/ think up a/an excuse/name
► make up/fabricate evidence

make up for sth phrasal verb (usu. approv.)

■ She made up for missing the penalty by scoring two great goals.

usu. approv. compensate • balance | esp. busin. offset

► make up/compensate for sth
► more make up for/ compensate for/balance/offset sth
● MAKE UP FOR STH OR COMPENSATE? Compensate is more formal but can be used in a wider range of structures, with or without for:
✔ Try to avoid overeating and then having to compensate by going on a strict diet. ✗ Try to avoid overeating and then having to make up by going on a strict diet.

man noun

1 [C] ■ Over 150 men responded to the survey.

infml guy | fml gentleman • male | BrE, infml bloke | esp. AmE, slang dude

► OPP woman
► a/an young/old man/guy/ gentleman/male/bloke/dude
► a/an middle-aged/older man/ guy/gentleman/male/bloke
► a good/great/funny man/guy/ bloke/dude

2 [U] ■ They uncovered tools used by prehistoric man.

humanity • mankind • the human race • humankind

● WHICH WORD? Man can be used to refer to humans when compared with other animals; to describe the development of people through history; or to talk about all the people and societies of the world:
the relationship between man and nature • Stone Age man • all diseases known to man
This last use is becoming old-fashioned because many people now replace man and mankind with gender neutral words like humanity and humankind.

manage verb

1 [T, I] ■ We managed to find a solution.

succeed • achieve • reach • accomplish | BrE fulfil | AmE fulfill | infml pull sth off • get there | fml attain • effect

► manage/succeed in/achieve/ accomplish/fulfil a task

▶ manage/achieve/accomplish/pull off a **feat**

2 [I] ▪ *It's difficult to manage on such a small income.*

cope • get by • get on | *esp. BrE* **muddle through**

▶ manage/cope/get by/muddle through **without** sth
▶ manage/get by **on** sth
▶ manage/get by/muddle through **somehow**

● **MANAGE OR COPE?** The subject of **manage** in this meaning is always a person; the subject of **cope** may be a person, thing or system:
✓*In heavy rain the system can't cope.* ✗ *In heavy rain the system can't manage.*
People often have to *manage* without a particular thing that they need or usu. have, or *on* a limited amount of money.

3 [T] ▪ *The program helps you manage data efficiently.*

organize • arrange

▶ manage/organize/arrange sth **in** a particular way
▶ manage/organize/arrange **information/data/things**
▶ manage/organize/arrange your **affairs**

4 [T, I] ▪ *Who is going to manage the new project?*

run • control • be in charge • be responsible for sb/sth • administer • direct

▶ manage/run/control a/an **company/business/organization**
▶ manage/run/control be in charge of/be responsible for/administer/direct a **project**
▶ manage/run/be responsible for/ administer a **service**

● **MANAGE OR RUN?** Managing a business, department, etc. means making decisions about how it should operate and organizing other employees. **Run** emphasizes organizing the necessary tasks.

5 [T] ▪ *It's a book about how to manage stress.*

control • handle

▶ manage/control a **child**
▶ be **easy/difficult** to manage/ control/handle

management noun

1 [U] ▪ *The report blamed bad management.*

leadership • administration • supervision • regulation • direction

▶ **under** the management/ leadership/administration/ supervision/direction **of** sb

▶ **day-to-day** management/ administration/supervision
▶ **be responsible for** the management/administration/ supervision/regulation **of** sth

2 [U+sing./pl. v., C] ▪ *Union leaders are meeting with management.*

leadership • executive • administration • directorate

▶ the **new/current/existing** management/leadership/ executive/administration
▶ the **central** management/ leadership/executive/ administration/directorate
▶ the **college/hospital** management/administration

● **MANAGEMENT, EXECUTIVE OR ADMINISTRATION?** There are different levels of **management** including *top, senior, middle* and *junior management*, although **management** used alone often refers just to the top management. **Executive** can refer to the group of people who lead a political party or trade union; the *executive board* is the highest management group in a company. **Administration** is used esp. to refer to the people who run an organization that provides a service: *the school/college/hospital administration*

manager noun [C]
▪ *a bank/hotel manager*

director • employer • supervisor • superintendent • foreman | *esp. BrE* **governor** | *infml* **boss**

▶ work **for** a/an manager/director/ employer/boss
▶ work **under** a manager/ supervisor/superintendent/ foreman
▶ **have** a/an manager/director/ employer/supervisor/foreman/ governor/boss

● **MANAGER OR DIRECTOR?** Both **manager** and **director** can be used to talk about a person who is in charge of an activity or department within a company: *a sales manager/director*. However, in a large company, a **director** is often in charge of several **managers**.

manipulate verb [T] (disapprov.)
▪ *She uses her charm to manipulate people.*

turn sth to your advantage • steer | *infml* **pull strings** | *often disapprov.* **engineer** | *BrE, sometimes disapprov.* **manoeuvre** | *AmE* **maneuver**

▶ manipulate/manoeuvre sb **into** sth
▶ manipulate/engineer a **situation**
▶ turn a **situation** to your advantage

manner noun

1 [sing.] (fml) ■ She answered in a business-like manner.

way • style • approach

▶ a manner/way/style of (doing) sth
▶ in a (...) manner/way/style
▶ a traditional/conventional/ different/casual/informal/formal manner/way/style/approach
▶ have/adopt a/an manner/way/ style/approach

2 [sing.] ■ She has a friendly, relaxed manner.

air • appearance • look

▶ sb's general manner/air/ appearance
▶ a confident manner/air/ appearance
▶ have a ...manner/air/ appearance/look

3 manners [pl.] ■ It is bad manners to talk with your mouth full.

politeness • etiquette • courtesy • respect • grace • formality | fml civility

▶ good manners/grace
▶ show manners/politeness/ courtesy/respect

manufacture verb [T]

■ The company manufactures bicycle parts.

make • produce • mass-produce • turn sth out | infml, disapprov. churn sth out

▶ a factory that manufactures/ makes/produces cars/ mainframes/microchips
▶ manufacture/make/produce/turn out/churn out 900 cars a week
▶ manufactured/mass-produced goods
● MANUFACTURE OR PRODUCE? Manufacture is more often used in business contexts and emphasizes the process of making goods; produce emphasizes the finished product.

manufacturer noun [C]

■ He was a rich textile manufacturer.

maker • producer • builder • developer | often approv. craftsman

▶ a big/large/leading/major manufacturer/producer
▶ a car manufacturer/maker/ producer
▶ a computer manufacturer/maker
● MANUFACTURERER, MAKER OR PRODUCER? Manufacturer and maker are used esp. about goods such as cars that are put together from different parts; producer is used more about natural materials

such as oil that are grown or obtained and then processed. **Maker** is also used about products for which quality and skill are seen to be important, such as steel and wine.

manufacturing noun [U]

■ Many jobs in manufacturing have been lost.

industry • production • manufacture • making • construction • building • assembly

▶ commercial/industrial manufacturing/production/ manufacture/construction/ building
▶ car/textile manufacturing/ production/manufacture
▶ manufacturing/construction/ building companies/costs/firms/ jobs/materials/work
● MANUFACTURING, PRODUCTION OR MANUFACTURE? Manufacture and production emphasize the process of making goods; manufacturing emphasizes the business of making goods in large quantities: the manufacturing industry. Production can refer to growing food and obtaining raw materials as well as making goods; manufacturing only refers to making goods.

map noun [C]

■ You'll need a road map.

plan • atlas • chart • globe

▶ street/route map/plan/atlas
▶ look at/consult a/an map/plan/ atlas/chart
▶ find sth on a/the map/plan/ chart/globe

march noun [C]

■ The protest march moved slowly along the city streets.

demonstration • protest | BrE, infml demo

▶ a march/demonstration/protest/ demo against sth
▶ a/an anti-war/pro-democracy/ anti-government march/ demonstration/protest/demo
▶ hold/organize/stage/go on/ join/participate in/take part in a march/demonstration/protest/ demo

march verb

1 [I] (usu. used with an adv. or prep.) ■ Guards were marching up and down.

stride • pace • step • walk

▶ march/stride/step/walk to/ towards sb/sth
▶ march/pace/step/walk around/ round sth

▶ march/pace/walk **up and down**

2 [I] (always with an adv. or prep.)
■ *Ann marched straight over and demanded an apology.*

storm ◆ stalk | *infml* stomp | *written* flounce

▶ march/storm/stalk/stomp/flounce **off/away**
▶ march/storm/stalk/stomp/flounce **in/into/out of** (sth)

mark noun

1 [C] ■ *The kids left dirty marks on the wall.*

stain ◆ smear ◆ smudge ◆ spot ◆ streak ◆ fingerprint ◆ blot ◆ blemish ◆ speck

▶ a mark/stain/smear/smudge/spot/streak/fingerprint/blot/blemish/speck **on** sth
▶ **leave** a mark/stain/smear/smudge/streak/fingerprint/blot/speck
▶ **remove** a mark/stain/smear/smudge/spot/fingerprint/blemish/speck

2 [C] ■ *The horse had a white mark on its head.*

spot ◆ dot ◆ patch

▶ a mark/spot/dot/patch **on** sth
▶ **with** marks/spots/dots/patches
▶ a **blue, black, red, etc.** mark/spot/dot/patch

3 (*esp. BrE*) ■ *What's the pass mark?*

grade ◆ score ◆ result

▶ a **high/low/good/poor** mark/grade/score
▶ a **final** mark/grade/score/result
▶ **get** a mark/a grade/a score/your results

● **MARK OR GRADE?** In British schools a **mark** is often more precise than a **grade**, expressed as a particular number out of 10 or 100, for example; **grade** is often a letter such as A, B or C, covering a range of marks. However, in American schools a **grade** can be a letter or a number, and **mark** is not usu. used.

mark verb

1 [T] ■ *Prices are marked on the goods.*

label ◆ highlight ◆ flag | *BrE* tick | *AmE* check

▶ mark/label/highlight/flag/tick/check sth **with** sth
▶ mark/highlight sth **in** red, yellow, etc.
▶ mark/highlight/flag/tick/check **an item**
▶ mark/highlight/flag a/an **word/paragraph/passage/section/error**

● **MARK OR LABEL?** When you use **mark**, you usu. have to say how sth is marked; when sth is **labelled**, sb has written sth on it, for example to say what it is or who it belongs to: *The path is marked in red.* ◆ *All luggage must be clearly labelled.*

2 [T, I] (*BrE*) ■ *Have you marked our homework?*

correct | *esp. AmE* grade

▶ mark/correct/grade a/an/sb's **paper/essay/assignment/work/homework**
▶ mark/grade a/an **test/examination/project/student/pupil**
▶ grade/mark sb/sth **A/B/C, etc.**

marked adj. (esp. written)

■ *There has been a marked increase in profits.*

definite ◆ decided ◆ noticeable ◆ conspicuous ◆ unmistakable/unmistakeable ◆ sharp ◆ clear ◆ striking ◆ distinct | *esp. written* pronounced | *disapprov.* glaring

▶ a marked/definite/noticeable/sharp/clear/striking/distinct/pronounced **difference**
▶ a marked/definite/decided/noticeable/sharp/clear/striking/distinct **improvement**
▶ a marked/conspicuous/striking/distinct/pronounced **feature**

● **MARKED, DEFINITE OR PRONOUNCED?** Definite is used most often to talk about things that you can see or feel; **marked** is used most often in a business context; **pronounced** is used most often to talk about physical or personal characteristics: *a definite smell of gas* ◆ *a marked effect on sales* ◆ *a pronounced limp*

market noun

1 [sing.] ■ *They have 20% of the world market in coffee.*

trade ◆ business ◆ custom ◆ marketplace

▶ the market/a trade **in** sth
▶ (the) **foreign/international/global** market/business/trade/marketplace
▶ the market/business/trade **grows/is booming/picks up/declines**

2 [C] ■ *a dictionary for the Korean market*

audience ◆ public ◆ clientele

▶ a market/an audience **for** sth
▶ **reach** a/an market/audience/wide public
▶ **attract/build up** a/an market/audience/clientele

3 [sing.] (busin.) ■ *The market for large cars is declining.*

demand | infml (no) call for sth

▶ a market/demand/(no) call for sth
▶ (a) buoyant/changing/potential/falling market/demand
▶ stimulate/boost/increase the market/demand
● **DEMAND OR MARKET?** Market is a more specialist business term. People talk about the housing/labour market but they talk about demand for housing/labour. When a business has trouble producing enough goods because so many people want them, people talk about demand rather than the market:
✓*We're struggling to meet the demand.* ✗ ~~We're struggling to meet the market.~~

marriage noun [C, U]
■ *The marriage took place in a local church.*

wedding

▶ sb's first/second, etc. marriage/wedding
▶ a forthcoming/royal marriage/wedding
▶ attend/go to/celebrate a marriage/wedding
● **MARRIAGE OR WEDDING?** Marriage usu. refers to the state of being married; wedding refers to the occasion of getting married: *They had a long and happy marriage.* • *We went to Jim and Sue's wedding last week.*
Marriage can be used to refer to the occasion formally: *You are invited to the marriage of Mark Wallace and Rachel Bull.*

marry verb [T, I]
■ *She married a German.*

get married • remarry | old-fash. or journ. wed

▶ plan/want/hope/be going to marry/get married/remarry
▶ sb never married/got married/remarried/wed
● **MARRY OR GET MARRIED?** If there is no object it is more common to use get married, except in formal English; if there is an object, marry is more common: *We got married in May.* • *I should never have married him.*

marsh noun [C, U]
■ *Cows grazed on the marshes.*

swamp • wetland • bog

▶ drain a marsh/swamp/wetland/bog
▶ sink into the marsh/bog

● **MARSH OR SWAMP?** Both marshes and swamps can have plants growing in them, but only a swamp has trees.

mass adj. [only before noun]
■ *Their latest product is aimed at the mass market.*

large-scale • general • widespread • broad • wide • wholesale • extensive

▶ mass/large-scale/general/widespread/broad/wide/extensive support
▶ mass/general/widespread/broad/wide appeal
▶ mass/large-scale/general/widespread/wholesale/extensive destruction
● **MASS OR LARGE-SCALE?** Mass is used esp. when a lot of people are involved, esp. all together in one place; large-scale is used esp. to talk about business activities that need a lot of resources and affect a wide area: *a mass movement/audience/protest/demonstration* • *a large-scale enterprise/project/operation*

massacre noun [C, U]
■ *Nobody survived the massacre.*

slaughter • carnage • bloodshed • killing • extermination • genocide • the Holocaust

▶ (a/an) bloody/appalling/terrible massacre/slaughter/carnage
▶ be killed in the massacre/slaughter/carnage/bloodshed/genocide/Holocaust
▶ escape/survive the massacre/slaughter/carnage/genocide/Holocaust
▶ prevent a massacre/the slaughter/bloodshed/a killing/genocide

massive adj.
1 ■ *massive rock formations*

heavy • bulky | physics dense

■ **OPP** tiny
▶ a heavy/bulky item/object

2 ■ *a massive increase in spending*

huge • enormous • vast • tremendous • immense • great • colossal • giant • gigantic • monumental

■ **OPP** tiny
▶ a/an massive/huge/enormous/vast/tremendous/great/colossal amount of sth
▶ a/an massive/huge/enormous/tremendous/great/monumental task
▶ a/an massive/huge/enormous/great/giant/gigantic/monumental step

match noun [C] (esp. BrE)
■ I'll watch the match on TV.

game | BrE fixture • tie • test (match)
▶ a match/game/fixture/tie/test against/between/with sb
▶ a/an international/friendly match/game/fixture
▶ win/lose a match/game/fixture/ test/tie
● MATCH OR GAME? Game has a wider range of uses than match. In BrE **match** is used to talk about individual or team sports. In AmE **match** is used for individual sports, but **game** is used for team sports:
✔ (BrE) a football match • (BrE, AmE) a tennis match • a football game • a game of football ✗ a match of football

match verb

1 [T, I] ■ a blue scarf with gloves to match

mix • blend | esp. spoken go | fml coordinate
▶ sth matches/goes with/ coordinates with the curtains/ decor
▶ match/coordinate colours
▶ colours match/blend/go with each other/coordinate

2 [I, T] (not used in the progressive tenses) ■ The two sets of figures don't match.

correspond • agree • tie in • fit | fml correlate • coincide
▶ A corresponds/agrees/ties in/ correlate/coincides with B
▶ A and B match/correspond/ agree/correlate/coincide
▶ figures match/correspond/agree/ correlate/coincide
▶ sb's account/version matches/ corresponds/agrees/correlates/ coincides with sb else's

3 [T] ■ Can you match the quote to the person who said it?

relate • connect • associate | esp. journ. link
▶ match/relate/connect/link sth to sth
▶ match/connect/associate/link sth with sth
▶ match/relate/connect/associate/ link (sth) directly

material noun

1 [U, C] ■ What material is this dress made of?

fabric • cloth • textile
▶ woven/cotton/woollen material/ fabric/cloth/textiles
▶ furnishing/curtain/dress material/fabric

▶ a length/piece/strip/roll/scrap of material/fabric/cloth

2 [C, U] ■ Oil is the raw material for plastic.

substance • chemical | infml stuff | fml or physics matter
▶ a natural/toxic material/ substance/chemical
▶ organic/radioactive material/ substances/chemicals/matter
▶ waste material/chemicals/matter

3 [C, usu. pl.] ■ You have to buy your own art materials.

equipment • gear • kit | infml stuff
▶ basic materials/equipment/kit
▶ have the right materials/ equipment/gear/kit/stuff
▶ use the materials/equipment/ gear/kit

matter noun

1 [C] ■ We had important matters to discuss.

question • issue • concern • subject
▶ a/an matter/question/issue relating to/concerning sth
▶ a key/major/serious/general matter/question/issue/concern/ subject
▶ a political/moral/technical matter/question/issue/concern/ subject
▶ raise/deal with/address/tackle/ discuss/consider/examine/ explore/focus on a/an matter/ question/issue/concern/subject
● MATTER OR QUESTION? In many cases you can use either word. However, a **matter** is often sth practical, whereas a **question** may be sth more philosophical.

2 [sing.] (esp. spoken) ■ What's the matter?

problem • difficulty • issue | disapprov. trouble
▶ the matter/a problem/a difficulty/ an issue/trouble with sth

maximum adj.
■ For maximum effect, do the exercises every day.

utmost • supreme • extreme • intense

■ OPP minimum
▶ maximum/the utmost/supreme/ extreme importance
▶ maximum/the utmost/extreme care/difficulty
▶ maximum/extreme/intense pleasure/enjoyment

meal noun

1 [C] ■ *They sat down to a four-course meal.*

dinner • lunch • banquet • snack • something to eat • feed • feast

► a **great/sumptuous** meal/dinner/ banquet/feast
► a **four-course/five-course, etc.** meal/dinner/lunch/banquet
► **have** (a) meal/dinner/lunch/ banquet/snack/something to eat/ feed/feast

2 [C] ■ *Enjoy your meal.*

food • dinner • diet | *fml* refreshment | *written, esp. journ.* fare

► **(a/an) simple/traditional/ vegetarian/English/Chinese, etc.** meal/food/diet/fare
► **provide** a meal/food/dinner/a... diet/refreshment
► **eat** a meal/food/dinner/a...diet/ ...fare

mean verb

1 [T] (not used in the progressive tenses) ■ *What does this sentence mean?*

indicate • imply • mark | *fml* signify • denote | *esp. journ.* signal

► mean/indicate/imply/signify sth **to** sb
► mean/indicate/imply/signify **that...**
► mean/indicate/mark/signify/ denote/signal the **beginning/ start/arrival/end** of sth

2 [T] (not used in the progressive tenses) ■ *What do you mean by that remark?*

suggest • hint • imply | *spoken* what sb is getting/driving at | *fml* intend | *disapprov.* insinuate

► mean/suggest **by/as** sth
► mean/suggest/hint/imply/ insinuate **that...**
► **seem/appear** to mean/suggest/ hint/imply sth

3 [T] ■ *I didn't mean to hurt you.*

intend • plan • aim | *fml* propose

► mean/intend/plan/aim/propose **to do** sth
► sb **originally** meant/intended/ planned sth

4 [T, usu. passive] (not used in the progressive tenses) ■ *His father meant him to be an engineer.*

be intended • for/as/to be sth • design • be aimed at sth

► be meant/designed/intended **for/ as** sth
► be meant/designed/intended **to be/do** sth

5 [T] ■ *This order will mean working overtime.*

involve • entail • spell | *fml* necessitate • imply

► sth means/implies **that...**
► sth means/involves/entails/ necessitates/implies a/an **increase/reduction**
► sth **usually/inevitably/ necessarily/actually** means/ involves/entails/implies sth

mean adj.

1 (*BrE, disapprov.*) ■ *He was too mean to buy her a decent present.*

frugal | *AmE, infml, disapprov.* cheap | *infml, disapprov.* stingy | *approv.* thrifty

■ OPP generous
► mean/frugal/stingy **with** sth
● MEAN, CHEAP OR STINGY? Mean and stingy can describe a person or an amount of money; cheap can only describe a person.

2 (*esp. spoken*) ■ *Don't be so mean to your little sister!*

unkind • hurtful • unpleasant • obnoxious | *fml* objectionable | *esp. spoken* nasty

■ OPP generous
► be mean/unkind/hurtful/ unpleasant/obnoxious/ objectionable/nasty **to** sb
► be mean/unkind/nasty **of** sb (to do sth)
► a/an mean/unkind/hurtful/nasty **thing to say/do**

meaning noun

1 [C, U] ■ *Words often have several meanings.*

sense • significance

► the **original/exact/precise/ general/true** meaning/sense/ significance
► the **accepted/wide/narrow/ literal/figurative/metaphorical/ legal/technical** meaning/sense
► **have** a meaning/sense/ significance
► **grasp/understand** the meaning/ significance of sth

2 [U] ■ *Her life seemed to have lost all meaning.*

value • worth • merit

► **without** meaning/value/worth/ merit
► **great/real** meaning/value/ worth/merit
► **have** meaning/value/worth/merit

means noun [C]

■ *TV is a highly effective means of communication.*

method + way + system + mechanism + technique + process

▶ a means/method/system/mechanism/technique/process **for** (doing) sth
▶ a means/way/method/system/technique **of** (doing) sth
▶ **use** a means/method/system/technique/process
▶ **devise/develop** a means/method/way/system/technique/process

measurement noun [C, usu. pl.]
■ I'll need to take some measurements.

dimension + size + area + volume + capacity + extent

▶ the **exact** measurements/dimensions/size/area/extent
▶ **measure** the dimensions/size/area/volume of sth

the media noun [sing.+ sing./pl. v.]
■ The media was accused of influencing the decision.

the press + coverage + reporting + journalism	fml reportage

▶ **in/by** the media/press
▶ **(the) mainstream** media/press/coverage/reporting/journalism
▶ the **national/local/free/foreign** media/press

medicine noun

1 [U] ■ He is qualified in traditional Chinese medicine.

treatment + therapy + medical care

▶ **(a/an) alternative/orthodox/conventional** medicine/treatment/therapy

2 [U, C] ■ Have you taken your medicine?

drug + medication + remedy + antidote + prescription + cure

▶ **(a/an)** medicine/drug/medication/remedy/antidote/prescription/cure **for** sth
▶ **prescribe** medicine/drugs/medication/a remedy/a cure
▶ **take** your medicine/your medication/a remedy/the antidote

● MEDICINE, DRUG OR MEDICATION?
Drug emphasizes what the substance is made of; **medicine** and **medication** emphasize what it is used for.

mediocre adj. (disapprov.)
■ His performance was only mediocre.

indifferent + middling + not much of a... + undistinguished	infml so-so

■ OPP **excellent**

▶ a/an **mediocre/indifferent/so-so performance/result/start**
▶ a **mediocre/not much of a/a so-so player**
▶ **mediocre/indifferent/middling/so-so quality**

medium noun [C]
■ The Internet is the modern medium of communication.

vehicle + channel + catalyst	fml instrument

▶ a/an medium/vehicle/channel/catalyst/instrument **of/for** sth
▶ the **a/an main/important/major/effective** medium/vehicle/channel/catalyst/instrument
▶ **see/use** sb/sth **as** a/an medium/vehicle/channel/catalyst/instrument

meet verb

1 [I, T, no passive] ■ I hope we'll meet again soon.

infml run into sb + bump into sb	fml encounter

▶ meet/run into/bump into a **friend**

2 [I, T, no passive] ■ The committee meets on Fridays.

meet with sb + gather + mass + assemble + rally	infml get together + meet up	fml convene

▶ meet/meet with sb/gather/mass/assemble/rally/get together/meet up/convene **for** sth
▶ meet/get together/meet up **with** sb
▶ meet/meet with sb/gather/get together/convene **regularly**

3 [T] ■ Will you meet me at the airport?

greet + welcome	fml receive

▶ meet/greet/welcome/receive sb **with** a smile, etc.
▶ meet/greet/welcome/receive a **guest/visitor**
▶ **be there to** meet/greet/welcome/receive sb

4 [T, no passive, I] ■ Where did you two first meet?

get to know sb	fml make sb's acquaintance

▶ **first** meet/get to know/make the acquaintance of sb

5 [I, T] ■ The curtains don't meet in the middle.

touch + cross + join + merge

▶ rivers meet/join/merge
▶ roads/paths meet/cross/join
▶ **not quite/almost/nearly** meet/cross/touch

6 [T] ■ *How can we meet the needs of all these different groups?*

satisfy • serve • suit | *BrE, fml* **fulfil** | *AmE* **fulfill**

▶ meet/satisfy/serve/suit/fulfil a **requirement/need/purpose**
▶ meet/satisfy/suit/fulfil a **demand/condition**
▶ meet/satisfy/fulfil a/an **standard/obligation**
▶ meet/satisfy/fulfil the **terms/criteria**

meeting noun

1 [C] ■ *Dr Grey will chair the meeting.*

session • gathering • assembly • conference • convention • summit

▶ an **annual** meeting/session/gathering/assembly/conference/convention/summit
▶ **hold/attend** a/an meeting/session/gathering/assembly/conference/convention/summit
▶ **address** a/an meeting/session/gathering/assembly/conference/convention

2 [C] ■ *I was nervous at our first meeting.*

encounter • appointment • date • engagement • introduction

▶ a/an meeting/encounter/appointment/date/engagement **with** sb
▶ **have** a/an meeting/encounter/appointment/date/engagement
▶ **arrange** a/an meeting/appointment/date/introduction

melt verb [I, T]

■ *The snow showed no sign of melting.*

thaw • defrost • dissolve

■ **OPP** freeze
▶ melt/dissolve **away**
▶ **ice/snow** melts/thaws
▶ **completely** melt/thaw/dissolve

memory noun [C, U]

■ *I have a bad memory for names.*
■ *happy memories of childhood*

recall • reminiscence • mind | *fml* **recollection • remembrance**

▶ a memory/reminiscence/recollection **of** sb/sth
▶ **in** memory/remembrance **of** sb/sth
▶ a **vague/vivid/clear** memory/recollection
▶ **have** a ...memory/recall/recollection

mental adj. [usu. before noun]

■ *Mental performance is impaired by alcohol intake.*

psychological • intellectual

■ **OPP** physical
▶ a/an mental/psychological/intellectual **problem/concept**

mentally ill adj.

■ *She was severely stressed, but not mentally ill.*

disturbed • unstable | *esp. written* **insane • deranged • crazed** | *med.* **neurotic • psychotic**

▶ **seriously** mentally ill/disturbed/neurotic/psychotic
▶ **emotionally/mentally** disturbed/unstable

mention verb [T]

■ *No one mentioned anything to me about it.*

refer to sb/sth • speak • say • quote | *fml* **cite • allude to sb/sth**

▶ mention/refer to/speak of/quote/cite/allude to sb/sth **as** sb/sth
▶ mention/refer to/quote/cite a/an **example/case/instance**
▶ the example mentioned/referred to/quoted/cited/alluded to **above/earlier/previously**

mercy noun [U]

■ *The prisoners begged for mercy.*

forgiveness • grace | *fml* **pardon • clemency • charity**

▶ **divine** mercy/forgiveness/grace
▶ **ask** for mercy/(for) forgiveness/(for) pardon
▶ **show no/receive** mercy/forgiveness/charity

mess noun

1 [C, usu. sing.] ■ *The room was in a mess.*

muddle • jumble • clutter | *fml* **disorder**

▶ a mess/muddle/jumble/clutter **of** sth
▶ **in** a mess/a muddle/a jumble/disorder
▶ **be** a mess/muddle/jumble

2 [C, usu. sing.] ■ *The economy is in a mess.*

chaos • confusion • straits • predicament • plight | *infml* **shambles**

▶ **in** (a) mess/chaos/confusion/...straits/predicament/plight/shambles
▶ (a) **financial** mess/straits/predicament/plight
▶ (a) **complete/total** mess/chaos/confusion/shambles
▶ **cause/create** (a) mess/chaos/confusion

message noun

1 [C] • *Ricky left me a message.*

note • email • memo • text • text message • mail | *fml* **communication • memorandum**

▶ a/an **message/note/email/ memo/text/text message/mail/ communication from/to** sb
▶ a **brief message/note/email/ memo/communication**
▶ **send/receive** a/an **message/ note/email/memo/text/text message/mail/communication**

2 [C, usu. sing.] • *It's a film with a strong message.*

the thrust • substance • subject matter • content • thread • gist

▶ the **main message/thrust/ substance/subject matter/ content/thread** of sth
▶ the **general message/thrust/ content/gist** of sth
▶ **get/understand** the **message/gist** of sth

metaphor noun [C, U]

■ *The writer uses the game of football as a metaphor for the competitive struggle of life.*

image • imagery • allegory | *tech.* **simile • figure of speech**

▶ (a) **striking metaphor/image/ imagery/image**
▶ (a/an) **powerful/vivid/poetic metaphor/image/imagery**
▶ **use** (a/an) **metaphor/image/ imagery/simile/figure of speech**
● **WHICH WORD? Metaphor, allegory** and **simile** are all types of **figure of speech**. These words all refer to the words, phrases, figures or ideas used to create an **image** in the mind of the reader.

method noun [C]

■ *He's quite critical of modern teaching methods.*

technique • way • means • process • procedure • approach • system • mechanism | *fml* **methodology**

▶ a **method/technique/means/ process/procedure/system/ mechanism/methodology for** (doing) sth
▶ a **method/technique/way/ means/system/methodology of** (doing) sth
▶ **use** a/an **method/technique/ means/process/procedure/ approach/system/methodology**
▶ **devise/develop** a/an **method/ technique/way/means/process/ procedure/approach/system/ methodology**

the middle noun [sing.]

■ *a lake with an island in the middle*

centre

■ **OPP edge, end, side**
▶ the **middle/centre of** sth
▶ **in the middle/centre**
● **THE MIDDLE OR THE CENTRE? The centre** of an area may be a more precise area than the **middle:** *the centre of a circle* is the point in the exact middle. **Middle** but not **centre** can be used to describe a situation or a period of time:
✓*When they quarrel, I am often caught in the middle.* ✗ *When they quarrel, I am often caught in the centre.*

middle class adj. (sometimes disapprov.)

■ *a rather middle-class attitude*

sometimes disapprov. **bourgeois**

▶ a **middle-class/bourgeois family/ institution**
▶ **middle-class/bourgeois culture/ intellectuals/liberalism/values**
● **MIDDLE CLASS OR BOURGEOIS?** Both these words can be used to show disapproval of people and cities. However, in writing about history or politics **bourgeois** is also used in a neutral way to describe a social class.

mild adj.

1 ■ *a mild form of the disease*

gentle • light

■ **OPP severe**
▶ mild/light **punishment**
▶ (a) gentle/light **breeze/wind/rain**
▶ gentle/light **work/exercise**
● **MILD, GENTLE OR LIGHT? Mild** is used esp. to describe diseases, drugs, criticism, punishment and the weather. **Gentle** is used esp. to describe weather, temperature, work and exercise. **Light** is used esp. to describe weather, work, exercise and punishment.

2 ■ *an exceptionally mild spring day*

dry • clear | *approv.* **sunny • good** | *esp. BrE, approv.* **fine** | *tech.* **temperate**

■ **OPP cold, harsh**
▶ mild/dry/clear/sunny/good/fine **weather**
▶ a **mild/dry/clear/sunny/fine day/ morning/evening/afternoon**
▶ a **mild/temperate climate**

3 ■ *a mild curry/cheese*

disapprov. **bland • tasteless**

■ **OPP hot, strong**
▶ a **mild/bland taste/flavour**
▶ **food** is bland/tasteless

mind noun

1 [C, U] ■ *All kinds of thoughts ran through my mind.*

head ◆ brain ◆ soul ◆ spirit ◆ the/your subconscious | *psychology* ego

▶ the **human** mind/brain/soul/spirit
▶ a thought **enters** sb's mind/head
▶ **deep in** your mind/the brain/your subconscious

● MIND OR HEAD? **Head** is slightly more informal than **mind** in this meaning and is used esp. to talk about thoughts and ideas that *get into your head* or that you *can't get out of your head.*

2 [C, usu. sing.] ■ *His mind is as sharp as ever.*

intelligence ◆ intellect ◆ brain ◆ wits ◆ genius | *AmE, infml* smarts

▶ (a) **great** mind/intelligence/intellect/brain/genius
▶ **have** a …mind/intelligence/intellect/a …brain/…wits/genius/smarts
▶ **use** your mind/intelligence/brain/wits/smarts

mind verb

[T, I, no passive] (used esp. in question or with negatives; not used in the progressive tenses) (*esp. spoken*)
■ *I don't mind wet weather.*

care | *esp. BrE, spoken* be bothered

▶ mind/care/be bothered **about** sth
▶ mind/care/be bothered **that**…
▶ **not** mind/care/be bothered **what** people think

minor adj. [usu. before noun]

■ *There may be some minor changes to the schedule.*

slight ◆ small ◆ modest | *esp. spoken* little | *esp. written* insignificant ◆ unimportant ◆ marginal | *often disapprov.* trivial ◆ petty | *fml, esp. busin.* peripheral

■ OPP major, serious, severe

▶ minor/small/little/unimportant/trivial/petty/peripheral **things**
▶ minor/small/little/insignificant/unimportant/trivial **details**
▶ a minor/slight/small/little/trivial/petty **problem**
▶ minor/petty **crime/theft/criminals**

minute noun [C]

■ *Could I see you for a minute?*

moment ◆ second ◆ instant ◆ split second | *esp. BrE, esp. spoken* bit | *infml, spoken* sec

▶ **in/for** a/an minute/moment/second/instant/split second/bit/sec/instant

▶ **at/from that** minute/moment/second/instant

▶ **hang on/hold on/wait** a/an minute/moment/second/sec

● MINUTE, MOMENT OR SECOND? In many cases you can use any of these words: *Wait/Hang on/Just a minute/moment/second.* **Minute** is the most frequent in spoken English; it is more usual to use **moment** in written English, esp. when telling a story.

miracle noun [C] (*infml*)

■ *It's a miracle no one was killed in the accident.*

wonder ◆ marvel ◆ phenomenon | *infml* fluke

▶ It's a miracle/wonder/fluke **(that)** …
▶ a miracle/wonder/phenomenon **of** sth
▶ **work/perform** a miracle/wonders

mislead verb [T]

■ *The company has deliberately misled its customers.*

delude | *infml* kid ◆ string sb along ◆ lead sb on

▶ mislead/delude sb **about** sth
▶ **deliberately** mislead sb/lead sb on

misleading adj.

■ *They face prosecution if they provide false or misleading information.*

deceptive ◆ ambiguous ◆ spurious

▶ a misleading/an ambiguous **statement**
▶ a misleading/spurious **argument/claim/impression**
▶ **highly/dangerously** misleading/ambiguous/deceptive

● MISLEADING OR DECEPTIVE? Sth that is **misleading** gives the wrong idea about sth, esp. deliberately, but without actually lying. Sth that is **deceptive** usu. gives a false impression without meaning to: *deceptive appearances*

miss verb

1 [T] ■ *I think you're missing the most important point here.*

overlook

■ OPP notice

▶ miss/overlook a **point/fact/detail/feature**
▶ **be easy/hard/impossible to** miss/overlook sth
▶ **be easily** missed/overlooked

2 [T] ■ *She hasn't missed a game all year.*

shirk ◆ skip | *BrE, infml* skive | *AmE, infml* goof off

▶ miss/skip a **class/meal**
▶ miss/skip sth **altogether**

3 [T] ■ The exhibition was an opportunity not to be missed.

infml **pass sth up** • **lose out**

▶ miss/pass up/lose out on a/an **chance/opportunity**
▶ be too good to miss/pass up

mission noun [C]

■ Her mission in life was to work with the homeless.

vocation • **purpose**

▶ find your mission/vocation/purpose
▶ a **sense of** mission/vocation/purpose
▶ sb's mission/vocation/purpose **in life**

miss sb/sth out phrasal verb (BrE)

■ Have I missed anyone out?

esp. spoken **leave sb/sth out** • **leave sb/sth off (sth)** | *fml* **omit**

■ OPP **include**
▶ miss/leave sb/sth **out of** sth
▶ leave out/omit sb/sth **from** sth
▶ leave out/omit **the details/a reference**

mistake noun

1 [C] ■ Don't worry—we all make mistakes.

error • **blunder** • **gaffe** • **oversight** | *fml* **omission**

▶ sth happens **due to** a/an error/mistake/blunder/oversight/omission
▶ **make** a/an mistake/error/blunder/gaffe
▶ **realize/admit (to)** a/an mistake/error/blunder
▶ **correct** a/an mistake/error/blunder/omission

2 [C] ■ His essay is full of spelling mistakes.

error • **slip** • **misprint** • **inaccuracy** | *esp. BrE, infml* **howler**

▶ a/an mistake/error/slip/misprint/inaccuracy/howler **in** sth
▶ **make** a/an mistake/error/slip/howler
▶ **contain/be full of** mistakes/errors/misprints/inaccuracies/howlers

mistake sb/sth for sb/sth phrasal verb

■ I think you must be mistaking me for someone else.

confuse • **take** | *esp. spoken* **mix sb/sth up**

▶ mistake/take sb/sth **for** sb/sth
▶ be **easily** mistaken for/confused with sb/sth

mistaken adj.

■ It was a case of mistaken identity.

wrong • **false** • **inaccurate** • **incorrect** • **misguided** • **untrue**

■ OPP **correct**
▶ be mistaken/wrong **about** sth
▶ mistaken/wrong/false/inaccurate/incorrect/untrue **information**
▶ **give/get** a mistaken/the wrong/a false/an inaccurate **impression**

misunderstand verb [I, T]

■ Please don't misunderstand—I'm very grateful for your help.

misinterpret • **mistake** • **misread** • **misjudge** | *spoken* **get sb/sth wrong**

■ OPP **understand**
▶ misunderstand/misinterpret/mistake/misread sth **as** sth
▶ misunderstand/misinterpret/mistake/misjudge **what...**
▶ misunderstand/misinterpret/mistake sb's **meaning/intentions**

mix verb [T, I]

■ Mix all the ingredients together in a bowl.

blend • **combine** • **stir** • **beat** • **whip** • **whisk** | *written* **mingle**

■ OPP **separate**
▶ mix/blend/combine/mingle (sth) **with** sth
▶ mix/blend/stir/beat/whisk/mingle (sth) **into** sth
▶ mix/blend/stir/beat/whisk/mingle (A and B) **together**
● **MIX OR BLEND?** If you **blend** things when you are cooking you usu. combine them more completely than if you just **mix** them.

mixed adj. [only before noun]

■ a mixed-ability class

diverse • **assorted** • **miscellaneous** | *often approv.* **varied** | *fml* **heterogeneous** • **eclectic** | *esp. written, often disapprov.* **motley**

■ OPP **homogeneous**
▶ a/an mixed/diverse/assorted/miscellaneous/varied/heterogeneous/motley **group**
▶ a mixed/diverse/miscellaneous/varied/heterogeneous/motley **collection**
▶ **racially/ethnically/culturally/socially** mixed/diverse

mixture noun

1 [C, U] ■ The city is a mixture of old and new buildings.

combination • **blend** • **variety** • **range** • **array** • **assortment** • **diversity** • **composite** | *often approv.* **mix**

mix sb/sth up

▶ a/an **mixture/blend/ combination/variety/range/ array/assortment/diversity/ composite/mix** of sth
▶ a **wonderful mixture/blend/ combination/variety/range/ array/assortment/diversity/mix**
▶ an **interesting mixture/blend/ combination/variety/range/ array/assortment/mix**
▶ a/an **unusual/strange mixture/ blend/combination/assortment/ mix**
● **MIXTURE OR COMBINATION?** A **combination** of things has often been put together deliberately; a **mixture** of things often just happens.

2 [C, U] ■ *Add an extra egg to the cake mixture.*

mix • blend • alloy • cocktail • concoction | tech. **compound • solution • suspension**

▶ a **special mixture/mix/blend/ concoction**
▶ a **cake/spice mixture/mix**
▶ a/an **mixture/alloy/compound/ solution/suspension contains/ containing sth**
● **MIXTURE OR MIX?** A *cake* **mixture** is the substance you make by adding all the ingredients; a *cake* **mix** is a powder that you buy and to which you simply add liquid.

mix sb/sth up *phrasal verb*

1 ■ *Someone has mixed up all the application forms.*

jumble • shuffle | esp. BrE **muddle**

▶ **mix/jumble/muddle** things up
▶ be **mixed/jumbled/muddled** up
▶ **mix** up/**jumble** the **letters in a word/words in a sentence**
● **MIX STH UP, JUMBLE or MUDDLE?** You can **mix** things up or **jumble** them either by mistake or deliberately; things are always **muddled** by mistake:
  ✔*The words in these questions have been mixed/jumbled up.* ✗ *The words in these questions have been muddled up.*
  You can **mix** up or **muddle** papers or forms by getting them in the wrong order; things that are **jumbled** are usu. objects which are not in any order at all.

2 (esp. spoken) ■ *She always gets her left and right mixed up.*

confuse • mistake sb/sth for sb/sth • take

▶ **mix** sb/sth up/**confuse** sb/sth **with** sb/sth

model *noun*

1 [C] ■ *The architects produced a scale model of the proposed factory.*

copy • replica • mock-up • reconstruction • reproduction

▶ a/an **good/accurate model/ copy/reconstruction/reproduction**
▶ a **full-scale/life-size model/ replica/reconstruction**
▶ **make** a **model/copy/replica/ reconstruction/reproduction**

2 [C] ■ *The latest models will be on display at the motor show.*

brand • make • label

▶ a **model/brand/make of** car
▶ a **popular/leading/major/ famous/well-known model/ brand/make/label**
● **MODEL OR MAKE?** All cars made by one company are the same **make**. For each make there will be a range of different **models** (= designs): *We need to know the make, model and year of our car.*

3 [C] ■ *The nation's constitution provided a model that other countries followed.*

pattern • prototype • blueprint • template • precedent

▶ a **model/pattern/prototype/ blueprint/template/precedent for** sth
▶ **provide/serve as/act as** a **model/ prototype/blueprint/template/ precedent**
▶ **follow/copy** a **model/pattern/ blueprint/template/precedent**
● **MODEL OR PATTERN?** A **pattern** is always an excellent example, and one that people should follow; a **model** is an example that people do follow, usu. because it works well. A system or organization is/ provides a **model** but sets a **pattern**.

moderate *verb* [T, I] (fml)

■ *They agreed to moderate their original demands.*

tone sth down • modify | fml **temper**

▶ **moderate/tone down/modify** your **language**
▶ **moderate/tone down/modify** your **behaviour/demands/views**

modern *adj.*

1 [only before noun] ■ *Stress is a major problem of modern life.*

modern-day • present-day • contemporary • present • current • recent • latest • new

■ OPP **ancient**

▶ **modern/recent times/**the **present time**
▶ **modern/contemporary/present/ current/recent/**the **latest trends**

- ▶ modern/modern-day/present-day/contemporary/a new **society**
- ▶ (a) modern/contemporary/recent/new **literature/writer**

2 ■ *She has very modern ideas of education.*

modernist • futuristic • avant-garde • postmodernist • experimental

■ OPP old-fashioned
- ▶ modern/modernist/avant-garde/postmodernist/experimental **art/writing/works**
- ▶ a/an modern/modernist/futuristic/avant-garde **style**
- ▶ a modern/modernist/futuristic **building**

3 (usu. approv.) ■ *modern farming methods*

advanced • up to date • state of the art

■ OPP old-fashioned
- ▶ modern/advanced/up to date/state of the art **design/technology/techniques**
- ● MODERN OR ADVANCED? Both these words can be used in the contexts of technology and economics; **modern** can also be used in the contexts of social relations and culture.

modest *adj.* (approv.)

■ *She's very modest about her success.*

humble • unassuming • unpretentious

■ OPP vain, boastful
- ▶ a/an modest/humble/unassuming/unpretentious **person/man/woman**
- ▶ in a/an modest/humble/unassuming **way**

mom (*AmE*) (*BrE* mom) noun [C] (*infml, esp. spoken*)

■ *My mom says I can come to the party.*

mother • stepmother • parent • guardian | *AmE, infml, esp. spoken* **mommy** | *BrE, infml, esp. spoken* **mummy** | *esp. AmE, infml* **folks**
- ▶ a **good/bad** mom/mum/mother/parent
- ▶ sb's **new** mom/mum/mother/stepmother/parent
- ▶ **become** a/sb's mom/mum/mother/stepmother/parent/guardian
- ● MUM OR MOTHER? In spoken English **mom/mum** is much more frequent. It can sound formal to say *my mother.*

moment noun

1 [C] ■ *He thought for a moment before replying.*

minute • second • instant • split second | *esp. BrE, esp. spoken* **bit** | *infml, spoken* **sec**
- ▶ **in/for** a/an moment/minute/instant/second/split second/bit/sec
- ▶ **at/from that** moment/minute/instant/second
- ▶ **hang on/hold on/wait** a moment/minute/second/sec
- ● MOMENT, MINUTE OR SECOND? In many cases you can use any of these words: *Wait/Hang on/Just a moment/minute/second.* **Minute** is the most frequent in spoken English; it is more usual to use **moment** in written English, esp. when telling a story.

2 [sing.] ■ *At that very moment, the phone rang.*

instant • point • hour • time • occasion
- ▶ a moment/the point/sb's hour/a time **of** sth
- ▶ **at the** moment/that instant/that point/the time
- ▶ **for the** moment/time/occasion
- ▶ **the very/precise** moment/instant/hour/time

3 [C] (*esp. spoken*) ■ *I'm waiting for the right moment to tell him the bad news.*

chance • opportunity • occasion | *esp. busin.* **window**
- ▶ a **suitable** moment/opportunity/occasion
- ▶ **have** a/an moment/chance/opportunity/occasion
- ▶ **wait for** the moment/a chance/an opportunity/an occasion

money noun

1 [U] ■ *The hospital is raising money for a new kidney machine.*

funds • finance • capital • means | *infml* **cash**
- ▶ **government/public** money/funds/finance/capital/cash
- ▶ **have/lack** the money/funds/finance/capital/means/cash (**to do** sth)
- ▶ **be short of** money/funds/capital/cash

2 [U] ■ *I counted the money carefully.*

cash • change
- ▶ **draw out/get out/take out/withdraw** money/cash
- ▶ **ready** money/cash (= money that you have available to spend immediately)
- ● MONEY OR CASH? If it is important to contrast money in the form of coins and notes with money in other forms, use **cash**:

✔Payments can be made by cheque or in cash. ✘ ~~Payments can be made by cheque or in money.~~

3 [U] ■ *He lost all his money on the stock market in 2008.*

wealth • fortune | *often approv.*
prosperity | *sometimes disapprov.*
affluence | *lit.* **riches**

▶ **have/possess/accumulate/
acquire/inherit** money/wealth/a
fortune/riches
▶ **bring** money/wealth/prosperity/
affluence/riches
▶ **make** money/a fortune (on/out of
sth)

---

monitor *verb* [T, often passive]
■ *The animals' heartbeat and
temperature are regularly monitored.*

**track • watch • keep track of sb/sth
• keep an eye on sb/sth |** *infml* **keep
tabs on sb/sth**

▶ **monitor/track/watch/keep an eye
on** (sb/sth) **for** sth
▶ **monitor/track/watch/keep track
of/keep tabs on what/where...**
▶ **monitor/track/watch/keep track
of** sth/keep tabs on **how...**
▶ **monitor/track/watch/keep track
of/keep tabs on sb/sth's
movements**
▶ **monitor/watch/keep an eye on/
keep tabs on a situation**
● **MONITOR OR TRACK?** You **monitor**
sth because the information is
necessary and you may need to
take action; you **track** sth because
what you find out might be
interesting.

---

mood *noun*

1 [C] ■ *She's in a good mood today.*

spirits • frame of mind • morale

▶ **in (a) good/better, etc. mood/
spirits/frame of mind**
▶ **in the mood/frame of mind for** sth
▶ **in the mood/frame of mind to do**
sth

2 [sing.] ■ *The film captures the mood
of the interwar years perfectly.*

**atmosphere • climate • spirit •
feeling • feel • aura • tone |** *BrE*
flavour | *AmE* **flavor**

▶ **the general** mood/atmosphere/
climate/spirit/feeling/feel/tone/
flavour
▶ **create a/an** mood/atmosphere/
climate/spirit/feeling/feel/aura/
flavour
▶ **capture the** mood/atmosphere/
spirit/feeling/tone/flavour of sth
● **MOOD OR ATMOSPHERE?** A **mood**
belongs to a group of people at a
particular time and may change as
time passes; an **atmosphere**
belongs esp. to a place, and may

---

stay the same over a period of
time:
✔*a leader who successfully gauged
the popular mood* ✘ ~~a leader who
successfully gauged the popular
atmosphere~~
✔*The hotel offers a friendly
atmosphere.* ✘ ~~The hotel offers a
friendly mood~~

---

moody *adj.* (*disapprov.*)
■ *Moody people can be difficult to live
with.*

**irritable • bad-tempered •
unpredictable • sulky |** *sometimes
disapprov.* **volatile |** *usu. disapprov.*
temperamental | *disapprov.* **sullen |**
infml, disapprov. **grumpy |** *written*
morose • petulant

▶ **a/an moody/irritable/bad-
tempered/unpredictable/sullen/
grumpy/morose man/woman/
person**
▶ **(a/an) unpredictable/volatile
character/personality/behaviour**
▶ **look moody/sulky/sullen/
grumpy/morose/petulant**

---

moral *adj.*

1 [only before noun] ■ *It's a moral
issue.*

ethical

▶ **a moral/an ethical question/
issue/problem/dilemma**
▶ **moral/ethical ideas/values/
standards/principles/practices**
● **MORAL OR ETHICAL? Moral** is used
esp. about individual people's
feelings of what is right and wrong;
ethical is used esp. in the context
of business, politics or society in
general. **Ethical** can sound more
formal and less forceful than
moral.

2 ■ *He led a very moral life.*

**principled • good • virtuous •
ethical • scrupulous**

■ OPP **immoral**
▶ **a moral/principled/good/
virtuous/scrupulous person**
▶ **a moral/good/virtuous life**
▶ **moral/good/ethical behaviour/
practices/principles**

---

morality *noun* [U]
■ *He seems to have no personal
morality at all.*

**morals • ethics • principle •
standards • values • goodness •
purity • right • good |** *fml* **virtue |**
fml, esp. religion **righteousness**

■ OPP **immorality**
▶ **personal** morality/ethics/
principles/standards/values/virtue
▶ **public** morality/morals/ethics/
values/virtue

▶ a **matter of** morality/ethics/
principle

mostly adv.

■ People mostly call him by his
surname.

usually • generally • normally •
most of the time • as a rule •
commonly • often • more often
than not/as often as not | *esp.
written* in general

■ OPP rarely
▶ mostly/usually/generally/
commonly/often **known as…**
▶ mostly/usually/generally/
normally/commonly/often
called/found…
▶ mostly/usually/generally/
normally/commonly/often **used**

mother noun [C]

■ She's the proud mother of twins.

parent • stepmother • guardian |
BrE, infml, esp. spoken mum •
mummy | *AmE, infml, esp. spoken*
mom • mommy | *esp. AmE, infml*
folks

▶ a **good/bad** mother/parent/
mum/mom
▶ sb's **new** mother/parent/
stepmother/mum/mom
▶ **become** a/sb's mother/parent/
stepmother/guardian/mum/mom
● **MOTHER OR MUM?** In spoken
English **mum/mom** is much more
frequent. It can sound formal to
say *my mother.*

motor noun [C]

■ The machine has an electric motor.

engine

▶ a **powerful** motor/engine
▶ **build/make** a motor/an engine
▶ **operate/run/install** a motor/
**switch on/switch off/turn on/
turn off** a motor/an engine
● **MOTOR OR ENGINE? Engine** is usu.
used to talk about vehicles which
use thermal (= heat) energy from
petrol, diesel or steam; **motor** is
used to talk about machines which
run on electricity.

mountain noun [C]

■ They took three days to climb the
mountain.

hill • peak • summit • ridge •
highlands • foothills • fell | *esp. BrE*
moor • moorland

■ OPP valley
▶ **on** a mountain/a hill/a peak/the
summit/a ridge/the fells/the
moors
▶ **in** the mountains/hills/highlands/
foothills/fells
▶ **climb** a mountain/hill/peak/
ridge/fell

mourn verb [T, I]

■ He was still mourning his brother's
death.

grieve | *written* pine

▶ mourn/grieve **for** sb/sth
▶ mourn/grieve the **death** of sb
▶ mourn/grieve **over** a **loss**
● **MOURN OR GRIEVE? Grieve** refers
just to sb's feeling of sadness that
sb has died; **mourn** refers both to
this and also to behaviour which
shows this, for example, in many
countries, wearing black.

move verb

1 [I, T] ■ Don't move—stay perfectly
still. ■ Don't move that box—leave it
just where it is.

stir • shift | *infml* budge | *fml*
dislodge

▶ move/stir/shift/budge/dislodge
(sth) **from** sth
▶ move/shift (sth) **from** sth **to** sth
▶ **won't/wouldn't/refuse to** move/
stir/shift/budge

2 [I] (always used with an adv. or
prep.) ■ She moved towards the
window.

go • travel • run • make your way •
make for sth • head • get • pass •
advance | *fml* proceed

▶ move/go/travel/run/make your
way/get/pass/advance/proceed
from… to…
▶ move/go/travel/run/make your
way/head/advance/proceed
towards sb/sth

3 [I] (always used with an adv. or
prep.) ■ The project is not moving
forward as fast as we had hoped.

develop • progress • advance •
improve • evolve • mature | *infml* come along/on | *esp.
journ.* shape up

▶ move/develop/progress/evolve/
mature **from** sth
▶ move/develop/progress/evolve to
sth
▶ move/develop/progress/
advance/evolve **towards/beyond**
sth

4 [I, T] ■ I'm moving to Scotland.

move out • relocate • leave • quit •
emigrate • migrate

▶ move/move out/relocate/
emigrate/migrate **from… to…**
▶ **decide/plan/want to** move/move
out/relocate/leave/quit/emigrate

5 [T] ■ He was deeply moved by her
story.

affect • touch • impress • take sb's
breath away • dazzle

move in 290

▶ move/impress/dazzle sb **with** sth
▶ it moves/touches/impresses sb to **see/hear** sth
▶ move/affect/touch/impress sb **deeply**

● MOVE, TOUCH OR AFFECT? You can be **moved** by sth that happens to sb else, esp. sth sad; you can be **touched** by what sb else does, esp. a small act of kindness they do for you; you are **affected** by sth that happens to you, or to sb else, but the emphasis is on the effect it has on you.

move in, move into sth
phrasal verb

■ Our new neighbours moved in last week.

settle | *BrE* **set up home**

● OPP **move out**
▶ move in/set up home **together**

movement *noun* [C, U]

■ Don't make any sudden movements.

move + gesture + wave + motion

▶ a little/slight movement/gesture/ wave/motion
▶ make a movement/move/ gesture/motion
▶ sb's every movement/move

move out *phrasal verb*

■ Local people were forced to move out of their homes.

move + leave + relocate + quit + emigrate + migrate

● OPP **move in**
▶ move out/leave/relocate/ emigrate/migrate **from... to...**
▶ threaten to move out/leave/quit
▶ decide/plan/want to move out/ move/leave/quit/relocate/ emigrate

movie *noun*

1 [C] (*esp. AmE*) ■ Have you seen that new Chinese movie?

video + DVD | *esp. BrE* **film**

▶ in a movie/video/film
▶ make/produce/direct a movie/ video/film
▶ see/watch a movie/video/DVD/ film

● MOVIE OR FILM? **Movie** is used esp. in *AmE*; **film** is used esp. in *BrE*. **Movie** can suggest that a film is just entertainment without any artistic value. In *AmE* **film** can suggest that a film has artistic value:

✔ an art film ✘ an art movie

2 movies [pl.] (*esp. AmE*) ■ I've always wanted to work in movies.

film | *esp. BrE* **cinema**

▶ work in movies/film/cinema
▶ the movie/film/cinema **industry**

moving *adj.*

■ His performance was very moving.

touching + poignant + haunting + stirring + uplifting

▶ a/an moving/touching/ poignant/haunting/uplifting **story**
▶ a moving/touching/poignant **moment/tribute**
▶ a/an moving/haunting/uplifting **experience**

mud *noun* [U]

■ The car got stuck in the mud.

soil + earth + ground + dust + clay + peat | *esp. AmE* **dirt**

▶ wet/soft mud/soil/earth/ ground/clay/peat/dirt
▶ dry mud/soil/earth/ground/ dust/clay/peat/dirt
▶ dig the mud/soil/earth/ground/ clay/peat

multiply *verb* [I, T]

■ The problems facing us are multiplying.

build up + accumulate + mount up + pile up | *fml* **accrue**

■ OPP **diminish**, (*fml*) **decrease**
▶ multiply/build up/mount up **to** sth
▶ problems multiply/build up/ accumulate

mum (*BrE*) (*AmE* **mom**) *noun* [C] (*infml, esp. spoken*)

■ My mum says I can come to the party.

mother + stepmother + parent + guardian | *BrE, infml, esp. spoken* **mummy** | *AmE, infml, esp. spoken* **mommy** | *esp. AmE, infml* **folks**

▶ a good/bad mum/mom/mother/ stepmother/parent
▶ sb's new mum/mom/mother/ stepmother/parent
▶ become a/sb's mum/mom/ mother/stepmother/parent/ guardian

● MUM OR MOTHER? In spoken English **mum/mom** is much more frequent. It can sound formal to say *my mother*.

mundane *adj.* (*disapprov.*)

■ mundane matters of household organization

everyday + day-to-day + daily | *disapprov.* **routine + humdrum** | *written, disapprov.* **prosaic**

▶ mundane/everyday/day-to-day/ daily/routine/humdrum **activities/tasks/work**

► a mundane/everyday/day-to-day/
daily/a humdrum **life**
► mundane/everyday/day-to-day/
routine **stuff/matters**

murder noun [C, U]
■ *He was charged with the attempted murder of his wife.*

killing + assassination + slaughter + massacre | *law* **manslaughter** | *esp. AmE, law* **homicide** | *esp. AmE, journ.* **slaying**

► a double/mass **murder/killing/
slaying**
► **commit** murder/manslaughter/
homicide
► **carry out** a/an **murder/killing/
assassination/slaughter/massacre**
● **MURDER OR KILLING?** Killing is usu.
used in the plural about acts
committed during a war, or by
extreme political groups or
organized groups of criminals;
murder more often refers to the
killing of one person.

murder verb [T]
■ *She denies murdering her lover.*

kill + assassinate + shoot | *infml* **take
sb/sth out** | *infml, humorous* **bump sb
off** | *fml* **eliminate** | *esp. AmE, esp.
journ.* **slay**

► **murder/kill/assassinate/shoot sb
in cold blood**
► **brutally** murder/kill/shoot/slay sb

music noun [U]
■ *pop/dance/classical music*

singing + song + melody + harmony

► (a) **beautiful** music/singing/
song/harmony/melody
► **listen to/hear** music/singing/a
song/the melody/the harmony

musician noun [C]
■ *The musicians came back on stage
and bowed.*

**performer + singer + artist + artiste +
entertainer**

► a **talented/famous** musician/
performer/singer/artist/
entertainer

mysterious adj.
■ *He died in mysterious circumstances.*

**strange + odd + uncanny + curious +
bizarre** | *BrE or fml* **peculiar** | *esp.
spoken* **funny + weird**

► a **mysterious/strange/odd/
uncanny/curious/bizarre/
peculiar/funny/weird way**
► mysterious/strange/odd/curious/
bizarre/peculiar **behaviour**
► a **mysterious/strange/odd/
peculiar person/man/woman**

mystery noun [C]
■ *They couldn't solve the mystery of the
missing murder weapon.*

**puzzle + enigma + problem +
paradox + secret**

► a **mystery/puzzle/paradox about**
sth
► a **mystery/puzzle/enigma to** sb
► **solve/remain** a/an **mystery/
puzzle/enigma/problem**
► **explain** a mystery/a problem/a
paradox/the secrets of sth
● **MYSTERY, PUZZLE OR ENIGMA?** A
puzzle always has a solution if you
can work it out. A **mystery** may
have a solution or it may deal with
deeper and wider issues: *the
mysteries of life/death/science*
An **enigma** is usu. sth that cannot
be solved.

Nn

naive (also **naïve**) adj. (disapprov.)
■ *It was so naive of you to trust him!*

**inexperienced + innocent +
impressionable** | *disapprov.* **gullible** |
often approv. **trusting**

■ OPP **sophisticated**
► a naive/an innocent **belief**
► a/an **inexperienced/
impressionable/gullible/trusting
person**
► an **innocent/impressionable child**

naked adj.
■ *The prisoners were stripped naked.*

**bare + nude + undressed + in the
nude**

■ OPP **clothed, dressed**
► sb's naked/bare **skin/flesh/
shoulder/thigh/torso**
► **completely/almost** naked/bare/
nude

name noun [C]
■ *What's your name?* ■ *Do you know
the name of this flower?*

**title + surname + family name + last
name + first name + middle name +
full name + maiden name + label +
nickname + pseudonym + alias**

► a/an **name/title/first name/label/
nickname/pseudonym/alias for**
sb/sth
► **use** a/an/your **name/title/
surname/family name/first name/
nickname/maiden name/
nickname/pseudonym/alias**
► **choose/decide on** a **name/title/
first name/middle name**
► **change** sb/sth's **name/title/
surname**

name verb

1 [T] ■ *He named his son Jack.*

call ∙ entitle ∙ nickname ∙ christen ∙ dub | *fml* **term ∙ designate**

▸ name/call/nickname/christen/dub sb **Mary/Jack, etc.**
▸ **officially** named/called/entitled/christened/dubbed/termed/designated

2 [T] ■ *The victim has not yet been named.*

identify ∙ recognize

▸ name/identify/recognize sb/sth **as sb/sth**

narrow adj.

1 ■ *I love walking down the narrow streets in the old city.*

thin ∙ fine

■ OPP **wide, broad**
▸ a narrow/thin/fine **crack/strip**
▸ narrow/thin **shoulders**
▸ (a) thin/fine **hair/thread/layer**
● NARROW OR THIN? **Narrow** describes sth that is a short distance from side to side; **thin** describes sth that has a short distance through it from one side to the other:
✔*a narrow street/bed/gap* ✗ *a thin street/bed/gap*
✔*a thin layer/shirt* ✗ *a narrow layer/shirt*

2 [usu. before noun] ■ *He had a narrow escape when his car skidded on the ice.*

close ∙ near ∙ hard-fought | *esp. BrE* **marginal**

▸ a narrow/close **vote**
▸ a narrow/hard-fought **win/victory**
▸ a narrow/marginal **lead**

3 ■ *She only has a narrow circle of friends.*

limited ∙ restricted

■ OPP **wide, broad**
▸ narrow/limited/restricted **in scope**
▸ a narrow/limited/restricted **range/scope/vocabulary**
▸ (a) narrow/limited **objective/horizons**

nation noun

1 [C] ■ *the main industrial nations*

country ∙ state ∙ power ∙ superpower | *lit.* **land**

▸ a **foreign** nation/country/state/power/land
▸ a/an **great/major/leading/industrial/colonial** nation/country/state/power
▸ **rule** a nation/country/state/land
● NATION, COUNTRY OR STATE? You can use all these words to refer to a country as a political unit or to its government. **Nation** and **country** can also refer to an area where people live, its economy, culture, etc. **Country** is the only word which can be used to refer to a country as a geographical area: *a newly independent nation/country/state* ∙ *a wealthy nation/country/state* ∙ *a hot country*

2 the nation [sing.] ■ *The savage murder shocked the entire nation.*

the country ∙ the public ∙ community ∙ society ∙ population

▸ the nation/the country/the public/the community/society/the population **at large/as a whole**
▸ **shock** the nation/country/public/community
● THE NATION OR THE COUNTRY? **The country** is used slightly more when talking about political and economic issues; **the nation** is used slightly more when talking about cultural issues.

national adj.

1 [usu. before noun] ■ *The country has a national debt of 80% of GNP.*

domestic ∙ nationwide ∙ internal ∙ civil | *esp. BrE* **home**

■ OPP **international, local**
▸ national/domestic/home **news**
▸ national/domestic **politics/law**
▸ a national/nationwide **campaign/survey/strike**
● NATIONAL OR DOMESTIC? **National** contrasts with both *international* and *local*; **domestic** contrasts with *international* (or *foreign*) but not with *local*. **Domestic** is mostly used when talking about business and politics; **national** has a wider range.

2 [usu. before noun] ■ *So-called 'hunter's stew' is the national dish.*

native ∙ cultural ∙ ethnic ∙ folk ∙ racial ∙ tribal | *fml* **indigenous**

▸ a/an national/cultural/racial/tribal/indigenous **group**
▸ a/an national/native/ethnic/tribal/indigenous **language**
▸ national/native/ethnic/folk/tribal **dress/costume**

3 [usu. before noun] ■ *The collection is housed at the national museum.*

state ∙ federal ∙ public

▸ national/state/federal/public **authorities/funding/expenditure/investment**
▸ the national/federal **government**

natural adj.

1 ■ *It's natural that he would want to see his own son.*

► natural/obvious/understandable/
logical **that...**
► the natural/obvious/logical **thing
to do/choice/conclusion/
solution**
● **NATURAL OR OBVIOUS?** Obvious is
used esp. to describe a decision,
choice or course of action. Natural
can be used in the same way, but is
more frequently used to describe
feelings: *a natural feeling/desire/
fear.* When obvious is used with
these words it does not mean 'as
you would expect', but 'easy to
notice':
✔Children have a natural desire for
affection. ✗ Children have an obvious
desire for affection.
George ignored Lucy's obvious desire
to be left alone.

2 ■ *Hunting is one of a cat's natural
instincts.*

**innate • instinctive • congenital •
hereditary • genetic • intuitive**

■ **OPP** acquired
► a/an natural/innate/genetic
characteristic
► a/an natural/innate/instinctive/
intuitive **ability/understanding/
response**
► natural/innate/intuitive
intelligence

nature noun

1 [U] ■ *Take time to appreciate the
beauties of nature.*

**the natural world • the
environment • the wild • life •
wildlife • ecosystem • habitat**

► in nature/the environment/the
wild/an ecosystem/a habitat
► (a/an/the) marine/terrestrial/
aquatic **environment/life/wildlife/
ecosystem/habitat**
► protect the natural world/the
environment/... life/wildlife/
habitats

2 [C,U] ■ *It's not in her nature to be
unkind.*

**character • personality •
temperament • self • make-up** | *fml*
disposition • persona

► by nature/temperament
► in sb's nature/character
► a **violent** nature/character/
personality/temperament
► a **generous** nature/character/
disposition
● **WHICH WORD?** Nature is used about
sb's normal way of behaving;
character is used esp. about sb's
moral behaviour. personality is
used esp. about whether sb is
confident, shy, etc. with other
people.; temperament is mostly

used about whether sb normally
stays calm, or gets angry, etc.

3 [sing.] ■ *It's difficult to define the
exact nature of the problem.*

character • essence • stuff • spirit

► in nature/character/essence/spirit
► the **very** nature/character/
essence/stuff/spirit of sth
► **preserve/capture/convey/reflect**
the nature/character/essence of
sth
● **NATURE OR CHARACTER?** Use nature
to talk about the basic qualities of
abstract things, such as society or
risks; use character to talk about
the qualities of buildings, places
and other physical things, esp.
qualities that make a place or thing
seem different or special.

naughty adj.

■ *You've been a very naughty boy!*

**bad • disobedient • rebellious •
defiant**

■ **OPP** good
► a naughty/bad/disobedient/
rebellious/defiant **child**
► a naughty/bad/disobedient **boy/
girl**
► naughty/bad/disobedient/
rebellious/defiant **behaviour**

nearly adj.

■ *I've worked here for nearly two years.*

**almost • virtually • more or less •
not quite** | *esp. spoken* **practically •
about • pretty much/well**

► nearly/almost/virtually/more or
less/not quite/practically/pretty
much **all/every**
► nearly/almost/virtually/more or
less/practically **always**
► nearly/almost/virtually/more or
less/not quite/practically **empty**
● **NEARLY OR ALMOST?** Nearly is more
common with numbers; only
almost can be used before *any,
anybody* and *anything*:
✔There were nearly 200 people at
the meeting. • They'll eat almost
anything. ✗ They'll eat nearly
anything.
In *BrE* you can use *very* and *so*
before *nearly*:
✔He was very nearly caught.

neat adj. (usu. approv.)

■ *He sorted his papers into a neat pile.*

ordered • orderly • uncluttered |
esp. BrE **tidy**

■ **OPP** untidy, (*fml*) **disorderly**
► neat/orderly/tidy **rows**
► a/an neat/orderly/tidy
arrangement

▶ a/an neat/uncluttered/tidy
house/room

● NEAT, ORDERLY OR TIDY? Neat is the
most general of these words and
can describe sb's appearance, a
place or an arrangement of things
such as a *row* or *pile*; **tidy** usu.
describes a place such as a *room* or
desk; **orderly** usu. describes the
way things are arranged in rows or
piles.

necessary adj.

1 ▪ It's not necessary to buy any
special equipment.

essential • vital • crucial • critical •
indispensable | *infml* of the essence
| *fml* imperative • compulsory •
mandatory • obligatory • requisite

▪ OPP unnecessary
▶ necessary/essential/vital/crucial/
critical/indispensable/of the
essence/imperative/requisite for
sth
▶ necessary/compulsory/
mandatory/obligatory for sb to do
sth
▶ necessary/essential/vital/crucial/
critical/imperative/compulsory/
mandatory/obligatory to do sth
▶ necessary/essential/vital/crucial/
critical/imperative that...

2 [only before noun] ▪ This is a
necessary consequence of progress.

inevitable • unavoidable •
inescapable | *fml* inexorable

▪ OPP avoidable
▶ a/an necessary/inevitable/
unavoidable consequence
▶ a/an necessary/inevitable/
inescapable conclusion/fact

need noun

1 [sing., U] ▪ There is an urgent need
for qualified teachers.

essential • necessity | *fml*
requirement • want

▶ a need/necessity/requirement for
sth
▶ basic needs/essentials/necessities/
requirements
▶ human/bodily needs/wants
▶ have/meet/satisfy (sb's) needs/
requirements/wants

2 [C, U] ▪ She felt the need to talk to
someone.

urge • impulse • temptation •
inclination • want | *esp. written* wish
• desire • compulsion | *often
disapprov.* whim

▶ a/an need/urge/inclination/
wish/desire for sth
▶ the need/urge/impulse/

temptation/inclination/wish/
desire/compulsion to do sth
▶ have (a/an) need/urge/impulse/
temptation/inclination/wants/
wish/desire/compulsion

● NEED, URGE OR DESIRE? A need or
an urge is often a strong feeling
that seems to come from the body
rather than the mind: *an instinctive
need/urge*. An **urge** may be very
strong and you may want to try to
control it. **Desire** describes a less
strong feeling, although it can be
combined with strong adjectives
such as *great, burning*, etc.

3 [U] ▪ The charity provides help to
people in need.

poverty • hardship • deprivation •
destitution | *fml* privation

▶ in need/poverty/hardship/
destitution
▶ need/poverty/hardship/
destitution among...
▶ great poverty/hardship/
deprivation/privation

need verb [T] (not usu. used in the
progressive tenses)

▪ Babies need large amounts of love.

rely on/upon sb/sth • call for sth •
demand | *esp. spoken* want | *fml*
require

▶ really need/call for/want/
demand/require sth
▶ just need/want/require sth

negative adj.

1 ▪ The crisis had a negative effect on
trade.

damaging • bad • ill • destructive |
fml harmful • detrimental •
pernicious

▪ OPP positive
▶ a negative/damaging/bad/
destructive/harmful/detrimental/
pernicious effect/ill effects
▶ a negative/damaging/bad/
destructive/pernicious influence
▶ negative/damaging/bad/harmful
publicity

2 ▪ He's been rather negative about
the idea.

pessimistic • gloomy • bleak • dark •
depressing • miserable • black |
infml downbeat

▪ OPP positive
▶ negative/pessimistic/miserable
about sth
▶ a negative/pessimistic/gloomy/
bleak outlook
▶ negative/gloomy/dark/
depressing/black thoughts
▶ paint a negative/pessimistic/
gloomy/bleak/depressing picture
(of sb/sth)

neglect noun [U, sing.]
■ The building is crumbling from years of neglect.

disrepair | *esp. BrE* disuse
■ OPP care, attention
▶ sth happens through neglect/disuse
▶ fall into/be in disrepair/disuse
▶ a period of neglect/disuse

negotiate verb [I]
■ The government is willing to negotiate with the rebels.

hold talks • bargain • do a deal • deal with sb/sth • haggle
▶ negotiate/hold talks/bargain/do a deal/deal/haggle with sb/sth
▶ negotiate/hold talks/do a deal on sth

negotiator noun [C]
■ Union negotiators are meeting management today.

go-between • peacemaker | *fml* mediator • intermediary • arbitrator
▶ a/an peacemaker/mediator/intermediary between A and B
▶ an independent mediator/intermediary/arbitrator
▶ act as (a/an) go-between/peacemaker/mediator/intermediary

neighbourhood (*BrE*) neighborhood (*AmE*) noun
1 [C] ■ They both grew up in the same neighbourhood.

district • quarter • area • part • zone
▶ the whole/entire neighbourhood/district/area/zone
▶ a residential neighbourhood/district/quarter/area/zone
▶ an urban neighbourhood/district/area/zone

2 [C] ■ We searched the neighbourhood for the missing boy.

fml vicinity • locality • proximity
▶ in the neighbourhood/vicinity/locality
▶ in the neighbourhood/vicinity/proximity of sth
▶ the immediate neighbourhood/vicinity/locality/proximity

nervous adj.
1 ■ I was very nervous before the exam.

worried • anxious • uneasy • afraid • frightened • agitated • flustered | *infml* scared | *fml* apprehensive • fearful
■ OPP relaxed
▶ nervous/worried/anxious/uneasy/frightened/agitated/

---

flustered/scared/apprehensive/fearful about sth
▶ nervous/worried/anxious/afraid/frightened/scared/apprehensive/fearful that...
▶ get nervous/worried/anxious/frightened/scared/apprehensive

2 ■ He's not the nervous type.

neurotic • on edge | *infml* edgy • jittery
■ OPP relaxed
▶ a nervous/neurotic man/woman
▶ feel nervous/on edge/edgy/jittery

network noun
1 [C] ■ The company has a network of regional offices.

system • web | *fml* apparatus
▶ a/an network/system/apparatus for sth
▶ in/within a network/a system/a web/the apparatus
▶ create a network/system/web

2 [C] ■ the main US television networks

channel • station
▶ a television network/channel/station
▶ a radio network/station

new adj.
1 ■ These ideas aren't new.

fresh | *often approv.* novel
■ OPP old
▶ a new/fresh/novel idea/approach/way
▶ a new/novel concept/design/feature/form/method
▶ completely/entirely/totally/relatively new/fresh/novel

2 ■ Let me show you my new dress.

brand new • untried
■ OPP old
▶ new/brand new/untried technology
▶ a new/brand new product/computer/house
▶ relatively new/untried

3 ■ I was fairly new to teaching at that time.

unfamiliar with sth • unused to sth | *fml* unaccustomed to sth
▶ new/unused/unaccustomed to sth

news noun [U]
■ Have you heard the news? Pat's coming home! ■ I saw it on the news.

word • report • bulletin • story • item

▶ news/word/a report/a bulletin/a story/an item **about/on** sb/sth
▶ news/word/a report of sb/sth
▶ **have/get/receive/hear** news/word/a report/a bulletin

newspaper noun [C]

■ a national newspaper

paper • newsletter • daily • weekly | BrE **broadsheet |** sometimes disapprov. **tabloid**

▶ a **local** newspaper/paper/newsletter/daily/weekly/tabloid
▶ a **national** newspaper/paper/daily/broadsheet
▶ **read** a newspaper/paper/newsletter
● NEWSPAPER OR PAPER? Newspaper can only be shortened to **paper** when it is clear what is being talked about:
✔ a scrapbook of newspaper cuttings
✗ a scrapbook of paper cuttings

next adj. [only before noun]

■ The next train to Bath will be at 12.20.

the following • coming • future • later | AmE **upcoming |** fml **subsequent • forthcoming • prospective**

■ OPP **last, past**
▶ the **next/following month/decade/generation**
▶ the **next event**
▶ **future/later/upcoming/subsequent/forthcoming events**
▶ sb's **next/future/later/upcoming/subsequent/forthcoming book/marriage**

nice adj.

1 (esp. spoken) ■ Have a nice day!

pleasant • enjoyable | esp. spoken **good |** esp. BrE, esp. spoken **lovely |** fml **pleasurable**

■ OPP **nasty**
▶ It's **nice/pleasant/good/lovely to be/feel/find/have/know/meet/see...**
▶ It would be **nice/pleasant/good/lovely if...**
▶ It's **nice/good/lovely that...**
● NICE, PLEASANT OR GOOD? All these words can describe times, events, feelings and the weather. Nice and **pleasant** can also describe places, and **nice** can describe sb's appearance.

2 (esp. spoken) ■ Our new neighbours are very nice.

charming • friendly • pleasant • good-natured • engaging | esp. BrE **likeable |** esp. AmE **likable |** infml **wonderful |** esp. BrE, esp. spoken **lovely • sweet**

■ OPP **nasty**
▶ a/an **nice/charming/friendly/pleasant/good-natured/engaging/likeable/wonderful/lovely/sweet man/woman**
▶ a/an **nice/charming/friendly/pleasant/engaging/likeable/wonderful/lovely/sweet personality**

nickname noun [C]

■ We had nicknames for all our teachers.

pseudonym • alias

▶ a **nickname/pseudonym/alias for** sb
▶ **use/adopt** a/an **nickname/pseudonym/alias**

night noun

1 [U, C] ■ Where did you spend the night?

night-time • the middle of the night • midnight • the early hours | infml **the small hours**

■ OPP **day**
▶ **in** the night/night-time/middle of the night/early hours/small hours
▶ **at** night/night-time/midnight
▶ **(well) into** the night/early hours/small hours
● NIGHT, NIGHT-TIME OR THE MIDDLE OF THE NIGHT? A **night** can be seen as either a completed or a continuing period of time; **night-time** is seen as a continuing, not a completed period; **the middle of the night** is a point in time during the night:
✔ I lay awake all night. • during the night/night-time ✗ during the middle of the night

2 [U, C] ■ She came round for dinner last night.

evening • dusk • twilight • sunset | esp. AmE, esp. written **sundown |** lit. **nightfall**

■ OPP **morning**
▶ **at** night/dusk/twilight/sunset/sundown/nightfall
▶ **tomorrow/yesterday/Monday** night/evening
▶ night/evening/dusk **falls**
● NIGHT OR EVENING? Evening emphasizes the earlier hours, from about 6pm onwards; night emphasizes the later part of the evening and can include the early hours of the next day: We were up late last night and didn't get to bed till 2 am.
Night can also mean the whole time till it gets light: I'm going to my sister's for the evening (= and coming back later in the evening). • I'm going to my sister's for the night (= and not coming back until the morning).

nightmare noun [C]
■ Losing a child is most people's worst nightmare.

horror • hell • ordeal • trauma
▶ a/an nightmare/ordeal/trauma for sb
▶ suffer a/an nightmare/horror/ordeal/trauma
▶ survive a/an nightmare/ordeal/trauma

nod verb [I, T]
■ She nodded at him to begin speaking.

signal | written gesture
▶ nod/gesture/signal to sb
▶ nod/gesture/signal towards/at/in the direction of sb/sth
▶ nod/gesture/signal (for) sb to do sth

noise noun [C, U]
■ Don't make so much noise.

sound
▶ a big/deafening/loud/high-pitched/low noise/sound
▶ hear/listen to/make/produce a noise/sound
▶ a noise/sound comes from sth/a place
▶ a noise/sound becomes/gets louder, closer, etc.
● NOISE OR SOUND? Sound is anything you hear. A noise is usu. loud and unpleasant:
✔the soft sound of rustling leaves
✗ the soft noise of rustling leaves

noisy adj. (often disapprov.)
■ The field was full of noisy children running around.

loud • deafening • roaring • ear-splitting
■ OPP quiet
▶ a/an loud/deafning/roaring/ear-splitting noise
▶ a loud/deafening crash/roar/cheer

nonsense noun [U, sing.]
■ How can you believe such nonsense?

gibberish • lies | BrE, infml rubbish | esp. AmE, infml garbage | esp. AmE, slang bull | taboo, slang bullshit • crap
■ OPP sense
▶ nonsense/lies/rubbish/garbage/bull/bullshit/crap about sth
▶ talk nonsense/gibberish/rubbish/bullshit/crap
▶ a load/lot of nonsense/rubbish/garbage/bull/bullshit/crap

normal adj.
1 ■ The help desk is available during normal office hours.

ordinary • average • typical • common
■ OPP abnormal, exceptional, strange, odd, weird
▶ normal/common for sb to do sth/for sth to happen
▶ the normal/ordinary/average/common man
▶ a/an normal/ordinary/average/typical working day
▶ in the normal/ordinary course of events/business/things
● NORMAL OR ORDINARY? Sth that is normal is as it should be or as you would expect; the word ordinary makes no comment about how things should be, only about how things are, whether this is good or bad:
✔Her temperature was normal.
✗ Her temperature was ordinary.
✔It's normal to feel tired after such a long journey. ✗ It's ordinary to feel tired after such a long journey.

2 ■ No normal person would do a thing like that.

sane • rational • in your right mind
■ OPP abnormal
▶ a normal/sane/rational person
▶ perfectly/quite/completely/otherwise normal/sane/rational
● NORMAL OR SANE? Sane can be used to talk about yourself in a rather humorous way; normal is always used about other people:
✔Having a laugh helps me to stay sane. ✗ Having a laugh helps me to stay normal.

normally adv.
■ The journey normally takes an hour.

usually • generally • as a rule • mostly • commonly • most of the time • more often than not • as often as not • often | esp. written in general
▶ normally/usually/generally/mostly/commonly/often called/found...
▶ normally/usually/generally/mostly/commonly/often used
▶ normally/usually/generally/commonly/often happen
● NORMALLY OR USUALLY? Usually gives information about what happens in most cases; normally is often used in the context of a particular case: It's normally much warmer than this in July (= but this July is unusually cold). • He normally stayed in luxury hotels (= but this time he could not afford to do so).

note noun [C]
■ I left a note for Diana on her desk.

message • memo • letter | *fml*
memorandum • communication

▶ a note/message/memo/letter/
memorandum/communication
from/to sb
▶ a **brief** note/message/memo/
letter/communication
▶ **send/receive** a note/message/
memo/letter/memorandum/
communication
▶ **write** a note/message/memo/
letter/memorandum

notice noun

1 [U] ▪ *Susan brought the problem to my notice.*

attention

▶ **careful/public** notice/attention
▶ **attract/bring sth to/come to/
escape** sb's notice/attention

2 [C] ▪ *A notice on the board said the class was cancelled.*

**poster • placard • handout • flyer •
circular • leaflet**

▶ sth is **on** a notice/poster/placard/
handout/flyer/circular
▶ **display** a notice/poster/placard
▶ **put up/stick up** a notice/poster

3 [C] ▪ *The notice read 'Keep off the grass'.*

sign • board • plaque

▶ **on** a notice/sign/board/plaque
▶ **put up/see/read** a notice/sign/
board/plaque
▶ a notice/sign/board/plaque
appears/goes up
▶ a notice/sign/plaque **says/reads**
sth
● **NOTICE OR SIGN?** A notice always
gives its information in words; a
sign often uses pictures or
symbols:
✔ a road/traffic/shop/pub sign ✗ a
road/traffic/shop/pub notice

4 [U] ▪ *Prices may be altered without notice.*

warning

▶ notice/warning **of** sth
▶ notice/warning **that…**
▶ **adequate/advance/ample/prior/
written** notice/warning

notice verb [T, I] (not usu. used in the progressive tenses)

▪ *I didn't notice Rob leaving.*

**note • take sth in • see • spot •
catch • detect • look** | *fml* **observe •
witness • perceive**

▶ notice/note/see/detect/observe/
perceive **that…**
▶ notice/note/see/spot/detect/

observe/perceive **how/what/
where/who…**
▶ notice/see/observe/witness sth
happen/sb do sth
▶ **suddenly** notice/see/spot/catch/
detect/perceive sb/sth

noticeable adj.

▪ *Her scars are hardly noticeable now.*

**visible • conspicuous • definite •
decided • distinct • in evidence** | *esp.
written* **marked • pronounced** | *fml*
discernible

▶ **OPP inconspicuous**
▶ noticeable/visible/conspicuous/
discernible **to/in** sb/sth
▶ a noticeable/visible/definite/
distinct/marked/pronounced/
discernible **difference**
▶ a noticeable/visible/definite/
marked/pronounced/discernible
effect

novel noun [C]

▪ *the novels of Jane Austen*

book • title • work • text | *fml*
volume

▶ a novel/book/work/text/volume
about sb/sth
▶ a novel/book/title/work/text/
volume **by** sb
▶ **read/write** a novel/book/work/
text/volume

nuisance noun [C, usu. sing.]
(disapprov.)

▪ *Don't be such a nuisance!*

inconvenience | *infml* **pain •
headache**

▶ a **real** nuisance/pain/headache

number noun

1 [C] ▪ *Think of a number and multiply it by two.*

figure

▶ a **high/low/round** number/figure
▶ **exact/approximate** numbers/
figures
▶ **add/multiply/subtract/divide**
numbers/figures

2 [C] ▪ *He lives at number 12.*

figure • digit

▶ a **binary/decimal** number/figure/
digit
▶ **bear/be marked with/have** a
number/figure
▶ a **sequence/series/set/string** of
numbers/figures/digits

3 [C] ▪ *Huge numbers of animals have died.*

amount • quantity • volume • sum

▶ the number/amount/quantity/
volume **of** sth

▶ a number/quantity of **people/things**
▶ a/an amount/quantity/volume of **information**
▶ an amount/a sum of **money**
● NUMBER, AMOUNT OR QUANTITY?
Number is used with plural countable nouns; **amount** is usu. used with uncountable nouns: a number of books/dogs/people • a large amount of time/money/information

Quantity can be used with both countable and uncountable nouns and is slightly more formal.

Oo

obey verb [T, I]
■ He refuses to obey rules.

follow • respect • carry sth out • act on/upon sth • comply | fml abide by sth • adhere to sth • observe

■ OPP disobey, break
▶ obey/follow/respect/comply with/abide by/adhere to/observe **conventions/rules/regulations/law**
▶ obey/follow/respect/comply with/abide by sb's **will/wishes**
▶ obey/follow/carry out/act on **instructions/orders**

object noun [C]
■ Plastic objects lined the shelves.

thing • item | infml, spoken **thing** | fml **article** • **entity** | tech. **artefact/artifact**

▶ a **precious/valuable** object/thing/item/artefact
▶ **everyday/household** objects/items
▶ **produce/manufacture** a/an object/thing/item/article/artefact
● OBJECT OR THING? **Thing** is a much more general word than **object**. **Object** is used esp. when you do not know exactly what sth is or when you are talking about a whole group of things. An **object** is usu. a solid thing.

object verb [I, T]
■ If nobody objects, we'll postpone the meeting.

protest • complain • disapprove | disapprov. **grumble** | infml, disapprov. **moan**

▶ object/protest/complain/grumble/moan **to sb**
▶ object/protest/complain/grumble/moan **that...**

objective noun [C]
■ What is the main objective of this project?

goal • target • purpose • aim • object • plan • idea • point | fml **end**

▶ objectives/goals/targets/aims/plans **for sth**
▶ **achieve/reach** a/an objective/goal/target/purpose/aim/end
▶ **set/agree on/identify/reach/meet/exceed** a/an objective/goal/target
● OBJECTIVE, GOAL OR TARGET? **Goals** usu. relate to a person or organization's long-term plans. **Targets** are usu. specific figures, such as a number of sales, that are set officially, for example by an employer or a government committee. People often set their own **objectives** that they wish to achieve, for example as part of a project, campaign or piece of writing.

objective adj.
■ It's hard to be objective about your own child.

impartial • neutral • disinterested • non-partisan • unbiased/unbiassed

■ OPP subjective
▶ objective/neutral **about sb/sth**
▶ a/an objective/impartial/neutral/disinterested/unbiased **observer**
▶ a/an objective/impartial/neutral/unbiased **opinion/assessment/analysis**

observation noun [U, C]
■ The suspect is being kept under observation.

surveillance • inspection • examination • survey • check

▶ (a) **close** observation/surveillance/inspection/examination/check
▶ **carry out/do** (a/an) observation/surveillance/inspection/examination/survey/check
▶ a/an observation/inspection/examination/survey/check **reveals/shows/confirms** sth

observe verb
1 [T] (not used in the progressive tenses) (fml) ■ Have you observed any changes lately?

notice • note • take sth in • see • witness • detect | fml **perceive**

▶ observe/notice/note/see/detect/perceive **that...**
▶ observe/notice/note/see/detect/perceive **how/what/where/who...**
▶ observe/notice/witness **sth happen/sb do sth**

obsession

2 [T, I] (not used in the progressive tenses) (*fml*) ■ *The patients were observed over several months.*

watch ♦ look | *fml* **contemplate ♦ regard ♦ view**

▶ **observe/watch/look/ contemplate/regard/view (sb/sth) from** somewhere
▶ **observe/watch what/who/ how...**
▶ **observe/watch/look/ contemplate/regard/view (sb/sth) with** amazement/surprise/ disapproval, etc.

obsession noun [U, C] (*usu. disapprov.*)

■ *She has an unhealthy obsession with her diet.*

preoccupation ♦ mania ♦ fixation ♦ complex | *infml* **hang-up** | *med.* **neurosis**

▶ a/an **obsession/preoccupation/ fixation/complex/hang-up/ neurosis about** sb/sth
▶ a/an **obsession/preoccupation/ mania/fixation for** sb/sth
▶ a/an **obsession/preoccupation/ fixation with** sb/sth
▶ **develop** a/an **obsession/ complex/neurosis**

obstacle noun [C]

■ *We overcame all obstacles put in our path.*

barrier ♦ hurdle ♦ handicap ♦ hindrance | *fml* **impediment** | *esp. journ.* **stumbling block** | *AmE, esp. journ.* **roadblock**

▶ a/an **obstacle/barrier/hurdle/ handicap/impediment/stumbling block to** sb/sth
▶ a **major obstacle/barrier/hurdle/ handicap/impediment/stumbling block**
▶ **remove** a/an **obstacle/barrier/ impediment/stumbling block/ roadblock**
▶ **overcome** a/an **obstacle/barrier/ hurdle/handicap/impediment/ roadblock**
● **OBSTACLE OR BARRIER?** A **barrier** makes sth impossible to do or achieve; an **obstacle** makes sth difficult but not impossible.

obtain verb [T] (*esp. written*)

■ *Further details can be obtained from the secretary.*

get hold of sth ♦ take ♦ extract | *esp. spoken* **get** | *esp. written* **gain** | *infml* **pick up sth** | *fml* **acquire ♦ procure ♦ secure**

▶ **obtain/take/extract/get/gain/ pick up/acquire/procure/secure from** sb/sth

▶ **obtain/get hold of/take/get/ gain/pick up/acquire/procure information**
▶ **obtain/get hold of/get/pick up/ acquire/procure a ticket**
▶ **obtain/take/extract/get water/ oil/minerals**

obvious adj.

1 ■ *It's obvious that something is wrong.*

clear ♦ plain ♦ apparent ♦ evident ♦ self-evident ♦ noticeable ♦ distinct ♦ definite ♦ conspicuous | *esp. written* **marked ♦ pronounced** | *disapprov.* **blatant ♦ glaring**

▶ **obvious/clear/plain/apparent/ evident/self-evident/noticeable/ conspicuous to/in** sb/sth
▶ **obvious/clear/plain/apparent/ evident/self-evident/noticeable from** sb/sth
▶ **obvious/clear/plain/apparent/ evident who/where/why...**
● **OBVIOUS, CLEAR OR PLAIN?** You make sth **clear** or **plain** deliberately, but you make sth **obvious** without meaning to:
✔*I hope I make myself clear/plain.*
✗*I hope I make myself obvious.*
✔*Try not to make your dislike so obvious.* ✗*Try not to make it so clear/plain.*

2 ■ *She was the obvious choice for the job.*

natural ♦ logical ♦ understandable

▶ **obvious/natural/logical/ understandable that...**
▶ the **obvious/natural/logical thing to do/choice/solution/ conclusion**
▶ the **obvious/a natural/an understandable temptation**

occasion noun

1 [C] ■ *They've been seen together on several occasions.*

time ♦ date ♦ moment

▶ **on that occasion/date**
▶ **for the occasion/time/moment**
▶ a/an **memorable/emotional occasion/time/moment**

2 [C] ■ *The concert was a very special occasion.*

event ♦ celebration ♦ party ♦ function | *infml* **get-together**

▶ a **special occasion/event/ celebration/party**
▶ a **family occasion/event/ celebration/party/get-together**
▶ a **social occasion/event/function**

occasional adj. [only before noun]

■ *Occasional gunshots could still be heard.*

intermittent | *written* **sporadic** | *esp. spoken* **the odd...**

■ OPP **regular, frequent**
▶ occasional/intermittent/sporadic **contact/attacks/bursts** of sth
▶ on a/an **intermittent/sporadic basis**
▶ the occasional/odd **bit/bout/spot** of sth

occasionally *adv.*
■ *We occasionally meet for a drink after work.*

once in a while • sometimes • at times • from time to time • now and again/then • on occasion(s) • every so often

■ OPP **regularly, frequently**
▶ **appear/wonder** occasionally/sometimes/at times/from time to time
▶ **happen** occasionally/sometimes/at times/from time to time/now and again
▶ **crop up** occasionally/from time to time

occupied *adj.*
■ *She's fully occupied with a life in politics.*

involved • busy • active • at work | *fml* **engaged**

■ OPP **at leisure**
▶ occupied/involved/busy **with** sth
▶ occupied/involved/active/engaged **in** sth
▶ **keep sb** occupied/involved/busy/active
● **OCCUPIED OR INVOLVED?** Involved usu. suggests a personal or emotional connection; **occupied** suggests that sb has a lot to do.

occupy *verb*

1 [T] ■ *Teaching occupies half her time.*

take sth up • fill • spend • pass • devote sth to sth • while sth away

▶ time is occupied/taken up **with** sth
▶ occupy/take up/fill/spend/pass/devote/while away (the) **time**
▶ occupy/take up/fill/spend/pass/devote/while away **an hour/a couple of hours**

2 [T] (*fml*) ■ *He occupies an office on the 3rd floor.*

inhabit • live | *fml* **reside**

▶ occupy/inhabit/live in/reside in a **house**
▶ occupy/inhabit/live in a **building**

3 [T] ■ *Soldiers occupied the capital.*

invade • seize • capture • take

▶ occupy/invade/seize/capture/take a **town/city**

▶ occupy/invade/seize a **country/region**
▶ occupy/seize/capture/take a **building**
▶ **troops/soldiers** occupy/invade/seize/capture/take a place

occur *verb*

1 [I] (*fml*) ■ *Something unexpected occurred.*

happen • take place • come up • come about • present itself • crop up | *fml* **arise**

▶ a **change** occurs/happens/takes place/comes about/arises
▶ a **situation** occurs/happens/comes about/presents itself/arises
▶ an **event/accident** occurs/happens/takes place

2 [I] (*fml*) (not used in the progressive tenses; used with an adv. or prep.)
■ *Sugar occurs naturally in fruit.*

exist • be found | *fml* **prevail**

▶ occur/exist/be found/prevail **in/among** sth
▶ **still** occur/exist/be found/prevail
▶ **never** occur/exist/be found

occur to sb *phrasal verb* [no passive] (not used in the progressive tenses)
■ *It never occurred to her to ask for help.*

cross your mind • come/spring to mind • dawn on sb • strike • come to sb | *infml* **hit**

▶ It occurs to/crosses sb's mind/dawns on sb/strikes sb/comes to sb/hits sb **that...**
▶ It occurs to/crosses sb's mind **to do sth**
▶ a/an **thought/idea** occurs to sb/crosses sb's mind/comes to mind/strikes sb/hits sb

ocean *noun* [C]
■ *Ocean levels are rising.*

sea • waters

▶ **by/on/across/beneath/under** the ocean/sea
▶ **in** the ocean/sea/... waters
▶ **cross/sail** the ocean/sea
● **OCEAN OR SEA?** The usual word in AmE is **ocean**; in BrE it is **sea**: (*BrE*) *a cottage by the sea* ◆ (*AmE*) *a house on the ocean*
For particular places you can only use one word: *the Pacific Ocean* ◆ *the Mediterranean Sea*

odd *adj.*
■ *There's something odd about that man.*

odour

302

strange • unusual • curious •
uncanny • bizarre • eccentric •
mysterious | *esp. spoken* funny •
weird | *BrE or fml* peculiar

■ OPP normal
▶ odd/strange/unusual/curious/
uncanny/bizarre/funny/weird/
peculiar that...
▶ odd/strange/curious/uncanny/
funny/weird/peculiar how/
what...
▶ something odd/strange/unusual/
curious/uncanny/bizarre/
mysterious/funny/weird/peculiar
● ODD OR STRANGE? Sb/sth that is
strange can be mysterious or
frightening. Sb/sth that is odd is
hard to understand or not right in
some way, but odd people probably
won't hurt you, whereas strange
people might.

odour (BrE) (AmE odor) noun [C]
(esp. written)

■ Use this spray to remove household
odours.

smell • reek • whiff | *infml* stink |
esp. written or lit. stench

▶ a/an odour/smell/reek/whiff/
stink/stench of sth
▶ a foul/putrid/powerful odour/
smell/stench
▶ give off a/an odour/smell/whiff
of sth/stench
▶ a/an odour/smell/stink/stench
comes from sth

offence (BrE) (AmE offense) noun
[C]

■ New legislation makes it an offence
to carry a gun.

crime • sin • outrage • atrocity | *BrE,
fml* misdemeanour | *AmE, law*
misdemeanor • felony | *fml* wrong

▶ a/an offence/crime/sin/outrage/
atrocity against sb/sth
▶ commit a/an offence/crime/sin/
outrage/atrocity/misdemeanour/
felony
▶ forgive a/an offence/crime/sin/
outrage/misdemeanour/wrong
● OFFENCE OR CRIME? In everyday
language crime is used more often
than offence for more serious
illegal acts, such as murder or rape.
Offence is used more frequently
for illegal activities such as driving
too fast, carrying a gun or using
drugs. However, in legal contexts,
offence is the preferred technical
term for all illegal acts.

offend verb [T, often passive, I]

■ Many people were deeply offended
by his jokes.

insult • shock

▶ feel offended/insulted/shocked
▶ deeply offended/insulted/
shocked
● OFFEND OR INSULT? To insult sb is
to do or say sth rude to them, usu.
deliberately. To offend sb is to
upset them, either because you
have insulted them, or because you
have been rude or thoughtless
about sb/sth that is important to
them.

offensive adj.

■ The programme contained offensive
language.

insulting • abusive • coarse • bad •
foul • filthy | *esp. BrE* rude

■ OPP inoffensive
▶ offensive/insulting/abusive to sb
▶ offensive/insulting/abusive/bad/
foul/filthy/rude language
▶ a/an offensive/insulting/abusive/
coarse/filthy/rude word
▶ a/an offensive/abusive/rude
gesture/remark/comment

offer noun

1 [C] ■ Thank you for your kind offer of
help.

proposal • approach • overture •
advances

▶ an offer/a proposal/an approach/
overtures/advances to sb
▶ an offer/a proposal of marriage
▶ make/receive an offer/a
proposal/an approach/overtures/
advances
▶ accept/decline/refuse/turn
down an offer/a proposal

2 [C] ■ They made an offer of £3 000.

esp. bus. or journ. bid | *esp. BrE,
busin.* tender

▶ a/an offer/bid/tender for sth
▶ put in/receive/accept an offer/
bid/tender
▶ invite offers/bids/tenders

offer verb

1 [T] ■ Jill offered to do the dishes.

volunteer • bid • hold sth out

▶ offer/volunteer/bid for sth
▶ offer/volunteer to do sth
▶ offer/bid £2000/a sum

2 [T] ■ The hotel offers excellent
facilities for families.

hold out sth | *fml* extend • tender |
written volunteer

▶ offer/hold out the hope/
possibility/prospect of sth
▶ offer/extend an invitation/a
welcome/hospitality/sympathy/
congratulations/aid/credit
▶ offer/tender advice/your
apologies/your resignation

▶ offer/volunteer **information/a suggestion/an opinion**

office noun

1 [C] ■ *Are you going to the office today?*

work ◆ **headquarters** ◆ **base** | *esp. busin. or journ.* **workplace**

▶ (a/an) **permanent/temporary/ main/local/regional/ administrative** office/ headquarters/base
▶ **go to/come to/arrive at/get to/ leave** the office/work/ headquarters
▶ **have/establish/set up** an office/ headquarters/a base

2 [C] ■ *Come into my office.*

study ◆ **studio** ◆ **workroom**

▶ a **large/small** office/study/studio/ workroom

3 [C] (usu. in compounds) ■ *You can get a map at the tourist office.*

agency ◆ **bureau** ◆ **service** ◆ **ministry**

▶ **do sth through** a/an office/ agency/bureau/service
▶ a **government/federal/public/ state** office/agency/bureau/ service/ministry
▶ a/an **local/employment/press/ information/intelligence/ security/advisory** agency/ bureau/service

4 [U, C] ■ *She held office as a cabinet minister for ten years.*

power ◆ **authority** ◆ **role** ◆ **capacity** | *esp. BrE* | *fml* **position**

▶ **sb's** office/role/capacity/post/ position **as**
▶ **take up** office/your role/your post/your position
▶ **give up/relinquish** office/power/ authority/your role/your post/ your position
▶ **leave** office/power/your role/your post/your position

officer noun [C]

■ *Drug squad officers raided a warehouse.*

police officer ◆ **policeman/ policewoman** ◆ **detective** ◆ **constable** | *BrE* **PC/WPC** | *AmE* **trooper** | *infml* **cop**

▶ a **uniformed** officer/police officer/ policeman/cop
▶ a **plain clothes** officer/police officer/policeman/detective/cop
▶ a/an **officer/police officer/ policeman/detective/constable/ cop arrrests sb/investigates sth**
▶ a/an **officer/police officer/ policeman/cop patrols** sth
● OFFICER, POLICE OFFICER OR POLICEMAN? Policeman is the most

frequent of these words. **Officer** and **police officer** are used in more formal contexts and to avoid referring to the gender of the person.

official noun [C]

■ *A senior official issued a statement.*

officer ◆ **civil servant** ◆ **commissioner** ◆ **secretary** ◆ **mayor** ◆ **councillor** | *AmE also* **councilor** | *AmE* **councilman/councilwoman** | *often disapprov.* **bureaucrat**

▶ a **senior** official/officer/civil servant/councillor/bureaucrat
▶ a **government** official/officer/ bureaucrat
▶ **appoint** a/an official/officer/ commissioner
● OFFICIAL OR OFFICER? **Official** is a general word for sb in a position of authority; **officer** is often part of a job title: *government/bank/Olympic officials* ◆ *an environmental health officer* ◆ *the chief medical officer*

official adj. [usu. before noun]

■ *She was in Berlin on official business*

formal ◆ **authorized** ◆ **licensed** ◆ **accredited**

■ OPP **unofficial**
▶ official/formal/authorized/ licensed/accredited **institutions**
▶ a/an official/formal/authorized **body**
▶ an **official/a formal announcement/request/inquiry/ complaint/protest/apology/ agreement**

offspring noun [C, usu. pl.]

■ *Badgers give birth to up to five offspring.*

young ◆ **baby** ◆ **litter** ◆ **brood**

▶ **produce/rear/raise** offspring/ young/babies/a litter/a brood
▶ **give birth to** offspring/young/a baby/a litter
● OFFSPRING, BABY OR YOUNG? **Offspring** and **young** are more scientific, technical words than **baby**. The parent animal must be mentioned or understood when using them:
✔*The females stay close to their offspring/young.* ◆ *Oh, look! That one's just a baby!* ✗ *Oh, look! That one's just an offspring/a young.*

often adv.

1 ■ *Your should come and see us more often.*

frequently ◆ **routinely** ◆ **habitually** | *infml, esp. spoken* **a lot**

■ OPP **rarely, seldom**

▶ often/routinely **available**
▶ **happen** often/frequently/a lot
▶ **wear sth** often/frequently/
habitually/a lot
▶ **How** often/frequently?
● **OFTEN OR FREQUENTLY?** Frequently
is more formal than **often** and is
used esp. to talk about things that
affect people generally; **often** is
used more to talk about things that
affect sb personally: *I've often
wondered what he looked like.* •
*Passengers complained that the
trains were frequently cancelled.*

2 ■ *Old houses are often damp.*

commonly • **usually** • **generally** •
mostly | *esp. written* **in general**

■ OPP **rarely, seldom**
▶ often/commonly/usually/
generally/mostly **known as/
called/found...**
▶ often/commonly/usually/
generally/mostly **used**
▶ often/commonly/usually/
generally **happen**

oil noun [U]
■ *Several companies are drilling for oil
in the region.*

petroleum • **diesel** • **fuel** • **fossil fuel**
| *BrE* **petrol** • *AmE* **gas** • **gasoline**

▶ sth **runs on** oil/diesel/fuel/petrol/
gas/gasoline
▶ the oil/petroleum/fuel/
gas/gasoline **industry**
▶ oil/petroleum/fuel/fossil fuel
reserves
▶ a/an oil/fuel/petrol/gas/gasoline
tanker

OK (also **okay**) adj.
1 [not usu. before noun] (*infml, esp.
spoken*) ■ *Write and let me know
you're OK.*

safe • **unharmed** • **unhurt** •
uninjured • **alive and well** • **secure** |
esp. spoken **all right** | *written*
unscathed | *infml* **in one piece**

▶ **remain** OK/safe/unharmed/alive
and well/secure/all right/
unscathed/in one piece
▶ **perfectly** OK/safe/secure/all right
▶ **otherwise** OK/unharmed/
unhurt/secure/all right
● **OK OR ALL RIGHT?** Both these words
are rather informal but **OK** is
slightly more informal than **all
right**.

2 [not before noun] (*infml, spoken*)
■ *He should be OK for the game on
Saturday.*

esp. BrE **fit** | *esp. spoken* **all right** •
well • **fine**

▶ OK/fit/all right **for sth**
▶ OK/fit/all right **to do sth**

▶ **feel/look** OK/fit/all right/well/
fine
▶ **perfectly** OK/fit/all right/well/
fine
● **OK OR ALL RIGHT?** These words are
slightly less positive than the other
words in this group; **OK** is slightly
more informal than **all right**.

3 [not usu. before noun] (*infml, esp.
spoken*) ■ *Is it OK if I leave now?*

acceptable • **fair** • **satisfactory** •
reasonable | *esp. spoken* **all right** •
fine • **not bad** | *fml* **in order**

▶ OK/fair/acceptable/satisfactory/
reasonable/all right/fine/in order
to do sth
▶ OK/fair/acceptable/satisfactory/
reasonable/all right/fine/in order
that...
▶ That's OK/all right/fine **by me**.

old adj.
1 ■ *He's getting old—he's 75 next
year.*

elderly • **mature** • **long-lived** | *fml*
aged

■ OPP **young**
▶ a/an old/elderly/mature/long-
lived/aged **man/woman**
▶ a/an old/elderly/mature/aged
gentleman/lady/couple
▶ sb's old/elderly/aged **father/
mother/aunt/uncle/relative**

2 ■ *It's one of the oldest parts of the
castle.*

ancient • **historic** • **antique** • **long-
standing**

■ OPP **new**
▶ a/an old/ancient/historic
building/monument
▶ an old/ancient/antique **chair/
clock/coin**
▶ a/an old/ancient/long-standing
**tradition/belief/method/
problem**
▶ an old/ancient **custom/way/
ritual/city/civilization**

3 ■ *We had more room in our old
house.*

former • **then** • **ex-**

■ OPP **new**
▶ sb's old/former/then/ex-**partner/
boyfriend/girlfriend**
▶ a/an old/former/ex-**lover/
colleague/member**
▶ a/an old/former/ex-**student/
colony**

old-fashioned adj. (*sometimes
disapprov.*)
■ *The room was full of heavy, old-
fashioned furniture.*

sometimes disapprov. **obsolete** • **out-
of-date** • **outdated** | *disapprov.*
dated • **antiquated**

■ OPP **modern**
▶ an old-fashioned/obsolete/
outdated/antiquated **system**
▶ old-fashioned/outdated/dated/
antiquated **attitudes/ideas/views**
● **become** old-fashioned/obsolete/
out-of-date/dated

▶ a/an open/direct/honest/
sincere/truthful **person**

opening noun [C, usu. sing.]
■ I got tickets for the opening
ceremony.

premiere ◆ **first night** | esp. busin.
launch

■ OPP **closing**
▶ at the opening/premiere/first
night/launch
▶ **go to/attend** the opening/
premiere/first night/launch
▶ **get ready for/announce/speak
at/delay/postpone** the opening/
launch

open verb

1 [T] ■ I opened the letter and read it.

undo ◆ **unwrap** ◆ **untie** ◆ **unzip**

▶ open/undo/unwrap/untie a
parcel/package
▶ open/unwrap a **present**
▶ open/unzip a **bag**

2 [I, T] ■ What if the parachute doesn't
open?

unfold ◆ **spread** ◆ **lay sth out** ◆ **lay** ◆
unroll

■ OPP **close**
▶ open/spread/lay out/lay sth **on**
sth
▶ open/spread/lay out **out**
▶ open/unfold/spread out/lay out a
map

3 [T] ■ Police have opened an
investigation.

begin ◆ **start** | esp. busin. or journ.
launch | fml **embark on/upon sth** ◆
commence ◆ **initiate** ◆ **institute**

■ OPP **close**
▶ open/begin/start/launch/embark
on/commence/initiate/institute
a/an **campaign/inquiry**
▶ open/begin/start/initiate a
discussion/conversation
▶ open/begin/start a **story/letter/
sentence/day/year/meeting**

open adj.

1 ■ an open display of affection

overt ◆ **clear** ◆ **obvious** | infml **under
sb's nose** | disapprov. **blatant** ◆
glaring

■ OPP **secret, covert**
▶ a/an open/overt/clear/obvious/
blatant **attempt**
▶ open/overt/blatant
discrimination

2 (approv.) ■ He was quite open about
his reasons for leaving.

direct ◆ **blunt** ◆ **forthright** | often
approv. **frank** ◆ **straight** ◆ **honest** ◆
candid | approv. **straightforward** ◆
sincere ◆ **truthful**

■ OPP **secretive**
▶ open/direct/forthright/frank/
straight/honest/candid/
straightforward/sincere/truthful
about sth
▶ open/direct/blunt/frank/
straight/honest/candid/
straightforward/sincere/truthful
with sb

operate verb

1 [I] (usu. used with an adv. or prep.)
■ Most domestic freezers operate at
below -18°C.

run ◆ esp. spoken **work** ◆ **go** | fml
function

▶ operate/run/work/function
**efficiently/satisfactorily/
smoothly/succesfully/normally**
▶ operate/work/function
effectively/properly/correctly
▶ operate/run **continuously**
● OPERATE OR FUNCTION? Function is
used more to talk about whether
sth works or how well or badly it
works; operate is used more to talk
about the conditions required for
sth to work: We now have a
functioning shower. ◆ Solar panels
can only operate in sunlight.

2 [T] ■ They were trained to operate
the machinery safely.

run ◆ **control** | esp. spoken **work** | fml
manipulate

▶ operate/run/control/work a
machine
▶ operate/run/control a/an
engine/motor
▶ operate/run **machinery**
▶ operate/manipulate the **controls/
levers**
● OPERATE, RUN OR CONTROL? A
person operates or runs a
machine; machines are often
controlled by the controls, such as
a computer, knob or lever.

3 [T] ■ The airline operates flights to
25 countries.

run ◆ **organize** | written **mount** ◆
orchestrate

▶ operate/run/organize/mount/
orchestrate a **campaign**
▶ operate/run/organize sth
efficiently/effectively/well

operation noun

1 [C] ■ *She had an operation on her lung to remove a tumour.*

surgery • treatment

► an operation/surgery/treatment **for** sth
► an operation/surgery/treatment **on** sb/sth
► **have/undergo/need/require** an operation/surgery/treatment
● **perform** an operation/surgery
● **OPERATION OR SURGERY?** Operation is countable; **surgery** is uncountable: *She's had three operations in the past two years.* • *The doctor recommended surgery.*

2 [C] ■ *A major rescue operation was launched.*

exercise • enterprise • undertaking • venture • project • process • activity

► a **major/successful/joint** operation/exercise/enterprise/undertaking/venture/project/process/activity
► **set up/run/support** a/an operation/enterprise/venture/project/process/activity
► **carry out/supervise** a/an operation/exercise/project/process/activity

opinion noun [C, U]

■ *In my opinion he should resign.*

view • point of view • belief • idea • feeling • judgement • point • attitude • stance • position • line • conviction | fml sentiment

► sb's opinion/view/beliefs/ideas/feelings/judgement/point/conviction/sentiments **about** sb/sth
► sb's opinion/view/ideas/feelings/stance/position/line **on** sb/sth
► **have** an opinion/view/point of view/belief/idea/feeling/attitude/line/conviction
► **express** your opinion/view/point of view/beliefs/ideas/feelings/conviction/sentiments

opponent noun

1 [C] ■ *He was greatly respected, even by his political opponents.*

enemy • rival • competitor • the opposition • the competition | fml adversary | old-fash. or fml foe

■ OPP **ally**

► **against** an opponent/an enemy/a rival/a competitor/the opposition/the competition/an adversary/a foe
► the **main** opponent/enemy/rival/competitor/opposition/competition/adversary

► **face** an opponent/an enemy/the opposition/the competition/a foe

2 [C] ■ *a leading opponent of reforms*

dissident • rebel • protester • demonstrator

■ OPP **supporter**, (*fml*) **proponent**

► a **political** opponent/dissident/demonstrator
► opponents/dissidents/protesters/demonstrators **call for/demand** sth

opportunity noun [C, U]

■ *You'll have an opportunity to ask questions later.*

chance • possibility • occasion • start | infml break | esp. spoken turn • moment | BrE, spoken go | esp. busin. window

► the opportunity/a chance/your turn **to do** sth
► an opportunity/possibilities/an occasion **for** sth
► **have** a/an opportunity/chance/break/turn/moment/go/window
► **get/give sb** a/an opportunity/chance/start/break/turn/moment/go/window
● **OPPORTUNITY OR CHANCE?** Opportunity tends to be more formal. In some cases only one of the words can be used:
✔ *I won't give him a second chance.*
✗ *I won't give him a second opportunity.*
✔ *job/equal opportunities* ✗ *job/equal chances*

oppose verb [T]

■ *I would oppose changing the law.*

resist • fight • combat • defy • go against sb/sth • stand up to sb • flout

■ OPP **support, propose**

► oppose/resist/fight a **plan/proposal**
► oppose/fight/defy/flout a **ban**
► oppose/fight/defy/stand up to the **government**
► oppose/defy/go against/flout sb's **wishes**

opposed adj.

■ *They are totally opposed to the new policies.*

be against sb/sth • hostile • resistant | fml antagonistic

■ OPP **in favour of** sth

► opposed/hostile/resistant/antagonistic **to** sth
► opposed to/against/hostile to/resistant **to the idea** of sth
► **openly/bitterly/fiercely** opposed/hostile/antagonistic

opposite noun [C]

■ *Hot and cold are opposites.*

contrast • the contrary | *esp. written* the reverse | *tech.* antonym

▶ **be** the opposite/a contrast/the reverse
▶ **do** the opposite/contrary/reverse
▶ **quite** the opposite/contrary/ reverse/**quite a** contrast

opposite *adj.* [usu. before noun]
■ *Unfortunately their attempts to calm him had the opposite effect.*

reverse • contrary • inverse • opposed

■ **OPP** same
▶ the opposite/reverse **direction/ side/order/effect**
▶ the opposite/contrary **view/ opinion**
▶ Their **views/opinions** are opposed.

opposition *noun* [U]
■ *Delegates expressed strong opposition to the plans.*

protest • resistance • objection • hostility

■ **OPP** support
▶ opposition/resistance/objection/ hostility **to** sth
▶ **provoke/meet with/face** opposition/protests/resistance/ objections/hostility
▶ **express** your opposition/ resistance/objections/hostility

optimistic *adj.*
■ *She's not very optimistic about the outcome of the talks.*

hopeful • positive | *esp. busin.* bullish • upbeat

■ **OPP** pessimistic
▶ optimistic/hopeful/positive/ bullish/upbeat **about** sth
▶ optimistic/hopeful **that...**
▶ a/an optimistic/hopeful/positive/ bullish **view**
▶ a/an optimistic/positive/bullish/ upbeat **mood/note**

option *noun* [C, U]
■ *As I see it, we have two options.*

choice • alternative • possibility

▶ (a/an) **real/realistic/viable/ practical/obvious** option/choice/ alternative/possibility
▶ (a) **good/healthy/preferred/ cheap/expensive** option/choice/ alternative
▶ **have** the option/choice **of doing** sth
▶ **have/give sb/offer (sb)** several options/choices/alternatives/ possibilities
● **OPTION, CHOICE OR ALTERNATIVE?** Alternative is slightly more formal than **option** or **choice**, and is more frequently used to talk about

choosing between two things rather than several.

order *noun*

1 [U, C] ■ *The names are listed in alphabetical order.*

sequence • series • chronology

▶ **in** a/an ...order/sequence/series
▶ **in/out of** order/sequence
▶ a **random** order/sequence/series

2 [U] ■ *The lack of order in the household made her feel uncomfortable.*

organization • structure • discipline | *fml* coherence

■ **OPP** chaos, (*fml*) disorder
▶ **bring** order/structure/discipline/ coherence **to** sth
▶ **have/lack** order/organization/ structure/discipline/coherence
▶ **impose** order/structure/ discipline/coherence **on** sth
● **ORDER OR ORGANIZATION?** Order is a state that can be *created*, or that sth can be *put into*; organization is a quality that either *has* or *lacks*:
  ✓*Get your ideas into some sort of order.* ✗*Get your ideas into some sort of organization.*
  ✓*creating order out of chaos* ✗*creating organization out of chaos*

3 [U] ■ *The army was brought in to maintain order.*

law and order • the rule of law • peace • calm

■ **OPP** *fml* disorder
▶ **maintain/establish/preserve/ restore/enforce** order/law and order/the rule of law/peace
▶ order/law and order/the rule of law/peace/calm **prevails**
▶ order/law and order/the rule of law **breaks down**

4 [C] ■ *The general gave the order to advance.*

command • instruction • decree • directive | *law* injunction

▶ **under** sb's orders/instructions/a decree/a directive/an injunction
▶ **in accordance with** an order/ instructions/a decree/a directive
▶ **issue/obey/ignore** an order/a command/instructions/a decree/ a directive/an injunction
▶ **give/receive/carry out** an order/a command/instructions

5 [C] ■ *He placed an order for ten copies of the book.*

request • application • demand

▶ a/an order/request/application/ demand **for** sth
▶ **on** order/request/application/ demand

order

▶ put in/receive a/an order/
request/application/demand

order verb

1 [T] ■ *The officer ordered them to fire.*

command ◆ instruct ◆ tell ◆ rule ◆
dictate ◆ decree | *fml* direct

▶ order/command/instruct/tell/
direct sb to do sth
▶ order/command/instruct/rule/
dictate/decree/direct that...
▶ do sth as ordered/commanded/
instructed/told/directed
● ORDER OR COMMAND? Command is
a slightly stronger word than order
and is the normal word to use
about an army officer; it is less likely
to be used about a parent or
teacher.

2 [T, I] ■ *I'll order a taxi for you.*

reserve ◆ charter | *esp. BrE* book |
esp. AmE rent | *BrE* hire

▶ order/reserve/charter/book/rent/
hire sth
▶ order/reserve/book sth for sb
▶ order/reserve/book sth for eight
o'clock/midday/this evening, etc.
▶ reserve/book a place/seat/table/
ticket
▶ reserve/book/rent/hire a room/
hall
▶ rent/hire a car/bicycle/boat/
van/movie

ordinary adj.

1 ■ *We were an ordinary family.*

normal ◆ average ◆ typical ◆
common

■ OPP extraordinary
▶ the ordinary/normal/average/
common man
▶ a/an ordinary/normal/average
person
▶ a/an ordinary/normal/average/
typical working day
▶ in the ordinary/normal course of
events/business/things
● ORDINARY OR NORMAL? Sth that is
normal is as it should be or as you
would expect; the word ordinary
makes no comment about how
things should be, only about how
things are, whether this is good or
bad:
✓*Her temperature was normal.*
✗ *Her temperature was ordinary.*
✓*It's normal to feel tired after such a
long journey.* ✗ *It's ordinary to feel
tired after such a long journey.*

2 (*disapprov.*) ■ *The meal was very
ordinary.*

unremarkable | *often disapprov.*
average | *often approv.* plain ◆
simple

■ OPP special

▶ an ordinary/average sort of
person/thing
▶ a/an ordinary/unremarkable/
average/simple person
▶ ordinary/average players

organization (*BrE also* -isation)
noun

1 [C] ■ *voluntary organizations
working with the homeless*

institution ◆ institute ◆ association ◆
society ◆ federation ◆ union ◆ club ◆
guild | *BrE* centre | *AmE* center

▶ a/an organization/institution/
institute/association/society/
club/centre for sth
▶ a national organization/institute/
association/society/federation/
union/club
▶ a government organization/
institution/institution
▶ a research/training organization/
institution/institute/centre

2 [U] ■ *An event on this scale takes a
lot of organization.*

planning ◆ arrangement ◆
preparation ◆ coordination ◆
provision

▶ organization/planning/
arrangements/preparations/
provision for sb/sth
▶ do the organization/planning/
preparation/coordination
▶ a lack of organization/planning/
preparation/coordination/
provision

3 [U] ■ *She's intelligent, but her work
lacks organization.*

order ◆ structure | *fml* coherence

▶ have/lack organization/order/
structure/coherence
● ORGANIZATION OR ORDER? Order is a
state that can be *created*, or that
sth can be *put into*; organization
is a quality that sth either *has* or *lacks*:
✓*Get your ideas into some sort of
order.* ✗ *Get your ideas into some
sort of organization.*
✓*creating order out of chaos*
✗ *creating organization out of chaos*

organize (*BrE also* -ise) *verb*

1 [T] ■ *He organized the school disco.*

arrange ◆ plan ◆ run ◆ operate | *esp.
spoken* sort sth out | *written* mount ◆
orchestrate

▶ organize/plan/run/operate/
mount/orchestrate a campaign
▶ organize/plan/run/mount an
operation/event
▶ organize/arrange/plan/mount an
exhibition

2 [T] ■ *Try to organize your time
better.*

manage • **arrange** • **set sth out** | *esp. spoken* **sort sth out**

▶ organize/manage/arrange/sort out (your) **things**
▶ organize/manage/arrange/set out **information/data**
▶ organize/arrange/set out/sort out your **thoughts/ideas**
▶ organize/set out your **work**

organized (BrE also -ised) adj.

■ The new chairman is a highly organized man.

efficient • **methodical** • **systematic** • **orderly** • **businesslike**

■ **OPP** disorganized

▶ organize/efficient/methodical/ systematic/businesslike **in** sth
▶ **in** a/an organized/efficient/ methodical/systematic/orderly/ businesslike **fashion**
▶ a/an organized/efficient/ methodical/systematic/orderly/ businesslike **approach/way**

organizer (BrE also -iser) noun [C]

■ The organizers of the race met to discuss safety.

administrator • **planner**

▶ an organizer/administrator **for** sth
▶ a **good** organizer/administrator/ planner
▶ a/an **area/local/regional** organizer/administrator/planner

origin noun

1 [C, U] ■ The series examines the origins of life on earth.

root • **source** • **starting point** • **cause** • **beginnings**

▶ (a) **common** origins/roots/source/ starting point/cause/beginnings
▶ **have** (a) origins/roots/source/ starting point/cause/beginnings
▶ **find** the origin/root/source/ starting point/cause of sth
▶ **locate/discover/investigate/ trace** the origins/roots/source/ cause of sth

● **ORIGIN OR ROOT?** Use **origin** to talk about when, where and how sth started; use **root** to talk about the cause of a problem: *the origin of life/the universe/species* • *We need to get to the root of the problem.* The word **roots** can suggest an emotional or cultural attachment; **origins** is more scientific. *Social origins* refers to sb's social class, but *cultural roots* refers to the beliefs and customs of their family or country.

2 [C, U] ■ people of German origin

birth • **roots** • **background** • **parentage** • **ancestry** • **family** • **pedigree** | *fml* **descent** • **blood** • **lineage**

▶ **by** origin/birth/descent
▶ **ethnic/racial/social/cultural, etc.** origin/roots/background/ ancestry/pedigree/descent
▶ **African/Scottish/Italian, etc.** origin/roots/background/ parentage/ancestry/family/ descent/blood/lineage

original adj.

1 [only before noun] ■ The land was returned to its original owner.

first • **initial** • **earliest** • **preliminary** | *fml or tech.* **primary**

■ **OPP** final

▶ the original/first/initial/ preliminary **estimate/draft/ version**
▶ original/first/initial/preliminary **remarks**
▶ the original/initial/preliminary **study/findings**

2 (*usu. approv.*) ■ It's an original and challenging film.

imaginative • **inventive** • **innovative** • **novel** • **ingenious** • **creative**

■ **OPP** conventional, unimaginative

▶ a/an original/imaginative/ inventive/innovative/novel/ ingenious/creative **idea/design/ solution**
▶ original/imaginative/innovative/ creative **thinking**
▶ a/an original/innovative/creative **thinker**

● **WHICH WORD?** *Original*, *imaginative* and *inventive* are often used in artistic contexts; *innovative* is used more in business or practical contexts. *Original/imaginative ideas* are interesting whether they work in practice or not; things that are *ingenious* are clever and do work, but may not be as big or important as things that are *innovative* or *original*.

ornament noun [C]

■ a few china ornaments on a shelf

trinket • **decoration** • **accessory** | *sometimes disapprov.* **knick-knack**

▶ a **little** ornament/trinket/ decoration/knick-knack
▶ a **glass** ornament/decoration
▶ a **Christmas (tree)** ornament/ decoration

outline noun

1 [C] ■ This is a brief outline of the events.

summary • **overview** • **sketch** • **synopsis** | *esp. spoken* **rundown** | *tech.* **abstract**

outline

▶ a/an outline/summary/overview/
sketch/synopsis/rundown/
abstract **of** sth
▶ **in** outline/summary
▶ **give** sb a/an outline/summary/
overview/sketch/synopsis/
rundown
▶ **provide** a/an outline/summary/
overview/sketch/synopsis/
abstract
● **OUTLINE, SUMMARY OR OVERVIEW?** A
summary is always made after the
full version of sth has been written
or recorded. An **outline** can be
given before the full version has
been worked out: *Draw up an
outline for the essay before you start.*
An **overview** is similar to an
outline, but the emphasis is more
on the fact that sb wants to look
for general trends across a wide
area, rather than that the details
are still to be worked out.

2 [C] ■ *We could see the dim outline of
an island.*

shape + silhouette + profile + form +
line | *written* contour
_____
▶ **in** outline/shape/silhouette/
profile/form
▶ **make out/see** a/an outline/
shape/silhouette/form
▶ **trace** the outline/shape/line/
contours

outline verb [T]
■ *He roughly outlined the plot of the
opera.*

sketch + set sth out | *esp. AmE* lay sth
out
_____
▶ outline/sketch/set out/lay out sth
for sb
▶ outline/sketch/set out/lay out a
plan/programme
▶ outline/sketch/set out/lay out the
details

output noun [U, sing.]
■ *Manufacturing output has increased
by 8%.*

production + productivity + yield
_____
▶ a **high/low** output/productivity/
yield
▶ **manufacturing/industrial**
output/production/productivity
▶ **boost/improve/increase/raise/
reduce** output/production/
productivity/yields
● **OUTPUT OR PRODUCTION?** Output
can belong to a country, company,
person or machine; you cannot use
production in this way:
✓*the country's/company's total
output* ✗ *the country's/company's
total production*

outrageous adj.
■ *He protested that her behaviour was
outrageous.*

shocking + disgraceful + scandalous
+ criminal + unforgivable + shameful
| *fml* deplorable
_____
▶ outrageous/shocking/disgraceful/
scandalous/shameful/
unforgivable/deplorable **that...**
▶ outrageous/shocking/disgraceful/
scandalous/criminal/shameful/
deplorable **behaviour**
▶ a/an outrageous/shocking/
disgraceful/scandalous/shameful
waste
● **OUTRAGEOUS OR SHOCKING?** For a
very serious situation, use
shocking; for an unfair situation,
use **outrageous**: *the shocking truth
about heroin addiction* ◇ *It's
outrageous that you should get paid
more than me.*

outstanding adj.
■ *She's an outstanding young cellist.*

excellent + first-rate + wonderful +
superb + tremendous | *infml* great +
fantastic + terrific | *BrE, esp. spoken*
marvellous | *AmE, esp. spoken*
marvelous | *BrE, infml, spoken*
brilliant
_____
■ **OPP** mediocre
▶ a/an outstanding/excellent/first-
rate/wonderful/superb/
tremendous/great/fantastic/
terrific/marvellous/brilliant
performance/job
▶ a/an outstanding/excellent/first-
rate/wonderful/superb/
tremendous/great/fantastic/
terrific **service**
▶ a/an outstanding/excellent/
wonderful/superb/tremendous/
great/fantastic/terrific/
marvellous/brilliant **achievement**

oven noun [C]
■ *Take the cake out of the oven.*

microwave (oven) + furnace + kiln +
range | *esp. AmE* stove | *BrE* cooker
_____
▶ **in** the oven/microwave/furnace/
kiln
▶ **on** the range/stove/cooker
▶ a/an **gas/electric** oven/furnace/
kiln/range/stove/cooker
▶ **cook** sth in/on the oven/
microwave/stove/cooker

overall adj. [only before noun]
■ *One person will have overall
responsibility for the project.*

global + across-the-board + general +
broad + inclusive + umbrella +
blanket | *BrE* all-round | *AmE* all-
around | *finance* gross
_____
▶ the/a/an overall/general/broad
context/heading

- a/an overall/general/umbrella title
- overall/gross income/profit/turnover

overcome verb [T]

■ *She overcame her fear of flying.*

control • bring/get/keep sth under control • get over sth | *infml* beat | *written* conquer

- overcome/control/get over/beat/conquer a **problem**
- bring/get/keep a **problem** under control
- overcome/control/get over/conquer a **fear**
- overcome/get over a **difficulty/hurdle**

overhear verb [T]

■ *I overheard him say he was going to Russia.*

monitor • eavesdrop • listen in • tap • bug

- eavesdrop/listen in **on** sth
- overhear/monitor/eavesdrop on/listen in to/bug a **conversation**

overthrow noun [sing.]

■ *A republic was declared following the overthrow of the monarchy.*

downfall • fall

- bring about/lead to sb's overthrow/downfall/fall

overthrow verb [T]

■ *The president was overthrown in a military coup.*

bring sb down • remove | *written* oust • depose | *fml* usurp | *esp. journ.* topple

- overthrow/bring down/remove/oust/depose/topple a **president/regime/government**
- overthrow/oust/depose/topple a **leader/dictator**
- overthrow/bring down **communism/capitalism**

overturn verb [T]

■ *Councillors overturned the decision.*

reverse • override • overrule • set sth aside | *written* quash

■ OPP uphold

- overturn/reverse/override/overrule/set aside a **decision**
- overturn/reverse/override/quash a **ban**
- overturn/reverse/set aside/quash a **conviction/verdict**

overwhelm verb [T]

■ *The office was overwhelmed by the volume of work.*

swamp • flood • inundate • bombard

- overwhelm/swamp/flood/inundate/bombard sb/sth **with** sth
- be swamped/flooded/inundated/bombarded **with complaints/requests**
- ● OVERWHELM OR SWAMP? People are typically **overwhelmed** by the *amount, number* or *volume* of a thing; they are **swamped** by the things themselves—*complaints, requests, offers* or *enquiries.*

own verb [T] (not used in the progressive tenses)

■ *I don't own anything of value.*

have | *esp. BrE, esp. spoken* have got | *fml* hold • possess

- own/have/have got/possess a **car/house**
- own/have/have got a **company**
- have/have got/hold a **driving licence/passport**
- own/hold sth **legally/jointly**

own adj.

■ *I have my own room at last.*

personal • individual • private | *sometimes disapprov.* subjective

- sb's own/personal/individual/private/subjective **experience**
- sb's own/personal/private/subjective **opinion**
- sb's own/personal/individual **needs/requirements/objectives/freedom**

Pp

pace noun

1 [sing., U] ■ *We set off at a leisurely pace.*

speed • rate • momentum | *written* tempo

- **at** a ... pace/speed/rate
- **increase** the pace/speed/rate/momentum/tempo
- **maintain** the pace/speed/rate/momentum

2 [C] ■ *She took two paces forward.*

step • stride • footstep

- take a few paces/steps/strides **back/forward/to** sth/**towards** sth
- take a pace/step **backwards**
- take a pace/step/stride

pack verb

1 [I, T] ■ *He packed his bag and left.*

---

fill • load

► OPP **unpack**
► pack/fill/load sth **with/in/into** sth

2 [I, T] ■ *Fans packed the hall to see the band.* ■ *Pack wet shoes with newspaper to help them dry.*

---

cram • stuff • jam • squeeze • crowd • wedge

► pack/cram/stuff/jam/squeeze/ crowd/wedge sb/sth **in/into** sth
► pack/cram/stuff/jam/squeeze/ wedge sb/sth **between** sth and sth else
► be packed/crammed/jammed/ squeezed/crowded/wedged **together**

● PACK, CRAM, STUFF OR JAM? Pack and **cram** are very similar, although **cram** suggests less order and more force. If you **stuff** or **jam** sth into a space you put it there in a quick or careless way.

packet noun

■ *a packet of biscuits/crisps/cigarettes*

esp. *AmE* **pack** | *AmE* **package** | *BrE* **sachet**

► a packet/pack/package/sachet **of** sth
► **in** a packet/pack/package/sachet
► **open** a packet/pack/package/ sachet

● WHICH WORD? The usual words used are **packet** in *BrE* and **pack** or **package** in *AmE*: these all mean a paper or cardboard container in which goods are packed or wrapped for selling. A **packet** in *AmE* (or **sachet** in *BrE*) is a closed paper or plastic container, like a small envelope, that contains a small amount of liquid or powder: *a packet/sachet of ketchup*

page noun [C]

■ *Read both pages before you answer.*

sheet • side • slip

► **on** a/the page/sheet/side/slip
► **in** the middle/at the bottom/at the top of the page/sheet
► a/an **blank/loose/printed/ separate/A4/A5, etc.** page/sheet

pain noun

1 [U, C] ■ *He felt a sharp pain in his knee.*

ache • suffering • agony | *fml* discomfort

► **in** pain/agony/discomfort
► (a) **back/stomach** pain/ache
► **cause** pain/suffering/discomfort
► **relieve/ease** the pain/suffering/ agony/discomfort

2 [U] ■ *The pain of separation remained intense.*

suffering • distress • misery • agony | *infml* hurt • torture | *fml* anguish

► **in** pain/distress/misery/agony/ anguish
► **physical/emotional** pain/ suffering/distress/agony/hurt/ torture/anguish
► **endure** the pain/suffering/ distress/misery/agony/torture
► **cause** (sb) pain/suffering/distress/ misery/agony/hurt/anguish

● PAIN, DISTRESS OR SUFFERING? These are all words for a feeling of great unhappiness. **Distress** can also be a feeling of worry. **Pain** is often used when the hurt is individual and the cause more personal, such as the death of a loved one. **Suffering** often refers to sth on a large scale that affects many people, such as a war or natural disaster.

painful adj.

1 ■ *Is your knee still painful?*

sore • tender • itchy • inflamed • raw • burning • excruciating

► OPP **painless**
► a painful/burning **sensation**
► a painful/an excruciating **death**
► sore/itchy/inflamed **eyes**
► itchy/inflamed/raw **skin**

2 ■ *The letter brought back painful memories.*

upsetting • distressing • sad • traumatic • harrowing • agonizing • heartbreaking

► painful/upsetting/distressing/ sad/traumatic/heartbreaking **for** sb
► painful/upsetting/distressing/ sad/heartbreaking **to do** sth
► a/an painful/upsetting/ distressing/sad/traumatic/ harrowing/heartbreaking **experience**
► a painful/an agonizing **decision**

paint verb [T]

■ *The walls were painted yellow.*

stain • dye • tint | *BrE* colour | *AmE* color

► paint/stain/dye/tint/colour sth **with** sth
► paint/stain/dye/tint/colour sth **red/yellow/green, etc.**
► paint/stain **wood**

painting noun [C]

■ *a collection of paintings by American artists*

picture • portrait • landscape • print • artwork

▶ do a painting/picture/portrait/
landscape
▶ paint a picture/portrait/landscape
▶ frame/hang/show/display/
exhibit a painting/picture/
portrait/landscape/print

palace noun [C]
■ *Protesters have overrun the
presidential palace.*

mansion • manor (house) • villa | *BrE*
stately home • country house | *from
French* château

▶ a magnificent palace/mansion/
country house/villa
▶ an ancient/royal palace/
mansion/manor
▶ a medieval palace/manor/
château

pale adj.
1 (*often disapprov.*) ■ *His face went
pale with shock.*

white • sallow | *BrE, disapprov.* grey |
AmE gray | *written* ashen • wan

■ OPP flushed, rosy
▶ pale/white/grey/ashen with
anger/fear/shock/pain, etc.
▶ a/an pale/white/sallow/grey/
ashen/wan face
▶ look pale/white/sallow/grey/
ashen/wan
▶ turn pale/white/grey

2 ■ *The bedroom walls are pale blue.*

light • soft • pastel • neutral | *usu.
approv.* cool

■ OPP dark, deep
▶ a pale/light/soft/pastel/neutral/
cool colour/shade
▶ pale/light/soft/pastel/cool
green/blue
▶ pale/light/soft/pastel pink
▶ sth is pale/light/neutral in colour
● PALE OR LIGHT? Both words can
describe colours. Pale can also
describe a kind of light that
contains a lot of white and is not
bright:
✓*a pale light/glow/sky* ✗ ~~a light
light/glow/sky~~

pan noun [C]
■ *Remove the pan from the heat.*

saucepan • frying pan • wok •
casserole (dish) | *esp. AmE* pot •
skillet | *BrE* tin

▶ a pan/saucepan/pot of sth
▶ a large pan/saucepan/frying pan/
wok/casserole/pot/skillet/tin
▶ a heavy pan/saucepan/frying
pan/casserole/pot/skillet
● PAN, SAUCEPAN OR POT? Pan is the
most general of these words.
Saucepan can be used for a deep
pan with a long handle and a lid.
Pot is often preferred in *AmE* for a
deep pan, either with two short

handles or no handles at all; it is
usu. used in compounds or in the
phrase *a pot of sth*. Pots and pans
means several different containers
that you use to cook food: *I washed
all the pots and pans after dinner.*

panel noun [C+sing./pl. v.]
■ *The designs will be judged by a panel
of experts.*

committee • board • jury • body •
council • commission • task force

▶ a panel/committee/commission/
task force on sth
▶ a/an advisory/consultative
panel/committee/board/body/
council
▶ chair a panel/committee/board/
body/council/commission
▶ be on/serve on/sit on a panel/
committee/board/jury/body/
council/commission

panic noun [U, C, usu. sing.]
■ *Office workers fled in panic as the fire
took hold.*

fear • alarm • fright • hysteria •
terror • dread

▶ in panic/fear/alarm/fright/terror/
dread
▶ panic/fear/alarm/fright/terror/
dread that...
▶ absolute/pure/sheer panic/
hysteria/terror/dread
▶ be filled with panic/fear/alarm/
terror/dread

panic verb [T]
■ *I panicked when I saw smoke coming
out of the engine.*

lose your nerve | *infml* freak out |
infml, disapprov. chicken out | *written*
take fright

▶ just panic/lose your nerve/freak
out

paper noun
1 [C] ■ *The papers soon got hold of
the story.*

newspaper • daily • weekly •
journal | *BrE* broadsheet | *sometimes
disapprov.* tabloid

▶ a local paper/newspaper/daily/
tabloid
▶ a national paper/newspaper/
daily/broadsheet
▶ publish/read a paper/newspaper/
daily/weekly/journal
● PAPER OR NEWSPAPER? Newspaper
can only be shortened to paper
when it is clear which one is talked
about:
✓*a scrapbook of newspaper cuttings*
✗ ~~a scrapbook of paper cuttings~~

2 papers [pl.] ▪ *I signed all the necessary papers.*

document + **paperwork** + **deed** + **file** + **archive** | *fml* **dossier**

▶ (a) **personal/secret** papers/documents/file/dossier
▶ (a/an) **official/government/state** papers/document/file/archive
▶ **keep** papers/a document/the paperwork/the deeds/a file/an archive/a dossier
▶ **leak/release** papers/a document/a file

3 papers [pl.] ▪ *We had to show our papers at the border.*

documentation + **ID** + **authorization** + **permit** + **credentials** + **certificate** | *BrE* **licence** | *AmE* **license**

▶ (an) **official** papers/documentation/authorization/permit/credentials/certificate/licence
▶ **have** (a) papers/documentation/ID/authorization/permit/credentials/certificate/licence
▶ **see/check** sb's papers/documentation/ID/authorization/permit/credentials/certificate/licence
▶ **show/present** your papers/documentation/ID/credentials/certificate/licence

4 [C] ▪ *a recent paper in the Journal of Medicine*

essay + **article** + **thesis** + **dissertation** + **assignment** | *fml* **treatise** + **monograph** | *sometimes disapprov.* **tract**

▶ a/an paper/essay/article/thesis/dissertation/treatise/monograph/tract **on** sth
▶ a/an paper/essay/article/thesis/dissertation/treatise/monograph **about** sth
▶ **write/read** a/an paper/essay/article/thesis/dissertation/assignment/treatise/monograph/tract

parent noun [C, usu. pl.]
▪ *He's forty but still living with his parents.*

mother + **father** + **step-parent/stepmother/stepfather** + **guardian** | *infml, esp. spoken* **dad** + **daddy** | *BrE, infml, esp. spoken* **mum** + **mummy** | *AmE, infml, esp. spoken* **mom** + **mommy** | *esp. spoken* **mom** + **folks**

▶ a **good/bad/caring/loving/doting/devoted/proud** parent/mother/father/dad/mum/mom
▶ a **stern/strict** parent/mother/father/step-parent/guardian
▶ **become** a/sb's parent/mother/father/step-parent/guardian/dad/mum/mom

park noun [C]
▪ *They went for a walk in the park.*

gardens + **playground** | *esp. AmE* **garden**

▶ **at/in** the park/gardens/playground/garden
▶ **visit** the park/gardens/garden

park verb [I, T]
▪ *You can park in front of the house.*

stop + **pull up** + **pull** (sb/sth) **over** | *esp. written* **halt**

▶ **park/stop/halt** a **car**
▶ a **car/driver** parks/stops/pulls up/pulls over

parliament noun [C+sing./pl. v., usu. sing.]
▪ *She was elected as a member of the Dutch parliament in 2006.*

assembly + **congress** + **senate** + **council** + **house** + **chamber** | *fml* **legislature**

▶ **elect** a/an parliament/assembly/congress/council
▶ **elect sb to** parliament/an assembly/congress/the senate/a council
▶ the parliament/assembly/congress/senate/council/house/chamber/legislature **votes** (for/on) sth
● **PARLIAMENT OR CONGRESS?** A **parliament** makes laws, which are then put into effect by a group of people selected from within it; a **congress** makes laws, which are put into effect by a separate group of people.

parody noun [C, U]
▪ *a parody of a horror film*

impersonation + **impression** + **imitation** | *infml* **spoof** | *sometimes disapprov.* **caricature**

▶ a/an parody/impersonation/impression/imitation/spoof/caricature of sb/sth
▶ **do** a/an parody/impersonation/impression/imitation/spoof
▶ **write** a parody/spoof

part noun

1 [C] ▪ *spare parts for the motorbike* ▪ *your part of the bargain*

piece + **element** + **component** + **section** + **unit** + **module** + **ingredient** + **strand** + **side** + **aspect** + **end**

▶ a/an part/element/component/strand/side/aspect **to** sth
▶ an **individual** part/piece/element/component/unit/module/ingredient/strand/aspect
▶ **component/constituent** parts/elements/modules

2 [C] (usu. followed by *of*) ■ *Apples grow in many parts of the world.*

area • region • zone • belt • district • quarter | *BrE* neighbourhood | *AmE* neighborhood

▶ (a/an) **eastern/northern/ southern/western** parts/area/ region/zone/district/quarter
▶ a **remote** part/area/region

3 [C] ■ *The story was originally published in 25 weekly parts.*

episode • chapter • unit • issue • volume • edition • instalment | *esp. BrE* instalment | *AmE* installment

▶ a/the **first/second/next** part/ episode/chapter/unit/issue/ volume/edition/instalment
▶ **produce** a/an part/episode/issue/ volume/edition/instalment
▶ a/an part/issue/edition **appears/ is out/comes out**

4 [C] ■ *Who played the part of Juliet?*

role • character

▶ the part/role/character **of** sb
▶ a part/role **in** sth
▶ a **major/minor** part/role/ character
▶ **play** a part/role/character

take **part** *phrase*
■ *How many countries took part in the Olympics?*

have/play a part • be/get involved • join in (sth) • join • share • compete • *fml* participate • engage in sth • enter into sth • enter

▶ take part/play a part/get involved/join/share/compete/ participate/engage **in** sth
▶ **actively/directly** take part/ compete/participate/engage in sth
● **WHICH WORD?** You **take part** or **participate** in a particular activity or event; **be/get involved** refers more generally to the kind of activity that you are involved with: *She took part in a debate.* ◆ *She's involved in politics.*
Engage in sth often refers to kinds of activity that are considered bad in some way: *Even in prison he engaged in criminal activities.*

partial *adj.*
■ *It's only a partial solution to the problem.*

incomplete • unfinished | *fml* fragmentary...

■ OPP **total, complete**
▶ partial/incomplete **information**

participant *noun* [C]
■ *Enrolment will be limited to 35 participants.*

entrant • contestant • competitor • contender • challenger • candidate

▶ a/an **participant/entrant/ contestant/competitor/ contender/challenger/candidate in** sth
▶ a **likely/possible** participant/ contender/candidate

particular *adj.*

1 [only before noun] ■ *The policy discriminates against particular groups of people.*

specific • certain • special • distinct • distinctive • separate • individual • single • unique • respective • peculiar

■ OPP **general**
▶ particular/specific/unique/ peculiar **to...**
▶ a particular/specific/certain/ distinct/separate/individual/single **category/region/regions**
▶ a particular/specific/certain/ distinct/distinctive/separate/ individual/unique **type** of sth
● **PARTICULAR OR SPECIFIC?** A **particular** person, group or thing is that one and not a different one: John, not Mary. A **specific** group or thing is a particular one in all its details, not the general group or type of which this is one example: school children with learning difficulties, not school children in general.

2 [only before noun] ■ *This data is of particular interest.*

special • exceptional | *fml* extraordinary

■ OPP **ordinary**
▶ of particular/special **concern/ importance/interest**
▶ take particular/special **notice** of sb/sth

partly *adv.*
■ *He was only partly responsible for the accident.*

partially • up to a point • half • somewhat | *esp. written* in part • to some extent • moderately

■ OPP **completely, totally**
▶ partly/partially/moderately **successful**
▶ partly/partially/in part/to some extent **because...**
▶ **only** partly/partially/up to a point/half/to some extent/ moderately
● **PARTLY, PARTIALLY OR IN PART?** Partly and in part are used esp. about the reason for sth; partially is often used about permanent physical conditions: *I didn't enjoy the trip,*

partly because of the weather. • a
service for blind and partially sighted
people

partner noun

1 [C] ■ Come to the New Year disco
and bring your partner.

**girlfriend • boyfriend • wife •
husband • man • fiancé/fiancée** |
esp. AmE **date** | fml or law **spouse** |
becoming old-fash. **sweetheart**

▶ sb's **new** partner/girlfriend/
boyfriend/wife/husband/man
▶ **have** a partner/girlfriend/
boyfriend/wife/husband/man/
fiancé/fiancée/spouse
▶ **find** a partner/girlfriend/
boyfriend/man
● WHICH WORD? A **partner** is usu. sb
you live with but are not married to
and suggests a more long-term
relationship. Young people often
prefer to use the words **girlfriend/
boyfriend**. **Partner** can also refer
to a husband or wife, esp. if you do
not know, or it is not important, if a
couple is married or not. **Partner** is
also used when you do not know
or are not interested in what sex
sb's partner is.

2 [C] ■ He is a senior partner in a law
firm. ■ Choose a partner for the next
activity.

**colleague • collaborator • co-
worker • teammate • contact • ally •
associate** | esp. BrE **workmate**

▶ a **business** partner/colleague/
contact/ally
▶ a **junior/senior** partner/
colleague/associate
▶ a **close** partner/colleague/
collaborator/contact/ally/
associate

partnership noun [C, U]

■ Marriage should be an equal
partnership.

**relationship • cooperation •
collaboration • alliance • bond • tie
• link • association** | fml **affiliation** |
esp. busin. **contact**

▶ (a/an) partnership/relationship/
cooperation/collaboration/
alliance/bond/ties/link/
association/affiliation/contacts
with sb/sth
▶ (a/an) partnership/relationship/
cooperation/collaboration/
alliance/bond/ties/links/
association/affiliation **between** A
and B
▶ **have** (a/an) partnership/
relationship/alliance/bond/ties/
link/association/affiliation/
contacts

party noun

1 [C+sing./pl. v.] ■ the Democratic
Party

faction • camp • lobby

▶ **rival/opposing** parties/factions/
camps
▶ the **socialist** party/camp
▶ **belong to** a party/faction/camp

2 [C] ■ They threw a huge party to
celebrate the end of term.

**celebration • reception • dance •
ball • rave** | BrE **disco** | AmE **shower** |
infml, esp. journ. **bash**

▶ **at** a party/celebration/reception/
dance/ball/rave/disco/shower/
bash
▶ **have/hold/go to/attend** a party/
celebration/reception/dance/
ball/rave/disco/shower/bash

3 [C+sing./pl. v.] ■ a coach party of
tourists

**group • band • contingent • team •
crew • squad • gang • detachment** |
fml **company** | often disapprov. **pack**

▶ a party/group/band/contingent/
team/crew/squad/gang/
detachment/pack of sth
▶ **in** (a) party/group/band/team/
crew/squad/gang/company/
pack
▶ **join** a party/band/team/crew/
gang

pass verb

1 [T, I] ■ The bus pulled out to pass a
truck.

BrE **overtake**

● PASS OR OVERTAKE? In BrE you can
use both these words about going
past sb/sth that is moving but
overtake is more common: (BrE)
It's dangerous to overtake on a bend.
In AmE **pass** is the normal word.

2 [T] ■ Pass the salt, please.

give • hand • hand sb/sth over

▶ pass/give/hand/hand over sth **to**
sb
▶ **just** pass/give/hand/hand over
sth
● PASS, GIVE OR HAND? **Hand** is used
esp. in written, literary English.
Pass is used esp. in spoken requests
and also in written, literary English.
Give is used frequently in both
spoken and written English.

3 [I] ■ Six months passed without any
news of them.

go by • tick away | written **wear on •
elapse • progress**

▶ **hours/days** pass/go by/elapse
▶ (a) **season/year/time** passes/goes
by/elapses
▶ the **minutes/seconds** pass/go by/
tick away/elapse

fill • while sth away • spend • devote sth to sth • occupy • take up sth

▶ pass/fill/while away/spend/ devote/occupy/take up (the) **time**
▶ pass/fill/while away/spend/ devote/occupy/take up **an hour/a couple of hours**

5 [I, T] ■ *I passed the test.*

graduate | *esp. BrE* **qualify** | *infml* **sail through (sth)** | *BrE, infml* **get through (sth)**

■ OPP **fail**

▶ pass/graduate **with sth**
▶ pass/sail/graduate/get through **a/ an course/exam/test**
▶ **students** pass/graduate/qualify/ sail through

passage *noun*

1 [C] ■ *A secret underground passage connected the two houses.*

hall • walkway • aisle | *esp. BrE* **corridor** | *esp. AmE* **passageway • hallway**

▶ **in/along/down** the passage/hall/ walkway/aisle/corridor/ passageway/hallway
▶ **through** the passage/hall/ corridor/passageway/hallway
▶ **at/to the end of** the passage/hall/ walkway/aisle/corridor/hallway

2 [C] ■ *Read the passage and answer the questions below.*

extract • excerpt • paragraph • scene • reading

▶ a/an passage/extract/excerpt/ paragraph/scene/reading **from sth**
▶ **read/quote** a/an passage/ extract/paragraph/scene
▶ a/an passage/extract/excerpt/ reading **is taken from** sth (e.g. a book)

passenger *noun* [C]

■ *The car was carrying three passengers.*

commuter | *esp. BrE* **traveller** | *AmE* **traveler**

▶ a **regular** passenger/commuter/ traveller
▶ **rail** passengers/commuters/ travellers
▶ passenger/commuter **fares/ services/traffic/trains**

passive *adj.*

■ *He was just a passive observer of events.*

docile • submissive • meek | *esp. written, approv.* **amenable** | *written, often disapprov.* **compliant**

■ OPP **active**

▶ a passive/submissive/compliant **role**
▶ passive/meek **obedience**

pass sth on *phrasal verb*

1 ■ *I passed your message on to my mother.*

repeat • send • transmit • spread • break • communicate • convey • relay • get sth across | *fml* **impart**

▶ pass on/repeat/send/transmit/ spread/break/communicate/ convey/relay/get across/impart **sth to sb**
▶ pass on/repeat/send/transmit/ spread/communicate/convey/ relay/get across/impart a **message**
▶ pass on/spread/break/convey **the news**

2 ■ *The disease is passed on by mosquitoes.*

spread • infect | *esp. spoken* **give** | *fml* **transmit**

▶ pass on/spread/give/transmit sth **to sb**
▶ pass on/spread/infect sb with/ give sb/transmit a/an **disease/ infection/virus**

3 ■ *These skills were passed on from father to son.*

hand sth down • leave | *fml* **bequeath**

▶ pass on/hand down/leave/ bequeath sth **to sb**
▶ pass on/hand down **skills/ knowledge**
▶ pass on/leave/bequeath **your property/your estate/a legacy**

past *noun*

1 the past [sing.] ■ *It all happened in the distant past.*

history | *infml* **the old days**

▶ **in** the past/(sth's) history/the old days
▶ sth's **colourful/rich/chequered/ glorious** past/history
▶ **(the/sth's) recent/ancient/ medieval** past/history

2 [C, usu. sing.] ■ *She didn't tell them about her boyfriend's criminal past.*

background • record • history • track record • life history • upbringing • origins

■ OPP **future**

▶ a **colouful/chequered** past/ history

past

▶ sb's **criminal** past/background/
record/history

past adj.

1 [usu. before noun] ■ *In past years
the industry received large subsidies.*

previous • **former** • **old** • **distant** •
remote | *fml* **prior** | *written* **bygone**

■ OPP **present**
▶ (a) past/previous/former/distant/
remote/bygone **era**/**times**
▶ (a) past/previous/former **experience**/
history/**life**
▶ a past/previous/former **owner**/
president/**prime minister**
● **PAST, OLD OR FORMER?** Use **past** or
former to talk about times gone
by; use **old** to talk about things
from your own life: *my old school/
colleagues/friends.* **Former** can also
describe sth that has changed: *the
former Yugoslav republic.* A *former
friend* is sb who is no longer your
friend; an *old friend* is sb you have
known for a long time.

2 [only before noun] ■ *I've not seen
her in the past few weeks.*

last • **previous** | *fml* **preceding**

■ OPP **next**
▶ the past/last/previous/preceding
few days/**week**/**month**/**year**/
decade/**century**
▶ the past/last/previous **weekend**/
season/**round**/**hundred years**
● **PAST OR LAST?** You can only use
past about a period of time that
has just gone by; it must be used
with *the* or a determiner such as
this:
✓*The past week has been very busy.*
• *Last week was very busy.*
Past is not used about particular
dates, or about things:
✓*The critics hated her last book.*
✗ *The critics hated her past book.*

pat verb [T]

■ *She patted the dog on the head.*

tap • **clap**

▶ pat/tap/clap sb **on the back**/
shoulder
▶ pat/tap/clap **gently**/**lightly**/
affectionately

patch noun [C]

■ *There were damp patches on the
wall.*

mark • **spot** • **dot**

▶ a **patch**/**mark**/**spot**/**dot on** sth
▶ **with** patches/marks/spots/dots

path noun

1 [C] ■ *a garden path* ■ *Follow the
path through the woods.*

---

trail | *esp. BrE* **track** • **footpath** | *BrE*
pavement | *AmE* **sidewalk**

▶ a path/trail/track/footpath
through/**to** sth
▶ a path/trail/track/footpath **leads
to** sth

2 [C] ■ *The diagram shows the path of
the satellite.*

course • **route** • **line** • **way** •
direction • **orbit** | *tech.* **bearing**

▶ a/the path/course/route/line/
way **from**... **to**...
▶ a/the path/course/route/line/
way **through**/**along**/**across** sth
▶ follow a/an path/course/route/
line/way/orbit

3 [C] ■ *Everyone has to find their own
path in life.*

road • **route** • **course** • **direction**

▶ a/the path/road/route **to** sth
▶ **on** a path/road/route/course
▶ **take** a/the... path/road/route/
course/direction
● **PATH, ROAD OR ROUTE?** Path is often
more personal than road: *her path
in life* (= the one that a particular
person follows) but *the road to
stardom* (= the one that all stars
must follow). **Route** may be used
in both personal and general ways
but is used esp. to report things in
a more factual, less emotional way:
the route to economic stability

patience noun [U]

■ *I have run out of patience with her.*

tolerance • **resignation**

■ OPP **impatience**
▶ patience/tolerance **for** sb/sth
▶ **with** patience/tolerance/
resignation
▶ **have**/**lack**/**require**/**show**/
exercise/**learn** patience/tolerance

patient noun [C]

■ *The hospital has over 800 patients.*

victim • **sufferer** • **case** • **invalid** •
the sick • **the dying**

▶ a/an **cancer**/**AIDS** patient/victim/
sufferer/case
▶ **care for** a patient/a sufferer/an
invalid/the sick/the dying
▶ **treat** a/the patient/victim/
sufferer/case/sick

patient adj.

■ *You'll just have to be patient and
wait till I've finished.*

calm • **controlled** • **composed** • **cool**
• **relaxed** • **placid** • **easy-going** |
infml **laid-back**

■ OPP **impatient**
▶ patient/calm/cool/easy-going/
laid-back **about** sth

patronizing (BrE also -ising) adj. (disapprov.)

■ I didn't mean to sound patronizing.

superior • snobbish | infml snooty | esp. written condescending • haughty

▸ patronizing/superior/snobbish/ snooty **about** sth
▸ patronizing/condescending **to/ towards** sb
▸ a patronizing/superior/ condescending/haughty **attitude/ tone/smile/manner**
● PATRONIZING, SUPERIOR OR CONDESCENDING? People who are **patronizing** or **condescending** talk in a way that they think is kind, but which shows that they do not consider the other person to be their equal; sb whose manner is **superior** shows their feeling of superiority by keeping apart from other people and not being too friendly.

pattern noun

1 [C] ■ changing patterns of behaviour/work/weather

rhythm • cycle

▸ a/an regular/irregular pattern/ rhythm/cycle
▸ break a pattern/rhythm/cycle
● PATTERN, RHYTHM OR CYCLE? Pattern is used esp. about people's work and behaviour; cycle is used esp. about events in the natural world; rhythm is used esp. about how people's bodies adapt to changing conditions.

2 [C, usu. sing.] ■ This system sets the pattern for others to follow.

model • prototype • blueprint • template • precedent

▸ a pattern/model/prototype/ blueprint/template/precedent **for** sth
▸ set a pattern/precedent
▸ follow/copy a pattern/model/ blueprint/template/precedent
● PATTERN OR MODEL? A pattern is always an excellent example and one that people should follow; a model is an example that people do follow, usu. because it works well.

3 [C] ■ He wore a shirt with a floral pattern.

design • motif • decoration

▸ a pattern/design/motif/ decoration **on** sth
▸ **in** a pattern/design
▸ have/make a pattern/design/ motif
▸ print/produce/weave a pattern/ design
● PATTERN OR DESIGN? A pattern is regular and repeated, and is either

created deliberately or formed by chance; a design is either repeated or single, and is always created deliberately.

pause noun [C]

■ There was a long pause before he replied.

break • gap • lull • interruption

▸ a/an pause/break/gap/lull/ interruption **in** sth
▸ **after** a/an pause/break/gap/lull/ interruption
▸ fill a pause/gap

pause verb [I]

■ She paused for a moment and looked back.

hesitate | esp. written break off | esp. BrE, disapprov. dither

▸ pause/hesitate/break off (for) a moment
▸ pause/hesitate briefly/ momentarily/a little
▸ pause/break off abruptly

pay noun [U]

■ The job is hard, but the pay is good.

wage/wages • salary • income • earnings

▸ (a/an) high/low/basic/good/ meagre/average pay/wage/ wages/salary/income/earnings
▸ receive pay/a wage/wages/a salary/an income/earnings
▸ earn your pay/a wage/wages/a salary/an income
● PAY, WAGES OR SALARY? Pay is the most general of these words. If you work in a factory, shop, etc. you usu. get your wages each week. Office workers and professionals such as doctors, teachers, etc. receive a salary that is paid monthly or twice a month. It is expressed as an annual figure: She's on a salary of over $80 000.

pay verb [I, T]

■ Have you paid the hotel bill?

give • settle • meet • clear | fml defray

▸ pay/settle/meet/clear your **debts**
▸ pay/settle/meet a **bill**
▸ pay/settle/defray the **cost** of sth

pay attention phrase

■ Can you all pay attention, please?

listen | fml heed

■ OPP ignore

▸ pay attention/listen **to** sb/sth
▸ pay attention/listen to a **conversation**

pay sb back (sth)

▶ pay attention to/listen to/heed sb's words/what sb says

pay sb back (sth), pay sth back *phrasal verb*

■ *I'll pay you back next week.*

repay ◆ **refund** ◆ **compensate** | *fml* **reimburse**

▶ pay back/repay/refund/ compensate/reimburse sb **for** sth
▶ pay back/repay/refund/reimburse sth **to** sb
▶ pay back/repay/refund/reimburse **money**
● **PAY SB BACK OR REPAY?** Repay is used in more formal English and more formal situations than pay sb back.

payment *noun* [C, U]

■ *He agreed to make monthly payments of £50.*

premium ◆ **contribution** ◆ **subscription** ◆ **repayment** ◆ **deposit** ◆ **settlement** | *esp. BrE* **instalment** | *AmE* **installment**

▶ a payment/premium/ subscription/repayment/deposit/ settlement **for** sth
▶ a/an payment/ repayment/deposit/instalment **on** sth
▶ **meet/keep up (with)** the payments/premiums/ repayments/instalments
▶ a/an payment/premium/ subscription/repayment/ settlement/instalment **is due**

peace *noun*

1 [U, sing.] ■ *The two communities now live together in peace.*

order ◆ **calm** ◆ **law and order** ◆ **the rule of law**

■ **OPP war, conflict**
▶ an uneasy peace/calm
▶ **maintain/establish/preserve** peace/order/law and order/the rule of law
▶ peace/order/calm/law and order/ the rule of law **prevails**

2 [U] ■ *She was enjoying the peace of a soft summer evening.*

calm ◆ **quiet** ◆ **hush** ◆ **silence** | *esp. BrE* **tranquillity** | *AmE usu.* **tranquility**

■ **OPP noise**
▶ **in** peace/silence/tranquillity
▶ **absolute/total** peace/calm/ quiet/silence/tranquillity
▶ **break** the peace/calm/quiet/ silence

peaceful *adj.*

■ *It's so peaceful out in the countryside.*

calm ◆ **quiet** ◆ **sleepy** ◆ **silent** | *written* **tranquil**

■ **OPP noisy**
▶ a peaceful/quiet/sleepy/silent/ tranquil **place/village/town**
▶ a peaceful/calm/quiet/tranquil **day/night/morning/evening**
▶ a peaceful/calm/quiet/tranquil **life/setting**

peak *noun*

1 [C, sing.+ sing./pl. *v.*] ■ *She's at the peak of her career.*

height ◆ **top** ◆ **high point** ◆ **climax** ◆ **prime** ◆ **highlight** ◆ **heyday** | *esp. written* **culmination** | *busin. or journ.* **high**

■ **OPP trough**
▶ the peak/height/top/high point/ climax/prime/highlight/ culmination/heyday **of** sth
▶ **at** its peak/its height/the top/a high point/its climax/its culmination/a high
▶ **reach** its peak/its climax/its high point/its height/the top/a high point/its climax/its culmination/a high
● **PEAK OR HEIGHT?** Peak is used before other nouns (*peak hours/ demand/fitness*) but height is not. A person can be *at the peak/height of their career/powers*, but otherwise *height* is not used to talk about a person. You can talk about a *peak* of a particular number or level but not a *height* of a number or level.

2 [C] ■ *a mountain peak*

summit ◆ **ridge** ◆ **mountain**

▶ **on** a/the peak/summit/ridge/ mountain
▶ **climb** a peak/ridge/mountain
● **PEAK OR SUMMIT?** A mountain can have more than one peak; only the highest peak is the **summit**. A whole mountain can be called a **peak**; only the top is called the **summit**.

people *noun*

1 [pl.] ■ *She doesn't care what people think of her.*

infml **folk** | *esp. AmE, infml* **folks**

▶ **young/elderly/old/rich/poor/ black/white** people/folk
▶ **common/ordinary/working/ working-class/everyday** people/ folk
▶ **city/country/local** people/folk

2 [C] ■ *We campaign for the rights of tribal peoples.*

race ◆ **nationality** ◆ **ethnic group** ◆ **clan** | *sometimes offens.* **tribe**

▶ **between** peoples/races/ nationalities/ethnic groups/clans/ tribes

► different/other peoples/races/
nationalities/ethnic groups/clans/
tribes

perfect adj.

1 ■ *He smiled, revealing a perfect set of
teeth.*

pristine • faultless • flawless •
impeccable • exemplary •
immaculate • unspoiled

■ OPP imperfect
► pristine/impeccable/
immaculate **condition**
► a/an perfect/faultless/flawless/
impeccable/exemplary/
immaculate **performance**
► perfect/flawless/impeccable
English/French

2 ■ *This farm is a perfect example of
sustainable agriculture.*

excellent • outstanding • wonderful
• classic • first-rate • prime • superb
| *infml* fantastic • terrific | *BrE, esp.
spoken* marvellous | *AmE, esp. spoken*
marvelous

■ OPP mediocre
► a/an perfect/excellent/
outstanding/wonderful/first-rate/
superb/fantastic/terrific/
marvellous **performance/job**
► a/an perfect/excellent/
outstanding/wonderful/classic/
prime/superb/fantastic/terrific/
marvellous **example**

3 ■ *It was the perfect day for a picnic.*

ideal • optimum • tailor-made |
spoken just right

► perfect/ideal/tailor-made/just
right **for** sb/sth
► a/an perfect/ideal **opportunity/
solution/candidate**
► absolutely perfect/ideal
● **PERFECT OR IDEAL?** Perfect is slightly
more informal. A *perfect day for sth*
is one with very good weather; an
ideal day for sth is a very convenient
day.

perfectly adv. (esp. spoken)

■ *To be perfectly honest, I don't like the
colour.*

completely • totally • utterly • fully
• entirely | *esp. BrE* quite | *esp. spoken*
absolutely

► perfectly/completely/totally/
entirely/quite/absolutely **normal**
► perfectly/completely/quite/
absolutely **still**
► perfectly/completely/totally/
fully/quite **understand**
● **WHICH WORD?** The main differences
between these words are in register
not meaning. **Completely**, **entirely**
and **fully** are used more in written
and formal English. **Totally**,
absolutely and **perfectly** are used
more in spoken and informal

English. **Utterly** is often used to
express failure or impossibility: *She
utterly failed to convince them.*

perform verb

1 [T] (*esp. written*) ■ *A computer can
perform many tasks at once.*

do • carry sth out • go through sth •
commit | *fml* conduct • undertake |
BrE, fml practise | *AmE, fml* practice

► perform/do/carry out/conduct/
undertake a/an **work/
activity/investigation/
assessment**
► perform/do/carry out/undertake
a **task/job**
► perform/do/carry out/practise
surgery
● **PERFORM OR CARRY STH OUT?**
Perform often emphasizes the skill
involved in doing sth; carry sth out
often emphasizes the amount of
work involved:
✓perform miracles ✗ ~~carry out
miracles~~
Perform is not used about negative
actions:
✓carry out an attack ✗ ~~perform an
attack~~

2 [T] ■ *The play was first performed in
2007.*

play • act • put sth on • produce |
esp. spoken do | *written* stage •
present

► perform/play/act in/put on/
produce/stage/present a
play/show
► perform/play/do a **piece**
► perform/play/do sth **live/in
public**

3 [I] ■ *The company has performed
poorly over the past year.*

esp. BrE get on/along | *esp. spoken* do
• go | *esp. written* fare

► perform/get on/do/go/fare **well**
► perform/get on/do/go
brilliantly/excellently/badly
● **PERFORM OR FARE?** A person or
company that *performs well* is
successful because of what they
do; a person or group that *fares
well* is successful because they are
lucky or because conditions are
right. These two words cannot be
used about these events:
✓*The interview went well.* ✗ ~~The
interview performed/fared well.~~

performance noun [C]

■ *They gave a magnificent
performance of Ravel's String Quartet.*

show • production • display • act •
spectacle

performer

► a **live** performance/show/
production/act
► **do** a/an performance/show/
production/act
► **put on/stage** a performance/
show/production/display

performer noun [C]
■ *Allan became a circus performer.*

**artist • actor • actress • entertainer •
musician • singer • dancer •
comedian** | *esp. AmE* **movie star** | *BrE*
film star | *esp. BrE, sometimes ironic*
artiste

► a **young** performer/artist/actor/
actress/entertainer/musician/
singer/dancer/comedian/artiste
► a **famous** performer/artist/actor/
actress/entertainer/musician/
singer/dancer/comedian/movie
star/film star

period noun

1 [C] ■ *There has been a 2% increase
this month compared with the same
period last year.*

**time • season • while • term • spell •
interval • run • stint • span** | *esp. BrE,
infml* **patch**

► a/an period/time/season/term/
spell/interval/run/stint/span/
patch **of** sth
► a period/time/season/term/spell/
stint **as** sth
► **for** a/an period/time/season/
while/term/spell/interval/stint/
span
► **have** a …period/time/season/
spell/run/patch
● **PERIOD OR TIME? Time** is more
about the feeling of time passing;
period is more about the amount
of time that has passed:
✓*The factory will be closed down
over a period of two years.* ✗ *The
factory will be closed down over a
time of two years.*
✓*I lived in Egypt for a time.* ✗ *I lived
in Egypt for a period.*

2 [C] ■ *This textbook covers the post-
war period.*

**time • age • day • century •
generation • decade • era** | *fml*
epoch

► **in** a period/the time of…/times/
the age of…/ …day(s)/the …
century/a generation/a decade/
an era/an epoch
► **(the) present** period/time/day/
century/generation/decade/era/
epoch
► **medieval/Victorian/post-
war, etc.** period/days/time/era

permanent adj.
■ *No permanent damage was done.*

lasting | *written* **enduring • eternal •
immortal**

■ OPP **temporary**
► permanent/lasting/enduring/
eternal **value**
► a/an permanent/lasting/enduring
relationship/solution/legacy

permission noun [U]
■ *He took the car without his father's
permission.*

**approval • agreement • clearance •
consent • authorization • authority**
| *fml* **leave • assent** | *infml, esp. journ.*
the go-ahead

► permission/approval/agreement/
clearance/consent/authorization/
authority/assent **for** sth
► **without** sb's permission/approval/
agreement/consent/
authorization/authority/leave/
assent
► permission/approval/clearance/
consent/authorization/authority/
leave/the go-ahead **to do** sth
● **PERMISSION OR CONSENT?**
Permission is often official, given
by sb in authority; **consent** is often
given more personally, by the
person that sth is being done to, esp. in
the context of medical treatment
or sexual relations: *You'll need to get
permission from the Council before
you can start building.* ◆ *Patients
must sign a consent form before the
operation can go ahead.*

permit verb

1 [T] *(fml)* ■ *The banks were not
permitted to invest overseas.*

**allow • let • grant • authorize •
license • entitle • clear** | *infml* **OK** |
fml **sanction • empower**

■ OPP **ban, forbid,** *(fml)* **prohibit**
► permit/allow/authorize/license/
entitle/clear/empower **sb to do**
sth
► **let** sb **do** sth
► be **legally** permitted/allowed/
authorized/entitled/sanctioned/
empowered

2 [I, T] *(fml)* ■ *We hope to visit the
cathedral, if time permits.*

allow • enable

■ OPP **prevent**
► permit/allow/enable **sb to do** sth
► permit/allow/enable **access**
► permit/allow/enable the
**creation/development/
expansion of** sth
● **PERMIT OR ALLOW? Permit** is more
formal than **allow** and is used esp.
in the fixed phrases *if time permits*
and *weather permitting.*

person noun [C]
■ *The price is $40 per person.*

individual • human • human being • figure • soul • character | *infml* **type** | *spoken thing* | *humorous* **mortal**

▶ a/an **average/normal/ordinary** person/individual/human/human being/mortal
▶ a/an **key/powerful/independent** person/individual/figure
▶ the person/individual **concerned/responsible**

personal adj.

1 [only before noun] ■ *Of course this is just my personal opinion.*

own • individual • private • exclusive | *sometimes disapprov.* **subjective**

▶ sb's personal/own/individual/private/subjective **experience**
▶ sb's personal/own/private/exclusive **property**
▶ sb's personal/own/individual **needs/requirements/objectives/freedom**
● **PERSONAL OR PRIVATE? Personal** things, details, etc. belong to a particular individual person and not any other individual person. **Private** things belong to a particular person or group, or are for them to use; they are not for people in general.

2 ■ *The letter was marked 'Personal'.*

private • confidential • secret • intimate

▶ personal/private/confidential/secret **information**
▶ a personal/private/confidential **letter**
▶ sb's personal/private **life**
● **PERSONAL OR PRIVATE?** You can usu. use either word to describe sth that is not connected with your work or official position, except: ✓*a personal friend of mine* ✗ *a private friend of mine*

personality noun

1 [C] ■ *The three children have very different personalities.*

character • nature • temperament • self • make-up | *fml* **disposition • persona**

▶ a **violent** personality/character/nature/temperament
▶ a/an **outgoing/charming** personality/character/disposition
▶ sth **reflects** sb's personality/character/nature
● **WHICH WORD? Personality** is used esp. about whether sb is confident, shy, etc. with other people; **character** is used esp. about sb's moral behaviour; **nature** is used esp. about sb's normal way of behaving; **temperament** is used

esp. about whether sb normally stays calm, or gets angry, etc.

2 [U] *(approv.)* ■ *We need someone with lots of personality to head the project.*

character • charisma • charm • presence

▶ lack personality/character/charisma/charm

3 [C] ■ *He was voted TV Personality of the Year.*

celebrity • star • name • legend • icon • idol • public figure | *infml* **superstar • great**

▶ a **famous/top** personality/celebrity/star/name
▶ a **television/TV/media** personality/celebrity/star
▶ a **sporting/sports** personality/star/legend/icon

persuade noun

1 [T, I] ■ *Can you persuade him to come to the party?*

convince • get • talk sb into sth • win sb over • coax • cajole | *BrE, infml* **get round** | *esp. AmE, infml* **get around** | *infml, often humorous* **convert**

■ OPP **dissuade**

▶ persuade sb/convince sb/get sb/be coaxed/be cajoled **to do sth**
▶ persuade/talk/coax/cajole sb **into** (doing) sth
▶ **try to** persuade sb/convince sb to do sth/get sb to do sth/talk sb into sth/win sb over/coax sb
● **PERSUADE OR CONVINCE?** You can **persuade** sb to do sth in many different ways, for example by providing good reasons or by giving them sth in return, but you usu. **convince** sb to do sth only by making them believe it is the right thing to do: *She persuaded/convinced me to get some legal advice. ◆ He was persuaded by bribes to reverse his judgement.*

2 [T] ■ *No one was persuaded by his arguments.*

convince • satisfy

▶ persuade/convince/satisfy sb **of** sth
▶ persuade/convince/satisfy sb **that**...
▶ persuade/convince/satisfy **yourself**

perverse adj.

■ *Are you being deliberately perverse about this?*

awkward • difficult • unhelpful • uncooperative • obstructive

petrol

▶ **deliberately** perverse/awkward/
obstructive

petrol noun [U] (BrE)
■ Does your car run on unleaded
petrol?

fuel • **diesel** | AmE **gas** • **gasoline**

▶ **unleaded** petrol/fuel/gas/
gasoline
▶ sth **runs on** petrol/fuel/gas/
gas/gasoline
▶ **fill** the car **up with** petrol/diesel/
gas
▶ **run out of** petrol/fuel/diesel/gas

philosophy noun [C]
■ a Buddhist philosophy of life

values • **doctrine** • **teaching** • **belief**
• **code** • **ethic** | fml **ethos** | sometimes
disapprov. **ideology**

▶ sb's **moral** philosophy/values/
doctrine/teaching/beliefs/code
▶ sb's **political** philosophy/values/
doctrine/beliefs/ethic/ethos/
ideology
▶ **subscribe to** (a/an) philosophy/
values/doctrine/teaching/code/
ethic/ideology

phone verb [I, T] (BrE, esp. spoken)
■ I'm phoning about your ad in the
newspaper.

call • **reach** • **dial** | esp. AmE, infml
call sb up | esp. BrE, fml **telephone** |
BrE, esp. spoken **ring**

▶ phone sb/call sb/call sb up/
telephone sb/ring sb **about** sth
▶ phone sb/call sb/telephone/ring
sb **from** somewhere
▶ phone/call/telephone/ring **to do**
sth
● **PHONE, CALL OR RING?** Call is the
only one of these three words used
in AmE. Ring and phone are the
most frequent terms in spoken BrE,
but call is preferred in an
emergency: Call the police/fire
brigade.
You **call/ring/phone** a person,
place or institution; you **call** a cab/
a taxi/an ambulance.

photograph noun [C]
■ some black and white photographs
of the city

photo • **picture** • **shot** • **snapshot** •
slide • **print** | BrE, infml **snap**

▶ a **colour** photograph/photo/
picture/slide/print/snap
▶ **take** a photograph/photo/
picture/shot/snapshot/snap
▶ a photograph/photo/picture/
shot/snapshot/slide/snap **shows**
sb/sth

● **PHOTOGRAPH, PHOTO OR PICTURE?**
Photo is more informal than
photograph. Picture is used esp.
about photographs in newspapers,
magazines and books.

phrase noun [C]
■ His favourite phrase was 'so it goes'.

expression • **idiom** • **word** • **term**

▶ a **technical/colloquial** phrase/
expression/word/term
▶ **use** a/an phrase/expression/
idiom/word/term
▶ **coin** a/an phrase/expression/
word/term

pick verb
1 [T] (infml) ■ Names were picked at
random out of a hat.

choose • **select** • **decide** • **opt** •
single sb/sth out • **adopt** | infml **go**
for sth

▶ pick/choose/select/single out A
from B
▶ pick/choose/select/decide
between A and B
▶ pick/choose/select/single out/
adopt/go for sb/sth **as** sb/sth
▶ pick/choose/select/single out sb/
sth **for** sth
● **PICK, CHOOSE OR SELECT?** When you
select sth you usu. choose it
carefully, unless you actually say
that it is selected randomly/at
random. Pick is a more informal
word that describes a less careful
action. Choose is the most general
of these words and the only one
that can be used without an
object:
✔You choose—I can't decide ✗ You
select/pick—I can't decide.

2 [T] ■ They picked some blackberries
from the hedgerow.

harvest | lit. **gather**

▶ pick/harvest/gather **fruit**
▶ harvest/gather a **crop**

pick sb/sth up phrasal verb
1 ■ He picked the baby up gently.

lift • **scoop** • **hoist** • **heave** | esp.
written **raise**

■ OPP **put sb/sth down**
▶ pick/lift/scoop/hoist/raise sth **up**
▶ pick up/lift/hoist/heave a **bag/
basket**
▶ pick up/lift the **phone/
telephone/receiver**
● **PICK SB/STH UP OR LIFT?** Pick sb/sth
up is usu. used about things or
people that are not very heavy; lift
suggests the person or thing is
quite heavy. Lift is used about
movement in different directions;
pick sb/sth up is only used about
upwards movement.

2 (*esp. spoken*) ■ *I'll pick you up from the station.*

collect | *esp. spoken* get | BrE, *esp. spoken* fetch

▶ pick up/collect/get/fetch sb/sth **from** sth/somewhere
▶ pick up/collect/get/fetch sth **for** sb
▶ go/come to pick up/collect/get/fetch sb/sth

picture *noun*

1 [C] ■ *The children drew pictures of their pets.*

painting ◆ drawing ◆ sketch ◆ image ◆ portrait ◆ print ◆ cartoon ◆ design ◆ diagram ◆ graphics ◆ artwork

▶ draw a picture/portrait/sketch/cartoon/design/diagram
▶ paint a picture/portrait
▶ show/display/exhibit a picture/painting/drawing/portrait/print

2 [C] ■ *There's a picture of you in the local paper.*

photograph ◆ photo ◆ shot ◆ snapshot ◆ print ◆ slide | BrE, *infml* snap

▶ a **colour** picture/photograph/photo/print/slide/snap
▶ take a picture/photograph/photo/shot/snapshot
▶ a picture/photograph/photo/shot/snapshot/slide/snap **shows** sb/sth

● **PICTURE, PHOTOGRAPH OR PHOTO?** Picture is used esp. about photographs in newspapers, magazines and books. In AmE *take a picture* is more common than *take a photo*. Photo is more informal than photograph.

3 [C] ■ *The report paints a gloomy picture of the economy.*

description ◆ profile ◆ portrait ◆ portrayal ◆ representation | *fml* depiction ◆ evocation

▶ a/an picture/description/profile/portrait/portrayal/representation/depiction/evocation **of** sb/sth
▶ a **vivid** picture/description/portrayal/representation/depiction/evocation
▶ give a picture/description/representation
▶ draw/paint a picture/portrait

4 [C] ■ *She had formed a picture in her mind of how the house would look.*

image ◆ idea ◆ thought ◆ prospect

▶ a picture/an idea/an image/the prospect/the thought **of** sb/sth
▶ a **clear** picture/image/idea/thought
▶ **have** a/an picture/image/idea/thought

▶ a/an picture/image/idea/thought **forms**

● **PICTURE OR IMAGE?** Picture often suggests an imagining of a whole scene including various details and/or events; an image often suggests a mental picture of only one person or thing at one particular time.

piece *noun*

1 [C] ■ *He cut himself a large piece of cheese.*

slice ◆ chunk ◆ lump ◆ hunk ◆ wedge ◆ slab ◆ cube ◆ length ◆ block ◆ sliver | *esp. BrE* bit

▶ a piece/slice/chunk/lump/hunk/wedge/sliver/bit of **cheese**
▶ a piece/chunk/lump/hunk/slab/bit of **meat**
▶ a piece/lump/slab/block of **ice**
▶ **cut** sth into pieces/slices/chunks/wedges/cubes/lengths/bits
▶ **cut (off)** a piece/slice/length/bit

2 [C] ■ *There were tiny pieces of glass all over the road.*

fragment ◆ sliver ◆ scrap ◆ shred ◆ speck ◆ particle ◆ morsel ◆ splinter ◆ chip | *esp. BrE* bit | *written* shard

▶ a piece/fragment/sliver/scrap/shred/speck/particle/morsel/splinter/bit/shard of sth
▶ a **small/tiny** piece/fragment/sliver/scrap/speck/particle/morsel/bit
▶ a piece/fragment/sliver/splinter/bit/shard of **glass**
▶ a piece/scrap/bit of **paper/information/news**
▶ **smash** sth to pieces/bits

3 [C] ■ *He took the clock to pieces.*

part ◆ component ◆ section ◆ element | *esp. BrE* bit

▶ an **individual** piece/part/component/section/element/bit

4 [C] ■ *The orchestra performed pieces by Ravel and Haydn.*

work ◆ masterpiece | *fml* composition ◆ oeuvre

▶ a piece/work/masterpiece/composition **by** sb
▶ a/an **orchestral/choral** piece/work/masterpiece/composition
▶ **perform** a piece/work/composition

● **PIECE, WORK OR COMPOSITION?** Piece and composition are used mostly to talk about music. Work is used to talk about any type of art, literature or music.

pile *noun* [C]

■ *I found it under a pile of papers on my desk.*

heap • stack • mound • mass

▶ a pile/**heap/stack/mound/mass of** sth
▶ **in/into** a pile/**heap/stack/mound**
▶ **make** a pile/**heap/mound**
▶ **put** sth **on** a pile/**heap**

pipe noun [C]

■ Both hot and cold water pipes should be properly insulated.

tube • hose • main • duct • line • pipeline

▶ **through** a pipe/**tube/hose/duct/pipeline**
▶ a **plastic/metal** pipe/**tube/hose**
▶ a **gas** pipe/**main/duct/pipeline**
▶ an **oil** pipe/**pipeline**
● PIPE OR TUBE? Pipe emphasizes the function; tube emphasizes the shape.

pitch noun [C] (BrE)

■ The game ended in chaos with fans invading the pitch.

field • playing field • stadium • arena | BrE **ground** | AmE **park • ballpark**

▶ **on/off** the pitch/**field/playing field**
▶ a **sports** pitch/**field/ground/stadium/arena**
▶ a **football/cricket/rugby** pitch/**field/ground/stadium**
▶ a **baseball** stadium/**field/park**
● PITCH, FIELD OR GROUND? Both field and pitch are used to talk about the area of land where a sport is played. Ground also includes the buildings, seating, etc. around the place where a game is played.

pity noun

1 [U] ■ She was full of pity for the unfortunate young man.

compassion • sympathy

▶ pity/**compassion/sympathy for** sb/sth
▶ **feel/be full of** pity/**compassion/sympathy**
▶ **have** pity/**compassion/sympathy** (for sb/sth)
● PITY OR COMPASSION? Compassion is a warm, kind feeling that suggests that you understand what sb is suffering. If you feel pity you do not necessarily have this understanding.

2 a pity [sing.] (esp. spoken) ■ It's a pity that you can't stay longer.

unfortunate | esp. spoken **a shame • too bad** | fml **regrettable**

▶ It's a pity/**a shame/too bad about** sb/sth.

▶ a pity/unfortunate/**a shame/too bad/regrettable that...**
▶ a **great/real/terrible** pity/**shame**
▶ **What** a pity/**shame!**

take place phrase

■ The film festival takes place in October.

happen • materialize • come about | fml **occur • arise**

▶ an **event/accident** takes place/**happens for** sth
▶ a **change** takes place/**happens/comes about/occurs/arises**

place noun

1 [C] ■ This is a good place for a picnic.

location • spot • site • scene • venue • point • area • position • whereabouts

▶ a (good, etc.) place/**location/spot/site/venue/position for** sth
▶ **at** a place/**location/spot/site/scene/venue/point/position**
▶ **in** a/an place/**location/venue/area/position**

2 [C] ■ Sit next to me—I've saved you a place.

seat

▶ a/an **good/empty** place/**seat**
▶ **take/book/reserve** a place/**seat**
▶ **save** sb a place/**seat**

place verb

1 [T] (always used with an adv. or prep.) ■ He placed a hand on her shoulder.

lay • put • set • position • plant • settle | infml **dump • stuff • stick** | esp. BrE, infml **pop**

▶ place/**lay/put/set/dump/stick/pop** sth **on** sth
▶ place/**put/set/dump/stuff/stick/pop** sth **in/into** sth
▶ place/**lay/put** sth **carefully**
● PLACE OR LAY? Place is usu. more deliberate; lay is usu. more gentle. You place things but not people; you can lay things or people:
✓A bomb had been placed under the seat. ✗ A bomb had been laid under the seat.
✓She laid the baby on the bed. ✗ She placed the baby on the bed.

2 [T] ■ We place a high value on punctuality.

put • attach • lay

▶ place/**put/attach/lay** sth **on** sth
▶ place/**put/attach/lay (the) blame**
▶ place/**put/attach/lay responsibility/emphasis**
● PLACE OR PUT? Put does not collocate with importance and is

not usu. used in the passive in this meaning:
✓Great importance is placed on education. ✗ ~~Great importance is put on education.~~

plain noun [C]
■ the flat coastal plain of the Yucatan peninsular

grassland • plateau • lowland • prairie • savannah • steppe • pampas

▶ on the **plains/grasslands/plateau/ prairie/savannah/steppes/pampas**
▶ the **open plains/grasslands/ plateau/prairie/savannah**
▶ the **rolling plains/grasslands/ plateau/prairie**

plain adj.
1 ■ He made it very plain that he wanted us to leave.

clear • obvious • apparent • evident • self-evident • explicit

▶ plain/clear/obvious/apparent/ evident/self-evident **to sb/sth**
▶ plain/clear/obvious/apparent/ evident/self-evident **from/in sb/ sth**
▶ make sth plain/clear/obvious/ apparent/evident/explicit
● **PLAIN, CLEAR OR OBVIOUS?** If you make sth **clear/plain**, you do so deliberately, but if you make sth **obvious**, you do so without meaning to:
✓I hope I make myself clear/plain. ✗ ~~I hope I make myself obvious.~~
✓Try not to make your dislike so obvious. ✗ ~~Try not to make it so clear/plain.~~

2 ■ The plain fact is that nobody really knows.

simple • bare • bald | fml **unequivocal |** usu. disapprov. **stark**

▶ the plain/simple/bare/bald/ unequivocal/stark **truth**
▶ a/an plain/simple/bare/bald/ unequivocal/stark **fact/statement**
▶ a/an plain/simple/unequivocal **answer**

3 ■ Let's be plain about this: we will need to make some cuts.

honest • direct • blunt • forthright | approv. **open • straight • straightforward**

▶ plain/honest/direct/blunt/ forthright/open/straight/ straightforward **about sth**
▶ plain/honest/direct/blunt/open/ straight/straightforward **with sb**
▶ To be/Let's be plain/honest/ blunt...

4 ■ a plain white shirt

bare | usu. approv. **simple • austere |** often disapprov. **severe • stark**

■ OPP **fancy**
▶ a/an plain/simple/austere **design**
▶ a plain/bare/simple **interior**
▶ a plain/bare/simple/stark **white...**
▶ a plain/simple/severe/stark **black...**

plan noun
1 [C] ■ The plan is to build new offices.

intention • idea • aim • objective • goal • target • purpose • object • end | fml or law **intent**

▶ the plan/intention/idea/aim/ objective/goal/target/object **is to do sth**
▶ sb's **original** plan/intention/idea/ aim/objective/goal/target/ purpose
▶ **have** a/an plan/intention/idea/ aim/objective/goal/target/ purpose/object/end
● **PLAN OR INTENTION?** Your **plans** are what you have decided or arranged to do, often, but not always, in the longer term; your **intentions** are what you want to do, esp. in the near future.

2 [C] ■ The government has announced plans to create 50 000 new jobs.

policy • proposal • initiative • strategy • platform • manifesto | esp. BrE **scheme |** BrE **programme |** AmE **program**

▶ a/an plan/policy/proposal/ initiative/strategy/platform/ manifesto/scheme/programme **for sth**
▶ a/an plan/policy/proposal/ initiative/strategy/scheme/ programme **to do sth**
▶ **propose** a plan/policy/proposal/ scheme
▶ **have/adopt** a plan/policy/ proposal/strategy/scheme

3 [C] ■ a street plan of the city

map

▶ on a plan/map
▶ **look at/consult** a plan/map
▶ a plan/map **shows sth**

4 [C] ■ A spy stole the plans for the new aircraft.

design • blueprint • draft

▶ a plan/design/blueprint/draft **of sth**
▶ a plan/design/blueprint/draft **for sth**
▶ **draw up/produce** a plan/design/ draft

plan verb

1 [T, I] ■ *It took a year to plan the expedition.*

organize • arrange | *esp. spoken* **sort sth out** | *written* **orchestrate**

▶ plan/arrange for sth
▶ plan/arrange/sort out how/who/when/where...
▶ plan/organize/orchestrate a **campaign**

2 [I, T] ■ *We're planning to go to Scotland this summer.*

intend • aim • have sb/sth in mind | *esp. spoken* **mean** | *fml* **propose**

▶ plan/intend/aim/have in mind/mean/propose to do sth
▶ sb **originally** planned/intended/meant sth

3 [T] ■ *You should plan your essay before you start writing it.*

design • make • formulate

▶ plan/design/make/formulate sth **to do sth**
▶ plan/design/formulate a **strategy**

planning noun [U]

■ *Planning for the future is very important.*

preparation • arrangement • organization • provision • logistics • coordination

▶ planning/preparations/arrangements/organization/provision for sb/sth
▶ planning/preparations/arrangements/provision to do sth
▶ need/require planning/preparation/provision/coordination

plant verb [T]

■ *Many farmers have planted cash crops.*

cultivate • grow

▶ plant/cultivate **the land**
▶ plant/cultivate/grow **crops**

plate noun [C]

■ *He barely touched the food on his plate.*

dish • bowl • platter

▶ a plate/dish/bowl/platter of sth
▶ on a plate/dish/bowl/platter
▶ fill a plate/dish/bowl/platter

platform noun [C]

■ *a concert platform*

stage • podium • pulpit • dock • box | *esp. written* **dais**

▶ on a platform/the stage/the podium/the dais

▶ a raised platform/stage/podium/dais
▶ mount the platform/stage/podium/pulpit/dais

play noun

1 [U] ■ *the happy sounds of children at play*

fun • amusement • entertainment • pleasure • recreation • relaxation

▶ do sth for fun/amusement/entertainment/pleasure/recreation/relaxation

2 [C] ■ *a play by Shakespeare*

drama • comedy • tragedy • farce • sketch

▶ a play/drama/comedy/tragedy/farce/sketch **about** sth
▶ **perform** a play/drama/comedy/sketch
▶ **see** a play/drama/comedy/sketch

play verb

1 [I, T] ■ *There's a time to work and a time to play.*

enjoy yourself • have fun • celebrate | *infml* **have a good/great time • party • live it up**

▶ Let's play/enjoy ourselves/have fun/celebrate/have a good time/party/live it up.

2 [T, I] ■ *He plays football in a local team.*

compete • go in for sth • enter

▶ play/compete **in** a competition, etc.
▶ play/compete **against** sb

3 [T, I] ■ *Who played the part of Juliet?* ■ *I could hear a band playing in the distance.*

perform • act | *esp. spoken* **do**

▶ play/perform/do a **piece**
▶ play/act a **role/part**
▶ a **band/musician** plays/performs/does sth
● PLAY OR ACT? When you are talking about drama **act** can be used with an object (*act a part*) as well as without (*He just can't act.*); **play** can only be used with an object (*play a part*) and is more commonly used in this way than **act**.

player noun [C]

■ *She's one of the country's top tennis players.*

athlete • runner | *esp. BrE* **sportsman • sportswoman • sportsperson** | *AmE, infml, sometimes disapprov.* **jock**

▶ a **top/great/keen** player/athlete/runner/sportsman, etc.
▶ a/an **all-round/amateur/professional** player/athlete/sportsman, etc.

▶ a/an player/athlete/runner/sportsman, etc. **competes** (in sth)

pleasant adj.

1 ■ *It's nice to live in pleasant surroundings.*

enjoyable | *esp. spoken* **nice** • **good** | *esp. BrE, esp. spoken* **lovely** | *fml* **pleasurable**

■ OPP **unpleasant**
▶ a/an pleasant/enjoyable/nice/good/lovely/pleasurable **experience/thing (to do)**
▶ a/an pleasant/enjoyable/nice/good/lovely **time/evening/party**
▶ It's pleasant/nice/good/lovely to be/feel/find/have/know/meet/see…
● PLEASANT, NICE OR GOOD? All these words can describe times, events, feelings and the weather. Pleasant and nice can also describe places, and nice can also describe sb's appearance.

2 ■ *He seemed a pleasant young man.*

friendly • **warm** • **good-natured** • **charming** • **approachable** • **personable** | *esp. BrE* **likeable** | *esp. AmE* **likable** | *esp. spoken* **nice** | *esp. BrE, esp. spoken* **lovely** | *written* **amiable** • **genial**

■ OPP **unpleasant**
▶ pleasant/friendly/charming/nice **to sb**
▶ a/an pleasant/friendly/warm/good-natured/charming/approachable/likable/nice/lovely/amiable/genial **person**
▶ a/an pleasant/friendly/warm/charming/nice/lovely/amiable/genial **manner**

please verb [T, I]

■ *I did it to please my parents.*

satisfy • **delight** | *esp. spoken* **make sb's day** | *written* **gratify**

■ OPP *fml* **displease**
▶ It pleased/satisfied/delighted/gratified **sb that…**
▶ It pleased/delighted/gratified sb **to find/hear/know/see/think…**
▶ You can't please/satisfy **everybody/everyone.**
● PLEASE OR SATISFY? Sth that satisfies you is just good enough, but sth might please you very much:
✔ *The result pleased us enormously.*
✗ *The result satisfied us enormously.*

pleased adj. [not before noun]

■ *She was pleased with her exam results.*

glad • **happy** • **satisfied** • **content** • **contented** • **proud** • **delighted** • **relieved**

---

plot

■ OPP **disappointed**, (*fml*) **displeased**
▶ pleased/glad/happy/satisfied/proud/delighted/relieved **about sth**
▶ pleased/glad/happy/satisfied/content/contented/delighted **with sth**
▶ pleased/glad/happy/delighted/relieved **for sb**
● PLEASED, GLAD OR HAPPY? Feeling **pleased** can suggest that you have judged sb/sth and approve of them or that sth has happened that is particularly good for you. Feeling **glad** can be more about feeling grateful for sth. **Happy** can mean glad, pleased or satisfied.

pleasure noun

1 [U] ■ *Reading for pleasure and reading for study are not the same.*

enjoyment • **fun** | *esp. spoken* **good time** • **great time** | *AmE, infml* **blast**

▶ do sth **for pleasure/enjoyment/fun**
▶ do sth **with pleasure/enjoyment**
▶ **get/derive pleasure/enjoyment from sth**
● PLEASURE OR ENJOYMENT? Pleasure can come either from sth you do or sth that happens; enjoyment usu. comes from sth you do:
✔ *He beamed with pleasure at seeing her.* ✗ *He beamed with enjoyment at seeing her.*

2 [U] ■ *Are you in Paris on business or pleasure?*

entertainment • **amusement** • **play** • **fun** • **recreation** • **relaxation**

▶ do sth **for pleasure/entertainment/amusement/fun/recreation/relaxation**

3 [C] ■ *the pleasures and pains of everyday life*

delight • **joy** • **pride** • **privilege** | *BrE* **honour** | *AmE* **honor** | *esp. spoken* **treat**

■ OPP **pain**
▶ the pleasures/delights/joys **of sth**
▶ It's a great pleasure/joy **to me that…**
▶ It's a pleasure/delight/joy/privilege/honour/treat **to do sth**
● PLEASURE, DELIGHT OR JOY? A **delight** or **joy** is greater than a **pleasure**; a person, esp. a child, can be a **delight** or a **joy**, but not a **pleasure**.

plot noun

1 [C] ■ *It's a conventional plot about love and marriage.*

storyline • **story** | *fml* **narrative** | *esp. written* **tale**

plot

▸ a **plot/storyline/story/narrative/ tale about** sb/sth
▸ a/an **good/amusing plot/ storyline/story/tale**
▸ a **dramatic/romantic/complicated plot/story/tale**

2 [C] ■ *He was the victim of an elaborate murder plot.*

conspiracy • scheme | *esp. written* **intrigue**

▸ a/an **plot/conspiracy/intrigue against** sb
▸ a **plot/conspiracy/scheme to do** sth
▸ **be involved in** a/an **plot/ conspiracy/scheme/intrigue**
▸ **uncover** a **plot/conspiracy/ scheme**

plot verb [I, T]
■ *They were plotting to overthrow the government.*

scheme • collude | *fml* **conspire • connive**

▸ **plot/scheme/conspire against** sb
▸ **plot/collude/connive with** sb
▸ **plot/conspire/collude together**
▸ **plot/scheme/conspire/ connive to do** sth

point noun

1 [C] ■ *I take your point but I still disagree with you.*

point of view • view • opinion • idea • feeling • belief

▸ sb's **point/point of view/view/opinion/idea/ feeling/belief about** sb/sth
▸ the **point/point of view/ opinion/idea/feeling/belief that...**

2 [C] ■ *I think there are two important points we need to consider.*

factor • consideration • fact • detail | *fml* **particular**

▸ (a) **point/considerations/fact/ detail/particulars about/relating to** sth
▸ the **point/consideration/fact that...**
▸ an **important point/factor/ consideration/fact/detail/ particular**
▸ **points/factors/considerations/ facts/details to be taken into account**

3 [sing.] ■ *I'll come straight to the point: we need more money.*

crux • heart • core

▸ the **main point/core of** sth
▸ **get to the point/crux/heart/core (of** sth**)**

4 [U, sing.] (*usu. disapprov.*) ■ *What's the point of all this violence?*

idea • purpose • aim • objective • object • intention

▸ the **whole point/idea/object**
▸ **have** a/an **point/purpose/aim/ objective/object/intention**
● **POINT OR IDEA?** Point is a more negative word than idea:
✓ *There's no point in going.* ✗ *There's no idea in going.*
You might **miss the point of** sth (= fail to understand) but **get the idea** (= understand).

5 [C] ■ *Many people suffer from mental illness at some point in their lives.*

time • occasion • date • moment • hour • instant

▸ the **point/a time/a moment/sb's hour of** sth
▸ **at that point/the time/the moment/that instant**
▸ **from/until that point/time/date/ moment**

6 [C] ■ *It's the point where the river divides.*

place • spot • position • location • site • area

▸ **at** a **point/place/spot/position/ location/site**
▸ the **point/place/spot/position/ location/site where...**
▸ the/sb/sth's **exact/precise point/ place/spot/position/location/site**

7 [C] ■ *The point of the pencil made a hole in the paper.*

tip • spike

▸ a **sharp point/tip/spike**

point verb

1 [I, T] ■ *She pointed to the spot where the house used to stand.*

show | *fml* **indicate**

2 [T] ■ *He pointed the gun at the target.*

aim • direct • focus • turn

▸ **point/aim/direct (sth) at** sb/sth
▸ **point/aim/focus a camera**
▸ **point/aim a gun at** sb
▸ **turn a gun on** sb

point sth out phrasal verb
■ *She pointed out to him the dangers of going alone.*

draw attention to sb/sth **• stress • emphasize • underline • highlight • point to** sth | *fml* **point sth up** | *esp. AmE, esp. busin.* **underscore**

▸ **point out/stress/emphasize/ underline/highlight/point to/ underscore how...**
▸ **point out/draw attention to/**

stress/emphasize/underline/ highlight/point to/point up underscore the **fact that...**

▶ point out/draw attention to/ stress/emphasize/underline/ highlight/point to/point up/ underscore the **importance/ difference**

poison noun [C, U]

■ Some mushrooms contain a deadly poison.

toxin ◆ **venom**

▶ a **powerful** poison/toxin
▶ **contain** poison/toxins
▶ **produce** poison/toxins/venom

poison verb [T]

■ He was accused of poisoning his wife.

drug ◆ **lace** | *infml* **dope**

▶ poison/drug/lace/dope sb/sth **with** sth
▶ poison/lace sb's **drink**

policeman, policewoman noun [C]

■ A policeman chased after the man.

police officer ◆ **officer** ◆ **detective** ◆ **constable** | *infml* **cop** | *BrE* **PC/WPC** | *AmE* **trooper**

▶ a **uniformed** policeman/police officer/officer/cop
▶ a/an policeman/police officer/ officer/detective/constable/cop **arrests** sb/**investigates** sth
▶ a/an policeman/police officer/ officer/constable/cop **patrols** sth
● POLICEMAN, POLICE OFFICER OR OFFICER? **Policeman** is the most frequent of these words. **Police officer** and **officer** are used in more formal contexts and to avoid referring to the gender of the person.

policy noun [C, U]

■ the government's policy on education

strategy ◆ **initiative** ◆ **plan** ◆ **proposal** ◆ **platform** ◆ **manifesto** | *esp. BrE* **scheme** | *BrE* **programme** | *AmE* **program**

▶ a/an policy/strategy/initiative/ plan/proposal/platform/ manifesto/scheme/programme **for** sth
▶ a/an policy/strategy/initiative/ proposal **on** sth
▶ **propose** a policy/strategy/plan/ scheme
▶ **have/adopt** a policy/strategy/ plan/scheme
▶ **develop** a/an policy/strategy/ initiative/plan/proposal/ programme

polite adj. (usu. approv.)

■ Please be polite to our guests.

civil | *approv.* **courteous** ◆ **respectful** ◆ **gracious** ◆ **gentlemanly** | *esp. written* **deferential**

■ OPP **rude, impolite**
▶ polite/civil/courteous/respectful/ gracious/deferential to sb
▶ a polite/civil/courteous/ respectful/gentlemanly **manner**
▶ polite/courteous **behaviour**

politician noun [C]

■ The affair led to the resignation of two leading politicians.

statesman ◆ **MP** ◆ **Member of Parliament** ◆ **senator** ◆ **Congressman/Congresswoman** ◆ **Representative** | *fml* **legislator** | *esp. AmE, esp. journ.* **lawmaker**

▶ a **Labour/Conservative/Liberal Democrat, etc.** politician/MP/ Member of Parliament
▶ a **Democratic/Republican, etc.** senator/Congressman/ Representative/legislator/ lawmaker
▶ an **opposition** politician/MP/ Member of Parliament/legislator/ lawmaker
▶ **elect** a/an politician/MP/senator/ Congressman/Representative

pool noun [C]

■ The waterfall cascades into a small pool below.

pond ◆ **lake**

▶ a **deep** pool/pond/lake
▶ the **edge/surface/bottom/ middle** of a pool/pond/lake

poor adj.

1 ■ They were too poor to buy shoes for the kids.

needy ◆ **impoverished** ◆ **deprived** ◆ **disadvantaged** ◆ **destitute** | *infml* **hard up** ◆ **broke** | *lit.* **penniless**

■ OPP **rich, wealthy, affluent**
▶ poor/needy/impoverished/ deprived/disadvantaged/ destitute/hard up **people/families**
▶ poor/needy/impoverished/ deprived/disadvantaged/destitute **children**
▶ poor/needy/impoverished/ deprived/disadvantaged **groups/ areas**
▶ a/an poor/impoverished/ deprived/disadvantaged **background**
● WHICH WORD? **Poor** is the most general of these words. **Needy** is used to describe groups of people, not individuals. **Impoverished** is used to talk about poor countries and their people. To talk about

poor areas in rich countries use **deprived**.

2 ■ *The work was of poor quality.*

bad • cheap • low • second-rate • inferior | *infml* **dismal** | *BrE, infml* **hopeless** | *BrE, taboo, slang* **crap** • **shit** | *AmE, taboo, slang* **crappy** • **shitty**

■ **OPP fine**
▶ a/an poor/bad/cheap/second-rate/inferior **copy/imitation**
▶ poor/bad/low/second-rate/inferior **quality**
▶ a/an poor/bad/inferior/dismal/crap/shit/crappy/shitty **performance**
● **POOR OR BAD? Bad** is used more in informal spoken English; **poor** is more frequent in written English. Some words do not collocate with both:
✔ *a poor standard of living* ✘ *a bad standard of living*
✔ *I don't think it's a bad school.* ✘ *I don't think it's a poor school.*

3 ■ *He's a good teacher but a poor manager.*

incompetent • inept • inadequate • *esp. spoken* **bad** | *infml* **useless • rotten**

■ **OPP good**
▶ poor/inept/bad/useless/rotten **at** sth
▶ a/an poor/incompetent/bad/useless/rotten **teacher/driver**

popular *adj.*

1 ■ *This is one of our most popular designs.*

in demand • appealing • attractive • *infml* **hot** | *fml* **desirable**

■ **OPP unpopular**
▶ **highly** popular/attractive/desirable
▶ **immediately/enormously** popular/appealing/attractive

2 ■ *By popular demand, the tour has been extended by two weeks.*

common • collective • public

▶ popular/common/collective/public **opinion**

porch *noun* [C] (*esp. AmE*)

■ *We sat on the front porch and talked for hours.*

deck • balcony • terrace • patio

▶ a **covered** porch/deck/balcony/terrace/patio
▶ **sit on** a porch/deck/balcony/terrace/patio
▶ a porch/deck/balcony/terrace/patio **overlooking** sth

port *noun* [C]

■ *The ship spent four days in port.*

dock • marina | *BrE* **harbour** | *AmE* **harbor**

▶ **in** port/dock/the marina/harbour
▶ **enter/leave** port/the dock/harbour

portion *noun* [C]

■ *Giles ordered a double portion of ham and eggs.*

helping | *esp. written* **serving**

▶ a portion/helping/serving **of** sth
▶ a **large/small/generous** portion/helping/serving
▶ **have** a portion/helping/serving of sth

pose *verb*

1 [T] ■ *The task poses no special problems.*

present • create • cause • represent | *fml* **constitute • give rise to sth**

▶ pose/present/create/cause/represent/constitute/give rise to a **problem/danger**
▶ pose/present/create/represent/constitute a **risk/challenge**
▶ pose/present/represent/constitute a **threat**

2 [I] ■ *The gang entered the building posing as workmen.*

impersonate • pass sb/yourself off as sb/sth • imitate

▶ pose **yourself off as** sb/sth
▶ pose as/impersonate/pass yourself off as/imitate **somebody**
▶ pose as/impersonate/pass yourself off as a **journalist/customer/doctor/police officer, etc.**

position *noun*

1 [C, U] ■ *These plants will grow well in a sheltered position.* ■ *The dancers all got into position.*

location • place • spot • site • point • whereabouts

▶ a (good, etc.) position/location/place/spot/site **for** sth
▶ **at** a position/location/place/spot/site/point
▶ **in** a position/location/place
▶ the/sb/sth's **exact/precise** position/location/place/spot/site/point/whereabouts

2 [C, U] ■ *Can you get into a sitting position?*

pose • posture • stance

▶ a **relaxed** position/pose/posture/stance
▶ **adopt/take up/keep/maintain** a position/pose/posture/stance
▶ **change** your position/pose/posture/stance

3 [C, usu. sing.] ■ *What would you do in my position?*

situation ♦ circumstances ♦ conditions ♦ state of affairs | *infml, esp. spoken* things

▶ in (a) particular position/ situation/circumstances/state of affairs
▶ the general/current/present/real position/situation/circumstances/ conditions/state of affairs
▶ describe/explain (the) position/ situation/circumstances/state of affairs/things

4 [C] ■ *Our party's position on education is very clear.*

stance ♦ line ♦ stand ♦ attitude ♦ perspective ♦ view ♦ point of view ♦ angle ♦ outlook

▶ a/an position/stance/line/stand/ perspective/view/angle/outlook on sth
▶ from the position/perspective/ point of view/angle of sb/sth
▶ take a/an position/stance/line/ stand/attitude/perspective/view/ point of view/angle
● POSITION OR STANCE? A stance can be more temporary and/or more personal than a position, in reaction to a new issue in current affairs. A position may be more long-term and/or official and concerns how sb acts on a particular issue, rather than what they say.

5 [C, U] ■ *Her position within the company was not very high.*

level ♦ rank ♦ status ♦ standing ♦ grade ♦ ranking ♦ class

▶ sb's position/level/rank/status/ standing/ranking in/within sth
▶ a/the high/higher position/level/ rank/status/standing/grade/ ranking
▶ improve your position/status/ standing/ranking

6 [C] (*fml*) ■ *I would like to apply for the position of art editor.*

job ♦ role ♦ vacancy ♦ opening ♦ work ♦ employment ♦ occupation ♦ *esp. BrE* post ♦ posting ♦ appointment

▶ (a) permanent/full-time/part-time position/job/role/vacancy/ work/employment/occupation/ post/appointment
▶ apply for a/an position/job/ vacancy/post/posting
▶ offer sb/take a/an position/job/ post/posting

positive *adj.*

1 ■ *She tried to be more positive about her new job.*

optimistic ♦ hopeful | *esp. busin.* bullish ♦ upbeat

■ OPP negative
▶ positive/optimistic/hopeful/ bullish/upbeat about sth
▶ a/an positive/optimistic/hopeful/ bullish view
▶ a/an positive/optimistic/bullish/ upbeat mood/note

2 ■ *We got very positive feedback on the idea.*

good ♦ approving ♦ appreciative ♦ complimentary ♦ glowing | *BrE* favourable | *AmE* favorable

■ OPP negative
▶ positive/complimentary about sb/ sth
▶ a/an positive/good/approving/ appreciative/complimentary/ favourable comment
▶ a positive/good/favourable opinion/impression/reaction/ response
▶ show sb/sth in a positive/good/ favourable light

3 ■ *He made a positive contribution to the debate.*

helpful ♦ valuable ♦ good ♦ constructive ♦ worthwhile | *BrE* favourable | *AmE* favorable | *fml* beneficial

■ OPP negative
▶ positive/helpful/valuable/good/ constructive suggestions/advice
▶ a positive/valuable/good/ constructive/worthwhile/ beneficial experience
▶ a positive/good/constructive/ beneficial effect

4 (*esp. spoken*) ■ *'Are you sure?' 'Positive.'*

sure ♦ certain ♦ convinced ♦ confident ♦ clear ♦ satisfied

▶ positive/sure/certain/convinced/ confident/clear about sth
▶ positive/sure/certain/convinced/ confident/clear/satisfied that…
▶ feel positive/sure/certain/ convinced/confident/satisfied

5 ■ *We have no positive evidence that he was involved.*

concrete ♦ absolute ♦ firm ♦ hard ♦ definite ♦ definitive ♦ final ♦ proven | *fml* categorical

▶ positive/concrete/absolute/firm/ hard/definite/definitive evidence
▶ positive/concrete/absolute/firm/ definite/definitive/final proof

possess *verb*

1 [T] (not used in the progressive tenses) (*fml*) ■ *This is the only coat I possess.*

possession

have • own | esp. BrE, esp. spoken have got | fml hold

▸ possess/have/own/have got a **car/house**
▸ have/own/have got a **company**
▸ have/own/hold a **driving licence/passport**

2 [T] (not used in the progressive tenses) (fml) ▪ He doesn't possess a sense of humour.

have | esp. BrE, esp. spoken have got | fml enjoy • be endowed with sth | esp. written be blessed with sth

▸ possess/have/have got/be blessed with **charm/talent/charisma**
▸ possess/have/have got/enjoy/be endowed with/be blessed with an/the **ability to do sth**
▸ possess/have/have got/be endowed with/be blessed with a **talent (for sth)**

possession noun [C, usu. pl.]
▪ Prisoners were allowed no personal possessions.

belongings • valuables • property | infml stuff • gear | esp. BrE, infml things | infml, disapprov. junk | busin. asset | esp. written or law goods

▸ **personal** possessions/belongings/ property/stuff/things/assets
▸ **collect/gather/pack** possessions/ belongings/stuff/things
▸ **sell** your possessions/belongings/ valuables/property/stuff/things/ assets/goods

possibility noun

1 [U, C] ▪ There is a real possibility of a tax increase.

chance • prospect • probability • likelihood • odds

▸ a possibility/a chance/the prospect/the probability/the likelihood/the odds **of** sth
▸ a possibility/a chance/the prospect/the probability/the likelihood/the odds **that...**
▸ **increase/reduce** the possibility/ chance/probability/likelihood/ odds

2 [C] ▪ We need to explore a wide range of possibilities.

option • choice • alternative

▸ (a/an) **real/realistic/viable/ practical/obvious** possibility/ option/choice/alternative
▸ **look at/limit** the possibilities/ options/choices/alternatives
▸ a **number/range of** possibilities/ options/choices/alternatives

3 [C, usu. pl.] ▪ The class offers a range of exciting possibilities.

opportunity • chance • occasion | esp. busin. window

▸ possibilities/the opportunity/the occasion **for** sth
▸ **take advantage of** the possibilities/an opportunity/the chance/a window
● POSSIBILITY OR OPPORTUNITY? Note that you cannot say 'a/the possibility to do sth'; in these cases use **opportunity** or **chance**:
✓I had the opportunity/chance to spend a year in Paris. ✗ I had the possibility to spend a year in Paris.

possible adj.

1 ▪ Use public transport whenever possible.

practical • feasible • realistic • workable • achievable | esp. busin. viable

■ OPP **impossible**
▸ be practical/feasible/realistic **to do sth**
▸ a practical/feasible/realistic/ workable/viable **solution/policy/ plan**
▸ **perfectly** possible/practical/ feasible/viable

2 ▪ She is a possible future president.

potential • likely • prospective | esp. written probable

▸ possible/likely/probable **that...**
▸ a possible/potential/likely/ prospective/probable **site**
▸ a possible/potential/likely/ probable **cause/effect/ consequence/outcome**

3 ▪ There are several possible explanations.

plausible • credible • conceivable • imaginable • believable

■ OPP **impossible**
▸ possible/plausible/credible/ conceivable/imaginable/ believable **that...**
▸ a possible/plausible/credible/ believable **explanation/excuse**
▸ **sound** possible/plausible/ credible/believable
▸ **barely/hardly/scarcely** possible/ credible/conceivable/imaginable/ believable

post noun

1 [U] (BrE) ▪ Have you opened your post yet?

mail • letter | fml correspondence

▸ post/mail/a letter/ correspondence **from/to** sb
▸ **open** the post/the mail/a letter
▸ the post/the mail/a letter **arrives**

2 [C] ▪ The wall had a high roof supported by wooden posts.

pillar • column • support • girder

► **tall** posts/pillars/columns

► a/an **iron/steel** post/pillar/column/support/girder

► a **wooden** post/pillar/column/support

► a post/pillar/column/girder **supports** sth

post verb [T] (BrE)

■ *Could you post this letter for me?*

send • **forward** | *esp. AmE* **mail** | *fml, esp. busin.* **dispatch**

► post/send/forward/mail/dispatch sth **to sb**

► post/send/forward/mail/dispatch a **letter/document**

► post/send/mail a/an **invitation/package/parcel/postcard/reply**

poster noun [C]

■ *Posters all over town advertised the concert.*

notice • **placard** • **banner**

► sth is **on** a poster/notice/placard

► **display** a poster/notice/placard

► **put up/stick up** a poster/notice

pot noun

1 [C] (*esp. AmE*) ■ *A large pot was simmering on the stove.*

pan • **saucepan** • **casserole** • **cauldron**

► a pot/pan/saucepan **of** sth

► a **large** pot/pan/saucepan/casserole/cauldron

► a **heavy** pot/pan/saucepan/casserole/cauldron

● **POT, PAN OR SAUCEPAN?** Pan is the most general of these words. Saucepan can be used for a deep pan with a long handle and a lid. Pot is often preferred in *AmE* for a deep pan, either with two short handles or no handles at all; it is usu. used in compounds or in the phrase *a pot of sth. Pots and pans* means several different containers that you use to cook food: *I washed all the pots and pans after dinner.*

2 [C] (*esp. BrE*) ■ *a pot of jam/honey/yogurt*

jar • **tub**

► **open** a pot/jar/tub

► a pot/jar/tub **contains** sth

potential noun [U]

■ *She has great potential as an artist.*

possibilities • **prospects** • **promise**

► potential/possibilities/prospects **for** sth

► sb/sth **with** potential/possibilities/prospects/promise

► **commercial/development/economic** potential/possibilities/prospects

► **have** potential/possibilities/prospects/promise

● **POTENTIAL OR POSSIBILITIES?** People or things can have **potential**, esp. people; things, but not usu. people, can have **possibilities**.

potential adj. [only before noun]

■ *First identify the actual and potential problems.*

possible • **likely** • **prospective** | *esp. written* **probable**

■ OPP **actual**

► a potential/possible/likely/prospective/probable **site**

► a potential/possible/likely/probable **cause/effect/consequence/outcome**

► a potential/possible/likely/prospective **candidate**

● **POTENTIAL OR PROSPECTIVE?** Both words can be used to talk about people who might become buyers, employees, etc. **Prospective** is used to describe sb who has already shown some interest in sth; **potential** is used to talk about people in general who might become interested in a product or service.

pour verb

1 [I] (always used with an adv. or prep.) ■ *Tears poured down his cheeks.*

flow • **run** • **stream** • **gush** • **pump** | *written* **cascade**

► pour/flow/stream/gush/pump/cascade **out**

► pour/flow/run/stream/gush/cascade **into/down** (sth)

► **water** flows/runs/streams/gushes/cascades

► **blood** pours/flows/runs/streams/gushes/pumps

► **light** pours/flows/streams

2 [I] (always used with an adv. or prep.) ■ *The rain continued to pour down.*

rain • **fall** • **come down**

► **It's** pouring/raining.

► **rain** pours down/falls/comes down

3 [I] (always used with an adv. or prep.) ■ *Commuters poured off the train.*

flood • **stream** • **surge** | *infml* **pile** | *often disapprov.* **swarm**

► pour/flood/stream/surge/pile/swarm **into** sth

► pour/flood/stream/swarm **out of** sth

► **come** pouring/flooding/streaming **in/out**

poverty

● **POUR OR FLOOD?** Flood places more emphasis on the large numbers of people involved; pour emphasizes that the action continues over a period of time.

poverty noun [U]
■ Land reform could alleviate rural poverty.

need ◆ hardship ◆ deprivation ◆ destitution | *fml* **privation**

■ OPP **wealth**
▶ **in** need/poverty/hardship/ destitution
▶ need/poverty/hardship/ deprivation **among...**
▶ **endure/suffer** poverty/ deprivation/privation

power noun

1 [U] ■ He seized power in a military coup.

control ◆ authority ◆ command ◆ rule ◆ office ◆ hold | *fml* **jurisdiction**

▶ power/control/authority/ command/rule/a hold/jurisdiction **over sb/sth**
▶ **in** power/control/authority/ command/office
▶ **absolute/complete** power/ control/authority/command/rule
▶ **have** power/control/authority/ command/a hold over sb/sth/ jurisdiction
▶ **take** power/control/command/ office

2 [U, C, usu. pl.] ■ The president has the power of veto over all legislation.

authority ◆ right ◆ privilege | *esp. BrE, fml* **entitlement**

▶ **the** power/authority/right/ entitlement **to do sth**
▶ **have** a/an/the power/authority/ right/privilege/entitlement
▶ **use/exercise** your powers/ authority/right/privilege/ entitlement
● **POWER OR AUTHORITY?** (to have) the authority to do sth usu. refers to what sb is allowed to do within a company or other organization; the power to do sth or special powers often refer to what sb is allowed to do within the law or government of a country:
✓Only the manager has the authority to sign cheques. ✗ ~~Only the manager has the power to sign cheques.~~
✓The powers of the police must be clearly defined. ✗ ~~The authority of the police must be clearly defined.~~

3 [U] (used in compounds) ■ the country's military power

influence ◆ weight | *fml* **leverage**

▶ **considerable/political** power/ influence/weight/leverage
▶ **economic/financial** power/ weight/leverage
▶ **have/use/exercise/exert** (your) power/influence/leverage

4 [U] ■ Wind power drives the machinery.

energy

▶ **electrical/nuclear/atomic/solar/ wind/tidal** power/energy
▶ **generate/produce/provide/ supply/use/harness** power/ energy
▶ a power/an energy **supply**
▶ a **source** of power/energy
● **POWER OR ENERGY?** Energy is the source of power: the fuel, the light and heat from the sun or a nuclear reaction, etc. Power is energy that has been collected and used to produce electricity, etc. The energy supply is all the power that has not yet been used up; the power supply is the continuous flow of power to where it is being used: The world's energy supply is heading for crisis. ◆ interruptions in the power supply

5 [U] ■ the sheer physical power of the man

strength ◆ force | *fml or lit.* **might**

▶ **physical** power/strength/force
▶ **use** your power/your strength/ force/your might

powerful adj.

1 ■ She is one of the most powerful women in politics.

influential ◆ important ◆ great ◆ dominant ◆ high-powered | *approv.* **strong**

■ OPP **weak, powerless**
▶ a/an powerful/influential/ important/great/dominant/ strong **figure/leader/position**
▶ a/an powerful/influential/ important/dominant **individual/ group**
▶ a/an powerful/important/great/ dominant/strong **influence**
● **WHICH WORD?** Powerful people such as politicians use their position to control events. Influential people change other people's opinions or behaviour because people respect and listen to them. Important people influence other people or events because people respect them or because their position means their actions have a great effect. Strong people are confident and have leadership qualities.

2 (*esp. written, usu. approv.*) ■ He was lithe and powerful as an athlete.

strong ◆ muscular

■ OPP **weak**

▶ (a) **powerful/strong/muscular**
  build/body/arms/legs
▶ **powerful/strong muscles/jaws**

practical adj.

1 ■ *There are some obvious practical applications of the research.*

applied • experimental | *infml*
hands-on | *fml* **empirical**

■ **OPP theoretical**
▶ **practical/applied/experimental/
  empirical knowledge**
▶ **practical/hands-on experience**
▶ **a/an practical/experimental/
  empirical investigation**

2 ■ *We need to find a practical solution.*

**realistic • feasible • workable •
achievable • possible** | *esp. busin.*
viable

■ **OPP impractical**
▶ **a practical/realistic/feasible/
  workable/viable solution/policy/
  plan**
▶ **a practical/realistic/feasible/viable
  means**
▶ **a practical/realistic/workable/
  viable alternative**

3 ■ *It's a practical little car—ideal for the city.*

convenient • useful • functional |
infml **handy**

■ **OPP impractical**
▶ **practical/useful/handy tips/hints**
▶ **highly practical/convenient/
  useful/functional**

4 (*usu. approv.*) ■ *Let's be practical and work out the cost.*

**realistic • no-nonsense • matter-of-
fact • down-to-earth • level-headed** |
esp. written **pragmatic**

■ **OPP impractical**
▶ **be practical/realistic/matter-of-
  fact/down-to-earth/pragmatic
  about sth**
▶ **a practical/realistic/no-nonsense/
  matter-of-fact/down-to-earth/
  level-headed approach**
▶ **a practical/down-to-earth/level-
  headed person**

practice noun

1 [U] ■ *the theory and practice of teaching*

application • exercise • use

▶ **effective/proper/continued/
  normal practice/application/
  exercise/use**
▶ **common/current/correct/safe/
  commercial/industrial/clinical
  practice/application/use**
▶ **limit/regulate/justify the
  practice/exercise/use of sth**

2 [U, C] ■ *a guide to best practice for employers*

**convention • custom • tradition •
norms**

▶ **(an) established practice/
  convention/custom/tradition/
  norms**
▶ **a local/British practice/custom/
  tradition**
▶ **follow a practice/convention/
  custom/tradition/…norms**

3 [U, C] ■ *We have choir practice every Friday.*

training • rehearsal • drill

▶ **football/hockey, etc. practice/
  training**
▶ **have practice/training/rehearsals/
  a drill**
▶ **do practice/training/rehearsals**
▶ **a practice/training/rehearsal
  session/schedule**

practise (*BrE*) (*AmE* practice) verb
[I, T]

■ *He's practising for his piano exam.*
■ *I've been practising my tennis serve.*

**rehearse • go over sth • run
through sth • train**

▶ **practise/rehearse/train for sth**
▶ **practise/rehearse/go over sth/run
  through sth again**
▶ **practise/rehearse/train regularly**

praise noun [U]

■ *The movie won high praise from the critics.*

**credit • acclaim • approval •
admiration • flattery** | *infml* **a pat on
the back** | *fml* **adulation • esteem**

■ **OPP criticism**, (*fml*) **censure**
▶ **praise/credit/acclaim/approval/a
  pat on the back for (doing) sth**
▶ **universal/widespread praise/
  acclaim/approval**
▶ **deserve praise/credit/acclaim/a
  pat on the back**
▶ **earn/win praise/acclaim/
  approval**
● **PRAISE OR CREDIT? Praise** describes
what you actually say, for example:
Well done! That's wonderful!
Credit refers to an opinion or
feeling of admiration; it can also
suggest a reward: *We should give
credit to the organizers.* ◆ *Credit is
given in the past for good spelling.*

praise verb [T]

■ *He praised the team for their performance.*

**congratulate • compliment •
acclaim • flatter** | *fml* **applaud •
celebrate • commend** | *esp. journ.*
hail • rave | *often disapprov.* **glorify**

■ OPP **criticize**
■ praise/congratulate/applaud/commend sb **for** (doing) sth
► congratulate/compliment/commend sb **on** sth
■ praise/applaud/commend/hail a **decison/plan**
► be **highly/widely/universally** praised/acclaimed/commended
● PRAISE OR CONGRATULATE? The object of the word **praise** can be a person, or their qualities, abilities or achievements; the object of **congratulate** must be a person:
✔ I praised his ability to stay calm. ✗ <del>I congratulated his ability to stay calm.</del>
You **praise** sb you are responsible for or have authority over, but not sb who has authority over you or is your equal:
✔ He praised/congratulated his son/class/team. • He congratulated his colleague on his promotion.

pray verb [I, T]
■ They knelt down and prayed.

worship • praise | fml venerate
► pray **to**/worship/praise **God**

precaution noun [C]
■ Safety precautions must be taken to prevent injury.

safeguard | BrE defence | AmE defense
► a precaution/safeguard/defence **against** sth
► **as** a precaution/safeguard/defence
► an **adequate** precaution/safeguard/defence

precise adj.
■ She gave precise details of the incident.

exact • specific • accurate
■ OPP **imprecise**
► precise/accurate/specific **about** sb/sth
► precise/exact/accurate/specific **instructions/details**
► precise/exact/accurate **measurements**
● PRECISE, EXACT OR ACCURATE? A description that is *not very precise/exact* lacks details; if it is *not very accurate* it has details, but they are wrong.

predict verb [T]
■ What is needed is a reliable method of predicting earthquakes.

forecast • foresee • prophesy | esp. spoken say | esp. busin. project

► predict/forecast/foresee/prophesy **that...**
► predict/forecast/foresee/prophesy/say **what/how/when/where/who/whether...**
► be predicted/forecast/projected **to do sth**
► predict/forecast/foresee/prophesy the **future**
● PREDICT OR FORECAST? Sb **predicts** what will happen based on the information available, their opinions or using religious or magical powers; sb **forecasts** sth based on the information available and often using scientific methods.

predictable adj.
1 ■ It was predictable that people would complain.

unsurprising • to be expected | esp. written foreseeable
■ OPP **unpredictable**
► predictable/unsurprising/to be expected/foreseeable **that...**
► a/an predictable/unsurprising/foreseeable **result**
► predictable/foreseeable **consequences**

2 (disapprov.) ■ Rock music has become boring and predictable.

uneventful | disapprov. flat • tame • uninspiring • unexciting
■ OPP **unpredictable**

prefer verb [T] (not used in the progressive tenses)
■ I'd prefer to stay at home.

esp. spoken would rather... | BrE favour | AmE favor

preference noun [U, sing.]
■ Most people expressed a strong preference for the original plan.

taste • liking • weakness | approv. love • passion
► a preference/taste/liking/weakness/passion **for** sth
► **have** a preference/taste/liking/weakness/love/passion for sth
► **show** a preference/liking for sth
● PREFERENCE OR TASTE? A **preference** is always a choice between two or more things, places, people, etc.; a **taste** is not: *a taste for French bread* • *a preference for red wine* (= rather than white wine)

preparation noun [U, C, usu. pl.]
■ We're making the final preparations for the conference.

arrangement • planning • organization • provision • coordination • logistics
► preparations/arrangements/

planning/organization/provision for sb/sth
▶ preparations/arrangements/ planning/provision to do sth
■ make preparations/ arrangements/provision

object but a **gift** may be a sum of money, or sth such as *the gift of love/life.*

present verb

1 [T] ■ *The local MP presented the prizes to the winners.*

give ◆ award ◆ transfer | *fml* **confer ◆ bestow**

▶ present/give/award/transfer sth to sb
▶ present/give/bestow gifts/an award
▶ present/give/award a prize

2 [T] ■ *They are going to present the new model at the trade fair.*

show ◆ display ◆ produce ◆ launch ◆ *journ.* **unveil**

▶ present/show/display/launch/ unveil a new product/model
▶ present/show/display your wares
▶ present/show/unveil plans

3 [T] ■ *Eight options were presented to the president for her consideration.*

submit ◆ hand sth in ◆ send sth in ◆ put sth in ◆ file | *BrE* **table** | *fml* **lodge ◆ register**

▶ present/submit/hand in/send in/ put in sth to sb
▶ present/send in/put in/file/ submit/lodge/register an application
▶ present/submit/put in/file/ lodge/register a claim/complaint
▶ present/submit/table a bill/ motion/resolution

4 [T] (not usu. used in the progressive tenses) ■ *The company wants to present a more modern image.*

show ◆ portray | *fml* **depict ◆ represent**

▶ present/show/portray/depict/ represent sb/sth as sth
▶ present/show/portray/depict/ represent sb/sth accurately

5 [T] (*BrE*) ■ *She used to present a gardening show on TV.*

host | *esp. spoken* **introduce**

▶ present/host/introduce a programme/show

6 [T] (written) ■ *Compass Theatre Company presents a new production of 'King Lear'.*

put sth on ◆ produce ◆ perform ◆ act | *esp. spoken* **do** | *written* **stage**

▶ present/put on/produce/ perform/act in/do/stage a play/ show
▶ present/put on/do/stage a/an performance/concert/exhibition

---

prepare verb

1 [T] ■ *You will need to prepare a report for the meeting.*

draw sth up ◆ put sth together ◆ draft | *esp. spoken* **get sth ready**

▶ prepare/draw sth up/put sth together/draft/get sth ready for sth
▶ prepare/draw up/put sth together/ draft a list/report/paper/plan/ programme/strategy
▶ prepare/draw up/draft a document/contract/budget/ treaty/will

2 [I, T] ■ *I was preparing to leave.*

esp. spoken get ready | *fml* **provide for sth** | *esp. journ.* **gear (yourself) up**

▶ prepare/get ready/provide/gear up for sth
▶ prepare/get ready/gear up to do sth
▶ prepare yourself/gear yourself up

3 [T] (*esp. written*) ■ *The women were busy preparing the wedding feast.*

make ◆ cook ◆ brew | *esp. spoken* **get** | *esp. AmE* **fix**

▶ prepare/make/brew sth from sth
▶ prepare/cook/make/get/fix breakfast/lunch/dinner
▶ prepare/cook/make a dish

---

prepared adj.

■ *I was not prepared for all the problems it caused.*

ready ◆ be waiting ◆ set

■ OPP **unprepared**

▶ prepared/ready/be waiting/set for sb/sth
▶ prepared/ready/be waiting/set to do sth
▶ fully prepared/ready/set

---

present noun [C]

■ *a birthday present*

gift ◆ donation ◆ contribution ◆ tip | *fml* **gratuity** | *often disapprov.* **handout**

▶ a present/gift/donation/ contribution/tip/gratuity/ handout for/from sb
▶ present/gift/donation/ contribution to sb/sth
▶ give (sb) a present/gift/donation/ tip
● **PRESENT OR GIFT?** Especially in *BrE* **gift** is more formal than **present** and is used more in business contexts. A **present** is usu. an

present

▶ a **company** presents/puts on/produces/does/stages a play/show

● **PRESENT, PUT STH ON OR STAGE?** You can **present**, **put on** or **stage** a live *performance, show, play, concert* or *exhibition*. You can **present**, but not **stage** or **put on**, a film or recorded *programme*. **Put sth on** is used esp. to talk about amateur (= not professional) performances.

present *adj.* [usu. before noun]
■ *The present owner of the house is a Mr T Grant.*

current • latest • immediate • present-day • contemporary

■ OPP past
▶ the present/current/latest/immediate/present-day/contemporary **situation**
▶ the present/current **climate**
▶ present/current/immediate **needs**

presentation *noun* [C]
■ *The manager gave a presentation on the new products.*

demonstration | *infml* demo

▶ a **sales/product** presentation/demonstration/demo
▶ **give/watch** a presentation/demonstration/demo
● **PRESENTATION OR DEMONSTRATION?** A **presentation** can be of a thing or an idea; a **demonstration** is always practical, either of a thing or a technique.

presenter *noun* [C] (*BrE*)
■ *Anne McKay, presenter of 'The Week in Politics'*

announcer • anchorman/anchorwoman • broadcaster • newscaster | *esp. AmE* anchor • host | *esp. BrE* commentator | *BrE* newsreader

▶ a **radio/television/TV** presenter/announcer/anchorman/broadcaster/newscaster/anchor/host/commentator/newsreader
● **WHICH WORD?** A **presenter** (in *BrE*) or **announcer** (in *AmE*) presents any type of television or radio show. An **anchor** presents news programmes. In *BrE* a **host** presents an entertainment show; in *AmE* **host** can also describe sb who presents more serious shows. A **broadcaster** may talk on a variety of shows but is not the presenter for a particular show.

preserve *verb*
1 [T] ■ *We are naturally anxious to preserve our reputation.*

maintain • keep sth up • sustain • extend • prolong | *esp. spoken* keep sth going | *fml* perpetuate | *often disapprov., esp. busin.* prop sth up

▶ preserve/maintain/keep up/sustain **standards/a relationship**
▶ preserve/maintain/sustain/extend/prolong (sb's) **life**
▶ preserve/maintain/keep up a **tradition**

2 [T, often passive] ■ *a perfectly preserved stretch of Roman road*

maintain • keep sth up

▶ preserve/maintain/keep up a **house**
▶ **have/keep sth** preserved/maintained
▶ **well/fully** preserved/maintained

3 [T] ■ *They try to preserve endangered species from extinction.*

protect • save • defend • guard • shield • shelter • rescue • secure | *fml* safeguard

▶ preserve/protect/save/defend/guard/shield/shelter/rescue/secure/safeguard sb/sth **from** sth
▶ preserve/protect/save/safeguard **jobs**
▶ preserve/protect/save a **species**

president (also President) *noun*
1 [C] ■ *President Obama*

head of state • prime minister • chancellor • governor | *journ.* premier

▶ the **acting/deputy** president/head of state/prime minister/governor/premier
▶ the **interim/incoming/outgoing** president/prime minister/governor
▶ **elect sb (as)/serve as/be sworn in (as)** president/head of state/prime minister/chancellor/governor

2 [C] ■ *She was elected president of the student union.*

head • leader • director • manager • chief executive • chairman/chairwoman • chair | *BrE* managing director • governor | *infml* boss | *esp. journ.* chief

▶ be **appointed (as)** president/head/leader/director/manager/chief executive/chairman/chair/managing director/governor/chief
▶ be **elected (as)** president/head/leader/chairman/chair
▶ **resign/stand down/step down as** president/head/leader/director/manager/chief executive/chairman/chair/managing director/governor/chief
● **WHICH WORD?** **President** is a title given to the most senior person in some companies. The **chairman** is the most senior member of the board of directors of a company.

The **chief executive** or **managing director** makes decisions about how a company is run and is often also the **chairman**.

the **press** noun [sing.+ sing./pl. v.]

■ The story was reported in the press and on television.

the media • coverage • reporting • journalism

▶ **in/by** the press/media
▶ **(the) mainstream** press/media/coverage/reporting/journalism
▶ press/media **reports/coverage**

press verb

1 [T, I] ■ Press any key to restart your computer.

push • squeeze

▶ press/push/squeeze **on** sth
▶ press/push a **bell/button/key/bell/switch**
▶ press/push/squeeze (sth) **hard/gently**
● **WHICH WORD? Press** is the most general word. You can **press** with your finger, hand or foot. **Push** is mostly used with the word **button**. You **squeeze** sth by bending your finger(s) around it.

2 [T] ■ Even senior officials are pressing for his resignation.

push • demand • insist • call for sth | esp. AmE pressure | BrE pressurize | clamour | AmE clamor | infml twist sb's arm | fml coerce

▶ press/push/demand/pressurize/coerce sb **into** (doing) sth
▶ press sb/push sb/pressure sb/pressurize sb/twist sb's arm **to do sth**
▶ press/push/call/clamour **for** sth
● **PRESS OR PUSH? Push** can be more forceful than **press**: you **press** people to do things that you want them to do; you might **push** sb to do sth that you think they would actually enjoy or benefit from:
✓My teacher pushed me to enter the competition. ✗ My teacher pressed me to enter the competition.

pressure noun

1 [U, C] ■ The nurse applied gentle pressure to his arm to stop the bleeding.

strain • stress • weight • load

▶ **under** the pressure/strain/stress/weight/load
▶ **high/low** pressure/stress
▶ **put** pressure/stress/strain/weight **on** sth
● **PRESSURE, STRAIN OR STRESS? Pressure** can be heavy, firm, gentle or light. Both **strain** and **stress** usu. suggest that there is too much pressure.

2 [U] ■ My parents never put any pressure on me to work in the family business.

force | fml coercion • compulsion

▶ pressure/compulsion **on** sb
▶ **under** pressure/coercion/compulsion
▶ pressure/compulsion **to do** sth

3 [U, pl.] ■ How can anyone enjoy the pressures of city life?

stress • strain • demands • tension | infml, esp. journ. heat

▶ be **under** pressure/stress/strain
▶ pressure/stress/demands/heat **on** sb
▶ **cope with** the pressure/stress/strain/demands/tension
● **PRESSURE OR STRESS?** It is common to say that sb is suffering from **stress**; **pressure** may be the thing that causes **stress**.

presumably adv. (esp. spoken)

■ Presumably this is where the accident happened.

probably • most likely • no doubt | esp. spoken (the) chances are... | written in all probability... • doubtless

● **PRESUMABLY OR PROBABLY?**
Probably suggests a conclusion based on what is likely to be true; **presumably** suggests a conclusion based on particular evidence. **Presumably** can be used to confirm sth; **probably** can be used to agree with sb or to comfort sb:
✓You'll be taking the car, presumably? ✗ You'll be taking the car, probably?
✓You're probably right. ✗ You're presumably right.
✓It'll probably be OK. ✗ It'll presumably be OK.

pretence (BrE) (AmE **pretense**) noun [U, sing.]

■ She was unable to keep up the pretence that she loved him.

act • front • cover • façade | lit. mask

▶ **put on** a/an pretence/act/front/mask
▶ **maintain** a pretence/front/cover/façade
▶ **keep up** a/an pretence/act/front

pretend verb

1 [I, T] ■ He pretended to be asleep.

act • bluff • fake • put sth on | fml feign • adopt • assume

▶ pretend **to do** sth
▶ fake/feign **illness/injury**
▶ pretend/feign/assume **interest/indifference**

pretension

2 [T, I] ■ *The children pretended they were on a desert island.*

imagine

▶ pretend/imagine that...
▶ Just pretend/imagine.

pretension *noun* [C, usu. pl., U] (*disapprov.*)
■ *She was charmed by his lack of pretension.*

snobbery • airs • affectation

▶ without pretension/affectation
▶ intellectual/social pretensions/ snobbery

pretty *adj.*

1 ■ *She's a very pretty girl.*

beautiful • attractive • good-looking • striking • handsome | *esp. BrE* lovely | *infml* gorgeous • stunning | *esp. AmE, infml* cute

■ OPP plain
▶ a/an pretty/beautiful/attractive/ good-looking/striking/ handsome/gorgeous/ stunning/cute girl/woman
▶ a/an pretty/beautiful/attractive/ good-looking/handsome/lovely/ gorgeous/cute boy
▶ a/an pretty/beautiful/attractive/ good-looking/striking/ handsome/lovely/cute face

2 ■ *Lydia—what a pretty name!*

beautiful • attractive • picturesque • scenic • charming • exquisite | *esp. BrE* lovely

▶ a/an pretty/beautiful/attractive/ picturesque/charming place/ town/village
▶ a/an pretty/beautiful/attractive/ exquisite/lovely design
▶ a/an pretty/beautiful/attractive/ charming/exquisite/lovely voice

pretty *adv.* (*AmE or infml, BrE*)
■ *I was pretty sure I'd seen him somewhere before.*

fairly • reasonably | *esp. BrE* quite • rather

▶ pretty/fairly/reasonably/quite/ rather good/successful/high/ large/common/confident
▶ pretty/fairly/reasonably/quite/ rather well/soon/easily
▶ pretty/fairly/quite/rather bad/ big/new/tired/dull/difficult/ expensive/dangerous

prevent *verb* [T]
■ *These strategies are aimed at preventing crime.*

stop • avoid • keep sb from sth • rule sb/sth out • thwart • frustrate | *fml* preclude | *written* avert • restrain | *esp. journ.* foil

■ OPP allow
▶ prevent/stop/keep/preclude/ restrain sb from doing sth
▶ prevent sb/stop/avoid (sb)/ preclude (sb) doing sth
▶ prevent/stop/avoid/avert av/an crisis/accident
● PREVENT OR STOP? Prevent is a more formal word. It suggests action that sb plans in advance so that sth does not even start; stop often suggests action taken to end sth already in progress.

previous *adj.*

1 [only before noun] ■ *She is his daughter from a previous marriage.*

past • former • old • distant • remote | *fml* prior | *written* bygone

■ OPP current, future
▶ (a) previous/past/former/distant/ remote/bygone era/times
▶ (a) previous/past experience/ history/life
▶ a previous/past/former owner/ president/prime minister

2 [only before noun] ■ *We dealt with this topic in the previous chapter.*

last • past | *fml* preceding

■ OPP the following
▶ the previous/last/past/preceding few days/week/month/year/ decade/century
▶ the previous/last/past weekend/ season/hundred years
▶ the previous/last/preceding paragraph/section

price *noun* [C, U]
■ *The price includes dinner.*

cost • value • rate • charge • expense • fee • worth

▶ increase/reduce the price/cost/ value/rate/charge/expense/fee
▶ the real/true/market/net price/ cost/value/rate/worth
▶ raise/double/lower the price/ cost/value/rate/charge/fee
● COST, PRICE OR VALUE? The price is what sb asks you to pay for an item or service:
✓ to ask/charge a high price ✗ to ask/charge a high cost/value
Obtaining sth may have a cost; the value of sth is how much money people would pay for it:
✓ house prices • the cost of moving house • The house now has a market value of twice what we paid for it.

price *verb* [T, usu. passive, I]
■ *These goods are priced too high.*

value • assess • cost • put a price on sth

▶ be priced/valued/assessed/costed **at** $500
▶ be priced/valued/assessed/costed **between** £15 and £35

pride noun

1 [U, sing.] ■ We take great pride in our nation's success in sport.

satisfaction • happiness • contentment	BrE **fulfilment**	AmE **fulfillment**

■ OPP shame
▶ pride/satisfaction/happiness/contentment/fulfilment **in** sth
▶ **bring** sb pride/satisfaction/happiness/contentment/fulfilment
▶ **take** pride/satisfaction in sth

2 [U] ■ I'm sorry if I hurt your pride.

dignity • self-esteem • self-respect • feelings	sometimes disapprov. **ego**

▶ injured/personal pride/dignity/self-esteem
▶ **hurt** sb's pride/feelings
▶ **restore** sb's pride/dignity/self-esteem/self-respect

3 [U] (disapprov.) ■ Male pride forced him to suffer in silence.

egoism • vanity • arrogance	esp. written **conceit**	lit. **hubris**

■ OPP humility, modesty
▶ **appeal to** sb's pride/vanity

principle noun

1 [C, usu. pl., U] ■ It's against my principles to lie.

morals • morality • ethics • standards • values • ideal

▶ **personal** principles/morality/standards/values/ethics
▶ **have** (no/high, etc.) principles/morals/standards/values/ideals
▶ **compromise** your principles/standards/values/ideals

2 [C, U] ■ The principle behind this method is very simple.

theory • law • rule	tech. **theorem**

▶ the principle/theory/law/rule/theorem that...
▶ a **basic/fundamental** principle/theory/law/rule/theorem
▶ a **scientific** principle/theory/law/rule
▶ **prove** a principle/theory/law/rule/theorem

3 [C, U] ■ Their policy is based on the principle that free education should be available to all.

rule • law	fml **tenet**

▶ the principle/rule/law/tenet that...

▶ a **basic/fundamental** principle/rule/law/tenet
▶ a **moral** principle/rule/law
▶ **accept** a principle/rule/tenet

print verb [T]

■ They printed 30 000 copies of the book.

publish • issue • release

▶ print/publish/issue/release a **book/report/details/document/statement/description**
▶ print/publish/issue a/an **booklet/brochure/newsletter/leaflet/pamphlet/apology**
▶ print/publish a **picture/photo/article**
▶ print/issue **banknotes**

priority noun [C, U]

■ Her family takes priority over her work.

precedence • emphasis • stress

▶ priority/precedence **over** sb/sth
▶ (a) **particular/special/equal** priority/emphasis/stress
▶ **give** sb/sth priority/precedence/emphasis
● PRIORITY OR PRECEDENCE? People or things usu. *take precedence* on the basis of rank; they are *given priority* on the basis of need: *The speakers came onto the platform in the order of precedence. • Homeless families will be given priority.*

prison noun [C, U]

■ He was sent to prison for six years.

jail	BrE **detention centre**	AmE **detention center** • **penitentiary** • **jailhouse** • **correctional facility**

▶ **in** prison/jail
▶ **in** a prison/jail/detention centre/penitentiary/jailhouse/correctional facility
▶ **go to/be sent to/be released from/get out of** prison/jail
● JAIL OR PRISON? In BrE there is little difference between these words. **Prison** can be used to describe the system, as well as the buildings or institution:
✓the prison service/system ✗ ~~the jail service/system~~
In AmE a **jail** is usu. smaller than a **prison**.

prisoner noun

1 [C] ■ prisoners serving life sentences

convict • inmate

▶ an **escaped** prisoner/convict
▶ **release** a/an prisoner/convict/inmate
▶ a/an prisoner/convict/inmate **serves** a sentence

2 [C] ■ He was taken prisoner by rebel soldiers.

---

hostage • **prisoner of war** • **POW** • **detainee** | lit. **captive**

▶ a **political** prisoner/hostage/detainee
▶ **hold/keep/take** sb prisoner/hostage/captive
▶ **free/release** a prisoner/hostage/prisoner of war/POW/detainee/captive
● **PRISONER OR CAPTIVE?** Captive is used in historical contexts, and also when talking about organizations holding people against their will. **Prisoner** is used more to talk about people who have been captured in war.

privacy noun [U] (approv.)
■ She longed for peace and privacy.

---

approv. **solitude** • **seclusion** | disapprov. **loneliness** • **isolation**

▶ **in** privacy/solitude/seclusion/isolation
▶ **experience/suffer/feel** loneliness/isolation
▶ **need/enjoy** privacy/solitude

private adj.
1 ■ All bedrooms have private bathrooms.

---

personal • **own** • **exclusive** • **individual**

■ OPP **public**
▶ sb's private/personal/own/individual **experience**
▶ sb's private/personal/own **opinion**
▶ sb's private/personal/own/exclusive **property**
● **PRIVATE OR PERSONAL?** Private things belong to a particular person or group, or are for them to use; they are not for people in general. **Personal** things, details, etc. belong to a particular individual person and not any other individual person.

2 ■ Senior defence officials held private talks.

---

personal • **secret** • **confidential** • **classified** • **undisclosed** • **intimate**

■ OPP **public**
▶ private/personal/secret/confidential/classified/undisclosed **information**
▶ private/personal/secret/confidential/classified **documents**
▶ sb's private/personal **life**
● **PRIVATE OR PERSONAL?** You can usu. use either word to describe sth that is not connected with your work or official position, except:
✔a personal friend of mine ✗ a private friend of mine

---

prize noun [C]
■ He was awarded the Nobel Prize for Literature.

---

award • **reward** • **title** • **medal** • **trophy** • **cup** | BrE **honour** | AmE **honor**

▶ a/an prize/award/reward/medal/trophy/cup for sth
▶ a **coveted/prestigious** prize/award/title/trophy
▶ a/an **top/academic** prize/award/honour
▶ **win** a/an prize/award/reward/title/medal/trophy/cup/honour

probable adj. (esp. written)
■ The probable cause of the fire was an electrical fault.

---

likely • **possible** • **potential** • **prospective**

■ OPP **improbable**
▶ be probable/likely/possible **that**…
▶ a probable/likely/possible/potential **cause/effect/consequence/outcome**
▶ a probable/likely/possible **explanation**
● **PROBABLE OR LIKELY?** Probable is much more frequent in writing than in spoken English. Likely is very frequent in both, and used in a far wider range of structures and registers than probable:
✔sb/sth is likely to do sth ✗ sb/sth is probable to do sth

probably adv.
■ You're probably right.

---

most likely • **no doubt** | esp. spoken **presumably** • **the chances are**… | written **in all probability** • **doubtless**

● **PROBABLY OR PRESUMABLY?** Probably suggests a conclusion based on what is likely to be true; presumably suggests a conclusion based on particular evidence. Presumably can be used to confirm sth; probably can be used to agree with sb or to comfort sb:
✔You'll be taking the car, presumably? ✗ You'll be taking the car, probably?
✔You're probably right. ✗ You're presumably right.
✔It'll probably be OK. ✗ It'll presumably be OK.

problem noun [C]
■ Unemployment is a real problem for graduates now.

---

difficulty • **issue** • **trouble** • **complication** | esp. spoken **the matter** | usu. approv. **challenge**

▶ (a/an/the) problem/difficulty/trouble/complication/issue/matter **with** sth

▶ **have** problems/difficulties/issues/
trouble
▶ **cause/avoid** problems/
difficulties/trouble/complications
▶ **create/bring/run into** problems/
difficulties/trouble
● **PROBLEM OR DIFFICULTY?** To talk
about one thing that is difficult to
deal with use **problem**; to talk
about more than one thing use
either word: *The problem first arose
in 2008. ◆ The project has been
fraught with problems/difficulties
from the start.*

procedure noun [C, U]
■ *He was not aware of the correct
procedure.*

process ◆ routine ◆ method ◆
measure ◆ step

▶ the **normal/usual** procedure/
process/routine/method
▶ **adopt** a procedure/routine/
method/measure
▶ **follow** the procedure/routine/
method/steps
▶ a **matter of/change in** procedure/
routine

proceed verb [I]
■ *Work is proceeding slowly.*

continue ◆ go on with sth/go on
doing sth ◆ press ahead | *esp. spoken*
keep ◆ carry (sth) on | *infml* stick
with sth/sb | *fml* pursue

▶ proceed/continue/go on/press
ahead/keep on/carry on/stick
with sth
▶ proceed/continue/go on/press
ahead/carry on/pursue (with)
the/your **work**
▶ proceed/continue/carry on/
pursue (with) an **investigation**

process noun
1 [C] ■ *Getting things changed will be
a slow process.*

operation ◆ exercise ◆ procedure ◆
routine

▶ a **major/successful/joint** process/
operation/exercise
▶ **go through** a/an process/
exercise/procedure/routine
▶ **carry out/supervise** a/an process/
operation/exercise/procedure

2 [C] ■ *advanced manufacturing
processes*

method ◆ technique ◆ system ◆
mechanism ◆ way | *fml*
methodology

▶ a **process/method/technique/
system/mechanism/methodology
for** (doing) sth
▶ **use** a process/method/technique/
system/way/methodology
▶ **devise/develop** a process/

method/technique/system/
methodology

produce verb
1 [T] ■ *a factory that produces
microchips*

manufacture ◆ make ◆ mass-
produce ◆ turn sth/sb out | *infml,
disapprov.* churn sth out

▶ a factory that produces/
manufactures/makes **cars/
mainframes/microchips**
▶ produce/manufacture/make/turn
out/churn out **900 cars a week**
▶ produce/turn out/churn out
books/articles
● **PRODUCE OR MANUFACTURE?**
Manufacture is more often used in
business contexts and emphasizes
the process of making goods;
produce emphasizes the finished
product.

2 [T] ■ *Our cat produced a litter of four
kittens.*

have ◆ breed ◆ give birth ◆
reproduce | *fml* or *lit.* bear

▶ produce/breed sth **from** sth
▶ produce/have/give birth to/bear
a/an **child/son/daughter/heir**
▶ produce/have/give birth to a
baby/litter
▶ produce/bear **fruit**

3 [T] ■ *He produced a delicious meal
out of leftovers.*

make ◆ create ◆ generate ◆ develop |
esp. spoken do

▶ produce/make/create/generate
sth **from/out of** sth
▶ produce/make/create a **meal**
▶ produce/create/generate
income/profits/wealth
▶ produce/generate **electricity/
heat/power**

4 [T] ■ *A phone call to the manager
produced the desired result.*

bring sth about ◆ result in sth ◆ lead
(sth) to sth ◆ cause ◆ create ◆
prompt ◆ provoke ◆ set sth off | *fml*
give rise to sth | *approv.* stimulate

▶ produce/bring about/result in/
lead to/cause/prompt/give rise to
a/an **change/increase/shift**
▶ produce/result in/lead to/cause/
create/give rise to **problems/
difficulties**
▶ produce/lead to/cause/create/
prompt/provoke/give rise to/
stimulate **speculation**

5 [T] ■ *She produces the school play
every year.*

put sth on | *esp. spoken* do | *esp.
written* present ◆ stage

producer

▶ produce/put on/do/present/
stage a **play/show**
▶ a **company** produces/puts on/
does/presents/stages a play/show

producer noun [C]

■ *The country is one of the world's largest oil producers.*

maker • manufacturer

▶ a car **producer/maker/
manufacturer**
▶ a **steel/wine producer/maker/
manufacturer**
● PRODUCER, MAKER OR
MANUFACTURER? Maker and
manufacturer are used esp. when
talking about goods such as cars
that are put together from different
parts; producer is used more when
talking about natural materials
such as food or oil that are grown
or obtained and then processed.
Maker is also used about products
for which quality and skill are seen
to be important, such as steel and
wine.

product noun [C, U]

■ *meat/pharmaceutical products*

goods • merchandise • produce |
economics **commodity**

▶ **consumer/industrial** products/
goods/commodities
▶ **household** products/goods
▶ **sell/market/buy/purchase/
produce** a product/goods/
merchandise/a commodity

production noun

1 [U] ■ *Production of the new model starts next year.*

**manufacturing • manufacture •
industry • making • construction •
building • assembly**

▶ **commercial/industrial**
production/manufacturing/
manufacture/construction/
building
▶ **car/textile** production/
manufacturing/manufacture
▶ production/manufacturing/
construction/building/assembly
**methods/processes/systems/
techniques**
▶ a production/an assembly **line**
● PRODUCTION, MANUFACTURING, OR
MANUFACTURE? Manufacture and
manufacturing emphasize the process
of making goods; manufacturing
emphasizes the business of making
goods in large quantities: *the
manufacturing industry.* Production
can refer to growing food and
obtaining raw materials as well as
making goods; manufacturing
only refers to making goods.

2 [U] ■ *Production will drop by 6 000 next year.*

output • productivity • yield

▶ **agricultural** production/output/
productivity/yields
▶ **manufacturing/industrial**
production/output/productivity
▶ **boost/improve/increase/raise/
reduce** production/output/
productivity/yields
● PRODUCTION OR OUTPUT? Output
can belong to a country, company,
person or machine; you cannot use
production in this way:
✓the country's/company's total
output ✗ *the country's/company's
total production*

productive adj.

■ *highly productive farming land*

fruitful • prolific • fertile • rich

■ OPP **unproductive**
▶ a productive/fruitful
**collaboration/discussion/
meeting**
▶ productive/fertile/rich **land/soil**
▶ **highly** productive/fertile

profession noun [C]

■ *Alan's a teacher by profession.*

**career • occupation • vocation • job
• practice • work • employment •
trade**

▶ sb's **chosen** profession/career/
occupation/vocation/job/work/
employment/trade
▶ **have/pursue** (a/an) profession/
career/occupation/work/
employment/trade
▶ **take up** (a/an) profession/career/
occupation/...practice/work/
employment/trade

professor noun [C]

■ *my professor at Harvard*

lecturer • fellow • tutor | *BrE* **don**

▶ a professor/lecturer/fellow/tutor/
don **at** Oxford University, Brighton,
etc.
▶ a professor/lecturer **in** Economics,
Music, etc.
▶ a/an **senior/honorary** professor/
lecturer/fellow
▶ **be made/appointed** professor/
lecturer/fellow

profit noun [C, U]

■ *The company made a profit of £6m last year.*

**interest • proceeds • return •
surplus • earnings • income •
revenue • dividend |** *often disapprov.*
gain

■ OPP **loss**
▶ (a/an) profit/interest/proceeds/
return/surplus/earnings/income/
dividend/revenue/gain **from** sth

- ▶ (a) profit/interest/return/surplus/
  earnings/dividend/gain **on** sth
- ▶ **generate** (a/an) profit/interest/
  return/surplus/earnings/income/
  revenue
- ▶ **make** (a/an) profit/return/
  surplus/income/gain

programme (BrE) (AmE program) noun

1 [C] ■ *The university is to launch a new research programme.*

plan + initiative + proposal + policy + strategy + platform + manifesto | *esp. BrE* **scheme**

- ▶ a/an programme/plan/initiative/
  proposal/policy/strategy/
  platform/manifesto/scheme **for** sth
- ▶ a programme/plan/initiative/
  proposal/policy/strategy/scheme
  to do sth
- ▶ **develop** a programme/plan/
  initiative/proposal/policy/strategy
- ▶ **implement** a programme/plan/
  proposal/policy/strategy/
  manifesto/scheme

2 [C] ■ *She presents a programme on Channel 4.*

show + broadcast + podcast + webcast + showing + transmission

- ▶ **be on** a programme/show
- ▶ a **radio/television/TV**
  programme/show/broadcast/
  transmission
- ▶ a **live** programme/show/
  broadcast/webcast/transmission
- ▶ **see/watch** a programme/show/
  broadcast/podcast/webcast/
  showing/transmission
- ● **PROGRAMME OR SHOW?** In *BrE*
  programme is the more general
  word; **show** is used about fairly
  informal TV or radio and is usu.
  used in compounds. In *AmE* **show**
  is the more general word; **program**
  is used about more serious TV and
  radio and is usu. used in
  compounds: (*AmE*) *What time is
  that show on?* • *She hosts a news
  program on TV.*

3 [C] ■ *a programme of lectures*

schedule + timetable + itinerary

- ▶ a **busy/full/packed/detailed**
  programme/schedule/timetable/
  itinerary
- ▶ a **hectic/demanding** programme/
  schedule/timetable
- ▶ **agree on/draw up/follow/
  change** a programme/
  schedule/timetable/itinerary
- ▶ **keep/stick/adhere to** a
  programme/schedule/timetable

progress noun [U] (often approv.)

■ *We have made great progress in our research.*

advance + development + rise + progression | *fml* **advancement**

- ▶ progress/an advance/
  development/advancement **in** sth
- ▶ **achieve** progress/advances/
  development/progression
- ▶ **chart/halt** the progress/
  development/rise/advancement
  of sth

progress verb [I]

■ *Students progress at their own speed.*

develop + advance + move | *infml*
come along/on | *esp. journ.* **shape up**

- ▶ progress/develop/move **from/to**
  sth
- ▶ progress/develop/advance/move
  towards/beyond sth
- ▶ a **war/campaign** progresses/
  develops

project noun

1 [C] ■ *They set up a project to computerize the library.*

operation + venture + enterprise + undertaking + exercise + activity

- ▶ a **major/successful/joint** project/
  operation/venture/enterprise/
  undertaking/exercise/activity
- ▶ **set up/run/support** a project/
  operation/venture/enterprise/
  activity
- ▶ **be involved in** a/an project/
  operation/venture/enterprise/
  exercise/activity

2 [C] ■ *The class is doing a project on Roman Britain.*

assignment + homework + task + essay + work

- ▶ (a/an) project/homework/essay
  on sth
- ▶ (a) **geography/history/biology,
  etc.** project/assignment/
  homework
- ▶ **do** a project/an assignment/your
  homework/a task/an essay/some
  work

promise noun

1 [C] ■ *He broke every single promise he ever made me.*

commitment + guarantee + word + vow + assurance + oath | *esp. journ.
or politics* **pledge**

- ▶ a/an promise/commitment/
  guarantee/your word/vow/oath/
  pledge **to do** sth
- ▶ a/an promise/guarantee/your
  word/vow/assurance/oath/
  pledge **that…**
- ▶ **make** a promise/commitment/
  guarantee/vow/pledge
- ▶ **keep** your promise/commitment/
  word/vow

▶ **break** a promise/your commitment/your word/a vow/a pledge

2 [U] ∎ *Her work shows great promise.*

potential ♦ **possibilities** ♦ **prospects**

▶ sb/sth **with** promise/potential/possibilities/prospects
▶ **show** promise/potential
▶ **fulfil** sb/sth's promise/potential

---

promise *verb* [T, I]
∎ *I promise not to tell anyone.*

guarantee ♦ **swear** ♦ **pledge** ♦ **commit** ♦ **assure** | *esp. written* **vow** | *fml or busin.* **undertake**

∎ **OPP**
▶ promise/guarantee/swear/pledge/vow/undertake **to do sth**
▶ promise/guarantee/swear/pledge/vow **that…**
▶ promise/guarantee/pledge your **support**

● **PROMISE OR GUARANTEE?** When you **promise**, you make a personal commitment to do sth. **Guarantee** is less personal; when you **guarantee**, you mean that you will make sure that it happens. You have a moral duty to do what you have promised, but you may also have a legal duty to do what you have guaranteed.

---

promising *adj.*
∎ *The weather doesn't look very promising.*

encouraging ♦ **hopeful** ♦ **heartening** | *fml* **auspicious** | *esp. journ. or busin.* **bright** ♦ **rosy**

∎ **OPP** unpromising
▶ be/look promising/encouraging/hopeful/auspicious/bright/rosy **for** sb/sth
▶ a/an promising/encouraging/hopeful/auspicious/bright **start**
▶ a/an promising/encouraging/hopeful/bright/rosy **future/prospect/outlook/life**

● **PROMISING OR ENCOURAGING?** Use **promising** to talk about sb's career; use **encouraging** to talk about people's reactions to things: *a promising career/candidate/young player* ♦ *The response from readers was extremely encouraging.*

---

promote *verb*
1 [T] ∎ *The church tries to promote racial harmony.*

foster ♦ **encourage** ♦ **further** ♦ **advance** ♦ **spur**

▶ promote/foster/encourage/further/advance **understanding** of sth

---

▶ promote/further/advance sb's **interests/career**
▶ promote/foster/encourage/spur **development/growth**
● **WHICH WORD?** **Foster** is usu. used to talk about encouraging sth that does not yet exist or is just starting. **Further** and **advance** are used to talk about helping sth to develop more. **Promote** and **encourage** are used in both contexts.

2 [T] ∎ *She came on the show to promote her new book.*

advertise ♦ **market** | *infml* **push** ♦ **plug** | *infml, disapprov.* **hype** | *busin.* **merchandise**

▶ promote/advertise/market/push/plug/hype/merchandise sth **as** sth
▶ promote/advertise/market/merchandise sth **through** sth
▶ promote/advertise/market/push/plug/merchandise a **product**
▶ promote/advertise/market/plug/hype a/an **book/film/movie/CD/album**

---

promotion *noun* [U, C]
∎ *His promotion to Sales Manager took everyone by surprise.*

progression ♦ **rise** | *fml* **advancement**

∎ **OPP** demotion
▶ sb/sth's promotion/progression/rise/advancement **to** sth
▶ (a) **rapid** promotion/progression/rise/advancement
▶ **achieve** promotion/progression

---

prompt *verb*
1 [T] ∎ *What prompted you to choose us?*

lead ♦ **make** ♦ **motivate** | *fml* **induce** ♦ **predispose**

▶ prompt/lead/motivate/induce/predispose **sb to do sth**
▶ **make** sb **do sth**

2 [T] ∎ *The news prompted speculation about further price rises.*

provoke ♦ **trigger** ♦ **set sth off** ♦ **cause** ♦ **lead** (sth) **to** sth | *esp. journ.* **spark**

▶ prompt/provoke/trigger/set sth off/cause/lead to/spark a **debate/reaction**
▶ prompt/provoke/trigger/cause/lead to/spark **discussions/controversy**
▶ prompt/provoke/trigger/lead to/spark **demonstrations**
▶ prompt/provoke/cause/lead to/spark **anger**

---

prompt *adj.*
1 ∎ *Prompt action was required as the fire spread.*

■ OPP slow, delayed
► a/an prompt/immediate/instant/ instantaneous **reaction/response/ return**
► a/an prompt/immediate/instant **action/attention/reaction/relief**
► a prompt/an immediate **start/ stop**
● WHICH WORD? Prompt describes sth that you do; **instantaneous** describes sth that happens; **immediate** and **instant** can describe either. Prompt does not suggest quite as much speed of reaction as the other words:
  ✔ a very/fairly prompt response
  ✗ a very/fairly immediate/instant/ instantaneous response

2 [not before noun] ■ *Please be prompt when attending this class.*

punctual • on time

■ OPP late
► very/always prompt/punctual

prone *adj.* [not before noun]
■ *Tired drivers are prone to accidents.*

inclined • liable • likely • susceptible | *fml* **subject to sth**

► be prone/inclined/liable/ susceptible/subject **to** sth
► be prone/inclined/liable/likely **to do** sth

pronunciation *noun* [U, C]
■ *He corrected our French pronunciation.*

accent • speech • voice | *phonetics* **intonation**

► have (a/an) **excellent/good/poor** pronunciation/accent/intonation
► (a) **clear** pronunciation/speech/ voice
► (a/an) **English/foreign** pronunciation/accent/intonation

proof *noun* [U]
■ *There is no proof that the knife belonged to her.*

evidence • support • demonstration | *fml* **testimony**

► proof/evidence/a demonstration/ testimony **that...**
► (a) **clear/convincing** proof/ evidence/support/ demonstration/testimony
► **provide/give** proof/evidence/ support/a demonstration/ testimony
● PROOF OR EVIDENCE? Evidence is what makes you believe that sth is true; proof shows that sth is true in a way that no one can argue against.

proper *adj.*

1 (*esp. BrE*) ■ *Please follow the proper procedures.*

correct • right

► the proper/correct/right **way/ method/approach/decision/ judgement/conclusion**
● PROPER, CORRECT OR RIGHT? People can be **correct** or **right** about sth, but not **proper**:
  ✔ You're right to be cautious.
  ✗ You're proper to be cautious.
  ✔ Am I correct in thinking...? ✗ Am I proper in thinking...?
  Correct and **proper** are more often used to talk about methods; **right** is more often used to talk about beliefs and decisions.

2 [only before noun] (*BrE, spoken*)
■ *It's time you got a proper job!*

real • true • genuine

► a/the proper/real/true/genuine **real**

property *noun* [U]
■ *The equipment is government property.*

possession • belongings • valuables | *infml* **stuff** | *esp. BrE, infml* **things** | *esp. written or law* **goods** | *busin.* **asset • holding**

► **personal** property/possessions/ belongings/stuff/things/assets/ holdings
► **private** property/possessions/ belongings/goods/assets/ holdings
► **acquire** property/possessions/ belongings/goods/stuff/things/ assets/your holdings
► **sell** your property/possessions/ belongings/valuables/goods/ stuff/things/assets/holdings

proportion *noun* [U, pl.]
■ *The head is out of proportion with the body.*

ratio • scale

► the proportion/ratio of A to B
► **out of** proportion/scale
► a **high/low** proportion/ratio

proposal *noun* [C]
■ *I welcome the proposal to reduce taxes for the low-paid.*

recommendation • suggestion • proposition • motion • plan • initiative

► a/an proposal/recommendation/ suggestion/motion/plan/initiative **for** sth
► a/an proposal/recommendation/ suggestion/motion/initiative **on** sth

▶ **accept/support/reject/discuss** a/
an **proposal/recommendation/
suggestion/proposition/motion/
plan/initiative**
▶ **put forward** a/an **proposal/
recommendation/suggestion/
motion/plan/initiative**

propose verb

1 [T] ■ *He proposed a solution to the
problem.*

**suggest • put sth forward •
recommend • present** | *fml* **move •
advance • moot**

▶ **propose/suggest/be put forward/
recommend/move/be proposed
that...**
▶ **propose/suggest/put forward/
recommend/present/move/moot
an idea**
▶ **propose/suggest/put forward/
present an alternative**
▶ **propose/suggest/put forward a
change/measure**
● PROPOSE, SUGGEST OR PUT
FORWARD? **Propose** and **put
forward** are used in more formal
situations than **suggest**.

2 [I] (*fml*) ■ *What do you propose to
do?*

**intend • plan • aim • have sb/sth in
mind** | *esp. spoken* **mean**

▶ **propose/intend/plan/aim/have in
mind/mean to do sth**
▶ **propose/intend doing sth**

prospect noun

1 [U, sing.] ■ *There is no reasonable
prospect of peace.*

**chance • possibility • likelihood •
probability • odds**

▶ **a/the prospect/chance/
possibility/likelihood/probability/
odds of sth**
▶ **a/the prospect/chance/
possibility/likelihood/probability/
odds that...**
▶ **There is little/no prospect/
chance/possibility/likelihood of
sth.**

2 prospects [pl.] ■ *They want a
reasonable salary and good career
prospects.*

possibilities • potential • promise

▶ **prospects/possibilities/potential
for sth**
▶ **have prospects/possibilities/
potential/promise**
▶ **assess/examine/consider/
discuss/explore sb's prospects/
possibilities/potential**

protect verb [T, I]

■ *Troops protected the aid workers
from attack.*

**defend • guard • shield • shelter •
save • preserve • secure** | *fml*
safeguard

■ OPP **expose**
▶ **protect/defend/guard/shield/
shelter/save/preserve/secure/
safeguard sb/sth from sth**
▶ **protect/defend/guard/secure/
safeguard sth against sth**
▶ **protect/defend/save yourself**
▶ **protect/preserve a species**

protection noun [U]

■ *He asked to be put under police
protection.*

security • cover | *BrE* **defence** | *AmE*
defense

▶ **protection/defence from/of/
against sth**
▶ **adequate** protection/security/
defence
▶ **provide** protection/security/
cover/defence

protest noun

1 [U, C] ■ *The announcement raised a
storm of protest.*

**opposition • resistance • objection •
hostility**

▶ **in protest/opposition/objection**
▶ **widespread/strong/fierce
protests/opposition/resistance/
objection/hostility**
▶ **provoke/meet with/face
protests/opposition/resistance/
objection/hostility**

2 [C] ■ *A massive anti-war protest was
planned.*

demonstration • march | *BrE, infml*
demo

▶ **a protest/demonstration/march/
demo against sth**
▶ **a/an anti-war/pro-democracy/
anti-government protest/
demonstration/march/demo**
▶ **hold/organize/stage/go on/
join/participate in/take part in a
protest/demonstration/march/
demo**
● PROTEST OR DEMONSTRATION? A
demonstration can be for or
against sb/sth; a **protest** is always
against sb/sth. A **demonstration** is
usu. about a more public, wider
issue that may affect a whole
country; a **protest** can be about a
more private matter, for example
by workers against their employers.

protest verb [I, T]

■ *He protested that he would not
receive a fair trial.*

object • complain

- ▶ protest/complain **about/at** sth
- ▶ protest/object/complain **to** sb
- ▶ protest/object/complain **that...**

protester noun [C]
■ *200 anti-nuclear protesters were arrested at the military base.*

demonstrator • opponent • rebel • dissident
___
- ▶ a protester/demonstrator/rebel **against** sth
- ▶ **angry/peaceful** protesters/ demonstrators
- ▶ protesters/demonstrators/ opponents/rebels **call for/ demand** sth
- ● **PROTESTER OR DEMONSTRATOR? Demonstrator** is used more frequently than **protester** to describe sb who is walking in a group to show opposition to sth; **protester** often refers to sb who is protesting in other ways: *30000 demonstrators marched to the parliament building.* • *Protesters threw paint at the prime minister.*

proud adj.
1 ■ *She was very proud of her achievements.*

pleased • delighted • happy
___
- ▶ proud/pleased/delighted/happy **that...**
- ▶ proud/pleased/delighted/happy **to see/hear/find/know...**
- ▶ proud/pleased/delighted/happy **to say (that...)**

2 (disapprov.) ■ *He was too proud to admit that he was wrong.*

arrogant • vain • conceited • pompous • self-important • boastful • superior | *infml* cocky | *esp. written* haughty
___
■ OPP humble, modest
- ▶ a/an proud/arrogant/vain/ conceited/pompous/self-important/haughty **man**
- ▶ a/an proud/arrogant/vain/ conceited/haughty **woman**

3 (often approv.) ■ *They were a proud and independent people.*

self-respecting | approv. dignified
___
- ▶ a proud/self-respecting/dignified **man/woman**

prove verb [T]
■ *New evidence proved his innocence.*

show • demonstrate • illustrate • indicate
___
■ OPP disprove
- ▶ prove/show/demonstrate/ indicate **to** sb
- ▶ prove/show/demonstrate/ illustrate/indicate **that/what/ how...**

- ▶ **figures/studies** prove/show/ demonstrate/illustrate sth
- ▶ **research** proves/shows/ demonstrates/illustrates sth
- ● **PROVE OR SHOW? Prove** is often preferred to **show** to give a stronger sense of justice being done.

provide verb [T]
■ *We are here to provide a service for the public.*

give • supply • issue • lend | *esp. busin.* yield • put sth up
___
- ▶ provide/supply/issue sb **with** sth
- ▶ provide/supply/put sth up **for** sb
- ▶ provide/give/supply/issue **equipment/details/information**
- ▶ provide/give/supply/put up **funds**
- ● **PROVIDE OR GIVE ? Provide** is often used when sth is being made available to people in general; **give** is more often used about a particular person: *The hospital aims to provide the best possible medical care.* • *We want to give you the best possible care.*

provide for sb phrasal verb
■ *Local authorities must do more to provide for children in need.*

support • maintain • serve • cater for sb/sth | *BrE* keep
___
- ▶ provide for/support/maintain/ keep a/your **family/children/ wife/husband**
- ▶ provide for/support/maintain/ keep **yourself**
- ● **WHICH WORD?** You can provide for sb on a continuous basis or by making one large payment. If you **keep, maintain** or **support** sb you provide for them on a continuous basis over a period of time.

provoke verb [T]
■ *Her laughter provoked him to fury.*

sting • prod | *esp. written* goad
___
- ▶ provoke/sting/prod/goad sb **into (doing)** sth
- ▶ provoke/sting/prod/goad sb **to do** sth
- ▶ provoke/sting/prod/goad sb **into action**

proximity noun [U]
■ *a house in the proximity of the airport*

vicinity • locality | *BrE* neighbourhood | *AmE* neighborhood
___
- ▶ **in** the proximity/vicinity/ neighbourhood **of** sth

pub

▸ **in** the vicinity/locality/
neighbourhood
▸ the **immediate** proximity/vicinity/
locality/neighbourhood

pub noun [C] (BrE)
■ We went to the pub for a drink.

bar | BrE, infml **local** | BrE, fml **public
house** | (in the past) **inn • tavern •
saloon**

▸ **go to** a bar/the pub/a public
house/an inn/a tavern/a saloon

the public noun [sing.+ sing./pl. v.]
■ The government should inform the
public of the risks.

**population • the country • the
nation • community • society**

▸ **(the)** public/population/country/
nation/community/society **at
large/as a whole**
▸ the **general** public/population/
community
▸ a **member** of (the) public/
population/community/society

public adj.

1 [only before noun] ■ The
government had to bow to public
pressure.

popular • social • civic

▸ public/popular/social **awareness/
pressure/support/unrest**
▸ public/popular **opinion**
▸ public/social **issues/values/
policy/welfare**

2 [only before noun] ■ He was
charged with destroying public
property.

common • communal • collective

■ OPP **private**
▸ public/common/communal/
collective **property**
▸ public/common/communal **land**

3 [only before noun] ■ Schools are
worried about public spending cuts.

state • national • federal

■ OPP **private**
▸ public/state/national/federal
**authorities/funding/
expenditure/investiture**
▸ public/state/federal **control/
institutions/officials/funds/
spending**
▸ public/state **education/hospitals/
enterprise/ownership**
▸ the **public/state sector**

publicity noun

1 [U] ■ The event attracted a great
deal of publicity.

**attention • exposure • fame •
celebrity**

▸ **international** publicity/attention/
exposure/fame/celebrity
▸ **attract** publicity/attention

2 [U] ■ There has been a lot of
advance publicity for the new film.

**promotion • advertising •
advertisement** | infml **plug** | infml,
disapprov. **hype**

▸ **(a/an)** publicity/promotion/
advertising/advertisement/plug/
hype **for sth**

publish verb

1 [T, I] ■ It's a company that publishes
reference books.

issue • print • release

▸ publish/issue/print/release a **book**
▸ publish/issue/print a **booklet/
brochure/newsletter/leaflet/
pamphlet**
▸ publish/issue/release a new **title/
edition**

2 [T] ■ The report will be published on
the Internet.

**issue • release • print • circulate •
publicize • advertise**

▸ publish/issue/release/print/
circulate a **report/details**
▸ publish/issue/release/print a
**document/statement/
description**
▸ publish/print a **picture/photo/
article**
● PUBLISH, ISSUE OR RELEASE? Use any
of these words to talk about
information being formally made
available to the public. **Issue** has
the widest range of collocates and
is used esp. with words relating to
announcements and legal notices.
Publish, but not **issue** or **release**, is
also used to talk about letters and
articles.

pull verb

1 [I, T] ■ Don't pull my hair!

tug • jerk | infml **yank**

■ OPP **push**
▸ pull/tug/yank **on/at** sth
▸ pull/tug/yank sb/sth **toward/
towards/out of** sth
▸ pull/tug (at) sb's **hair/elbow/arm**

2 [T] (usu. used with an adv. or
prep.) ■ She pulled his boots off.

tear • pluck • lever | esp. BrE **prise/
prize** | AmE **pry** | fml **extract** | written
wrench

▸ pull/tear/pluck/prise/pry/
extract/wrench sth **from** sb/sth
▸ pull/tear/pluck/lever/prise/pry/
wrench sb/sth **out/out of** sth

▶ pull/tear/pluck/prise/pry/wrench
sth **off**/**open**/**apart**

3 [T] ■ *Ponies were used to pull the
coal trucks.*

**drag • haul • tow • tug • trail |
written draw**

■ OPP push
▶ pull/drag/haul/tow/tug/trail/
draw sth **along**/**down**/**towards**
sth
▶ pull/drag/haul/tow/tug/trail/
draw sb **behind** you
▶ pull/drag/haul/draw a **cart**/
sledge/**sled**
▶ pull/haul/tow a **truck**

pump verb [T, I] (usu. used with an
adv. or prep.)
■ *An engine pumped water out of the
mine.*

**extract • siphon/syphon | written
draw**

▶ pump/extract/siphon/draw sth
from sth
▶ pump/extract/siphon/draw
water from sth
▶ pump/extract/siphon **oil**/**liquid**/
gas from sth

punch verb [T]
■ *They kicked and punched him as he
lay on the ground.*

**hit • thump • beat • pound •
pummel | infml sock • whack | fml
strike**

▶ hit/punch/thump/strike sb **in the
stomach**/**chest**
▶ hit/punch sb **on the nose**
▶ hit/punch/thump/beat/sock/
strike sb **hard**

punish verb [T]
■ *He was punished for refusing to
answer their questions.*

**discipline • penalize • sentence |
infml come down on sb**

■ OPP reward
▶ punish/discipline/penalize/
sentence/come down on sb **for
doing sth**
▶ punish/penalize/sentence/come
down on an **offender**
▶ punish/penalize (bad,
unacceptable, etc.) **behaviour**

punishment noun [U, C]
■ *Do harsher punishments deter
criminals?*

penalty • sentence | fml retribution

■ OPP reward
▶ (a) punishment/penalty/
sentence/retribution **for** sth
▶ a/an **heavy**/**harsh**/**severe**/
appropriate punishment/penalty/
sentence

▶ **impose** a punishment/penalty/
sentence

pupil noun [C] (esp. BrE, becoming
old-fash.)
■ *The school has over 850 pupils.*

**student • schoolboy • schoolgirl •
schoolchild**

▶ a/an **good**/**bright**/**outstanding**/
star/**disruptive** pupil/student
▶ a **primary school**/**junior school**/
secondary school pupil/student
▶ **teach** pupils/students/
schoolboys/schoolgirls/
schoolchildren

purchase verb [T] (fml)
■ *Please ensure that you purchase your
ticket in advance.*

**buy • take | esp. spoken get | infml
pick sth up • snap sth up | fml
acquire**

▶ purchase/buy/get/pick up/snap
up/acquire sth **for £10**, **$2 million**,
etc.
▶ purchase/buy/get/acquire sth
from sb
▶ purchase/buy/get/snap up/
acquire (a) **property**/**company**/
house
▶ purchase/buy/get/acquire **land**/
premises/**a site**/**tickets**

pure adj.

1 ■ *These shirts are 100% pure cotton.*

solid • refined

▶ pure/solid/refined **gold**/**silver**
▶ pure/refined **oil**

2 ■ *The mountain air was sweet and
pure.*

clean • sterile • spotless

▶ pure/clean/sterile (**drinking**)
water
▶ pure/clean **air**

3 ■ *They met by pure chance.*

**sheer • complete • total • utter •
unqualified • unconditional •
unmitigated**

▶ pure/sheer/complete/total/utter
joy/**bliss**
▶ pure/sheer/complete/total
coincidence
▶ pure/sheer **luck**/**chance**

purpose noun

1 [C] ■ *The main purpose of the
campaign is to raise money.*

**aim • objective • object • point •
idea • goal • target • intention •
plan • end | fml or law intent**

▶ **with** the purpose/aim/objective/

object/idea/goal/intention/intent **of** doing sth
▶ sb's purpose/aim/intention/plan/intent **that...**
▶ **have** a/an purpose/aim/intention/plan/intent

2 [C] ■ *The building is used for religious purposes.*

function • use

▶ a **useful** purpose/function
▶ **have** a purpose/function/use
▶ **serve/fulfil** a purpose/function

3 [C, U] ■ *Volunteer work gives her life a sense of purpose.*

vocation • mission

▶ **find** your purpose/vocation/mission
▶ a **sense of** purpose/vocation/mission
▶ sb's purpose/vocation/mission **in life**

push verb

1 [T, I] (often used with an adv. or prep.) ■ *He pushed the key into the lock.*

stick • drive • force • ram • poke • press | *infml* **shove** | *written* **thrust**

■ OPP **pull**

▶ push/stick/drive/force/ram/poke/press/shove/thrust **into** sth
▶ push/stick/drive/force/ram/poke/shove/thrust sth **through** sth
▶ push/force/shove/thrust sb/sth **away**

2 [I, T] (usu. used with an adv. or prep.) ■ *A boy pushed his way through the crowd.*

shove • barge • shoulder • elbow • jostle

■ OPP **pull**

▶ push/shove/barge/shoulder/elbow **past** sb
▶ push/barge/elbow **through** sth
▶ push/shove/shoulder/elbow sb **aside/out of the way**

3 [T] ■ *Push the red button to open the door.*

press • squeeze

▶ push/press/squeeze **on** sth
▶ push/press a **bell/button/key/switch**
▶ push/press/squeeze (sth) **hard/gently**

● **WHICH WORD?** Press is the most general word. You can **press** sth with your finger, hand or foot. **Push** is mostly used with the word *button*. You **squeeze** sth by bending your finger(s) around it.

4 [T] ■ *No one pushed you to take the job, did they?*

press | *BrE* **pressurize** | *esp. AmE* **pressure** | *infml* **twist sb's arm** | *fml* **coerce**

▶ push/press/pressurize/pressure/coerce sb **into** (doing) sth
▶ push sb/press sb/pressurize sb/pressure/coerce sb/twist sb's arm **to do sth**
▶ push/press sb **for** sth

5 [T] (*usu. approv.*) ■ *Lucy should push herself harder.*

work | *sometimes disapprov.* **drive** | *disapprov.* **overwork**

▶ push/work/drive sb **hard**
▶ push/drive sb **too far/to the limit**

push sb around/about
phrasal verb

■ *She's wrong if she thinks she can push me around.*

bully • order sb around/about • dictate to sb • lay down the law | *written* **tyrannize**

▶ sb **will not be** pushed around/bullied/dictated to/tyrannized (by sb)
▶ **allow yourself to be** pushed around/bullied/dictated to
▶ sb **thinks they can** push/order sb around

● **PUSH SB AROUND, ORDER SB AROUND OR DICTATE TO SB?** These expressions all mean to tell sb what to do, because you believe you are more important or powerful than they are. Sb who **pushes sb around/about** may use threats or violence. Sb who **orders sb around/about** may or may not be obeyed.

put verb

1 [T] (always used with an adv. or prep.) ■ *Put the cases down there, please.*

lay • place • set • position • settle • plant | *infml* **stuff • dump • stick** | *esp. BrE, infml* **pop**

▶ put/lay/place/set/position/dump/stick/pop sth **on** sth
▶ put/place/set/stuff/dump/stick/pop sth **in/into** sth
▶ put/lay/set sth **down**

2 [T] (always used with an adv. or prep.) ■ *We're not allowed to put posters on the walls.*

attach • fasten • stick | *esp. BrE* **fix**

▶ put/fasten/stick/fix sth **on** sth

3 ■ *The incident put her in a bad mood.*

set • place

▶ put/set sb/sth **at ease/in motion**

► put/place sb in charge/in sb's care/under command/under arrest

put sth forward *phrasal verb*
■ *Several fund-raising ideas were put forward.*

suggest • recommend • present | *fml* **propose • advance • move • moot**

► be put forward/suggest/ recommend/proposed/move/be mooted that…
► put forward/suggest/ recommend/propose/ advance/moot a **plan**
► put forward/suggest/ recommend/present/propose/ move/moot an **idea**
► put forward/suggest/ recommend/present/propose an **alternative**
● **PUT FORWARD, SUGGEST OR PROPOSE?** Propose and put forward are used in more formal situations than suggest.

put sth off *phrasal verb*
■ *He keeps putting off going to the dentist.*

delay • postpone • reschedule • shelve • suspend | *fml* **defer**

■ OPP **bring sth forward**
► put off/delay/postpone/shelve/ suspend/defer **for** a few days/ the time being, etc.
► put off/delay/postpone/defer sth **until** sth
► put off/delay/postpone/defer **doing sth**
► put off/delay/postpone/ reschedule/defer a **visit**
► put off/delay/postpone/defer a **decision**

put sth on *phrasal verb*
■ *Hurry up! Put your coat on.*

wear • have (got) sth on • get dressed • change

■ OPP **take sth off**
► put on/wear/have on a **coat/ jacket/suit/hat/ring/badge/ watch**
► put on/wear/have on your **glasses**
► put on/wear/have on **make-up/ lipstick**

put sth out *phrasal verb*
■ *Put your cigarette out.*

blow sth out • snuff • douse | *fml* **extinguish**

■ OPP **light**
► put out/blow out/snuff (out)/ douse/extinguish a **flame/flames**
► put out/blow out/snuff (out)/ extinguish a **candle**
► put out/douse/extinguish a **fire/ blaze**

► put out/extinguish a **cigarette/ light**

put sth together *phrasal verb*
■ *They put together a strong case for the defence.*

prepare • draw sth up • get sb/sth ready • draft

► put together/prepare/draw up/ get ready/draft sth **for** sth
► put together/prepare/draw up/ draft a **list/report/paper/plan/ strategy**
► put together/prepare a **show/get a show ready**

put sth up *phrasal verb*
■ *They put up posters all over town.*

hang • display

► put up/hang/display a **picture/ painting**
● **PUT STH UP OR HANG?** You hang a *painting* in a frame, that hangs on a hook; you put up a *notice* or *poster* that has no frame and is just stuck to the wall.

put up with sb/sth *phrasal verb (esp. spoken)*
■ *I don't know how she puts up with his drinking.*

stand • bear • take • tolerate | *fml* **endure**

► (can't/not) put up with/stand/ bear **sb/sth doing sth**
► put up with/stand/bear/endure **pain**
► sb **has to** put up with/bear/ endure/tolerate sth

Q q

qualify *verb*
1 [I] (*esp. BrE*) ■ *She qualified as a doctor last year.*

graduate • pass

► qualify/graduate **as** sth
► **students** qualify/graduate/pass

2 [T] ■ *The training will qualify you for a better job.*

BrE **fit** | *esp. busin.* **equip**

► qualify/fit/equip sb **for** sth
► be qualified/fitted/equipped **to do sth**
► be **well/perfectly** qualified/fitted/ equipped for sth

quality *noun*
1 [U, C] ■ *The goods are of very poor quality.*

standard • grade • level | *BrE* calibre | *AmE* caliber

▶ **be of** a/the ... quality/standard/ grade/level/calibre
▶ **high/highest/low** quality/ standard/grade/level/calibre
▶ **raise/improve** the quality/ standard/grade/level/calibre
▶ **maintain** the quality/the standard/ grade/level/calibre

2 [U] ■ *We provide quality at reasonable prices.*

value • excellence • merit • worth • distinction • meaning

▶ sb/sth **of** quality/value/ excellence/merit/worth/ distinction
▶ **great/real** quality/value/merit/ worth/distinction/meaning
▶ **have** quality/value/merit/worth/ distinction/meaning

3 [C, U] ■ *personal qualities such as honesty and generosity*

characteristic • feature • trait • point • attribute | *fml or tech.* property

▶ a/an **essential/desirable/ individual** quality/characteristic/ feature/trait/attribute/property
▶ a/an **important/natural/special/ useful** quality/characteristic/ feature/attribute/property
▶ **possess/display/share** (a) quality/characteristic/feature/ trait/... points/attribute/property

quantity *noun* [C, U]

■ *It is a product that is cheap to produce in large quantities.*

number • amount • volume

▶ **the** quantity/number/amount/ volume **of** sth
▶ a/an quantity/number/amount **of** sth
▶ a **quantity/number of people/ things**
▶ a/an quantity/amount/volume **of information**

● **QUANTITY, NUMBER OR AMOUNT? Number** is used with plural countable nouns; **amount** is usu. used with uncountable nouns: *a number of books/dogs/people* • *a large amount of time/money/ information*
Quantity can be used with both countable and uncountable nouns and is slightly more formal.

queen *noun* [C]

■ *The Queen of Denmark hosted the banquet.*

empress • monarch • ruler • the crown • regent | *fml* sovereign

▶ **under** a/an queen/empress/ monarch/ruler
▶ **become** queen/empress/ monarch/ruler/regent
▶ a/an queen/empress/monarch **reigns/rules**

question *noun*

1 [C] ■ *She refused to answer questions about her private life.*

enquiry/inquiry • query

▶ a/an question/enquiry/query **about/as to/concerning/on** sth
▶ **address/direct** a/an question/ enquiry/query **to** sth
▶ **have/deal with/handle/reply/ respond to/answer** a/an question/enquiry/query

2 [C] ■ *The new play poses some challenging questions.*

matter • issue • concern • subject • theme • topic

▶ a/an **important/key/major/ serious/general** question/matter/ issue/concern/subject/theme/ topic
▶ a/an **political/ethical** question/ matter/issue/concern/subject/ theme/topic
▶ a/an **technical/practical** question/matter/issue/concern/ subject/topic
▶ **discuss/consider/deal with/ tackle/examine/explore/focus on** a/an question/matter/issue/ concern/subject/theme/topic
● **MATTER OR QUESTION?** In many cases you can use either word. However, a **matter** is often sth practical, whereas a **question** may be sth more philosophical.

3 [U] ■ *Her version of events was accepted without question.*

doubt • uncertainty • a question mark over/against sth • confusion

▶ **in** question/doubt/uncertainty
▶ **beyond/without** question/doubt
▶ **come into/be open to** question/ doubt

question *verb*

1 [T] ■ *Police are questioning a suspect.*

interview • interrogate • cross-examine • grill | *esp. journ.* quiz

▶ question/interview/interrogate/ cross-examine/grill/quiz sb **on/ about** sth
▶ question/interview/interrogate/ cross-examine a **witness**
▶ question/interview/interrogate a **suspect**

2 [T] ■ *No one has ever questioned her judgement.*

query • doubt • challenge • dispute • contest

► question/query/doubt/
challenge/dispute/contest
whether...
► question/doubt/challenge/
dispute/contest the **validity** of sth
► question/query/challenge/
dispute/contest a **decision**
● QUESTION OR QUERY? **Query** is often
used to express doubts about the
details of sth, such as a bill or
report. **Question** expresses
stronger doubt, including the
doubt that sth exists at all:
✔ I question the existence of life on
other planets. ✗ I query the existence
of life on other planets.

quick adj.

1 ■ She gave him a quick glance.

rapid • fast • hurried • speedy •
short • brief | *often disapprov.* hasty |
written swift • fleeting

■ OPP slow
► a quick/rapid/fast/hurried/hasty/
swift **exit**
► a quick/rapid/fast/speedy/hasty/
swift **decision**
► a quick/rapid/short/swift
answer/reply/descent
► a quick/rapid/swift/brief/fleeting
look/glance

2 ■ He's a very quick worker.

fast • brisk • high-speed • express •
supersonic

■ OPP slow
► quick/fast **at** doing sth
► a quick/fast/brisk **movement/
pace/walk/run**
► a quick/fast **reader/worker/
learner/rhythm/walk/run**
● QUICK OR FAST? Use **fast** to talk
about travelling:
✔ a fast road/car ✗ a quick road/car
A person may be **fast** or **quick**, but
fast is not used in expressions
where sb does sth in a short time:
✔ a fast/quick reader/runner/learner
• The kids were quick to learn ✗ The
kids were fast to learn.

quiet adj.

1 ■ We could hear quiet footsteps
outside.

soft • faint • inaudible • hushed •
muffled | *written* dull

■ OPP loud
► a/an quiet/soft/faint/inaudible/
hushed/muffled **voice**
► a/an quiet/soft/faint/inaudible/
hushed **whisper**
► a quiet/soft/faint/muffled/dull
sound

2 ■ They lead a quiet life.

peaceful • calm • sleepy • silent |
written tranquil

■ OPP busy

► a quiet/peaceful/sleepy/silent/
tranquil **place/village/town**
► a quiet/peaceful/calm/sleepy/
tranquil **atmosphere**
► a quiet/peaceful/calm/tranquil
day/night/morning/evening

3 ■ She was quiet and shy, and rarely
spoke in class.

reserved • shy • silent | *fml* reticent •
taciturn

► a quiet/reserved/shy/silent/
reticent **person/man**
► He's the quiet/silent **type**.
► strangely quiet/silent/reticent

quite adv.

1 (*esp. BrE*) (not used in negative
sentences) ■ He plays quite well.

fairly • reasonably • moderately |
esp. BrE rather | *AmE or infml, BrE*
pretty

► quite/rather **a/an...**
► quite/fairly/reasonably/
moderately/rather/pretty
successful/high/well
► quite/fairly/reasonably/rather/
pretty **good/large/common/
pleased/confident/quickly/
easily**
► I quite/rather **like** sth

2 (*esp. BrE*) ■ quite delicious/amazing/
perfect

completely • totally • fully • entirely
• utterly | *infml* dead | *esp. spoken*
absolutely • perfectly

► quite/completely/totally/fully/
utterly/dead/absolutely/perfectly
sure
► quite/completely/totally/entirely/
absolutely/perfectly **normal**
► quite/completely/totally/entirely/
utterly **agree**
● WHICH WORD? The main differences
between these words are in register
not meaning. **Completely**, **entirely**
and **fully** are used more in written
and formal English. **Totally**, **quite**,
absolutely and **perfectly** are used
more in spoken and informal
English. **Utterly** is often used to
express failure or impossibility: *She
utterly failed to convince them.*

3 (usu. used with adjectives and
adverbs) ■ I can see it quite clearly.

very • extremely • highly • truly •
desperately | *esp. spoken* really • so |
fml most

► quite/very/extremely/highly/
really/so **successful/intelligent/
competitive/critical**
► quite/very/extremely/really/so/most
anxious/concerned/

quotation

disappointed/unhappy/
important
▶ quite/very/extremely/
desperately/truly/really/so sorry

quotation noun

1 [C, U] (fml) ■ The book began with a quotation from Goethe.

infml quote | fml citation

▶ a quotation/quote/citation
(taken) from sb/sth
▶ This quotation/quote/citation
comes from...

2 (fml) ■ You should get a written quotation from builders before they start work.

estimate • valuation | BrE costing | infml quote

▶ a/an quotation/estimate/quote
for a piece of work
▶ a high/low quotation/estimate/
valuation/quote
▶ give/provide/get/obtain/accept
a/an quotation/estimate/
valuation/quote

quote verb [T, I]

■ He quoted a passage from the president's speech.

repeat • recite • say | fml cite

▶ quote/repeat/recite/cite a
passage
▶ quote/repeat/recite/say a line
▶ quote/recite (a) poem/speech/
poetry

Rr

race noun

1 [C] ■ He took part in a 10-mile road race.

event • contest • competition

▶ a/an major/international race/
event/contest/competition
▶ hold/organize/enter/compete
in/win a/an race/event/contest/
competition

2 [C, U] ■ This custom is found in people of all races throughout the world.

people • ethnic group • nationality
• clan | sometimes offens. tribe

▶ a race/clan/tribe of sth
▶ from a/an race/ethnic group/
clan/tribe
▶ between peoples/races/ethnic
groups/nationalities/clans/tribes
▶ belong to a/an race/ethnic
group/nationality/clan/tribe

race verb [I] (always used with an adv. or prep.) (written)

■ We all raced back to the camp.

run • sprint • tear • charge • gallop •
bound • stampede

▶ race/run/sprint/charge/gallop/
bound towards/after sb/sth
▶ race/run/sprint/tear/gallop/
bound off/along (sth)
▶ race/run/tear/charge around/
round

racism noun [U] (disapprov.)

■ a victim of racism

chauvinism • xenophobia •
apartheid • bigotry • discrimination
• prejudice • intolerance | usu.
approv. patriotism • affirmative
action

▶ fight racism/apartheid/
discrimination/prejudice
▶ a form of racism/chauvinism/
apartheid/discrimination/
prejudice/patriotism

radical adj. [usu. before noun]

■ He proposed a radical solution to the problem. ■ the radical wing of the party

revolutionary | usu. approv.
progressive | usu. disapprov. extreme

■ OPP conservative, moderate

▶ radical/revolutionary/progressive/
extreme ideas/views
▶ radical/revolutionary proposals/
solutions
▶ a radical/revolutionary leader

rain noun [U, sing.]

■ Don't go out in the rain.

shower • drizzle • downpour •
rainfall • monsoon

▶ (a) heavy rain/shower/
downpour/rainfall
▶ (a) light rain/shower/drizzle/
rainfall
▶ be/get caught in the rain/a
shower/a downpour

rain verb [I]

■ It had been raining all night.

fall • come down • pour • drizzle

▶ It's raining/pouring/drizzling.
▶ rain/fall heavily/lightly/steadily
● RAIN, FALL OR COME DOWN? Rain is
the most frequent verb and is used
with the subject it. Fall and come
down are used with a subject such
as rain or snow: 70 millimetres of
rain fell in just a few hours. • The rain
came down in torrents.

raise verb

1 [T] (usu. used with an adv. or prep.) (esp. written) ■ He raised a hand in greeting.

lift • pick sb/sth up • hoist • heave • scoop

■ OPP lower

▸ raise/lift/pick/hoist/scoop sb/sth up
▸ raise/lift your hand/arm/head/chin/face/eyes/eyebrows
● RAISE, LIFT OR PICK SB/STH UP? Lift can mean to move sb/sth in a particular direction, not just upwards; pick sb/sth up is usu. used about sb/sth that is not very heavy and is only used for upwards movement; raise is used esp. about parts of the body: He lifted the suitcase down from the rack. • He picked up the phone and dialled the number. • She raised her eyebrows.

2 [T] ■ The government has promised not to raise taxes.

increase • heighten • intensify • step sth up | often approv. boost | often disapprov. inflate | esp. busin. maximize

■ OPP lower

▸ raise/increase/step up/boost/inflate sth by 15%, 250, £100, a third, etc.
▸ raise/increase/step up/boost/inflate from/to 150, $500, etc.
▸ raise/increase/boost/inflate/maximize prices
▸ raise/increase/heighten/boost awareness/interest
▸ raise/increase/intensify step up the pressure
● RAISE OR INCREASE? Increase is used slightly more often about numbers, prices and figures; raise is often used about feelings and qualities.

3 [T] ■ The sale raised over £3 000 for charity.

collect • make • bring sth in • fetch

▸ raise/collect money for sth
▸ raise/collect/make/bring in money
▸ raise/collect/make/bring in/fetch $200/£300000

4 [T, often passive] (esp. AmE) ■ I was born and raised a city boy.

bring sb up • rear • be born and bred • adopt | esp. BrE foster

▸ raise/bring up/rear/adopt/foster a child
▸ raise/bring up/rear/adopt a daughter/son/family
▸ raise/rear young/animals/sheep/chickens/poultry

random adj. [usu. before noun]
■ The names are listed in random order.

unsystematic | disapprov. haphazard • indiscriminate • disorganized

■ OPP systematic, predetermined

▸ in a random/unsystematic/haphazard way
▸ a random/haphazard approach
▸ random/indiscriminate attacks

range noun

1 [C, usu. sing.] ■ There is a full range of activities for children.

variety • choice • selection • assortment • array • diversity

▸ a wide range/variety/choice/selection/assortment/array/diversity
▸ offer/provide a/an range/variety/choice/assortment/array/diversity (of sth)
▸ choose from a/an range/variety/choice/selection/assortment/array of sth
● RANGE OR VARIETY? Range emphasizes the (often large) number of things available; variety emphasizes the amount of difference between the types of a particular thing.

2 [C, usu. sing., U] ■ This was outside the range of his experience. ■ Most of the students are in the 17–20 age range.

scope • reach • breadth • spectrum • bracket

▸ within/beyond/outside the range/scope/reach of sb/sth
▸ the entire/full/whole/complete range/scope/breadth/spectrum
▸ the broad/narrow range/scope/spectrum of sth
▸ expand/extend/widen/limit/narrow/restrict/define the range/scope/reach/breadth/spectrum

rank noun [C, U]
■ He was promoted to the rank of major. ■ people of high social rank

level • grade • position • class • status • standing

▸ the top rank/level/grade
▸ a high/higher rank/level/grade/position/status/standing
▸ a low/lower rank/level/grade/position/class/status/standing
▸ sb's social rank/position/class/status/standing

rank verb [T, I] (not used in the progressive tenses)
■ The criteria are ranked in order of importance.

grade • rate • place • put | fml order

▸ rank/grade/rate/order sb/sth according to sth
▸ rank/grade/order sb/sth by sth
▸ rank/rate/place/put/order sb/sth above/below sb/sth

rape

▶ rank/grade/rate/place/put sb/sth **in order of** sth

rape verb [T]

■ She had been raped in her own home.

assault • abuse • molest

▶ brutally rape/assault/abuse sb
▶ sexually assault/abuse/molest sb

rapid adj. [usu. before noun]

■ There has been a rapid rise in sales.

quick • fast • speedy • high-speed • brisk • hurried • express | written swift | often disapprov. hasty

■ OPP slow
▶ a rapid/quick/fast/swift/hasty **change**
▶ a rapid/quick/fast/speedy/brisk **rate**
▶ a rapid/quick/fast/brisk/swift **movement**
▶ a rapid/quick/fast/hurried/swift/hasty **exit**

rare adj.

■ He suffers from a rare bone disease.

uncommon • infrequent

■ OPP common, frequent
▶ rare/uncommon/infrequent **words**
▶ a rare/an uncommon **experience/feature/occurrence**
▶ rare/infrequent **occasions/use**

rarely adv.

■ He rarely spoke.

seldom • hardly ever • infrequently

■ OPP often, frequently
▶ rarely/seldom/hardly ever/infrequently **used**
▶ rarely/seldom/hardly ever **available/the case**
▶ rarely/seldom/hardly ever **happen/speak**
● **RARELY OR SELDOM?** Rarely is slightly more formal than not often and seldom is slightly more formal than rarely.

rate noun

1 [C] ■ At the rate you're working, you'll never finish!

speed • pace • momentum | written tempo

▶ at a...rate/speed/pace
▶ a fast/slow/steady rate/speed/pace
▶ increase the rate/speed/pace/momentum/tempo
▶ maintain the rate/speed/pace/momentum

---

2 [C] ■ The job has a low hourly rate of pay.

terms • charge • price • fee • rent • rental • fare

▶ the rate/terms/charge/price/fee/rent/rental/fare **for** sth
▶ **at** a rate/charge/price/fee/rent/rental/fare of...
▶ a **high/low** rate/charge/price/fee/rent/rental/fare
▶ (a) **reasonable** rate/terms/charge/price/fee/rent/rental/fare

rate verb

1 [T] (not used in the progressive tenses) ■ How did you rate her speech?

assess • evaluate • judge • gauge

▶ rate/assess/evaluate/judge sb/sth **as** sth
▶ rate/assess/evaluate/judge sb/sth **on/according to** sth
▶ rate/assess/evaluate/judge/gauge **how...**

2 [T, usu. passive] (not used in the progressive tenses) ■ She is currently rated number two in the world.

rank • grade • place • put | fml order

▶ rate/rank/grade/order sb/sth **according to** sth
▶ rate/rank/place/put/order sb/sth **above/below** sb/sth
▶ rate/rank/grade/place/put sb/sth **in order of** sth

rather adv. (esp. BrE)

■ It's rather a difficult question.

fairly • reasonably • moderately • somewhat | esp. BrE quite | AmE or infml, BrE pretty

▶ rather/quite **a/an**...
▶ rather/fairly/reasonably/moderately/somewhat/quite/pretty **successful/high**
▶ rather/fairly/reasonably/moderately/quite/pretty **well**
▶ rather/fairly/reasonably/quite/pretty **good/large/common/pleased/confident/soon/quickly/easily**
▶ I rather/quite **like** sth

ratio noun [C]

■ What is the ratio of men to women in the department?

proportion • scale

▶ the ratio/proportion of A to B
▶ a ratio/scale **of** 1:25, etc.
▶ a **high/low** ratio/proportion

rational adj.

■ There is no rational explanation for his actions.

logical • reasoned • reasonable • valid • well founded • good • sound • solid • scientific • coherent

■ OPP irrational

▶ a rational/reasoned/reasonable/ valid/good/sound/scientific/ coherent **argument**
▶ a rational/reasoned/reasonable/ valid/good/sound/scientific/ coherent **explanation**
▶ rational/logical/reasoned/ scientific/coherent **thought**

raw adj.

■ These fish are often eaten raw.

uncooked

■ OPP cooked

▶ raw/uncooked **food/meat/fish/ eggs/vegetables**
● RAW OR UNCOOKED? Raw describes fresh food that is usu. eaten cooked, such as meat, fish, eggs and vegetables; uncooked is more often used to describe that has been prepared in some way but not yet cooked, such as pastry, dough or ham.

reach noun [U]

■ Victory is now out of her reach.
■ Such matters are beyond the reach of the law.

grasp • scope • range

▶ within the reach/grasp/scope/ range of sb/sth
▶ out of our reach/grasp
▶ beyond/outside the reach/ scope/range of sb/sth
▶ expand/extend/widen/limit/ narrow/restrict/define the reach/scope/range of sth

reach verb

1 [T] (esp. written) ■ It took them three hours to reach the shore.

arrive | esp. spoken get • make • make it | infml hit

▶ reach/arrive/get/make it here/ there/home
▶ reach/arrive at/get to/make it to your **destination**
▶ reach/get to/make/make it to the **summit**
▶ reach/arrive at/get to/make it to/ hit the **border**

2 [T] ■ Politicians again failed to reach an agreement.

arrive at sth • achieve • accomplish | BrE fulfil | AmE fulfill | infml pull sth off • get there | fml attain • effect

▶ reach/achieve/accomplish/fulfil/ attain a **goal/objective**
▶ reach/achieve/fulfil/attain a **target**
▶ reach/arrive at/achieve a/an **agreement/result**
▶ reach/pull off/attain a **deal**

3 [I, T] ■ Is the cable long enough to reach the power supply?

stretch • go • extend • lead

▶ reach/stretch/go/extend/lead **beyond/across** sth
▶ reach/stretch/go/extend/lead **from** sth **to** sth

react verb [I]

■ Local residents have reacted angrily to the news.

respond • take • receive • meet sth with sth | esp. written greet

▶ react/respond **by doing** sth
▶ react/respond/meet sth/greet sth **with anger**
▶ react/receive/meet sth/greet sth **with dismay**
▶ react/respond/take sth/receive sth **well/badly**
● REACT OR RESPOND? Respond often describes more detached, less emotional behaviour. Respond is used more frequently with adverbs like immediately, promptly and quickly; react is used more frequently with adverbs like angrily, violently and strongly.

reaction noun [C, U]

■ What was his reaction to the news?

response • reception • welcome • feedback

▶ a reaction/response/reception/ welcome **to** sth
▶ in reaction/response **to** sth
▶ (a/an) instant/negative/ appropriate reaction/response/ feedback
▶ give (sth)/get/have (a)... reaction/response/reception/ welcome/feedback
● REACTION OR RESPONSE? Your response is what you decide to do or say about it; your reaction is often less considered or is simply the feeling that sth produces in you: My immediate reaction was of one shock.

read verb [I, T]

■ Just read through what you've written.

scan • skim • look through sth • flick through sth • leaf through sth • dip into sth | BrE plough through sth | AmE plow through sth | fml peruse

▶ read/look through/flick through/ leaf through/dip into/plough through/peruse a **book**
▶ read/scan/skim/look through/ flick through/leaf through/peruse a **newspaper/paper**
▶ read/look through/plough through/peruse a **report**

ready *adj.* [not before noun]
■ *I'm just getting the kids ready for school.*

prepared • set • waiting

▶ ready / prepared / set / waiting for sb/sth
▶ ready / prepared / set / waiting to do sth

real *adj.*

1 [usu. before noun] ■ *It wasn't a ghost: it was a real person.* ■ *Her real name was Norma Jean Baker.*

true • actual • genuine • authentic | *BrE,* spoken **proper**

■ OPP **imaginary, pretend**
▶ a real / the true / the actual / a genuine / a proper **reason**
▶ the real / true / actual **cost** of sth
▶ a/an real / true / genuine / authentic **work of art**
● **REAL OR TRUE?** In many cases you can use either word: *You're a real / true friend.* • *He's a real / true gentleman.*
However, **real** looks at the necessary qualities of sth in a more practical way; **true** looks at those qualities in a more romantic way.

2 ■ *I had no real interest in politics.*

genuine • sincere • deep • heartfelt | *approv.* **wholehearted**

■ OPP **superficial**
▶ real / sincere / genuine / deep / heartfelt **sympathy / concern**
▶ real / sincere / genuine / deep **affection / respect / regret**
▶ a real / genuine / deep **sense** of sth

3 [only before noun] (*esp.* spoken) ■ *He looks like a real idiot.*

complete • total • utter • perfect | *esp.* spoken **absolute • positive** | *esp.* spoken, usu. disapprov. **downright**

▶ a/an real / complete / total / utter / absolute **disaster**
▶ a/an real / complete / total / absolute **mess**
▶ a real / complete / total **idiot**

realistic *adj.*

1 (*usu. approv.*) ■ *We have to be realistic about our chances.*

no-nonsense • matter-of-fact | *usu. approv.* **pragmatic • practical • down-to-earth • level-headed**

■ OPP **unrealistic**
▶ realistic / matter-of-fact / pragmatic / practical / down-to-earth **about** sth
▶ a realistic / non-nonsense / matter-of-fact / pragmatic / practical / down-to-earth / level-headed **approach**

▶ a realistic / pragmatic / practical **solution**

2 ■ *We must set realistic goals.*

possible • achievable • feasible • practical • workable | *esp.* busin. **viable**

■ OPP **unrealistic**
▶ be realistic / possible / feasible **to do** sth
▶ a realistic / feasible / practical / workable / viable **solution / policy / plan**
▶ a realistic / an achievable **goal / objective / target**

3 ■ *a realistic drawing of a horse*

authentic • lifelike

▶ look realistic / authentic / lifelike

reality *noun* [U]
■ *Outwardly she seemed confident but in reality was very nervous.*

fact • the truth • real life • the real world

■ OPP **fantasy**
▶ in reality / fact / real life / the real world
▶ face / accept / ignore reality / the fact / the truth

realize (*BrE also* **-ise**) *verb* [T] (not used in the progressive tenses)
■ *I didn't realize you were so unhappy.*

know • appreciate

▶ realize / know / appreciate **that...**
▶ realize / know / appreciate **what / how / why...**
▶ begin / come to realize / know / appreciate
● **REALIZE OR KNOW?** To realize sth means to become or be aware of it. To **know** sth is to be aware of it; **know** can mean 'become aware' if it happens in a single moment. However, if the process of becoming aware takes any time, use **realize**:
✔ *The moment I walked in the room I realized / knew something was wrong.* • *I soon / quickly / gradually realized my mistake.* ✗ *I soon / quickly / gradually knew my mistake.*

really *adv.* (*esp.* spoken)
■ *This is a really nice place.*

very • highly • quite • well • truly • extremely • desperately | *esp.* spoken **so** | *fml* **most**

▶ really / very / highly / quite / extremely / so **successful / intelligent / competitive / critical**
▶ really / very / quite / extremely / desperately / so / most **anxious / concerned / disappointed / unhappy / important**
▶ really / very / quite / truly / extremely / desperately / so **sorry**

● **REALLY, VERY OR SO?** Very is the most frequent and most neutral of these words. Really and so are more informal and can be stronger. Really and so can be used with both weak and strong adjectives; very is not used with strong adjectives:

✔ so/really/very good (= weak) • so/really wonderful (= strong) ✗ very wonderful

reason noun

1 [C, U] ■ I'd like to know the reason why you're so late.

explanation • motive • need • cause • grounds • basis • argument • case • excuse • justification • pretext

▶ (a/an) reason/explanation/motive/need/cause/grounds/basis/argument/case/excuse/justification/pretext for sth
▶ the reason/motive behind sth
▶ the reason/grounds/basis/argument/excuse/justification/pretext that...
▶ (a) good/valid reason/explanation/motive/cause/grounds/argument/case/excuse/justification
▶ give/offer (sb) a/an reason/explanation/excuse/justification/pretext

2 [U] ■ I can't get her to listen to reason.

logic • rationality • reasoning

▶ the reason/logic/rationality in sth
▶ see/defy reason/(the) logic

reasonable adj.

1 ■ It seems a perfectly reasonable request to make.

fair • just • plausible • equal • even-handed | fml equitable

■ **OPP** unreasonable
▶ be reasonable/fair/just/plausible/equitable that...
▶ be reasonable/fair/just to do sth
▶ a/an reasonable/fair/just/equal/equitable division/distribution/share of sth

2 ■ The furniture is in reasonable condition.

fair • acceptable • satisfactory • adequate • decent | esp. spoken all right • not bad | infml, esp. spoken OK

▶ be reasonable/fair/acceptable/satisfactory/all right/OK to do sth
▶ be reasonable/fair/acceptable/satisfactory/all right/OK that...
▶ a/an reasonable/fair/acceptable/satisfactory solution
▶ a/an reasonable/fair/acceptable/satisfactory/adequate/decent level/standard of sth

3 ■ We sell good quality food at reasonable prices.

affordable • inexpensive • economical • cheap | esp. busin. competitive

■ **OPP** unreasonable
▶ reasonable/affordable/economical/cheap/competitive prices/rates/fares
▶ affordable/inexpensive/economical/cheap/competitive products/services

reasoning noun [U]

■ Could you explain the reasoning behind this decision?

thinking • reason • logic • thought • reflection

▶ the reasoning/thinking/reasons/logic/thought behind sth
▶ reasoning/thinking/thought/reflections on sth
▶ a line of reasoning/thinking/thought

reassure verb [T]

■ The doctor reassured him that there was nothing seriously wrong.

put/set sb's mind at rest • encourage • cheer sb up • comfort

■ **OPP** alarm
▶ reassure sb/put sb's mind at rest/encourage sb/cheer sb up/comfort sb with sth
▶ reassure/comfort yourself/cheer yourself up
▶ do little/nothing/much to reassure sb/put sb's mind at rest

rebel verb [I]

■ The colonies rebelled against the king.

revolt • mutiny • fight • resist • defy • oppose • stand up to sb • go against sb/sth • disobey • flout | fml rise

▶ rebel/revolt/mutiny/fight/go/rise against sth
▶ rebel against/defy/disobey/flout authority
▶ the people rebel/revolt/resist sth/defy sb/rise
● **REBEL OR REVOLT?** Rebel often describes opposition to authority by people who already have some political power and does not always involve violence; revolt usu. describes the actions of ordinary people against unfair authority and nearly always involves violence: 136 MPs rebelled against the government's proposals. • The peasants revolted against high taxes and the losses of the war.

rebuild verb [T, I]

■ *After the earthquake, the people set about rebuilding their homes.*

reconstruct • reassemble • remodel • redevelop • renovate • restore • refurbish • redecorate • revamp

▶ rebuild/remodel/renovate/restore/refurbish/redecorate a **house**
▶ reconstruct/remodel/renovate/restore/refurbish a **building**
▶ remodel/renovate/redecorate a **room**

recall verb [T, I] (not used in the progressive tenses) (*fml*)

■ *I can't recall meeting her before.*

remember • look back • think back • bear sb/sth in mind • reminisce | *fml* recollect

■ OPP forget

▶ recall/remember/bear in mind/recollect **that...**
▶ recall/remember/bear in mind/recollect **how/what/where/when...**
▶ as far as I can recall/remember/recollect

receive verb

1 [T] (*esp. written*) ■ *I've just received this letter from an old friend.*

collect • accept | *esp. spoken* get | *esp. written* reap | *fml* derive sth from sth

▶ receive/collect/accept/get/reap/derive sth **from** sb/sth
▶ receive/collect/accept/get a/an **medal/award/prize**
▶ receive/collect/accept/get a/an **reply/letter/shock/impression/prison sentence**
● RECEIVE OR GET? Receive is a more formal word; get is the more usual word in spoken English. You can get or receive a sudden feeling such as a *shock* or an *impression*, but feelings that you experience over a period of time such as *enjoyment* and *satisfaction* you usu. get.

2 [T] (*esp. written*) ■ *Several passengers received severe injuries.*

have • take | *esp. spoken* get | *esp. written* suffer • experience • undergo

▶ receive/get/have/suffer an **injury**
▶ receive/get/have/suffer a/the **shock**
▶ receive/get/have/experience/undergo **treatment**
● RECEIVE OR SUFFER? You can receive or suffer an *injury*. Suffer gives more emphasis to the bad effects experienced.

3 [I] ■ *The play was well received by the critics.*

meet sth with sth • take • respond • react | *esp. written* greet

▶ receive sth/meet sth/react/greet sth **with dismay**
▶ receive/take sth/respond/react **well/badly**
▶ receive/respond/react/greet sth **coolly/enthusiastically**

recent adj. [usu. before noun]

■ *Recent developments have changed the situation.*

latest • new • current • present • modern • contemporary • modern-day • present-day

■ OPP long-standing

▶ recent/modern **times**/ the present time
▶ recent/current/present/contemporary/present-day **events**
▶ recent/the latest/current/present/modern/contemporary **trends**

reception noun

1 [U] (*esp. BrE*) ■ *We arranged to meet in reception at 6.30.*

lobby • foyer • entrance

▶ in reception/the lobby/the foyer/the entrance
▶ at reception
▶ (a) hotel reception/lobby/foyer

2 [C] ■ *The wedding reception was held at a local hotel.*

celebration • party • function • festivities • event • occasion | *infml* bash

▶ at a/an/the reception/celebration/party/function/festivities/event/bash
▶ (a) wedding reception/celebrations/party
▶ (a/an) reception/celebrations/party/function/festivities /event/bash **is/are held**

3 [U] ■ *The audience gave her a warm reception. ■ The town set up facilities for the reception of injured soldiers.*

welcome • response • reaction • feedback • hospitality | *esp. written* greeting

▶ a reception/a welcome/a response/a reaction/feedback/hospitality/a greeting **from** sb
▶ (a) **warm/friendly** reception/welcome/response/greeting/hospitality
▶ **give** sb (a) ...reception/welcome/response/reaction/feedback/hospitality
▶ **get/have** (a) ...reception/welcome/response/reaction/feedback

● RECEPTION OR WELCOME? A
reception is more likely than a
welcome to be described using
negative adjectives: *a lukewarm/
frosty/cool reception*

recession *noun* [C, U]

■ *These industries have been hit hard
by the recession.*

depression | *esp. busin.* **slump** +
slowdown + **trough**

■ OPP **boom, upturn**
► **in (a) recession/depression/
slump/trough**
► **a major/serious/severe
recession/depression/slump**
► **go into recession/depression/
slump**
● WHICH WORD? A **recession** affects a
whole industry or a country's
whole economy, and it can last for
years; a **slowdown**, **slump** or
trough might just describe one
particular business or industry and
might only last months.
Depression is sometimes used to
suggest the negative effects of
recession on ordinary people.

reckless *adj.* (*usu. disapprov.*)

■ *He showed a reckless disregard for
his own safety.*

irresponsible + **rash** + **hasty** +
careless | *esp. written* **foolish** +
unwise | *esp. AmE, infml* **crazy** | *esp.
BrE, infml* **mad**

■ OPP **cautious, responsible**
► **It can be reckless/irresponsible/
rash/foolish/unwise/crazy/mad
to do sth.**

reckon *verb*

1 [T, I] (not used in the progressive
tenses) (*esp. BrE, infml*) ■ *I reckon
(that) I'm going to get that job.*

think + **believe** + **feel** + **make sth of
sb/sth** + **be under the impression
that...** | *fml* **hold**

► **reckon/think/believe/feel/be
under the impression/hold that...**
► **It is reckoned/thought/believed
that...**
► **be reckoned/thought/believed/
felt/held to be sth**

2 [T, usu. passive] (not used in the
progressive tenses) (*esp. BrE, infml*)
■ *The show was generally reckoned a
success.*

consider + **regard** + **count** + **see** +
view + **call** + **describe** + **find**

► **be reckoned/considered/seen/
found to be sth**
► **reckon/consider that...**
► **reckon/consider/regard/count/
see/view/describe yourself (as)
sth**

3 [T, often passive] ■ *The age of the*

*earth is reckoned to be about 4.6
billion years.*

estimate + **judge** + **gauge** + **calculate**
+ **guess** | *fml* **extrapolate** | *esp. AmE,
infml* **figure**

► **reckon/estimate/calculate/judge
at sth**
► **reckon/estimate/judge/calculate/
guess/extrapolate/figure that...**
► **reckon/estimate/judge/gauge/
calculate/guess/figure sth to be
sth**

recognition *noun* [U]

■ *He received the award in recognition
of his success over the year.*

appreciation + **admiration** + **respect**
+ **acknowledgement** | *fml* **esteem**

► **recognition/admiration/respect
for sb**
► **do sth in recognition/
appreciation/admiration/
acknowledgement**
► **deserve recognition/admiration/
respect/acknowledgement**
► **win/gain recognition/admiration/
respect**

recognizable (*BrE also* -isable)
adj.

■ *Even after thirty years she was still
immediately recognizable.*

identifiable + **distinguishable**

■ OPP **unrecognizable**
► **recognizable/identifiable/
distinguishable as sb/sth**
► **recognizable/identifiable/
distinguishable by sth**
► **recognizable/identifiable to sb**
● RECOGNIZABLE OR IDENTIFIABLE?
People, places and things are
recognizable from experience,
because you have seen or heard
them before; places and things are
identifiable either from experience
or because you have studied them
or been told about them.

recognize (*BrE also* -ise) *verb*

1 [T] (not used in the progressive
tenses) ■ *I recognized him by the
way he walked.*

know + **identify** + **place** + **pick sb/sth
out** + **make sb/sth out** | *fml* **discern**

► **recognize/know/identify sb/sth
by sth**
► **recognize/identify sb/sth as sb/
sth**
► **recognize/know/identify/make
out/discern who/what/how...**
● RECOGNIZE OR KNOW? **Know** is used
esp. to talk about sounds, or when
sb recognizes the quality or
opportunity that sb/sth represents,
as in the phrase *sb knows a...when
they see one:*

✓*I know that voice/laugh/tune!* • *He knows a lady when he sees one.*
Recognize can also be used in this way but sounds slightly more formal. **Know** is not usu. used to talk about people:
✓*I recognized him as soon as he came in.* ✗ *I knew him as soon as he came in.*

2 [T] (not used in the progressive tenses) ■ *The directors recognize that there is a serious problem.*

3 [T] (not used in the progressive tenses) ■ *These qualifications are internationally recognized.*

approve • confirm • ratify • certify | *fml* **validate**

▶ recognize/approve/confirm/ratify/certify/validate sth **as** sth
▶ recognize/approve/validate a **course**
▶ **officially** recognize/approve/confirm/ratify sth

recommend *verb*

1 [T] ■ *Can you recommend a good hotel?*

suggest • nominate • endorse

▶ recommend/suggest/nominate sb/sth **for/as**
▶ recommend/suggest sb/sth **to** sb
▶ recommend/nominate **sb to do sth**

2 [T] ■ *He recommended reading the book before seeing the movie.*

advise • suggest • urge | *fml* **advocate • propose**

▶ recommend/advise/suggest/urge/advocate/propose **that...**
▶ It is recommended/advised/suggested/urged/advocated/proposed **that...**
▶ recommend/advise/urge **sb to do sth**
▶ recommend/advise/suggest/advocate **doing sth**
● **RECOMMEND OR ADVISE?** Advise is stronger than **recommend**. Use **advise** about sb in a position of authority:
✓*Police are advising fans without tickets to stay away.* ✗ *Police are recommending fans without tickets to stay away.*

Use **recommend** about possible benefits; use **advise** about possible dangers:
✓*I recommend reading the book before seeing the movie.* ✗ *I advise reading the book before seeing the movie.*
✓*I would advise against going out on your own.* ✗ *I would recommend against going out on your own.*

record *noun*

1 [C] ■ *You should keep a record of your expenses.*

log • minutes • diary • journal • blog

▶ **in** a/the record/log/minutes/diary/journal/blog
▶ a **daily** record/log/diary/journal/blog
▶ **keep** a record/log/diary/journal/blog

2 [sing.] ■ *The report criticizes the government's record on housing.*

track record • history • background • past

▶ sb has a record/track record/history/background **of** sth
▶ sb has a record/track record/background **in** sth
▶ a/an **proven/impressive/excellent/poor** record/track record

record *verb* [T]

■ *The discussion was recorded in detail in his diary.*

document • chart • log • register • enter • *esp. BrE* **minute**

▶ record/document/log/register/enter/minute sth **as** sth
▶ record/document/register/enter sth **in**
▶ record/document/chart **how...**
▶ record/document/minute **that...**

recover *verb*

1 [I] ■ *He's still recovering from his operation.*

get better • get well • heal • survive • pull through • make it • shake sth off • come through (sth) | *fml* **recuperate • convalesce**

■ OPP **relapse**

▶ recover/recuperate **from** sth
▶ **gradually** recover/get better/heal
▶ **completely/partially** recover/heal

2 [T] ■ *The police eventually recovered the stolen paintings.*

get sth back • reclaim • regain | *fml* **recoup • retrieve**

▶ recover sth/get sth back/reclaim/recoup/retrieve sth **from** sb/sth
▶ recover/get back/reclaim/recoup/retrieve your **money**

▶ recover/get back/reclaim/regain **the lead**

▶ recover/regain **consciousness**

recruit noun [C]

■ All army recruits are trained in first aid.

trainee • apprentice • cadet | *AmE* intern | *esp. AmE, infml* rookie

▶ a young/19-year-old recruit/trainee/apprentice/cadet/intern/rookie

▶ train a recruit/an apprentice

reduce verb [T]

■ Costs have been reduced by 20% over the past year.

cut • lower • cut sth back/cut back on sth • cut sth down/cut down on sth • bring sth down • discount • minimize • turn sth down | *fml* decrease | *esp. AmE or busin.* scale sth back | *journ.* slash

■ **OPP** increase

▶ reduce/cut/lower/cut back/cut down/bring down/decrease/scale back/slash sth **from** 100 **to** 75

▶ reduce/cut/lower/cut back/cut down/bring down/discount/decrease/scale back/slash sth **by** half, 50, etc.

▶ reduce/cut/lower/cut back (on)/cut down (on)/bring down/minimize/decrease/slash the **number/amount/level/cost** of sth

reduction noun [C, U]

■ This year has seen a 33% reduction in the number of hospital beds available.

cut • fall • decline • drop • cutback • discount • downturn • slump | *fml* decrease

■ **OPP** increase

▶ a reduction/cut/fall/decline/drop/cutback/downturn/slump/decrease **in** sth

▶ a reduction/cut/fall/decline/drop/cutback/discount/decrease **of** 20%

▶ see a reduction/fall/decline/drop/downturn/decrease

● REDUCTION OR CUT? Reduction can be used for things that become less or smaller by themselves, or things that are reduced deliberately by sb. A **cut** is usu. a negative thing and happens at one point in time; a **reduction** can be gradual:

✓job/salary/pay cuts • a gradual reduction in output ✗ a gradual cut in output

reference noun

1 [C, U] ■ In an obvious reference to

the president, she talked of corruption in high places.

mention | *infml* quote | *fml* allusion • quotation • citation

▶ in a reference/an allusion **to** sb/sth

▶ make no reference to/mention of sb/sth

▶ be full of references/allusions to sth

● REFERENCE OR MENTION? Reference is usu. countable; the uncountable form is mostly used in fixed expressions in formal writing. Mention is more often uncountable; the countable form can be slightly informal, as in the phrase *get a mention*.

2 [C] ■ You should supply a reference from your current employer.

recommendation • testimonial • endorsement

▶ a/an reference/recommendation/testimonial/endorsement **from** sb

▶ a reference/an endorsement **for** sb/sth

▶ a glowing reference/testimonial/recommendation/endorsement

● REFERENCE OR RECOMMENDATION? Reference is the usual word for a letter written by sb to say that another person is suitable for sth such as a new job. A reference can be from a former employer or other suitable person, but a recommendation is usu. from a former employer.

refer to sb/sth phrasal verb

1 ■ I promised not to refer to the matter again.

mention • speak • quote | *fml* allude to sb/sth • cite

▶ refer to/mention/speak of/quote/allude to/cite sb/sth **as** sb/sth

▶ refer to/mention/quote/cite a/an **example/case/instance** of sth

2 ■ This paragraph refers to the events of last year.

apply • relate to sb/sth • deal with sth • concern • be concerned with • be about sth • have/be to do with sth • treat

▶ a rule/law refers to/applies to/relates to/deals with/concerns sth

▶ a chapter/poem refers to/deals with/is concerned with/is about sth

▶ specifically/directly refer to/apply to/relate to/deal with/be concerned with/be about/have to do with sth

3 ■ Please refer to the Food Guide for nutrition recommendations.

look sth up • consult

▶ refer to/consult a **dictionary**/
guide/**map**/**timetable**/**website**
▶ refer to/consult your **notes**
● **WHICH WORD? Look sth up** is
slightly informal. The object of
look sth up is the information you
want to find, rather than the place
where you look: *Please refer to/
consult the Help file for further
information.* • *Try looking it up on
the Internet.*

reform verb [T, I]

■ *The president has promised to reform
the welfare system.*

**overhaul • improve • fix •
reorganize • reshape • revise •
revamp • make sth over** | *esp. journ.*
shake sth up

▶ reform/overhaul/improve/fix/
reorganize/reshape/revamp/
shake up a **system**
▶ reform/overhaul/fix/reorganize/
reshape/revamp the **economy**
▶ reform/overhaul/revise the **law**

refuge noun [C]

■ *He regarded his room as a refuge
from the demands of the outside
world.* ■ *The marshes are a wetland
refuge for seabirds.*

**shelter • sanctuary • hiding place •
hideout • haven • retreat • safe
house**

▶ a refuge/sanctuary/hiding place/
haven/retreat from the **demands**
▶ a **secret** refuge/hiding place/
hideout/retreat
▶ an **animal** refuge/shelter/
sanctuary
▶ a **mountain** refuge/hideout/
retreat

refugee noun [C]

■ *There has been a steady flow of
refugees from the war zone.*

**asylum seeker • exile • evacuee •
immigrant • migrant • expatriate •
emigrant**

▶ a **political** refugee/asylum seeker/
exile
▶ refugees/asylum seekers/exiles/
evacuees/migrants/emigrants/
expatriates **return**
▶ a **flow/flood of** refugees/
immigrants/migrants/emigrants

refusal noun [U, C]

■ *There was no reason given for the
refusal of the application.*

rejection • denial • veto • no | *fml*
rebuff

■ **OPP agreement, acceptance,
consent**

▶ a refusal/rejection/no/rebuff from
sb
▶ a refusal/rejection/veto/rebuff **by**
sb
▶ **receive/be met with** a refusal/
rejection/rebuff

refuse verb [I, T]

■ *The government has refused all
demands for a public inquiry.*

**reject • turn sb/sth down • veto •
throw sb out** | *fml* **decline • deny •
disallow** | *fml, often disapprov.* **rebuff**

■ **OPP agree, accept**
▶ refuse/reject/turn down/veto/
throw out/decline a **proposal**
▶ refuse/reject/turn down/decline/
rebuff a/an **offer/request**
▶ refuse/reject/turn down/decline
a/an **chance/opportunity/
invitation**
▶ refuse/deny sb **access to** sth

regard verb [T] (not used in the
progressive tenses)

■ *I came to regard him as a friend.*

**consider • see • view • look at sb/
sth • count • call • think** | *esp. BrE,
infml* **reckon**

▶ regard/consider/see/view/look
at/count/call/think of sb/sth **as**
sth
▶ regard/consider/see/view/look at
sb/sth **from** a particular point of
view
▶ regard/see/view/look at sb/sth
with sth

● **REGARD OR CONSIDER?** In this
meaning **consider** must be used
with a complement or clause. You
can *consider sb/sth as sth/to be sth.*
Often the *to be* or *as* is left out:
✓*They are considered a high-risk
group.*
You can *regard sb/sth as sth* but not
to be sth, and as cannot be left out:
✓*I regard him as a friend.* ✗ *I regard
him to be a friend.* • *I regard him a
friend.*

region noun [C]

■ *Soil erosion is particularly serious in
dry tropical regions.*

**area • part • zone • climate • belt •
district • province**

▶ (a/an) **eastern/northern/
southern/western** region/area/
parts/zone/district/province
▶ the **whole/entire** region/area/
zone/district/province
▶ a **border/coastal** region/area/
zone/district/province
● **REGION OR AREA?** A **region** refers to
a large area of a country or
continent, esp. in terms of its
geographical, political or economic
importance. **Area** has a wide range
of meaning and can refer to a part

of sth as large as a continent or smaller than a room.

register noun [C]

■ Could you sign the hotel register, please?

list • listing • roll • index • directory • catalogue • inventory

▶ in a/an register/list/listing/index/directory/catalogue/inventory
▶ on a/an register/list/roll/inventory
▶ compile a/an list/listing/index/directory/inventory
▶ keep a/an register/list/index/inventory

register verb [T, I]

■ All students must be registered with a local doctor. ■ The company's logo has been registered as a trademark.

record • enter • log | esp. BrE enrol | AmE usu. enroll

▶ register/record/enter/log/enrol sb/sth as sth
▶ register/record/enter/enrol sb/sth in sth
▶ register/record/enter/log the details of sth

regret noun

1 [U, C] ■ He gave up teaching in 2007, much to the regret of his students.

disappointment • sadness • unhappiness • grief | fml sorrow | lit. melancholy

■ OPP satisfaction, happiness
▶ regret/disappointment/sadness/unhappiness/grief/sorrow/melancholy at/about/over sth
▶ regret/sadness/grief/sorrow for sth
▶ to your regret/disappointment/grief/sorrow
▶ with regret/sorrow/sadness

2 [U, C] ■ She expressed deep regret at the incident.

remorse • shame • guilt | fml, esp. religion repentance

■ OPP pride
▶ regret/remorse/shame/guilt at sth
▶ regret/remorse/repentance for sth
▶ feel (no) regret/remorse/shame/guilt

regret verb [T, I] (fml, esp. written)

■ The airline regrets any inconvenience.

apologize | esp. BrE, fml, spoken beg sb's pardon

▶ regret/apologize that…
▶ apologize/beg sb's pardon for sth
▶ apologize/beg sb's pardon if…
● REGRET OR BEG SB'S PARDON? Regret is used in writing and in formal

announcements, esp. on behalf of a company or organization; beg sb's pardon is also formal but it is more personal, used by an individual speaking to another individual.

regular adj.

1 ■ A light flashed at regular intervals.

steady • even • constant • consistent | usu. approv. stable

■ OPP irregular
▶ a regular/steady/constant supply
▶ regular/steady/even breathing
▶ (a) regular/steady/stable relationship/employment
● REGULAR OR STEADY? Both these words can be used to describe a job, work, employment, an income, the supply of sth or a relationship that continues for a long time and that you can rely on. A regular job is sometimes used in contrast to another job that is not regular:
✓I decided to give up the freelance work and concentrate on my regular job. ✗ I decided to concentrate on my steady job.
✓If you want money, get a regular/steady job.

2 ■ There were regular disputes over boundaries. ■ They have been regular customers for many years.

frequent • habitual • continual • repeated • recurrent • periodic

■ OPP irregular
▶ regular/frequent/habitual/continual/repeated use
▶ regular/frequent/continual/repeated/recurrent attacks
▶ a regular/frequent visitor
▶ a regular/habitual drinker/offender
● REGULAR OR FREQUENT? Use regular in more active examples, when you are talking about people doing things, rather than things that happen:
✓Eat a healthy diet and take regular exercise. ✗ Take frequent exercise.

regulate verb [T]

■ The activities of credit companies are regulated by law.

police • supervise • oversee | fml administer • superintend

▶ regulate/supervise/oversee/administer the affairs of sb/sth
▶ be properly/effectively regulated/policed/supervised/administered

regulation noun

1 [C, usu. pl.] ■ It's against safety regulations to drink in the laboratory.

rule • law • act • statute

- ▶ the regulations/rules/laws **on** sth
- ▶ **under/within** the regulations/rules/act/statute
- ▶ **against** the regulations/rules/law

2 [U] ■ *There are calls for tighter regulation of the industry.*

supervision • administration • management • government

- ▶ regulation/supervision **by** sb
- ▶ **effective** regulation/supervision/administration/management/government
- ▶ **be responsible for** the regulation/supervision/administration/management of sth

rein noun [C, usu. pl.]
■ *She pulled gently on the reins.*

bridle • halter • harness • tether | *esp. AmE* leash | *BrE* lead

- ▶ **pull on** the reins/leash/lead
- ▶ **attach** a halter/harness/leash/lead

reject verb
1 [T] ■ *He urged the committee to reject the plans.*

refuse • turn sb/sth down • veto • throw sth out | *fml* decline • deny • disallow | *written, often disapprov.* rebuff

- ■ OPP **approve, accept**
- ▶ reject/refuse/turn down/veto/throw out/decline a **proposal**
- ▶ reject/refuse/turn down/decline/rebuff an/a an **offer/request**
- ▶ reject/refuse/turn down/decline an/a an **chance/opportunity/invitation**
- ▶ reject/refuse/turn down/veto/decline/disallow an **application**

2 [T] ■ *The lioness rejected the smallest cub, which died.*

disown • turn your back on sb/sth • disinherit • wash your hands of sb/sth

- ■ OPP **accept**
- ▶ His **father/family** rejected/disowned/disinherited him.
- ▶ Her **friends/mother** rejected/disowned her.

relate verb [T]
■ *Pay increases will be related to productivity.*

connect • associate • link • match

- ▶ relate/connect/link/match sth **to** sth
- ▶ connect/associate/link/match sth **with** sth
- ▶ relate/connect/associate/link/match (sth) **directly**
- ● RELATE, CONNECT OR ASSOCIATE?

When you **associate** two things in your mind, it just happens, often because of experiences you have already had. When you **relate** or **connect** two things in your mind, it requires more of an effort because the connection is not so obvious or natural to you:

✓ *I always associate the smell of baking with my childhood.* ✗ ~~I always relate/connect the smell of baking with my childhood.~~

✓ *I found it hard to relate/connect the two ideas in my mind.* ✗ ~~I found it hard to associate the two ideas in my mind.~~

related adj.
■ *Much of the crime is related to drug abuse.*

connected • resulting • consequent | *esp. busin.* associated | *fml* attendant • resultant

- ■ OPP **unrelated**
- ▶ connected/associated **with** sth
- ▶ related/resulting/consequent/associated/attendant/resultant **problems/changes**
- ▶ related/consequent/associated/attendant/resultant **costs/effects**
- ▶ **closely** related/connected/associated
- ● RELATED OR ASSOCIATED? Related often describes more general things; associated is used esp. in business contexts and to talk about risks: *a related issue/question/problem/field/area/matter/theme • the risks associated with taking drugs*

relate to sb/sth phrasal verb
1 (not used in the progressive tenses)
■ *The second paragraph relates to the situation in Scotland.*

refer to sb/sth • have/be to do with sth • concern • be concerned wth sth • apply • be about sth • deal with sth • treat

- ▶ a rule/law relates to/refers to/concerns/applies to/deals with sth
- ▶ **specifically/directly** relate to/refer to/have to do with/be concerned with/apply to/be about/deal with sth

2 (not used in the progressive tenses)
■ *Many adults can't relate to children.*

identify with sb/sth • empathize • understand

- ▶ **can/could/be able to/be unable to** relate to/identify with/empathize with/understand sb/sth
- ● RELATE TO SB/STH OR IDENTIFY WITH SB/STH? Relate to sb/sth is often used to talk about personal relationships between people who

actually know each other. **Identify with sb/sth** often describes people's positive feelings towards characters in a book or film or famous people: *He's a successful and popular teacher because he really relates to the children.* • *Which character do you identify with most, the father or his son?*

relation noun [U, C]

■ *Its brain is small in relation to its body.*

relationship • connection • link • association • correlation | *fml* interdependence

▶ the relation/relationship/ connection/link/association/ correlation/interdependence **between** A and B
▶ the relation/relationship of A to B
▶ a **close/significant/direct/clear/ strong/definite/possible** relation/relationship/connection/ link/association/correlation
▶ **have/find/show/examine** a/an/ the relation/relationship/ connection/link/association/ correlation

relationship noun

1 [C, U] ■ *I have a good working relationship with my boss.*

relations • partnership • bond • rapport • tie • link • association | *esp. busin.* contact

▶ (a/an) relationship/relations/ partnership/bond/rapport/ties/ link/association/contacts **with** sb/ sth
▶ (a/an) relationship/relations/ partnership/bond/rapport/ties/ links/association **between** A and B
▶ (a) **close** relationship/relations/ partnership/bond/rapport/ties/ links/association/contacts
▶ **have/develop** (a/an) relationship/relations/ partnership/bond/rapport/ties/ links/association/contacts
● **RELATIONSHIP OR RELATIONS?** **Relations** is often used to talk about how good or bad the relationship between people, groups or countries is: *strained/ difficult/cordial/harmonious/ improved relations*
Relationships are often more personal than **relations**: *international/race/cultural relations* • *interpersonal/one-to-one/parent- child relationships*

2 [C] ■ *He was not married but he was in a stable relationship.*

romance • affair • love affair | *fml* liaison

▶ a/an relationship/romance/affair/ love affair/liaison **with** sb

▶ a/an relationship/romance/affair/ love affair/liaison **between** A and B
▶ a **brief/long/passionate** relationship/romance/affair/love affair
▶ **have** a/an relationship/romance/ affair/love affair/liaison

relative noun [C]

■ *She cares for an elderly relative.*

relation • family • connections | *fml* kin

▶ (a) **close/near/distant/female/ male** relative/relation/kin
▶ **have/stay with/visit** relatives/ relations/family
▶ **friends and** relatives/relations/ family
● **RELATIVE OR RELATION?** **Relative** is often used when the exact relationship is not known or does not matter; **relation** is often used when stating or asking the degree of relationship between people: *On his death the house will pass to the nearest surviving relative.* • *What relation is Rita to you?*

relative adj.

■ *You must consider the relative merits of the two plans.*

comparative • respective • corresponding • comparable • proportional | *fml* proportionate • analogous

▶ relative/comparative/ corresponding/comparable/ proportional/proportionate/ analogous **to** sth
▶ a relative/corresponding/ comparable/proportional/ proportionate **increase**
▶ relative/comparative/comparable **size**

relax verb

1 [I] ■ *Just relax and enjoy the movie.*

unwind • take it/things easy • sit back • put your feet up • rest | *infml* chill (out) • hang out | *BrE* potter | *AmE* putter

▶ **try to/help sb (to)** relax/unwind/ rest
▶ **just** relax/unwind/take it easy/sit back/rest/hang out/potter/putter

2 [I] ■ *Relax! Everything will be OK.*

calm down • cool • pull yourself together

▶ **calm/cool down**
▶ **things** calm down/cool off
● **RELAX OR CALM DOWN?** People can **relax**; people or a situation can **calm down**. To **relax** is to stop feeling worried. **Calm down** is more about behaviour than

feelings: you may still feel worried but you manage to behave in a calm way.

3 [I, T] ■ *He relaxed his grip on her arm.*

loosen • slacken • release

■ OPP tighten, tense
► relax/loosen/slacken/release your grip/hold
► relax/loosen/slacken your grip/hold
► loosen/slacken a knot/tie/belt

relaxed *adj.*

1 ■ *She appeared relaxed and confident before the match.*

calm • cool • composed • unfazed • unperturbed • easy-going • laid-back • placid

■ OPP nervous, agitated
► relaxed/calm/cool/easy-going/laid-back about sth
► unfazed/unperturbed by sth
► a/an relaxed/calm/cool/easy-going/laid-back manner
● RELAXED, CALM OR COOL? Relaxed describes how you feel about sth. Cool is used more to describe how sb behaves when they don't let their feelings affect their behaviour. Calm can describe feelings or behaviour.

2 ■ *It's a family-run hotel with a relaxed atmosphere.*

informal • casual

■ OPP formal
► a relaxed/an informal atmosphere
► informal/casual dress

3 ■ *I take a relaxed attitude towards what the kids wear to school.*

sometimes disapprov. casual | disapprov. offhand • blasé

► relaxed/casual/offhand/blasé about sth
► a relaxed/casual/blasé attitude

release *verb*

1 [T] ■ *The kidnappers have agreed to release the hostages by 12 noon.*

free • set sb/sth free • let sb go • liberate • ransom • let sb/sth loose | *fml* emancipate

■ OPP imprison
► release/free/set free/liberate/emancipate sb from sth
► release/free/set free/let go/liberate/ransom a prisoner/hostage
► release/free an animal/a bird into the wild
● RELEASE, FREE OR SET SB/STH FREE? Free emphasizes the decision to let sb go; release emphasizes the physical act of letting sb go. Set

sb/sth free is often used when sb/sth is freed by force, not authority: *Rioters stormed the prison and set all the prisoners free.*

2 [T] ■ *Firefighters took two hours to release the driver from the wreckage.* ■ *He refused to release her arm.*

free • let (sb/sth) go • cut • disentangle | *fml* disengage

► release/free/cut/disentangle/disengage sb/sth from sth
► release/free/disentangle/disengage **yourself** from sth
► release/free/let go of/disentangle/disengage your/sb's **arm/hand**

3 [T] ■ *Police have released no further details about the accident.*

issue • publish • print • publicize • circulate

► release/issue/publish/print/circulate a **report/details**
► release/issue/publish/print a **document/statement/description**
► release/issue/publish a new **title/edition**

relevant *adj.*

■ *These comments are not directly relevant to this inquiry.*

applicable | *approv.* to the point | *fml* pertinent | *fml or law* material

■ OPP irrelevant
► relevant/applicable/pertinent/material **to/for** sb/sth
► relevant/pertinent **to do** sth
► a relevant/pertinent/material **point/fact/factor**

reliable *adj.*

1 (often approv.) ■ *We are looking for someone who is reliable and hard-working.*

responsible • trustworthy • dedicated • committed • loyal • faithful • true • staunch • trusted

■ OPP unreliable
► a reliable/trustworthy/loyal/faithful/true/staunch/trusted **friend**
► a reliable/committed/loyal/faithful/staunch **supporter**
► reliable/trustworthy/dedicated/committed/trusted **staff**

2 ■ *These tests are a reliable indicator for future performance.*

authoritative • accurate • verifiable • factual • authentic

■ OPP unreliable
► a/an reliable/authoritative/accurate/factual/authentic **account** (of sth)
► reliable/authoritative/accurate/verifiable/factual **information**

► reliable/authoritative/verifiable/
factual **evidence**
► a/an reliable/authoritative/
verifiable/authentic **source** (of
information)

relief noun

1 [U, sing.] ■ We all breathed a sigh of
relief when he came back safely.

reassurance + **comfort** + **consolation**

► a relief/comfort/consolation **to** sb
► relief/reassurance/comfort/
consolation **in** sth
► **seek/find/bring/offer** (sb) relief/
reassurance/comfort/consolation

2 [U] ■ We raised £5 000 for famine
relief.

aid + **help** + **charity** + **welfare** |
sometimes disapprov. **handout**

► relief/aid/charity/welfare/help/
handouts **for** sb
► **immediate/direct/emergency/
medical/financial** relief/aid/help
► **get/receive** relief/aid/help/
charity/welfare/handouts
► **provide/send/promise** relief/aid/
help

● **RELIEF OR AID?** **Aid** is used esp. to
talk about money given to
countries in financial need. **Relief**
refers to money, medicine, food,
etc. given in response to a sudden
emergency such as a war or natural
disaster.

religion noun [U, C]

■ Is there always a conflict between
science and religion?

faith + **theology** + **Church** + **sect** | *fml*
denomination | *often disapprov.* **cult**

► a **religious** faith/sect/cult
► **practise** your religion/faith
► **belong to** a the Church/sect/
denomination/cult

religious adj. [only before noun]
■ religious beliefs/faith

sacred + **holy** + **theological**

■ OPP **secular**
► religious/sacred **music/art**
► a sacred/holy **shrine/temple/
relic/river/book/thing**

reluctant adj.

■ She was reluctant to admit she was
wrong.

unwilling + **grudging**

■ OPP **eager**
► reluctant/unwilling **to do** sth
► reluctant/unwilling/grudging
acceptance
► (a) reluctant/grudging
admiration/admission

rely on/upon sb/sth *phrasal
verb*

■ Can I rely on you to keep this secret?

depend on/upon sb/sth + **trust** +
count on sb/sth + **have confidence
in sb/sth** + **pin your hopes on sb/sth**
+ **believe in sb** | *sometimes disapprov.*
take sb/sth for granted

► rely on/depend on/trust/count on
sb **to do** sth
► rely on/trust/have confidence/
believe in **yourself**
► rely on/trust/have confidence in
sb's **judgement**
► rely on/depend on/count on sb's
support

● **RELY ON/UPON SB/STH, DEPEND ON/
UPON SB/STH OR TRUST?** You can
trust a person, but not a thing or a
system:
✓The local transport system can't be
relied/depended on. ✗ The local
transport system can't be trusted.
Rely on is used esp. with *you can/
could* or *you should* to give advice
or a promise:
✓You can't really rely on his
judgement. ✗ I don't really rely on his
judgement.

remain verb

1 [I, T] (not usu. used in the
progressive tenses) (*fml*) ■ For a
long time he remained motionless.

stay + **keep** + **be left** + **stand** + **last** |
esp. written **continue** + **live** | *written*
linger

► remain/stay/keep **awake/calm/
cheerful/cool/dry/fine/healthy/
quiet/silent**
► remain/stay **alert/asleep/
loyal/safe/the same/a secret/
shut/sober/upright**
► sb's **memory** remains/lives (on)/
lingers

2 [I] (usu. used with an adv. or prep.)
(*fml*) ■ They remained in Mexico
until June.

stay | *esp. written* **linger** | *infml* **hang
around** + **stick around** + **stay put** |
BrE, infml **stop** | *sometimes disapprov.*
loiter

► remain/stay/linger/hang around/
stick around/stop **for a few
minutes/weeks/years**, etc.
► remain/stay/linger/hang around/
stick around/stop **here**
► remain/stay/stop **at home/
indoors/behind**

remains noun

1 [pl.] ■ the remains of a sandwich

remnant + **scraps** + **leftover**

► remains/remnants/scraps/
leftovers **from/of** sth

▶ the **last** remains/remnants/scraps

● **REMAINS OR REMNANTS?** Remains is
used esp. to describe what is left of
sth that has been mostly eaten or
burnt; **remnant** is mostly used to
describe much larger things that
have become smaller, either in the
course of history or because of
some great event: *the remains of a
meal/breakfast/lunch • the remnants
of a forest/an empire/an army*

2 [pl.] ■ *The museum has an
impressive collection of prehistoric
remains.*

ruin/ruins • wreckage • wreck • rubble • debris

▶ the remains/ruins/wreckage/
wreck **of** a building/vehicle, etc.
▶ **in/amid/among/amongst** the
remains/ruins/wreckage/rubble/
debris
▶ **ancient/Roman** remains/ruins

remark noun [C]

■ *He made a number of rude remarks
about the food.*

comment • statement • declaration | fml observation

▶ a/an remark/comment/
statement/declaration/
observation **about** sth
▶ a **casual** remark/comment/
observation
▶ **make** a/an remark/comment/
statement/declaration/
observation
● **REMARK, COMMENT OR
OBSERVATION?** A **comment** can be
official or private. An **observation**
may be more considered than a
remark, but both are always
unofficial.

remark verb [I, T]

■ *Critics remarked that the play was
not original.*

comment | fml observe • note

▶ remark/comment **on** sth
▶ remark/comment/observe **to** sb
▶ remark/comment/observe/note
that...
▶ remark/comment/observe/
note **how...**
● **REMARK, COMMENT OR OBSERVE?**
You can only use **refuse to** with
comment:
✔*He refused to comment until after
the trial.* ✗ *He refused to remark/
observe until after the trial.*

remarkable adj.

■ *The interior of the house was
remarkable for its beauty.*

exceptional • unique • extraordinary • phenomenal • amazing • astonishing • miraculous | infml incredible • unbelievable • staggering • stunning | written unusual

■ **OPP** unremarkable

▶ a/an remarkable/exceptional/
unique/extraordinary/
phenomenal/amazing/
astonishing/incredible/staggering
achievement
▶ a/an remarkable/extraordinary/
phenomenal/amazing/
astonishing/miraculous/
incredible/stunning/unusual
success
▶ remarkable/exceptional/unique/
extraordinary/astonishing/
incredible/unbelievable/stunning
beauty

remember verb [T, I] (not usu. used in the progressive tenses)

■ *This is Carla. Do you remember her?*

bear sb/sth in mind • look back • think back • reminisce | fml recall • recollect

■ **OPP** forget

▶ remember/bear in mind/recall/
recollect **that...**
▶ remember/bear in mind/recall/
recollect **how/what/where/
when...**
▶ remember/bear in mind/recall the
facts

remind sb of sb/sth phrasal verb (not used in the progressive tenses)

■ *You remind me of your dad when you
say that.*

take sb back • conjure sth up | written evoke | fml recall

▶ remind sb of/take sb back to/
conjure up/evoke/recall **the past/
past times**
▶ conjure up/evoke a/an **memory/
picture/image/feeling**
▶ **vividly** remind sb of sth/conjure
sth up/evoke sth

remove verb

1 [T] ■ *Remove the pan from the heat.*

take • strip

■ **OPP** replace

▶ remove/take/strip sth **from** sb/sth
▶ **simply/easily/quickly/carefully/
forcibly/illegally** remove/take/strip

2 [T] ■ *She removed her glasses and
rubbed her eyes.*

take sth off • strip • undress • get undressed

■ **OPP** put sth on

▶ remove/take off/strip off your

clothes/jacket/coat/shirt/
sweater/jeans/gloves

3 [T] ■ *What is the best way to remove grease stains?*

get rid of sb/sth • eliminate • dispose of sb/sth | *fml* **discard**

▶ remove/get rid of/eliminate sth **from** sth
▶ remove/get rid of/eliminate/ dispose of/discard **waste**
▶ remove/get rid of/eliminate/ dispose of a **problem**

4 [T] ■ *After his arrest he was immediately removed as party president.*

overthrow • bring sb/sth down | *written* **oust • depose** | *fml* **usurp** | *esp. journ.* **topple**

▶ remove/oust/depose sb **as** leader, chairman, etc.
▶ remove/oust sb **from power**
▶ remove/overthrow/bring down/ oust/depose/topple a **president/ regime/government**

reorganize (*BrE* also **-ise**) *verb* [T, I]

■ *The laboratory was reorganized as a separate establishment.*

rearrange • reshape • redesign • reshuffle • reform | *esp. busin.* **restructure** | *esp. journ.* **shake sth up**

▶ reorganize/reshape/redesign/ reform/restructure a **system**
▶ reorganize/reshape/reshuffle/ reform/restructure the **government**
▶ reorganize/restructure a **company**

repair *noun* [C, usu. pl., U]

■ *Janet took her bike in for repair.*

maintenance • service • upkeep | *esp. BrE* **servicing**

▶ essential/car maintenance/servicing
▶ take sth in for repair/a service
▶ sb is responsible for repairs/the maintenance/the upkeep of sth
▶ repair/maintenance/servicing **costs/work**

repair *verb*

1 [T] ■ *We need to get the roof repaired.*

fix • patch sth up • overhaul • patch | *esp. BrE* **mend**

▶ repair/fix/mend a **road/fence/ roof/fault/puncture**
▶ repair/fix a **car/television/fault/ defect/leak**
▶ repair/patch/mend **shoes/clothes**
▶ have/get sth **repaired/fixed/ overhauled/mended**
● **REPAIR OR FIX?** The most general word in *BrE* is **repair**. **Fix** is less formal and used to talk about

repairing machines and equipment. In *AmE* **fix** is the usual word to talk about repairing sth that is damaged or broken, and **repair** sounds rather formal.

2 [T] ■ *They moved quickly to repair relations between the two countries.*

mend • patch sth up • resolve • straighten sth out | *esp. BrE, esp. spoken* **sort sth out • sort**

▶ repair/mend/patch up a **rift/the damage/relations**
▶ resolve/straighten out/sort out a **problem/situation**
▶ repair/mend/patch up/resolve/ straighten out/sort out/sort **things**

repay *verb* [T]

■ *He lost his job and was unable to repay his debts.*

pay sb back (sth) • pay sth back • refund • compensate | *fml* **reimburse**

▶ repay/pay sb back/refund/ compensate/reimburse sb **for** sth
▶ repay/pay sb back/refund sth **to** sb
▶ repay/pay back/refund/reimburse **money**
● **REPAY OR PAY SB BACK?** Repay is used in more formal English and more formal situations than **pay sb back**.

repeat *verb*

1 [T] ■ *I can only repeat what I've already told you.*

fml **reiterate • restate** | *esp. written* **echo**

▶ repeat/reiterate/restate **that...**
▶ repeat/reiterate/echo a **warning/ sentiment**
▶ repeat/reiterate a **request**

2 [T, I] ■ *Try not to repeat your mistakes.*

redo • duplicate • reproduce | *fml* **replicate**

▶ repeat/reproduce/replicate the **results**
▶ merely/simply repeat/duplicate/ reproduce/replicate sth
▶ repeat/duplicate/reproduce/ replicate sth **exactly**

3 [T] ■ *Don't repeat a word of this to anyone.*

pass sth on • tell • relay • convey • communicate

▶ repeat/pass on/relay/convey/ communicate sth **to** sb
▶ repeat/tell/relay/convey/ communicate (to) sb **that...**
▶ repeat/tell/relay/convey/ communicate (to) sb **what...**

▸ repeat/relay/convey/communicate a **message**

4 [T] ■ *Listen and repeat the sentence after me.*

say • recite • quote

▸ repeat/say/recite/quote a **line**
▸ repeat/recite/quote a **passage**

replace verb

1 [T] ■ *She replaced her husband as the local doctor.*

stand in for sb/sth • substitute for sb/sth • cover for sb/sth • relieve | *esp. AmE* **fill in for sb/sth |** *fml* **deputize**

▸ stand in/substitute/cover/fill in/deputize **for** sb
▸ replace/stand in for/cover for/fill in for a **colleague**

2 [T] ■ *They had to replace the old carpets.*

change • substitute • switch • swap/swop • exchange

▸ replace/change/substitute A **with** B
▸ change/substitute/switch/swap/exchange B **for** A
▸ replace/change a **battery/bulb/fuse/tyre/wheel**

3 [T] ■ *I replaced the cup carefully in the saucer.*

put sth back • return

▸ replace/put sth back **on** sth
▸ replace/put back a **lid**
▸ replace/put back the **(telephone) receiver**

replacement noun [C] (often used as an adjective)

■ *replacement windows* ■ *We need to find a replacement for Sue.*

substitute • surrogate • stand-in • cover • relief | *fml or law* **proxy**

▸ a replacement/substitute/surrogate/stand-in/cover/proxy **for** sb/sth
▸ **act as** a replacement/substitute/surrogate/stand-in/proxy
▸ **appoint** a replacement/substitute/proxy

reply noun [C, U]

■ *I haven't received a reply yet.*

answer • response • acknowledgement | *written* **retort**

▸ a/an reply/answer/response/retort **to** sb/sth
▸ a/an reply/response/acknowledgement **from** sb
▸ **in** reply/answer/response **to** sth
▸ **get/receive** a/an reply/answer/response/acknowledgement

▸ give/write/elicit/produce/wait for a reply/answer/response **to** sb/sth

● **REPLY, RESPONSE OR ANSWER? Response** is slightly more formal than **answer** and **reply**. It is used esp. in written or business English.

reply verb [I, T]

■ *She didn't reply to my question.*

answer • acknowledge • respond • write back | *infml* **get back to sb |** *written* **retort**

▸ reply/respond/write back/get back to sb
▸ reply/answer/acknowledge sth/respond/get back to sb/retort **with** sth
▸ reply to/answer/to acknowledge/respond to a **question/letter/email**
▸ reply to/answer/respond to an **ad/advertisement/accusation**

● **REPLY, ANSWER OR RESPOND?** You can **answer** sb/sth or just **answer**, but not 'answer to sb/sth'; you can **reply/respond** to sb/sth or just **reply/respond**, but not 'reply/respond sb/sth'. For some uses you can only use **answer**:
✓**answer** the phone/the door/sb's prayers ✗ *reply/respond to the phone/the door/sb's prayers*
You can **answer/respond** to a call but not 'reply to a call'.

report noun

1 [C] ■ *Are these newspaper reports true?*

story • account • bulletin • item • version | *esp. BrE* **commentary**

▸ a/an report/story/bulletin/item **about** sth
▸ a/an report/story/account/item/version **is based on** sth
▸ **give** a report/an account/your version/a commentary

2 [C] ■ *Can you give us a progress report?*

statement • return

▸ **in** a/the report/statement/return
▸ an **annual** report/statement/return
▸ a **monthly/quarterly/financial** report/statement
▸ **prepare/complete/do/submit/file** a report/statement/return

3 [C] ■ *He commissioned a report on the health service.*

study • review • survey • investigation

▸ a/an report/survey/investigation **into** sth
▸ a/an **government/official/independent** report/study/review/survey/investigation

▶ **commission** a report/study/review/survey
▶ **publish/receive/read** a/an report/study/review/survey/investigation

4 [C] ■ *There are unconfirmed reports of a shooting in the district.*

talk | *BrE* **rumour** | *AmE* **rumor** | *fml* **hearsay** | *disapprov.* **scandal + gossip**

▶ the reports/talk/rumours/hearsay/scandal/gossip **about** sb/sth
▶ reports/talk/rumours/gossip **that...**
▶ **hear/believe** reports/talk/rumours/gossip
▶ **deny/confirm** reports/rumours

report *verb*

1 [I, T] ■ *The pilot reported engine trouble soon after take-off.*

tell + fill sb in | *AmE* **inform + brief** | *fml* **notify** | *esp. written or humorous* **enlighten**

▶ report/tell sb/inform sb/brief sb/notify sb **that...**
▶ report/fill sb in/brief sb/enlighten sb **on** sth
▶ report/tell sb/inform/notify sb **officially/immediately**

2 [T, I] ■ *The stabbing was reported in the local press.*

tell + describe + cover + relate + chronicle

▶ report/tell/describe/recount/relate **what/how...**
▶ report/tell/describe/recount/relate **that...**
▶ report/describe/cover/recount/relate/chronicle **events/a series of events**

reporter *noun* [C]

■ *I spoke to a reporter from the 'New York Times'.*

journalist + correspondent + columnist + editor + writer | *disapprov.* **hack**

▶ a **newspaper/magazine/news/sports/financial** reporter/journalist/correspondent/columnist/editor
▶ an **investigative** reporter/journalist
▶ **tell** reporters/journalists

represent *verb*

1 *linking verb (not used in the progressive tenses) (written)* ■ *The results represent a breakthrough in AIDS research.*

pose + amount to sth | *fml* **constitute**

▶ represent/pose/amount to/constitute a **challenge/threat**

▶ represent/pose/constitute a **problem/danger/risk**
▶ represent/amount to/constitute a/an **failure/increase/breach**
▶ a/an **result/activity/action** represents/constitutes sth
● **REPRESENT OR CONSTITUTE? Represent** is used esp. with words relating to change; **constitute** is used to talk about more dangerous or negative situations or acts: *This represents a change/turning point/decline.* • *This constitutes a crime/nuisance/refusal.*

2 [T, no passive] ■ *The artist uses doves to represent peace.*

symbolize + embody + typify + epitomize | *fml* **exemplify**

▶ represent/symbolize/embody/epitomize the **spirit/essence** of sth
▶ represent/embody/exemplify a/an **idea/ideal/principle**
● **REPRESENT, SYMBOLIZE OR EMBODY?** Sometimes you can use any of these words: *He came to represent/embody/symbolize his country's struggle for independence.* **Embody** is used to talk about real people becoming the basis for other people's hopes. You use **symbolize** to talk about objects being used to give the idea of sth. **Represent** is the most general word and can be used to mean 'express': *The comments represent the views of the majority.*

representative *noun* [C]

■ *The committee includes representatives from industry.*

delegate + spokesman/spokeswoman/spokesperson + messenger + envoy + ambassador

▶ a/an representative/delegate/spokesman/messenger/ambassador **for** sb/sth
▶ a/an representative/delegate/spokesman/messenger/envoy/ambassador **from** sb/sth
▶ a/an **government/official** representative/delegate/spokesman/envoy
▶ **elect** a representative/delegate/spokesman
● **REPRESENTATIVE OR DELEGATE? Representative** is a more general word than **delegate**. A **delegate** is always sb who represents their group or organization at a meeting.

repression *noun* [U]

■ *There was a campaign of repression against minorities.*

oppression + persecution + tyranny + bullying + dictatorship

▶ repression/oppression/persecution **against** sb
▶ **political/religious** repression/oppression/persecution/dictatorship
▶ **state/police** repression/oppression/persecution
▶ **suffer** repression/oppression/persecution/tyranny

● REPRESSION, OPPRESSION OR PERSECUTION? **Repression** is the use of force by those in power to control people in an unfair way. **Oppression** is the unfair use of power to stop one group of people from having the same rights and freedoms as others. **Persecution** can include the harm and even death of a group of people who are different in a way that is considered offensive by others or by those in power.

repressive adj.
■ It was one of the world's most repressive regimes.

oppressive • tyrannical • totalitarian • autocratic • undemocratic • dictatorial • authoritarian

▶ a/an repressive/oppressive/tyrannical/totalitarian/autocratic/undemocratic/dictatorial/authoritarian **regime**
▶ a/an repressive/tyrannical/totalitarian/autocratic/dictatorial/authoritarian **government**
▶ a/an repressive/oppressive/tyrannical/totalitarian/autocratic/dictatorial **power**

reproduce verb
1 [T] ■ It is illegal to reproduce this material.

copy • photocopy • duplicate

▶ reproduce/copy **from** sth
▶ reproduce/copy/photocopy/duplicate a **letter/document**
▶ reproduce/copy a **painting**

2 [T] ■ The computer program reproduces the effects of earthquakes on buildings.

simulate • recreate • reconstruct | fml **replicate** | computing or tech. **model**

▶ reproduce/recreate/reconstruct sth **from** sth
▶ reproduce/simulate/replicate/model sth **closely**
▶ reproduce/recreate/reconstruct/replicate/model sth **accurately**

reputation noun [C, U]
■ The school has a good reputation.

name • image • profile • status • prestige | BrE **honour** | AmE **honor** | fml **stature** • **character**

▶ sb's reputation/name/image/status/stature **as** sth
▶ **gain** a/an reputation/name/image **as/for** sth
▶ **defend** sb's reputation/image/status/honour
▶ **restore** sb's reputation/image/status/prestige/honour

request noun [C]
■ Catalogues are available on request.

application • appeal • order • claim • demand • petition | fml **plea** | esp. journ. **call**

▶ a/an request/application/appeal/order/claim/demand/petition/plea/call **for** sth
▶ **make** a/an request/application/appeal/claim/demand/plea
▶ **receive** a/an request/application/appeal/order/claim/demand/petition/plea
▶ **refuse/reject** a/an request/application/claim/demand/petition

request verb [T] (fml)
■ He requested permission to film inside the palace.

ask • apply • appeal • claim • petition | fml **seek** • **invite** | esp. journ. **call for** sth

▶ request/ask/appeal for/claim/petition/seek/invite/call for sth **from** sb
▶ request/ask/appeal/petition/invite/call for **sb to do** sth
▶ request/ask **that…**

require verb
1 [T] (not usu. used in the progressive tenses) (fml) ■ This condition requires urgent treatment.

need • call for sth • demand • rely on/upon sb/sth | esp. spoken **want**

▶ **really** require/need/call for/demand/want sth
▶ **urgently** require/need/want sb/sth
▶ **clearly/obviously** require/need/call for/demand sth

2 [T, often passive] (not usu. used in the progressive tenses) (fml) ■ All candidates are required to take a short test.

demand • expect • insist • ask | fml **stipulate**

▶ require/demand/expect/ask sth **from/of** sb
▶ require/demand/expect/insist/ask/stipulate **that…**
▶ require/expect/ask **sb to do** sth
▶ require/demand/expect/insist **on high standards**

requirement noun

1 [C] (*fml*) ■ *Our immediate requirement is extra staff.*

need • necessity • essential | *fml* **want**

▸ a requirement/need/necessity **for** sth
▸ **basic** requirements/needs/necessities/essentials
▸ **meet/satisfy** sb's requirements/needs/wants

2 [C] (*fml*) ■ *Be sure to check visa requirements before travelling.*

condition • terms • provision • qualification | *BrE* **the small print** | *AmE* **the fine print** | *fml* **proviso • prerequisite**

▸ (a) requirement/condition/terms/provision/prerequisite **for** sth
▸ **lay down** requirements/conditions/terms/provisions
▸ **accept/observe/comply with** the requirements/conditions/terms/provisions

rescue verb [T]

■ *He jumped into the river to rescue the child.*

save • bail sb out | *fml, religion* **redeem**

▸ rescue/save/redeem sb/sth **from** sth
▸ rescue/save/redeem a **situation**
▸ rescue sb/bail sb out **financially**

research noun [U] (also **researches** [pl.])

■ *He's done a lot of research into renewable energy.*

analysis • study • enquiry/inquiry • exploration • examination | *fml* **scrutiny**

▸ research/enquiry **into** sth
▸ **carry out/conduct/undertake** (a/an) research/analysis/study/exploration/examination
▸ research/analysis/the study/exploration/examination/scrutiny **reveals** sth

● **RESEARCH OR ANALYSIS?** When you do **research** you try to find out new information; when you do **analysis** you make a detailed study of the information you already have, in order to understand it better.

research verb [T, I]

■ *They are researching new ways of improving people's diets.*

investigate • explore • look into sth • enquire/inquire into sth • study • delve into sth | *esp. journ.* **probe**

▸ research/look/enquire/delve/probe **into** sth
▸ research/investigate/explore/look

into/enquire into/study **what/why/how/whether...**
▸ research/investigate/explore/look into/enquire into/study a **problem/matter**
▸ research/investigate/explore/look into/study/delve into a **subject**

resent verb [T]

■ *He bitterly resented being treated like a child.*

begrudge • take exception to sth

▸ resent/begrudge **(sb) doing** sth
▸ resent/begrudge/take exception **to the fact that...**

resentment noun [U, C]

■ *She could not conceal the deep resentment she felt at the unfair way she had been treated.*

bitterness • grudge • bad feeling • *esp. AmE* **bad feelings** | *fml* **acrimony**

▸ resentment/a grudge **against** sb
▸ do sth **without** resentment/bitterness/acrimony
▸ **harbour** resentment/bitterness/a grudge
● **RESENTMENT OR BITTERNESS?**
Bitterness can be sudden and can last a long or short time: *She felt touched with a momentary/sudden bitterness.* ● *The long occupation of the island has left a legacy of bitterness.*
Resentment may be a less obvious feeling: people try or fail to hide it. It grows more slowly, but it may be shared by many people: *his growing/increasing/mounting/smouldering resentment • popular/public/widespread resentment*

reserve noun [C, usu. pl.]

■ *The country has huge untapped reserves of coal and gas.*

stockpile • stock • supply • store • resource • bank • pool • hoard • arsenal

▸ a/an reserve/stockpile/stock/supply/store/bank/pool/hoard/arsenal **of** sth
▸ reserves/stockpiles/stocks/supplies **of coal**
▸ **build up** reserves/a stockpile/a stock/a supply/a store/resources/a bank/an arsenal

reserve verb

1 [T] ■ *They rang the hotel and reserved a room for the night.*

order • charter | *esp. BrE* **book** | *BrE* **hire** | *esp. AmE* **rent**

▸ reserve/order/charter/book/hire/rent sth **for** sb

► reserve/book a **place/seat/table/ticket**
► reserve/order/book sth **for eight o'clock/this evening/midday, etc.**
● **RESERVE OR BOOK?** Reserve means to ask for sth to be kept for you and does not usu. require payment in advance. You can also say *make a reservation*. **Book** usu. means to make a firm arrangement to have sth, including making a payment in advance.

2 [T, usu. passive] ■ *These seats are reserved for special guests.*

save | *esp. BrE* keep | *fml* hold

► reserve/save/keep sth **for sb/sth**
► reserve/save/keep a **seat/place** for sb
● **RESERVE, SAVE OR KEEP?** Reserve is used when sth is officially saved for sb/sth; **save** and **keep** are used when sth is reserved unofficially: *reserve a place on a course • Paolo saved/kept me a seat next to him.*

resident noun [C]
■ *Local residents have complained about the noise from the building site.*

inhabitant • citizen • local • native | *fml* householder | *written* dweller

► local residents/inhabitants/citizens/householders
► city/urban residents/dwellers
► permanent residents/inhabitants
● **RESIDENT OR INHABITANT?** Resident is the most general word here, but usu. refers to sb who lives in a city, town or village in a modern society; **inhabitant** can refer to people (or animals) living a more basic life either in the past or in a wilder environment: *the inhabitants of the rainforest*

resist verb
1 [T] ■ *The prime minister resisted pressure to change the law.*

oppose • fight • stand up to sb • defy • go against sb/sth • flout • disobey • rebel

► resist/oppose/fight a **plan/proposal**
► fiercely/bitterly/strongly resist/oppose sth

2 [I, T] ■ *He tried to push me to the ground, but I resisted.*

struggle • hold/stand your ground • hold/keep sb/sth at bay • hold out against sb/sth

■ OPP give in, submit
► resist/hold out against an **attack/pressure**

3 [T] ■ *A healthy diet should help your body to resist infection.*

stand • stand up to sth • absorb • tolerate | *fml* withstand

► resist/stand/tolerate/withstand **high temperatures/heat**
► resist/stand up to/withstand **stress/wear**
► resist/withstand **attack/damage**

resistance noun [U, sing.]
■ *Resistance to change has destroyed the industry.*

opposition • hostility • protest • objection

► resistance/opposition/hostility/objection **to sth**
► widespread/strong/fierce resistance/opposition/hostility/protests/objections
► provoke/meet/meet with/face resistance/opposition/hostility/protests/objections

resolve verb [T]
■ *Where can people get help with resolving family problems?*

settle • solve • repair • mend | *infml* patch sth up | *esp. BrE, esp. spoken* sort sth out • sort

► resolve/settle/mend/patch up **your differences**
► resolve/settle/solve/sort out a/an **dispute/argument/crisis/matter/issue**
► resolve/mend **matters**

resource noun
1 [C, usu. pl.] ■ *the exploitation of minerals and other natural resources*

supply • reserve • stock • store • stockpile • pool • bank • hoard • arsenal

► (a/an) vast resources/supply/reserve/stock/store/stockpile/bank/hoard/arsenal
► build up (a/an) resources/supply/reserves/stock/store/stockpile/bank/arsenal
► use up/exhaust (the) resources/supply/reserves/stock/store

2 [C] ■ *We have plenty of teaching resources in the college library.*

facilities • service • amenity | *esp. AmE* utility

► public/basic/local resources/facilities/services/amenities/utilities
► the resources/facilities/services/amenities **available**
► provide/lack resources/facilities/services/amenities

respect noun
1 [U, sing.] ■ *I have the greatest respect for your brother.*

admiration • appreciation • recognition • awe | *fml* esteem

▶ respect/admiration/recognition for sth
▶ have a lot of, no, etc. respect/ admiration/appreciation (for sb/ sth)
▶ win/gain/deserve respect/ admiration/appreciation
● RESPECT OR ADMIRATION? Admiration suggests that you like sb and would like to be like them. You can have respect for sb even if you do not like them: *She had a lot of respect for him as an actor, but she didn't like the way he behaved in public.*

2 [U, sing.] ■ *Everyone has the right to be treated with respect.*

politeness • courtesy • manners • etiquette • grace • formality | *fml* civility

■ OPP disrespect, contempt
▶ with respect/politeness/courtesy/ grace/civility
▶ out of respect/politeness/courtesy
▶ show respect/politeness/ courtesy/manners

respect *verb*

1 [T] (not used in the progressive tenses) ■ *She is always honest with me and I respect her for that.*

admire • appreciate • esteem • look up to sb • be/stand in awe of sb/sth

▶ respect/admire/appreciate/ esteem/look up to sb as/for sth
▶ respect/admire the way sb does sth
▶ a respected/an esteemed writer/ teacher/scientist
● RESPECT OR ADMIRE? You admire a person or their good qualities, but not their opinions. You can respect a person or their opinions, but not their good qualities:
✓*I really admire her (for her) courage.* ✗ *I admire Jack's opinion on most subjects.*
✓*I respect Jack's opinion on most subjects.* ◆ *I respect him for his honesty.* ✗ *I respect his honesty.*

2 [T] ■ *The new leader has promised to respect the constitution.*

obey • follow • comply | *fml* adhere to sth • abide by sth • observe

■ OPP violate
▶ respect/obey/follow/comply with/adhere to/abide by/observe the conventions/rules/ regulations/law
▶ respect/obey/follow/comply with/abide by sb's will/wishes

respectable *adj.*

■ *You should get yourself a respectable job.*

decent • reputable • law-abiding | *BrE* honourable | *AmE* honorable

■ OPP disreputable
▶ (a/an) respectable/decent/law-abiding/honourable man/ woman/people
▶ (a) respectable/decent/law-abiding citizen/member of the community/folk
▶ a respectable/reputable firm/ organization

respond *verb*

1 [I, T] ■ *I asked him his name, but he didn't respond.*

answer • reply • write back • acknowledge | *infml* get back to sb | *written* retort

▶ respond/reply/write back/get back to sb/sth
▶ respond/answer/reply/ acknowledge sth/get back to sth
▶ respond/answer/reply/write back/retort that...
● RESPOND, ANSWER OR REPLY? You can answer sb/sth or just answer, but not 'answer to sb/sth'; you can respond/reply to sb/sth or just respond/reply, but not 'respond/ reply sb/sth'. For some uses you can only use answer:
✓answer the phone/door/sb's prayers ✗ *respond/reply to the phone/the door/sb's prayers*
You can answer/respond to a call but not 'reply to a call'.

2 [I] ■ *Members of the public responded immediately to the charity's appeal for funds.*

react • take • receive • meet sth with sb | *esp. written* greet

▶ respond/react by doing sth
▶ respond/react/meet sth with sth
▶ respond/react/meet sth with/greet sth with anger
● RESPOND OR REACT? Respond often describes more detached, less emotional behaviour. Respond is used more frequently with adverbs like immediately, promptly and quickly; react is used more frequently with adverbs like angrily, violently and strongly.

response *noun*

1 [C, U] ■ *Customers should receive a response within 10 days.*

answer • reply • retort | *written* acknowledgement

▶ a/an response/answer/reply/ retort to sb/sth

> ▶ a/an response/answer/reply/
>   acknowledgement **from** sb
> ▶ **in** response/answer/reply **to** sb/
>   sth
> ▶ **get/receive** a/an response/
>   answer/reply/acknowledgement
> ▶ **make no** response/answer/reply
> ● RESPONSE, ANSWER OR REPLY?
>   Response is slightly more formal
>   than answer and reply. It is used
>   esp. in written or business English.

2 [C, U] ■ *The product was developed
in response to customer demand.*

**reaction • reception • welcome •
feedback**

> ▶ (a) response/reaction/reception/
>   welcome/feedback **from** sb
> ▶ a response/reaction/reception/
>   welcome **to** sth
> ▶ (a) **positive/favourable** response/
>   reaction/reception/feedback
> ▶ (an) **immediate** response/
>   reaction/welcome/feedback
> ● RESPONSE OR REACTION? Your
>   response to sth is what you decide
>   to do or say and it; your reaction
>   is often less considered or is simply
>   the feeling that sth produces in
>   you: *My immediate reaction to the
>   news was one of shock.*

responsibility *noun*

1 [U, C] ■ *It is your responsibility to see
that the rules are enforced.*

**duty • charge • burden • obligation
• commitment** | *infml* **job** | *fml*
accountability | *esp. busin. or law*
liability

> ▶ a responsibility/duty **towards** sb
> ▶ responsibility/accountability/
>   liability **for** sth
> ▶ **have** a responsibility/a duty/
>   charge/an obligation/a
>   commitment/the job/liability
> ▶ **accept** responsibility/a duty/the
>   burden/an obligation/liability

2 [U] ■ *The bank refuses to accept
responsibility for the error.*

fault • blame • guilt

> ▶ the responsibility/blame/guilt **for**
>   sth
> ▶ **bear/accept/share/absolve** sb
>   **from/shift** the responsibility/
>   blame/guilt
> ▶ the responsibility/blame/fault
>   **lies/rests with** sb
> ● RESPONSIBILITY OR FAULT? People
>   typically accept/share/admit/claim/
>   deny responsibility for sth:
>   ✗ *The bank refuses to accept fault for
>   the error.*
>   Fault is usu. used in the phrases
>   my/your/his/her/our/their/sb's
>   (own) fault or sb is at fault:
>   ✔ *It was her fault that we were late.*

✗ *It was her responsibility that we
were late.*

responsible *adj.*

1 [not before noun] ■ *Who's
responsible for all this mess?*

**to blame • at fault • in the wrong •
guilty**

> ▶ responsible/to blame/at fault **for**
>   sth
> ▶ **feel** responsible/to blame/guilty
> ▶ **consider/hold** sb responsible/to
>   blame/at fault/guilty

2 ■ *Clare has a mature and
responsible attitude to her work.*

approv. **reliable • dedicated •
committed • trustworthy • trusted**

> ● OPP **irresponsible**
> ▶ a responsible/dedicated/
>   committed/trusted **member** (of
>   sth)

be responsible for sb/sth
phrase

■ *Pat is responsible for the business
side of the project.*

**be in charge of • run • manage •
administer • control • direct •
command**

> ▶ be responsible for/be in charge of/
>   manage/control/direct
>   **operations**
> ▶ be responsible for/run/manage/
>   administer/control/direct a
>   **project**
> ▶ be responsible for/run/manage a
>   **department**

rest *noun*

1 the rest [sing.+ sing./pl. v.] ■ *Take
what you want and throw the rest
away.*

balance • difference • excess | *fml*
the remainder

> ▶ the rest/balance/remainder **of** sth
> ▶ **pay** the rest/balance/difference/
>   excess/remainder
> ▶ **find/make up/pocket** the rest/
>   balance/difference/remainder

2 [C, U] ■ *You need a rest from all your
hard work.*

break • breathing space | *infml* **time
out • breather** | *fml* **respite**

> ▶ (a) rest/break/time out/respite
>   **from** sth
> ▶ **have/take** (a) rest/break/time
>   out/breather
> ▶ **need** a rest/a break/some time
>   out/respite

rest *verb*

1 [I, T] ■ *The doctor told me to go
home and rest.*

relax • unwind • take it/things easy • put your feet up • sit back | *infml* chill (out) • hang out | *BrE* potter | *AmE* putter

▶ try to/help sb (to) rest/relax/unwind
▶ just rest/relax/unwind/take it easy/sit back/hang out/potter
▶ rest/relax/sit back **a little/a bit**

2 [T, I] (always used with an adv. or prep.) ▪ *He rested his chin in his hands.*

lean • prop • stand • balance • poise • steady

▶ rest/lean/prop/stand/balance (sth) **on** sth
▶ rest/lean/prop/stand/steady (sth) **against** sth

restless *adj.*
▪ *The audience was becoming restless.*

impatient • unsettled

▪ OPP calm
▶ become/feel/look restless/impatient/unsettled
▶ get restless/impatient

restore *verb* [T]
▪ *His job is restoring old paintings.*

renovate • refurbish • redecorate • revamp • remodel • rebuild • reconstruct

▶ restore/renovate/refurbish/redecorate/remodel/rebuild a **house**
▶ restore/renovate/refurbish/remodel/reconstruct a **building**
▶ newly/recently restored/renovated/refurbished/redecorated/rebuilt
● RESTORE OR RENOVATE? Restore is used more to talk about furniture and works of art; **renovate** is used more to talk about buildings.

restraint *noun* [U]
▪ *He exercised considerable restraint in ignoring the insults.*

self-control • self-discipline • composure • cool • poise • calm

▶ show restraint/self-control/self-discipline/composure/poise
▶ exercise restraint/self-control
▶ keep/lose your self-control/composure/cool/poise
▶ a lack of restraint/self-control/composure
● WHICH WORD? Self-control, composure, cool, and poise are qualities that you *have* and can *keep* or *lose* on particular occasions; **restraint** is more a matter of behaviour: you can *exercise restraint* but it is not sth that you have, keep or lose:
✔ *She struggled to keep her self-*

control. ✗ *She struggled to keep her restraint.*

restrict *verb* [T]
▪ *We restrict the number of students per class to ten.*

limit • control • curb • check • rein sth in • hold/keep sth in check | *esp. BrE* cap | *written* contain • suppress

▶ restrict/limit/control/curb/check/rein in/cap **spending**
▶ restrict/limit/control/curb/check **growth/your speed**
▶ restrict/limit/control the **size/number/extent/amount** of sth
● RESTRICT OR LIMIT? Limit is used both about controlling what people can do and also about controlling the effects of sth; **restrict** is used more often about controlling what people can do:
✔ *to limit carbon dioxide emissions*
✗ *to restrict carbon dioxide emissions*

restricted *adj.*

1 ▪ *There is only a restricted range of goods available.*

limited | *usu. disapprov.* narrow

▪ OPP unlimited
▶ restricted/limited/narrow **in** scope/range/amount/approach, etc.
▶ a restricted/limited/narrow **range/scope/vocabulary**

2 ▪ *The tournament is restricted to players under the age of 23.*

limited • controlled

▶ be restricted/limited **to** sth
▶ restricted/limited/controlled **access**
▶ highly/tightly restricted/controlled

restriction *noun* [C]
▪ *Speed restrictions are in operation due to poor visibility.*

limit • control • constraint • restraint • limitation • curb • ceiling • check

▶ restrictions/limits/controls/constraints/restraints/limitations/curbs/a ceiling/checks **on** sth
▶ without restrictions/limits/controls/constraints/restraints/limitations/checks
▶ impose restrictions/limits/controls/constraints/restraints/limitations/curbs/a ceiling/checks
● WHICH WORD? A restriction is a rule or law. A **constraint** is sth that exists, rather than sth that is made, although it may exist as a result of sb's decision. A **restraint** is also sth that exists, often as an idea of what is acceptable behaviour. A

limitation can be a rule, fact or condition that exists.

result noun [C]

■ *The decision had immediate results.*

outcome • consequence • upshot • effect • impact • implication • product | written **the fruit/fruits of sth** • repercussion

▶ with the result/outcome/ consequence **that...**
▶ as a result/consequence
▶ have a result/an outcome/ consequences/effects/an impact/ implications/repercussions
● **RESULT OR OUTCOME?** A **result** is usu. directly caused by sth else; an **outcome** is what happens at the end of a process. **Result** is often used after an event to talk about what happened; **outcome** is often used before an action or process to talk about what is likely to happen.

result verb [I] (not used in the progressive tenses)

■ *The job losses resulted from changes in production methods.*

follow • stem from sth | fml **arise** • ensue

▶ result/follow/stem/arise/ensue **from** sth
▶ result/follow/arise **out of** sth
▶ sth results/follows/stems/arises **from the fact that...**

result in sth phrasal verb

■ *Closure of the factory could result in the loss of thousands of jobs.*

cause • lead (sth) to sth • bring sth about • produce • create • trigger • make | fml **give rise to sth** • induce

▶ result in/cause/lead to/bring about/produce/give rise to a/an **change/shift/increase**
▶ result in/cause/lead to/bring about/produce a **reduction** in sth
▶ result in/cause/lead to/produce/ create/give rise to **problems/ difficulties**

retire verb [I]

■ *He retired after 23 years with the company.*

leave • resign • step down • stand down • give/hand in your notice | infml **quit** | AmE or busin. **depart**

■ **OPP** stay on
▶ retire/resign/step down/stand down **from** a post/position
▶ retire/resign/step down/stand down/quit/depart **as** director/ chief executive, etc.
▶ retire from/leave/resign from/step

down from/stand down from/ quit/depart a **post/position**

return verb

1 [I] ■ *When did she return home from Italy?*

come back • go back • get back • turn back

■ **OPP** set out
▶ return/come back/go back/get back **to/from/with** sth
▶ return/come back/go back/get back/turn back **again**
▶ return/come back/go back/get back **home/to work**

2 [T] ■ *She returned the books to the library.*

take sth back • give sth back • put sth back • hand sth back • replace | fml **restore**

■ **OPP** keep
▶ return/take sth back/give sth back/hand sth back/restore sth **to** sb/sth
▶ return/give back/put back/hand back/replace **money**
▶ return/take back/give back/put back/replace a **book**
▶ return/take back **faulty/ unwanted goods**

return to sth phrasal verb (esp. written)

■ *He returns to the topic later in the report.*

continue • restart • reopen | esp. spoken **go on** • take sth up | fml **resume** | esp. journ. **renew**

▶ return to/continue/restart/ reopen/resume/renew **talks**
▶ return to/continue/reopen/ resume a **discussion**
▶ return to/continue/take up/ resume a **conversation**
▶ return to/continue/take up/ resume/renew the **attack**

reveal verb [T]

■ *Her expression revealed nothing.*

disclose • expose • uncover • betray • give sb/sth away • bring sth to light | fml **divulge** | journ. **leak**

■ **OPP** hide, (fml) **conceal**
▶ reveal/disclose/expose/betray/ give away/divulge/leak sth **to** sb
▶ reveal/disclose/expose/uncover sb/sth **as** sb/sth
▶ reveal/disclose/betray/give away/ divulge **that...**
▶ reveal/disclose/betray/divulge **what/how/who/where/ whether...**

revenge noun [U]

■ *He swore to take revenge on his enemies.*

retaliation | *fml* **vengeance** | *written* **reprisal**

▶ revenge/retaliation/vengeance/ reprisals **for** sth
▶ **in** revenge/retaliation/ vengeance/reprisal
▶ **take** revenge/vengeance **on** sb
▶ **want/vow/swear/exact/wreak** revenge/vengeance
● WHICH WORD? Revenge is the most general of these words. It often refers to a personal act that is done in response to sth that has been done to you personally.
Retaliation and reprisals are often taken by a group, such as a military force, against another group who may not be responsible for the first crime: *They fear reprisals against aid workers in the region.*
Vengeance is extreme, violent and often personal.

revenue *noun* [U, C]

■ *The company's annual revenues rose by 30% last year.*

income ∙ **takings** ∙ **proceeds** ∙ **profit** | *busin.* **turnover** ∙ **receipts** ∙ **earnings** | *esp. AmE, busin.* **take**

▶ the revenue/income/takings/ proceeds/profit/turnover/ receipts/earnings/take **from** sth
▶ **gross/net/total** revenue/income/ takings/proceeds/profit/ turnover/receipts/earnings/take
▶ **increase/boost/reduce** (your) revenue/income/profit/earnings/ turnover
● INCOME OR REVENUE? These words are very similar but revenue is used when talking about tax. Income, but not revenue, is also used to talk about the money that a person earns.

reverse *verb*

1 [T] (*esp. written*) ■ *Nothing can reverse the economic decline.*

undo

▶ reverse/undo **effect/damage/ reforms/years of hard work,** **neglect, etc.**
▶ **completely** reverse/undo sth

2 [T] ■ *The Court of Appeal reversed the decision.*

override ∙ **overrule** ∙ **set sth aside** | *written* **quash** | *esp. journ.* **overturn**

▶ reverse/override/overrule/set aside/quash/overturn a **decision**
▶ reverse/override/quash/overturn a **ban**
▶ reverse/set aside/quash/overturn a **conviction/verdict**

3 [T] ■ *They reversed the traditional roles of husband and wife.*

switch ∙ **swap/swop/exchange** ∙ **change**

▶ reverse/switch/swap/exchange A and B
▶ reverse/switch/swap/exchange **roles**

review *noun* [C, U]

■ *I always read the film reviews.*

critique ∙ **criticism** ∙ **commentary** ∙ **write-up**

▶ **in** a review/critique/commentary/ write-up
▶ **give** a review/critique
▶ **write** a review/critique/ commentary

review *verb* [T]

■ *Staff performance is reviewed annually.*

examine ∙ **study** ∙ **survey** ∙ **discuss** | *BrE* **analyse** | *AmE* **analyze** | *esp. spoken* **go into** sth

▶ review/examine/study/survey/ discuss/analyse/go into **what/ how/whether...**
▶ review/examine/study/survey/ discuss/analyse the **situation**
▶ review/examine/study/discuss/ analyse a/an **proposal/idea**

revise *verb*

1 [T] ■ *I had to revise my opinions of his work.*

modify ∙ **adjust** ∙ **amend** ∙ **change** ∙ **alter** ∙ **qualify** ∙ **shift**

▶ revise/modify/adjust/change/ alter your **ideas**
▶ revise/modify/adjust/change/ alter/shift your/sb's **attitude/ opinion**
▶ revise/modify/amend/change/ alter a **text**

2 [T] ■ *Have you got the revised edition of this book?*

edit ∙ **rewrite** ∙ **rephrase**

▶ revise/edit/rewrite a **text/report/ book**
▶ revise/edit a **document/ manuscript**
▶ revise/rewrite a **theory**

3 [T, I] (*BrE*) ■ *She's revising for exams at the moment.*

study ∙ **learn** | *esp. AmE* **review**

▶ revise/study/review (sth) **for** sth
▶ revise/study/learn/review a **subject**
▶ revise/study/learn/review **geography/biology, etc.**

revision noun [U, C]

■ He made some minor revisions to the report.

change • amendment • adjustment • modification • alteration

▶ a/an revision/change/amendment/adjustment/modification/alteration to sth
▶ make a/an revision/change/amendment/adjustment/modification/alteration
▶ need/require a/an revision/change/amendment/adjustment/modification/alteration

revolution noun

1 [C, U] ■ The shooting of 30 people started a revolution.

coup • uprising • revolt • rebellion • mutiny | fml insurgency

▶ a/an revolution/coup/uprising/revolt/rebellion against sb/sth
▶ (a) violent revolution/uprising/rebellion
▶ stage/lead a revolution/coup/revolt/rebellion/mutiny

2 [C] ■ A technological revolution is taking place.

reversal • turnaround • a change of heart | written sea change | infml, esp. journ. U-turn

▶ a revolution/reversal/turnaround/sea change/U-turn in sth
▶ undergo a revolution/change of heart/sea change
▶ represent a revolution/reversal/turnaround/change of heart
▶ bring about a revolution/reversal/change of heart

reward noun [C, U]

■ You deserve a reward for being so helpful.

award • prize | BrE honour | AmE honor

■ OPP punishment, penalty
▶ a/an reward/award/prize for sth
▶ earn a/an reward/award/prize
▶ win/receive/accept a/an reward/award/prize/honour

rhythm noun

1 [U, C] ■ The dancers moved to the rhythm of the music.

beat • time | music tempo | BrE, tech. metre | AmE meter

▶ to the rhythm/beat
▶ in rhythm/time
▶ a slow/fast rhythm/beat/tempo

2 [C] ■ the rhythm of the tides

cycle • pattern

▶ a/an regular/irregular rhythm/cycle/pattern
▶ a natural rhythm/cycle
▶ break a rhythm/cycle/pattern
▶ the rhythm/cycle of the seasons
● RHYTHM, CYCLE OR PATTERN? Pattern is used esp. about people's work and behaviour; cycle is used esp. about events in the natural world; rhythm is used esp. about how people's bodies adapt to changing conditions.

rich adj.

■ She is one of the richest women in the world.

wealthy • well off • prosperous • affluent • comfortable | infml loaded | sometimes disapprov. privileged

■ OPP poor
▶ a/an rich/wealthy/well off/prosperous/affluent/privileged family
▶ a/an rich/wealthy/well off/prosperous man/woman
▶ a/an rich/wealthy/prosperous/affluent country/city/suburb
● RICH OR WEALTHY? Rich is more frequent than wealthy and can be used in some fixed phrases where wealthy cannot:
✓a resort for the rich and famous ✗ a resort for the wealthy and famous

ride noun [C]

■ We went for a ride in Jo's new car.

drive • flight | BrE lift

▶ a ride/drive/flight/lift in sth
▶ a ride/drive/flight/lift back/home
▶ take/go on a ride/drive/flight
▶ give sb/hitch a ride/lift

ridiculous adj.

■ You look ridiculous in that hat!

absurd • ludicrous • laughable | esp. spoken silly | esp. written foolish

■ OPP sensible
▶ ridiculous/absurd/ludicrous/silly that...
▶ a/an ridiculous/absurd/ludicrous/silly/foolish idea/notion
▶ a/an ridiculous/absurd/silly/foolish question
● RIDICULOUS OR ABSURD? Sth that is ridiculous invites unkind laughter; sth that is absurd is often completely illogical. Absurd is slightly more formal and is more frequent in BrE than AmE.

get rid of sb/sth phrase

■ We got rid of all the old furniture.

dispose of sth • throw sth away/out • dump • scrap • remove • eliminate • eradicate | esp. spoken do away with sth | fml discard • dispense with sb/sth | esp. journ. shed

■ OPP keep, (*infml*) hang on to sth
▸ get rid of/remove/eliminate/
eradicate sth **from** sth
▸ get rid of/dispose of/dump/
remove/eliminate/discard **waste**
▸ get rid of/dispose of/remove/
eliminate a **problem**

right noun

1 [U, C, usu. pl.] ■ *She doesn't
understand the difference between
right and wrong.*

good • goodness • purity | *fml*
virtue | *fml, esp. religion*
righteousness

■ OPP **wrong**
▸ do **right/good**
● **RIGHT OR GOOD?** Questions of **right**
and wrong are about treating
people in a fair way, not an unfair
way. Matters of **good** and evil are
about treating people in a kind
way, not a cruel way.

2 [C] ■ *Everyone has the right to a fair
trial.*

**claim • power • authority • liberty •
due • privilege** | *BrE, fml* **entitlement** |
law **title**

▸ a/an **right/claim/entitlement/title
to** sth
▸ the **right/power/authority/
entitlement to do** sth
▸ have a/an **right/claim/
power/authority/privilege/
entitlement/title**
▸ use/exercise your **right/powers/
authority/privilege/entitlement**

right adj.

1 [not usu. before noun] ■ *Hunting
may be legal, but that doesn't make
it right.*

**acceptable • good • proper •
justified • justifiable • decent** | *fml*
due

■ OPP **wrong**
▸ right/acceptable/good/proper/
justified/justifiable **to do** sth
▸ right/acceptable/good/proper
in doing sth
▸ right/acceptable/good/proper
that...
▸ do the **right/proper/decent thing**

2 ■ *I got about half the answers right.*

correct • true

■ OPP **wrong**
▸ right/correct **about** sth
▸ the **right/correct/true answer**
▸ the **right/correct time**
● **RIGHT OR CORRECT?** Correct is more
formal than **right** and is more likely
to be used in official instructions or
documents.

3 ■ *He's definitely the right man for
this job.*

**good • appropriate • suitable •
convenient • apt • fit** | *infml* **cut out
for/to be** sth | *fml* **fitting**

■ OPP **wrong**
▸ right/good/appropriate/suitable/
convenient/apt/fit/cut out/fitting
for sb/sth
▸ right/good/appropriate/suitable/
convenient/apt/fit/fitting **that...**
▸ right/good/appropriate/suitable/
convenient/apt/fit/fitting **to do** sth
● **WHICH WORD?** How **good,
appropriate** or **suitable** sb/sth is is
a matter of judgement; how **right**
sb/sth is is more a matter of fact:
✔*Do you think she would be a/an
good/appropriate/suitable person to
ask?* ✗ *a right person to ask*
✔*She's definitely the right person to
ask.* ✗ *She's definitely the good/
appropriate/suitable person to ask.*

4 ■ *You're right to be cautious in this
situation.*

correct | *esp. BrE* **proper**

■ OPP **wrong**
▸ right/correct **about** sb/sth
▸ right/correct **to do** sth
▸ right/correct **in thinking/
believing/saying** sth
▸ the **right/correct/proper
decision/judgement/conclusion/
way/method/approach**
● **RIGHT, CORRECT OR PROPER?** People
can be **right** or **correct** about sth,
but not **proper**:
✗ *You're proper to be cautious.*
Correct and **proper** are more often
used to talk about methods; **right**
is more often used to talk about
beliefs and decisions.

ring noun [C]

■ *a key ring*

circle • hoop • disc | *esp. AmE* **disk**

▸ **in** a ring/circle
▸ **through** a ring/circle/hoop
▸ **concentric** rings/circles

ring verb

1 [T, I] (*BrE, esp. spoken*) ■ *I'll ring you
later.*

call • dial • reach | *esp. AmE, infml*
call sb up | *esp. BrE, fml* **telephone** |
BrE, esp. spoken **phone**

▸ ring sb/call sb/call sb up/
telephone sb/phone sb **about** sth
▸ ring/call/telephone/phone **to do**
sth
▸ ring/call/dial/telephone/phone a
**number/a hotline/the
switchboard/reception**
▸ ring/call/telephone/phone the
**doctor/fire brigade/police/
hospital**
● **RING, CALL OR PHONE?** Call is the

only one of these three words used in *AmE*. Ring and phone are the most frequent words in spoken *BrE*, but call is preferred in an emergency: *Call the police/fire brigade.*
You **call/ring/phone** a person, place or institution; you **call** *a cab/ a taxi/an ambulance.*

2 [T, I] ■ *Someone was ringing the doorbell.* ■ *The church bells rang.*

sound • buzz • strike • jangle • clang • ping • tinkle • jingle | *lit.* toll

▸ the **bell** rings/sounds/chimes/ jangles/clangs/tinkles/jingles/tolls
▸ the **doorbell** rings/sounds/ buzzes/chimes/jangles
▸ the **clock** rings/sounds/chimes/ strikes

rise noun

1 [C] ■ *The industry is feeling the effects of recent price rises.*

increase • growth • surge • gain • spiral • upturn • inflation | *AmE* raise | *esp. journ.* hike

■ OPP fall, decline, drop
▸ (a/an) rise/increase/growth/ surge/gain/spiral/upturn/ inflation/hike in sth
▸ (a/an) rise/increase/growth/ surge/gain/inflation/hike of 20%, etc.
▸ (a) tax/price/wage rise/increase/ growth/inflation/raise/hike
▸ see (a/an) rise/increase/growth/ surge/gain/upturn/inflation/hike
● INCREASE, RISE OR GROWTH? Growth is used more often about sth positive; increase and rise are used more often about sth negative: *the growth in earnings/employment • an alarming increase/rise in violent crime*
Rise is used more for sth that happens to rise, rather than deliberate increases; increase is used in both these ways.

2 [sing.] ■ *The film traces the rise of fascism in Europe.*

development • advance • promotion • progression | *often approv.* progress | *fml* advancement

■ OPP fall
▸ sb/sth's rise/promotion/ progression/advancement to sth
▸ chart/halt the rise/development/ progression/the progress of sth
▸ assist the rise/development/ progress/advancement of sth

rise verb

1 [I] ■ *rising fuel bills/divorce rates*

increase • grow • climb • escalate • jump • rocket | *esp. spoken* go up | *written* soar | *disapprov.* spiral • shoot up | *often approv.* leap | *esp. busin.* surge

■ OPP fall, drop, sink
▸ rise/increase/grow/jump/go up/ shoot up/soar in price, number, etc.
▸ rise/increase/grow/go up/climb/ jump/rocket/shoot up/soar (by) 10%, 200, etc.
▸ rise/increase/grow/go up/climb/ escalate/jump/rocket/shoot up/ soar from 2% to 5%
● RISE, INCREASE OR GROW? Rise is the most frequent of these verbs. It is used most often about the number or level of sth; grow and increase can also be used about size and strength: *Profits/Numbers have risen/grown/increased.* • *Her confidence/fear grew/increased.*

2 [I] ■ *From the river the ground rises steeply towards the north.*

slope • climb

■ OPP drop away
▸ rise/slope/climb towards sth
▸ rise/slope climb steeply
▸ rise/slope gently/slightly

risk noun

1 [C, U] ■ *There is still a risk that the whole deal will fall through.*

danger • threat • fear

▸ the risk/danger/threat/fear of sth happening
▸ the risk/danger/threat/fear that sth will happen
▸ put sth at risk/in danger/under threat

2 [C] ■ *The group is considered to be a risk to national security.*

threat • danger • hazard • menace

▸ a risk/threat/danger/hazard/ menace to sb/sth
▸ a great/serious risk/threat/ danger/hazard/menace
▸ pose a risk/threat/danger/ hazard/menace
● WHICH WORD? A danger is the possibility of physical or moral harm and can come from a person or a thing; a threat or hazard is the threat of physical harm from a thing but not a person. A threat is usu. a probability, not just a possibility, and is most often used in the phrase *a threat to sth.*

3 [C] (usu. used in the phrase take a risk) ■ *You have no right to take risks with other people's lives.*

chance • gamble

▸ take a risk/chance/gamble on sth
▸ take a risk/chance with sth
▸ take a risk/chance/gamble

● **RISK, CHANCE OR GAMBLE?** Risk is used esp. when there is danger to life or sb's safety; **gamble** is used about less serious danger, or when you risk money. When you decide to give/not to give sb the opportunity to do sth, you *take a chance/take no chances*.

risk verb

1 [T] ■ *Don't risk your job for my sake.*

endanger • **threaten** | *written* **jeopardize**

▶ risk/endanger/threaten sb's/your **life/health**
▶ risk/threaten/jeopardize sb's/your **job/career**
● **WHICH WORD?** People usu. choose to **risk** sth that's their own, such as their *life*, in the hope of gaining sth else; it is not used about things outside your control:
✔ *The survival of the species is being endangered/threatened/jeopardized by overdevelopment.* ✗ ~~The survival of the species is being risked by overdevelopment.~~

2 [T] ■ *He risked a glance at her furious face.*

dare • **hazard** | *infml* **chance** • **stick your neck out** | *usu. approv.* **pluck up (the/your) courage** | *fml* **venture** • **presume**

▶ dare/pluck up courage/venture/presume **to do sth**
▶ risk/chance **doing sth**
▶ risk/chance a **look** (at sth)
▶ risk/chance **it**

at risk phrase

■ *Poorer nations are particularly at risk from the effects of global warming.*

endangered • **vulnerable** • **exposed** • **open to sth** • **helpless** | *BrE* **defenceless** | *AmE* **defenseless**

▶ **feel** at risk/vulnerable/exposed/helpless/defenceless
▶ **leave** sb/sth at risk/vulnerable/exposed/open to sth/helpless/defenceless

rival noun [C]

■ *The Japanese were their biggest economic rivals.*

competitor • **opponent** • **enemy** • **the competition** • **the opposition** | *fml* **adversary** | *old-fash. or fml* **foe**

■ **OPP** partner, ally
▶ a rival/competitor **for** sth
▶ **against** a/an/the rival/competitor/opponent/enemy/competition/opposition/adversary/foe
▶ **have** a/an rival/competitor/opponent/enemy/foe

role

river noun [C]

■ *A new bridge was built across the River Thames.*

waterway • **stream** • **tributary** • **canal** | *AmE, AustralE* **creek**

▶ a **narrow** river/waterway/stream/canal
▶ a river/stream/tributary/canal/creek **flows**
▶ a river/stream/canal/creek **runs**

road noun [C]

■ *She lives on a very busy road.*

street • **lane** • **avenue** • **alley** | *esp. AmE* **highway** | *AmE* **boulevard** | *BrE* **terrace**

▶ **in** the road/street/lane/avenue/alley
▶ **on** a road/street/highway
▶ **cross** the road/street/highway
● **ROAD OR STREET?** In a town or city, **street** is the most usual word, although streets are often called **Road**, esp. in BrE; in the countryside the usual word is **road**: *a street map of London* • *a road map of Britain* • *205 Woodstock Road*

rob verb [T]

■ *An armed gang has robbed three banks.*

hold up sb/sth • **raid** • **break into sth** • **loot** | *BrE* **burgle** | *AmE* **burglarize** | *fml* **plunder**

▶ to be robbed/plundered **of** sth
▶ rob/raid/break into/loot/burgle/burglarize a **building/shop/store**
▶ rob/raid/break into/burgle/burglarize a **house**
▶ rob/hold up a **bank**

rock noun [U, C]

■ *They drilled through several layers of rock to reach the oil.*

stone • **boulder** • **pebble**

▶ **solid** rock/stone
▶ **throw** a rock/stone/boulder/pebble
● **ROCK OR STONE?** Rock [U] is still a part of the ground; stone [U] has been dug up from the ground:
✔ *houses built of stone* ✗ ~~houses built of rock~~
✔ *the rock walls of the cave* ✗ ~~the stone walls of the cave~~
In BrE people **throw stones** and a **rock** is sth too big to pick up and throw. In AmE **rock** is the usual word for a small piece of rock that you can pick up.

role noun

1 [C] ■ *Even after she retired, she retained her role as social secretary.*

roll

place • office • capacity | *fml*
position

▶ sb's role/office/sb's capacity/sb's
position **as** sth
▶ a role/place/position **in** sth
▶ **take up** your role/your place/
office/position

2 [C] ■ He played the role of Hamlet.

character • part

▶ the role/character/part **of** sb
▶ a role/part/part **in** sth
▶ **play** a role/character/part

3 [C] ■ Regional managers have a
crucial role to play in developing the
strategy.

part • stake • interest • contribution
• input • participation •
involvement | *fml* engagement | *esp.
journ.* **hand**

▶ a/(an) role/part/stake/interest/
involvement/engagement/hand
in sth
▶ **have** a/an role/part/stake/
interest/input/hand **in** sth
▶ **have** a role/part **to play**
● **ROLE OR PART?** Role is slightly more
formal and is more common in
business contexts, esp. with
adjectives such as *key, essential* and
primary; part is used mainly in
phrases: *have/play a part in* sth.

roll noun [C]
■ Wallpaper is sold in rolls.

bundle • wad • reel | *esp. AmE* spool

▶ a roll/bundle/wad/reel/spool **of**
sth
▶ **in** a roll/bundle/wad/reel/spool
▶ **on** a roll/reel/spool

roll verb

1 [I, T] ■ He rolled over onto his back.

turn (sth) over • flip • overturn • tip
(sth) over • capsize

▶ roll/turn/flip/tip sth **over**
▶ roll/overturn/capsize **a** car
▶ overturn/capsize **a** boat

2 [T, I] (usu. used with an adv. or
prep.) ■ I rolled the string into a ball.

wind • wrap sb/sth around/round
sb/sth • curl • coil

■ OPP unroll
▶ roll sth/wind sth/curl **into** a ball
▶ roll/curl/coil **up**

room noun [U]
■ Is there room in the car for me?

space • headroom • legroom

▶ room/space **for/between** sth
▶ room/space **to do** sth

▶ leave/make/create/save/take up
room/space
● **ROOM OR SPACE?** Room is usu.
space that you have or need for
some practical purpose; space can
be used in the same way, or it can
mean a feeling of space that you
enjoy for its own sake:
✓The bright colours give a lovely
feeling of space. ✗ *The bright colours
give a lovely feeling of room.*

root noun

1 [C] ■ We have to get to the root of
the problem. ■ Flamenco has its
roots in Arabic music.

origin/origins • cause • source •
starting point • beginnings

▶ (a) **common** roots/origin/cause/
source/starting point
▶ **have** (a) roots/origins/cause/
source/starting point/beginnings
▶ **locate/discover/investigate/
trace** the roots/origin/cause/
source of sth
● **ROOT OR ORIGINS?** Root is used esp.
about the cause of a problem; use
origin to talk about when, where
and how sth started:
✗ *We have to get to the origin of the
problem.*
✓the origin of the universe ✗ *the root
of the universe*
Roots can suggest an emotional or
cultural attachment; **origins** is
more scientific.

2 [pl.] ■ I'm proud of my African roots.

origin/origins • background •
ancestry • parentage • pedigree •
family | *fml* blood • descent •
lineage

▶ **ethnic/racial/social/cultural**
roots/origin/background/
ancestry/pedigree/descent
▶ **African, Scottish, Italian, etc.**
roots/origin/background/
ancestry/parentage/descent
▶ **trace** your roots/origin/ancestry/
pedigree/family/lineage

rope noun [C, U]
■ They tied his hands together with
rope.

cord • string • cable

▶ **tie** sth with rope/cord/string
▶ **coil** the rope/cable
▶ **wind** the cord/string/cable
▶ a rope/cord/string/cable **breaks**

rotten adj.
■ The fruit is starting to go rotten.

bad • stale • sour • rancid | *BrE* off •
mouldy | *AmE* moldy

■ OPP fresh
▶ rotten/stale/mouldy **food**
▶ rotten/bad **eggs**
▶ stale/mouldy **bread**

▶ go rotten/bad/stale/sour/rancid/off/mouldy

rough adj.

1 ■ *The car is designed for travelling over rough ground.*

uneven • bumpy • rutted • rocky • rugged

■ OPP **smooth**

▶ a/an rough/uneven/bumpy/rocky **surface**
▶ a/an rough/uneven/bumpy/rutted **road**
▶ rough/uneven/bumpy/rocky **ground/terrain**

2 ■ *The skin on her hands was hard and rough.*

coarse • leathery • scaly • scratchy • bristly • prickly

■ OPP **soft**

▶ rough/coarse/leathery/scaly **skin**
▶ rough/coarse/scratchy **cloth/fabric/material**
● ROUGH OR COARSE? Coarse is a more literary word than **rough** for talking about skin or fabric. Coarse, but not **rough**, can also describe hair, sand, salt or gravel.

3 ■ *There were about 20 people there, at a rough guess.*

vague • imprecise • broad | *esp. written* approximate

■ OPP **exact**

▶ a/an rough/vague/broad/approximate **idea**
▶ a rough/an approximate **calculation/figure/estimate/guide/translation**
● ROUGH OR APPROXIMATE? Rough more often describes an *estimate*, *idea* or *guess* of sth; **approximate** most often describes the *number*, *amount*, *cost*, etc. of sth. **Rough**, but not **approximate** can describe a piece of writing or a drawing:
✔*a rough draft/sketch of sth* ✘ *an approximate draft/sketch of sth*

4 ■ *They complained of rough handling by the guards.*

violent • aggressive • brutal

■ OPP **gentle**

▶ rough/violent/brutal **treatment**
▶ get rough/violent/aggressive

5 ■ *It was too rough to sail that night.*

stormy • violent • choppy • turbulent • raging

■ OPP **calm**

▶ a rough/stormy/violent/choppy/turbulent/raging **sea**
▶ rough/stormy/violent/choppy/turbulent **conditions**
▶ rough/stormy/violent **weather**

6 ■ *Life was rough on the streets.*

tough • difficult • hard • bad | *fml* adverse • *BrE, fml* unfavourable | *AmE, fml* unfavorable

■ OPP **easy, pleasant**

▶ rough/tough/hard **on** sb
▶ rough/tough/difficult/hard/bad/adverse/unfavourable **conditions**
▶ a rough/tough/difficult/hard/bad **time/day/week/year**
▶ a rough/tough/difficult/hard/bad **life/childhood**

roughly adv.

■ *The trip takes approximately seven hours.*

approximately • about • around • round about • something like • more or less • imprecisely

■ OPP **exactly**

round noun [C]

■ *Italy qualified for the second round of the tournament.*

heat • leg • lap • hole • game • set • innings • inning • half • quarter

▶ in a/an round/heat/leg/game/set/innings/inning/half/quarter
▶ the **first/second, etc.** round/heat/leg/lap/hole/game/set/innings/inning/half/quarter
▶ win a round/heat/leg/hole/game/set
● ROUND OR HEAT? Round is a more general word to describe a stage of a competition between teams or individuals; the whole competition may take place over several days, weeks or even months. **Heats** is used esp. to describe the first round of a race between individuals, such as in running or swimming, in which the winners of each heat then compete in the semi-final or final.

route noun

1 [C] ■ *It's the best route into the city from the south.*

way • course • path • line • direction • orbit

▶ a/the route/way/course/path/line **from... to...**
▶ a/the route/way/course/path/line **through/along/across** sth
▶ **follow** a/an route/course/path/line/orbit

2 [C] ■ *Education was the traditional route out of poverty.*

path • road • course • direction

▶ a/the route/path/road **to** sth
▶ **on** a/the route/path/road/course
▶ **take** a/the ...route/path/road/course/direction
● ROUTE, PATH OR ROAD? Route may

be used about a particular person or people in general, but is used esp. to report things in a more factual, less emotional way; **path** is often more personal than **road**: *the route to economic stability • her path in life • the road to stardom*

routine *noun* [C, U]
■ *We are trying to get the baby into a routine for feeding and sleeping.*

procedure • process

▶ a routine/procedure/process **for** sth
▶ the **usual/normal** routine/ procedure/process
▶ **go through** a routine/procedure/ process

routine *adj.*

1 [usu. before noun] ■ *The fault was discovered during a routine check.*

standard • regular • usual • traditional • habitual • general

▶ be routine/usual/traditional **to do** sth
▶ routine/usual/traditional **for** sb/ sth
▶ the routine/standard/regular/ usual/traditional/habitual/general **procedure/practice**

2 [usu. before noun] *(often disapprov.)* ■ *I have little patience with routine tasks such as washing the dishes.*

everyday • day-to-day • daily | *disapprov.* **mundane • humdrum |** *written, disapprov.* **prosaic**

▶ routine/everyday/day-to-day/ daily/mundane/humdrum **activities/existence/tasks/work**
▶ routine/everyday/day-to-day/ mundane **stuff/things/matters/ situations/affairs/aspects**

row *noun* [C]
■ *The vegetables were planted in rows.*

line • rank • file • cordon | *BrE* **queue**

▶ a row/line/rank/file/queue **of** sb/ sth
▶ **in** a row/(a) line/single file/a queue
▶ (an) **orderly** row/line/ranks/ queue
● **ROW OR LINE?** People or things in a **row** are next to each other from side to side. People or things in a **line** can be next to each other from side to side, but are more often one behind the other from front to back. People or vehicles in a **row** are not usu. waiting for anything; those in a **line** usu. are: *a row of parked cars • a line of traffic waiting at the lights*

In *BrE* the usual word for people waiting in a line is **queue**; in *AmE* it is **line**.

rubbish *noun*

1 [U] *(esp. BrE)* ■ *The streets were littered with rubbish.*

waste • litter • scrap | *AmE* **garbage • trash |** *fml* **refuse • debris**

▶ **household/domestic** rubbish/ waste/garbage/trash/refuse
▶ **dump** rubbish/waste/garbage/ trash/refuse/debris
▶ **produce** rubbish/waste/garbage/ trash/debris
● **WHICH WORD?** Use **rubbish** in *BrE* and **garbage** or **trash** in *AmE* for the everyday things that we throw away. **Waste** is used esp. to talk about large amounts and in the context of industry.

2 [U] *(BrE, infml, disapprov.)* ■ *Their new album's complete rubbish.*

infml **trash |** *AmE, infml* **garbage |** *taboo, slang* **crap**

▶ **absolute/complete/total** rubbish/trash/garbage/crap
▶ **read/watch/listen to** rubbish/ trash/garbage
▶ **eat** rubbish/crap
▶ **a load of** rubbish/trash/crap

3 *(BrE, infml, disapprov.)* ■ *That idea's absolute rubbish.*

nonsense • lie • story • fiction | *esp. AmE, infml* **garbage |** *esp. AmE, slang* **bull |** *taboo, slang* **bullshit • crap**

▶ rubbish/nonsense/lies/stories/ garbage/bull/bullshit/crap **about** sth
▶ **believe** that/those rubbish/ nonsense/lies/story/fiction/ garbage/bull/bullshit/crap
▶ **a load/lot** of rubbish/nonsense/ garbage/bull/crap

rude *adj.* *(disapprov.)*
■ *Why are you so rude to your mother?*

disapprov. **disrespectful • impolite • impertinent • insolent • churlish |** *fml, disapprov.* **discourteous |** *BrE, esp. spoken, disapprov.* **cheeky |** *often approv.* **irreverent**

● **OPP** polite
▶ rude/disrespectful/impolite/ discourteous/cheeky **to** sb
▶ rude/impolite/impertinent/ churlish **to do** sth

ruin *noun* [C] *(also* **ruins** *[pl.])*
■ *the ruins of a Norman castle*

remains • wreckage • rubble • debris • wreck

▶ the ruins/remains/wreckage/ wreck **of** a building/vehicle, etc.
▶ **in/amid/among/amongst** the

ruins/remains/wreckage/rubble/
debris
► ancient/Roman ruins/remains
► reduce sth to ruins/rubble

ruin verb [T]
■ The bad weather ruined our trip.

spoil • wreck • mar

► ruin/spoil/wreck sth **for** sb
► ruin/spoil/wreck/mar sb's **career**
► ruin/spoil/wreck **things/
everything**
► ruin/spoil/wreck sb's **plans/day/
life/chances**
► ruin/wreck sb's **health/**sb's
marriage/the economy
● **RUIN OR SPOIL? Ruin** is stronger
than **spoil**. If sth is **ruined** it is
completely **spoiled**. If sth is
spoiled it may just be less good
than it was before.

rule noun
1 [C] ■ Tackling a player without the
ball is against the rules.

**regulation • law • legislation • act •
statute • commandment**

► the rules/regulations/laws **on** sth
► **against** the rules/regulations/laws
► **obey** a rule/the regulations/a law/
a commandment
► **break** a rule/regulation/law/
commandment

2 [U] ■ The country was in the process
of a return to civilian rule.

**control • power • authority •
command** | fml **jurisdiction**

► rule/control/power/authority/
command/jurisdiction **over** sb/sth
► be **under** sb's rule/control/
authority/command/jurisdiction
► **direct** rule/control/authority/
command

rule verb
1 [T,I] ■ Henry VII ruled for 24 years.

govern • be in power • reign

► rule/reign **over** sth
► rule/govern a **country**
► a (political) **party** rules/governs/is
in power
► a **king/queen/monarch** rules/
reigns

2 [T,I] ■ The court ruled that the deal
was illegal.

**order • decree • lay sth down •
prescribe • dictate • command** | fml
legislate • direct

► rule/legislate **on/against** sth
► rule/order/decree/prescribe/
dictate/command/legislate/direct
that...
► rule/order/decree/prescribe/
dictate/direct **how/what/who...**

rule sb/sth out phrasal verb
■ The proposed solution was ruled out
as too expensive.

**eliminate • exclude • reject •
dismiss**

► rule out/eliminate/exclude/
reject/dismiss sb/sth **as** sth
► rule out/eliminate/exclude/
reject/dismiss a/an **possibility/
explanation**
► rule out/eliminate sb **as a suspect**

ruler noun [C]
■ The country was finally united under
one ruler.

**king • queen • emperor • monarch •
sovereign • regent**

► **under** a/an ruler/king/queen/
emperor/monarch
► a **great/strong** ruler/king/queen/
emperor/monarch
► a/an **hereditary/absolute** ruler/
monarch/sovereign

rumble verb [I]
■ Thunder rumbled in the distance.

boom • thunder • roar • roll

► thunder rumbles/booms/roars/
rolls
► **traffic** rumbles/thunders/roars
► rumble/boom/thunder/roar/roll
loudly

rumour (BrE) (AmE rumor) noun
[C, U]
■ There are widespread rumours of job
losses.

report • talk • hearsay | infml **dirt** |
sometimes disapprov. **scandal •
gossip**

► rumours/reports/talk/hearsay/
dirt/scandal/gossip **about** sb/sth
► rumours/reports/talk of sth
happening
► **spread** rumours/reports/gossip
► **hear/believe** rumours/reports/
talk/gossip
► **deny/confirm** rumours/reports

run verb
1 [I, T] ■ He ran to catch the bus.

**sprint • tear • charge • jog • bound •
pound • trot • gallop • stampede** |
written **race**

► run/sprint/charge/jog/bound/
pound/trot/gallop/race **towards**
sb/sth
► run/sprint/charge/bound/
pound/trot/gallop/race **after** sb/
sth
► run/sprint/tear/bound/pound/
trot/gallop/race **along** (sth)
► run/sprint/bound/race **away**

2 [T] ■ *She ran a small business for many years.*

---

manage • control • be in charge • be responsible for sb/sth • administer • direct

▶ run/manage/control a/an **company/business/organization**
▶ run/manage/control/be in charge of/be responsible for/administer/direct a **project**
▶ run/manage/be responsible for/administer a **service**
● **RUN OR MANAGE?** Managing a business, department, etc. means making decisions about how it should operate and organizing other employees. **Run** emphasizes organizing the necessary tasks.

3 [T, I] ■ *Could you run the engine for a moment?* ■ *Stan had the chainsaw running.*

---

operate • control | *esp. spoken* work • go | *fml* function • manipulate

▶ run/operate/control/work a **machine**
▶ run/operate/control a/an **engine/motor**
▶ run/operate **machinery**
▶ run/operate/work/function **efficiently/reliably/smoothly/normally**
● **RUN, OPERATE OR CONTROL?** A person **operates** or **runs** a machine; machines are often **controlled** by the controls, such as a computer, knob or lever.

4 [I] ■ *The buses run every ten minutes.*

---

go • come • travel

▶ run/go/come/travel **from/to sth**

5 [I] ■ *Tears ran down her cheeks.*

---

flow • pour • stream • gush • circulate • trickle | *written* cascade

▶ run/flow/pour/stream/gush/trickle **out of sth**
▶ run/flow/pour/stream/gush/cascade/trickle **down** (sth)
▶ **water** runs/flows/pours/streams/gushes/circulates/trickles/cascades
▶ **blood** runs/flows/pours/streams/gushes/circulates/trickles

---

run away *phrasal verb* (*esp. spoken*)

■ *I ran away as fast as I could.*

---

make off • bolt • run for it | *esp. BrE* run off | *infml* take off | *esp. written* flee

▶ run away/bolt/flee **from sb/sth**
▶ run away/bolt/run off/flee **to sb**
▶ run away/make off/run off/take off **with sb/sth**
● **RUN AWAY OR RUN OFF?** Run away

can mean to make a sudden journey to escape from a situation: *Why don't we run away to Paris?* When sb physically **runs away** it is because they are frightened; they may **run off** through fear or just to get away from sth. In *AmE* **run away** is used in both meanings.

---

runner *noun* [C]

■ *He's a keen marathon runner.*

---

athlete • player | *esp. BrE* sportsman/sportswoman

▶ a **top/great/keen** runner/sportsman/player/sportsman/sportswoman/
▶ a/an **average/good/world-class** runner/athlete/player
▶ a/an runner/athlete/player/sportsman/sportswoman **trains/practises/competes**

---

rush *verb*

1 [I, T] ■ *We've got plenty of time; there's no need to rush.*

---

hurry • dash • fly • run | *infml, spoken* get a move on | *esp. written* hasten

▶ rush/hurry/fly/hasten **to do sth**
▶ rush/hurry a **meal**

2 [T] (always used with an adv. or prep.) ■ *He was rushed to hospital immediately.*

---

bundle • hustle • haul • drag | *infml* pack sb off

▶ rush/bundle/hustle/haul/drag sb **out of** sth
▶ rush/bundle/hustle/haul sb **into** sth

---

ruthless *adj.* (*usu. disapprov.*)

■ *He's a violent, ruthless man who will stop at nothing.*

---

cruel • hard • callous • heartless • coldblooded • brutal | *esp. written* merciless

● **OPP** merciful, compassionate
▶ a ruthless/cruel/hard/callous/heartless **man/woman**
▶ a ruthless/coldblooded/merciless **attack**

Ss

sack *verb* [T, often passive] (*esp. BrE, infml*)

■ *She was sacked for refusing to work on Sundays.*

---

fire • dismiss • lay sb off • let sb go | *BrE* make sb redundant | *esp. BrE, infml* give sb the sack | *fml* discharge | *journ.* (*BrE* axe | *AmE* ax)

▶ sack sb/fire sb/dismiss sb/lay sb

off/make sb redundant/give sb the sack/discharge sb **from** a job
▶ sack/fire/dismiss/lay off/axe **staff/workers/employees**
▶ make **staff/workers/empoyees** redundant
▶ let **staff/employees** go

sad adj.

1 ■ I felt so sad that she had to go.

unhappy • miserable • gloomy • glum • depressed • heartbroken | infml **down** | esp. written mournful • despondent | lit. melancholy

■ OPP happy
▶ sad/unhappy/miserable/gloomy/ glum/depressed/heartbroken/ despondent **about** sth
▶ sad/unhappy/miserable/ depressed/heartbroken **when/ that...**
▶ **feel** sad/unhappy/miserable/ gloomy/depressed/despondent
▶ **look** sad/unhappy/miserable/ mournful/gloomy/glum/ depressed
● SAD OR UNHAPPY? You usu. feel **unhappy** about sth that has happened to you; you feel **sad** about sth that has happened to sb else. A period of your life can be **unhappy**; sth that you see or hear can be **sad**: an unhappy childhood ◇ sad news

2 ■ The sad truth is, he never loved her.

pathetic • painful • upsetting • distressing • tragic • heartbreaking
▶ sad/painful/upsetting/ distressing/tragic/heartbreaking **for** sb
▶ sad/painful/upsetting/ heartbreaking **to do** sth
▶ a sad/pathetic/tragic/ heartbreaking **story**

sadness noun [U, sing.]

■ His memories were tinged with sadness.

regret • unhappiness • grief • heartache • heartbreak • depression | infml **the blues** | fml sorrow | lit. melancholy

■ OPP happiness
▶ sadness/regret/unhappiness/ grief/heartache/heartbreak/ sorrow/melancholy **at/about/ over** sth
▶ sadness/regret/sorrow/grief **for** sth
▶ **be filled with/full of/overcome with** sadness/regret/ unhappiness/grief/heartache/ heartbreak/sorrow/melancholy
▶ **express/show/hide** your sadness/ regret/unhappiness/grief/sorrow

safe adj.

1 [not usu. before noun] ■ The girl was eventually found safe and well.

unharmed • alive and well • unhurt • uninjured • secure • out of harm's way | esp. spoken **all right** | infml, esp. spoken **OK** • **in one piece** | written unscathed

▶ safe/secure **from** sth
▶ **remain** safe/unharmed/alive and well/secure/all right/OK/in one piece/unscathed
▶ **perfectly** safe/secure/all right/OK

2 ■ Is the water safe to drink?

harmless | fml or med. benign

■ OPP dangerous, unsafe
▶ a harmless/benign **substance**
▶ **environmentally** safe/harmless/ benign

safety noun

1 [U] ■ There was concern for the missing boy's safety.

security • welfare • wellbeing

▶ **for** safety/security
▶ **improve** safety/security/sb's welfare/sb's wellbeing
▶ **promote** the safety/welfare/ wellbeing of sb/sth
● SAFETY OR SECURITY? Use **safety** to talk about protection from physical harm or danger; use **security** to talk about being or feeling financially or emotionally protected.

2 [U] ■ I managed to swim to safety.

refuge • shelter • cover | fml sanctuary

▶ a **place** of safety/refuge/sanctuary

sail verb [T, I]

■ He sailed the boat between the rocks.

navigate • pilot • steer • handle | BrE manoeuvre | AmE maneuver

▶ sail/navigate/steer/manoeuvre sth **into/out of** sth
▶ sail/navigate/steer **across/ through** sth
▶ sail/navigate/pilot/steer/handle/ manoeuvre a **boat/ship**

salary noun [C]

■ He gets a basic salary plus commission.

wage/wages • pay • earnings • income

▶ (a) **high/low/basic** salary/wage/ pay/earnings/income
▶ **receive** (a/an) salary/wage/pay/ earnings/income
▶ **pay/give sb** (a/an) salary/wage/ income

● SALARY, WAGES OR PAY? **Pay** is the most general of these words. If you work in a factory, shop, etc. you usu. get your **wages** each week. Office workers and professionals such as doctors, teachers, etc. receive a **salary** that is paid monthly or twice a month. It is expressed as an annual figure: *She's on a salary of over $80000.*

for **sale** phrase
■ *They've put their house up for sale.*

on the market • on sale • available
▶ **now/still** for sale/on the market/on sale/available
▶ **go** on the market/on sale

the **same** adj.
■ *The same thing happened to me last week.*

identical • equal • uniform • indistinguishable • synonymous
■ OPP **different**
▶ **exactly** the same/identical/equal/synonymous
▶ **almost** the same/identical/equal/uniform/indistinguishable/synonymous
▶ **roughly** the same/equal/synonymous

sane adj.
■ *No sane person would do a thing like that.*

normal • rational • in your right mind
■ OPP **insane**
▶ a sane/normal/rational **person**
▶ **perfectly/quite/completely/otherwise** sane/normal/rational
● SANE OR NORMAL? **Sane** can be used to talk about yourself in a rather humorous way; **normal** is always used about other people: ✔ *Having a laugh helps me to stay sane.* ✗ *Having a laugh helps me to stay normal.*

satisfaction noun [U]
■ *She had the satisfaction of seeing her book become a best-seller.*

pride • happiness • contentment | BrE fulfilment | AmE fulfillment
■ OPP **regret, dissatisfaction**
▶ satisfaction/pride/happiness/contentment/fulfilment **in** sth
▶ **feel** satisfaction/pride/happiness/contentment
▶ **bring** sb satisfaction/pride/happiness/contentment/fulfilment
▶ **take** satisfaction/pride **in** sth
● WHICH WORD? You feel **happiness** when things give you pleasure; you feel **contentment**, which is a

quieter feeling than **happiness**, when you have learned to find pleasure in things. You can feel **satisfaction** at achieving almost anything, small or large; you feel **fulfilment** when you do sth useful and enjoyable with your life.

satisfactory adj.
■ *He couldn't give us a satisfactory explanation.*

adequate • acceptable • reasonable • decent • respectable • fair | esp. spoken all right • not bad | infml, esp. spoken OK | fml in order
■ OPP **unsatisfactory**
▶ satisfactory/acceptable/reasonable/fair/all right/OK/in order **to do sth**
▶ satisfactory/acceptable/reasonable/fair/all right/OK/in order **that...**
▶ satisfactory/adequate/acceptable/reasonable/all right/not bad/OK **for** sb/sth
▶ a/an satisfactory/adequate/acceptable/reasonable/decent/respectable/fair **level/degree/standard**

satisfied adj.
1 ■ *She's never satisfied with what she's got.*

happy • content • contented • pleased • glad • proud
■ OPP **dissatisfied**
▶ satisfied/happy/pleased/glad/proud **about** sth
▶ satisfied/happy/content/contented/pleased **with** sth
▶ **feel** satisfied/happy/content/contented/pleased/glad/proud

2 [not before noun] ■ *I'm satisfied that he's telling the truth.*

confident • persuaded • convinced • certain • sure | esp. spoken positive
▶ satisfied/confident/persuaded/convinced/certain/sure **of** sth
▶ satisfied/confident/persuaded/convinced/certain/sure **that...**
▶ satisfied/certain/sure **who/what/how...**

satisfy verb
1 [T] (not used in the progressive tenses; often used in negative sentences) ■ *The plans satisfied no one.*

please | esp. spoken make sb's day | written gratify
▶ It satisfied/pleased/gratified sb **that...**
▶ **You can't** satisfy/please everybody/everyone.
▶ **Nothing** satisfies/pleases sb.
● SATISFY OR PLEASE? Sth that

satisfies you is just good enough, but sth might **please** you very much:

✔ The result pleased us enormously.
✘ The result satisfied us enormously.

2 [T] ■ She failed to satisfy the requirements for entry to the college.

meet • serve • suit • fml **fulfil |** BrE **fulfil |** AmE **fulfill**

► satisfy/meet/serve/suit/fulfil a **requirement/need/purpose**
► satisfy/meet/suit/fulfil a **demand/condition**
► satisfy/meet/suit/fulfil **a standard/an obligation/the terms/the criteria**

3 [T] (not used in the progressive tenses) ■ His answer didn't satisfy the jury.

convince • persuade

► satisfy/convince/persuade sb **of** sth
► satisfy/convince/persuade sb **that...**
► satisfy/convince/persuade **yourself**

satisfying adj.

■ It's satisfying to play a game well.

rewarding • fulfilling • pleasing | fml **gratifying**

► satisfying/rewarding/pleasing/gratifying **to do** sth
► a satisfying/rewarding/fulfilling/gratifying **experience**
► (a) satisfying/rewarding/fulfilling **job/career/work**
● **SATISFYING, REWARDING OR FULFILLING? Satisfying** and **fulfilling** are used more to talk about personal happiness; **rewarding** is used to talk about a feeling of doing sth important or useful for others.

save verb

1 [T] ■ They launched a campaign to save the school from closure.

rescue • preserve • protect • defend • safeguard • bail sb out | fml, religion **redeem**

■ OPP **endanger**

► save/rescue/preserve/protect/defend/redeem sb/sth **from** sth
► save/redeem **sinners/mankind**
► save/preserve/protect/safeguard **jobs**
► save/preserve/protect a **species**

2 [I] ■ I'm saving up for a new car.

budget • economize • skimp | infml **tighten your belt**

■ OPP **spend**

► save up/budget **for** sth
► economize/skimp **on** sth

3 [T] ■ I've saved almost £100 so far.

put/set sth aside • deposit • bank

■ OPP **waste**

► save/put aside/deposit/bank **money, £100, etc.**
► save/deposit **cash**

4 [T] ■ I'll save you a seat.

reserve • hold | esp. BrE **keep**

► save/reserve/hold/keep sth **for** sb/sth
► save/reserve/hold/keep a **seat/place** for sb/sth
► save/keep some **food** for sb
● **SAVE, RESERVE OR KEEP?** Reserve is used esp. when sth is officially saved for sb/sth. **Keep** and **save** are more often used if sth is saved for you unofficially, for example by a friend.

5 [T, I] ■ We'll take a cab to save time.

fml **conserve**

■ OPP **waste**

► save/conserve **energy/water/fuel**

say verb

1 [T] ■ I didn't believe a word she said.

speak • talk

► say/speak/talk **to** sb
► say/speak/talk **about** sth

2 [T] ■ I said a quiet prayer to myself.

repeat • recite • quote

► say/repeat/recite/quote a **line**

3 [T] ■ It's hard to say why he left.

express • voice • air • put • phrase • state | esp. journ. **indicate**

► express/voice/air your **thoughts/opinions/views/concerns**
● **SAY OR EXPRESS?** Express is often followed by a noun describing a feeling or emotion; **say** cannot be used in this way: to express your dissatisfaction/fear/horror/gratitude • to say that you are dissatisfied/afraid/horrified/grateful

4 [T, I] (used esp. in negative sentences and questions) (esp. spoken) ■ It's difficult to say when it will be finished.

predict • forecast • foresee • prophesy | esp. busin. **project**

► say/predict/forecast/foresee/prophesy **what/how/when/who/where/whether...**
► be **difficult/impossible** to say/predict/forecast/foresee/project
► say/forecast/predict sth **in advance**

5 [T, no passive] (esp. spoken) ■ Say you lose your job. What then?

suppose • imagine

saying

▶ say/suppose/imagine that…
▶ let's just/let us say/suppose/ imagine that…

saying noun [C]

■ 'Accidents will happen,' as the saying goes.

proverb • maxim • motto • catchphrase | *disapprov.* **platitude**

▶ the saying/proverb/maxim/motto that…
▶ a/an **well-known/old** saying/ proverb/maxim
● **SAYING OR PROVERB?** A saying is any kind of phrase used to express an idea that people believe to be wise or true. A proverb is a traditional saying that is usu. expressed as a metaphor (= in terms of sth else): *'Don't count your chickens before they are hatched' is a proverb.*

scale noun

1 [U, sing.] ■ *It was impossible to take in the full scale of the disaster.*

extent • size • level • degree • proportions | *fml* **magnitude**

▶ the **full** scale/extent/size of sth
▶ the **sheer** scale/extent/size/ magnitude of sth
▶ **assess/judge** the scale/extent/ size/level/degree/magnitude of sth
▶ the scale/extent/size/magnitude **of the problem**
● **SCALE OR EXTENT?** The scale of sth is how large it is; the extent is how far it goes. Some qualities, such as *knowledge*, are considered as being wide rather than large, and so have extent rather than scale:
✔*I was amazed at the extent of his knowledge.* ✗ ~~I was amazed at the scale of his knowledge.~~
You are more likely to try to *measure/calculate* the extent of sth, while you usually try to *comprehend/grasp* the scale of sth.

2 [C] ■ *a salary/pay scale*

hierarchy • ladder • level • rankings • line | *infml* **pecking order**

▶ **on** a/the scale/ladder
▶ **in** the hierarchy/rankings/pecking order
▶ **move up** the scale/hierarchy/ ladder/rankings/pecking order
▶ be **at the top/bottom** of the scale/hierarchy/ladder/rankings/ pecking order

3 [C, U] ■ *The map is drawn to a scale of 1:25 000.*

ratio • proportion

▶ a scale/ratio **of 1:25, etc.**

▶ **out of** scale/proportion

scarce adj.

■ *Land suitable for building on is scarce.*

in short supply • few and far between • short • low • limited

■ OPP **plentiful**
▶ **resources** are scarce/in short supply/short/low/limited
▶ **food** is scarce/in short supply/ short
▶ **time** is short/limited
● **WHICH WORD? Scarce** and **in short supply** are used about resources that are not generally available; **short** is used esp. about *time* and *money*; **low** is used esp. about your supplies when you have not got much left.

scare noun [C]

■ *There was a bomb scare at the airport.*

fright • shock

▶ **get/have/give sb** a scare/fright/ shock

scare verb [T]

■ *It scared me to think I was alone in the building.*

frighten • alarm • terrify • traumatize | *infml* **spook**

▶ scare/frighten sb/sth **away/off**
▶ scare/frighten/terrify sb **into** doing sth
▶ It scares/frightens/alarms/terrifies me **that…**
● **SCARE OR FRIGHTEN? Scare** is more common in spoken English. Both words can be used without an object: *He doesn't scare/frighten easily.*, but it would be more natural to say: *Nothing scares/ frightens him.*

scared adj.

■ *The thieves got scared and ran off.*

afraid • frightened • startled • alarmed • terrified • petrified • intimidated | *fml* **fearful**

▶ scared/afraid/frightened/ terrified/petrified/fearful **of** sb/sth
▶ scared/afraid/frightened/ terrified/petrified/fearful **that…**
▶ scared/afraid/frightened/fearful **about** sth
● **SCARED, AFRAID OR FRIGHTENED? Scared** is more informal, more common in speech, and often describes small fears. **Afraid** cannot come before a noun:
✔*a frightened child* • *a scared expression* ✗ ~~an afraid child/ expression~~

scatter verb [T]

■ *Scatter the grass seed over the lawn.*

strew • sprinkle • spread • shower • rain

▶ scatter/strew/sprinkle/spread/spray/strew/shower/rain sth **on/onto/over** sth
▶ scatter/strew/spread/spray sth **across** sth
▶ scatter/sprinkle/spread **seeds**
▶ scatter/shower/rain **ash**

scene noun

1 [C, usu. sing.] ■ *The police arrived at the scene of the accident.*

location • site • place • spot • area

▶ **at** a/the scene/location/site/place/spot
▶ the scene/location/site/area **of** sth

2 [C] ■ *The movie opens with a scene in a New York apartment.*

clip • extract • excerpt • passage

▶ (a/an) scene/clip/extract/excerpt/passage **from** sth
▶ the **opening** scene/passage

3 [C] ■ *It was a picturesque rural scene.*

view • panorama • sight

▶ a **beautiful/breathtaking** scene/view/panorama/sight
▶ **enjoy** the scene/view/panorama/sight
▶ **take in** the scene/view/sight

scepticism (BrE) (AmE skepticism) noun [U]

■ *Other scientists have expressed scepticism about these results.*

doubt • disbelief • suspicion • distrust | *often disapprov.* **cynicism**

▶ scepticism/suspicion/distrust/cynicism **towards** sth
▶ scepticism/doubt/suspicion/cynicism **about** sth
▶ **express** scepticism/doubt/disbelief/suspicion/distrust

schedule noun [C, U]

■ *We're working to a tight schedule.*

timetable • itinerary • diary • calendar • agenda | *BrE* **programme** | *AmE* **program**

▶ be/put sth **in** the/your schedule/timetable/itinerary/diary/calendar/programme
▶ **on** the schedule/timetable/itinerary/calendar/agenda/programme
▶ a **busy/full/packed** schedule/timetable/diary/calendar/agenda/programme
▶ **check/consult** the/your schedule/timetable/diary/calendar
● SCHEDULE OR TIMETABLE? A

schedule is usu. a plan of what must happen; a **timetable** is often a plan of what you hope will happen: *work/production schedules • the government's timetable for the peace talks*

schedule verb [T, usu. passive]

■ *The meeting is scheduled for Friday afternoon.*

set • fix • time • book • set sth up • line sb/sth up | *esp. BrE* **timetable**

▶ schedule/set/fix/time/book/set up/line up/timetable sth **for** sth
▶ schedule/set/fix/time/book/set up/line up/timetable **sb/sth to do** sth
▶ schedule/set/fix/time/set up/timetable a **meeting**
▶ schedule/set/fix/book a **time/date/day**

scheme noun

1 [C] (*esp. BrE*) ■ *Over 10 000 people joined the training scheme.*

initiative • plan • strategy • policy | *BrE* **programme** | *AmE* **program**

▶ a/an scheme/initiative/plan/strategy/policy/programme **for** sth
▶ a/an scheme/initiative/plan/strategy/policy/programme **to do** sth
▶ **have/propose/adopt** a scheme/plan/strategy/policy
▶ **launch** a/an scheme/initiative/plan/programme

2 [C] ■ *Police uncovered a scheme to steal two Picasso paintings.*

conspiracy • plot | *esp. AmE* **sting** | *esp. written* **intrigue**

▶ a scheme/conspiracy **to do** sth
▶ **be involved in** a scheme/conspiracy/plot/sting/intrigue
▶ **uncover** a scheme/conspiracy/plot

scholar noun [C]

■ *She's an eminent scholar of the Enlightenment.*

academic • intellectual • theorist • thinker

▶ a **great/leading** scholar/academic/intellectual/theorist/thinker/philosopher
▶ a/an **distinguished/eminent** scholar/academic/philosopher

school noun [C]

■ *My sister and I went to the same school.*

academy • college • university • seminary

▶ **at/in** school/college/university

scold

▶ **at** a/an/the school/academy/college/university/seminary
▶ **go to/attend** school/an academy/college/university/a seminary

scold verb [T] (written)
■ Rose scolded the child gently for her behaviour.

esp. BrE, spoken **tell sb off** | fml **rebuke • reprimand • chide • castigate • berate • reproach** | disapprov. **lecture**

▶ scold/tell sb off/rebuke/reprimand/chide/castigate/berate/reproach sb **for sth**
▶ scold/rebuke/chide/castigate/berate/reproach yourself
▶ scold/tell sb off/rebuke/reprimand/castigate/berate sb **severely**
▶ scold/rebuke/chide/castigate/berate sb **gently**
● **SCOLD OR TELL SB OFF?** There is no verb for telling sb that you disapprove of their actions that is neither formal nor informal. **Scold** is used esp. in written stories; **tell sb off** is the most frequent word in spoken BrE.

score noun [C]
■ The final score was 4–3.

result • point • grade | esp. BrE **mark**

▶ a high/low/good/poor score/result/mark/grade
▶ the final score/result/mark/grade
▶ get a score/your results/a point/a mark/a grade

scratch noun [C]
■ Her hands were covered in scratches from the roses.

cut • graze • gash • injury • wound

▶ a deep scratch/cut/gash/wound
▶ suffer scratches/cuts/a gash/an injury/a wound
▶ cuts and scratches/grazes

scratch verb

1 [T, I] ■ She scratched at her attacker's face.

claw

▶ scratch/claw **at sth**
▶ scratch/claw sth **with sth**
▶ scratch/claw sth **frantically**

2 [T] ■ Be careful not to scratch the furniture.

scrape • graze • scuff • rub

▶ scratch/scrape/graze a **surface**
▶ scratch sth/scrape sth/graze sth/scuff sth/rub **on sth**
▶ scrape/graze your **knee/knuckles/elbow/shin**

● **SCRATCH OR SCRAPE?** If you scratch a surface you make a long thin line on it; if you scrape it, you make a wider mark.

scream verb

1 [I] ■ She screamed in pain.

shriek • screech • cry out • squeal • howl • wail • yelp

▶ shriek/screech/cry out/squeal/howl/wail/yelp **at sb**
▶ shriek/screech/cry out/squeal/howl/wail/yelp **in/with pain/terror, etc.**
▶ brakes/tyres scream/shriek/screech/squeal

2 [I, T] ■ He screamed at me to stop.

shout • yell • cry out (sth) • bellow • cheer | AmE, infml **holler** | written **cry • roar** | disapprov. **bawl**

▶ scream/shout/yell/bellow/holler/roar/bawl **at sb**
▶ scream/shout/yell/cry out/bellow/holler/roar **in pain/anguish/rage, etc.**
▶ scream/shout/cry out **for joy/excitement/delight, etc.**

script noun [C]
■ That line isn't in the original script.

text • screenplay • manuscript • lines • lyrics | music **libretto**

▶ in the script/text/screenplay/manuscript/lines/lyrics/libretto
▶ write/read a/the script/text/screenplay/manuscript/line/lyrics/libretto
▶ the script/text/screenplay/lyrics is/are **based on sth**

scruffy adj. (esp. BrE, disapprov.)
■ He looked scruffy in his old jeans.

AmE **messy** | fml **unkempt** | lit., BrE **dishevelled** | AmE **disheveled**

■ OPP **smart**

▶ a/an scruffy/messy/unkempt/dishevelled **appearance**
▶ a/an scruffy/unkempt/dishevelled **man/woman/child**

● **SCRUFFY, MESSY OR DISHEVELLED?** A messy man/woman/child is sb who makes a mess, not sb who looks untidy. A **scruffy** person, or sb with a **messy** appearance, is untidy because they have not taken care of their appearance; a **dishevelled** person has become untidy as a result of sth, for example a strong wind. **Scruffy** clothes are old and often dirty or with holes, etc.; **messy** clothes are untidy (in AmE) or dirty (in BrE).

(the) sea noun [U, C]
■ He was in the navy so he spent much of his life at sea.

(the) ocean • waters

■ OPP land

▶ by/on/across/beneath/under the sea/ocean
▶ in the sea/the ocean/… waters
▶ cross/sail the sea/ocean
● SEA OR OCEAN? In BrE the usual word for the mass of salt water that covers most of the earth's surface is **sea**; in AmE it is **ocean**: (BrE) a cottage by the sea • (AmE) a house on the ocean
For particular places you can only use one word: the Pacific Ocean • the Mediterranean Sea

seal noun [C]

■ The letter bore the president's seal.

stamp • crest • arms • coat of arms • emblem • logo • trademark

▶ the royal seal/crest/arms/coat of arms/emblem
▶ an official seal/stamp
▶ bear/carry a/an the seal/stamp/crest/arms/coat of arms/emblem/logo
● SEAL OR STAMP? A **stamp** may show any kind of information, such as a date, a few words or a symbol; a **seal** is likely to appear on legal documents. Both words can be used to show that sth has been approved: (fig.) The project has the government's seal/stamp of approval.

seal verb [T, often passive]

■ The unit is sealed to prevent dust from getting in.

block (sth up) • plug • stop • clog • choke

▶ seal/block/plug/stop/clog/choke sth up
▶ seal/block/plug/stop/clog/choke sth with sth
▶ seal/block (up)/plug a hole

search noun [C]

■ The police found the gun after a long search.

look | written pursuit • quest | esp. journ. hunt

▶ a search/look/quest/hunt for sb/sth
▶ in search/pursuit/quest of sth
▶ begin/launch/help in a search/quest/hunt

search verb [I, T]

■ He searched everywhere for his passport.

look • hunt • scout | fml seek | written forage • cast about/around for sth

▶ search/look/hunt/scout/seek/forage for sth
▶ search/look/hunt for clues

▶ police/detectives search/look for/seek/hunt sb/sth

seat noun

1 [C] ■ He sat back in his seat and tried to relax.

chair • sofa • bench • armchair • stool • pew • throne | esp. AmE couch

▶ in/into/out of a/an seat/chair/armchair/pew
▶ on/onto/off a/an seat/chair/sofa/bench/armchair/stool/pew/throne/couch
▶ sit (down) on/in a/an seat/chair/sofa/bench/armchair/stool/pew/throne/couch
● SEAT OR CHAIR? A **chair** is a piece of furniture designed for sitting on; a **seat** is anywhere that you can sit: ✔ a set of dining/kitchen chairs ✘ a set of dining/kitchen seats
✔ We used the old tree stump as a seat. ✘ We used the old tree stump as a chair.
Seat is also used for the place where you sit in a vehicle: ✔ the passenger seat/driver's seat (= in a car) • an aisle/a window seat (= in a bus/plane/train)

2 [C] ■ I reserved two seats for a performance of 'King Lear'.

place

▶ a/an good/empty place/seat
▶ take/book/reserve a place/seat
▶ save sb a place/seat

second noun [C]

■ She can run 100 metres in 12 seconds. ■ Hang on a second while I find my keys.

moment • minute • instant • split second | esp. BrE, infml bit | infml, spoken sec

▶ in/for a/an second/moment/minute/instant/split second/bit/sec
▶ at/within that second/moment/minute/instant
▶ hang on/hold on/wait a second/moment/minute/sec
● SECOND, MOMENT OR MINUTE? In many cases you can use any of these words: Wait/Hang on/Just a second/moment/minute.
Minute is the most frequent in spoken English; it is more usual to use **moment** in written English, esp. when telling a story.

secret noun [C]

■ The two leaders held secret talks.

confidential • private • classified • undisclosed • personal • intimate

■ OPP open

▶ secret/confidential/private/
classified/undisclosed/personal
information
▶ secret/confidential/private/
classified/personal **documents**
▶ **keep** sth secret/confidential/
private

secret adj. [only before noun]
■ He was a secret agent during the
war.

undercover • underground | fml
covert | fml, usu. disapprov.
clandestine

▶ secret/undercover/underground/
covert/clandestine **activity**
▶ a secret/clandestine **meeting/
relationship/affair**
▶ a secret/an undercover **agent**

secretive adj. (often disapprov.)
■ He's very secretive about his work.

conspiratorial • stealthy | sometimes
disapprov. **secret** | esp. written,
disapprov. **furtive** | written
surreptitious

▶ be secretive/secret **about** sth

section noun

1 [C] ■ The shed comes in sections
that you assemble yourself.

**part • piece • component • unit •
module**

2 [C] ■ The book is divided into three
sections.

**part • unit • chapter • paragraph •
clause** | law **article**

▶ **in** (a particular) section/part/unit/
chapter/paragraph/clause/article
▶ **under** (a particular) section/
paragraph/clause/article
▶ **include/add/amend/
contravene/be in breach of** a/an
section/paragraph/clause/article

sector noun [C]
■ the manufacturing/service sector

**area • field • domain • sphere •
realm**

▶ **within/outside** the sector/area/
field/domain/sphere/realm of sth
▶ **the public/private/domestic**
sector/domain/sphere/realm
▶ **work in** the sector/area/field/
domain of sth

secure adj.

1 ■ Data is stored so that it is secure
from accidental deletion.

safe • out of harm's way | esp.
spoken **all right** | infml, esp. spoken
OK

▶ **secure/safe from/against** sth
▶ **remain** secure/safe/all right/OK

2 ■ The aerial doesn't look very secure
up there.

firm • steady • stable

▶ a secure/firm/steady/stable
foundation
▶ a secure/firm/stable **base**

security noun

1 [U] ■ Airport security has been
tightened.

protection • cover | BrE **defence** |
AmE **defense**

▶ **adequate** security/protection/
defence
▶ **provide** security/protection/
defence/cover

2 [U] ■ The plan offers your family
financial security in the event of your
death.

safety • welfare • well-being

▶ **for** security/safety
▶ **economic/financial/material**
security/welfare/well-being
▶ **improve** security/safety/sb's
welfare/sb's well-being
● **SECURITY OR SAFETY?** In this
meaning **security** is used esp.
about financial or emotional
protection; **safety** is used esp.
about protection from physical
harm or danger.

see verb

1 [T] (not used in the progressive
tenses) ■ Did you see what
happened?

**notice • spot • catch • take sth in •
note • detect • witness** | fml **observe
• perceive** | written **glimpse • sight**

▶ see/notice/note/detect/observe/
perceive **that...**
▶ see/notice/note/spot/detect/
observe/perceive **how/what/
where/who...**
▶ see/notice/observe **sth
happen/sb do sth**
▶ **suddenly** see/notice/spot/catch/
detect/perceive/glimpse sb/sth

2 [T] (not used in the progressive
tenses) ■ We went to see a movie.

watch | fml **view** | esp. AmE, infml
catch

▶ see/watch/view/catch a **film/
movie/show/programme**
▶ see/watch/catch a **match/game/
fight**

3 [T] ■ You should see a doctor.

visit • go to sth • consult

▶ see/visit/consult a/the **doctor/
dentist**
▶ **come/go to** see/visit sb
▶ **come/go and** see/visit sb

4 [T] (used esp. in the progressive tenses) ∎ *Are you seeing anyone at the moment?*

go out | *esp.* AmE **date** | *esp. spoken* **be together** | *old-fash.* **court ∙ woo**

● SEE, GO OUT WITH SB or DATE? These expressions are all commonly used in the progressive tenses with time expressions such as *how long, for three months*, etc. This suggests a temporary relationship that may or may not become permanent.

5 [I, T] (not used in the progressive tenses) (*esp. spoken*) ∎ *Oh yes, I see what you mean.*

understand ∙ grasp ∙ follow | *infml, esp. spoken* **get ∙ catch on** | *fml* **comprehend**

▶ see/follow/understand/grasp/get/catch on to/comprehend **what/how...**
▶ see/understand/grasp/comprehend **that...**
▶ **can/can't** see/follow/understand/grasp/comprehend **sth**
▶ be **easy/difficult/hard** to see/follow/understand/grasp/comprehend

6 [T] (not used in the progressive tenses) ∎ *Try to see it from her point of view.*

look at sth ∙ consider ∙ view | *fml* **regard**

▶ see/look at/consider/view/regard **sb/sth** as sth
▶ see/look at/consider/view/regard sb/sth **from** a particular point of view
▶ see/look at/view/regard/consider **with** sth

7 [T] (not used in the progressive tenses) ∎ *I can't see her changing her mind.*

imagine ∙ picture ∙ visualize ∙ envision | *esp. BrE* **envisage** | *fml* **conceptualize**

▶ see/imagine/picture/visualize/envision/envisage/conceptualize **sb/sth** as sth
▶ see/imagine/picture/visualize/envision/envisage (sb) **doing sth**
▶ see/imagine/picture/visualize/envision/envisage **who/what/how...**

seek *verb*

1 [I, T] (*fml*) ∎ *Police are seeking witnesses.*

look ∙ search ∙ hunt | *written* **cast around/about for sth**

▶ seek/look/search/hunt **for sth**
▶ seek/look/search for/cast around for a/an **alternative/way**
▶ **police/detectives** seek/look for/search for/hunt **sb/sth**

---

select

2 [T, I] (*fml*) ∎ *She is seeking work in the charity sector.*

go after sth | *fml* **pursue**

▶ seek/go after a **job**
▶ **actively/successfully** seek/pursue **sth**
▶ be **currently** seeking/pursuing **sth**

3 [T] (*fml*) ∎ *She sought help from a neighbour.*

ask ∙ appeal ∙ apply ∙ claim ∙ demand | *fml* **request** | *esp. journ.* **call for sth**

▶ seek/ask for/appeal for/claim/request/call for sth **from** sb
▶ **formally** seek/ask for/apply for/claim/request/call for sth

seem *linking verb* (not used in the progressive tenses)

∎ *He seems a nice man.*

appear ∙ look ∙ sound ∙ feel ∙ come across ∙ come over ∙ strike sb (as sth)

▶ seem/appear/look/sound/feel **odd/OK/nice**, etc.
▶ seem/appear/look **to be** sth
▶ seem/look/sound/feel **like** sth
▶ seem/look/sound/feel **as if/as though...**

seize *verb* [often passive] (*esp. journ.*)

∎ *Officers seized a large quantity of drugs.*

confiscate ∙ commandeer ∙ impound | *fml* **appropriate ∙ requisition**

▶ seize/confiscate/appropriate/requisition **land**
▶ seize/confiscate/appropriate **assets/funds/property**
▶ the **government** seizes/confiscates/commandeers/requisitions sth
▶ the **authorities** seize/commandeer/requisition/impound sth

select *verb* [T, often passive]

∎ *He hasn't been selected for the team.*

choose ∙ decide ∙ single sb/sth out | *infml* **pick ∙ go for sth**

▶ select/choose/decide/pick **between** A and/or B
▶ select/choose/single out/pick/go for **sb/sth** as sb/sth
▶ select/choose/single out/pick sb/sth **for** sth
▶ select/choose/single out/adopt/pick/go for sb/sth **to do sth**
● CHOOSE, SELECT OR PICK? When you **select** sth you usu. choose it carefully, unless you actually say that it is *selected randomly/at*

random. **Pick** is a more informal word that describes a less careful action. **Choose** is the most general of these words and the only one that can be used without an object:

✔ You choose—I can't decide ✗ You select/pick—I can't decide.

selection noun

1 [U] ■ *The final team selection will be made tomorrow.*

choice • nomination | *infml* pick

▶ sb's selection/nomination as/for sth
▶ **make** a selection/choice/nomination
▶ **secure/win** selection/the nomination

2 [C] ■ *A selection of readers' comments is published here.*

choice | *esp. AmE, infml* pick

▶ sb's selection/choice/pick as sth
▶ a/an **excellent/good/popular/fine/obvious** selection/choice

3 [C] ■ *There is a wide selection of kitchens on offer.*

choice • range • variety • assortment • array

▶ a **wide** selection/choice/range/variety/assortment/array
▶ a/an **good/interesting/limited** selection/choice/range/variety
▶ **have/offer/provide** (a/an) selection/choice/range/variety/array/assortment (**of** sth)

selfish adj. (disapprov.)

■ *It was selfish of him to leave all the work to you.*

self-serving | *BrE* self-centred | *AmE* self-centered | *esp. written* egotistical • egocentric

■ OPP unselfish, selfless

▶ a/an selfish/self-centred/egotistical/egocentric **person/man**
▶ a/an selfish/self-centred/egocentric **nature**
▶ a/an selfish/self-serving/egotistical **way**

sell verb

1 [T, I] ■ *I sold my car to Jim for £800.*

sell sth off • auction sth off • sell up | *esp. BrE* auction | *finance* liquidate

▶ sell/sell sth off/auction sth off/auction sth **to** sb/a place
▶ sell/sell sth off/auction sth off/auction sth **for** £100, $47, etc.
▶ sell/sell off/auction/liquidate **property/assets**

2 [T] ■ *The shop sells a range of products.*

trade • deal in sth • export • import • handle • stock • carry | *busin.* retail | *old-fash.* or *disapprov.* peddle • hawk

▶ sell/trade/deal in/export/import/handle/stock/retail **goods**
▶ sell/trade/deal in **shares/futures/stocks/bonds/securities**
▶ sell/deal in **furniture/antiques/property**
▶ sell/carry/stock/retail a **range/line** of goods

3 [I] ■ *The painting sold for £8 000 at auction.*

cost • go | *busin.* trade • retail | *esp. spoken* be

▶ sth sells/trades/retails **at** £9.95
▶ sth sells/goes/retails **for** £9.95

send verb

1 [T] ■ *I sent Amy a postcard.*

address • forward • send sth on | *BrE* post | *esp. AmE* mail | *fml, esp. busin.* dispatch

▶ send/address/forward/send on/post/mail/dispatch sth **to** sb
▶ send/address/forward/send on/post/mail/dispatch a **letter**
▶ send/address/post/mail a/an **invitation/package/parcel/postcard/reply**

2 [T] ■ *Such behaviour sends the wrong message to young people.*

convey • communicate • relay • get sth across • pass sth on • transmit • spread • repeat | *fml* impart

▶ send/convey/communicate/relay/get across/pass on/transmit/spread/repeat/impart sth **to** sb
▶ send/convey/communicate/relay/get across/pass on/transmit/spread/repeat/impart a **message**

3 [T] ■ *She was sent to prison for two years.*

post • station • assign • put • place | *fml* dispatch

▶ send/post/assign/dispatch sb **to** a place
▶ send/assign/dispatch sb **to do** sth
▶ send/station/assign/dispatch a **force**
▶ send/post/station sb **abroad/overseas**

senior adj.

■ *I'd like a more senior position.*

superior • high-ranking • high • top • chief • leading

■ OPP junior

▶ a senior/superior/high-ranking/
top/chief/leading **officer**
▶ a senior/top/chief/leading
adviser/aide/economist/lawyer
▶ a senior/high-ranking/leading
figure/member
● **SENIOR OR SUPERIOR?** Superior is
used more than senior where there
is a strong sense of status, for
example in the army: *I'll need to
check with my superior officer.*
In everyday situations it is more
usual to talk about a *senior
colleague/adviser/teacher,* etc.

sense noun

1 [C] (often followed by *of*) ▪ *He felt
a strong sense of loss.*

feeling • impression • idea | *esp.
written* sensation

▶ a strong sense/feeling/
impression/idea/sensation
▶ a/an **wonderful/warm/
uncomfortable** sense/feeling/
sensation
▶ **have** the sense/feeling/sensation
that...
▶ **get/give** sb/**leave** sb with/
convey a sense/feeling/
impression/idea

2 [sing.] ▪ *Babies have an innate
sense of rhythm.*

understanding • conception • grasp
• comprehension • appreciation

▶ sb's sense/understanding/
conception/grasp/
comprehension/appreciation **of**
sth
▶ a/an sense/understanding/
conception/appreciation **that...**
▶ **have** a/an sense/understanding/
conception/grasp/
comprehension/appreciation

3 ▪ *You should have the sense to take
advice.*

common sense • realism • sanity •
sometimes ironic wisdom | *fml*
pragmatism

■ **OPP** nonsense
▶ sense/realism/wisdom/
pragmatism **in** (doing) sth
▶ **have** the sense/common sense/
wisdom **to do** sth
▶ **show** (great) sense/common
sense/wisdom

4 [C] ▪ *The word 'love' is used in
different senses by different people.*

meaning • significance

▶ the **original/exact/precise/
general/true** sense/meaning/
significance
▶ the **accepted/narrow/literal/
metaphorical/legal/technical**
sense/meaning of sth
▶ **have** a sense/meaning/
significance

● **SENSE OR MEANING?** Sense is used
more in technical or formal
contexts.

sensible adj.

1 ▪ *Be sensible for once!*

wise • prudent

■ **OPP** stupid
▶ a sensible/wise/prudent **person/
man/woman**
● **SENSIBLE OR WISE?** Sensible
describes sb who makes the right
decisions in practical matters; wise
often describes sb older who is
respected for the knowledge they
have gained by experience.

2 ▪ *The sensible thing would be to take
a taxi home.*

wise • best • advisable

■ **OPP** stupid
▶ be sensible/wise/best/advisable
to do sth
▶ a sensible/a wise/the best **choice/
thing to do/of** sth/**course (of
action)/investment**

sensitive adj.

1 (approv.) ▪ *He's very sensitive to
other people's feelings.*

sympathetic • understanding •
gentle • compassionate • humane •
soft

■ **OPP** insensitive
▶ sensitive/sympathetic/
understanding/gentle/
compassionate **towards** sb
▶ a sensitive/sympathetic/gentle/
compassionate/humane **manner/
man**
▶ (in) a sensitive/sympathetic/
gentle/compassionate/humane
way

2 (sometimes disapprov.) ▪ *You're far
too sensitive.*

often disapprov. touchy | *BrE, infml,
often disapprov.* prickly

▶ sensitive/touchy/prickly **about** sth
● **WHICH WORD?** Sb who is **sensitive**
or **touchy** is likely to get upset or to
cry. Sb who is **prickly** is more likely
to be aggressive than to cry.

3 ▪ *Her health is a sensitive issue.*

delicate • awkward • problematic •
emotive | *infml* tricky

▶ a/an sensitive/delicate/awkward/
problematic/tricky **matter/
situation**
▶ a/an sensitive/delicate/awkward/
emotive/tricky **question/subject**
▶ the sensitive/delicate/
problematic/emotive **nature** of sth

separate verb

1 [I, T] ■ *It is impossible to separate belief from emotion.*

disentangle • sort sth out • filter sth out | *fml* **divorce**

▶ separate/disentangle/sort out/divorce sth **from** sth
▶ separate/disentangle the **strands** of sth
▶ be **totally/easily** separated/divorced from sth

2 [I, T] ■ *The war separated many families.*

break (sth) up • scatter • isolate • cut sb/sth off | *written* **disperse** | *fml* **part • divide • segregate**

▶ separate/isolate/cut off/part/divide/segregate sth **from** sb/sth else
▶ a **crowd** scatters/disperses/parts

3 [T] ■ *A high wall separated the school from the park.*

divide • partition • mark sth off • fence sth off • cordon sth off • seal sth off

▶ separate/divide/partition sth into different **sections/areas**
▶ separate/divide/partition/mark off/fence/cordon/seal off **an area**
▶ a **wall** separates/divides sth from sth else

4 [I] ■ *He separated from his wife last year.*

split (up) • break up • divorce • get divorced

▶ separate/split (up) **from** sb
▶ split (up)/break up **with** sb
▶ a **couple** separates/splits (up)/breaks up/divorces/gets divorced

separate adj.

■ *They lead totally separate lives.*

distinct • individual • single • respective • particular • specific

■ OPP **joint, communal**
▶ a/an separate/distinct/individual/single/particular/specific **category/region**
▶ respective **categories/regions**
▶ a separate/single/particular/specific **event/incident/occasion**

separated adj. [not usu. before noun]

■ *Her parents are separated but not divorced.*

divorced | *fml* **estranged** | *esp. BrE, esp. written* **lone**

▶ be separated/divorced/estranged **from** sb

▶ a separated/divorced/lone **man/woman/parent/mother/father**
▶ a separated/divorced **couple**

separation noun [U, sing.]

■ *He argued for the need for a clear separation between Church and State.*

isolation • division • segregation • split • partition | *fml* **dissolution**

▶ separation/isolation/division/segregation **from** sb/sth
▶ separation/division/segregation/split **between** A and B
▶ separation/division/segregation/split **into** parts

● SEPARATION OR ISOLATION? **Isolation** is used of a country or its politics: *diplomatic/geographical/political/international isolation* This kind of **isolation** is usu. seen as a bad thing. **Separation** is a more general word and is often seen as a good thing.

series noun [C] (always followed by of)

■ *This is the first in a series of articles about rock 'n' roll legends.*

sequence • succession • string • order • chain • line • chronology | *esp. BrE* **catalogue** | *AmE also* **catalog**

▶ a series/sequence/string/chain/line/chronology/catalogue **of** sth
▶ a/an **long/endless/continuous/unbroken** series/sequence/succession/string/chain/line
▶ **the first/last/latest** in a series/sequence/succession/string/line

● SERIES OR SEQUENCE? A **series** of things is usu. a set of individual items that are similar in some way. It does not have to be in any logical order. **Sequence** suggests that each number or event is connected in some way to the previous one.

serious adj.

1 ■ *These explosives pose a serious threat to security.*

severe • critical • acute • extreme • drastic • desperate • life-threatening | *fml* **grave** | *esp. BrE, fml* **dire** | *esp. spoken* **bad**

■ OPP **minor**
▶ a/an serious/severe/critical/acute/desperate/life-threatening/grave/bad **problem**
▶ a/an severe/serious/acute/extreme/desperate/dire **shortage**
▶ a/an serious/severe/critical/acute/life-threatening/grave **illness**
▶ serious/severe/acute/extreme/grave **danger**

● SERIOUS OR SEVERE? **Serious** is not used to describe weather conditions:

Serious is used to describe medical conditions in everyday English; in medical English **severe** is used.

2 ■ *Please give this matter some serious thought.*

deep • profound

■ OPP **trivial, superficial**
▶ a serious/deep/profound **question/issue/analysis**
▶ a serious/deep **conversation/discussion**

3 ■ *She looked at him with a serious expression.*

solemn • earnest | *written* sober • grave | *BrE,* written sombre | *AmE, written* somber, *BrE, disapprov.* humourless | *AmE, disapprov.* humorless

■ OPP **light-hearted**
▶ a/an serious/solemn/earnest/sober/grave/sombre **expression**
▶ a serious/solemn/sombre **mood/atmosphere**
▶ on a serious/sober/sombre **note**

servant *noun* [C]
■ *They treat their mother like a servant.*

maid • footman • valet • housekeeper • butler • cleaner

▶ a **personal** servant/maid
▶ **have** a servant/maid/footman/valet/housekeeper/butler/cleaner

serve *verb*

1 [T, I] ■ *Lunch is served from 12 to 2.30 p.m.* ■ *This dish will serve four hungry people.*

feed • nourish • cater • dish (sth) up

▶ serve/feed/nourish sb/sth with sth
▶ serve/dish up a **meal**

2 [T] ■ *How can we serve the needs of our clients?*

satisfy • meet • suit | *BrE, fml* fulfil | *AmE* fulfill

▶ serve/satisfy/meet/suit/fulfil a **requirement/need/purpose**
▶ serve/satisfy/suit/fulfil sb/sth's **interest**

3 [T] ■ *The town is well served with buses.*

cater for sb/sth • provide for sb

▶ sb/sth is **well** served/catered for/provided for
▶ serve/cater for/provide for sb/sth **adequately**

service *noun*

1 [C] ■ *Essential services will be maintained.*

facilities • amenity • resource | *esp. AmE* utility

▶ **public/basic/local** services/facilities/amenities/resources/utilities
▶ **provide/lack** services/facilities/amenities/resources
▶ **have access to** services/facilities/amenities/resources

2 [C] ■ *She works for the prison service.*

agency • office • bureau • ministry

▶ **do sth through** a/an service/agency/office/bureau
▶ a **government/federal/public/state** service/agency/office/bureau/ministry
▶ a/an **local/employment/press/information** service/agency/office/bureau

3 [U] ■ *She has just celebrated 25 years' service with the company.*

work | *BrE* labour | *AmE* labor | *disapprov.* drudgery | *lit.* toil

▶ **hours/years/a lifetime** of service/work/labour/drudgery/toil

4 [C] ■ *He always attends morning service.*

ceremony • prayers • ritual • rite • liturgy

▶ **at (a)** service/ceremony/ritual/rite/prayers
▶ a **religious** service/ceremony/ritual/rite
▶ **attend (a)** service/ceremony/prayers
▶ **hold** a service/ceremony

session *noun*

1 [C] ■ *The training includes weekly practice sessions.*

class • lesson • seminar • workshop • tutorial • period

▶ a session/class/lesson/seminar/workshop/tutorial **on sth**
▶ **in/during** a session/class/lesson/seminar/workshop/tutorial/period
▶ **at** a session/class/lesson/seminar/workshop/tutorial

2 [C] ■ *a session of the UN General Assembly*

meeting • gathering • assembly • conference • convention • summit

▶ an **annual** session/meeting/gathering/assembly/conference/convention/summit
▶ **hold/attend** a/an session/meeting/gathering/assembly/conference/convention/summit
▶ **address** a/an session/meeting/

gathering/assembly/conference/convention

set noun [C]
■ *a set of six matching chairs*

group • collection • cluster • bunch • clump
► a set/group/collection/cluster/bunch/clump **of** sth
► **in** a set/group/cluster/bunch/clump
► **form** a set/group/cluster/clump
► **divide** sth into sets/groups/clusters

set verb
1 [T] (always used with an adv. or prep.) ■ *She set the tray down on the table.*

put • lay • place • position • settle • plant | *infml* **stick** | *esp. BrE, infml* **pop**
► set/put/lay/place/position/stick/pop sth **on** sth
► set/put/lay/place/stick/pop sth **in/into** sth
► set/put/lay sth **down**

2 [T] ■ *Her manner set everyone at ease.*

put • place
► set/put/place sb/sth **at ease/in motion**

3 [T] ■ *Have they set a date for the wedding?*

fix • schedule • book | *esp. BrE* **timetable**
► set/fix/schedule/book/timetable sb/sth **to do** sth
► set/fix/schedule/book a **time/date/day**
► set/fix/schedule/timetable a **meeting**

4 [T] ■ *She's set herself a difficult task.*

allocate • assign • allot
► set/allocate/assign/allot sth **for** sth
► set/allocate/assign **work**
► set/assign **homework**

set adj. [usu. before noun]
■ *Each person was given set jobs to do.*

fixed • predetermined • prearranged
► set/fixed/predetermined **rules**
► a set/fixed/predetermined **number/level/quantity/pattern**
► a set/fixed **price**

set off phrasal verb
■ *We set off at dawn.*

start • take off • be off • set sail • leave | *fml* **depart** | *esp. written* **set out**

■ OPP **arrive**
► set off/start/take off/set sail/leave/depart/set out **for/from** sth
► set off/start (out)/take off/be off/set sail/set out **on** a journey
► set/start/take off/leave/depart/set out **early**

settle verb
1 [T, I] ■ *Talks will be held in an attempt to settle the dispute.*

resolve • solve • repair • mend | *infml* **patch** sth **up** | *esp. BrE, esp. spoken* **sort** sth **out**
► settle/patch up sth **with** sb
► settle/resolve/solve/mend/patch up/sort out **your differences**
► settle/resolve/solve/sort out a/an **dispute/argument/crisis/matter/issue**

2 [T] ■ *It's all settled—we're leaving on the nine o'clock plane.*

agree • negotiate • do a deal • understand • broker • hammer sth **out** | *infml* **thrash** sth **out** | *fml* **conclude**
► settle/agree/negotiate/do a deal/broker/hammer out/thrash out/conclude (sth) **with** sb
► settle/agree sth/negotiate sth/be understood/broker sth/hammer sth out/conclude sth **between** A and B
► settle/agree/negotiate/do/broker/hammer sth out/conclude a **deal**

3 [T, often passive] ■ *Bob will be there? That settles it. I'm not coming.*

decide • clinch • confirm
► settle/decide/clinch an **argument**
► finally settle/decide/clinch/confirm sth
► That settles/clinches **it**.

4 [I] (always used with an adv. or prep.) ■ *He settled in Vienna after his wife's death.*

move in | *BrE* **set up home**
► settle/set up home **in** a district/city/country, etc.

set sth **up** phrasal verb
1 ■ *Police set up roadblocks in the city.*

put sth **up • build • construct** | *fml* **erect**

■ OPP **take** sth **down**
► set up/put up/build/construct/erect a **barrier**
● **SET STH UP OR PUT STH UP?** Set sth up is not used for permanent buildings. You can set up or put up

a fence/barrier/shelter. You set up camp, but put up a tent.

2 ■ *The meeting took months to set up.*

---

schedule • fix • line sb/sth up | *esp. BrE* **timetable**

▸ set up/schedule/fix/timetable/ line up sth **for** sth
▸ set up/schedule/fix/timetable a **meeting**
▸ set up/schedule/fix an **appointment**
▸ set up/schedule/timetable an **event**

3 ■ *He plans to set up his own business.*

---

start • form | *esp. written* **establish • found**

▸ set up/start/form/establish/found a **group/society/company/ movement**
▸ set up/start/establish/found a **business/firm/programme**
▸ set up/form/establish a **government/committee/team/ database**

---

severe adj.

1 ■ *Strikes have caused severe disruption to services.*

---

serious • critical • acute • extreme • drastic • desperate • life-threatening | *fml* **grave** | *esp. BrE, fml* **dire** | *infml, esp. spoken* **bad**

■ OPP **minor**
▸ a/an severe/serious/critical/ acute/desperate/life-threatening/ grave/bad **problem**
▸ a/an severe/serious/critical/ acute/life-threatening/grave **illness**
▸ severe/serious/acute/extreme/ grave **danger**
▸ severe/serious/acute/extreme/ desperate/dire **poverty**
● **SEVERE OR SERIOUS?** Serious is used to describe medical conditions in everyday English; in medical English severe is used.

2 ■ *It was an unusually severe winter.*

---

harsh • hard • bleak

■ OPP **mild**
▸ a severe/harsh/hard/bleak **winter**
▸ severe/harsh **weather/conditions**
▸ a severe/hard **climate**
▸ a severe/hard **frost**

3 ■ *a severe punishment for drug use*

---

tough • strict | *usu. disapprov.* **harsh** | *often approv.* **firm** | *fml* **punitive**

■ OPP **lenient, soft**
▸ severe/tough/strict/harsh/firm **with** sb/sth
▸ severe/tough/strict/harsh **on** sb/ sth

▸ severe/tough/strict/harsh/firm **discipline**
▸ a severe/tough/harsh **penalty/ sentence**

---

shade noun [C]

■ *a delicate shade of blue*

---

tint • tinge | *BrE* **colour** | *AmE* **color** | *lit. or tech.* **hue**

▸ a shade/tinge of blue/green, etc.
▸ a **warm/rich** shade/tint/colour/ hue
▸ a **bright/dark/pastel/subtle** shade/colour/hue
▸ **have** a shade/tint/tinge/colour/ hue

---

shadow noun

1 [C] ■ *His figure cast a shadow on the wall.*

---

shape • silhouette • form • figure

▸ a **tall** shadow/shape/silhouette/ form/figure
▸ a **black/dark** shadow/shape/ silhouette/figure
▸ a **ghostly** shadow/shape/form/ figure

2 [U] ■ *Her face was deep in shadow.*

---

shadows • shade • darkness • the dark | *lit.* **gloom**

▸ **in** shadow/shade/darkness/ gloom
▸ **in/into/out of** the shadows/ shade/darkness/dark/gloom
▸ be **shrouded in/plunged into** shadows/darkness/gloom

---

shake verb

1 [I, T] ■ *Shake the bottle before use.*

---

rattle • vibrate • shudder • wobble • jolt • jar | *infml* **jiggle** | *esp. journ.* **rock**

▸ shake/rattle/vibrate/shudder/jar/ rock **with**
▸ shake/rattle/vibrate/shudder/ rock (sth) **violently**
▸ shake/vibrate/rock (sth) **gently**

2 [I] ■ *I was shaking like a leaf.*

---

tremble • shudder • shiver • twitch • convulse

▸ shake/tremble/shiver/be convulsed **with** fear
▸ shake/tremble/shiver **with** cold
▸ sb's **hands** shake/tremble/twitch
▸ sb's **legs** shake/tremble

3 [T] (not used in the progressive tenses) ■ *He was badly shaken by the news.*

---

unnerve | *written* **agitate • fluster • disconcert**

▸ be shaken/unnerved/agitated/ flustered/disconcerted **by** sth

shame

shame noun

1 [U] ■ She hung her head in shame.

guilt + **regret** | *esp. written* **remorse** | *fml, esp. religion* **repentance**

► shame/guilt/regret/remorse **at** sth
► do sth **without** shame/guilt/
regret/remorse/repentance
► **feel** (no) shame/guilt/regret/
remorse
► **have** no shame/regret/remorse
● **SHAME OR GUILT?** You feel **guilt**
when you have done sth you
believe to be wrong; you feel
shame when other people know
that you have done sth wrong or
stupid: *He could not bear the guilt of
knowing it was his fault.* ♦ *He could
not bear the shame of his family
knowing what he had done.*

2 a shame [sing.] (*esp. spoken*)
■ What a shame he couldn't come.

unfortunate | *esp. spoken* **a pity** +
too bad | *fml* **regrettable**

► It's a shame/a pity/too bad **about**
sb/sth.
► a shame/a pity/unfortunate/too
bad/regrettable **that...**
► a **great/real/terrible** shame/pity.
► **What** a shame/pity.

3 [U] ■ His greed brought shame on
the party.

disgrace | *fml* **discredit** + **disrepute** |
BrE, fml **dishonour** | *AmE, fml*
dishonor

■ **OPP** honour

► **bring** shame/disgrace/discredit/
dishonour **on** sth.
► **There is no** shame/disgrace/
dishonour in sth.
● **WHICH WORD?** All these words are
used to talk about a public loss of
respect. **Disgrace** is also used to
talk about the loss of respect of
people who are close to you.

shape noun

1 [C, U] ■ The building has a
rectangular shape.

form + **figure** + **outline** + **shadow** +
silhouette + **profile** + **line** | *written*
contour

► **in** shape/form/outline/silhouette/
profile
► a **tall** shape/form/sigure/
shadow/silhouette
► a **black/dark** shape/figure/
outline/shadow/silhouette/profile
► **make out/see** a/an shape/form/
figure/outline/silhouette

2 [U] ■ The economy is still in good
shape. ■ How do you manage to
stay in shape?

state + **condition** + **repair** + **health**

► **in** (a) ... shape/state/condition/
repair/health
► a) **good/poor/bad** shape/state/
condition/ (state of) repair/health
► **keep** sth **in** (a) ... shape/state/
condition/repair
► **get** (sth) **into** (a) ... shape/state/
condition

shape verb

1 [T] ■ Shape the dough into balls.

form + **sculpt** + **carve** + **cast** | *BrE*
mould | *AmE* **mold** | *written* **fashion**

► shape/form/sculpt/carve/mould/
fashion sth **into** sth
► shape/form/sculpt/carve/cast/
mould/fashion sth **from/out of**
sth
► shape/sculpt/carve/fashion **wood**
► shape/sculpt/mould/fashion **clay**
► sculpt/carve **stone/marble**

2 [T] ■ She helped to shape party
policy.

form + **decide** + **govern** | *fml*
determine

► shape/form/decide/govern/
determine **how...**
► shape/decide/determine the
outcome/result (of sth)
► shape/determine the **course/
direction/future** (of sth)
► a **factor** shapes/decides/governs/
determines sth
● **SHAPE OR FORM?** Both these words
can be used to talk about the
influences on sth.
✔ to shape/form sb's character/
ideas/attitude/opinions
Shape, but not **form**, can be used
to talk about influencing sb's
behaviour or a course of events:
✔ the power of religion to shape
behaviour ✗ the power of religion to
form behaviour
✔ Historical events helped to shape
the town. ✗ Historical events helped
to form the town.

share noun [C, usu. sing.]

■ How much was your share of the
winnings?

ration + **quota** + **cut** + **percentage** +
allocation

► a share/ration/quota/cut/
percentage/allocation **of** sth
► **get** your share/ration/quota/cut/
percentage/allocation
► **have** your share/ration/quota
● **SHARE, RATION OR QUOTA?** **Share**
and **quota** can be used to talk
about such things as *luck, laughs,
work* or *blame*. **Share** is more
frequent and **quota** is used more in
formal or written English. **Ration** is
used to talk about food, or sth nice
that you must not expect too
much of.

share verb [T, I]

■ *She shares a house with two other students.*

divide • split • pool | *disapprov.* **carve sth up**

▶ share/divide/split/carve up sth **between/among** different people
▶ share/split/pool sth **with** sb
▶ share/split/divide **the money/work**

● **SHARE, DIVIDE OR SPLIT?** Things are **shared** between people; things are **divided** between people, uses or places; things are **split** between people, things or places. **Divide** is often used about very important things; **share** is used about less important things:
✓He shared his sweets out among his friends. ✗ He divided his sweets among his friends.
✓The story is about a father who divides his property among his sons.

sharp adj.

1 ■ *Use a really sharp knife.*

jagged • serrated

■ OPP **blunt**

▶ a sharp/jagged/serrated **edge**
▶ a sharp/serrated **blade/knife**
▶ (a) sharp/jagged **rock/teeth**

2 [usu. before noun] ■ *There has been a sharp rise in crime.*

sudden • dramatic • abrupt

■ OPP **gradual**

▶ a/an sharp/sudden/dramatic/abrupt **increase/rise** (in sth)
▶ a sharp/sudden/dramatic **drop/fall/change/improvement/deterioration** (in sth)

3 [usu. before noun] ■ *In sharp contrast to her mood, the sun shone in a clear blue sky.*

striking • distinct • definite • clear | *esp. written* **marked • pronounced**

▶ a/an sharp/striking/distinct/definite/clear/marked/pronounced **difference**
▶ a/an sharp/striking/distinct/definite/clear/marked **improvement**
▶ a sharp/striking/distinct/clear/marked **contrast**
▶ a sharp/striking/definite/marked/pronounced **increase**

4 (usu. *disapprov.*) ■ *He was sharp with me when I was late.*

usu. *disapprov.* **curt • brusque |** *sometimes disapprov.* **short • abrupt • terse • clipped**

▶ sharp/curt/brusque/short/abrupt **with** sb
▶ a sharp/curt/brusque/terse/clipped **voice**
▶ a sharp/curt/brusque/clipped **tone**

5 ■ *The fruit had a sharp taste.*

sour • acid • bitter • pungent • acrid

■ OPP **sweet**

▶ a/an sharp/sour/acid/bitter/pungent/acrid **taste/flavour/smell/odour**
▶ a/an sharp/sour/acid/bitter **fruit**
▶ a/an sharp/bitter/pungent/acrid **scent**

● **WHICH WORD?** A **bitter** taste is usu. unpleasant, but some people enjoy the bitter flavour of coffee or chocolate; no other word can describe this flavour. A **sharp** or **pungent** flavour is more strong than unpleasant, esp. when describing cheese. **Sharp**, **sour** and **acid** all describe the taste of a lemon or a fruit that is not ripe. An **acrid** smell is strong and unpleasant, esp. the smell of smoke or burning, but not the smell of food.

shave verb [T, I]

■ *He shaved off his beard.*

cut • trim • snip • shear • clip • crop

▶ shave/cut/trim/snip/shear/clip sth **off**
▶ shave/cut/snip/shear/clip sth **from** sth
▶ shave/cut/trim/snip/shear/clip/crop **hair**

shed noun [C]

■ *a garden/tool shed* ■ *a cowshed*

barn • outbuilding • stable • hut • shack • cabin • shelter

▶ a wooden shed/hut/shack/cabin/shelter
▶ build a shed/barn/stable/hut/shack/cabin/shelter

sheet noun [C]

■ *Take a clean sheet of paper.*

page • side • slip

▶ a sheet/slip **of paper**
▶ **on** a sheet/page/side/slip
▶ **in the middle/at the bottom/at the top of** the sheet/page
▶ a/an blank/loose/printed/separate/A4/A5, etc. **sheet/page**

shelter noun [U]

■ *They had to find shelter for the night.*

refuge • cover • safety • asylum | *fml* **sanctuary**

▶ shelter/refuge/asylum/sanctuary **from** sth
▶ **temporary** shelter/refuge/asylum/sanctuary
▶ **seek/find** shelter/refuge/asylum/sanctuary

shelter verb [T]

■ Trees shelter the house from the wind.

protect • shield • guard | fml **safeguard**

► shelter/protect/shield/guard/safeguard sb/sth **from** sth

shift verb [I, T] (esp. written)

■ He shifted uncomfortably in his chair.

move • stir | infml **budge |** fml **dislodge**

► shift/move/stir/budge/dislodge (sth) **from** sth
► won't/wouldn't/refuse to shift/move/stir/budge
► hardly/barely shift/move/stir/budge

shine verb [I]

■ The could see a light shining in the distance.

gleam • glow • sparkle • twinkle • glitter • glisten • glint | written **shimmer**

► shine/gleam/glow/sparkle/twinkle/glitter/glisten/glint/shimmer **with** sth
► shine/gleam/sparkle/glitter/glisten/glint/shimmer **in the sunlight**
► a **light** shines/gleams/glows
► the **stars** shine/twinkle/glitter
► sb's **eyes** shine/gleam/glow/sparkle/twinkle/glitter/glint

ship noun [C]

■ They boarded a ship bound for India.

boat • cruiser • yacht • ferry • submarine | infml **sub |** fml **vessel • craft**

► on/onto/off a ship/boat/cruiser/yacht/ferry/submarine/vessel/craft
► aboard/on board a ship/boat/cruiser/yacht/ferry/submarine/vessel/craft
► a ship/boat/cruiser/yacht/ferry/vessel/craft **sails/sets sail**
► a ship/boat/cruiser/yacht/ferry/submarine/vessel/craft **floats/capsizes/sinks/goes down**
● **SHIP OR BOAT?** You can use **boat**, but not **ship**, as a general term for any vehicle that travels on water; but a **ship** only travels by sea.

shiver noun [C]

■ A shiver of fear went through him.

shudder • tremor • tremble • shaking • spasm • twitch | esp. written **quiver |** fml **convulsion**

► feel a shiver/shudder/tremor/tremble/twitch/spasm/quiver
► send a shiver/shudder/tremor/spasm/quiver down/through, etc. sth
► a shiver/shudder/tremor/tremble/quiver **goes/runs through** sb/sth

shiver verb [I]

■ Don't stand outside shivering.

shake • shudder • tremble • twitch | fml **convulse**

► shiver/shake/tremble/be convulsed **with** fear
► shiver/shake/tremble **with** cold
► shiver/shudder/tremble **at a** thought/memory, etc.

shock noun

1 [U] ■ The team were in shock after their first round defeat.

dismay • horror

► shock/dismay/horror **at** sth
► **in/with** shock/dismay/horror

2 [C] ■ The news of his death came as a shock to us all.

scare • fright

► get/have/give sb a shock/scare/fright

3 [C, U] ■ The shock of the explosion was felt six miles away.

impact • force

► the shock/force of the **impact/explosion**
► **feel** the shock/impact/force of sth
► **absorb** the shock/impact of sth

shock verb

1 [T, often passive] (not used in the progressive tenses) ■ We were all shocked at the news of Michael's death.

horrify • scandalize • dismay • repel | BrE **sicken • appal |** AmE **appall |** infml **rock**

► shocked/horrified/scandalized/dismayed/appalled **at** sth
► shock/horrify/scandalize/dismay/sicken/appal sb **that...**
► shock/horrify/scandalize/dismay/sicken/appal sb **to think/see/hear/find/learn...**

2 [I, T] ■ The film deliberately sets out to shock.

offend • disgust • insult • abuse

► feel shocked/offended/disgusted/insulted
► **deeply** shocked/offended/insulted

shocking adj.

■ What a shocking waste of money!

outrageous • disgraceful • scandalous • criminal • unforgivable • shameful | *fml* deplorable

▶ shocking/outrageous/disgraceful/ scandalous/unforgivable/ shameful/deplorable **that...**
▶ shocking/outrageous/disgraceful/ scandalous/criminal/shameful/ deplorable **behaviour**
▶ a/an shocking/outrageous/ disgraceful/scandalous/criminal/ shameful **waste**
▶ a shocking/disgraceful/ scandalous/shameful/deplorable **situation/condition**
● **SHOCKING OR OUTRAGEOUS?** For a very serious situation, use **shocking**; for an unfair situation, use **outrageous**: *the shocking truth about heroin addiction* ◇ *It's outrageous that you should get paid more than me.*

shoot verb

1 [I, T] ■ *Don't shoot—I surrender.*

fire • open fire • launch

▶ shoot/fire **at** sb/sth
▶ shoot/fire **blanks/bullets/arrows**
▶ a **gun** shoots/fires

2 [I, T] (always used with an adv. or prep.) ■ *A cat shot out into the road in front of the car.*

fly • flash • streak • hurtle • speed | *esp. BrE* career | *infml* zoom | *infml, esp. BrE* past | *infml, esp. AmE* whizz

▶ shoot/fly/flash/streak/hurtle/ speed/career/zoom/whizz **down/across**
▶ shoot/fly/flash/streak/hurtle/ speed/career/zoom/whizz **past** (sb/sth)
▶ shoot/fly/hurtle/speed/career/ zoom **off**

shop noun [C] (esp. BrE)

■ *a pet/gift/flower shop*

store • supermarket • boutique • salon | *AmE* grocery store | *busin.* outlet

▶ an **expensive/exclusive** shop/ store/boutique/salon
▶ a **specialist** shop/store/outlet/ boutique
▶ a/an shop/store/supermarket/ boutique/salon/grocery store/ outlet **sells/offers** sth
▶ **own/have** a/an shop/store/ salon/supermarket/boutique/ grocery store/outlet
● **SHOP OR STORE?** In *BrE* **shop** is the usual word; it is only used in *AmE* about small, specialist shops. In *AmE* **store** is the usual word; it is only used in *BrE* about large shops, esp. in business English, journalism and advertising.

short adj.

1 ■ *He was a short, fat little man.*
■ *She ran as fast as her short legs would carry her.*

stubby • stunted | *fml* diminutive | *approv.* petite | *disapprov.* dumpy

■ **OPP** tall, long
▶ a short/diminutive/petite/dumpy **woman/figure**
▶ a short/diminutive **man**
▶ short/stubby **fingers**

2 ■ *Professor Ogawa gave a short talk on solar eclipses.*

temporary • short-lived • passing | *esp.* written brief • fleeting • momentary

■ **OPP** long
▶ a short/brief/passing **moment**
▶ a short/temporary/brief **stay**
▶ a short/brief/momentary **silence/pause**
● **SHORT OR BRIEF?** Short is used more in informal and spoken English. Short, but not brief, is used to describe books, lists, projects, etc. that take only a short time. Brief is used more to describe a *look, glance, glimpse, smile* or *sigh.*

3 [not before noun] ■ *When food was short they picked berries in the woods.*

scarce • in short supply • low • limited • few and far between

■ **OPP** plentiful
▶ **resources** are short/scarce/in short supply/limited
▶ **food** is short/scarce/in short supply
▶ **time** is short/limited
● **WHICH WORD?** Short is used esp. about *time* and *money*. Scarce and in short supply are used about resources that are not generally available. Low is used esp. when you have not got much left.

4 ■ *She kept her answers short.*

brief • concise • economical • abbreviated | *approv.* succinct • pithy | *sometimes disapprov.* terse | *usu. disapprov.* curt • brusque

■ **OPP** long
▶ a/an short/brief/concise/ abbreviated/succint/terse **account**
▶ a short/brief/concise/succint/ terse **summary/answer/statement**
● **SHORT OR BRIEF?** A mention is usu. brief; an *answer* is more likely to be short. Brief is used about speech: ✓*Please be brief.* ✗*Please be short.*

shout verb [I, T]

■ *Stop shouting and listen!*

yell • scream • cry out (sth) • bellow • cheer • call • raise your voice | AmE, infml holler | written cry • roar | disapprov. bawl

■ OPP whisper
► shout/yell/cry out/call/raise your voice/holler/cry **to** sb
► shout/yell/scream/bellow/holler/roar **at** sb
► shout/yell/scream/cry out/bellow/holler/roar **in** pain/anguish/rage, etc.

show noun

1 [C] ■ *His one-man show had the audience falling about with laughter.*

performance • production • act • display • spectacle

► **in** a/an performance/production/act/display/spectacle
► **at** a show/performance/production/display/spectacle
► **do** a/an performance/production/act
► **put on/stage** a show/performance/production/display

2 [C] ■ *a late-night radio show*

broadcast • webcast • showing • transmission | BrE programme | AmE program

► a show/broadcast/programme **about** sth
► **be on** a show/programme
► **in** a show/broadcast/webcast/transmission/programme
► a radio/television/TV show/broadcast/transmission/programme
● **SHOW OR PROGRAMME?** In BrE **programme** is the more general word; **show** is used about fairly informal TV or radio and is usu. used in compounds. In AmE **show** is the more general word; **program** is used about more serious TV and radio and is usu. used in compounds: *(AmE) What time is that show on?* • *She hosts a news program on TV.*

3 [C, U] ■ *They hold a fashion show twice a year.*

display • trade show/fair | esp. BrE exhibition | AmE exhibit • fair

► **be on** show/display/exhibition/exhibit
► **see** a/an show/display/exhibition/exhibit
► **attend/go to/visit** a/an show/display/fair/trade show/exhibition/exhibit
● **SHOW OR EXHIBITION?** An **exhibition** usu. contains works of art, or items of cultural or scientific interest that may be on display for a long time. **Show** is a more general word and usu. refers to a temporary event.

show verb

1 [T] ■ *Opinion polls show that the government's popularity is declining.*

prove • demonstrate • indicate • illustrate

► show/prove/demonstrate/indicate sth **to** sb
► show/prove/demonstrate/indicate/illustrate **that/what/how…**
► **figures/studies** show/prove/demonstrate/indicate/illustrate sth
● **SHOW OR PROVE?** **Prove** is often preferred to **show** to give a stronger sense of justice being done.

2 [T] ■ *You have to show your ticket as you go in.*

reveal • expose

► show/reveal sth **to** sb

3 [T, I] ■ *Show me how to do it.*

teach • train • coach | fml instruct

► show/teach sb **how to** do sth
► show/teach sb **that…**

4 [T] ■ *He showed me our location on the map.*

point • indicate

5 [T] ■ *You'll need someone to show you the way.*

guide • take • go with sb • escort • walk • drive • lead • usher • direct | fml accompany

► show/guide/take/escort/walk/drive/lead/usher/direct/accompany sb **to/out of/into** sth
► show/guide/take/escort/walk/drive/lead sb **around/round**
► show/guide/take/escort/lead/usher sb **in/out**

6 [T, I] ■ *Her expression showed her disappointment.*

reflect • express • display • demonstrate

► show/demonstrate **that…**
► show/reflect/express/display/demonstrate **interest**
► show/reflect/express/display (your) **feelings/emotions**

7 [I, T] ■ *The cloth was folded so that the stain didn't show.*

appear • emerge • come out | fml manifest itself

► **suddenly** show/appear/emerge/come out

8 [T] (not usu. in the progressive tenses) ■ *The picture shows St George slaying the dragon.*

present • portray | fml depict • represent

▶ show/present/portray/depict/ represent sb/sth **as** sth
▶ show/present/portray/depict/ represent sb/sth **accurately**
▶ show/present/portray/depict sb/ sth **clearly/vividly**

9 [I, T] ■ She plans to show her paintings early next year.

display • present • produce • launch | journ. unveil

▶ show/display/present/launch/ unveil a new **product/model**
▶ show/display/present **your wares**
▶ show/display a **painting/your work/a collection/a trophy**

shower noun

1 [C] ■ He's in the shower just now.

bath • wash

▶ **in** the shower/bath
▶ **need/have** a shower/bath/wash
▶ **take** a shower/bath

2 [C] ■ We got caught in a heavy shower.

downpour • rain • drizzle

▶ (a) **heavy** shower/downpour/rain
▶ a **sudden** shower/downpour
▶ **be/get caught in** a shower/a downpour/the rain

3 [C, usu. sing.] (usu. followed by of) (written) ■ The fire sent out a shower of sparks.

volley | written hail

▶ a shower/volley/hail of **arrows/ bullets/stones**

shower verb

1 [I] ■ He showered and dressed and went downstairs.

freshen (yourself) up | esp. BrE wash | BrE bath | AmE bathe • wash up • clean yourself up

▶ shower/wash **quickly**
▶ shower/wash/bath/bathe and **change/dress**

2 [T] ■ The roof collapsed, showering us with dust.

rain • scatter • spray • sprinkle

▶ shower/rain/scatter/spray/ sprinkle sth **with** sth
▶ shower/rain/scatter/spray/ sprinkle **on/onto/over** sth
▶ shower/rain/scatter **ash**

show off phrasal verb (infml, disapprov.)
■ They drove around in their new cars, showing off to their friends.

boast • brag • gloat

▶ show off/boast/brag/gloat **about** sth

▶ show off/boast/brag/gloat **to** sb

show up phrasal verb (infml)
■ When she failed to show up by eight we got worried.

arrive • appear • land | esp. spoken turn up • get | infml roll in • hit • show | esp. written reach

▶ show up/arrive/appear/land/turn up **in/at/on** a place
▶ show up/arrive/appear/land/turn up/get/reach **here/there**
▶ **be the first/last** to show up/ arrive/appear/land/turn up/get here/roll in

shrewd adj. (often approv.)
■ My mother was a shrewd judge of character.

canny | approv. astute • perceptive • incisive • discriminating • discerning

▶ a/an shrewd/canny/astute **businessman/politician/move**
▶ a/an shrewd/astute/perceptive **observer/observation**
▶ a/an shrewd/perceptive/incisive **comment**

shrink verb [I, T]
■ The market for their products is shrinking.

contract • narrow • shorten

■ OPP **grow**
▶ shrink/contract/narrow/shorten (sth) **to** a particular size
▶ shrink/contract/narrow/shorten (sth) **by** a particular amount
▶ a **market/the economy** shrinks/ contracts
● **SHRINK OR CONTRACT?** A market or economy **shrinks** or **contracts**. Glass, metal and muscles **contract**, and words can be **contracted**. Most other things, including clothes and fabric, **shrink**.

shut verb [T, I]
■ I can't shut my suitcase—it's too full.

close • slam • draw • lock • bolt

■ OPP **open**
▶ shut/close/slam/lock/bolt a **door/gate**
▶ shut/close/lock a **window/ drawer/case/suitcase**
▶ shut/close a/an/your **box/lid/ eyes/mouth/flap/valve/book/ umbrella**
▶ close/draw the **curtains/blinds**
● **SHUT OR CLOSE?** Close often suggests a more slow or gentle action than **shut**: Close your eyes and go to sleep.

shut sb/yourself in (sth)
phrasal verb

■ Her brothers used to shut her in the cellar.

**lock sb/yourself in (sth) • coop sb/
sth up • cage • pen • trap • confine**

▶ be shut/locked/cooped up/
caged/penned/trapped/confined
in sth
▶ be shut/locked/cooped up/
caged/penned/trapped/confined
with sb/sth

shy *adj.*

■ Don't be shy—come and say hello.

**coy • embarrassed • awkward •
self-conscious • introverted •
reserved • inhibited • insecure** | *esp.
written* **timid • diffident**

■ **OPP confident**

▶ shy/coy/embarrassed/awkward/
self-conscious/inhibited/insecure/
timid/diffident **about** sth
▶ a/an shy/reserved/insecure/timid
(young) **man/woman/child**
▶ a/an shy/coy/embarrassed/self-
conscious/diffident **smile**

sick *adj.*

1 ■ Her mother's very sick.

**not (very) well • unwell • sickly •
unhealthy** | *esp. BrE* **ill** | *esp. spoken*
bad | *fml* **ailing**

■ **OPP well**

▶ sick/unwell/ill **with** flu, a fever,
etc.
▶ a sick/an ailing **mother/father/
parent/husband/wife**
▶ sick/sickly/unhealthy/seriously ill
children
▶ become/get/fall sick/ill
● **SICK OR ILL?** In *BrE* the usual word is
ill, unless you are taking time off
work because of illness:
✓Ellie is off sick/called in sick today.
✗Ellie is off ill/called in ill today.
In *AmE* the usual word is **sick**; **ill** is
only used about very serious
illnesses.

2 [not usu. before noun] ■ Whenever
I think about the exams I feel
physically sick.

---

queasy | *fml* **nauseous**

▶ sick/queasy/nauseous **with** fear
▶ feel sick/queasy/nauseous
▶ make sb sick/queasy/nauseous

3 sick of sth [not before noun]
(*infml*) ■ I'm sick and tired of your
moaning.

---

bored | *infml* **fed up**

▶ sick/bored/fed up **of** sth
▶ get sick/bored/fed up
▶ sick/bored **to death (of** sb/sth**)**

---

side *noun*

1 [C] ■ A van was parked at the side of
the road.

---

edge • end • perimeter

■ **OPP the middle**

▶ **at/on** the side/edge/end/
perimeter
▶ **along/around** the sides/edge/
perimeter
▶ the **northern/eastern/southern/
western** side/edge/end
● **SIDE, EDGE OR END?** The **edge** of an
object goes all the way around it. The
ends or **sides** are the parts of the
edge that are opposite each
other. **Ends** have the longest
distance between them.

2 [C] ■ You need to listen to both sides
of the argument.

**point of view • perspective • view •
opinion • attitude • position • angle
• stance • line**

▶ **different/various** sides/points of
view/perspectives/views/
opinions/attitudes/positions/
angles
▶ **take** a/an side/point of view/
perspective/view/attitude/
position/stance/line
▶ **change** (your) sides/point of view/
perspective/view/opinion/
attitude/position/stance

3 [C] ■ It's good you can see the funny
side of the situation.

---

aspect • dimension • strand • end

▶ a/an side/aspect/dimension/
strand **to** sth
▶ the **political/cultural/historical/
spiritual/human** side/aspect/
dimension of sth
▶ **consider** a/an side/aspect/
dimension of sth

4 [C+sing./pl. v.] (*BrE*) ■ He led his
side to victory.

---

team • squad • line-up | *BrE* **club**

▶ a football/rugby/cricket side/
team/squad/club
▶ a/an **Irish/French, etc.** side/team/
squad/club
▶ the **England/Ireland, etc.** side/
team/squad/line-up
▶ a side/team/club **plays/wins/
loses** (a game/match)
● **SIDE, TEAM OR CLUB?** Club refers to
the organization that includes
players, owner and manager; **team**
and **side** usu. refer just to the
players, often at a particular time:
This team is arguably even better
than the Welsh side of the seventies.

---

sight *noun*

1 [U] ■ He caught sight of a car behind
him.

---

glimpse • look • glance

► catch sight/a glimpse of sb/sth

2 [U] ■ *He looked, but there was no one in sight.*

---

view • vision

► in/out of sight/view
► in/within sight/view **of** sth
► come into/disappear from sight/ view/sb's vision
● SIGHT, VIEW OR VISION? Use **view** to say how well you can see:
  ✓ *I had a good view of the stage.* ✗ *i had a good sight/vision of the stage.*
  Vision must always be used with a possessive pronoun: *my/his/her, etc.* (field of) vision

3 [C] ■ *It's a spectacular sight as the birds fly off.*

---

view • scene • panorama

► a beautiful/breathtaking sight/ view/scene/panorama
► a magnificent/spectacular sight/ view/scene/panorama
► enjoy the sight/view/scene/ panorama

---

sign noun

1 [C, U] ■ *Headaches may be a sign of stress.*

---

indication • signal • symptom • mark • pointer • hint • clue • trace • suggestion • symbol | *esp. busin.* **indicator** | *esp. journ.* **hallmark**

► a/an sign/indication/signal/ symptom/mark/hint/trace/ suggestion/symbol/indicator/ hallmark **of** sth
► a/an sign/indication/signal/ symptom/hint/suggestion/ indicator **that...**
► have (the) signs/symptoms/ marks/traces/hallmarks of sth
● SIGN, INDICATION OR SIGNAL? An **indication** often comes in the form of sth that sb says; a **sign** is usu. sth that happens or that sb does. **Signal** is often used for sth that suggests to sb that they should do sth. **Sign** is not usu. used in this way:
  ✓ *Reducing prison sentences would send the wrong signals to criminals.* ✗ *Reducing prison sentences would send the wrong signs to criminals.*

2 [C] ■ *Follow the signs for the Arts Centre.*

---

board • plaque • notice • plate

► on a sign/board/plaque/notice/ plate
► put up/see/read a sign/board/ plaque/notice/plate
► a sign/board/plaque/notice/plate **appears/goes up**
● SIGN OR NOTICE? A **notice** always gives its information in words; a **sign** often uses pictures or symbols:

✓ a road/traffic/shop/pub sign ✗ ~~a road/traffic/shop/pub notice~~

3 [C] (used in compounds) ■ *a plus/ minus/sign*

---

symbol • mark | *fml or tech.* **character**

► the sign/symbol/character **for** sth
► a sign/symbol/character **means/ indicates** sth
● SIGN OR SYMBOL? A **symbol** usu. refers to a shape or small picture, or the letters representing chemical elements. A **sign** is usu. sth more simple, such as a *dollar sign*.

---

signal noun [C]

■ *When I give the signal, run!*

---

sign • cue

► a sign/signal/cue **for** sb/sth
► give sb a signal/sign/cue
► wait for/miss a/your signal/sign/ cue
► understand/misunderstand a signal/sign

---

signal verb [I, T]

■ *Don't fire until I signal.*

---

nod • wave • beckon | *written* **gesture**

► signal/nod/wave/beckon/gesture **to** sb
► signal/nod/gesture **for** sb **to do** sth
► signal/gesture **that** sb should do sth/it is time to do sth, etc.

---

significant adj.

■ *This is a highly significant discovery.*

---

important • momentous • great | *infml* **big** | *fml* **notable**

► OPP insignificant
► significant/important **for/to** sb/ sth
► significant/important/notable **that...**
► significant/important/great/ momentous/big/notable **events/ changes/developments**
► a/an significant/important/great/ big/notable **difference/feature/ achievement/success**
● SIGNIFICANT OR IMPORTANT? **Important** is a more general word. Things that are **significant** are important from a particular point of view, have been measured in some way, or are great in degree:
  ✓ *These figures are statistically significant.* ✗ ~~These figures are statistically important.~~
  ✓ *a significant proportion of the population* ✗ ~~an important proportion of the population~~

silence noun [U]

■ *A cry broke the silence of the night.*

peace • quiet • hush • calm | *esp. BrE, written* **tranquillity** | *AmE usu.* **tranquility**

■ OPP **noise**

▶ **in** silence/peace/tranquillity
▶ **absolute/total** silence/peace/quiet/calm/tranquillity
▶ **break** the silence/peace/quiet/calm

silent adj.

1 ■ *The crowd remained silent.*

speechless • dumb | *lit.* **mute**

▶ speechless/dumb **with rage/anger**

2 [only before noun] ■ *He's the strong, silent type.*

quiet • reserved | *fml* **reticent • taciturn**

▶ a silent/quiet/reserved/reticent **person/man**
▶ He's the silent/quiet **type.**
▶ **strangely** silent/quiet/reticent

3 ■ *The streets were silent and deserted.*

quiet • peaceful • calm | *written* **tranquil**

■ OPP **noisy**

▶ a silent/quiet/peaceful/calm/tranquil **place/village/town**

4 ■ *She said a silent prayer.*

inaudible • quiet

▶ silent/quiet **laughter**

silly adj.

1 (*esp. spoken, usu. disapprov.*) ■ *That was a silly thing to do!*

stupid • idiotic • irresponsible | *infml* **insane** | *esp. BrE, infml* **mad** | *esp. AmE, infml* **crazy • dumb** | *esp. written* **foolish • unwise**

■ OPP **sensible**

▶ silly/stupid/idiotic/irresponsible/insane/mad/crazy/dumb/foolish/unwise (of sb) **to do sth**
▶ a/an silly/stupid/idiotic/insane/mad/crazy/dumb/foolish **idea/thing to do**
▶ a/an silly/stupid/idiotic/dumb/foolish **mistake**
● **WHICH WORD?** Silly, stupid, dumb and foolish describe people or their actions. Crazy usu. describes a person, but it can also be used to describe a deliberate and dangerous action. All these words are usu. disapproving and can be offensive.

2 (*esp. spoken*) ■ *I feel silly in this hat.*

---

ridiculous • absurd • ludicrous | *esp. written* **foolish**

▶ silly/ridiculous/absurd/ludicrous **that...**
▶ It would be silly/ridiculous/absurd/ludicrous **to do sth.**
▶ a silly/foolish **comment/remark/smile/grin**

similar adj.

■ *We have very similar interests.*

like • close • alike

■ OPP **different,** (*fml*) **dissimilar**

▶ similar/close **to sth**
▶ similar/like sth/close/alike **in size, amount, etc.**
▶ **look** similar/like sth/alike
▶ **feel/sound/taste** similar/like sth

similarity noun [U, C]

■ *The report highlights the similarities between the two groups.*

resemblance • likeness • parallel • correspondence • comparison • analogy • uniformity | *fml* **equivalence • affinity**

■ OPP **difference,** (*fml*) **dissimilarity**

▶ (a/an) similarity/resemblance/likeness/parallel/correspondence/comparison/analogy/equivalence/affinity **between** A and B
▶ a/an similarity/resemblance/likeness/parallel/comparison/analogy/equivalence **to sth**
▶ **bear** (a/an) similarity/resemblance/likeness/comparison/affinity

simple adj.

1 ■ *The machine is simple to use.*

easy • straightforward • uncomplicated • plain sailing | *written* **undemanding**

■ OPP **complicated**

▶ simple/easy/straightforward/plain sailing **for sb**
▶ simple/easy/straightforward/plain sailing **to do sth**
▶ a/an simple/easy/straightforward **matter/decision/test/question**
▶ **There's no** simple/easy/straightforward **answer.**
● **SIMPLE OR EASY?** Easy means 'not difficult': an *easy test/task* is one that causes you no difficulties because you have the ability to do it. Simple means 'not complicated': a *simple task* is one that needs only very few, basic actions and does not usu. depend on people's abilities.

2 (*esp. written, usu. approv.*) ■ *a simple meal of soup and bread*

plain | *esp. written* **bare • austere**

■ OPP **fancy**

3 [only before noun] ■ *The simple fact is I can't afford it.*

plain • bare • bald | *fml* **unequivocal** | *often approv.* **honest • straightforward** | *esp. written, usu. disapprov.* **stark**

► the simple/plain/bare/unequivocal/honest/stark **truth**
► a/an simple/plain/bare/unequivocal/stark **fact**
► a/an simple/plain/bare/unequivocal/honest/straightforward **statement**
► a/an simple/plain/unequivocal/honest/straightforward **answer**
● **SIMPLE OR PLAIN?** Simple is used with more collocations and structures than **plain**. Expressions with **simple** often suggest impatience with other people's behaviour: *No one wanted to believe the simple truth.*

4 [usu. before noun] ■ *They were simple country people.*

unremarkable | *often approv.* **plain** | *disapprov.* **ordinary** | *often disapprov.* **average**

► a/an simple/unremarkable/plain/ordinary/average **person**
► simple/plain **ignorance/common sense**
● **SIMPLE OR PLAIN?** Simple is used more about people and **plain** about qualities. When used about people **simple** tells you how other people see sb; **plain** tells you more about how sb sees him/herself.

simulate *adj.* [T]
■ *Role-play is a way of simulating real-life situations.*

reproduce • reconstruct • recreate | *fml* **replicate** | *computing or tech.* **model**

► simulate/reproduce/model sth **closely**

sincere *adj.*

1 (*approv.*) ■ *I'd like to express our sincere gratitude.*

genuine • real • deep • heartfelt • from the heart • wholehearted

■ OPP **insincere**
► sincere/genuine **about** sth
► sincere/genuine/real/deep/heartfelt **sympathy/concern**
► sincere/real/deep **affection/respect/regret**
● **SINCERE OR GENUINE?** Sincere is more likely to be used by sb about their own feelings and intentions; **genuine** is more likely to be used to express a judgement on sb else's feelings and intentions:

✔Please accept our sincere apologies.
✗ ~~Please accept our genuine apologies.~~
✔He made a genuine attempt to improve the situation.

2 (*approv.*) ■ *He seemed sincere in his offer of help.*

approv. truthful • open • straightforward | *often approv.* **honest • frank • candid**

■ OPP **insincere, hypocritical**
► sincere/truthful/open/straightforward/honest/frank/candid **about** sth
► sincere/honest/frank/candid **in** your views/criticism, etc.
► a/an sincere/truthful/open/honest **person**

sing *verb* [I, T]
■ *Sing us a song.*

chant • hum • whistle

► sing/chant/whistle **at** sb/sth
► sing/whistle **to** sb/sth
► sing/hum/whistle a **song/tune**

singer *noun* [C]
■ *the band's lead singer*

vocalist • musician • artist • performer • entertainer

► a talented/famous singer/vocalist/musician/artist/performer/entertainer

singing *noun* [U]
■ *There was singing and dancing all night.*

song • music • harmony • melody

► beautiful singing/music/harmony
► hear singing/music
► listen to singing/music/the harmony/the melody

single *adj.*

1 [only before noun] ■ *What is the single most important factor here?*

individual • particular • specific • separate • distinct

► a single/individual/particular/specific/separate/distinct **category/region**
► a single/particular/specific/separate **event/incident/occasion**
► a single/particular/specific/distinct **objective/purpose**

2 ■ *The apartments are ideal for single people living alone.*

unmarried • divorced • widowed • separated | *esp. BrE, esp. written* **lone**

■ OPP **married**
► a/an single/unmarried/divorced/widowed/separated/lone **man/woman/parent/mother/father**

sip noun [C]

■ *She took another sip of her drink.*

drop • drink • gulp | *infml* **swig**

▶ a sip/drop/drink/gulp/swig **of** sth
▶ **take** a sip/drop/drink/gulp
▶ **have** a sip/drop/drink/gulp/swig

sit verb [I]

■ *May I sit here?*

sit down • take a seat • perch • sprawl | *fml* **be seated • recline**

■ OPP **stand (up)**
▶ sit/sit down/take a seat/perch/
sprawl/be seated/recline **on** sth
▶ sit/sit down/take a seat/sprawl/
be seated **in** sth

site noun [C]

■ *They've chosen a site for the new school.*

place • position • location • spot • scene • venue • area

▶ a (good, etc.) site/place/position/
location/spot/venue **for** sth
▶ **at** a site/place/position/location/
spot/scene/venue
▶ the site/place/position/location/spot/
venue **where…**
▶ a/an **interesting/beautiful/
convenient/remote** site/place/
position/location/spot

situation noun [C]

■ *Consider the current economic situation.*

state of affairs • position • conditions • circumstance • the case | *infml, esp. spoken* **things**

▶ **in** (a) particular situation/state of
affairs/position/conditions/
circumstances
▶ the **general/current/present/real**
situation/state of affairs/position/
conditions/circumstances
▶ **describe/explain** (the) situation/
state of affairs/position/
circumstances/things
● SITUATION OR STATE OF AFFAIRS?
State of affairs is mostly used with
this and with adjectives such as
happy, *sorry*, *shocking*, *present* and
current: *How did this unhappy state
of affairs come about?*
Situation is much more frequent
and used in a wider variety of
contexts.

size noun

1 [U, C] ■ *It's an area the size of Wales.*

measurement • dimension • area • volume • capacity • extent • bulk

▶ **in** size/area/volume/capacity/
extent/bulk

▶ the **exact** size/measurements/
dimensions/area/extent
▶ **measure** the size/dimensions/
area/volume of sth

2 [U] ■ *It was hard to grasp the size of the problem.*

scale • extent • level • degree • proportions | *fml* **magnitude**

▶ the **true** size/extent/level
▶ **assess/judge** the size/scale/
extent/level/degree/magnitude of
sth
▶ **realize** the size/scale/extent/
level/degree of sth

skill noun

1 [U] ■ *The job requires considerable skill.*

expertise • competence • proficiency • technique • dexterity | *infml* **know-how** | *fml* **prowess** | *esp. written* **artistry**

▶ skill/expertise/competence/
proficiency/know-how/prowess **in** sth
▶ **do** sth with skill/expertise/
competence/dexterity/artistry
▶ **have** skill/expertise/competence/
technique/dexterity/know-how
▶ **demonstrate/show** your skill/
expertise/competence/
proficiency/technique/know-
how/prowess

2 [C] ■ *We need people with practical skills like carpentry.*

ability • talent • art • gift • aptitude • flair | *infml* **knack**

▶ (a) **great** skill/ability/talent/gift/
aptitude/flair
▶ **demonstrate** a skill/an ability/a
talent/an aptitude/flair
▶ **develop** a skill/an ability/a talent/
the art/a gift/the aptitude/a flair/
the knack
▶ **master/perfect** a skill/the art
● SKILL OR ART? Skills are usu.
practical or technical things; an **art**
is more about expressing yourself
and/or relating to other people: *the
art of fiction/poetry/film* • *the art of
conversation/negotiation/listening*

skilled adj.

■ *We need more skilled engineers.*

good • able • competent • proficient • capable • expert • talented • accomplished | *BrE* **skilful** | *AmE* **skillful** | *esp. spoken* **great**

■ OPP **unskilled**
▶ skilled/good/competent/
proficient/expert/accomplished/
skilful/great **at** sth
▶ skilled/good/competent/expert/
great **with** sb/sth
▶ a/an **skilled/good/able/
competent/skilful/great**
teacher

sky noun [C, U]

■ *The sky went dark.*

air • atmosphere • airspace | *lit.* **the heavens**

▶ **in/into** the sky/air/atmosphere/ sb's airspace/the heavens
▶ **through** the sky/air/atmosphere/ sb's airspace

sleep verb [I]

■ *Try not to sleep during the day.*

doze • nap | *infml* **snooze** | *lit.* **slumber**

▶ sleep/doze **lightly/fitfully**

slice noun [C]

■ *Another slice of cake, anyone?*

piece • slab • wedge | *esp. BrE* **bit** | *BrE* **rasher**

▶ a slice/piece/wedge/bit of **cheese/lemon**
▶ a slice/piece/slab/bit of **meat**
▶ a slice/piece/bit/rasher of **bacon**
▶ a slice/piece/bit of **cake/ham/ pizza/pie/bread**

slice verb [T, I]

■ *Slice the cucumber thinly.*

cut • chop • carve

▶ slice/cut/chop/carve sth **into** sth
▶ slice/cut/chop **off** sth
▶ slice/cut/chop/carve **meat**
▶ slice/cut **bread/cake**
▶ slice/chop **an onion**

slide verb [I, T] (usu. used with an adv. or prep.)

■ *A tear slid down his cheek.*

roll • glide • slither

▶ slide/roll/glide/slither **into/out of/along/on** (sth)
▶ slide/roll/glide **past** sth
▶ slide/roll/glide/slither **to** the floor/bottom, etc.

slight adj.

■ *The damage was slight.*

small • modest • minimal • minor • marginal | *esp. written* **negligible • insignificant** | *esp. spoken* **little**

■ OPP **big, major**
▶ a/an slight/small/modest/ minimal/minor/marginal/ insignificant/little **change/ difference/improvement**
▶ a/an slight/small/minor/ insignificant/little **problem**
▶ a slight/small/minor/little **error/ mistake/defect/accident**
▶ a slight/small/minimal **chance**
● **SLIGHT OR SMALL?** Use either word to talk about changes or problems. Use **slight** but not **small** to talk about medical problems, feelings or things that affect the senses; use

small but not **slight** to talk about amounts: *a slight cold/headache/ movement/touch • a small amount/ number/quantity, etc.*

slip verb

1 [I] ■ *He slipped on the ice.*

skid | *esp. written* **fall** | *esp. spoken* **fall over**

▶ slip/skid/fall/fall over **on** the ice/ wet grass, etc.

2 [I] (always used with an adv. or prep.) ■ *I slipped away before the end of the performance.*

creep • slink • tiptoe • pad • slide | *usu. disapprov.* **sneak**

▶ slip/creep/slink/tiptoe/pad/ slide/sneak **away/in/out**
▶ slip/creep/tiptoe/sneak **up to** sb/ sth
▶ slip/creep/pad **silently**

3 [T] ■ *Anna slipped her hand into his.*

slide • insert • tuck • slot

▶ slip/slide/insert/tuck/slot sth **into** sth
▶ slip/slide/tuck sth **under** sth
▶ slip/slide/insert/tuck/slot sth **quickly** into sth
● **SLIP OR SLIDE?** These words are very close in meaning and use. **Slip** may emphasize that sth is being done secretly; **slide** emphasizes that sth is done with a smooth movement.

slogan noun [C]

■ *The company used catchy advertising slogans.*

motto • catchphrase • mantra • formula

▶ **come up with** a slogan/formula
▶ **coin/adopt** a slogan/motto
▶ **use** a slogan/motto/catchphrase/ mantra/formula

slope noun

1 [C] ■ *We sat on a grassy slope.*

bank • ramp | *fml or tech.* **incline**

▶ a **steep** slope/bank/ramp/incline
▶ a **gentle** slope/incline
▶ **climb (up)** a/an slope/bank/ ramp/incline

2 [sing., U] ■ *the slope of the roof*

angle | *esp. BrE* **gradient** | *esp. AmE* **grade**

▶ **at** a/an slope/angle/gradient
▶ a **slight/steep/gentle** slope/ angle/gradient

slope

slope verb

1 [I] (usu. used with an adv. or prep.)
■ *The path sloped gently down.*

dip • rise • climb • descend • drop

▶ a road/path slopes/dips/climbs/
descends/drops
▶ slope/dip/rise/climb/descend/
drop **steeply**
▶ slope/dip/rise **gently**

2 [T] (usu. used with an adv. or
prep.) ■ *It was an old house with
sloping walls.*

lean • slant • tilt • tip • angle

▶ slope/lean/slant/tilt/tip/angle
(sth) **towards/away from**
▶ slope/slant/tilt/tip/angle (sth)
up/down

slow adj.

1 ■ *a slow driver/walker/reader*
■ *Progress was slower than
expected.*

gradual • measured • leisurely |
written unhurried | *written, often
disapprov.* sluggish

■ OPP fast, quick
▶ a slow/gradual **improvement/
change/acceptance**
▶ a/an slow/measured/leisurely/
unhurried **pace**
▶ slow/measured **steps**

2 ■ *They were slow in paying me.*

late | *written* belated

■ OPP quick
▶ slow/late **in doing sth**

slump verb [I] (busin.)

■ *Profits slumped by over 50%.*

fall • drop • decline | *esp. busin.*
plunge • plummet • tumble • sink

■ OPP jump, surge
▶ slump/fall/drop/decline/plunge/
plummet/tumble/sink **by** 100,
25%, a half, etc.
▶ slump/fall/drop/decline/plunge/
plummet/tumble/sink **from** 1 500
to 250
▶ **prices/profits/sales** slump/fall/
drop/decline/plunge/plummet/
tumble/sink
▶ slump/plunge **dramatically/
suddenly**

small adj.

1 ■ *That dress is too small for you.*

little • tiny • miniature • compact •
minute • microscopic

■ OPP large, big
▶ a small/little/tiny/miniature
house/town/room
▶ a small/little/tiny/minute/
microscopic **detail**

▶ a small/little/tiny **baby/child**
● SMALL OR LITTLE? Small is the most
usual opposite of *big* or *large*. Little
is often used to show how you feel
about sb/sth, esp. after other
adjectives such as *ugly*, *nice* or *cute*.

2 [usu. before noun] ■ *I've made a
few small changes to the report.*

slight • minor • modest • minimal •
marginal | *esp. spoken* little | *esp.
written* negligible • unimportant

■ OPP big, major
▶ a small/slight/minor/modest/
minimal/marginal/little **change/
difference/improvement**
▶ a small/modest/minimal/
negligible **amount**
▶ a small/slight/minor/little **error/
mistake/defect/accident/
problem**
● SMALL OR SLIGHT? Use either word to
talk about changes or problems.
Use slight but not small to talk
about medical problems, feelings
or things that affect the senses; use
small but not slight to talk about
amounts: *a slight cough/headache/
movement/touch* • *a small amount/
number/quantity*, etc.

smart adj.

1 (*esp. BrE, approv.*) ■ *You look very
smart in that suit.*

elegant • stylish • fashionable •
graceful • classic • well-dressed |
infml classy

■ OPP scruffy
▶ a/an smart/elegant/stylish/
fashionable/graceful/well-dressed
woman
▶ a/an smart/elegant/fashionable/
well-dressed **man**
▶ a/an smart/elegant/stylish/
fashionable/classic **dress**
▶ a/an smart/elegant/stylish/
fashionable/classy **restaurant**

2 (*esp. AmE*) ■ *She's smarter than her
brother.*

intelligent • bright • brilliant | *esp.
BrE, sometimes disapprov.* clever

■ OPP dumb, stupid
▶ a/an smart/intelligent/bright/
brilliant/clever **child/boy/girl/
man/woman**
▶ a/an smart/intelligent/brilliant/
clever **thing to do/move**

smash verb

1 [T, I] ■ *The glass smashed into a
thousand pieces.*

shatter • break • break (sth) up •
splinter

▶ smash/shatter/break a **window/
windscreen**
▶ a **glass** smashes/shatters/breaks/
splinters

► sb's smashed/shattered/broken/
splintered **bones**

● **SMASH OR SHATTER?** People smash
things deliberately; things get
shattered as a result of explosions,
stones, etc.: *The thief smashed a
window.* • *Windows were shattered
in the blast.*

2 [I, T] ■ *The stolen car smashed into a
wall.*

**crash • slam • bang into sth • wreck
| BrE write sth off • plough into sth |
AmE plow into sth | esp. AmE, infml
total**

► smash/crash/slam/bang/plough
into sth
► smash/crash/slam sth **into** sth
► smash/crash/wreck/write off/
total a car/truck/vehicle

● **SMASH, CRASH OR SLAM?** When
used to talk about vehicles **smash**
and **slam** always take a prep., but
crash does not have to:
✓*We're going to crash!* ✗ *We're
going to smash/slam!*

smell noun

1 [C, U] ■ *Do you like the smell of
coffee?*

scent • aroma • fragrance • whiff

► a smell/the scent/an aroma/the
fragrance/a whiff **of**
► **have/give off** a/an smell/scent/
aroma/fragrance/whiff
► a/an smell/scent/aroma **hangs/
lingers/comes/wafts** somewhere

2 [sing.] ■ *What's that terrible smell?*

**reek | BrE odour | AmE odor | infml
stink | esp. written or lit. stench**

► a/an smell/reek/odour/stink/
stench **of** sth
► a **foul/powerful/putrid** smell/
odour/stench
► **give off** a/an smell/odour/stench

smelly adj. (disapprov.)
■ *He's got smelly feet.*

**stale • dank • musty | disapprov.
stinking**

► a smelly/dank/musty **room**
► (a) stale/dank/musty **smell/air**
► **smell** stale/dank/musty

smile verb [I, T, no passive]
■ *She smiled with pleasure.*

**grin • beam | disapprov. smirk •
simper**

■ **OPP frown**

► smile/grin/beam/smirk/simper **at**
sb/sth
► smile/grin/beam/smirk **with** sth
► smile/grin/beam **broadly/
widely/happily/cheerfully/from
ear to ear**

smoke noun [U]
■ *The room was thick with smoke.*

fumes • exhaust • smog

► toxic/poisonous smoke/fumes
► emit/produce/give off smoke/
fumes
► a **cloud of** smoke/fumes

smooth adj. (often approv.)
■ *The water was as smooth as glass.*

flat • level • horizontal

■ **OPP rough**

► a smooth/flat/level/horizontal
surface
► a smooth/flat/level **road/floor**
► a smooth/flat **rock/stone**

smug adj. (disapprov.)
■ *What are you looking so smug
about?*

**complacent • self-satisfied • self-
righteous • sanctimonious**

► smug/complacent/self-satisfied/
self-righteous/sanctimonious
about sth
► a smug/complacent/self-satisfied
smile

snack noun [C]
■ *There's just time for a quick snack.*

something to eat • refreshments

► (a) **light** snack/refreshments
► **have/grab** a snack/something to
eat
► **stop for** a snack/something to
eat/refreshments

snow noun [U]
■ *Snow was falling heavily.*

**sleet • slush • snowfall • snowflake
• snowdrift • hail • hailstone**

► **in/through** the snow/sleet/slush/
hail
► (a) **heavy/light** snow/snowfall
► snow/sleet/snowflakes/hail/
hailstones **falls/fall**
► snow/slush/snowflakes **melts/
melt**

soak verb [T, I]
■ *Rain soaked the spectators.*

**drench • douse • wet • flood | fml
immerse**

► soak/drench/douse/wet sth **with**
sth
► soak/drench/douse/immerse sth/
yourself **in** sth
► rain soaks/drenches/floods sb/sth
► be soaked/drenched **with** blood/
sweat
● **SOAK OR DRENCH?** In many cases
you can use either word. **Soak** but

not **drench** is used when you deliberately put sth in water.

soar verb [I] (written)
■ *Unemployment has soared to 18%.*

rocket • jump • rise | *often approv.* leap | *disapprov.* spiral • shoot up | *esp. journ., esp. busin.* surge

■ **OPP** tumble, plummet
▶ soar/jump/rise/shoot up in price, number, etc.
▶ soar/rocket/jump/rise/leap/ shoot up/surge (by) 60%, 2 000, etc.
▶ soar/rocket/jump/rise/leap/ shoot up from 2% to 75%
▶ the price soars/rockets/jumps/ rises/leaps/spirals/shoots up/ surges

sociable adj. (approv.)
■ *She's a sociable child who'll talk to anyone.*

gregarious • outgoing • extrovert | *esp. AmE, approv.* social

■ **OPP** unsociable, antisocial
▶ a/an sociable/gregarious/ outgoing/extrovert/social person
▶ a/an sociable/gregarious/ outgoing/social nature
● **SOCIABLE OR GREGARIOUS?** Sociable is an approving term to describe sb's character, behaviour or mood. **Gregarious** is neither approving or disapproving; it describes sb's character or behaviour but not their mood:
✔*I'm not feeling very sociable this evening.* ✗ *I'm not feeling very gregarious this evening.*

social adj. [only before noun]
■ *It was a time of social unrest.*

public • popular • civic
▶ social/public/popular awareness/ pressure/support/unrest
▶ social/public/civic responsibility
▶ social/public issues/values/ policy/welfare

society noun
1 [U] ■ *The clinic deals with a wide cross-section of society.*

community • population • the public • the country • the nation
▶ society/the community/the population/public/the country/ the nation at large/as a whole
▶ the wider society/community/ population/public
▶ a section/cross-section/member of society/the community/the population/the public

2 [C, U] ■ *the problems of Western society*

culture • world • civilization • community • race
▶ (the) Western society/culture/ world/civilization
▶ a/an the ancient/modern/ contemporary society/culture/ world/civilization
▶ a primitive society/culture/ community/race
▶ create a society/culture/ civilization

3 [C] (esp. in names) ■ *the Royal Society for the Protection of Birds* ■ *Local societies opposed the idea.*

club • association • organization • institute
▶ form/set up/belong to/join a/an society/club/association/ organization/institute
▶ a/an society/club/association/ organization meets
▶ a member of a/an society/club/ association/organization/institute
● **SOCIETY, CLUB OR ASSOCIATION?** These words are all used for groups of people who have a shared interest or purpose. Often, but not always, a **club** relates to leisure interests, a **society** to academic interests, and an **association** to professional interests. A **club** can be quite informal.

soft adj.
1 ■ *a soft cheese with a hard rind*

spongy | *infml* squishy | *often approv.* moist | *usu. disapprov.* soggy • mushy • slimy | *infml, usu. disapprov. or approv.* gooey

■ **OPP** firm, hard
▶ a soft/spongy/soggy/gooey mass
▶ a soft/gooey/slimy substance
▶ a soft/spongy texture

2 ■ *He chose some soft background music and and lit the candles.*

quiet • faint • hushed • muffled • inaudible | *written* dull

■ **OPP** loud
▶ a/an soft/quiet/faint/hushed/ muffled/inaudible voice
▶ a soft/quiet/faint/muffled/dull sound
▶ a soft/faint/muffled/dull noise/ thud/thump

soil noun [U, C]
■ *Plant the seedlings in damp soil.*

earth • mud • clay • ground • land | *esp. AmE* dirt
▶ dry soil/earth/mud/clay/ground/ land/dirt
▶ wet/soft soil/earth/mud/clay/ ground/dirt

- **dig** the soil/earth/mud/clay/ground/land
- **cultivate/till/fertilize/drain** the soil/ground/land

soldier noun [C]

■ *Many brave soldiers lost their lives.*

serviceman/servicewoman + fighter + mercenary + guerrilla | *fml* warrior + combatant

- a/an **experienced/wounded/dead** soldier/warrior
- a **good/great/trained** soldier/fighter/warrior
- a soldier/serviceman/servicewoman/mercenary/guerrilla/warrior/combatant **fights/is killed**

solid adj.

1 ■ *The stream was frozen solid.*

hard + stiff + rigid | *approv.* firm

■ OPP **liquid**
- solid/stiff/rigid **material**
- a solid/hard/firm **surface**

2 ■ *She always gives solid and practical advice.*

good + sound + valid + logical + well founded

■ OPP **flimsy**
- a solid/good/sound/valid/logical **reason/basis**
- solid/good/sound/valid **evidence**
- solid/good/sound **advice**

3 [only before noun] ■ *a bracelet made of solid gold*

pure + refined

■ OPP **hollow**
- solid/pure/refined **silver/gold**

solitary adj.

■ *Tigers are solitary animals.*

introverted + reclusive + withdrawn + unsociable | *usu. disapprov.* antisocial

■ OPP **gregarious**
- a solitary/reclusive **figure/man**
- **feel** unsociable/antisocial
- ● WHICH WORD? **Solitary** and **introverted** describe sb's character; **reclusive** and **withdrawn** describe sb's behaviour. **Unsociable** and **antisocial** describe behaviour, often a temporary state: *Why are you being so unsociable/antisocial when we've got guests?*

solution noun [C]

■ *There's no simple solution to the problem.*

answer + remedy + way out + key + resolution | *infml* fix

- the solution/answer/remedy/key/resolution/fix **to** sth
- **look for** a solution/an answer/the key/a fix
- **find/provide** a solution/an answer/a remedy/the key/a resolution

solve verb

1 [T] ■ *You can't solve your difficulties by running away.*

resolve + settle + straighten sb/sth out | *esp. BrE, esp. spoken* sort sth out + sort

- solve/resolve/settle/straighten out/sort out a **problem/situation/dispute/crisis**
- solve/resolve/settle **things**
- straighten/sort **things out**

2 [T] ■ *The mystery has not yet been solved.*

do + clear sth up + crack | *esp. BrE, esp. spoken* work sth out | *esp. AmE, esp. spoken* figure sb/sth out

- solve/do/work out a/an **puzzle/equation**
- solve/clear up/crack a **case/mystery**
- solve/clear up a/an **crime/murder/investigation**

sometimes adv.

■ *I sometimes walk to work in the summer.*

occasionally + at times + from time to time + now and again/then + on occasion(s) + once in a while + every so often + off and on/on and off

- **appear/wonder** sometimes/occasionally/at times/from time to time
- **happen** sometimes/occasionally/at times/from time to time/now and again
- **think** sometimes/at times/from time to time that...

son noun [C]

■ *He's the son of a teacher.*

boy + child | *infml* kid | *esp. BrE, infml* lad | *fml* offspring

■ OPP **daughter**
- a **newborn** son/boy/child
- sb's **eldest/oldest/youngest** son/boy/child/kid/lad
- **bring up/raise** a son/boy/child/kid

song noun [C]

■ *She sang her favourite song.*

track + tune + melody + theme + number

- a song/track/tune/melody/theme/number **by** sb

▶ **sing** a song/tune/number
▶ **play** a song/track/tune/melody/theme/number
▶ **record** a song/track/theme

sophisticated adj. (often approv.)

■ Mark is a smart and sophisticated young man.

experienced | often approv. suave • urbane

■ OPP **naive**
▶ a/an sophisticated/experienced/suave/urbane **man/manner**

sordid adj. (disapprov.)

■ It was a shock to hear about his sordid past.

seedy • squalid • disreputable | BrE unsavoury | AmE unsavory | infml sleazy

▶ a sordid/seedy/squalid/sleazy **affair**
▶ sb's sordid/squalid/disreputable/unsavoury **past**
▶ a sordid/unsavoury **business/story**
▶ the sordid/squalid **details**

sore adj.

■ He had a sore throat and a high temperature.

inflamed • raw • burning • itchy • painful

▶ sore/inflamed/itchy **eyes**

sorry adj.

1 [not before noun] ■ I'm sorry to hear that he's lost his job.

upset • dismayed • distressed

■ OPP **glad, happy**
▶ sorry/upset/distressed **about sth**
▶ sorry/upset/dismayed/distressed **that…**
▶ sorry/dismayed/distressed **to see/hear/find, etc.…**

2 [not before noun] ■ She was sorry that she'd lost her temper.

apologetic • ashamed • guilty | spoken bad • I'm afraid

▶ sorry/apologetic/ashamed/guilty/bad **about sth**
▶ I'm sorry/afraid **that…**
▶ feel sorry/ashamed/guilty/bad **that…**

sort noun [C] (esp. BrE)

■ What sort of music do you like?

kind • type • form • variety • style • brand • nature • category • class | fml genre

▶ a sort/kind/type/form/variety/

style/brand/category/class/genre **of** sth
▶ a different/the same sort/kind/type/form/variety/style/brand/nature/category/class/genre
▶ various sorts/kinds/types/forms/styles/categories/genres
▶ a/the/that sort/kind/type **of thing**
● **SORT, KIND OR TYPE?** Kind is the most frequent word in this group; sort is used more in BrE. Type is slightly more formal and used more in official, scientific or academic contexts.

sort verb [T]

■ The documents were sorted by age and type.

organize • group • categorize • classify • class • file

▶ sort/organize/group/categorize/classify sb/sth **according to sth**
▶ sort/organize/group/categorize/classify sb/sth **into/by sth**
▶ sort/group/categorize/classify/class/file sb/sth **under sth**

sort sb/sth out phrasal verb

1 (infml) ■ Have you sorted your clothes out yet?

organize • arrange

▶ sort out/organize/arrange (your) **things**
▶ sort out/organize/arrange your **things**

2 (esp. BrE, esp. spoken) ■ I'll try to sort this out.

solve • straighten sb/sth out • resolve • settle | esp. BrE, esp. spoken sort

▶ sort out/solve/resolve/settle a/an **dispute/argument/crisis/matter/issue/problem/situation**
▶ sort/straighten **things out**
▶ resolve/settle **things**
▶ get sth sorted out/straightened out/resolved/settled/sorted

soul noun [C]

■ His poetry deals with the dark side of the human soul.

spirit • mind • the/your subconscious | psychology ego

▶ the **human** soul/spirit/mind
● **SOUL OR SPIRIT?** Spirit is a more positive word than soul. We talk about lost/tormented/troubled souls but the power of the human spirit.

sound noun

1 [C] ■ I heard the sound of footsteps outside.

noise

▶ a big/deafening/loud/high-pitched/low sound/noise

► hear/listen to/make/produce a sound/noise
► a sound/noise comes from sth/a place
► a sound/noise becomes/gets louder, closer, etc.
● SOUND OR NOISE? Sound is anything you hear. A noise is usu. loud and unpleasant.
  ✔ the soft sound of rustling leaves
  ✗ the soft noise of rustling leaves

2 [U] ■ Could you turn the sound down?

volume

► the sound/volume on sth
► turn up/turn down/increase/reduce the sound/volume

sound verb

1 linking verb (not used in the progressive tenses) ■ Leo made it sound so easy.

seem • appear • look • feel • strike

► sound/seem/appear/look/feel odd/OK/nice, etc.
► sound/seem/look/feel like sth
► sound/seem/look/feel as if/as though...

2 [I] ■ A bell sounded for the end of class.

ring • chime • clang • buzz • jangle • strike | lit. toll

► the bell sounds/rings/chimes/clangs/jangles/tolls
► the doorbell sounds/rings/chimes/buzzes/jangles
► the clock sounds/rings/chimes/strikes

sour adj.

1 ■ The wine tasted sour.

sharp • acid • bitter • pungent • acrid

■ OPP sweet
► a/an sour/sharp/acid/bitter/pungent/acrid taste/flavour/smell/odour
► a/an sour/sharp/acid/bitter fruit
► taste sour/sharp/bitter
● WHICH WORD? A bitter taste is usu. unpleasant, but some people enjoy the bitter flavour of coffee or chocolate; no other word can describe this flavour. A sharp or pungent flavour is more strong than unpleasant, esp. when describing taste. Sharp, sour and acid all describe the taste of a lemon or a fruit that is not ripe. An acrid smell is strong and unpleasant, esp. the smell of smoke or burning, but not the smell of food.

2 ■ The milk had turned sour.

bad • rancid • rotten • stale | BrE off • mouldy | AmE moldy

■ OPP fresh
► go sour/bad/rancid/rotten/stale/off

source noun [C]

■ We need to obtain more energy from renewable sources.

origin/origins • root • cause • starting point • beginnings

► (a) common source/origin/roots/cause/starting point
► have (a) source/origins/roots/cause/starting point/beginnings
► find the source/origin/root/cause/starting point of sth
► locate/discover/investigate/trace the source/origin/roots/cause of sth

space noun

1 [U] ■ That desk takes up too much space.

room • headroom • legroom

► space/room for/between sth
► space/room to do sth
► leave/make/create/save/take up space/room
● SPACE OR ROOM? Room is usu. space that you have or need for some practical purpose; space can be used in the same way, or it can mean a feeling of space that you enjoy for its own sake:
  ✔ The bright colours give a lovely feeling of space. ✗ The bright colours give a lovely feeling of room.

2 [C] ■ a parking space

gap • opening • hole • slot | fml or tech. aperture

► a/an gap/opening/hole/slot/aperture in sth
► a space/gap between A and B
► leave a/an space/gap/opening/hole

3 [U] ■ the first woman in space

outer space • universe • the cosmos

► through/in space/outer space/the universe/the cosmos
► go into space/outer space
● SPACE OR OUTER SPACE? There is not much difference between these words. Space is used in compounds such as space station, space travel. Outer space can be used for emphasis.

spacious adj. (approv.)

■ The rooms are spacious and comfortable.

large • big • extensive | usu. approv. roomy • airy | written cavernous

spare

428

■ OPP **cramped**
▶ a/an **spacious/large/big/airy/cavernous room**
▶ a **spacious/large/big/roomy/cavernous kitchen**
▶ a **spacious/large/big/roomy house**

spare adj.

1 [usu. before noun] ■ *I haven't got any spare cash.*

surplus • excess • superfluous • leftover

▶ spare/surplus/excess **cash/capacity/energy**
● SPARE, SURPLUS OR EXCESS? Spare is the most informal and common of these words. Surplus is often used in business contexts: *surplus stock/products, surplus capital/income.* To talk about an extra amount that is seen as a bad thing, excess is often used: *excess fat/baggage*

2 ■ *He's studying music in his spare time.*

free • available

▶ spare/free/available **time**
▶ a spare/free **morning/afternoon/weekend/moment**

speak verb

1 [I] ■ *Can I speak to Paddy?*

talk • chat • discuss • communicate • consult • debate | *fml* **confer**

▶ speak/talk/chat/discuss sth/communicate/consult/debate/confer **with** sb
▶ speak/talk/chat **to** sb
▶ speak/talk **of** sth
● SPEAK OR TALK? Speak can suggest a more formal level of communication than talk. You talk to sb in order to be friendly or to ask their advice. You speak to sb to try to achieve a particular goal or to tell them to do sth: *'What were you two talking about?' 'Oh, this and that.'* • *Have you talked to your parents about the problems you're having?* • *I've spoken to Ed about it and he's promised not to let it happen again.*

2 [I] ■ *Please speak more slowly.*

talk • say

▶ speak/talk/say sth **to** sb
▶ speak/talk/say sth **about** sth
▶ They were speaking/talking **(in)** French.
● SPEAK OR TALK? If sb *can't speak* they are physically unable to speak because of illness, disability or emotion. If you are talking about a baby who has not learned to talk yet, use talk.

3 [I] ■ *She speaks of him with great affection.*

mention • refer to sb/sth | *fml* **allude to sb/sth**

▶ speak of/mention/refer to/allude to sb/sth **as** sth
▶ sb is **frequently/often** spoken of/mentioned/referred to/alluded to

speaker noun

1 [C] ■ *He is a brilliant public speaker.*

lecturer | *fml* **orator**

▶ a **good/brilliant** speaker/lecturer/orator
▶ the **principal** speaker/lecturer
▶ a **visting/guest** speaker/lecturer

2 [C] ■ *a native speaker of English*

talker • communicator

▶ a **good/great** speaker/talker/communicator
▶ an **effective/excellent** speaker/communicator

special adj.

1 [usu. before noun] ■ *Journalists were given no special privileges.*

exceptional • particular | *fml* **extraordinary**

■ OPP **ordinary**
▶ a special/an exceptional **case/situation**
▶ special/exceptional **circumstances**
▶ of special/particular **concern/importance/interest**

2 ■ *She has a special way of smiling.*

unique • distinctive • peculiar • idiosyncratic | *usu. approv.* **individual**

▶ sth special/unique/distinctive/individual **about** sth
▶ a/an special/unique/distinctive/peculiar/idiosyncratic/individual **style/character**
▶ sb's/sth's special/unique/distinctive/peculiar **brand** of sth

specialist noun [C]

■ *He's a noted specialist in his field.*

expert • authority • connoisseur | *infml, esp. journ.* **guru**

▶ a/an specialist/expert/authority **in/on** sth
▶ a/an specialist/expert/authority **in the field** (of sth)
▶ a/an **recognized/independent/outside** specialist/expert/authority
▶ a **financial/technical/computer/media** specialist/expert/guru

specific adj.

1 ■ *I gave you specific instructions.*

precise • exact • accurate

■ OPP **vague**

▶ specific/precise/accurate **about sb/sth**

▶ specific/precise/exact/accurate **instructions/details**

2 [usu. before noun] ■ *The money was collected for a specific purpose.*

particular • certain • individual • distinct • separate • single • respective

■ OPP **general**

▶ a/an specific/particular/certain/ individual **person**

▶ a/an specific/particular/certain/ separate/single **event/incident/ occasion**

▶ a/an specific/particular/certain/ individual/distinct/separate **type** of sth

● SPECIFIC OR PARTICULAR? A **particular** person, group or thing is that one and not a different one: John, not Mary. A **specific** group or thing is a particular one in all its details, not the general group or type of which this is one example: school children with learning difficulties, not school children in general.

speculation noun [U, C]

■ *His private life is the subject of much speculation.*

conjecture • guesswork • guess • assumption • presumption | *fml, often disapprov.* presupposition

▶ speculation/conjecture/ guesswork/a guess/an assumption/a presumption/a presupposition **about** sth

▶ speculation/the conjecture/a guess/the assumption/the presumption/the presupposition **that...**

▶ pure/sheer speculation/ conjecture/guesswork

speech noun

1 [C] ■ *She gave a short acceptance speech.*

address • lecture • talk • sermon

▶ a/an inaugural/farewell/keynote speech/address/lecture

▶ write/prepare/give/deliver/hear a/an speech/address/lecture/ talk/sermon

● SPEECH OR ADDRESS? A **speech** can be given on a public or private occasion; an **address** is always public.

2 [U] ■ *His speech was slurred—he was clearly drunk.*

pronunciation • voice | *phonetics* intonation

▶ (a) clear speech/pronunciation/ voice

speed noun

1 [C, U] ■ *Students can progress at their own speed.*

rate • pace • momentum | *written* tempo

▶ at a... speed/rate/pace

▶ increase the speed/rate/pace/ momentum/tempo

▶ gain/lose/pick up speed/ momentum

▶ a change of speed/pace/tempo

2 [U] ■ *The accident was due to excessive speed.*

rapidity | *fml* haste | *tech. or fml* velocity

▶ increasing speed/rapidity/velocity

▶ alarming/amazing/bewildering/ remarkable speed/rapidity

▶ reckless speed/haste

speed (sth) up phrasal verb

■ *The train soon speeded up.*

accelerate | *written* speed • hasten • quicken

■ OPP **slow (sth) down**

▶ speed up/accelerate/speed/ hasten/quicken the **pace/progress** (of sth)

▶ speed up/accelerate/speed/ hasten the **development** (of sth)

● SPEED UP OR SPEED? **Speed** is more formal than **speed sth up**. It is used to talk about making things happen faster but not vehicles moving faster:

✗ *The train soon speeded.*

spend verb

1 [T, I] ■ *She spent £100 on a new dress.*

pay • give • invest

▶ spend/invest (money) **on** sth

▶ spend/pay/give/invest **money/ £1000**

▶ spend/pay/give/invest **a lot**

2 [T] ■ *I spend too much time watching TV.*

pass • occupy • fill • devote sth to sth • while sth away | *sometimes disapprov.* take up sth

▶ spend/pass/occupy/fill/devote/ while away/take up (the) **time**

▶ spend/pass/take up/devote/ while away/take up an **hour/a couple of hours**

spicy adj.

■ *a plate of spicy chicken wings*

hot • strong | *BrE* savoury | *AmE* savory

■ OPP **mild, bland**

spin

- a spicy/hot/strong/savoury **flavour**
- a spicy/strong/savoury **taste**
- a spicy/savoury **food/dish/sauce**

spin verb

1 [I, T] ■ *The dancers spun round and round.*

turn • rotate • revolve • circle • roll • swivel • orbit • twist | *esp. spoken* **go around/round (sth)** | *written* **whirl • twirl**

- spin/turn/rotate/revolve/circle/roll/orbit/go/whirl **round/around (sth)**
- spin/turn/rotate/revolve/circle/swivel **on sth**
- spin/turn/rotate/circle/whirl **faster (and faster)**

2 [I, T] (always used with an adv. or prep.) ■ *She spun on her heel and walked out.*

turn • turn (sb/sth) round/around • swing • twist • pivot | *written* **whirl • wheel • swivel**

- spin/turn/swing/twist/pivot/whirl/wheel/swivel **round/around**
- spin/turn/swing/whirl/wheel/swivel **back/away**
- spin/turn/turn around/swing/twist/whirl around/wheel/swivel **to face sb/sth**

spirit noun

1 [C] ■ *He is dead, but his spirit lives on.*

soul • mind • the/your subconscious | *psychology* **ego**

- ▶ **human** spirit/soul/mind
- ● SOUL OR SPIRIT? **Spirit** is a more positive word than **soul**. We talk about *lost/tormented/troubled souls* but *the power of the human spirit.*

2 **spirits** [pl.] ■ *She was tired and in low spirits.*

morale • mood • frame of mind

- ▶ **in** (a) good/better, etc.) spirits/mood/frame of mind
- ▶ sb's spirits are/morale is **high/low**
- ▶ **lift/raise** sb's spirits/morale

3 [U] (*approv.*) ■ *Show some fighting spirit.*

determination • perseverance • persistence • purpose | *fml* **resolve • tenacity**

- ▶ **great** spirit/determination/perseverance/persistence/purpose/resolve/tenacity
- ▶ **show** (your) spirit/determination/persistence/resolve/tenacity
- ▶ **have** spirit/determination/perseverance/persistence/purpose/tenacity

---

4 [C] ■ possessed by evil spirits

ghost | *esp. written* **apparition**

- ▶ **see** a/an spirit/ghost/apparition
- ▶ a/an spirit/ghost/apparition **haunts** sb
- ▶ a spirit/ghost **appears**

spirit noun

1 [C] ■ *A damaging split within the party has occurred.*

rift • division | *fml* **schism • estrangement • disunity**

- ▶ a split/a rift/division/a schism/estrangement/disunity **between** people or groups
- ▶ a split/a rift/division/a schism/disunity **within** a group
- ▶ a split/rift **with** sb
- ▶ **cause/lead to** a split/a rift/divisions/a schism
- ● SPLIT OR RIFT? A **rift** is a serious disagreement that can lead to a **split**, when people or groups actually separate.

2 [sing.] ■ *He demanded a 50–50 split in the profits.*

division • separation • segregation

- ▶ a split/division/separation/segregation **between** A and B
- ▶ (a) split/division/separation/segregation **into** parts
- ▶ a **clear** split/division/separation

split verb

1 [I, T] ■ *The debate has split the country.*

divide • separate

- ▶ **be** split/divided **over** sth
- ▶ **increasingly** split/divided/separated
- ▶ **deeply** split/divided
- ● SPLIT OR DIVIDE? **Divide** suggests a disagreement between two or more people that may be temporary; **split** suggests it may be permanent.

2 [I, T] ■ *She split the class into groups of four.*

divide • break (sth) up • split (sb) up • cut sth up • separate (sth) out • subdivide

- ▶ split/divide/break/cut sth **up**
- ▶ split/divide/break up/subdivide sth **into parts**
- ▶ split/divide/split up/subdivide sth **into groups**
- ● SPLIT, DIVIDE, OR BREAK UP? **Divide** is slightly more formal. Things often **break up** because people or circumstances have forced them to. When sth has **broken up** it is no longer one whole thing: *The empire was broken up into four parts* (= it was no longer one empire). ◆ *The empire was divided/split into different parts* (= it was still one*

empire but contained separate areas).

Things usu. **divide** or **split** because it is natural for them to do so.

3 [T] ■ *She split the prize money with her brother.*

divide • share | *disapprov.* carve sth up

▶ split/divide/share/carve up sth **between/among** different people
▶ split/divide/share the **money/ work**
▶ split/divide your **time**
● **SPLIT, DIVIDE OR SHARE?** Things are **shared** between people; things are **divided** between people, uses or places; things are **split** between people, things or places. **Divide** is often used about very important things; **share** is used about less important things:
  ✔*He shared his sweets out among his friends.* ✗ *He divided his sweets among his friends.*

4 [I, T] ■ *Her dress had split along the seam.*

tear • rip

▶ split/tear/rip your **trousers/ pants/jeans**

split up *phrasal verb*

■ *The couple split up last year.*

break up • separate • divorce • get divorced • disband | *infml, esp. journ.* split

■ **OPP** get together
▶ split up/break up/split **with** sb
▶ split up/separate/split **from** sb
▶ a **couple** splits up/breaks up/ separates/divorces/gets divorced/ splits
▶ a **group** splits up/breaks up/ disbands/splits
● **SPLIT UP OR BREAK UP?** Only people can **split up**, but a relationship (personal or business) or people can **break up**: *My parents split up when I was five.* • *The company broke up last year.*

spoil *verb* [T]

■ *I don't want to spoil your fun, but it's time to go.*

ruin • wreck • mar

▶ spoil/ruin/wreck sth **for** sb
▶ spoil/ruin/wreck **things/ everything**
▶ spoil/ruin sb's **plans/day/ evening/life/chances/hopes**
● **SPOIL OR RUIN?** Ruin is stronger than spoil. If sth is **ruined** it is completely spoiled. If sth is **spoiled** it may just be less good than it should be.

spokesman, spokeswoman *noun* [C]

■ *A government spokesman denied the rumours.*

spokesperson • representative • delegate • messenger • envoy • ambassador

▶ a/an spokesman, etc./ representative/delegate/ messenger/ambassador **for** sb/sth
▶ a/an spokesman, etc./ representative/delegate/ messenger/envoy/ambassador **from** sb/sth
▶ **appoint** a/an spokesman, etc./ representative/delegate/envoy/ ambassador

sponsor *noun* [C]

■ *The race organizers are trying to attract sponsors.*

patron • donor | *fml* benefactor | *esp. busin.* backer

▶ the **main/principal** sponsor/ patron/donor/benefactor/backer
▶ a **major/potential** sponsor/ patron/donor/benefactor/backer
▶ **look for/seek/find/get** a sponsor/patron/donor/backer

spontaneous *adj.*

■ *The audience burst into spontaneous applause.*

impromptu • impulsive | *infml* off-the-cuff

▶ a spontaneous/an impulsive **gesture/reaction/act**
▶ a spontaneous/an off-the-cuff **remark**

sport *noun*

1 [U] (*BrE*) (*AmE* **sports** [pl.]) ■ *facilities for sport and recreation*

exercise • workout • aerobics | *BrE* PE | *AmE* P. E.

▶ **do** sport/exercises/a workout/ aerobics/PE

2 [C] ■ *skiing, skating and other winter sports*

game

▶ **play/take part** in a sport/game
▶ **team** sports/games

spot *noun*

1 [C] ■ *a white dress with red spots*

dot • patch • mark

▶ a spot/dot/patch/mark **on** sth
▶ **with** spots/dots/patches/marks
▶ a **blue/black/red/etc.** spot/dot/ patch/mark

2 [C] ■ *His coat was covered with spots of mud.*

mark • speck • blot • stain

▶ a spot/mark/speck/blot/stain **on** sth
▶ a spot/speck/blot of sth
▶ an ink spot/mark/blot/stain
▶ a grease spot/mark/stain

spray verb [T, I]

■ *The crops are sprayed with pesticide.*

squirt • splash • spatter

▶ spray/squirt/splash/spatter sth **on/over** sth
▶ be sprayed/splashed/spattered **with** sth
▶ spray/splash/spatter **water**
▶ spray/splash **paint**

spread verb

1 [T] ■ *He spread the map out on the floor.*

lay sth out • lay • unfold • open • unroll

▶ spread/lay out/lay/open sth **on** sth
▶ spread/lay/open sth **out**
▶ spread out/lay out/unfold/open a **map**

2 [T] ■ *Papers were spread out on the desk.*

scatter • strew

▶ spread/scatter/strew sth **on/onto/over/across** sth
▶ spread/scatter **seeds**

3 [I, T] ■ *The disease spreads easily.*

pass sth on • hand sth down • infect | *esp. spoken* give | *fml* transmit

▶ spread sth/pass sth on/hand sth down/give sth/transmit sth **to** sb
▶ spread sb/pass on/infect sb **with**/give sb/transmit a/an **disease/infection/virus**
▶ spread/pass on/transmit **information/a message**
▶ spread/pass on/hand down **knowledge**

4 [T, I] (usu. used with an adv. or prep.) ■ *She spread butter on a piece of toast.*

cover • coat • smear • rub • daub

▶ spread/cover/coat/smear/rub/daub sth **with** sth
▶ spread/smear/rub/daub sth **on** sth
▶ be spread/covered/coated with **chocolate**

spring verb [I] (usu. used with an adv. or prep.)

■ *The cat crouched ready to spring.*

jump • leap | *infml* hop

▶ spring/jump/leap/hop **up/down/out**
▶ spring/jump/leap/hop **out of bed**
▶ spring/jump/leap **to your feet/into action/into the air**
● **WHICH WORD? Jump** is used most often for quick body movements (*jump up/to your feet*). **Leap** is used most for longer distances and more figurative actions (*leap into action/to sb's defence*). **Spring** is used esp. about animals. **Hop** is usu. used for getting into or out of vehicles.

square noun [C]

■ *The hotel is just off the main square.*

marketplace • piazza • courtyard | *BrE* yard | *fml* quadrangle

▶ **in/across** the square/marketplace/piazza/courtyard/yard/quadrangle
▶ the **central/main** square/courtyard/yard/quadrangle
▶ a **cobbled** square/courtyard/yard

squeeze verb [T, I]

■ *He slowly squeezed the trigger.*

press • push

▶ squeeze/press/push **on** sth
▶ squeeze/press/push (sth) **hard/gently**
● **WHICH WORD? Press** is the most general word. You can **press** sth with your finger, hand or foot. **Push** is mostly used with the word **button**. You **squeeze** sth by bending your finger(s) around it.

stable adj.

1 ■ *This ladder doesn't seem very stable.*

steady • secure • firm

■ OPP **unstable**
▶ a stable/steady/secure/firm **foundation**
▶ a stable/secure/firm **base**

2 (usu. approv.) ■ *Children need a stable home life.*

steady • regular • consistent • even • constant | *written* unchanging | *sometimes disapprov., esp. busin.* static

■ OPP **unstable**
▶ a/an stable/steady/even/constant **temperature**
▶ stable/steady/regular **employment**
▶ a stable/steady/regular **relationship**

staff noun [C, pl.]

■ *All medical staff are tested for the virus.*

workforce • workers • employees • manpower • sales force | *BrE* members of staff | *esp. AmE* staff members | *busin.* personnel • human resources

▶ (a/an) **skilled/unskilled/ qualified/trained** staff/ workforce/workers/employees/ personnel
▶ (a/an) **female/male/experienced** staff/workforce/workers/ employees/members of staff/staff members/personnel
▶ a **10-strong, 2-000 strong, etc.** staff/workforce/sales force
▶ **train** staff/the workforce/workers/ employees/members of staff/staff members
▶ **reduce/increase** staff/the workforce/personnel

stage noun

1 [C] ■ *This product is at the design stage.*

phase • step • round • leg

▶ a **stage/phase/round/step/leg of** sth
▶ the **early** stages/phases/rounds/ steps
▶ **begin/enter/reach/finish** a stage/phase/round/leg
● **STAGE OR PHASE?** A **phase** is always a period of time with a beginning and an end, such as a planned part of a project; a **stage** is similar but can also refer to a moment or state within a period of time:
✔*At one stage in the game it looked as though they would win.* ✗ *At one phase in the game it looked as though they would win.*

2 [C] ■ *The performers went on stage.*

platform • podium | *esp. written* dais

▶ **on** the/a stage/platform/ podium/dais
▶ a **raised** stage/platform/podium/ dais
▶ **mount/approach** the stage/ platform/podium/dais

stall noun [C]

■ *a flower stall at the market*

booth • stand | *esp. BrE* kiosk

▶ a **hot-dog** stall/stand
▶ **have/run** a stall/booth/stand/ kiosk
▶ **set up/man** a stall/stand

stamp noun [C]

■ *The passports, with the visa stamps, were waiting at the embassy.*

seal • emblem • logo

▶ an **official** seal/stamp
▶ **bear/carry** a/an seal/stamp/ emblem/logo
● **SEAL OR STAMP?** A **stamp** may

show any kind of information, such as a date, a few words or a symbol; a **seal** is likely to appear on legal documents. Both words can be used to show that sth has been approved: (fig.) *The project has the government's seal/stamp of approval.*

stand verb

1 [I] ■ *She was too weak to stand.*

stand up • get up • be on your feet • pick yourself up | *written* get to your feet | *fml* rise

■ **OPP** sit, sit down
● **STAND, STAND UP OR GET UP? Stand** means 'to be in/get into a standing position'. **Get up** is the most frequent way of saying 'get into a standing position', and this can be from a sitting, kneeling or lying position. **Stand up** is used esp. to tell sb or a group of people to get into a standing position.

2 [T, no passive] (not used in the progressive tenses; used with *can/ could* in negative sentences and questions) ■ *She couldn't stand being kept waiting.*

bear • take | *esp. written* tolerate • *esp. spoken* put up with sb/sth | *fml* endure

▶ (can't/not) **stand/bear/endure doing** sth
▶ (can't/not) **stand/bear/put up with sb/sth doing** sth
▶ **stand/bear/put up with/endure pain**
▶ **not stand/take/tolerate any nonsense**
● **STAND OR BEAR? Bear** is slightly stronger and more formal than **stand**. **Stand** is used with *can/could* in negative statements and questions, but not in positive statements:
✔*She bore it with her usual patience.* ✗ *She stood it with her usual patience.*

3 can't stand [T, no passive] (not used in the progressive tenses) (esp. spoken) ■ *I can't stand his wife.*

can't bear • hate • loathe • detest | *fml* abhor

▶ I **can't stand/can't bear/hate/ loathe/detest doing** sth
▶ I **can't stand/can't bear/hate it when...**
▶ I **really can't stand/can't bear/ hate/detest sb/sth**

4 [T] (not used in the progressive tenses; used esp. with *can/could*) ■ *His heart can't stand the strain.*

tolerate • resist • stand up to sth | *fml* withstand

▶ stand / tolerate / resist / withstand
high temperatures / heat
▶ stand / tolerate / withstand (harsh,
dry, etc.) **conditions**
▶ stand / withstand **pressure / strain /
weight**

standard noun

1 [C, usu. pl.] ■ The journey was quick
by any standards.

criterion ∙ measure ∙ benchmark ∙
yardstick ∙ guide ∙ guideline ∙ norm

▶ by any standard / criteria / measure /
yardstick
▶ **provide** a standard / criterion /
measure / benchmark / yardstick /
guide
▶ **set / establish** a standard / criteria /
the benchmark / **norms**

2 [C, U] ■ There are concerns about
falling standards in schools.

level ∙ quality ∙ grade | BrE calibre |
AmE caliber

▶ be of a / the ...standard / level /
grade / quality / calibre
▶ **high / highest / low** standard /
level / grade / quality / calibre
▶ **raise / improve** the standard / level /
quality / calibre of sth

3 standards ■ a woman of high moral
standards

principle ∙ ideal ∙ values ∙ morality ∙
morals ∙ ethics

▶ **personal** standards / principles /
values / morality / morals / ethics
▶ **have (no / high, etc.)** standards /
principles / ideals / values / morals
▶ **compromise** your standards /
principles / ideals / values

standard adj.

■ Calls will be charged at the standard
rate.

usual ∙ regular ∙ general ∙ routine ∙
traditional ∙ habitual

■ OPP non-standard
▶ the standard / usual / regular /
general / routine / traditional
procedure / practice
▶ the standard / usual / regular /
general / routine / traditional /
habitual **way**

stand up phrasal verb

■ He stood up and put on his coat.

get up ∙ stand ∙ pick yourself up |
written get to your feet | fml rise

■ OPP sit down, sit
▶ stand up / get up / pick yourself up /
rise **from** sth
● STAND UP, GET UP OR STAND? Stand
means 'to be in / get into a standing
position'. **Get up** is the most

frequent way of saying 'get into a
standing position', and this can be
from a sitting, kneeling or lying
position. **Stand up** is used esp. to
tell sb or a group of people to get
into a standing position.

stand up for sb/sth phrasal
verb [no passive]

■ Always stand up for your friends.

defend ∙ justify | infml stick up for
sb/sth

▶ stand up for / defend / justify / stick
up for **yourself**
▶ stand up for / defend / stick up for
sb's **rights**

star noun

1 [C] ■ I wanted to be a pop star when
I was a teenager.

celebrity ∙ superstar ∙ legend ∙ idol
∙ icon ∙ name ∙ personality ∙ hero |
infml great

▶ a famous / top star / celebrity /
name / personality
▶ a showbiz star / celebrity / legend /
personality
▶ a film / pop star / superstar / legend /
idol / icon / hero
▶ a sports star / legend / icon /
personality / hero

2 [C] ■ She was the star of many TV
series.

lead ∙ hero ∙ heroine | fml
protagonist

▶ a young star / hero / heroine /
protagonist
▶ a male / female star / lead /
protagonist
▶ the star / lead **role**

star verb [I, T, passive]

■ Johnny Depp stars in a new movie.

feature ∙ appear ∙ figure

▶ star / feature / appear / figure **in** sth
▶ star / feature / appear / figure **as** sb /
sth
▶ star / feature / appear in a **film /
movie**
▶ a film / movie stars / features sb

stare noun [C]

■ He fixed the officer with a hard stare.

look ∙ glare ∙ gaze

▶ a / an **hard / angry** stare / look / glare
▶ a **cold / penetrating / piercing /
curious / quizzical** stare / look / gaze
▶ **fix** sb with a stare / look / glare

stare verb [I]

■ I screamed and everyone stared.

glare ∙ gaze ∙ peer ∙ look | infml
gawk

▶ stare / glare / gaze / peer / look / gawk
at sb / sth

▸ stare/gaze/gawk in surprise/
amusement, etc.
▸ stare/glare/peer/look
suspiciously

start noun [C, usu. sing.]

■ We'll miss the start if we don't hurry.

beginning • opening • birth | *fml*
outset • onset | *lit.* **dawn** | (in
football) **kick-off**

● OPP **finish**

▸ **at** the start/beginning/opening/
outset/onset/birth/dawn (of sth)
▸ **from** the (very) start/beginning/
outset
▸ **mark** the start/beginning/
opening/onset/birth/dawn (of
sth)
● START OR BEGINNING? Compare:
✔ We missed the beginning of the
movie (= the first few scenes). •
We'll miss the start of the game (=
the moment when it starts; the
kick-off). • from start to finish ✘ *from
beginning to end* ✘ *from start to end*
• *from beginning to finish*
✔ the beginning of the day/
week/year/century/a new era • at
the beginning of July/summer (the
90s ✘ *at the start of July/summer/the
90s*
✔ I want to make an early start.
✘ *I want to make an early beginning.*

start verb

1 [T, I] ■ He's just started a new job.

**begin • open • take sth up • set
about sth • go about sth • start sth up
• set/put sth in motion** | *fml*
**commence • embark on/upon sth •
initiate • institute** | *esp. busin. or
journ.* **launch**

● OPP **finish, stop**

▸ start/begin/take up/set about/go
about/commence **doing sth**
▸ start/begin **to do sth**
▸ start/begin/open/embark on/
initiate/institute/launch a/an
campaign/inquiry
▸ start/begin/set in motion/embark
on/initiate/institute/set up/
launch a **scheme**
● START OR BEGIN? Compare:
✔ 'Ladies and gentlemen,' he began.
✘ *'Ladies and gentlemen,' he started.*
✔ Who started the fire? • I can't start
the car. ✘ *Who began the fire?* • *I
can't begin the car.*

2 [I] ■ When does the class start?

begin • start • open | *infml* **kick
off** | *fml* **commence**

● OPP **finish**

▸ start/begin/start off/open/kick
off/commence **with** sth
▸ start/begin/start off/open/kick
off/commence **by** doing sth
▸ a **campaign/competition/match/**

meeting starts/begins/starts off/
opens/kicks off/commences
▸ a **film/book/chapter** starts/
begins/starts off

3 [T, I] ■ Start the engines!

**start sth up • turn sth on • switch
sth on**

● OPP **stop**

▸ start/start up/turn/switch on a
machine/motor/engine
▸ start/turn/switch on the
ignition
● START OR START UP? Only **start** is
used in the phrases *get sth started*
and *sth won't start*. Use **start sth up**
to talk about computers.

4 [I] ■ They started out early for
Saigon.

set off • take off • set sail • leave |
fml **depart** | *esp. written* **set out**

▸ start/set off/take off/set sail/
leave/depart/set out **for/from** sth
▸ start/set off/take off/set out
on a journey, voyage, etc.
▸ start/set off/take off/leave/
depart/set out **early**

state noun

1 [C] ■ There are concerns about the
current state of the economy.

condition • shape • repair

▸ (a) **good/poor/bad**
condition/(state of) repair/shape
▸ sb's/sth's **financial/economic** state/
condition/shape
▸ **keep** sth in (a) … state/condition/
repair/shape
▸ **get** (sth) into (a) … state/
condition/shape
● STATE OR CONDITION? Condition is
mainly used to talk about the
appearance or working order of
sth; state is a more general word
used to describe the quality sth has
at a particular time.

2 [C] ■ an independent sovereign state

**nation • country • power •
superpower** | *lit.* **land**

▸ a **foreign** state/country/nation/
power/land
▸ **rule** a state/country/nation/land
▸ **govern** a state/country/nation/land
● STATE, NATION OR COUNTRY? You
can use all these words to refer to a
country as a political unit or to its
government. **Country** and **nation**
can also refer to an area where
people live, its economy, culture,
etc. **Country** is the only word
which can be used to refer to a
country as a geographical area: *a
newly independent nation/country/
state • a wealthy nation/country • a
hot country*

3 [C] ■ *The hurricane swept across the southern states of the US.*

province • county • district • region • zone

▶ **in** a state/province/county/district/region/zone
▶ a **border/coastal** state/province/county/district/region/zone
▶ the **northern/southern, etc.** states/provinces/counties/districts/region/zone
● **STATE, COUNTY OR PROVINCE?** Britain and Ireland are both divided into **counties**, but in Ireland these counties are organized into four large **provinces**. The US is divided into **states**, and nearly all these states are divided into counties. Canada is divided into **provinces**, but only some of these provinces are divided into counties.

state *verb* [T]
■ *He stated his intention to run for election.*

declare • announce • express • say | *fml* **proclaim • pronounce |** *esp. journ.* **indicate**

▶ state/declare/announce/express/say/proclaim/pronounce/indicate sth **to** sb
▶ state/declare/announce/say/proclaim/pronounce/indicate **that...**
▶ state/declare/announce/express/proclaim/indicate your **intention** to do sth

state *adj.* [only before noun]
■ *The law only applies to schools within the state system.*

public • federal • national

■ OPP **private**

▶ state/public/federal/national **authorities/funding/expenditure/investment**
▶ state/public/federal **power/control/institutions/employees/funds**
▶ state/public **education/hospitals/enterprise/ownership**
▶ the state/public **sector**

statement *noun* [C]
■ *He made a brief statement to the press.*

announcement • declaration • comment • remark • observation

▶ a/an statement/announcement/declaration/comment/remark/observation **about** sth
▶ a/an statement/observation/comment **on** sth
▶ a/an **public/official** statement/announcement/declaration/comment

▶ **make** a/an statement/announcement/declaration/comment/remark/observation

station *noun*
1 [C] ■ *Get off at the next station.*

stop • bus stop • terminus • terminal • destination | *AmE* **depot**

▶ a **rail/railway/railroad** station/terminus/terminal
▶ a **train** station/terminus/depot
▶ a **bus** station/terminus/terminal/depot
▶ **arrive at** the station/the stop/the bus stop/the terminal/your destination

2 [C] (often in compounds) ■ *a local radio/TV station*

channel • network | *tech.* **frequency**

▶ a **television** station/channel/network
▶ a **radio** station/network/frequency
▶ **tune to** a station/channel/frequency

status *noun*
1 [U, C, usu. sing.] ■ *the struggle for equal status in society*

position • rank • standing • ranking • class • rating • grade • level

▶ sb's status/position/rank/standing/ranking/class/level **in/within** sth
▶ a/the **high/higher** status/position/rank/standing/ranking/rating/grade/level
▶ a/the **low/lower** status/position/rank/standing/ranking/class/rating/grade/level
▶ sb's **social** status/position/rank/standing/ranking/class

2 [U, C, usu. sing.] ■ *The job brings status and a high income.*

prestige • reputation | *BrE* **honour |** *AmE* **honor |** *fml* **stature**

▶ **social** status/prestige
▶ **gain/bring/lose/seek** status/prestige/honour
▶ status/prestige/honour **is attached to** sth

stay *noun* [C]
■ *I enjoyed my stay in Sydney.*

visit • tour • stopover • call

▶ **during** sb's stay/visit/tour
▶ **make** a stay/visit/call
▶ **cut short** a stay/visit/tour
▶ an **overnight** stay/stopover

stay *verb*
1 [I] ■ *Stay there and don't move!*

fml **remain** | *infml* **hang around** + **stick around** + **stay put** | *BrE, infml* **stop** | *esp. written* **linger** | *sometimes disapprov.* **loiter**

■ **OPP go**
▶ stay/remain/hang around/stick around/stop/linger **for** a few minutes/weeks/years, etc.
▶ stay/remain/hang around/stick around/stop/linger **here**
▶ stay/remain/stop **at home/indoors/behind**

2 [I] ■ *I can't stay awake any longer.*

keep | *fml* **remain** | *esp. written* **continue** + **linger** + **live**

▶ stay/keep/remain **awake/calm/cheerful/cool/dry/fine/healthy/quiet/silent**
▶ stay/remain **alert/alive/asleep/loyal/safe/the same/a secret/shut/sober/upright**
▶ stay/keep **close/still/warm**

3 [I] ■ *She's staying with her sister.*

visit + **stop over**

▶ stay/visit/stop over **for** two nights, a week, etc.
▶ stay/visit/stop over **in/at** a place
▶ **come/go** to stay/visit

stay away *phrasal verb*
■ *Stay away from those children!*

avoid + **steer clear** + **keep your distance** + **boycott** | *written* **shun**

▶ deliberately stay away from/avoid/steer clear of sb/sth

steady *adj.*

1 ■ *He made slow but steady progress.*

regular + **constant** + **consistent** + **unchanging** + **even** | *usu. approv.* **stable** | *sometimes disapprov., esp. busin.* **static**

▶ a/an steady/constant/even/stable **temperature**
▶ a steady/constant/consistent **trend/rate**
▶ (a) steady/regular/stable **relationship/employment**
● **STEADY OR REGULAR?** Both these words can be used to describe a job, work, employment, an income, the supply of sth or a relationship that continues for a long time and that you can rely on. A *regular* job is sometimes used in contrast to another job that is not regular: ✔*I decided to give up the freelance work and concentrate on my regular job.* ✗ *I decided to concentrate on my steady job.* ✔*If you want money, get a regular/steady job.*

2 ■ *The work requires a steady hand.*

stable + **firm** + **secure**

■ **OPP unsteady**
▶ a steady/stable/firm/secure **foundation**

steal *verb* [I, T]
■ *Thieves stole jewellery worth over $10000.*

take + **shoplift** + **embezzle** + **rob** + **loot** | *esp. BrE* **poach** | *fml* **plunder** | *BrE, infml* **nick**

▶ steal/take/shoplift/embezzle/loot/poach/nick (sth) **from** sb/a place
▶ steal/take/nick sb's **bag/purse/passport**
▶ steal/take **food/goods/items**

step *noun*

1 [C] ■ *I took a step forward.*

pace + **stride** + **footstep**

▶ take a few steps/paces/strides **(back/forward/to sth/towards sth)**
▶ take a step/pace **(backwards)**
▶ hear (sb's) steps/footsteps

2 [C] ■ *This was a first step towards a united Europe.*

move + **measure** + **action** + **act** + **procedure** + **gesture**

▶ a/an step/move/measure/action/act/gesture **by** sb
▶ **make** a step/move/gesture **(towards** sb)
▶ **take** steps/measures/actions

3 ■ *I'll explain it step by step.*

stage + **round**

▶ the **first/initial/preliminary/opening/second/final/last** step/stage/round
▶ **successive** steps/stages/rounds
▶ a/an **important/critical/crucial/key/difficult** step/stage

stern *adj.*
■ *His voice was suddenly stern.*

grim | *esp. written* **severe** + **steely** | *disapprov.* **hard** + **unforgiving** + **dour**

▶ a stern/grim/severe/steely/hard **look/voice**
▶ a stern/grim/severe/hard/dour **expression/face**
▶ a stern/grim/severe **warning**

stick *verb*

1 [T, I] (always used with an adv. or prep.) ■ *She stuck a pin in the balloon.*

push + **press** + **poke** + **ram** + **force** + **drive** | *infml* **shove** | *written* **thrust**

▶ push/stick/press/poke/ram/force/shove/thrust sth **into** sth

▶ stick/push/poke/force/drive/shove/thrust sth **through** sth

2 [T, I] (always used with an adv. or prep.) ■ *Stick a stamp on the envelope.*

put • **attach** • **glue** • tape • fasten • *esp. BrE* **fix** | *fml* **secure**

▶ stick/attach/glue/tape/fasten/fix/secure sth **to** sth
▶ stick/put/glue/tape/fasten/fix sth **on** sth
▶ stick/glue/tape/fasten/fix sth **together**

stiff *adj.*
■ *Scrub it with a stiff brush* ■ *The windows were stiff and she couldn't get them open.*

rigid • **hard** • taut • tight | *approv.* **firm**

■ **OPP flexible**
▶ stiff/rigid **material**
▶ go stiff/hard

still *adj.*
■ *Stay absolutely still.*

stationary • **at a standstill** | *fml* **inert** | *written* **motionless** • **immobile**

■ **OPP moving**
▶ remain still/stationary/inert/motionless/immobile
▶ stay/lie still/inert/motionless/immobile
▶ sit/stand still/motionless/immobile

stimulate *verb* [T] (approv.)
■ *The article stimulated discussion among the students.*

arouse • **inspire** • **excite** • encourage | *esp. written* **stir** | *disapprov.* **incite**

■ **OPP suppress**
▶ stimulate/arouse/excite/encourage/stir (sb's) **interest**
▶ stimulate/arouse/excite/encourage **curiosity**
▶ stimulate/arouse/excite/encourage/incite **speculation**

sting *verb* [I, T]
■ *Her eyes were stinging.*

burn • **tingle** • **hurt**

▶ your **eyes** sting/burn/hurt
▶ your **skin/flesh** stings/burns/tingles/hurts
▶ It stings/tingles/hurts.

stir *verb* [T]
■ *Stir in the milk until the sauce thickens.*

beat • whip • whisk • blend • mix

▶ stir/beat/whisk/blend/mix sth **into** sth
▶ stir/beat/whisk/blend/mix A and B **together**
▶ stir/beat/whisk/blend/mix **ingredients**
▶ beat/whip/whisk **cream/eggs/egg whites**

stock *noun* [U, C]
■ *Food stocks are running low.*

supply • **store** • reserve • resource • pool • stockpile

▶ a stock/supply/store/reserve/pool/stockpile **of** sth
▶ have sth **in** stock/supply
▶ a stock/a supply/stores of **food**
▶ stocks/supplies/reserves/stockpiles of **coal**

stomach *noun* [C]
■ *Lie on your stomach.*

belly • **gut** • paunch | *infml* **tummy** • **insides** | *fml or med.* **intestine** • **abdomen**

▶ **in** the/your stomach/belly/gut/tummy/insides/intestine/abdomen
▶ **on** your stomach/belly/tummy
▶ a/an **fat/flat/empty/full** stomach/belly/tummy

stone *noun* [U, C]
■ *a stone bridge/floor/carving*

rock • **boulder** • **pebble**

▶ **solid** stone/rock
▶ **throw** a stone/rock/boulder/pebble
● **STONE OR ROCK?** Rock [U] is still a part of the ground; stone [U] has been dug up from the ground:
  ✓*houses built of stone* X *houses built of rock*
  ✓*the rock walls of the cave* X *the stone walls of the cave*
  In BrE people **throw stones** and a **rock** is sth too big to pick up and throw. In AmE **rock** is the usual word for a small piece of rock that you can pick up.

stop *noun*

1 [C] ■ *Work came to a stop.*

esp. written, esp. busin. **halt** • **standstill**

▶ a/an **abrupt/sudden/complete/total** stop/halt/standstill
▶ a/an **brief/unscheduled/immediate** stop/halt
▶ **come/bring** sth to a stop/halt/standstill
▶ **draw/jolt/screech/shudder/skid** to a stop/halt
● **STOP OR HALT?** A **stop** is gentler than a **halt** and more likely to be planned:
  ✓*a lunch stop* • *a stop for*

refreshments ✗ ~~a lunch halt~~ • ~~a halt for refreshments~~

You can **bring** a vehicle *to a stop/ halt* or it can **come** *to a stop/halt.* You can **put** a stop *to sth* that is wrong or **call** a halt *to sth* that is not worth doing.

2 ■ *I'm getting off at the next stop.*

station • bus stop • destination

▸ **arrive at** *the/your stop/station/ bus stop/destination*
▸ **get off at** *a stop/station*

stop *verb*

1 [I, T] ■ *The car stopped in front of the house.*

park • pull up • pull (sb/sth) over | *esp. written* **halt**

▸ **stop/park/halt** *a car*
▸ **stop/park/halt** *a bus/cab/vehicle*
▸ *a car/driver* **stops/parks/pulls up/ pulls over**
▸ *a train* **stops/halts**

2 [T, I] ■ *The phone never stops ringing!*

give sth up • abandon • drop | *infml* **leave off • knock off (sth) • pack sth in |** *esp. AmE, infml* **quit |** *fml* **cease • discontinue**

■ OPP **start**

▸ **stop/give up/leave off/quit/cease doing** *sth*
▸ **stop/give up/abandon/drop/ leave off/quit/cease what you are doing**
▸ **stop/give up/leave off/abandon/ knock off/quit/cease work**

3 [I, T] ■ *When will this fighting stop?*

end • finish | *fml* **conclude • terminate**

■ OPP **start**

▸ **almost/nearly/effectively stop/ end/finish/conclude/terminate**
▸ **virtually/all but/never stop/end/ finish/conclude/terminate**
▸ **stop/end/finish/conclude/ terminate at last/eventually/ finally**
● **STOP, END, FINISH OR CONCLUDE?** End, finish and conclude are used esp. about things that you do not expect to start again: *The war ended in 1945.* • *The concert should finish by 10 o'clock.* • *She concluded her speech with a quotation from Shakespeare.*
Stop is used about things that may or will start again: *The rain stopped for a couple of hours.*

4 [T] ■ *Doctors couldn't stop the bleeding.*

halt • stem • put a stop to sth • suspend

■ OPP **start**

---

439   **store**

▸ **stop/halt/stem/suspend the flow** *(of sth)*
▸ **stop/halt/stem the progress/ development/advance/ expansion/spread/decline/slide** *(of sth)*
▸ **stop/halt/put a stop to/suspend the plans/an activity/a practice**

5 [T] ■ *Protesters failed to stop the tests from going ahead.*

prevent • keep sb from sth • thwart • frustrate • avoid • rule sb/sth out | *written* **restrain • avert |** *fml* **preclude |** *esp. journ.* **foil**

▸ **stop/prevent/keep/restrain/ preclude sb/sth from doing sth**
▸ **stop/prevent sb/sth/keep/ avoid (sb/sth)/preclude (sb/sth) doing sth**
▸ **stop/prevent/avoid/avert/a an crisis/accident**
● **STOP OR PREVENT? Prevent** is a more formal word. It suggests action that sb plans in advance so that sth does not even start; **stop** often suggests action taken to end sth already in progress.

store *noun* [C]

■ *a health food/liquor store* ■ *a department store*

supermarket • boutique • salon | *esp. BrE* **shop |** *AmE* **grocery store |** *busin.* **outlet**

▸ **an expensive/exclusive store/ shop/boutique/salon**
▸ **a specialist store/shop/outlet/ boutique**
▸ **a/an store/shop/supermarket/ boutique/salon/grocery store/ outlet sells/offers sth**
▸ **own/have a/an store/shop/ salon/supermarket/boutique/ grocery store sells sth**
● **SHOP OR STORE?** In *BrE* **shop** is the usual word; **store** is only used about large shops, esp. in business, journalism and advertising. In *AmE* **store** is the usual word; **shop** is only used about small, specialist shops.

store *verb*

1 [T] ■ *The squirrels are storing up food for the winter.*

keep • hoard • stockpile • stock up | *infml* **stash**

▸ **store/stash sth away**
▸ **store/keep/hoard/stockpile/stock up on food**
▸ **store/keep/stockpile weapons**

2 [T] ■ *how information is stored in the brain*

hold • keep | *fml* **retain**

▶ store/hold/keep/retain **information/data**
▶ store/retain **facts**

storm noun

1 [C] ■ *Fierce storms lashed the country.*

gale ◆ thunderstorm ◆ snowstorm ◆ blizzard ◆ hurricane ◆ cyclone ◆ typhoon ◆ tornado | *AmE, infml* twister

▶ a storm/thunderstorm/blizzard/ hurricane/cyclone/typhoon/ tornado/twister **hits/strikes** sth
▶ a storm/gale/blizzard/hurricane/ tornado **warning**
▶ the **eye** of a storm/hurricane/ cyclone

2 [C] (*infml, esp. journ.*) ■ *His comments created a storm of protest in the media.*

outcry ◆ uproar ◆ fuss | *BrE* furore | *esp. AmE* furor

▶ a/an storm/outcry/uproar/fuss/ furore **over** sth
▶ a **political** storm/outcry/uproar/ furore
▶ **cause** a/an storm/outcry/uproar/ fuss/furore
▶ **provoke** a/an storm/outcry/ uproar

story noun

1 [C] ■ *I always read the children a bedtime story.*

tale ◆ anecdote ◆ saga ◆ narrative ◆ fairy tale ◆ fable ◆ legend ◆ myth ◆ plot ◆ storyline

▶ a/an story/tale/anecdote/saga/ narrative/fairy tale/fable/legend/ myth/plot/storyline **about** sth
▶ a **long** story/tale/anecdote/saga/ narrative
▶ an **ancient** story/legend/fable/ epic
▶ **tell** (sb) a story/tale/anecdote/ fairy tale/fable/legend

2 [C] ■ *The police didn't believe her story.*

account ◆ report ◆ version ◆ item ◆ news

▶ a story/a report/an item/news **about** sth
▶ a/an story/account/report/ version/item **is based on** sth
▶ a **true/false/conflicting** story/ account/report/version

3 the story of sth [C, usu. sing.] ■ *He told us the story of his life.*

history ◆ chronicle

▶ **read/write** the story/a history/a chronicle of sth

▶ **tell** (sb)/**recount/relate** the story/ history of sth
● STORY OR HISTORY? The **story** of sth is usu. more popular and less academic than a **history**.

stove noun [C] (*esp. AmE*)

■ *She put a pan of water on the stove.*

oven ◆ microwave (oven) | *BrE* cooker ◆ hob

▶ **on** the stove/cooker/hob
▶ **in** the oven/microwave
▶ a/an **gas/electric** stove/oven/ cooker/hob

strain noun

1 [U, C] ■ *Their marriage is under great strain.*

stress ◆ pressure ◆ tension ◆ demands | *infml, esp. journ.* heat

▶ be **under** strain/stress/pressure
▶ **cope with** the strain/stress/ pressure/tension/demands
▶ **relieve/release** the strain/stress/ pressure/tension

2 [U, C] ■ *The rope broke under the strain.*

stress ◆ pressure ◆ weight ◆ load

▶ **under** the strain/stress/pressure/ weight/load
▶ **put** strain/stress/pressure/ weight/load **on** sth
▶ **bear** the strain/stress/weight/load of sth
● STRAIN, STRESS OR PRESSURE? **Pressure** can be *heavy*, *firm*, *gentle* or *light*. Both **strain** and **stress** usu. suggest that there is too much pressure.

strange adj.

1 ■ *A strange thing happened this morning.*

odd ◆ mysterious ◆ curious ◆ bizarre ◆ uncanny ◆ unusual | *esp. spoken* funny ◆ weird | *BrE or fml* peculiar

■ OPP **normal**
▶ strange/odd/curious/bizarre/ uncanny/unusual/funny/weird/ peculiar **that...**
▶ strange/odd/curious/bizarre/ uncanny/funny/weird/peculiar **how/ what...**
▶ a/an strange/odd/mysterious/ curious/bizarre/uncanny/unusual/funny/ weird/peculiar **thing**
▶ a/an strange/odd/curious/ bizarre/uncanny/unusual/funny/ weird/peculiar **feeling**
● STRANGE OR ODD? Sb/sth that is **strange** can be mysterious or frightening. Sb/sth that is **odd** is hard to understand or not right in some way, but *odd* people probably won't hurt you, whereas *strange* people might.

unfamiliar • unknown | *written* **alien**

■ **OPP familiar**

▸ strange/unfamiliar/unknown/alien **to sb**
▸ a/an strange/unfamiliar/unknown/alien **place**
▸ a/an strange/unfamiliar/alien **environment**
● **STRANGE OR UNFAMILIAR?** In this meaning **strange** usu. describes people and places. If it is used to describe other things such as *words, sounds,* etc. it usu. means 'unusual'; if you mean 'not known' use **unfamiliar**.

strangle *verb* [T]

■ *He strangled her to death.*

throttle • suffocate • choke

▸ almost/half/nearly strangle/throttle/suffocate/choke **sb**
▸ strangle/throttle/suffocate/choke **sb to death**
● **STRANGLE OR THROTTLE?** These words are very similar but **throttle** is slightly more informal. Both can be used humorously: *I felt like strangling/throttling him!*

strategy *noun* [C, U]

■ *a strategy for dealing with unemployment*

initiative • policy • plan • proposal • proposition • scheme | *BrE* **programme** | *AmE* **program**

▸ a/an strategy/initiative/policy/plan/proposal/scheme/programme **for sth**
▸ a/an strategy/initiative/policy/plan/proposal/proposition/scheme/programme **to do sth**
▸ **have/adopt** a strategy/policy/plan/proposal/scheme
▸ **develop** a/an strategy/initiative/policy/plan/proposal/programme

stream *noun*

1 [C] ■ *We waded across a little mountain stream.*

river • tributary | *AmE, AustralE* **creek**

▸ a/an **narrow/underground** stream/river
▸ a stream/river/tributary/creek **flows**
▸ a stream/river/creek **runs**

2 [C] ■ *I've had a steady stream of visitors.*

flow • trickle

▸ a stream/flow (of sb/sth) **into/through** sth
▸ a **steady/constant** stream/flow/trickle
▸ a/an **continuous/endless** stream/flow

3 [C] (always followed by *of*) ■ *She had to deal with a constant stream of enquiries.*

flood • torrent • barrage | *written* **outpouring**

▸ a stream/flood/torrent of **words**
▸ a stream/torrent/barrage of **abuse**
▸ a stream/flood of **calls**

street *noun* [C]

■ *I walked up the street.*

road • avenue • lane • alley | *esp. AmE* **highway** | *AmE* **boulevard**

▸ **in** the street/road/avenue/lane/alley
▸ **on** a street/road/highway
▸ **cross** the street/road/highway
● **STREET OR ROAD?** In a town or city, **street** is the most usual word, although streets are often called **Road**, esp. in *BrE*; in the countryside the usual word is **road**: *a street map of London ◆ a road map of Britain ◆ 205 Woodstock Road*

strength *noun*

1 [U] ■ *His physical strength won him the title.*

power • force | *fml or lit.* **might**

▸ **physical** strength/power/force
▸ **brute** strength/force
▸ **use** (your) strength/power/force/might

2 [U, sing.] ■ *She has remarkable inner strength.*

resilience • endurance • stamina • resistance

■ **OPP weakness**

▸ the strength/resilience/stamina **to do sth**
▸ **have** strength/resilience/endurance/stamina/resistance
▸ **show** strength/resilience/endurance

3 [C] ■ *Consider your strengths and weaknesses.*

merit • asset • virtue • good point • benefit • advantage | *infml* **plus**

■ **OPP weakness**

▸ **considerable/great/real/relative** strengths/merits/virtues/benefits/advantages

strengthen *verb* [I, T]

■ *Repairs are necessary to strengthen the bridge.* ■ *Their attitude only strengthened his resolve to fight on.*

reinforce • bolster • cement • shore sth up

■ **OPP weaken**

▸ strengthen/reinforce a **view**
▸ strengthen/bolster/cement the **case** (for sth)

stress

▶ strengthen/bolster/shore up the **economy**

stress noun

1 [U, C, usu. pl.] ■ *the stresses and strains of public life*

pressure • **strain** • **tension** • **demands**

▶ be under stress/pressure/strain
▶ cope with the stress/pressure/strain/tension/demands
▶ release/relieve the stress/pressure/strain/tension
▶ suffer from stress/tension
● PRESSURE OR STRESS? It is common to say that sb *is suffering from stress*; pressure may be the thing that causes **stress**.

2 [U, C] ■ *An injury can put stress on other parts of the body.*

strain • **pressure** • **weight** • **load**

▶ under the stress/strain/pressure/weight/load
▶ considerable/enormous/great/immense stress/strain/pressure/weight
▶ put stress/strain/pressure/weight on sth
● STRESS, PRESSURE OR STRAIN? Pressure can be *heavy, firm, gentle* or *light*. Both **strain** and **stress** usu. suggest that there is too much pressure.

stress verb [T]

■ *She stressed the importance of exercise.*

emphasize • **underline** • **highlight** • **point sth out** | *esp. AmE, esp. busin.* **underscore**

▶ stress/emphasize/underline/highlight/point out **how...**
▶ stress/emphasize/underline/point out **that...**
▶ stress/emphasize/underline/underscore **the fact that...**
▶ stress/emphasize/underline/underscore the **importance/extent/necessity** of sth
● STRESS OR EMPHASIZE? Emphasize is slightly more formal and is used more in written and academic English, esp. when the subject is not human: *The report emphasizes....* Stress is used more in spoken English and journalism, esp. when the subject is human: *I must stress....*

stressed adj.

■ *He was feeling stressed and tired.*

strained • **tense** • **under pressure** | *infml* **stressed out** • **uptight**

■ OPP **relaxed**

stressful adj.

■ *It was a stressful time for all of us.*

tense • **strained** • **anxious** • **nerve-racking/nerve-wracking** • **worrying** • **unsettling** • **upsetting** • **traumatic** | *esp. BrE* **fraught**

■ OPP **relaxing**

▶ a/an stressful/tense/anxious/worrying/unsettling/upsetting/traumatic/fraught **time**
▶ a stressful/tense/worrying/fraught **situation**
▶ a stressful/tense/fraught **meeting**

stretch noun [C]

■ *an unspoilt stretch of coastline*

expanse • **tract** • **field**

▶ a/an stretch/expanse/tract/field of sth
▶ a great/large/huge/vast stretch/expanse/tract/field
▶ a/an wide/broad/continuous/open/empty/barren/deserted stretch/expanse

stretch verb

1 [I, T] ■ *This sweater has stretched.*

expand • **enlarge** • **widen** • **broaden** • **lengthen** • **extend**

■ OPP **shrink**

▶ stretch/expand/enlarge/widen/lengthen/extend (sth) **to** a particular amount

2 [I] (always used with an adv. or prep.) ■ *The road stretched ahead for miles.*

continue • **extend** • **lead** • **go** • **reach** • **span**

▶ stretch/continue/extend/lead/go/reach/span **beyond/across** sth
▶ stretch/continue/extend/lead/go/reach **from** A **to** B
▶ stretch/continue/extend/reach **for** sth

strict adj.

■ *There are strict regulations regarding hours of work.*

tough • **severe** | *fml* **stringent** • **punitive** | *often approv.* **firm** | *usu. disapprov.* **harsh** • **rigid**

■ OPP **lenient**

▶ strict/tough/severe/firm/harsh **with** sb/sth
▶ strict/tough/severe/harsh **on** sb/sth
▶ strict/tough/severe/firm/harsh/rigid **discipline**
▶ strict/stringent/firm/rigid **controls**

strike noun [C]

■ *Devastating air strikes took place.*

attack • **raid** • **assault** • **offensive**

▶ a/an strike/attack/raid/assault/offensive **against** sb/sth

► a/an strike/attack/assault/
offensive **on** sb/sth
► **plan/launch** a/an strike/attack/
raid/assault/offensive

strike verb

1 [T] (fml) ■ *The ship struck a rock.*

hit • knock | infml **bash**

► strike/hit the ground/floor/wall

2 [T] (fml) ■ *She struck him hard
across the face.*

**hit • punch • thump • beat • batter •
slap • spank •** esp. BrE **smack •** infml
whack • sock

► strike/hit/beat/batter/whack sb/
sth **with** sth
► strike/hit/thump/whack sb **over
the head**
► beat/batter sb **around/about the
head**
► strike/hit/punch/thump sb **in the
stomach/chest**

3 [I, T] ■ *Planes struck targets in the
city.*

attack • raid • charge • storm

► strike/charge **at** sth
► strike/attack/charge **the enemy**
► aircraft strike/attack/raid sth

4 [I, T] (written, esp. journ.) ■ *tragedy/
disaster strikes* ■ *The area was struck
by an outbreak of cholera.*

attack | esp. journ. or spoken **hit**

► a/an **earthquake/hurricane/
storm** strikes/hits (sth)
► a **disease/virus** strikes/hits/attacks sb/
sth

5 (not used in the progressive
tenses) ■ *An awful thought has just
struck me.*

**occur to sb • cross your mind •
dawn on sb • come to sb • come/
spring to mind** | infml **hit**

► It strikes sb/occurs to sb/crosses
sb's mind/dawns on sb/comes to
sb/hits sb **that...**
► a/an **thought/idea** strikes sb/
occurs to sb/crosses sb's mind/
comes to sb/comes to mind/hits
sb
► **suddenly** strike/occur to/dawn
on/come to/hit sb

6 [T] ■ *His reaction struck me as odd.*

**come across • come over • seem •
appear**

► strike sb/come across/come over
as (being) etc.
► It strikes sb/seems/appears **that...**

striking adj.

■ *She bears a striking resemblance to
her sister.*

**conspicuous • distinct • noticeable •
unmistakable • sharp • clear •
definite • decided** | esp. written
marked • pronounced | disapprov.
glaring

■ OPP **inconspicuous**

► a **striking/distinct/noticeable/
sharp/clear/definite/marked/
pronounced difference**
► a **striking/distinct/noticeable/
sharp/clear/definite/decided/
marked improvement**
► a **striking/conspicuous/distinct/
marked/pronounced feature**

string noun [U, C]

■ *The key hangs on a string by the
door.*

cord • rope • thread • yarn

► **tie** sth **with** string/cord/rope
► **wind** the string/cord/thread/yarn
► a string/cord/rope/thread **breaks**
► a **length/piece** of string/cord/
rope/thread

strip noun [C]

■ *Cut a strip of paper.*

band • ribbon • stripe

► a strip/band/ribbon **of** sth
► a **narrow/broad** strip/band/
ribbon/stripe
► a **wide** strip/band/ribbon
► a **horizontal/vertical** strip/band/
stripe

strip verb [I, T]

■ *He was stripped naked and left in a
cell.*

undress • get undressed • take sth
off | written **remove**

■ OPP **dress, get dressed**

► strip off/take off/remove your
**clothes/jacket/coat/shirt/
sweater/jeans/gloves**
● **STRIP OR UNDRESS?** To **strip** is a
quicker and less gentle action. A
guard might order a prisoner to
strip, but a doctor would ask a
patient to **undress** or **take off** their
clothes.

stroke verb [T]

■ *He stroked her hair tenderly.*

caress • fondle | esp. AmE **pet** |
disapprov. **grope**

► stroke/pet a **dog/cat/horse**
► stroke/caress/fondle sb's **hair/
ears/face/neck**
► stroke/caress sb/sth **gently/
lightly/tenderly/absently**

strong adj.

1 ■ *He's strong enough to lift a car!*

muscular | *esp. written, usu. approv.*
powerful

■ OPP **weak**
▶ (a) strong/muscular/powerful **build/body/arms/legs**
▶ strong/powerful **muscles/jaws**

2 ■ *Stay indoors when the sun is strongest.*

bright • dazzling • brilliant • bold • intense | *disapprov.* **harsh • glaring**

■ OPP **weak**
▶ strong/bright/dazzling/brilliant/intense/harsh/glaring **light**
▶ strong/bright/dazzling/brilliant/bold/harsh/glaring **colours**
▶ strong/bright/dazzling/brilliant/glaring **sunshine**

3 (approv.) ■ *The country needs a strong leader.*

powerful • important • influential • great • dominant

■ OPP **weak**
▶ a/an strong/powerful/important/influential/great/dominant **figure/leader/position**
▶ a/an strong/powerful/influential **lobby**
▶ a/an strong/powerful/important/great/dominant **influence**
● WHICH WORD? **Strong** people are confident and have leadership qualities. **Powerful** people such as politicians use their position to control events. **Important** people influence other people or events because people respect them or because their position means their actions have a great effect. **Influential** people change other people's opinions or behaviour because people respect and listen to them.

4 ■ *You have a strong case for getting your job back.*

convincing • persuasive • forceful • compelling | *fml* **cogent**

■ OPP **weak**
▶ a strong/convincing/persuasive/forceful/compelling/cogent **argument**
▶ strong/convincing/persuasive/compelling/cogent **evidence**
▶ a strong/convincing/persuasive/compelling/cogent **reason/case**

5 ■ *You need vitamins to keep you strong and healthy.*

healthy • good | *esp. BrE* **fit** | *esp. spoken* **well • fine**

■ OPP **weak**
▶ **get** strong/fit/well
▶ **physically** strong/healthy/fit/well
▶ **fit and** strong/healthy/well

6 ■ *strong cheese/coffee*

---

hot • spicy

■ OPP **mild, weak**
▶ a strong/hot/spicy **flavour**
▶ a strong/spicy **taste**
▶ strong/hot **mustard**

structure noun

1 [C] ■ *the structure of human societies throughout history*

framework • organization • composition • form • fabric • construction | *esp. spoken or journ.* **make-up**

▶ the **basic** structure/framework/organization/composition/form/fabric/construction of sth
▶ a **complex/flexible** structure/framework/organization/form
▶ a **simple/coherent/rigid** structure/framework/form
▶ the **economic/political/social** structure/framework/organization/composition/fabric/make-up of sth
▶ **create/devise/establish/provide** a structure/framework for sth

2 [C] ■ *The pier is a wooden structure, built in 1867.*

building • construction

▶ a/an **imposing/magnificent/brick/stone** structure/building
▶ **erect/demolish/put up/pull down** a structure/building

3 [U, C] ■ *Children need structure in their lives.*

order • coherence • organization

▶ **bring/give** structure/order/coherence to sth
▶ **have/lack** structure/order/coherence/organization
▶ a **lack of** structure/order/coherence/organization

struggle noun

1 [C] ■ *It is an epic tale of the struggle between good and evil.*

battle • fight • war • crusade • campaign • drive

▶ the struggle/battle/fight/war/crusade/campaign/drive **for/against** sth
▶ **lead/continue** the struggle/battle/fight/campaign/drive
▶ **win/lose** the struggle/battle/fight/war

2 [C] ■ *He was injured in the struggle.*

fight • scuffle • tussle • brawl | *journ.* **clash**

▶ a struggle/fight/scuffle/tussle/brawl/clash **with** sb
▶ a struggle/fight/scuffle/tussle/brawl/clash **between** people
▶ a struggle/fight/scuffle/tussle/brawl/clash **over** sth

▶ in a struggle/fight/scuffle/tussle/ brawl/clash
▶ a violent struggle/fight/clash

3 [sing.] ■ *It was a real struggle to be ready on time.*

effort • hard work • exertion | *BrE* endeavour | *AmE* endeavor
▶ (a) great struggle/effort/exertion/ endeavour
▶ (a) physical/mental struggle/ effort/exertion

struggle *verb*

1 [I, I] ■ *She struggled to pay her bills.*

try | *fml* strive | *BrE, fml* endeavour | *AmE, fml* endeavor
▶ struggle/try/strive/endeavour **to do** sth
▶ struggle/try/strive **for/against** sth
▶ struggle/try/strive **desperately/in vain**

2 [I] ■ *He struggled against cancer for two years.*

resist • hold out against sb/sth • hold/stand your ground • hold/ keeep sb/sth at bay
▶ struggle/hold out/hold your ground **against** sb/sth
▶ resist/hold out against **pressure/ an attack**

3 [I] ■ *I struggled and screamed for help.*

fight • wrestle • grapple • scuffle
▶ struggle/fight/wrestle/grapple/ scuffle **with** sb
▶ struggle/fight **against** sb
▶ struggle/fight **fiercely/furiously**

4 [I] ■ *The two men struggled for control of the party.*

fight • compete • vie | *esp. journ.* battle
▶ struggle/fight/compete/vie/ battle **for** sth
▶ struggle/compete/vie/battle **with** sb
▶ struggle/fight/compete/vie for **power**
▶ struggle/fight/vie/battle for **control**

stubborn *adj.*

■ *He's too stubborn to admit that he's wrong.*

obstinate • strong-willed | *esp. BrE* wilful | *AmE usu.* willful | *esp. written* headstrong

■ OPP compliant
▶ a/an stubborn/obstinate/wilful **child**
▶ a/an stubborn/obstinate **man/ woman**
▶ a/an stubborn/obstinate/wilful **refusal**

student *noun*

■ *He was an outstanding student.*

learner • schoolboy • schoolgirl • schoolchild | *esp. BrE, becoming old-fash.* pupil
▶ a/an good/bright/outstanding/ star student/pupil
▶ a disruptive student/pupil
▶ older/younger students/learners/ pupils
▶ a primary school/junior school/ secondary school student/pupil
▶ teach students/learners/ schoolboys/schoolgirls/ schoolchildren/pupils

study *noun*

1 [U] ■ *It's important to develop good study skills.*

learning • training • education | *fml* schooling
▶ formal study/learning/training/ education/schooling
▶ compulsory study/training/ education/schooling
▶ private study/education/ schooling

2 [U, C] ■ *a scientific study of American dialects*

examination • research • analysis • exploration • enquiry/inquiry | *fml* scrutiny
▶ (a) detailed/scientific study/ examination/research/analysis/ exploration/enquiry/scrutiny
▶ do a study/research/analysis
▶ carry out/conduct/undertake a study/an examination/research/ analysis/an exploration
● STUDY OR EXAMINATION? An **examination** is often practical, in order to make a decision about sth; **study** is usu. academic, in order to find out about a subject.

3 [C] ■ *A recent study revealed unacceptable levels of pollution.*

investigation • survey • report • review
▶ a/an government/official/ public/independent study/ investigation/survey/report/ review
▶ publish/release/read a study/ survey/report/review
▶ a/an study/investigation/survey/ report/review **finds/shows/ reveals/suggests** sth

4 [C] ■ *Giles is working in his study.*

office • studio • workroom
▶ a large/small study/office/studio/ workroom

study verb

study verb

1 [I, T] ■ Nell studied at York University.

learn + train + do | BrE revise | esp. AmE review

► study/revise/review (sth) for sth
► study/learn/train to be sth
► study/learn/do/revise/review geography/biology, etc.

2 [T] ■ Fran was studying the menu.

scan + survey | esp. written scrutinize

► study/scan/survey/scrutinize for sth
► study/scan/scrutinize sb's face
► study/survey/scrutinize sth in detail/thoroughly

3 [T] ■ Study the report carefully before you make a decision.

examine + review | BrE analyse | AmE analyze | esp. spoken go into sth

► study/examine/review/analyse/ go into what/how/whether…
► study/examine/review/analyse the situation
► study/examine/review/analyse/ go into sth in depth/in detail
● STUDY OR EXAMINE? You examine sth in order to understand it or to help other people understand it, for example by describing it in a book; you study sth in order to understand it yourself.

stuff noun

1 [U] (infml) ■ What's that sticky stuff on the carpet?

substance + material + liquid + solid | fml or physics matter

► (a) sticky stuff/substance/liquid/ solid

2 [U] (infml) ■ Where's all my stuff?

property + possessions + belongings + equipment + kit | infml gear | esp. BrE, infml things | infml, disapprov. junk

► personal stuff/property/ possessions/belongings/ equipment/gear/things
► collect/gather/pack your stuff/ possessions/belongings/ equipment/gear/things
► search sb's stuff/property/ belongings/things

3 [U] (infml) ■ I've got loads of stuff to do today.

things

► a lot/lots/loads of stuff/things
► stuff/things to do/say

stumble verb

stumble verb [I] (always used with an adv. or prep.)
■ We stumbled around in the dark.

stagger + lurch + reel + lumber + hobble + limp

► stumble/stagger/lumber/hobble/ limp along
► stumble/stagger/hobble/limp a few steps
► stumble/stagger/lurch/lumber to your feet
► stagger/lurch/reel drunkenly

stupid adj.

stupid adj.

1 (usu. disapprov.) ■ She made a stupid mistake.

idiotic + reckless | esp. spoken silly | infml insane | esp. AmE, infml crazy + dumb | esp. BrE, infml mad | esp. written foolish

■ OPP sensible

► stupid/idiotic/reckless/silly/ insane/crazy/dumb/mad/foolish to do sth
► stupid/idiotic/reckless/silly/ insane/crazy/dumb/mad/foolish of sb to do sth
► a/an stupid/idiotic/silly/insane/ crazy/dumb/mad/foolish thing to do/idea
► Are you stupid/insane/crazy/ dumb/mad?
● WHICH WORD? Stupid, silly, foolish and dumb describe people or their actions. Crazy usu. describes a person, but it can also be used to describe a deliberate and dangerous action. All these words are usu. disapproving and can be offensive.

2 (esp. spoken) ■ I felt completely stupid.

fml obtuse | esp. AmE, infml dumb | BrE, infml thick

■ OPP intelligent, smart, clever

► look stupid/dumb/thick
► totally/completely stupid/dumb/ thick
► Don't be so/How can you be so stupid/obtuse/dumb!

style noun

style noun

1 [C] ■ I don't like his style of management.

way + approach | fml manner

► a style/way/manner of (doing) sth
► in a (…) style/way/manner
► a/an traditional/conventional/ different/casual/informal/formal style/way/approach/manner
► have/adopt a/an style/way/ approach/manner
● STYLE OR WAY? Style tells you how sb usu. does sth; way tells you how sb does sth on a particular occasion.

2 [C, U] ■ *Short skirts are back in style.*

fashion • trend • look | *written* **vogue**

▶ **in** style/fashion/trend/vogue
▶ **set a** style/fashion/trend
▶ **create a** style/trend/look/vogue

3 [U] (*approv.*) ■ *She does everything with style and grace.*

elegance • flair • class • grace • glamour

▶ **do sth with** style/elegance/flair/grace
▶ **have/lack** style/elegance/flair/class/grace/glamour
▶ **add** style/elegance/flair/class/glamour

4 [C, U] ■ *different styles of architecture*

kind • type • form | *esp. BrE* **sort** | *fml* **genre**

▶ **a** style/kind/type/form/sort/genre **of** sth
▶ **of a/the ...** style/kind/type/form/sort
▶ **various/different** styles/kinds/types/forms/sorts/genres

subject *noun*

1 [C] ■ *Let's change the subject.*

topic • theme • matter • issue • question

▶ **on a/an** subject/topic/theme/matter/issue/question
▶ **a/an important/key/major/serious/general** subject/topic/theme/matter/issue/question
▶ **deal with/tackle/discuss/consider/examine/explore a/an** subject/topic/theme/matter/issue/question

2 [C] ■ *Biology is my favourite subject.*

field • area | *fml* **discipline**

▶ **scientific** subjects/fields/disciplines

substance *noun* [C]

■ *chemical substances that act on the brain*

material • chemical • liquid • solid • gas | *infml* **stuff** | *fml or tech.* **matter • fluid** | *chemistry* **element**

▶ **a natural** substance/material/chemical/gas
▶ **a chemical** substance/material/element
▶ **a toxic** substance/material/chemical/liquid/gas/element
▶ **organic** substances/material/chemicals/liquid/matter/elements

substantial *adj.*

■ *Substantial sums of money were involved.*

considerable • large • big • great • extensive • sizeable/sizable • hefty • huge • massive • vast • enormous | *approv.* **handsome**

■ **OPP insubstantial, negligible**

▶ **a/an** substantial/considerable/large/big/great/extensive/sizeable/huge/massive/vast/enormous/handsome **amount**
▶ **a/an** substantial/considerable/large/big/great/sizeable/hefty/huge/massive/vast/enormous/handsome **sum/profit**
▶ **a/an** substantial/considerable/big/great/extensive/huge/massive/vast/enormous **change/improvement/influence**

● **SUBSTANTIAL OR CONSIDERABLE?**
Considerable is not used to talk about solid things, such as meals or buildings. Substantial is not used to talk about emotions or personal qualities, such as anger, concern or efficiency:
✔*He ate a substantial breakfast.* ✘ *a considerable breakfast*
✔*Caring for elderly relatives requires considerable moral courage.*
✘ *substantial moral courage*

substitute *noun* [C]

■ *The bus service was a poor substitute for their car.*

replacement • surrogate • stand-in • exchange • cover • understudy | *esp. BrE* **reserve** | *fml or law* **proxy**

▶ **a/an** substitute/replacement/surrogate/stand-in/understudy/reserve/proxy **for** sb/sth
▶ **a good/poor** substitute/replacement/exchange
▶ **a/an satisfactory/suitable/possible/ideal** substitute/replacement
▶ **act as a/an** substitute/replacement/surrogate/stand-in/understudy/proxy

substitute *verb* [T]

■ *Margarine can be substituted for butter in this recipe.* ■ *Butter can be substituted with margarine.*

replace • change • switch • exchange • swap/swop

▶ **substitute/change/switch/exchange/swap** A **for** B
▶ **substitute/replace/switch** B **with** A
▶ **simply substitute/replace/change/switch/exchange** sth

substitute for sb/sth *phrasal verb*

■ *A colleague agreed to substitute for her.* ■ *Nothing can substitute for the advice your doctor gives you.*

replace • stand in for sb/sth • cover for sb • relieve | *esp. AmE* fill in for sb/sth | *fml* deputize

▶ substitute/stand in/cover/fill in/ deputize for sb
▶ stand in for/cover for/replace/fill in for a **colleague**

succeed *verb*

1 [T] ■ *He succeeded in getting a place at art school.*

achieve • manage • accomplish • reach | *BrE* fulfil | *AmE* fulfill | *infml, spoken* get there | *fml* attain

■ OPP fail

▶ succeed in/achieve/accomplish/ reach/fulfil/attain a/an **goal**/ **objective**
▶ succeed in/achieve/accomplish/ fulfil an **aim**
▶ succeed in/achieve/manage/ accomplish/fulfil a **task**

2 [I] ■ *You have to work hard to succeed in this business.*

make it • make your/a mark • make a name for yourself • achieve | *esp. spoken* get on | *infml* arrive

■ OPP fail

▶ succeed/make it/make your mark/ make a name for yourself **in** sth
▶ succeed/make it/make your mark/ arrive/make a name for yourself/ get on **as** sth

success *noun* [C]

■ *The party was a great success.*

hit • best-seller | *infml* winner

■ OPP failure

▶ a big **success/hit/winner**
▶ an instant **success/hit/best-seller**
▶ have a **success/hit**

successful *adj.*

1 ■ *The successful candidate will manage a new project.*

effective • winning | *esp. written* victorious • triumphant

■ OPP unsuccessful, failed

▶ successful/effective/victorious/ triumphant **in** sth
▶ successful/effective/victorious **in doing** sth
▶ a/an successful/effective/ victorious/triumphant **campaign**/ **challenge**
▶ the successful/winning **side**

2 ■ *The company has had another successful year.*

profitable • lucrative • thriving • commercial • profit-making | *busin.* buoyant

■ OPP unsuccessful

▶ a successful/profitable/lucrative/ thriving/profit-making **business**
▶ a successful/profitable/lucrative/ profit-making **enterprise**
▶ a successful/profitable/lucrative **investment/career/year**

successive *adj.* [only before noun]

■ *This was their third successive win.*

consecutive • straight • in a row

▶ the second/third/fourth successive/consecutive/straight sth
▶ the second/third/fourth sth in a row
▶ sb's second, etc. successive/ consecutive/straight **win/victory/ defeat**
▶ sb's second, etc. **win/victory/ defeat** in a row
▶ two, etc. successive/consecutive/ straight **days/weeks/months/ years**
▶ two, etc. **days/weeks/months/ years** in a row

sudden *adj.*

■ *Don't make any sudden movements.*

abrupt • sharp • dramatic

■ OPP gradual

▶ a/an sharp/abrupt/sudden/ dramatic **increase/rise** (in sth)
▶ a sharp/sudden/dramatic **drop/ fall/change/improvement/ deterioration** (in sth)
▶ a sharp/an abrupt **disappearance/ departure/movement/stop/halt**

suffer *verb* [T] (*esp. written*)

■ *The company suffered huge losses.*

have • take • feel • go through sth | *esp. written* receive • experience • encounter • undergo

▶ suffer/have/receive/experience/ encounter a **setback**
▶ suffer/have/feel/receive/ experience a/the **shock**
▶ suffer/go through/experience/ undergo an **ordeal**
● SUFFER OR RECEIVE You can **suffer** or **receive** an **injury**. **Suffer** gives more emphasis to the bad effects experienced.

suffer from sth *phrasal verb* [no passive]

■ *She suffers from asthma.*

have • get • develop • catch • come down with sth | *esp. BrE, esp. spoken* have got | *fml* contract

▶ suffer from/have/get/develop/ catch/have got/contract a/an **disease/illness**
▶ suffer from/have/get/catch/come down with/have got a **bug/cold**
▶ suffer from/have/get/catch/come

down with/have got/contract the flu
▶ suffer from/have/get/catch/have got/contract a **virus/HIV/malaria**

suffering *noun*

1 [U, pl.] ■ *Death brought an end to her suffering.*

pain • **agony** • **ache** | *fml* **discomfort**

▶ cause suffering/pain/discomfort
▶ inflict suffering/pain
▶ relieve/ease the suffering/pain/agony/discomfort

2 [U, pl.] ■ *Bullying can cause intense mental suffering.*

pain • **distress** • **misery** • **agony** | *infml* **hurt** • **torture** | *fml* **anguish**

▶ physical/emotional suffering/pain/distress/agony/hurt/torture/anguish
▶ endure the suffering/pain/distress/misery/agony/torture
▶ cause (sb) suffering/pain/distress/misery/agony/hurt/anguish
● SUFFERING, PAIN OR DISTRESS? These are all words for a feeling of great unhappiness. Distress can also be a feeling of worry. Pain is often used when the hurt is more individual and the cause more personal, such as the death of a loved one. Suffering often refers to sth on a large scale that affects many people, such as a war or natural disaster.

suggest *verb*

1 [T] ■ *I suggested going in my car.*

propose • **put sth forward** • **recommend** | *fml* **move** • **advance** • **moot**

▶ suggest/propose/put forward/recommend/advance/moot sth as sth
▶ suggest/propose/be put forward/recommend/move/be mooted that...
▶ suggest/propose/put forward/recommend/move/moot an **idea**
▶ suggest/propose/put forward/recommend a/an **alternative/change/measure**
● SUGGEST, PROPOSE OR PUT FORWARD? Propose and put forward are used in more formal situations than suggest.

2 [T] ■ *Who would you suggest for the job?*

recommend • **nominate**

▶ suggest/recommend/nominate sb/sth for/as sth
▶ suggest/recommend sb/sth to sb
▶ suggest/recommend/nominate a **sb to do sth**
▶ suggest/recommend/nominate a **candidate**

3 [T] ■ *All the evidence suggests (that) he stole the money.*

imply • **indicate** • **point** • **mean** | *fml* **signify** • **denote**

▶ suggest/imply/indicate/mean/signify sth to sb
▶ suggest/imply/indicate/mean/signify **that...**
▶ suggest/imply/indicate/point to/mean a **great deal/high degree/lack** of sth
● SUGGEST OR IMPLY? Imply is often used to talk about how facts show the need for sth or the existence of sth; suggest is often used to talk about how a piece of research, etc. shows a link between things: *The data implies an imminent healthcare crisis.* • *Research suggests a strong link between state of mind and the body's immune system.*

suggestion *noun*

1 [C] ■ *Can I make a suggestion?*

proposal • **recommendation** • **proposition** • **motion**

▶ a suggestion/proposal/recommendation/motion **for/on** sth
▶ a suggestion/proposal/recommendation/proposition/motion **that...**
▶ accept/support/reject/discuss a suggestion/proposal/recommendation/proposition/motion
▶ submit/put forward/oppose a suggestion/proposal/recommendation/motion

2 [U, C, usu. pl.] ■ *There was no suggestion of a rift.*

hint • **indication** • **sign** • **clue** • **pointer**

▶ a suggestion/hint/indication/sign/clue/pointer **as to how/what/why**, etc.
▶ a/an suggestion/hint/indication/sign **that...**
▶ an **obvious** suggestion/hint/indication/sign/clue/pointer

suit *verb* [T, no passive] (not used in the progressive tenses)

■ *Choose a computer to suit your particular needs.*

meet • **satisfy** • **serve** | *BrE, fml* **fulfil** | *AmE* **fulfill**

▶ suit/meet/satisfy/serve/fulfil a **requirement/need/purpose**
▶ suit/satisfy/serve/fulfil sb/sth's **interests**
▶ suit/meet/satisfy/fulfil the **conditions**

suitable *adj.*

■ *The film is not suitable for children.*

suitcase

appropriate • right • good • convenient • apt • fit | *infml* cut out for sth/to be sth | *fml* fitting

■ OPP unsuitable
▶ suitable/appropriate/right/good/convenient/apt/fit/cut out/fitting for sb/sth
▶ suitable/appropriate/good as sb/sth
▶ suitable/appropriate/right/good/convenient/apt/fit/fitting that...
● WHICH WORD? How **appropriate** or **suitable** sb/sth is depends on your judgement. How **good** sth/sb is depends on what you like yourself or what is convenient. How **right** sth/sb is depends more on the facts:
✔Do you think she would be a/an good/appropriate/suitable person to ask? ✗ ~~a right person to ask~~
✔She's definitely the right person to ask. ✗ ~~She's definitely the good/appropriate/suitable person to ask.~~
Good, **suitable** and **right** can all be used when sth is correct for a particular purpose, but **appropriate** is only used about people or situations.

suitcase noun [C]

■ The suitcases were too heavy for her to carry.

bag • luggage • baggage • backpack | *BrE* case • rucksack | *old-fash.* or *AmE* knapsack

▶ carry (a) suitcase/bag/luggage/baggage/backpack/case/rucksack/knapsack
▶ pack/unpack a suitcase/bag/backpack/case/rucksack/knapsack
▶ check (in) your/search sb's suitcase/bag/luggage/baggage

sum noun [C]

■ She inherited a large sum of money from her father.

amount • number • quantity

▶ a sum/an amount of money
▶ tiny sums/amounts/numbers/quantities
▶ a reasonable/considerable/large/small sum/amount/number/quantity

summarize (BrE also -ise) verb [T, I]

■ To summarize, the main conclusions are...

sum (sth) up • condense | *esp. spoken* recap

■ OPP elaborate, expand on sth
▶ summarize/sum sth up as sth
▶ Let me summarize/sum up/recap.
▶ To summarize/sum up/recap...

summary noun [C]

■ Here is a summary of the news.

outline • overview • sketch • synopsis | *esp. spoken* rundown | tech. abstract

▶ a/an summary/outline/overview/sketch/synopsis/rundown/abstract of sth
▶ in summary/outline
▶ give sb a/an summary/outline/overview/sketch/synopsis/rundown
▶ provide a/an summary/outline/overview/sketch/synopsis/abstract
● SUMMARY, OUTLINE, OR OVERVIEW? A **summary** is always made after the full version of sth has been written or recorded. An **outline** can be given before the full version has been worked out: *Draw up an outline for the essay before you start.* An **overview** is similar to an **outline**, but the emphasis is more on the fact that sb wants to look for general trends across a wide area, rather than that the details are still to be worked out.

(the) sun noun [sing., U]

■ This room gets the sun in the morning.

sunlight • daylight • natural light | approv. sunshine

■ OPP shade
▶ in sun/sunlight/daylight/natural light/sunshine
▶ hot/direct/morning/afternoon/spring/summer, etc. sun/sunlight/sunshine
▶ the sun/sunlight/daylight/sunshine **floods (into)** a place
● SUN OR SUNSHINE? **Sunshine** is always a good thing; it is possible to have too much **sun**:
✔It's too hot in the sun. ✗ ~~It's too hot in the sunshine.~~

sunny adj. (approv.)

■ The weather was fine and sunny.

dry • clear | approv. glorious • good | esp. BrE, approv. fine

■ OPP cloudy
▶ sunny/dry/clear/glorious/good/fine weather
▶ sunny/dry/clear/good/fine (weather) conditions
▶ a sunny/dry/clear/glorious/fine day/morning/afternoon/evening

superior adj.

1 ■ This model is far superior to its competitors.

better • preferable

■ OPP inferior
▶ superior/preferable to sb/sth

► better **than** sb/sth
► far/greatly/vastly/infinitely superior/better/preferable

2 ■ *superior downtown apartments*

excellent • high quality • quality • prime • first-rate • fine | *esp. BrE, fml* sterling

■ **OPP inferior**
► (of) superior/excellent/prime/ fine/sterling **quality**
► a/an superior/excellent/high quality/first-rate/fine/ sterling **performance/service**

3 ■ *I need to check with my superior officer.*

senior • chief • high-ranking • top • leading

■ **OPP inferior, junior**
► a/an senior/chief/high-ranking/top/leading **officer**
● **SUPERIOR OR SENIOR?** Superior is used more than **senior** where there is a strong sense of status, for example in the army: *I'll need to check with my superior officer.* In everyday situations it is more usual to talk about a *senior colleague/adviser/teacher*, etc.

supply noun

1 [C] ■ *The water supply is unsafe.*

stock • store • reserve • resource • stockpile • pool • bank • hoard • arsenal

► a/an supply/stock/store/reserve/ stockpile/pool/bank/hoard/ arsenal **of** sth
► be/have sth **in** supply/stock
► build up (a/an) supply/stock/ store/reserves/resources/ stockpile/bank/arsenal
► use up/exhaust (the) supply/ stock/store/reserves/resources

2 supplies [pl.] ■ *We were running short of supplies.*

stores • provisions • rations

► emergency supplies/provisions/ rations
► military/medical supplies/stores
► buy/stock up on supplies/ provisions
► run out of supplies/provisions/ rations

supply verb [T]
■ *He supplied the rebels with arms.*

provide • issue • give • lend | *esp. busin.* put sth up

► supply/issue/give/lend sth **to** sb
► supply/provide/issue sb **with** sth
► supply/provide/issue/give **equipment/details/information**
► supply/provide/give/put up **funds**

support noun

1 [U] ■ *He needed constant emotional support.*

help • backup • cooperation • service | *fml* assistance • aid

► support/help/cooperation/ assistance **in** doing sth
► mutual support/help/ cooperation/assistance/aid
► get support/help/backup/ cooperation/sb's services/ assistance/aid
► offer/need support/help/sb's cooperation/sb's services/ assistance

2 [C] ■ *The supports under the bridge were cracked.*

pillar • post • buttress • column • beam • girder • rafter • joist

► a wooden support/pillar/post/ beam/rafter
► a steel support/pillar/post/ column/beam/girder/joist
► a stone pillar/buttress/column

3 [U] ■ *The statistics offered support for the theory.*

evidence • proof

► support/evidence **for** sth
► clear/convincing/conclusive support/evidence/proof
► find/provide/give support/ evidence/proof

support verb

1 [T] ■ *He supported the party loyally.*

back • stand for sth • vote • second • champion • side with sb | *BrE* (be) in favour of (sb/sth) | *AmE* (be) in favor of (sb/sth) | *fml* subscribe to sth

■ **OPP oppose**
► support/back/vote for/side with sb **in** sth
► support/back/stand for/ champion/be in favour of/ subscribe to an **idea**
► support/back/vote for/second/be in favour of a **proposal/plan/ motion/resolution**

2 [T] ■ *The group supports people with AIDS.*

help • help (sb) out • cooperate • lend (sb) a hand | *fml* assist • aid | *law or humorous* aid and abet

► support/help/cooperate/assist/ aid (sb) **in** sth
► actively support/help/cooperate with/assist sb/sth
► be ably supported/assisted by sb

3 [T] ■ *A major company supported the project.*

supporter

fund • finance • sponsor • back • subsidize • endow | *esp. AmE, infml* bankroll

▶ support/fund/finance/sponsor/back/subsidize/bankroll a **project/programme**
▶ support/fund/finance/sponsor/back/bankroll a **campaign**
▶ support/fund/finance/sponsor/back/subsidize **research**

4 [T] ■ *I can't support a family on my salary.*

maintain • provide for sb | *BrE* keep

▶ support/maintain/provide for/keep a/your **family/children/wife/husband**
▶ support/maintain/provide for **yourself**
▶ support/maintain sb **financially**
● **WHICH WORD?** If you **provide for sb** you do so either on a continuous basis or by making one large payment. If you **keep**, **maintain** or **support** sb you provide for them on a continuous basis over a period of time.

5 [T] ■ *Support the baby's head when you hold her.*

hold sb/sth up • bear • hold • prop sth up • carry

▶ support/bear/hold/carry the **weight** of sb/sth

6 [T] ■ *The witness's story was not supported by the evidence.*

confirm | *fml* substantiate • validate • corroborate

■ OPP contradict, undermine
▶ support/confirm/substantiate/corroborate **what...**
▶ support/confirm/substantiate/validate/corroborate a **claim/theory**
▶ support/confirm/substantiate/validate an **argument**
▶ support/confirm/substantiate/validate/corroborate a **story**

supporter noun

1 [C] ■ *He is an active supporter of democratic change.*

follower • voter • backer • disciple • advocate • champion • promoter • campaigner • exponent | *fml* proponent

■ OPP opponent
▶ a **loyal** supporter/follower/voter/disciple
▶ a **leading** supporter/follower/disciple/advocate/campaigner/proponent
▶ **attract** supporters/followers/voters/backers/disciples

2 [C] (*BrE*) ■ *a keen Arsenal supporter*

fan • follower | *sometimes disapprov.* fanatic

▶ a **keen** supporter/fan/follower
▶ a **big** supporter/fan

suppose verb

1 [T] (not used in the progressive tenses) ■ *Prices will go up, I suppose.*

assume • imagine • presume | *esp. spoken* take it | *esp. BrE, spoken* expect • I dare say | *esp. AmE, spoken* guess

▶ suppose/assume/imagine/presume/take it/expect/dare say/guess **that...**
■ **Let's/let us** suppose/assume/imagine/presume/take it...
■ **can only** suppose/assume/imagine/presume/take it (that)...

2 [T] ■ *Suppose you win—what then?*

presume • speculate | *esp. spoken* say | *fml* postulate • presuppose

▶ suppose/presume/speculate/say/postulate/presuppose **that...**
▶ suppose/presume/postulate/presuppose **the existence of** sth
■ **let's just/let us** suppose/say (that...)

suppress verb

1 [T] (*written, disapprov.*) ■ *The rebellion was brutally suppressed.*

crush • put sth down • persecute | *written* quell • repress • oppress | *fml* subdue

▶ suppress/crush/put down/quell/repress a **rebellion**
▶ suppress/crush/put down/quell a/an **uprising/revolt**
▶ **army/troops/police** (are used/called in, etc. to) suppress/crush/put down/quell/subdue sb/sth
● **WHICH WORD?** All these words are disapproving and suggest an unfair use of power. **Suppress** is the most general word; **subdue** is a more formal word to refer to bringing opposition under control. **Crush** and **put sth down** both refer to using force, and **crush** suggests the use of particularly violent methods.

2 [T] ■ *He could hardly suppress his anger.*

repress • stifle • restrain • hold sth back • control • curb • keep from sth • rein sth in | *written* contain • check

■ OPP arouse
▶ suppress/repress/restrain/hold back/control/contain/check your **anger**
▶ suppress/repress/stifle/control/contain/check a/an **feeling/emotion**
▶ suppress/stifle/restrain/control a **smile**

● **SUPPRESS OR REPRESS?** Suppress describes an effort to prevent your feelings being seen by other people; **repress** is slightly stronger, often suggesting you do not want to express your inner feelings even to yourself.

sure *adj.*

1 [not before noun] ■ *Are you sure about that?*

certain • confident • convinced • clear • satisfied | *esp. spoken* positive

■ OPP unsure

▶ sure/certain/confident/ convinced/clear/positive **about** sth
▶ sure/certain/confident/ convinced/satisfied **of** sth
▶ sure/certain/confident/ convinced/clear/satisfied **that...**
▶ sure/certain/clear/satisfied **who/ what/how, etc...**
● **SURE OR CERTAIN?** Certain is slightly more formal and less frequent than **sure**. Both words are often used in negative statements and questions.

2 ■ *It's sure to rain.*

certain • bound • guaranteed | *esp. spoken* definite | *written* assured | *fml* destined

▶ sure/certain/assured **of** sth
▶ sure/certain/bound/guaranteed/ destined **to do** sth
▶ **by no means** sure/certain/ guaranteed/definite/assured

make **sure** *phrase*

1 ■ *Make sure (that) no one finds out.*

ensure • see to it that ... • guarantee • assure

▶ make sure/ensure/see to it/ guarantee **that...**
▶ make **absolutely** sure
▶ absolutely ensure/guarantee/ assure sth

2 ■ *Make sure (that) the door's locked.*

check | *fml* verify • assure yourself

▶ make sure/check/verify/assure yourself **that...**
▶ **go and** make sure/check
▶ **always** make sure/check/verify sth

surge *verb* [I] (always used with an adv. or prep.)
■ *The crowd surged forward.*

pour • flood • stream | *infml* pile | *often disapprov.* swarm

▶ surge/pour/flood/stream/pile/ swarm **into** sth
▶ pour/flood/stream/pile/swarm **out of** sth
▶ surge/pour/stream/swarm **through/across** sth

surgery *adj.*

1 [U] ■ *She requires surgery on her knee.*

operation • treatment

▶ surgery/an operation/treatment **for** sth
▶ surgery/an operation **on** sb/sth
▶ have/undergo/need/require surgery/an operation/treatment
▶ perform surgery/an operation
● **SURGERY OR OPERATION?** Operation is countable; **surgery** is uncountable: *She's had three operations in the past two years.* • *The doctor recommended surgery.*

2 [C] (*BrE*) ■ *I phoned the surgery to make an appointment.*

esp. spoken doctor's • *AmE* doctor's office • clinic | *BrE* health centre

▶ **at** the surgery/doctor's/doctor's office/clinic/health centre
▶ a **local** surgery/clinic/health centre
▶ **go to** the doctor's/a clinic

surname *noun* [C] (*esp. BrE*)
■ *Most women still take their husband's surname on marriage.*

name • last name • family name • maiden name

▶ use sb's surname/a name/your family name/your maiden name
▶ address/call sb by their surname/ last name
▶ have/bear a surname/last name/ family name

surprise *verb* [T]
■ *It surprises me how popular he is.*

startle • amaze • astonish • astound • stagger • stun | *written* take sb aback

▶ It surprises/startles/amazes/ astonishes/astounds/staggers/ stuns sb/takes sb aback
▶ What surprises/startles/amazes/ astonishes/astounds/staggers/ stuns sb **is...**
▶ surprise/startle/amaze/astonish/ astound/stun sb **that...**
▶ surprise/startle/amaze/astonish/ astound/stun sb **to know/find/ learn/see/hear...**

surprising *adj.*
■ *It's surprising how quickly rumours spread.*

unexpected • extraordinary • remarkable • unpredictable • unforeseen • unforeseeable • amazing • astonishing

■ OPP unsurprising

▶ surprising/unexpected/ extraordinary/remarkable/

unpredictable/unforeseen/
amazing **events/effects/changes**
▶ surprising/unexpected/
extraordinary/remarkable/
unpredictable/amazing/
astonishing **results**
▶ a/an surprising/unexpected/
extraordinary/remarkable/
unforeseen/amazing/astonishing
development

surround verb [T]
■ *The lake is surrounded by trees.*

enclose • line • flank | written
encircle • border

▶ be surrounded/enclosed/lined/
flanked/encircled/bordered **by/
with** sth
▶ sth surrounds/encloses a **town/
city**
▶ **walls/fences** surround/enclose/
encircle sth

surroundings noun [pl.]
■ *Paintings can't capture the beauty of
the surroundings.*

setting • environment •
background | written backdrop

▶ **in** surroundings/a setting/an
environment
▶ (a/an) **attractive/perfect**
surroundings/setting/
environment/background/
backdrop
▶ **provide/create** (a/an)
surroundings/setting/
environment/background/
backdrop

survey noun
1 [C] ■ *The charity did a survey of
people's attitudes to the disabled.*

investigation • poll • review •
report • study • inquiry/enquiry

▶ a/an survey/investigation/poll/
report/inquiry **into** sth
▶ **in** a/an survey/poll/review/
report/study/inquiry
▶ **carry out** a/an survey/
investigation/poll/study/
inquiry
▶ a/an survey/investigation/poll/
review/report/study/inquiry
finds/shows/reveals sth

2 [C] ■ *They carried out an aerial
survey of the mountains.*

inspection • examination •
observation

▶ a **detailed** survey/inspection/
examination/observation
▶ **carry out/do** a/an survey/
inspection/examination/
observation
▶ a/an survey/inspection/

examination/observation **reveals/
shows/confirms** sth

survey verb
1 [T] ■ *Next day we surveyed the
damage.*

examine • review • study • scan |
esp. written scrutinize

▶ survey/examine/study/scan/
scrutinize sth **for** sth
▶ survey/examine/review/study/
scan/scrutinize sth **carefully**
▶ survey/examine/review/study/
scrutinize sth **in detail/thoroughly**

2 [T] ■ *87% of the smokers surveyed
would like to give up.*

poll • canvass • ballot | tech. sample

▶ survey/canvass **opinion**

survive verb [I, T]
■ *Only two people survived the crash.*

live • make it • come through (sth) •
weather • recover

▶ survive/live **on** (a diet of) sth
▶ survive/live **for** a few days/many
years, etc.
▶ survive/live **without** food/money,
etc.
▶ survive/live/make it/come
through sth
▶ survive/weather a **storm/crisis/
recession**

suspect verb
1 [T] (not used in the progressive
tenses) ■ *As she had suspected, he
was not a real policeman.*

suppose • imagine • assume •
presume | esp. spoken take it | esp.
BrE, spoken expect • I dare say | esp.
AmE, spoken guess

▶ suspect/suppose/imagine/
assume/presume/take it/expect/
dare say/guess **that...**
▶ be suspected/supposed/
imagined/assumed/presumed **to
be** sth
▶ I suspect/suppose/imagine/
assume/presume/expect/guess
so.

2 [T] (not used in the progressive
tenses) ■ *He resigned after being
suspected of theft.*

doubt | written distrust | fml
disbelieve

▶ suspect/distrust sb's **motives**
▶ **still/never** suspect/doubt/
distrust/disbelieve sb
▶ **have (no) reason to** suspect/
doubt/distrust/disbelieve sb
● **SUSPECT OR DISTRUST?** Distrust is
more general than **suspect**: you
can *distrust* sb's motives or *distrust*
sb/sth. You can *suspect*, but not

distrust sb 'of' a particular action or crime.

suspicion noun

1 [U, C] ■ *She was reluctant to voice her suspicions.*

doubt • misgiving • uncertainty • second thoughts

▶ suspicions/doubts/misgivings/ second thoughts **about** sth
▶ express suspicions/doubts/ misgivings
▶ raise/arouse/voice suspicions/ doubts

2 [C] ■ *I had a horrible suspicion that I'd got it wrong.*

feeling • idea • hunch • instinct • intuition • inkling | *esp. written* **premonition • foreboding**

▶ a/an suspicion/feeling/idea/ hunch/instinct/intuition/inkling/ premonition/foreboding **about** sth
▶ have a/an suspicion/feeling/idea/ hunch/instinct/intuition/inkling/ premonition/foreboding
▶ confirm sb's suspicion/feeling/ hunch/intuition

3 [U] ■ *Their offer was greeted with some suspicion.*

distrust • disbelief | *BrE* **scepticism** | *AmE* **skepticism** | *often disapprov.* **cynicism**

▶ suspicion/distrust/scepticism/ cynicism **towards** sth
▶ suspicion/scepticism/cynicism **about** sth
▶ express suspicion/distrust/ disbelief/scepticism

suspicious adj.

1 ■ *Many were suspicious of reform.*

incredulous • disbelieving | *BrE* **sceptical** | *AmE* **skeptical** | *often disapprov.* **cynical**

■ OPP **trusting**
▶ suspicious/incredulous/sceptical/ cynical **about** sth
▶ suspicious/incredulous/sceptical **of** sth
▶ a/an suspicious/incredulous/ disbelieving/sceptical/cynical **look**

2 ■ *He died in suspicious circumstances.*

dubious • questionable | *infml* **fishy • shady • shifty** | *BrE, infml* **dodgy** | *esp. journ.* **suspect**

■ OPP **innocent**
▶ a suspicious/dubious/ questionable/shady/shifty/ suspect **character**
▶ suspicious/dubious/questionable **circumstances**
▶ There's **something** suspicious/ fishy/shady/shifty/suspect **about** sb/sth.

swear verb

1 [I] ■ *He fell over and swore loudly.*

curse • blaspheme | *infml, spoken* **damn**

▶ swear/curse loudly/quietly/ softly/silently/**under your breath**
● SWEAR OR CURSE? Swear is used more than curse in spoken English. You can **curse** but not **swear** a person or thing.

2 [T, I, no passive] ■ *She made him swear not to tell anyone.*

promise • guarantee • pledge | *esp. written* **vow** | *fml or busin.* **undertake**

▶ swear/vow **to** sb that...
▶ swear/promise/guarantee/ pledge/vow/undertake **to do** sth
▶ swear/promise/guarantee/ pledge/vow **that**...

sweet adj.

1 (*esp. BrE, esp. spoken, approv.*) ■ *What a sweet little kitten!*

cute • lovable/loveable • endearing | *esp. BrE* **lovely** | *BrE* **dear old/little...** | *esp. AmE* **adorable** | *infml* **cuddly**

▶ a/an sweet/cute/lovable/ endearing/lovely/dear/adorable **little...**
▶ a/an sweet/cute/lovely/ adorable/cuddly **baby**
▶ a/an sweet/cute/adorable **girl/ boy/child/kid**
● SWEET OR CUTE? You can usu. use either word; **cute** is more frequent in *AmE*.

2 (*esp. spoken*) ■ *It's sweet of you to offer to help.*

kind • thoughtful • considerate | *esp. spoken* **good • nice** | *esp. BrE, esp. spoken* **lovely**

■ OPP **horrible**
▶ sweet/kind/thoughtful/ considerate/good **of** sb (to do sth)
▶ a sweet/kind/thoughtful/nice/ lovely **man/woman/person**

swell verb [I, T]

■ *Cook the lentils until they swell and soften.*

bloat | *esp. spoken* **blow sth up** | *esp. written* **inflate**

▶ swell/inflate sth **with** sth
▶ blow up/inflate a **balloon/tyre**

swelling noun [U, C]

■ *Use ice to reduce the swelling.*

inflammation • lump • bump • abscess • boil | *BrE* **tumour** | *AmE* **tumor**

swing noun [C]

- a/an swelling/lump/abscess/boil/tumour **on** a part of the body
- (a/an) swelling/inflammation/lump/abscess/tumour **in** a part of the body
- **have** (a/an) swelling/inflammation/lump/bump/abscess/boil/tumour

swing noun [C]

■ He is liable to abrupt mood swings.

change • variation • fluctuation • alternation | esp. journ. **shift**

- (a/an) swing/change/variation/fluctuation/alternation/shift **in** sth
- **cause** (a) swing/change/variation/fluctuations/shift
- (a) swing/change/variation/fluctuation/shift **occurs**

swing verb [I, T]

■ The rope swung in the breeze.

sway • rock | physics **oscillate**

- swing/sway/rock/oscillate backwards and forwards
- swing/sway/rock **back and forth/from side to side/to and fro**
- swing/sway/rock/oscillate **violently/wildly/gently**

switch noun [C]

■ Which switch do I press?

button • key • control • lever • knob • handle • dial

- (a) switch/button/key/the controls/lever/knob/handle/dial **on** sth
- the **on/off/on-off** switch/button
- **press** a switch/button/key/lever
- **push** a switch/button/lever/handle
- **pull** a switch/lever/handle

symbol noun

1 [C] ■ The dove is a symbol of peace.

sign • emblem • representation

- a/an symbol/sign/emblem/representation of sth
- a/an **clear/obvious/powerful** symbol/sign

2 [C] ■ a chemical symbol

sign • mark • figure • letter • number | fml or tech. **character**

- **write** sth in symbols/figures/letters/numbers
- the symbol/sign/character **for** sth
- a symbol/sign/character **means/indicates** sth
- a **sequence/series/set/string** of symbols/figures/letters/numbers/characters
- **SYMBOL OR SIGN?** A symbol usu. refers to a shape or small picture, or the letters representing chemical

elements. A **sign** is usu. sth more simple, such as a dollar sign.

sympathetic adj. (approv.)

■ The helpline provides a sympathetic listener.

sensitive • understanding • compassionate • humane • gentle • soft

■ OPP **unsympathetic**

- sympathetic/sensitive/understanding/compassionate/gentle **towards** sb
- a sympathetic/sensitive/compassionate/humane/gentle **manner/man**
- (in) a sympathetic/sensitive/compassionate/humane/gentle **way**

sympathy noun [U, C, usu. pl.]

■ Their plight aroused considerable sympathy.

compassion • pity • understanding • empathy • condolence • concern • humanity

- sympathy/compassion/pity/empathy/concern **for** sb/sth
- **do** sth **with** sympathy/compassion/understanding/empathy/concern/humanity
- **show** (sb) sympathy/compassion/pity/understanding/empathy/concern/humanity

system noun

1 [C] ■ This is an effective system for storing data.

method • means • way • mechanism • technique • process | fml **methodology**

- a system/method/means/mechanism/technique/process/methodology **for** (doing) sth
- a system/method/way/technique/methodology **of** (doing) sth
- **use** a system/method/means/technique/process/methodology
- **devise/develop** a system/method/means/way/technique/process/methodology

2 [C] ■ the educational/justice system

organization • apparatus • structure • framework • network • web • workings

- a/an system/apparatus/structure/framework/network **for** sth
- **in/within** a/an system/apparatus/structure/framework/network/web
- **create** a system/structure/framework/network/web
- **understand/explain** a system/the organization/structure/workings of sth

Tt

table noun [C]

■ *Table 2 shows how prices have increased over the last 5 years.*

list ‹ diagram ‹ chart ‹ graph ‹ index | written figure

▶ **in** a/an table/list/diagram/chart/graph/index/figure
▶ **draw** a table/diagram/chart/graph
▶ **draw up** a table/list ‹ **handle**
▶ a table/an index **lists** sth

tackle verb

1 [T] ■ *The government is determined to tackle inflation.*

deal with sb/sth ‹ get to grips with sth ‹ set about sth ‹ handle ‹ go about sth ‹ approach | esp. written grapple | fml address

▶ tackle/deal with/get to grips with/set about/handle/go about/approach/address a **task**
▶ tackle/deal with/get to grips with/handle/approach/grapple with/address a **problem**
▶ tackle/deal with/handle/approach/grapple with/address a/an **question/issue**

2 [T] ■ *I tackled him about the money he owed me.*

confront ‹ face ‹ challenge

▶ tackle/confront/challenge sb **directly**

tact noun [U] (approv.)

■ *Settling the dispute required tact and diplomacy.*

sensitivity | esp. written diplomacy ‹ discretion

▶ the **utmost** tact/sensitivity/discretion
▶ **require** tact/sensitivity/diplomacy/discretion
● **TACT OR DIPLOMACY? Tact** is a natural quality that some people have; **diplomacy** is a skill that can be learned through practice.

tactic noun [C, usu. pl.]

■ *They tried all sorts of tactics to get us to go.*

device ‹ strategy | BrE manoeuvre ‹ AmE maneuver | often disapprov. ploy ‹ ruse

▶ a tactic/device/strategy/ploy/ruse **for** (doing) sth
▶ a tactic/device/strategy/manoeuvre/ploy/ruse **to do sth**
▶ **use** a tactic/device/strategy/manoeuvre/ploy

take verb

1 [T] ■ *Remember to take your bag with you.*

bring ‹ deliver ‹ carry ‹ transport ‹ ship ‹ fly ‹ ferry

▶ take/bring/deliver/carry/transport/ship/fly/ferry sb/sth **to/from** sb/sth
▶ take/bring/carry/transport/ship/fly/ferry sb/sth **back/home**
▶ take/bring/deliver/carry/transport/ferry sb/sth **by car, rail, truck, etc.**
● **TAKE OR BRING? Take** is used from the point of view of the person who is going somewhere with sth; **bring** is used from the point of view of sb who is already in the place the person is going to.

2 [T] ■ *The boy took us to our rooms.*

lead ‹ escort ‹ show ‹ walk ‹ guide ‹ usher ‹ drive | fml accompany

▶ take/lead/escort/show/walk/guide/usher/drive/accompany sb **to/out of/into**
▶ take/lead/escort/show/walk/guide/usher/drive/accompany sb **there/somewhere**
▶ take/lead/escort/show/walk/guide/drive sb **round/around**

3 [T] ■ *I passed him the rope and he took it.*

grab ‹ snatch ‹ catch | esp. written seize

▶ take/grab/snatch/catch/seize sth **from** sb
▶ take/grab/catch/seize **hold of** sb/sth
▶ take/grab/snatch/catch/seize sth **suddenly/quickly**

4 [T] (always used with an adv. or prep.) ■ *The sign must be taken down.*

remove ‹ strip

▶ take/remove/strip sth **from** sb/sth
▶ **simply/easily/quickly/carefully/forcibly/illegally** take/remove sth

5 [T] ■ *Someone has taken my scarf.*

steal | infml pinch | BrE, infml nick

▶ take/steal/pinch/nick (sth) **from** sb/a place
▶ take/steal/pinch/nick **money**
▶ take/steal (sb's) **purse/bag/passport/food/goods/items**

6 [T] ■ *Scientists took samples from the river.*

extract | esp. spoken get | esp. written obtain

▶ take/extract/get/obtain sth **from** sb/sth

take care of sb/sth

> ► take/extract/get/obtain **water/ oil/minerals/samples** (from sth)
> ► take/get/obtain a/an **extract/ example**

7 [T] ■ *The rebels succeeded in taking the town.*

capture • conquer • seize • occupy • invade | *fml* annex

> ► take/capture/conquer/seize/ occupy/invade a **town/city**
> ► take/capture/seize/occupy a **building**
> ► **troops/soldiers** take/capture/ seize/occupy/invade a place

8 [T] ■ *He was taken prisoner.*

arrest • catch • capture | *fml* apprehend

> ► take/arrest/apprehend sb **for** sth

9 [T] ■ *Take this medicine for your cough.* ■ *He doesn't smoke, drink or take drugs.*

use | *infml* do

> ► take/use/do **drugs**
> ► take/use **heroin**

10 [T] ■ *If they offer me the job, I'll take it.*

accept • take sb/sth on • take sth up • take sb up on sth

> ■ OPP refuse, *(fml)* decline
> ► take/accept/take on a **job/post/ position/role/responsibility**
> ► take/accept/take on **new clients**
> ► take/accept/take up an **offer**

11 [T] ■ *Take the opportunity to travel while you can.*

grab • jump at • seize on/upon sth | *esp. journ.* seize

> ► take/grab/jump at/seize on/seize a/an **chance/opportunity**
> ► take/grab/seize the **initiative**
> ► take/seize on sth **immediately/ eagerly**

12 [T] ■ *Why should I take the blame?*

accept • carry • shoulder | *fml* bear • assume

> ► take/accept/carry/shoulder/ bear/assume sth **for** sb/sth
> ► take/accept/carry/shoulder/ bear/assume the **responsibility**
> ► take/accept/carry/shoulder/bear the **blame**
> ► take/accept/bear the **consequences**

13 [T, I] ■ *The journey takes an hour.*

last

> ► take/last **a few minutes/an hour/ all day/years**, etc.

take care of sb/sth *phrase*

■ *Celia will take care of the travel arrangements.*

deal with sb/sth • handle • tackle | *esp. BrE* look after sth | *fml* address | *spoken* see to sth

> ► take care of/deal with/handle/ tackle/look after/address/see to **the matter**
> ► take care of/deal with/handle/ tackle/look after/address a **problem**
> ► take care of/deal with/handle/ tackle/look after/address a **problem**
> ► take care of/deal with/handle/ tackle/look after the **paperwork**

take care of yourself *phrasal verb*

■ *He's old enough to take care of himself.*

fend for yourself • stand on your own (two) feet | *esp. BrE* look after yourself

> ► **be able to** take care of yourself/ fend for yourself/stand on your own feet/look after yourself
> ► **be capable of** taking care of yourself/fending for yourself/ looking after yourself
> ● TAKE CARE OF YOURSELF, FEND FOR YOURSELF OR LOOK AFTER YOURSELF? Take care of yourself and look after yourself are used to talk about care, health and safety. Fend for yourself is used for more practical matters, such as finding food, money or accommodation, and is used about animals as well as people.

take (sth) off *phrasal verb*

1 ■ *The plane took off an hour late.* ■ *We took off for the beach.*

set off • start • leave | *fml* depart | *esp. written* set out

> ■ OPP land
> ► take off/set off/start/leave/ depart/set out **for/from** sth
> ► take off/set off/start (out)/set out **on** a journey, voyage, etc.

2 ■ *Take off your wet clothes.*

strip • undress • get undressed | *written* remove

> ■ OPP put sth on
> ► take off/strip off/remove your **clothes/jacket/coat/shirt/ sweater/jeans/gloves**
> ► **quickly** take sth off/strip off/ undress/get undressed/remove sth

take (sth) over *phrasal verb*

■ *Fast food outlets seem to be taking over the world.*

corner | *often disapprov.* dominate • monopolize | *infml, disapprov.* hog

▶ take over / corner / dominate / monopolize the **market**

▶ take over / dominate / monopolize **the conversation / an industry**

▶ a **company** takes over / corners / dominates / monopolizes a market, industry, etc.

take part *phrase*

■ *How many countries took part in the Olympics?*

have/play a part • be/get involved • join in (sth) • join • share • compete | *fml* participate • engage in sth • enter into sth • enter

▶ take part / play a part / get involved / join sb / share / compete / participate / engage in sth

▶ actively / directly take part / compete / participate / engage in sth

● WHICH WORD? You **take part** or **participate** in a particular activity or event; **be/get involved** refers more generally to the kind of activity that you are involved with: *She took part in a debate. • She's involved in politics.*
Engage in sth often refers to kinds of activity that are considered bad or illegal in some way: *Even in prison he was engaged in criminal activities.*

take place *phrase*

■ *The film festival takes place in October.*

happen • materialize • come about | *fml* occur • arise

▶ an **event** / **accident** takes place / happens

▶ a **change** takes place / happens / comes about / occurs / arises

talk *noun*

1 [C] ■ *I had a long talk with my boss.*

conversation • discussion • chat • gossip

▶ a talk / conversation / discussion / chat / gossip **about** sth

▶ a talk / conversation / discussion / chat / gossip **with** sb

▶ have a talk / conversation / discussion / chat / gossip

2 [C] ■ *He gave a talk about his visit to China.*

lecture • speech • address • sermon

▶ a **formal** talk / lecture / speech

▶ an **informal** talk / lecture

▶ give / deliver / hear / write / prepare a/an talk / lecture / speech / address / sermon

▶ attend / go to a talk / lecture

talk *verb*

1 [I, T] ■ *Stop talking and listen!* ■ *She talks a lot of sense.*

express • say

▶ talk / express yourself **openly** / **freely**

2 [I] ■ *All they talk about is football.*

speak • chat • chatter • discuss • communicate • debate • consult | *fml* confer | *sometimes disapprov.* gossip

▶ talk / speak / chat / chatter / discuss sth / communicate / debate / consult / confer / gossip **with** sb

▶ talk / speak / chat / chatter / gossip **to** sb

▶ talk / speak to sb / chat / chatter / gossip / consult sb / confer **about** sth

● TALK OR SPEAK? **Speak** can suggest a more formal level of communication than **talk**. You **talk** to sb in order to be friendly or to ask their advice. You **speak** to sb to try to achieve a particular goal or to tell them to do sth: *'What were you two talking about?' 'Oh, this and that.' • Have you talked to your parents about the problems you're having? • I've spoken to Ed about it and he's promised not to let it happen again.*

3 [I, T] ■ *Olivia can't talk yet—she's only just one year old.*

speak • say

▶ talk / speak / say sth **to** sb

▶ talk / speak / say sth **about** sth

▶ They were talking / speaking **(in)** French.

talkative *adj.*

■ *He's not very talkative.*

forthcoming | *esp. BrE, infml* chatty

● OPP *fml* taciturn, reticent

▶ be **in** a talkative / chatty **mood**

tall *adj.*

1 ■ *She's tall and thin.*

often disapprov. lanky | *approv.* willowy | *infml, often approv. but sometimes offens.* leggy

■ OPP short

▶ a tall / lanky **man** / **teenager** / **youth** / **figure**

▶ a tall / leggy **woman**

2 ■ *the tallest building in the world*

high • high-rise • towering | *fml or lit.* lofty

▶ a tall / high / towering / lofty **mountain** / **cliff**

▶ a tall / high / high-rise / lofty **tower** / **building**

▶ tall / high **trees** / **grass**

● TALL OR HIGH? Common collocations are: *a high mountain /*

peak/cliff/wall • (a) *tall building/
tower/tree/grass*
Compare: *The room has high
windows* (= the windows are at the
top of the wall near the ceiling). •
The room has tall windows (= the
windows stretch from the bottom
of the wall to the top).

tank *noun* [C]
■ *a/an fuel/petrol/fish/oil/hot water
tank*

**vat • drum • barrel • cylinder •
canister**

▶ a tank/vat/drum/barrel/cylinder/
canister **of** sth
▶ a 5-gallon, 50-litre, etc. tank/
drum/barrel/canister
▶ an **oil** tank/drum/barrel
▶ a **gas** tank/cylinder/canister
▶ **fill** a tank/vat/drum/barrel/
cylinder

tap *verb* [I, T]
■ *He was tapping his feet to the music.*

knock • drum • rap • pat • clap

▶ tap/knock/rap **at** sth
▶ tap/knock/rap/rap **on/with** sth
▶ tap/pat/clap sb **on the back/
shoulder**

target *noun* [C]
■ *Set yourself targets that you can
reasonably hope to achieve.*

**goal • objective • object • aim • plan
• purpose** | *fml* **end**

▶ targets/goals/objectives/aims/
plans **for** sth
▶ **set/agree on/identify/reach/
meet/exceed** a/an target/
objective/goal
▶ **achieve** a/an target/goal/
objective/aim/purpose/end
● **TARGET, GOAL OR OBJECTIVE?** Targets
are usu. specific figures, such as a
number of sales, that are set
officially, for example by an
employer or a government
committee. **Goals** usu. relate to a
person or organization's long-term
plans. People often set their own
objectives that they wish to
achieve, for example as part of a
project, campaign or piece of
writing.

task *noun* [C]
■ *Our first task will be to set up a
communications system.*

**job • assignment • duty • chore •
mission • project • work • business
• housework • errand**

▶ (a) **routine** task/job/assignment/
chore/duties/mission/work/
business

▶ **do** a task/a job/an assignment/a
chore/a project/your work/
business/the housework/an errand
▶ **give** sb a task/a job/an
assignment/their duties/a chore/a
mission/some work/an errand
● **TASK OR JOB?** A **job** may be one of
several small things you have to
do, esp. in the home; a **task** may
be more difficult and may require
more thought.

taste *noun*
1 [C, U] ■ *The drink left a bitter taste
in his mouth.*

tang | *BrE* **flavour** | *AmE* **flavor**

▶ a **delicious/rich/spicy/bitter/
sour/sweet** taste/flavour
▶ a **sharp/salty/distinctive** taste/
tang/flavour
▶ **have/give/add** taste/flavour
▶ **enhance/spoil** the taste/flavour of
sth
● **TASTE OR FLAVOUR?** Use either word
to talk about how a meal tastes.
Use **taste** for food you can find in
nature. Use **flavour** for food that
has been created by sb: *The
tomatoes give extra taste/flavour to
the sauce.* • *I don't like the taste of
olives.* • *Which flavour of ice cream
would you like?*

2 [C, U] ■ *She had acquired a taste for
foreign travel.*

preference • liking • weakness |
approv. **love • passion**

▶ a taste/preference/liking/
weakness/passion **for** sth
▶ **have** a taste/preference/liking/
weakness/love/passion **for** sth
▶ sth is **to** sb's taste/liking
▶ **too** big, small, sweet, etc. **for** sb's
taste/liking
● **TASTE OR PREFERENCE?** A
preference is always a choice
between two or more things,
places, people, etc.; a **taste** is not:
a taste for French bread • *a
preference for red wine* (= rather
than white wine)

taste *verb*
1 [T] ■ *Taste it and see if there's
enough salt.*

try • test | *written* **sample**

▶ taste/try/sample **food/wine**

2 [T] ■ *I've never tasted anything quite
like it.*

eat • have | *fml* **consume**

▶ taste/eat/have/consume some
meat/fruit

tax *noun* [C, U]
■ *the tax on cigarettes*

duty • customs • tariff • rates

► (a) tax/(a) duty/a tariff/rates **on**
sth
► pay an amount of money **in** tax/
duty/customs/rates
► increase/raise/reduce taxes/
duty/tariffs/rates

teach verb

1 [I, T] ■ *He teaches at our local
school.*

lecture • tutor • prepare • educate

► teach/lecture (sb) **about** sth
► teach/lecture/tutor/prepare/
educate (sb) **effectively**

2 [T] ■ *My mother taught me to swim.*

train • coach • show • educate | *fml*
instruct | *journ.* **groom**

► teach/train/groom sb **to do** sth
► teach/show sb **how to** do sth
► teach/train/educate a **teacher/
doctor/nurse/student**
► teach/coach **athletics/football,**
etc.
► train/coach a/an **athlete/
footballer,** etc.

teacher noun [C]

■ *I used to work as a history teacher.*

**tutor • instructor • lecturer •
professor • governess** | *esp. BrE*
educationalist/educationist | *fml*
educator | *becoming old-fash.*
schoolteacher

► a teacher/tutor/governess **to** sb
► a/an **qualified/experienced**
teacher/tutor/instructor
► a **part-time/full-time/private**
teacher/tutor
► a **history/chemistry,** etc. teacher/
tutor/lecturer/professor
► a **university** teacher/tutor/
lecturer/professor

teaching noun

1 [U] ■ *What made you go into
teaching?*

education • training | *BrE* **coaching** |
esp. AmE **tutoring** | *fml* **instruction •
tuition • schooling**

► teaching/education/training/
coaching/tutoring/instruction/
tuition/schooling **in** sth
► **private** teaching/education/
coaching/tutoring/tuition/
schooling
► **formal** teaching/education/
training/coaching/tutoring/
instruction/tuition/schooling

2 [U, C, usu. pl.] ■ *They studied the
teachings of Confucius.*

**philosophy • doctrine • belief •
values** | *sometimes disapprov.* **ideology**

► sb's **religious** teaching/

philosophy/doctrine/beliefs/
values/ethos/ideology
► sb's **moral** teaching/philosophy/
doctrine/beliefs/values
► **subscribe to** (a/an) teaching/
philosophy/doctrine/values/
ideology

team noun

1 [C+sing./pl. v.] ■ *What team do you
support?*

squad • line-up | *BrE* **side • club**

► a/an **Irish/French** team/squad/
side/club
► the **England/Ireland** team/squad/
line-up/side
► a team/side/club **plays/wins/
loses** (a game/match)
► a **member** of a team/squad/line-
up/side/club
● **TEAM, SIDE OR CLUB? Club** refers to
the organization that includes
players, owner and manager; **team**
and **side** usu. refer just to the
players, often at a particular time:
*This team is arguably even better
than the Welsh side of the seventies.*

2 [C+sing./pl. v.] ■ *They worked
together as a team.*

**gang • party • band • crew • squad
• detachment • corps • ring**

► a team/gang/party/band/crew/
squad/detachment/corps **of** sth
► **in** a team/gang/party/band/
crew/squad
► a team/gang/squad/ring **leader**
► **join** a team/gang/party/band/
crew/corps

tear verb

1 [T, I] ■ *I tore my jeans on the fence.*

rip • split • shred • pull sth apart

► tear/rip sth **from/out of** sth
► tear/rip/pull sth **apart**
► tear/rip/shred **paper**
► tear/rip/split your **trousers/
pants/jeans**

2 [T] (usu. used with an adv. or
prep.) ■ *I tore a sheet from the
notebook.*

pull • pluck | *fml* **extract** | *written*
wrench

► tear/pull/pluck/extract/wrench
sth **from** sb/sth
► tear/pull/tear/wrench sb/sth
out/out of sth
► tear/pull/tear/wrench sth **off/
open/apart**

technique noun

1 [C] ■ *You will learn techniques for
dealing with difficult customers.*

► tell / report / convey / break the news

method • way • system • process • mechanism • means | *fml* **methodology**

► a technique / method / system / process / mechanism / means / methodology **for** (doing) sth
► a technique / method / way / system / means / methodology **of** (doing) sth
► **devise / develop** a technique / method / way / system / process / means / methodology

2 [U, sing.] ■ *Her technique has improved a lot recently.*

skill • expertise • proficiency • competence • dexterity | *infml* **know-how** | *esp. written* **artistry**

► **have** the technique / skill / expertise / competence / dexterity / know-how
► **need / lack** the technique / skill / expertise / competence / know-how
► **demonstrate / show** your technique / skill / expertise / proficiency / competence / artistry

technology *noun* [U]
■ *The company has invested in the latest technology.*

machinery • hardware | *tech.* **plant**

► **current / the latest / basic / advanced / complex / sophisticated** technology / machinery / hardware
► **have / use / invest in** technology / machinery / hardware / plant
► **supply / install / update** technology / machinery / hardware

telephone *verb* [I, T] (*esp. BrE, fml*)
■ *I was about to telephone the police.*

call • dial | *BrE, esp. spoken* **ring • phone** | *esp. AmE, infml* **call sb up**

► **telephone** sb / **call** sb / **ring** sb / **phone** sb / **call** sb up **about** sth
► **telephone / call / dial / ring / phone a number / a hotline / the switchboard / reception**
► **telephone / call / ring / phone the doctor / fire brigade / police / hospital**

tell *verb*

1 [T] ■ *He told everyone the news.*

report • inform • fill sb in • convey • communicate • relay • repeat • break • brief | *fml* **notify • impart** | *esp. written or humorous* **enlighten**

► **tell** sb / **report / inform** sb / **brief** sb / **notify** sb **that...**
► **report / inform / communicate / relay / repeat / break** it **to** sb **that...**
► **tell / inform / brief / enlighten** sb **about** sth

2 [T] ■ *Are you telling the truth?*

report • describe | *fml* **recount • relate • narrate • chronicle** | *lit.* **weave**

► **tell / report / describe / recount / relate what / how...**
► **tell / recount / relate / narrate / weave a story / tale**

3 [I] (*infml, esp. spoken, often disapprov.*) ■ *Promise you won't tell.*

disapprov. **betray** | *fml, often disapprov.* **inform on sb** | *infml, disapprov.* **blab** | *BrE* **turn King's / Queen's evidence** | *AmE* **turn State's evidence** | *AmE, infml* **finger** | *BrE, slang, disapprov.* **grass** | *infml, approv., esp. journ.* **blow the whistle on sb**

► **tell / inform / grass / blow the whistle on** sb
► **tell on / betray / inform on** a **friend**

4 [T] ■ *He was told to sit and wait.*

instruct • order • command | *fml* **direct**

► **tell / instruct / order / command / direct** sb **to do sth**
► **tell / instruct / order / command / direct** sb **that...**
► **do sth as** told / instructed / ordered / commanded / directed

5 [T, no passive] (not used in the progressive tenses) ■ *I can't tell one twin from the other.*

distinguish | *esp. written* **differentiate**

► **tell / distinguish / differentiate** A **from** B
► **distinguish / differentiate between** A **and** B
► **easily tell / distinguish / differentiate** sb / sth

tell sb off *phrasal verb* (*esp. BrE, spoken*)
■ *I told the boys off for making so much noise.*

written **scold** | *fml* **rebuke • reprimand • chide • castigate • berate • reproach** | *disapprov.* **lecture**

► **tell** sb **off / scold / rebuke / reprimand / chide / castigate / berate / reproach** sb **for** sth
► **tell** sb **off / scold / rebuke / reprimand / castigate / berate** sb **severely**
● **TELL SB OFF OR SCOLD?** There is no verb for telling sb that you disapprove of their actions that is neither formal nor informal. **Scold** is used esp. in written stories; **tell sb off** is the most frequent word in spoken *BrE*.

temper noun [C, usu. sing., U]
■ She broke the plates in a fit of temper.

tantrum • **rage** • **mood** • **sulk** | BrE also **the sulks** | infml **huff**

▶ be in a temper/rage/huff at/about/over sth
▶ have a temper/a tantrum/the sulks
▶ fly into a temper/rage

lose your **temper** idiom
■ She lost her temper and started shouting.

get angry • **lose patience** • **go berserk** | BrE, infml **go mad** | AmE, infml **get mad**

■ OPP keep your temper
▶ lose your temper/get angry/lose patience/get mad with sb
▶ lose your temper/get angry/get mad at sth
▶ lose your temper/get angry over sth
● LOSE YOUR TEMPER OR GET ANGRY? If you **lose your temper** you show it in your behaviour; if you **get angry** the emphasis is more on your feelings and less on your behaviour.

temporary adj.
■ The job's only temporary.

short-lived • **passing** • **short** • esp. written **brief** • **momentary** • **fleeting**

■ OPP permanent
▶ a temporary/short/brief stay
▶ a temporary/short-lived/passing/momentary interest
▶ a temporary/short-lived/brief success

tempt verb [T]
■ I was tempted by the dessert menu.

entice • **attract** | written **seduce** | usu. disapprov. **lure**

▶ tempt/entice/attract/seduce/lure sb into sth
▶ be tempted/enticed/attracted/seduced/lured by sth
▶ tempt/entice sb to do sth

tenant noun [C]
■ They had evicted their tenants for non-payment of rent.

guest | esp. BrE **lodger** | fml **resident** • **householder** | esp. written **occupant**

▶ a new tenant/lodger/occupant
▶ the previous/current/sole tenant/occupant

tendency noun [C]

1 [C] ■ This fabric has a tendency to shrink.

bias • **bent** | fml **propensity** • **orientation**

▶ a/an tendency/bias/orientation toward/towards sth
▶ a tendency/propensity to do sth
▶ a natural tendency/bias/bent/propensity
▶ have a/an tendency/bias/bent/propensity/orientation

2 [C] ■ There is a growing tendency among employers to hire casual workers.

trend • **movement** • **drift**

▶ a tendency/trend/movement/drift towards sth
▶ a tendency/trend to do sth
▶ a general tendency/trend/movement/drift

tense adj.
■ She sounded tense and angry.

stressed • **strained** • **under pressure** • **fraught** • **stressful** | infml **stressed out** • **uptight**

■ OPP relaxed
▶ get tense/uptight
▶ sth makes sb tense/uptight
▶ a tense/strained/fraught atmosphere/silence/relationship
▶ a tense/fraught/stressful meeting/situation/time

tension noun

1 [U, C, usu. pl.] ■ There is mounting tension along the border.

hostility • **animosity** • **aggression** • **enmity** | fml **antipathy** | written **antagonism**

▶ tension/hostility/animosity/enmity/antipathy/antagonism between A and B
▶ feel the tension/hostility/animosity/antipathy/antagonism

2 [U, C, usu. pl.] ■ Exercise helps to release tension.

pressure • **stress** • **strain** | esp. journ. **heat**

▶ cause tension/stress/strain
▶ cope with/relieve/release the tension/pressure/stress/strain
▶ feel the tension/pressure/strain/heat
▶ suffer from tension/stress

term noun

1 [C] ■ technical/legal/scientific terms

word • **expression** • **phrase** • **idiom**

▶ a/an new/ambiguous term/word/expression/phrase
▶ use a/an term/word/expression/phrase/idiom
▶ a/an term/word/expression/phrase/idiom means sth

2 [C] ■ *the president's first term of/in office*

period • time • spell • stint • season

▶ a term/period/time/spell/stint/season **of/as** sth
▶ **for/during/after** a term/period/time/spell/stint/season
▶ **do** a term/spell/stint

term *verb* [T, usu. passive] (*fml*)
■ *REM sleep is termed 'active' sleep.*

call • name • entitle • dub • nickname | *sometimes disapprov.* label | *fml* designate

▶ **officially** termed/called/named/entitled/dubbed/labelled/designated
▶ **aptly** termed/called/named/entitled/nicknamed
▶ **commonly** termed/called/named/called/labelled

terrible *adj.*

1 ■ *What terrible news!*

bad • nasty • grim • *esp. spoken* awful • horrible | *esp. BrE, esp. spoken* dreadful | *infml* vile • horrendous • ghastly | *written* wretched

■ OPP good, wonderful
▶ terrible/nasty/grim/awful/horrible/dreadful **for** sb
▶ a/an terrible/bad/nasty/awful/horrible/dreadful/vile **thing/business**
▶ a/an terrible/bad/nasty/awful/horrible/dreadful **thought/feeling**
▶ terrible/bad/nasty/grim/awful/horrible/dreadful/vile/ghastly **weather**
▶ terrible/bad/grim/awful/dreadful/ghastly **news**

2 ■ *There's been a terrible accident.*

awful • horrible • dreadful • horrific • horrifying • gruesome | *BrE or fml, AmE* appalling

▶ a/an terrible/awful/horrible/dreadful/horrific/horrifying/gruesome/appalling **scene/sight**
▶ a/an terrible/awful/horrible/dreadful/horrific/horrifying/appalling **accident/incident**
▶ terrible/awful/horrible/dreadful/horrific/appalling **pain/suffering**
● **TERRIBLE, AWFUL OR APPALLING?** Awful is more often used to describe events or experiences. In *BrE* appalling is used to describe accidents, crimes and their results, and also bad social conditions. You can use terrible for all of these, although appalling is stronger.

3 (*infml*) ■ *We had a terrible meal at that restaurant.*

abysmal • atrocious | *infml* lousy

■ OPP excellent, wonderful
▶ a/an terrible/abysmal/atrocious/lousy **record**
▶ a/an terrible/atrocious/lousy **performance**
▶ terrible/atrocious/lousy **weather**

4 [only before noun] (*infml, esp. spoken*) ■ *The room's in a terrible mess.*

awful

■ OPP a bit of a
▶ a terrible/an awful **mistake/mess/nuisance/disappointment**
▶ a terrible/an awful **fool/snob**

territory *noun* [U, C]

■ *There are reports of heavy fighting in the disputed territory.*

region • colony • enclave | *fml* possession • dominion

▶ (a) **British/Spanish, etc.** territory/colony/enclave/possession
▶ a **self-governing** territory/colony/dominion
▶ (a) **former** territory/colony/possession
▶ **overseas** territory/possessions

test *noun*

1 [C] ■ *an end of year test*

exam • assessment | *esp. AmE* quiz | *BrE* paper | *fml* examination

▶ a/an test/exam/quiz/examination **on** sth
▶ a/an test/exam/assessment/examination **in** sth
▶ a **chemistry/geography, etc.** test/exam/quiz/paper/examination
▶ **take/pass/fail** a/an test/exam/assessment/quiz/paper/examination
● **TEST OR EXAM?** An exam is an important test at school or college, usu. at the end of a year, semester or course of study; a test is sth that students might be given at any point, covering only part of the material. Test is also usu. used for tests of practical skill or physical or mental ability rather than academic knowledge: *an IQ test* • (*BrE*) *a driving test* • (*AmE*) *a driver's test*

2 [C] ■ *a/an eye/blood/pregnancy test*
■ *The software is still at the test stage.*

experiment • testing • trial • pilot study

▶ a test/an experiment/testing/a trial **on** sth
▶ **scientific/practical/clinical/medical** tests/experiments/testing/trials
▶ **do/run** a/an test/experiment/trial/pilot study
▶ **carry out/conduct** a test/an

experiment/testing/a trial/a pilot study

test verb

1 [T, I] ■ *Students are tested in English.*

assess | *AmE* **quiz** | *fml* **examine**

▶ test/assess/quiz/examine sb on sth
▶ test/examine sb in sth

2 [T] ■ *Our products are not tested on animals.*

try sth out • experiment • pilot • put sth to the test • screen • try

▶ test (sb/sth)/try sth out/screen sb for sth
▶ test sth/try sth out/experiment on sb/sth
▶ test/screen **patients**

text noun

1 [U] ■ *The headings should be in plain text.*

writing • literature

▶ publish text/writing/literature
▶ read text/writing/literature
▶ a piece of text/writing/literature

2 [C] ■ *The paper printed the full text of his speech.*

script • screenplay • manuscript • lyrics | *music* **libretto**

▶ in the text/script/screenplay/ manuscript/lyrics/libretto
▶ write/read a text/script/ screenplay/manuscript/lyrics/ libretto
▶ the text/script/screenplay/lyrics is/are **based on** sth

3 [C] ■ *one of the most difficult literary texts*

work • book • textbook

▶ a text/work/book/textbook about/on sb/sth
▶ a text/work/book **by** sb
▶ read/write a text/work/book/ textbook

texture noun [C, U]

■ *the soft texture of velvet*

the feel • touch • consistency

▶ a/the smooth • soft texture/feel/ consistency
▶ a/the silky/firm texture/feel
▶ a thick/creamy texture/ consistency
▶ have/give sth a … texture/ consistency

thanks noun [pl.]

■ *How can I ever express my thanks?*

gratitude • appreciation

▶ thanks/gratitude **for** sth

▶ **in/with** thanks/gratitude/ appreciation
▶ **express/show/deserve** thanks/ gratitude/appreciation

theatre (*BrE*) (*AmE* theater) noun

1 [C] ■ *How often do you go to the theatre?*

hall • auditorium • arena | *BrE* **amphitheatre** | *AmE* **amphitheater**

▶ a 500-seat theatre/hall/ auditorium/arena/amphitheatre
▶ a **crowded/packed** theatre/hall/ auditorium/arena
▶ an **open-air** theatre/auditorium/ arena/amphitheatre

2 [U] ■ *an evening of music and theatre*

drama • acting • the stage • the performing arts • show business | *infml* **showbiz**

▶ study theatre/drama/acting
▶ a/an theatre/drama/acting/ stage/performing arts **school**
▶ a theatre/drama **critic**

theft noun [U, C]

■ *A number of thefts have been reported.*

robbery • burglary • break-in • embezzlement • shoplifting • raid | *esp. AmE, infml* **heist** | *AmE or old-fash., BrE, law* **larceny**

▶ **commit** a theft/robbery/burglary/ larceny
▶ **carry out** a theft/robbery/ burglary/raid
▶ **report/investigate** a theft/ robbery/burglary/break-in/raid

theme noun [C]

■ *The theme of this evening's lecture is…*

topic • subject • motif | *esp. journ. or politics* **keynote**

▶ **on** a theme/topic/subject
▶ a/an **important/key/major/ serious/general** theme/topic/ subject
▶ a **central** theme/topic/motif
▶ **discuss/consider/deal with/ examine/explore/look at/focus on/touch on/tackle** a theme/ topic/subject

theory noun

1 [C, U] ■ *Einstein's theory of relativity*

principle • law • rule | *tech.* **theorem**

▶ the theory/law/rule/theorem **about** sth
▶ the theory/principle **behind** sth
▶ a **basic/fundamental/ mathematical** theory/principle/ law/rule/theorem

▶ a **scientific** theory/principle/law/rule

▶ **prove** a theory/principle/law/rule/theorem

2 [C, U] ■ *I have this theory that most people prefer work to home life.*

hypothesis • **thesis** | *fml* **premise** • **proposition**

▶ a theory/hypothesis/thesis/premise/proposition **about** sth

▶ a theory/hypothesis/thesis/premise/proposition **that…**

▶ **support/test** a theory/hypothesis/thesis/premise/proposition

thick adj.

■ *a thick book/carpet/slice of bread*

wide | *often approv., esp. written* **broad**

■ OPP **thin**

● WHICH WORD? **Wide** usu. describes measurement from one side to another; **thick** describes measurement between surfaces: *a wide road/river • Thick walls kept the house cool in summer.*
Broad is often used to suggest that sth is wide in an attractive way: *a broad avenue lined with trees*

thief noun [C]

■ *Thieves made off with jewellery worth over £2 million.*

robber • **burglar** • **pickpocket** • **shoplifter** • **looter** • **raider** • **poacher** • **bandit** • **pirate**

▶ **catch** a thief/robber/burglar/pickpocket/shoplifter/looter/poacher

▶ a thief/robber/burglar/pickpocket/shoplifter/looter/raider/pirate **takes/steals** sth

▶ a thief/robber/burglar/looter **escapes/gets away/makes off** with sth

▶ a **gang of** thieves/robbers/pickpockets/shoplifters/looters/raiders

thin adj.

1 ■ *Cut the vegetables into thin strips.*

narrow • **fine**

■ OPP **thick**

▶ a thin/narrow/fine crack/strip

▶ thin/narrow shoulders

▶ a thin/fine hair/thread/layer

● THIN OR NARROW? **Narrow** describes sth that is a short distance from side to side; **thin** describes sth that has a short distance through it from one side to the other:
✔ *a narrow street/bed/gap* ✘ *a thin street/bed/gap*

✔ *a thin layer/shirt* ✘ *a narrow layer/shirt*

2 ■ *She was looking pale and thin.*

slight | *approv.* **slim** | *written, approv.* **slender** • **lean** | *often disapprov.* **underweight** | *infml, usu. disapprov.* **skinny**

■ OPP **fat**

▶ a thin/slight/slim/slender/lean/skinny **woman/man/boy**

▶ a thin/slight/slim/slender/skinny **girl**

▶ sb's thin/slight/slim/slender/lean/skinny **body/figure**

▶ thin/slight/slim/slender/lean/skinny **arms/legs/fingers**

thing noun

1 [C] ■ *He's bought one of those exercise things.*

item • **object** | *fml* **entity** • **commodity** | *infml, spoken* **thingy** | *tech.* **artefact/artifact**

▶ a **precious/valuable** thing/item/object/commodity/artefact

▶ a **separate** thing/item/object/entity

▶ **produce/manufacture** a/an thing/item/object/commodity/artefact

2 **things** [pl.] (*esp. BrE, infml*) ■ *I'll help you pack your things.*

belongings • **possessions** • **property** • **valuables** • **equipment** • **kit** | *infml* **stuff** • **gear** | *infml, disapprov.* **junk** | *esp. written or law* **goods**

▶ **personal** things/belongings/possessions/property/equipment/stuff/gear

▶ **collect/gather/pack** your things/belongings/possessions/equipment/stuff/gear

▶ **sell** your things/belongings/possessions/property/valuables/equipment/stuff/gear/goods

3 [C] ■ *I've got lots of things to do.*

infml **stuff**

▶ a **lot/lots/loads of** things/stuff

▶ things/stuff **to do/say**

4 **things** [pl.] (*infml, esp. spoken*) ■ *I'd like to think things over.*

situation • **circumstance** • **state of affairs**

▶ **describe/explain** things/the situation/circumstances/state of affairs

▶ **look at/review** things/the situation/circumstances

think verb

1 [T] (not used in the progressive tenses) ■ *I think it looks good.*

believe • feel • consider • find • be under the impression that... • make sth of sb/sth | *esp. BrE, infml* reckon | *fml* hold

▶ think/believe/feel/consider/find/be under the impression/reckon/hold that...
▶ be thought/believed/felt/reckoned/held to be sth
▶ think/believe/feel/make sth of sb/sth

● **THINK OR BELIEVE?** When you are talking about an idea of what is true or possible, use **believe** to talk about other people and **think** to talk about yourself: *Police believe (that) the man may be armed.* • *I think this is their house, but I'm not sure.*
Use **believe** to talk about matters of principle; use **think** to talk about practical matters or matters of personal taste: *I believe we have a responsibility towards the less fortunate in society.* • *I think we should reserve seats in advance.* • *I don't think he's funny at all.*

2 [I] ■ *All Sam ever thinks about is money.*

consider • wonder • reflect • mull sth over • look at sth | *esp. written* ponder | *fml* deliberate • contemplate • meditate

▶ think/wonder/ponder/contemplate **about** sth
▶ think/mull/ponder/deliberate/meditate **over** sth
▶ think/consider/wonder/reflect/look at/ponder/deliberate/contemplate **how/what/whether...**
▶ think/consider/reflect **that...**

3 [T, no passive, I] ■ *Just think—this time tomorrow we'll be lying on a beach.*

imagine • picture • visualize • pretend | *esp. BrE* envisage | *fml* envision

▶ think/imagine/picture/visualize/envisage/envision **who/what/how...**
▶ think/imagine/visualize/envisage/envision/pretend **that...**
▶ **Just** think/imagine/pretend.

4 [T] ■ *The job took longer than we thought it would.*

expect • anticipate | *infml* bargain for/on sth

▶ think/expect/anticipate **that...**
▶ **It is** thought/expected/anticipated **that...**

thinking *noun* [U]
■ *What is the current thinking on this?*

thought • reflection • logic | *written* reasoning

▶ thinking/thought/reflections/reasoning **on** sth
▶ the thinking/thought/logic/reasoning **behind** sth
▶ current/traditional/logical/scientific/political thinking/thought/reasoning

think sth up *phrasal verb* (*infml*)
■ *Can't you think up a better excuse?*

come up with sth • devise • hatch • work sth out • invent • make sth up | *infml* hit on sth • dream sth up | *fml* conceive • conceive of sth

▶ think up/come up with/devise/hatch/work out/hit on/dream up/conceive a **plan/scheme**
▶ think up/come up with/hatch/hit on/dream up/conceive an **idea/the idea of doing sth**
▶ think up/come up with/invent/make up/dream up an **excuse**

thorough *adj.*

1 ■ *The police carried out a thorough search.*

detailed • rigorous • exhaustive • comprehensive • careful • close • minute • in-depth • full-scale

■ OPP cursory, superficial
▶ a/an thorough/detailed/rigorous/exhaustive/comprehensive/careful/close/minute/in-depth **analysis**
▶ a/an thorough/detailed/rigorous/exhaustive/comprehensive/careful/close/in-depth/full-scale **study/investigation**
▶ a/an thorough/detailed/rigorous/exhaustive/comprehensive/careful/close/minute **examination**

2 [not usu. before noun] ■ *He was always thorough in his research.*

meticulous • painstaking

▶ thorough/meticulous **in** sth

thought *noun*

1 [C] ■ *I don't like the thought of you walking home alone.*

idea • concept • notion • prospect

▶ a/an thought/idea/concept/notion **about** sth
▶ the thought/idea/concept/notion **that...**
▶ **have** a/an thought/idea/concept/notion

2 [U] ■ *Give the matter some thought.*

consideration • reflection | *fml* deliberation • meditation • contemplation

▶ **after** (some, etc.) thought/consideration/reflection/deliberation/contemplation

▶ **quiet** thought/consideration/
reflection/deliberation/
meditation/contemplation
▶ be **deep/lost in** thought/
meditation/contemplation

3 [U] ■ *the history of scientific thought*

thinking | *written* **reasoning**

▶ thought/thinking/reasoning **on**
sth
▶ the thought/thinking/reasoning
behind sth
▶ **current/traditional/logical/
scientific/political** thought/
thinking/reasoning

thoughtful *adj.*

1 ■ *You're looking very thoughtful.*

introspective | *written* **reflective +
pensive**

▶ a/an thoughtful/introspective/
reflective/pensive **mood**
▶ a thoughtful/pensive **expression/
look**
▶ a thoughtful/reflective **silence**

2 (*approv.*) ■ *It was very thoughtful of
you to look after the flowers.*

considerate + kind + generous | *esp.
spoken* **good + sweet + nice**

■ OPP **thoughtless**
▶ be thoughtful/considerate/kind/
generous/good/sweet/nice **of** sb
(to do sth)
▶ a thoughtful/considerate/kind/
generous/sweet/nice **person**
▶ a thoughtful/considerate/kind/
generous **gesture**
● THOUGHTFUL OR CONSIDERATE?
Thoughtful is more often used
when sb does a particular thing for
sb else without being asked to.
Considerate is used more about
sb's general character and their
attitude towards people.

thread *noun* [C]

■ *the delicate threads of a spider's
web* ■ *Have you got a needle and
thread?*

strand + hair + yarn + cotton | *BrE*
fibre | *AmE* fiber

▶ a **long/single** thread/strand/hair/
fibre
▶ a **fine** thread/strand/hair
▶ **delicate/cotton** threads/fibres

threat *noun*

1 [U, C, usu. sing.] ■ *There is a real
threat of war.*

risk + danger

▶ a threat/risk/danger **of** sth
happening
▶ a threat/risk/danger **that** sth will
happen

▶ **pose** a threat/risk/danger
▶ **put** sth **under** threat/**at** risk/**in**
danger

2 [C, usu. sing.] ■ *Drug abuse poses a
threat to society.*

risk + danger + hazard + menace

▶ a threat/risk/danger/hazard/
menace **to** sb/sth
▶ a **potential** threat/risk/danger/
hazard/menace
▶ **pose** a threat/risk/danger/
hazard/menace
● WHICH WORD? A **danger** is the
possibility of physical or moral
harm and can come from a person
or a thing; a **risk** or **hazard** is the
threat of physical harm from a
thing but not a person. A **threat** is
usu. a probability, and is most often used
in the phrase *a threat to sth.*

threaten *verb*

1 [T] ■ *The attacker threatened him
with a gun.*

intimidate + warn sb off (sth) + scare
sb into (doing) sth | *written* **cow**

▶ threaten/intimidate sb **with** sth
▶ **try to** threaten sb/intimidate sb/
warn sb off/scare sb into doing sth

2 [I, T] ■ *A storm was threatening.* ■
The clouds threatened rain.

promise | *written* **herald + bode well/
ill**

▶ threaten/promise **to do** sth
▶ threaten/promise/herald **rain**
▶ promise/herald a (new) **beginning**

3 [T] ■ *Pollution is threatening marine
life.*

endanger + risk | *written* **jeopardize**

▶ threaten/endanger/risk sb's/your
life/health
▶ threaten/risk/jeopardize sb's/your
job/career
▶ threaten/endanger/jeopardize the
survival of sth
▶ a **threatened/an endangered
species**

threatening *adj.*

■ *threatening letters and obscene
phone calls*

ominous + sinister + forbidding

▶ a threatening/sinister/forbidding
look
▶ a/an threatening/ominous/
sinister **tone**
▶ threatening/ominous **black/dark
clouds**

throw *verb* [T, I]

■ *He threw the ball up into the air.*

toss + hurl + fling + bowl + pitch |
infml **lob | *esp. BrE, infml* chuck**

■ OPP **catch**
- ► throw/toss/hurl/fling/bowl/pitch/lob/chuck sth **at/to** sb/sth
- ► throw/toss/fling/chuck sth **aside/away**
- ► throw/toss/hurl/fling/bowl/pitch/lob/chuck a **ball**
- ► throw/toss/hurl/fling/bowl/pitch/lob/chuck sth **stones/rocks/a brick**

throw sth away *phrasal verb*

1 ■ *Throw those old shoes away.*

throw sth out • **scrap** • **get rid of sth** • **dump** • **dispose of sb/sth** | *infml* **chuck sth away/out** | *fml* **discard**

■ OPP **keep**
- ► throw away/throw out/dump/dispose of/chuck away/discard **rubbish/garbage/trash**

2 (*infml, disapprov.*) ■ *I threw away all my chances in life.*

squander • **waste** • **lose** • **splurge** | *infml* **blow**

- ► throw away/squander/waste/lose/splurge/blow sth **on** sth
- ► throw away/squander/waste/lose/splurge/blow **money**
- ► throw away/squander/waste/lose/blow a/an **fortune/chance/opportunity**
- ► throw away/squander/waste your **life**
- ● THROW AWAY, SQUANDER OR BLOW? **Blow** is used mostly to talk about money and in the phrases *blow your chances* and *blow it*. **Throw away** is used more to talk about things other than money. **Squander** is more formal than **throw away** or **blow**.

throw sb out *phrasal verb*

■ *She threw him out of the house.*

evict • **expel** • **deport** • **drop** | *esp. BrE* **move sb on** • **exclude** | *infml* **kick sb out** | *esp. AmE, infml* **chuck sb out** | *fml* **eject** • **ostracize**

- ► throw/kick/chuck sb **out of** a place
- ► evict/expel/deport/drop/eject sb **from** a place
- ► a **landlord** throws sb out of/evicts sb/kicks sb out/chuck sb out/ejects sb

thug *noun* [C]

■ *A gang of thugs attacked him.*

gangster • **hooligan** | *BrE* **lout** | *esp. AmE* **mobster** | *infml* **heavy** | *esp. AmE, infml* **goon**

- ► an **armed** thug/gangster/mobster
- ► **set** your thugs/heavies/goons (on sb)
- ► a **gang** of thugs/hooligans/heavies/goons

thwart *verb* [T, often passive]

■ *She was thwarted in her attempt to take control.*

disappoint • **stop** • **prevent** • **dash sb's hopes** • *esp. written* **frustrate** | *esp. journ.* **foil** • **derail**

- ► be thwarted/disappointed/frustrated/foiled **in** sth
- ► thwart/disappoint/dash/frustrate sb's **hopes**
- ► thwart/frustrate/foil/derail sb's **plans**
- ► thwart/stop/prevent/foil a **plot/raid/coup**

tidy *verb* [T, I] (*esp. BrE*)

■ *I spent all day tidying the house.*

clean (sth) up • **clear (sth) up** | *infml* **sort sth out/sort through sth**

- ► tidy up/clean up/clear up **after** sb
- ► tidy up/clear up/sort out a **house/room**
- ► tidy up/sort out a **cupboard/your desk**
- ► tidy up/clean up/clear up the **mess**

tidy *adj.* (*esp. BrE, usu. approv.*)

■ *The room was clean and tidy.*

neat • **orderly** • **uncluttered**

- ■ OPP **untidy**
- ► tidy/neat/orderly **rows**
- ► a tidy/neat **person**
- ► a/an tidy/neat/uncluttered **house/room**
- ► **leave** sth tidy/neat/uncluttered
- ● TIDY, NEAT OR ORDERLY? **Neat** is the most general of these words and can describe sb's appearance, a place or an arrangement of things such as a *row* or *pile*; **tidy** usu. describes a place such as a *room* or *desk*; **orderly** usu. describes the way things are arranged in rows or piles.

tie *noun* [C, usu. pl.]

■ *The firm has close ties with an American corporation.*

link • **bond** • **relationship** • **relations** • **association** • **partnership** | *fml* **affiliation** | *esp. busin.* **contact**

- ► (a/an) ties/link/bond/relationship/relations/association/partnership/affiliation/contact **with** sb/sth
- ► (a/an) ties/links/bond/relationship/relations/association/partnership/affiliation **between** A and B
- ► **build/establish/foster** (a) ties/links/bond/relationship/relations/partnership/contacts
- ● LINK OR TIE? A **link** is less strong than a **tie**. **Link** is used more

frequently about practical rather
than emotional connections:
✔trade/business links ◆ family ties
✗ ~~family links~~

tie verb

1 [T] (usu. used with an adv. or
prep.) ■ *The label was tied on with
string.*

attach • fasten • strap | *esp. BrE* fix |
fml secure

■ OPP untie
▸ tie/attach/fasten/strap/fix/secure
  sth **to** sth
▸ tie/fasten/strap/fix sth **on** sth
▸ tie/fasten/strap/fix sth **together**
▸ tie/fasten/fix **back**

2 [T, I] ■ *The robe ties at the waist.*

fasten • do (sth) up

■ OPP untie
▸ tie/fasten/do sth **up**
▸ tie/fasten/do sth **up at** the neck,
  waist, etc.
▸ tie/do up your **laces/shoelaces**

tie sb up *phrasal verb*
■ *The gang tied up a security guard.*

fml bind | *esp. written* tether

▸ tie up/bind/tether sb/sth **to** sth
▸ tie up/bind sb **with** sth
▸ **firmly** tie up/bind/tether sb/sth

tight adj.
■ *He kept a tight grip on her arm.*

taut | *often approv.* firm | *often
disapprov.* stiff

■ OPP loose
▸ a tight/firm **grip/hold**
▸ a **rope/wire** is tight/taut

tighten verb [I, T]
■ *His mouth tightened into a thin line.*

clench • tense • grit your teeth •
screw your eyes/face up

■ OPP relax, loosen, slacken
▸ tighten/clench/tense/grit your
  teeth/screw your eyes up **with/in**
  pain/irritation, etc.
▸ tighten/clench your **hand/fist/
  jaw**
▸ tighten/tense your **muscles**
▸ your **jaw/hand** tightens/
  clenches/tenses
▸ your **fist/stomach** tightens/
  clenches

time noun

1 [U, C] ■ *It's time for lunch.* ■ *When
was the last time you saw her?*

occasion • moment • point • hour •
date • instant

▸ **at** the time/the moment/that
  point/that instant
▸ **from/until** that time/moment/
  point/date
▸ **choose/pick** your time/moment
▸ the time/moment/hour **comes/
  arrives**

2 [C] ■ *It all happened a long time
ago.*

period • while • season • spell •
term • interval • run • stint • span |
esp. BrE, infml patch

▸ **a/an** time/period/season/spell/
  term/interval/run/stint/span/
  patch **of**
▸ **for** a/an time/period/while/
  season/spell/term/interval/run/
  stint/span
▸ **after** a/an time/period/while/
  season/spell/term/interval/run/
  stint/... patch
▸ **have** a ...time/period/season/
  spell/run/patch
● TIME OR PERIOD? Time is more
  about the feeling of time passing;
  period is more about the amount
  of time that has passed:
  ✔I lived in Egypt for a time. ✗ ~~I lived
  in Egypt for a period.~~
  ✔The factory will be closed down
  over a period of two years. ✗ ~~The
  factory will be closed down over a
  time of two years.~~

3 times [U, pl.] ■ *The story is set in
Victorian times.*

day • period • era • age | *fml* epoch

▸ **in** the time of.../... times/...
  day(s)/a period/an era/the age
  of.../an epoch
▸ (the) **present** time/day/period/
  era/epoch
▸ (the) **medieval/Victorian/post-
  war**, etc. time/days/period/era
● WHICH WORD? Era, age and epoch
  are used more often to mean a
  period in history. Time and day are
  often used, esp. in the plural, to
  talk about the present: modern
  times ◆ these days
  When time or day means a period
  in history, it is often used after a
  person's name: The family was very
  poor in my great grandmother's
  time.

timetable noun [C]
■ *I have a busy timetable this week.*

schedule • itinerary • agenda •
calendar | *BrE* diary • programme |
AmE program

▸ **be/put** sth **in** the/your timetable/
  schedule/itinerary/calendar/
  diary/programme
▸ **on** the timetable/schedule/
  itinerary/agenda/calendar/
  programme
▸ a **busy/full/packed** timetable/

► **check/consult** the/your timetable/schedule/calendar/diary
● **TIMETABLE OR SCHEDULE?** A **schedule** is usu. a plan of what must happen; a **timetable** is often a plan of what you hope will happen: *work/production schedules* • *the government's timetable for the peace talks*

tin noun [C] (*BrE*)
■ *She opened a tin of soup.*

can • **jar** • **pot**
► a **tin/can** of **beans/paint**
► a **jar/pot** of **honey/jam/marmalade**
● **CAN OR TIN?** In *AmE* use **can**. In *AmE* you can also use **tin** for food, paint, etc. but not for drinks:
✔ *a can of Coke* ✘ *a tin of Coke*

tiny adj.
■ *Only a tiny minority hold such extreme views.*

minute • **microscopic** • **miniature** • **little** • **small** • **compact**
■ **OPP** huge, enormous
► tiny/minute/microscopic/little/small **particles/organisms/creatures**
► a tiny/miniature/little/small **house/town/room**
► a tiny/minute/microscopic/little/small **detail**
► a tiny/minute/little/small **amount/quantity/trace/fraction**

tip verb [I, T] (usu. used with an adv. or prep.)
■ *Suddenly the boat tipped to one side.*

tilt • **lean** • **angle** • **slant** • **slope** • **bank**
► tip/tilt/lean/angle/slant/slope (sth) **towards/away** from sth
► tip/tilt/lean (sth) **forwards/back/backwards/to one side**
► tip/tilt/angle/slant/slope (sth) **up/down**
► tip/tilt/angle your **head**

tire verb [I, T]
■ *His legs were beginning to tire.*
■ *Long conversations tired her.*

exhaust • **wear sb/yourself out** • **weaken** | *esp. spoken* **tire sb/yourself out**
► tire/exhaust **yourself**
► wear/tire **yourself** out

tired adj.
1 ■ *I'm too tired to think.*

worn out • **weary** • **exhausted** • **drained** • **sleepy** • **drowsy** | *fml* **fatigued** | *BrE, infml* **shattered** | *esp. AmE, infml* **pooped**
► **feel** tired/worn out/weary/exhausted/drained/sleepy/drowsy/fatigued/shattered
► **look** tired/worn out/weary/exhausted/drained/sleepy/fatigued/shattered/pooped
► **leave sb** tired/exhausted/drained
► **physically/mentally** tired/exhausted/drained

2 ■ *He began with a few tired old jokes.*

trite • **stale** • **hackneyed** • **clichéd** | *infml* **corny**
► a tired/trite/hackneyed/clichéd **phrase**
► tired/stale/corny **jokes**
● **TIRED OR TRITE?** Tired *phrases, jokes* and *advice* make the listener feel *bored*; trite *observations, questions* and *remarks* make the listener feel *contemptuous* (= lacking respect).

title noun [C]
■ *This book's title is 'Oxford Learner's Pocket Thesaurus'.* ■ *His job title is Projects Officer.*

name
► a **name/title** for sb/sth
► **under** the **name/title** (of)...
► **choose/decide on** a **name/title**

toilet noun [C] (*BrE*)
■ *The toilet is upstairs.*

AmE **bathroom** • **restroom** • **ladies' room** • **men's room** | *BrE, infml* **loo** | *BrE, fml* **lavatory**
► a **public** toilet/bathroom/restroom/loo/lavatory
► **use/go to** the toilet/bathroom/restroom/ladies' room/men's room/loo/lavatory
► **need** the toilet/bathroom/loo/lavatory
● **TOILET OR BATHROOM?** In *BrE* **bathroom** means a room with a bath or shower in it. It may also contain a toilet. In *AmE* **bathroom** often means a room with a toilet in it, even if there is no bath or shower. In *AmE* **toilet** is used only for the toilet itself, not for the room in which it is found.

tolerant adj. (*approv.*)
■ *She had become more tolerant of others.*

permissive • **easy-going** | *usu. approv.* **open-minded** • **liberal** • **enlightened** | *usu. disapprov.* **indulgent**
■ **OPP** intolerant

tolerate

- a/an **tolerant**/permissive/easy-going/open-minded/liberal/enlightened **attitude**
- a/an **tolerant**/permissive/liberal/enlightened **society**
- a **tolerant**/easy-going/open-minded/enlightened **person**/**man**/**woman**

tolerate verb

1 [T] (*esp. written*) ■ *There is a limit to what one person can tolerate.*

stand • bear • take | *esp. spoken* **put up with sb/sth** | *fml* **endure**

- not **tolerate**/stand/take any **nonsense**
- **tolerate**/take **criticism**
- sb can **no longer** tolerate/stand/bear/endure sth

2 [T] ■ *Few plants will tolerate sudden changes in temperature.*

stand • resist • stand up to sth | *fml* **withstand**

- **tolerate**/stand/resist/withstand **high temperatures**/**heat**
- **tolerate**/stand/withstand (harsh, dry, etc.) **conditions**

tone noun

1 [C] ■ *She answered him in a businesslike tone.*

voice • accent | *phonetics* **intonation**

- speak in a/an ... **tone**/voice/accent
- a **rising**/**falling** tone/intonation

2 [sing.] ■ *The article was moderate in tone.*

mood • atmosphere • spirit • feeling • feel | *BrE* **flavour** | *AmE* **flavor**

- the **general** tone/mood/atmosphere/spirit/feeling/feel/flavour
- **reflect** the tone/mood/atmosphere/spirit/feeling (of sth)
- **capture** the tone/mood/atmosphere/spirit/feeling/flavour (of sth)

3 [C] ■ *the rich tone of the cello*

sound | *fml* **timbre**

- a **deep**/**rich** tone/timbre

tool noun [C]

■ *a set of garden tools*

instrument • device • gadget • aid | *fml* **implement • utensil**

- a **useful** tool/device/gadget/aid
- a **sharp**/**metal** tool/instrument/implement
- a **drawing**/**writing** tool/instrument/aid/implement

- a **teaching**/**training**/**research** tool/device/aid

top noun

1 [sing.] ■ *She's at the top of her profession.*

peak • height • climax • high point

■ **OPP** bottom

- the **top**/peak/height/climax/high point **of** sth
- **at** the **top**/its peak/its height/its climax/the high point
- **reach** the **top**/its peak/its height/its climax/a high point

2 [C] ■ *Where's the top of my pen?*

cap • lid

- a **screw** top/cap
- a **pen** top/cap
- **put on**/**screw on**/**take off**/**screw off** the top/cap/lid

top adj. [usu. before noun]

■ *He's one of our top players.*

high-ranking • leading • elite • senior • chief • superior • high • first | *infml* **number one** | *esp. written* **foremost** | *esp. written or journ.* **premier**

■ **OPP** bottom

- a **top**/high-ranking/leading/senior/chief/superior **officer**
- a **top**/leading/senior/chief **adviser**/**aide**/**economist**/**lawyer**
- the **top**/**first**/**premier** **division**/**prize**

topic noun [C]

■ *The topic for tonight's discussion is...*

subject • theme • issue • matter • question

- **on** a/an **topic**/subject/theme/issue/matter/question
- a/an **important**/**key**/**major**/**general**/**serious** **topic**/subject/theme/issue/matter/question
- **deal with**/**tackle**/**discuss**/**consider**/**examine**/**explore** a/an **topic**/subject/theme/issue/matter/question

total adj.

1 [usu. before noun] ■ *The total profit was more than £500.*

full • whole • entire

- (a) **total**/**full** **membership**
- the **total**/**whole**/**entire** **population**

2 [only before noun] ■ *The room was in total darkness.*

complete • utter • perfect • outright • unqualified • unmitigated • pure • sheer | *infml* **positive** | *esp. spoken* **real • absolute** | *usu. disapprov.* **downright**

■ **OPP** partial

► a/an total/complete/real/
absolute/utter/unmitigated
disaster
► total/complete/absolute/utter/
pure/sheer **rubbish/nonsense**
► total/complete/absolute/utter/
perfect **silence**
► a/an total/complete/absolute/
outright **ban**
● **TOTAL OR COMPLETE?** In most cases
you can use either of these words,
although *total war* is a fixed
collocation that cannot be
changed. **Total** is only used before
a noun.

totally *adv.*

■ *His behaviour is totally unacceptable.*

**completely • utterly • entirely •
fully** | *esp. BrE* **quite** | *esp. spoken*
absolutely • perfectly | *infml* **dead**

► totally/completely/utterly/
entirely/fully/quite/absolutely/
perfectly/**dead sure**
► totally/utterly/quite/absolutely/
perfectly **miserable**
► totally/completely/fully/quite/
absolutely **agree**
● **WHICH WORD?** The main differences
between these words are in register
not meaning. **Completely**, **entirely**
and **fully** are used more in written
and formal English. **Totally**, **quite**,
absolutely and **perfectly** are used
more in spoken and informal
English. **Utterly** is often used to
express failure or impossibility: *She
utterly failed to convince them.*

touch *verb*

1 [T] ■ *I touched him on the arm.*

brush • feel | *written* **graze**

► touch/brush/feel/graze **sb/sth
with sth**
► touch/brush **sb/sth gently/lightly**
► **accidentally** touch/brush **sb/sth**

2 [I, T] ■ *Make sure the wires don't
touch.*

meet • cross

► **not quite/almost/nearly** touch/
meet/cross

3 [T] ■ *I had been touched by his
kindness to my aunts.*

move • affect • impress

► it touches/moves/mpresses **sb to
see/hear sth**
► touch/move/affect/impress **sb
deeply**
● **TOUCH, MOVE OR AFFECT?** You can
be **moved** by sth that happens to
sb else, esp. sth sad; you can be
touched by what sb else does, esp.
a small act of kindness they do for
you; you are **affected** by sth that
happens to you, or to sb else, but
the emphasis is on the effect it has
on you.

tough *adj.*

1 ■ *He had a tough childhood.*

**hard • difficult • bad • rough •
adverse** | *fml* **disadvantageous** | *BrE,
fml* **unfavourable** | *AmE, fml*
unfavorable

■ **OPP easy**

► tough/hard/difficult/bad/
disadvantageous/unfavourable **for
sb**
► tough/hard/difficult/bad/rough/
adverse/unfavourable **conditions**
► a/an tough/hard/difficult/bad/
rough/unfavourable **situation**
► a tough/hard/difficult/bad/rough
time/day/week/year

2 ■ *He's going to get tough on crime*

hard • strict • stern • severe | *often
approv.* **firm** | *usu. disapprov.* **harsh •
rigid** | *fml* **stringent • punitive**

■ **OPP soft**

► be tough/hard/strict/firm/harsh
with sb/sth
► be tough/hard/strict/firm/harsh **on
sb/sth**
► tough/strict/severe/firm/harsh/
rigid **discipline**
► tough/strict/firm/rigid/stringent
controls

tour *noun*

1 [C] ■ *We're going on a tour of
Provence.*

**trip • excursion • expedition •
journey • travels • outing** | *esp. BrE*
day out | *BrE* **holiday** | *AmE* **vacation**

► a/an tour/trip/excursion/
expedition/journey/outing/day
out **to sth/somewhere**
► a **bus/coach** tour/trip/journey
► **go on** (a/an) tour/trip/excursion/
expedition/journey/outing/day
out/holiday/vacation

2 [C] ■ *a guided tour of the castle*

visit

► **during** sb's tour/visit
► **go on/cut short/cancel** a tour/
visit

tour *verb* [T, I]

■ *We spent six weeks touring in India.*

explore • go backpacking

► tour/explore **by car**
► **go** touring/exploring/
backpacking

tourist *noun* [C]

■ *A busload of tourists arrived at the
site.*

**visitor • sightseer • backpacker •
pilgrim** | *BrE* **holidaymaker •
traveller** | *AmE* **traveler • vacationer**

marks, a smell, objects left behind by sb/sth or a series of clues.

trade noun

1 [U, A] ■ *International trade is increasing.*

business • trading • commerce • enterprise • operation • dealing • trafficking • market • marketplace

▶ trade/business/trading/ commerce/enterprise/dealing/ trafficking **between** people/ countries
▶ trade/business/trading/ commerce/dealing **with** sb/a country
▶ **encourage/promote** trade/ business/commerce/enterprise
▶ trade/business/the market **grows/is booming/picks up/ declines**
● **TRADE OR BUSINESS?** Trade is used slightly more to talk about buying and selling goods rather than services. Business is used when sb is trying to emphasize the more personal aspects, such as discussing things and working together to provide goods or services.

2 [C] ■ *He's in the building trade.*

business • industry • service

▶ be in/work in a particular trade/ business/industry/service
▶ the **book/tourist/car/catering/ hotel/construction** trade/ business/industry
▶ the **timber/fur/wool/wine/ motor/building** trade/industry

3 [C] ■ *Jim's a carpenter by trade.* ■ *My parents wanted me to leave school and learn a trade.*

occupation • profession • vocation • job • work • employment

▶ a) **skilled/manual** trade/ occupation/work/employment
▶ **have/pursue/take up** (a/an) trade/occupation/profession/ work/employment

trade verb [I, T]

■ *They began trading in flour, sugar and leather.*

deal in sth • sell • export • import • handle • do business • stock • carry | busin. retail | old-fash. or disapprov. peddle • hawk

▶ trade/do business **with** sb
▶ trade/deal in/sell/export/import/ handle/stock/retail/peddle/hawk goods
▶ trade/deal in/sell **shares/futures/ stocks/bonds/securities**
● **TRADE IN STH OR DEAL IN STH?** Trade in is often used to talk about buying and selling raw materials such as *animals*, *coal* and *sugar*, as

---

town noun [C]

■ *The nearest town is ten miles away.*

city • village • borough • metropolis | fml municipality • conurbation

▶ **in** a town/city/village/borough/ metropolis/municipality/ conurbation
▶ a **small** town/city/village/ borough/municipality
▶ a **major** town/city/metropolis/ conurbation
▶ a **provincial** town/city
● **TOWN OR CITY?** A city is usu. bigger and more important than a town.

trace noun

1 [C, U] ■ *They found no trace of the boy.*

sign • indication • mark

▶ a/an trace/sign/indication/mark **of** sth
▶ **have/bear** the traces/signs/marks
▶ **no/any** trace/sign/indication of sth

2 [C] (always followed by of) ■ *She spoke with no trace of bitterness.*

hint • touch • element • tinge

▶ **detect** a/an trace/hint/touch/ element/tinge of sth
▶ a trace/hint/touch of **humour/ irony/sarcasm**
▶ a/an trace/hint/touch/element/ tinge of a/an **smile/accent**

trace verb [T]

■ *We finally traced him to an address in Chicago.*

track sb/sth down • find • search sb/sth out • locate | infml sniff sb/ sth out

▶ trace/track down/find the **killer/ location**
▶ trace/track down/locate sb's **whereabouts**
▶ trace/track down/find/locate the **missing...**

track noun [C, usu. pl.]

■ *We saw the bear's tracks in the snow.*

trail • footprint

▶ **fresh** tracks/footprints
▶ **leave/make** tracks/a trail/ footprints
▶ **follow** tracks/a trail
● **TRACK OR TRAIL?** A track is always marks on the ground; a trail can be

well as textiles; **deal in sth** is used about manufactured products such as *cars* and *antiques*. **Deal in sth** also often refers to criminal buying and selling; typical collocates are *drugs, guns* and *stolen goods*.

tradition verb [C, U]

■ *He followed the family tradition of joining the navy.*

practice • custom • convention • norms

▶ by tradition/custom/convention
▶ a tradition/custom/convention that...
▶ follow a tradition/practice/custom/convention...norms
▶ break with a tradition/practice/convention

traditional adj.

1 ■ *Haggis is a traditional Scottish dish.*

customary • usual • habitual

▶ traditional/customary/usual to do sth
▶ sb's traditional/customary/usual/habitual role/manner/way
▶ the traditional/customary/usual procedure/practice

2 (sometimes disapprov.) ■ *Traditional attitudes were changing.*

conventional • orthodox • conservative • traditionalist • classical • mainstream

■ OPP modern
▶ the traditional/conventional/orthodox/conservative/classical/mainstream view
▶ traditional/conventional/orthodox/classical/mainstream theories/methods/approaches/economics
▶ traditional/conventional/conservative/classical/mainstream ideas/thinking
● TRADITIONAL OR CONVENTIONAL? Traditional emphasizes how old a method or idea is; conventional emphasizes how usual it is now. Traditional medicine is actually a form of alternative medicine, which is the opposite of modern conventional medicine.

traffic noun [U]

■ *I was stuck in heavy traffic.*

congestion • traffic jam • bottleneck • gridlock

▶ urban traffic/congestion
▶ increase/reduce traffic/congestion
▶ be stuck/caught in traffic/a traffic jam

trail noun [C]

■ *a trail of blood/footprints*

track • footprint • scent

▶ leave/make a trail/tracks/footprints/your scent
▶ follow a trail/tracks/the scent
▶ be on the trail/track/scent of sb/sth
● TRAIL OR TRACK? A **track** is always marks on the ground; a **trail** can be marks, a smell, objects left behind by sb/sth or a series of clues.

train verb

1 [T, I] ■ *All staff are trained in first aid.*

coach • teach • tutor • show • prepare | fml instruct • educate | journ. groom

▶ train/coach/instruct/educate sb in sth
▶ train/coach/prepare/groom sb for sth
▶ train/coach a/an athlete/footballer, etc.
▶ teach/coach athletics/football, etc.
● TRAIN OR COACH? You can **train** but not **coach** people in skills for a job; you can **train** but not **coach** animals:
✗ *All staff are coached in first aid.*
✔ *They train dogs to sniff out drugs.*
✗ *They coach dogs to sniff out drugs.*
You can **coach** a person or sport, but you can only **train** a person:
✔ *He coaches basketball.* ✗ *He trains basketball.*

2 [I, T] ■ *athletes training for the Olympics*

exercise • work out • warm up | BrE practise | AmE practice • keep fit

▶ train/exercise/warm up properly
▶ train/exercise/work out/practise regularly
▶ train/exercise a horse/dog

training noun

1 [U] ■ *New recruits undergo six weeks' basic training.*

tuition • teaching • education • learning | BrE coaching | esp. AmE tutoring | fml instruction

▶ training/tuition/teaching/education/coaching/tutoring/instruction in sth
▶ training/tuition/teaching/education/coaching for sth
▶ have/get/receive training/tuition/an education/coaching/instruction

2 [U] ■ *Phillips is in training for the Olympics.*

practice • exercise • rehearsal • drill

▶ training/practice/rehearsal for sth

traitor noun [C] (disapprov.)

■ *She was accused of being a traitor.*

collaborator • defector • deserter | *fml* **renegade**

▶ an **alleged** traitor/collaborator

tramp noun [C] (*sometimes disapprov.*)

■ *An old tramp was sitting on the bench.*

beggar • esp. AmE drifter • esp. AmE, infml bum • fml or law vagrant

▶ an **old** tramp/beggar/bum
● **WHICH WORD?** All these words are disapproving. Neutral terms are **homeless person/man/woman** and **the homeless** [pl.]: *the plight of the homeless in the city*

trance noun [C, usu. sing.]

■ *She drove in a trance, hardly aware of anything.*

daze • stupor • daydream • dream | *fml or lit.* **reverie**

▶ be **in** a trance/daze/stupor/ daydream/dream/reverie
▶ **go/fall into** a trance/stupor

transform verb [T]

■ *It was an event that would transform my life.*

change • turn • convert | *fml* **metamorphose** | *biology* **evolve • mutate**

▶ transform sth/change/turn/ convert/metamorphose/evolve/ mutate (**from** sth) **into** sth
▶ transform sth/change/turn/ convert/evolve/mutate **rapidly**
▶ transform sth/change/turn/ convert/evolve **quickly/slowly/ gradually**

transparent adj.

■ *The insect's wings are almost transparent.*

clear • see-through | *BrE* **colourless** | *AmE* **colorless** | *written* **translucent**

■ **OPP opaque**
▶ transparent/clear/translucent **glass**
▶ transparent/clear/see-through **plastic**
▶ transparent/clear/colourless **varnish**
● **TRANSPARENT OR CLEAR? Clear** is the word most often used to describe water. **Transparent** is used to describe solid things or materials, not liquids (except **varnish**).

transport noun

1 [U] (*esp. BrE*) ■ *The region has good transport links.*

traffic • shipping | *esp. AmE* **transportation**

▶ **international** transport/traffic/ shipping/transportation
▶ **local/urban/city/air/rail/river/ road** transport/traffic/ transportation
▶ **private/public** transport/ transportation
▶ a **means/form/mode of** transport/transportation

2 [U] (*esp. BrE*) ■ *We need stricter controls on the transport of live animals.*

delivery • freight • transit • shipment • shipping | *esp. AmE* **transportation** | *BrE* **haulage** | *fml* **handling** | *busin.* **distribution**

▶ **for** transport/delivery/freight/ shipment/shipping/ transportation/haulage/ distribution
▶ transport/delivery/freight/ shipping/transportation/haulage/ handling/distribution **costs**
▶ a transport/delivery/freight/ shipping/transportation/haulage/ distribution **company/business**
▶ the transport/freight/transit/ shipping/transportation/haulage **industry**

transport verb [T, often passive]

■ *Too many goods are transported by road.*

carry • deliver • take • bring • ferry • ship

▶ transport/carry/deliver/take/ bring/ferry/ship sb/sth **to/from** sb/sth
▶ transport/carry/take/bring/ferry/ ship sb/sth **back/home**
▶ transport/carry/deliver/take/ bring/ferry sb/sth **by car/rail/ truck**, etc.
● **TRANSPORT OR CARRY? Carry** is used esp. to talk about people, **transport** to talk about goods.

trap verb [T, usu. passive]

■ *He was trapped in the burning building.*

confine • cage • pen • lock sb in (sth) • shut sb in (sth)

▶ be trapped/confined/caged/ penned/locked/shut **in** sth
▶ be trapped/confined/caged/ penned/locked/in/shut **in with** sb/sth

travel noun

1 [U] ■ *My interests include music and foreign travel.*

tourism • sightseeing | *esp. BrE* travelling | *AmE usu.* traveling
> ▶ travel/travelling **by** sth
> ▶ a day's travel/sightseeing/travelling
> ▶ travel/travelling **costs/expenses/arrangements**
● **TRAVEL OR TRAVELLING?** Travel is used more to talk about journeys made by people in general; travelling is used more to talk about journeys made by a particular person: *The pass allows unlimited bus travel.* • *My job involves a lot of travelling.*

2 travels [pl.] ■ *When are you off on your travels?*

journey • trip • tour • expedition | *esp. written* voyage | *BrE* holiday | *AmE* vacation
> ▶ **go/be on** your travels/a journey/a trip/a tour/an expedition/a voyage/holiday/vacation
> ▶ **set out/set off on** your travels/a journey/a trip/a tour/an expedition/a voyage
> ▶ **come back/return from** your journey/a trip/a tour/an expedition/a voyage/a holiday/a vacation

travel verb

1 [I, T] ■ *We travelled across the US.*

go • fly • drive • come • cover | *esp. AmE* ride
> ▶ travel/go/fly/drive/come/ride **from/to** sth
> ▶ travel/go/fly/drive/come/ride **with** sb
> ▶ travel/go/fly/drive/come/cover/ride **50 miles/1000 km**

2 [I] (usu. used with an adv. or prep.) ■ *The car was travelling north.*

go • move • head • run • pass | *fml* proceed
> ▶ travel/go/move/run/proceed **from...to...**
> ▶ travel/go/move/head/proceed **to** sb/sth
> ▶ travel/go/move/run/proceed **towards** sb/sth

traveller (*esp. BrE*) (*AmE usu.* traveler) noun [C]
■ *Rail travellers complained about the rise in fares.*

passenger • commuter
> ▶ a regular traveller/passenger/commuter
> ▶ rail travellers/passengers/commuters
> ▶ passenger/commuter **fares/services/traffic/trains**

travelling (*esp. BrE*) (*AmE usu.* traveling) adj.
■ *The travelling exhibition is currently in Moscow.*

nomadic | *fml* itinerant | *tech.* migratory
> ▶ travelling/nomadic **people**
> ▶ a travelling/an itinerant **preacher**

treat verb

1 [T] ■ *She was treated for sunstroke.*

nurse | *BrE* dose | *fml* tend | *esp. written* care for sb
> ▶ treat/nurse/tend to/care for the **sick**
> ▶ treat/nurse/tend to an **injury**
> ▶ treat/nurse a **cold**

2 [T, often passive] ■ *The crops are treated with pesticide.*

process
> ▶ treat/process **waste**
> ▶ be **routinely/efficiently** treated/processed

treatment noun [U, C]
■ *He is receiving treatment for shock.*

medical care • therapy • surgery • operation • medicine • nursing • healing • cure
> ▶ treatment/therapy/surgery/an operation **for** sth
> ▶ (a/an) **alternative/orthodox/conventional** treatment/therapy/medicine
> ▶ **have/need/require** treatment/medical care/therapy/surgery/an operation

trend noun

1 [C] ■ *an upward trend in sales*

tendency • movement • drift
> ▶ trend/tendency/movement/drift **towards** sth
> ▶ trend/movement/drift **away from** sth
> ▶ a **general** trend/tendency/movement/drift

2 [C] ■ *You seem to have set a new trend.*

fashion • style • look • craze | *written* vogue | *disapprov.* fad
> ▶ a trend/fashion/style/vogue/fad **for** sth
> ▶ the **latest** trend/fashion/style/look/craze/fad
> ▶ **set/follow** a trend/fashion/style

trial noun

1 [U, C] ■ *He's on trial for murder.*

hearing • case • prosecution • court martial • action • proceedings

▶ a murder/rape/fraud trial/case
▶ (a) libel trial/hearing/case/
action/proceedings
▶ face trial/a hearing/prosecution/
court martial/proceedings

2 [C, U] ■ *The drug is undergoing
clinical trials.*

**test • testing • experiment • pilot
study**

▶ a trial/a test/testing/an
experiment on sth
▶ carry out/conduct a trial/a test/
testing/an experiment/a pilot
study
▶ trials/tests/testing/experiments/
pilot studies **show/shows** sth

---

trick *noun* [C]
■ *She won't fall for such a stupid trick.*

**trap • tactic • device • bluff • prank
• joke** | *BrE* **manoeuvre** | *AmE*
maneuver | *esp. journ.* **hoax** | *often
disapprov.* **ploy** | *infml, usu. disapprov.*
set-up | *written, sometimes disapprov.*
ruse

▶ a **clever** trick/trap/joke/
manoeuvre/ploy/ruse
▶ **use** a trick/tactic/device/
manoeuvre/ploy
▶ **resort** to a trick/tactic/device/
ploy
▶ a trick/trap/tactic/device/bluff/
prank/joke/manoeuvre/ploy/ruse
works

---

trick *verb* [T] (*sometimes disapprov.*)
■ *He tricked me into giving him £100.*

**cheat • con • fool • take sb in • dupe
• deceive • swindle • defraud** | *esp.
AmE, infml* **bilk** | *slang* **screw**

▶ trick/cheat/con/dupe/swindle/
defraud/bilk/screw sb **out of** sth
▶ trick/cheat/con/fool/dupe/
deceive sb **into doing/believing**
sth
▶ trick/cheat/con **your way into** sth

---

trickle *verb* [I, T] (*usu. used with
an adv. or prep.*)
■ *Water trickled through the cracks.*

dribble • drip • run • flow

▶ blood/water trickles/dribbles/
drips/runs/flows
▶ tears trickle/drip/run/flow
▶ sweat trickles/drips/runs

---

trip *noun* [C]
■ *We went on a trip to the mountains.*

**journey • tour • expedition •
excursion • outing • pilgrimage •
travels** | *esp. BrE* **day out**

▶ a/an trip/journey/tour/
expedition/excursion/outing/

---

pilgrimage/day out **to** sth/
somewhere
▶ go on/be on/come back from/
return from a/an trip/journey/
tour/expedition/excursion/
outing/pilgrimage/your travels/
day out
▶ make a/an trip/journey/tour/
expedition/excursion/outing/
pilgrimage
● **TRIP OR JOURNEY?** A **trip** is usu. a
journey to a place and back again
and is used esp. when you travel
for pleasure or for a particular
purpose; a **journey** is usu. one-
way, and is often used when the
travelling takes a long time and is
difficult: *a day/school/business trip* ■
*It was a difficult journey across the
mountains.*

---

trip *verb* [I] (*usu. used with an adv.
or prep.*)
■ *She tripped over a rock and cut her
knee.*

stumble • slip | *esp. spoken* **fall over** |
esp. written **fall**

▶ trip/stumble/fall **over** sth

---

trouble *noun*

1 [U, C] ■ *The trouble with you is you
don't want to work.*

**problem • difficulty • issue •
complication** | *esp. spoken* **the
matter**

▶ (a/an/the) trouble/problem/
difficulty/complication/issue/
matter **with** sth
▶ **have** trouble/problems/
difficulties/issues
▶ **cause/avoid** problems/
difficulties/complications

2 [U] (*usu. used after* in *or into*) ■ *The
company ran into trouble last year.*

hardship | *fml* **misfortune •
adversity**

▶ **great/real** trouble/hardship/
misfortune/adversity
▶ **cause** trouble/hardship
▶ **in times of** trouble/hardship/
adversity

3 [U] ■ *Drunken youths were causing
trouble.*

**disturbance • unrest • agitation •
anarchy** | *fml* **disorder**

▶ trouble/disturbances/unrest/
agitation/disorder **among** sb
▶ **cause** trouble/a disturbance/
unrest
▶ trouble/a disturbance/unrest/
disorder **occurs**

4 [U] ■ *I hope the children weren't too
much trouble.*

difficulty | *BrE* **job** | *infml* **hassle** | *esp.
BrE, esp. spoken* **bother**

► the trouble/difficulty/hassle/
bother **with** sth
► **without** any trouble/difficulty/
hassle/bother
► **have** trouble/difficulty/a job
► **cause** (sb) trouble/difficulty/
hassle/bother

truck noun [C] (*esp. AmE*)
■ *a truck loaded with timber*

van • vehicle | *BrE* lorry

► **by** truck/van/lorry
► a **heavy** truck/vehicle/lorry
► **drive** a truck/vehicle/van/lorry

trudge verb [I, T] (usu. used with
an adv. or prep.)
■ *They trudged wearily into town.*

plod • trail • traipse • tramp • trek •
troop

► trudge/plod/traipse/tramp/trek
through the snow, etc.
► trudge/plod/trail **slowly/wearily**
► trudge/tramp **the streets**

true *adj.*

1 ■ *Is it true that she's leaving?*

right • correct • factual • accurate •
real-life • authentic

■ OPP untrue, false
► the true/right/correct **answer**
► a/an true/factual/accurate/real-
life/authentic **account**

2 ■ *You're a true friend.*

real • actual • genuine • authentic |
BrE, spoken proper

► a/the true/real/actual/genuine/
authentic/proper **reason**
► the true/real/actual **cost** of sth
► a/an true/real/genuine/authentic
work of art
● **TRUE OR REAL?** In many cases you
can use either word: *You're a true/
real friend. • He's a true/real
gentleman.*
However, **real** looks at the
necessary qualities of sth in a more
practical way; **true** looks at those
qualities in a more romantic way.

trust noun [U]
■ *It has taken years to earn their trust.*

faith • confidence • belief

■ OPP distrust
► trust/faith/confidence/belief **in**
sb/sth
► **have/show** trust/faith/confidence
► **lose** sb's trust/faith/confidence
► **destroy** sb's trust/faith/
confidence/belief

trust verb [T]
■ *You can't trust anyone these days.*

depend on/upon sb/sth • rely on/
upon sb/sth • count on sb/sth •
believe in sb • have confidence in
sb/sth

■ OPP distrust
► trust/depend/rely on/count on
sb **to do** sth
► trust/believe/have confidence **in**
sb/sth
► trust/rely on/have confidence **in**
sb's **judgement**
● **TRUST, DEPEND ON/UPON SB/STH OR
RELY ON/UPON SB/STH?** You can
trust a person, but not a thing or a
system:
✔ *The local transport system can't be
depended on/relied on.* ✗ ~~The
local transport system can't be
trusted.~~
Rely on is used esp. with *you can/
could* or *you should* to give advice
or a promise:
✔ *You can't really rely on his
judgement.* ✗ ~~I don't really rely on
his judgement.~~

truth noun

1 the truth [sing.] ■ *The awful truth
finally dawned on her.*

fact • the case • reality

■ OPP lies
► the truth/fact (of the matter)/case
is that...
► **face/accept/ignore** the truth/the
fact/reality
► be **based on** the truth/the fact

2 [U] ■ *There is no truth in the
rumours.*

good faith • sincerity

■ OPP *fml* falsehood
► **in** truth/good faith/sincerity
► **say** sth with truth/sincerity
► **doubt** the truth/good faith/
sincerity of sth

try verb

1 [I, T] ■ *She tried her best to solve the
problem.*

attempt • struggle | *infml* have a go
| *fml* seek • strive | *BrE, fml*
endeavour | *AmE, fml* endeavor

► try/attempt/struggle/seek/strive/
endeavour **to do** sth
► try/attempt/struggle/seek/strive
desperately/in vain
► try/struggle/strive **hard**
● **TRY OR ATTEMPT?** Attempt is more
formal than **try** and places the
emphasis on the act of starting to
do sth rather than on the effort of
achieving it.

2 [T] ■ *Try this new coffee—it's really
good.*

taste • try sth out • test | *written*
sample

▶ try/try out/test/sample a **new product**
▶ try/taste/sample **food/wine**

tumour *(BrE)* *(AmE* **tumor**) *noun* [C]
■ He had a malignant brain tumour.

growth • lump • swelling
▶ a/an tumour/lump/swelling **on/ in** a part of the body
▶ **have** a/an tumour/lump/swelling

tune *noun* [C]
■ He was humming a familiar tune.

melody • theme • song • number
▶ a tune/melody/theme/song/ number **by** sb
▶ a **folk** tune/melody/song
▶ **play** a tune/melody/theme/ song/number

turn *noun*

1 [C] ■ The lane was full of twists and turns.

bend • corner • twist
▶ a **sharp** turn/bend/corner/twist
▶ a **left-hand/right-hand** turn/ bend/corner
▶ **negotiate** a turn/bend/corner

2 [C] *(esp. spoken)* ■ Please wait your turn.

chance • opportunity | *BrE, spoken* go
▶ **your** turn/a chance/the opportunity **to do sth**
▶ **have/miss** a turn/your chance/an opportunity/a go
▶ **get/give** sb a/an turn/chance/ opportunity/go

turn *verb*

1 [I, T] ■ She turned the steering wheel quickly.

rotate • revolve • spin • circle • roll • swivel • twist • orbit | *esp. spoken* go around/round (sth) | *written* whirl • twirl
▶ turn/rotate/revolve/spin/circle/ roll/orbit/go/whirl **round/around** (sth)
▶ turn/rotate/revolve/spin/circle/ swivel **on sth**
▶ turn/rotate/spin/circle/whirl **faster (and faster)**

2 [I, T] *(usu. used with an adv. or prep.)* ■ Anne turned her head away.

turn (sb/sth) round/around • spin • swing • twist • pivot | *written* wheel • swivel • whirl
▶ turn/spin/swing/twist/pivot/ wheel/swivel/whirl **round/around**

▶ turn/spin/swing/wheel/swivel/ whirl **back/away**
▶ turn/twist/swivel your **head**
▶ turn/spin/swing/ twist/wheel/swivel/whirl around **to face sb/sth**

3 [I, T] *(always used with* into *or from and* to*)* ■ The witch turned him into a frog.

change • transform • convert • translate | *fml* metamorphose | *biology* mutate • evolve
▶ turn/change/transform sth/ convert/translate/ metamorphose/mutate/evolve **into sth**
▶ turn/change/transform sth/ convert/metamorphose/mutate/ evolve **from sth into sth**
● **TURN OR CHANGE?** Change is only used in cases where sth occurs naturally, automatically or by magic. Turn can also be used when people use their effort or skill to change one thing or situation into sth different, or when circumstances change a situation:
✔ There are plans to turn the old station into a hotel. ✗ *There are plans to change the old station into a hotel.*
✔ A minor disagreement turned into a major crisis. ✗ *A minor disagreement changed into a major crisis.*

4 [I] *(usu. used with an adv. or prep.)* ■ The river turns north at this point.

wind • twist • bend • curve | *written* snake
▶ turn/curve/bend **(to the) left/ right/south/north, etc.**
▶ the **road/path** turns/winds/ twists/bends/curves/snakes
▶ the **river** turns/winds/bends/ curves/snakes

5 *linking verb* ■ She turned white when she heard the news.

become • go • grow • get
▶ turn/become/go/grow/get **cold**
▶ turn/become/grow/get **warm/ chilly**
▶ turn/become/go **red/white/ blue, etc.**
▶ turn/go **bad/sour**

turn sb/sth down *phrasal verb*

1 ■ He asked her to marry him but she turned him down.

refuse • reject • throw sth out • veto | *fml* decline • deny • disallow | *fml, often disapprov.* rebuff
● OPP **take sth up, take sb up on sth**
▶ turn down/refuse/reject/throw out/veto/decline a **proposal**
▶ turn down/refuse/reject/decline/ rebuff a/an **offer/request**

► turn down/refuse/reject/decline a/an **chance/opportunity/invitation**

2 ■ *Please turn the volume down.*

lower • reduce

■ OPP **turn sth up**
► turn down/lower/reduce the **volume/sound**
► turn sth down/reduce sth **slightly**

turning point noun [C, usu. sing.]

■ *The peace process has reached a turning point.*

crossroads • head • crisis • landmark | *esp. written* **watershed**

► at a turning point/crossroads
► a turning point/crossroads/crisis/ watershed/landmark **in** sth
► **reach** a turning point/crossroads/ crisis/watershed

turn sth off phrasal verb

■ *Turn the lights off when you leave.*

switch sth off • turn sth out • unplug | *esp. written* **disconnect** | *esp. written or tech.* **shut sth off**

■ OPP **turn sth on**
► turn off/switch off/unplug/ disconnect the **machine/phone**
► turn off/switch off/disconnect/ shut off the **power/electricity supply**
► turn off/disconnect/shut off the **gas/water**
► turn off/switch off the **motor/ ignition/wipers/alarm/torch/ computer**

turn sth on phrasal verb

■ *She turned her computer on.*

switch sth on • start • start sth up • plug sth in | *esp. spoken* **put sth on**

■ OPP **turn sth off**
► turn on/switch on/start/start up/ plug in a **machine**
► turn on/switch on/start/start up/ plug in a **computer**
► turn on/switch on/put on/plug in the **light/television/radio/heater**
► turn on/switch on/put on the **gas/heating/oven/headlights/ wipers**

turn out phrasal verb

■ *It turned out that she was a friend of my sister.*

emerge • come out • come to light | *fml* **transpire**

► **It** (now) turns out/emerges/ transpires **that...**
► turn out/emerge/come out/come to light/transpire **later**

| 481 | **twist** |

turn (sth) over phrasal verb

■ *She turned over and went to sleep.*
■ *The car skidded and turned over.*

roll • flip • overturn • tip (sth) over • capsize

► turn/roll/flip/tip sth **over**
► a **car** turns over/flips over/ overturns
► a **boat** turns over/flips over/ overturns/capsizes

turn round, turn around phrasal verb

■ *She turned round to face me.*

turn • spin • swing • twist • pivot | *written* **whirl • wheel • swivel**

► turn round/turn/spin/swing/ twist/whirl around/wheel/swivel **to face** sb/sth
► turn round/turn/spin/swing/ whirl/wheel **suddenly**
► turn round/turn/twist **slowly**

turn up phrasal verb (*esp. spoken*)

■ *She was surprised when they turned up on her doorstep.*

appear • arrive • land | *infml* **show up • roll in**

► turn up/appear/arrive/land/show up **at/in/on** a place
► turn up/appear/arrive/land/show up/show **here/there**
► **be the first/last to** to turn up/ appear/arrive/land/show up/roll in
► turn up/appear/arrive **late**

twist noun [C]

■ *the twists and turns of a mountain road*

turn • bend • corner • zigzag | *BrE* **hairpin bend** | *AmE* **hairpin curve/ turn**

► a **sharp** twist/turn/bend/corner

twist verb

1 [T, I] ■ *He twisted my arm behind my back.* ■ *Twist the wire to form a circle.*

bend • deform • buckle • warp • distort

► be **slightly** twisted/bent/ deformed/buckled/warped/ distorted
► be twisted/bent **out of shape**

2 [I] ■ *The road twists and turns along the coast.*

wind • bend • turn • zigzag • curve | *written* **snake**

► twist/wind/bend/curve/snake **around/round** sth
► twist/wind/zigzag/curve/snake **through/across** sth

▶ the road/path twists/winds/
bends/turns/zigzags/curves/
snakes

twisted adj.

■ The car was mass of twisted metal.

**bent • crooked • gnarled •
deformed**

▶ twisted/gnarled roots/branches
▶ a twisted/crooked smile
▶ get twisted/bent

type noun [C]

■ What type of car do you drive?

**kind • form • variety • style • brand
• category • class • version • nature**
| esp. BrE **sort** | fml **genre**

▶ a type/kind/form/variety/style/
brand/category/class/version/
sort/genre of sth
▶ of a/the... type/kind/form/
variety/style/nature
▶ the same type/kind/form/variety/
style/brand/category/class/
version/nature/sort/genre
▶ a/the/that type/kind/sort of
thing
● TYPE, KIND OR SORT? Kind is the
most frequent word in this group;
sort is used more in BrE. Type is
slightly more formal and used
more in official, scientific or
academic contexts.

typical adj.

1 ■ a typical example of Roman
pottery

**characteristic • representative •
classic** | written **archetypal** | fml
quintessential | often disapprov.
stereotypical

■ OPP atypical
▶ typical/characteristic/
representative of sb/sth
▶ a/an typical/characteristic/
representative/classic/archetypal
example of sth
▶ typical/characteristic/stereotypical
behaviour
● TYPICAL OR CHARACTERISTIC? When
it is used to mean that sb behaves
as you would expect, typical often
shows disapproval;
characteristic usu. shows approval:
It was typical of her to forget. ◆ Such
kindness was characteristic of Mike.

2 ■ Describe your typical working day.

average • normal • ordinary • usual

■ OPP atypical
▶ a/an typical/average/normal/
ordinary working day
▶ pretty/fairly typical/average/
normal/ordinary

Uu

ugly adj.

■ The room was full of heavy, ugly
furniture.

unsightly • grotesque | esp. spoken
hideous | esp. written **unattractive •
plain**

■ OPP beautiful
▶ a/an ugly/grotesque/hideous/
plain face
▶ a/an ugly/unattractive/plain girl/
woman
▶ a/an ugly/unattractive man
▶ look ugly/unsightly/grotesque/
hideous/unattractive

unacceptable adj.

■ Such behaviour is totally
unacceptable.

**intolerable • unreasonable •
unbearable • insufferable** | BrE, infml
out of order | esp. AmE, infml **out of
line**

■ OPP acceptable
▶ unacceptable/intolerable to sb
▶ unacceptable/intolerable/
unreasonable/unbearable that...
▶ unacceptable/intolerable/
unreasonable/unbearable/out of
order to do sth
▶ unacceptable/intolerable/
unreasonable behaviour/
demands/interference/levels

unattractive adj.

■ He was an unattractive character:
selfish and arrogant.

unappealing • unappetizing | esp.
BrE, infml **off-putting**

■ OPP attractive
▶ unattractive/unappealing/off-
putting to sb
▶ an unattractive/unappealing
quality/prospect/character/
personality
▶ distinctly unattractive/
unappealing/unappetizing/off-
putting

unaware adj. [not before noun]

■ She was completely unaware of the
whole affair.

**ignorant • oblivious • in the dark •
blind** | esp. written **unsuspecting •
unwitting**

■ OPP aware
▶ unaware/ignorant/oblivious of sth
▶ oblivious/blind to sth
▶ totally unaware/ignorant/
oblivious/blind/unsuspecting
▶ blissfully unaware/ignorant

uncertain _adj._

1 [not usu. before noun] ■ _I'm still uncertain about what to do next._

unsure • **undecided** • **hesitant** • **doubtful** • **dubious** • **in doubt** | _esp. written_ **ambivalent**

■ OPP **certain, sure**
► uncertain/unsure/undecided/ hesitant/doubtful/dubious/in doubt/ambivalent **about** sth
► uncertain/unsure/undecided/ doubtful/dubious/in doubt **as to** sth
► uncertain/unsure/hesitant/ doubtful/dubious **of** sth
► uncertain/unsure/undecided **what...**

2 ■ _Our future looks uncertain._

unsettled • **variable** | _fml_ **fluid** | _disapprov., esp. journ._ **fickle** | _esp. busin. or politics_ **volatile** • **unstable**

■ OPP **certain**
► the uncertain/fluid/fickle/volatile/ unstable **nature** of sth
► a/an uncertain/fluid/volatile/ unstable **situation**
► a/an uncertain/variable/fluid/ unstable **environment**
► uncertain/unsettled/fickle **weather**

unclear _adj._

■ _Our plans are unclear at the moment._

uncertain • **in doubt** • **undecided** • **in the balance** | _fml_ **unresolved**

■ OPP **clear**
► unclear/uncertain **what/ whether...**
► **remain** unclear/uncertain/in doubt/undecided/in the balance/ unresolved
► **leave** sth unclear/uncertain/in doubt/unresolved

uncomfortable _adj._

■ _He looked uncomfortable when the subject was mentioned._

embarrassed • **awkward** • **self-conscious** • **sheepish**

■ OPP **comfortable**
► uncomfortable/embarrassed/ awkward/self-conscious/sheepish **about** sth
► an uncomfortable/embarrassed/ awkward **silence**
► **feel/look** uncomfortable/ embarrassed/awkward/self-conscious/sheepish
● UNCOMFORTABLE, AWKWARD OR EMBARRASSED? **Embarrassed** is used esp. to describe how sb feels; **uncomfortable** can describe a situation; **awkward** often describes sb's personality or usual behaviour.

unconscious _adj._

■ _the depths of the unconscious mind_ ■ _The brochure is full of unconscious humour._

subconscious • **unintended** • **unintentional** • **unplanned**

■ OPP **conscious, deliberate**
► an unconscious/unintended/ unplanned **action**
► **at** an unconscious/a subconscious **level**
► an unconscious/a subconscious **desire/feeling/fear/memory**
● UNCONSCIOUS OR SUBCONSCIOUS? Feelings may be **unconscious** or **subconscious**, but actions can only be **unconscious**. In pyschology **unconscious** is the more technical term.

uncontrollable _adj._

■ _I had an uncontrollable urge to laugh._

overwhelming • **irresistible** • **unmanageable** | _fml_ **intractable**

► an uncontrollable/overwhelming/ irresistible **urge/impulse**
► an overwhelming/irresistible **force/influence/pressure/ temptation/desire**

undermine _verb_ [T]

■ _The director saw this move as an attempt to undermine his authority._

weaken • **sap** • **wear sb/sth down** • **erode**

■ OPP **strengthen**
► undermine/weaken/sap/erode sb's **confidence/morale**
► undermine/weaken/erode sb's **position**
► weaken/wear down sb's **resistance**

understand _verb_

1 [T, I] (not used in the progressive tenses) ■ _I just don't understand!_

grasp • **follow** • **take sth in** | _esp. spoken_ **see** | _infml, esp. spoken_ **get** • **catch on** | _fml_ **comprehend**

■ OPP **misunderstand**
► understand/grasp/follow/take in/ see/get/catch on to/comprehend **what/why/how...**
► understand/grasp/take in/see/ comprehend **that...**
► **can/can't** understand/grasp/ follow/take in/see/comprehend sth
► **be easy/difficult/hard** to understand/grasp/take in/see/ comprehend sth

2 [T, I] ■ _Nobody understands me._

relate to sb/sth • **identify with sb/ sth** • **empathize**

understanding

- OPP **misunderstand**
- ▶ can/could/be able to/be unable to understand/relate to/identify with/empathize with sb/sth

understanding noun

1 [U, sing.] ■ *She shows no understanding of the problems.*

grasp • sense • conception • appreciation | *esp. written* comprehension | *often approv.* insight • depth

- OPP **misunderstanding**
- ▶ sb's understanding/grasp/sense/ conception/appreciation/ comprehension **of** sth
- ▶ **beyond** sb's understanding/ grasp/conception/comprehension
- ▶ **have** (a/an) understanding/ grasp/sense/conception/ appreciation/comprehension/ insight/depth
- ▶ a **lack** of understanding/ appreciation/comprehension/ insight/depth

2 [U, sing.] ■ *Try to show a little more understanding.*

sympathy • empathy • compassion • pity • concern • humanity

- ▶ do sth **with** understanding/ sympathy/empathy/compassion/ concern/humanity
- ▶ **great** understanding/sympathy/ empathy/compassion/concern/ humanity
- ▶ **show (sb)** understanding/ sympathy/empathy/compassion/ pity/concern

3 [U, C] ■ *My understanding of the situation is…*

interpretation • reading • definition

- ▶ (a) **clear/precise/narrow/broad/ conventional** understanding/ interpretation/definition
- ▶ a **literal** understanding/ interpretation/reading
- ▶ **different** understandings/ interpretations/readings/ definitions
- ● **UNDERSTANDING, INTERPRETATION OR READING?** Understanding is used esp. about understanding how sth works or what problems are involved; interpretation is used esp. about understanding what happened or what sth means; reading is used esp. about understanding a written text: *an understanding of a process/a relationship/an issue • interpretation of data/results/events/the law/ dreams • a different reading of the text/story*

understate verb [T] (*esp. written*)

■ *The figures understate the real unemployment rate.*

make light of sth • minimize | *esp. journ.* play sth down | *usu. disapprov.* trivialize

- OPP **overstate, exaggerate**
- ▶ understate/minimize/play down the **importance/extent** of sth
- ▶ mkae light of/play down a **problem**
- ▶ play down/trivialize an **issue**

undo verb [T]

■ *He undid his coat and took it off.*

open • untie • unfasten • unbutton • unzip • unwrap

- OPP **do sth up**
- ▶ undo/open/untie/unwrap a **parcel/package**
- ▶ undo/untie a **knot/rope/string/ ribbon/lace/shoelace**
- ▶ undo/unfasten/unbutton/unzip a **jacket/coat/fly**
- ▶ undo/unfasten a **belt/button/ clip/strap/zip/buckle/catch/seat belt**

undoubted adj. [usu. before noun]

■ *The event was an undoubted success.*

undisputed • unchallenged • uncontested • undeniable • indisputable | *fml* unquestioned • unquestionable

- OPP **doubtful**
- ▶ an undoubted/undisputed/ uncontested/undeniable/ indisputable/unquestionable **fact**
- ▶ undisputed/unchallenged/ uncontested/undeniable/ indisputable/unquestionable **evidence**
- ▶ undisputed/unchallenged/ unquestioned **authority**

unemployed adj.

■ *Almost 3 million are now registered unemployed.*

out of work | *BrE* redundant | *BrE, infml* on the dole | *esp. AmE* on welfare | *journ.* jobless

- OPP **employed, in work**
- ▶ unemployed/jobless **people**
- ▶ unemployed/redundant **workers**
- ▶ **currently/still** unemployed/out of work
- ● **UNEMPLOYED OR OUT OF WORK?** Out of work is used more in everyday conversation and sounds less permanent than unemployed.

unexpected adj.

■ *I had an unexpected visitor this morning.*

surprising • unpredictable • unforeseen • unforeseeable

■ OPP expected, predictable
► unexpected/surprising/unpredictable/unforeseen **events/effects/changes**
► a/an unexpected/surprising/unforeseen **development**
► unexpected/unpredictable/unforeseen **demands/problems**

unfortunate adj.

1 ■ an unfortunate accident ■ He was unfortunate to lose in the final round.

unlucky • out of luck | written ill-fated

■ OPP fortunate
► unfortunate/unlucky **for sb**
► unfortunate/unlucky **in sth**
► unfortunate/unlucky **that...**
► unlucky/unfortunate **for sb in sth/that ...**
► unfortunate/unlucky **(not) to do sth**

2 ■ It was unfortunate that she couldn't speak English.

esp. spoken a pity • a shame • too bad | fml regrettable • sorry | often disapprov. sad

■ OPP fortunate
► unfortunate/a pity/a shame/too bad/regrettable **that...**
► It's a pity/a shame/too bad **about sb/sth.**
► an unfortunate/sorry/sad **sight/state (of affairs)/affair/business/episode/saga/tale/plight**
● UNFORTUNATE OR REGRETTABLE? Sth that is **unfortunate** is usu. the result of bad luck; sth that is **regrettable** is usu. the result of sb's actions: The loss of jobs is highly regrettable.

unfriendly adj.

■ He shot her an unfriendly glance.

cool • cold • chilly • frosty • impersonal • remote • distant | written aloof

■ OPP friendly
► a/an unfriendly/cool/cold/frosty/impersonal/aloof **manner**
► a/an unfriendly/cool/cold/frosty **look**
► a/an unfriendly/cool/cold **voice**

unhappiness noun [U]

■ A marriage break-up can cause a lot of unhappiness.

sadness • grief • regret • heartache • heartbreak • depression | infml the blues | fml sorrow | lit. melancholy

■ OPP happiness
► unhappiness/sadness/grief/regret/heartache/heartbreak/

sorrow/melancholy **at/about/over sth**
► be filled with/full of/overcome with unhappiness/sadness/grief/regret/heartache/heartbreak/sorrow/melancholy
► express/show/hide your unhappiness/sadness/grief/regret/sorrow

unhappy adj.

1 ■ She felt alone and unhappy.

sad • miserable • depressed • gloomy • glum • heartbroken | infml down | esp. written mournful • dejected • despondent | lit. melancholy

■ OPP happy
► unhappy/sad/miserable/depressed/gloomy/glum/heartbroken/despondent **about sth**
► unhappy/sad/miserable/depressed/heartbroken/despondent **when/that...**
► feel unhappy/sad/miserable/depressed/gloomy/down/dejected/despondent
► look unhappy/sad/miserable/mournful/depressed/gloomy/glum
● UNHAPPY OR SAD? You usu. feel **unhappy** about sth that has happened to you; you feel **sad** about sth that has happened to sb else. A period of your life can be **unhappy**; sth that you see or hear can be **sad**: an unhappy marriage • sad news

2 ■ We were unhappy with our accommodation.

dissatisfied • discontented • disappointed • frustrated • disgruntled | fml displeased • aggrieved

■ OPP happy
► unhappy/dissatisfied/discontented/disappointed/frustrated/disgruntled/displeased **with sth**
► unhappy/disappointed/frustrated/disgruntled/displeased/aggrieved **at sth**
► feel unhappy/dissatisfied/disappointed/frustrated/disgruntled/aggrieved

unhealthy adj.

■ Too many teenagers adopt an unhealthy lifestyle.

bad • damaging • unhygienic | fml harmful | esp. BrE, fml insanitary | AmE, fml unsanitary

■ OPP healthy
► an unhealthy/a bad **diet**

unimportant

▶ unhealthy/unhygienic/insanitary **conditions**

● **UNHEALTHY OR BAD?** Bad is used esp. in the collocations *bad for you/ your health, etc.* and *bad diet.* **Unhealthy** has a wider range of collocations, but is slightly more formal.

unimportant adj. (esp. written)

■ *Don't worry about unimportant details.*

minor | *esp. written* **insignificant** | *often disapprov.* **petty • trivial** | *fml, esp. busin.* **peripheral**

■ OPP **important**

▶ unimportant/minor/petty/trivial/ peripheral **things**
▶ unimportant/minor/insignificant/ trivial **details**
▶ a/an unimportant/insignificant/ trivial **fact**

union noun [C]

■ *The union threatened strike action.*

association • alliance • league • guild • federation • coalition • syndicate • group • club • society • organization

▶ a **national** union/association/ league/federation/coalition/ group/club/society/organization
▶ a **trade** union/association/guild/ federation
▶ **belong** to a/an union/ association/alliance/guild/ federation/group/club/society/ organization

unique adj.

1 ■ *The pattern of stripes is unique to each individual animal.*

peculiar • special • distinctive • particular • idiosyncratic | *usu. approv.* **individual**

▶ sth unique/special/distinctive/ individual **about** sth
▶ sb's **own** unique/peculiar/special/ distinctive/particular/individual…
▶ the unique/peculiar/special/ distinctive/particular/ idiosyncratic/individual **nature** of sth

● **UNIQUE OR PECULIAR?** Unique is often a more positive word than **peculiar**, suggesting that sth is special or rare. **Peculiar** is used more to talk about places; **unique** is used more about individuals.

2 ■ *a unique opportunity to study in Vienna*

extraordinary • remarkable • exceptional • outstanding | *infml* **incredible**

▶ a/an unique/extraordinary/

remarkable/exceptional/ outstanding/incredible **achievement**
▶ a/an unique/extraordinary/ exceptional/incredible **opportunity**
▶ a/an unique/extraordinary/ remarkable/exceptional/ outstanding/incredible **talent/ skill**

unit noun

1 [C] ■ *The basic unit of society is the family.*

component • module • section • part • piece • element

▶ a **basic** unit/component/module/ part/element
▶ **core** unit/component/module/ element
▶ **major/important/fundamental** unit/component/element

2 [C] ■ *She was taken to the intensive care unit.*

department • division • arm • wing

▶ a **research** unit/department/ division/arm
▶ a **political** unit/department/arm/ wing
▶ a **military** unit/arm/wing

unite verb [I, T]

■ *The two countries united in 1887.*
■ *His aim was to unite Italy.*

unify • join • combine • integrate • merge | *fml or tech.* **fuse** | *busin. or tech.* **consolidate**

■ OPP **divide, separate**
▶ unite/unify/join/combine/ integrate/merge/fuse/consolidate (sth) **with** sth
▶ unite/join/combine/merge/fuse **to form** sth
▶ unite/unify a/an **country/area**
● **UNITE OR UNIFY?** Use either word to talk about a group or area in which individuals are brought together. Use **unite** but not **unify** to talk about the individuals who are brought together. Use **unify** but not **unite** to talk about joining together the parts of a system: *to unite/unify the country/the party • to unite two political parties/the two Germanies • to unify the tax/ transport system*

universe noun [C, usu. sing.]

■ *a theory of how the universe began*

the cosmos • space • outer space

▶ **through/in** the universe/the cosmos/space/outer space
▶ the **entire** universe/cosmos

university noun [C, U]

■ *I'm a graduate of Exeter University.*

► **at/in** university/college/school
► **go to/attend/finish/leave/quit**
university/college/school
► **study at/graduate from** a/an
university/college
● **UNIVERSITY OR COLLEGE? College** is
used in BrE and AmE to describe a
place where you do further study
after leaving school. In BrE the
usual word for an institution where
you study for a degree is
university; in AmE it is **college**:
(BrE) He's at university. • (AmE) He's
in college.
Some British universities, such as
Oxford and Cambridge, are
divided into **colleges**: Emmanuel
College, Cambridge

unjustified adj. (sometimes
disapprov.)
■ Her fear of failure is unjustified.

**unnecessary + gratuitous +
undeserved + unfounded +
groundless + irrational +
unjustifiable** | fml **unwarranted +
untenable**

■ OPP **justified**
► an unjustified/unnecessary/
unjustifiable/unwarranted
interference/intrusion/risk
► unjustified/gratuitous/
undeserved/unwarranted **criticism**
► a/an unjustified/unnecessary/
gratuitous **comment**
► sb's **fears** are unjustified/
unnecessary/unfounded/
groundless/irrational/
unwarranted

unkind adj.
■ It would be unkind to go without her.

**mean + hurtful + unpleasant +
obnoxious** | fml **objectionable** | esp.
spoken **nasty**

■ OPP **kind**
► be unkind/mean/hurtful/
unpleasant/obnoxious/
objectionable/nasty to sb
► be unkind/mean/nasty **of** sb (**to
do sth**)
► a/an unkind/mean/hurtful/nasty
thing to say/do

unknown adj.
■ a species previously unknown to
science

unfamiliar + strange

■ OPP **known**
► unknown/unfamiliar/strange **to** sb
► a/an unknown/unfamiliar/strange
place

unlike prep., adj. [not before noun]
■ Music is quite unlike any other art
form.

---

different + contrasting + unequal |
fml **dissimilar + disparate**

■ OPP **like**
► **look** unlike sth/different/dissimilar
► **very** unlike/different/dissimilar/
unequal/dissimilar
► **not altogether/not entirely**
unlike/different/dissimilar

unlikely adj.

1 ■ It's unlikely that she'll arrive before
seven.

esp. written **doubtful + improbable**

■ OPP **likely**
► be unlikely/doubtful/improbable
that...
► **seem/look/make** sth unlikely/
doubtful/improbable

2 [only before noun] ■ It was a most
unlikely story.

**far-fetched + implausible +
unconvincing + weak** | written
improbable

■ OPP **likely, believable**
► a/an unlikely/far-fetched/
implausible/unconvincing
explanation
► a/an unlikely/far-fetched/
unconvincing/improbable **story**
► an unlikely/improbable **situation**

unlucky adj.
■ She was unlucky not to win.

unfortunate + out of luck | written
ill-fated

■ OPP **lucky**
► unlucky/unfortunate **for** sb
► unfortunate/unlucky **in** sth
► unfortunate/unlucky **that...**
► unfortunate/unlucky **(not) to do**
sth

unnecessary adj.
■ We must avoid unnecessary expense.

avoidable + preventable | esp.
written **needless + redundant** | esp.
busin. **expendable**

■ OPP **necessary**
► a/an unnecessary/avoidable/
preventable/needless **death**
► unnecessary/avoidable/needless
risk/suffering/distress
► an unnecessary/avoidable **cost/
delay**

unofficial adj.
■ According to unofficial estimates
about 200 died.

unlicensed + off the record | fml
unauthorized

■ OPP **official**
● **UNOFFICIAL OR UNAUTHORIZED?** An
unofficial action or statement has

not yet been approved by sb in
authority, although it may be
approved later. An **unauthorized**
action may already have been
refused permission.

unpleasant adj.

1 ■ There was an unpleasant
atmosphere in the room.

uncomfortable ◆ bad ◆ nasty ◆ grim
| infml **ghastly** | esp. spoken **horrible** |
written **wretched**

■ OPP **pleasant**
▶ a/an unpleasant/uncomfortable/
bad/nasty/grim/ghastly/horrible
situation
▶ a/an unpleasant/uncomfortable/
bad/nasty/ghastly/horrible
experience/feeling
▶ a/an unpleasant/uncomfortable/
nasty/grim/ghastly/wretched/
horrible **thought**
▶ a/an unpleasant/bad/nasty/
horrible **taste/smell**

2 ■ She said some very unpleasant
things about him.

unkind ◆ hurtful ◆ obnoxious | fml
objectionable | esp. spoken **nasty ◆
mean**

■ OPP **pleasant**
▶ unpleasant/unkind/hurtful/
obnoxious/objectionable/nasty/
mean **to sb**
▶ a/an unpleasant/obnoxious/nasty
little man

unrealistic adj.

■ It's unrealistic to expect so much.

impractical ◆ unworkable

■ OPP **realistic**
▶ It is unrealistic/impractical **to do
sth.**
▶ an unrealistic/impractical/
unworkable **plan**
▶ **prove/become/make sth**
unrealistic/impractical/
unworkable

unreasonable adj.

■ The job made unreasonable
demands on her free time.

**unacceptable ◆ unfair ◆ excessive ◆
intolerable ◆ unbearable** | infml,
spoken **too much**

■ OPP **reasonable**
▶ unreasonable/unacceptable/
unfair/intolerable/unbearable
that...
▶ unreasonable/unacceptable/
unfair/intolerable/unbearable/too
much **to do sth**
▶ unreasonable/unacceptable/
excessive/intolerable **demands/
interference/levels**

▶ unreasonable/unacceptable/
intolerable **behaviour**

unsuccessful adj.

■ Unsuccessful applicants will be
informed by post.

failed ◆ losing

■ OPP **successful**
▶ a/an unsuccessful/failed/losing
bid
▶ an unsuccessful/a failed **attempt/
experiment/policy/venture/
coup/candidate/company**
▶ an unsuccessful/a losing **team/
battle**

unsure adj. [not before noun]

■ He was unsure of what to do next.

**uncertain ◆ undecided ◆ hesitant ◆
doubtful ◆ dubious ◆ in doubt** | esp.
written **ambivalent**

■ OPP **sure**
▶ unsure/uncertain/undecided/
hesitant/doubtful/dubious/in
doubt/ambivalent **about** sth
▶ unsure/uncertain/undecided/
doubtful/dubious/in doubt **as to**
sth
▶ unsure/uncertain/hesitant/
doubtful/dubious **of** sth
● **UNSURE OR UNCERTAIN?** Unsure is
more frequent; uncertain is slightly
more formal. Use **uncertain** to talk
about facts or situations that are
not definite or decided.

untidy adj. (esp. BrE, sometimes
disapprov.)

■ Try not to make the place untidy.

**messy ◆ cluttered ◆ out of place ◆
jumbled** | infml **all over the place** |
fml **disordered**

■ OPP **tidy**
▶ a/an untidy/messy/cluttered
house
▶ an untidy/a cluttered **room/desk**
▶ a/an untidy/messy/jumbled
heap/pile of sth
● **UNTIDY OR MESSY?** Untidy is the
most frequent word in this
meaning in BrE; messy is the most
frequent in AmE.

unusual adj.

■ She has a very unusual hobby.

**atypical ◆ unorthodox ◆ out of the
ordinary ◆ eccentric ◆ strange ◆ odd
◆ curious** | often approv.
unconventional | esp. spoken
different ◆ funny | infml **offbeat** | BrE
or fml **peculiar**

■ OPP **usual, common**
▶ unusual/atypical/unorthodox/
eccentric/strange/odd/curious/
unconventional/peculiar
behaviour
▶ unusual/unorthodox/eccentric/
strange/odd/curious/

unconventional/funny/peculiar ways

▶ unusual/unorthodox/eccentric/
strange/odd/unconventional/
funny/peculiar **ideas**
▶ an unusual/unorthodox/
unconventional **approach**

unwanted adj.

■ It is very sad when children feel unwanted.

unwelcome • unsolicited • uninvited • undesirable • unpopular • unloved

■ OPP wanted
▶ an unwanted/unwelcome/
uninvited **change/effect**
▶ unwanted/unwelcome/uninvited
guest/visitor
▶ unwanted/unsolicited **calls/
advice/goods/material**
● UNWANTED OR UNWELCOME? Guests, visitors, intruders, attention, publicity, changes or effects can be either unwanted or unwelcome. Children, babies, pregnancies, goods or advice can be unwanted. News, facts or the truth can be unwelcome.

unwilling adj.

■ She was unable, or unwilling, to help.

reluctant • grudging

■ OPP willing
▶ unwilling/reluctant **to do sth**
▶ unwilling/reluctant/grudging
acceptance
▶ an unwilling/a reluctant
participant

upright adj.

■ Keep the bottle upright.

vertical • on end • straight | fml erect

■ OPP horizontal
▶ an upright/a vertical **position**
▶ sth **stands** upright/on end
▶ sb **stands** upright/up straight/
erect
▶ **sit** upright/straight/erect
▶ **hold** sth upright/vertical/straight/
erect

upset verb [T]

■ Try not to let him upset you.

hurt • distress • break sb's heart | fml sadden • pain | written sting | lit. wound

■ OPP comfort
▶ It upsets/hurts/distresses/
saddens/pains me **to see/think/
know...**
▶ It **breaks my heart to** see/think/
know...
▶ It upset/hurt/distressed/
saddened/pained me **that...**
▶ upset/distress **yourself**

▶ **not want/not mean** to upset/
hurt/distress/wound sb
● UPSET OR HURT? Hurt is used esp. to talk about sb you like or trust doing sth to make you unhappy. Being **upset** can be sth that sb does partly willingly:
✔ Don't upset yourself about it.
✗ ~~Don't hurt yourself about it.~~
✔ Try not to let him upset you. ✗ ~~Try not to let him hurt you.~~

upset adj. [not before noun]

■ The incident left him angry and upset.

hurt • distressed • distraught • dismayed • sorry

▶ upset/hurt/distressed/dismayed
by sth
▶ upset/hurt/distressed/distraught/
dismayed/sorry **that...**
▶ **feel** upset/hurt/distressed/
dismayed/sorry

upsetting adj.

■ He finds the whole experience too upsetting to talk about.

painful • distressing • traumatic • harrowing

▶ be upsetting/painful/distressing/
traumatic **for sb**
▶ be upsetting/painful/distressing **to
do sth**
▶ be upsetting/distressing **that...**
▶ a/an upsetting/painful/
distressing/traumatic/harrowing
experience

urge noun

■ I felt a sudden urge to hit him.

impulse • need • inclination • temptation | esp. written compulsion • desire

▶ a/an urge/impulse/need/
inclination/temptation/
compulsion/desire **to do sth**
▶ **have/feel** a/an urge/impulse/
need/inclination/temptation/
compulsion/desire
▶ **resist/fight** a/an urge/impulse/
temptation/desire

urge adj.

1 [T] ■ He urged the government to take action.

encourage • spur • egg sb on | fml exhort

▶ urge/encourage/spur/egg on/
exhort sb **to do sth**
▶ urge/encourage/exhort sb **not to
do sth**
▶ **constantly/repeatedly** urge/
encourage/exhort sb to do sth

2 [T] ■ The UN is urging caution.

advise • recommend | *fml* advocate

▶ urge/advise/recommend/advocate **that…**
▶ urge/advise/recommend/advocate **sb to do sth**
▶ urge/advise/recommend/advocate **caution**
▶ urge/advise/advocate **restraint**

urgent *adj.*

■ The situation calls for urgent action.

burning | *esp. written* pressing • compelling

▶ a/an urgent/burning/pressing/compelling **desire/need**
▶ a/an urgent/burning/pressing **issue/question**
▶ an urgent/a pressing **problem/matter/task**

use *noun*

1 [U, sing.] ■ The software is designed for use in schools.

application • exercise • practice

▶ effective/proper/continued/normal use/application/exercise/practice
▶ sth has a use/an application
▶ limit/regulate/justify the use/exercise/practice of sth

2 [C, U] ■ The chemical has a wide range of industrial uses.

function • purpose

▶ sth's **main/primary** use/function/purpose
▶ a **useful** function/purpose
▶ **have** a use/function/purpose

use *verb*

1 [T] ■ Don't ask me—just use your common sense!

make use of sb/sth • apply • resort to sth • fall back on sb/sth • exert | *fml* employ • exercise • draw on/upon sth • utilize

▶ use/make use of/resort to/fall back on/employ/draw on/utilize sth **to do sth**
▶ use/make use of/apply/fall back on/employ/exercise/draw on/utilize a **skill**
▶ use/make use of/apply/resort to/fall back on/employ/utilize a **method/technique**

2 [T] ■ The heater uses a lot of electricity.

use sth up • get through sth • absorb • exhaust • drain | *fml* consume • expend • deplete

▶ use/use up/absorb/exhaust/drain/consume/expend/deplete **resources**

▶ use/use up/exhaust/deplete a **supply/supplies** of sth
▶ use/use up/absorb/exhaust/drain/consume/expend **energy**

used to (doing) sth *adj.*

■ I'm not used to eating so late.

familiar with sth | *fml* accustomed to sth

■ OPP unused to sth
▶ get/grow used/accustomed to sth

useful *adj.*

■ a useful book/gadget

convenient • practical • functional • usable | *infml* handy • great for sth | *fml* of use

■ OPP useless
▶ useful/of use **to sb**
▶ be useful/convenient/handy/great **for doing sth**
▶ useful/practical/handy **tips/hints**
▶ **come in** useful/handy

useless *adj.*

■ It was useless to protest.

pointless • futile • hopeless • fruitless • unusable | *written* (in) vain

■ OPP useful, valuable
▶ be useless/pointless/futile/hopeless/fruitless/vain **to do sth**
▶ be useless/pointless/futile **doing sth**
▶ a useless/pointless/futile/fruitless **exercise**

usual *adj.*

■ He made all the usual excuses.

standard • routine • regular • habitual • traditional • general

■ OPP unusual
▶ be usual/routine/traditional **to do sth**
▶ the usual/standard/routine/regular/traditional/general **procedure/practice**
▶ sb's usual/habitual/general **behaviour**

usually *adv.*

■ The journey usually takes an hour.

normally • generally • as a rule • mostly • commonly • most of the time • more often than not • as often as not • often | *esp. written* in general

■ OPP unusually, exceptionally
▶ usually/generally/mostly/commonly/often **known as…**
▶ usually/normally/generally/mostly/commonly/often **called/found…**
▶ usually/normally/generally/mostly/commonly/often **used**
● **USUALLY OR NORMALLY?** Usually gives information about what

happens in most cases; **normally** is often used in the context of a particular case: *It's normally much warmer than this in July* (= but this July is unusually cold). • *He normally stayed in luxury hotels* (= but this time he could not afford to do so).

V v

vacation noun

1 [U, C] (*AmE*) ■ *The job includes two weeks' paid vacation.*

break • leave • time off • day off • recess • sabbatical | *BrE* holiday

► **during** the vacation/break/recess/ sabbatical/holidays
► be **on** vacation/leave/holiday
► **spend** your vacation/leave/time off/day off/sabbatical/holiday doing sth

2 [C] (*AmE*) ■ *We're going on a ski vacation.*

break • trip | *BrE* holiday | *infml* getaway

► a **summer/winter** vacation/ break/trip/holiday/getaway
► a vacation/holiday **destination/ home/resort/spot**
► **take** a vacation/break/trip/ holiday

vague adj.

■ *Her plans for next year are a little vague.*

imprecise • indistinct • inexact • rough | *esp. written* approximate • indeterminate | *disapprov.* ill-defined

■ OPP **clear, precise**

► vague/imprecise **about** sth
► a/an vague/rough/approximate **idea**
► a/an vague/imprecise/ill-defined **term**

valley noun [C]

■ *a small town set in a valley*

gorge • canyon • ravine • glen

■ OPP **hill**

► a **deep/steep/narrow** a valley/ gorge/canyon/ravine

valuable adj.

1 ■ *Spinach is a valuable source of iron.*

helpful • good • worthwhile • constructive • positive • fruitful • advantageous | *fml* beneficial

■ OPP **useless**

► valuable/helpful/good/ advantageous/beneficial **for** sb/ sth
► valuable/helpful/good/ worthwhile/fruitful/ advantageous/beneficial **to do sth**
► a valuable/helpful/worthwhile/ constructive/positive/beneficial **contribution**
► a valuable/good/worthwhile/ constructive/positive/beneficial **experience**

2 ■ *Thieves stole valuable jewellery.*

precious • priceless • irreplaceable

■ OPP **worthless**

► valuable/precious/priceless/ irreplaceable **to** sb
► valuable/precious/priceless/ irreplaceable **possessions**
► valuable/precious/priceless **antiques/jewels/jewellery/gems**

valuation noun [C, C]

■ *Experts set a high valuation on the painting.*

estimate | *BrE* costing | *fml* quotation | *infml, esp. spoken* quote

► a **high/low** valuation/estimate/ quotation/quote
► a **stock/market/share** valuation/ quotation/quote
► **give/provide/get/obtain/accept** a/an valuation/estimate/ quotation/quote

value noun

1 [U, C] ■ *Property values are rising fast.*

worth • price • cost • rate

► a **high** value/price/cost/rate
► the **real/true/market/net** value/ worth/price/cost
► **put/set** a value/price **on** sth
● VALUE, PRICE OR COST? The **price** is what sb asks you to pay for an item or service:
  ✓*to ask/charge a high price* ✗ *to ask/charge a high cost/value*
  Obtaining sth may have a **cost**; the **value** of sth is how much money people would pay for it:
  ✓*house prices* • *the cost of moving house* • *The house now has a market value of twice what we paid for it.*

2 [U] (*esp. BrE*) ■ *Charter flights are good value for money.*

bargain • good buy

► be **good value/a bargain/a good buy at** a particular price

3 [U] ■ *The value of regular exercise is well known.*

worth • merit • excellence • distinction • quality • meaning

▶ sb/sth **of value/worth/merit/
excellence/distinction/quality**
▶ **value/merit/excellence/
distinction** in sth
▶ **have value/worth/merit/
distinction/quality/meaning**

4 values [pl.] ■ *religious/moral/
political/social/cultural* **values**

**principle • ethic • standards • ideal •
doctrine • philosophy • code •
belief • teaching • morality** |
sometimes disapprov. **ideology** | *fml*
ethos

▶ **have (a/an) values/principles/
ethics/standards/ideals/doctrine/
philosophy/code/beliefs/
ideology/ethos**
▶ **subscribe to (a/an) values/
principles/ethic/standards/
ideals/doctrine/philosophy/
teaching/ideology**
▶ **go/be against** sb's **values/
principles/doctrine/philosophy/
code/beliefs/teaching/ethos**

value verb

1 [T] (not used in the progressive
tenses) ■ *She's a valued member of
staff.*

appreciate • prize • treasure | *fml*
cherish • esteem

▶ **value/prize** sb/sth **as/for** sth
▶ **value/prize/treasure** sb's
friendship
▶ **value/prize/treasure** sb/sth
highly
● **VALUE OR APPRECIATE?** Use **value**
for things that are important to
you, for example your *friends*,
health or *freedom*. If you **appreciate**
sb/sth, you recognize its value,
even if it is not important to you
personally.

2 [T, usu. passive] ■ *The property is
valued at over $2 million.*

assess • cost • price • put a price on
sth

▶ **be valued/assessed/costed/priced
at** *$500*
▶ **be valued/assessed/costed/priced
between** *£15* and *£35*

vandalize (*BrE* also **-ise**) verb
[T, usu. passive]

■ *The station had been vandalized
overnight.*

wreck • sabotage • deface | *infml*
trash • smash up

▶ **vandalize/wreck/sabotage/trash/
smash up equipment**
▶ **vandalize/wreck/trash/smash up
cars**
▶ **vandalize/wreck/deface a
building**

variable adj.

■ *Polar habitats are harsh and highly
variable.*

uneven • unsettled | *fml* **fluid** | *usu.
disapprov.* **irregular • inconsistent •
uncertain** | *disapprov., esp. busin. or
politics* **volatile • unstable** | *usu.
disapprov., esp. journ.* **fickle** | *usu.
approv., esp. busin.* **dynamic**

■ OPP **constant**

▶ **variable/uneven/inconsistent
quality**
▶ **a/an variable/fluid/uncertain/
unstable/dynamic environment**
▶ **variable/unsettled/uncertain/
fickle weather**

variation noun

1 [C, U] ■ *The dial records slight
variations in pressure.*

**fluctuation • change • swing •
alternation** | *written* **variability** | *esp.
journ.* **shift**

▶ **(a/an) variation/fluctuation/
change/swing/alternation/
variability/shift in** sth
▶ **(a/an) variation/fluctuation/
alternation/shift between** A and B
▶ **show (a/an) variation/
fluctuation/change/swing/
alternation/variability/shift**

2 [C, U] ■ *There may be striking
variations within a species.*

**difference • contrast • distinction •
imbalance** | *fml* **variance •
divergence • disparity**

▶ **a/an variation/difference/
contrast/distinction/imbalance/
variance/divergence/disparity
between** A and B
▶ **a/an variation/difference/
contrast/imbalance/variance/
divergence/disparity in** sth
▶ **show a/an variation/difference/
contrast/distinction/imbalance/
variance/divergence/disparity**
▶ **see/be aware of/look at a**
variation/difference/contrast/
distinction

varied adj. (*often approv.*)
■ *a wide and varied programme of
entertainment*

**diverse • wide-ranging • mixed •
assorted • miscellaneous** | *fml*
heterogeneous • eclectic | *often
disapprov.* **motley**

■ OPP **uniform**

▶ **a/an varied/diverse/mixed/
assorted/miscellaneous/
heterogeneous/motley group**
▶ **a varied/diverse/wide-ranging/
mixed/miscellaneous/
heterogeneous/motley collection**
▶ **racially/ethnically/culturally/
socially varied/diverse/mixed**

variety noun

1 [sing.] ■ *There is a wide variety of dishes on offer.*

range ◆ choice ◆ selection ◆ assortment ◆ array ◆ diversity ◆ mixture ◆ mix

▶ a **wide** variety/range/choice/ selection/assortment/array/ diversity
▶ **offer/provide** a/an variety/ range/choice/selection/ assortment/array/diversity/ mixture/mix (of sth)
▶ **choose from** a/an variety/range/ selection/assortment/array of sth
● **VARIETY OR RANGE? Range** emphasizes the (often large) number of things available; **variety** emphasizes the amount of difference between the types of a particular thing.

2 [C] ■ *a rare variety of orchid*

kind ◆ type ◆ form | *esp. BrE* **sort |** *fml* **genre ◆ nature**

▶ **of a/the…** variety/kind/type/ form/sort/nature
▶ **different** varieties/kinds/types/ forms/sorts/genres
▶ **every/any** variety/kind/type/ form/sort/nature

vary verb

1 [I] ■ *The students' work varies in quality.*

differ ◆ range | *fml* **diverge**

▶ vary/differ/range/diverge **in** size, shape, etc.
▶ vary/differ/range **between** things/A and B
▶ vary/differ **according to** sth

2 [I] ■ *The menu varies with the season.*

change ◆ alter ◆ fluctuate ◆ alternate | *esp. journ.* **shift ◆ swing**

▶ vary/alternate/fluctuate/swing **between** A and B
▶ vary/change/fluctuate **according to** sth
▶ vary/change/alter/fluctuate/ shift/swing **dramatically/sharply**

3 [T] ■ *The instructor varies the routine each week.*

change ◆ alter ◆ adapt

▶ vary/change/alter the **emphasis**
▶ vary/change/adapt your **routine**

vast adj.

■ *To the south lay a vast area of wilderness.*

huge ◆ enormous ◆ massive ◆ great ◆ immense ◆ giant ◆ gigantic ◆ tremendous ◆ monumental ◆ colossal ◆ considerable ◆ extensive

■ **OPP tiny, minute**

▶ a/an vast/huge/enormous/ massive/great/tremendous/ colossal/considerable **amount**
▶ a/an vast/huge/enormous/ massive/great/considerable/ extensive **area**
▶ **on a/an** vast/huge/enormous/ massive/great/colossal/ monumental **scale**

venture noun [C]

■ *a disastrous business venture*

enterprise ◆ project ◆ operation ◆ undertaking ◆ exercise ◆ activity

▶ a **major/successful/joint** venture/ enterprise/project/operation/ undertaking/exercise/activity
▶ **set up/run/support** a/an venture/enterprise/project/ operation/activity
▶ **be involved in** a/an venture/ enterprise/project/operation/ exercise/activity

version noun

1 [C] ■ *the latest version of the Mini*

form ◆ brand ◆ variety ◆ style ◆ type ◆ kind | *esp. BrE* **sort |** *fml* **genre**

▶ a version/form/brand/variety/ style/type/kind/sort/genre **of** sth
▶ **another** version/form/brand/ variety/style/type/kind/sort
▶ a **particular** version/form/brand/ variety/style/type/kind/sort/ genre

2 [C] ■ *She gave us her version of what had happened.*

account ◆ report ◆ story

▶ a/an version/account/report/ story **is based on** sth
▶ a **true/false/conflicting** version/ account/report/story
▶ **give** your version/an account/a report

vertical adj.

■ *The cliff was almost vertical.*

upright ◆ straight ◆ on end | *fml* **erect**

■ **OPP horizontal**

▶ a vertical/an upright **position**
▶ **hold** sth vertical/upright/straight/ erect

very adj. [only before noun]

■ *Those were her very words.*

actual ◆ exact ◆ precise

▶ the very/actual/exact/precise **moment**
▶ sb's very/actual/exact **words**
▶ the very/exact **same** sth

very adv.

■ This room is very small/hot/useful.

extremely + quite + highly + well +
truly + desperately | fml most | esp.
spoken really + so | BrE, taboo, spoken
bloody

▶ very/extremely/quite/highly/
really/so **successful/intelligent/
competitive/critical/sensitive**
▶ very/extremely/quite/highly/
really/so **ill/sick/
tired/poor/lonely/hard/close**
▶ very/extremely/quite/really/so
bloody **good/hot/well**
● VERY, SO OR REALLY? **Very** is the
most frequent and most useful of
these words. **Really** and **so** are
more informal and can be
stronger. **Really** and **so** can be
used with both weak and strong
adjectives; **very** is not used with
strong adjectives:
✓so/really/very good (= weak) • so/
really wonderful (= strong) ✗ very
wonderful

vicious adj.

1 ■ He was attacked by vicious thugs.

brutal + savage + barbaric +
inhuman + cruel + sadistic | esp.
written merciless

▶ vicious/brutal/savage/barbaric/
inhuman/cruel/sadistic
treatment/acts
▶ a vicious/brutal/savage/merciless
attack
▶ a vicious/brutal/savage/barbaric
murder

2 ■ He was vicious in his criticism.

malicious + vindictive + spiteful |
infml bitchy

▶ a vicious/malicious/vindictive/
spiteful **attack**
▶ a vicious/malicious/spiteful/bitchy
remark
▶ vicious/malicious **gossip/rumours**

victim noun

1 [C] ■ murder/rape/accident/
earthquake/famine victims

casualty + fatality

▶ a victim/casualty/fatality **of** sth
▶ **accident** victims/casualties
▶ a **war** victim/casualty

2 [C] ■ a new programme to assist
stroke victims

sufferer + patient + case

▶ a **long-term** victim/sufferer/
patient
▶ a/an **cancer/AIDS** victim/sufferer/
patient/case
▶ **treat** a victim/sufferer/patient/
case

● VICTIM OR SUFFERER? In many cases
you can use either word: cancer/
AIDS/leukemia victims/sufferers
Sufferer is often used with long-
term conditions: asthma/arthritis/
dementia sufferers

3 [C] ■ They were victims of a cruel
hoax.

scapegoat | fml dupe | esp. AmE,
infml fall guy | esp. AmE, infml,
disapprov. sucker + patsy

▶ a **poor** victim/scapegoat/dupe/
sucker
▶ **make** sb a victim/scapegoat/fall
guy/patsy

victory noun [C, U]

■ We celebrated a 3–2 victory over
Wales.

win + landslide | BrE, infml result

■ OPP defeat
▶ a victory/win/landslide/result **for**
sb
▶ a **stunning/surprise** victory/win/
result
▶ **clinch/secure/score/gain/earn** a
victory/win
▶ **win** a victory/by a landslide

video noun [U, C]

■ The school made a short promotional
video.

DVD | esp. BrE film | esp. AmE movie

▶ **in** a video/film/movie
▶ **on** video/DVD
▶ **see/watch** a video/film/movie/
DVD
▶ **produce/direct** a video/film/
movie

view noun

1 [C] ■ The two leaders have widely
differing views.

opinion + point of view + belief +
idea + feeling + judgement/
judgment + point + conviction | fml
sentiment

▶ sb's view/opinion/beliefs/ideas/
feelings/judgement/point/
conviction/sentiments **about** sb/
sth
▶ sb's view/opinion/point of view/
ideas/feelings **on** sb/sth
▶ **express** your view/opinion/point
of view/beliefs/ideas/feelings/
conviction/sentiments

2 [C] ■ I have a pretty optimistic view
of life.

attitude + perspective + outlook +
point of view + stance + position

▶ a/an/sb's view/attitude/
perspective/outlook/stance/
position **on** sth
▶ **take** a/an view/attitude/
perspective/point of view/stance/
position

► change your view/attitude/perspective/outlook/point of view/stance/position

3 [U, sing.] (*esp. written*) ■ The sun disappeared from view.

sight • vision

► in/out of view/sight
► in/within view/sight of sth
► come into/disappear from view/sight/sb's vision
● VIEW, SIGHT OR VISION? Use **view** to say how well you can see:
✓I had a good view of the stage. ✗I had a good sight/vision of the stage.
Vision must always be used with a possessive pronoun: *my/his/her, etc. (field) of vision*

4 [C] ■ The hotel has a spectacular sea view.

sight • scene • panorama

► a view/panorama of sth
► a beautiful/breathtaking view/sight/scene/panorama
► enjoy the view/sight/scene/panorama

villain noun [C] (*disapprov.*)

■ He plays the part of the villain.

criminal • brute • monster | *infml* crook | *taboo, slang* bastard

■ OPP **hero**
► an evil villain/criminal/monster/bastard
► an old villain/brute/bastard

violent adj.

1 ■ The crowd suddenly turned violent.

aggressive • rough • bloodthirsty • homicidal | *written* murderous | *esp. journ.* bloody

► violent/aggressive/homicidal/murderous **towards** sb
► (a) violent/aggressive/homicidal/murderous **attack/tendencies**

2 ■ The issue became the subject of violent controversy.

fierce • intense • heated • fiery • passionate • emotional

■ OPP **mild**
► a/an violent/fierce/intense/passionate **controversy**
► violent/fierce/intense **opposition**
► a/an violent/fierce/heated/passionate/emotional **argument**
► a violent/fierce/fiery/passionate **temper**

3 ■ The island was hit by a violent cyclone.

raging • turbulent • rough • stormy

■ OPP **mild, calm**
► violent/raging/turbulent/rough/stormy **sea**
► violent/turbulent/rough/stormy **conditions**

► violent/rough/stormy **weather**

virtually adv.

■ Virtually all students are exempt from the tax.

almost • nearly • more or less • not quite | *esp. spoken* practically • about • pretty much/well

► virtually/almost/nearly/more or less/not quite/practically/about/pretty much **all/every**
► virtually/almost/more or less/practically/about/pretty much **any/anything**
► virtually/almost/more or less/practically **impossible**

visible adj.

■ He showed no visible sign of emotion.

noticeable • apparent • conspicuous • in evidence • in view • on display | *esp. written* marked | *fml* discernible

■ OPP **invisible**
► noticeable/apparent/conspicuous/discernible **to/in** sb/sth
► a/an visible/noticeable/apparent/conspicuous/marked/discernible **difference/change**
► a visible/noticeable/conspicuous/discernible **feature**
► clearly visible/noticeable/apparent/in view/on display/discernible

vision noun

1 [U] ■ The man moved outside her field of vision.

sight | *esp. written* view

► come into/disappear from sb's vision/sight/view
► block sb's vision/view
► sb's **field of** vision/view
● VISION, SIGHT OR VIEW? Use **view** to say how well you can see:
✓I had a good view of the stage. ✗I had a good sight/vision of the stage.
Vision must always be used with a possessive pronoun: *my/his/her, etc. (field) of vision*

2 [C] (*esp. written*) ■ The idea came to her in a vision.

dream • illusion • hallucination • nightmare

► have a/an vision/dream/illusion/hallucinations/nightmare
► experience visions/dreams/hallucinations/nightmares
► a/an vision/dream/illusion **fades**

visionary noun [C] (*usu. approv.*)

■ Morris was a true visionary.

idealist • romantic | *often disapprov.* dreamer

> ▶ a great visionary/romantic/
> dreamer
> ▶ a true visionary/romantic

visit noun [C]
■ It was my first visit to New York.

stay • tour • call • stopover

> ▶ on a visit/tour/call
> ▶ make a visit/stay/call
> ▶ cut short a visit/stay/tour

visit verb

1 [T] ■ He's visiting his son in Texas.

see • go to sth • drop in/round/by •
stop by • look in on sb | esp. BrE call |
infml look sb up | fml attend | BrE,
infml pop in/round/over

> ▶ visit/see a the doctor/dentist
> ▶ go to the doctor's/dentist's
> ▶ come/go to visit/see sb
> ▶ come/go and visit/see sb

2 [I, T] ■ Give me a call next time you
visit Oxford.

stay • stop over

> ▶ visit/stay/stop over for two
> nights/a week, etc.
> ▶ come/go to visit/stay

visitor noun

1 [C] ■ We're expecting visitors this
weekend.

guest • caller | fml company

> ▶ a visitor/guest/caller at/from sth
> ▶ have visitors/guests/company
> ▶ be expecting/entertain/invite
> visitors/guests

2 [C] ■ The palace is open daily to
visitors.

tourist • sightseer | BrE
holidaymaker • traveller | AmE
traveler • vacationer

> ▶ visitors/tourists/sightseers/
> holidaymakers/travellers/
> vacationers from...
> ▶ foreign visitors/tourists/travellers/
> holidaymakers/vacationers
> ▶ attract visitors/tourists/sightseers/
> holidaymakers/vacationers

vital adj.
■ It is vital to keep accurate records.

essential • crucial • critical •
indispensable • of the essence •
decisive • necessary • important |
fml imperative

> ▶ vital/essential/crucial/critical/
> indispensable/of the essence/
> decisive/necessary/important/
> imperative for sth
> ▶ be vital/essential/crucial/critical/
> necessary/important/imperative
> that...
> ▶ be vital/essential/crucial/critical/

necessary/important/imperative
to do sth
> ▶ of vital/crucial/critical/decisive
> importance

vocabulary noun [C, U]
■ Reading will increase your
vocabulary.

language • wording • terms •
terminology • usage

> ▶ in... vocabulary/language/terms/
> terminology/usage
> ▶ formal/informal/everyday
> vocabulary/language/terms/
> usage
> ▶ use ... vocabulary/language/
> wording/terms/terminology

voice noun [C, U]
■ He recognized Sue's voice.

accent • speech • tone •
pronunciation | phonetics intonation

> ▶ speak in a/an... voice/accent/
> tone
> ▶ (a) clear voice/speech/
> pronunciation

volume noun

1 [U, C] ■ How do you measure the
volume of a gas?

size • capacity • bulk

> ▶ a volume/capacity of 30 litres, etc.
> ▶ in size/capacity/bulk
> ▶ measure/calculate the volume/
> size/capacity of sth

2 [U] ■ A high volume of traffic enters
the city.

amount • quantity • number

> ▶ the volume/amount/quantity/
> number of sth
> ▶ record/sufficient/growing/
> increasing volumes/amounts/
> quantities/numbers
> ▶ a limited/the total/the sheer
> volume/amount/quantity/
> number

3 [U] ■ She turned down the volume
on the car stereo.

sound

> ▶ the volume/sound on sth
> ▶ turn up/turn down/increase/
> reduce the volume/sound

voluntary adj.

1 ■ Attendance at classes is voluntary.

optional | fml discretionary

■ OPP involuntary, compulsory
> ▶ a voluntary/an optional course/
> procedure/scheme
> ▶ entirely voluntary/optional/
> discretionary
● VOLUNTARY OR OPTIONAL?
Voluntary puts the emphasis on
choosing to do or have sth without

being forced to; **optional** puts the emphasis on sth being available for you to choose when it is extra.

2 [usu. before noun] ■ *I do voluntary work at the local hospital.*

unpaid • honorary

▶ on a/an **voluntary/unpaid/honorary basis**
▶ **voluntary/unpaid work/service/overtime**
▶ a **voluntary/an unpaid worker/carer/helper**

vomit *verb* [I, T]
■ *The smell made her want to vomit.*

throw (sth) up | *esp. BrE* **be sick** | *infml* **puke** | *fml* **regurgitate** | *AmE, infml* **barf**

▶ **vomit/puke up** sth
▶ **vomit/throw up/regurgitate your food**
▶ **want to/make sb vomit/throw up/puke/barf**

vote *noun* [C]
■ *We took a vote on the issue.*

election • ballot • referendum • show of hands | *esp. journ.* **poll/the polls**

▶ a/an **vote/election/ballot/referendum/poll on** sth
▶ a **democratic/free vote/election/ballot/poll**
▶ **have** a/an **vote/election/ballot/referendum/show of hands/poll**

vote *verb* [I, T]
■ *They all voted for the new tax.*

support • back • elect

▶ **vote for/support/back** sb **in** sth
▶ **vote for/support/back/elect a candidate**
▶ **vote for/support/back a measure/proposal/plan/motion/resolution/move/scheme**

vulnerable *adj.*
■ *Older people are particularly vulnerable to the flu.*

at risk • endangered • exposed • open to sth **• helpless** | *BrE* **defenceless** | *AmE* **defenseless**

■ **OPP protected, invulnerable**
▶ **vulnerable/exposed/open to criticism, attack,** etc.
▶ **feel vulnerable/at risk/exposed/helpless/defenceless**
▶ **leave sb/sth vulnerable/at risk/exposed/open to** sth **/helpless/defenceless**

W w

wage *noun* [C] (also **wages** [pl.])
■ *There are extra benefits for people on low wages.*

pay • salary • earnings • income

▶ (a) **high/low/basic wage/pay/salary/earnings/income**
▶ **receive** (a/an) **wage/pay/salary/earnings/income**
▶ **pay/give sb** (a/an) **wage/salary/income**
● **WAGES, PAY OR SALARY?** Pay is the most general of these words. If you work in a factory, shop, etc. you usu. get your **wages** each week. Office workers and professionals such as doctors, teachers, etc. receive a **salary** that is paid monthly or twice a month. It is expressed as an annual figure: *She's on a salary of over $80 000.*

wait *verb*

1 [I, T] ■ *She rang the bell and waited.*

stay | *spoken* **hold on • hang on** | *infml* **hang around • stick around** | *esp. written* **sit tight • linger** | *fml* **remain** | *BrE, infml* **stop**

▶ **wait/stay/hold on/hang on/hang around/stick around/sit tight/linger/remain until** sth happens
▶ **wait/hold on/hang on a minute/second**

2 [I, T] ■ *It's the opportunity I've been waiting for.*

hope • expect • anticipate • look forward to sth | *fml* **await**

▶ **wait/hope for** sth
▶ **wait/hope/expect to do** sth
▶ **wait for/hope for/expect/anticipate/look forward to/await a reply**

wake up *phrasal verb*
■ *What time do you usually wake up?*

get out of bed • get up • come to | *BrE* **come round** | *AmE* **come around** | *written* **wake**

■ **OPP fall asleep, go to sleep**
▶ **wake up/come to/come round/come around/wake from** sth
▶ **wake up/get out of bed/get up/wake late/early/in the morning/at seven o'clock**

walk *noun* [sing.]
■ *He moved with a slow, hesitant walk.*

step • stride | *written* **gait • tread**

▶ **with** a/an... **walk/stride/gait/tread**

▶ a light/heavy **strep/tread**
▶ **have** a/an...**walk/gait**

walk verb

1 [I, T] (usu. used with an adv. or prep.) ■ *The door opened and Jo walked in.*

stride • stroll • pace • step • march | *BrE* **tread** | *written* **prowl**

▶ walk/stride/stroll/step/march **to/ towards** sb/sth
▶ walk/stroll/pace/step/march/ prowl **around/round** (sth)
▶ walk/pace/prowl the **streets/ corridors**

2 [I, T] (*esp. BrE*) ■ *We're going walking in Scotland.*

hike • trek

▶ **go** walking/hiking/trekking

wander verb [I, V] (usu. used with an adv. or prep.)
■ *She wandered aimlessly around.*

roam • drift • amble • saunter

▶ wander/roam/drift/amble/saunter **around/about** (sth)
▶ wander/roam/drift **aimlessly**
▶ wander/roam **freely**
▶ wander/roam the **streets**

want verb

1 [T] (*esp. spoken*) (not usu. used in the progressive tenses) ■ *Do you want some more wine?*

wish | *fml* **desire** | *fml, esp. spoken* **would like sth** | *infml, spoken* **feel like sth** | *BrE, infml, esp. spoken* **like sth** | **fancy**

▶ sb wants/wishes/desires/would like/likes **to do sth**
▶ **if you** want/wish/like
▶ sb **really** wants/wishes/desires/ would like/feels like/likes/fancies sth

2 [T] (not usu. used in the progressive tenses) ■ *What this house wants is a good clean.*

need • call for sth • demand | *fml* **require**

▶ **really** want/need/call for/ demand/require sth
▶ **just/urgently** want/need/require sb/sth

war noun [C]
■ *He fought in two world wars.*

warfare • conflict • combat • fighting • battle • campaign | *esp. journ.* **hostilities • action**

■ OPP **peace**
▶ (a) war/warfare/conflict/combat/ fighting/battle/campaign/

hostilities/action **with/against/ between** sb/sth
▶ **in** war/warfare/conflict/combat/ fighting/battle/hostilities/action
▶ the **outbreak** of war/conflict/ combat/fighting/hostilities

warehouse noun [C]
■ *Police are investigating a fire at a furniture warehouse.*

depot • store • storehouse | *fml* **repository**

▶ warehouse/depot/store/ storehouse/repository **for** sth
▶ a **storage/distribution** warehouse/depot
▶ a **grain** warehouse/store

warm verb [T, I]
■ *Come and warm yourself by the fire.*

heat • heat (sth) up • reheat | *esp. spoken* **warm (sth) up**

■ OPP **cool**
▶ warm/heat sth **through**
▶ warm/heat/warm up a **room/ house**
▶ warm sth/heat sth/heat sth up/ reheat/warm/warm sth up **in the oven/microwave**

warm adj.

1 ■ *Wash the dress in warm water.*

heated • hot • humid | *often disapprov.* **sultry** | *disapprov.* **stuffy**

■ OPP **cold, cool**
▶ warm/hot/humid/sultry **weather**
▶ warm/hot **sunshine/water**
▶ **keep** sth warm/heated/hot
▶ **nice and** warm/hot

2 ■ *The speaker was given a warm welcome.*

friendly • pleasant • welcoming • hospitable | *written* **amiable • genial** | *esp. BrE, esp. spoken* **lovely**

■ OPP **cold, cool**
▶ a/an warm/friendly/pleasant/ hospitable/amiable/genial/lovely **person**
▶ a/an warm/friendly/pleasant/ welcoming/hospitable/amiable/ genial **manner**
▶ a/an warm/friendly/pleasant/ welcoming/genial/lovely **smile**

warn verb [T, I]
■ *We were warned about pickpockets.*

alert | *infml* **tip sb off** | *fml* **caution**

▶ warn/caution (sb) **against** sth
▶ warn sb/tip sb off **about** sth
▶ warn/alert sb/tip sb off/caution **that...**

warning noun [C, U]
■ *People continue to ignore warnings about the dangers of sunbathing.*

notice • alert • alarm | *infml* tip-off | *fml* caution

▶ warning/notice **of** sth
▶ warning/notice **that**...
▶ a **flood/bomb/health** warning/alert
▶ **give/receive** warning/notice/a tip-off
▶ **sound** a/an warning/alert/alarm/note of caution

wash *verb*

1 [T, I] ■ *wash the car/dishes*

clean • rinse • cleanse • hose • mop • sponge • bathe • shampoo • scrub

▶ wash/clean/rinse/cleanse/bathe sth **in/with** sth
▶ wash/clean/mop/scrub the **floor**
▶ wash/rinse/shampoo your **hair**
▶ wash/clean/cleanse/bathe a **wound**

2 [I, T] (*esp. BrE*) ■ *I washed and changed before going out.*

shower • freshen (yourself) up | *AmE* wash up • clean yourself up • bathe | *BrE* bath

▶ wash/shower **quickly**
▶ wash/shower/bathe/bath **and change/dress**

waste *noun* [U]

■ *four million tons of industrial waste*

scrap • litter | *esp. BrE* rubbish | *AmE* garbage • trash | *fml* refuse • debris

▶ **household/domestic** waste/rubbish/garbage/trash/refuse
▶ **dump** waste/rubbish/garbage/trash/refuse/debris
▶ **produce** waste/rubbish/garbage/trash/refuse
▶ waste/rubbish/garbage/trash/refuse **disposal/collection**
● WHICH WORD? Use **rubbish** in *BrE* and **garbage** or **trash** in *AmE* for the everyday things that we throw away. **Waste** is used esp. to talk about large amounts and in the context of industry.

waste *verb* [T] (*disapprov.*)

■ *Why waste money on clothes you don't need?*

lose • throw away • squander | *infml* blow • splurge

▶ waste/lose/throw away/squander/blow/splurge sth **on** sth
▶ waste/lose/throw away/squander/blow/splurge **money**
▶ waste/lose/throw away/squander/blow a/an **fortune/chance/opportunity**

watch *noun* [sing., U]

■ *Police mounted a watch outside the house.*

guard • vigil • alert

▶ **on** watch/guard/alert
▶ a **round-the-clock** watch/guard/vigil
▶ **keep** watch/guard/a vigil

watch *verb*

1 [T, I] ■ *I watched the kids playing in the yard.*

look • see • witness | *infml* check sth out | *esp. AmE, infml* catch | *fml* observe • view • regard • contemplate

▶ watch/look/view/observe/regard/contemplate (sb/sth) **from** somewhere
▶ watch/observe **what/who/how**...
▶ watch/see/view/catch a **film/movie/show/programme**

2 [T] ■ *The new initiative is being closely watched by government regulators.*

monitor • track • keep an eye on sb/sth • keep track of sb/sth | *infml* keep tabs on sb/sth

▶ watch/monitor/track/keep an eye on (sb/sth) **for** sth
▶ watch/monitor/track/keep track of/keep tabs on **what/who/where**...
▶ watch/monitor/track **how**...

wave *noun*

1 [C] ■ *The wind made waves on the water.*

ripple • swell

▶ **make** waves/ripples
▶ **send** waves/ripples across sth
▶ a wave/swell **breaks/surges**

2 [C] ■ *A wave of violence swept the country.*

spate • rash • outbreak • epidemic

▶ a/an wave/outbreak/spate/rash/epidemic **of** sth
▶ the **recent/latest/renewed** wave/spate/outbreak (of sth)
▶ **lead to** a/an wave/spate/rash/outbreak/epidemic (of sth)

3 [C] ■ *A wave of guilt washed over her.*

surge • rush • thrill | *written* ripple

▶ wave/surge/rush/thrill/ripple of **excitement/pleasure/fear**
▶ wave/surge/rush of **desire/anger/emotion/relief**
▶ **feel/send** a wave/surge/rush/thrill/ripple of sth

way *noun*

1 [C] ■ *There's a simple way of doing this.*

method • **means** • **technique** • **system** • **process** • **mechanism**

▶ a way/method/means/technique/system **of** doing sth
▶ **devise/develop** a way/method/means/technique/system/process
▶ **find** a way/method/means/system

2 [C] ■ *Try to approach this in a sensible way.*

style • **approach** | *fml* **manner**

▶ a way/style/manner **of** (doing) sth
▶ **in** a (…) way/style/manner
▶ **have/adopt** a/an way/style/approach/manner
● **WAY OR STYLE?** **Way** tells you how sb does sth on a particular occasion; **style** tells you how sb *usu.* does sth.

3 [C, usu. sing.] ■ *He stopped to ask the way.*

route • **direction** • **path** • **line** • **course**

▶ the way/route/path/line/course **to/from/through/along/across** sth
▶ the **right/wrong** way/route/direction/path/course
▶ **block** the/sb's/sth's way/route/line/path
▶ **know** the way/route

way of life *phrase*

■ *They were hunter-gatherers with a nomadic way of life.*

lifestyle • **life** • **living** • **existence**

▶ a **traditional** way of life/lifestyle
● **WAY OF LIFE OR LIFESTYLE?** A **lifestyle** is often more modern; sb might have a *busy/hectic lifestyle* or choose a *healthy/alternative lifestyle*. A **way of life** is more likely to be *traditional/old* or *British/Western, etc.* and shared by the whole community.

weak *adj.*

1 ■ *She is still weak after her illness.*

frail • **feeble** • **infirm** • **delicate**

■ OPP **strong**
▶ weak/frail/feeble/delicate **health**
▶ **look** weak/frail/feeble/delicate

2 ■ *The case for the prosecution was rather weak.*

unconvincing | *fml* **implausible**

■ OPP **strong**
▶ a weak/an unconvincing **argument**

3 ■ *weak winter sunlight*

dim • **faint** | *lit.* **thin**

■ OPP **strong**

▶ weak/dim/faint/thin **light**
● **WEAK, DIM OR FAINT?** **Dim** describes light in a room or place when it is not bright enough to see clearly; **faint** describes a particular point of light which is hard to see; **weak** *usu.* describes sunlight that is not bright.

weakness *noun*

1 [C] ■ *A weakness of the organization is poor communication.*

shortcoming • **limitation** • **failing**

■ OPP **strength**
▶ a weakness/shortcoming/limitation/failing **in** sth
▶ **have/suffer from** weaknesses/shortcomings/limitations
▶ **expose/reveal/identify/highlight** the weaknesses/shortcomings/limitations/failings of sth
● **WEAKNESS OR SHORTCOMING?** A **weakness** is often sth that makes sth fail to be as good as it should be for its own sake; a **shortcoming** is *usu.* sth that makes sth fail in its duty to other people: *We need to highlight any potential weaknesses in the proposal* (= or the proposal may not be accepted). • *The report highlights the shortcomings of the prison service* (= where it is failing prisoners/society).

2 [C, U] ■ *He regarded asking for help as a sign of weakness.*

fault • **inadequacy** • **failing** • **flaw** | *fml* **frailty**

■ OPP **strength**
▶ (a) weakness/fault/inadequacies/failing/flaw **in** sb
▶ **human** weakness/faults/failings/frailty
▶ **personal** weakness/inadequacy/failings
▶ **have** weaknesses/inadequacy/flaws
● **WEAKNESS OR FAULT?** A **fault** is often more serious than a **weakness**. You can see a **weakness** in yourself, but a **fault** in sb else.

wealth *noun* [U]

■ *The purpose of industry is to create wealth.*

money • **fortune** | *often approv.* **prosperity** | *sometimes disapprov.* **affluence** | *lit.* **riches**

■ OPP **poverty**
▶ **growing/increasing/rising** wealth/prosperity/affluence
▶ **have/possess/accumulate/acquire/inherit** wealth/money/a fortune/riches
▶ **bring** wealth/money/prosperity/affluence/riches

wealthy adj.

■ *The couple are said to be fabulously wealthy.*

rich • well off • prosperous • affluent • comfortable | *infml* **loaded** | *sometimes disapprov.* **privileged**

■ **OPP poor, needy**

▶ a/an wealthy/rich/well off/prosperous/affluent/privileged **family**
▶ a wealthy/rich/well off/prosperous **man/woman**
▶ a/an wealthy/rich/prosperous/affluent **country/city/suburb**
● **WEALTHY OR RICH? Rich** is more frequent than **wealthy** and can be used in some fixed phrases where **wealthy** cannot:
✓a resort for the rich and famous ✗ a resort for the wealthy and famous

weapon noun [C]

■ *Police haven't found the murder weapon.*

arms • armaments • munitions • weapons of mass destruction | *esp. journ.* **WMD**

▶ **nuclear/conventional** weapons/arms/armaments
▶ **carry** weapons/arms
▶ a/an weapons/arms/armaments/munitions **factory**

wear verb [T]

■ *Do I have to wear a tie?*

have (got) sth on • put sth on

▶ wear/have on/put on a **coat/jacket/suit/hat/tie/badge/watch**
▶ wear/have/put on your **glasses**
▶ wear/have/put on **make-up/lipstick**

weather noun [U]

■ *I'm not going out in this weather!*

climate • the elements

▶ **in/have** (a) good, mild, etc. weather/climate
▶ **brave** the weather/elements
▶ **open to/protected from/sheltered from** the weather/elements

wedding noun [C]

■ *We were invited to my cousin's wedding.*

marriage

▶ a **forthcoming/royal** wedding/marriage
▶ **attend/go to/celebrate** a wedding/marriage
● **MARRIAGE OR WEDDING? Marriage** usu. refers to the state of being married; **wedding** refers to the occasion of getting married: *They*

had a long and happy marriage. • *We went to Jim and Sue's wedding last week.*
Marriage can be used to refer to the occasion formally: *You are invited to the marriage of Mark Wallace and Rachel Bull.*

weight noun [U, C]

■ *It is about 76 kilos in weight.*

load • pressure • strain • stress | *physics* **mass • density**

▶ **under** the weight/load/pressure/strain/stress
▶ (a) **heavy** weight/load/pressure/strain/stress
▶ **bear** the weight/strain/stress/load

welcome noun [C, U]

■ *Ellen received a rapturous welcome on her return.*

reception • hospitality | *esp. written* **greeting**

▶ (a) welcome/reception/hospitality/greeting **from** sb
▶ a/an **rapturous/rousing/enthusiastic** welcome/reception
▶ **receive/expect/give sb/get/have/meet (with)** a … welcome/reception

welcome verb

1 [T, I] ■ *They were at the door to welcome us.*

greet • meet • entertain • accept | *fml* **receive**

▶ welcome/greet/meet/receive sb **with** a smile, etc.
▶ welcome/greet/meet/entertain/receive a **guest/visitor**
▶ **be there to** welcome/greet/meet/entertain/receive sb
● **WELCOME OR GREET? You greet** sb when you say hello to them. You **welcome** sb when they come to visit you or when they return after being away for a long time. You make a special effort to show them that you are happy they are with you.

2 [T] ■ *They welcomed the new volunteers with open arms (= with enthusiasm).*

accept | *fml* **receive**

▶ welcome/accept/receive sb **into** sth
▶ welcome/receive a **guest/visitor**
▶ welcome/accept/receive sb **with open arms**

3 [T] (not usu. used in the progressive tenses) ■ *I'd welcome your advice.*

appreciate

▶ welcome/appreciate sb's **support/
help/comments/view/
suggestion**
▶ welcome/appreciate the **chance/
opportunity**
▶ I'd welcome/appreciate…

well adj. [not usu. before noun]
(esp. spoken)
■ Is he well enough to travel?

healthy • strong | esp. BrE fit | esp.
spoken **fine** • **all right** | infml, spoken
OK | AmE, infml **good**

■ OPP **sick, ill, unwell**
▶ feel/look **well/healthy/strong/
fit/fine/all right/OK/good**
▶ keep (sb) **well/healthy/fit**
▶ get **well/strong/fit**

get **well** phrase
■ Get well soon!

get better • recover • come through
(sth) • pull through • shake sth off |
fml **recuperate**

▶ recover/recuperate **from** sth
▶ gradually get better/recover

well known adj.
■ She's married to a well-known actor.

famous • prominent • renowned |
written **famed** • **celebrated**

■ OPP **unknown, obscure**
▶ well known/famous/prominent/
renowned/famed/celebrated **as** sb
▶ well known/famous/prominent/
famed/celebrated **for** sth
▶ a well-known/famous/prominent/
renowned/celebrated **author/
actor/architect/artist/collection**
▶ a well-known/famous/prominent/
renowned/celebrated **politician/
personality**

wet adj.

1 ■ A car skidded on the wet road.

soaked • sodden • drenched | often
approv. **moist** | sometimes disapprov.
damp | written **saturated**

■ OPP **dry**
▶ wet/soaked/drenched/moist/
damp/saturated **with** sth
▶ sb's **clothes/hair** is/are wet/
soaked/sodden/drenched/damp/
saturated
▶ wet/sodden/moist/damp/
saturated **ground/earth**
▶ get wet/soaked/sodden/moist/
damp

2 ■ It was the wettest October for
years.

rainy • bad

■ OPP **dry**
▶ wet/rainy/bad **weather**
▶ a wet/rainy **day/morning/**

afternoon/evening/night/
month/season
▶ It's wet/rainy.

while noun [sing.]
■ They chatted for a while.

time • period • spell • stint
▶ for/after a while/time/period/
spell/stint
▶ a long/short while/time/period/
spell/stint
▶ a brief while/time/period/spell

whisper verb [I, T]
■ He whispered something in my ear.

murmur • mutter • mumble • mouth
■ OPP **shout**
▶ whisper/murmur/mutter/mumble
(sth) **to** sb
▶ whisper/murmur/mutter/mumble
about sth
▶ whisper/murmur/mutter/mumble
that…
▶ whisper/murmur/mutter/
mumble/mouth **something/an
apology**

whistle noun [C]
■ She attracted whistles and jeers from
the crowd.

boo • jeer • hiss • catcall
▶ whistles/jeers/hisses **of** sth
▶ whistles/boos/jeers/hisses/
catcalls **from** the crowd/audience
▶ be **met/greeted with** whistles/
boos/jeers/hisses/catcalls

whole adj. [only before noun]
■ We drank a whole bottle too.

entire • full • complete • total
▶ a/an whole/entire/full/complete
day/set
▶ the whole/full/complete **truth/
story**
▶ your whole/your entire/a full **life**
● WHOLE OR ENTIRE? Entire
emphasizes sth more strongly than
whole and is used esp. to
emphasize how bad sth is:
✓I wasted an entire/a whole day on
it. • We spent the whole day on the
beach. ✗ We spent the entire day on
the beach.

wide adj.

1 ■ The road is just wide enough for
two cars to pass.

thick | often approv., esp. written
broad

■ OPP **narrow**
▶ a wide/broad **road/street/river/
stream/staircase**
▶ a wide/broad **mouth/smile/grin**
● WHICH WORD? Wide usu. describes
measurement from one side to
another; thick describes

measurement between surfaces: *a wide road/river* • *Thick walls kept the house cool in summer.*

Broad is often used to suggest that sth is attractive in an attractive way: *a broad avenue lined with trees*

2 ■ *We stock a wide range of goods.*

broad • **extensive** • **widespread** • **general** • **universal** • **diverse** • **mass** • **large-scale** • **sweeping** • **far-reaching** | *written* **wide-ranging** | *often approv.* **varied**

■ OPP **narrow**
▶ a/an wide/broad/extensive/ diverse/varied **range**
▶ wide/broad/extensive/ widespread/general/universal/ mass **support**
▶ wide/broad/extensive/sweeping/ wide-ranging **powers**
● **WIDE OR BROAD?** Broad is used more to talk about the effect of sth on a large number of people:
✔*have a broad appeal* • *attract broad support*
Broad also often relates to knowledge, education and business:
✔*a broad curriculum* • *broad experience/knowledge*
Wide is used more to talk about *a choice* or *a range of things or people* and also for *a geographical area*:
✔*The festival attracts people from a wide area.* ✗ *The festival attracts people from a broad area.*

wife noun [C]

■ *This is my wife, Anna.*

partner | *fml* or *law* **spouse** | *infml, esp. spoken, often humorous* **missus/ missis** • **sb's other half**

■ OPP **husband**
▶ sb's **future** wife/spouse
▶ sb's **former/ex-** wife/partner/ spouse
▶ **have/find** a wife/partner

wild adj.

1 ■ *Those girls have been allowed to run wild.*

disruptive • **unruly** • **rowdy** | *fml* **disorderly**

▶ wild/disruptive/unruly/rowdy/ disorderly **behaviour**

2 ■ *The crowd were wild with excitement.*

mad • **crazy** • **frantic** • **furious** • **frenzied**

■ OPP **calm**
▶ a wild/mad/frantic/furious **rush**
▶ **go** wild/mad/crazy
▶ wild/mad/crazy **with excitement**

willing adj. [usu. before noun]

■ *There were plenty of willing helpers.*

helpful • **cooperative** | *fml* **obliging**

■ OPP **unwilling**
▶ **find** sb willing/helpful/ cooperative

win verb

1 ■ [I, T] ■ *He always wins at cards.*

win out • **come out on top** | *fml* **prevail** | *written* **triumph** | *written, esp. journ.* **win the day**

■ OPP **lose**
▶ win/prevail/win the day **against** sb
▶ win out/prevail/triumph **over** sb/ sth
▶ win/win out/prevail/triumph **in the end**

2 ■ [T] ■ *He won scholarship to study at Stanford.*

gain • **earn** • **land** | *fml* **secure**

▶ win/gain/earn/secure sth **by** (doing) sth
▶ win/gain/earn/secure **support/ approval**
▶ win/gain/earn **respect/ admiration**
▶ win/land/secure a **contract**

wind noun [C, U]

■ *Trees were swaying in the wind.*

breeze | *BrE* **draught** | *AmE* **draft**

▶ a **cold** wind/breeze/draught
▶ a **cool/warm/hot** wind/breeze
▶ a wind/breeze/draught **blows**

wind verb

1 ■ [I, T] (always used with an adv. or prep.) ■ *The path winds its way down to the beach.*

twist • **zigzag** • **turn** • **curve** • **bend** | *written* **snake**

▶ wind/twist/curve/bend/snake **around/round** sth
▶ wind/twist/zigzag/curve/snake **through/across** sth
▶ the **road/path** winds/twists/ zigzags/turns/curves/bends/ snakes
▶ the **river** winds/turns/curves/ bends/snakes

2 ■ [T] (usu. used with an adv. or prep.) ■ *She wound the bandage around my finger.*

wrap • **twist** • **roll** • **coil** • **curl** • **loop**

▶ wind/wrap/twist/coil/curl/loop (sth) **around/round** sb/sth
▶ wind/roll/curl (sth) **into a ball**

winner noun [C]

■ *The winner of the competition was announced last night.*

champion • prizewinner | written victor | BrE medallist | AmE medalist

■ OPP loser
▶ a **worthy** winner/champion/victor
▶ a **clear**/**comfortable**/**runaway** winner/victor
▶ **emerge** as (the) winner/champion/victor

wire noun [C, U]

■ *Watch out for bare wires.*

cable | BrE flex | esp. AmE cord

▶ **along**/**down** a wire/cable/flex
▶ an **electric**/**electrical** wire/cable/flex/lead/cord
▶ **connect**/**disconnect** a wire/cable/flex/lead/cord

wisdom noun [U] (sometimes ironic)

■ *She's not lacking in worldly wisdom.*

sense • common sense • realism • sanity | fml pragmatism

■ OPP stupidity, foolishness, folly
▶ wisdom/sense/realism/pragmatism **in** (doing) sth
▶ **political**/**economic** wisdom/sense/common sense/realism/pragmatism
▶ **question**/**doubt**/**have doubts about** the wisdom/sense/common sense/sanity of sth

wise adj.

1 ■ *a wise and experienced ruler*

sensible • prudent

■ OPP foolish
▶ a wise/sensible/prudent **person**/**man**/**woman**
● WISE OR SENSIBLE? **Wise** often describes sb older who is respected for the knowledge they have gained by experience; **sensible** describes sb who makes the right decisions in practical matters.

2 ■ *Locking the windows is a wise precaution.*

sensible • best • advisable

■ OPP unwise
▶ be wise/sensible/best/advisable **to do sth**
▶ a wise/a sensible/the best **choice**/**thing** to do/**use** of sth/**course** (of action)/**investment**

wish noun

1 [C] (*esp. written*) ■ *I understand her wish for secrecy.*

need • want • longing • craving • ambition • hope • dream • aspiration • urge • inclination | esp. written **desire** | often disapprov. whim

▶ (a/an) wish/need/longing/craving/hopes/aspirations/urge/inclination/desire **for** sth
▶ the wish/need/longing/craving/ambition/aspiration/urge/inclination/desire **to do** sth
▶ **have** (a/an) wish/need/wants/longing/craving/ambition/hopes/dream/aspirations/urge/inclination/desire
▶ **pander** to sb's wishes/wants/whims
● WISH, NEED OR DESIRE? These words all refer to sth you want. **Need** is the strongest and usu. refers to sth you feel you must have. When used with adjectives such as *deep*, *great*, *urgent*, etc. **desire** expresses a stronger feeling than **wish**.

2 [C] ■ *He refused to carry out her wishes.*

request | fml will

▶ a wish/request **for** sth
▶ sb's **particular**/**personal**/**dying** wish/request
▶ **obey**/**go against** sb's wishes/will

wish verb

1 [T] (not usu. used in the progressive tenses) ■ *I wish I were taller.*

want • like | fml desire | fml, esp. spoken **would like** sth

▶ sb wishes/wants/likes/desires/would like **to do** sth
▶ **if you** wish/want/like
▶ wish/want **desperately** to do sth

2 ■ *He has everything he could wish for.*

hope • aspire • wait • set your heart on sth | esp. journ. set your sights on sth

▶ wish/hope/wait **for** sth
▶ wish/hope **that...**
▶ **just**/**only** wish/hope

witch noun [C]

■ *He was turned into a rat by a wicked witch.*

wizard • magician | esp. written sorcerer • sorceress • enchantress

▶ an **evil** witch/wizard/magician/sorcerer/sorceress/enchantress
▶ a/an witch/wizard/magician/sorcerer/sorceress/enchantress **casts a spell**
● WHICH WORD? All these words describe people in stories who have magic powers. A **witch**, **sorcerer**, **sorceress** or **enchantress** is usu. evil; a **wizard** or **magician** may be good or evil. A **witch** is usu. an ugly

old woman; an **enchantress** is often a beautiful young woman; a **wizard** is often a grand or wise old man.

withdraw verb

1 [I, T] ■ The troops were forced to withdraw.

retreat • pull sb/sth out | fml retire

▶ withdraw/retreat/retire **to** a place
▶ withdraw/retreat/pull out **troops/forces**
▶ withdraw/retreat/retire to your **room/study**
▶ withdraw/retreat **into your shell**

2 [I, T] ■ She was forced to withdraw from the race.

pull out • back off • back out | written retreat

▶ withdraw/back off/retreat **from** sth
▶ withdraw from/pull out of (a) **project/tournament/tour/talks**

3 [T] (fml) ■ The newspaper withdrew the allegations the next day.

fml retract • recant | esp. spoken take sth back

▶ withdraw/retract a/an **claim/allegation/confession**

withstand verb [T] (fml)

■ The boat was built to withstand all weather conditions.

stand • stand up to sth • resist • tolerate • absorb

▶ withstand/stand/resist/tolerate **high temperatures/heat**
▶ withstand/stand up to/resist **stress/wear**
▶ withstand/stand the **pressure/strain/weight**

witness noun [C]

■ Police appealed for witnesses to the accident.

eyewitness • observer • onlooker • bystander • passer-by

▶ a/an witness/eyewitness/observer/onlooker/bystander/passer-by **sees** sb/sth
▶ a/an observer/onlooker/bystander/passer-by **witnesses** sth

woman noun [C]

■ a 24-year-old woman

lady | fml female

■ OPP man

▶ a/an **young/older/black/white** woman/lady/female
▶ a/an **middle-aged/old/elderly** woman/lady
▶ a/an **married/single/unmarried** woman/lady

wonder verb [I, T]

■ She was wondering what to do next.

think • consider • reflect | esp. written **ponder** | fml contemplate

▶ wonder/think/ponder/contemplate **about** sth
▶ wonder/think/consider/reflect/ponder/contemplate **how/what/whether...**

wonderful adj.

■ It's wonderful to see you!

delightful | infml great • fantastic • fabulous • terrific | esp. BrE, esp. spoken **lovely** | BrE, esp. spoken **marvellous** | AmE, esp. spoken **marvelous** | BrE, infml, spoken **brilliant** | lit. delicious

■ OPP awful

▶ a wonderful/delightful/great/fantastic/lovely/marvellous/delicious **feeling**
▶ (a) wonderful/delightful/great/fantastic/fabulous/terrific/lovely/marvellous/brilliant **experience/place**
▶ (a) wonderful/delightful/great/fantastic/lovely/marvellous **scenery/weather**
▶ have a wonderful/delightful/lovely/great/fantastic/fabulous/terrific/marvellous/brilliant **time**
▶ It's wonderful/great/lovely/marvellous **to be/feel/find/know/have/see...**
● WONDERFUL, DELIGHTFUL OR LOVELY? Lovely is the most frequent in spoken BrE. In AmE wonderful is the most frequent, both written and spoken. Delightful is used mostly to talk about times, events and places.

wood noun [C] (also woods [pl.])

■ We went for a walk in the woods.

woodland/woodlands • forest • plantation • jungle

▶ in a wood/woodland/forest/plantation/jungle
▶ a dense wood/woodland/forest/jungle

word noun [C]

■ What's the French word for 'duck'?

term • expression

▶ a word/term **for** sth
▶ a **new/ambiguous/technical/colloquial** word/term/expression
▶ **use/coin** a/an word/term/expression
▶ a/an word/term/expression **comes/derives/is derived from** sth

work noun

1 [U] ■ *He's been out of work for over a year.*

employment ◆ occupation ◆ job ◆ career ◆ profession ◆ trade ◆ practice | *esp.* BrE **post** | *fml* **position**

▸ **(a) full-time/part-time/permanent** work/employment/occupation/job/career/post/position
▸ **look for/seek/find** work/employment/an occupation/a job/a career/a post/a position
▸ **go back/return to** work/employment/a career/a profession/...practice

2 [U] ■ *Police work is mainly routine.*

duty/duties ◆ task ◆ business ◆ job ◆ chore

▸ **(a) routine/daily/day-to-day** work/duties/task/business/job/chore
▸ **household/domestic** work/duties/task/job/chore
▸ **carry out** the work/your duties/a task/a job
● **WORK OR DUTIES?** Your **duties** are a list of tasks that you have to do because they are your responsibility; your **work** is all the activities you do in the course of doing your job.

3 [U] (used without *the*) ■ *When do you leave for work?*

office ◆ headquarters ◆ base | *esp.* busin. *or journ.* **workplace**

▸ **go to/come to/arrive at/get to/leave** work/the office/headquarters

4 [U] ■ *Work continues on renovating the hotel.*

service | BrE **labour** | AmE **labor** | *disapprov.* **drudgery** | *infml, disapprov.* **slog** | *lit.* **toil**

▸ **(a) hard** work/labour/slog/toil
▸ **manual/physical/honest/unremitting** work/labour/toil
▸ **hours/years/a lifetime of** work/service/labour/drudgery/toil

5 [U] ■ *The art collection was his life's work.*

approv. **achievement** ◆ **accomplishment** ◆ **feat**

▸ **a/an impressive/notable** work/achievement/accomplishment/feat
▸ **your own** work/achievement/accomplishment
▸ **a/an literary/artistic/scientific** work/achievement/accomplishment

6 [C] ■ *The play is based on an early work by Jean Rhys.*

piece ◆ masterpiece ◆ work of art ◆ book ◆ novel ◆ text ◆ writings | *fml* composition ◆ opus ◆ oeuvre

▸ **a** work/piece/masterpiece/work of art/book/novel/text/composition **by sb**
▸ **a/an great/original** work/piece/masterpiece/work of art/book/novel/composition
▸ **a/an orchestral/choral** work/piece/masterpiece/composition
▸ **perform a** work/piece/composition
● **WORK, PIECE OR COMPOSITION?** Piece and composition are used mostly to talk about music. **Work** is used to talk about any type of art, literature or music.

work verb

1 [I, T] ■ *Doctors work very long hours.*

BrE, *esp. written* **labour** | AmE, *esp. written* **labor** | *esp. spoken, usu. disapprov.* **slave** | *lit.* **toil**

▸ work/labour/slave/toil **at sth**
▸ work/labour/toil **away**
▸ work/labour/toil **endlessly/long and hard/tirelessly**

2 [I] ■ *I've always worked in education.*

be employed ◆ have a job ◆ earn a/your living | BrE **be in work** ◆ practise | AmE **practice**

▸ work/be employed/have a job/earn a living/practise **as sth**
▸ work/be employed/have a job **at a place**

3 [I] ■ *She dedicated her life to working for peace.*

campaign ◆ lobby ◆ fight

▸ work/campaign/lobby/fight **for sth**
▸ work/campaign/lobby/fight **to do sth**
▸ work/campaign/lobby **actively/vigorously**

4 [I] (*esp. spoken*) ■ *The phone isn't working.*

operate ◆ run | *esp. spoken* **go** | *fml* **function**

▸ work/operate/run/function **efficiently/smoothly/independently/successfully/normally/reliably**
▸ work/operate/function **effectively/properly/correctly**

worker noun [C] (often in compounds)

■ *factory/manual/office workers*

employee • workman • workforce • manpower • staff | *esp. AmE* staff member | *BrE* member of staff • labourer | *AmE* laborer | *busin.* personnel

▶ a/an **full-time/part-time/key** worker/employee/staff member/ member of staff
▶ (a/an) **skilled/unskilled** worker/ employee/workforce/staff/ labourer/personnel
▶ (a/an) **female/male/experienced** worker/employee/workforce/ staff/staff members/members of staff/personnel
▶ **employ** a/an worker/employee/ workman/member of staff/staff member/labourer
▶ **dismiss/fire/sack** a/an worker/ employee/member of staff/staff member

working class *adj.*

■ She grew up in a working-class area.

often disapprov. **proletarian** | *often humorous* **lowly** | *lit.* or *humorous* **humble** | *BrE, often disapprov.,* often *humorous* **common**

● **OPP middle class, upper class**
▶ working class/humble/common **people**
▶ working class/lowly/humble **origins**
▶ a working class/proletarian/ humble **hero**

work sth out *phrasal verb*

1 ■ Have you worked out the answer yet?

calculate • tally • figure sth out | *AmE* figure | *infml, fml* compute | *BrE, infml* tot sth up

▶ work out/calculate/tally/figure out/figure/compute/tot up **how much/how many...**
▶ work out/calculate/figure out/ figure **that...**
▶ work out/calculate/tally/figure out/figure/compute/tot up the **number/amount/cost of sth**
● **WORK STH OUT, CALCULATE OR COMPUTE?** Calculate is the most frequent word in written English, but **work sth out** is the most frequent word in spoken English. **Compute** is used in formal, written English, esp. to describe calculations done by a machine.

2 (*esp. BrE, esp. spoken*) ■ I'm trying to work out how I could have spent £150 last night.

solve • do • clear sth up • crack | *esp. AmE, esp. spoken* figure sb/sth out

▶ work out/figure out **how/what/ where/how/why...**
▶ work out/solve/do a/an **puzzle/ equation**

▶ solve/clear up/crack a **case/ mystery**
● **FIGURE STH OUT OR FIGURE SB/STH OUT?** Figure sb/sth out is used more in *AmE* and **work sth out** is used more in *BrE*. However, if you are talking about understanding sb's character and behaviour, **figure sb out** is used in both: I've never been able to figure her out.

3 ■ I've worked out a new way of doing it.

come up with sth • devise • hatch | *infml* hit on sth • think sth up | *fml* conceive (of sth)

▶ work out/come up with/devise/ hatch/hit on/think up/conceive a **plan/scheme**
▶ work out/come up with/devise/ think up/conceive a **system/ theory**
▶ work out/come up with/devise/ hit on a **method/formula/means**

the **world** *noun* [sing.]

■ He's always wanted to sail around the world.

the earth • the globe • the planet

▶ around/across/all over the world/globe/planet
▶ save/destroy the world/earth/ planet
▶ the world/earth **turns/revolves**
● **THE WORLD OR THE EARTH?** Use the **world** when you are concerned with things that exist in the world and not outside it. Use the **earth** when our planet is being considered in relation to other planets, its place in space, or heaven.

worried *adj.*

■ Many parents are worried about the latest flu virus.

anxious • nervous • concerned • alarmed • uneasy • bothered | *fml* apprehensive | *written* disturbed • troubled

■ **OPP unconcerned**
▶ worried/anxious/nervous/ concerned/alarmed/uneasy/ bothered/apprehensive/ disturbed/troubled **about** sth
▶ worried/anxious/nervous/ concerned/alarmed/bothered/ apprehensive/disturbed **that...**
▶ a/an worried/anxious/nervous/ concerned/uneasy/apprehensive/ troubled **expression/look/smile**
● **WORRIED, ANXIOUS, OR NERVOUS?** **Worried** is the most frequent word; **anxious** is more formal and can describe a stronger feeling. **Nervous** can describe sb's personality; **worried** describes

feelings, not personality. **Anxious** describes feelings or personality.

worry noun [U, C]

■ family/financial worries

anxiety + concern + apprehension + unease + angst + agitation

▶ worry/anxiety/concern/apprehension/unease/angst over/about sth
▶ worry/anxiety/concern/apprehension/unease that...
▶ express your worries/anxiety/concern/apprehension/unease
● WORRY, ANXIETY OR CONCERN? Worry is a more informal word than concern and anxiety. Worry and anxiety are used to refer to personal matters; a concern often affects many people.

worry verb

1 [I] ■ Don't worry about me.

agonize + esp. BrE fret + infml sweat

▶ worry/agonize/fret about sth
▶ agonize/fret/sweat over sth
▶ Don't worry/fret.

2 [T] ■ What worries me is how I'm going to get another job.

concern + trouble + disturb + bother + alarm

▶ It worries/concerns/troubles/disturbs/bothers/alarms sb that...
▶ worry/concern/trouble/bother yourself about sth
▶ sth doesn't worry/concern/bother sb in the slightest/least
● WHICH WORD? Concern is the most formal of these words and is not usu. used in the progressive tenses. Bother is the most informal, esp. in spoken phrases like It doesn't bother me. and I'm not bothered.

worrying adj.

■ a worrying development/sign/trend

disturbing + unsettling + disconcerting + unnerving + alarming + stressful + upsetting + distressing

▶ worrying/disturbing/unsettling/disconcerting/unnerving/alarming/stressful/upsetting/distressing for sb
▶ a/an worrying/disturbing/alarming thought
▶ find sth worrying/disturbing/unsettling/disconcerting/unnerving/alarming/stressful/upsetting/distressing

worsen verb [I]

■ The economic situation is still worsening.

deteriorate + decline + weaken + degenerate + fail | esp. spoken get worse | esp. busin. slip

■ OPP improve
▶ sb's health worsens/deteriorates/declines/fails/gets worse
▶ a situation worsens/deteriorates/degenerates/gets worse
▶ the weather worsens/deteriorate/gets worse

worship verb [T, I]

■ They built temples to worship their gods.

praise + pray | fml venerate

▶ worship/praise/pray to God

worthy adj. (fml, often approv.)

■ Don is raising money for a very worthy cause.

fine + noble | BrE honourable | AmE honorable + deserving + admirable + creditable

■ OPP unworthy
▶ be worthy/deserving of sth
▶ a/an worthy/fine/noble/admirable man/woman
▶ a/an worthy/fine/noble/honourable/deserving cause

would like sth phrase (fml, esp. spoken)

■ Would you like a drink?

wish | esp. spoken want | fml desire | infml, esp. spoken feel like sth | BrE, infml, esp. spoken fancy

▶ sb would like/wishes/wants/desires to do sth
▶ feel like/fancy doing sth
▶ sb really would like/wishes/wants/desires/feels like/fancies sth

wound noun [C]

■ A nurse cleaned his wounds.

injury + cut + gash + graze + scratch

▶ (a/an) wound/injury/cuts/gash to a part of the body
▶ minor wounds/injuries/cuts
▶ suffer (a/an) wound/injury/cuts/gash/scratches

wound verb [T, often passive]

■ Two soldiers were wounded in the attack.

injure + hurt + maim

▶ be badly wounded/injured/hurt/maimed
▶ be severely/slightly/seriously wounded/injured/hurt
▶ accidentally wound/injure/hurt sb/sth

wounded adj.

■ The wounded soldiers were taken back to camp.

injured • hurt

▶ a wounded/an injured **arm/leg/ shoulder/knee**
▶ a wounded/an injured **man/ woman/person**
▶ **seriously** wounded/injured/hurt

wrapping noun [U] (also **wrappings** [pl.])

■ He tore the cellophane wrapping off the box.

wrapper • wrap • cover

▶ a **protective** wrapping/wrapper/ cover
▶ a **plastic** wrapping/wrapper/ wrap/cover
▶ **take off/remove** the wrapping/ wrapper/wrap/cover

wriggle verb [I, T]

■ The boy wriggled uncomfortably in his seat.

fidget • writhe • squirm • twist | infml **wiggle**

▶ wriggle/writhe/twist **about/ around**
▶ wriggle/writhe/squirm **in/with** pain/delight/embarrassment, etc.
▶ wriggle/wiggle **your toes**

write verb

1 [I, T] ■ Write clearly in black ink.

write sth down • put sth down • sign • copy • scribble • scrawl • transcribe

▶ write/write sth down/put sth down/sign/scribble/scrawl **on** sth
▶ write/write sth down/put sth down/scribble/scrawl **in** sth
▶ write/write down/put down/ copy/scribble/scrawl/transcribe some **notes**
▶ write/write down/put down/ sign/scribble/scrawl your **name**

2 [T, I] ■ Who wrote 'Moby Dick'?

dash sth off | fml **compose**

▶ write/dash off/compose a/an **letter/essay**
▶ write/compose a/an **novel/ poem/speech/song/opera/ symphony**
▶ write/compose **music**
▶ write/compose **a note**

writer noun [C]

■ a travel/cookery/science writer

author • journalist • novelist • poet • playwright • dramatist • scriptwriter • screenwriter • biographer • scribe

▶ a/an **famous/aspiring/award- winning** writer/author/journalist/ novelist/poet/playwright/ screenwriter

▶ a **best-selling/romantic** writer/ author/novelist/poet
▶ a/an **writer/author/journalist/ novelist/poet/playwright/ dramatist/scriptwriter/ screenwriter/biographer/journalist** writes sth

writing noun

1 [U] ■ The review is a brilliant piece of writing.

literature • text

▶ writing/literature **on** sth
▶ **feminist/scientific/English** writing/literature
▶ a **piece** of writing/literature/text

2 **writings** [pl.] ■ the writings of Susan Sontag

work | fml **oeuvre**

▶ sb's **complete/collected** writings/ works

wrong adj.

1 ■ I got all the answers wrong.

incorrect • false • mistaken • inaccurate • misguided • untrue

■ OPP **right**
▶ be wrong/mistaken **about** sth
▶ wrong/incorrect/false/mistaken/ inaccurate/untrue **information**
▶ **give/get** the wrong/a false/a mistaken/an inaccurate **impression**

2 (esp. spoken) ■ There's something wrong with my car.

faulty • defective | infml, spoken **up**

■ OPP **right**
▶ There's something wrong/up with sb/sth.
▶ faulty/defective **goods/ equipment/parts/workmanship**
▶ **seriously** wrong/defective

3 ■ It was the wrong thing to say.

inappropriate • unsuitable • awkward • inconvenient • bad

■ OPP **right**
▶ wrong/inappropriate/unsuitable/ awkward/inconvenient **for** sb/sth
▶ wrong/inappropriate/unsuitable/ inconvenient **to do** sth
▶ the wrong/an inappropriate/an awkward/an inconvenient/a bad **time**

4 [not usu. before noun] ■ Paying people such low wages is simply wrong.

unfair • unjust • immoral • unethical • improper | fml **inequitable**

■ OPP **right**

▶ wrong / unfair / unjust / improper **of** sb

▶ wrong / unfair / unjust / immoral / unethical / improper **to do sth**

▶ be wrong / unfair / unjust **that...**

go wrong *phrase*

■ The marriage started to go wrong when he lost his job.

break down • fail • collapse • backfire • fall through • get/go nowhere • come to nothing | *fml* founder

▶ a **plan** goes wrong / fails / backfires / falls through / comes to nothing / founders

▶ a **relationship / marriage** goes wrong / breaks down / fails / collapses

▶ a **deal** goes wrong / collapses / falls through

Y y

yard *noun*

1 [C] (*BrE*) ■ The prisoners lined up in the yard.

courtyard • compound • square • quad | *fml* quadrangle • precinct

▶ **in** the yard / courtyard / compound / square / quad / quadrangle / precincts

▶ **across** the yard / courtyard / compound / square / quad / quadrangle

▶ the **central / main** yard / courtyard / square / quadrangle

2 [C] (*AmE*) ■ She cut the grass in the yard.

grounds | *BrE* garden | *AmE* backyard

▶ **in** the yard / grounds / garden / backyard

▶ **(a) beautiful / landscaped** yard / grounds / garden / backyard

▶ the **front / back** yard / garden

young *noun* [pl.]

■ a mother bird feeding her young

offspring • baby • litter • brood

▶ **produce / rear / raise** young / offspring / babies / a litter / a brood

▶ **give birth to** young / offspring / a baby / a litter

● YOUNG, OFFSPRING OR BABY? Young and **offspring** are more scientific, factual words than **baby**. The parent animal must be mentioned or understood when using them: ✔The females stay close to their young/offspring. • Oh, look! That one's just a baby! ✗ ~~Oh, look! That one's just a young/an offspring.~~

young *adj.*

■ a team full of talented young players

adolescent • junior • teenage | *esp. AmE, infml* teen | *fml or law* juvenile

■ OPP old, elderly, aged

▶ a/an young / adolescent / teenage **boy / girl**

▶ a **juvenile offender**

▶ a young / teenage **fan**

youth *noun*

1 [U, sing.] ■ He spent much of his youth in Hong Kong.

adolescence • teens • childhood

■ OPP old age

▶ **in / during / since / throughout** (sb's) youth / adolescence / teens / childhood

▶ a/an **happy / unhappy** youth / childhood

▶ **spend** your youth / adolescence / teens / childhood

2 [C] (*often disapprov.*) ■ a fight started by a gang of youths

teenager • adolescent | *infml* kid | *esp. BrE, infml* lad | *esp. AmE, infml* teen | *sometimes offens.* girl | *fml or law* juvenile

▶ an **older** youth / teenager / girl

▶ a **local** youth / teenager / lad / girl

▶ youth / juvenile **crime / unemployment**

● YOUTH, TEENAGER OR LAD? A **teenager** is a boy or girl between the ages of 13 and 19; **youth** and **lad** are less specific about age, but always refer to boys or young men. When talking about young people in general, **youth** is more common than **teenagers**: *unemployed/ modern youth*

Z z

zone *noun* [C]

■ Aid workers had to leave the war zone.

area • region • district • quarter • part

▶ a/an **eastern / northern / southern / western** zone / area / region / district / quarter / parts

▶ an **industrial** zone / area / region / district / quarter

▶ a **border / coastal / geographical / military** zone / area / region / district